THE PAPERS OF
THOMAS JEFFERSON

THE PAPERS OF
Thomas Jefferson

Volume 26
11 May to 31 August 1793

JOHN CATANZARITI, EDITOR

EUGENE R. SHERIDAN, SENIOR ASSOCIATE EDITOR

J. JEFFERSON LOONEY, ASSOCIATE EDITOR

ELIZABETH PETERS BLAZEJEWSKI, EDITORIAL ASSISTANT

JEAN-YVES M. LE SAUX, CONSULTING EDITOR

PRINCETON, NEW JERSEY

PRINCETON UNIVERSITY PRESS

1995

DEDICATED TO THE MEMORY OF

ADOLPH S. OCHS

PUBLISHER OF THE NEW YORK TIMES

1896-1935

WHO BY THE EXAMPLE OF A RESPONSIBLE

PRESS ENLARGED AND FORTIFIED

THE JEFFERSONIAN CONCEPT

OF A FREE PRESS

ACKNOWLEDGMENTS

As INDICATED in the first volume, this edition was made possible by a grant of $200,000 from The New York Times Company to Princeton University. Since this initial subvention, its continuance has been assured by additional contributions from The New York Times Company and The New York Times Company Foundation; by grants of the Ford Foundation, the National Historical Publications and Records Commission, and the National Endowment for the Humanities; by grants of the Andrew W. Mellon Foundation, the Pew Charitable Trusts, and the Charles E. Culpeper Foundation to Founding Fathers Papers, Inc.; by benefactions from the Charlotte Palmer Phillips Foundation, Time Inc., the Dyson Foundation, the Lucius N. Littauer Foundation; and by gifts from James Russell Wiggins, David K. E. Bruce, and B. Batmanghelidj. In common with other editions of historical documents, THE PAPERS OF THOMAS JEFFERSON is a beneficiary of the good offices of the National Historical Publications and Records Commission, tendered in many useful forms through its officers and dedicated staff. For these and other indispensable aids generously given by librarians, archivists, scholars, and collectors of manuscripts, the Editors record their sincere gratitude.

GUIDE TO EDITORIAL
APPARATUS

1. TEXTUAL DEVICES

The following devices are employed throughout the work to clarify the presentation of the text.

[. . .], [. . . .]   One or two words missing and not conjecturable.

[. . .]¹, [. . . .]¹   More than two words missing and not conjecturable; subjoined footnote estimates number of words missing.

[   ]   Number or part of a number missing or illegible.

[roman]   Conjectural reading for missing or illegible matter. A question mark follows when the reading is doubtful.

[*italic*]   Editorial comment inserted in the text.

⟨*italic*⟩   Matter deleted in the MS but restored in our text.

2. DESCRIPTIVE SYMBOLS

The following symbols are employed throughout the work to describe the various kinds of manuscript originals. When a series of versions is recorded, *the first to be recorded is the version used for the printed text.*

Dft   draft (usually a composition or rough draft; later drafts, when identifiable as such, are designated "2d Dft," &c.)

Dupl   duplicate

MS   manuscript (arbitrarily applied to most documents other than letters)

N   note, notes (memoranda, fragments, &c.)

PoC   polygraph copy

PrC   press copy

RC   recipient's copy

SC   stylograph copy

Tripl   triplicate

All manuscripts of the above types are assumed to be in the hand of the author of the document to which the descriptive symbol pertains. If not, that fact is stated. On the other hand, the following types of manuscripts are assumed *not* to be in the hand of the author, and exceptions will be noted:

FC   file copy (applied to all contemporary copies retained by the author or his agents)

Lb   letterbook (ordinarily used with FC and Tr to denote texts copied into bound volumes)

Tr   transcript (applied to all contemporary and later copies except file copies; period of transcription, unless clear by implication, will be given when known)

3. LOCATION SYMBOLS

The locations of documents printed in this edition from originals in private hands and from printed sources are recorded in self-explanatory form in the descriptive note following each document. The locations of documents printed from originals held by public and private institutions in the United States are recorded by means of the symbols used in the National Union Catalog in the Library of Congress; an explanation of how these symbols are formed is given in Vol. 1: xl. The symbols DLC and MHi by themselves stand for the collections of Jefferson Papers proper in these repositories; when texts are drawn from other collections held by these two institutions, the names of those collections will be added. Location symbols for documents held by institutions outside the United States are given in a subjoined list. The lists of symbols are limited to the institutions represented by documents printed or referred to in this volume.

CSmH   The Huntington Library, San Marino, California
Ct   Connecticut State Library, Hartford
CtY   Yale University Library
DLC   Library of Congress
DNA   The National Archives, with identifications of series (preceded by record group number) as follows:

         AL   American Letters
         CD   Consular Dispatches
         DCI   Diplomatic and Consular Instructions
         DCLB   District of Columbia Letter Book
         DD   Diplomatic Dispatches
         DL   Domestic Letters
         LGS   Letters from the Governors of the States
         MD   Miscellaneous Dispatches
         MDC   Miscellaneous Duplicate Consular and Diplomatic Dispatches
         MLR   Miscellaneous Letters Received
         MTA   Miscellaneous Treasury Accounts
         NFC   Notes from Foreign Consuls

	NL	Notes from Legations
	NWT	Northwest Territory Papers
	PBG	Public Buildings and Grounds
	PCC	Papers of the Continental Congress
	SDC	State Department Correspondence: Copy books of George Washington's Correspondence with the Secretaries of State
	SWT	Southwest Territory Papers
	TR	Transcribed Reports

DP   United States Patent Office, Arlington, Virginia

G-Ar   Georgia State Department of Archives and History, Atlanta

ICHi   Chicago Historical Society

InU   Indiana University, Bloomington

MHi   Massachusetts Historical Society, Boston

MdAA   Maryland Hall of Records, Annapolis

MdHi   Maryland Historical Society, Baltimore

MoSHi   Missouri Historical Society, St. Louis

NHi   New-York Historical Society, New York City

NN   New York Public Library

NNC   Columbia University Library

NNP   Pierpont Morgan Library, New York City

Nc-Ar   North Carolina State Department of Archives and History, Raleigh

NjMoHP   Morristown National Historical Park, Morristown, New Jersey

NjP   Princeton University Library

O   Ohio State Library, Columbus

PHarH   Pennsylvania Historical and Museum Commission, Harrisburg

PHi   Historical Society of Pennsylvania, Philadelphia

PP   Free Library of Philadelphia

PPAmP   American Philosophical Society, Philadelphia

PWacD   David Library of the American Revolution, Washington Crossing, Pennsylvania

RPAB   Annmary Brown Memorial Library, Providence, Rhode Island

ScHi   South Carolina Historical Society, Charleston

Vi   Virginia State Library, Richmond

ViU   University of Virginia Library, Charlottesville

ViW   College of William and Mary Library, Williamsburg, Virginia

The following symbols represent repositories located outside of the United States:

AGI   Archivo General de Indias, Seville
AHN   Archivo Histórico Nacional, Madrid
AMAE   Archives du Ministère des Affaires Étrangères, Paris, with identification of series as follows:
           CPEU   Correspondance Politique, États-Unis
PRO   Public Record Office, London, with identification of series as follows:
           FO   Foreign Office
RSAS   Royal Swedish Academy of Sciences, Stockholm

4. OTHER SYMBOLS AND ABBREVIATIONS

The following symbols and abbreviations are commonly employed in the annotation throughout the work.

Second Series   The topical series to be published as part of this edition, comprising those materials which are best suited to a topical rather than a chronological arrangement (see Vol. 1: xv-xvi)

TJ   Thomas Jefferson

TJ Editorial Files   Photoduplicates and other editorial materials in the office of *The Papers of Thomas Jefferson*, Princeton University Library

TJ Papers   Jefferson Papers (applied to a collection of manuscripts when the precise location of an undated, misdated, or otherwise problematic document must be furnished, and always preceded by the symbol for the institutional repository; thus "DLC: TJ Papers, 4: 628-9" represents a document in the Library of Congress, Jefferson Papers, volume 4, pages 628 and 629. Citations to volumes and folio numbers of the Jefferson Papers at the Library of Congress refer to the collection as it was arranged at the time the first microfilm edition was made in 1944-45. Access to the microfilm edition of the collection as it was rearranged under the Library's Presidential Papers Program is provided by the *Index to the Thomas Jefferson Papers* [Washington, D.C., 1976])

RG   Record Group (used in designating the location of documents in the National Archives)

SJL   Jefferson's "Summary Journal of Letters" written and received for the period 11 Nov. 1783 to 25 June 1826 (in DLC: TJ Papers). This register, kept in Jefferson's hand, has been checked against the TJ Editorial Files. It is to be assumed that all outgoing letters are recorded in SJL unless there is a note to the contrary. When the date of receipt of an incoming letter is recorded in SJL, it is incorporated in the notes. Information and discrepancies revealed in SJL but not found in the letter itself are also noted. Missing letters recorded in SJL are, where possible, accounted for in the notes to documents mentioning them or in related documents. A more detailed discussion of this register and its use in this edition appears in Vol. 6: vii-x

SJPL   "Summary Journal of Public Letters," an incomplete list of letters and documents written by TJ from 16 Apr. 1784 to 31 Dec. 1793, with brief summaries, in an amanuensis's hand. This is supplemented by six pages in TJ's hand, compiled at a later date, listing private and confidential memorandums and notes as well as official reports and communications by and to him as Secretary of State, 11 Oct. 1789 to 31 Dec. 1793 (in DLC: TJ Papers, Epistolary Record, 514-59 and 209-11, respectively; see Vol. 22: ix-x). Since nearly all documents in the amanuensis's list are registered in SJL, while few in TJ's list are so recorded, it is to be assumed that all references to SJPL are to the list in TJ's hand unless there is a statement to the contrary

V   Ecu
ƒ   Florin
£   Pound sterling or livre, depending upon context (in doubtful cases, a clarifying note will be given)
s   Shilling or sou (also expressed as /)
d   Penny or denier
₶   Livre Tournois
℗   Per (occasionally used for pro, pre)

5. SHORT TITLES

The following list includes only those short titles of works cited frequently, and therefore in very abbreviated form, throughout this edition. Since it is impossible to anticipate all the works to be cited in very abbreviated form, the list is appropriately revised from volume to volume.

Adams, *Diary*   L. H. Butterfield and others, eds., *Diary and Autobiography of John Adams*, Cambridge, Mass., 1961, 4 vols.
Adams, *Works*   Charles Francis Adams, ed., *The Works of John Adams*, Boston, 1850-56, 10 vols.
AHA   American Historical Association

AHR   *American Historical Review*, 1895-

Ammon, *Genet Mission*   Harry Ammon, *The Genet Mission*, New York, 1973

Ammon, *Monroe*   Harry Ammon, *James Monroe: The Quest for National Identity*, New York, 1971

Annals   *Annals of the Congress of the United States: The Debates and Proceedings in the Congress of the United States . . . Compiled from Authentic Materials*, Washington, D.C., Gales & Seaton, 1834-56, 42 vols. All editions are undependable and pagination varies from one printing to another. The first two volumes of the set cited here have "Compiled . . . by Joseph Gales, Senior" on the title page and bear the caption "Gales & Seatons History" on verso and "of Debates in Congress" on recto pages. The remaining volumes bear the caption "History of Congress" on both recto and verso pages. Those using the first two volumes with the latter caption will need to employ the date of the debate or the indexes of debates and speakers.

APS   American Philosophical Society

Archives Parlementaires   *Archives Parlementaires de 1787 à 1860: Recueil Complet des Débats Législatifs & Politiques des Chambres Françaises*, Paris, 1862- , 222 vols.

ASP   *American State Papers: Documents, Legislative and Executive, of the Congress of the United States*, Washington, D.C., Gales & Seaton, 1832-61, 38 vols.

Aulard, *Recueil*   F. A. Aulard, ed., *Recueil des Actes du Comité de Salut Public . . .*, Paris, 1889-1951, 28 vols.

Bear, *Family Letters*   Edwin M. Betts and James A. Bear, Jr., eds., *Family Letters of Thomas Jefferson*, Columbia, Mo., 1966

Bemis, *Jay's Treaty*   Samuel Flagg Bemis, *Jay's Treaty: A Study in Commerce and Diplomacy*, rev. ed., New Haven, 1962

Bemis, *Pinckney's Treaty*   Samuel Flagg Bemis, *Pinckney's Treaty: America's Advantage from Europe's Distress, 1783-1800*, rev. ed., New Haven, 1960

Berkeley, *Beckley*   Edmund Berkeley and Dorothy Smith Berkeley, *John Beckley: Zealous Partisan in a Nation Divided*, Philadelphia, 1973

Betts, *Farm Book*   Edwin M. Betts, ed., *Thomas Jefferson's Farm Book*, Princeton, 1953

Betts, *Garden Book*   Edwin M. Betts, ed., *Thomas Jefferson's Garden Book, 1766-1824*, Philadelphia, 1944

Biog. Dir. Cong.   *Biographical Directory of the United States Congress, 1774-1989*, Washington, D.C., 1989

Bowman, *Neutrality*   Albert H. Bowman, *The Struggle for Neutral-*

ity: Franco-American Diplomacy During the Federalist Era, Knoxville, Tenn., 1974

Brant, *Madison*   Irving Brant, *James Madison*, Indianapolis, 1941-61, 6 vols.

Brigham, *American Newspapers*   Clarence S. Brigham, *History and Bibliography of American Newspapers, 1690-1820*, Worcester, Mass., 1947, 2 vols.

Bryan, *National Capital*   W. B. Bryan, *History of the National Capital*, New York, 1914-16, 2 vols.

Burnett, *Letters of Members*   Edmund C. Burnett, ed., *Letters of Members of the Continental Congress*, Washington, D.C., 1921-36, 8 vols.

Butterfield, *Rush*   L. H. Butterfield, ed., *Letters of Benjamin Rush*, Princeton, 1951, 2 vols.

Childs, *French Refugee Life*   Frances S. Childs, *French Refugee Life in the United States, 1790-1800: An American Chapter of the French Revolution*, Baltimore, 1940

Coker and Watson, *Indian Traders*   William S. Coker and Thomas D. Watson, *Indian Traders of the Southeastern Spanish Borderlands: Panton, Leslie & Company and John Forbes & Company, 1783-1847*, Pensacola, 1986

Correspondance   [Edmond Charles Genet], *Correspondance entre le Citoyen Genet, Ministre Plenipotentiaire de la Republique Française pres les Etats-Unis, et les Membres du Gouvernement Féderal, Precedee des Instructions données à ce Ministre par les Autorités constituées de la France*, Philadelphia, 1794

Correspondence   [Edmond Charles Genet], *The Correspondence between Citizen Genet, Minister of the French Republic, to the United States of North America, and the Officers of the Federal Government; to which are Prefixed the Instructions from the Constituted Authorities of France to the Said Minister. All from Authentic Documents*, Philadelphia, 1793

Counter Case   *The Counter Case of Great Britain as Laid before the Tribunal of Arbitration, Convened at Geneva, under the Provisions of the Treaty between the United States of America and Her Majesty the Queen of Great Britain, Concluded at Washington, May 8, 1871*, U.S. House of Representatives, Executive Documents, 42d Cong., 2d Sess., Vol. XVI, No. 324, Washington, D.C., 1872

CVSP   William P. Palmer and others, eds., *Calendar of Virginia State Papers . . . Preserved in the Capitol at Richmond*, Richmond, 1875-93, 11 vols.

DAB   Allen Johnson and Dumas Malone, eds., *Dictionary of American Biography*, New York, 1928-36, 20 vols.

DeConde, *Entangling Alliance*   Alexander DeConde, *Entangling Alliance: Politics & Diplomacy under George Washington*, Durham N.C., 1958

Dexter, *Yale*   Franklin B. Dexter, *Biographical Sketches of the Graduates of Yale College with Annals of the College History*, New York, 1885-1912, 6 vols.

DNB   Leslie Stephen and Sidney Lee, eds. *Dictionary of National Biography*, 2d ed., New York, 1908-09, 22 vols.

DSB   Charles C. Gillispie, ed., *Dictionary of Scientific Biography*, New York, 1970-80, 16 vols.

Duane, *Decree*   *Decree on the Admiralty Side of the District Court of New-York . . . By Judge Duane, in the Case of the Catharine, on the 28th January, 1794*, New York, 1794

Evans   Charles Evans, Clifford K. Shipton, and Roger P. Bristol, comps., *American Bibliography: A Chronological Dictionary of all Books, Pamphlets and Periodical Publications Printed in the United States of America from . . . 1639 . . . to . . . 1820*, Chicago and Worcester, Mass., 1903-59, 14 vols.

Federal Cases   *The Federal Cases; Comprising Cases Argued and Determined in the Circuit and District Courts of the United States . . .*, St. Paul, Minn., 1894-97, 30 vols.

Fitzpatrick, *Writings*   John C. Fitzpatrick, ed., *The Writings of George Washington*, Washington, D.C., 1931-44, 39 vols.

Ford   Paul Leicester Ford, ed., *The Writings of Thomas Jefferson*, Letterpress Edition, New York, 1892-99, 10 vols.

Franklin, *Papers*   Leonard W. Labaree, William B. Willcox, Barbara B. Oberg, and others, eds., *The Papers of Benjamin Franklin*, New Haven, 1959- , 30 vols.

Freeman, *Washington*   Douglas Southall Freeman, *George Washington*, New York, 1948-57, 7 vols.; 7th volume by J. A. Carroll and M. W. Ashworth

Goebel, *Supreme Court*   Julius Goebel, Jr., *The Oliver Wendell Holmes Devise History of the Supreme Court of the United States, Volume 1: Antecedents and Beginnings to 1801*, New York and London, 1971

Hardie, *Phila. Dir.*   James Hardie, *The Philadelphia Directory and Register . . .*, Philadelphia, 1793

HAW   Henry A. Washington, ed., *The Writings of Thomas Jefferson*, New York, 1853-54, 9 vols.

Heitman, *Register*   Francis B. Heitman, *Historical Register of Officers of the Continental Army during the War of the Revolution, April, 1775, to December, 1783*, new ed., Washington, D.C., 1914

Hening   William Waller Hening, ed., *The Statutes at Large; Being a Collection of All the Laws of Virginia*, Richmond, 1809-23, 13 vols.

Henry, *Henry*   William Wirt Henry, *Patrick Henry, Life, Correspondence and Speeches*, New York, 1891, 3 vols.

Humphreys, *Humphreys*   F. L. Humphreys, *Life and Times of David Humphreys*, New York, 1917, 2 vols.

Hunt, *Madison*   Gaillard Hunt, ed., *The Writings of James Madison*, New York, 1900-10, 9 vols.

Hyneman, *Neutrality*   Charles S. Hyneman, *The First American Neutrality*, Urbana, Ill., 1934

JAH   *Journal of American History*, 1964-

JCC   Worthington C. Ford and others, eds., *Journals of the Continental Congress, 1774-1789*, Washington, D.C., 1904-37, 34 vols.

Jefferson Correspondence, Bixby   Worthington C. Ford, ed., *Thomas Jefferson Correspondence Printed from the Originals in the Collections of William K. Bixby*, Boston, 1916

JEP   *Journal of the Executive Proceedings of the Senate of the United States . . . to the Termination of the Nineteenth Congress*, Washington, D.C., 1828

JHD   *Journal of the House of Delegates of the Commonwealth of Virginia* (cited by session and date of publication)

JHR   *Journal of the House of Representatives of the United States*, Washington, D.C., Gales & Seaton, 1826, 9 vols.

JS   *Journal of the Senate of the United States*, Washington, D.C., Gales, 1820-21, 5 vols.

JSH   *Journal of Southern History*, 1935-

Kimball, *Jefferson, Architect*   Fiske Kimball, *Thomas Jefferson, Architect*, Boston, 1916

L & B   Andrew A. Lipscomb and Albert E. Bergh, eds., *The Writings of Thomas Jefferson*, Washington, D.C., 1903-04, 20 vols.

Library Catalogue, 1783   Jefferson's MS list of books owned or wanted in 1783 (original in Massachusetts Historical Society)

Library Catalogue, 1815   *Catalogue of the Library of the United States*, Washington, D.C., 1815

Library Catalogue, 1829   *Catalogue: President Jefferson's Library*, Washington, D.C., 1829

List of Patents   *A List of Patents granted by the United States from April 10, 1792, to December 31, 1836*, Washington, D.C., 1872

Madison, *Papers*   William T. Hutchinson, Robert A. Rutland, J. C. A. Stagg, and others, eds., *The Papers of James Madison*, Chicago and Charlottesville, 1962- , 21 vols.

Malone, *Jefferson*   Dumas Malone, *Jefferson and his Time*, Boston, 1948-81, 6 vols.

Marshall, *Papers*   Herbert A. Johnson, Charles T. Cullen, Charles F. Hobson, and others, eds., *The Papers of John Marshall*, Chapel Hill, 1974- , 7 vols.

Mathews, *Andrew Ellicott*   Catharine Van Cortlandt Mathews, *Andrew Ellicott, His Life and Letters*, New York, 1908

Mayo, *British Ministers*   Bernard Mayo, ed., "Instructions to the British Ministers to the United States 1791-1812," American Historical Association, *Annual Report*, 1936

MB   James A. Bear, Jr., and Lucia C. Stanton, eds., *Jefferson's Memorandum Books: Accounts, with Legal Records and Miscellany, 1767-1826*, Princeton, forthcoming as part of *The Papers of Thomas Jefferson*, Second Series

Message   A Message of the President of the United States to Congress Relative to France and Great-Britain. Delivered December 5, 1793. With the Papers therein Referred to. To Which Are Added the French Originals. Published by Order of the House of Representatives*, Philadelphia, 1793

Miller, *Treaties*   Hunter Miller, ed., *Treaties and other International Acts of the United States of America*, Washington, D.C., 1931-48, 8 vols.

Mirsky and Nevins, *Eli Whitney*   Jeannette Mirsky and Allan Nevins, *The World of Eli Whitney*, New York, 1952

Mitchell, *Hamilton*   Broadus Mitchell, *Alexander Hamilton*, New York, 1957-62, 2 vols.

Morris, *Diary*   Beatrix C. Davenport, ed., *A Diary of the French Revolution by Gouverneur Morris, 1752-1816*, Boston, 1939, 2 vols.

Morris, *Papers*   E. James Ferguson, John Catanzariti, and others, eds., *The Papers of Robert Morris, 1781-1784*, Pittsburgh, 1973- , 7 vols.

MVHR   *Mississippi Valley Historical Review*, 1914-64

National State Papers   Eileen D. Carzo, ed., *National State Papers of the United States, 1789-1817. Part II: Texts of Documents. Administration of George Washington, 1789-1797*, Wilmington, Del., 1985, 35 vols.

Neel, *Phineas Bond*   Joanne L. Neel, *Phineas Bond: A Study in Anglo-American Relations, 1786-1812*, Philadelphia, 1968

Notes, ed. Peden   Thomas Jefferson, *Notes on the State of Virginia*, ed. William Peden, Chapel Hill, 1955

Nussbaum, *Commercial Policy*   Frederick L. Nussbaum, *Commercial Policy in the French Revolution: A Study of the Career of G. J. A. Ducher*, Washington, D.C., 1923

OED   Sir James Murray and others, eds., *A New English Dictionary on Historical Principles*, Oxford, 1888-1933

Ott, *Haitian Revolution*   Thomas O. Ott, *The Haitian Revolution, 1789-1804*, Knoxville, 1973

Pa. Archs.   Samuel Hazard and others, eds., *Pennsylvania Archives. Selected and Arranged from Original Documents in the Office of the Secretary of the Commonwealth*, Philadelphia and Harrisburg, 1852-1935, 119 vols.

Peterson, *Jefferson*   Merrill D. Peterson, *Thomas Jefferson and the New Nation*, New York, 1970

PMHB   *Pennsylvania Magazine of History and Biography*, 1877-

Randall, *Life*   Henry S. Randall, *The Life of Thomas Jefferson*, New York, 1858, 3 vols.

Randolph, *Domestic Life*   Sarah N. Randolph, *The Domestic Life of Thomas Jefferson, Compiled from Family Letters and Reminiscences by His Great-Granddaughter*, 3d ed., Cambridge, Mass., 1939

Scott and Rothaus, *Historical Dictionary*   Samuel F. Scott and Barry Rothaus, eds., *Historical Dictionary of the French Revolution, 1789-1799*, Westport, Conn., 1985, 2 vols.

Setser, *Reciprocity*   Vernon G. Setser, *The Commercial Reciprocity Policy of the United States*, Philadelphia, 1937

Shalhope, *Taylor*   Robert E. Shalhope, *John Taylor of Caroline: Pastoral Republican*, Columbia, S.C., 1980

Shipton-Mooney, *Index*   Clifford K. Shipton and James E. Mooney, comps., *National Index of American Imprints through 1800: The Short-Title Evans*, [Worcester, Mass.], 1969, 2 vols.

Sowerby   E. Millicent Sowerby, comp., *Catalogue of the Library of Thomas Jefferson*, Washington, D.C., 1952-59, 5 vols.

Sparks, *Morris*   Jared Sparks, *Life of Gouverneur Morris With Selections from His Correspondence and Miscellaneous Papers*, Boston, 1832, 3 vols.

Stein, *Sonthonax*   Robert L. Stein, *Léger Félicité Sonthonax: The Lost Sentinel of the Republic*, Rutherford, N.J., 1985

Syrett, *Hamilton*   Harold C. Syrett and others, eds., *The Papers of Alexander Hamilton*, New York, 1961-87, 27 vols.

Taxay, *Mint*   Don Taxay, *The U.S. Mint and Coinage: An Illustrated History from 1776 to the Present*, New York, 1966

Terr. Papers   Clarence E. Carter and John Porter Bloom, eds., *The Territorial Papers of the United States*, Washington, D.C., 1934- , 28 vols.

Thomas, *Neutrality*   Charles M. Thomas, *American Neutrality in 1793: A Study in Cabinet Government*, New York, 1931

TJR   Thomas Jefferson Randolph, ed., *Memoir, Correspondence, and Miscellanies, from the Papers of Thomas Jefferson*, Charlottesville, 1829, 4 vols.

Tucker, *Life*   George Tucker, *The Life of Thomas Jefferson*, Philadelphia, 1837, 2 vols.

Turner, *CFM*   Frederick Jackson Turner, "Correspondence of French Ministers, 1791-1797," American Historical Association, *Annual Report*, 1903, ii

U.S. Statutes at Large   Richard Peters, ed., *The Public Statutes at Large of the United States . . . 1789 to March 3, 1845*, Boston, 1855-56, 8 vols.

vmhb   *Virginia Magazine of History and Biography*, 1893-

Washington, *Diaries*   Donald Jackson and others, eds., *The Diaries of George Washington*, Charlottesville, 1976-79, 6 vols.

Washington, *Journal*   Dorothy Twohig, ed., *The Journal of the Proceedings of the President, 1793-1797*, Charlottesville, 1981

Washington, *Papers*   W. W. Abbot, Dorothy Twohig, and others, eds., *The Papers of George Washington*, Charlottesville, 1983- , 18 vols.

Whitaker, *Frontier*   Arthur P. Whitaker, *The Spanish-American Frontier: 1783-1795*, Boston, 1927

White, *Federalists*   Leonard White, *The Federalists: A Study in Administrative History*, New York, 1948

Windham Papers   *The Windham Papers: The Life and Correspondence of the Rt. Hon. William Windham, 1750-1810*, Boston, 1913, 2 vols.

wmq   *William and Mary Quarterly*, 1892-

Woodfin, "Genet Mission"   Maude H. Woodfin, "Citizen Genet and his Mission" (Ph.D. diss., University of Chicago, 1928)

Woods, *Albemarle*   Edgar Woods, *Albemarle County in Virginia*, Charlottesville, 1901

CONTENTS

·◄§ 1793 §►·

CONTENTS

CONTENTS

CONTENTS

CONTENTS

CONTENTS

CONTENTS

[xxv]

CONTENTS

[xxvi]

CONTENTS

CONTENTS

CONTENTS

CONTENTS

CONTENTS

CONTENTS

CONTENTS

CONTENTS

CONTENTS

CONTENTS

CONTENTS

ILLUSTRATIONS

Following page 340

EDMOND CHARLES GENET (1763-1834)

Jefferson initially welcomed Genet's arrival in Philadelphia in May 1793 as the harbinger of closer relations between the sister republics of France and the United States. But, much to Jefferson's dismay, the French Republic's first minister to the United States soon provoked the gravest crisis the Virginia statesman ever faced as Secretary of State. Adhering unswervingly to instructions from his Girondin superiors which called for a high level of American support for the French war effort against the allied coalition, the headstrong Genet insisted that France was entitled to commission privateers in American ports, enlist American citizens in French service, and exercise exclusive consular admiralty jurisdiction over French prizes. Despite the Washington administration's condemnation of these practices as violations of American neutrality, Genet persisted in them and sought to mobilize popular support for greater American assistance to France by aligning himself with the Republican opposition and by claiming a right to appeal from the President to Congress and to the American people. The resulting conflict between the French minister and the Washington administration led in August 1793 to an official American request for Genet's recall.

Engraving by Gilles Louis Chrétien, 1793. (*Courtesy of the Thomas Jefferson Memorial Foundation*)

GEORGE WASHINGTON (1732-99)

During the early stages of the Cabinet debates over the recall of Edmond Charles Genet, the President and the Secretary of State found themselves at odds with each other. Like Jefferson, Washington believed that the United States could best serve itself and the French cause as a neutral supplier of provisions to the French Republic and its West Indian colonies, and therefore he feared that Genet's efforts to bend American neutrality in a pro-French direction might provoke British retaliation. Unlike Jefferson, however, Washington resented Genet's alignment with the Republican party because he was apprehensive that the French minister would take advantage of the widespread popular support the French Revolution enjoyed in the United States to pave the way for the accession to power of what he perceived to be a factious opposition whose policies would be ruinous to the new American nation. Initially Washington favored a proposal by Alexander Hamilton to discredit the enthusiastically pro-Genet Republican opposition by accompanying the federal government's request for Genet's recall with a public statement to the American people explaining the full magnitude of the French minister's defiance of the President and his neutrality policy. However, Washington turned against Hamilton's initiative in part because of Jefferson's warning that the proposed statement would make the President himself appear to be a mere partisan leader.

Portrait by Charles Willson Peale, 1795. (*Courtesy of the New-York Historical Society*)

ILLUSTRATIONS

ALEXANDER HAMILTON (ca. 1755-1804)

Edmond Charles Genet's opposition to American neutrality predictably led to Hamilton's emergence as the leading proponent of the French minister's recall. The Secretary of the Treasury abhorred the radicalization of the French Revolution attendant upon the overthrow of the Bourbon monarchy and the establishment of the French Republic as a sustained exercise in political anarchy and wanted the United States to enter into closer relations with Great Britain. He also feared that Genet's repeated defiance of American neutrality would eventually involve the United States in hostilities with Great Britain that would endanger the whole edifice of Hamiltonian finance. Indeed, Hamilton was convinced that Genet's criticisms of American neutrality and alignment with the Republican opposition were parts of a deliberate revolutionary strategy designed to make the United States an active participant in the French war effort while subverting popular confidence in the Washington administration. By alerting the American public to the full extent of Genet's resistance to American neutrality and disrespect for the President, Hamilton was confident that Federalists could rally popular support for themselves as defenders of American sovereignty, discredit Republicans as tools of a foreign power inimical to American interests, and undermine American support for the French cause. Consequently Hamilton became the strongest advocate in the Cabinet of Genet's recall.

Portrait by Charles Willson Peale, ca. 1791. (*Courtesy of Independence National Historical Park*)

HENRY KNOX (1750-1806)

This Massachusetts Federalist leader was the strongest supporter in the Cabinet of Hamilton's call for Edmond Charles Genet's recall. Knox shared the same concerns as Hamilton about Genet's resistance to American neutrality and was even more extreme than the Treasury Secretary about the proper response to the French minister's defiant behavior. In addition to supporting Genet's recall and the immediate release of an explanatory statement to the American people, the Secretary of War also argued unsuccessfully that Genet either be expelled from the United States or forced to suspend his mission while the request for his recall was still pending. During the Cabinet debates over Genet's recall, Jefferson was particularly annoyed by Knox's habit of citing extreme Republican criticisms of the President in order to underscore for Washington the danger of the French minister's alignment with Republican opponents of the Washington administration. In fact, Jefferson was so contemptuous of Knox's unwavering support of Hamilton in the Cabinet that on more than one occasion he denounced Knox as a fool in private memorandums that later became part of the "Anas."

Posthumous portrait by Gilbert Stuart, 1810. (*Courtesy of the Museum of Fine Arts*)

EDMUND RANDOLPH (1753-1813)

Despite frequent oscillations between Hamiltonian and Jeffersonian positions in the Cabinet that infuriated the Secretary of State, Randolph provided critical support for Jefferson during the debates over Edmond Charles Genet's recall. Like Washington and Jefferson, Randolph valued the French alliance as a cornerstone of American diplomacy. He was especially sensitive to the political implications of the overwhelming popular support the French Revolution enjoyed in the United States but apprehensive about the "ardour of some, to transplant French politics, as fresh fuel for our own parties" (Opinion of Randolph, 6 May 1793, DLC: Washington Papers). In order to preserve the confidence of the American people, Randolph believed that the federal government had to avoid even the appearance of hostility to France. Therefore he supported Jefferson's effort to bring about Genet's recall in a way that was least offensive to the French Republic and its American supporters. Since the President relied increasingly on the Attorney General as a moderate voice in the Cabinet, Randolph was able to raise doubts in Washington's mind about the wisdom of Alexander Hamilton's proposed statement to the American people about the Genet affair.

Copy by Flavius J. Fisher of a missing portrait by an unidentified artist. (*Courtesy of the Virginia State Library*)

EDMOND CHARLES GENET TO THOMAS JEFFERSON

Replete with extensive revisions characteristic of Genet's drafts, this is the first page of a 23 May 1793 letter to Jefferson in which the French minister sought to begin negotiations for a far-reaching commercial treaty that, unbeknownst to the Secretary of State, would have made the United States a virtual partner in the French war effort against the allied coalition. Although Jefferson did not learn the full dimensions of the proposed treaty until Genet published a modified text of his instructions from the French government in December 1793, he favored entering into negotiations with the French minister in order to achieve his longstanding goal of strengthening the economic ties between France and the United States in order to end what he regarded as America's economic vassalage to Great Britain. But he was overruled by President Washington and his colleagues in the Cabinet, who opposed a new commercial treaty with France because they were satisfied with the extensive commercial concessions that the European war had already forced France to make to the United States, concerned that the French Republic might not survive internal opposition and the allied onslaught, and apprehensive that the new political links with France Genet alluded to in this letter might fatally compromise American neutrality. Jefferson was consequently obliged to resort to the polite diplomatic fiction of notifying Genet in conversation that the Senate's constitutional share of the treaty-making power made it advisable for him to delay any negotiations for a new commercial treaty until that body reconvened as scheduled later in 1793. By then, however, the Washington administration was awaiting the French response to its request for Genet's recall, and Jefferson was never able to achieve the treaty by which he had hoped to bring about a fundamental reordering of the political economy of the new American nation. (*Courtesy of the Library of Congress*)

GEORGE WASHINGTON TO THE PROVISIONAL EXECUTIVE COUNCIL OF FRANCE

The drafting of this letter, which was finally dated 24 May 1793, revealed important differences in the attitudes of Jefferson and the President toward the cause of the embattled French Republic. Washington asked Jefferson to draft a letter in his name to the Provisional Executive Council expressing the President's sentiments on the occasion of the termination of the diplomatic mission of

ILLUSTRATIONS

Jean Baptiste Ternant, Louis XVI's last minister to the United States. During a private meeting on 23 May 1793 Washington objected to Jefferson's use of the phrase "our republic" with respect to the United States because it seemed to be too redolent of Republican complaints about the alleged monarchism of Federalists and expressed reservations about Jefferson's use of the term "republic" in regard to France because the rapidly shifting situation in that country left the survival of the French Republic open to doubt. In accordance with the President's wishes, Jefferson deleted the offending words, so that the final text of the letter reflected Washington's wish to avoid too close a linkage between the American and French republics. (*Courtesy of the Library of Congress*)

THOMAS JEFFERSON TO ISAAC SHELBY

Written at the behest of Edmond Charles Genet, Jefferson's letter of 28 June 1793 to the governor of Kentucky introducing the distinguished French botanist André Michaux was a deliberately ambiguous response to a diplomatic dilemma. On the one hand, Jefferson's belief that Spanish intrigues with the Southern Indians threatened to provoke a war between Spain and the United States predisposed him to favor a Girondin-inspired plan by the French minister to liberate Louisiana from Spanish rule with an expeditionary force raised in part in Kentucky with the help of Michaux, who had already agreed to embark on a search for an all-water route to the Pacific under the aegis of the American Philosophical Society. On the other hand, Genet's increasing defiance of key elements of the Washington administration's neutrality policy inclined Jefferson to distance himself from the French minister as much as possible. Under the impact of these conflicting imperatives, Jefferson carefully revised the draft so as to encourage Shelby to assist Michaux's efforts without directly committing himself as Secretary of State to Genet's proposed expedition against Louisiana. (*Courtesy of the Library of Congress*)

EDMOND CHARLES GENET'S ADDRESS TO THE FRENCH PEOPLE OF LOUISIANA

In this pamphlet Genet called upon French settlers in Louisiana to rise up against Spanish rule and support a combined French and American land and naval expedition that was designed to create an independent Louisiana with close ties to France and the United States. Genet read this address to Jefferson during a meeting on 5 July 1793, emphasizing that he was doing so unofficially, and Jefferson refrained from informing the President or the Cabinet about it. Late in August 1793, however, Josef Ignacio de Viar and Josef de Jaudenes, the Spanish government's agents in Philadelphia, procured a copy of the pamphlet and sent it to Jefferson with a request that the Washington administration take steps to prevent any American participation in the projected assault on Louisiana. Jefferson duly submitted the Spanish agents' letter and its enclosure to Washington, without revealing his prior knowledge of Genet's address, and then instructed Governor Isaac Shelby of Kentucky in accordance with their wishes. (*Courtesy of the Library of Congress*)

THOMAS JEFFERSON TO GOUVERNEUR MORRIS

Jefferson's 16 Aug. 1793 letter to the American minister in Paris set forth the rationale for the Washington administration's request for Edmond Charles

Genet's recall. Jefferson's Cabinet colleagues advised him to emphasize Genet's challenge to American neutrality and his disrespect for constituted authority in the United States, and Hamilton also urged him to stress Genet's involvement in domestic politics as evidence of a calculated French design to subvert popular confidence in the Washington administration. Eager to avoid a diplomatic crisis with France, to comply with the President's preference for a statement that distinguished between the French nation and its minister, and to counteract Hamilton's efforts to associate Genet with the Republican party, Jefferson produced a masterful letter which defended American neutrality policy, arraigned Genet for repeatedly defying it, and absolved France of any responsibility for the French minister's actions, attributing them instead to Genet's personal willfulness. In this way Jefferson offered France a graceful way out of a difficult diplomatic situation, but at the unexpected cost of convincing the new Jacobin government in Paris that Genet was a key actor in an alleged Girondin plot against French republican liberty and unity. (*Courtesy of the Library of Congress*)

"A PEEP INTO THE ANTIFEDERAL CLUB"

Drawn by an anonymous American artist in New York City on 16 Aug. 1793, a few days after Edmond Charles Genet began a prolonged stay there in connection with his ultimately fruitless efforts to mount French expeditions against Canada and Louisiana, and offered for sale to a public increasingly agitated by reports of the French minister's defiance of presidential authority, this caricature represents a Federalist demonology of the Republican opposition. Attributing Satanic origins and anti-Federalist roots to the party, the caricature presents an imaginary conclave of Republicans dedicated to philosophical anarchism, moral relativism, unlimited popular sovereignty, and the overthrow of the federal government, and consisting of a motley assortment of politicians, savants, artisans, sailors, a black, and a revolutionary Frenchman. The figure standing on the table and dominating the group bears a strong resemblance to Jefferson, whom the artist could have met or seen when the Republican leader was serving as Secretary of State in New York City in 1790. The sentiments attributed to this figure were scarcely those of an aristocratic Virginia planter, but perhaps they were meant to satirize Jefferson's appeal to what many Federalists regarded as the lower orders of American society. (*Courtesy of the Library Company of Philadelphia*)

Volume 26

11 May to 31 August 1793

JEFFERSON CHRONOLOGY

1743 · 1826

1743	Born at Shadwell, 13 Apr. (New Style).
1760	Entered the College of William and Mary.
1762	"quitted college."
1762-1767	Self-education and preparation for law.
1769-1774	Albemarle delegate to House of Burgesses.
1772	Married Martha Wayles Skelton, 1 Jan.
1775-1776	In Continental Congress.
1776	Drafted Declaration of Independence.
1776-1779	In Virginia House of Delegates.
1779	Submitted Bill for Establishing Religious Freedom.
1779-1781	Governor of Virginia.
1782	His wife died, 6 Sep.
1783-1784	In Continental Congress.
1784-1789	In France as Minister Plenipotentiary to negotiate commercial treaties and as Minister Plenipotentiary resident at Versailles.
1790-1793	Secretary of State of the United States.
1797-1801	Vice President of the United States.
1801-1809	President of the United States.
1814-1826	Established the University of Virginia.
1826	Died at Monticello, 4 July.

VOLUME 26

11 May to 31 August 1793

15 May	Defines French violations of American neutrality.
16 May	Edmond Charles Genet arrives in Philadelphia.
2 June	Jacobins take control of the French government in Paris.
5 June	Announces that French privateers outfitted in Charleston must leave American ports.
8 June	Great Britain imposes restrictions on neutral trade with France.
20 June	Eli Whitney requests patent for cotton gin.
30 June	Instructions to William Carmichael and William Short on diplomatic crisis with Spain.
5 July	Edmond Charles Genet reveals proposed French expeditions against Canada and Louisiana.
5-12 July	Crisis over the *Little Sarah* affair.
15 July	Conference on William Thornton's plan for the Capitol.
18 July	Submits twenty-nine neutrality questions to the Supreme Court.
31 July	Notifies Washington that he plans to retire from office at the end of September.
1 Aug.	Cabinet agrees to request Edmond Charles Genet's recall.
3 Aug.	Cabinet approves neutrality rules.
7 Aug.	Announces that the United States will restore or make compensation for certain prizes captured by French privateers.
8 Aug.	Supreme Court declines to advise the Executive on neutrality.
11 Aug.	Advises James Madison on Republican party strategy.
11 Aug.	Notifies Washington of his willingness to remain in office until the end of the year.
16 Aug.	Letter to Gouverneur Morris requesting Edmond Charles Genet's recall.
20 Aug.	Cabinet approves the letter of recall.
23 Aug.	Indicates American interest in a new commercial treaty with France.
29 Aug.	Instructs Isaac Shelby to oppose French expedition against Louisiana.

THE PAPERS OF
THOMAS JEFFERSON

·◖━━━━━━◗·

From Nathaniel Anderson

DEAR SIR   Richmond May 11th 1793

Mr. Genet the french Embassador left this place this morning for Philadelphia. I think it probable that he may come on some terms with the President, for the payment of our debt to france in the Shipment of wheat flour &c, and that an Agent here will be wanting. I have therefore to request the favor of you to Mention me, If you think me worthy of the Appointment. I have one American Ship, and in A few days expect to Own another, and I can Negotiate Bills of Exchange on London, Bordeaux, Cadiz, and I believe any other Port in Europe, provided funds are placed to draw on, to the Satisfaction of William Anderson & Co. of London. I did not Mention the Subject to Mr. Genet. It was my intention, but my friend Colo. Robert Gamble having Spoken to him before prevented me, as it was not my wish to be his Competitor, he and myself have agree'd that if the Business here would be an Object for Us both, that we will be equally Concerned. Otherwise it would be my desire that he should have the preference. The above Mentioned Ships will load immediately here with Tobacco for London and return with fall goods, when I could send them to Any port in france. Your friendship in this or any other Business you may think proper to Mention my Name in, Shall be ever Acknowledged by Dear Sir your very respectfull hble Servt   NATHL. ANDERSON

RC (DLC); at head of text: "Thomas Jefferson Esqr"; endorsed by TJ as received 18 May 1793 and so recorded in SJL.

From David M. Clarkson

St. Eustatius, 11 May 1793. He acknowledges receipt of his consular commission for this island from the President, as well as his instructions and the laws of the United States, but notes that he is unable to exercise this office because to his surprise the governor of the island has informed him that the

States General has ordered all Dutch governors in their American colonies not to acknowledge consuls from the United States.

RC (DNA: RG 59, MLR); 1 p.; at foot of text: "The Honable Thomas Jefferson Esqr. Secretary of State"; endorsed by TJ as received 25 May 1793 and so recorded in SJL. Enclosed in TJ to George Washington, 27 May 1793.

David M. Clarkson (1765-1821), the son of Matthew Clarkson, mayor of Philadelphia from 1792 to 1796, was a shipper on St. Kitts for six years before being appointed United States consul at St. Eustatius in February 1793. See J. Robert T. Craine, comp., and Harry W. Hazard, ed., *The Ancestry and Posterity of Matthew Clarkson (1664-1702)* [n.p., 1971], 18, 27.

From Tench Coxe

Saturday [11 May 1793]

Mr. C. has the honor to send to the Secretary of State a copy of a letter received this day. The names of the persons, to and from whom the letter is, have been omitted, because they will be both known to the Secretary. Mr. C. thinks it his duty to the writer, respectfully to request, that the matter may be confined to the P. and himself.

RC (DLC); partially dated; endorsed by TJ as received 11 May 1793 and so recorded in SJL. FC (PHi: Coxe Papers); subjoined to RC of enclosure. Enclosure: [William Seton] to Coxe, New York, 10 May 1793, reporting that Albion Cox failed soon after the establishment of the Bank of New York; that a knowledgeable acquaintance of Cox's describes him as "a man of the most superior abilities in his line or profession as a Smelter or refiner of Metals," but one who lacks prudence and regularity and whose conduct before and since his failure does not say much for his integrity; and that he wishes his name and those of his friends to remain confidential (Tr in DLC; in Coxe's hand, with signature omitted and initials used for Cox's name).

On 8 May 1793, two days after TJ showed the President a letter from Thomas

Pinckney announcing that he had engaged Albion Cox to serve as assayer of the United States Mint, Coxe, undoubtedly acting in response to a request for information from TJ, wrote a letter to William Seton, a New York City merchant who was cashier of the Bank of New York, and asked him for an evaluation of Cox's business failure in New York and personal character, noting that Cox was under consideration for a sensitive public office and that the information requested was intended for the head of a department and an even more important official—a clear reference to the Secretary of State and the President (PHi: Coxe Papers; Washington, *Journal*, 129). TJ and Director of the Mint David Rittenhouse conveyed the substance of Seton's evaluation of Cox to the President on 16 May 1793, with the result described in note to Pinckney to TJ, 12 Mch. 1793.

To Samuel Freeman

SIR   Philadelphia May 11. 1793.

I received yesterday the honour of your letter of the 1st. inst. covering an application from a number of the inhabitants of Portland to have the laws of the Union published in the gazette of that place, and think it my duty to give them the earliest explanation of the footing on which the law has placed those publications. The act of Congress makes it the duty of the Secretary of state, on the passage of a law, to have it published in 'at least three of the public newspapers printed within the US.' It appeared evident from this expression that the law did not mean that the public should be at the expence of a publication in every state; and that it contemplated a number somewhere about *three*, tho' not less.

New Hampshire
* Massachusetts
Rhode island
Connecticut
* New York
Vermont
New Jersey
* Pennsylvania
Delaware
Maryland
* Virginia
Kentucky
North Carolina
* South Carolina
Georgia.

On the supposition therefore that the papers of a state may have some circulation in the adjoining state on each side, I concluded to have five publications, and that these should be in the states marked thus* in the margin, as being most likely to give some communication to every state in the union. It is certain that if our citizens were to depend on this mode of communication alone, it would be quite inadequate; and doubtful whether newspaper publication is not altogether too partial, and too perishable to answer the purpose. But these are considerations for the legislature, and not for an executive officer, who as long as something like a measure is prescribed to him, is bound to follow it according to his best discretion and judgment. It would have given me great pleasure to have been able to fulfill the wishes of the citizens of Portland on this occasion, but on comparing the law with the plan on which I have executed it, I am persuaded they will perceive that I have not abridged the views of the legislature, and that it is from them the remedy must proceed. I have the honor to be with the greatest respect to them & to yourself, Sir, their & your most obedt. humble servt

TH: JEFFERSON

PrC (DLC); at foot of first page: "Mr. Samuel Freeman. Portland." FC (Lb in DNA: RG 59, DL).

From Thomas Pinckney

My dear Sir   Great Cumberland Place London 11 May 1793

Mr. Harriott is so obliging as to take charge of your news papers up to the present date—with these I inclose a copy of the instructions given to the commanders of Vessels carrying letters of Marque, on which it will be necessary for our Merchants to observe that the property of all persons resident in the Dominions of France is liable to capture and the decisions of the British Courts of Admiralty last war established that if a partner of any mercantile house is a resident in France his proportion of any property belonging to the house which may be captured is liable to condemnation.

On the subject of impressments I am referred till the arrival of answers to enquiries directed to be made by Mr. Bond for the conclusion of permanent regulations: in the mean [time]¹ impressment has not fallen so heavy on our trade as on former occasions, the masters of some of our Vessels have informed me that they had not been boarded by any press gang during their stay here and I inclose a copy from a mercantile house at Leith which shews that though some irregularities have taken place it has not met with the countenance of Government. I am informed by Mr. Van staphorst that he has two large packets of news papers for me from America but does not know how to forward them as they are too bulky for the post. I shall esteem it a favor if you will in future direct my papers to be sent to the Consul at either of the Ports of this kingdom with directions to forward them immediately by the mail coach which is an expeditious and not expensive mode of conveyance. I have the honor to be with sincere respect My dear Sir Your most faithful and obedient Servant   THOMAS PINCKNEY

RC (DNA: RG 59, DD); at foot of text: "The Secretary of State"; endorsed by TJ as received 3 Aug. 1793 and so recorded in SJL. PrC (ScHi: Pinckney Family Papers). Tr (Lb in DNA: RG 59, DD). Enclosures: (1) *Instructions for the Commanders of such Merchant Ships or Vessels Who shall have Letters of Marque and Reprisals* [London, 1793] (printed pamphlet in same, with notations by Pinckney on third page giving 14 Feb. 1793 as date of instructions; Tr, with numerous copying errors, in Lb in same). (2) Ramsay, Williamson & Company to Pinckney, Leith, 3 May 1793, advising that impressment officers here distressed American vessels so much that they sought and obtained relief from the Judge Admiral for Scotland, and that the Admiralty has now given an order that will prevent future trouble (Tr in same, in the hand of William A. Deas; Tr in Lb in same, with penciled note in a clerk's hand: "The original not found"). Enclosed in John Harriott to TJ, 1 Aug. 1793.

Phineas Bond had recently returned to America to assume the office of British consul general for the middle and southern states. During his stay in England he prepared a report on the SUBJECT OF IMPRESSMENTS for Lord Grenville, the British foreign minister, in which he defended the continuance of this practice as essential for the security of British navigation, while suggesting the use of certificates of citizenship and registries of crews to protect American seamen from its worst abuses. Upon instructions from TJ, Pinckney rejected these proposals during a subsequent conference with Bond prior to his departure for America, and there is no other evidence that Bond was under formal instructions from his superiors to make ENQUIRIES about impressment after his return to America (Bond to Grenville, 1 Feb. 1793, AHA, *Annual Report* [1897], p. 524-7; Pinckney to TJ, 13 Mch. 1793; Neel, *Phineas Bond*, 95-8; Samuel F. Bemis, "The London Mission of Thomas Pinckney, 1792-1796," AHR, XXVIII [1922-23], 233-5; Charles R. Ritcheson, "Thomas Pinckney's London Mission, 1792-1796, and the Impressment Issue," *International History Review*, II [1980], 529-34). TJ submitted this letter to the President on 3 Aug. 1793 and received it back two days later (Washington, *Journal*, 213, 214).

Pinckney also wrote another letter to TJ this day, introducing John Harriott—whose acquaintance he had enjoyed since his arrival in England and who was removing with his family to settle in some part of the United States—and asking TJ to arrange for Harriott to pay his respects to the President in person (RC in DNA: RG 59, DD, in the hand of William A. Deas, with complimentary close and signature by Pinckney, at foot of text: "The Secretary of State"; Tr in Lb in same).

[1] Word supplied.

From Edward Stevens

DEAR SIR   Alexandria 11th May 1793

Your favour of the 18th. Ulto. was delivered to me three or four days agoe, And at a time, Just as I was seting out on a Tour through part of my Survey upon publick business; But so soon as I return home your request shall be complied with, as far as it Lays in my Power, For in Genl. Gates defeat, I was unfortunate enough to loose all my Baggage and Papers. I am with great esteem Dear Sir your very hum: Servt

EDWARD STEVENS

RC (MoSHi: Bixby Collection); endorsed by TJ as received 16 May 1793 and so recorded in SJL.

To John Wayles Eppes

DEAR SIR   Philadelphia May. 12. 1793

I have just received from Donald & Burton the invoice of your books. Thinking you would be impatient to hear something of them, I inclose you the invoice. They have been shipped from Dublin on board the Young eagle, Elias Lord. The four last in the invoice came here under the care of Mr. Marshal, who told me he would have them delivered to me as soon as they could be come at in the ship. They shall be sent on to you the moment they are landed. I believe I never rendered any account of the money deposited in my hands for your use while here. You know my constant employment and will therefore excuse it. It is to supply the omission that I have now gone over my memorandums and made out a statement. Be so good as to compare it with your own notes and correct mine wherever wrong, for I cannot answer for perfect exactness.—Your friends here complain that you have written to none of them. We do not know whether you are gone or going to Wms. burg. You have missed seeing what has highly gratified the great mass of Philadelphians, British prizes brought in by French armed vessels. Thousands and thousands collected on the beach when the first came up, and when they saw the British colours reversed and the French

[7]

flying above them they rent the air with peals of exultation. I have got off my furniture &c. to Virginia, so as to be in readiness for flight the moment I find an apt occasion. My friendly respects to Mr. & Mrs. Eppes & family, & am Dear Sir your's affectionately

TH: JEFFERSON

PrC (DLC); at foot of text: "Mr. J. W. Eppes." Tr (MHi); 19th-century copy. Enclosures: (1) Invoice of Donald & Burton to Whieldon & Butterworth, 30 Dec. 1792, for eighteen books purchased in Dublin and four bought in London, all itemized by title, except an unnamed "upper book in the parcel," and by price, the whole totaling £25.16.0 (PrC of Tr in DLC: TJ Papers, 85: 14773; entirely in TJ's hand; with letter of Donald & Burton to Whieldon & Butterworth at foot of list: "Since our last we have received your invoice from Ireland, and find the three last articles not charged, therefore conclude they have not been printed there, or that our correspondent has neglected sending them"; at foot of text: "The above is a copy of the invoice sent by Donald & Burton to Th:J. and by him sent to J.W. Eppes. May. 12. 1793"; enclosed in Donald & Burton to TJ, 9 Mch. 1793, recorded in SJL as received 6 May 1793, but not found). (2) TJ's Account with Eppes, n.d., containing entries for 20 Apr. 1791-5 Apr. 1793 (PrC in CSmH; entirely in TJ's hand).

For the law BOOKS TJ had ordered for Eppes, see enclosure to TJ to Alexander Donald, 11 Oct. 1792. Except for the unnamed work, the twenty-one titles listed there match those named in the enclosed INVOICE.

From Joseph Fenwick

SIR   Bordeaux 12 May 1793.

Herewith is a copy of my last letter. The chanels now left to write you from this country render it imprudent to say anything on the subject of politics. We are perfectly quiet here and in the neighbourhood of this Department. The government of France continues their uniform protection and favor to the American Commerce, and the Trading people have much confidence in and pay higher freights to American vessels than to any other neutral ones.

I enclose you a third Copy of a Bond required of the Consuls, least those that preceded it have not reached you. Mr. John Mason of George Town Potomack will procure the security required.

I annex a note of the prices of American produce, and the freights of American Ships now here and remain with the greatest respect Sir your most obedient and humble Servant   JOSEPH FENWICK

Freights for W. Indias—30 a 34 Dollars per Ton of 4 hhds Wine & ten per Ct.

for Isle france   40–Dlrs. per do and as much back—Dto.
for Holland & Hans Towns 4 £rs Str per ton   & Dto.
for the Baltic   5 a 5. 10/ do: per do.

Foreign Wheat 7/ Str per American Bushel
flower 35/ Str per Barrel
Tobacco 60 a 90^{tt} per Ct.
Whale Oil 65^{tt} per Ct.
liver Dto. 75^{tt} per Ct.
Whale Bone 200 a 250 per Ct.
Beef 100^{tt} per Barrel
Pork 120 a 130^{tt} per Dto. Exchange London 4d Str per livre

RC (DNA: RG 59, CD); addressed: "The Honble The Secretary of State Philadelphia"; franked and postmarked; noted in pencil by TJ above first paragraph: "Extract of lre dated Bordeaux 12. May. 93."; endorsed by TJ as received 25 July 1793 and so recorded in SJL. Enclosures: (1) Fenwick to TJ, 14 Apr. 1793 (recorded in SJL as received 25 July 1793, but not found). (2) Fenwick's consular bond, 20 Nov. 1792 (Tripl in DNA: RG 59, CD; in Fenwick's hand). The last three sentences of the first paragraph of the letter were published in the 27 July 1793 issue of the *National Gazette* and the postscript in its 31 July 1793 issue.

From Josef de Jaudenes and Josef Ignacio de Viar

Mui Señor nuestro   Philadelphia 12. de Mayo de 1793.

Las mismas miras que tubimos en pasar à manos de V.S. Copia del tratado concluido entre España, y la Nacion Creeke el año de 1784, nos inducen ahora à remitir à V.S. adjunta otra Copia del que se concluyò el año proximo pasado por nuestro Governador de Natches con las Naciones Chactaws, y Chicachas, y nos lisonjeamos que enterado el Presidente de los Estados Unidos de sus contenidos, se valdrà de los medios mas oportunos, y que puedan contribuir à evitar el que los Estados Unidos entren en Convenios con los precitados Indios que sean opuestos à los que tienen estipulados con nosotros, rectificando al mismo tiempo los de esta naturaleza concluidos anteriormente por el Govierno de V.S. Nos repetimos à la disposicion de V.S. con la mas fina voluntad, y respeto, quedando, Señor Los mas obedtes. y humdes. servs. Q.B.L.M. de V.S.

JOSEF DE JAUDENES   JOSEF IGNACIO DE VIAR

E D I T O R S'   T R A N S L A T I O N

Our very dear Sir   Philadelphia 12 May 1793

The same purpose we had in transmitting to your hands a copy of the treaty concluded between Spain and the Creek Nation in 1784 induces us now to send you enclosed another copy of the treaty concluded last year by our Governor of

Natchez with the Choctaw Nation and the Chickasaws, and we flatter ourselves with the belief that the President of the United States, once informed of its contents, will avail himself of the most appropriate means conducive to keeping the United States from entering into accords with the aforementioned Indians that may conflict with those they have reached with us as well as at the same time revising such accords previously reached by your government. Again we place ourselves at your disposition with all good will and respect, remaining, Sir, your most obedient and humble servants. Respectfully yours,

JOSEF DE JAUDENES JOSEF IGNACIO DE VIAR

RC (DNA: RG 59, NL); in Jaudenes's hand, signed by Jaudenes and Viar; at foot of text: "Sor. Dn. Thomas Jefferson &ca."; endorsed by TJ as received 14 May 1793 and so recorded in SJL. Tr (AHN: Papeles de Estado, legajo 3895); attested by Jaudenes and Viar. Enclosure: Treaty of Natchez between Spain and the Chickasaw and Choctaw Indians, 14 May 1792 (Tr in DNA: RG 59, NL, in Spanish, attested by Jaudenes and Viar; Tr in same, English translation in TJ's hand, misdated 14 May 1790; Tr in same, English translation in a clerk's hand, misdated 14 May 1790; Tr in DNA: RG 46, Senate Records, 3d Cong., 1st sess., English translation in a clerk's hand, misdated 14 May 1790; English translation misdated 14 May 1790 printed in ASP, Foreign Relations, I, 280; correctly dated Spanish text printed in Manuel Serrano y Sanz, ed., Documentos Históricos de La Florida y La Luisiana Siglos XVI al XVIII [Madrid, 1912], 436-9).

The Treaty of Natchez was an outgrowth of Spain's policy of fortifying strategic points on the Mississippi to serve as barriers against American westward expansion. In accordance with this strategy, Manuel Gayoso de Lemos, governor of the Natchez District, began construction in 1791 of Fort Nogales on the site of what is now Vicksburg, so as to frustrate the settlement plans of the Yazoo Company of South Carolina. Not only was this fort located about a hundred miles north of the southern boundary claimed by the United States, but it initially aroused opposition among the Choctaws, who opposed the building of a Spanish post near their hunting grounds. However, under the terms of the enclosed treaty negotiated by Governor Gayoso, the Chickasaws and Choctaws pledged friendship with Spain and ceded to her the land on which Fort Nogales was situated in return for gifts worth about $2,000 (Jack D. L. Holmes, Gayoso: The Life of a Spanish Governor in the Mississippi Valley, 1789-1799 [Baton Rouge, 1965], 137-8, 145-50).

TJ submitted the above letter and enclosures, as well as the fourth letter of this date from Viar and Jaudenes with its enclosures, to the President on 18 May 1793 and formally replied to the Spanish agents three days later, the day after the President returned the documents (Washington, Journal, 143, 144; TJ to Viar and Jaudenes, 21 May 1793).

From Josef de Jaudenes and Josef Ignacio de Viar

MUI SEÑOR NUESTRO   Philadelphia 12. de Mayo de 1793.

Adjuntas tenemos la honrra de pasar à manos de V.S. Copias de una Carta escrita por el Governador de Sn. Agustin à Dn. Diego Seagrove incluyendole la de un Memorial que se le presento por cinco habitantes de aquella Plaza quexandose de que haviendoseles huido cinco Esclavos de su propriedad al Estado de Georgia, se los han detenido en dicho Estado: Asimismo và à continuacion Copia de algunos pasos que se tomaron en el particular, y tambien la respuesta de Don Diego Seagrove al mencionado Governador.

Se servirà V.S. informar de todo al Presidente de los Estados Unidos, quien no dudamos tendrà à bien dar las ordenes correspondientes para que no se detengan por el Estado de Georgia à los Esclavos en question, ni à otro alguno que pasase de las Posesiones del Rey, pues lo contrario serà faltar à la reciproca correspondencia que tan justamente reclama la escrupulosidad con que se conduce el Governador de Sn. Agustin sobre este, y demas puntos, y darà motivo à que en lo venidero siga dicho Governador el exemplo del Estado de Georgia su vecino. Nos ofrecemos como siempre à la obediencia de V.S. con las veras de la mas sincera estimacion, y respeto, con que somos Señor Los mas obedtes. y humdes. Servs. Q.B.L.M. de V.S.

JOSEF DE JAUDENES   JOSEF IGNACIO DE VIAR

EDITORS' TRANSLATION

OUR VERY DEAR SIR   Philadelphia 12 May 1793
We have the honor to put into your hands copies, enclosed, of a letter written by the Governor of St. Augustine to Mr. James Seagrove, including the copy of a memorandum presented to him by five residents of that place complaining that five slaves of theirs that had escaped to the State of Georgia had been detained in that state: likewise, attached to that document is the copy of certain steps that were taken regarding the matter, as well as Mr. James Seagrove's answer to the aforementioned Governor.

Please be so kind as to pass all this information to the President of the United States, who we do not doubt will gladly issue the pertinent orders not to detain the slaves in question or any other person who might cross from the King's possessions, for not to do so would be to disregard the principle of reciprocity that so rightly has invoked the scrupulousness with which the Governor of St. Augustine has conducted himself in this and other matters, and it would give grounds in the future for the said Governor to follow the example of his neighbor the State of Georgia. We place ourselves as always at your disposal, with the most sincere expressions of esteem and respect, as we remain, Sir, your most obedient and humble servants. Respectfully yours,

JOSEF DE JAUDENES   JOSEF IGNACIO DE VIAR

RC (DNA: RG 59, NL); in Jaudenes's hand, signed by Jaudenes and Viar; at foot of text: "Sor. dn. Thomas Jefferson &ca."; endorsed by TJ as received 14 May 1793 and so recorded in SJL. Tr (AHN: Papeles de Estado, legajo 3895); attested by Jaudenes and Viar. PrC of another Tr (DLC); in a clerk's hand. Enclosures: (1) Governor Juan Nepomuceno de Quesada to James Seagrove, St. Augustine, 20 Feb. 1793, stating that he was enclosing a petition from Spanish subjects in his jurisdiction concerning five slaves legally belonging to them who are detained in Georgia, and three papers by Leonard Marbury concerning them; that Marbury's position concerning the slave belonging to Mrs. Marshall was of no force in the case, and that his deposition with regard to the slave originally owned by Mr. Gibbons was no more satisfactory, for property declared by the British government to be legitimate spoils of the late war and purchased as such by a Spaniard cannot be reclaimed by the original owner; that three of the slaves were in the possession of Richard Lake in Frederica, Glynn County, Georgia, and that he has been informed by Richard Lang, who last year had been commissioned by their owners to bring them back from Georgia, that he thought two of the slaves were being concealed by citizens of Frederica, though he did not know the whereabouts of a third; that Seagrove must bring about the return of all these slaves in order to maintain the scrupulous reciprocity required by their agreement on this issue; that failure to do so will lead him to detain fugitive slaves from their state until he receives instructions from his government or ascertains the attitude of the United States government through the king's agents in Philadelphia; and that he had recently ordered the return of a slave offered for sale here, apparently by a Georgian, which slave claimed that he had run away last year from his true owner, General Barnwell of South Carolina. (2) Memorial of Domingo Martinely, Juan Bauló, Manuel Solana, Lorenzo Llanes, and Manuel Marshal of St. Augustine to Quesada, 31 Jan. 1793, asking Quesada to order the return of their respective slaves, who fled to Georgia and have not been returned, despite the memorialists' claims and Quesada's representation, and who are reportedly in Frederica, most of them in Richard Lake's possession. (3) Three papers by Leonard Marbury, Justice of the Peace in Glynn County, Georgia, the first, dated 22 Aug. 1792, authorizing Richard Lang to call upon all persons for assistance in seizing and bringing before him or another magistrate certain slaves in the county who had fled from their owners in East Florida, at the same time informing their possessors to appear and give cause, if any, why they should not be returned; the second, dated 25 Aug. 1792, ordering Martin Palmer to take any slaves, particularly three named in No. 2, into custody and deliver them to Lang, if Lang satisfied the legal rights of their possessors; and the third, dated 25 Aug. 1792, advising Lang that the slave he claimed as the property of Mrs. Marshall was being held by the chief constable of Glynn County because of Marbury's claim against another person, that another slave appeared to be the property of her original owner, Mr. Gibbons, from whom she had been taken by a posse to Florida, but that if this ownership was not established he would do all in his power to return her to Mr. Solana. (4) Seagrove to Quesada, St. Marys, 4 Mch. 1793, stating that he would bring Quesada's demand for the return of the fugitive slaves to the attention of the governments of Georgia and the United States and communicate to him in due course the results of his efforts to obtain justice and preserve harmony with Spain (Trs in DNA: RG 59, NL, in Spanish, attested by Jaudenes and Viar; PrCs of other Trs in DLC, in a clerk's hand). Enclosed in TJ to Edward Telfair, 22 May 1793.

TJ laid this and the next letter from Jaudenes and Viar on the subject of slaves stolen from East Florida by residents of Georgia before the President on 21 May 1793 with his own reply to the Spanish agents (Washington, *Journal*, 145-6; TJ to Viar and Jaudenes, 21 May 1793). On the following day TJ also referred both letters to the governor of Georgia (TJ to Edward Telfair, 22 May 1793). For the agreement on the rendition of fugitive slaves between Governor Quesada of East Florida and James Seagrove, the United States agent to the Creeks, which provided the basis for the Spanish demand for the return of the five slaves mentioned above, see enclosures to TJ to the Governors of Georgia and South Carolina, 15 Dec. 1791.

From Josef de Jaudenes and Josef Ignacio de Viar

MUI SEÑOR NUESTRO   Philadelphia 12. de Mayo de 1793.

La Carta escrita por el Procurador general del Estado de Georgia Don Juan Young Noel al Secretario del Govierno de Sn. Agustin Don Carlos Howard (de que tenemos la honrra de pasar à V.S. adjunta una Copia baxo el No. 1.) impondrà à V.S. de los pasos que se tomaron en la Georgia con los complices en el robo de los cinco Esclavos pertenecientes à Vasallos de S.M.C.; pero como por dicha Carta aparece que se dexò pasar la primera Junta del tribunal superior sin resolver conclusivamente sobre el objeto, y ès de temer que en la otra Junta de dicho tribunal que debe haverse celebrado el 15. de Enero proximo pasado, se haya tomado por efugio para no determinar el no haverse presentado el querellante, ô su apoderado; pedimos à V.S. con este motivo se sirva informar nuevamente al Presidente de los Estados Unidos sobre este objeto para que tenga à bien dar las ordenes que Juzgase convenientes à fin de que no se dilate la desicion de la causa, y la restitucion consequente de los Esclavos robados por habitantes del Estado de Georgia à Vasallos de S.M., con la competente recompensa por los graves perjuicios causados à sus verdaderos Dueños.

A maior abundamiento pasamos à V.S. tambien copia baxo el No. 2. de la respuesta que dio el mencionado Dn. Carlos Howard à Dn. Juan Young Noel. Nos reiteramos de V.S. con el mas sincero afecto, y veneracion Señor Los mas obedtes. y humdes. servs. Q.B.L.M. de V.S.

JOSEF DE JAUDENES   JOSEF IGNACIO DE VIAR

EDITORS' TRANSLATION

OUR VERY DEAR SIR   Philadelphia 12 May 1793

The letter written by the Attorney General of the State of Georgia, Mr. John Young Noel, to the Secretary of the government of St. Augustine, Mr. Carlos Howard (of which we have the honor to enclose a copy for you under No. 1), will inform you of the steps that were taken in Georgia regarding those involved in the theft of the five slaves belonging to vassals of His Catholic Majesty; but since it appears from said letter that the first session of the supreme court was allowed to pass without resolving the matter conclusively, and it is to be feared that in the next session of the said court, which was to have taken place the 15th of January last, the fact that neither the plaintiff nor his representative appeared may have served as a subterfuge for not reaching a decision, we for this reason beg you once more kindly to inform the President of the United States regarding this matter, so that he may see fit to issue such orders as he deems appropriate with the object of not further delaying a decision in the case and of returning the slaves stolen by inhabitants of the State of Georgia from His Majesty's vassals, together with adequate recompense for the serious damages inflicted upon their true owners.

Further, we transmit to you also a copy under No. 2 of the answer given by the aforesaid Mr. Carlos Howard to Mr. John Young Noel. We assure you again of our most sincere regard and respect, Sir, your most obedient and humble servants JOSEF DE JAUDENES JOSEF IGNACIO DE VIAR

RC (DNA: RG 59, NL); in Jaudenes's hand, signed by Jaudenes and Viar; at foot of text: "Sor. Dn. Thomas Jefferson &ca."; endorsed by TJ as received 14 May 1793 and so recorded in SJL. Tr (AHN: Papeles de Estado, legajo 3895); attested by Jaudenes and Viar. PrC of another Tr (DLC); in a clerk's hand. Enclosures: (1) John Young Noel to Carlos Howard, Savannah, 28 Dec. 1792, stating that he was writing by instruction of Governor Telfair to reveal the steps being taken to bring to trial David Rees and others accused of taking slaves owned by a resident of East Florida and bringing them to Georgia; that as a result of the governor's representation the Georgia department of justice had the accused men taken into custody and brought to trial before the Liberty County Superior Court; that for want of time the court postponed the trial until its next session beginning 15 Jan. 1793; that the aggrieved party or a representative must be present and produce witnesses because written depositions do not constitute proof in criminal cases; and that the state's judicial and executive branches are determined to investigate the matter fully and do everything allowed by the law to render justice. (2) Howard to Noel, St. Augustine, 20 Mch. 1793, stating that he received Noel's abovementioned letter on 16 Feb. 1793 and communicated it to Governor Quesada; that even if this letter had been delivered promptly it would not have

given John Blackwood time enough to appear before the Liberty County court by 15 Jan.; that the letter portrayed David Rees as the main culprit, when in fact Blackwood's and Quesada's memorandums to the governor of Georgia showed that Rees, a justice of the peace, and William Irwin were merely accomplices of Thomas Harrison; that Quesada reiterated the demand made in that memorandum for the return of the five slaves and was still willing to leave to Georgia authorities the responsibility for punishing those who had taken them from East Florida; that TJ had informed the king's ministers at the Congress on 3 July 1792 that he had referred this matter to the governor of Georgia and would notify them of the result; and that Noel's letter and this reply would be sent to those ministers so that the issue could be settled in Philadelphia (Trs in DNA: RG 59, NL, in Spanish, attested by Jaudenes and Viar; PrCs of other Trs in DLC, in a clerk's hand). Enclosed in TJ to Edward Telfair, 22 May 1793.

For TJ's response to this letter, see note to preceding document. For further information on the theft of the five slaves belonging to John Blackwood of East Florida by Thomas Harrison and other Georgians, see Viar and Jaudenes to TJ, 26 June 1792; TJ to Edward Telfair, 3 July 1792; and TJ to Viar and Jaudenes, 3 July 1792.

From Josef de Jaudenes and Josef Ignacio de Viar

MUI SEÑOR NUESTRO Philadelphia 12. de Mayo de 1793.

Acavamos de recivir varios avisos del Governador de Sn. Agustin relativos à la disposicion que prevalece actualmente entre los Indios Creekes, las atrosidades que han cometido estos ultimamente, y otras noticias que aclaran bastante la conducta amistosa, y pacifica hacia los Americanos, è Indios que se desea seguir de parte de nuestro govierno, y la mui diferente que observa el Superintendente de los Estados Unidos Don Diego Seagrove hacia los Españoles, y dichos Salvages.

De todos nos hà parecido oportuno pasar Copias à V.S. con el fin de que se entere el Presidente de los Estados Unidos de sus contenidos, y convencerle al mismo tiempo del interes que tomamos en todo quanto puede contribuir à la conservacion de la buena harmonia, y perfecta amistad que felizmente reina entre España, y los Estados Unidos. Tenemos la honrra de subscrivirnos à la disposicion de V.S. con la mas sincera voluntad y sumo respeto, Señor Los mas obedtes., y humdes. servs. Q.B.L.M. de V.S.   JOSEF DE JAUDENES   JOSEF IGNACIO DE VIAR

EDITORS'   TRANSLATION

OUR VERY DEAR SIR   Philadelphia 12 May 1793
We have just received several communications from the Governor of St. Augustine concerning the situation prevailing at present among the Creek Indians, the atrocities these Indians have committed recently, and other pieces of information that do much to explain the peaceful and friendly behavior our government desires to follow towards the Americans and Indians, and the very different behavior observed by the United States Superintendent, Mr. James Seagrove, towards the Spaniards and those savages.

It has seemed to us appropriate to forward copies of all these communications to you with the object of informing the President of the United States of their contents, and of convincing him, at the same time, of the interest we take in everything that can contribute to maintaining the good harmony and perfect friendship that happily reigns between Spain and the United States. We have the honor of placing ourselves at your disposition with our best will and complete respect, Sir, your most obedient and humble servants. Respectfully yours,
JOSEF DE JAUDENES   JOSEF IGNACIO DE VIAR

RC (DNA: RG 59, NL); in Viar's hand, signed by Jaudenes and Viar; at foot of text: "Sor. Dn. Thomas Jefferson &ca."; endorsed by TJ as received 14 May 1793 and so recorded in SJL. Tr (AHN: Papeles de Estado, legajo 3895); attested by Jaudenes and Viar. Enclosures: (1) A Reliable Person of the Creek Nation to Governor Juan Nepomuceno de Quesada, St. Marys River, 18 Feb. 1793, stating that, according to Mr. Fowler, at the beginning of the month an Indian in Coweta threw at the feet of John M. Holmes, James Seagrove's deputy, the scalp of a man he had found on the Creek side of the boundary along the Oconee; that Fowler witnessed nine Shawnee chiefs and a white man at Coweta attempt to persuade the Creeks to make war on the Americans, but the Creeks deferred making a decision until the full moon; that Fowler also saw Upper and Lower Creeks returning every day from Cumberland and Kentucky with horses, slaves, and scalps; that the writer himself had recently seen several Indians seemingly displeased with the boundary drawn in St. Marys; and that the Indians charged that the old chief Maletkie had accepted bribes to allow American surveyors to draw the boundary for the Treaty of New York as they wished. (2) Same to same, 13 Mch. 1793, describing attacks the previous evening by a party of ten young braves on Robert Seagrove's store at the head of the St. Marys and on Gascoigne's depot nearby, as well as one the same night by another party of ten young braves on James Cashen's depot on the Satilla. (3) Quesada to A Reliable Person of the Creek Nation, St. Augustine, 16 Mch. 1793, stating that he regretted these Indian attacks on Americans;

that steps should be taken to allay the resultant fears of Spanish subjects; that American refugees from Indian cruelty should be welcomed in East Florida but kept away from the St. Marys; and that he would respond to any Indian complaints by pointing out that Indians rightly defended with zeal any white man who took refuge with them. (4) A Reliable Person of the Creek Nation to Quesada, 19 Mch. 1793, stating that the Indians on the Satilla had attacked three families on their way to East Florida, not Cashen's store; that James Seagrove had behaved cowardly while in pursuit of the offending Indians and Seagrove's men had promised to make this public in a Savannah newspaper; that Seagrove sold for private profit the goods Congress sent him for the Indians; that Seagrove probably incited the Indians to attack Panton, Leslie & Company and had ordered a letter to be published blaming the Spanish for the Indian attacks; that Seagrove had become highly unpopular because of his rough methods in carrying out the Treaty of New York; and that American refugees would be assisted according to Quesada's instructions; with postscript of 20 Mch. 1793 advising that he has just learned that Indians were murdering and raiding all along the Georgia frontier. (5) Quesada to A Reliable Person of the Creek Nation, 22 Mch. 1793, stating that there was no truth to the charge that the government of East Florida had encouraged the Indians to attack the Georgians and that the world would soon be convinced of a certain person's responsibility for this calamity; that it was unwise to cross the St. Marys; and that American refugees were still to be received. (6) A Reliable Person of the Creek Nation to Quesada, 28 Mch. 1793, stating that thirteen Shawnee chiefs were conferring with the Creeks in an effort to make them declare war against the Americans immediately; that squads had been sent to different parts of Georgia in quest of booty and horsemen; that a messenger sent to this town about eighteen or twenty days ago by Timothy Barnes, James Seagrove's deputy, had probably been killed by the same Indians who sacked in Satilla; that two of Cashen's employees had just gone to the Creeks with a load of goods; that Alexander McGillivray died two months ago in Pensacola at Panton's house; and that he would welcome American refugees. (7) Same to same, 8 Apr. 1793, stating that the Creeks were divided over war and peace; that since his last letter murders and robberies had been committed on the Altamaha, with all the stores on it having been looted; that Cashen's employees reported that the Creeks were at odds with the Choctaws and Chickasaws and that three Creek towns had united unanimously with the Shawnees; that Juan Canard could not convince the Creeks that the war was unjust; that James Seagrove had been invited to appear before the Creek nation and had received an order that Lachua chief Thomas Pain should keep his people in their area; and that rumors of an increase in the number of savages between the St. Marys and the Satilla seemed true because Indians had crossed over to Georgia eight miles from Seagrove's store. (8) Same to same, 20 Apr. 1793, stating that since his last letter twenty-five or thirty Indians, probably from Lachua, came to Mac-Girtt's ford apparently to move on to the Altamaha; and that since Indians moved through East Florida on their expeditions against Georgia, Quesada should ask the chiefs in St. Augustine to instruct their braves to keep to the established roads and settlements on the St. Marys, so as to avoid destruction of the few cattle owned by Spanish subjects along the river, reduce American distrust of the government of East Florida, and prevent the Indians from learning that Americans were routinely informed of their movements by East Floridians. (9) Declaration of James Dearment to Quesada, St. Augustine, 18 Apr. 1793, attesting to the veracity of his three attached and undated reports, the first of which stated that he had been informed by white and red men that the Shawnees had visited the Creeks to remind them of the alliance the two tribes had concluded at Fuguebatche in 1786, to argue that the Creeks were impoverishing themselves through land cessions to the United States, and to urge that these cessions contravened the 1786 agreement between the two tribes, and that it was believed that several Creek towns would adopt the northern accord in February after their hunts; the second of which stated that, according to an important Indian named Fuckfuloke, the Creeks at a recent treaty signing in St. Marys with James Seagrove had responded to Seagrove's denigration of the Spaniards by praising them for being peaceful where they settled, generous with presents for Indians, and not covetous of Indian lands, and cited Fuckfuloke as asserting that he would never visit Americans again because of a deceptive statement Seagrove made to him; and the third of which stated that, according to the half-breed Juan Canard, the Chiaha Indian excesses began after the Distant King learned from a woman from the Chattahoochee that some Creeks went to war against upper Georgia because northern savages had said that if the Creeks did not do this their northern friends would twist off their ears and noses and regard them as old men (Trs in DNA: RG 59, NL, in Spanish, in Viar's hand, attested by Jaudenes and Viar; Trs in AHN: Papeles de Estado, legajo 3895; in Viar's hand, attested by Jaudenes and Viar).

Apparently unknown to Jaudenes and Viar, Governor Quesada's carefully disguised correspondent, far from being a Creek Indian, was in fact John Forrester, a district alcalde who at the time of the resumption of the Creek attacks on Georgia was in the process of closing a trading post on the St. Marys River that he had operated on behalf of Panton, Leslie & Company, the powerful mercantile firm that controlled Spanish trade with the Southern Indians (Coker and Watson, *Indian Traders*, 32, 190).

For TJ's immediate response to this letter, see note to the first letter from Viar and Jaudenes of this date. The Washington administration's reaction to the outbreak of hostilities between elements of the Creek nation and Georgia is set forth in Cabinet Opinion on the Creek Indians and Georgia, 29 May 1793. For an analysis of the origins of the Creek attacks on Georgia, which emphasizes the importance of Shawnee promises of British assistance to the Creeks and the wanton intrusion on Creek lands of Georgians seeking game for themselves and pasturage for their cattle and horses, see Randolph C. Downes, "Creek-American Relations, 1790-1795," JSH, VIII (1942), 356-63. See also same, "Creek-American Relations, 1782-1790," *Georgia Historical Quarterly*, XXI (1937), 142-84, for a discussion of the longstanding conflict between the Creeks and Georgia frontiersmen.

Note on the Public Debt

May. 12. Lear called on me to-day. Speaking of the lowness of stocks (16/) I observed it was a pity we had not money to buy on publick account.—He said yes, and that it was the more provoking as 2 millions had been borrowed for that purpose and drawn over here, and yet were not here. That he had no doubt those would take notice of the circumstance whose duty it was to do so.—I suppose he must mean the President.

MS (DLC); entirely in TJ's hand; partially dated; written on same sheet as "Anas" entries for 6 and 7 May 1793. Entry in SJPL: "[Notes] on money improperly drawn from Europe." Included in the "Anas."

To Martha Jefferson Randolph

My dear Martha   Philadelphia May. 12. 1793.

I have at length found time to copy Petit's list of the packages sent to Richmond. Tho' I have not heard of their arrival there, I take for granted they must be arrived. I inclose you the list wherein I have marked with an * the boxes which must remain at Richmond till they can be carried up by water, as to put them into a waggon would be a certain sacrifice of them. They are the Nos. 2. 5. 10. 18. 19. 22. 23. 25. 26. 27. 28. Such of the others as contain any thing that you think would be convenient immediately, you may perhaps find means of having brought up. As to the rest, they may lie till I can have waggons of my own or find some other oeconomical means of getting them up. In any way it will be expensive, many of the boxes being enormously large.—I got a person to write to Scotland for a mason and house-joiner for me. I learn that they were engaged, and only waited for a ship. They will be delivered at Richmond to the address of Mr. Brown. A person who is come here, and knows them personally, says they are fine characters, will be very useful to have on a farm; it is material therefore that they do not remain 24. hours in Richmond to be spoiled. I shall write to Mr. Brown to send them off instantly and shall be obliged to Mr. Randolph to have an eye to the same object. How to employ them will be the subject of consideration. It will be puzzling till my return. It is one of the great inconveniences I experience by having been persuaded by my friends[1] to defer carrying into execution my determination to retire. However when I see you, it will be never to part again. In the mean time my affairs must be a burthen to Mr. Randolph.—You have never informed me whether the box containing the servant's clothes, which were sent in December last, have been received. I am anxious to hear, because if it has not, I will prosecute the captain.—Maria's brain is hard at work to squeeze out a letter for Mr. Randolph. She has been scribbling and rubbing out these three hours, and this moment exclaimed 'I do not think I shall get a letter made out to-day.'—We shall see how her labours will end. She wonders you do not write to her. So do I. Present me most affectionately to Mr. Randolph and be assured of my unceasing love to yourself. Kiss the dear little ones for me. Yours &c.

Th: Jefferson

RC (NNP); at foot of first page: "Mrs. Randolph"; endorsed by Mrs. Randolph. PrC (ViU: Edgehill-Randolph Papers); second page only. Tr (MHi); 19th-century copy.

The person TJ got to write to scotland was probably James Traquair (see Memorandum on Traquair, 5 Dec. 1792).

[1] Preceding three words interlined.

Adrien Petit's List of Packages Sent to Richmond

[ca. 12 May 1793]

No. 1. deux tables de la bibliotheque
plusieurs petites caisses de verre
12. rechauds argentés.

  *2. 4. bustes de terre cuite, & 3. pieds pour les bustes.

   3. une petite table ronde [à trois fins.]
2 petites tables quarrés. [Pembroke.]
plusieurs pieds de table.
deux presses. [for cutting paper]
le dessus du pié du Compas pour le telescope.

   4. le poele de la salle à manger
une partie de petit poele et des tuyaux [. . .]

 *5. 4 petites caisses. viz. 1 de petite figure qui etoit dans [le] salon, et son
verre
2. de verreries
1. de plusieurs ferments de physique.

   6. une caisse contenant 5. petites caisses. viz
3. de verres de physique
1. de 4 sceaux argentés
4. moules à glace.
4. croix plaqués
un petit sucriere.
12 moules à chocolat—une petite sonnette.
1. deux bras de cheminée dorés.
une moule à Macaroni
un petit rechaud à esprit de vin.
un chandelier double
deux petites porte-chandelles du petit pupitre.

   7. une grande caisse contenant
un Sopha. [ses?] 2 [oreillers son?] coussin. table de nuit
les queues du Compas pour le telescope.
1. petite caisse de verres de physique.
1. petite table pour se laver la figure.
un petit bois de lit [du Moustier's]
2 morceaux des petits tables de marbre.
un petit marche-pied. —une bassinoir.
plusieurs tuyaux de poele.
une fontaine d'etain avec sa cuvette.
un petit paquet de garniture des flambeaux de Mademoiselle.—un
vieux matelas.

   8. 5. caisses de bougie verte. deux pieds des poeles.

   9. une grande caisse contenant l'Ottomane de votre bibliotheque
votre petite necessaire rempli de cartons.
une presse—dont sa boete entourée de drap. [copyg press.]
deux tables.—une grande carte de geographie
un Matelas.

 *10. le dessus de marbre de la Commode de la chambre à coucher.
le marbre de la grande table.—une Console en marbre.

11. Caisse contenant un petit poele pour l'Alembique et plusieurs tuyaux de poele.
12. un petit barrique rempli d'un parti de l'Alembique.
13. une caisse de tableaux qui etoient dans la bibliotheque, et autres de la salle a manger.
14. une grande caisse des tableaux du Salon.
15. une caisse des tableaux de la salle à manger.
16. une caisse de tableaux.
17. une caisse de tableaux.
*18. une caisse de plusieurs tableaux celui de Louis XVI. et celui de Monsieur avec leurs verres. [that done by Williams in crayons]
*19. une caisse de 4. glaces. [chimney glasses]
20. une poele et plusieurs poeles à frire.
21. une malle rempli d'habits
*22. une caisse contenant.

    5. [petites] caisses. viz. une du verre de la machine de votre lit.— une des verres de physique de votre lit.—une de huit flambeaux & deux girandoles—une d'une fontaine á thé plaquée et 2. flambeaux—une des 2 pieds des machine & plusieurs autres petites choses.

*23. une caisse.—2 pieds de buste—une boéte d'acajou avec une machine qui est la boule du monde & autres petites choses.
24. un forté piano [viz. the Spinet]
*25. une grande glace.
*26. une grande glace.
*27. une glace à demi-ovale.
*28. glaces. [round]
29. une grande caisse rempli de plusieurs tableaux du salon et celui du lit de Monsieur.
30. une poele, et les plaques de la cheminée de Monsieur.
31. to 41. deux chaises dans chaque.
42. [un] fauteuil.
43. une grande caisse rempli de tableaux.
44. le tour c'est a dire[1] les planches rondes. caisse de[2] Cartes qui etoit sur deux tretteaux.
45. Casseroles. une presse. [the great copying press.]
46. le Side-board et une caisse.
47. [la com]mode et les jalousies, et un bois-de-lit.
48. [le dessu]s du buffet rempli de cartons.
49. le bas du buffet.
50. une caisse rempli de tableaux.
51 [. . .] rempli d'une partie du tour, une carte,[3] des barres du lit de Monsr. Eppes.

PrC of Tr (ViU: McGregor Library); undated; consists of two pages entirely in TJ's hand, with asterisks and two words added in ink; badly faded in part and torn at folds and edges, resulting in the partial loss of several lines; brackets editorially supplied except for French words describing package No. 3 and English words throughout; printed literally.

[1] Preceding three words interlined.
[2] Preceding two words interlined.
[3] Preceding two words added or enhanced in ink.

From James Currie

Hble. Sir   Richmond May. 13th. 1793

From the last letter I had the honor of receiving from you I was informed that my suit vs. Griffin had lain by from the Gentleman to whom it was formerly intrusted having left off the practice of the Law and that it would be determined at the april term. I have every thing to hope from your friendly attention to the business and will be glad as soon as convenient to be informed of its Situation if you please. I have taken the liberty to inclose a letter to my friend Mr. Wm. McKenzie, (who is connected with Swanwick & Coy.) upon a very particular business and shall hold myself under a great Obligation; if you will contrive it him as soon as possible after receiving it. Your Old friend Colo. T. M. Randolph has been dangerously ill, with a complicated Complaint of Gout Dropsy and Asthma but contrary to every expectation of mine he is seemingly in a fair way of recovery. Mr. T. Randolph and his Lady and children have been there during his illness, all very well. We have no news here that can in the least entertain you. I therefore, (with every sentiment of respectfull regard & the highest esteem) subscribe myself Sir yr most Obt Hble Servt   JAS. CURRIE

RC (MHi); endorsed by TJ as received 18 May 1793 and so recorded in SJL. Enclosure not found.

From Robert Gamble

Sir   Richmond May 13. 1793

I had this honor the 10th. inst. since which Mr. N. Anderson has informed me he has wrote you on the same subject—And solicits your patronage, provided the Agency is an object worth attention, but if it will only be a trifling matter, he does not wish to deprive me of a trifle. He mentioned his *desire to me*, and urged as a motive, Why I ought to let him Join in the business of purchasing and shipping supplies to France—That he had two American Vessells ready to Load. As I have *of my own*, as much Flour as would Complete both Cargoes without a moments delay, The oportunity of two ships to Carry provisions to our suffering allies, was to my mind a desireable acquisition, But when on enquiry I am informed that those two Ships are the Powhatan and Hariet, both sent out from London for the express purpose of taking off two Cargoes of Tobacco, which is Consigned to Mr. Andersons friends there, and are actually loading—And No Ships till these are to make the Voyage, and probably return, *or not*, as Wm. Anderson & Co. thinks proper—I am astonished. The present moment was what I had in View. Two agents at this place can do no more than *one*—We should only be in each others way, and probably rivals to raise the Flour, &c. in price. I forbear to give any opinion of what might be construed as the motives of my friend whom I respect. I troubled you on the occasion as a Virginian and friend to Human liberty, And having Trespassed, on your time, the reasons which occurs in this letter will apologize for this second intrusion. I can only *repeat* that no person here will execute Such a commission (as is presumeable will be given to some person here) with more Zeal and oeconomy, than I will endeavor to do; I have as much in my power as my Neighbor, And if Government will advance the Money in whole or in part, And Guarantee Mr. Genets Bills, so as to give them a credit, all will be then wanting, *is a few Vessells* to obtain from this River handsome Aid in provisions &c. for Our friends.

Having established at Norfolk and Alexandria Correspondants of ability and integrity all the supplies from Virginia can with promptness be procured—Norfolk and Suffolk, is the place for Naval stores.

Did I think it necessary on this occasion I would have Wrote to the President and obtained from Gentlemen of the highest responsibility letters of Assurance to him and you. But at this eventful Moment when the Minds of all and especially *His* must be deeply engaged, I did not wish to intrude a matter that in Some respects are of a secular nature *when* he can have little liesure for things of a private tendency. Therefore having taken the liberty with you, *you will* if Necessary Mention me to the President. If any security is required I named some Gentlemen to you, And can add to the Number. I confide in your disposition *to oblige*, and as much as Government can do Will I trust meet your *Zealous Concurrence*. A Measure of this kind will give relief abroad— And add fresh Motives to Industry amongst our Virginia farmers *at home*. I am with highest sentiments of respect Your Mo. Obt Hu St

RO. GAMBLE

RC (DLC); at foot of text: "Mr. Jefferson"; endorsed by TJ as received 18 May 1793 and so recorded in SJL.

From Alexander Hamilton

Philadelphia May 8. [i.e. 13] 1793.

The Secretary of the Treasury has the honor to transmit, for the information of the Secretary of State, the Copy of a letter of the 23rd. of April last from the Collector of the District of Nantucket to the Register of the Treasury. Copies of the declarations on the Registers, therein referred to, are also transmitted.   A HAMILTON

RC (DLC); in a clerk's hand, signed by Hamilton; endorsed by TJ as received 13 May 1793 and so recorded in SJL. Enclosures: (1) Joseph Nourse to Hamilton, Treasury Department, Register's Office, 10 May 1793, enclosing certified copies of Nos. 2-4 (RC in DLC). (2) Stephen Hussey to Nourse, Collector's Office, District of Nantucket, 23 Apr. 1793, enclosing the registers of the *Beaver* and the *Washington*, which had been returned to his office for cancellation because of the Spanish declarations written on the back of them; stating that the captain of the Spanish frigate *Hare*, which encountered the *Beaver*, Captain Paul Worth, on a whaling voyage twelve leagues off the coast of Peru in thirteen degrees latitude, informed Worth that he had no right to sail in these waters because he lacked a passport from the Spanish king and wrote a declaration in Spanish on the back of the *Beaver*'s register that it was subject to seizure, but after ascertaining that it was not on a trading voyage released the ship and warned Worth to leave the Peruvian coast or risk the loss of the ship as a prize to another armed Spanish vessel; reporting that upon putting into Lima in distress because of the sickness of the crew and the lack of supplies Worth was ordered by a Spanish officer to leave port as soon as possible for want of a passport from the king; and concluding that these circumstances showed that participation in "the Whale Fishery in the Southern Ocean must be lost to American Vessels unless some Credentials can be obtaind sufficient to protect them against Insults and Injuries from Spanish armed vessels" (Tr in DLC; in Nourse's hand and attested by him; notation by TJ next to Hussey's name: "Collector of the district of Nantucket"). (3) Ship Register, issued at Sherbourne, Nantucket County, 3 Sep. 1791, to the *Washington*, Captain George Bunker, with

declaration on verso in Spanish by Nicolas Lobato, Callao, 18 July 1792, stating that he had informed Bunker, whose ship had taken on supplies at this port the previous night, that navigating this sea was prohibited and that any Spanish warship may seize any ship found therein. (4) Ship Register issued at Sherbourne, Nantucket County, 7 Oct. 1791, to the *Beaver*, Captain Paul Worth, with declaration on verso in Spanish by Tomas Geraldino, on board the *Hare*, 10 July 1792, stating that he had informed Worth, whose ship had taken in 900 of an intended 1,300 barrels of oil on a whaling voyage, that Spain forbade all nations to navigate or fish in these seas and that his ship would be detained and confiscated if he did not leave this coast; and another by Luis Lasqueti, Callao, 4 Aug. 1792, stating that the *Beaver* was not allowed to enter this port, there being no necessity for it, and that he had informed Worth that his ship may be detained by any Spanish warship in this sea (Trs in DLC: TJ Papers, 85: 14763-6; with accompanying English translations of Spanish declarations, all attested by Nourse).

Hamilton could not have written this letter before 10 May, when Nourse sent him the enclosures from Hussey, and it seems more likely that he actually wrote it on the 13th, the day TJ received it.

Although the *Beaver* and the *Washington* were the first American whaling ships to venture into the Pacific, TJ and Hamilton evidently took no further action on Stephen Hussey's plea for federal intervention to protect American whalers from Spanish interference (Edouard A. Stackpole, *Whales & Destiny: The Rivalry between America, France, and Britain for Control of the Southern Whale Fishery, 1785-1825* [Amherst, Mass., 1972], 130).

Memorandum from Alexander Hamilton and Edmund Randolph

[ca. 13-15 May 1793]

A Perhaps the Secretary of State, revising the expression of this member of the sentence, will find terms to express his idea still more clearly and may avoid the use of a word of doubtful propriety "Contraventions"

B "but be attentive"

C "mere" to be omitted

D Considering that this Letter[1] will probably become a matter of publicity to the world is it necessary to be so strong?
Would not the following suffice as a substitute?
"but our unwillingness to believe that the French Nation could be wanting in respect or friendship to us upon any occasion suspends our assent to and conclusions upon these statements 'till further evidence."   It will be observed that the words "conclusions upon" are proposed to be added to indicate that some further measure is contemplated, conformably to the declaration to Mr. Hammond [. . .][2] measures will be taken [. . .][3] may be in lieu of General Knox's amendment

E Suppose the words "bay of" were omitted—

F "Expectation" is proposed to be substituted to "*desire*"

G For the sentence between [ ][4]   It is proposed to substitute this—
"They consider the rigorous exercise of that virtue as the surest means of preserving perfect harmony between the U States and the Powers at War"

A HAMILTON
EDM: RANDOLPH

MS (DLC: TJ Papers, 95: 16289); in Hamilton's hand, signed by Hamilton and Randolph; undated; part of two lines torn away; endorsed by TJ.

This document consists of observations by the Secretary of the Treasury and the Attorney General on a missing draft of TJ to Jean Baptiste Ternant, 15 May 1793. Their suggested revisions undoubtedly arose from a consideration of TJ's draft at some point during the Cabinet meetings held on 13, 14, and 15 May to discuss various complaints by George Hammond of French violations of American neutrality (Washington, *Journal*, 132, 137). For the revisions TJ made in response to these suggestions, insofar as they can be identified in the absence of the draft, see notes to TJ to Ternant, 15 May 1793.

[1] Word interlined.
[2] Estimated five words missing.
[3] Two or three words missing.
[4] Brackets in MS.

From Henry Lee

Sir   Richmond May 13th. 1793.

I do myself the honor to transmit to you a letter addressed to me by the British Consul residing at Norfolk with an Affidavit enclosed therein. The subject to which they relate will no doubt receive the Consideration of the President of the United States. I have the honor to be sir with the sentiments of the most perfect respect your ob: ser

HENRY LEE

RC (DNA: RG 59, LGS); in a clerk's hand, with complimentary close and signature by Lee; endorsed by TJ as received 18 May 1793 and so recorded in SJL. FC (Vi: Executive Letter Book). Enclosures: (1) John Hamilton to Lee, Norfolk, 5 May 1793, stating that several armed vessels cruising off the capes and in the bay under French colors but manned by British or American sailors have fired on vessels putting into this port in the last two days; that many merchant ships feared to sail from Hampton Roads lest they be captured; that it would be advisable to empower Commodore Taylor of the revenue cutter or someone else to arm and man his vessel in order to prevent further insults to the British and American flags by suspicious vessels off the capes or in the bay; that he was confident that the United States would adhere to a strict neutrality on this occasion and punish those who disturbed good relations with Great Britain; that British cruisers were expected to arrive very soon to protect British trade; and that he was enclosing the report of Captain Tucker, who has just arrived (RC in DNA: RG 59, LGS). (2) Affidavit of Henry Tucker, Norfolk, 5 May 1793, stating that on 29 Apr. 1793 the schooner *Eunice*, seventeen days out of New Providence under his command, was captured at 35° 50′ north latitude in 27 fathoms of water by the schooner *Sans Culotte*, a French privateer three days out of Charleston, armed with two four- and two three-pounders,

manned by seventeen Frenchmen and thirty Americans and Englishmen, officered entirely by Americans and Britons, except for Captain Jean Baptiste André Ferey and the boatswain, and owned by John Oper, an American citizen from Cambridge, Maryland; that after both ships moved within the Capes of Virginia and spent two days at Hawkins Hole near Hampton, the *Eunice* was sent to Baltimore or a nearby creek on 1 May with Oper as prize master, its name having been erased from the stern; that on the night of 2 May while "some distance above the light House" in Chesapeake Bay the *Sans Culotte* detained the brig *Union*, Captain Potter, which first described itself as a Bristol vessel but proved to be an American vessel with a British cargo; that Tucker and four of his crew were put aboard the brig after being paid part of their salaries; and that another privateer from Charleston under a Captain Connoley with a crew of fifty and four guns is also cruising off the Capes of Virginia (MS in same; signed by Tucker and witnessed by Hamilton).

TJ submitted this letter to the President on 21 May 1793 while obtaining his approval of TJ's response to Lee bearing that date (Washington, *Journal*, 146 and n, where Enclosure No. 1 is confused with Hamilton's 7 May 1793 letter to Governor Thomas Sim Lee, which the latter enclosed to TJ on 20 May 1793).

To James Madison

Th:J. to J. Mad.   [13 May 1793]

I wrote you on the 5th. covering an open letter to Colo. Monroe. Since that I have received yours of Apr. 29.—We are going on here in

the same spirit still. The Anglophobia has seised violently on three
members of our council. This sets almost every day on questions of
neutrality. H. produced the other day the draught of a letter from himself to the Collectors of the customs, giving them in charge to watch
over all proceedings in their districts contrary to the laws of neutrality
or tending to infract our peace with the belligerent powers, and particularly to observe if[1] vessels pierced for guns should be built, and to inform *him* of it. This was objected to 1. as setting up a system of espio-
nage, destructive of the peace of society. 2. transferring to the Treasury
Departmt. the conservation of the laws of neutrality and our peace with
foreign nations. 3. it was rather proposed to intimate to the judges that
the laws respecting neutrality being now come into activity, they should
charge the grand juries with the observance of them; these being constitutional and public informers, and the persons accused *knowing* of what
they should do, and having an opportunity of justifying themselves.
E.R. found out a hair to split, which, as always happens, became the
decision. H. is to write to the collectors of the customs, who are to convey their information to the Attornies of the districts, to whom E.R. is
to write to receive their information and proceed by indictment. The
clause respecting the building vessels pierced for guns was omitted. For
tho' 3. against 1. thought it would be a breach of neutrality, yet they
thought we might defer giving a public opinion on it as yet. Every thing
my dear Sir, now hangs on the opinion of a single person, and that the
most indecisive one I ever had to do business with. He always contrives
to agree in principle with one, but in conclusion with the other. Anglophobia, secret[2] Antigallomany, a federalisme outrée, and a present ease
in his circumstances not natural, have decided the complexion of our[3]
dispositions, and our proceedings towards the Conspirators against
human liberty and the Assertors of it, which is unjustifiable in principle,
in interest, and in respect to the wishes of our constituents. A manly
neutrality, claiming the liberal rights ascribed to that condition by the
very powers at war, was the part we should have taken, and would I
believe have given satisfaction to our allies. If any thing prevents it's
being a mere English neutrality, it will be that the penchant of the P. is
not that way, and above all, the ardent spirit of our constituents. The
line is now drawing so clearly as to shew, on one side, 1. the fashionable
circles of Phila., N. York, Boston and Charleston (natural aristocrats),[4]
2. merchants trading on British capitals. 3. paper men, (all the old tories
are found in some one of these three descriptions). On the other side are
1. merchants trading on their own capitals. 2. Irish merchants, 3.
tradesmen, mechanics, farmers and every other possible description of
our citizens.—Genest is not yet arrived tho' hourly expected.—I have
just heard that the workmen I had desired from Europe were engaged

and about to embark. Another strong motive for making me uneasy here. Adieu my dear Sir.

RC (DLC: Madison Papers); undated, but recorded under this date in SJL and so described in TJ to Madison, 19 May 1793; addressed: "Mr. Madison"; endorsed, probably by Madison: "—1793." PrC (DLC: TJ Papers, 85: 14790-1); with penciled notation by Nicholas P. Trist. Tr (DLC); 19th-century copy.

Madison's letter to TJ OF APR. 29. concerning "political sentiments of Va.," which is recorded in SJL as received from Orange on 8 May 1793, has not been found (Madison, *Papers*, xv, 11). For the Secretary of the Treasury's DRAUGHT OF A LETTER, see Notes on Alexander Hamilton and the Enforcement of Neutrality, 6 May 1793, and note. Edmund Randolph was the SINGLE PERSON TJ found INDECISIVE.

¹ TJ here canceled "armed."
² Word interlined.
³ TJ here canceled "proceedings."
⁴ Parenthetical phrase interlined.

To Sir John Temple

SIR   Philadelphia May 13. 1793.

I received from Mr. Beckley the inclosed commission with a request to have it recorded in my office, without giving you the trouble of coming to this place. This trouble may certainly be spared to you as being unnecessary, but it is our usage, where a nation has a minister here, to receive the Consular commissions through him only. If therefore you will be so good as to inclose your commission to Mr. Hammond, he will of course present it, and an Exequatur will be made out immediately. Not knowing whether Mr. Beckley would be in N. York, I have thought it better to return the commission to yourself directly, and have the honor to be Sir Your most obedt & most humble servt

TH: JEFFERSON

PrC (DLC); at foot of text: "Sr. John Temple." Tr (DLC); 19th-century copy. Enclosure: Sir John Temple's commission as British consul general for New York and New England, 8 Feb. 1793 (Tr in DNA: RG 59, NFC).

In March 1793, as part of a general reorganization of its consular service in America, the British government appointed Sir John Temple consul general for New York and New England and Phineas Bond consul general for the Middle and Southern states. Upon receipt of TJ's letter, Temple, who hitherto had been serving as British consul general for the United States, wrote a letter to George Hammond asking him to submit his new consular commission to the Secretary of State. As a result, the Department of State approved Temple's exequatur on 17 May 1793 (Exequatur for Temple, 17 May 1793, FC in DNA: RG 59, Exequaturs, with George Washington and TJ as signatory and countersignatory). See also Lord Grenville to Temple, 8 Mch. 1793, Temple to Bond, 10 May 1793, Temple to Hammond, 14 May 1793, Temple to Grenville, 18 May 1793, all in PRO: FO 5/2; Memorandum Book of the Department of State, 17 May 1793, DNA: RG 360, PCC; Washington, *Journal*, 142; Neel, *Phineas Bond*, 96-7.

From George Washington

May 13th. 1793.

The President requests that the Secretary of State will have the enclosed letter from the Governor of So. Carolina taken into consideration, with the other matters which are to be weighed.

RC (DLC); in the hand of Tobias Lear; endorsed by TJ as received 14 May 1793. Recorded in SJPL. Enclosure: William Moultrie to Washington, 26 Apr. 1793, expressing hope that the President would approve his decision to erect a few cannon to defend Charleston and asking for guidance in dealing with unspecified conflicting provisions in the treaties between the United States and some of the countries involved in the European war (RC in NjMoHP; in a clerk's hand, signed by Moultrie; endorsed as received 13 May 1793). Neither TJ nor Washington replied to Moultrie.

From George Washington

DEAR SIR   Philadelphia May 13th. 1793.

Sometime last fall I sent to Mr. Young transcripts of the accounts respecting the Agriculture of this Country, which I had collected from Gentlemen of the best information on this subject, with whom I was acquainted in the middle States, New York and Virginia.

The account which you had the goodness to draw up was among the number.

I have lately received from Mr. Young a letter in reply to mine which accompanied these accounts—in which he makes the observations and queries relative to the Virginia Statement, which you will find enclosed.

As I wish this matter to be brought before Mr. Young in as clear a light as the nature of it will admit—you will oblige me by giving, when convenient,[1] such answers to the queries and such solution of the difficulties stated by him as your knowledge of the Subject may enable you to do, that I may[2] give him the most satisfactory information in my power. I am always, with much truth & sincerity—Yr. Affecte Servt

GO: WASHINGTON

RC (DLC); at foot of text: "Mr. Jefferson." Dft (DLC: Washington Papers); in the hand of Tobias Lear; endorsed by Washington. FC (Lb in same); follows Dft. Recorded in SJL as received 14 May 1793.

Washington had written Arthur Young on 18-21 June 1792, not LAST FALL, enclosing the account TJ had HAD THE GOODNESS TO DRAW UP, as well as the other ACCOUNTS of American agriculture (Notes on Arthur

Young's Letter to George Washington, 18 June 1792, and note). For two related letters that the President wrote to the noted English agricultural reformer in the fall of 1792, see Fitzpatrick, *Writings*, XXXII, 192, 250-1.

[1] Preceding two words interlined in Dft in place of "at your leisure."

[2] In Dft Lear here wrote "⟨be able⟩ in my next letter to that Gentleman."

Extracts from Arthur Young to George Washington

Extract of a Letter From Arthur Young Esquire To The
President of the US. dated 17. Jan. 1793.

"Your information has thrown me affloat on the high-Seas. To analyse your Husbandry has the difficulty of a problem. I cannot understand it, and the more I know of it, the more surprising it appears. Is it possible that the Inhabitants of a great Continent not new settlers, who of course live only to hunt, to eat and to drink, can carry on farming and planting as a business, and yet never calculate the profit they make by *per centage* on their capital? Yet this seems to be the case."

After making observations on the Accounts from Bucks County, Pittsburgh and maryland he says—

Extract of a Letter From Arthur Young Esquire to The
President of the US. dated 17. Jan: 1793.

"The[1] Virginia calculation comes much nearest the point; but I can not admit it. It[2] reckons £60 a year increasing value of negroes, and £156 a year rise in the value of land. These articles may be fact in certain circumstances, but they will not do for comparisons, either with other States or with Europe. To have a considerable value invested in Slaves, is a hazardous capital; and there is no man who would not give £60 a year on 6000 acres[3] to change slaves to Cows and Sheep: he can not otherwise command labour and therefore must keep them; but the profit in any other light than labourers is inadmissible. As to the rise on lands it may be fair, but taking place equally perhaps in Europe or other States, it must not come into the account. During the last ten years land in England has risen $\frac{1}{3}$d. in value. Correcting then the Account from Virginia, it's[4] capital pays 11 per Cent. There are however many deductions to be made—as wear and tear of implements; Carriage; team; Seed; repairs of buildings; white servants, Overseers &c. These ought, as I conjecture, to amount to near £200 a year; which, if so, would reduce the profit in the gross to about 8 per Cent.

But I have a heavier objection than this and which bears upon the pith of the subject. How can be produced[5] annually 5000 bushels of wheat worth £750; by means of a Cattle product of only £125? I do not want to come to America to know that this is simply impossible. At the commencement of a term it may do; but how long will it last? This is the management that gives such products as 8 and 10 bushels an acre. Arable land can yield wheat only by means of Cattle and sheep. It is not dung that is wanted so much, as a change of products, and repose under grass, which is the soul of management; all cleaning and tillage to be given in the year that yields green winter food. In such a system you may produce by means of 40 oxen and 500 sheep, 5000 bushls. of wheat; and if you raise the oxen to 60 and the Sheep to 600, you may have so much more wheat. It is only by increasing Cattle that you can increase wheat *permanently*. £125 from Cattle, to £751 from wheat, would reduce the finest farm in the world to a caput mortuum that is to say, to 10 bs. an acre, which must be from a caput mortuum. I should however, be greatly obliged by an explanation[6] on these points.

This subject is that which is most in the dark—the *demand* for Cattle and Sheep products? The prices your Correspondents note are ample. I should desire no higher. It is the quantity to be sold that makes the difficulty. The demand must be very great or encouragement will be wanting. Have the goodness to excuse my begging further explanations on this most interesting topic.[7]

The account of the back parts of Virginia seem to me so flattering that I have taken the further liberty of adding a few more queries, for which I hope your pardon.

District. In the map prefixed to Mr. Jefferson's Virginia, the County of Bottetourt as traced by the mountains forms nearly a triangle. From the Southern point of that triangle draw 2 lines; one to Alexandria, and the other to Fort Pitt, and you enclose a Country nearly of this form and size,

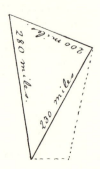

by extending it to the dotted lines it will strike the bend in the Fluvanna near *Toher*, *Randolph*, and *Snowden*, and include a Country which I suppose is gentle slopes rising to the mountains. This large District ought upon *theory* to be the best Sheep Country in America.

Queries.

I.   It includes only three degrees of latitude from $37\frac{1}{2}$ to $40\frac{1}{2}$ and therefore ought to vary very little in climate. Is this the case? or do the positions of the Mountains or other causes make much difference?

II.   What is the climate respecting the heats in summer, and the cold of winter? and particularly as to sudden changes?

III.   Does snow lay long, and where? in the vallies or only on the hills? For how many months or weeks is the ground so covered or so frozen that Sheep or Cattle cannot support themselves abroad without provision of fodder? Would the frost destroy turnips, or lock them up so as not to be got at? The latitude ought to preclude such; but see eels frozen to death at Charleston S. Carol. in a Kitchen chimney. *Gov. Glen Desc. S. C.*

IV.   The Pennsylvania Account[8] mentions the heats burning up all the pasturage near Philadelphia. How far is this the case in this District? and in what parts?

V.   How far are these Mountains inhabited? By settlers? By Indians? How far and how securely removed from their depredations and incursions?

VI.   In a small angle of this District the waters flow westward, does that circumstance mark any difference in Climate?

VII.   What is the face of the Country? Woodland with under wood? or trees and lawns? Rocks? Bogs? Marshes? Any Savannas or natural sheep walks cloathed with Clovers?

VIII.   Is the soil in the vallies generally dry or wet? and on the Mountains rocky? or loamy? or sandy?

IX.   The price of land? distinguishing that cultivated? that fit for culture, and that which is considered as waste? The district between the west ridge and the blue ridge *on navigation* is noted to be 22/6 to 27/6 Sterling; and at Pittsburgh 16/8, but not mentioned if sterling."

Tr (DLC: Washington Papers); consists of five pages in the hand of Bartholomew Dandridge, Jr., the last four consisting of the second extract; with variations in wording, spelling, and punctuation from RC of Young's letter in same, including appendices A-E, the most significant being recorded below.

Washington sent similar extracts of the above to Richard Peters on 16 May 1793, but the repetition of the heading above the second extract sent to TJ, which begins a new page, suggests that they each received the first extract followed by different sections of Young's letter, a hypothesis consistent with Peters's response (Fitzpatrick, *Writings*, XXXII, 459-60; Peters to Washington, 20 June 1793, enclosing undated "Observations on an Extract of a Letter dated 17. Jany. 1793 from Arthur Young Esqr. to The President," in DLC: Washington Papers, and printed in Arthur Young, *Letters from His Excellency General Washington, to Arthur Young, Esq. F. R. S.* [London,

1801], 136, 141-55). For TJ's response, see TJ to Washington, 28 June 1793.

CAPUT MORTUUM: "worthless residue." The description of EELS FROZEN TO DEATH AT CHARLESTON on a bitterly cold night in 1747 is in [James Glen], *A Description of South Carolina . . .* (London, 1761), 28.

[1] Sentence to this point in RC: "Mr. Jeffersons."

[2] Sentence to this point in RC: "He."

[3] Here Tr omits "be able to."

[4] Sentence to this point in RC: "Correcting thus Mr. Jeffersons account his."

[5] Sentence to this point in RC: "How can Mr. Jefferson produce."

[6] Remainder of sentence in RC: "from Mr. Jefferson."

[7] Tr to this point extracted from body of RC; next paragraph of Tr taken from postscript following appendix D, the remainder of Tr from appendix E.

[8] Sentence to this point in RC: "Mr. Peters."

Edmund Randolph's Opinion on the *Grange*

The attorney general of the U.S. has the honor of submitting to the secretary of state his opinion concerning the seizure of the ship Grange.

The essential facts are,

that the river Delaware takes its rise within the limits of the U.S:

that in the whole of its descent to the Atlantic ocean, it is covered on each side by the territory of the U.S:

that from tide water to the distance of about Sixty miles from the Atlantic ocean, it is called the *river* Delaware:

that at this distance from the sea, it widens, and assumes the name of the *bay* of Delaware, which it retains to the mouth:

that its mouth is formed by the Capes Henlopen and May; the former belonging to the state of Delaware in property and jurisdiction; the latter to the state of New Jersey:

that the Delaware does not lead from the sea to the dominions of any foreign nation:

that from the establishment of the British provinces on the banks of the Delaware to the American revolution, it was deemed the peculiar navigation of the British empire:

that by the treaty of Paris on the 3d. day of September 1783, his Britannick Majesty relinquished, with the privity of France, the sovereignty of those provinces, as well as of the other provinces and colonies:

and that the Grange was arrested *in* the Delaware, *within the capes*, before she had reached the sea, after her departure from the port of Philadelphia.

It is a principle, firm in reason, supported by the civilians, and tacitly approved in the document, transmitted by the French minister, that to attack an enemy in a neutral territory is absolutely unlawful.

Hence the inquiry is reduced to this simple form, whether the place of seizure was in the territory of the U.S.?

From a question, originating under the foregoing circumstances is obviously and properly excluded every consideration of a dominion over the *Sea*. The solidity of our neutral right does not depend in this case, on any of the various distances, claimed on that element, by different nations, possessing the neighbouring shore. But if it did, the field would probably be found more extensive, and more favorable to our demand, than is supposed by the document, above-referred to. For the *necessary* or *natural* law of nations, unchanged as it is in this instance by any compact or other obligation of the U.S., will perhaps, when combined with the treaty of Paris in 1783, justify[1] us in attaching to our coasts an extent into the sea, beyond the reach of cannon-shot.

In like manner is excluded every consideration, how far the spot of seizure was capable of being defended by the U.S. For, altho' it will not be[2] conceded, that this could not be done; yet will it rather[3] appear, that the mutual rights of the states of New Jersey and Delaware up to the middle of the river[4] supersede the necessity of such an investigation.

No. The corner-stone of our claim is, that the U.S. are proprietors of the lands on both sides of the Delaware from its head to its enterance into the sea.

The high ocean *in general*,[5] it is true, is unsusceptible of becoming property. It is a gift of nature, manifestly destined for the use of all mankind—inexhaustible in its benefits—not admitting metes and bounds. But rivers may be appropriated; because the reverse is their situation. Were they open to all the world, they would prove the inlets of perpetual disturbance and discord; would soon be rendered barren by the number of those, who would share in their products; and moreover may be defined.

"A river, considered merely as such, is the property of the people, thro' whose lands it flows, or of him, under whose jurisdiction that people is." Grot: b.2. c.2. §12.

"Rivers might be held in property; tho' neither where they rise, nor where they discharge themselves, be within our territory, but they join to both or the sea. It is sufficient for us, that the larger part of water, that is, the sides, is shut up in our banks, and that the river, in respect of our land, is itself small and insignificant." Grot: b.2. c.3. §.7. And Barbeyrac in his note subjoins, that neither of these is necessary.

—"Rivers may be the property of whole states." Puff: b.3. c.3. §4.

"To render a thing, capable of being appropriated, it is not strictly necessary, that we should inclose it, or be able to inclose it within artificial bounds, or such as are different from its own substance; it is sufficient, if the compass and extent of it can be any way determined. And therefore Grotius hath given himself a needless trouble, when, to prove rivers, capable of property he useth this argument, that altho' they are bounded by the land at neither End, but united to the other rivers or the sea; yet it is enough, that the greater part of them, that is, their sides, are inclosed. Puff: b.4. c.5. §.3.

"When a nation takes possession of a country in order to settle there, it possesses every thing included in it, as lands, lakes, rivers" &c. Vattel. b.1. c.22. §.266.

To this list might be added Bynkershoek and Selden. But the dissertation of the former de dominio maris cannot be quoted with advantage in detachment; and the authority of the latter *on this* head may, in the judgment of some, partake too much of Affection for the hypothesis of mare clausum. As Selden, however, sinks in influence on this question; so must Grotius rise, who contended for the mare liberum; and his accurate commentator, Rutherforth, confirms his principles in the following passage. "A nation, by settling upon any tract of land, which at the time of such settlement had no other owner, acquires, in respect of all other nations, an exclusive right of full or absolute property, not only in the land, but in the waters likewise, that are included within the land, such as rivers, pools, creeks or bays. The absolute property of a nation, in what it has thus seized upon, is its right of territory." 2. Ruth: b.2. c.9. §.6.

Congress too have acted on these ideas, when, in their collection-laws, they ascribe to a state the rivers, wholly within that state.

It would seem, however, that the spot of seizure is attempted to be withdrawn from the protection of these respectable authorities, as being in the *bay* of Delaware, instead of the *river* Delaware.

Who can seriously doubt the identity of the *river* and *bay* of Delaware? How often are different portions of the same stream denominated differently. This is sometimes accidental; sometimes for no other purpose, than to assist the intercourse between man and man by easy distinctions of space. Are not this river and this bay fed by the same springs from the land, and the same tides from the ocean? Are not both doubly [6] flanked by the territory of the U.S.? Have any local laws at any time provided variable [7] arrangements for the river and the bay? Has not the jurisdiction of the contiguous states been exercised equally on both?

But suppose that the *river* was dried up, and the *bay* alone remained. Grotius continues the argument of the 7th. Section, of the 3d. chapter of the 2d. book above cited, in the following words.

"By this instance it seems to appear, that the property and dominion of the sea might belong to him, who is in possession of the lands on both sides, tho' it be open above, as a gulph, or above and below, as a straight; provided it is not so great a part of the sea, that, when compared with the lands on both sides, it cannot be supposed to be some part of them. And now, what is thus lawful to one king or people, may be also lawful to two or three, if they have a mind to take possession of a sea, thus inclosed within their lands; for 'tis in this manner, that a river, which separates two nations, has first been possessed by both, and then divided."

"The gulphs and channels or arms of the sea are, according to the regular course, supposed to belong to the people, with whose lands they are encompassed." Puff. b.4. c.5. §.8.

Valin, in b. 5. tit: 1. p. 685. of his commentary on the marine ordonnance of France, virtually acknowledges, that *particular* seas may be appropriated. After reviewing the contest between Grotius and Selden, he says. "S'il (Selden) s'en fût donc tenu là, ou plutôt, s'il eût distingué l'ocean des mers particuliers, et même dans l'ocean, l'etendue de mer, qui doit être censée appartenir aux souverains des côtes, qui en sont baignées, sa victoire eût été complette."

These remarks may be enforced by asking, what nation can be injured in its rights, by the Delaware being appropriated to the U.S.? And to what degree may not the U.S. be injured on the contrary ground? It communicates with no foreign dominion; no foreign nation has, ever before, exacted a community of right in it, as if it were a main sea; under the former and present governments, the exclusive jurisdiction has been asserted; by the very first collection-law of the U.S. passed in 1789, the county of Cape May, which includes Cape May itself, and all the waters thereof, theretofore [8] within the jurisdiction of the state of New Jersey, are comprehended in the district of Bridgetown; the whole of the state of Delaware, reaching to Cape Henlopen is made one district; nay unless these positions can be maintained, the bay of Chesapeak, which in the same law is so fully assumed to be within the U.S., and which for the [9] length of the Virginia territory is subject to the process of several counties to any extent, will become a rendezvous to all the world, without any possible controul from the U.S. Nor will the evil stop here: It will require but another short [10] link in the process of reasoning, to disappropriate the mouths of some of our most important rivers. If, as Vattel inclines to think in the 294th. Section of his first book, the Romans were free to appropriate the mediterranean, merely because they secured by one single stroke the immense range of their coast; how much stronger must the vindication of the U.S. be, should they adopt maxims for prohibiting foreigners from gaining, without permission, access into the heart of their country.

This inquiry might be enlarged by a minute discussion of the practice of foreign nations in such circumstances. But I pass it by; because the U.S. in the commencement of their career ought not to be precipitate in declaring their approbation of any usages, (the precise facts concerning which we may not thoroughly understand) until those usages shall have grown into principles, and are incorporated into the law of nations; and because no usage has ever been accepted, which shakes the foregoing principles.

The conclusion then is, that the Grange has been seized on neutral ground. If this be admitted, the duty arising from the illegal act, is restitution.

EDM: RANDOLPH

May 14. 1793.

RC (DLC); endorsed by TJ and George Taylor, Jr. FC (DNA: RG 59, Letters from and Opinions of the Attorneys General); in a clerk's hand; at foot of text in Taylor's hand: "True copy Geo. Taylor Jr." PrC of Tr (DLC); in a clerk's hand. Tr (DLC: Genet Papers). Tr (same); in French. Tr (AMAE: CPEU, xxxvii); in French. Printed in *Message*, 18-20. Enclosed in TJ to Jean Baptiste Ternant, 15 May 1793, TJ to Gouverneur Morris, 13 June 1793, and TJ to Thomas Pinckney, 14 June 1793.

This document consists of the Attorney General's response to the defense of the legality of the capture of the British merchant ship *Grange* by the *Embuscade* contained in the enclosure to Jean Baptiste Ternant to TJ, 9 May 1793, the DOCUMENT, TRANSMITTED BY THE FRENCH MINISTER, which denied American jurisdiction over the part of Delaware Bay where the incident occurred. The President had directed TJ on the 9th to submit these documents to Randolph for a legal opinion (Washington, *Journal*, 132). For further information on this case and the significance of Randolph's assertion of American jurisdiction over Delaware Bay, see note to Memorial from George Hammond, 2 May 1793.

BARBEYRAC: Hugo Grotius, *De Jure Belli ac Pacis . . . . Notulas denique additit Joannes Barbeyrac* (Amsterdam, 1720) and later editions; first French translation by Barbeyrac (Amsterdam, 1724) and later editions. BYNKERSHOEK: Cornelius van Bynkershoek, *De Dominio Maris Dissertatio* (The Hague, 1703; conjoined to Bynkershoek's treatise on Rhodian law) and later editions. SELDEN: John Selden, *Mare Clausum, seu De Dominio Maris Libri Duo* (London, 1635) and later editions and translations. RUTHERFORTH: Thomas Rutherforth, *Institutes of Natural Law, being the Substance of a Course of Lectures on Grotius De Jure Belli et Pacis . . .*, 2 vols. (Cambridge, Eng., 1754-56; 2d ed., Cambridge, 1779). VALIN: René Josué Valin, *Nouveau commentaire sur l'ordonnance de la marine, du mois d'août 1681 . . .*, 2 vols. (La Rochelle, 1760). FIRST COLLECTION-LAW: see U.S. Statutes at Large, I, 29-49, esp. 32-3.

[1] Randolph here canceled "on our part."

² Preceding three words interlined in place of "ought not to be admitt."
³ Word interlined.
⁴ Preceding seven words interlined in place of canceled and illegible word.
⁵ Preceding two words interlined.

⁶ Word interlined.
⁷ Word interlined in place of "different."
⁸ Word interlined.
⁹ Randolph here canceled "whole."
¹⁰ Word interlined.

From George Washington, with Jefferson's Note

Tuesday Noon May 14th: 1793.

The President of the United States requests that the Secretary of State will lay the enclosed letter before the Gentlemen who are to meet today—that it may be taken into consideration with the other matters which may be before them.

[*Note by TJ:*]
viz. a letter from T. Newton.

RC (DLC); in the hand of Tobias Lear; with note by TJ at foot of text; endorsed by TJ as received 14 May 1793. Recorded in SJPL. Enclosures: (1) Thomas Newton, Jr., and William Lindsay to Washington, Norfolk, 5 May 1793, stating that the schooners *Sans Culotte*, commanded by Mr. Ferey, and the *Eagle*, fitted out with four guns apiece in Charleston, were cruising off the capes as privateers under French commissions, damaging trade and violating the law of nations by stopping ships "within our territories"; that the *Eagle* was manned mostly by American and English seamen and had only one Frenchman on board; that one of the privateers belonged to Mr. Hooper of Cambridge, Maryland, who had taken Captain Tucker's vessel as a prize to that place; that a fraud may be intended because the captors erased the prize's name from its stern; and that Washington should refer to Tucker's report for details (RC in DNA: RG 59, MLR, in Newton's hand, signed by Newton and Lindsay; PrC of Tr in same, in a clerk's hand; PrC of another Tr in DLC, in a clerk's hand; Tr in Lb in DNA: RG 59, DL). (2) Summary of the reports of Captain Lindsay of the schooner *Greyhound* and Captain Tucker of the schooner *Eunice*, n.d., the first reporting that on his arrival at Norfolk from Jamaica on 3 May he was hailed while less than half a mile from Cape Henry by the pilot boat *Ranger* commanded by Mr. Latimer, that a small schooner privateer was within hearing, and that he escaped capture by the subterfuge of claiming his was a Norfolk ship coming from St. Eustatius; the second reporting that after leaving New Providence the *Eunice* was captured on 29 Apr. 1793 by the *Sans Culotte* at 36° latitude in 27 fathoms of water, that the ship's name was erased from the stern and Hooper was placed on board as prize master, that the ship was laid up in a Maryland creek while Hooper went to Philadelphia on business, leaving Major Ganset of New England as marine officer and lieutenant on the privateer in Hooper's absence, that after staying in Hampton Road for two days both the privateer and its prize left on a cruise, that Hooper owned the *Eagle*, which was originally fitted in Cambridge and plied between Norfolk and Georgia and Charleston as a packet, and that the privateers intended to seize vessels in Chesapeake Bay (MS in DNA: RG 59, MLR, in Newton's hand; PrC of Tr in DLC: TJ Papers, 87: 15003, 236: 42398, in a clerk's hand; Tr in Lb in DNA: RG 59, DL).

From George Washington

May 14th: 1793.

The President sends to the Secretary of State the enclosed Extract which he has just received from a respectable Gentleman in this City—who informs him that the writer is a person of respectability and good information in London. The President wishes it to be shewn to the Gentlemen if they are still together.

RC (DLC); in the hand of Tobias Lear; endorsed by TJ as received 14 May 1793.

Although the enclosed letter is unsigned, and although the President evidently sought to conceal the identity of the author, TJ may have recognized John Vaughan's handwriting. There is no evidence of the reaction to Vaughan's letter by the GENTLE-MEN of the Cabinet, who met on 13, 14, and 15 May to consider TJ's response to George Hammond's complaints about French violations of American neutrality (Washington, *Journal*, 132, 137; Memorandum from Alexander Hamilton and Edmund Randolph, printed under 13 May 1793; TJ to Hammond, 15 May 1793; TJ to Jean Baptiste Ternant, 15 May 1793).

ENCLOSURE

John Vaughan to George Washington

May 14. 1793.

"America and all that belongs to it is Still viewed with Jealousy in England and be assured that if this war of Kings succeeds, Spain and England will jointly quarrel with America, So as to shake your funds to their roots—Be assured the War will daily open cases of Jeopardy and dispute to compromise your peace. The publick is a little Cooled in its rage for War and adverse events would quickly make it unpopular."

The above extract Comes from, and is taken from a letter written by, a warm friend to America, his fears may be too strong but as he is in the way of information, it may be proper not to suffer them to pass by Unnoticed or unreflected upon.

RC (DLC); in Vaughan's hand, unsigned and unaddressed; dateline at foot of text; identity of author and recipient established from Washington, *Journal*, 137.

From Tench Coxe

SIR   May 15th. 1793

I find Mr. J. is a collector of Money, tho not in a very large way, for several persons of reputation, the Episcopal Church and one or two Charitable Institutions—that he has been employed by several others and it is generally understood that he has conducted himself with regularity and honesty. This recommendation has therefore a certain degree of weight when he speaks of Mr. C. as an honest man notwithstanding his misfortunes. I am of opinion however, that Mr. C. has been a very inattentive man both to the characters of the persons with whom he had considerable transactions, and to the conduct of those whom he employed in his trade. His skill in the line for which he is wanted is probably sufficient, but his steadiness and discretion do not appear to be insisted upon as real by any body. The impressions at New York, against his principles, are somewhat lessened by the representation of Mr. J. If it shall be found necessary to employ him, it will be much to be wished that there were more favorable Circumstances in his past story. I have the honor to be with great respect, Sir your most obedient & humble Servant   TENCH COXE

RC (DLC); at head of text: "(Private)"; at foot of text: "The Secretary of State"; erroneously endorsed by TJ as a letter of 16 May 1793 received that day and so recorded in SJL.

MR. J. has not been identified, but MR. C. was Albion Cox, who was being considered for a position at the Mint. See Tench Coxe to TJ, [11 May 1793], and note.

To George Hammond

SIR   Philadelphia May 15. 1793.

Your several Memorials of the 8th. instant, have been laid before the President, as had been that of the 2d. as soon as received. They have been considered with all the attention and the impartiality which a firm determination could inspire to do what is equal and right between all the belligerent powers.

In one of these, you communicate on the information of the british Consul at Charleston, that the Consul of France, at the same place, had condemned, as legal prize, a british vessel, captured by a french Frigate, and you justly add, that this judicial act is not warranted by the usage of nations, nor by the stipulations existing between the United States and France. I observe further, that it is not warranted by any law of the Land. It is consequently a mere nullity, as such it can be respected in no Court, can make no part in the title to the Vessel, nor give to the purchaser any other security than what he would have had without it. In short, it is so absolutely nothing as to give no foundation of just concern to any person interested in the fate of the vessel, and in this point of view, Sir, I am in hopes you will see it. The proceeding, indeed, if the British Consul has been rightly informed, and we have no other information of it, has been an act of disrespect towards the United States, to which its Government cannot be inattentive: A just sense of our own rights and duties and the obviousness of the principle are a security that no inconveniences will be permitted to arise from repetitions of it.

The purchase of arms and military accoutrements by an agent of the french Government, in this Country, with an intent to export them to France, is the subject of another of the memorials. Of this fact, we are equally uninformed, as of the former. Our Citizens have been always free to make, vend, and export arms. It is the constant occupation and livelihood of some of them. To suppress their callings, the only means perhaps of their subsistance because a war exists in foreign and distant countries, in which we have no concern, would scarcely be expected. It would be hard in principle, and impossible in practice. The law of nations, therefore, respecting the rights of those at peace, does not require from them such an internal derangement in their occupations. It is satisfied with the external penalty pronounced in the President's proclamation, that of confiscation of such portion of these arms as shall fall into the Hands of any of the belligerent powers on their way to the ports of their enemies. To this penalty our Citizens are warned that they will be abandoned, and that even private contraventions may work no inequality between the parties at war, the benefit of them, will be left equally free and open to all.

The capture of the British Ship Grange, by the French frigate l'Embuscade, has, on inquiry been found to have taken place within the Bay of Delaware and Jurisdiction of the United States, as stated in your Memorial of the 2d: instant. The Government is therefore, taking measures for the liberation of the Crew and restitution of the Ship and cargo.

It condemns in the highest degree the conduct of any of our citizens, who may personally engage in committing hostilities at sea against any of the nations, parties to the present war, and will exert all the means with which the laws and constitution have armed them to discover such as offend herein and bring them to condign punishment. Of these dispositions I am authorized to give assurances to all the parties, without reserve. Our real friendship for them all, our desire to pursue ourselves the path of peace as the only one leading surely to prosperity, and our wish to preserve the morals of our Citizens from being vitiated by courses of lawless plunder and murder, may assure you that our proceedings in this respect will be with good faith, fervor and vigilance. Instructions are consequently given to the proper law officer to institute such proceedings as the laws will justify, for apprehending and punishing certain individuals of our Citizens suggested to have been concerned in enterprises of this kind, as mentioned in one of your memorials of the 8th. instant.

The practice of commissioning, equipping and manning vessels, in our ports to cruise on any of the belligerent parties, is equally and entirely disapproved, and the Government will take effectual measures to prevent a repetition of it. The remaining point in the same memorial, is reserved for further Consideration.

I trust, Sir, that in the readiness with which the United States have attended to the redress of such wrongs as are committed by their citizens, or within their Jurisdiction, you will see proofs of their justice and impartiality to all the parties, and that it will ensure to their Citizens pursuing their lawful business, by Sea or by Land, in all parts of the world a like efficacious interposition of the governing powers to protect them from injury, and redress it, when it has taken place. With such dispositions, on both sides vigilantly and faithfully carried into effect, we may hope that the blessings of peace, on the one part, will be as little impaired, and the evils of War on the other, as little aggravated, as the nature of things will permit: and that this should be so is we trust the prayer of all. I have the honor to be, with sentiments of respect, Sir, Your most obedient and most humble servant

PrC (DLC); in the hand of George Taylor, Jr., unsigned; at foot of first page: "The minister plenipo. of Gt. Britain." PrC of Tr (DNA: RG 59, MD); in Taylor's hand. FC (Lb in same, DL). Tr (Lb in PRO: FO 116/3). Tr (same, 5/1). Tr (NHi: Rufus King Papers). Enclosed in George Washington to TJ, 15 May 1793, TJ to Gouverneur Morris, 13 June 1793, and TJ to Thomas Pinckney, 14 June 1793.

TJ dispatched this key official statement on American neutrality policy after it had been reviewed by the Cabinet and approved by the President. The testimony of Hammond, who was regularly informed of Cabinet proceedings by the Secretary of the Treasury, and other evidence suggest that Cabinet members discussed the contents of this letter between 13 and 15 May 1793, at the end of which time they approved its main points (Hammond to Lord Grenville, 17 May 1793, PRO: FO 5/1; Henry Knox to Washington, 16 May 1793, DLC: Washington Papers; Washington, *Journal*, 132, 137). The President himself returned the letter to TJ this day with his approval, but Hammond did not receive it until the evening of the following day because TJ did not dispatch it until after the President had approved on the 16th TJ's letter of this date to Jean Baptiste Ternant (Washington to TJ, 15 May 1793; TJ to Washington, 16 May 1793; Hammond to Grenville, 17 May 1793, PRO: FO 5/1; Washington, *Journal*, 137, 138-41). See also notes to Memorials from Hammond, 2, 8 May 1793.

The REMAINING POINT to be resolved was Hammond's request for the restoration of the British merchant ships captured by the privateers Edmond Charles Genet had commissioned at Charleston (see Opinion on the Restoration of Prizes, 16 May 1793).

To William Rawle

SIR   Philadelphia May 15. 1793

By the inclosed papers you will perceive there is reason to believe that certain citizens of the United States have engaged in committing depredations on the property and commerce of some of the nations at peace with the United States. I have it in charge to express to you the desire of the Government that you would take such measures for apprehending and prosecuting them as shall be according to law. I am not able to point out to you the individuals against whom suggestions have been made but take the liberty of referring you to Mr. Deblois and Mr. Sharpe Delany who may give you information on the subject. I am with great esteem Sir Your most obedient and Most humble servant

PrC (DLC); in a clerk's hand, except for place and dateline in the hand of George Taylor, Jr., with day added in ink; unsigned; at foot of text: "Mr. Rawle." PrC of Tr (DNA: RG 59, MD); in a clerk's hand. FC (Lb in same, DL). Enclosures: (1) Memorial from George Hammond, 8 May 1793, on French privateers commissioned in Charleston. (2) Enclosures to George Washington to TJ, 14 May 1793. Letter enclosed in Washington to TJ, 15 May 1793, TJ to Gouverneur Morris, 13 June 1793, and TJ to Thomas Pinckney, 14 June 1793.

TJ dispatched this letter to the federal district attorney in Pennsylvania only after the Cabinet had approved it and he had submitted it to the President this day and received his approval (Washington, *Journal*, 139-40; Washington to TJ, 15 May 1793). Rawle promptly instituted legal proceedings against the Massachusetts mariner Gideon Henfield (see Memorial from Edmond Charles Genet, 27 May 1793, and note). Lewis DEBLOIS appeared as a prosecution witness in this case (*Federal Cases*, XI, 1115).

From Peyton Short

DEAR SIR   Woodford County (Kentucky) May 15th 1793

I return you my thanks for your obliging favor enclosing a Letter from my Brother, which came to hand a few days past and in consequence of your friendly offer, take the liberty of enclosing an Answer to your Care.

I was a good deil disappointed on hearing that several Letters of which you take notice in your last had not come to hand.

To insure a paper from this to your Metropolis, in the present State of our affairs is worth a policy of 50 per Ct.

Should it ever happen that my Services might be of any Value to you in this distant quarter of the Continent, I beg you will command them— for I am, Dr. Sir, with the most unfeigned respect—Yr. much obliged Hble. Servt   PEYTON SHORT

RC (MHi); at foot of text: "Mr. Jefferson"; endorsed by TJ as received 21 June 1793 and so recorded in SJL. Enclosure not found.

To Jean Baptiste Ternant

Sir Philadelphia May 15th. 1793.

Having received several Memorials from the British Minister on subjects arising out of the present War, I take the liberty of enclosing them to you, and shall add an explanation of the determinations of the government thereon. These will serve to vindicate the principles on which it is meant to proceed, and which are to be applied with impartiality to the proceedings of both parties. They will form, therefore, as far as they go, a rule of action for them and for us.

In one of these memorials, it is stated, that arms and military accoutrements are now buying up by a French agent in this Country with an intent to export them to France. We have answered that our citizens have been always free to make, vend and export arms: that it is the constant occupation and livelihood of some of them. To suppress their callings, the only means, perhaps of their subsistence, because a War exists in foreign and distant countries, in which we have no concern, would scarcely be expected. It would be hard in principle and impossible in practice. The law of nations, therefore, respecting the rights of those at peace, has not required from them such an internal derangement in their occupations. It is satisfied with the external penalty pronounced in the President's proclamation, that of confiscation of such portion of these arms as shall fall into the hands of any of the belligerent powers, on their way to the ports of their enemies. To this penalty our Citizens are warned that they will be abandoned; and that the purchases of arms here,[1] may work no inequality between the parties at war, the liberty to make them will be enjoyed equally by both.

Another of these Memorials complains that the Consul of France at Charleston, has condemned, as legal prize, a British vessel captured by a French frigate, observing that this judicial act is not warranted by the usage of nations nor by the stipulations existing between the United States and France. It is true, that it is not so warranted, nor yet by any law of the Land: that, therefore, it is a mere nullity, can be respected in no Court, make no part in the title to the vessel, nor give to the purchaser any other security than what he would have had without it; that consequently it ought to give no concern to any person interested in the fate of the vessel. While we have considered this to be the proper answer, as between us and Great Britain, between us and France, it is an act, to which we cannot but be attentive.[2] An assumption of jurisdiction by an Officer of a foreign power, in cases which have not been permitted by the nation within whose limits it has been exercised, could not be deemed an act of indifference. We have not full evidence that the case has happened, but on such an hypothesis, while we should be disposed to view it, in this instance, as an error in judgment in the particular officer, we should rely, Sir, that you would interpose efficaciously, to prevent a repetition of the error by him, or any other of the Consuls of your nation.

Our information is not perfect on the Subject matter of another of these memorials, which states that a vessel has been fitted out at Charleston, manned there, and partly too, with Citizens of the United States, received a Commission there, to cruize against Nations at peace with us, and has taken and sent a British vessel into this port. Without taking all these facts for granted, we have not hesitated to express our highest disapprobation of the conduct of any of our Citizens who may personally engage in committing hostilities at sea against any of the Nations, parties to the present war; to declare that if the case has happened, or that should it happen, we will exert all the means with which the Laws and Constitution have armed us, to discover such offenders, and bring them to condign punishment, and that the like conduct shall be observed, should the like enterprises be attempted against your nation, I am authorized to give you the most unreserved assurances. Our friendship for all the parties at war; our desire to pursue ourselves the path of peace, as the only one leading surely to prosperity, and our wish to preserve the morals of our Citizens from being vitiated by courses of lawless plunder and murder, are a security that our proceedings, in this respect, will be with good faith, fervor, and vigilance. The arming of Men and Vessels within our territory, and without consent or consultation on our part, to wage war on Nations with which we are in peace, are acts, which we will not gratuitously impute to the public Authority of France. They are stated indeed with positiveness in one of the Memorials. But our unwillingness to believe that the French nation could be wanting in respect or friendship to us, on any occasion, suspends our assent to, and conclusions upon these statements till further evidence.[3] There is still a further point in this memorial, to which no answer has been yet given.

The capture of the British Ship Grange, by the French frigate l'Embuscade, within the[4] Delaware, has been the subject of a former letter to you. On full and mature consideration, the Government deems the capture to have been unquestionably within it's jurisdiction, and that according to the rules of neutrality and the protection it owes to all persons while within it's limits, it is bound to see that the crew be liberated and the vessel and cargo restored to their former owners. The Attorney General of the United States, has made a statement of the grounds of this determination, a copy of which I have the honor to enclose you. I am, in consequence charged by the President of the United States to express to you his expectation,[5] and at the same time his confidence that you will be pleased to take immediate and effectual measures for having the ship Grange and her Cargo restored to the British owners, and the persons taken on board her, set at liberty.

I am persuaded, Sir, you will be sensible on mature consideration, that in forming these determinations, the Government of the United States, has listened to nothing but the dictates of immutable Justice:[6] they consider the rigorous exercise of that virtue as the surest means of preserving perfect harmony between the United States and the powers at War. I have the honor to be, with sentiments of great respect Sir Your most obedient and most humble servant   TH: JEFFERSON

PrC (DLC); in the hand of George Taylor, Jr., signed by TJ; at foot of first page: "M. Ternant minister plenipo. of France." PrC of Tr (DLC); in a clerk's hand; final page missing. PrC of Tr (DNA: RG 59, MD); in Taylor's hand; final page missing. Tr (NNC: Gouverneur Morris Papers). PrC of Tr (PRO: FO 97/1); in a clerk's hand. Tr (DNA: RG 46, Senate Records, 3d Cong., 1st sess.). FC (Lb in DNA: RG 59, DL). Tr (DLC: Genet Papers). Tr (same); in French. Tr (AMAE: CPEU, XXXVII); in French. Printed in *Message*, 16-17. Enclosures: (1) Memorial from George Hammond, 2 May 1793. (2) Last three memorials from same, 8 May 1793. (3) Edmund Randolph's Opinion on the *Grange*, 14 May 1793. Letter enclosed in TJ to Gouverneur Morris, 13 June and 16 Aug. 1793, and TJ to Thomas Pinckney, 14 June 1793.

As with his letter of this date to the British minister, TJ dispatched this official statement on American neutrality policy only after a draft of it had been reviewed by the Cabinet, and the final version had been approved by the President on 16 May 1793, the same day TJ submitted it to him (TJ to Washington, 16 May 1793; Washington,

Journal, 140-1). For the comments of the Secretary of the Treasury and the Attorney General on the missing draft, see Memorandum from Alexander Hamilton and Edmund Randolph, printed under 13 May 1793; insofar as possible, the textual notes below describe TJ's response to these remarks.

[1] Preceding five words possibly substituted for "even private contraventions" in response to Hamilton and Randolph. For the passage as it may have appeared in TJ's missing draft, see the last sentence in the third paragraph of TJ to George Hammond, 15 May 1793.

[2] Hamilton and Randolph called the preceding three words to TJ's attention, but it is not clear if they wanted them added or deleted.

[3] Preceding sentence added at the suggestion of Hamilton and Randolph.

[4] TJ here omitted "bay of" in response to Hamilton and Randolph.

[5] TJ rejected Hamilton and Randolph's suggestion that he change this word to "desire."

[6] Remainder of sentence added in response to Hamilton and Randolph.

From George Washington, with Jefferson's Note

May 15th: 1793

The President of the United States approves of the enclosed Letter to Mr. Hammond, and likewise of that to Mr. Rawle.

[*Note by TJ:*]
viz the letter of May 15. 93.

RC (DLC); in the hand of Tobias Lear; addressed: "The Secretary of State"; with subjoined note by TJ. Enclosures: (1) TJ to George Hammond, 15 May 1793. (2) TJ to William Rawle, 15 May 1793. Recorded in SJPL.

From Tench Coxe

Sir   May 16. 1793

Mr. Stephen Kingston, a merchant of this city, by birth an Irishman, but now a citizen of the U. S. has applied to me on a subject, which he refrains, for a time, to act upon from public Considerations. The prize-master of one of the prizes taken by "*the Citizen Genet*" privateer is a debtor to him. He wishes to arrest the man, but is apprehensive, that it may produce some public difficulty: and he has requested me to ask you whether there is any circumstance in the state of things or in the rules prevailing in these cases, which renders it adviseable that a citizen of the U. S. should not cause a debtor on board of a prize in the capacity of a prizemaster to be arrested for debt. I have the honor to be with great respect, Sir your most obedt. Servant   Tench Coxe

RC (DLC); at head of text: "(Private)"; endorsed by TJ as received 16 May 1793 and so recorded in SJL.

From Fenwick, Mason & Company

Sir   Bordeaux 16 May 1793.

Herewith you will receive an Invoice of 14 cases wine you ordered last winter but no opportunity offering for either Richmond or Philadelphia we profit of the present and send them to the care of Mr. Archibald Campbell merchant in Baltimore who will give them what direction you desire. If you have retired from public business, he will forward them on without further directions to Richmond to the care of Mr. Henry Heith (Brown of the House of Donnald & Burton we presume

[45]

must have experienced the same fate of that House). We therefore have drawn on you for the amount and balance of your former account as ℔ note within, payable in Philadelphia or Richmond, instead of Donnald & Burton as you desired—which hope will be agreeable and the note of the amount found right.

We had this wine bottled in the strongest bottles to be had here—and we hope the quality will correspond with what you described—it is of the vintage of 1788 and such as cost formerly about 600ᵗᵗ ℔ Ton and such as was used in the best french Houses for vin ordinaire—the price it now costs you here is, bottle included, 20ᵗᵗ effective ℔ bottle, the freight is extreemly high on account of the war and the advantageous neutrality of the Americans. We have the honor to be Sir your most obedient Servts.   FENWICK MASON & CO.

RC (MHi); in the hand of Joseph Fenwick; at head of text: "Thomas Jefferson Esquire"; endorsed by TJ as received 16 Aug. 1793 and so recorded in SJL. Enclosed in Archibald Campbell to TJ, 13 Aug. 1793.

The INVOICE has not been found, but see TJ to Archibald Campbell, 18 Aug. 1793. For the amount of the NOTE WITHIN, which has not been found, see MB, 11 Dec. 1793.

From Edmond Charles Genet

Philadelphie le 16 Mai 1792 [1793].
L'an 2e. de la République francaise.

J'ai l'honneur de vous communiquer, Monsieur, une copie des lettres de créance qui m'ont été délivrées par le Conseil éxécutif de la République française; Je vous prie de vouloir bien les mettre Sous les yeux du Président des Etats unis et de me faire connoitre l'heure à laquelle Je pourrai les lui presenter ainsi qu'une lettre que la convention-nationale à chargé son Président de lui ecrire.

FC (DLC: Genet Papers); below dateline: "Le Citoyen Genet Ministre plénipotentiaire de la République française près les Etats-unis d'amerique, à Monsieur Jefferson Secretaire d'Etat des Etats-unis"; at foot of text: "Translated." FC (same); in English. Recorded in SJL as received 16 May 1793.

With this letter Edmond Charles Genet (1763-1834), the first minister to the United States appointed by the French Republic, began what was destined to be a tumultuous and short-lived diplomatic relationship with TJ and the Washington administration. Born in Versailles, Genet was the only son of Edmé Jacques Genet,

the chief of the Bureau of Interpretation in the French Ministry of Foreign Affairs. A gifted linguist with a keen interest in science, Genet became a clerk in the Bureau at the age of fourteen, translating documents relating to the American Revolution and making the acquaintance of such noted American diplomats as John Adams and Benjamin Franklin. Upon the death of his father in 1781, Genet became chief of the Bureau and held this position until the agency was abolished in 1787 for reasons of economy. With the patronage of Marie Antoinette, whom one of his sisters served as a lady in waiting, Genet served in Russia for the next five years, first as secretary of legation to the French ambassador, the Comte de Ségur, and then, after Ségur's return to France in 1789, as the French government's chargé d'affaires in St. Petersburg, until at length he was expelled by Catherine the Great in July 1792 on account of his enthusiastic support for the French Revolution. Genet's diplomatic experience and zeal for the revolutionary cause commended him to the Girondin ministry that came to power after the overthrow of the Bourbon monarchy and led to his appointment as French minister to the United States in November 1792. Genet did not leave Paris until late January 1793, having been delayed by an abortive Girondin plan to avert the execution of Louis XVI by exiling the king and the royal family to the United States, and his ship did not sail for America until the following month, landing him in Charleston, South Carolina, in April (DAB; Meade Minnigerode, *Jefferson, Friend of France, 1793: The Career of Edmond Charles Genet* . . . [New York, 1928]). For an overview of his mission to the United States and its collapse, see Editorial Note on the recall of Edmond Charles Genet, at 16 Aug. 1793.

Genet presented the French text of the enclosed LETTRES DE CRÉANCE to the President on 18 May 1793 (Washington, *Journal*, 143). At that time he probably also presented two letters addressed to Washington by the French government. The first was a letter from the president of the CONVENTION-NATIONALE of 22 Dec. 1792 which proclaimed the establishment of the French Republic, justified the abolition of the monarchy, ascribed the French court's support of American independence to deceitful motives, declared that by its solitary struggle for liberty against the coalition of kings France has shown itself worthy of American brotherhood, compared the successes of French armies to the American victories at Saratoga, Trenton, and Yorktown, gave thanks for American assistance to France's colonies, and expressed eagerness to strengthen the political and commercial ties between the two nations, now that they shared the same principles and interests, if the United States had the courage to hasten the time when commerce would rest, not on exclusive interests, but on the joint interests of all nations and the nature of things (Dft in AMAE: CPEU, XXXVI, in French; printed in *Archives Parlementaires*, 1st ser., LV, 353-4; translation printed in *National Gazette*, 2 Mch. 1793; see also TJ to Washing-

ton, 22 Aug. 1793). Genet probably also produced a letter of [13] Jan. 1793 from the Provisional Executive Council to the President expressing confidence that the establishment of the French Republic would lead to closer relations between France and the United States, noting that Genet came with extensive powers to agree with anyone authorized by Washington on articles designed to consolidate on the most liberal and durable basis the ties of friendship and commerce between the two nations, and expressing satisfaction that Genet's success would depend in great part on a virtuous and talented President who had frequently manifested friendly sentiments toward France (Tr in DNA: RG 59, NL; in the hand of George Taylor, Jr., and bearing month and year of date only, with "Translation" at head of text; Tr in same, consisting of draft translation in a clerk's hand, except for revisions by TJ, partial date and salutation in Taylor's hand, and endorsement by Tobias Lear; Dft in AMAE: CPEU, XXXVII, in French, in a clerk's hand, unsigned, bearing date of 13 Jan. 1793, with "[. . .] Washington [Pré]sident des Etats unis de l'Amerique. A Philadelphie" at head of text). For the manner in which Genet was received, see Genet to the Minister of Foreign Affairs, 7 Oct. 1793, Turner, *CFM*, 245.

The present letter is the first of the approximately 80 surviving letters and memorials that Genet wrote to TJ in his capacity as Secretary of State. Although, according to TJ's own later testimony, recipient's copies were on file in the Department of State when he retired from office at the end of 1793, only two have survived (Genet to TJ, 30 Sep. 1793, which TJ returned for the correction of clerical errors; Note from Genet, [ca. 30 Oct. 1793], which TJ preserved among his papers; see also Deposition of TJ, [ca. 9 Feb. 1809]). In view of this significant gap in the inventory of Genet's communications, the following guidelines have been adopted for their presentation. Letters and memorials written by Genet between 27 May and 25 July 1793 and enclosed in TJ's 16 Aug. 1793 letter to Gouverneur Morris requesting the French minister's recall have been printed from press copies of transcripts made from the missing recipient's copies by a clerk working in the State Department under TJ's aegis and preserved by TJ among his own papers. Except for occasional anomalies and transparent slips of the pen, internal evidence indicates that these texts are faithful copies of the letters and memorials the Secretary of State received from Genet. Whenever possible, all other letters and memorials TJ received from the French minister, whether written before or after 25 July 1793, have been printed from authorial texts that survive among Genet's papers in the Library of Congress and the New-York Historical Society. Some of these texts were drafted by the French minister and bear clerical additions; others were prepared by Genet's clerks and revised by him. When these authorial texts are unavailable, clerical file copies in Genet's papers or clerical transcripts in the Archives du Ministère des Affaires Étrangères, both derived from authorial texts, have been employed. In all cases, the most significant emendations and variations derived from the collation of extant manuscript texts are recorded in textual notes.

The political controversy generated by the French minister's diplomatic mission and the request for his recall, documented in this and the next volume, led the President on 5 Dec. 1793 to transmit to Congress copies of the relevant correspondence and enclosures that Genet exchanged with TJ. On the recommendation of the Secretary of State, supported decisively by Washington, a selection of TJ's correspondence with George Hammond and Thomas Pinckney on British violations of the peace treaty and American neutrality was also sent with Washington's message (see Notes of a Cabinet Meeting on the President's Messages to Congress, 28 Nov. 1793; Fitzpatrick, *Washington*, XXXIII, 170-3). The House of Representatives ordered the publication of all this material in pamphlet form, the documents from Genet being presented in English translation with a separately paginated appendix of French texts (see *Message*). Genet in turn published a smaller selection of his correspondence with TJ and related documents, first in English (see *Correspondence*) and then in French (see *Correspondance*). The descriptive notes to the relevant documents on French and British relations in this and the next volume record their publication in these pamphlets. Citations to Genet's communications and their enclosures in the *Message* will include page references both for the appended French texts and English translations, in that order. Translations printed in the *Message* are also printed in ASP, *Foreign Relations*, I, 142-88. The infrequent discrepancies between the manuscript texts and the pamphlets have been recorded in textual notes.

For earlier correspondence with the British minister printed in the *Message* in a separate pagination, see TJ to Hammond, 29 Nov. 1791; Hammond to TJ, 30 Nov. and 6 Dec. 1791; TJ to Hammond, 13 Dec. 1791; Hammond to TJ, 14 Dec. 1791; TJ to Hammond, 15 Dec. 1791, and enclosures; Hammond to TJ, 19 Dec. 1791, and 5 Mch. 1792, and enclosures; TJ to Hammond, 30 Mch. 1792; Hammond to TJ, 6 Apr. 1792; TJ to Hammond, 29 May 1792, and enclosures; and Hammond to TJ, 2 June 1792.

ENCLOSURE

Letter of Credence from the Provisional Executive Council of France

In the name of the French Republic.

In virtue of the law of the 15th. of Aug. last which attributes to the Executive Provisory council all the functions of the Executive power, and of the Decree of the National Convention of the 21st. Sep. following, which continues the public authorities which were in activity at this last epoch.

We citizens forming THE EXECUTIVE PROVISORY COUNCIL OF THE REPUBLIC TO THE UNITED STATES OF NORTH AMERICA.

VERY DEAR, GREAT FRIENDS AND ALLIES. Having resolved to give a successor to the citizen Ternant, minister plenipotentiary of the French republic near you, we have chosen, to replace him, in the same quality, the Citizen Genet, Adjutant General and Colonel in the service of the republic. The marks of zeal and patriotism which he has given until now persuade us that he will conduct himself in a manner to render his person agreeable to you. We pray you, very dear, great friends and allies, to add entire faith to whatsoever he shall be charged to say to you on the part of the republic, above all, when he shall assure you of our dispositions to concur to the advantage and prosperity of the US. We have no doubt he will employ all his attention to convince you of the desire of the French nation to strengthen more and more the bonds of friendship and fraternity which ought to unite two free people, made for reciprocal esteem, and to consolidate between them the most perfect harmony.　　　Written at Paris the 30. Dec. 1792. the 1st. year of the republic

the citizens forming the Provisory Executive council of the republ. of France
signed. LE BRUN. CLAVIERE. GARAT. ROLAND. PACHE. MONGE.
By the Provisory Executive council　　　　　　　　GROUVELLE

Tr (DNA: RG 59, Communications from Heads of Foreign States); translation in TJ's hand. MS (same); in French; signed by all six members of the Council and Grouvelle, with seal affixed; addressed: "À Nos très-chers, grands Amis et Alliés Les Etats-Unis de l'Amérique Septentrionale"; endorsed by George Taylor, Jr., in part: "Credence to Mr. Genet." Translation printed in *Correspondence*, 8-9; printed in *Correspondance*, 13-14. Translation enclosed in Tobias Lear to TJ, 20 May 1793.

From Henry Lee

DEAR SIR　　　　　　　　　　　　　　Richmond May 16th. 93

The enclosed resolution of the G. assembly I very much wish to see fitly and ingeniously executed and feel a thorough sterility of genius on the subject.

Nor have I been able to obtain aid here.

Thus circumstanced I resort to your goodness and pray you will be pleased to favor me with a plan. The execution can be effected in this city. I have the honor to be Sr with every sentiment of the highest respect Your ob: st.　　　　　　　　　　　　　HENRY LEE

RC (DLC); endorsed by TJ as received 23 May 1793 and so recorded in SJL.

The text TJ received of the Virginia General Assembly's RESOLUTION of 17 Dec. 1792 instructing the governor to have new ceremonial maces made for the Senate and the House of Delegates has not been found, but the original motion had declared that it was "inconsistent with the principles of a republican government, that any badge or appendage of kingly pomp should remain therein" (JHD, Oct.-Dec. 1792, p. 178, 184, 194).

Opinion on the Restoration of Prizes

The facts suggested, or to be taken for granted, because the contrary is not known, in the case now to be considered, are, that a vessel was purchased at Charleston and fitted out as a privateer by French citizens, manned with foreigners chiefly, but partly with citizens of the US. the command given to a French citizen by a regular commission from his government, that she has made prize of an English vessel in the open sea, and sent her in to Philadelphia. The British minister demands restitution, and the question is Whether the Executive of the US. shall undertake to make it?

This transaction may be considered 1. as an offence against the US. 2. as an injury to Great Britain.

In the 1st. view it is not now to be taken up, the opinion being that it has been an act of disrespect to the jurisdiction of the US. of which proper notice is to be taken at a proper time.

Under the 2d. point of view, it appears to me wrong on the part of the US. (where not constrained by treaties) to permit one party in the present war to do what cannot be permitted to the other. We cannot permit the enemies of France to fit out privateers in our ports, by the 22d. article of our treaty. We ought not therefore to permit France to do it, the treaty leaving us free to refuse, and the refusal being necessary to preserve a fair and secure neutrality.[1] Yet considering that the present is the first case which has arisen, that it has been in the first moment of the war, in one of the most distant ports of the US. and before measures could be taken by the government to meet all the cases which may flow from the infant state of our government and novelty of our position, it ought to be placed by Great Britain among the accidents of loss to which a nation is exposed in a state of war, and by no means as a premeditated wrong on the part of the government. In this last light it cannot be taken, because the act from which it results placed the US. with the offended, and not the offending party. Her minister has seen himself that there could have been on our part neither permission nor connivance. A very moderate apology then from the US. ought to satisfy Great Britain. The one we have made already is ample, to wit, a pointed disapprobation of the transaction, a promise to prosecute and punish according to law such of our citizens as have been concerned in it, and to take effectual measures against a repetition. To demand more, would be a wrong in Gr. Britain: for to demand satisfaction *beyond* what is adequate, is a wrong. But it is proposed further to take the prize from the captors and restore her to the English. This is a very serious proposition.

The dilemma proposed in our conferences, appears to me unanswerable. Either the commission to the commander of the privateer was good, or not good. If not good, then the tribunals of the country will take cognisance of the transaction, recieve the demand of the former owner, and make restitution of the capture: and there being, on this supposition, a regular remedy at law, it would be irregular for the government to interpose.—If the commission be good, then the capture having been made on the high seas, under a valid commission from a power at war with Gr. Britain, the British owner has lost all his right, and the prize would be deemed good even in his own courts, were the question to be brought before his own courts. He has now no more claim on the vessel than any stranger would have who never owned her, his whole right being transferred by the laws of war to the captor.

The legal right then being in the captor, on what ground can we take it from him? Not on that of *right*, for the right has been transferred to him. It can only be by an act of *force*, that is to say, of reprisal for the offence committed against us in the port of Charleston. But the making reprisal on a nation is a very serious thing. Remonstrance and refusal of satisfaction[2] ought to precede; and when reprisal follows, it is considered as an act of war, and never yet failed to produce it in the case of a nation able to make war.—Besides, if the case were important enough to require reprisal, and ripe for that step, Congress must be called on to take it; the right of reprisal being expressly lodged with them by the constitution, and not with the executive.

I therefore think that the satisfaction already made to the *government* of Great Britain is quite equal to what ought to be desired in the present case: that the property of the British *owner* is transferred by the laws of war to the *captor*; that for us to take it from the captor would be an act of force or reprisal which the circumstances of the case do not justify, and to which the powers of the Executive are not competent by the constitution.

TH: JEFFERSON

May. 16. 1793.

MS (DLC: Washington Papers); entirely in TJ's hand; endorsed by Bartholomew Dandridge, Jr. PrC (DLC); partially overwritten in a later hand. Tr (Lb in DNA: RG 59, SDC); at head of text: "The heads of Departments & the Attorney General of the US. having been called upon by the President of the US. to give their opinions on the subject of the Government of the US. interfering, to cause restoration to be made of certain vessels taken as prizes by a French privateer, fitted out at Charleston, & brought into the Port of Philadelphia, The Secretary of State gave the following opinion." Entry in SJPL: "Opn on an English prize taken by French privateer & brot here."

This opinion stemmed from the inability of the Cabinet to agree on a neutrality issue raised in one of the series of memorials George Hammond had written to TJ on 8 May 1793—whether the United States government was obliged to restore to their original owners British merchant ships captured and brought into American ports by the French privateers commissioned by Edmond Charles Genet at Charleston. Pursuant to the President's direction, the Cabinet met without him and considered this question on 15 May 1793. During this meeting the Cabinet divided equally, with TJ and the Attorney General opposed to the restoration of these prizes and the Secretaries of Treasury and of War in favor of it. Unable to present the President with a unanimous opinion on this question, the Cabinet members agreed to submit separate written opinions. TJ submitted his opinion against restoration to the President this day, and the Attorney General wrote a concurring opinion on the following day. The Secretary of the Treasury and the Secretary of War also transmitted their opinions in favor of restoration to the President this day, arguing that since Genet's commissions clearly violated American neutrality, restoring the prizes was necessary to preserve that neutrality and avoid giving Great Britain a *casus belli* against the United States (Alexander Hamilton to Washington, 15 May 1793, Syrett, *Hamilton*, XIV, 454-60; Henry Knox to Washington, 16 May 1793, DLC: Washington Papers; Edmund Randolph to Washington, 17 May 1793, same; Washington, *Journal*, 141).

The President then attempted, through the Attorney General, to probe mercantile opinion in Philadelphia on this issue before coming to a decision. Randolph advised Washington that the majority of the people clearly opposed restitution, but despite one report that ninety percent of the merchants were in agreement, he insisted that most of them necessarily supported restitution because "the existence of our poor mercantile capitals is so interwoven with those of Great Britain, that the pleasure of the British merchants must always be a rule of action to ours." He also informed Washington that on 17 May he had urged the Secretary of State, as they were leaving the President's house, "to discover from Mr. Genest his temper upon this subject, and his participation in the affair of the commission. He expressed his hope, that something might result from a communication with him, which might lessen the present embarrassment. Perhaps an intimation to Mr. J. might induce him to be more earnest in this pursuit" (Randolph to Washington, 18 May 1793, "private," DLC: Washington Papers). What ensued from the Attorney General's suggestion is not known, but by 21 May the President had resolved the conflict of opinion in the Cabinet in favor of TJ and Randolph, although the Secretary of State waited another two weeks before officially informing the British minister that the federal government would not restore the prizes taken by the privateers Genet had commissioned in Charleston (TJ to William Vans Murray, 21 May 1793; Hammond to TJ, 31 May 1793; TJ to Hammond, 5 June 1793; Hammond to Lord Grenville, 10 June 1793, PRO: FO 5/1; Washington, *Journal*, 159). For the related issue of whether the privateer and its prizes should be expelled from American ports, see Notes on the *Citoyen Genet* and Its Prizes, 20 May 1793.

The editorial caption for this opinion in Ford, VI, 257, has misled some scholars into believing that the English PRIZE in question was the *Little Sarah* (see Thomas, *Neutrality*, 191; Malone, *Jefferson*, III, 100). In fact, the two ships under consideration in the present opinion were the privateer *Citoyen Genet*, which had been commissioned by Edmond Charles Genet and outfitted at Charleston, and the *William*, a British prize it had captured on the high seas on 3 May 1793 and sent to Philadelphia. The *William* arrived on 12 May, and the *Citoyen Genet* and its second prize, the *Active*, captured on 9 May 1793, reached Philadelphia two days later (Hammond, "List of British Ships captured on the coast of America," n.d., enclosed in Hammond to Lord Grenville, 17 May 1793, PRO: FO 5/1; "Statement of British vessels captured and brought as prizes into the . . . ports of the United States," n.d., enclosed in Hammond to Grenville, 5 Nov. 1794, *Counter Case*, 610; *National Gazette*, 15 May 1793; *General Advertiser*, 15 May 1793; Woodfin, "Citizen Genet," 603-4; TJ to William Rawle, 15 May 1793, and note; and Hammond to TJ, 5 June 1793). For the case of the *Little Sarah*, see Memorial from Benjamin Holland and Peter Mackie, 24 May 1793; Edmund Randolph to TJ, 26 May 1793; and Cabinet Opinions on the *Little Sarah*, 8 July 1793, and note.

The United States government's MODERATE APOLOGY was contained in TJ to Hammond, 15 May 1793.

[1] TJ first wrote "a fair neutrality" and then altered it to read as above.

[2] Preceding four words interlined.

From Martha Jefferson Randolph

I recieved your kind letter of April the 28 a week ago and should have answered it imediately but that the house was full of company at the time. The subject of it has been one of infinite anxiety both to Mr. Randolph and my self for many months and tho I am too sensible of the iliberality of extending to one person the infamy of an other, to fear one moment that it can reflect any real disgrace upon me in the eyes of people of sense yet the generality of mankind are weak enough to think otherwise and it is painful to an excess to be obliged to blush for so near a connection. I know it by fatal experience. As for the poor deluded victim I believe all feel much more for her than she does for her self. The villain having been no less successfull in corrupting her mind than he has in destroying her reputation. Amidst the distress of her family she alone is tranquil and seems proof against every other misfortune on earth but that of a separation from her vile seducer. They have been *tried* and acquited tho I am sorry to say his Lawers gained more honour by it than they did as but a small part of the world and those the most inconsiderable people in it were influenced in there opinion by the dicision of the court. In following the dictates of my own heart I was so happy as to stumble upon the very conduct you advised me to, before I knew your opinion. I have continued to behave with affection to her which her errors have not been able to eradicate from my heart and could I suppose her penitent, I would redouble my attentions to her though[1] I am one of the few who have allways *doubted* the truth of the report. As the opinion I had of R. R. was most exalted would to heaven my hopes were equal to my fears but the latter often to often[2] preside. The divisions of the family encrease daily. There is no knowing where they will end. The old gentleman has plunged into the thickest of them governed by the most childish passions he lends the little weight his imprudence has left him to widen the breaches it should be his duty to close. Mr. R—s conduct has been such as to conciliate the affections of the whole family. He is the Link by which so many discordant parts join. Having made up his difference with David Randolph there is not one individual but what Looks up to him as one, and the only one who has been uniform in his affection to them. My Little cherubs are both in perfect health. Anna was very much delighted with the *yather* and *fasty old bosselor* enclosed in it. She talks incessantly of you and Aunt Polly. Your chess nuts are all alive but *one* and the *acasia*'s all dead but one. But that is very much grown and flourishing. Bergere has aded one to the number of genuine shepherds. The mungrels encrease upon us daily. My garden is in good order and would really cut a figure but for the worms and[3] catipillars which abound so every where this year that they destroy the seed before it comes up and even the Leaves of the trees. Adieu my dear Papa. We are all impatient to see you. My love to Dear Maria and believe me ever yours,   M. RANDOLPH

RC (ViU: Edgehill-Randolph Papers); minimal punctuation supplied; endorsed by TJ as received 25 May 1793 and so recorded in SJL.

THE POOR DELUDED VICTIM was Ann Cary Randolph and HER VILE SEDUCER was Richard Randolph; for a different interpre-

tation of this controversial episode, see note to TJ to Martha Jefferson Randolph, 28 Apr. 1793. THE OLD GENTLEMAN: Thomas Mann Randolph, Sr.

[1] Word interlined.
[2] Preceding two words interlined.
[3] Preceding two words interlined.

From Thomas Mann Randolph, Jr.

DEAR SIR   Monticello May 16: 1793.

I thank you most heartily for the information your last letter contained and beg you to favor me with communications concerning the French whenever you have leisure as we may expect the grossest misrepresentations in the papers and I feel myself warmly interested in their affairs. Their late misfortunes have excited a general sorrow in this part of the country: all persons with whom I have intercourse except those in the towns sympathize strongly with them and wish it were possible to give them aid. The antipathy to Englishmen seems to become more violent and more general, with good reason too in my opinion for to the former causes of hatred, their insults and oppressions their hostilities and rapine, are now added their present persecution of truth and justice and their late base endeavor to undermine that free government the establishment of which they could not hinder with force, by giving countenance and aid to our profligate citizens in their treasonable schemes.

The English traders in Richmond have been so loud in their applauses of our aristocratic faction and so bold in expressing their abhorrence of the French doctrines that they have at length brought out some menaces in the papers of that place. It is certainly not consistent with Liberty to inforce silence on any man but when the cause of Liberty itself is in danger, her friends will not have their ears assailed by clamors against her. It is at least as reasonable for men to be irritated at the contemptuous treatment of their political opinions when evidently founded in truth and nature as at the ridicule of their manners or unjust censure of their morals. Your most aff. friend & hble Servt.

TH: M. RANDOLPH

Patsy and the children are in good health and we are extremely impatient to know the season of your visit this year.

RC (MHi); endorsed by TJ as received 25 May 1793 and so recorded in SJL.

To George Washington

May. 16. 1793.

Th: Jefferson presents his respects to the President and submits to his approbation a letter to Mr. Ternant, in conformity to that to Mr. Hammond. It has been submitted to the Secretaries of the treasury and War[1] and Attorney General, and corrected by them. If the President approves the letter he asks the favor of him to stick a wafer in it, and the bearer will proceed to deliver that and Mr. Hammond's at the same time, as Th:J. thinks they should be.—He knows of the arrival of Mr. Genest, and thinks this letter had better be delivered to Mr. Ternant before Genest is announced, or several days delay, and a new moulding of the business, might take place. For this reason Th:J. thinking the letter might find the President at table, supposed the importance of the case would justify his desiring it to be opened even in that situation.

RC (DNA: RG 59, MLR); addressed: "The President of the US. to be opened immediately"; endorsed by Tobias Lear. Tr (Lb in same, SDC). Not recorded in SJL. Enclosure: TJ to Jean Baptiste Ternant, 15 May 1793.

[1] TJ first wrote "Secretary of the treasury" before altering the passage to read as above.

From Brothers Coster & Company

SIR   Newyork 17th. May 1793.

Our Brig Resolution Commanded by John H: Shackerly, which sailed from the Texel on the 17th. of february last, was on the next day boarded by a french Privateer call'd the young-Mary Commanded by Phil Everaert belonging to the Port of Dunkirk, and carried by force to the Port of Ostende; The french Consul there examined his Papers, but having no Power to decide would have transmitted them to Paris; Our Capt. was advised by the House of John Buchanan & Co. and several other Merchants, to make a small sacrifice to the Privateer and Pursue his voyage immediately; he paid therefore some Money and was released the next day. We take the Liberty to inclose two Letters of the french Consul and two Protest of our Capt., which will explain this Transaction more fully, likewise a receipt of the Money the Capt. has paid, and also a bill of the loss sustained by the interruption of his voyage.

We ask the favor Sir! that you will be pleased to take this business in your consideration, and expect as Citizens of the united States, to be indemnified for the loss we have Suffered on account of the unlawfull proceedings of the above mentioned Privateer. We have the honor to be with all Respect, Sir Your most Ob: & Hle: Servants

BROTHERS COSTER & COMPY

RC (DNA: RG 76, France, Unbound Records); at head of text: "Thomas Jefferson Esqr. Philadelphia"; endorsed by TJ as received 18 May 1793 and so recorded in SJL. Enclosures not found.

Brothers Coster & Company, a mercantile firm at 35 Little Dock Street, New York City, flourished during the French Revolutionary and Napoleonic wars thanks in part to good contacts in the Netherlands. The principals were Henry Arnold Coster (d. 1821) and John Gerhard Coster (d. ca. 1841), natives of Haarlem in the Netherlands, who immigrated to New York around the time of the American Revolution ([Joseph A. Scoville], *The Old Merchants of New York City*, 2d ser. [New York, 1864], 190-5; *Wealth and Biography of the Wealthy Citizens of New York City . . .*, 6th ed. [New York, 1845], 8, facsimile reprint in Henry W. Lanier, *A Century of Banking in New York, 1822-1922* [New York, 1922]; Pieter J. van Winter, *American Finance and Dutch Investment, 1780-1805: With an Epilogue to 1840*, rev. and trans. with the assistance of James C. Riley, 2 vols. (New York, 1977), I, 442, 467n; *New York Genealogical and Biographical Record*, CXI [1980], 14).

From Tench Coxe

SIR   May 17th. 1793

An application has been made to me, since I had the honor of seeing you, to know whether it will be illegal, or, in any respect, improper for a Citizen of the United States to accept the business and to perform the service of an agent for the prizes sent and to be sent into the port of Philadelphia by the French ships of war, *public* and *private*. I have promised the applicants information upon the Subject, who will forbear to engage or to act until they receive an answer, and I have no doubt but that they will conform to what may be thought a proper line of conduct in the premises. With great respect, I have the Honor to be, Sir, your most Obedt Servant   TENCH COXE

RC (DLC); in a clerk's hand, signed by Coxe; at foot of text: "The Secretary of State"; endorsed by TJ as received 17 May 1793 and so recorded in SJL. Dft (PHi: Coxe Papers).

From Tench Coxe

Sir   Treasury Department Revenue office May 17th. 1793.

I have the honor to transmit you a note of all the Sea letters received by me, and of the Disposition thereof. A communication of similar import has been made to the Secretary of the Treasury that he may know for how many the Collectors of the Customs are to be held responsible. With great respect, I have the honor to be, Sir, Your most Obedient Servant   TENCH COXE
           Commissioner of the Revenue

Sea letters, considered as received; Seventy seven. (including seven transmitted thro the Messenger of the Department of State to the Collector of Philadelphia on or about the 30th. of April 1793   }   77

Transmitted to the Collector of Boston		11	
Ditto	of New York	13	
Ditto of Philada. (including the above seven),		37	
Ditto	of Baltimore	9	
Ditto	of Alexandria	7	77

RC (DLC); in a clerk's hand, signed by Coxe; below signature: "The Secretary of State"; endorsed by TJ as received 17 May 1793 and so recorded in SJL.

The COMMUNICATION OF SIMILAR IMPORT to Alexander Hamilton has not been found.

To George Washington

           May 18. 93.

Th: Jefferson has the honor to inform the President that having, from a slight expression of Mr. Genet's yesterday, doubted whether he did not chuse to wait upon the President separately from Mr. Ternant, he called on the latter yesterday evening, but he was not at home. He called again this morning, and left it to himself and Mr. Genet to come together or separately as they should chuse. Ternant now writes that he will wait on the President precisely a quarter before two, consequently separately from Mr. Genet.

RC (DNA: RG 59, MLR); addressed: "The President of the US."; endorsed by Tobias Lear. Tr (Lb in same, SDC). Not recorded in SJL.

According to SJL, on 17 May 1793 TJ received a letter of the previous day from Jean Baptiste Ternant pertaining to his recall as French minister to the United States. This missive, not found, was obviously distinct from the letter Ternant NOW WRITES about his meeting with the President, which is not recorded in SJL and has not been found.

To George Washington

May 18. 1793.

Th: Jefferson presents his respects to the President and will take the liberty of waiting on him at half after one, as well that he may get through some long papers he has to communicate to him, as that he may be sure of being there when Mr. Genet comes.

RC (DNA: RG 59, MLR); addressed: "The President of the US."; endorsed by Tobias Lear. Tr (Lb in same, SDC). Not recorded in SJL.

For the LONG PAPERS in question, see Tobias Lear to TJ, 20 May 1793.

To Nathaniel Anderson

DEAR SIR   Philadelphia May 19. 1793.

Two or three days before the receipt of your favor of the 11th. inst. (which I received yesterday only) I had received a letter from Colo. Gamble asking me to patronize his proposals to Mr. Genet on the same subject with what is mentioned in your letter. I do not know that I can be of use to either of you in this case, tho I wish to be so in this and every other case. I do not know what will be Mr. Genet's plan: however if it should admit of communications between him and me, you may rely on my rendering the justice due both to yourself and Colo. Gamble. I rather imagine that the operations for the last crop are pretty well over. I am with great esteem Dear Sir Your most obedt. humble servt

TH: JEFFERSON

PrC (DLC); at foot of text: "Mr. N. Anderson." Tr (DLC); 19th-century copy.

To Mary Barclay

DEAR MADAM   Philadelphia May 19. 1793.

I recieved yesterday your favor of the 9th. Colo. Humphreys has been instructed to proceed a second time to Gibraltar and to settle the affairs of Mr. Barclay with the public, and as it is not probable he had any others there than with the public, this settlement will go to the whole. I think you may be assured that Colo. Humphreys will render you every service in his power, and[1] recommendations to him to that effect shall certainly not be wanting. Colo. Humphreys is in habits of connection with the Bulkeleys, the correspondents of Mr. J. Barclay, which will facilitate the delivery to him of Mr. Barclay's private effects. In this and every other particular in which I can render you any service, I shall do it with the utmost pleasure and zeal, being with sentiments of most sincere esteem Dear Madam Your most obedt. & most humble servt

Th: Jefferson

PrC (DLC); at foot of text: "Mrs. Barclay." Tr (DLC); 19th-century copy.

¹ TJ here canceled "my."

To Robert Gamble

Dear Sir   Philadelphia May 19. 1793.

I have to acknolege the receipt of your favors of the 10th. and 13th. inst. and shall with great pleasure render you any service in my power with Mr. Genet. The footing on which Mr. Anderson places his views, with the priority of your application to Mr. Genet as well as the patronage under which it was presented, will, no doubt, have their weight. I do not think that these purchases will be made by bills, and consequently their security will not come into question. The course of the business will probably be for our government to pay the cash through their collectors in the states where the purchases will be made, so that they will be cash purchases. I wish to heaven the spirit of mill-building and manufacturing which you mention to have taken place in Augusta &c. could spread itself into Albemarle. We are miserably circumstanced there as to the disposal of our wheat. We can neither manufacture nor sell it there. And tho we have fine mill seats at the head of the navigation of the Rivanna, we cannot get mills built. We are however, under these discouragements, going entirely into the culture of wheat, and shall be able to furnish a great deal. I hope it will in time draw the attention of some of you spirited gentlemen of commerce. With every assurance of my dispositions to serve you, I am Dr Sir Your most obedt. humble servt   Th: Jefferson

PrC (DLC); at foot of text: "Colo. Gamble." Tr (DLC); 19th-century copy.

To Edmond Charles Genet

Sunday May 19. 93.

Th: Jefferson presents his respectful compliments to Mr. Genet. He will be at his office at half past after eight tomorrow morning, and must be with the President precisely at nine. If this short interval will suit Mr. Genet, Th:Jefferson will be happy to devote it to him. If not, the length of time he will be engaged with the President is so uncertain that he could not give him a fixed rendezvous till the next morning.

RC (AMAE: CPEU, Supplément, xx); addressed: "The Minister Plenipotentiary of the French republic." Not recorded in SJL.

From David Humphreys

SIR   Lisbon May 19th. 1793.

I have received on the 9th. instant the letter which you did me the honour to write to me on the 30th. of March. Although two Packets have arrived from England since that letter came to hand, I have received no news of Captn. Cutting. In the mean time, I pray you will assure the President on my part, that I am making preparations for proceeding in the proposed business, in order that there may be as little delay as possible; and that I shall not fail to use every exertion in my power to have the attempt attended with success. Still I entreat it may be remembered that the difficulties and obstacles which I have heretofore pointed out to him are neither removed or surmounted; and that as yet I have not been able to find any neutral vessel which could be chartered for the purpose, or any other safe mode of conveyance. I shall however hold myself personally ready to set out at a moment's notice, and will not omit to keep you advised of the circumstances; being with sentiments of perfect consideration & esteem Sir Your Most obedient & Most humble Servant   D. HUMPHREYS

RC (DNA: RG 59, DD); at head of text: "(No. 72.)"; at foot of text: "The Secretary of State"; endorsed by TJ as received 17 July 1793 and so recorded in SJL. Tr (Lb in same).

To John Garland Jefferson

DEAR SIR   Philadelphia May 19. 1793.

I have for some days delayed answering your letter of Apr. 27. to see whether any prospect would open of my complying with your desires from this quarter: but I assure you it is out of my power. A very capital disappointment in a sum of money, my share of which was 1000£. due under judgment and execution, and to have been received at Richmond in February last as was expected, has been delayed by some further evasions as I learn. Depending on this I had ventured to go here beyond my ordinary resources, so as to place me under embarrasments here. I have no doubt but Mr. Shelton could furnish your wants cheaper than

Colo. Bell, and should have preferred your taking things of him, especially as you live with him, but that my means happen to be in the one place and not in the other. However reluctantly therefore, I am obliged still to refer you to Colo. Bell.—As far as I am a judge, the district of practice you mark out in your letter is well chosen: but my long absence from my own country makes me a very incompetent judge. On this subject however I shall be able to confer with you vivâ voce, before you will commence the execution of your plan. I am with great esteem Dear Sir Yours affectionately   TH: JEFFERSON

PrC (DLC); at foot of text: "Mr. J. Garland Jefferson." Tr (ViU: Carr-Cary Papers); 19th-century copy.

To James Madison

TH:J. TO J. MAD.   Phila May 19. 1793.

I wrote you last on the 13th. Since that I have received yours of the 8th. I have scribbled on a separate paper some general notes on the plan of a house you inclosed. I have done more. I have endeavored to throw the same area, the same extent of walls, the same number of rooms, and of the same sizes, into another form so as to offer a choice to the builder. Indeed I varied my plan by shewing what it would be with alcove bedrooms, to which I am much attached.—I dare say you will have judged from the pusillanimity of the proclamation, from whose pen it came. A fear lest any affection should be discovered is distinguishable enough. This base fear will produce the very evil they wish to avoid: for our[1] constituents seeing that the government does not express their mind, perhaps rather leans the other way, are coming forward to express it themselves. It was suspected that there was not a clear mind in the P's consellors to receive Genet. The citizens however determined to recieve him. Arrangements were taken for meeting him at Gray's ferry in a great body. He escaped that by arriving in town with the letters which brought information that he was on the road. The merchants i.e. Fitzsimmons & Co. were to present an address to *the P*. on the neutrality proclaimed. It contained much wisdom but no affection. You will see it in the papers inclosed. The citizens determined to address *Genet*. Rittenhouse, Hutcheson, Dallas, Sargeant &c. were at the head of it. Tho a select body of only 30. was appointed to present it, yet a vast concourse of the people attended them. I have not seen it: but it is understood to be the[2] counter address.—Ternant's[3] hopes of employment in the French army turn out to be without grounds. He is told by the minister of war expressly that the places of Marechal de camp are all full. He thinks it more prudent therefore to remain in America. He delivered yesterday his letters of recall, and Mr. Genet presented his of credence. It is impossible for any thing to be more affectionate, more magnanimous than the purport of his mission. 'We know that under present circumstances we have a right to call upon your for the guarantee of our islands.[4] But we do not desire it. We wish you to do nothing but what is for your own good, and we will do all in our power to promote it. Cherish your own peace and prosperity. You have expressed a willingness to enter into a more liberal treaty of commerce with us; I bring full powers (and he produced them) to form such a treaty, and a preliminary decree of the National convention to lay open our country and it's colonies to you for every purpose of utility, without your participating the burthens of maintaining and defending them. We see in you the only persons on earth who can love us sincerely and merit to be so loved.' In short he offers every thing and asks nothing. Yet I know the offers will be opposed, and suspect they will not be accepted. In short, my dear Sir, it is impossible for you to concieve what is passing in our conclave: and it is evident that one or two at least, under pretence of avoiding war on the one side have no great antipathy to run foul of it on the other, and to make a part in the confederacy of princes against human liberty.—The people in the Western parts of this state have been to the excise officer and threatened to burn his house &c. They were blacked and otherwise disguised so as to be unknown. He has resigned, and H. says there is no possibility of getting the law executed there, and that probably the evil will spread. A proclamation is to be issued, and another instance of my being forced to appear to approve what I have condemned uniformly from it's first conception.—I expect every day to receive from Mr. Pinckney the model of the Scotch threshing machine. It was to have come in a ship which arrived 3. weeks ago, but the workman had not quite finished it. Mr. P. writes me word that the machine from which my model is taken threshes 8. quarters (64. bushels) of oats *an hour*, with 4. horses and 4. men. I hope to get it in time to have one erected at Monticello to clean out the present crop.—I inclose you the pamphlet you desired. Adieu.

RC (DLC: Madison Papers). PrC (DLC).

In his letter of 8 May 1793 Madison had evidently enclosed a plan of a house for his brother William and asked for TJ's comments. Neither that plan nor the GENERAL NOTES and alternative design with which TJ responded have been found (Madison to TJ, 19 June 1793; see also Elizabeth C. Norfleet, *Woodberry Forest: The Extended View* [Orange, Va., 1979], 178-83). THE PROCLAMATION: Washington's Proclamation of Neutrality. The address of the Philadelphia MERCHANTS favoring this proclamation was presented to the President on 17 May 1793, the same day that THE CITIZENS delivered to Genet their COUNTER ADDRESS professing attachment to the cause of France (both addresses are printed in *National Gazette*, 22 May 1793; the former had already appeared in the 18 May 1793 issues of the

Gazette of the United States and the *General Advertiser*).

Benjamin Wells was THE EXCISE OFFICER who had been THREATENED by a mob in April. In fact he RESIGNED neither then nor when a second mob seized his commission and official papers in November 1793. Despite Alexander Hamilton's urging that a proclamation BE ISSUED, none was, sparing TJ from ANOTHER INSTANCE OF MY BEING FORCED TO APPEAR TO APPROVE the excise (Washington, *Journal*, 141, 142n; Thomas P. Slaughter, *The Whiskey Rebellion: Fron-*

tier Epilogue to the American Revolution [New York, 1986], 150-1, 158; for the earlier instance, see George Washington to TJ, 15 Sep. 1792, and note).

The enclosed PAMPHLET is discussed in note to Notes on Stockholders in Congress, 23 Mch. 1793.

[1] Word written over "their," erased.
[2] Word written over "a."
[3] TJ here canceled "fair."
[4] Sentence thus in manuscript.

To John Mason

DEAR SIR   Philadelphia May 19. 1793.

I have been longer without answering your favor of Apr. 26. than I would have been if the answer could be of any consequence. I knew also that the same information was handed you thro another channel, which I have now to give, and give only in respect to your letter. The government of the US. will not meddle with the investment of the monies they will pay to France. They will pay the cash to the order of the French minister, and leave it to him to make the purchases of flour in what places, and through what agents he pleases. You will therefore perceive that nothing can be done for you in the way proposed. Had there been room for it, no one would render you a service with more pleasure than Dear Sir Your most obedt. humble servt   TH: JEFFERSON

PrC (DLC); at foot of text: "Mr. John Mason." Tr (DLC); 19th-century copy.

Tobias Lear sent Mason THE SAME IN-FORMATION on 6 May 1793 (Fitzpatrick, *Writings*, XXXII, 450n).

On 7 June 1793 Mason wrote TJ a brief letter enclosing his and James Fenwick's

joint consular bond for Stephen Cathalan, Jr., in accordance with TJ's directions when he was in Philadelphia a few days ago (RC in DNA: RG 59, MLR; at foot of text: "Thomas Jefferson Esqr"; endorsed by George Taylor, Jr., as received 11 June 1793). The bond has not been found.

From Robert Quarles

SIR   Virginia, Columbia May 19th. 1793

Altho' I have Not the honor of a Personal Acquaintance with you, Yet from the recommendation of those who have, I have taken the liberty to trouble you with the Negotiation of a small matter of business.

Some time in the Course of the last year, I left in the hands of a Mr. Dunscomb in Richmond, an Account of the Claims I have against the

Public as a Lieutenant in the late Continental Army. He tells me he carried them to the Proper Office for their Adjustment in Philadelphia, with a Certificate accompanying them from a Magistrate before whom I had made Oath to their propriety; and that a Variety of difficulties was Started so as to prevent their liquidation, therefore he left the papers in the Office to be farther Operated on. Now Sir I wish you would so far interest yourself as to Apply to the Office, and do me the favor of letting me know the result thereof, in doing which you will confer an Obligation on Sir your very Obt. & Hble. Servt   ROBERT QUARLES

RC (DLC); endorsed by TJ as received 3 June 1793 and so recorded in SJL.

Robert Quarles (1763-1827) of Columbia, Virginia, served as ensign and regimental quartermaster of the First Virginia Regiment in the Continental Army from 15 May 1782 to the end of the Revolution, his rank of LIEUTENANT apparently having been a brevet award. He held the rank of major in the Albemarle County militia in the late 1780s and was superintendent of the state arsenal at Point of Fork from August 1793 until it closed in 1801 (National Society of the Daughters of the American Revolution, *DAR Patriot Index* [Washington, D.C., 1966], 553; Heitman, *Register*; CVSP, III, 615, IV, 546, VI, 515-17, 576, IX, 183-4, 202, X, 148, 445-7; Edgar E. Hume, ed., *Papers of the Society of the Cincinnati in the State of Virginia 1783-1824* [Richmond, 1938], 4, 116-17, 226-7).

To Thomas Mann Randolph, Jr.

DEAR SIR   Philadelphia May 19. 1793.

Your favor of the 8th. came to hand yesterday. I received one at the same time of May 13. from Dr. Currie expressing his hope that Colo. T. Randolph would get the better of his complaints. This circumstance with that of your being all returned to Monticello in good health is most pleasing to my mind. Maria appears entirely recovered. At least I am relieved from apprehensions as to the nature of her disease.—The general war which has taken place among other powers, and the cautions which are necessary to keep ourselves clear of it, produce daily incidents which add much to my occupations. I am now quite unable to pay that[1] attention to my own affairs, which to be of any use should be followed up. I had entertained hopes of running up one flank of my house this fall. But I now apprehend we shall have to weather another winter in it as it is. Were it adviseable to continue the carpenters at their occupation in that line, I believe with you it would be better to employ one to work with them. In this case he should undertake to find work enough in the neighborhood to pay his own share, and to accept these debts as *payment*. For I know nothing which our peace of mind requires so carefully to be avoided as money-engagements in a country where the money-circulation is so dull as in Virginia. But I doubt whether it would not be better (as I scarcely expect now[2] to do any thing to the house this fall) to devote this season to my canal. It is a great object, and enters materially into my plan of renting my estate. To carry it on with vigour will require that all our force be concentered on it, and every thing else laid by for it. When the canal is once done, the water visibly brought to the place and the fall demonstrated, the greatest obstacle to renting it will be removed. Till this be done also, I cannot begin my pot-ash plan, which I have also at heart as a resource for money subsidiary to the farm. The motives then are very powerful for getting the canal out of hand, and if this summer could accomplish it, I should think it a great acquisition in itself, and that my way would be cleared for other interesting objects. To this therefore I would rather now point all our efforts. My ideas on the subject I expressed in my letter to you of Feb. 3.   I shall take the first vacant time in my power to go to Brandy-wine and the head of Elk, to find land tenants and a mill tenant. And to settle with them the season of their removal. This will fix a term *beyond which* at least my stay here cannot be continued. I have reason to expect daily the arrival at Richmond of a mason and house joiner from Scotland. The person is now here who engaged them before he came away, and says they would come in the first ship bound to Richmond. It becomes necessary to think of something which may employ them till I come home. I would wish in the first place that they should not stay one day in Richmond: as even an hour may give them ideas which may destroy their utility to me afterwards. The mason may be employed in cutting columns for the porticoes, exactly like those now standing. 6 more will be wanting. I intend Moses to be his disciple. As the raising and bringing up such large peices of stone will require considerable force, this will occasion so far an interruption of the canal. It will be the less if he is first employed in making the bases and Capitels, because these peices are small, and will yet give him a great deal of work.—As to the house joiner, I mean Johnny (Betty Heming's son) to work with him. The first plain and simple job for him will be to make 10. window frames, exactly of the size of those now in the house and of the same mouldings, but without entablatures. The poplar stocks 9. feet long and sawed into peices 8. I. square, mentioned in the memorandum I left when I came from Monticello, were intended for these. Before he could get through this I could add another job of time. He will have to vamp up my old set of tools and make the most of them, and what is necessary in addition to these, and cannot be made by himself and George, I will send from hence, on his notifying them. As I destine the stone house for workmen, the present inhabitants must remove into the two nearest of the new log-houses, which were intended for them; Kritty taking the nearest of the whole, as oftenest wanted about the house.—With these general views, be so good as to marshal the troops and their employment as you please. If they are always employed, the order in which things are done will be less material.

The horse you have purchased for me I shall take with pleasure. I should not propose to trouble you with such a commission and to leave the purchase on your hands if on trial it was not found to answer. Besides if he fulfills my wishes in other points, his being rather delicate is a motive of preference rather than of rejection. My next return to Monticello is the last long journey I shall ever take, except the last of all for which I shall not want horses. I should propose some time hence to send Tarquin with a servant to George town where he may meet one with the new purchase, exchange and return. Tarquin's hoofs (wherein is his whole complaint, and only in those of the fore-feet) have been more tender this spring than ever, insomuch that for some time I could not ride him at all, and now he cannot go fast. But he is getting better.—The moment I receive the model of the threshing machine, I will forward it to Monticello. I wish it may be in time to have one erected for this crop. My love to my dear daughter and kiss the little ones for me. I am dear Sir your's with constant affection   TH: JEFFERSON

RC (DLC); at foot of first page: "Mr. Randolph." PrC (MHi).

The PERSON . . . HERE who engaged the stone mason and house joiner was James Traquair (Memorandum on James Traquair, 5 Dec. 1792). TJ gave his instructions on sawing the POPLAR STOCKS in Memorandums for Manoah Clarkson, [23 Sep. 1792].

[1] Word written over "any."
[2] Word interlined.

From Tobias Lear

May 20th: 1793

T. Lear has the honor, by the President's command, to return to the Secretary of State the following letters &ca. which were laid before the President on Saturday the 18th. currt.

A Letter from Mr. Short of the 6th. of March.

Copy of Letters to and from the Governor of St. Augustine.

Copy of treaties between the Spaniards and several of the Indian Nations.

Copy of a letter to the Minister of France—of 15th. Curt.

Translation of Mr. Genet's letter of Credence.

Do.   of Mr. Ternant's letter of recall.

There is also enclosed a letter from Mr. Vall Travers to the President, which he wishes the Secretary of State to peruse and give thereto such an Answer as may be proper.

RC (DLC); endorsed by TJ as a letter from Washington received 20 May 1793. Recorded in SJPL as a letter from Washington. Enclosures (1) William Short to TJ, 6 Mch. 1793. (2) Enclosures to fourth letter of Josef de Jaudenes and Josef Ignacio de Viar to TJ, 12 May 1793. (3) Treaty of Pensacola between Spain and the Creek Indians, 1 June 1784 (see note to Viar and Jaudenes to TJ, 7 May 1793). (4) Treaty of Natchez between Spain and the Chickasaw and Choctaw Indians, 14 May 1792 (see note to first letter of Jaudenes and Viar to TJ of 12 May 1793). (5) TJ to Jean Baptiste Ternant, 15 May 1793. (6) Translation of the Letter of Credence from the Provisional Executive Council of France, 30 Dec. 1792 (enclosure to Genet to TJ, 16 May 1793). (7) Rodolph Vall-Travers to Washington, 16 Mch. 1793 (see note to Vall-Travers to TJ, 29 Mch. 1793). The letter recalling Ternant has not been found.

TJ did not reply to the enclosed letter from Vall-Travers to the President.

From Thomas Sim Lee

Sir   In Council Annapolis May 20.[1] 1793

We have been honoured with your letter of the 26th. Ulto. covering the Proclamation issued by the President of the United States, respecting the conduct to be observed towards the powers at War in Europe; and we have issued a Proclamation conformably to the Sentiments contained in that of the President. Since that time we have received from Mr. Hamilton British Consul at Norfolk, the letter of which the enclosed is a copy.[2] The Captured Vessel is, contrary to Mr. Hamilton's information, in Choptank river on the Eastern Shore, and will probably be given up to Capt. Tucker by the Naval Officer of that District, who has, as we are informed, taken her into his Care upon her being abandoned by the Captors. We have acquainted the Consul with our incompetency in point of authority to interfere, even Supposing the Capture to be illegal, and have advised him that it can only be obtained from the general government. Esteeming the Situation of the United States with Regard to the powers at War to be extremely critical, and conceiving that the greatest circumspection will be requisite to keep them from being involved with some of the parties, We have thought it proper to make you this communication; and[3] if any Measures can be pointed out by which[4] we may aid the Views of the President in so important a concern we shall be happy to adopt them. With the greatest Consideration We have the honor to be, Sir, Yr Mo. Obedt. & Mo. Hble Servts.

Tho. S. Lee

RC (DNA: RG 59, MLR); in a clerk's hand, with signature and part of complimentary close by Lee; at foot of text: "The Honble Thomas Jefferson Esqr. Secretary of State"; endorsed by TJ. Dft (MdAA: Maryland State Papers); in Lee's hand, with some revisions in a clerk's hand (see notes 3-4 below); only the most important emendations are noted below. FC (MdAA: Letterbooks of Governor and Council of Maryland). Recorded in SJL as received 23 May 1793. Enclosure: John Hamilton to

Lee, Norfolk, 7 May 1793, soliciting his interference to prevent any unlawful condemnation in his state of the British-owned schooner *Eunice* of New Providence, Henry Tucker master, bound for Philadelphia with 2,000 dollars in specie and a few boxes of sugar when it was captured on 29 Apr. 1793 off Virginia in latitude 36° north in water 27 fathoms deep by an American-built armed schooner which sailed under French colors and was said to be French property but was manned largely by Americans; reporting that Tucker's captors put him on an American vessel bound for Norfolk while sending his ship as a prize to Baltimore; and requesting justice and protection for Tucker, who will deliver this letter (Tr in DNA: RG 59, MLR).

The NAVAL OFFICER who had taken charge of the *Eunice* was Jeremiah Banning (William Vans Murray to TJ, 9 May 1793).

[1] Reworked from "19" in Dft.

[2] In Dft Lee here canceled "We have advised Capt. Tucker to."

[3] Word substituted in Dft by clerk for Lee's original passage: "and would be glad to be informed of any measures by which we may aid the ⟨wise intentions⟩ views of the President in ⟨this particular⟩ so important a concern." Remainder of sentence added by clerk below Lee's original complimentary close.

[4] In Dft the clerk here canceled "in the case of more events of this nature."

From Gouverneur Morris

DEAR SIR   Sain port near Paris 20 May 1793

I have the Honor to transmit herewith the copy of mine (No. 29) of the nineteenth of last Month. You will see by the Gazettes the State of Affairs as given to the Public but much Allowance must be made, as I have already had occasion to mention. It is however clear that the greater Part of those Troops which adhered to Dumouriez have return'd to their Country and many to their Standards. It is evident also that the Prince de Cobourg's Conduct in holding out again the old Constitution has been disapprov'd of by his Masters and their Associates, since he has found it proper to recall that Proclamation; but whether for what is there said as to the Government or as to the Territory of France may admit of Doubt: perhaps there may be a little of both in the objections made against it. The Delay to be noticed in the Operations of the Allied Armies proves in my Opinion two important Facts. One that they mean to leave as little as possible to Chance and therefore wait the Arrival of all their Forces and the other that the original Plans of the Campaign are to be steadily pursued. Hence I infer that the supposed Disunion mention'd in my last does not exist in any essential Degree. It seems that the Austrian Artillery was not come up untill very lately so as to open the Trenches against Condé which hitherto has been rather invested than beseiged. It seems also that the Hanoverian Troops have come on so slowly as to have given every advantage to the french Armies in Holland if the Successes of the Prince de Cobourg in Flanders had not rendered the proposed Invasion abortive. However the Period being now arriv'd about which it might reasonably be expected that the Weather would permit of offensive Operations and the Country afford Resources to the Cavalry of the Armies we shall soon know somewhat of the comparative Strength of Parties. On the northern Frontier they have to beseige not only Conde but Valenciennes Bouchain and Cambray in order to open a Road in the direct Line of Advance besides which it would seem that they want Douay and Arras on the Right with Bavay and Maubeuge on the left to cover their Flanks. Hence results the Formation of seven Seiges after Condé in order to open the Road fairly to Paris while on the Sea Coast they would want only Dunquerque and Calais after which they might march securely along the Coast taking Possession of the Ports and erecting slight Works to cover their Retreat should Retreat become necessary. I am persuaded therefore that the main Efforts will be made still in that last Direction, unless Intelligences are established in the Towns on the other Route. I learn, but on slender Authority, that the Citizens of Valenciennes and the regular Troops are not dispos'd to resist. The Militia or Volontaires are however well determind. I know that the Government are very apprehensive as to Normandy, and I still beleive in a descent there, and consequent Revolt. You will have seen that the Insurgents on the Southwest of the Loire have had hitherto very great Success altho the Gazettes have teemed with Accounts of the victories obtaind over them. That they have hitherto receivd no Succor from abroad confirms me in the Opinion that the main Blow is to be struck on the Side of Normandy, unless indeed the Enemies of France are absolutely blind. I learn that the Army of Biron has suffered very severely in the Defeats, all published as Victories gaind over the Piedmontese. However as yet the french Territory (notwithstanding the numerous Foes) remains untouchd, though on all Sides greatly menaced.

Enclosed you have Copies of my Letters of the twenty eighth of April and fourteenth Instant to Mr. Lebrun the Minister of foreign Affairs, with that of his Answer of the seventeenth and my Reply of to Day. These Pieces require no Comment. With sincere Esteem & Respect I have the Honor to be Dear Sir your obedient Servant

GOUV MORRIS

RC (DNA: RG 59, DD); at head of text "No. 30."; at foot of first page: "Thomas Jefferson Esqr. Secretary of State Philadelphia"; endorsed by TJ as received 5 Sep. 1793 and so recorded in SJL. FC (Lb in DLC: Gouverneur Morris Papers). Tr (DNA: RG 46, Senate Records, 3d Cong., 1st sess.). PrC (DNA: RG 59, MD). Tr (Lb in same, DD). Enclosures: (1) Morris to TJ, 19 Apr. 1793. (2) Same to Lebrun, 28 Apr. 1793, complaining about a resolution of the municipality of Dunkirk preventing Captain Alexander Frazer of the Fame, an American ship owned by Thomas Dickenson of Boston, from carrying 182 pipes of brandy from Dunkirk to Altona for Joshua

Johnson, the American consul in London—which resolution was first justified by the supposition that the brandy was intended for England and then (when Altona was accepted as the true destination) by the scarcity of brandy in Dunkirk—and requesting restitution of the cargo. (3) Same to same, 14 May 1793, predicting that a 9 May 1793 decree of the National Convention, which authorized French warships and privateers to seize neutral vessels carrying food from neutral countries to an enemy port and declared enemy merchandise carried on such vessels as lawful prize, would be adopted as to foodstuffs by France's maritime enemies, thereby leaving the success of such shipments in the future to naval superiority between the belligerents, and suggesting that it be modified by a supplementary decree to make it conform to France's treaty of commerce with the United States. (4) Lebrun to Morris, 17 May 1793, stating that the Committee of Public Safety will demand that the National Convention amend its decree of 9 May to accord with the treaty of commerce with the United States, advising that the Provisional Executive Council has determined that Dunkirk's dangerous situation justified its precaution in blocking the exportation of brandy, and transmitting the Council's decree providing for indemnification of the captain of the *Fame*. (5) Extract from the Register of the Provisional Executive Council, 16 May 1793, declaring that it approved the detention of the *Fame*'s cargo of brandy by the city of Dunkirk because of the danger of immediate attack by land and sea and the consequent need to maintain supplies for the troops, but ordering the city to reimburse the captain for the expenses incurred in loading and unloading the brandy, as well as for the resultant delay, and directing Lebrun to inform Morris why the Council could not comply with his request for the return of the brandy. (6) Morris to Lebrun, 20 May 1793, declaring that it was only natural for Dunkirk to secure supplies and suspend the general laws of commerce under threat of a siege, expressing pleasure that the Council has ordered indemnification and rejoicing in these "proceedings of a free people," asking that the order be executed with dispatch, and noting that he was informing the United States government that the decree of 9 May would be amended in a few days in the manner Lebrun described

(Trs of Enclosures Nos. 2-6 in DNA: RG 59, DD, in French, in Morris's hand; Trs in DNA: RG 46, Senate Records, 3d Cong., 1st sess., in French with English translations in the hand of George Taylor, Jr.; PrCs in DNA: RG 59, MD; Trs in Lb in same, DD, in French and English).

Morris's eventual vindication of an American treaty right violated by the National Convention in its decree of 9 May 1793 (see Enclosures Nos. 3 and 4 above) proved to be a short-lived French concession to American sensibilities. Under the terms of Article 23 of the 1778 treaty of commerce, France and the United States agreed to the principle that free ships make free goods, which in practice meant among other things that, with the exception of contraband (which was specifically defined in Article 24 to exclude provisions), neutral American ships carrying provisions or enemy goods were not liable to seizure by the French (Miller, *Treaties*, II, 21-2). However, in retaliation for British captures of American and other neutral ships bound for France with provisions, the National Convention's 9 May decree authorized French warships and privateers to capture and take into French ports neutral vessels bringing provisions to an enemy port or carrying merchandise owned by an enemy. In addition to confiscating enemy merchandise as lawful prize for the captor, the decree also provided that the provisions were to be paid for at the price they would have received at their intended place of destination and that after having unloaded their forbidden cargoes the captured ships would be permitted to depart with an allowance for the costs of freight and detention. Finally, the decree announced that these measures would cease as soon as enemy powers agreed that they would not seize neutral vessels bearing food for France or carrying merchandise owned by the French government or its citizens (ASP, *Foreign Relations*, I, 377-8). Although the Convention passed a decree on 23 May 1793 which exempted United States ships from this measure, it did so on the basis of Article 16 of the treaty of commerce, which dealt with the restoration of ships and mechandise rescued from pirates or robbers on the high seas. But the imperatives of war soon took precedence over French treaty obligations to a neutral ally. The Convention successively revoked this exemption on 28 May, restored it on 1 July, and revoked it again on 27 July 1793. Thereafter the United States remained subject to the provisions of the 9 May decree, with its attendant spoliation of American shipping, until January 1795, when the Convention finally nullified this measure five months after British repeal of a June 1793 order in council calling for the seizure of neutral ships carrying corn, flour, or meal to any French port or any port occupied by French armies (Morris to TJ, 1 June 1793, and note; ASP, *Foreign Relations*, I, 240, 642-3; Miller, *Treaties*, II, 16; Bowman, *Neutrality*, 108-15, 185-6; Samuel F. Bemis, "Washington's Farewell Address: A Foreign Policy of Independence," AHR, XXXIX [1934], 250-5).

TJ submitted this letter to the President on 5 Sep. 1793, and Washington returned it the same day (Washington, *Journal*, 238).

Notes on the *Citoyen Genet* and Its Prizes

Qu. shall the Privateer fitted out at Charleston, and her prizes be ordered out of the ports of the US.?   May 20. 93.

I. As PUNISHMENT.

explain circumstance which drove Genet into the Southern passage

induced him to land at Charleston

Fr. citizens solliciting commission to arm.—Governr. winking at it.

words of XXII. art. *shall not* be lawful for enemies of Fr. fit out privateers

IMPLICATION that it *shall* be lawful for French.

so understood universally. by every one here—by ourselves at Charleston—by Genet.

still true that is not EXPRESSLY PERMITTED—may be forbidden.

but till forbidden must be slight offence.

the Prohibition to be future, not RETROSPECTIVE.

II. RIGHT.

What RIGHT to order away?

XVII. makes LAWFUL to enter with prizes and stay.

in whom is the RIGHT to these privateers and prizes?

Fr. citizens retain fidelity in foreign country

have right to return to defence of country by sea or land.

may confer on that, associate, contribute money

may buy vessel with own money—man her themselves

ON CONDITION commit no hostility *within limits* of US.

as soon as out of limits themselves and vessel free as any other.

Fr. citizens *ante-residents*, on same footing as *new visitants*.

[71]

when take a vessel at sea, property transferred by laws of war.

this point understood at former conference.

for if not transferred should be given up.

if right transferred then XVIIth. article authorises entry

no HALF-WAY ACT justifiable.

obj. it is PUNISHMENT for the offence.

ans. NO offence till FORBIDDEN.—looks only to FUTURE.

III. POLICY of this TOUCHINESS.

Minister newly arrived

FIRST FROM the REPUBLIC

POPULARITY of French nation and cause.

Proposals he brings

no call of GUARANTEE

FREE TRADE to islands⎫
                to France⎭ by treaty

shall such a mission be received with reprimand?

and for whom. for England?

for confederated princes?

our reward the CYCLOPS' boon to Ulysses. LAST DE-VOURED. OD. *ι*. 369

are we playing the part England plaid? force France to attack us?

that we may take SIDE with the Confederated princes?

the party wishing that is very small.

[*On verso:*]

H. and K. were of opinion for giving up the prize, but if that could not be, then to order away the privateer and prize; and if that could not be, then to order away the privateer.

T.J. of opinion that neither could be given up or ordered away.

E.R. for ordering away the privateer and nothing more.

The President confirmed the last opinion and it seemed to be his own.

MS (DLC); entirely in TJ's hand, with all but the final four paragraphs written on recto and the rest at another time on verso (see note below). Entry in SJPL: "Notes on proposn to order away a privateer fitted out at Charleston." Included in the "Anas."

This document consists of two sections evidently written at different times on 20 May 1793. The first part, containing all but the four paragraphs written on verso, consists of notes of points TJ planned to make at

a Cabinet meeting on the subject of the *Citoyen Genet*, THE PRIVATEER FITTED OUT AT CHARLESTON by direction of the new French minister, Edmond Charles Genet, and the *William* and the *Active*, the British PRIZES it had brought to Philadelphia (see note to Opinion on the Restoration of Prizes, 16 May 1793). Since TJ did not date the second part, which consists of the notes on the Cabinet's deliberations on this subject that he set down on verso—the only known record of this meeting—the tentative presumption is that this session took place on 20 May 1793. Soon thereafter TJ orally informed Genet of the President's decision that French privateers commissioned in the United States had to be withdrawn from American ports in order to preserve the nation's neutrality, a determination he confirmed in writing for the French minister some two weeks later in response to Genet's defense of the validity of his privateering commissions (Genet to TJ, 27 May 1793; TJ to Genet, 5 June 1793).

From F. P. Van Berckel

MONSIEUR   à Philadelphie Ce 20e. Mai 1793.

J'ai l'honneur de Vous envoyer Ci joint un Exemplaire imprimé du Manifeste que Leurs Hautes Puissances ont jugé à propos de publier à l'occasion de la Guerre qui Leur a été déclarée par la France.

Je m'acquitte par la des ordres que je viens de recevoir à Cet égard, ayant l'honneur d'etre avec les Sentimens de la plus parfaite Consideration Monsieur Votre très humble & très Obeïssant Serviteur.

F: P: VAN BERCKEL

RC (DNA: RG 360, PCC); at foot of text: "à Monsieur Jefferson Secretaire d'Etat &c. a Philadelphie"; endorsed by TJ as received 20 May 1793 and so recorded in SJL. Enclosure: *Manifeste. Les Etats Généraux des Provinces-Unies* [n.p., n.d.], a manifesto of the States General, 20 Feb. 1793, written in the form of a reply to a proc-lamation addressed to the people of the Netherlands by Charles François du Périer Dumouriez, commander of the invading French forces, denouncing his call for the overthrow of the Prince of Orange and calling upon the Dutch people to repel the French invasion (pamphlet in same).

From Willink, Van Staphorst & Hubbard

SIR   Amsterdam 20 May 1793.

We have your respected favor of 19 March remitting us Hd. Cy. ƒ99.000. in a Bill drawn by the Treasury of the United States to your order on ourselves, which we shall credit to an account with the Secretary of the united States of America, That will in future be charged with the drafts of Mr. Short, Mr. Carmichael, Col: Humphreys, and Mr. Dumas for their salaries and allowances. We shall await the explanations you promise us by a Subsequent conveyance, to debit the above account with the Salaries and expences paid the above mentioned gentlemen from the first day of July 1790, that we may do it in the manner most agreable to your wishes.

You omitted to endorse the Bill to us Please therefore send us a Second properly transferred to us. With the assurances of our earnest desire, to render you the usefull and agreable offices in our Power We remain respectfully Sir Your most obedient Hble Servants.

WILHEM & JAN WILLINK

N. & J. VAN STAPHORST & HUBBARD

Dupl (DLC); at head of text: "Copy"; at foot of text: "The Hble Th: Jefferson Esqr."; endorsed by TJ as received "Aug."

To Brothers Coster & Company

GENTLEMEN   Philadelphia May 21. 1793.

I have duly received and considered your favor of the 17th. inst. complaining that the French privateer, the young Mary, commanded by Phil. Everaert, seised your vessel, the brig Resolution commanded by John H. Shackerly, carried her into Ostend, and there detained her some time, and praying an indemnification.   As it is to be presumed the French privateer had orders to cruize on the *enemies* of France only, any violation committed on the vessel of a *friend*, as that complained of by you, would be out of her orders, and not imputable to her sovereign. It is of the nature of a trespass, and states are not answerable for the unauthorized trespasses committed by their citizens. All that can be asked of them is to punish them. This we have a right to expect will be done on your prosecution of the matter. Nations however, in their treaties, take another measure to guard their citizens against the irregularities of privateers. They stipulate with each other that no commission shall be issued by either to a privateer without sufficient security taken to indemnify the sufferers by their irregularities. There is such a stipulation in our treaty with France, and we have no doubt that Capt. Everaert has given security in the port from which he issued, to which you can resort for indemnification. It would only be in the case that no such security has been taken, or that justice shall be refused you in resorting to it, that the US. could make it a subject of national complaint. For my own, as well as your greater satisfaction, I have communicated your papers to the Atty. Genl. of the US. who concurs with me in the above opinions. I am with great respect Gentlemen your most obedt. humble servt.   TH: JEFFERSON

PrC (DLC); at foot of text: "Messrs. Coster, freres & co." FC (Lb in DNA: RG 59, DL).

To Henry Knox, with Proposed Circular to the Governors of the States

Sketch of a letter proposed to be written by the Secretary of war to the governors of the states, according to the ideas understood to have been expressed on the subject.

Sir

A case which has lately presented itself here, and may do the same in other parts of the union, renders it necessary for the General government to provide a remedy which may be prompt, adequate and always within reach. An armed vessel of one of the powers engaged in the present war captured the ship of another, lying within the bay of Delaware, and consequently under the protection of the US. Both duty and honor required that the government should cause the capture to be restored which the minister, residing here, of the power whose vessel committed the aggression has very readily undertaken to have done. But as this remedy may not be adapted to every case, and especially to distant ones, some other is to be resorted to of more universal application. Capture being generally the consequence of attack and combat, and that by an armed and foreign force, is, in it's nature, a military aggression, to be repressed by the military force of the nation; and the rather as the aggressors are generally, both in power and position, beyond the coercive means of the civil authority. The standing military of the union is it's militia, and this is every where at hand to meet every violation of the public protection. To your Excellency therefore, as the head of the militia within your state, the President of the US. commits the charge of interposing in all cases of hostility committed between the belligerent parties, within the protection of your state; desiring that you will be pleased with the aid of your militia to detain the parties first aggressing, till you can communicate the case to the President, with evidence in writing which may establish the facts for his ultimate decision thereon. This you may be assured of recieving on every occasion with all the dispatch circumstances will admit.

Th: Jefferson presents his respectful compliments to Genl. Knox and sends him the preceding sketch, drawn according to what he understood to be the sentiments of gentlemen on the subject.
May 21. 93.

PrC (DLC); overwritten by TJ. Recorded in SJPL.

The ARMED VESSEL was the French frigate *Embuscade* and its prize was the British merchant SHIP *Grange*. The decision to send a circular to the governors of the states was presumably made by the Cabinet, perhaps at one of the meetings of 13-15 May at which the neutrality issues raised by the capture of the *Grange* were considered (Memorial from George Hammond, 2 May 1793, and note; TJ to Hammond, 15 May 1793). Knox adopted TJ's draft with only minor changes in wording. The Cabinet approved this revised version, probably the next day, for TJ's papers contain a copy of the modified letter bearing that date (Tr in DLC; in the hand of a State Department clerk, unsigned; dated "War department May 22d. 1793"). At the same meeting the Cabinet evidently approved the draft of a letter by the Secretary of War to the governors instructing them to prevent the commissioning, arming, or equipping of privateers in their jurisdictions, and to detain any vessel thus illegally fitted out. Indicating that both letters were intended only for the governors of "the several Atlantic States," Knox obtained the President's approval for the circulars on 23 May. The letter printed above was sent under that date, while the one concerning privateers was dated a day later (Washington, *Journal*, 147; Knox to Washington, [23?] May 1793, DLC: Washington Papers; and the texts sent to the governor of Virginia in cvsp, i, 377, 379).

To Henry Lee

Sir   Philadelphia May 21. 1793.

I have been duly honored with your favor of May 8. covering the letter of Mr. Newton, and that of May 13. with the letter of the British consul at Norfolk and the information of Henry Tucker, all of which have been laid before the President.

The putting the several harbours of the US. into a state of defence having never yet been the subject of deliberation and decision with the legislature, and consequently the necessary monies not having been appropriated or levied, the President does not find himself in a situation competent to comply with the proposition on the subject of Norfolk.

Mr. Newton supposes that by the treaties with France and Holland, those powers are authorised to arm vessels within our ports. A careful examination of the treaties will shew however that no such permission has been stipulated therein. Measures are accordingly taken to correct this error as to the past, and others will be taken to prevent a repetition of it. Prosecutions are ordered against Mr. Hooper and other American citizens who have participated in any hostilities against nations at peace with the US. and circular instructions are given to the District attornies of the US. to institute like prosecutions in all future similar cases. The bringing vessels to, of whatever nation, while within the limits of the protection of the US. will be pointedly forbidden; the government being firmly determined to enforce a peaceable demeanor among all the parties within those limits, and to deal to all the same impartial measure. I have the honor to be with the most perfect respect Your Excellency's most obedient & most humble servt   Th: Jefferson

RC (Herbert R. Strauss, Chicago, 1952); addressed: "His Excellency Governor Lee Richmond"; franked, stamped, and postmarked; endorsed by Lee. PrC (DLC). FC (Lb in DNA: RG 59, DL).

TJ obtained the President's approval of this letter on this day (Washington, *Journal*, 146).

To William Vans Murray

DEAR SIR   Philadelphia May 21. 1793.

I duly received your favor of the 9th inst. and communicated it's contents to the President, with other information received from other quarters on the same subject. The case has been fully considered: the Executive views the fitting out privateers in our ports as inadmissible in fair neutrality; they have taken measures for correcting what is past, and preventing the like in future, and most particularly for punishing our own citizens who have engaged, or shall engage, in hostilities against nations at peace with the US. On mature deliberation however they did not think they could order a restitution of the prizes taken by those privateers.—The part we have to act is delicate and difficult, not with respect to the other powers, who are temperate, forbearing, and without designs on us, but with respect to that nation which from her overbearing pride, constant course of injustice and propensity to eternal war, seems justly to have obtained for herself the title of hostis humani generis. No moderation, no justice, on our part can secure us against the violence of her character, and that we love liberty is enough for her to hate us. That any line of conduct either just or honorable will secure us from war on her part, is more to be wished than counted on. I am with sincere esteem Dear Sir your friend & servt   TH: JEFFERSON

PrC (DLC); at foot of text: "Mr. Murray." Tr (DLC); 19th-century copy.

HOSTIS HUMANI GENERIS: "enemy of the human race."

From Hans Rodolph Saabÿe

Copenhagen, 21 May 1793. Since his last letter of 22 Dec., which was accompanied by his security and an account of all American ships passing by this place for the last half of 1792, the great demand for corn in the Mediterranean, Spain, Portugal, and France and the resulting high prices for it confirm his remarks about grain shipments from America. Corn and munitions mostly animate trade, business being otherwise stagnant because of mercantile failures in Russia, Poland, Germany, Holland, Spain, England, as well as in Denmark, where only parliamentary intervention prevented more mischief. Already eight ships from the United States have arrived here this year and several others have passed by on their way to the Baltic, a list of which he will send at the end of next month. Besides the case of Captain Vredenburgh mentioned in his last letter, another American ship, the brig *Betsy*, Captain Joseph Chandler of Boston, was also cast away on the coast of Jutland, the mate and three crew members of which he has sent back to America with Captain Ambrose of New York. He encloses the register, received from Fabritius & Wever here, of the *Minerva* of Petersburg, which was sold in Europe. The good cause might yet succeed if depraved French manners and the resultant home broils do not prevent it. England's interference in the war is contrary to her interests, and the division of Poland may teach the English how their action promoted untoward consequences. It is probable that reasonable terms would lead to a speedy peace between England and France. Denmark and Sweden remain strictly neutral, despite efforts to make them follow a contrary course. The English and French governments have ended the recent molestation of Danish ships by their privateers, and now the Danish flag is respected. A few frigates and smaller armed vessels have been equipped to protect commerce.

RC (DNA: RG 59, CD); 4 p.; endorsed by TJ as received 17 July 1793 and so recorded in SJL. Enclosure not found.

TJ submitted this letter to the President on 17 July 1793 (Washington, *Journal*, 201-2).

To Josef Ignacio de Viar and Josef de Jaudenes

GENTLEMEN   Philadelphia May 21. 1793.

Your several favors of the 7th. and 12th. instant were duly received and laid before the President. I have to thank you for the intelligence relative to the Creek Indians contained in one of the latter, and forwarded to you by Governor Quesada: and I must do that gentlemen the justice to say that, as far as our information goes, we have no reason to believe that any thing has been done on his part to disturb the peace of the US. with the Indians. I repeat to you the assurance that the orders of the President have been, and continue to be, to the officers of the US. in all parts, to cultivate the peace of your colonies adjoining us with the Indian nations: and as I find, in the papers communicated, a charge against Mr. Seagrove[1] of exciting the Indians against them, I hope he has in no instance been guilty of it. The expression of his which ascribes the late hostilities to our neighbors, I suppose must allude to the governors in the Western quarter, against whom my former letters have informed you that we had well grounded motives of discontent. But these and all others will we hope be brought to an end by the negociations now going on at Madrid, which circumstance also renders unnecessary any observations on the treaties with the Creeks, Choctaws and Chickasaws, which you were so kind as to inclose to me.

I will reserve to myself a further communication to you on the subject of the two cases respecting slaves between Georgia and East Florida, when more complete information shall be obtained of the state of those proceedings. I have the honor to be with sentiments of the most perfect respect & esteem, Gentlemen, your most obedt. & most humble servt

TH: JEFFERSON

PrC (DLC); at foot of text: "Messrs. Viar & Jaudenes." FC (Lb in DNA: RG 59, DL). Tr (AHN: Papeles de Estado, legajo 3895); in Spanish; attested by Jaudenes and Viar.

TJ submitted this letter to the President on this day (Washington, *Journal*, 145-6).

[1] Preceding three words interlined.

From Robert Aitken

SIR   Philada. 22d. May 1793

The inclosed piece for the Philosophical Transactions, ordered to be printed end of Vol. 3—It has been unfortunately gnawed by mice. As you are acquainted with the performance—perhaps you will do me the kindness to Supply Some defects in the reading—I cannot, with propriety make it out as it now stands. I am Sir Your Most Obedt. & humble Servant

ROBT. AITKEN

NB I will Send for it to morrow.

RC (DLC); at foot of text: "His Excellency Thomas Jefferson"; endorsed by TJ as received 23 May 1793 and so recorded in SJL.

Robert Aitken (1734-1802), a native of Scotland who came to Philadelphia before the Revolution and published the first complete English Bible in America in 1782, was a noted printer, bookseller, and engraver at 22 High Street (DAB; Hardie, *Phila. Dir.*, 1). The INCLOSED PIECE was probably John Cooke's paper, "A Description of a new Standard for Weights and Measures," which the author sent to George Washington in a letter of 28 Mch. 1791. For TJ's acquaintance WITH THE PERFORMANCE, see Vol. 19: 626-7.

From Edmond Charles Genet

MONSIEUR   Philadelphie le 22.[1] mai 1793 l'an 2e. de la Repe. f.

Le Conseil éxécutif de la Republique françoise ayant Consideré que le Commerce étranger est une des bases principales de la richesse des nations et que sous ce rapport le soin de suivre ses progrès, de faciliter ses operations et de proteger ses agents est un des devoirs les plus importants des Ministres de la Rep. françoise auprès des puissances Etrangeres a Jugé convenable de supprimer la place de Consul general auprès des Etats unis de l'Amerique et de réunir au même centre d'observations les rapports politiques et Commerciaux de la Repe. avec Ces Etats. En Conséquence le Conseil a arrêté que Je serois chargé en Chef de toutes les affaires consulaires de la République et que quatre Consuls seulement[2] départis dans les ports de Boston de New york et de Charles Town rempliroient sous ma direction les fonctions attribuées Jusqu'à présent aux Consuls de france qui ont résidé dans ces ports. Le Conseil éxécutif a supprimé toutes les autres places de Consuls et de Vice Consuls payées par la nation en Amerique; mais comme il a pensé qu'il seroit possible[3] que l'intérêt de l'état éxigeat que l'on en rétablisse dans certains ports éloignés de la résidence des Consuls Il m'a chargé de lui faire incessamment un rapport sur cet objet et[4] il m'a autorisé en attendant à nommer provisoirement à ces emplois, de Concert avec les Consuls, les citoyens francois ou americains qui[5] paroitront dignes d'être revêtus de ce titre.

Les Changements survenus dans la forme du gouvernement en france ont éxigé, M., le renouvellement de la plupart des fonctionnaires publics dans les pays Etrangers; Ce principe général a été appliqué aux officiers Consulaires de france en Amerique. Un seul des anciens consuls Conservera le poste qui lui a été Confié, c'est le Citoyen Mangourit Consul à Charles Ton. Les trois autres Consulats seront remplis par les Citoyens dupont, hauterive et Dannery le premier à Philadelphie, le second à New york et le troisieme à Boston.

J'aurai l'honneur, M., de vous presenter successivement les[6] provisions qui ont été données à ces fonctionnaires publics[7] par le Conseil éxécutif; et Je vous prierai de vouloir bien les faire reconnoitre et de leur faire obtenir à cet éffet l'éxéquatur du président des Etats unis. Je ne doute point que nos nouveaux consuls ne Justifient par leur conduite la Confiance que le gouvernement de la République françoise leur accorde et qu'ils ne reunissent tous leurs éfforts pour meriter celle du gouvernement[8] des Etats auprès des quels Ils seront accredités.

Dft (DLC: Genet Papers); in Genet's hand, except for part of the dateline (see note 1 below) and two minor additions in a clerical hand; unsigned; above salutation: "Le Citoyen Genet Mtre plenipotentiaire de la Rep. françoise à M. Jefferson secretaire d'Etat des Etats unis de l'Amerique"; at head of text: "Consulats"; at foot of text: "à Philadelphie le ⟨22.⟩ mai 1793. l'an 2e."; only the most important emendations are noted below. FC (same). FC (same). Recorded in SJL as received 23 May 1793.

The Provisional Executive Council's 4 Jan. 1793 instructions to Genet on the reorganization of the French consular service in the United States, parts of which the French minister incorporated verbatim in his letter, are in Aulard, *Recueil*, I, 394-7.

In accordance with his intention of presenting the PROVISIONS given to French consuls by the CONSEIL ÉXÉCUTIF, Genet on this day also wrote TJ a letter about François Dupont's exequatur as French consul at Philadelphia, and on 26 May 1793 he wrote him another one about the exequatur of Alexandre Maurice d'Hauterive as French consul at New York. These letters, recorded in SJL as received 23 and 28 May 1793, have not been found. The Department of State approved Dupont's exequatur on 25 May and Hauterive's on 29 May 1793 (Exequaturs for Dupont and Hauterive, 25 and 29 May 1793, FCs in DNA: RG 59, Exequaturs, with Washington and TJ as signatory and countersignatory). See also Washington, *Journal*, 149, 150, 155; and Memorandum Book of the Department of State, DNA: RG 360, PCC. French texts of the Provisional Executive Council's consular commissions to Dupont, dated 19 Dec. 1792, and to Hauterive, dated 28 Dec. 1792, are in DNA: RG 360, PCC. Concerning Thomas Dannery, who evidently did not arrive in the United States for several more months, see TJ to Genet, 2 Oct. 1793.

TJ submitted this letter to the President on 24 May 1793, at which time Washington requested a translation of it, though none has been found (Washington, *Journal*, 148).

[1] Digits inserted by a clerk in space left blank by Genet.
[2] Word written in the margin.
[3] Preceding four words written in the margin.
[4] Genet here canceled "de lui proposer ce qu."
[5] Genet first wrote "les personnes qui leur" and then altered it to read as above.
[6] Genet first wrote "Je Joins ici, M., ⟨un modele⟩ une copie des" and then altered it to read as above.
[7] Word written in the margin.
[8] In Dft Genet here canceled "particulier."

From Edmond Charles Genet

M.   Philadelphie le [22][1] mai 1793. l'an 2e.

Le Ministre des affaires Etres. de la République françoise vient de m'informer par sa dépêche du 10. mars dernier que les officers municipaux de la ville de Dunkerque ont fait retirer les bouées qui indiquoient les passages dans la rade du port de cette ville. Vous Jugerés sans doute M.,[2] qu'il est très instant de prévenir les navigateurs americains de ce changement.

Dft (DLC: Genet Papers); unsigned; partially dated, with day supplied from SJL; above salutation: "Le M &c à M Jefferson"; at head of text: "Bouées retirées de Dunkerque." Recorded in SJL as a letter of 22 May 1793 received the following day.

In response to this letter TJ inserted the following notice in the 25 May 1793 issue of the *National Gazette*: "*Department of State, to wit*. Official information has been received that the municipality officers of the city of Dunkirk have withdrawn the Buoy which marked the entrance into the road of that harbour. Notice thereof is hereby given to all masters of vessels of the United States, mariners and others whom it may concern. Given under my hand this 24th day of May 1793. Th. Jefferson."

Genet also wrote a letter to TJ this day enclosing a form for French letters of marque. This letter, recorded in SJL as received 23 May 1793, has not been found, but TJ apparently sent a French text of the enclosure to District Attorney William Rawle for use in the trial of Gideon Henfield

(see note to Memorial from Genet, 27 May 1793) with this certification: "Department of State, to wit: I hereby certify, that the aforegoing is one of the blank forms of commissions, issued by the French Republic, communicated to me officially by the Minister of France. In testimony whereof, I have caused my seal of office to be hereto affixed. Given under my hand, this first day of June, 1793. Th. Jefferson" (MS not found; printed in *Federal Cases*, XI, 1101n). TJ had an English translation of the form printed in the 25 May 1793 issue of the *National Gazette* with this prefatory notice: "*Department of State, to wit*. I hereby certify all whom it may concern that I have received an official communication of the form adopted for letters of marque by the French Republic of which form the following is a translation. Given under my hand and seal of office this 24th day of May 1793. Th. Jefferson."

[1] Date supplied for blank space in manuscript.
[2] Preceding three words interlined in place of "comme moi Citoyen."

From Edmond Charles Genet

MONSIEUR   Philadelphie le 22.[1] mai 1793. l'an 2e. de la Repe. françoise

Le Conseil éxécutif de la République françoise a appris par[2] mon predécesseur le Citoyen Ternant l'Empressement[3] avec le quel le gouvernement des Etats unis de l'amerique[4] s'est prêté à[5] faciliter les achats[6] que ce Ministre a été chargé de faire dans les Etats unis pour le Compte de la République francoise[7] ainsi que l'acquitement des traites des colonies auquel des circonstances imperieuses l'ont obligé de pourvoir. Le Conseil éxécutif, M., m'a recommandé[8] d'éxprimer au gouvernement Americain la reconnoissance que lui inspirent toutes les marques d'amitié qu'Il a donne à ce sujet au[9] peuple francois et pour lui prouver la reciprocité de nos sentiments Il[10] s'est déterminé a imprimer sur le champ un grand mouvement au Commerce de la France avec l'amérique en tirant désormais des Etats unis la plus grande partie des subsistances et des approvisionnements[11] nécessaires pour les Armées les flottes et les Colonies de la République françoise.

Le Conseil éxécutif m'a confié la direction de[12] ces grandes et utiles operations et il m'a donné des pouvoirs particuliers renfermés dans les rapports et dans les arrêtés ci Joints en vertu des quels Je suis autorisé par le Conseil et par la trésorerie nationale de france à employer les sommes dont les Etats unis pourront effectuer[13] le payement sur leur dette envers la france, ou celles que Je me procurerai sur mes traites personnelles payables par la Caisse de la trésorerie nationale, à acheter des subsistances, des munitions navales et à remplir d'autres services particuliers Conformément aux ordres qui m'ont été donnés par les Ministres de l'Interieur, de la guerre, de la Marine et des affaires Etrangeres.

Le gouvernement des Etats unis est trop éclairé pour ne point sentir les avantages immenses qui résulteront de cette mesure pour le peuple Americain et Je ne puis douter que connoissant les difficultés[14] que differentes circonstances pourroient opposer dans ce moment ci à l'éxécution des[15] commissions pressées qui m'ont été données s'il ne se prêtoit point encore a nous faire toucher de nouveaux fonds[16] par anticipation Il ne trouve dans sa sagesse et dans les rapports ci joints du Ministre des contributions publiques de france des mesures propres a remplir nos vues et à satisfaire nos besoins.

Il ne m'appartient point de Juger si le Président des[17] Etats unis est revêtu de pouvoirs suffisants pour acquiescer à notre demande sans le concours du Corps législatif;[18] mais Je me permettrai de vous observer, M., que les derniers payements anticipés qui ont eu lieu[19] le prouvent et que cette question paroit[20] également résolue par l'acte du Congrès qui autorise le pouvoir éxécutif à ne changer[21] l'ordre des remboursements de la dette Etrangere des Etats unis que lorsqu'il y trouvera[22] un avantage évident. Or quel avantage plus sensible[23] pouvons nous vous offrir que celui de vous acquiter envers nous avec vos propres denrées, sans éxporter votre numeraire, sans recourir aux operations onereuses[24] des banquiers. C'est vous fournir[25] à la fois[26] le moyen de payer vos dettes et d'enrichir vos Concitoyens: c'est enfin augmenter la valeur de vos productions et par conséquent de vos terres en[27] etablissant une concurrence nécessaire[28] entre nous et une nation[29] qui s'est pour ainsi dire reservé avec beaucoup d'art et de sacrifices[30] le monopole de[31] vos propres denrées. Il est tems M., que cette revolution Commerciale que Je regarde comme[32] le complément de votre immortelle revolution politique s'accomplisse d'une manière solide; et la france[33] me paroit être la seule puissance qui puisse[34] operer ce bien incalculable. Elle le desire vivement; les sages dispositions[35] dont Je viens de vous rendre compte en sont le garant. C'est donc à votre gouvernement maintenant à seconder les vues qui nous sont suggerées par[36] notre constante[37] amitié[38] pour nos freres les americains et par le desir que nous avons de resserrer les liens qui nous unissent à eux. Je me ferai un devoir bien doux de me conformer dans l'administration qui m'est confiée[39] à ces sentiments de la[40] nation françoise pour tous les Etats unis et afin que chacun d'eux participe à l'éxtension de nos rapports commerciaux J'aurai soin de répartir mes achats entre les differents Etats de l'union autant que le permettront les productions naturelles de leur sol et la nature de leur commerce. Je ne négligerai rien non plus pour que le mode[41] qui m'est préscrit pour passer les marchés mette non seulement les négociants Americains et françois;[42] mais aussi les[43] proprietaires des terres et les fermiers en mesure de profiter des benefices qui pourront résulter de nos approvisionnemens.

Dft (DLC: Genet Papers); in Genet's hand, except for part of dateline (see note 1 below) and one revision in a clerical hand; unsigned; above salutation: "Le Citoyen Genet Mtre. &c à M. Jefferson secretaire d'Etat des Etats unis de l'amerique"; at head of text: "Liquidation de la dette des Etats unis envers la france"; contains numerous emendations, only the most important being noted below. Tr (AMAE: CPEU, XXXVIII); with minor variations. FC (DLC: Genet Papers); in English. Recorded in SJL as received 23 May 1793, and initially as a letter of that date before TJ corrected the entry. Enclosures: (1) First Report of the Minister of Public Contributions to the Provisional Executive Council on the American debt to France, Paris, 2 Jan. 1793, stating that Genet has been charged with requesting advance payment of the balance of this debt to purchase war supplies and provisions in the United States and empowered to dispose of the entire balance, or the approximately 17,000,000 livres needed by the departments of the interior, war, marine, and foreign affairs, for this purpose; recommending, in the unlikely event the United States followed a hostile course by refusing payment, that he draw bills of exchange at two months' sight on the French treasury to pay for these purchases up to the amount authorized, after first offering as an inducement to the American government, if it cannot pay the debt in specie or bank notes, the option of furnishing it in interest-bearing securities that would pass at par among those to whom Genet may have to make payment on the French Republic's account; and setting forth procedures for drawing the bills and orders (PrC of Tr in DLC: TJ Papers, 86: 14895-901, in French, with "Copie Dette Americain Per. Rapport" at head of text and record of Council approval on 4 Jan. 1793 by secretary Philippe Antoine Grouvelle, countersignature by Foreign Minister Lebrun, and 22 May 1793 certification by Genet at foot of text, all in a clerk's hand with corrections by George Taylor, Jr.; Tr in DNA: RG 59, NL, English translation in Taylor's hand with corrections by him; PrC in DLC: TJ Papers, 80: 13939-44, lacking some corrections; Tr in DNA: RG 46, Senate Records, 3d Cong., 1st sess., in English, lacking some corrections). (2) Extract from the Registers of the Provisional Executive Council, 4 Jan. 1793, approving draft instructions for Genet on his mission to the United States Congress pertaining to the reorganization of consular affairs in the United States and payment of the American debt to France in accordance with No. 1 (PrC of Tr in DLC: TJ Papers, 86: 14891-4, in French, partly faded, with certifications by Grouvelle and Genet, all in Taylor's hand; Tr in DNA: RG 59, NL, English translation in Taylor's hand with corrections by him; PrC in DLC: TJ Papers, 80: 13945-8, lacking two corrections; Tr in DNA: RG 46, Senate Records, 3d Cong., 1st sess., in English, lacking two corrections). (3) Second Report of the Minister of Public Contributions to the Provisional Executive Council on the liquidation of the American debt to France, 4 Jan. 1793, stating that Genet had been given information of the offers by Colonel Smith to procure reimbursement of what remains of the American debt, under a proposed rate of converting livres to dollars, and to purchase with it army supplies and provisions for the Republic, that the balance of the debt will have been reduced before Genet's arrival by American advances to Ternant on behalf of Saint-Domingue, that a law of Congress authorizes reimbursement by anticipation only if it would be advantageous to the United States, and that Hamilton's proposal for establishing the rate of specie exchange between livres and dollars is more advantageous to France than that suggested by Smith; and recommending that the Council authorize Genet to solicit payment of the principal and interest of this debt from the United States, to give as the reason the necessities of the French Republic in defending its liberty and independence just as the United States defended theirs when the sum was lent, to promise the American government, in view of the law requiring an advantage to the United States, that he would use these funds solely to purchase supplies produced in the United States, and to accept the proposed conversion of livres to dollars in a manner agreeable to the laws of both nations (PrC of Tr in DLC: TJ Papers, 86: 14902-9, in French, with "dette americain 2d. Rapport" at head of text and record of Council approval on 4 Jan. 1793 by President Gaspard Monge and countersignature by Lebrun at foot of text, all in a clerk's hand with a correction by Taylor; Tr in DNA, RG 59, NL, English translation in Taylor's hand with corrections by him; PrC in DLC: TJ Papers, 80: 13949-55, lacking some corrections; Tr in DNA: RG 46, Senate Records, 3d Cong., 1st sess., in English, lacking some corrections). (4) Commissioners of the French National Treasury to the President of the Provisional Executive Council, 8 Jan. 1793, acknowledging receipt of No. 2 and stating their readiness to facilitate Genet's mission to the United States by accepting any sum sent to them in the name of Congress, or orders furnished by Genet to the United States treasury, as payment on account of the American debt to France, and, in the event of any deficiencies in American reimbursements, by expediting payment of any notes issued by Genet at two months' sight (PrC of Tr in DLC: TJ Papers, 86: 14910-13, in French, with subjoined certifications, one of 17 Jan. 1793 by all six members of the Council stating that the letter was written in consequence of the mission they had given to Genet, and another by Genet, all in a clerk's hand; Tr in DNA: RG 59, NL, English translation in Taylor's hand with corrections by him; PrC in DLC: TJ Papers, 81: 14022-4, lacking some corrections). Letter and enclosures with translations printed in *Message*, 1-8 (App.), 5-14; translations printed in ASP, *Foreign Relations*, I, 142-6. TJ submitted French texts of this letter and its enclosures to the President on 24 May 1793, at which time Washington requested translations that TJ supplied three days later (Washington, *Journal*, 148; TJ to Washington, 27 May 1793). French texts intended for the Secretary of the Treasury were enclosed in TJ to Washington, 30 May 1793, 3 June

1793. See also Washington to Alexander Hamilton, 3 June 1793.

The Washington administration ultimately rejected Genet's request for advance payment of the balance of the American debt to France—a sum estimated by French finance minister Etienne Clavière to amount to about 26,560,145 livres as of 1 July 1792—despite Genet's stipulation that the money would be used to purchase provisions and supplies in the United States for the armies, fleets, and colonies of the French Republic (see F. A. Aulard, "La Dette Américaine envers la France," *Revue de Paris*, xxx [1925], 537; and Editorial Note and documents on Jefferson and the American debt to France, at 3 June 1793).

The ACTE DU CONGRÈS was the 1790 act relating to the payment of the foreign debt of the United States, which authorized the President to borrow up to $12,000,000 to discharge this debt "if it can be effected upon terms advantageous to the United States" (*Annals*, II, 2304).

[1] Digits inserted by a clerk in space left blank by Genet.
[2] Preceding two words interlined in place of "instruit par." Following them, in the margin, Genet canceled the following passage: "avec ⟨la plus vive reconnaissance⟩ plaisir par les rapports de."
[3] Genet here canceled an interlined "et le zêle."
[4] Genet here canceled "⟨avoit⟩ a bien voulu se."
[5] Genet here canceled "pourvoir par des payements anticipés sur le remboursement de la dette de la Republique Americaine envers celle de france à l'acquitement du."
[6] Preceding two words substituted for "par tous les moyens qui étoient en son pouvoir ⟨les operat⟩ les approvisionnements." In the margin, next to the last line of this passage, Genet wrote and then canceled "le payement ⟨du⟩ que ce Ministre."
[7] Genet here canceled "et les payements" and added the next eight words, interlining the first four and writing the last four in the margin.
[8] Word interlined in place of "prié."
[9] Genet first wrote "inspire un procédé aussi amical," which he revised to "inspirent tous les sentiments d'amitié dont Il ne cesse de donner des preuves au" before altering the passage to read as above.

[10] Genet here canceled "m'a préscrit de vous Informer, M."
[11] Preceding three words interlined.
[12] Preceding three words written in the margin.
[13] Word interlined in place of "encore avancer."
[14] Word interlined in place of "obstacles."
[15] Genet here canceled "ordres."
[16] Genet first wrote "un nouveau fonds" and then altered it to read as above.
[17] Preceding two words interlined in place of "gouvernement."
[18] Preceding six words written in the margin.
[19] Preceding four words interlined.
[20] Word interlined in place of "est."
[21] Preceding two words, in the margin, substituted for "n'interve[n]," which Genet had interlined in place of "n'accelerer."
[22] Word altered from "trouverait."
[23] Genet first wrote "Quel avantage plus précieux l." He then altered it to read in succession "Cet avantage se trouve incontestablement" and "Or quel avantage plus précieux" before altering the text to read as above.
[24] Genet here canceled "ruineuses."
[25] Word interlined in place of "offrir."
[26] *Message*: "en même temps."
[27] Preceding seven words written in the margin.
[28] Word interlined in place of "utile dans les differents Etats ⟨unis⟩ de l'union."
[29] Genet here canceled a heavily emended passage which in its final form appears to read "à laquelle d'anciennes habitudes de la part de vos négociants et d'immenses capitaux du sien ont pour."
[30] Preceding seven words interlined.
[31] Genet here canceled "votre commerce."
[32] Preceding three words interlined in place of "qui sera."
[33] Preceding three words interlined in place of "mais notre gouvernement."
[34] AMAE Tr: "⟨qui⟩ capable de."
[35] Genet first wrote "ce bien incalculable par des dispositions aussi sages que celles" and then altered it to read as above.
[36] Genet here first wrote "le desir ⟨qu'elle a⟩ que nous avons de resserer tous les liens qui unissent les peuples de france et d'amerique" and then changed the latter clause to "qui nous unissent au peuple Americain" before canceling the entire

passage to adopt the modified version which follows above.

[37] Word interlined in place of "ferme et."

[38] Remainder of sentence inserted interlinearly and in the margin.

[39] Genet first wrote "Je ⟨me propose⟩ tacherai, M., dans l'administration qui m'est confiée de ⟨donner des preuves par-

ticul⟩ me conformer" before a clerk altered the passage to read as above.

[40] Genet here canceled "Republique."

[41] Genet here canceled "d'achat."

[42] Preceding three words written in the margin.

[43] Genet here canceled what appears to be "bon."

TRANSLATION

SIR   Philadelphia May 22. 1793. 2d. year of the French republic.

The Executive council of the French republic has learnt through my predecessor, the citizen Ternant, the readiness with which the government of the US. of A. attended to the facilitation of the purchases which that minister was charged to make in the US. on account of the French republic, as also the acquittal of the draughts of the colonies for which imperious circumstances obliged it to provide. The Executive council, Sir, has charged me to express to the American government the acknolegement inspired by all the marks of friendship which it has given on this subject to the French nation; and to prove to it the reciprocity of our sentiments it has determined to give at once a great movement to the commerce of France with America, in drawing henceforth from the US. the greatest part of the subsistence and stores necessary for the armies, fleets and colonies of the French republic.

The Executive council has entrusted me with the direction of these great and useful operations, and has given me particular powers comprehended in the reports, and in the resolutions now inclosed, in virtue of which I am authorized by the council and by the national treasury of France to employ the sums of which the US. can effect the paiment (towards their debt to France) or those which I can procure on my personal draughts payable by the national treasury in purchasing provisions, naval stores, and in fulfilling other particular services, conformably to the orders which have been given to me by the ministers of the Interior, of war, of the Marine, and of foreign affairs.

The government of the US. is too enlightened not to perceive the immense advantages which will result from this measure to the people of America, and I cannot doubt that, knowing the difficulties which different circumstances might oppose at this moment to the execution of the pressing commissions which have been given to me, if it should not facilitate to us still the receipt of new sums by anticipation, it will find in it's wisdom and in the reports, now inclosed, of the Minister of the public contributions of France, measures proper to answer our views, and to satisfy our wants.

It does not belong to me to judge if the President of the US. is invested with powers sufficient to accede to our request, without the concurrence of the legislative body: but I will permit myself to observe to you, Sir, that the last anticipated payments, which took place, prove it, and that this question appears equally decided by the act of Congress which authorizes the Executive power not to change the order of the reimbursements of the foreign debt of the US. unless it shall find therein an evident advantage. Now what advantage more sensible can we offer to you, than that of discharging your debt to us with your own productions, without exporting your cash, without recurring to the burthensome operations of bankers? It is furnishing you at the same time with the means of paying your debts, and of enriching your citizens: in short it is to raise the value of your productions, and consequently of your lands, in establishing a necessary competition between us and a nation which has in a measure reserved with a great deal of art and of sacrifices, the monopoly of your own productions. It is time, Sir, that this commercial revolution, which I consider as the completion of your immortal political revolution, should accomplish itself in a solid manner; and France appears to me to be the only power which can operate this incalculable good. She desires it ardently. The wise arrangements of which I have now given you an account, are the proof of it. It remains then with your government to second the views which are suggested to us by our constant friendship for our brethren the Americans, and by the desire we have to strengthen the bonds which unite us to them. It will be a pleasing duty to me, Sir, to conform myself, in the administration which is confided to me, to these sentiments of the French nation for all the US. and in order that every one of them may participate in the extension of our commercial relations, I will take care to distribute my purchases among the different states of the union, as much as the natural productions of their soil, and the nature of their commerce will permit. I will neglect no means, moreover, in order that the modes of purchase prescribed to me may enable not only the American and French merchants, but also the landholders and farmers to take advantage of the benefits which may result from our purchases.   GENET

Tr (DNA: RG 59, NL); entirely in TJ's hand; above salutation: "The Citizen Genet, Min. plen. of the French republic to Mr Jefferson secretary of state of the US. of America"; at head of text: "Liquidation of the debt of the US. to France." PrC (DLC); partly overwritten in a later hand. Tr (DNA: RG 46, Senate Records, 3d Cong., 1st sess.).

From Thomas Mann Randolph, Jr.

DEAR SIR   Monticello May: 22. 1793.

Since I wrote last a parcel of bonds to the amount of 560 £ have been deposited with me for you by Bowling Clarke. Those taken by Mr. Hylton for Elkhill have not yet come into my hands: according to your desire I should have brought them up with me but I left Richmond with an expectation of returning in a day or two, which did not happen.

We are apprehensive of great loss in our grain from the Weevil this year. They have appeared allready in vast numbers on the farm of young Mr. Lewis at the foot of Monticello: some stacks of Wheat which he neglected to thresh during the Winter are full of the fly and the grain in them is allmost entirely destroyed.

I made a small experiment in the culture of Barley on the red land last fall: it has succeeded (from the appearance now) beyond my expectation and has convinced me that our soil is not more favorable to the Wheat and Rye than to that plant which has been thought to delight most in low situations and black light soils. You will be astonished when you come to spend a spring at home at the progress of the white clover: there is more of it I am convinced within this inclosure at present than there was in all your lands the first summer I lived here. I am not so fortunate with Edgehill: there are scarcely a hundred plants on it.

I cannot omit to announce to you the arrival of the mocking-bird another pleasant guest. I told you that I heard it last summer but we concluded I must have mistaken for its voice that of the fox-colored thrush: we have now more music from it than all the feathered tribe besides and see it frequently.

Patsy and the children are well. We pray you to assure Maria of our affection. Your friend and hble Servt   TH: M. RANDOLPH

P.S. If you have among your books two late pamphlets one written by a Mr. Christie and published just before the Vindiciae Gallicae the other intitled The constitutional interests of Ireland with respect to the popery laws Dublin 1791 you will add to the favors (allready past computation) you have conferred on me by lending them to me. They are written I believe by two of my old College acquaintances.   TH:M.R

RC (ViU: Edgehill-Randolph Papers); addressed: "Thomas Jefferson, Secretary of state Philada."; franked; endorsed by TJ as received 3 June 1793 and so recorded in SJL.

The TWO LATE PAMPHLETS were Thomas Christie, *Letters on the Revolution of France, and on the New Constitution established by the National assembly . . .* (London, 1791), and *The Constitutional Interests of Ireland, with respect to the Popery Laws, Impartially Investigated* (Dublin, 1791), an anonymous work printed by J. Moore arguing that Irish Catholics should be given political rights. English and Irish editions of James Mackintosh's VINDICIAE GALLICAE, which like Christie's pamphlet defended the French Revolution, appeared in 1791, followed the next year by a Philadelphia edition (see Sowerby, no. 2545). Randolph had taken classes in anatomy while attending the University of Edinburgh from 1784-88, and his two COLLEGE ACQUAINTANCES were Christie and possibly James Moore, physician and brother of Lieutenant General Sir John Moore, whom Randolph could easily have confused with the Dublin printer. Christie and Moore both attended medical lectures at Edinburgh in the 1780s (William H. Gaines, Jr., *Thomas Mann Randolph: Jefferson's Son-in-Law* [Kingsport, Tenn., 1966], 13-22; DNB).

From James Simpson

Gibraltar, 22 May 1793. He wrote on 30 Apr. by the American brig *Holebrooke* bound for Philadelphia upon learning that Muley Suliman had arrived at Alcázar from Mequinez, where deputies from the midland provinces invited him to accompany them in force to Morocco. Since then, instead of coming to Tetuán and Tangier, Muley Suliman yielded to these deputies to the extent that on 28 Apr. he left Alcázar for Rabat, where he invited all the provinces to send deputies to meet with him on 12 May, the date of the grand feast at the end of Ramadan, and announced that he would be guided in his future operations by the numbers attending. Since Muley Yezid's death Muley Suliman has acted on the principle that he would assume the office of Emperor if the people chose him, but it is doubtful that he will personally assist in a military conquest of any part of Morocco. Matra, the English consul general at Tangier, wrote to him on 16 May that Muley Suliman would proceed southward only if the center provinces sent all their deputies to Rabat to feast on the holy days with him. He will communicate precise news on this subject to TJ as soon as he learns it. The Swedish consul writes him that Muley Abderhaman has been proclaimed king of Sus and will likely prove a formidable opponent to any who try to go there. The war in Europe grows more serious by the day. Lately France has so effectively severed all its communications, except "in hostile measures," that little is known of what happens there. Contrary to expectations that France would not send her grand fleet to sea, letters by the last post from Spain report that 24 sail of the line had left Toulon, with Leghorn or Genoa feared as their destination. Twenty-six Spanish ships of the line have sailed from Cartagena, 7 English warships are now here, and Lord Hood is daily expected with a large force. The English frigate *Iris* was badly damaged during a battle with a 40-gun French frigate off Cape Finisterre on 13 May, but evidently because of her own loss of men the French ship sailed away without taking advantage of the crippled warship.

RC (DNA: RG 59, CD); 4 p.; at foot of first page: "The Honble Thomas Jefferson &ca"; endorsed by TJ as received 29 July 1793 and so recorded in SJL.

To Edward Telfair

SIR   Philadelphia May 22. 1793.

I have the honor to inclose you two letters, with the papers which accompanied them, from the Spanish commissioners here to myself. One of them is relative to the slaves taken forcibly from E. Florida, by Harrison, Rees, and others, which was the subject of a letter I had the honor of writing you on the 3d. of July 1792. The other respects some fugitive slaves from that government into your state, reclaimed and not rendered. These having been laid before the President of the US. I am to assure you of his confidence that justice will be done by your state on both subjects, and that you will see it expedient for the general tranquility of the US. and more particularly for that of your own, that in giving the satisfaction sought by a neighbor, you will go beyond rather than stop short of the line of strict justice. I must ask the favor of your information of the present state of these cases, to enable me to give a present answer on the subject, and a fuller one when they shall be finally acted on, to be given as a final answer. I have the honor to be with perfect respect, Your Excellency's Most obedt. & most humble servt

TH: JEFFERSON

PrC (DLC); at foot of text: "H.E. the Governor of Georgia." FC (Lb in DNA: RG 59, DL). Enclosures: Second and third letters of Josef de Jaudenes and Josef Ig- nacio de Viar to TJ, 12 May 1793, and their enclosures. Letter enclosed in TJ to George Washington, 22 May 1793.

To Jean Baptiste Ternant, with Jefferson's Notes on Diplomatic Medals

SIR   Philadelphia May 22d: 1793.

The President of the United States in a letter addressed to the provisory executive Council of the french republic, has expressed his sense of your merit and his entire approbation of your conduct while here. He has also charged me to convey to yourself the same sentiments on his part. It is with pleasure I obey this charge, in bearing witness to the candour and integrity of your conduct with us, and to the share you may justly claim in the cultivation of harmony and good understanding between the two nations by a ready accomodation to circumstances, whenever offices of friendship or duty were to be claimed or rendered on either side.

To the homage thus paid to truth and justice permit me to add sincere wishes that in whatever line you may engage for the good of either or both republics, your course may be marked with success and prosperity.

As a testimony of the regard of the United States we shall take an early occasion to ask your acceptance of a medal and chain of gold on their part. I have the honor to be with sentiments of great respect, Sir, Your most obedient and most humble servant

[*Subjoined to PrC of draft:*]
Notes on the subject of the present.

It was proposed that the medal should always contain 150. dollars worth of gold; it was presumed the gentlemen would always keep this.

The chain was to contain 365 links always, but these to be proportioned in value to the time the person had been here, making each link worth 3. dimes for every year of residence. No expence to be bestowed on the making because it was expected they would turn the chain into money.—On this plan

Luzerne's chain for $8\frac{1}{4}$ years residence @	$2\frac{1}{2}$ D. a link	with the medal worth	$1062.\frac{1}{2}$ D.
Van Berckel's	5.	$1\frac{1}{2}$ D.	697.
De Moustier's	3.	9 dismes	$478\frac{1}{2}$
Ternant's	$1\frac{3}{4}$ (say 2.)	6 dismes	369.
			2,607

PrC (DLC); in a clerk's hand, unsigned; at foot of text: "Mr. Ternant"; lacks notes supplied from PrC of Dft. PrC of Dft (DLC); in TJ's hand, unsigned; with notes subjoined; slightly faded, illegible digits being supplied from FC. FC (Lb in DNA: RG 59, DL); with notes subjoined. Tr (DLC); 19th-century copy; lacks subjoined notes. Draft with subjoined notes enclosed in TJ to Washington, 22 May 1793.

Concerning the practice of granting a PRESENT to diplomats taking leave of the United States, see Editorial Note and documents on Jefferson's policy concerning presents to foreign diplomats, Vol. 16: 356-68.

Ternant may have replied to TJ in a letter of 26 May 1793, which is recorded in SJL as received 3 June 1793 but has not been found.

From F. P. Van Berckel

Fait à Philadelphie Ce 22e. May 1793.

Le Soussigné Resident de Leurs Hautes Puissances les Seigneurs Etats Generaux des Provinces Unies a l'honneur d'informer Monsieur le Secretaire d'Etat du fait Suivant: Un Vaisseau marchand Americain *the Hope* s'etant trouvé dans le port de Rotterdam a l'epoque de l'embargo general, qui fut mis Sur tous les Batimens dans les ports de la Republique, a l'occasion de la guerre declarée par la France, le Patron de Ce Batiment *John Miller* s'est adressé par Requête à Leurs Hautes Puissances, reclamant l'Article 8e. du Traité d'Amitié et de Commerce qui Subsiste entre Elles et les Etats Unis, en vertu du quel il pretendoit devoir être excepté de Cet ordre General, priant a cette fin, que l'embargo fut oté de Son Batiment, et qu'il Lui fut permis de Se rendre a Sa destination. Leurs Hautes Puissances ont jugé devoir le lui refuser, avec assurance cependant, qu'il ne Seroit detenu qu'aussi longtemps que les Circonstances le rendroient indispensable, et q'ayant Surtout égard a la bonne intelligence et l'amitié existant entre Elles et les Etats Unis, Elles feroient tout Ce qui seroit en Leur pouvoir, pour rendre Sa detention aussi Courte que possible.

Leurs Hautes Puissances ayant toujours en vuë de Cultiver la bonne harmonie entre les deux Republiques, ont Cru devoir Chercher a prevenir l'impression erronnée à laquelle Ce refus pourroit donner lieu, Si les motifs qui ont necessité Ce refus etoient ignorés, d'autant plus qu'un Article du Traité a formé la base de la priere qui Leur a été faite, Elles ont donné ordre au Soussigné de declarer au Gouvernement des Etats Unis, que loin de vouloir s'ecarter des engagemens Solemnels d'un Traité, dont la foi Leur Sera toujours Sacrée, Elles n'ont rien plus a Coeur que de les observer Strictement, et qu'Elles pensent que les mesures prises à Cette Occasion Sont parfaitement legitimées à l'Epoque d'une invasion inattendue d'un Voisin aussi puissant que la France, attaquant Leur paisible Republique Sans aucune provocation, et que dans des Circonstances où la nécessité justifieroit une Suspension de toute Loi, une explication forcée d'un Article du Traité n'a du porter aucun Changement à de telles mesures.

Le Soussigné Se flatte, que le Gouvernement des Etats Unis considerera l'exposé qu'il vient de faire, Comme une nouvelle preuve de la

Sincerité des Sentimens de Ses Maitres, et Servira à raffermir les liens d'amitié qui unissent les deux Republiques.   F: P: van Berckel

RC (DNA: RG 360, PCC); endorsed by TJ as received 23 May 1793 and so recorded in SJL.

TJ submitted this letter to the President on 24 May 1793 (Washington, *Journal*, 148). See also Rodolph Vall-Travers to TJ, 29 Mch. 1793.

To George Washington

May 22. 1793.

Th: Jefferson has the honor to submit to the President a letter to the Govr. of Georgia, and two others on the occasion of Mr. Ternant's recall. He sends at the same time the letters which were written on the recall of Mr. De Moustier, as it is necessary to preserve a certain proportion between the expressions used on these occasions.

RC (DNA: RG 59, MLR); addressed: "The President of the US." Tr (same, Lb in SDC). Not recorded in SJL. Enclosures: (1) George Washington to the King of France, 2 Mch. 1791 (Vol. 19: 425-6n). (2) TJ to Moustier, 2 Mch. 1791. (3) TJ to Edward Telfair, 22 May 1793. (4) Draft of TJ to Jean Baptiste Ternant, with Jefferson's Notes on Diplomatic Medals, 22 May 1793. (5) Draft of Washington to the Provisional Executive Council of France, 24 May 1793. See Washington, *Journal*, 147.

To James Brown

Dear Sir   Philadelphia May 23. 1793.

I have yet to acknolege the receipt of your two favors of Apr. 10. and 15. I have learnt from Baltimore that the 3. pipes of wine are reshipped from thence to Richmond to your address, where I hope them safely arrived as well as the packages of furniture sent from this place. Mr. Donald had shipped for me from Dublin a box of books by the Young eagle Elias Lord. The note said she was bound to Philadelphia. But on enquiry, no such vessel has come, or belongs, to this port. From this circumstance, as well as that the orders were that they should be shipped to Richmond to your address, I presume the vessel has gone there. The books were for Mr. Eppes.—Mr. Donald likewise sends to you by the Camilla, Service, a small box for me containing a Mathematical instrument, to be stored with my other effects till called for.—I had got a person here, who had connections at Edinburgh, to engage a mason and house-joiner to come to me. They also were desired to be addressed to you, a liberty I had taken on so many other occasions till I should come home and be in a position to do my own business. I should be very glad that these men could be sent on, with some of the waggons, to Monticello, the moment of their arrival, as a very short stay in Richmond would suffice to debauch them from my service. I know they were engaged and only waited some vessel coming to James river, so that they may very possibly be arrived. To whom do you consign my tobacco? I have so much confidence in my friend Mr. Donald that I would rather he should have the selling it than any body, and I learn that this would be the case if consigned to a Mr. John Younger, heretofore a clerk in the house of D. & B. I also understand that Havre is a fine market for tobacco at present. I shall leave this to your decision, but shall be glad to hear from you on the subject, as also to recieve the line promised for Mr. Short, when you shall have a little leisure. He cannot but be under the greatest anxiety on the accident which has happened. I am with great esteem Dr. Sir Your friend & servt

TH: JEFFERSON

PrC (DLC); at foot of first page: "Mr. James Brown."

From Stephen Cathalan, Jr.

Marseilles, 23 May 1793. He wrote on 19 Mch. about the unfortunate fate of the *Aurora*, André Lewis Burgain master, belonging to Zacharie, Coopman & Company of Baltimore. Burgain was finally discharged from prison yesterday after the proper administrative and judicial authorities had examined and found wanting the evidence brought against him by his chief accuser, Captain Neel, the French commander of the privateer *Patriote*. In consequence of Cathalan's importunities at the head of the merchants trading with the United States, Burgain's consignees, Captain Roger Robins of the American brig *Bacchus* (the bearer of this letter), and others who knew Burgain in Baltimore, the departmental and district authorities on 19 May unanimously rejected the accusation that Burgain was an émigré, as he had left France before there was any law against emigration, gave him the right to seek compensation from Neel in a court of justice for his cruel treatment, and listened with great interest when Cathalan criticized Neel in his presence for inhumanity and reclaimed Burgain as a United States citizen. Cathalan does not know what compensation would suffice for a man detained in irons in a ship's hold for twenty-two days and in prison for more than two months because of the calumniating reports of another man. He hopes that when the ship and cargo come up for judgment on 29 May the authorities will not award them as a prize to the privateer. In this city law is observed and the public spirit of the people has completely changed compared to last year. The "hangs Mens or Lanthernors" were judged and guillotined last week. The prisons are filled with the chief intriguers who were "contriving for anarchy, Murders, and Plunder." They will soon receive their reward, and three of them committed suicide four days ago. The Duke of Orléans, suspected to be the head of the anarchists, is confined and will soon be judged here. Robins, the same person previously reported to have been carried into Cette, is an able and learned man who will inform TJ of all he saw here and describe the great advantages awaiting American ships in the Mediterranean. Robins returns to Philadelphia with an enormous freight, and fifty such vessels could now obtain the same kind. He has insured Robins individually for 2,100 dollars at 4 percent to pay his ransom if he is captured by the barbarian powers. As long as the war continues American merchants will control the West Indian trade. Foreign exchanges are the great regulators of import prices here, with £3ᵗ in assignats worth only 7½ pence sterling in London and Spanish dollars sold at £13ᵗ 10s. to 14ᵗ in assignats. Tobacco now sells for £90ᵗ per quintal marc and will soon rise to £100ᵗ. Owing to military operations, flour will continue in great demand; there is none from the United States. Flour and wheat now fetch £125 to 130ᵗ—a situation that promises to last another year. West Indian coffee is now worth 50s. to 3ᵗ per pound Marseilles weight. News just arrived that a small English fleet entered the straits of Gibraltar and that a Spanish squadron lies at anchor at Barcelona. The French squadron is fitting out at Toulon, where unfortunately the anarchist spirit still reigns. For want of naval protection Marseilles has lost a large number of richly loaded merchant vessels coming from the straits since news of the war reached Gibraltar and the Spanish ports, but privateers have brought a good number of prizes here, though of "a very Short value." It is now impossible for any French merchant vessel to pass the straits in either direction. He lately received TJ's 31 May 1792 letter with the printed laws of Congress, a boon for his chancery. He has ordered Robins to show TJ the passport he gave him and the certificates sworn by the loaders that the goods on board Robins's ship belong solely to American citizens. The belligerent powers will respect the American flag, but the barbarian powers will not do likewise, and he hopes they may be forced to soon. [*30 May.*] On 27 May tobacco was purchased here for £100, the 28th at £110ᵗ and yesterday at 115 and 120ᵗ per quintal. The purchaser was unable to obtain all of it, the remainder being unsold at £130 to 150ᵗ while others will not sell at all. The exchanges remain as described in the annexed letter. No judgment has been given on the *Aurora.*

RC (DNA: RG 59, CD); 5 p.; at foot of first page: "The Secretary of State at Philadelphia"; postscript supplied from Dupl; endorsed by TJ as received 17 Aug. 1793 and so recorded in SJL. Dupl (same); in a clerk's hand, signed by Cathalan; at head of text: "Copy"; contains minor variations and signed postscript of 30 May 1793 in Cathalan's hand on verso of last page.

TJ submitted this letter to the President on 19 Aug. 1793, and Washington returned it the same day (Washington, *Journal*, 225).

From Tench Coxe

Sɪʀ   May 23d. 1793

I have the honor to inform you that the house of Pragers & Co. will supply some Bills on Amsterdam at 3/ Pennsa. Money, or 36 ninetieths of a dollar. The Treasury bills supplied for the use of the Department of State on the last occasions were at $36\frac{4}{11}$ Ninetieths, which the Merchants consider as *the par.*

Not being in trade I would recommend an Application to Mr. Vaughan in regard to Messrs. Pragers bills, which however I consider as among the best at all times.

If you wish to have the matter completed I shall be ready to make the Enquiry and to procure the bills on your favoring me a note of the number of Dollars to be invested.

British bills are to be procured at 70 ⅌Cent, or 2 ⅌Cent premium. With great respect, I have the honor to be, Sir Your most obedt. servt.

TENCH COXE

RC (DLC); endorsed by TJ as received 23 May 1793 and so recorded in SJL.

From William Foushee

DR. SIR   Richmond 23d. May 1793

I have taken the Liberty of Inclosing a Letter, and also of forwarding to your address, a Box, for Citizen Genet the French Minister. The Box contains (just one cubic foot as) a Sample of our *Timber* for *Shipbuilding* with some Leaves from the same Tree—these are Sent in consequence of a short Conversation with the Minister on his Way to Phila., who expressed a great desire to obtain information of the Texture and true Species of Such Wood, in Virginia. The quality we consider as most excellent indeed, for Ships built with Timber from this Forrest, upwards of Twenty years ago are now running. Our mutual friend D. L. Hylton will explain to you the Company and Purchase we have made of a large Tract of Extraordinary Oak Timber, situated on Warwick River, a Branch of James. Should the Minister Consider this Business as an Object he is refer'd to you for an acquaintance with Some of the Partners, and the probability of a Compliance with any Contract they may make.

As your Disposition (and I hope that of every real American) will, I am Satisfied, lend every proper aid to a nation to whom we are much indebted on the Score of gratitude, and with whom sound Policy, in my Judgment, ought ever to Connect us; an assurance of your good wishes and exertions in every thing which may tend to the Benefit of this State; as well as your friendly disposition in general and particularly to Some of the Partners, are the reasons offered in Excuse, for the Liberty now taken in troubling you. With much respect & Esteem, Am, Dr. Sir, Your mo. Obt Servt.   W FOUSHEE

RC (MHi); with penciled notation in TJ's hand underneath signature: "Saw bridge"; endorsed by TJ as received 5 June 1793 and so recorded in SJL. Enclosed in William Hylton to TJ, 25 May 1793.

The enclosed LETTER, not found, was forwarded in TJ to Edmond Charles Genet, 6 June 1793.

From Edmond Charles Genet

M.   Philadelphie le 23.[1] mai 1793. l'an 2e. de la Repe. frse.

Seule contre des hordes innombrables[2] de tyrans et d'ésclaves[3] qui menacent sa liberté naissante, la nation francoise[4] seroit en droit de reclamer[5] les obligations qu'imposent aux Etats unis les traités qu'ils ont contractés avec elle et qu'elle a cimentés de son sang;[6] mais forte de la grandeur de[7] ses moyens et de la puissance de ses[8] principes non moins redoutables à ses énnemis que les armes victorieuses[9] qu'elle oppose à leur rage, elle vient dans le tems même ou des emissaires de nos ennemis communs faisoient d'inutiles éfforts[10] pour neutraliser la reconnoissance, refroidir le zêle, racourcir ou obscurcir[11] la vue de vos Concitoyens, Elle vient dis je cette nation genereuse,[12] Cette amie fidele de travailler encore à accroitre leur prosperité à augmenter le bonheur dont elle se plait à les voir Jouir.[13]

Des obstacles élevés dans[14] des intentions liberticides par les Ministres perfides du despotisme[15] des obstacles dont le but étoit d'arrêter[16] les progrès rapides[17] du Commerce des Americains et l'éxtension de leurs maximes bienfaisantes[18] n'existent plus. La République francoise ne voyant en eux que des freres, leur a ouvert par les décrets ci Joints[19] tous ses ports dans les deux mondes, leur a accorde toutes les faveurs[20] dont Jouissent ses propres citoyens dans ses vastes possessions, les a invités à partager les bénefices de sa navigation en accordant à leurs Vaisseaux les mêmes droits qu'aux siens et m'a chargé de proposer à votre gouvernement de Consacrer dans un veritable pacte de famille dans un pacte national les bases libérales et fraternelles[21] sur les quelles[22] elle désire voir reposer le système commerical et politique[23] de deux peuples dont tous les interêts se Confondent. Je suis revêtu, M., des pouvoirs nécéssaires pour entamer cette importante négociation[24] dont les tristes[25] annales de l'humanité avant l'Ere brillante qui s'est enfin ouverte pour elle, n'offrent, aucun éxemple.

Dft (DLC: Genet Papers); heavily emended text in Genet's hand, except for part of dateline (see note 1 below) and several words added in clerical hands; unsigned; above salutation: "Le &c a Mr. Jefferson &c."; at head of text: "Nouvelles preuves ⟨*de fraternité*⟩ d'amitié données par la france aux Etats unis"; only the most important emendations are noted below. Tr (AMAE: CPEU, xxxvii); with minor variations; certified by Genet. Recorded in SJL as received 23 May 1793. Enclosure: Decree of the National Convention, 19 Feb. 1793, liberalizing American trade with France and its colonies (see note to Joseph Fenwick to TJ, 25 Feb. 1793); with an accompanying statement by Genet announcing the suspension of a 15 May 1791 law inhibiting Americans from introducing, selling, and arming their ships in France and from enjoying the advantages allowed to vessels built in France (Tr in DNA: RG 59, NL, English translation in the hand of George Taylor, Jr.; PrC in DLC: TJ Papers, 82: 14172, 14228; Tr in DNA: RG 46, Senate Records, 3d Cong., 1st sess., in English). Letter and enclosure with translations printed in *Message*, 8 (App.), 15-16;

translations printed in *Correspondence*, 11-13; printed in *Correspondance*, 15-17; translations printed in ASP, *Foreign Relations*, I, 147. Translations of letter and enclosure enclosed in TJ to Washington, 27 May 1793.

TJ could not have begun to appreciate the full dimensions of Genet's proposal for a PACTE NATIONAL between France and the United States, the details of which involved far more than the new French-American commercial treaty that was its ostensible object, until the French minister published a partial text of his instructions from the Girondin-dominated Provisional Executive Council in December 1793, on the eve of TJ's retirement as Secretary of State (*Correspondence*, 1-7). Envisioning a political and economic agreement strengthening the ties between France and the United States and facilitating American support for Girondin plans to liberate Louisiana and Canada from Spanish and British rule, the Executive Council authorized Genet to negotiate a new treaty of commerce with the United States that was to include four major provisions: an agreement by both parties to exclude from their ports the vessels of nations with closed commercial and colonial systems—a clear call for American economic retaliation against Great Britain; a reciprocal exemption of American and French vessels from the payment of tonnage duties; a mutual naturalization of American and French citizens with respect to commercial matters; and a renewed United States guarantee to defend French possessions in America in return for free trade with France and the French West Indies and a French guarantee to protect America and its trade, including the stationing of French forces in American ports. Except for the last, these provisions were based on proposals TJ had made to previous French diplomatic representatives in the United States and thus were calculated to appeal to his well-known desire for a new commercial agreement with France in order to end American economic dependence on Britain (*Correspondence*, 3, 6; Turner, *CFM*, 204, 209-10; TJ to Gouverneur Morris, 28 Apr. 1792, and note; Bowman, *Neutrality*, 39-46; Peter P. Hill, *French Perceptions of the Early American Republic, 1783-1793* [Philadelphia, 1988], 118, 121-2).

TJ delivered Genet's letter and its enclosure to the President on 24 May 1793, at which point Washington, citing uncertainty about the outcome of the French Revolution, impressed upon him the need to give deliberate consideration to this and other proposals from Genet because the government "ought not to go faster than it was obliged; but to walk on cautious ground." Three days later TJ supplied Washington with English translations of these documents, and thereafter the President and the Cabinet periodically considered opening negotiations for the proposed treaty during the summer of 1793, with TJ alone favoring it (Washington, *Journal*, 148, 151; TJ to James Madison, 2 June 1793; Notes on Relations with France, 23 Aug. 1793). During this time TJ hinted in conversation with Genet that he could not take up the treaty until the Senate reconvened in the fall. But this was merely a polite fiction to mask the Washington administration's reluctance to conclude a new treaty because of its satisfaction with the sweeping commercial concessions the French Republic had already made to the United States, its uncertainty about the republican regime's prospects for survival, and its apprehensions that the political ties hinted at in Genet's letter would compromise American neutrality. For these reasons, as well as the administration's decision in August 1793 to seek Genet's recall, TJ was unable to overcome Cabinet opposition to Genet's overtures and never entered into negotiations with him for the treaty that he hoped would fundamentally transform the American political economy (TJ to Gouverneur Morris, 16 and 23 Aug. 1793; Notes of Cabinet Meeting on a Commercial Treaty with France, 23 Aug. 1793; Hill, *French Perceptions*, 114-29; Setser, *Reciprocity*, 81-92, 119-26; Merrill D. Peterson, "Thomas Jefferson and Commercial Policy, 1783-1793," WMQ, 3d ser., XXII [1965], 584-610; Turner, *CFM*, 258).

[1] Digits inserted by a clerk in a space left blank by Genet.

[2] Genet first wrote "une horde innombrable" and then altered it to read as above.

[3] Preceding two words interlined in place of "⟨d'Esclaves⟩ de barbares."

[4] Preceding two words written in the margin in place of "france" and an addition which reads "après avoir ⟨versé⟩ repandu ses trésors et s."

[5] Genet here canceled "l'éxécution des traités qui."

[6] Preceding eight words written in the margin.

[7] Preceding three words written in the margin in place of an interlined "l'immensité de ses."

[8] Preceding six words interlined in place of "et de la Justice de sa cause de ses."

[9] Word interlined.

[10] Genet first wrote "ou ⟨de prétendus politiques mettoient en action tous les ressorts de leur imagination,⟩ l'on faisoit d'inutiles éfforts" before a clerical hand revised the passage to read as above. In the emending process, "l'on" was inadvertently left uncanceled.

[11] Preceding two words written in the margin.

[12] Preceding three words written in the margin in a clerical hand.

[13] Genet here canceled "⟨au milieu meme des dangers qui l'environnent⟩ sans s'occuper de ses propres intérêts."

[14] Word interlined in place of "à dessein."

[15] Word interlined by a clerical hand in place of "dernier Roi des francois."

[16] Preceding eight words altered by Genet from "pour arrêter."

[17] Word added in the margin, but omitted in *Correspondance*.

[18] Preceding eight words interlined in place of "Etats unis avec les françois." *Message*: "de leurs principes."

[19] Preceding five words written in the margin.

[20] AMAE Tr and *Correspondance*: "toutes les faveurs."

[21] Preceding three words interlined.

[22] Genet here canceled "doit reposer" and wrote the next four words in the margin.

[23] Preceding two words interlined.

[24] Genet here canceled "et Je recueillerai avec bien du plaisir par l'organe d'un ami aussi sincere que vous des fo."

[25] Word written in the margin.

T R A N S L A T I O N

SIR   Philadelphia May 23. 1793. 2d. year of the Republic

Single against innumerable hordes of tyrants and slaves who menace her rising liberty, the French nation would have a right to reclaim the obligations imposed on the US. by the treaties she has contracted with them and which she has cemented with her blood: but strong in the greatness of her means, and of the power of her principles not less redoutable to her enemies than the victorious arms which she opposes to their rage, she comes, in the very time when the emissaries of our common enemies are making useless efforts to neutralize the gratitude, to damp the zeal, to weaken or cloud the view of yours fellow citizens, she comes, I say, that generous nation, that faithful friend, to labour still to increase the prosperity, and add to the happiness which she is pleased to see them enjoying.

The obstacles raised with intentions hostile to liberty by the perfidious ministers of despotism, the obstacles whose object was to stop the rapid progress of the commerce of the Americans, and the extension of their principles, exist no more. The French republic, seeing in them but brothers, has opened to them by the decrees now inclosed, all her ports in the two worlds, has granted them all the favors which her own citizens enjoy in her vast possessions, has invited them to participate the benefits of her navigation in granting to their vessels the same rights as to her own, and has charged me to propose to your government to establish in a true family compact, that is, in a national compact, the liberal and fraternal bases on which she wishes to see raised the commercial and political system of two people all whose interests are confounded.

I am invested, Sir, with the powers necessary to undertake this important negociation, of which the sad annals of humanity offer no example before the brilliant aera at length opening on it.   GENET

Tr (DNA: RG 59, NL); translation in TJ's hand containing minor inaccuracies; addressed: "The Citizen Genet, Min. plen. of the French republic to Mr. Jefferson, Secretary of state for the US." PrC (DLC). Tr (DNA: RG 46, Senate Records, 3d Cong., 1st sess.).

From Alexander Hamilton

SIR   Treasury Department May 23. 1793.

I have the honor of your note, transmitting the copy of one from Mr. Genet of yesterday.

As our laws stand, no transfer of any part of her cargo from one vessel to another within our Ports, can take place 'till after a regular entry and the paying or securing the payment of the duties. You are sensible, Sir, that I have no discretion to dispense with their requisitions.

If the wines are be carried to any foreign port and there landed, a drawback of the duties, essentially, may be obtained, under the usual securities for their due transportation to the place for which they are destined. I have the honor to be very respectfully, Sir your obedient Servant.   ALEX. HAMILTON

PrC of Tr (DLC); in a clerk's hand; at foot of text: "The Secretary of State." Tr (DNA: RG 59, DL). Enclosed in TJ to Edmond Charles Genet, 24 May 1793.

TJ's NOTE to Hamilton has not been found and is not recorded in SJL. The ONE of 22 May 1793 from Edmond Charles Genet, recorded in SJL as a letter of 23 May 1793 received that day, has also not been found, but it evidently concerned a cargo of wine belonging to the Philadelphia merchant James Vanuxem.

To Harry Innes

DEAR SIR   Philadelphia May 23. 1793.

I am in your debt for several letters received and not yet acknoleged. One of these is particularly to be noticed, as it was interesting to you; I mean that which concerned your slaves carried off by the Indians. I knew that the channel proposed in your letter would effect nothing. I therefore concluded to take the opportunity which I knew was to occur, of endeavoring to serve you through the Commissioners who were to go to the treaty with the Indians. Those of the very towns where you supposed your negroes to be were to be at the treaty. A clause would of course be inserted in the treaty for the restoration of all captives of every condition. As Mr. Beverley Randolph was appointed a commissioner, and passed by this place, I put into his hands your letter and description of the slaves, that the moment the treaty should be concluded, he being on the spot with those Indians might avail himself of the opportunity to find out yours and take means for their restoration to you. This he promised me he would do, and it appears to me at least the best chance of recovering them which I have been able to seize.—It is very interesting to the US. to see how this last effort for living in peace with the Indians will succeed. If it does not, there will be a great revolution of opinion here as to the manner in which they are to be dealt with. If war is to follow, the event of this campaign will probably fix the kind of instruments to be used. I suspect that your state might farm the conduct of this war from us with great advantage to both parties. I fear we are to have it on our Southern quarter also. It is very necessary for us then to keep clear of the European combustion, *if they will let us*. This they will do probably if France is successful: but if great successes were to attend the arms of the kings, it is far from being certain they might not chuse to finish their job completely, by obliging us to change in the form of our government at least, a change which would be grateful to a party here, not numerous, but wealthy and influential.—The late retreat of the French from the Netherlands, tho' a check, is little decisive. As long as they can be tolerably unanimous internally, they can resist the whole world. The laws of nature render a large country unconquerable if they adhere firmly together and to their purpose. This summer is of immense importance to the future condition of mankind all over the earth: and not a little so to ours. For tho' it's issue should[1] not be marked by any direct change in our constitution, it will influence the tone and principles of it's administration so as to lead it to something very different in the one event from what it would be in the other. I am with great & sincere esteem Dear Sir Your friend & servt   TH: JEFFERSON

RC (DLC: Innes Papers); addressed: "Harry Innes esquire Kentuckey"; franked, stamped, and postmarked. PrC (DLC). Tr (DLC); 19th-century copy.

The SEVERAL LETTERS RECEIVED AND NOT YET ACKNOLEGED were Innes to TJ, 30 May, 27 Aug., 30 Sep. 1791, and missing letters of 30 June 1792 and 8 Feb. 1793 (see TJ to Beverley Randolph, 28 Apr. 1793, and TJ to John Adams, 1 Mch. 1793, respectively). Evidently the letter of 30 June 1792 dealt with Innes's SLAVES CARRIED OFF BY THE INDIANS.

[1] TJ originally wrote "it should" and then altered the phrase to read as above.

From James Monroe

DEAR SIR   Albemarle May 23. 1793.

I have just replaced myself at home where I hope to enjoy for a while repose. I did not see Mr. Pope at Richmond and of course could not execute the other objects of your commission. I shall however soon be able to communicate with him thro' some one of the gentlemen who practice in the Louisa Cty. court and will then apprize you of the result.

At Richmond I was requested by Mr. Robert Gamble to mention to you his desire to be employed as an agent for the French in the purchase of flour &ca. I am well satisfied from his connection with the country from Richmond to Staunton, his great industry, and other suitable qualifications, that a more judicious appointment could not be made. Indeed considering his political principles I should deem it a desirable object with Mr. Genet to enlist him in the business.

Your letter to the care of Mr. Madison has this moment been put into my hands. It shall be noticed by the next post. I saw Mr. and Mrs. R. yesterday in good health. Very sincerely I am your friend & servant

JAS. MONROE

RC (DLC); endorsed by TJ as received 3 June 1793 and so recorded in SJL.

YOUR LETTER TO THE CARE OF MR. MADISON: TJ to Monroe, 5 May 1793. MR. AND MRS. R.: Thomas Mann Randolph, Jr., and Martha Jefferson Randolph.

Notes of a Conversation with George Washington

1793. May 23. I had sent to the President yesterday, draughts of a letter from him to the Provisory Exec. council of France, and of one from myself to Mr. Ternant, both on the occasion of his recall. I called on him to-day. He said there was a word in one of them which he had never before seen in any of our public communications, to wit 'our republic.' The letter prepared for him to the Council began thus 'the citizen Ternant has delivered to me the letter wherein you inform me that, yielding &c. you had determined to recall him from his mission as your Min. plen. to *our republic*.' He had underscored the words *our republic*. He said that certainly ours was a republican government, but yet we had not used that stile in this way: that if any body wanted to change it's form into a monarchy he was sure it was only a few individuals, and that no man in the US. would set his face against it more than himself: but that this was not what he was afraid of: his fears were from another quarter, that there was more danger of anarchy being introduced. He adverted to a peice in Freneau's paper of yesterday, he said he despised all their attacks on him personally, but that there never had been an act of the government, not meaning in the Executive line only, but in any line which that paper had not abused. He had also marked the word republic thus √ where it was applied to the French republic. [see the original paper][1] He was evidently sore and warm, and I took his intention to be that I should interpose in some way with Freneau, perhaps withdraw his appointment of translating clerk to my office, but I will not do it: his paper has saved our constitution which was galloping fast into monarchy, and has been checked by no one means so powerfully as by that paper. It is well and universally known that it has been that paper which has checked the career of the Monocrats, and the President, not sensible of the designs of the party, has not with his usual good sense, and sang froid, looked on the efforts and effects[2] of this free press, and seen that tho some bad things had passed thro' it to the public, yet the good had preponderated immensely.

MS (DLC); entirely in TJ's hand, with one sentence added at another time (see note 1 below); clipped at bottom, probably by TJ when he revised the "Anas" later in life, with possible loss of text; brackets in original. Recorded in SJPL under 24 May 1793 beneath entry for draft of George Washington to the Provisional Executive Council of France, 24 May 1793: "note on its being scored by the Presidt." Included in the "Anas."

For a discussion of the President's objections to TJ's wording of the draft of this letter, see note to George Washington to the Provisional Executive Council of France, 24 May 1793. The PEICE IN FRENEAU'S PAPER was probably the intemperate article by "An Old Soldier" in the *National Gazette* of 22 May 1793 lauding the enthusiastic popular reception of Edmond Charles Genet in Philadelphia, attacking the Philadelphia merchants who had lately addressed Washington in support of the Proclamation of Neutrality as "the mercenary band, who bask in the sun-shine of court-favour," and giving thanks that in America "the *sovereignty* still resides with THE PEOPLE, and that neither proclamations, nor *royal demeanor and state* can prevent them from exercising it."

[1] Preceding sentence interlined in a different ink.
[2] Preceding three words interlined in place of "proceedings."

From Joseph Ravara

MONSIEUR   23. Mai. 1793.

J'ose, et je dois même me flatter, Monsieur, que dans un Pays, celebre, et respectable par ses bonnes loix, et sa justice on ne permettra pas la ruine totale d'un Innocent.

Il est bien malheureux de me voir depuis dix jours dans une Prison, sans entendre qu'on s'occupe de developper quelque intrigue, qui sans doute existe. J'ai pitié de mon pauvre Peruquier, que l'on me dit se trouver aussi en prison, et je declare qu'il souffre sans raison, comme sa famille qui est dans la Misere par cet affaire.

Il a été bien dommage que la Justice n'ait pas fait ses demarches d'une façon differente, et plus secrete: Si lorsque le Peruquier fut à la Poste, on l'eut suivi sans fracas, l'on l'auroit vu entrer chez moi: allors j'aurois dit, qu'un Étranger m'avoit laissé les noms en question: il seroit revenu pour ses reponses, et il auroit été arreté: Mais le bruit, et la Publicité l'on mis en fuite sans doute.

L'on m'a accusé de ce que ce soir la j'ai entré chez le Peruquier: il est vrai, et cela etoit tout naturel, puisque j'avois entendu qu'il étoit dans des Embarras par rapport a moi qui l'avoit tout bonnement envoyé à la Poste chercher des lettres pour un Étranger, lettres que je croiois devoir arriver de dehors.

L'on m'accuse de ce que j'ai evité moi même les Constables: oui cela est vrai; je les ai evité *Le Soir*, ne voulant pas m'exposer: Mr. Oellers fut chez moi, et il me dit qu'il y avoit des Constables à ma poursuite; je lui repondis que je n'avois rien fait, mais que le lendemain matin ils me trouveroient chez-moi: En effet j'ai gardé ma parole; j'ai envoié cherché une voiture, et je me suis présenté; et me voila depuis ce moment, en Prison, n'ayant pas pu trouver une Caution, puisque tout Citoyen etoit épouvanté puisque on debitoit, et on debite que je suis un grand Criminel.

Depuis que je suis ici, personne ne s'occupe de moi, et il paroit que les portes de la Justice, du devoir, de l'humanité, et de l'hospitalité sont fermées. Il y a Cependant des Circonstances, que si l'on se donnoit la peine d'examiner, et d'approffondir, comme on devroit le faire, l'on trouveroit assez de quoi connoître la verité: Je prendrai la liberté de n'en citer que deux.

1ere: Mr. van Berckel a eté me voir, et il m'a dit, que dans une lettre anonyme adressée a Mr. Hammond on lui demandoit une réponse adresée a un tel Nom, mais dit Mr. van Berckel que ce Nom n'est pas aucun de deux que l'Étranger me donna, que j'ai donné au Peruquier, et qui sont actuellement chez Mr. Baker.

2de. Mr. Dallas, et le Dr. Ross m'ont dit l'autre jour, qu'une lettre a etée adressé à la Poste, écrite dans le même gout des autres anonymes, declarant que Ravara souffre innocement. Il paroit que cela demande, Monsieur, quelque perquisition.

J'implore, votre Assistance, comme Étranger, comme habitant des États-Unis, et comme homme. Je vous prie en outre d'exposer mon Cas, et cette lettre au President, puisque j'entends que beaucoup des faussetés ont eté debité sur mon Compte. Il me doit être permis d'observer que mon Caracter etoit très bien connu ici, et que je n'ai jamais fait que du Bien.

Quelle Situation, Monsieur! quel triste Sort! quel Cahos de

Malheurs! J'ai voyagé depuis 12. ans: j'ai resté 4. Ans a Philadelphie: j'ai reçu il est peu de jours des lettres des plus flatteuses d'Europe: j'avois la plus belle prospective du Monde, et j'avois choisi cette Ville pour ma residence, et y passer en paix le reste de mes jours. J'ai formé des liaisons; j'attends un Associé sous peu, j'allois, enfin être heureux. Mais voila qu'un seul Moment defait le tout: me perd, me ruine, et m'opprime.

Où puis-je aller où je ne sois pas connu? en outre les Gazettes portent de Pays en Pays cette histoire, et qu'elle soit crue, ou non, cela me fait toujours du tort.

Il n'y a jamais eu au Monde des plus grands malheurs. Mes affaires sont arretés: mon Credit, mon honneur, perdu, et engagé encore dans des fraix pour me deffendre d'une chose que je ne connois pas. Grand Dieu, comment me peut-on croire capable à ecrire des lettres anonymes? Il falloit être fou, Sot, ou Scelerat; Et personne, personne ne prend ma deffense: tout homme s'excuse.

Il faudra que je quitte ce Pays, que j'avois choisi dans le Monde entier pour ma Residence: oui il faudra que je m'en aille, malgré ne savoir où aller; puisque Ce Coup me ruine effectivement: j'étois bien: j'allois être mieux, et je suis ruiné.

Mr. Carmichael a Madrid informera le Ministre de Génes, et mon Oncle de ce cas, qui passera de Pays en Pays: Patience si je fusse Criminel, mais il est trop dur d'être exposé de cette façon étant innocent! J'espere enfin qu'on se donne quelque peine, et que l'on remede en part au tort qu'on m'a fait.

Je Suplie, aussi de m'indiquer ce que je dois faire par rapport à la Commission, ou *exequatur*, que j'ai reçu du President, par vos mains, ne pouvant guere combiner comment la garder, si l'on ne s'occupe plus de moi.

Enfin, Monsieur: n'oubliez pas mon histoire; Pesez cette relation, et ayez la bonté d'agir de façon, que ou votre reponse, ou le ressultat m'annoncent qu'on s'est occupé de moi. Si je ne fusse pas innocent, je ne vous aurois pas écrit, soyez-en sur Monsieur, aussi-bien que des Sentiments de respect et Consideration avec les quels j'ai l'honneur d'etre, Monsieur Votre très-hble & très-Obst   JOSEPH RAVARA

RC (DNA: RG 59, NFC); addressed: "Honble: Thomas Jefferson. Secretary of State"; endorsed by TJ as received 23 May 1793 and so recorded in SJL.

Joseph Ravara, a Genoese-born merchant, first came to the United States in 1789 and settled in Philadelphia, where he became associated with the firm of Willing, Morris & Swanwick and served as consul general for Genoa from 25 Oct. 1791, when TJ formally presented him to the President (Exequatur for Ravara, 25 Oct. 1791, FC in DNA: RG 59, Exequaturs, with Washington and TJ as signatory and countersignatory). A patron and promoter of Jean Pierre Blanchard's aeronautical experiments, Ravara at this time was in prison awaiting trial following a hearing in the United States Circuit Court for the District of Pennsylvania in April 1793 at which he pleaded not guilty to the charge of having written threatening anonymous letters to the British minister George Hammond and the Philadelphia merchant Benjamin Holland with the intent of extorting $200 from each of them. Despite his claims that these letters had actually been written by a mysterious stranger from Parma named Vidal, Ravara was convicted of attempted extortion at a trial in April 1794. After his conviction he received a pardon from the President, reportedly on condition that he relinquish his consular office (Joseph Ravara, *A Statement of Facts, Concerning Joseph Ravara, Written by Himself* [Philadelphia, 1793], Sowerby, No. 3171, as well as notes by an unidentified hand in the copy in PP; Washington's pardon of Ravara, 25 Apr. 1793 [1794], DNA: RG 59, Petitions for Pardon; *Federal Cases*, XXVII, 713-15; PMHB, LXVII [1943], 56, 57; John D. Gordan III, *"United States v. Joseph Ravara*: 'Presumptuous Evidence,' 'Too Many Lawyers,' and a Federal Common Law Crime," in Maeva Marcus, ed., *Origins of the Federal Judiciary: Essays on the Judiciary Act of 1789* [New York, 1992], 106-72).

To Edmond Charles Genet

May 24. 1793.

Th: Jefferson having forwarded to the Secretary of the Treasury the application of Mr. Genet on behalf of Mr. Vanuxem, has now the honor to inclose to Mr. Genet the answer he has received, and of assuring him of his respect.

PrC (DLC). FC (Lb in DNA: RG 59, DL). Enclosure: Alexander Hamilton to TJ, 23 May 1793.

To John Harvie

DEAR SIR   Philadelphia May 24. 1793.

The bearer hereof, Mr. Bayley, is an English gentleman who has studied the laws of that country as the basis of ours, and proposes now to take up ours, as he means to engage in the practice in Virginia. Supposing it will take him a twelvemonth to complete this part of his study, he finds it necessary in aid of his finances to become tutor in some private family, or clerk in some office, if any such place can be obtained. I am not personally acquainted with him, but Colo. Smith of N.Y. recommends him to me strongly and on that foundation I think myself authorized to ask your patronage and notice of him, and to render him such services within the line he has marked out for himself as you can with convenience, which will be considered as an obligation on Dear Sir your friend & servt   TH: JEFFERSON

PrC (DLC); at foot of text: "Colo. John Harvie." Tr (DLC); 19th-century copy.

Memorial from Benjamin Holland and Peter Mackie

To Thomas Jefferson Esqr., Secretary of State

The Memorial of Benjamin Holland and Peter Mackie, Citizens of
Philadelphia

Respectfully Sheweth

That your Memorialists on the[1] 4th. day of April last past, engaged freight on board the Brigantine Little Sarah, Joseph Lowrey, master, for between three and four hundred barrels of flour &c., to be shipped by them, and on their own account and risk, to Kingston in the Island of Jamaica. That in consequence of this Engagement, they did on the day following, Viz. the 5th. of April, purchase from Jacob Downing Two hundred barrels Flour, and on the same day from Philip Cave, One hundred barrels Flour, for this purpose. That the said Three hundred barrels Flour were accordingly shipped, on board the said Brig Little Sarah, by your Memorialists, together with Nineteen barrels of Indian corn Meal to fill up by your Memorialist Peter Mackie. That those Shipments were actually, and bona fide, made before your Memorialists had any certain Intelligence of War between France and Great Britain. That the said Brig Little Sarah was detained in this port sometime after she was compleatly loaded, owing to some of the Sailors having left her; That she actually sailed on her intended voyage on the 17th. of April. That she had not proceeded many leagues from the Capes of the Delaware, before she was captured by the French ship of War L'Embuscade, commanded by Citizen Bompard, and sent into this Port, where she now remains with her cargo.

That your Memorialists flatter themselves the Government of the United States, as well as the Minister from the Republic of France, are disposed to put the most favorable construction on the Existing Treaties between the Two Nations, and that as these Shipments were really made before your Memorialists had any certain information of the present War, and before the Proclamation of the President of the United States was promulgated, they hope that the said Flour and Meal may be restored to them.

Your Memorialists therefor respectfully Pray, that the Premises may be submitted to the Consideration of the President of the United States, and that they may receive such an answer thereto, as in Equity and Justice may be right.

Philadelphia

24th. May 1793

BENJ. HOLLAND

PETER MACKIE

RC (DNA: RG 76, France, Case Files); in a clerk's hand, signed by Holland and Mackie; with marginal note by TJ (see note 1 below); notation in margin in unidentified hand: "No: 12."; endorsed by TJ as received 25 May 1793 and so recorded in SJL.

Benjamin Holland and Peter Mackie were Philadelphia merchants located, respectively, at 3 North Front Street and 119 South Front Street (Hardie, *Phila. Dir.*, 66, 87).

[1] TJ here inserted an asterisk to serve as a key to a note he wrote in the margin: "The declaration of war by France was on the 1st. of February."

From Daniel L. Hylton

MY DEAR SIR   Richmond Virga. May 24th. 1793

In conjunction with Mr. Miles King Doctor Wm. Foushee and my Brother Mr. Wm. Hylton we have made a purchase of Mr. Wilson Miles Cary for his plantation call'd Rich Neck situated on Warwick river to carry on the lumber business in its various branches. The french minister citizen Genet as he passd through this place had some conversation with my friend Dr. Foushee on this subject and at his request we have taken the liberty of forwarding to your care a Cubic foot of the Oak with the leaf of the tree for his inspection. Should he approve the texture of the wood and is willing to enter into contract with us for any quantity either cut or standing, I only wish you to give him such assurance of our abilities for the performance on our part he may think necessary. Its our wish (not from Interest alone) but gratitude we owe that nation whose friendly aid we are at this moment indebted to for the free enjoyment we now exercise of our property and liberty. As individuals of this great community we have every desire to render them all the aid in promoting their navy within the reach of our power and flatter myself the confidence you have hitherto repos'd me is such, as induces me to take the liberty of requesting the favour of your friendly assistance in a negotiation with the Minister as may eventualy prove reciprocal to both. I am with every wish for your health & happiness Your Sincere Frd

DANL L HYLTON

RC (ViU: Carr-Cary Papers); opening parenthesis supplied; endorsed by TJ as a letter of 21 May 1793 received 5 June 1793 and so recorded in SJL. Enclosed in William Hylton to TJ, 25 May 1793.

To Jean Baptiste Le Roy

DEAR SIR   Philadelphia May 24. 1793.

You may remember that I had the honour of presenting to you at Paris my ingenious countryman Mr. Rumsey, as the discoverer of a simple and advantageous method of propelling vessels thro' the water by steam. You first mentioned to me the step which Bernoulli had advanced towards the same discovery. Mr. Rumsey is since dead, and the bearer hereof Mr. Barnes, a citizen of the United states, goes to Europe to save the benefit of Mr. Rumsey's discoveries to those entitled to them. I lodged in the hands of M. de Condorcet the titles of Mr. Rumsey to this discovery. Permit me my dear Sir, to ask your patronage of Mr. Barnes's pursuits in this business, as far as shall be just, and I am sure he will press them no further. He is a man of worth and talents, well known to me and well meriting any good offices you can render him in this way. I have with pleasure given him this line to you, because it gives me an opportunity of recalling myself to your recollection, of repeating to you assurances of the satisfaction with which I recall the memory of my acquaintance with you, and of declaring the constant esteem with which I shall ever remain Dear Sir Your most obedt. & most humble servt   TH: JEFFERSON

PrC (DLC); at foot of text: "M. Le Roy." Tr (DLC); 19th-century copy.

For TJ's efforts AT PARIS on behalf of inventor James RUMSEY, see Le Roy to TJ, [30 Apr. 1789], and note. Joseph BARNES promoted RUMSEY'S DISCOVERIES both before and after the latter died in 1792 (Barnes to TJ, 2 July 1790, 17 Aug. 1793).

To Gouverneur Morris

DEAR SIR   Philadelphia May 24. 1793.

The bearer hereof, Mr. Barnes, is, as I understand, the representative of the company concerned in the steam navigation of the late Mr. Rumsey, was the attorney of Mr. Rumsey here, and goes now to Europe to secure the benefit of his discoveries to those entitled to them. In times like these he may need your protection as a stranger, and at all times would merit it as a man of worth and talents. As such I take the liberty of recommending him to your good offices, and particularly so far as shall be necessary for securing the benefit of the discoveries in which himself, and those for whom he acts, are interested. To these titles to your patronage he adds that of being a citizen of the US. I am with great & sincere esteem Dear Sir your most obedt. & most humble servt

TH: JEFFERSON

PrC (DLC); at foot of text: "Mr. G. Morris." Tr (DLC); 19th-century copy.

This day TJ wrote an almost identical letter to Thomas Pinckney (PrC in DLC, at foot of text: "Mr. Pinckney"; Tr in DLC, 19th-century copy).

From John Nicholas, Jr.

DEAR SIR   May [24-31][1] 1793

As the only friend and acquaintance I have now remaining in Philadelphia, I take the liberty to enclose to your care, for publication, an Advertisement, trusting from your general disposition to oblige, that you will excuse the liberty, when I inform you, that it proceeds from a desire in me to procure the best price I can, on account of those Lands being the principal part of the fortune given by your friend my father to two of his Daughters.

The reason for advertising it in the Northern papers, is, the superior propensity those people have for mineral pursuits, to our own Countrymen; and the reason of my taking the liberty of referring those inclined to purchase, to you, the difficulty perhaps there would be in persuaiding any one to come such a distance on so precarious an adventure, without some other assurances than those which could come from one so totally unknown as myself.

The mineral spoken of is the one formerly sought for by Col. Chiswell, and which I observe is slightly touched on in your Notes. From this circumstance and the intimacy of your father and my Grandfather Fry, I suspect you have had better information on the subject of that experiment than I have. I am well assured however that Col. Chiswell established the fact of the existence of a large quantity of copper—tho' he was obliged from the situation of his funds, or some other circumstance, with which perhaps you are also better acquainted than myself, to desist in the pursuit.

I am now in Richmond attending the debates on the subject of the British debts—on the ultimate desision, of which, various conjectures are formed; tho' from my own observations, arising out of the questions propounded by the Court to the bar, I am inclined to think that they will deside on the General question, viz. the payment of the debts, in favour of the creditors; and on the payments into the treasury, in favour of the debtors. This is all the news we have at present in this quarter. Heaven grant that what we received by the yesterday's mail from the North, of the success of the French, may be true. It has already struck a damp on the tory party in this place; and will I make no doubt, if true, assist in lowering the heads of all the friends to monarchy in America. This, aided by your continuance in Office, which has not only pleased your personal friends, but given universal satisfaction to all the friends of republicanism, will I trust tend in time to place the Government of America, in that point of view, in its operation, it was intended to be seen in.[2]

Mr. Randolph's family and all your friends in Alble. were well a few days ago. Yours with friendship & respect   JOHN NICHOLAS

RC (DNA: RG 59, MLR); partially dated (see note 1 below), with incorrect day—"5"—added by a later hand and accepted in Vol. 16: 140n; addressed: "The Honorable Thos: Jefferson Esqr Sectry: of State"; endorsed by TJ as received 4 June 1793 and so recorded in SJL.

While Nicholas only dated this letter "May   1793" and TJ so endorsed it, the reference to the Richmond trial on THE BRITISH DEBTS establishes that it was written no earlier than 24 May, when the United States District Court there began hearing the case of Ware v. Hylton (Marshall, *Papers*, V, 295-6).

The enclosed ADVERTISEMENT, which offered for sale 1,360 acres of Amherst County land suitable for farming and probably containing "an abundance of metals," has not been found, but TJ had it printed in the 8 June 1793 issues of both the *National Gazette* and the *Gazette of the United States* (TJ to Nicholas, 8 June 1793). TJ had SLIGHTLY TOUCHED ON the COPPER at this site in *Notes*, ed. Peden, 27.

[1] Editors' conjecture for space left blank in manuscript.
[2] Preceding three words interlined in place of "have."

George Washington to the Provisional Executive Council of France

VERY GREAT AND GOOD FRIENDS & ALLIES   [24 May 1793]

The citizen Ternant has delivered to me the letter wherein you inform me that yielding to his desire to serve his country in the military line, you had determined to recall him from his mission as your[1] Minister plenipotentiary to[2] the US. His conduct during the time of his residence in this country has been such as to meet my entire approbation and esteem; and it is with great pleasure I render him the justice of this testimony. In whatever line of service you may hereafter think proper to employ him, I have no doubt he will so conduct himself as to merit well of his country and to obtain it's favor and protection.

I assure you, with a sincere participation, of the great[3] and constant friendship which these US. bear to the French nation,[4] of the interest they feel in whatever concerns their happiness and prosperity,[5] and of their wishes for a perpetual fraternity with them, and I pray god to have them and you, very great and good friends and allies, in his holy keeping.

Written at Philadelphia this   [6] day of May in the year of our lord 1793 and of the independence of the US. the 17th.[7]

Dft (DLC); unsigned and partially dated text written by TJ ca. 22 May 1793 and then revised by him on 23 or 24 May 1793; with three markings in pencil by Washington—two of them described in the "Anas" entry of 23 May 1793—three revisions by TJ made at the President's behest, and two additions by George Taylor, Jr. (see notes below); at foot of text by TJ and encircled in pencil, presumably by the President: "To the Provisory Executive council of the republic of France." PrC (DLC); lacks all but two of the revisions in Dft; written at head of text in ink by TJ, probably on one of the occasions later in life when he reviewed or reorganized his papers: "See among my official reports &c. the original of which this is a press-copy, scored by the President, and altered to his views." Recorded in SJPL under 24 May 1793: "draught of lre from the Presidt. to the Exve of France. Ter[nant]." Enclosed in TJ to Washington, 22 May 1793; final text enclosed in TJ to Gouverneur Morris, 13 June 1793.

The drafting of this letter reflects the difference between TJ's enthusiasm for the cause of the French Republic and the President's more restrained attitude toward it. On 17 May 1793, the day after Jean Baptiste Ternant wrote to TJ about his recall by the Provisional Executive Council of France, the French minister wrote privately to Washington requesting an expression of his "personal and private assurance" that he had faithfully discharged his official duties in the United States "notwithstanding the violent agitations, and great vicissitudes experienced by the government of my country" (Ternant to Washington, 17 May 1793, DLC: Washington Papers; note to TJ to Washington, 18 May 1793). Washington drafted a personal letter to Ternant expressing approval of his conduct in the United States, but then decided that it would be impolitic to send it because the Provisional Executive Council had not explained its motives for recalling the last French minister to the United States appointed by Louis XVI (Washington to Ternant, [ca. 17] May 1793, and his note thereto, DLC: Washington Papers). In the meantime, having been asked by Washington to draft for him a letter to the Provisional

Executive Council expressing his sentiments on the occasion of the end of Ternant's diplomatic mission, TJ submitted a draft of the above letter to the President on 22 May 1793. During a conversation with the Secretary of State on the following day, Washington criticized TJ's use in the draft of the phrase "our republic" with respect to the United States because it seemed to reflect Republican complaints about the alleged monarchism of Federalists, and also objected to TJ's use of the term "republic" with respect to France, possibly because of the rapidly changing political situation in that country (see Notes of a Conversation with George Washington, 23 May 1793). Washington apparently also challenged the form of address TJ had inscribed at the foot of the draft. TJ altered the draft in accordance with the President's wishes (notes 2, 4-5 below), and the next day Washington signed the final text containing these revisions (Washington, *Journal*, 147, 148). The text sent to the Provisional Executive Council has not been found, but retained copies, dated 24 May 1793, indicate that it included one minor change in wording not recorded in TJ's Dft and that it was signed by Washington alone (FC in Lb in DLC: Washington Papers, addressed: "The Provisionary Executive Council of France"; FC in Lb in DNA: RG 59, Credences). For the phrase "our republic" as it was later considered by the President, see Notes of a Cabinet Meeting on the President's Messages to Congress, 28 Nov. 1793.

[1] Word interlined.

[2] Remainder of sentence interlined in Dft in place of "our republic," which Washington had underscored in pencil.

[3] TJ here canceled "friendship."

[4] Word interlined in Dft in place of "republic," which Washington had flagged with a penciled check mark.

[5] In Dft TJ first wrote "the happiness and prosperity of the nation" and then altered it to read as above.

[6] In Dft George Taylor, Jr., later inserted "24" in the blank space left by TJ.

[7] Below the body of the letter in Dft Taylor later added: "signed Go. Washington
By the President
Th: Jefferson."

From Stephen Cathalan, Jr.

Marseilles, 25 May 1793. European political affairs, embroiled by the revolutions in France, will require TJ's continuance in office because he is perhaps better able than anybody in France to judge the current situation, having left during the first year of the Revolution and subsequently kept in contact through public or private correspondence. By land strong armies surround all of France's frontiers and by sea the war with England and Spain has cost Marseilles all but one of the vessels coming from the straits. The city's Levant trade is conducted by convoy, and he now learns that an English fleet has passed the straits while a Spanish fleet is near Barcelona; some think the latter is intended to assist the recent Spanish incursion into Roussillon, others that it is going to help the king of Sardinia to reconquer Nice. It is hoped the natural situation of Marseilles will prevent a siege by sea, but it could be easily blockaded and deprived of incoming shipping. He refers TJ to the newspapers for the National Convention and other news; a hot summer lies ahead. Trade at sea has been badly protected, the Toulon squadron is unready, and sailors are insubordinate now that merchant captains are their officers. Tired of anarchy, the people here brought about a revolution a fortnight ago, guillotining three "chiefs of the anarchist," leading three others to commit suicide, and imprisoning many others who will receive their just reward. The Duc d'Orléans is here and the people apparently want to try and judge him as he deserves, if he is guilty of everything of which he is accused. Until peace is concluded and a good constitution takes effect, France will be in a critical situation, but one that will benefit the United States, which now controls the West Indian trade and which should protect its Mediterranean trade either with frigates or through a treaty with the barbarian powers. Captain Roger Robins, the very able young man bearing this letter who seeks employment as an American merchant ship captain, will report what is happening in these parts. Robins will say that all is perfectly well at Marseilles and that American vessels will do well if they come here, his own brig having obtained for Philadelphia 40 hard dollars with ten percent freight, half of it payable in advance here in effective Spanish money—terms on which Cathalan could freight thirty American vessels. Tobacco, now at £85 to 90, will very soon be at 100 and 120^{tt} per quintal; wheat and flour, which will be greatly wanting for at least a year, £120 per charge. Foreign exchanges are very ruinous for remittances, but cargoes suitable for the United States and the French West Indies can be procured. He refers to a letter he writes to Pinckney about the olive trees. [P.S.] The exchange rate with Amsterdam is $20\frac{1}{4}$, with London $9\frac{5}{8}$ to $\frac{1}{2}$. Spanish dollars equal £14^{tt} in assignats.

RC (DNA: RG 59, CD); 4 p.; addressed: "Thos. Jefferson Esqr. Pr. the Brig Bacchius Capn. Rogr. Robbins"; endorsed by TJ as received 17 Aug. 1793 and so recorded in SJL.

From J. P. P. Derieux

Charlottesville, 25 May 1793. He acknowledges TJ's letter of 10 Mch. and thanks him for the eggplant seeds which accompanied it. The plant is rare here and difficult to raise, for only two or three of those he sowed have escaped destruction by flies, and only by covering them in gauze can he hope to keep the survivors. He wrote Fenwick asking for information about his bills of exchange, but hopes that before his reply Gamble will learn that what happened was the fault of the bearer at Bordeaux, who on 6 Nov. had yet to inform his London correspondent that he cashed the sum at the end of September. He asks TJ to inquire about the success of his merchandise in Philadelphia and advise him whether the sale will be completed soon, his impatience being so great because he is anxious to satisfy creditors who are pressing him. From what TJ wrote about the uncertain sale of some items, he expects that flowers, plumes, and laces especially will lag behind and entail losses. If TJ thinks it proper and advantageous, he suggests that Vaughan be asked to exchange all or some of the slow-selling objects for goods likely to do well in Virginia, such as heavy brown cloth for Negroes, spinning cotton, nankeen, blue-striped ticking, and some good fine cloth. This proposition would not appear reasonable in general, but he believes this is a special case and that because luxury items are as sought after in Philadelphia as necessities, the trade might benefit one party without hurting the other. If the plan is feasible and dangerous delays in selling some of his goods are likely, he asks TJ to make the exchange, acting with as much freedom as if he were concerned personally but remembering his pressing need for money and how essential it would be for his business affairs here to be able to obtain at once the remittances which can be collected for items already sold. He hopes that TJ will pardon his frequent requests, forced upon him by his press-ing circumstances. Many false speculations have upset his business affairs, and he is impatient to get back into things and not make any more. Madame De-rieux sends respects and asks TJ to choose from the merchandise some lengths of ribbon correct for her age, without flattery, and bring them on his next visit.

RC (MHi); 3 p.; in French; addressed: "The Honble. Ths. Jefferson Esqr Secretary of State Philadelphia"; franked and postmarked; endorsed by TJ as received 3 June 1793 and so recorded in SJL.

From C. W. F. Dumas

The Hague, 25 May 1793. We receive neither letters nor papers from France and hear from there and elsewhere only what they wish us to know or delude us about. In Germany, as in Poland, the big despots are overwhelming the little ones and seizing peoples like flocks of sheep. All around him, commerce over-thrown, treasury exhausted, imminent vexations to refill it, hypocrisy on the throne and all around. His only consolation is the conviction that God, as he unceasingly prays, will protect our fortunate states.

RC (DNA: RG 59, MLR); in French; 1 p.; at head of text: "No. 98. A S. E. Mr. . . . Secretaire d'Etat, & pour les Affes. Etr. en Congres genl. des Et. Un. d'Am." Dupl (same, MDC); endorsed by TJ as received 9 Sep. 1793 and so recorded in SJL.

According to SJL, Dumas wrote four let-ters to TJ during the next three months that have not been found. Two dated 22 June 1793 were received 24 Oct. and 2 Dec. 1793, respectively, although it is possible that the second was merely a duplicate of the first. One dated 13 July 1793 and another dated 14 Aug. 1793 were received 24 Oct. and 9 Nov. 1793, respectively.

From Jean Antoine Gautier

Monsieur   Paris 25e May 1793.

J'eus l'honneur de répondre au mois d'octobre dernier à la lettre que vous avies pris la peine de m'écrire. Je vous fis part, Monsieur, des circonstances qui empêchoient Mr. Romilly de pouvoir promettre une montre telle que celle que vous desiriés plutôt que dans l'espace de huit à neuf mois et je vous priai de vouloir bien me donner vos ordres à ce Sujet, ainsi que pour le prix qu'il fixoit à 35 Louis.

Le Change Sur Londres ayant considerablement baissé depuis Décembre, ce prix Seroit devenu très mediocre; mais Mr. Romilly que j'ai depuis cette époque diverses fois entretenu de cette Commission; m'a témoigné qu'il ne pouvoit S'en occuper, et en effet, outre les circonstances publiques, il a éprouvé des chagrins domestiques qui l'ont fort détourné de tout objet d'application: Il m'a témoigné d'ailleurs qu'il Se fût fait un vrai plaisir de travailler pour un aussi bon apppréciateur du bon ouvrage et de l'industrie, et qu'il regrettoit d'autant plus de ne pouvoir faire cette montre pour le présent.

Je puis, Monsieur, vous donner de bonnes nouvelles de la Santé de Messs. et Mes. Grand et de Monsr. Le Veillard. Ces familles vous prient d'agréer leurs obeissances: Le fils de Mr. Le Veillard Se dispose à partir pour Philadelphie, où il prendra part à un des Etablissemens de Commerce que des maisons Françoises y projettent.

Les amis de l'humanité, Si cruellement affectés par les maux qu'elle éprouve en Europe, trouvent au moins de la douceur à penser qu'au delà des mers, il est une grande nation qui prospère par les arts de la paix et qui est heureuse par les Sages institutions qu'elle S'est données. Veuillés agréer les Sentimens respectueux avec lesquels j'ai l'honneur d'etre Monsieur Votre très humble & très obeissant Serviteur

J: A: GAUTIER

RC (DLC); endorsed by TJ as received 2 Oct. 1793 and so recorded in SJL. Enclosed in Benjamin Bankson to TJ, 23 Sep. 1793.

From Grand & Cie.

Monsieur   Paris 25e May 1793

Son Excellence l'Honorable Monsieur Hamilton Sécrétaire de la Trésorerie, nous ayant demandé la Suite du Compte des Etats-Unis qui étoit ci devant Sous votre direction, ainsi que la Spécification des articles qui composent le débit de ce Compte et de celui qui a précédé; nous avons, Monsieur, l'honneur de vous informer que nous lui addressons aujourd'hui la Suite de ce Compte, pour Solde duquel nous restons redevables à ce jour de £48339:14. Nous y joignons les détails et les éclaircissemens demandés par Monsieur Hamilton.

Nous avons aussi, Monsieur, l'honneur de vous transmettre une copie de la Suite dudit Compte et l'extrait de celui de l'Etat de Virginie Soldé à ce jour par £6931.9.6. que nous avons portées au débit de votre compte particulier et nous accompagnons ce compte des détails des Titres pour les articles au débit.

Nous y joignons, Monsieur, l'extrait de votre Compte Soldé par £18392.5.6. que nous avons pris la liberté de porter au débit du Compte des Etats-Unis Sauf votre approbation et celle de Monsieur Hamilton. Monsieur Short vous aura Sans doute, Monsieur, donné dans le tems connoissance des mandats qu'il a fournis Sur nous et qui forment en partie le débit du Compte que nous avons l'honneur de vous remettre.

Nous apprendrons avec plaisir que ces divers Comptes auront été trouvés en règle, et nous Serons toujours heureux d'avoir des occasions de vous témoigner notre dévouement à vos ordres. Nous avons l'honneur d'être avec les Sentimens d'un veritable respect Monsieur Vos très humbles & très obeissans Serviteurs GRAND & CO

RC (DLC); at foot of first page: "Son Excellence l'Honorable Monsieur Thomas Jefferson Sécrétaire au Département des affaires Etrangères à Philadelphie"; endorsed by TJ as received 2 Oct. 1793 and so recorded in SJL. Tripl (DLC); in a clerk's hand, signed by Grand & Cie.; at head of text: "Triplicat"; enclosed in Dupl of Grand & Cie. to TJ of 24 Mch. 1795 and endorsed by TJ as received 11 Aug. 1795. Enclosures: (1) "Les Etats-Unis D'Amérique son compte courant avec Grand & Co.," Paris, 25 May 1793, containing entries from 6 Aug. 1787 to 25 May 1793 (MS in DLC: TJ Papers, 86: 14964-5; in a clerk's hand, unsigned; endorsed by TJ: "Grand's acct. agt. the US. continuation from Aug. 7. 1787"). (2) "L'Etat de Virginie Son Compte Courant avec Grand & Co. à Paris," 25 May 1793, containing entries from 17 July 1785 to 14 Dec. 1792 (MS in same, 100: 17090, in a clerk's hand, signed by Grand & Cie., with later annotations by TJ consisting of an explanatory note for each debit entry and a signed certification of 20 Mch. 1796; Tr in Vi, fair copy made ca. 15 May 1802 by an unidentified hand, with note at foot of text in another hand: "A Copy. The original sent to Mr. Jefferson with the expectation that it will be returned"; Tr in DLC: TJ Papers, 96: 16499, consisting of abstract in English in TJ's hand written ca. 1796 on verso of Tr of No. 4). (3) "Titres à l'appui du Compte de l'Etat de Virginie," consisting of a descriptive list of instruments for the debit entries in No. 2 above (MS in same, 86: 14928-9; in a clerk's hand; undated, but bearing certification by Grand & Cie. of 25 May 1793). (4) "Son Excellence Monsieur Ths. Jefferson Son Compte Courant avec Grand & Co.," 25 May 1793, containing entries from 12 Oct. 1789 to 25 May 1793 (MS in same, 14957, in a clerk's hand, signed by Grand & Cie., and endorsed by TJ: "Grand's acct. agt. Th: Jefferson beginning 1789. Oct. 12"; Tr in same, 96: 16499, consisting of abstract in English of entries from 12 Oct. 1789 to 27 Apr. 1792 written by TJ ca. 1796 on verso of abstract of No. 2). Enclosed in Benjamin Bankson to TJ, 23 Sep. 1793.

From Grand & Cie.

Monsieur   Paris ce 25e May 1793

Nous avons l'honneur de vous addresser aujourd'hui le relevé du Compte de l'Etat de Virginie, la copie de celui des États-Unis et l'extrait du Compte qui étoit Sous votre nom particulier; nous avons aussi, Monsieur, l'honneur de vous faire part que nous portons le débit de votre Compte à celui des États Unis, que nous addressons à Son Excellence Monsieur Hamilton, le tout Soumis à votre approbation et à la Sienne.

Nous Sommes d'autre part dépositaires depuis le 28 Decembre 1789 d'une Somme de £66000 nous disons Soixante Six mille livres Tournois, que Monsieur Short nous remit contre notre reconnoissance et dont il nous avoit fait espérer qu'il disposeroit peu après, pour payer la rançon de quelques prisonniers. Comme ces dispositions n'ont pas encore eu lieu, il eut été à Souhaiter d'après l'evénement, que cette Somme eût été laissée preférablement entre les mains de Messieurs Willink & van Staphorst, vû que les Billets de la Caisse d'Escompte, dans lesquels cette Somme nous a été payée et qui faisoient la monnoie de Paris depuis le 16e Août 1788, ont été retirés de la circulation à la fin de l'année derniere, en conséquence d'un décret de la Convention et remplacés par Somme pareille d'assignats, auxquels ces Billets avoient été assimilés par un décret de l'Assemblée Nationale Constituante dès le mois d'Avril 1791.

Cette Somme nous ayant été remise pour un objet particulier par Monsieur Short, nous présumons qu'elle ne doit pas être mentionnée dans les comptes que nous avons l'honneur de vous addresser, ainsi qu'à Monsieur Hamilton et c'est ce qui nous engage à en faire l'objet de cette lettre. Nous continuons à attendre les ordres de Monsieur Short pour ces £66000. Nous avons l'honneur d'etre avec les Sentimens d'un Sincere respect Monsieur vos très humbles & tres obeissans Serviteurs

GRAND & Co.

RC (DLC); at foot of first page: "Son Excellence Monsieur Thomas Jefferson Secretaire au Departement des affaires Etrangères à Philadelphie"; endorsed by TJ as received 2 Oct. 1793 and so recorded in SJL. Dupl (DLC); in a clerk's hand, signed by the firm; conjoined to Dupl of Grand & Cie. to TJ of 24 Mch. 1795. Tr (DLC); in a clerk's hand; at head of text: "(Copie)"; conjoined to RC of Grand & Cie. to TJ of 24 Mch. 1795. Tr (DLC); in a clerk's hand; enclosed in Grand & Cie. to TJ of 11 Sep. 1795. Later texts contain minor variations from the RC. Enclosed in Benjamin Bankson to TJ, 23 Sep. 1793.

QUELQUES PRISONNIERS: the officers and crews of the American merchant ships *Maria* and *Dauphin*, who had been held captive by the Algerines since 1785 (see TJ to John Paul Jones, 1 June 1792).

From William Hylton

SIR Hampton Virginia 25 May 1793

An opportunity from hence this morning enables me to forward the Letters inclosed—with two samples of Rich Neck oak. One of them (from the haste in which they have been procured, by an ignorant plantation Carpenter) appears to be from a young Tree; and has a large portion of Sap; with a Dote in it. But as the Forest abounds with this species of *any requisite* size for the navy—no doubt their *specific gravity* will increase with their age and size.

Permit me sir to add herewith, a few of the Circular Letters, I have had suddenly printed for the Company; to be transmitted abroad. Your honoring them with your aid to such purpose will be most gratefully acknowledged by them and particularly by sir Your very obliged obt. svt.   WM. HYLTON

RC (MHi); endorsed by TJ as received 5 June 1793 and so recorded in SJL.

The LETTERS INCLOSED were William Foushee to TJ, 23 May 1793, and Daniel L.

Hylton to TJ, 24 May 1793. DOTE: decay in wood or timber. The CIRCULAR letter has not been found.

To Thomas Sim Lee

SIR   Philadelphia May 25. 1793.

I am honoured with your Excellency's letter of the 20th. and have duly laid the same before the President. Measures had been already taken for prosecuting such American citizens as had joined in the capture therein mentioned, a letter to that effect having been written to the Attorney of the US. in the state of Maryland. With respect to the prize, the government did not think itself authorised to do any thing. Your Excellency will have been informed by a letter from the Secretary at war, addressed to you as the head of the militia of your state, of the measures proposed for preventing the fitting out privateers in our ports in future, as well as for the preservation of peace within our limits. I have the honor to be with great respect & esteem your Excellency's most obedt. & most humble servt.   TH: JEFFERSON

RC (Facsimile in R. M. Smythe, Auction No. 82, 26 Oct. 1989, Lot 245); at foot of text: "H. E. the Governor of Maryland." PrC (DLC). FC (Lb in DNA: RG 59, DL).

The orders FOR PROSECUTING SUCH AMERICAN CITIZENS as bore arms with the

European belligerents were given in a 12 May 1793 circular letter from Attorney General Edmund Randolph to the United States District Attorneys (see note to Notes on Alexander Hamilton and the Enforcement of Neutrality, 6 May 1793). Henry Knox sent the state governors a circular let-

ter on PREVENTING THE FITTING OUT PRIVA-
TEERS on 24 May and another one on THE
PRESERVATION OF PEACE WITHIN OUR LIM-
ITS a day earlier (Washington, *Journal*,
147; see also TJ to Knox, with Proposed
Circular to the Governors of the States, 21
May 1793, and note).

To Joseph Ravara

SIR   Philadelphia May. 25. 1793.

I sincerely lament the situation in which you are unhappily placed.
Though circumstances have worn such an aspect as to render it necessary in the opinion of the magistrate to subject them to a legal enquiry,
yet I hope they will be found finally inconclusive. But till that enquiry,
there is no power in this country which can withdraw you from the
custody of the law, nor shorten it's duration. I learn that your cause will
be taken care of by able counsel and I am sure you will have upright
judges. Under such circumstances, innocence has nothing to fear; and
that that innocence may be yours is the sincere hope of Sir Your very
humble servant   TH: JEFFERSON

PrC (DLC); at foot of text: "Mr. Ravara."
FC (Lb in DNA: RG 59, DL).

Ravara wrote again to TJ on 29 May
1793, reiterating that he was innocent of the
charge against him and complaining about
having to remain in prison until he came to
trial, stating that he was now falsely believed to have written a letter to "Mr. Cra-
mond" against the English (RC in DNA:
RG 59, NFC; in French; above postscript:
"Mr. T. Jefferson"; endorsed by TJ as received 31 May 1793 and so recorded in
SJL). TJ did not reply to the Genoese consul general, and no other letters subsequently passed between them.

From Josef Ignacio de Viar and Josef de Jaudenes

SIR   Philada. May 25. 1792. [1793]

We received with due respect your letter of the 21st. inst. and have
this new assurance of the sincere desire of the President of the US. to
preserve the peace and harmony subsisting between Spain and the US.

For the same reason which prevented your making any reflections on
the treaties with the Creeks, Choctaws and Chickasaws, we avoid at
present transmitting you a voluminous relation, well authenticated, of
the judicious and very opportune steps taken by the Baron de Carondelet (whom you censure) after his arrival in Louisiana, to preserve
peace and friendship between Spain, and the US. and the Indian nations
without exposing the known interests of the last, which otherwise
would probably be sacrificed.

Nevertheless we cannot avoid inclosing you a copy of the exhortations given by the same Baron de Carondelet to the chiefs of the Cherokee nation, which not only contradict the opinion formed in these states of his character, but manifest that he has used prudent reasons only, not proposing to require from the Indians a decisive answer whether they would take arms against the US. in case that Spain should enter into war against them, as Govr. Blunt required from the various Indian chiefs, and particularly from Ugulayacabe when by dint of persuasions, and offering him to establish a store near Bear creek, and other promises he made him go to Cumberland, where he asked lands from him, and whether he would assist the Americans in case these should fight with Spain; and afterwards dismissed him for his obstinacy in refusing the lands, and declaring that in such case he would remain neuter.

As little has the Baron de Carondelet created Grand-Medal chiefs as Govr. Blount has practised, nor do we know if there have been distributed on our part, to various chiefs, medals of silver, as those which the US. have distributed with the effigy of the president, and at the bottom, *George Washington President 1792.* and others with the legend *Friendship and trade without end.*

In fine as we rely that there will be established in the negociation now on foot between Spain and the US. a fixed system of conduct with the Indians, for both parties, we omit producing other different proofs, which are in our possession, in vindication of the government of New Orleans; and we flatter ourselves that your government will use the most convenient means to avoid taking measures with the various nations of Indians (pending the negociation) which might have disagreeable results. We have the honor to be &c.

JOSEPH IGNATIUS DE VIAR   JOSEPH DE JAUDENES

PrC of Tr (DLC); translation in TJ's hand, with incorrect date added in ink by TJ after its submission to the President (see below); at head of text: "translation"; at foot of text: "Mr. Jefferson." RC (DNA: RG 59, NL); in Spanish; in Viar's hand, signed by Viar and Jaudenes; dated 25 May 1793; at foot of text: "Señor Don Thomas Jefferson"; endorsed by TJ as received 25 May 1793 and so recorded in SJL. Tr (AHN: Papeles de Estado, legajo 3895); in Spanish; attested by Jaudenes and Viar. Tr (DLC: William Short Papers); in Spanish; lacks year. PrC (DLC). Tr (DNA: RG 46, Senate Records, 3d Cong., 1st sess.); in English; misdated 25 May 1792. Tr (Lb in same, TR); in English; misdated 25 May 1792. Translations of letter and enclosure

enclosed in TJ to Washington, 27 May 1793, the former without date (Washington, *Journal*, 153). Spanish texts of letter and enclosure enclosed in TJ to William Carmichael and William Short, 31 May 1793, and TJ to James Blake, 12 July 1793.

The enclosed EXHORTATIONS of Baron de Carondelet, the governor of Louisiana and West Florida, to a delegation of Chickamauga Cherokees during a conference in New Orleans with various Southern Indians were not as guileless as the Spanish agents portrayed them. In fact they were part of a deliberate strategy by Carondelet to entice the Cherokees into joining a confederation of Southern tribes—under Spanish auspices and located in territory claimed by the United States under the Treaty of Paris—that would serve in effect as a barrier state between the United States and Spain's North American dominions. With respect to the Cherokees, this policy, which Carondelet began to implement soon after taking office on 30 Dec. 1791, sharply differed from that of his predecessors, who had made no effort after the Revolutionary War to include this tribe in Spain's system of Indian alliances (Arthur P. Whitaker, "Spain and the Cherokee Indians, 1783-98," *North Carolina Historical Review*, IV [1927], 252-60).

ENCLOSURE

Carondelet's Speech to the Cherokee Nation

To the chiefs, warriors and others of the Cherokee nation.

Brothers. I have seen with much satisfaction the chiefs Respiracion, Chickamoga Charles, and the Bloody-fellow warrior of your nation: I have heard their words, which I will preserve in my heart. The losses and misfortunes of your nation have afflicted me, and I desire sincerely to relieve them.

I transmit to the great king of the Spains whatever your messengers have said to me. His Majesty keeps in his heart all the coloured people, he desires their happiness, and that all of them should live in peace, and preserve their lands. The great king will employ with pleasure his mediation between your nation and those of the North your allies, with the US. his friends, for the reestablishment of peace between both, and that all may be content.

Brothers. Your messengers will tell you what they have seen and heard, the good counsels which I have given them, the strict union which I procure for the happiness of the coloured men our good friends, and to keep at a distance from them in future the miseries of war. Let your nation suspend all hostility against the US. keeping themselves within their lands on the defensive, while the good king treats of peace between you and the Americans your neighbors, and obtains from them the lands necessary for your habitations, with a demarcation of limits which may leave no more room for contest.

You will let me know your claims as to limits that I may immediately inform the great king of them, and if the other nations of the North, your allies, will let me know theirs, I will procure that they may be comprised in the same treaty, which shall terminate your differences with the US.

Given, these presents, signed with my hand, sealed with the seal of my arms, in the city of New Orleans the 24th. of Nov. 1792.

the Baron of Carondelet
by order of his Seignory
Andrew Lopez de Arnesto
(signed) THE BARON OF CARONDELET

PrC of Tr (DLC: TJ Papers, 79: 13697-8), translation in TJ's hand; partially overwritten in a later hand. Tr (DNA: RG 59, NL); in Spanish; in Viar's hand, attested by Jaudenes and Viar. Tr (DLC: William Short Papers); in Spanish. Tr (DNA: RG 46, Senate Records, 3d Cong., 1st sess.); in English. Recorded in SJPL under 24 Nov. 1792.

From Nathaniel Anderson

Dear Sir Richmond May 26th 1793

I duly received your Esteemed favor of the 19th Current, and return you my Sincere thanks for your friendly disposition to Serve me, which encourages me to make a further request, that is to give me your Opinion from time to time of the Neutrality of the United States of America, in the present European War, As I have lately Ventured to lay out a large Sum of Money in two American Ships, and am Now in treaty for another, which I shall not Close with, untill I can hear from you. A report prevails here that, the french Embassador's demands are of such a Nature that it must involve America in the War, particularly in that of his requiring us to comply with that part of our treaty with france to Guarantee their West India Islands. This report is said to be founded in a Letter from Mr. Saml. Griffin who is at present in Philadelphia. I am with very great Esteem Dear Sir, your Mo: Obdt.

NATHL. ANDERSON

RC (DLC); at head of text: "Thomas Jefferson Esqr."; endorsed by TJ as received 3 June 1793 and so recorded in SJL.

From Edmund Randolph

Sir Philadelphia May 26. 1793

The 14th. article of our treaty with France has shut out all general reasoning from the law of nations, on the memorial of Benjamin Holland and Peter Mackie.

The flour and meal were actually shipped *after* the declaration of war, made by France on the 1st. of february 1793. If the inquiry was to depend on their knowledge of the declaration, their relief would be very doubtful at least. But as two months had passed *after* the declaration and *before* the shipment, it is impossible for the government of the United States, to wrest the property from the captors. I have the honor, sir, to be with sincere esteem & respect yr. mo. ob. serv.

EDM: RANDOLPH

RC (DLC); at foot of text: "The Secretary of State"; endorsed by TJ as received 27 May 1793 and so recorded in SJL. PrC of Tr (DLC); in a clerk's hand; at foot of text: "(Copy)." Enclosed in TJ to Benjamin Holland and Peter Mackie, 27 May 1793, and TJ to George Washington, 27 May 1793.

The 14th ARTICLE of the 1778 treaty of amity and commerce between France and the United States provided that "whatever shall be found to be laden by the Subjects and Inhabitants of either Party on any Ship belonging to the Enemys of the other or to their Subjects, the whole although it be not of the Sort of prohibited Goods may be confiscated in the same manner, as if it belonged to the Enemy, except such Goods and Merchandizes as were put on board such Ship before the Declaration of War, or even after such Declaration, if so be it were without knowledge of such Declaration," adding that "the Term of two Months being passed after the Declaration of War, their respective Subjects, from whatever Part of the World they come, shall not plead the Ignorance mentioned in this Article" (Miller, *Treaties*, ii, 14-15).

To Martha Jefferson Randolph

My dear Martha   Philadelphia May 26. 1793.

Your and Mr. Randolph's welcome favors of the 16th. came to hand yesterday, by which I perceive that your post-day for writing is the Thursday. Maria is here and, tho not in flourishing health, is well. I will endeavour to prevail on her to write, and perhaps may succeed, as the day is too wet to admit her saunters on the banks of the Schuylkill, where she passes every Sunday with me. We are in sight both of Bartram's and Gray's gardens, but have the river between them and us.—We have two blind stories here. The one that Dumourier is gone over to the Austrians. The authority for this is an English paper. No confidence in DuMourier's virtue opposes it, for he has none: but the high reputation he has acquired is a pledge to the world, which we do not see that there were any motives on this occasion to induce him to forfeit. The other story is that he has cut off 10,000 Prussians, and among them the K. of Prussia and D. of Brunswick. The latter we know is out of command, and the former not in DuMourier's way. Therefore we concluded the story fabricated merely to set off against the other. It has now come thro' another channel and in a more possible form to wit that Custine has cut off 10,000 Prussians without naming the King or Duke. Still we give little ear to it.—You had at your Convent so many -courts (as terminations of names) that I wish the following paragraph of a newspaper may involve none of them. 'A few days ago several rich and respectable inhabitants were butchered at Guadaloupe. The following are the names of the unfortunate victims. Madame Vermont &c Madame Meyercourt. Monsr. Gondrecourt, three daughters just arrived from France from 11. to 18. years of age. Messrs. Vaudrecourt &c.' Maria thinks the Gondrecourts were at the convent.—The French minister Genet told me yesterday that matters appeared now to be tolerably well settled in St. Domingo. That the Patriotic party had taken possession of 600 aristocrats and monocrats, had sent 200 of them to France, and were sending 400. here: and that a coalition had taken place among the other inhabitants. I wish we could distribute our 400 among the Indians, who would teach them lessons of liberty and equality. Give my best affections to Mr. Randolph and kiss the dear little ones for me. Adieu my very dear Martha. Your's constantly & affectionately

                                                        Th: Jefferson

RC (NNP); at foot of first page: "Mrs. Randolph"; endorsed by Mrs. Randolph. PrC (DLC). Tr (DLC); 19th-century copy.

THREE DAUGHTERS of the Gondrecourt family were indeed among Martha's school-mates at her Paris CONVENT, the Abbaye Royale de Panthemont, although they were apparently not part of her circle of close friends (Thomas Jefferson Memorial Foundation, *Report of the Curator* [1960], illus. facing p. 11; note to TJ to Martha Jefferson Randolph, 20 Jan. 1791).

To Hugh Rose

DEAR SIR   Philadelphia May. 26. 1793.

I received yesterday your favor of the 13th. and I hasten to answer it, tho' a long interruption of my attention to questions of law renders it necessary for me to give opinions on them with great diffidence, and especially where the Virginia laws come into consideration, as they have been so much changed since I knew any thing of them. As these stood when I left Virginia in 1784. you might bring suits against the persons for whom you have been bail in any of the state courts: and if they are not changed you may do the same now if you can find any property in the state. By the act of Congress 1789. c.20.§.11. if you can find their persons in Virginia you may sue them either in the state courts, or the federal circuit courts; if not to be found there, you may sue them wherever they can be found, either in the state courts, or federal court of the state where found. The judgment of Amherst court is a sufficient foundation for the suit in any other court which can take cognizance of the action.—We have a story here that DuMourier is gone over to the Austrians. Another that Custiné has cut off 10,000 Prussians. Little attention is paid to either.—I presume you receive Freneau's paper regularly, and therefore add nothing further of news. I have a complaint against your son here, for not coming to see me. His cousin is kind enough to do it.—My best compliments to Mrs. Rose & am with great sincerity Dear Sir your affectionate friend & servt   TH: JEFFERSON

PrC (DLC); at foot of text: "Colo. H. Rose." Tr (DLC); 19th-century copy; with lacunae.

The FAVOR of 13 May 1793, described in SJL as a letter received on 25 May 1793 from Charles Rose, has not been found, and the Editors have been unable to clarify TJ's apparent confusion of him with his brother Hugh (see Lenora H. Sweeny, *Amherst County, Virginia In the Revolution Including Extracts from the "Lost Order Book" 1773-1782* [Lynchburg, Va., 1951], 2n).

To George Wythe

TH: JEFFERSON TO G. WYTHE   [26 May 1793]

I duly received, my Dear Sir, the note you inclosed for the 64. dollars which was paid.—We have two blind stories here of which as yet we make nothing. The one is that DuMourier is gone over to the Austrians. The credit of this stands on an English paper only. It is opposed (not by the virtue of the man; he has none, but) by the great forfeit of reputation which he has acquired with the world, and which there seems to have been no sufficient motive for him to throw away. The 2d. story is that he had cut off 10,000 Prussians and among them the K. of Prussia and D. of Brunswick. We know the latter to be out of command, and the former out of the way of DuMourier, and therefore supposed the story made to balance the former one. But it now comes through another *captain of a ship*, and in better form, to wit that Custine has cut off 10,000 Prussians, without naming the K. of Prussia or D. of Brunswick. Still it is little attended to. Adieu, my dear Sir.

PrC (DLC: TJ Papers, 86: 14966); undated but recorded under this date in SJL. Tr (same, 87: 14999); 19th-century copy.

Wythe's note for 64. DOLLARS was enclosed in an undated letter to TJ, of which only the address cover has been found (RC in MHi; addressed: "Thomas Jefferson, sec-retary of state, Philadelphia"; postmarked: "RICHMOND, MAY 8"; franked; endorsed by TJ as received 14 May 1793 and so recorded in SJL; notation by TJ: "it covered Hoops's order on John Barclay for 64. D."). TJ immediately "lodged it in bank for collection" (MB, 14 May 1793).

From Edmond Charles Genet

Philadelphie le 27 Mai 1793.
MONSIEUR   l'an 2e. de la Republique française

Mon prédécesseur m'a remis la lettre que vous lui aves[1] ecritte le 15 de ce mois[2] en lui communiquant differens mémoires de l'envoyé[3] du roi d'angleterre et les décisions que le Gouvernement americain s'est empressé de prendre d'après les plaintes de ce Ministre.

Le premier de ses griefs que vous rapportes dans votre lettre, Monsieur, porte sur un fait faux;[4] Je n'ai aucune connaissance des acquisitions d'armes en question et dans tous les cas la reponse que vous aves faitte à Mr. Hammond lui demontreroit le vuide de ses observations si la bonne foi les avait dictées; mais il est vraisemblable que sa démarche n'a d'autre but que de préparer diplomatiquement aux vaisseaux de guerre anglais des prétextes pour assujetir les batimens americains, à l'ombre même de leur modeste neutralité a des visites et detentions arbitraires.

Le second grief de l'envoyé[5] de George 3 Monsieur,[6] est fondé sur la vente des prises envoyées dans le Port de Charleston par la Fregatte de la Republique française, l'Embuscade.

Je ne repondrai, Monsieur, que par des faits et un raisonnement fort simple aux representations de Mr. Hammond sur ce point.

Le Traité de commerce[7] de 1778. autorise exclusivement[8] tous les vaisseaux de guerre français ou americains[9] armés par les deux Etats ou par des particuliers à conduire en toute liberté ou bon leur semblera les prises qu'ils auront faittes sur leurs ennemis sans être obligés à aucun droit soit des amirautés ou d'aucuns autres sans qu'aussi les dits vaisseaux ou les dites prises entrant dans les Ports de France ou d'Amerique puissent etre arretés ou saisis, ni que les officiers des lieux puissent prendre connaissance de la validité des dittes prises. Cette faculté est interdite aux ennemis de l'une des deux nations qui se trouverait en guerre: les deux parties contractantes[10] se sont expressement engagées de ne permettre à aucun corsaire étranger,[11] lequel aurait une commission de la part d'un prince ou d'une puissance en guerre avec l'une des deux nations d'armer leurs vaisseaux dans les ports de l'une des deux parties, ni d'y vendre[12] les prises qu'il aurait faittes, ni decharger en autre maniere quelconque les vaisseaux; marchandises ou aucune partie de leur cargaison. Ces privilèges que les deux nations se sont reservées exclusivement,[13] ces restrictions severes et clairement definies contre leurs ennemis communs prouvent evidemment qu'en vertu des traités que J'ai cites nous avons seuls aujourdhui le droit d'amener nos prises[14] dans les ports americains, et d'en disposer à notre gré comme d'une propriété sur la validité de la quelle les officiers civils ou judiciaires des[15] Etats Unis n'ont rien à connoitre tant que les droits[16] des Etats Unis ne sont pas lesés.[17] C'est pour acquerir des informations sur cet objet important que la publicité de la vente des prises autorisée par les officiers consulaires de la République[18] est nécessaire et si en remplissant ce devoir prescrit par l'amitié et par notre respect pour le droit des nations, le Consul de la République française à Charleston a fait usage de quelque formalité ou de quelque expression dont on ait pu inferer qu'il s'arrogeait une jurisdiction qui ne lui etait pas accordée par les traités et par les loix des Etats Unis, J'aurai soin, Monsieur, que cette erreur soit evitee à l'avenir et que toutes les procédures relatives a la vente de nos prises conformement à l'esprit du traité[19] portent l'empreinte d'une transaction nationale particuliere et de l'aliénation pure et simple d'une proprieté acquise par le droit de la guerre[20] reconnue légale par les officiers de la nation française.

La troisieme plainte qui a été faite a votre Gouvernement, Monsieur, par le Ministre anglais est relative aux armemens qui ont eu lieu à Charleston[21] sous le pavillon de la République française. Le Gouvernement americain, Monsieur, a donné une nouvelle preuve de sa sagesse et de sa confiance dans nos sentimens[22] en n'admettant pas aveuglément les assertions de Mr. Hammond. Je n'y repondrai encore que par des faits. Il est certain que plusieurs batimens ont été armés à Charleston, qu'ils ont reçu de moi des commissions de la République conformes aux modeles que J'ai eu l'honneur de vous communiquer et que ces batimens mis en mer avec une grande célérité ont fait beaucoup de prises ont condamné à l'inaction par la terreur qu'ils ont rependue parmi les anglais presque tous les matelots et les batimens[23] de cette nation qui se trouvaient dans les Ports des Etats Unis et ont fait hausser par leurs succès d'une maniere tres sensible le fret des navires americains. Tout cela, J'en conviens, doit deplaire à Mr. Hammond, à sa Cour et à ses amis,[24] mais ce n'est pas la ce qu'il s'agit d'examiner.

Je dois par un exposé sincère de ma conduite[25] vous mettre à même[26] de juger si J'ai porté atteinte a la souveraineté de la nation américaine, à ses loix et aux principes de son Gouvernement.

Les batimens armés a Charleston appartiennent à des maisons françaises. Ils sont commandés et montés[27] par des citoyens français ou par des americains qui, au moment ou ils sont entrés au service de France[28] pour deffendre[29] leurs freres et leurs amis,[30] ne connaissaient que les traités[31] et les loix des Etats Unis[32] dont aucune disposition ne leur a encore fait la penible deffense de nous abandonner au milieu des dangers qui nous entourent.

Il est donc évident, Monsieur, que ces armemens ne peuvent etre imputés aux citoyens des[33] Etats Unis[34] et que ceux qui se trouvent a bord de[35] nos vaisseaux ont renoncé à la protection immediate[36] de leur patrie en prenant[37] parti parmi nous. Il sagit maintenant d'examiner si les maisons francaises de Charleston ont pu armer des vaisseaux qui leur appartenaient.

J'ai soumis cette question au Gouverneur de la Caroline du Sud,[38] avant de delivrer des lettres[39] de marque a nos armateurs. Je lui ai rappellé[40] que la liberté consistait à faire[41] ce que la loi ne defendait pas; que Je croyais[42] qu'il n'existait pas[43] de loi qui put priver les[44] citoyens français dans les ports des Etats Unis de la faculté de[45] mettre leurs navires en Etat de deffense, de prendre en tems de guerre de nouvelles commissions et de servir leur[46] patrie en faisant courir hors des Etats Unis[47] sur les batimens de ses ennemis;[48] qu'il n'y en avait pas non plus qui donnat au Gouvernement[49] le droit de soumettre les[50] operations particulieres des negotians[51] à une inquisition d'Etat,[52] et qu'il me semblait qu'il ne pouvait[53] ni autoriser ni empecher les dits armemens. Son avis m'a paru se rapprocher du mien et nos navires ont mis en mer[54] malgré toutes les intrigues que les partisans de l'angleterre ont fait agir pour s'y opposer.

Voila la verité, Monsieur, voila[55] la marche, J'ose dire respectueuse,[56] que J'ai suivie et Je connois trop les sentimens d'équité[57] du Gouvernement fédéral pour ne pas me livrer à la douce esperance de le voir revenir des premieres impressions que paroissent avoir faittes sur lui les rapports du Ministre du roi d'angleterre.

Le dernier point qui me reste à traiter, Monsieur, est relatif à la prise du navire anglais le Grange par la fregatte l'Embuscade.

Les savantes[58] conclusions du Procureur Général des Etats Unis et les deliberations du Gouvernement Américain ont été sur cet objet la regle de ma conduite. J'ai fait rendre la prise et quoique sa valeur fut assés considerable mes braves freres les matelots de l'Embuscade se sont empressés de concourir a une mesure que Je leur ai présenté comme un moyen propre a convaincre le Gouvernement americain de notre deference et de notre amitie.

Les Republicains[59] français, Monsieur, connoissent[60] les devoirs auxquels sont soumises[61] les nations entr'elles: éclairés sur les droits de l'homme ils ont des idees justes des loix générales de la sociabilité, comprises[62] sous la dénomination commune[63] de droit des gens; instruits sur[64] les interets de leur patrie, ils savent distinguer ses ennemis et ses amis et vous pouves assurer le Gouvernement americain que collectivement et individuellement ils saisiront toutes les occasions de montrer au peuple souverain des Etats Unis[65] leur respect pour ses loix et leur desir sincere de maintenir[66] avec lui la plus parfaite harmonie.

GENET

PrC of Tr (DLC); in a clerk's hand, with several corrections by TJ in ink; above salutation: "Le Citoyen Genet Ministre Plenipotentiaire de la République française à Monsieur Jefferson Sécrétaire d'Etat des Etats Unis." Dft (DLC: Genet Papers); unsigned; dated 28 May 1793; heavily emended, only the most important alterations being noted below. Tr (AMAE: CPEU, XXXVII); dated 28 May 1793; with variations. Tr (NNC: Gouverneur Morris Papers); dated 27 May 1793. PrC of another Tr (PRO: FO 97/1); in a clerk's hand; dated 27 May 1793. FC (DLC: Genet Papers); in English; dated 28 May 1793. FC (same); in English; dated 28 May 1793. FC (same); in English; dated 28 May 1793; draft translation of preceding FCs. Tr (DNA: RG 46, Senate Records, 3d Cong., 1st sess.); in English; dated 27 May 1793. Recorded in SJL as a letter of 27 May 1793 received 28 May 1793. Printed with translation in *Message*, 9-10 (App.), 20-2; translation printed in ASP, *Foreign Relations*, I, 149-50. Enclosed in TJ to Gouverneur Morris, 16 Aug. 1793.

This letter was Genet's first official exposition to TJ of his opposition to three of the key elements of the Washington administration's neutrality policy. Written as a reply to TJ's 15 May 1793 statement of that policy to Jean Baptiste Ternant, his PRÉDECESSEUR as French minister to the United States, it upheld the right of French consular courts to exercise admiralty jurisdiction over French prizes brought into American ports, the right of the French to commission and arm privateers in such ports, and the right of Americans to enlist in French service while their nation was in a state of neutrality. Genet's insistence on maintaining these rights was one of the major reasons for the Washington administration's decision in August 1793 to request his recall by the French government (see Editorial Note on the recall of Edmond Charles Genet, at 16 Aug. 1793).

Article 17 of the 1778 TRAITÉ DE COM-
MERCE between the United States and
France gave French warships and priva-
teers the right to bring enemy prizes into
American ports without being subject to
duties, seizure, search, arrest, or examina-
tion into the legality of prizes, but did not
mention any role for French consular courts
(Miller, *Treaties*, II, 16-17). For the SAVAN-
TES CONCLUSIONS DU PROCUREUR GÉNÉRAL
DES ETATS UNIS, see Edmund Randolph's
Opinion on the *Grange*, 14 May 1793. See
also Memorial from George Hammond, 2
May 1793, and note.

[1] In Dft Genet first wrote "avés fait
l'honneur de lui écrire" and then altered it
to read as above.
[2] In Dft Genet here canceled "Je l'ai lue
avec la plus grande attention."
[3] Preceding three words interlined in
Dft in place of "du Ministre."
[4] Remainder of paragraph in Dft heavily
revised from a passage that, with some intermediate cancellations reproduced here,
reads "⟨sur une prétention injuste⟩ sur une
inquisition maladroite et offensante même
pour la plus modeste neutralité, vous l'avés
senti et votre réponse concluante mettroit
sans doute un terme à de pareilles ⟨trompe-
ries⟩ reclamations si le but de ceux qui les
font n'etoit point evidemment ⟨de motiver
en apparence des recherches⟩ de forger des
pretextes pour soumettre les batimens
americains, à l'ombre même de leur neutralité, aux recherches les plus ⟨rigoureu-
ses⟩ arbitraires et à des ⟨saisies illegales⟩ detentions arbitraires. Et que peut la logique
contre de pareils désseins?"
[5] Preceding three words interlined in
Dft in place of "du Ministre."
[6] In Dft Genet here canceled "semble indiquer qu'il ⟨ne considere point⟩ se croit
fondé à ne plus considerer ⟨les traités⟩
comme éxistans les traités qui unissent les
Républiques de france et d'amerique."
[7] In Dft Genet first wrote "L'article
XVII du traité de Commerce" and then altered it to read as above.
[8] Word interlined in Dft.
[9] Preceding two words written in the
margin in Dft.
[10] Sentence to this point altered in Dft
from a heavily revised passage that, with
some intermediate cancellations reproduced here, reads "⟨Le même traite d⟩ Cette
⟨faveur⟩ prerogative non seulement est in-

terdite expressement à tout batiment de
guerre qui n'appartiendroit point aux Etats
unis ou à la france; mais encore Il leur est
defendu d'armer leurs Vaisseaux dans les
ports de l'une des deux parties ⟨sur toutes⟩
et Il leur est expressement."
[11] In Dft Genet here canceled "non appartenant à ⟨quelque sujet⟩ ⟨aucun⟩ ⟨quelque
Citoyen de l⟩ à des Americains libres ou à
des francois."
[12] Preceding four words underscored in
Dft.
[13] In Dft Genet here canceled "pour le
cas où l'une d'elle seroit seule engagée dans
une guerre."
[14] In Dft Genet first wrote "le droit
d'amener et de vendre nos prises et que" in
the margin and then altered it to read as
above.
[15] Preceding five words interlined in
Dft.
[16] Dft and AMAE Tr: "les droits des Citoyens."
[17] In Dft Genet here canceled "soit par le
fait même de la prise."
[18] Preceding eight words written in the
margin in Dft.
[19] Dft and AMAE Tr: "des traités."
[20] Preceding seven words written in the
margin in Dft.
[21] In Dft Genet here canceled "Vous
avés eu raison, M., de suspendre votre
Jugement sur ce fait et de ne point ⟨embras-
ser⟩ écouter les."
[22] Preceding seven words written in the
margin in Dft.
[23] Dft and AMAE Tr: "tous les batiments et tous les matelots," with last four
words written in the margin in Dft.
[24] Preceding four words written in the
margin in Dft.
[25] In Dft Genet here canceled "(car c'est
moi M., qui en vertu de mes instructions ai
favorisé ces armements) Je dois dis je."
[26] Word interlined in Dft in place of
"portée."
[27] Preceding two words written in the
margin in Dft.
[28] Preceding seven words interlined in
Dft in place of "ils se sont embarques d."
[29] In Dft Genet here first wrote "notre
cause," which he altered to "la cause de"
and then canceled.
[30] Preceding clause interlined and written in the margin in Dft after the next two
words. AMAE Tr follows Dft.
[31] In Dft Genet here canceled "de Com-

merce et d'Alliance, nos interêts communs."

[32] Preceding three words interlined in Dft in place of "de leur pays." Genet wrote the remainder of the sentence in the margin of Dft in place of "⟨*n'écoutant*⟩ qui ne pouvoient entendre que la voix de la reconnoissance, qui ne croyoient fermement que la seule politique qui convient à Ce pays étoit de contenir à quelque prix que ce puisse être la cause de la liberté seule base de leur prosperité."

[33] Preceding two words altered in the margin of Dft from "sujets des."

[34] Remainder of sentence written in the margin in Dft.

[35] In Dft Genet here canceled "leurs."

[36] Word interlined in Dft.

[37] Word interlined in Dft in place of "se rangeant lib."

[38] In Dft Genet here canceled a passage that in its final state read "et le sens de la reponse de ce Républicain a été" and then wrote the remainder of the sentence in the margin.

[39] Word substituted in Dft for "commissions."

[40] Word interlined in Dft in place of "fait sentir."

[41] Dft and AMAE Tr read "à pouvoir faire," with "pouvoir" interlined in Dft by a clerk.

[42] Preceding three words written in the margin in Dft.

[43] In Dft Genet here canceled "encore," as well as "en l'Amerique" interlined above it.

[44] In Dft Genet here canceled "vaisseaux de propriet."

[45] Preceding three words written in the margin in Dft in place of a passage that in its final state reads "de pourvoir à leur sureté et à celle de leurs concitoyens."

[46] Preceding two words interlined in Dft in place of "défendre sa."

[47] Dft and AMAE Tr: "des eaux des Etats unis."

[48] Preceding clause written in the margin in Dft.

[49] Preceding two words interlined in Dft.

[50] Word interlined in Dft in place of "leurs."

[51] Preceding three words and "Etrangers" interlined in Dft. "Etrangers" not in AMAE Tr.

[52] In Dft Genet here canceled a passage that in its final state appears to read "et à une surveillance effective des ports."

[53] Preceding six words interlined in Dft in place of "ne devoit en aucune maniere."

[54] In Dft Genet here canceled "aux risques et perils de leurs armateurs."

[55] In Dft Genet here canceled "les principes qui m'ont dirigé voila."

[56] Preceding clause written in the margin in Dft, which adds "le" before "dire." AMAE Tr follows Dft.

[57] Preceding eight words altered in Dft from two consecutive canceled passages that in their final state appear to read: "Maintenant le Gouvernement Fédéral prendra sur cet objet le parti que ce me semble sa sagesse lui fera envisager comme le plus" and "et J'ai trop de Confiance dans ses sentiments et dans son équité pour Supposer."

[58] Word interlined in Dft.

[59] Word interlined in Dft.

[60] Remainder of sentence up to "droits des gens" written in the margin in Dft in place of "trop bien aujourdhui les droits de l'homme et par conséquent le droit des gens qui n'est qu'une application des lois de la nature ⟨*aux lois de*⟩ à la sociabilite generale et vous pouvés être assuré que collectivement ⟨*par l'organe de leurs représentants et individuellement Ils vous prouveront dans tous les cas qu'ils*⟩ ils connoissent."

[61] Dft and AMAE Tr: "assujeties."

[62] AMAE Tr: "et de la sociabilité comprise."

[63] Word interlined in Dft.

[64] Dft and AMAE Tr: "éclairés sur."

[65] In Dft Genet first wrote "aux Etats unis" and then altered it to read as above.

[66] Dft and AMAE Tr: "maintenir au moins."

Memorial from
Edmond Charles Genet

Philadelphie 27.[1] mai 1793. L'an 2e. de la Republique Française.

Le Soussigné Ministre plenipotentiaire de la Republique Française a l'honneur d'informer Monsieur le Secretaire d'etat Jefferson que le Citoyen Gedeon Henfield né à[2] Salem[3] officier à bord du[4] Corsaire de la République Francaise[5] le Citoyen Genet a été arreté et mis[6] en prison en vertu, dit-on,[7] d'un mandat de l'alderman Baker de cette ville qui l'accuse d'avoir[8] enfreint, en s'embarquant à bord du dit batiment la neutralité que les Etats-Unis veulent observer avec les puissances Européenes actuellement en guerre. Le soussigné observe à Monsieur le Secretaire d'Etat que cet officier a été admis au service de france en s'embarquant sur le dit Corsaire,[9] ainsi qu'il appert par le role d'équipage et[10] par le certificat ci joint du Consul de[11] la République française à Philadelphie et que si cet officier en embrassant la deffense de la cause que soutient la france, s'est exposé sans avoir pu le prévoir à des poursuites dans le sein des Etats Unis, il a mérité l'appui et la protection de la République française.

Le[12] soussigné le réclame donc comme étant au service de la Republique[13] et prie en consequence Monsieur le Secretaire d'Etat Jefferson d'employer ses bons offices pour obtenir promptement son élargissement. (signed) GENET

Tr (DLC); in the hand of George Taylor, Jr., with date altered by him (see note 1 below). PrC (DLC); with date altered in ink. Dft (DLC: Genet Papers); in Genet's hand except for dateline; dated "Du 29 Mai," with "9" written over "7"; at head of text by Genet and a clerk: "Note relative à l'Emprisonnement fait en vertu d'un ordre du Président des officiers du corsaire le Citoyen genet." Tr (AMAE: CPEU, XXXVII); with minor variations; dated "Du 29 May." FC (DLC: Genet Papers); in English; dated 29 May 1793. FC (same); in English; dated 29 May 1793. FC (same); in English; dated 29 May 1793; draft translation of preceding FCs. Recorded in SJL as a letter of 27 May 1793 received 28 May 1793. Enclosure: Statement by François Dupont, 27 May 17[9]3, certifying that Gideon Henfield of Salem, about forty years of age, had been in the service of the French Republic on board the *Citoyen Genet*, commanded by Captain Pierre Johanene, Lieutenant of the French Republic, since 17 Apr. 1793 (Tr in DLC, in French, in Taylor's hand; PrC in same).

The Washington administration decided to prosecute Gideon HENFIELD as a test case of the Proclamation of Neutrality's ban on American enlistments in belligerent service during the current European war. A seaman from Salem, Massachusetts, Henfield had recently arrived in Philadelphia as prize master of the *William*, a Scottish merchant ship captured in the Delaware River on 3 May 1793 by the *Citoyen Genet*, a French privateer commissioned by Genet at Charleston, where Henfield had enlisted on it in return for a promise from the captain that he would be appointed master of its first prize (*Federal Cases*, XI, 1101, 1112, 1113, 1116; *National Gazette*, 3 Aug. 1793; Memorial from George Hammond, 21 June 1793, and enclosures). The Cabinet's unanimous decision to prosecute Henfield led to an open conflict between the Washington administration and Genet, who insisted on the right of American citizens to enlist in French service so that he could carry out his instructions from the Provisional Executive Council to fit out French privateers in the United States and obtain American support for French expeditions against Louisiana and Canada. Although no act of Congress expressly forbade American citizens to enlist in belligerent service while the nation was at peace, Attorney General Edmund Randolph advised TJ that Henfield's service on the *Citoyen Genet* and his participation in the capture of the *William* were indictable not only under federal law—because they violated the American treaties which guaranteed peace with three of the countries then at war with France (Great Britain, the Netherlands, and Prussia) and were the supreme law of the land under the Constitution—but also under the common law because they had disturbed the peace of the United States (Opinion on the Case of Gideon Henfield, 30 May 1793). Failing to avert legal action against Henfield, Genet hired three lawyers—Peter S. Du Ponceau, Jared Ingersoll, and Jonathan Dickinson Sergeant—to defend him when his case came before a special session of the United States Circuit Court of Pennsylvania which convened in Philadelphia on 22 July 1793. Five days later District Attorney William Rawle obtained a grand jury indictment, drafted by Randolph and possibly amended by Alexander Hamilton, charging that Henfield's actions violated the law of nations as well as the peace and dignity of the United States. It remains unclear whether the latter formulation was intended to charge Henfield with a transgression of common law, though in his argument to the jury Rawle maintained that Henfield's actions infringed the law of nations, threatening the United States with reprisals from and even war with France's enemies, and violated common law, which gave the American government alone the right to wage war. Henfield's attorneys, while admitting that he had performed the acts of which he stood accused, argued that the seaman had renounced American citizenship upon entering French service, that the charges against him did not include an offense under the common law, that if the Proclamation of Neutrality created such an offense, his actions preceded it, that the treaty with France did not forbid the enlistment of Americans in its service, and that there was no statutory basis for the court's jurisdiction in the case. Despite a charge to the jury by Supreme

Court Justice James Wilson upholding the prosecution's contention that Henfield's actions clearly violated the law of nations as well as laws of the United States, on 29 July 1793, after dividing eleven to one in favor of acquittal, the jurors finally found him not guilty on all counts (*Federal Cases*, XI, 1105-22; *National Gazette*, 31 July, 3 Aug. 1793; Turner, *CFM*, 204-5, 207-9, 211; Genet to TJ, 1 June 1793; TJ to Genet, 1 June 1793; TJ to James Monroe, 14 July 1793; TJ to James Madison, 11 Aug. 1793; TJ to Gouverneur Morris, 16 Aug. 1793, and note; Randolph's later and somewhat confused recollections on the common law aspects of the case in Madison, *Papers*, XVII, 283-5; Goebel, *Supreme Court*, 624-7, which argues that the prosecution was not grounded in the common law). Although Genet hailed the jury's decision as a vindication of his right to enlist Americans in French service, the Washington administration continued to maintain its ban on American enlistments in belligerent service, and in June 1794 Congress finally provided a statutory basis for this policy by passing the so-called Neutrality Act (*Annals*, IV, 1461-4; Hyneman, *Neutrality*, 131-2, 155-6; Thomas, *Neutrality*, 173-6, 186-8).

[1] Digit written over what appears to be "9"; it is overwritten in ink in PrC.
[2] Preceding two words written in the margin in Dft in place of "de."
[3] In Dft Genet here canceled "enseigne."
[4] In Dft Genet here canceled "batiment."
[5] Preceding four words written in the margin in Dft.
[6] Dft and AMAE Tr: "arrêté et conduit."
[7] Preceding two words interlined in Dft.
[8] In Dft Genet here canceled "contrevenu aux loix des Etats unis en prenant les armes contre."
[9] Preceding seven words written in the margin in Dft.
[10] Preceding six words interlined in Dft as "par les rôles d'équipage et."
[11] In Dft Genet here canceled "france."
[12] In Dft Genet here canceled "Citoyen."
[13] Preceding eight words written in the margin in Dft in place of "en Consequence."

To Benjamin Holland and
Peter Mackie

[GENTLE]MEN   Philadelphia May 27. 1793.

Your memorial claiming a part of the cargo on board the brigantine Little Sarah, a British vessel taken by the French frigate L'Embuscade, having been referred to the Attorney General of the US. I now inclose you a copy of his answer by which you will perceive it to be his opinion that you are not entitled to restitution. I have therefore rendered you the only service which the nature of the case admits, by a prompt attention and answer to your application. With wishes that it could have been more satisfactory, I am, Gentlemen, your most obedt. [& most] humble servt   TH: JEFFERSON

PrC (DLC); at foot of text (with last two words overwritten in ink): "Messrs. Holland & Mackie"; clipped and faded words supplied from FC. FC (Lb in DNA: RG 59, DL). Enclosure: Edmund Randolph to TJ, 26 May 1793. Letter and enclosure enclosed in TJ to George Washington, 27 May 1793.

To James Madison

May 27. 1793.

I wrote you last on the 19th. The doubts I then entertained that the offers from the Fr. rep. would be declined, will pretty certainly be realized. One[1] person represents them as a snare into which he hopes we shall not fall. His second of the same sentiment of course. He whose vote for the most part, or say always, is casting, has by two or three private conversations or rather disputes with me,[2] shewn his opinion to be against doing what would be a mark of predilection to one of the parties, tho not a breach of neutrality in form. And an opinion of still more importance is still in the same way. I do not know what line will be adopted; but probably a procrastination, which will be immediately seen through.—You will see in the papers two blind stories, the one that DuMourier is gone over to the Austrians; the other that he has cut to peices 10,000 Prussians, and among them the K. of Prussia and D. of Brunswick. The latter has come through another channel, placing Custine instead of Dumourier, and saying nothing of the K. and Duke. But no attention is paid to either story.—We want an intelligent prudent native, who will go to reside at N. Orleans as a secret correspondent, for 1000.D. a year. He might do a little business, merely to cover his real office. Do point out such a one. Virginia ought to offer more loungers equal to this and ready for it, than any other state. Adieu. Yours affectionately.

[132]

RC (DLC: Madison Papers); unsigned. PrC (DLC). Tr (DLC); 19th-century copy.

ONE PERSON: Alexander Hamilton. HIS SECOND: Henry Knox. HE WHOSE VOTE

... IS CASTING: Edmund Randolph. AN OPINION OF STILL MORE IMPORTANCE: that of George Washington.

[1] Word written over "two," erased.
[2] Preceding two words interlined.

From James Madison

DEAR SIR   May 27. 1793

I have received your letter with the unsealed one for Monroe and have forwarded the latter. Your subsequent one, which I calculate to have been written on the 12th. inst: came to hand two days ago. I feel for your situation but you must bear it. Every consideration private as well as public require a further sacrifice of your longings for the repose of Monticello. You must not make your final exit from public life till it will be marked with justifying circumstances which all good citizens will respect, and to which your friends can appeal. At the present crisis, what would the former think, what could the latter say? The real motives, whatever they might be would either not be admitted or could not be explained; and if they should be viewed as satisfactory at a future day, the intermediate effects would not be lessened, and could not be compensated. I am anxious to see what reception Genest will find in Philada. I hear that the fiscal party in Alexa. was an overmatch for those who wished to testify the American Sentiment. George Town it is said repaired the omission. A public dinner was intended for him at Fredericksburg, but he passed with such rapidity that the compliment miscarried. It would not be amiss, if a knowledge of this could in a proper mode get to him. I think it certain that he will be misled if he takes either the fashionable cant of the Cities or the cold caution of the Government for the sense of the public; and I am equally persuaded that nothing but the habit of implicit respect will save the Executive from blame if thro' the mask of Neutrality, a secret Anglomany should betray itself. I forgot when I requested your attention to my plows to ask the favor of you to pay for them, and to let me know the amount of your several advances. Yours always & affy.   Js. MADISON JR

The plows are to be consigned to the care of Mr. Jno. Anderson Merchant Fredg. Billy at Mrs. Houses was charged to look out for the first vessel that offers. If the Newspapers should present one to your eye be so good as to let him have notice that he put them on board.

RC (DLC: Madison Papers); endorsed by TJ as received 4 June 1793 and so recorded in SJL.

TJ's LETTER to Madison and THE UNSEALED ONE FOR MONROE were both dated 5 May 1793. The SUBSEQUENT ONE to Madison is printed under 13 May 1793.

From Phineas Miller

Sir   Mulberry Grove Georgia May 27th 1793

I am desired by Mrs. Greene, whose sensibility to the late unhappy accident in her family prevents her writing herself, to solicit the favor of your particular attention to the application of Mr. Whitney. He has resided in our family during the last winter—and amidst all the inconveniences which a situation in the country without tools and without workmen, could throw in his way, has invented a machine for ginning cotton which promises to be highly useful to the Southern States—and I shall not only speak the opinion of Mrs. Greene, but of others who have known Mr. Whitney in saying that his amiable character has a particular claim to private friendship and patronage, at the same time that his strong inventive genius deserves the encouragement of the Public. With perfect respect I am Sir Your Obedt. Servant   PHINS. MILLER

RC (ViW: Tucker-Coleman Collection); at foot of text: "The Honble. Thos. Jefferson"; endorsed by TJ as received 17 June 1793 and so recorded in SJL.

THE LATE UNHAPPY ACCIDENT was the death of George Washington Greene (Miller to TJ, 3 May 1793). On or shortly before this date Miller and Eli WHITNEY formalized an earlier understanding that in ex-change for financing the initial expenses, Miller would share equally in all profits derived from "patenting, making, vending, and working" Whitney's MACHINE FOR GINNING COTTON. Whitney petitioned TJ for a patent three days after presenting this letter of introduction (Mirsky and Nevins, *Eli Whitney*, 66-8; Petition from Whitney, 20 June 1793).

To George Washington

May 27. 1793.

Th: Jefferson has the honor to inclose to the President, (among other papers,) those relating to a commercial treaty with France, and to the reimbursement of the French debt, being translations of the communications of Mr. Genet on those subjects.

RC (DNA: RG 59, MLR); addressed: "The President of the US."; endorsed by Tobias Lear. Not recorded in SJL. Enclosures: (1) Translations of Edmond Charles Genet to TJ, 22 May (third letter) and 23 May 1793, and their enclosures. (2) Translations of Josef Ignacio de Viar and Josef de Jaudenes to TJ, 25 May 1793, and enclosure. (3) Henry Cooper to TJ, 1 May 1793. (4) David M. Clarkson to TJ, 11 May 1793. (5) Draft of TJ to F. P. Van Berckel, 25 May 1793 (not found; see note to TJ to Van Berckel, 29 May 1793). (6) Edmund Randolph to TJ, 26 May 1793. (7) TJ to Benjamin Holland and Peter Mackie, 27 May 1793. See Washington, *Journal*, 151-4.

From James Monroe

Dear Sir   Alb: May 28. 1793.

My last informed you that I had just received yours of the fifth, as I returned from a circuit of professional duties. It communicated to you likewise what I had to communicate respecting your own commissions in that line.

The European war becomes daily as it progresses more interesting to us. I was happy to find Mr. Genet whom I passed on the road between Fredbg. and Richmd. had made a most favorable impression on the inhabitants of the latter city. It furnishes a favorable presage of his impression on a more important tho' if possible not a more prejudic'd theatre.

There can be no doubt that the general sentiment of America is favorable to the French revolution. The minority compared with the strength of those in that interest, if the division could be properly drawn, would in my opinion, be as the aggregate of Richmond and Alexa. to Virginia—but general as this sentiment is I believe it is equally so in favor of our neutrality. And this seems to be dictated by the soundest policy even as it may respect the object in view, the success of the French revolution. For if we were to join France we should from that moment put it out of her power to derive any advantage from these States. We could neither aid her with men nor money. Of the former we have none; and of the latter our weak and improvident war with the Indians, together with the debts we have assumed will completely exhaust us. Our declaration would not be felt on the continent. It would produce no effect on the general combination of European powers—would not retard the movements of Brunswick, or any other invading army. It would in fact be simply a declaration against G. Britain, which would prove beneficial to her, and highly injurious to France, and ourselves. From the view I have of the subject it would relieve her from restraints growing out of the present state of things, which would be both gratifying and advantageous to her. For whilst the rights of neutrality belong to us some respect will be shewn to those rights, nor is it probable that an invasion of them by her will be countenanc'd by her other associates in the war. Under the protection of these rights the ports and the bottoms of America will be free to France; in addition to which every act of gratuity and favor which a generous and grateful people can bestow, without an infringement of them on the other side, will be shewn. France may greatly profit from this situation, for under a wise management immense resources may be gathered hence to aid her operations and support her cause. And America must flourish under it, if indeed it were generous to count her profits arising from the general misfortunes of mankind. Let it be notic'd as a posterior consideration, after estimating the effect our declaration or neutrality might produce upon the affairs of France. On the other hand I am persuaded our declaration in favor of France, would not only in a correspondent degree, injure that nation, and ourselves, but benefit the party we meant to injure. Freed from any embarrassing questions respecting the rights of neutrality, our commerce would be her lawful plunder, and commanding as I presume she will the seas, but little would escape her. Neither the vessels of France nor even our own, would be safe in our ports, unless we raised fortifications in each for their protection. I shall not therefore be surprised to find G. B. endeavoring to draw us into the war, even against her, by every species of insult and outrage which a proud, selfish, and vindictive nation, can impose; or that this disposition should shew itself in the impressment of our ships sailors, and other violations of our neutrality. Whether an appeal from such conduct should be made to the general sense even of the combined powers, with whom I see no reason why we should not stand on good terms, with a view of degrading her among all civilized nations, as the Algiers of Europe, or to any other means for the purpose of teaching her better principles and manners, I will not pretend to determine. Certain however I am, at least this is my present impression, that it is our duty to avoid by every possible dexterity a war which must inevitably injure ourselves and our friends and benefit our enemies.

One circumstance seems to press us at present, and which I fear will lessen, before any possible remedy can be applied, the benefits of our neutrality and to those for whom they are wished, I mean the scarcity of American bottoms. I am told such cannot be procured, and in consequence that our productions cannot be exported. The injury that must arise from such a cause will be universally felt. Can this be otherwise remedied than by allowing the American merchants to buy in the bottoms of other nations, for a limited time 12. months for instance? I can perceive no other cause at present which can make the meeting of Congress necessary before, or much before the time appointed; and the fact I hope does not exist, or so partially as will admit of a remedy under the regular operation of the existing law by the [great?] encouragement offered to American ships. If such an event should take place (a more early meeting of Congress) which is much spoken of here by letters from Phila., shall thank you to mention the time you think it will sit, as it will regulate me in my family and law concerns, and particularly whether I shall bring Mrs. M. with me or leave her behind. If such a call should be made, however injurious it may be to me, I shall obey it—for whilst I hold the present station, I shall always endeavor to perform its duties. I have troubled you with a long letter upon subjects very familiar to you, and upon which you have no doubt long since made up your mind. Mr. R. and family were well two days past—and the neigh-bourhood generally—except Mrs. M. who has been indisposed for a few days past. With great respect & esteem I am yr. affectionate friend & servant   JAS. MONROE

Is it not surprising that since my arrival in Virga. I have not received one of Freneau's papers, tho' Fenno's have come regularly. Perhaps they have not been sent—will you be pleased to enquire and direct them to be sent in case they are not. He should know that Davis is, if not in the opposit interest, yet so miserable a tool of it as not to be counted on in any respect. I enclosed for Beckley from Fredbg. for that paper a politi-cal Jeu de Esprit of a friend who wishes well to the republican cause. If Beckley should be absent, as the cover to him was intended meerly as one from you, to prevent your being troubled with it, could not this be mentioned to the Editor to authorize his stripping it off?

RC (DLC); one word illegible; endorsed by TJ as received 8 June 1793 and so re-corded in SJL.

MR. R.: Thomas Mann Randolph, Jr. DAVIS: Augustine Davis, the postmaster in Richmond.

Memorandum from Edmund Randolph

[ca. 28-30 May 1793]

Minutes of reasons, which operated with E. R. in advising the expul-sion of the Genet privateer.

1. That it is the prerogative of every[1] nation to prohibit acts of sover-eignty to be done[2] within its limits by another nation, except where treaties otherwise provide, or those acts relate to the privileges of minis-ters.

2. That it is the peculiar prerogative of every neutral nation,[3] to[4] prohibit such acts of sovereignty, going to the injury of one of the war-ring powers.

3. That the granting of a commission within the limits of the U.S. is an attack upon their sovereignty.

4. That the granting of a commission to citizens of the U.S. within their limits, who are liable to punishment, is an attack upon their sover-eignty.

5. That for an attack on their sovereignty, the U.S. are judges of the measure of satisfaction; and it seems to be a satisfaction, allied to the attack,[5] that the vessel, which has been thus illegally commis-sioned, and illegally manned in part,[6] should be put out of the protec-tion of the U.S.

6. That reasons of expediency may concur, to enforce these reasons of

right; as it is always adviseable for a neutral nation, to avoid even a suspicion of the faith of its neutrality.

MS (DLC: TJ Papers, 87: 15001); entirely in Randolph's hand; undated and unsigned; endorsed by TJ: "Randolph Edmund May.   1793."

Although the provenance of this document is unrecorded, this elaboration of the Attorney General's reasons for supporting a Cabinet decision of 20 May 1793 to expel from American ports French privateers commissioned in the United States was almost certainly prepared at TJ's request to provide guidance for his reply to a 27 May 1793 letter from Edmond Charles Genet disputing the decision, which TJ had conveyed orally to the French minister (see Notes on the *Citoyen Genet* and Its Prizes, 20 May 1793, and note). It seems unlikely that TJ would have solicited this communication prior to his receipt of Genet's letter on 28 May—though it is not clear whether he submitted the missive to Randolph for that purpose—or that Randolph would have set down these notes later than 30 May 1793, the day before TJ received the Attorney General's reaction to the draft of his reply to Genet, which incorporated some of the language used above by Randolph in arguing that the commissioning of French privateers in the United States was a serious violation of American neutrality (Randolph to TJ, 31 May 1793). For the approval of the draft by the President and the Cabinet, and for the final text of the reply to the French minister, see TJ to Genet, 5 June 1793, and note.

[1] Word interlined in place of "a neutral."
[2] Word interlined in place of "exercised."
[3] Randolph first wrote "of neutral nations" before altering the passage to read as above.
[4] Randolph here canceled "exclud."
[5] Word interlined in place of "offense."
[6] Preceding two words interlined.

Cabinet Opinion on the Creek Indians and Georgia

May 29th 1793

The President of the United States having assembled the heads of the respective departments and the attorney General, laid before them for their advice thereon, sundry communications from the Governor of Georgia, and others, relatively to the recent alarming depredations of the creek Indians upon the State of Georgia.

Whereupon after the subject was maturely considered and discussed it was unanimously advised

That the Governor of Georgia be informed that from considerations relative to foreign powers, and the pending treaty with the Northern Indians, it is deemed adviseable for the present, to avoid offensive expeditions into the Indian Country. But from the nature of the late appearances, it is thought expedient to encrease the force to be kept up for defensive purposes. The President therefore authorises, the calling into, and keeping in service, in addition to the troops heretofore stationed in Georgia, one hundred horse, and one hundred infantry, to be employed in repelling inroads as circumstances shall require. As it does not yet appear that the whole nation of the creeks, is engaged in hostility, it is confided that this force will be sufficient for the object designated. The case of a serious invasion of the territory of Georgia, by large bodies of Indians must be referred to the provisions of the constitution. The proceeding with efficacy in future requires absolutely, that no unnecessary expence should be incurred in the mean time.

The above corps of horse to be raised for any period of time not exceeding twelve Months[1] as may be found most practicable, subject to be dismissed at any time sooner as the government may think fit. The infantry to be called into service according to the course of the militia Laws endevoring to secure their continuance in service for the like time.

That General Pickens be invited to repair to the seat of Government, for the purpose of information and consultation; a proper compensation for his expences, and loss of time to be allowed.

That a further supply of one thousand arms with correspondent accoutrements be forwarded to the state of Georgia. Arms and accoutrements, for the cavalry to be also provided and forwarded.

That an agent be sent to the Creeks to endevor to adjust the surrender of those Indians who have lately committed murders on the citizens of Georgia; to conciliate, and secure such of the Indians as may be well disposed to the United States; in the event of a war with the Creek nation, and if possible to prevent that extremety.

TH: JEFFERSON

H KNOX

EDM: RANDOLPH

ALEXANDER HAMILTON

MS (DLC: Washington Papers); in the hand of an unidentified War Department clerk, with signatures added by TJ, Knox, and Randolph on 1 June and by Hamilton on 3 June 1793; contains alterations made on 1 June 1793 (see note 1 below); endorsed by Tobias Lear. Enclosed in Lear to TJ, 31 May 1793, TJ to Hamilton, 1 June 1793, Hamilton to TJ, 3 June 1793, and TJ to Washington, 4 June 1793.

The SUNDRY COMMUNICATIONS were: Governor Edward Telfair of Georgia to Secretary of War Knox, 22 and 29 Apr. 1793; Major John Habersham, the officer in charge of military stores at Savannah, to Knox, 23, 29 Apr., and 3 May 1793; Governor William Moultrie of South Carolina to George Washington, 11 May 1793; and documents accompanying these letters. All of this material dealt with "the alarming prospect of hostilities with the Creek & Cherokee Indians" (Washington, *Journal*, 149-50, 154; ASP, *Indian Affairs*, I, 364; Telfair's letters and their enclosures and the enclosures to Habersham's 3 May letter are printed in same, 368-9, 389-91).

The President and the Cabinet treated these reports of Creek attacks on Georgia with gravity because they believed that the Spanish authorities had incited them as part of a general plan to create an alliance of the Southern Indians as a buffer against American expansion into disputed border areas. Secretary of the Treasury Alexander Hamilton being detained in the country when the Cabinet met on 28 May 1793, it sent the documents under consideration to him for perusal and adjourned to the following day, when it agreed in substance to the above opinion. The text printed here was evidently prepared later, although the term of service of the cavalry to be raised was left unspecified (see note 1 below). On 31 May the President instructed the Secretary of State to have the blank filled in and the opinion signed at a Cabinet meeting the following day. Hamilton was not at that meeting, but he affixed his signature after receiving the document from TJ, who sent the signed opinion to the President on 4 June 1793 (Washington, *Journal*, 154, 155, 157, 159). Knox INFORMED Telfair of the Cabinet's decision in a letter of 30 May 1793 (ASP, *Indian Affairs*, I, 364).

A statute of March 1792 provided the authority for raising a CORPS OF HORSE for frontier service. The MILITIA LAWS of 2 May 1792 permitted the President to take state militia into federal service (*Annals*, III, 1345, 1370-2).

Adroit diplomacy by James Seagrove, the United States AGENT to the Creeks, ultimately led to a peaceful resolution of the crisis despite the bellicose stance assumed by Georgia (Daniel M. Smith, "James Seagrove and the Mission to Tuckaubatchee, 1793," *Georgia Historical Quarterly*, XLIV [1960], 47-55).

[1] At this point the clerk originally wrote "from   to   Months," but after the Cabinet meeting on 1 June 1793 he interlined "not exceeding" in place of "from   to" and inserted "twelve" in the second blank.

From David Humphreys

SIR   Lisbon May 29th. 1793

I had the honour of writing to you on the 19th by Capt. Orne, who was bound to Salem. In that letter I acquainted you with my having received yours of the 30th. of March, and that I should endeavour to make all the preparations in my power for the accomplishment of its object. No intelligence is received as yet of Captn. Cutting: nor is any vessel yet found that would be likely to answer the purpose.

The defection of Dumourier has not injured the French cause as much as was expected. Notwithstanding the parties and confusions in Paris, their armies seem to be in such force in different quarters that the combined Powers make little impression. The season for the campaign is passing without any thing decisive being done. The English are slow in getting to Sea. The Spanish have a fleet of twenty Sail cruising in the Mediterranean, said to be with a design of intercepting a convoy with wheat from Algiers to Marseilles. The Portuguese fleet of ten Sail have been out five days to Maneuvre and is returned. You will have seen the account of the division of Poland. The combination against freedom is formidable. Spain[1] proposed to England to make a common [cause][2] against the United States of America.[3] This information comes from a Person who had the means of knowing the fact, and who could have no interest in deceiving me. It does not appear the proposal was listened to. This may perhaps occasion a different subsequent conduct on the part of the proposer.

I forward this by way of St. Ubes, as there is not a single vessel here destined immediately for the U.S. I also send one of three Packets just received from Messrs. Carmichael and Short—the others noted to go by different conveyances. With sincere & great respect I have the honour to be Sir Your Most obedient & Most humble Servant

D. HUMPHREYS

RC (DNA: RG 59, DD); with sentence in code (see note 1 below); at head of text: "(No. 73.)"; at foot of text: "The Secretary of State &c. &c. &c."; endorsed by TJ as received 22 July 1793 and so recorded in SJL; filed with separate sheet bearing decipherment in a clerk's hand. Tr (Lb in same); entirely *en clair*, with deciphered sentence underscored.

The enclosed packet from William CARMICHAEL and William SHORT apparently contained texts of their letters to TJ of 18 Apr. and 5 May 1793, both of which TJ received on the same day as the above letter and submitted to the President on the following day with the dispatch from Humphreys (Washington, *Journal*, 205-6).

[1] This sentence is written in code, the text being supplied from the clerical decipherment filed with the RC and verified by the Editors against partially reconstructed Code No. 8, with one anomaly being noted below.

[2] Word encoded by Humphreys as "a" and deciphered as such both in the clerical decipherment filed with the RC and in the Tr. However, in the Tr an unidentified hand penciled "cause" above "a," an interpolation which undoubtedly represents the meaning intended by Humphreys.

[3] Preceding two words omitted in Tr.

From James Madison

DEAR SIR   Orange May 29. 93.

I wrote you two or three days ago with an inclosure of Newspapers &c since which I have been favored with yours of the 19th. I thank you for the plans and observations which far exceeded the trouble I meant to give you. The sentiments expressed by Genest would be of infinite service at this crisis. As a regular publication of them cannot be expected till the meeting of Congress, if then, it were to be wished they could in some other mode make their way to the press. If he expressed the substance of them in his verbal answer to the address, or announces them in open conversation, the Printers might surely hand them to the public. The affection to France in her struggles for liberty would not only be increased by a knowledge that she does not wish us to go to war; but prudence would give its sanction to a bolder enunciation of the popular sentiment. I inclose a letter to the French Minister of the Interior which has been written some time.[1] I pray you to look it over with an eye to every proper consideration, and if you find a particle in it wrong or doubtful not to seal and forward it, till I have an opportunity of making the requisite variations. I hope your model of the Threshing Machine is by this time arrived and answerable to expectation. You will have much use for it if your harvest should turn out according to the promises of our fields in this quarter. Wheat was never known to be more uniformly excellent. Adieu. Yrs. always & affy.   Js. MADISON JR

RC (DLC: Madison Papers); endorsed by TJ as received 6 June 1793 and so recorded in SJL. Enclosure: Madison to Jean Marie Roland de La Platière, French Minister of the Interior, April 1793, gratefully accepting the French citizenship conferred on him by the Legislative Assembly on 26 Aug. 1792, and avowing his wishes for the prosperity and glory of the French nation and the victory of liberty over the minds of its opponents (Dft in same; printed in Madison, *Papers*, xv, 4).

In recognition of their services to liberty, the Legislative Assembly in August 1792 bestowed French citizenship on three Americans, Madison, George Washington, and Alexander Hamilton—the last two of whom did not respond to the award—as well as on a number of European supporters of the French Revolution (*Archives Parlementaires*, 1st ser., xlix, 10).

¹ Preceding two words written over "recently."

From John Nixon

SIR   Wednesday May 29. 1793
    Mr. Henry Cruger left with you sometime past, Some papers belonging to his Brother respecting the Seizure of Capt. Burke on Hispaniola; that Gentleman has now directed me to Call for them and forward them on to him; I shall be therefore obliged to you to deliver them to the Bearer, as I mean to send them on this day. I am very Respectfully Your very hum Sert   JOHN NIXON

RC (DNA: RG 76, France, Unbound Records); at foot of text: "Thomas Jefferson Esqr"; endorsed by TJ as received 29 May 1793 and so recorded in SJL.

John Nixon (1733-1808) was a Philadelphia merchant and Revolutionary War veteran who served as city alderman from 1789 to 1796 and as president of the Bank of North America from 1792 until his death (DAB). The PAPERS may have been enclosed in Nicholas Cruger to TJ, 8 Apr. 1793, recorded in SJL as received 16 Apr. 1793 but not found. For further details of the SEIZURE of the schooner *York*, see Memorial from Nicholas Cruger and Others, 26 June 1793.

To John Nixon

SIR   Philadelphia May 29. 1793.
    When Mr. Cruger delivered his papers to me, it was concluded that as Mr. Genet was expected daily, it would be better to await his arrival and put the case into his hands, that he might adopt his own plan of redressing it, than to put it into the hands of Mr. Ternant, just then going out of office. We have not got into a train of business with Mr. Genet till within these few days, and these have been so occupied by more pressing questions between the two countries that I had still kept back Mr. Cruger's case. Consequently it has not been laid before Mr.

Genet. Not understanding from your note whether Mr. Cruger has asked for his papers with a view to decline moving in the case altogether, or on a supposition that they may have been communicated to the minister, I return them according to your desire. But if they were asked on the last supposition, it will be necessary for me to have them again in which case I shall immediately present the case to Mr. Genet. I have the honor to be with great respect Sir Your most obedt. humble servt TH: JEFFERSON

PrC (DLC); at foot of text: "John Nixon esq." Tr (DLC); 19th-century copy. Enclosures not found.

From John Nixon

SIR   Wednesday May 29. 1793

Mr. Cruger at present is desirous of having the [policys?] only, to Confer with his Underwriters on this Loss. The other papers he wished me to look into and give my Opinion, how far I might think his Underwriters bound to pay, in Case no Redress to be obtained of the French Government. I shall write Mr. Cruger by this post, and inform him of your Intention to apply Soon to Mr. Genet on this business. Should there be any Occasion for Mr. Burk or Indeed Mr. Cruger to Come here, I request you to Notify me of it. I have the honour to be with great Respect Your very hum Sevt JOHN NIXON

RC (DNA: RG 76, France, Unbound Records); one word illegible; at foot of text: "Thomas Jefferson Esqr"; endorsed by TJ as received 29 May 1793 and so recorded in SJL.

To F. P. Van Berckel

SIR   Philadelphia May 29th. 1793.

I am favored with your note of the 22d. instant, stating that under circumstances of invasion, and urgent danger, their High Mightinesses the States General of the United Netherlands had found it necessary to lay an embargo on all vessels in their Ports, and that an American Ship, the Hope, being involved in this general order, the master had claimed an exemption, under the eighth article of our Treaty, which it had been necessary to refuse him.

I have laid this Note before the President of the United States, and have it in charge from him to assure you that the United States, having the utmost confidence in the sincerity and good faith with which their

High Mightinesses will observe the Treaty between the two Countries, feel no dissatisfaction at the circumstance mentioned in your Note. They are sensible that in human affairs there are moments of difficulty and necessity to which it is the office of friendship to accommodate its strict rights.

The President considers the explanation, which their High Mightinesses have instructed you to give of this incident, as a proof of their desire to cultivate harmony and good understanding with these United States; and charges me to assure you that he has nothing more at heart than to convince their High Mightinesses of the same amicable sentiments on the part of this Country and of the certainty with which they may count on its justice and friendship on every occasion. I have the honor to be with great respect and esteem Sir, your most obedient & most humble Servant.

PrC (DLC); in a clerk's hand, unsigned; at foot of text: "Mr. Van Berckel." FC (Lb in DNA: RG 59, DL). Enclosed in TJ to Washington, 27 and 30 May 1793.

TJ prepared this letter in two stages. He first wrote a missing draft on 25 May 1793, which he submitted to the President two days later and which Washington then approved. Instead of dispatching that text to the Dutch minister, however, TJ composed a second draft that was designed, in the words of the President, "to leave an opening" for the captain or owners of the HOPE "to seek redress for any damage they may have sustained by the detention." Washington approved this draft on 30 May 1793, the same day TJ submitted it to him, and returned it to TJ the following day (Washington, *Journal*, 153, 155). See also TJ to Washington, 30 May 1793, for an indication of where the two drafts differed.

For the case of the HOPE, see Rodolph Vall-Travers to TJ, 29 Mch. 1793, and note. The EIGHTH ARTICLE of the 1782 treaty of amity and commerce between the Netherlands and the United States among other things forbade either of the contracting parties to seize or detain ships and cargoes belonging to subjects of the other without the consent of their owners, except for "debts or Crimes" (Miller, *Treaties*, II, 66-7).

From William Vans Murray

DEAR SIR   Cambridge 30th: May 1793.

I am very much obliged to you for the favor of an answer to my letter—as the matter would I thought receive its issue from a policy which might not be exactly then digested, I scarcely expected an answer so soon. I confess I almost dread the summum jus of the XIXth article of the Treaty with the Dutch—should judicial proceedings look that way. The error was certainly on the right side—and flow'd from a sentiment which in any other combination of things would be an agent of genuine patriotism when directed against the insolence of That Power whose movements are now associated with more amiable nations. Certainly Sir the difficulty will be great. While the Executive endeavors to discharge the general duties of neutrality it will be to be regretted if a sentiment is too much cooled which it is of infinite importance to preserve under a well regulated warmth.

I fear I did not explain with sufficient precision the idea I might perhaps have suggested, as to *restitution*. I never did suppose that the prize I alluded to would be restored—on the contrary, in some remarks which I published in the *Herald*—I observed that Captn. Ferey on application would without doubt have his prize, he showing his commission. I beg leave again Sir to thank you for your letter & to assure you that I am with sincere esteem & respect yr. mo. obt. Sert.   W. V. MURRAY

RC (ViW: Tucker-Coleman Collection); addressed: "The Honourable Thomas Jefferson, Esquire, Secretary of State—Philadelphia"; franked and postmarked; endorsed by TJ as received 12 June 1793 and so recorded in SJL.

SUMMUM JUS: "strict legal right." Article 19 of the 1782 TREATY WITH THE DUTCH provided that citizens of the United States should not take out letters of marque from any foreign nation at war with the Netherlands on pain of punishment as pirates (Miller, *Treaties*, II, 76-7). Murray was expressing concern that Americans who accepted French privateering commissions would be subject to such a penalty, since Great Britain was ASSOCIATED WITH MORE AMIABLE NATIONS, including the Netherlands, in its war with France.

Edmund Randolph's Opinion on the Case of Gideon Henfield

The Attorney general of the United States has the honor of submitting to the Secretary of State the following Opinion on the Case of Gideon Henfield, as represented by the Minister of France.

1. It may well be doubted, how far the Minister of France has a right to interfere. Henfield is a citizen of the United States; and it is unusual at least, that a foreign Power should interfere in a Question, whether as a citizen, a man has been guilty of a Crime? Nor can an authority be derived from Henfield being under the protection of the french Republic; because being still a citizen, he is amenable to the laws, which operate on citizens, and the very act, by which he is said to have been taken under such protection, is a violation of the sovereignty of the United States. If he be innocent, he will be safe in the hands of his countrymen: if guilty, the respect, due by one Nation, to the decrees of another, demands, that they be acquiesced in.

2. But Henfield is punishable; because treaties are the Supreme law of the land; and by treaties with three of the powers at war with France, it is stipulated, that there shall be a peace between their subjects, and the citizens of the United States.

3. He is indictable at the common Law; because his conduct comes within the description of disturbing the Peace of the United States.

EDM: RANDOLPH
May 30. 1793.

MS (DLC); in the hand of George Taylor, Jr., with signature and date by Randolph; endorsed by TJ as received 30 May 1793. PrC of Tr (DNA: RG 59, MLR); in a clerk's hand. PrC of another Tr (DLC); in a clerk's hand. Tr (DLC: Genet Papers). Tr (NNC: Gouverneur Morris Papers). Tr (PRO: FO 97/1). Tr (DNA: RG 46, Senate Records, 3d Cong., 1st sess.). Tr (DLC: John Trumbull Letterbook). Tr (DLC: Genet Papers); in French. Tr (same); in French; draft translation of preceding Tr. Tr (AMAE: CPEU, xxxvii); in French. Printed in *Message*, 25-6. Enclosed in TJ to Edmond Charles Genet, 1 June 1793, TJ

to Gouverneur Morris, 13 June and 16 Aug. 1793, and TJ to Thomas Pinckney, 14 June 1793.

For the case of Gideon Henfield AS REPRESENTED BY THE MINISTER OF FRANCE, see Memorial from Edmond Charles Genet, 27 May 1793, and note. The TREATIES WITH THREE OF THE POWERS AT WAR WITH FRANCE were the 1782 treaty of amity and commerce with the Netherlands, the 1783 peace treaty with Great Britain, and the 1785 treaty of amity and commerce with Prussia (Miller, *Treaties*, ii, 59-88, 151-83).

From Edmund Randolph, with Jefferson's Note

E. R. TO MR. J.   May 30. 1793.

The return of Warder's bills under protest has embarrassed me so much, as to make me request the favor of your name to the inclosed. You shall hear no more of it.

[*Note by TJ:*]

In consequence of the above I endorsed E.R's note for 1000 D. payable at 60. days sight.

RC (MHi); with TJ's note subjoined; addressed: "Mr. Jefferson"; endorsed by TJ as received 30 May 1793. Enclosure not found.

To George Washington

May 30. 93.

Th: Jefferson has the honor to inclose to the President *French* copies of the communications of Mr. Genet on the subject of our debt to France, as they will convey his sense perhaps more faithfully to the Secretary of the treasury should the President think proper to refer them to him.— He has changed the expression in the close of the 2d. paragraph of the letter to Mr. Van Berkel, so as to leave less room to doubt but that

indemnification to the individual may be required should the case require it, as such an indemnification will be *an accomodation of our strict
right.*

RC (DNA: RG 59, MLR); addressed:
"The President of the US."; endorsed by
Tobias Lear. Tr (Lb in same, SDC). Not
recorded in SJL. Enclosures: (1) Edmond

Charles Genet's third letter to TJ, 22 May
1793, and enclosures. (2) TJ to F. P. Van
Berckel, 29 May 1793.

From James Biddle

SIR   May 31. 1793

   I have taken proper measures to discover the person complained of
for the Insult to the national flag of France tending to provoke the french
Citizens to Acts of Outrage and breach of the publick peace—and have
issued a Warrant to apprehend the Offender which I doubt not will be
executed. While I am now sitting in Court an Application is made on
behalf of one John L. Steele Second Mate of the Ship Active Captn.
Blair who it is alledged was assaulted while peaceable in the street the
Night before last about ten o'Clock by a large body of the Crew of the
Ambuscade and taken and carried on board the Little Sally and from
thence to the Ambuscade where he has been and still is[1] kept confined
in Irons.

   I have requested Mr. Dunkin Merchant of this City who makes the
Complaint to apply to you for redress which I doubt not you will readily
obtain. I am Sir wth. great respect Your obedt. servt.

                                                                   JAMES BIDDLE

RC (DNA: RG 59, MLR); endorsed by
TJ as received 31 May 1793 and so recorded in SJL.

   James Biddle (1731-97), a lawyer who
had lived alternately in Philadelphia and
Reading, was President Judge of Pennsylvania's first judicial district, which included the city and county of Philadelphia
(James S. Biddle, ed., *Autobiography of
Charles Biddle . . . 1745-1821* [Philadel-
phia, 1883], 236n; John H. Martin, *Martin's Bench and Bar of Philadelphia* [Philadel-
phia, 1883], 49, 52).
   The INSULT TO THE NATIONAL FLAG OF
FRANCE probably occurred in Philadelphia on 26 May 1793, when the boatswain
of the British merchant ship *Grange*, who
had recently been released from French captivity, went on board the *Amiable*, Captain

Paul, which had just arrived from St. Vincent's, and tore down and trampled the
French colors that had been hoisted as a compliment to that nation (*General Advertiser*,
28 May 1793; *National Gazette*, 1 June
1793). TJ had apparently called on Biddle
after receiving a note from French minister
Edmond Charles Genet on 28 May 1793
complaining about the incident (see TJ to
Genet, 1 June 1793, and note). STEELE,
whose ship had been brought to Philadelphia as a prize of the *Citoyen Genet*, was one
of several English sailors confined on board
the French frigate *Embuscade* during
clashes with French seamen on 29 May
1793, although he was soon released (*General Advertiser*, 4 June 1793).

[1] Preceding three words interlined.

To William Carmichael and
William Short

GENTLEMEN   Philadelphia May 31st. 1793.

In my letters of Oct. 14. and Nov. 3. 1792, I communicated to you, papers and Observations, on the conduct of the Spanish Officers on our South Western frontier, and particularly of the Baron de Carondelet, the Governor of New Orleans. These made it evident that he had industriously excited the Southern Indians to war against us, and had furnished them with Arms and Ammunition, in abundance, for that express purpose. We placed this under the view of the Commissioners of Spain here, who undertook to communicate it to their Court, and also to write on the subject to the Baron de Carondelet. They have lately made us communications from both these Quarters; the aspect of which, however, is by no means such as to remove the causes of our dissatisfaction. I send you these communications, consisting of[1] Treaties between Spain, the Creeks, Choctaws, Chickasaws, and Cherokees, handed us by express order from their Court, a Speech of Baron de Carondelet, to the Cherokees, and a letter from Messrs. de Viar and Jaudenes, covering that Speech, and containing in itself very serious matter.

I will first observe to you, that the question stated in that letter, to have been proposed to the Cherokees, What part they would take in the event of a war, between the United States and Spain? was never proposed by authority from this Government. It's instructions to it's agents, have on the contrary, been explicitly to cultivate, with good faith, the peace between Spain and the Indians: and from the known prudence and good conduct of Governor Blount, to whom it is imputed, it is not believed to have been proposed by him. This proposition then you are authorized to disavow, to the Court of Madrid, in the most unequivocal terms.

With respect to the treaties, the Speech, and the letter, you will see that they undertake to espouse the concerns of Indians within our limits; to be mediators of boundary between them and us; to guaranty that boundary to them; to support them with their whole power; and hazard to us intimations of acquiescence to avoid disagreeable results. They even propose to extend their intermedlings to the northern Indians. These are pretensions, so totally inconsistent with the usages established among the white nations, with respect to indians living within their several limits; that it is believed no example of them can be produced, in times of peace; and they are presented to us in a manner, which we cannot deem friendly. The consequence is, that the Indians, and particularly the Creeks, finding themselves so encouraged, have passed, without the least provocation on our part, from a state of peace, which appeared to be well settled, to that of serious hostility. Their Murders and Depredations, which, for some months, we were willing to hope were only individual aggressions, now assume the appearance of unequivocal War. Yet, such is our desire of courting and cultivating the peace of all our Indian neighbors, that instead of marching at once into their Country, and taking satisfaction ourselves, we are peaceably requiring punishment of the individual Aggressors; and, in the mean time, are holding ourselves entirely on the defensive. But this state of things cannot continue. Our Citizens are entitled to effectual protection; and defensive measures are, at the same time, the most expensive, and least effectual. If we find then, that peace cannot be obtained by the temperate means we are still pursuing; we must proceed to those which are extreme, and meet all the consequences, of whatever nature, or from whatever quarter, they may be. We have certainly been always desirous to avoid whatever might disturb our harmony with Spain. We should be still more so, at a moment when we see that nation making part of so powerful a confederacy as is formed in Europe, and under particular good understanding with England, our other neighbor. In so delicate a position, therefore, instead of expressing our sense of these things, by way of answer to Messrs. Viar and Jaudenes, the President has thought it better that it should be done to you, and to trust to your discretion the moment, the measure, and the form, of communicating it to the Court of Madrid.   The actual state of Europe, at the time you will receive this, the solidity of the confederacy, and especially, as between Spain and England, the temper and views of the former, or of both, towards us, the state of your negotiation, are circumstances, which will enable you better to decide how far it may be necessary to soften, or even, perhaps, to suppress, the expressions of our sentiments on this subject. To your discretion therefore, it is committed, by the President, to let the Court of Spain see how impossible it is for us to submit, with folded arms, to be butchered by these Savages, and to prepare them to view, with a just Eye, the more vigorous measures we must pursue to put an end to their atrocities, if the moderate ones, we are now taking, should fail of that effect.

Our situation, on other accounts, and in other quarters, is critical. The President is, therefore, constantly anxious to know the state of things with you: and I entreat you to keep him constantly and well informed. Mr. Yznardi, the younger, lately appointed Consul of the United States, at Cadiz, may be a convenient channel of forwarding your letters. I have the honor to be with great esteem & respect, Gentlemen your most obedt. & most humble servt   TH: JEFFERSON

RC (DLC: Short Papers); in the hand of George Taylor, Jr., with complimentary close and signature by TJ and marginal note by Short (see note 1 below); at foot of first page: "Messrs. Carmichael & Short"; endorsed by Short. PrC (DLC); with complimentary close and signature added by TJ in ink. Intended RC (DLC); in Taylor's hand, unsigned, but not sent; written entirely in Code No. 10, except for *en clair* salutation and date; omits several words and letters because of encoding errors and contains slightly variant complimentary close; endorsed by TJ: "letter to Messrs. Carmichael & Short, cyphered, but afterwards sent by Mr. Blake uncyphered. In W S's cypher." PrC (DLC); with correction in ink by Taylor. FC (Lb in DNA: RG 59, DCI); entirely *en clair*. Recorded in SJPL. Enclosures: (1) Treaty of Pensacola between Spain and the Creek Indians, 1 June 1784 (see note to Josef Ignacio de Viar and Josef de Jaudenes to TJ, 7 May 1793). (2) Treaty of Natchez between Spain and the Chickasaw and Choctaw Indians, 14 May 1792 (see note to letter on this subject from Jaudenes and Viar to TJ, 12 May 1793). (3) Carondelet's Speech to the Cherokee Nation, 24 Nov. 1792 (printed as enclosure to No. 4). (4) Viar and Jaudenes to TJ, 25 May 1793.

On this day the Secretary of State submitted a draft of this letter to the President, who returned it the same day, authorizing TJ to lay it before the Cabinet if he saw fit and report to him the result of that body's deliberations. The Cabinet approved the draft during a meeting on 1 June 1793 that the President and the Secretary of the Treasury were unable to attend. TJ thereupon submitted the draft to Alexander Hamilton, who returned it with his approval on 3 June 1793 (Washington, *Journal*, 156-7, 159; TJ to Hamilton, 1 June 1793; Hamilton to TJ, 3 June 1793). But owing to the need to find a reliable courier to deliver this highly sensitive communication, TJ waited for nearly six weeks before dispatching the final version (TJ to James Blake, 12 July 1793).

TJ erred when he wrote that he was enclosing a Spanish treaty with the CHEROKEES. Spain had no treaty with this tribe, and the Spanish agents in Philadelphia had not mentioned one in any of the letters on Indian affairs they wrote to TJ in May 1793.

[1] Here Short drew a finger pointing to the next word to serve as a key to a note he wrote in the margin: "These treaties did not come. W.S." He also underscored two words—"Treaties" and "Cherokees"—later in the sentence.

From George Hammond

Sir   Philadelphia 31 May 1793

In your letter of the 15th curt., you mention that one of the points, stated in my memorial of the 8th of this month, has been reserved for future deliberation. That point appearing to me to be of the most serious magnitude, I shall be infinitely obliged to you, if you will have the goodness to inform me at what time I may expect to receive the determination of this government upon it; as my knowledge of that circumstance will regulate my conduct with regard to the departure of the June packet. I have the honor to be, with great respect, Sir, Your most obedient, humble Servant,   GEO. HAMMOND

RC (DNA: RG 59, NL); at head of text: "*Private*"; at foot of text: "Mr Jefferson"; endorsed by TJ as received 31 May 1793 and so recorded in SJL. Tr (Lb in same).

From Tobias Lear

May 31st: 1793

By the President's command T. Lear has the honor to return to the Secretary of State, the draughts and Copies of letters which he sent to the President this day—And to inform the Secretary, that the President is so much indisposed that he does not think he shall be able to meet the Gentlemen at his House tomorrow (the President having had a high fever upon him for 2 or 3 days past, and it still continuing unabated)—he therefore desires that the Secretary of State will request the Attendance of the other Heads of the Departments and the Attorney General at his Office tomorrow, and lay before them, for their consideration and opinion,[1] such matters as he would have wished to have brought to their view if they had met at the President's—and let the President know the results of their deliberations thereon.

The President likewise directs T. Lear to send to the Secrety. of State the Opinions of the Gentlemen expressed at their last meeting on the subject of Indian Affairs in Georgia, for their signature tomorrow, and to have the blank, which is left therein to limit the time of the service of the troops, filled up.

Also a note from the Attorney General relative to certain communications from Baltimore, which the President thinks should be laid before the Gentlemen.

TOBIAS LEAR
Secretary to the President
of the United States

RC (DLC); endorsed by TJ as received 31 May 1793. Dft (DNA: RG 59, MLR); with several emendations and minor variations. FC (Lb in same, SDC); wording follows Dft. Enclosures: (1) Enclosures to TJ's first letter to George Washington, 31 May 1793. (2) Cabinet Opinion on the Creek Indians and Georgia, 29 May 1793. (3) Edmund Randolph to Lear, [31 May 1793], urging that the President ask TJ to convene the Cabinet "at his office to morrow, upon the subject of the Baltimore papers, which E.R. has this moment sent to Mr. Jefferson by his messenger" (RC in DLC: TJ Papers, 87: 14994; dated "Friday P. M."). See Washington, *Journal*, 156-7.

The COMMUNICATIONS FROM BALTIMORE were enclosed in Edmund Randolph to TJ, 31 May 1793.

[1] Preceding two words interlined in Dft in place of "and decision."

From Edmund Randolph, with Jefferson's Note

E. R. TO MR. J.   May 31. 1793.

The requisition of departure is, in my judgment, expressed in the most accurate and satisfactory manner possible. It gives me real pleasure to find the strong measure capable of such a softening of feature, while it retains full nerve.

Were I to speak for myself, as an individual, I should assent with equal cordiality to the last clause. But I can't help believing, that it would accord better with a neutral situation, to omit the reciprocation of affection. The existence of this is too manifest in the people, to render any very warm expression of it on the part of the government, necessary to convince the French of our fidelity.

I forward some papers from Baltimore, which the President, thro' Mr. Lear, requested me to send to you. As he is unwell, I intend to desire, that we may assemble at your office to morrow 12 o'clock. Perhaps it may not be amiss, to authorize me to say *informally* to Colo. Smith, as I pass thro' Baltimore, that the President will, at the next session of congress, recommend the suppression of the sale of prizes in our ports.

[*Note by TJ:*]

The concluding clause of the letter objected to was in these words. 'The assurance conveyed in your letter of the friendship and attachment of your nation is received with sincere pleasure and returned with equal sincerity on the part of this country. That these may be long and firm no one wishes more cordially than he who has the honor to be with sentiments of esteem & respect Sir &c.'
The paragraph was struck out.

RC (DLC); with note on verso by TJ; endorsed by TJ as received 31 May 1793 and so recorded in SJL. Recorded in SJPL. Enclosures: (1) Otho H. Williams, Collector at Baltimore, to Alexander Hamilton, 28 May 1793, enclosing copies of his letter to the surveyor of the port about a French privateer and its prize lately arrived, the surveyor's report, and a translation of the French commission of the captain of the privateer, and, in view of the silence both of the laws of Congress and Hamilton's instructions, asking for advice about the proper course to follow in such a case (Syrett, *Hamilton*, xiv, 489). (2) Samuel Smith to same, n.d., concerning the fears aroused in Maryland by the prizes taken by French privateers fitted out in the United States (not found, but abstracted in Washington, *Journal*, 156).

The REQUISITION OF DEPARTURE from American ports of French privateers commissioned in the United States was contained in the draft of TJ to Edmond Charles Genet, 5 June 1793, on which TJ had obviously solicited the Attorney General's views prior to his submission of it to the President this day (see Memorandum from Randolph, printed under 28 May 1793; and Tobias Lear to TJ, 31 May 1793).

Washington had originally requested Randolph to lay the enclosed PAPERS FROM BALTIMORE concerning the French privateer *Sans Culotte* before TJ and to give their opinion on the steps the administration should take in the case, but the President acceded to Randolph's suggestion that the papers be laid before the Cabinet (Washington, *Journal*, 156). For the results of its deliberations, see Cabinet Memorandum on French Privateers, printed under 1 June 1793, and note.

The letter from Genet referred to in TJ's note was the French minister's long letter to the Secretary of State of 27 May 1793.

From Thomas Mann Randolph, Jr.

DEAR SIR   Monticello May 31: 1793

A report of your having resigned your office is in circulation here and
receives great credit from us mostly perhaps because we wish to have it
so but considerably too from our not having received letters as usual by
the two last posts: we conclude that the hurry of preparing for your
departure and the expectation of seeing us soon have prevented your
writing. We are strongly impressed with the thought of your being either actually on the way home or at least on the eve of seting out and
have the most sanguine hopes of seeing you before this letter can reach
Philada. Full of this idea I content myself with telling you that your
daughter and her children are well and happy and with assuring you of
the gratitude and affection of your most sincere friend & most obedt
hble Servt.   THS: M. RANDOLPH

RC (ViU: Coolidge Deposit); endorsed by TJ as received 19 June 1793 and so recorded in SJL.

From Edward Stevens

DEAR SIR   Culpeper Court House May 31st: 1793

I now do myself the pleasure to Transmit you herewith Copys of the
Letters (which I preserved) that passed between us during my Military
Services under your Administration, in the time of the American Revo-
lution. All those Prior to Genl. Gates defeat, I informed you before was
lost among my Baggage in that unlucky affair. And I discover some
Letters which I know I wrote you about the latter part of my Southern
service the Copys, are lost, or mislaid that I cant put my hands on them.
I am with every sentiment of Respect Dear Sir Your most hum: Servt

EDWARD STEVENS

RC (MoSHi: Bixby Collection); endorsed by TJ as received 11 June 1793 and
so recorded in SJL.

With this letter Stevens enclosed copys
of twenty-four letters he had exchanged
with TJ between 19 July 1780 and 8 Feb.
1781, all printed in this edition under their
respective dates.

From Francis Walker

SIR   Richmond May 31. 1793

Mr. Underwood of Goochland, requests me to inclose some certificates respecting his son. He has forwarded such to the war office, but

fearing the subscribers may not be so well known there as to yourself, solicits you to give them the weight they deserve. We both trust that our wish to promote a deserving soldier will be a sufficient apology for giving you this trouble. I am sir your obdt Servt.   FRAS: WALKER

RC (DLC); endorsed by TJ as received 25 June 1793 and so recorded in SJL. Enclosures not found.

MR. UNDERWOOD: probably Thomas Underwood, a friend of James Madison who represented Goochland County in the Virginia House of Delegates from 1777 to 1790. HIS SON was probably Thomas Un-

derwood, who waited almost two years for his appointment in February 1795 as a lieutenant in the Army Corps of Artillerists and Engineers (Madison, *Papers*, XII, 249n; TJ to Walker, 27 June 1793; JEP, I, 173, 174).

A missing letter from Walker to TJ, written from Richmond on 21 May 1793, is recorded in SJL as received 24 June 1793.

To George Washington

May 31. 93.

Th: Jefferson has the honor to send the President draughts of letters on the subjects discussed in his presence the other day, meant merely as a ground-work for the gentlemen to propose amendments to. He shall be able to send another in the course of to-day, so that the whole would be ready for consideration tomorrow, if the President should think proper to have them considered before the departure of the Attorney general.

RC (DNA: RG 59, MLR); addressed: "The President of the US."; endorsed by Tobias Lear. Tr (Lb in same, SDC). Not recorded in SJL. Enclosures: (1) Draft of TJ to Edmond Charles Genet, 1 June 1793. (2) Draft of TJ to William Carmichael and William Short, 31 May 1793, with copies of same to same, 14 Oct. and 3

Nov. 1792, and last two paragraphs of Report on Negotiations with Spain, 18 Mch. 1792. (3) Draft of TJ to Josef Ignacio de Viar and Josef de Jaudenes, 5 June 1793, but dated 1 June 1793 as submitted to Washington (Washington, *Journal*, 156-7).

To George Washington

May 31. 93.

Th: Jefferson has now the honor of inclosing to the President the draught of a letter to Mr. Genet on the subject of the departure of the privateer.—Also a letter just received from Colo. Humphreys.

RC (DNA: RG 59, MLR); addressed: "The President of the US."; endorsed by Tobias Lear as a letter of 1 June 1793. Tr (Lb in same, SDC). Not recorded in SJL. Enclosures: (1) Draft of TJ to Edmond Charles Genet, 5 June 1793. (2) David Humphreys to TJ, 4 Apr. 1793.

The President returned the second enclosure to TJ on this day and the first on the following day, when he also sent TJ a 4 Apr. 1793 letter he had just received from Humphreys (Washington, *Journal*, 156, 157, 158).

To Edmond Charles Genet

[May 1793?]

Thomas Jefferson présente Ses respects à Mr. Genet et lui renvoie les pamphlets marqués à rendre, avec mille remerciemens pour la lecture qu'il lui en a procuré.

On peut également renvoyer les autres si Mr. Genet en a le moindre besoin vu qu'après une lecture ils deviendront inutiles. On desirerait cependant garder *les Résultats du Commerce &ce.* qu'il serait bon de garder dans les Bureaux.

Tr (DLC: Genet Papers); undated; probably a translation, but unmentioned in TJ's extant correspondence with Genet, though presumably written not long after the French minister's arrival in Philadelphia on 16 May 1793. Not recorded in SJL. Enclosures not found.

RÉSULTATS DU COMMERCE: *Résultats du commerce de la nation françoise avec les Anglo-Américains, tant en Europe, qu'en Amérique, à trois époques distinctes, depuis leur scission avec l'Angleterre, jusqu'au moment de la révolution françoise* (n.p., [1789?]).

Cabinet Memorandum on French Privateers

[1 June 1793]

On the letters and papers from Genl. Williams and Colo. Smith.
It is the opinion that the writers be informed that[1] with respect to vessels armed and equipped in the ports of the US. before notice to the contrary was given, the President is taking measures for obliging them to depart from the ports of the US. and that all such equipments in future are forbidden: but that as to the prizes taken by them, no power less than that of the legislature can prohibit their sale.—That as the Attorney General is to pass through Baltimore shortly, it is better that this answer be given verbally by him, any[2] other gentleman being free to do the same in writing in his private capacity. Also that they be informed that[3] measures are taken for punishing such citizens as have engaged in hostilities by sea against nations at peace with the US.

MS (DLC); entirely in TJ's hand, unsigned; undated, but probably drafted on 1 June 1793 (see note below); notation added at foot of text by TJ at a later date: "May. [about the end of the month] 1793." Recorded in SJPL under 24 May 1793: "Opn on equipments in ports of US.—on selling prizes here." Enclosed in TJ to Alexander Hamilton, 1 June [1793], and Hamilton to TJ, 3 June 1793.

Despite TJ's notation on the manuscript and his entry in SJPL, which were undoubtedly made years later, the Secretary of State evidently prepared this document for a Cabinet meeting that he held on 1 June 1793 with Attorney General Edmund Randolph and Secretary of War Henry Knox to consider the LETTERS AND PAPERS submitted to the President by Secretary of the Treasury Alexander Hamilton relating to concerns that had arisen in Maryland over the threat to American neutrality posed by the sale in American ports of prizes captured by French privateers fitted out in the United States, and to report to the President their opinion on what action the federal government should take in the matter (for the documents and the antecedents to the meeting, see Randolph to TJ, 31 May 1793, and note). Although Randolph and Knox approved the memorandum in its final form at the meeting—hence the conjectural date assigned above—the President and the Secretary of the Treasury were unable to attend. Hamilton signified his approval two days later, and Washington's sanction can be inferred from a letter the Attorney General wrote to him describing a conversation with Congressman Samuel Smith in Baltimore on the "subject of his letter to Colo. Hamilton" (see descriptive note above; Randolph to Washington, 11 June 1793, DLC: Washington Papers).

The NOTICE forbidding the fitting out of foreign privateers in American ports was implied in Washington's Proclamation of Neutrality and made explicit in TJ's letters of 15 May 1793 to George Hammond and

Jean Baptiste Ternant. TJ announced the MEASURES FOR OBLIGING the privateers to depart from American ports in his 5 June 1793 letters to Hammond and Edmond Charles Genet. Randolph planned to PASS THROUGH BALTIMORE SHORTLY on a trip to Virginia undertaken at the President's behest to gauge public reaction to the Washington administration's neutrality policy (for his reports to the President, see Randolph to Washington, 11 and 24 June 1793, DLC: Washington Papers; see also John J. Reardon, *Edmund Randolph: A Biography* [New York, 1974], 232-4). For the measures taken against American citizens ENGAGED IN HOSTILITIES BY SEA, see TJ to William Rawle, 15 May 1793, and Memorial from Genet, 27 May 1793, and note.

Samuel Smith wrote a letter to TJ of 1 Aug. 1793 that is recorded in SJL as received from Baltimore on 7 Aug. 1793, but has not been found.

[1] TJ here canceled "the President is taking."
[2] Word added and remainder of sentence interlined.
[3] TJ here canceled "orders."

Cabinet Opinions on Sending an Agent to the Choctaw Indians

June 1. 1793.

That an Agent be sent to the Choctaw nation to endeavour secretly to engage them to support the Chickasaws in their present war with the Creeks, giving them for that purpose arms and ammunition sufficient: and that it be kept in view that if we settle our differences amicably with the Creeks, we at the same time mediate effectually the peace of the Chickasaws and Choctaws, so as to rescue the former from the difficulties in which they are engaged, and the latter from those into which we may have been instrumental in engaging them.   TH: JEFFERSON
H KNOX

Altho' I approve of the general[1] policy of employing Indians against Indians; yet I doubt greatly, whether it ought to be exercised under the particular existing circumstances with Spain; who may hold herself bound to take the part of the Creeks, and criminate the U. S. for some degree of insincerity.   EDM: RANDOLPH

My judgment ballanced a considerable time on the proposed measure; but it has at length decided against it, and very materially on the ground that I do not think the UStates can honorably or morally or with good policy[2] embark the Chocktaws in the War, without a determination to extricate them from the consequences even by force. Accordingly it is proposed that in settling our differences with the Creeks, "we *mediate effectually* the peace of the Chickesaws and Choctaws" which I understand to mean, that we are to insist with the Creeks on such terms of peace for them as shall appear to us equitable, and if refused will exert ourselves *to procure them by arms*. I am unwilling, all circumstances foreign and domestic considered, to embarrass the Government with such an obligation.   ALEX HAMILTON

MS (DLC: Washington Papers); date and first paragraph in TJ's hand, signed by TJ and Henry Knox; second paragraph and signature in the hand of Edmund Randolph; third paragraph and signature in the hand of Alexander Hamilton added between 3 and 5 June 1793; endorsed by Tobias Lear: "Opinion of the Heads of the Departmts. & Atty Genl. of the U.S. relative to sending an Agent to the Choctaws—June 1st: 1793." An entry in SJPL under 1 June 1793— "[G.W. to Th:J.] on sending agent to Choctaws & Chickasaws"—refers either to this document or to an otherwise unknown letter from the President to TJ on the same subject. Enclosed in TJ to Hamilton, 1 June [1793].

While its exact antecedents are unclear, this document was an outgrowth of the Cabinet's 29 May 1793 meeting on the issue of Creek hostilities with Georgia, with the proposed overture to the Choctaws being intended to relieve Creek pressure on the state (Cabinet Opinion on the Creek Indians and Georgia, 29 May 1793). Both the President and the Secretary of the Treasury missed this Cabinet meeting because of ill-

ness. After Hamilton added his opinion, TJ transmitted the document to the President on 5 June (Tobias Lear to TJ, 31 May 1793; TJ to Hamilton, 1 June [1793]; Hamilton to TJ, 3 June 1793; Washington, *Journal*, 157, 159, 161). With his advisors evenly divided on whether to send an agent to the Choctaw nation, Washington took no action. Energetic efforts by Spanish officials headed off the threat of a divisive war between the Creeks and the Chickasaws by June 1793, and at the Treaty of Nogales of 28 Oct. 1793 these nations joined the Choctaws and Cherokees in forming an offensive and defensive alliance under Spanish protection (Jack D. L. Holmes, *Gayoso: The Life of a Spanish Governor in the Mississippi Valley 1789-1799* [Baton Rouge, 1965], 150-5; D. C. Corbitt and Roberta Corbitt, trans. and eds., "Papers from the Spanish Archives Relating to Tennessee and the Old Southwest," East Tennessee Historical Society, *Publications*, XXXIII [1961], 75).

[1] Word interlined by Randolph.
[2] Preceding four words interlined by Hamilton.

To George Clinton

SIR   Philadelphia June 1. 1793.

The bearer hereof, Monsr. de Hauterive, appointed Consul at New York in the place of M. de Crevecoeur, having brought me some very particular recommendations from friends at Paris, who would not give them lightly, I comply with their desire in presenting him to your notice. In a short conversation which I had with him, I found him a man of literature, and a genuine republican, under which character I am sure he will be acceptable to your Excellency. The Minister here also seems to interest himself particularly for him. I therefore take the liberty of asking your countenance of him, both in the social and official line, and verily believe he will do justice to your attentions: which will also be considered as a favor conferred on Your Excellency's Most obedt. & most humble servt   TH: JEFFERSON

PrC (DLC); at foot of text: "H. E. Govr. Clinton." Tr (CtY); in the hand of and attested by DeWitt Clinton. Tr (DLC); 19th-century copy.

For one of the PARTICULAR RECOMMENDATIONS FROM FRIENDS AT PARIS, see Jean Baptiste Le Roy to TJ, 18 Feb. 1793. No other has been found.

To Edmond Charles Genet

SIR   Philadelphia June 1. 1793.

[. . .]¹ to correct an error of fact into [. . .]² being just led into it myself [. . .]³ concerning the trespass committed by [a British] sailor on the French flag on board the Amiable. I mentioned it to a gentleman present, who informed me that the sailor [who made the insult?] and another concerned in it, were in jail, [. . .]⁴ mentioned to you. I found on further enquiry that these two sailors were British, who had been committed for another assault on French [sailors?], and had not been concerned in the insult on board the Amiable. I immediately asked the attention of the [proper?] judge to the arrest and punishment of the offender on board the Amiable. I have this moment called on him again. [He informs?] me that he has discovered the name of the other [man?], that he had got on board a vessel bound to Halifax, which vessel [. . .]⁵ that he has reason to believe [that?] the offender [. . .],⁶ that the sheriff and some of his best officers [are now?] in pursuit of him, and he has no doubt he will be taken.—In order to support the civil power, I am informed the Governor has called for sufficient patroles of militias. So that I hope, [. . .] the [. . .]⁷ prepared for them, we shall soon be led by [these into all?] the measures necessary for the preservation of peace. I have the honor to be with great esteem & respect, Sir, your most obedient & most humble servt.   TH: JEFFERSON

PrC (DLC); very badly faded; at foot of text: "The Minister Plenipotentiary of France."

dealing with an "insult to French flag by Brit. sailor." See James Biddle to TJ, 31 May 1793, and note.

Genet's NOTE was a missing letter to TJ of 27 May 1793, recorded in SJL as received 28 May 1793 and there described as

¹ Estimated five words illegible.
² Estimated three or four words illegible.

[3] Estimated five or six words illegible.
[4] Estimated three words illegible.
[5] Estimated five words illegible.

[6] Estimated three words illegible.
[7] Estimated three or four words illegible.

From Edmond Charles Genet

Philadelphie le 1er. Juin 1793. l'an 2e. de la République Française.

Je viens d'etre informé, Monsieur, que deux officiers au service de la République française les Citoyens Gideon Henfield et John Singletary ont été arretés à bord du corsaire de la République française le Citoyen Genet, et conduits en prison. Le crime qu'on leur impute, le crime que mon ésprit ne peut concevoir et que ma plume se refuse presque à rapporter, c'est de servir la France et de deffendre avec ses enfans la cause commune et glorieuse de la liberté.

Ne connoissant pas de loi positive ni de traité qui interdise à des americains cette faculté et qui autorise des officiers de Police d'enlever arbitrairement des marins au service de France à bord de leurs navires, Je reclame votre intervention, Monsieur, et celle du President des Etats Unis pour obtenir l'elargissement immediat des officiers susmentionnes qui ont acquis par les sentimens qui les animent et par le fait de leur engagement, anterieur a tout acte à ce contraire, le droit de Citoyen français s'ils ont perdu celui de citoyens americains—je vous renouvelle, en meme tems, Monsieur, la requisition que Je vous ai faitte en faveur d'un autre officier français detenu pour la même cause et pour le même objet.

GENET

PrC of Tr (DLC); in a clerk's hand; at head of text: "Le Citoyen Genet Ministre Plenipotentiaire de la République française pres les Etats Unis à Mr. Jefferson Secretaire d'Etat des Etats Unis." Dft (NHi: Genet Family Papers); in a clerk's hand; docketed by Genet: "Nouvelle arrestation d'officiers de corsaires réclamés par le Cit. Genet." Tr (AMAE: CPEU, xxxvii); with minor variations. Tr (NNC: Gouverneur Morris Papers). PrC of another Tr (PRO: FO 97/1); in the hand of George Taylor, Jr. FC (DLC: Genet Papers); in English. FC (same); in English. FC (same); in English; draft translation of preceding FCs. Tr (DNA: RG 46, Senate Records, 3d Cong., 1st sess.); in English. Recorded in SJL as received 1 June 1793. Printed with translation in *Message*, 10 (App.), 25; translation printed in ASP, *Foreign Relations*, I, 151. Enclosed in TJ to Gouverneur Morris, 16 Aug. 1793.

SINGLETARY: John Singleterry, a native of Charleston, South Carolina, currently residing in Beaufort, North Carolina, who was one of two American citizens being prosecuted by the Washington administration for serving on the *Citoyen Genet*, a French privateer commissioned by Genet in Charleston. The outcome of his case is unknown (*Dunlap's American Daily Advertiser*, 3 June 1793; for the case of Gideon Henfield, see Memorial from Genet, 27 May 1793, and note).

To Edmond Charles Genet

SIR   Philadelphia June 1. 1793.

I have to acknowledge the receipt of your Note of the 27th. of May on the subject of Gideon Henfield, a citizen of the United States, engaged on board an armed vessel in the service of France. It has been laid before the President, and referred to the Attorney General of the United States, for his opinion on the matter of law, and I have now the honor of enclosing you a copy of that opinion. Mr. Henfield[1] appears to be in the custody of the civil magistrate, over whose proceedings the Executive has no controul.[2] The act with which he is charged will be examined by a Jury of his Countrymen, in the presence of Judges of learning and integrity, and if it is not contrary to the laws of the land, no doubt need be entertained that his case will[3] issue accordingly. The forms of the law involve certain necessary delays; of which, however, he will assuredly experience none but what are necessary.[4] I have the honor to be, with sentiments of perfect Esteem and respect, Sir, Your most obedient and Most humble servant   TH: JEFFERSON

P.S. After writing the above I was honored with your note on the subject of Singleterry on which it is in my power to say nothing more than in that of Henfeild.

PrC (DLC); in the hand of George Taylor, Jr., except for correction in ink, signature, and postscript by TJ; at foot of text: "M. Genet Minister plenipotentiary of France." Dft (DLC); entirely in TJ's hand, unsigned; lacks postscript and varies in other respects from PrC (see notes below); note written on verso by TJ at a later date: "A clause stood in the original draught in these words. 'It will give me great pleasure to be able to communicate to you &c.—animadversion' (see it still legible on the other side). E.R. objected to it as conveying a wish that the act might not be punisheable, and proposed it should be 'it will give me great pleasure to be able to communicate to you that on his examination he shall be found to be innocent.' ⟨The letter with this⟩ It was done. The letter with this alteration was sent into the country to Colo. Hamilton, who found the clause, even as altered, to be too strong and proposed it should be omitted. It was therefore struck out altogether. See his letter of June 3." PrC of Tr (DLC); in a clerk's hand. Tr (NNC: Gouverneur Morris Papers). PrC of another Tr (DNA:

RG 59, MD); in a clerk's hand. Tr (DNA: RG 46, Senate Records, 3d Cong., 1st sess.). PrC (PRO: FO 97/1). FC (Lb in DNA: RG 59, DL). Tr (DLC: Genet Papers). Tr (DLC: John Trumbull Letterbook); misdated 6 June 1793. Tr (DLC: Genet Papers); in French. Tr (same); in French; draft translation of preceding Tr; docketed and initialed by Genet. Tr (AMAE: CPEU, XXXVII); in French. Entry in SJPL: "Th:J. to Genet on Henfield's case. qu. if printed?" Printed in *Message*, 25. Enclosure: Edmund Randolph's Opinion on the Case of Gideon Henfield, 30 May 1793. Enclosed in TJ to Gouverneur Morris, 13 June and 16 Aug. 1793, and TJ to Thomas Pinckney, 14 June 1793; altered draft enclosed in TJ to Alexander Hamilton, 1 June [1793], and Hamilton to TJ, 3 June 1793.

Although it is clearly dated 1 June 1793, the final version of this letter could not have been completed before 4 June 1793. TJ laid a draft of the letter before a Cabinet meeting held in his office on 1 June 1793 that the

President and the Secretary of the Treasury were unable to attend. Attorney General Edmund Randolph and Secretary of War Henry Knox approved the substance of the draft, though in response to Randolph's suggestion TJ altered a sentence as recorded below in note 4. On the same day TJ sent the altered draft to Hamilton, whose further revisions, contained in a 3 June letter TJ received on the following day, are also reflected in the PrC as described in notes 3 and 4 below (Washington, *Journal*, 159).

¹ In Dft TJ here canceled "being in the."
² In Dft TJ began the next sentence with "He will" and then canceled the words.
³ In Dft TJ first wrote the remainder of

the sentence as "have the favorable issue you desire" and then, in response to a suggestion by Alexander Hamilton, altered it to read as above (see Hamilton to TJ, 3 June 1793).

⁴ As explained above, at this point in Dft TJ first wrote "It will give me great pleasure to be able to communicate to you that the laws (which admit of no controul) on being applied to the actions of Mr. Henfeild, shall have found in them ⟨nothing⟩ no cause of animadversion." Then, in response to an objection by Edmund Randolph, he lined out everything after "that" and interlined "on his examination he shall be found to be innocent." Finally, at the insistence of Alexander Hamilton, he eliminated the entire sentence.

To Alexander Hamilton

SIR   Philadelphia June 1. [1793].

I have the honor to inclose you the following papers.

Draught of a letter to Mr. Genet in answer to [his enquiry respecting Hen]field.

do.   to order away the privateers fitted out in our ports.

do. to Messrs. Carmichael and Short on the letter of Viar and Jaudenes.

do. to Viar and Jaudenes in answer to their letter.

With these are all the preceding letters respecting the same subjects.

The above are in the form approved by Genl. Knox, Mr. Randolph, and myself: and we have agreed to meet at my office on Monday at 12. aclock to consider of any alterations which you would wish to propose on my giving them previous notice.

I also inclose two other papers for signature. The third which relates to the letters of Genl. Williams [and Colo.] Smith is merely in the form of a memorandum to which no signature was thought to be requisite. I have the honor to be with great respect Sir Your most [obedt. humble Servt]   TH: JEFFERSON

PrC (DLC); badly faded; at foot of text: "The Secretary of the Treasury." Enclosures: (1) Enclosure No. 2 listed at Tobias Lear to TJ, 31 May 1793. (2) Enclosures to TJ to George Washington, 31 May 1793 (first letter). (3) Enclosure No. 1 listed at TJ to Washington, 31 May 1793 (second

letter). (4) Cabinet Opinions on Sending an Agent to the Choctaw Indians, 1 June 1793. (5) Cabinet Memorandum on French Privateers, [1 June 1793].

The PRECEDING LETTERS RESPECTING THE SAME SUBJECTS probably included TJ to Carmichael and Short, 14 Oct., 3 Nov. 1792; Viar and Jaudenes to TJ, 7, 25 May 1793; Jaudenes and Viar to TJ, 12 May 1793; and TJ to Viar and Jaudenes, 21 May 1793.

To Gouverneur Morris

DEAR SIR   Philadelphia June 1. 1793.

The bearer hereof Majr. Jackson formerly of the army, and afterwards of the President's family, is already too well known to you to need any recommendations from me. Yet a sense of his merit will not permit me to forbear mentioning that your attentions to him will confer an obligation on me. The circumstances of the times too may perhaps render the attentions of your office necessary for him, in which case, as one among our best citizens, I am sure he will have the benefit of them. I am happy in every occasion of expressing to you the sentiments of respect & esteem with which I am Dear Sir Your most obedt & most humble servt   TH: JEFFERSON

PrC (DLC); at foot of text: "Mr. Morris." Tr (DLC); 19th-century copy.

William JACKSON, the English-born South Carolina Revolutionary War officer who had served as secretary to the Constitutional Convention and as private secretary to President Washington, was about to embark for Europe as an agent to sell William Bingham's American lands. See Frederick S. Allis, Jr., *William Bingham's Maine Lands, 1790-1820* (Colonial Society of Massachusetts, *Publications*, XXXVI-XXXVII [Boston, 1954]), I, 92-3, 278-9.

From Gouverneur Morris

DR SIR   Sainport near Paris 1 June 1793

My last No. 30 was of the twentieth of May. I had the Honor to transmit therein Copies of my last Correspondence with the Minister of foreign Affairs. Herein I have the Pleasure to send a Copy of his Letter to me of the twenty sixth, covering Copy of the Decree of the twenty third.

I shall not say any Thing at present upon the State of public Affairs, but refer to what I have formerly said and the Developements contain'd in the Gazettes. With sincere Esteem & Respect I have the Honor to be Dr Sir your obedient Servant   GOUV MORRIS

RC (DNA: RG 59, DD); at head of text: "No. 31"; at foot of text: "Thomas Jefferson Esqr. Secretary of State"; endorsed by TJ as received 5 Sep. 1793 and so recorded in SJL. FC (Lb in DLC: Gouverneur Morris Papers). Tr (DNA: RG 46, Senate Records, 3d Cong., 1st sess). PrC (DNA: RG 59, MD). Tr (Lb in same, DD). Enclosures: (1) Lebrun to Morris, 26 May 1793, stating that the enclosed decree of the National Convention demonstrated anew the friendship of the French people for the

United States. (2) Decree of the National Convention, 23 May 1793, providing, in conformity with Article 16 of the 1778 treaty of commerce between France and the United States, that American ships were not comprehended in the Convention's decree of 9 May 1793 (Trs in DNA: RG 59, DD, in French; Trs in DNA: RG 46, Senate Records, 3d Cong., 1st sess., in French with English translations in the hand of George Taylor, Jr.; PrCs in DNA: RG 59, MD; Trs in Lb in same, DD, in French and English).

TJ submitted this letter to the President on 5 Sep. 1793 and received it back the same day (Washington, *Journal*, 238).

To William Short

DEAR SIR   Philadelphia June 1. 1793.

The bearer hereof is Major Jackson, formerly of the army, and afterwards of the President's family. Supposing it possible he may see you at Madrid, I with pleasure make him known to you, as a gentleman of information talents and worth. He merits well any attentions you can shew him, and I also will be thankful for them. Should he, from the circumstances of the times, need your official interferences, I am sure that, as one among our best citizens, he will have the benefit of them. I am with sincere and constant attachment Dear Sir Your affectionate friend   TH: JEFFERSON

RC (PHi: Society Collection); addressed: "Mr. Short Minister resident of the US. of America at the Hague and one of their Commissioners Plenipotentiary now at Madrid by Majr. Jackson"; endorsed by William Jackson: "from Mr. Jefferson to Mr. Short introducing WJ not presented as I did not go to Madrid." PrC (DLC). Tr (DLC); 19th-century copy.

As William Jackson's endorsement indicates, Short never received this letter. On this day TJ wrote a similar letter of introduction to William Carmichael, Short's fellow American commissioner in Madrid, which Jackson must also not have delivered (PrC in DLC, at foot of text: "Mr. Carmichael"; Tr in DLC, 19th-century copy).

From James Simpson

Gibraltar, 1 June 1793. Having been detained by contrary winds, the vessel this letter goes by also brings his letter of 22 May, to which he adds intelligence of the capture off Cape Gata by an Algerine row boat of an American schooner from Cartagena, the *Lark*, Captain Pulling, and the escape of her master and crew to Spain. Muley Suliman, to whom most provinces have sent deputies, remains at Rabat and has sent part of his army to Shauia or Tremecena to give the alcaides Benasser and Belarosi an opportunity to join him, they having been independent and uncommitted to any of the contending princes. When Spain supported Muley Ischem against Yezid and Slema it only had communication with the part of the empire under Ischem's dominion. Now Spanish vessels have received permission to trade as before with all the ports, and according to the best authority the court at Madrid will be one of the first to send an ambassador to Suliman as soon as he establishes himself at Morocco. The reported sailing of the Toulon fleet has not been confirmed. The allied army has entered France and is before Condé and Valenciennes.

RC (DNA: RG 59, CD); 2 p.; at foot of first page: "The honble Thomas Jefferson &ca &ca"; endorsed by TJ as received 29 July 1793 and so recorded in SJL.

TJ submitted this letter to the President on 30 July 1793 (Washington, *Journal*, 211).

From Fulwar Skipwith

SIR   Trinity, Martinique, 1 June 1793.

It is now a week since the Vessel in which I took my passage from Boston, came into this place, (a small port in the Windward part of the Island) where is exhibited the most terrible scene of distress and Confusion immaginable.

About a month ago it seems that the Planters were advised of the arrival of the British fleet, at Barbados, and at the same time they received Assurance that the object of this Armament was to invade the Island, to protect the Royalists, (composed entirely of Planters) and to bend their force against the Patriots, consisting of Townspeople of St. Pierre and Fort-Royal, and the Mulatoes with Mr. Rochambeau at their head. Indeed these two Parties have been thus secretly formed and distinguished previous to the Arrival of the british fleet—Professing however submission to the existing Government, and Keeping up the Appearance of tranquillity. But, immediately on the promise of this force from Barbados, the Planters threw of the mask, changed the flag, and dispatched Deputies to the Admiral of the british Fleet, with an offer of the Island. On the other hand, Mr. Rochambeau was active in assembling and arming his Adherents, and putting the towns of Fort-Royal and St. Pierre in a state of Defense. This done, hostilities soon commenced by frequent Skirmishes; The Planters, to defend their Plantations, and the Patriots, to possess themselves of them, in order to derive a supply for Fort-Royal of provisions. In these rencontres, the former generally lost ground, when, to complete the measure of their misfortunes, there sprung up a numerous band of Plunderers, Composed mostly of their own Negroes, who have been for fifteen days, and are now employed in murdering, burning and destroying. Already, upwards of forty of the most valuable Sugar-Estates are in ashes; many more are likely to share the same fate, and the Planters are closely confined to their two last strong holds, Gros-Morne and Case-Navira; and these must likewise fall, unless early assistance be afforded by the English; what their real intention may be at present, in regard to this unhappy Island, is perhaps a little problematical, altho' they have promised to receive it at the hands of the Planters, and have actually coalesced so far with them, as to receive into their fleet a french 74, and a frigate under the white flag (the vessels that took refuge some months since at Trinidad, with a number of their part, when Mr. Rochambeau assumed the Government). This fleet, in all said to be ten sails, have been a fortnight off the Island, but have not landed a Soldier, or done more than to cut off all Communication with Fort-Royal by water; hence American Vessels cannot go there; and unluckily every shilling to which I have any Claim, lays there.

From very respectable Authority I've just learned that five American Vessels have been seized by English Privateers, and carried into St. Kitts, for having on board french property. Such property I apprehend will be condemned, but the Vessels doubtless must be released. However I shall as much as may be in my power, Caution the American Flag against committing themselves in future.

A few days before my leaving Boston, I had the honor to receive from you a Packet containing the Laws of the United States, and your two favors of May 31. 1792 and March 21. 1793. Their several Contents I shall be strictly governed by, whenever I may be placed in a situation to fulfill any one of their purposes. At present, I've no more to say than to subscribe myself &ca.　　　　　　(signed) FULWAR SKIPWITH

Tr (DLC: Causten-Pickett Papers); at head of text: "The Secretary of State, United States of America"; made by John J. Pacaud, "Chancelor of the Commercial Agency of the United States of America," from a letterbook shown to him by Skipwith in Paris, 2 Jan. 1803, as described by Pacaud's signed attestation at foot of text with agency seal affixed. Not recorded in SJL and probably not received by TJ.

From Edward Telfair

SIR　　　　　　　　　　State House, Augusta 1st June 1793

Your Communication of the 26th. April last, with its enclosure being the Proclamation of the President of the United States, enjoining a strict neutrality with the European powers at War, came this day to hand; nothing has as yet been attempted in this State, except one case, on which immediate order was taken, which is herewith transmitted: I shall make every exertion to cause a due observance of the said neutrality. I have the honor to be Sir Your most obedt. Servt.

EDRD. TELFAIR

RC (MHi: Charles E. French Collection); in the hand of William Urquhart, signed by Telfair; at foot of text: "The Secretary of The United States"; endorsed by TJ as received 21 June 1793 and so recorded in SJL. Enclosure: Executive

Order, Augusta, 17 May 1793, referring the deposition of John Cerisier concerning the fitting out of an English privateer by William Oakman and others to the Department of the Attorney General to be dealt with according to law (Tr in DNA: RG 59,

LGS; in Urquhart's hand and attested by him).

TJ submitted this letter to the President on 21 June 1793 (Washington, *Journal*, 185).

From George Washington

Sir   Philadelphia June 1st 1793

To call upon Mr. Hammond without further delay for the result of the reference to his Court concerning the surrender of the Western Posts—or to await the decision of the trial at Richmond on the subject of British debts before it be done, is a question on which my mind has been divided[1] for sometime.

If your own judgment is not *clear* in favor of one, or the other, it is my desire, as the heads of the Departments are *now* together, that you would take their opinion thereupon, and act accordingly.

Go: Washington

RC (DLC); endorsed by TJ as received 1 June 1793. FC (Lb in DNA: RG 59, SDC); with one variation (see note 1 below). Recorded in SJPL.

TJ alone or in combination with the two Cabinet officers who met with him this day—Attorney General Edmund Randolph and Secretary of War Henry Knox—evidently decided to await the DECISION of the United States Circuit Court in Richmond in the case of Ware v. Hylton, news of which became known in Philadelphia on 19 June 1793, before asking George Hammond about the British government's reaction to TJ's demand in his letter to him of 29 May 1792 for the surrender of the western posts that British troops continued to occupy on United States soil in retaliation for American violations of the Treaty of Paris, particularly with respect to the payment of

prewar debts to the British (*Gazette of the United States*, 19 June 1793; TJ to Hammond, 19 June 1793; TJ to Washington, 19 June 1793; Cabinet Opinion on Relations with Spain and Great Britain, 20 June 1793; Washington, *Journal*, 159). The decision in this noted British debt case rejected all but one of the customary legal arguments advanced on behalf of Virginians sued for payment of prewar debts by British creditors, thereby opening the gates to a host of British suits for recovery in that state. It was not until 1796, however, that the Supreme Court ruled on the final appeal in the case (Charles F. Hobson, "The Recovery of British Debts in the Federal Circuit Court of Virginia, 1790 to 1797," VMHB, XCII [1984], 187-93).

[1] FC: "balanced."

From Delamotte

Le Havre, 2 June 1793. Our political position is still the same. The allied powers attack us from all sides by land and sea and until now we have resisted them passably. But in the last two days our enemies have apparently had some success, unconfirmed reports saying that they have taken Valenciennes and

Condé. Our internal troubles hurt us more than the efforts of foreigners. Despite constant talk of bringing minds together, they grow more and more embittered. The different factions forgive each other temporarily and then fight even more furiously, and if in the end we succumb, this will probably be the cause of our ruin. Even now Paris is in a state of extreme agitation, and what little is known about it makes us fear a new effusion of blood. The exchange on London is 9½d. Tobacco is worth 100# to 105#, rice 80#, pearl ashes 125#, and flour 100# per hundredweight. If those with an interest in the *Lawrence*—bound from Charleston to London under Captain White with a cargo of indigo and rice— have learned that it was brought into this port by a French privateer seeking to have the cargo condemned as enemy property, assure them that the cargo will be delivered to its destination because four or five days ago the National Convention exempted Americans alone from the measures taken under the 9 May decree on neutral cargoes. With our government showing a complete partiality for America, TJ can easily draw the possible consequences.

RC (DNA: RG 59, CD); 2 p.; in French; in a clerk's hand, signed by Delamotte; at foot of first page: "Mr. Le Secretaire d'Etat des E. U. d'amerique"; endorsed by TJ as received 7 Sep. 1793 and so recorded in SJL.

According to SJL, a private letter from Delamotte of 2 June 1793 was also received on 7 Sep. 1793, but it has not been found.

To James Madison

June 2. 1793.

I wrote you on the 27th. Ult. You have seen in the papers that some privateers have been fitted out in Charleston by French citizens, with their own money, manned by themselves, and regularly commissioned by their nation. They have taken several prizes and brought them into our ports. Some native citizens had joined them. These are arrested and under prosecution; and orders are sent to all the ports to prevent the equipping privateers by any persons foreign or native. So far is right. But the vessels so equipped at Charleston are ordered to leave the ports of the US. This I think was not right. Hammond demanded further a surrender of the prizes they had taken. This is refused, on the principle that by the laws of war the property is transferred to the captors. You will see, in a paper I inclose, Dumourier's address to his nation, and also Saxe Cobourg's. I am glad to see a probability that the constitution of 1791. would be the term at which the combined[1] powers would stop. Consequently that the reestablishment of that is the worst the French have to fear. I am also glad to see that the combiners adopt the slow process of nibbling at[2] the strong posts on the frontiers. This will give to France a great deal of time. The thing which gives me uneasiness is their internal combustion. This may by famine be rendered extreme. E.R. sets out, the day after tomorrow, for Virginia. I have no doubt he is charged to bring back a faithful statement of the dispositions of that state. I wish therefore he may fall into hands which will not deceive him. Have you time and the means of impressing Wilson Nicholas, (who will be much with E.R.) with the necessity of giving him a strong and perfect understanding of the public mind?[3] Considering that this journey may strengthen his nerves, and dispose him more favorably to the proposition of a treaty between the two republics, knowing that in this moment the division on that question is 4. to 1. and that the last news has no tendency to proselyte any of the majority, I have my self proposed to refer taking up the question till his return. There is too at this time a lowering disposition perceivable both in England and Spain. The former keeps herself aloof and in a state of incommunication with us, except in the way of demand. The latter has not begun auspiciously with C. and S. at Madrid, and has lately sent 1500. men to N. Orleans, and greatly strengthened her upper posts on the Missisipi. I think it more probable than otherwise that Congress will be convened before the constitutional day. About the last of July this may be known. I should myself wish to keep their meeting off to the beginning of October, if affairs will permit it. The invasion of the Creeks is what will most likely occasion it's convocation. You will see Mrs. House's death mentioned in the papers. She extinguished almost like a candle. I have not seen Mrs. Trist since, but I am told she means to give up the house immediately, and that she has suffered great loss in her own fortune by exertions hitherto to support it. Browse is not returned, nor has been heard of for some time.—Bartram is extremely anxious to get a large supply of seeds of the Kentucky coffee tree. I told him I would use all my interest with you to obtain it, as I think I heard you say that some neighbor of yours had a large number of the trees. Be so good as to take measures for bringing a good quantity if possible to Bartram when you come to Congress. Adieu yours affectionately.

RC (DLC: Madison Papers); unsigned. PrC (DLC).

In his ADDRESS TO HIS NATION of 2 Apr. 1793, General Charles François du Périer Dumouriez urged France to rally around him and restore the CONSTITUTION OF 1791, a goal seconded three days later in a proclamation by the Austrian General Friedrich Josias, Prince of Saxe-Coburg. Translations of both documents appeared in the *Federal Gazette*, 1 June 1793.

[1] Word interlined in place of "allied."

[2] TJ first wrote "taking all" before altering the phrase to read as above.

[3] TJ added this sentence in a smaller hand at the foot of the first page, canceling part of the first word of the next sentence and interlining it at the top of the next page.

To Thomas Mann Randolph, Jr.

DEAR SIR   Philadelphia June 2. 1793.

I have to acknolege the receipt of yours of May 16. with the information always pleasing of your being all well.—In addition to the news which you will see in the papers, we now have the certainty of Dumourier's operation. He had proposed an armistice to the Prince of Saxe Cobourg, which was agreed to on condition of his withdrawing his troops from the Netherlands. He did so. It was then agreed that he should march with his army (on whom he thought he could rely) to Paris and reestablish the constitution of 1791. on which Cobourg stipulated peace on the part of the Emperor and K. of Prussia. Dumourier's army knew nothing of this. He made them believe the deputies sent from the National assembly were to arrest and carry him to Paris to be tried for his defeat of the 18th. to the 22d. of March. They considered this as an injury to themselves, and really loved and confided in him. They set out with him, but very soon began to suspect his purpose was to overset the republic and set up a king. They began to drop off in parties, and at length in a body refused to go further. On this he fled with 2. regiments of horse, mostly foreigners, to the Austrians. His and Saxe-Cobourg's addresses to the French nation prove all this. Hostilities recommenced: and the combiners have determined not to attempt to march to Paris, as the last year, but to take all the strong places on the frontier. This will at least give time to the republic. The first thing to be feared for them is famine. This will infallibly produce anarchy. Indeed that, joined to a draught of soldiers, has already produced some serious insurrections.—It is still a comfort to see by the addresses of Dumourier and Saxe-Cobourg that the constitution of 1791. is the worst thing which is to be forced on the French. But even the falling back to that would give wonderful vigor to our Monocrats, and unquestionably affect the tone of administering our government. Indeed I fear that if this summer should prove disastrous to the French, it will damp that energy of republicanism in our new Congress from which I had hoped so much reformation.—We have had here for a considerable time past true winter weather, quite cold enough for white frost, tho that accident has not happened. Fires are still kept up, having been intermitted only for short intervals of very hot weather.—I have not yet received my model of the threshing mill. I wish it may come in time for the present crop. After so mild a winter as the last we must expect weavil. My love to my dear Martha, and kiss the little ones for me. Adieu my dear Sir. Your's with constant affection   TH: JEFFERSON

RC (DLC). PrC (DLC); at foot of first page in ink: "Randolph mr."

From James Sullivan

Boston June 2d 1793

I have a wish to serve the public and to oblige my friend. From the office you hold, and the character you support, I venture to attempt through you to do it. Mr. de L Etombe the consul of france for this state, has rendered himself very agreeable to the people here, and has been from the reduction of the Bastile to the present moment, a friend to liberty and the french revolution: and yet it has been represented to the present Government in france that he is against the revolution there. This has been done by men who are themselves violently opposed to it, and who wish to injure him because he has opposed his sentiments to theirs.

I give you this trouble, because I beleive, that if Mr. Genet is under any wrong impressions it is in your power to convince him. The line of opinion here with regard to the french revolution is exactly the same as that which formerly divided the Whigs and the Tories. Men who are opposed to the liberty of Mankind are generally, alike opposed to it under every appearance, and in every time and place. Should the Democratical principles of Mr. d'L Etombe be called in question, he can at once obtain the Evidence of our Governor and Lieutenant Governor, and of all our republicans in his favour. Should he need Testimonies in favour of his prudence and goodness, to theirs would be added the Testimonies of all the men of public characters in our state.

As this is intended to aid a friend who I conceive to be ardently engaged in a cause which you love, the cause of Liberty I hope you will pardon the freedom I take, and allow me to assure you with how much respect I am your Most Obedient and very Humble Sert

JA SULLIVAN

RC (MoSHi: Bixby Collection); at foot of text: "His Excellency Mr Jefferson"; endorsed by TJ as received 7 June 1793 and so recorded in SJL.

From James Brown

DEAR SIR   Richmond 3d: June 1793

I am favor'd with yours of the 23d: May. Your 3 Pipes Wine are lodged in my Own Cellar apparantly in good Order Where they Shall Remain for Your further commands. I have discovered the Books from Dublin paid the Duties and landed them at Osbornes subject to the Order of Young Mr. Eppes for whom they appear to have been intended. I will make enquiry after the Mathematical Instruments ⅌ the

Cammella, I expect they are lodged at the Naval Office. Your furniture was all lodged in a good Lumber House at Rockets, every care was taken of the Glasses and I fondly hope they and the Other furniture will be found free from Damage. You had as well empower me to Send the Whole up by Boats to Warren or some other landing on James River where Mr. Randolph can send your Waggons for them.

You may write Mr. Short that his Certificates and every Penny of Interest is Safe, the Certificates are now in his Own name, When I can Spare a little time I will write him with a full State of his Matters. As to your Tobacco I shall hold it Subject to your Orders. For the Present no Ships can be had to Any Port. The confidence You are Pleased to place in me on this Score shall not be misapplied. Donald & Burton have Settled Matters With their Creditors and obtained time to pay. When I hear that matters are fully adjusted I will conclude on future arrangements for their Joint Interest. I am sorry to discover Mr. Donald has Personal Views, that to enforce them he exculpates himself from all Blame of course Rests the failure on his Partners without giving them an oportunity to clear themselves from censure. This conduct every generous Mind will condemn and Suspend Opinions till both Sides are heard. Mr. Donald is also pleased to find fault with my conduct to some of his confidential friends, Without Writing me a Single line on the Subject, however I feel perfectly easy under the charge's, as I can Satisfy every liberal mind that they are groundless, and this manner of attack below the character of a Man.

When your Carpenter and Stone mason appears I will have them sent forward to Mounticello. With due Respect I am Dear Sir Your Very Hbl: Serv   JAMES BROWN

RC (MHi); addressed: "The Honble: Thomas Jefferson Esqr Philada:"; stamped and postmarked; endorsed by TJ as received 8 June 1793 and so recorded in SJL. Tr (ViW); consists of extract of first sentence of second paragraph in TJ's hand on same sheet with extract of Brown to TJ, 15 Apr. 1793; enclosed in TJ to William Short, 11 July 1793. PrC (DLC). Tr (ViU: Edgehill-Randolph Papers); 19th-century copy of extract.

TJ had expressed his solicitude for the safe carriage of his looking GLASSES in let-

ters to Brown of 7 and 10 Apr. 1793, and in a check dated 3 July 1793 drawn on the Bank of the United States he paid James Reynolds, a carver and gilder in Philadelphia, 99.53 dollars for framing them (Facsimile of printed form with blanks filled in and signed by TJ, in Jefferson Rarities Collection Catalogue No. 101, [1992], Lot 234; with preprinted "1792" altered by TJ). See also MB, 3 July 1793; and Hardie, *Phila. Dir.*, 15.

From Matthew Clarkson

Sir Philadelphia June 3d. 1793.

Having understood that it was Doctor Foulke who gave to Mr. Moissonier the names of the two persons who are represented in the Vice Consuls Memorial, as having excited the English Sailors to continue the Quarrel with the People of the Ambuscade, The Doctor has been so obliging as to call upon me, at my request, to inform me what he knew of the matter.

The following is the substance of what he told me, Vizt.

That on the 29th. ulto. at the time the riot happened, he was standing at his Door, when Mr. Moissonier represented to him, that he had seen Several persons encouraging the English Seamen to beat the French men; and occasioned great tumult, that he asked Mr. Moissonier if he could discover any of the persons who had been active in so doing, that Mr. Moissonier pointed out a person who he said was one of them; that he (the Doctor) knows him to be a man whose name is Peter, and is a domestick of the Spanish Chargé des'affaires; that he went to the said Peter and spoke to him, and told him that he had better go home and let the Frenchmen alone, or that he would get into trouble, to which he answered that "he knew what he was about," and went on with the crowd.

The Doctor says, that he also saw George Abbot a Hair-Dresser, running along side of the French-men; that he spoke to him, and desired him to go home; he answered "he would be damned if he did, for he intended to have a Crack at the French-men for beating one of his Comrades." That the Doctor told Mr. Moissonier his name, upon being asked who he was.

The Doctor adds that he hath mentioned to Mr. Viar what passed between his domestick, *Peter*, and him, and that he appeared Very much displeased with his Conduct. I am with much esteem Sir Your most obedt. humbl. Servt.

MATTH CLARKSON
Mayor

RC (DNA: RG 59, MLR); at foot of text: "Thomas Jefferson Secretary of State"; endorsed by TJ as received 4 June 1793 and so recorded in SJL.

Matthew Clarkson (1733-1800), a native of New York City, moved to Philadelphia as a child and spent the rest of his life there as a merchant and public official. He served as mayor of Philadelphia from 1792 to 1796, earning praise for his energetic and courageous efforts to combat the yellow fever epidemic of 1793, and was a long-standing member of the American Philosophical Society (John Hall and Samuel Clarkson, *Memoirs of Matthew Clarkson of Philadelphia . . . and of his Brother Gerardus Clarkson . . .* [Philadelphia, 1890], 17-80; APS, *Proceedings*, XXII, pt. 3 [1885], 33, 101, 110).

PETER: Petter Ardens, a Flemish native. See list of servants enclosed in Josef de Jaudenes and Josef Ignacio de Viar to TJ, 27 June 1792 (Vol. 24: 129n).

From James Currie

Richmond, 3 June 1793. He introduces Alexander Maitland, a young English gentleman formerly of the British Navy who has come to see America and amuse himself—having been recommended by Currie's friends in Europe, who say he is well connected in England and Jamaica, whence he lately came—and requests TJ's attention to him as he passes to the north.

RC (MHi); 1 p.; endorsed by TJ as received 14 June 1793 and so recorded in SJL.

From Alexander Hamilton

Sir   Treasury Department June 3d. 1793

It was not till within an hour, that I received your letter of the 1st with the papers accompanying it. I approve all the Drafts of letters, as they stand, except that I have some doubt about the concluding sentence of *that* on the subject of *Henfield*. If the *facts* are (as I presume they are) established—may it not be construed into a wish, that there may be found no law to punish a conduct in our citizens, which is of a tendency dangerous to the peace of the Nation and injurious to powers with whom we are on terms of peace and neutrality?

I should also like to substitute to the words "have the *favourable* issue you desire" these words "issue accordingly."

I retain till tomorrow the paper relating to an Agent to the Choctaws. My judgment is not intirely made up on the point—the state of my family's and of my own health for some days having prevented due reflection upon it. With great respect I have the honor to be, Sir Your obedient Servant   A Hamilton

RC (DLC); at foot of text: "The Secretary of State"; endorsed by TJ as received 4 June 1793. For the enclosures, see Enclosures Nos. 1-3 and 5 listed at TJ to Hamilton, 1 June [1793].

Jefferson and the
American Debt to France

EDITORIAL NOTE

The documents printed below have been grouped here in order to record more clearly, with the benefit of Jefferson's connecting commentary, the process by which the Washington administration rejected Edmond Charles Genet's request for a substantial advance payment of the American debt to France. On instructions from the Provisional Executive Council of France, Genet had pledged to use the advance to purchase provisions in the United States for the French Republic and its colonies—a strategy that reflected the broader Girondin plan of enlisting extensive American support for the French war effort against the allied coalition—but in contrast to other issues involving American relations with France during the neutrality crisis of 1793, there was general agreement in the administration over the advisability of rejecting his request. The only major point of disagreement between Jefferson and Alexander Hamilton in this respect was over how best to inform the French minister of this decision, and with the President's mediation the two great antagonists for once managed to reconcile their differences without much difficulty.

Jefferson immediately recognized the significance of Genet's proposal on the debt and sought a prompt response to it. On 24 May 1793, the day after he received Genet's letter of 22 May 1793 on this issue with its enclosures, Jefferson met with Washington, submitted the French texts of these documents to him, and promised to provide translations. During this meeting Washington revealed his own disinclination to approve Genet's request by informing Jefferson of his belief that the United States should respond cautiously to any overtures from the French Republic because "it was impossible to decide with precision what would be the final issue of the contest" in Europe (Washington, *Journal*, 148). Jefferson submitted translations of the relevant documents to Washington on 27 May and three days later sent copies in French for referral to Hamilton if the President thought fit to do so. But when on 31 May the President asked the Secretary of State to draft a letter on his behalf asking Hamilton for a report on these papers, he accepted instead Jefferson's suggestion that the Cabinet consider this matter when it met the next day. In Hamilton's absence, however, the Cabinet members who met on 1 June came to no decision on Genet's proposal, and Jefferson proposed to send the enclosures to the Treasury Secretary for his opinion. Washington, however, preferring to make the referral himself so that a report on the debt "might be given in answer to Mr. Genet & the proceedings in the business be regular," reiterated the same day his request to Jefferson for a letter in the President's name asking Hamilton for a report (TJ to Washington, 27, 30 May 1793; Tobias Lear to TJ, 31 May 1793; Washington, *Journal*, 151-3, 155, 156, 157, 159). Jefferson soon drafted a letter in which the President directed the Secretary of the Treasury to submit a report on Genet's proposal in accordance with a March 1793 Cabinet decision rejecting a similar proposition by William Stephens Smith, and to consider the possibility of paying in advance the remaining installments on the debt to France for 1793. Significantly, Washington omitted the latter suggestion in the text of the letter he actually sent to Hamilton (Documents I and II below).

The President's directive to the Secretary of the Treasury led to a short-lived difference of opinion between Jefferson and Hamilton that Washington resolved in Jefferson's favor. Hamilton submitted a draft report to the President recommending that the government summarily reject the French minister's proposal without offering any explanation for its decision (Document IV below). Finding this to be "rather too dry & abrupt an answer," Washington sent the report to Jefferson with an undated letter requesting the Secretary of State to meet with him early the next morning. Jefferson's endorsement indicates that he received the letter on 5 June, but the President's journal states that it was written a day later—a conflict in dating that, like similar disparities in Washington's journal relating to some of the later documents in this episode, is simply irreconcilable in light of the existing evidence (Document III below; Washington, *Journal*, 163). After reading Hamilton's report, Jefferson advised Washington that the Secretary of the Treasury could cite the deleterious financial consequences of Genet's proposal for the United States as reasons for rejecting it without offending the French, and suggested once again that the government make the small gesture of paying in advance the remaining 1793 installments on the debt if it could be done without risking war or double payment in the event that the French Republic was overthrown and the monarchy was restored (Document V below). Washington forwarded Jefferson's recommendations to Hamilton with his approval, and the Treasury Secretary, while ignoring Jefferson's support for a limited advance payment on the French debt, added a section to his draft report explaining that the United States could not comply with Genet's proposal because it was unable to contract the new foreign loans needed to make the payment in specie and was unwilling to risk its credit or that of France by making the payment in interest-bearing bonds. Washington submitted the revised report to Jefferson, who recommended to him that Hamilton delete everything in the report preceding his addition and explain why the French promise to purchase provisions in the United States with the advance was not a compelling inducement. As before, the President passed these recommendations on to Hamilton, who again revised his report (Documents VI and VII below; Washington, *Journal*, 163, 164). Thus, except for the limited advance on the debt urged by the Secretary of State, Hamilton's final report of 8 June, which he submitted to Washington two days later, generally accorded with Jefferson's wishes. The Secretary of State transmitted the report to Genet with a conciliatory letter of 11 June 1793. Despite the reasoned explanations in the final report, the administration's decision was a heavy blow to the French minister because the Girondin ministry that appointed him had anticipated that advances on the debt would provide the major source of income for his diplomatic mission (Documents VIII and IX below; Washington, *Journal*, 165; Ammon, *Genet Mission*, 71).

Jefferson carefully preserved many of the documents pertaining to this episode, and added explanatory comments to link some of them in what later became the "Anas," no doubt to underscore the contrast between his own sympathy for revolutionary France and Hamilton's antipathy to it. Although the President's mediation ensured that Hamilton's final report reflected Jefferson's solicitude for the French Republic, Washington's recourse to the Secretary of State on 4 June 1793 for an assessment of Hamilton's proposal to open a new foreign loan for an entirely different purpose initiated a parallel set of exchanges that continued beyond the present episode and elicited more vehement, though less successful, responses from Jefferson (see Washington to TJ, 4, 16 June 1793, and enclosures; and TJ's opinions of 5 and 17 June 1793).

I. Thomas Jefferson to George Washington

June[1] 3. 93.

Th: Jefferson with his respects to the President has the honor of inclosing him the draught of a reference to the Secretary of the Treasury, with the papers to be referred, on the subject of the French debt. The latter clause of the letter is inserted merely for the consideration of the President.

RC (DNA: RG 59, MLR); addressed: "The President of the US."; endorsed by Tobias Lear. Tr (Lb in same, SDC). Not recorded in SJL. Enclosures: (1) Document II below. (2) Edmond Charles Genet's third letter to TJ, 22 May 1793, and enclosures.

[1] Word interlined by an unidentified hand in place of "Mar."

II. George Washington to Alexander Hamilton

SIR

June 3. 1793.

The question of admitting modifications of the debt of the US. to France having been the subject of a consultation with the heads of the departments and the Attorney general, and an unanimous opinion given thereon which involves the inclosed propositions from the French minister, you will be pleased, under the form of a report to me, to prepare what may serve as an answer, making it conformeable to the opinion already given. If however the instalments of the present year can be made a matter of accomodation, and it be mutual, their near approach may perhaps admit it within the spirit of the opinion given.

PrC of Dft (DLC); entirely in TJ's hand, unsigned; at foot of text: "The Secretary of the Treasury." Entry in SJPL: "draught of a lre from G.W. to A.H. on paiments to France." Enclosed in Document I above.

TJ submitted the above letter to the President this day. Washington omitted the final sentence in the text he sent to Hamilton (Washington, *Journal*, 159; Fitzpatrick, *Writings*, XXXII, 485). For the UNANIMOUS OPINION of the Cabinet against a similar request by William Stephens Smith, see Cabinet Opinion on the American Debt to France, 2 Mch. 1793.

III. George Washington to Thomas Jefferson

DEAR SIR   [5 June 1793]

The Secretary of the Treasury left the enclosed to day (without my seeing him) and is to call to morrow morning to know how it is approved, or what alterations to make.

Whether to assign, or not to assign reasons for non-complying with the French Ministers proposals is one question—and the footing on which to decline doing it another. I wish you to consider these and if it is not convenient for you to take Breakfast with me at half past Seven tomorrow—to send in the Report, with your sentiments thereon by that time. I sent to your Office for this purpose to day but you had just left the City. Yours always   GO: WASHINGTON

RC (DLC: TJ Papers, 87: 15076); undated; addressed: "Mr: Jefferson"; endorsed by TJ as received 5 June 1793 and so dated conjecturally. Entry in SJPL under 5 June 1793: "G.W. to Th:J. with a report of A.H's on paimts to France." For conflicting evidence as to the date, see Washington, *Journal*, 163. Enclosure: Document IV below.

IV. Alexander Hamilton's Draft Report on the American Debt to France, with Jefferson's Commentary

[5 June 1793]

The Secy. of the Treasury, to whom were referred by the President of the US. sundry documents communicated by the Min. Plenipy. of the Republic of France, respectfully makes the following report thereupon.

The object of the communication appears to be to engage the US. to enter into arrangements for discharging the residue of the debt which they owe to France by an *anticipated* payment of the instalments not yet due, either in specie, bank bills of equal currency with specie, or Government bonds, bearing interest and payable at certain specified periods, upon condition that the sum advanced shall be invested in productions of the US. for the supply of the French dominions.

This object is the same which came under consideration on certain propositions lately made by Colo. W. S. Smith who appeared to have been charged by the Provisional Executive Council of France with a negociation concerning it; in reference to which it was determined by the President with the concurring opinions of the heads of department and the Attorney general that the measure was ineligible, and that the proposer should be informed that it did not consist with the arrangements of the government to adopt it.

The grounds of the determination were purely political. Nothing has hitherto happened to weaken them. The decision on the application of the Min. pleny. of France will therefore naturally correspond with that on the propositions of Col. Smith. This indeed is signified to be the intention of the President.

It consequently only remains to make known the determination to the Minister, in answer to his application with or without reasons.

The following considerations seem to recommend a simple communication of the determination without reasons, viz.

I. The US. not being bound by the terms of their contract to make the anticipated payments desired, there is no necessity for a specification of the motives for not doing it.

II. No adequate reasons but the true ones can be assigned for the non-compliance; and the assignment of these would not be wholly without inconvenience. The mention of them might create difficulties in some future stage of affairs, when they may have lost a considerable portion of their force.

The following answer in substance, is presumed then to be the most proper which can be given . . . . .

"That a proposition to the same effect was not long since brought forward by Col. Smith, as having been charged with a negociation on the subject, by the Provisional Executive Council of France. That it was then, upon full consideration, concluded not to accede to the measure, for reasons which continue to operate, and consequently lead at this time to the same conclusion. That an explanation of these reasons would with pleasure be entered into, were it not for the considerations that it could have no object of present utility, and might rather serve to occasion embarrasment in future."[1]

⟨*Which is humbly submitted.*⟩[2]

The above having been communicated by the President to me, I wrote the following letter.

Tr (DLC: TJ Papers, 87: 15039); entirely in TJ's hand, with commentary subjoined by him; undated; ellipsis in original. Recorded in SJPL under 5 June 1793: "A.H's report."

FOLLOWING LETTER: Document v below.

[1] Closing quotation mark supplied.
[2] For an explanation of this cancellation, see Document vi below.

V. Thomas Jefferson to George Washington

SIR   June 6. 1793.

I cannot but think that to decline the propositions of Mr. Genet on the subject of our debt, without assigning any reasons at all, would have a very dry and unpleasant aspect indeed. We are then to examine what are our good reasons for the refusal, which of them may be spoken out, and which may not.   1. want of confidence in the continuance of the present form of government, and consequently that *advances* to them might commit us with their successors. This cannot be spoken out. 2. since they propose to take the debt in produce, it would be better for us that it should be done in moderate masses yearly, than all in one year. This cannot be professed.   3. when M. de Calonne was minister of finance, a Dutch company proposed to buy up the whole of our debt, by dividing it into actions or shares. I think Mr. Claviere, now minister of finance, was their agent. It was observed to M. de Calonne that to create such a mass of American paper, divide it into shares, and let them deluge the market, would depreciate them, the rest of our paper, and our credit in general. That the credit of a nation was a delicate and important thing and should not be risked on such an operation. M. de Calonne, sensible of the injury of the operation to us, declined it. In May 1791,[1] there came, thro' Mr. Otto, a similar proposition from Schweizer, Jeanneret & Co. We had a representation on the subject from Mr. Short, urging this same reason strongly. It was referred to the Secretary of the Treasury, who in a letter to yourself assigned the reasons against it, and these were communicated to Mr. Otto, who acquiesced in them. This objection then having been sufficient to decline the proposition twice before, and having been urged to the two preceding forms of government (the antient and that of 1791) will not be considered by them as founded in objections to the present form.   4. the law allows the whole debt to be paid only on condition it can be done on terms *advantageous* to the US. The minister foresees this objection and thinks he answers it by observing the *advantage* which the paiment in *produce* will occasion. It would be easy to shew that this was not the sort of advantage the legislature meant, but a *lower rate of interest.* 5. I cannot but suppose that the Secretary of the Treasury, much more familiar than I am with the money operations of the treasury, would on examination be able to derive practical[2] objections from them. We pay to France but 5. per cent. The people of this country would never subscribe their money for less than 6. If to remedy this, obligations at less than 5. per cent were offered and accepted by Mr. Genet, he must part with them immediately at a considerable discount to indemnify the loss of the 1. per cent: and at a still greater discount to bring them down[3] to par with our present 6. per cents: so that the operation would be equally disgraceful to us and losing to them &c. &c. &c.

I think it very material myself to keep alive the friendly sentiments of that country as far as can be done without risking war, or double payment. If the instalments falling due in this year can be advanced, without incurring those dangers, I should be for doing it. We now see by the declaration of the Prince of Saxe-Cobourg on the part of Austria and Prussia that the ultimate point they desire is to restore the constitution of 1791. Were this even to be done before the pay-days of this year, there is no doubt in my mind but that that government (as republican as the present except in the form of it's executive) would confirm an advance so moderate in sum and time. I am sure *the nation* of France would never suffer their government to go to war *with us* for such a bagatelle, and the more surely if that bagatelle shall have been granted by us so as to *please* and not to *displease the nation*; so as to keep their affections engaged on our side. So that I should have no fear in advancing the instalments of this year at epochs convenient to the treasury, but at any rate should be for assigning reasons for not changing the form of the debt. These thoughts are very hastily thrown on paper, as will be but too evident. I have the honor to be with sentiments of sincere attachment & respect, Sir your most obedient & most humble servt

TH: JEFFERSON

RC (DNA: RG 59, MLR); at foot of first page: "the President of the US."; endorsed by Bartholomew Dandridge, Jr. PrC (DLC). Tr (Lb in DNA: RG 59, SDC). Recorded in SJPL.

This letter consists of TJ's observations on Document IV above.

For the 1786 proposal to transfer to a group of private Dutch investors the WHOLE OF OUR DEBT to France, see enclosure to TJ to Washington, 17 Oct. 1792, and note. The

SIMILAR PROPOSITION FROM SCHWEIZER, JEANNERET & CO. is discussed in Editorial Note on the debt to France, in Vol. 20: 175-97. The REPRESENTATION on this subject from William Short consisted of his 18 Dec. 1790 letter to Hamilton and its enclosures (Syrett, *Hamilton*, VII, 355-68). LETTER TO YOURSELF: no letter has been found from Hamilton to Washington discussing at length the REASONS AGAINST the proposed purchase by the Parisian bankers Schweitzer, Jeanneret & Cie. But Hamilton did write such a letter to TJ, who conveyed the substance of it to Louis Guillaume OTTO, the former French chargé d'affaires in the United States (Hamilton to TJ, 12 Apr. 1791, and TJ to Otto, 7 May 1791, in Vol. 20: 199, 203). For the section of the 4 Aug. 1790 public debt act relating to the payment of the foreign debt ON TERMS ADVANTAGEOUS TO THE US., see *Annals*, II, 2304.

[1] Sentence to this point interlined in place of "While we were at New York."
[2] Word interlined.
[3] Word interlined.

VI. Alexander Hamilton's Addition to His Draft Report, with Jefferson's Commentary

[6-7 June 1793]

The President concurring with the Preceeding letter, and so signifying to Colo. Hamilton he erased the words 'Which is humbly submitted' on the former report, and added on the same paper as follows.

If nevertheless the President should be of opinion that reasons ought to be assigned the following seem to [be][1] the best which the nature of the case will admit, viz.

'Two modes of reimbursing or discharging *by anticipation* the residue of the debt which the US. owe to France are proposed.

The first by a payment in specie, or bank bills having currency equal with specie which amounts to the same thing.

The second by Government bonds, bearing interest, and payable at certain specified periods.

With regard to the first expedient the resources of the Treasury of the US. do not admit of it's being adopted. The government has relied for the means of reimbursing the foreign debt of the country on loans to be made abroad. The late events in Europe have thrown a temporary obstacle in the way of these loans producing an inability to make anticipated payments of sums hereafter to grow due.

With regard to the second expedient, it has repeatedly come under consideration, and has uniformly been declined, as ineligible. The government has perceived, and continues to perceive great inconveniences to it's credit tending to the derangement of it's general operations of finance in every plan which is calculated to throw suddenly upon the market a large additional sum of it's bonds. The present state of things, for obvious reasons, would serve to augment the evil of such a circumstance; while the existing and possible exigencies of the US. admonish them to be particularly cautious, at the present juncture, of any measure which may in any degree serve to impair or hazard their credit.

[181]

These considerations are the more readily yielded to, from a belief that the utility of the measure to France might not on experiment prove adequate to the sacrifices which she would have to make in the sale of the bonds."

All which is humbly submitted.

This being put into my hands by the President I wrote the following note.

Tr (DLC: TJ Papers, 87: 15040); entirely in TJ's hand, including his commentary consisting of first and last paragraphs; undated, but conjecturally assigned to 6 or 7 June 1793. Entry in SJPL under 6 June 1793: "A. H's addition to his report."

THE PRECEEDING LETTER: Document V above. THE FORMER REPORT: Document IV above. THE FOLLOWING NOTE: Document VII below.

[1] Word supplied.

VII. Thomas Jefferson to George Washington

[June 7. 93.]

Th: Jefferson has the honor of returning to the President [the report of the Secretary of the Treasury on the proposition of Mr. Genet. He is of opinion that all may be omitted which precedes the words 'two modes of reimbursing or discharging &c.'] What follows [. . .] [the reasons which are proper] and not offensive. [The following passage should perhaps be] altered. 'It has repeatedly come under consideration and has uniformly been declined &c.' The present proposition varies from that repeatedly offered, in a circumstance, which is of some importance and is accordingly marked by the minister, viz. the offer to take the whole in the produce of the US.—A very short alteration will qualify this expression so as to accomodate it to the fact, without abating the force of the argument.

PrC (DLC); badly faded and illegible in part, with bracketed passages consisting of words overwritten in pencil by a later hand. Recorded in SJPL under 7 June 1793: "Th:J. to G.W. on [A. H's additions to his report]."

The REPORT OF THE SECRETARY OF THE TREASURY on the French debt, as revised by Hamilton, has not been found, but it can be reconstructed from Documents IV and VI above. For the final text of the report, which reflected most of TJ's suggestions, see Document VIII below.

VIII. Alexander Hamilton's Report on the American Debt to France

The Secretary of the Treasury to whom was referred a Communication from the Minister Plenipotentiary of the Republic of France, on the subject of the Debts of the United States to France, respectfully makes thereupon the following Report.

The object of this communication is to engage the United States to enter into an arrangement for discharging the residue of the debt which they owe to France; by an anticipated payment of the Installments not yet due, either in specie or bank bills of equal currency with specie, or in Government Bonds, bearing interest and payable at certain specified periods; upon condition that the sum advanced shall be invested in productions of the United States, for the supply of the French Dominions.

With regard to the first expedient, namely a payment in Specie or bank bills, the resources of the Treasury of the United States do not admit of its being adopted. The Government has relied for the means of reimbursing its foreign debt on new Loans to be made abroad. The late events in Europe have thrown a temporary obsticle in the way of these loans; producing consequently an inability to make payment, by anticipation, of the residue of the debt hereafter to grow due.

With regard to the second expedient, that of Government Bonds payable at certain specified periods; this in substance, though in other forms, has repeatedly come under consideration, and has as often been declined as inelegible. Great inconveniencies to the credit of the Government, tending to derange its general operations of finance have been, and must continue to be perceived, in every plan, which is calculated to throw suddenly upon the market a large additional sum of its bonds. The present state of things, for obvious reasons, would serve to augment the evil of such a circumstance; while the existing and possible exigencies of the United States admonish them to be particularly cautious, at this juncture, of any measure, which may tend to hazard or impair their Credit.

These considerations greatly outweigh the advantage which is suggested as an inducement to the measure (the condition respecting which is the principal circumstance of difference between the present and former propositions)—to arise from an investment of the sum to be advanced in the products of the Country; an Advantage on which perhaps little stress can be laid, in the present and probable state of foreign demand for these products.

The motives which dissuade from the adoption of the proposed measure, may, it is conceived, be the more readily yielded to, from the probability that the utility of it to France might not, on experiment, prove an equivalent for the sacrifices which she might have to make in the disposition of the bonds.

All which is humbly submitted

(Signed) ALEXANDER HAMILTON
Secy of the Treasy

Treasury Department
June 8th: 1793

Tr (DLC); in Tobias Lear's hand; at foot of text: "A True Copy—Tobias Lear Secretary to the President of the United States." Tr (AMAE: CPEU, Supplément, xx); in the hand of George Taylor, Jr. Tr (NNC: Gouverneur Morris Papers). Tr (DNA: RG 46, Senate Records, 3d Cong., 1st sess.). PrC (PRO: FO 97/1). Tr (Lb in DLC: Washington Papers). Tr (Lb in DNA: RG 59, DL). Tr (AMAE: CPEU, xxxvii, in French). Tr (DLC: Genet Papers); in French; draft translation of preced-

ing Tr. Printed in *Message*, 34-5. Enclosed in Document ix below, TJ to Edmond Charles Genet, 11 June 1793, TJ to Gouverneur Morris, 13 June and 16 Aug. 1793, and TJ to Thomas Pinckney, 14 June 1793.

Hamilton had enclosed this final state of his report in a letter to Washington of 8 June 1793 stating that it had been "altered in conformity to your desire" (Syrett, *Hamilton*, xiv, 523).

IX. George Washington to Thomas Jefferson

June 10th: 1793

The President sends to the Secretary of State the enclosed copy of a Report made by the Secretary of the Treasury to him—relative to the Debts of the United States to France, in order that it may be communicated to the Minister of the Republic of France.

RC (DLC); in the hand of Tobias Lear; address almost entirely torn away; endorsed by TJ as received 10 June 1793. Entry in SJPL: "duplicate of ante June 5." Enclosure: Document viii above.

From James Maury

Liverpool, 3 June 1793. He encloses a price current for this place and regards the prices affixed as nominal because for three months there has scarcely been a sale of consequence as a result of the stagnation of business arising from the distresses of the commercial part of the community.

RC (DNA: RG 59, CD); 1 p.; at foot of text: "Secretary of State to the United states of America Philadelphia"; endorsed by TJ as received 1 Aug. 1793 and so recorded in SJL. Enclosure: Price current of American produce at Liverpool, 3 June 1793, with subjoined extracts from Lloyd's list of quotations for stock, exchange with Paris, and gold and silver, 31 May 1793 (printed form in same; signed by Maury, with prices entered in his hand; endorsed by Maury: "For these three months past there have scarcely been any sales Owing to the Calamity of the Times, so that these Prices are rather Nominal. J.M.").

From John Nixon

Sir   Monday June 3d. 1793

By yesterdays post I received directions from Mr. Cruger to inform you, that Capt. Burke was in New York with the Condemnation of his Vessell and sundry other documents respecting her Seizure. That should you think it necessary that he (Mr. Cruger) or Capt. Burke should come forward at this time, they will immediately appear here to answer any Questions that may be thought necessary to Explain this business or will send the papers on for your Examination. I shall therefore thank you to let me know, what information I shall give Mr. Cruger on this Occasion, as he seems extremely anxious to know what he is to Expect from the determination, which may be taken here. I remain with great Respect Your most hum Servt   John Nixon

RC (DNA: RG 76, France, Unbound Records); at foot of text: "Thomas Jefferson Esqr."; endorsed by TJ as received 3 June 1793 and so recorded in SJL.

From David Rittenhouse

Sir   June 3d. 1793

I was unwilling to ask a further Sum of money on account of the Mint until the Treasurer had obtained a Settlement of his Accounts at the Comptrollers Office, which is now done, to the 1st. of April last. This has obliged me to advance considerably for the Expenditures of the Mint, and I must request you to apply to the President for his Warrant for 5000 Dollars, in favour of the Mint. In future I hope our expences will be greatly diminished, the Necessary Buildings and Machinery being nearly compleated. I have subjoined a Short State of the Mint Accounts at this day. I am, Sir, your most obedient Servant

DAVD. RITTENHOUSE, Direcr of the Mint

	Dollars
Mint in advance as ℔ Statement March 22d	1063.25
Paid Since, For Copper Since purchased, Vizt.	
11,353 ℔.	2624.99
Officers Salaries & Clerks pay, complete to March 31	2400.
Workmen employed at the Mint 10. Weeks	609.58
For Materials Carpenters & Millwrights Bills & other Expences	1455.02
	8152.84
Presidents Warrant of March 25th. 1793	5000.
Ballance, Mint in advance, June 3d. 1793	3152.84 Drs.

RC (DNA: RG 59, MLR); below signature: "Mr. Jefferson"; endorsed by Tobias Lear.

TJ sent this letter to the President this day with a brief covering note describing it as "containing a general statement of the expenditure of the last monies furnished, and an application of a further sum of 5000. D."

(RC in DNA: RG 59, MLR, addressed: "The President of the US.," endorsed by Bartholomew Dandridge, Jr.; Tr in Lb in same, SDC). Washington immediately instructed the Secretary of the Treasury to pay the desired sum (Washington to Hamilton, 3 June 1793, Syrett, *Hamilton*, XIV, 514; Washington, *Journal*, 160).

To George Washington

June 3. 93.

Th: Jefferson respectfully submits to the President the draught of a letter to Mr. Hammond on the subject of the prizes taken by the Charleston privateers. Mr. Randolph has read and approved it. He has had no opportunity of communicating it to the Secretaries of the Treasury and War. The former is still prevented from coming to town by the situation of his family.

RC (DNA: RG 59, MLR); addressed: "The President of the US."; endorsed by Bartholomew Dandridge, Jr. Tr (Lb in same, SDC). Not recorded in SJL. Enclosure: Draft of TJ to George Hammond, 3 June 1793 (see TJ to Hammond, 5 June 1793).

In reply to this communication, Washington informed TJ in a brief note of this date that he "approves the enclosed draught of a letter to the Minister Plenipo. from Great Britain" (RC in DLC; in the hand of Tobias Lear; addressed: "The Secretary of State"; recorded in SJPL).

To Nathaniel Anderson

SIR   Philadelphia June 4. 1793.

I am just now favored with yours of May 26th. The neutrality of the US. so far as depends on France is on the f[irmest] ground. Her minister has not only not required our guarantee of the W. India islands, but has declared that France does not wish to interrupt our peace and prosperity by doing it. She wishes [us] to remain in peace, and has opened all her ports in every part [of the] world to our vessels on the same footing as to her own. With respect to England, if she consults either justice, public[1] economy, or the private interest of her citizens, she will certainly leave us neutral.—You say you are about purchasing an *American* ship. The merchants seem not to have adverted sufficiently to the circumstance that [it] suffices that a vessel be *American-owned* to be entitled to the *protection of our flag*: if she be *American-built*, also, she has the additional title to pay *lower duties* at home.[2] But if a vessel *belong to Americans*, [no] foreigner has a right to touch her any more than they might [any] other American property. The Custom house officers have [been] accordingly instructed to give passports to all vessels bonâ fide *owned* by American citizens. Were we to depend on our *home-built* vessels only, much of our productions must remain on our hands. It would be well that this circumstance were made more known to the merchants. I am with great esteem Dear Sir your friend & servt

TH: JEFFERSON

PrC (DLC); with faded words supplied from Tr in PRO; at foot of text: "Mr. N. Anderson." Tr (PRO: FO 95/1); with extract of TJ to James Brown, 9 June 1793, on verso. Tr (DLC); 19th-century copy; with gaps for words faded in PrC filled by a different hand.

Anderson and fellow Richmond merchant James Brown, to whom a few days later TJ sent a similar statement of the recent decision to GIVE PASSPORTS to all American-owned ships, whether foreign-built or not,

evidently took TJ's hint and made this information KNOWN TO THE MERCHANTS, for on 20 June 1793 John Hamilton, the British consul at Norfolk, sent Lord Grenville a copy of this letter and an extract from that to Brown, which he described collectively as a "circular letter" to merchants in the United States (TJ to Brown, 9 June 1793; Hamilton to Grenville, 20 June 1793, PRO: FO 95/1).

[1] Word interlined in place of "or."
[2] Preceding two words interlined.

To James Currie

DEAR SIR   Philadelphia June 4. 1793.

Yours of the 13th. of May has been duly received. My former letters had informed you that by Mr. Barton's retiring from the bar, a term had been lost in your case. Mr. Serjeant to whom it was turned over, had at first a thought that it might possibly be repaired by running two measures into one. But on further enquiry he found it would not be permitted. It cannot therefore be finished till the September term.—I think the delays of justice in certain other states will hardly justify declamation, when in so commercial a place as Philadelphia it shall take two years and a half to get an uncontested case through the court into the hands of the sheriffs.—You remember you desired me to import a pipe of Termo wine for you, when I should do it for my self. I accordingly ordered three pipes, intending one of them for you, if you should continue in the mind (for you had mentioned it only once, and that in a course of conversation). They arrived at Baltimore, and have been sent thence to Mr. Brown in Richmond. You are perfectly free to take one or not, as you please, since it will be quite equal to me to keep the three, or only two: therefore follow your more mature determination as if you had never said a word on the subject.—Be assured that no other delay shall be permitted to happen to your suit against Griffin. I am with great esteem, Dear Sir your affectionate friend & servt   TH: JEFFERSON

PrC (DLC); at foot of text: "Doctr. Currie." Tr (DLC); 19th-century copy.

To Charles Lilburne Lewis

DEAR SIR   Philadelphia June 4. 1793.

The constant calls of public business, which scarcely ever permit me to turn to what is private, will I hope apologize for my late acknolegement of your letter of Mar. 23. on the subject of the claims of Anthony and Giovannini against Mr. Mazzei. With respect to Anthony, I always assured him that whenever I should have any money of Mr. Mazzei's in my hands, I would join him in referring his claim to any impartial judge, and do him justice as far as in my power. I am still in the same purpose. With respect to Giovannini, I have known him now 16. or 18. years. He lived a considerable time in my family, I have enjoyed his confidence and I believe his esteem, and never before heard of his having any claim against Mazzei. I have too much regard for him not to hope he will avoid the risk of any unfounded claim. However when I come home in the fall I will hear what he has to say, and do for him whatever justice and my powers will authorize.

I have little of news to add to what the news papers will give you. We have a good prospect of preserving our neutrality. Consequently we may hope open markets for our productions. I am afraid it will be difficult to quiet the Creek Indians; and an open war with them will be expensive and hazardous.—Be so good as to present my [sincere] love to my sister and the family, and to be assured of the esteem of Dear Sir Your friend & servt   TH: JEFFERSON

PrC (DLC); lower left corner partially torn away; at foot of text: "Colo. C. L. Lewis."

Neither Lewis's LETTER OF MAR. 23, described in SJL as a letter of 22 Mch. 1793 received from Buck Island on 1 Apr. 1793, nor a subsequent letter of 7 July 1793 recorded in SJL as received from Buck Island on 20 July 1793, have been found.

From Adam Lindsay

DEAR SIR   Norfolk 4th. June 1793

Last February I shipped you a quantity of Candles which the Skipper told me he delivered safe—at same time wrote you by post inclosing his receipt for them with a bill of parcels, but am afraid some mistake has happened as I have never received any answer. I will thank to inform me if you received my letter.

Respecting affairs in General here trade is extremely dull, owing to this port depending allmost on the British Shipping and that trade being stopped by the little pickeroons that has been on our Coast. The Merchants wait with patience to know what will be done with the prizes carried in to Phila. as on that determination much depends whether the trade of this place will revive or be anihilated. I Remain Dr. Sir Yr. Most Obt. & Hbl. Servt.   ADAM LINDSAY

RC (DLC); at head of text: "Thomas Jefferson Eqr"; endorsed by TJ as received 11 June 1793 and so recorded in SJL.

To James Monroe

DEAR SIR   Philadelphia June 4. 1793.

I am to acknolege the receipt of your favors of May 8. and 23. and to express my perfect satisfaction with what you have done in the case of Barrett. With respect to the interest from the date of the judgment it is a thing of course, and always as just as the judgment itself. If he swears that the account is unpaid, I shall be satisfied he believes it to be so, and in that case would always have paid it had he applied to me, because I do not possess equal evidence to the contrary. The original sum having been about 58. or 59£ with interest from Apr. 19. 1783. the order I gave you on Mr. Pope will be more than sufficient to cover it, and will render a delay till the fall unnecessary, as I may hope. The money too, coming to the hands of Mr. Pope, his own lawyer, will abridge the business.

I will certainly do justice to Mr. Gamble's competition for the French purchases of flour. I have written to him on that subject. I mean shortly to take a trip to Brandywine, and endeavor to engage a tenant for my mill, so as to produce some competition for the purchase of our flour. I shall go on also to Elkton to take arrangements of time with the tenants engaged for me there. On these may depend the time I see you in Albemarle, as I must precede them.—You should look to the possibility of being called to Philadelphia early in October, if matters with the Creek Indians continue to wear their present serious aspect. The times too are otherwise so pregnant of events that every moment may produce cause for calling you. France has explained herself generously. She does not wish to interrupt our prosperity by calling for our guarantee. On the contrary she wishes to promote it by giving us in all her possessions all the rights of her native citizens, and to receive our vessels as her vessels. This is the language of her new minister. Gr. Britain holds back with the most sullen silence and reserve. She has never intimated to our Minister a wish that we would remain neutral. Our correspondence with her consists in *demands* where she is interested, and *delays* where we are. Spain too is mysterious. Nothing promising at Madrid, and contrary symptoms on the Missisipi. Were the combination of kings to have a very successful campaign, I should doubt their moderation.—Parties seem to have taken a very well defined form in this quarter. The old tories, joined by our merchants who trade on British capital, paper dealers, and the idle rich of the great commercial towns, are with the kings. All other descriptions with the French. The war has kindled and brought forward the two parties with an ardour which our own interests merely, could never excite. I pray that the events of the summer may not damp the spirit of our approaching Congress to whom we look forward to give the last direction to the government in which we are embarked. Give my best affections to Mrs. Monroe, and accept them sincerely for yourself. Adieu.

RC (NN: Presidential Papers); unsigned; addressed: "Colo. James Monroe near Charlottesville"; franked, stamped, and postmarked. PrC (DLC). Tr (DLC); 19th-century copy.

The first of Monroe's FAVORS was actually dated 9 May 1793.

To John Nixon

Sir   Philadelphia June 4. 1793.

From the view I had of Mr. Cruger's papers, I had conceived his case to have been that of an arbitrary seizure of his vessel. I now perceive there has been a judicial condemnation of her. The proceedings of courts are so respected in every country that it is always difficult and often impracticable to get them revised. Nevertheless it is sometimes possible where their decision has been very palpably wrong. To effect this, it is necessary that Mr. Cruger should procure the strongest evidence his case admits, authenticated in the highest forms. On this subject he will be best advised by the gentlemen of the law on the spot. On sending to me these proofs, I will give them in to the French minister with a request to him to use his influence with the government of the island where the case happened, to have the proceedings of the court revised and corrected. I have the honor to be with great respect & esteem Sir Your most obedt. humble servt   Th: Jefferson

PrC (DLC); at foot of text: "John Nixon esq." Tr (DLC); 19th-century copy.

To Thomas Pinckney

Dear Sir   Philadelphia June 4. 1793.

I wrote you last on the 7th. of May, since which I have received yours of Mar. 12. Apr. 5. 6. 6. and 10.

Tho' the character of Mr. Albion Coxe here was not exactly what we would have wished, yet he will be received if he can give the security required by law. With respect to Mr. Holloway, my former letters will have informed you that the necessity of proceeding in our coinage would admit no longer delay in the appointment of officers; and that for this reason a day was fixed after which even Drost could not be received. The same reason operates more powerfully against Mr. Holloway; the office he desired cannot remain so long unfilled, and we shall be obliged to fill it immediately with some one of the candidates here, some of whom indeed are pretty good. The box of coins, which you mention to have forwarded from Mr. Digges, has not come to hand.

With respect to the advance of monies to Mr. Wilson, my letter of the 16th. of March has answered you fully, by observing that no money has been provided by law for advances in such cases, and that were it to be done in one, it must be done in all of the same kind, which would open a very wide feild indeed.—The register of the ship Philadelphia packet is received and shall be immediately returned to the Treasury.—Your

information that we are not likely to obtain any protection for our seamen in British ports, or against British officers on the high seas, is of a
serious nature indeed. It contrasts remarkeably with the multiplied applications we are receiving from the British minister here for protection
to their seamen, vessels and property within our ports and bays, which
we are complying with with the most exact justice. However I shall
hazard no further reflection on the subject thro the present channel of
conveyance. You will be pleased to bear in mind what I wrote you on
the subject of M. de la Fayette, to consider it as an object of interest in
this country, and to let me know what may be expected in the case. I
have the honor to be with great & sincere esteem Dr. Sir Your most
obedt. & most humble servt   TH: JEFFERSON

P.S. June 5. Your letter of Apr. 15. is this moment received, as also the
box of medals.

RC (CtY); at foot of first page: "Mr. Pinckney"; endorsed by Pinckney. PrC (DLC); with postscript added in ink. FC (Lb in DNA: RG 59, DCI). Enclosed in TJ to George Washington, 4 June 1793.

On 6 June 1793 Joseph Nourse, the Register of the Treasury, made out a receipt to TJ declaring that he had received from him by way of Pinckney "the Original certificate of Registry for the Ship Philadelphia Packet No. 12 issued at the port of Philadelphia February 10. 1791" and had canceled it (MS in DNA: RG 59, MLR; in a clerk's hand, signed by Nourse). This receipt is filed with a text of the certificate in an un-identified hand, on the verso of which TJ wrote: "Receipt for the Register of the ship Philadelphia packet, which Register was forwarded by Mr. Pinckney and given in by Th:J. to Mr. Nourse. To be lodged in the of-fice, and delivered to the Ship owners, if they call for it" (Tr in same). See also Pinck-ney to TJ, 10 Apr. 1793.

For WHAT I WROTE YOU on the captivity of the Marquis de Lafayette, see TJ to Gou-verneur Morris and Thomas Pinckney, 15 Mch. 1793.

To George Washington

June 4. 1793.

Th: Jefferson has the honor to inclose to the President a letter from Mr.
Pinckney covering proposals from a Mr. Holloway to come over as engraver to our mint. It does not appear that Mr. Holloway was very
eminent, as far as we can judge from the expressions in Mr. Pinckney's
letter: his idea of making it a kind of appointment for life seems inadmissible; and the delay to which his appointment would subject the commencement of our coinage of silver and gold, would be injurious. It
therefore appears adviseable to decline his proposition *by the packet now
about to sail.*   Th:J. has indeed received information from Mr. T.
Digges on the subject of coining which to him appears interesting. He
has put it into the hands of Mr. Rittenhouse; if he should find in it any

thing which can be useful, Th:J. will have the honor of laying it before the President.

RC (DNA: RG 59, MLR); addressed: "The President of the US."; endorsed by Bartholomew Dandridge, Jr. PrC (DLC). Tr (Lb in DNA: RG 59, SDC). Recorded in SJPL. Enclosure: Thomas Pinckney to TJ, 6 Apr. 1793, and enclosure.

David Rittenhouse evidently reported that the letters received from Thomas DIGGES were potentially USEFUL, possibly in a missing letter to TJ of 7 June 1793 recorded in SJL as received the same day, for TJ submitted them to the President in a note of 12 June 1793.

From George Washington

June 4th: 1793

The President returns to the Secretary of State Mr. Pinckney's letter enclosing Mr. Holloways proposals to come over to this country as engraver to our Mint—which proposals the President conceives are inadmissible.

RC (DLC); in the hand of Tobias Lear; addressed: "The S[. . .]"; endorsed by TJ as received 4 June 1793. Recorded in SJPL.

To George Washington

June 4. 1793.

Th: Jefferson has the honor to inclose to the President the draught of a letter to Mr. Pinckney. Also the paper sent to him for the signatures now put to it.

RC (DNA: RG 59, MLR); addressed: "The President of the US."; endorsed by Bartholomew Dandridge, Jr. Tr (Lb in same, SDC). Enclosures: (1) TJ to Thomas Pinckney, 4 June 1793. (2) Cabinet Opinion on the Creek Indians and Georgia, 29 May 1793.

From George Washington

Dear Sir   4th. June 1793.

If you see any objections to the propositions contained in the enclosed pray furnish me with them as soon as convenient as I want to return an answer with out delay. Yours &ca   Go: Washington

RC (DLC); endorsed by TJ as received 4 June 1793. Recorded in SJPL.

Alexander Hamilton to George Washington

S<small>IR</small>   Treasury department June 3. 1793.

The failure of the late enterprize against the United Netherlands may be expected to have made a favorable alteration in regard to the prospects of obtaining loans there for the US. Such an expectation is also countenanced by a late letter from our bankers at Amsterdam, which however as yet gives no certainty, that can be a basis of operation.

The existing instructions from the department to Mr. Short do not extend beyond 2. millions of florins. A comprehensive view of the affairs of the US. in various relations, appears to me to recommend a still further loan, if obtainable. Yet I do not think it adviseable to take the step, by virtue of the general powers from you, without your special approbation; particularly as there is little probability that the loan can be effected on better terms than 5. per cent interest and 4. per cent charges. The further loan which I should contemplate would embrace 3,000,000 of florins. With perfect respect & the truest attachment I have the honor to be Sir Your obedient servant   A. H<small>AMILTON</small>

Tr (DLC); entirely in TJ's hand; at head of text: "*Copy* of a letter from the Secy. of the Treasury to the President"; at foot of text: "The President of the US." PrC (DLC). Recorded in SJPL.

From Robert Gamble

S<small>IR</small>   Richmond June 5. 1793

I was duly honored with your esteemed favor of the 19th. ulto. for which, and the friendly sentiments you entertain for me I beg you to accept my sincere thanks.

In hopes that it would be in the power of Mr. Genet to furnish me with the means of purchasing and shipping Flour and Naval stores, I have continued to receive all that offered for sale. And have declined selling to British purchasers—of consequence I have a large quantity on hand. The great difficulty in procuring Vessells to carry the Flour I suppose is the principal reason Why we hear nothing further on the subject.

I am solicitous, that if any thing can be effected—That Virginia may not be forgot, and—if for particular reasons—Nothing can be done at present—I confide my Dear sir, That when occasion offers you will remind Mr. Genet—That this part of Virginia hopes for an oportunity of furnishing a proportion of the supplies that may be Needed for France. I am with sentiments of respect Your mo Obt Hle Svt.

R<small>O</small> G<small>AMBLE</small>

P.S. I have taken the liberty of enclosing a letter to Mr. Genet which you will please to hand him. You will excuse the trouble I give you on the occasion. Yours.   ROBERT GAMBLE

RC (DLC); endorsed by TJ as received 11 June 1793 and so recorded in SJL. Enclosure not found.

To Edmond Charles Genet

SIR   Philadelphia 5 June 1793.

In my letter of May 15th: to M. de Ternant, your predecessor, after stating the answers which had been given to the several memorials of the British Minister of May 8th: it was observed that a part remained still unanswered of that which respected the fitting out armed vessels in Charleston to cruise against nations with whom we were at peace.

In a conversation which I had afterwards the honor of holding with you, I observed, that one of those armed vessels, the Citizen Genet, had come into this Port with a prize; that the President had thereupon,[1] taken the case into further consideration, and after mature consultation and deliberation was of opinion that the arming and equipping vessels in the Ports of the United States to cruise against nations with whom they are at peace, was incompatible with the territorial sovereignty of the United States; that it made them instrumental to the annoyance of those nations, and thereby tended to compromit their peace, and that he thought it necessary as an evidence of good faith to them, as well as a proper reparation to[2] the Sovereignty of the Country,[3] that the armed vessels of this description should depart from the ports of the United States.

The letter of the 27th. instant, with which you have honored me, has been laid before the President, and that part of it which contains your observations on this subject has been particularly attended to. The respect due to whatever comes from you, friendship for the french nation, and justice to all, have induced him to reexamine the subject, and particularly to give to your representations thereon, the consideration they deservedly claim. After fully weighing again however all the principles and circumstances of the case, the result appears still to be[4] that it is the *right* of every nation to prohibit acts of sovereignty from being exercised by any other within its limits; and the *duty* of a neutral nation to prohibit such as would injure one of the warring powers: that the granting military commissions within the United States by any other authority than their own[5] is an infringement on their Sovereignty, and particularly so when granted to their own[6] citizens, to lead them to commit[7] acts contrary to the duties they owe their own country; that the departure of vessels thus illegally equipped, from the Ports of the United States, will be but an acknowledgment of respect analogous to the breach of it, while it is necessary on their part, as an evidence of their faithful neutrality. On these considerations Sir, the President thinks that[8] the United States owe it to themselves, and to the nations in their friendship, to expect this act of reparation, on the part of vessels marked in their very equipment with offence to the laws of the land, of which the law of nations makes an integral part.

The expressions of very friendly sentiment which we have already had the satisfaction of receiving from you leave no room to doubt that the conclusion of the President, being thus made known to you these vessels will be permitted to give no further umbrage by their presence in the Ports of the United States.[9] I have the honor to be with sentiments of perfect esteem and respect Sir, Your most obedient & Most humble servant

PrC (DLC); in a clerk's hand, unsigned; at foot of first page: "Mr. Genet, Minister Plenipotentiary of France." Dft (DLC); undated and unsigned text written entirely in TJ's hand between 28 and 31 May 1793, with final paragraph added in a different ink and subsequently canceled at Edmund Randolph's suggestion, and note of explanation added lengthwise in margin by TJ (see note 9 below); date added later in the hand of George Taylor, Jr.; only the most significant emendations have been noted below. PrC (DLC); with date added in ink by TJ; lacks one emendation (see note 2 below), final paragraph, and marginal note; note by TJ in ink at head of text, possibly added at a later date: "[r]ough prepared & approved ⟨May 31⟩." Tr (NNC: Gouverneur Morris Papers). PrC of another Tr (DNA: RG 59, MD); in a clerk's hand. PrC of another Tr (PRO: FO 97/1); in a clerk's hand. Tr (DNA: RG 46, Senate Records, 3d Cong., 1st sess.). FC (Lb in DNA: RG 59, DL). Tr (DLC: Genet Papers). Tr (DLC: same); in French. Tr (same); in French; draft translation of preceding Tr; revised, docketed, and initialed by Genet. Tr (AMAE: CPEU, xxxvii); in French. Recorded in SJPL. Printed in *Message*, 22-3. Enclosed in TJ to Gouverneur Morris, 13 June and 16 Aug. 1793, and TJ to Thomas Pinckney, 14 June 1793.

This letter reiterating the federal government's ban on the fitting out of French privateers in American ports, a critical point of conflict between the Washington administration and the French minister, underwent careful review by the President and the Cabinet before being dispatched. TJ first solicited the views of the Attorney General on Genet's LETTER OF THE 27TH. INSTANT defending this practice and then wrote a draft reply that drew heavily on Randolph's advice (see note 4 below). After making a press copy, TJ submitted the draft itself to the Attorney General for review, but not before adding a new concluding paragraph, which he subsequently expunged in light of Randolph's suggestion that it was too sympathetic to France (Randolph to TJ, 31 May 1793; note 9 below). Later the same day he submitted a text of the letter to Washington and was authorized to lay it before the Cabinet (Washington, *Journal*, 156, 157). In the absence of the President and the Secretary of the Treasury, the Cabinet could not make a final decision on TJ's letter when it met on 1 June, though the Attorney General and the Secretary of War did signify their general approval. Two days later, after receiving a text of the letter from TJ, Hamilton also gave his approval. Which text TJ submitted to the President and the Cabinet—the emended draft or the press copy without the offending paragraph—remains unclear (Washington, *Journal*, 159; TJ to Hamilton, 1 June [1793]; Hamilton to TJ, 3 June 1793).

[1] In Dft TJ here canceled "fully considered of the case, and after mature consult."

[2] Preceding two words—the first initially written in the plural—interlined in Dft in place of "⟨assertion⟩ vindication of." In PrC of Dft the second interlined word is lacking and "of" is not canceled.

[3] Word interlined in Dft in place of "US."

[4] The text from this point through "owe their own country" is adapted to a large extent from points made in Memorandum from Edmund Randolph, printed under 28 May 1793.

[5] Preceding seven words interlined in Dft.

[6] Word interlined in Dft.

[7] In Dft TJ first wrote "for the ⟨commi⟩ purpose of committing" before amending the passage to read as above.

[8] In Dft TJ here canceled "he owes it to."

[9] At this point in Dft, in response to Edmund Randolph's suggestion, TJ canceled the following paragraph: "The assurance conveyed in your letter of the friendship and attachment of your nation gives very sincere pleasure and is as sincerely returned on the part of our country. That these may continue long and firm, no one more ardently wishes than he who has the honor to be with sentiments of great esteem & respect Sir your mo. obedt. & mo. humble servt." With reference to this cancellation TJ added the following note in the margin of the Dft: "'The sentiments expressed in your letter of the friendship and attachment of your nation give very sincere pleasure, and are sincerely returned on the part of our country. That these may continue long and firm no one more ardently wishes than he who has the honor to be &c.' This letter being communicated to E.R. he disliked this concluding sentence as ⟨hardly n⟩ scarcely neutral. I therefore struck it out."

To George Hammond

Sir   Philadelphia, June 5.[1] 1793.

In the letter which I had the honor of writing you on the 15th. of May, in answer to your several memorials of the 8th. of that month, I mentioned that the President reserved, for further consideration, a part of the one which related to the equipment of two privateers in the port of Charleston. The part alluded to, was that wherein you express your confidence that the Executive Government of the United States would pursue measures for repressing such practices in future, and for restoring to their rightful owners any captures, which such privateers might bring into the ports of the United States.

The President, after a full investigation of this subject, and the most mature consideration, has charged me to communicate to you, that the first part of this application, is found to be just, and that effectual measures are taken for preventing repetitions of the act therein complained of: but that the latter part, desiring restitution of the prizes is understood to be inconsistent with the rules, which govern such Cases, and would, therefore, be unjustifiable towards the other party.

The principal Agents in this Transaction were French citizens. Being within the United States, at the moment a war broke out between their own and another country, they determine to go into it's defence; they purchase, arm, and equip, a vessel, with their own money, man it themselves, receive a regular Commission from their nation, depart out of the United States, and then commence hostilities, by capturing a vessel. If, under these circumstances, the Commission of the captors was valid, the property, according to the laws of War, was, by the capture, transferred to them, and it would be an aggression on their nation, for the United States to rescue it from them, whether on the high Seas or on coming into their ports. If the Commission was not valid, and, consequently, the property not transferred, by the laws of war, to the Captors, then the case would have been cognisable in our Courts of Admiralty, and the Owners might have gone thither for redress. So that on neither supposition, would the Executive be justifiable in interposing.

With respect to the united States, the transaction can in no wise be imputed to them. It was in the first moment of the War, in one of their most distant ports, before measures could be provided by the Government to meet all the cases, which such a state of things was to produce; impossible to have been known, and, therefore, impossible to have been prevented by that Government.

The moment it was known, the most energetic orders were sent to every state and port of the Union, to prevent a repetition of the accident. On a suggestion that Citizens of the United States had taken part in the act, one, who was designated, was instantly committed to prison, for prosecution; one or two others have been since named, and committed in like manner; and, should it appear, that there were still others, no measures will be spared to bring them to Justice.—The President has even gone further. He has required, as a reparation of their breach of respect to the United States, that the vessels, so armed and equipped, shall depart from our Ports.

You will see, Sir,[2] in these proceedings of the President, unequivocal proofs of the line of strict right, which he means to pursue. The measures now mentioned, are taken in justice to the one party; the ulterior measure, of seizing and restoring the prizes, is declined, in justice to the other: and the evil, thus early arrested, will be of very limited effects; perhaps, indeed,[3] soon disappear altogether. I have the honor to be, with sentiments of respect, Sir, Your most obedient and most humble servant

PrC (DLC); in the hand of George Taylor, Jr., except for addition by TJ (see note 1 below); unsigned; at foot of first page: "The minister plenipoy. of Gt. Britain." Dft (DLC); entirely in TJ's hand, unsigned; dated 3 June 1793; contains several variations. PrC of Tr (DNA: RG 360, PCC, AL); in a clerk's hand; incomplete; misfiled at Dec. 1790. FC (Lb in DNA: RG 59, DL). Tr (Lb in PRO: FO 116/3). Tr (same, 5/1). Tr (DLC: John Trumbull Letterbook). Recorded in SJPL under 3 June 1793. Enclosed in TJ to Gouverneur Morris, 13 June 1793, and TJ to Thomas Pinckney, 14 June 1793.

This document was a response to the British minister's letter to TJ of 31 May

1793, which sought to ascertain the Washington administration's position on RESTITUTION OF THE PRIZES captured by French privateers commissioned in Charleston by Edmond Charles Genet. TJ submitted Hammond's letter to the President on the following day and the draft of his reply two days later (Washington, *Journal*, 159). Then, after receiving Alexander Hamilton's approval of a related letter to the French minister on 4 June, he put both letters into final form on this day (Hamilton to TJ, 3 June 1793; TJ to Genet, 5 June 1793). See also Opinion on the Restoration of Prizes, 16 May 1793, and note.

[1] Digit added in ink by TJ in space left blank in manuscript.

[2] In Dft TJ first wrote "I am in hopes, Sir, you will see" and then altered the passage to read as above.

[3] In Dft TJ here canceled "may."

From George Hammond

SIR   Philadelphia 5th June 1793

I have received your letter of this date, upon which as well as on your former communication of the 15th. ulto., I shall have the honor of submitting to you some few observations in the course of two or three days. In the mean time I think it my duty to state to you a circumstance (connected with the subject of your letters) to the particulars of which I presume to request your immediate attention. The Ship William of Glasgow, Captain Leggett, was some time ago captured by a privateer Schooner named Le Citoyen Genêt fitted out at charleston, and was sent as prize to this port, but some doubts having been entertained with respect to the validity of the commission of the Schooner which made the capture (and which is now also in this harbour) a suit was instituted by the agent for the Owners of the Ship William in the district federal Court of this state, for the purpose of obtaining its opinion on this subject. Another point will also I understand be submitted to the court viz. that the Ship William was captured within the jurisdiction of the United States. Of the truth of this last mentioned fact of which I had prior information, I have now obtained such corroborating testimony as I am persuaded will be satisfactory to the general government of the United States, should the district Court deem itself incompetent either to the requisition or enforcement of the restitution of the vessel captured. In consequence of this suit the Ship William and the property on board are now under attachment by the Marshal of the district Court. The Court will give judgment on this question on Friday next. But if its decision be unfavorable to the restoration of the ship, I am apprehensive lest the attachment being taken off, the vessel may be sent to sea so speedily as to preclude the effect of any application relative to it which I may deem it expedient to make. I therefore venture to hope that the general government of the United States will either direct the attachment now subsisting to be continued or will adopt any other measures that may tend to prevent the vessel from departing, until it shall have investigated and formed some determination on the evidence, which I shall lay before it without delay, in order to substantiate the fact of the Ship William having been captured within the jurisdiction of the United States.

As I expect at the same time to be enabled to offer testimony establishing a similar state of facts relative to the brig Fanny Captain Pyle now lying in this harbour, as a prize to another privateer fitted out at Charleston named the Sans culottes, and also under an attachment from the Marshall of the district Court, I hope that the general government will prevent that vessel also from sailing until that point can be ascertained. I have the honor to be with great respect, Sir, Your most obedient humble servant, GEO. HAMMOND

RC (DNA: RG 59, NL); in the hand of Edward Thornton, signed by Hammond; at foot of first page: "Mr Jefferson"; endorsed by TJ as received 6 June 1793 and so recorded in SJL. FC (Lb in PRO: FO 116/3). Tr (same, 5/1). Tr (same, 115/2).

The capture of the British merchant vessels WILLIAM and FANNY, allegedly in American territorial waters, by French privateers commissioned in Charleston by Edmond Charles Genet, and the arrival of these prizes in Philadelphia, was another link in the chain of events that led to a historic definition of the maritime limits of the United States (see Memorial from Hammond, 2 May 1793, and note). In anticipation of TJ's announcement this day that the United States government would not restore British prizes captured by French privateers commissioned in America (TJ to Hammond, 5 June 1793), Hammond had prevailed upon the agents of the owners of the WILLIAM and the FANNY to file separate libels for their restitution in the United States District Court of Pennsylvania, a tribunal presided over by Judge Richard Peters which, in common with other federal district courts, had "cognizance of all crimes and offences . . . committed . . . upon the high seas . . . and . . . exclusive original cognizance of all civil causes of admiralty and maritime jurisdiction" (Hammond to Lord Grenville, 10 June 1793, PRO: FO 5/1; Annals, II, 2242). The libellants demanded restitution on the grounds that the CITOYEN GENET and the SANS CULOTTES had been commissioned invalidly and that they had captured the two British vessels "within the territorial jurisdiction, and under the pro-

tection of the United States" (Federal Cases, IX, 57, XVII, 942). Although Hammond doubted that the court would accept the first plea, he was more confident about its receptivity to the second, and even if it did not accept cognizance of the cases he was sure that this would not compromise a subsequent claim for restitution to the federal executive. Such a claim became necessary when Judge Peters ordered the William to be released from federal custody as part of his ruling on 21 June 1793 that the District Court lacked jurisdiction in the case because as the tribunal of a neutral nation it was not authorized "to decide in a matter growing out of the contests between belligerent powers." Later in the year, moreover, Peters issued the same ruling in the case of the Fanny (Federal Cases, IX, 57-62, XVII, 943-8; Hammond to Grenville, 10 June, 7 July 1793, PRO: FO 5/1).

Immediately after Judge Peters issued the first of these decisions, Hammond turned to the federal executive for redress (Memorials from Hammond, 21, 26 June 1793). During the summer of 1793 the Washington administration sought unsuccessfully to enlist the assistance of the United States Supreme Court in determining the federal government's obligation in regard to restoring belligerent prizes captured in American territorial waters and waited in vain for the United States District Court in Philadelphia to take up this issue again (Editorial Note and documents on the referral of neutrality questions to the Supreme Court, at 18 July 1793; Cabinet Opinions on Privateers and Prizes, 5 Aug. 1793). Ultimately, Hammond's persistence and Genet's incisive rejoinders forced the

Washington administration in November 1793 provisionally to proclaim a three-mile limit for the nation's maritime jurisdiction, a landmark development in international law (TJ to Genet, 8 Nov. 1793; Philip C. Jessup, *The Law of Territorial Waters and Maritime Jurisdiction* [New York, 1927], 3-7, 49-54).

Opinion on a New Foreign Loan

Instructions having been given to borrow 2. Millions of florins in Holland, and the Secretary of the Treasury proposing to open a further loan of 3. millions of florins, which, he says, 'a comprehensive view of the affairs of the US. in various relations, appears to him to recommend,' the President is pleased to ask Whether I see any objections to the proposition?

The power to borrow money is confided to the President by the two acts of the 4th. and 12th. of Aug. 90. and the monies when borrowed are appropriated to two purposes only: to wit, the 12. millions to be borrowed under the former are appropriated to discharge the arrears of interest and instalments of the foreign debt; and the 2. millions under the latter to the purchase of the public debt under direction of the Trustees of the sinking fund.

These appropriations render very simple the duties of the President in the discharge of this trust. He has only to look to the *payment* of the foreign debt, and *purchase* of the general one. And in order to judge for himself of the necessity of the loan proposed, for effecting these two purposes, he will need from the Treasury [1] the following statements.

A. a Statement of the Nett amount of the loans already made under these acts, adding to that the 2,000,000. florins now in a course of being borrowed. This will form the Debet of the trust.

The Credit side of the account will consist of the following statements, to wit.

B. Amount of the Principal and Interest of foreign debt, paid and payable, to the close of 1792.

C. do. payable to the close of 1793.

D. do. payable to the close of 1794. (For I think our preparations should be a year before hand.)

E. Amount of monies necessary for the Sinking fund to the end of 1794.

If the amount of the 4. last articles exceeds the 1st. it will prove a further[2] loan necessary, and to what extent. The Treasury alone can furnish these statements with perfect accuracy. But to shew that there is probable cause to go into the examination, I will hazard a statement from materials, which tho' perhaps not perfectly exact, are not much otherwise.

[Report of]³
Jan. 3. 1793.
new edition.
page. 4.

The Trust for Loans   Dr.

A. To nett amount of loans to June 1. 1792. as stated in the
Treasury report, to wit 18,678,000. florins @ 99   Dollars
florins to 40.D. the treasury-exchange   7,545,912.
To loan now going on for 2,000,000. florins   808,080.

8,353,992.

So that instead of an additional loan being necessary, the monies already borrowed will suffice for 387,474.64 D. to cover charges & errors. And as, on account of the unsettled state of the French dead interest & risk.—Perhaps it might be said that new monies must be borrowed for the loan for this purpose.—If it should be said that the monies heretofore borrowed are so far put out certainly I would rather borrow than fail in a payment. But if borrowing will secure a payment time, then we cannot get an additional sum in time.

The above account might be stated in another way, which might perhaps be more satisfactory.

The Trust for loans   Dr.

To the nett amount of loans to June 1. 1792   Dollars
18,678,000. florins @ 99.ƒ to 40.D.   7,545,912.

The Trust for loans   Dr.

Dollars.
To balance as per contra   1,688,581.10
To 2. millions florins new loan when effected   808,080.

2,496,661.10

Cr.

		florins s	
page 4. B.	By charges on remittances to France	10,073–1	
5.	By reimbursement to Spain	680,000.	
	By Interest paid to Foreign officers	105,000.	Dollars
		795,073–1 =	321,239.46
7.	By Principal paid to Foreign officers		191,316.90
	By amt. of French debt, Principl. &	livres	
	Intt. payable to end of 1791.	26,000,000.	
	By do. for 1792.	3,450,000.	
		29,450,000	5,345,171.
C.	By do. for 1793.	3,410,000.	618,915.
D.	By do. for 1794.	3,250,000	[589,875.][4]
E.	By necessary for Sinkg. fund @ 50,000.D. a month from		
	July 1. 93. to Dec. 31. 94.		900,000.
	Balance which will remain in hands of the Trust at end		Dollars
	of 1794.		387,474.64 8,353,992.

all the purposes to which they can be legally applied to the end of 1794. and leave a surplus of
government, it is not proposed to pay in advance, or but little so, any further sum would be lying at a
current domestic service of the year. To this I should answer that no law has authorised the opening a
of our power that we cannot command them before an instalment will be due: I should answer that
in time, the 2. millions of florins now borrowing are sufficient to secure it: if we cannot get this sum in

To wit:

Cr.

Report.		florins s	
page. 4.	By charges on remittances to France	10,073–1	
5.	By reimbursement to Spain	680,000.	
	By Interest paid to Foreign officers	105,000.	
		795,073–1	321,239.46
7.	By Principal paid to Foreign officers		191,316.90
		florins s	Dollars.
4.	By paiments to France	10,073,043.8	4,069,918.54
		livres	
7.	By do. to St. Domingo	4,000,000.	726,000.
	By do. to do.	3,000,000.	544,500.
	By do. to M. Ternant [I state		
	this by memory]	24,000.	4,356 5,344,774.54 dollars
	Balance in hand to be carried to new Debet		1,688,581.10 7,545,912.

Cr.

By the following payments when made, to wit.

Balance due to France to close the year 1792.		Dollars
(5,345,171 D – 5,344,774.54)		396.46
	livres	
Instalments & Interest to close of the year 1793.	3,410,000.	618,915.
do. 1794.	3,250,000.	589,875.
Necessary for Sinking fund from July 1. 93. to Dec. 31. 94.	900,000.	
Balance will then be in hand to be carried to new Debet		387,474.64 2,496,661.10

By this statement, it would seem as if all the paiments to France, hitherto made and ordered, would not quite acquit the year 1792. so that we have never yet been clear of arrears to her.

The amount of the French debt is stated according to the Convention, and the Interest is calculated accordingly.—Interest on the 10. million loan is known to have been paid for the years 84. 85. and is therefore deducted. It is not known whether it was paid on the same loan[5] for the years 86. 7. 8. 9. previous to the payment of Dec. 3. 1790. or whether it was included in that paiment. Therefore this is not deducted. But if in fact it was paid before that day, it will then have lessened the debt so much, to wit, 400,000. livres a year for 4. years, making $1,600,000^{tt} = 290,400.D.$ which sum would put us in advance near half of the instalments of 1793.[6]—Note: livres are estimated at $18\frac{15}{100}$ cents proposed by the Secretary of the Treasury to the French ministry as the[7] rate of conversion.

This uncertainty with respect to the true state of our account with France, and the difference of the result from what has been understood, shews that the gentlemen who are to give opinions on this subject must do it in the dark; and suggests to the President the propriety of having an exact statement of the account with France communicated to them, as the ground on which they are to give opinions. It will probably be material in that about to be given on the late application of Mr. Genet, on which the Secretary of the Treasury is preparing a report.

Th: Jefferson
June 5. 1793.

PrC (DLC: TJ Papers, 87: 15064, 15067-9); entirely in TJ's hand; brackets in original except where noted; letterpressed from one large sheet folded to make four pages, with the statement of account spread across the second and third pages. PrC of Tr (same, 87: 15065, 86: 14842-3, 87: 15066); in TJ's hand; with one variation in wording (see note 7 below) and minor differences in punctuation and capitalization. Tr (Lb in DNA: RG 59, SDC); wording and punctuation follow PrC. Enclosed in TJ to George Washington, 5 June 1793, and TJ to James Madison, 9 June 1793.

With this opinion TJ resumed his attempt to persuade the President that the Secretary of the Treasury's handling of foreign loans would not bear close scrutiny (Editorial Note and documents on Jefferson's questions and observations on the application of France, at 12 Feb. 1793; Editorial Note on Jefferson and the Giles

resolutions, at 27 Feb. 1793). On 3 June Alexander Hamilton had requested the President's special authorization to open a further loan of 3,000,000 florins in Holland because the interest and charges would be higher than those obtained for recent borrowings. Despite his caution in the aftermath of the Giles resolutions, Hamilton did not tell the President how the loan was to be grounded on, nor how the proceeds were to be applied in accordance with, the TWO ACTS OF THE 4TH. AND 12TH. OF AUG. 1790 under which Congress had authorized the President to borrow abroad. Perhaps mindful of the reflections that the earlier controversy over Hamilton's management of the Treasury had cast on his own stewardship, Washington immediately passed the Treasury Secretary's proposal to TJ (Washington to TJ, 4 June 1793, and enclosure). After TJ responded with the opinion printed above, the President asked Attorney General Edmund Randolph to review both documents. On 8 June, two days after Randolph submitted his "opinion & remarks," which have not been found, Washington, desiring "to make the subject clear to my mind" before any further steps were taken, asked Hamilton to indicate whether all the money already borrowed under the two August 1790 acts of Congress had been expended for the purposes authorized and to state the unexpended balance if it had not, to designate under which of the two acts he proposed to open the new loan, to give the balance remaining unborrowed under the acts, and to identify how the proceeds of the new loan were to be applied (Syrett, *Hamilton*, xiv, 521-2; Washington, *Journal*, 160, 161, 163). For Hamilton's response and the Secretary of State's reaction, see Washington to TJ, 16 June 1793, and enclosure, and Second Opinion on a New Foreign Loan, 17 June 1793, and note.

[1] Preceding three words interlined.
[2] Word interlined.
[3] Supplied from PrC of Tr.
[4] Supplied from Tr. PrC and PrC of Tr: "569, 875."
[5] Preceding eight words interlined in place of "to have been paid."
[6] Remainder of paragraph interlined.
[7] PrC of Tr here adds "par of the metals, to be the."

To Josef Ignacio de Viar and Josef de Jaudenes

GENTLEMEN   Philadelphia, June 5th. 1793.

I have laid before the President, the letter, which you did me the honor of writing on the 25th. of May. I had, on late, as well as former, occasions, had that of assuring you of the orders given by the President, for befriending your peace with the Indian nations, in your neighborhood: and I do, with the utmost sincerity, assure you, that the question of a contrary aspect, supposed, in your letter, to have been proposed to the Cherokees, has been unauthorized by the President, and unknown to him: and, from the good Opinion entertained of the discretion of Governor Blount, to whom it is imputed, and the whole tenor of his conduct, as far as known to the Government,[1] it is strongly presumed, there has been error in your information.

We remain firmly persuaded, that it is for the interest of both nations, to cultivate each other's peace, with the neighboring Indians, and we are acting faithfully on that principle, in expectation that your Government will prescribe the same rule to it's officers in our neighborhood, and take measures to be obeyed by them.

The other parts of your communications, have such relation to the subjects in negotiation at Madrid, that it is deemed more expedient to express the President's sense of them to our Commissioners there. I have the honor to be, with the most perfect respect Gentlemen, Your most obedient and most humble servant   TH: JEFFERSON

PrC (DLC); in the hand of George Taylor, Jr., signed by TJ; at foot of text: "Messrs. Viar & Jaudenes." Dft (DLC); in TJ's hand, unsigned, with date altered by Taylor from 1 to 5 June 1793. FC (Lb in DNA: RG 59, DL). Tr (AHN: Papeles de

Estado, legajo 3895); in Spanish; attested by Viar and Jaudenes. Recorded in SJPL. Draft enclosed in TJ to Alexander Hamilton, 1 June [1793], and Hamilton to TJ, 3 June 1793.

TJ first submitted the draft of this letter, dated 1 June 1793, to the President on 31 May 1793. With Washington's approval he submitted the draft on the following day to a Cabinet meeting unattended by the President and the Secretary of the Treasury. After securing the general approval of the Attorney General and the Secretary of War, TJ consulted with the President on the same day and sent the draft to the Secretary of the Treasury, who gave it his sanction in a letter TJ received on 4 June (Washington, *Journal*, 157, 159).

[1] Preceding fourteen words interlined in Dft.

To George Washington

5 June 1793

Th: Jefferson with his respects to the President has the honor to enclose him the answer to his note of yesterday. Should any article of it need explanation, he will be at the orders of the President for that purpose to do it either verbally or in writing.

Tr (Lb in DNA: RG 59, SDC). Not recorded in SJL. Enclosure: Opinion on a New Foreign Loan, 5 June 1793.

From William Carmichael and William Short

SIR   Aranjuez June 6. 1793

We have had the honor of writing to you jointly on the 19th. of feby.—18th. of April—and 5th of May. These letters were sent by duplicates, and went into very minute details of whatever had occurred here with respect to the business of our joint commission. Such conveyances as could with propriety be made use of have not presented themselves so as to admit of our writing more often—and the state of things did not appear to us such as to require the sending of special messengers.

These letters will have informed you of the delay which took place before the opening of the first conference with M. de Gardoqui on the 23d. of March—of the manner in which our ideas on the navigation of the Mississipi and territorial limits were recieved by him—of his ideas on the same subjects being so divergent therefrom, and expressed to us in such a manner, as to shew beyond all kind of doubt, that they could not then be brought within the circle of negotiation—of the embarassing postion in which this placed us, on account of the changes which

had taken place in the foreign relations of this country since your instructions had been drawn up, and particularly those which it was probable they were then forming with England—and finally, of our determination therefore not to push the negotiation until some change should
turn up; or until we should hear further from you, after the President
should have been made acquainted with the events which had thrown
England and this country into the same scale, and that, the one in which
most of the military and maritime powers of Europe were already
placed, and the rest of them likely to enter either of themselves or by
force.

According to our calculation of the time when you would probably
have recieved from your ministers at London and Paris, the intelligence
of this posture of European politics, we flattered ourselves that we
should have heard from you in pursuance thereof before this: and we
have found that we were not mistaken in the time we allowed, as M. de
Gardoqui has already recieved letters from the Spanish commissaries
informing him of the arrival in America, of the news of the execution of
Lewis the 16th.—of the declaration of war between France and England, and the certain expectation of the same between France and this
country. We still suppose it impossible you should not have done us the
honor to have written to us after being informed of a revolution of that
kind—whether the intention of the President should have been that the
negotiation should be accomodated to the effects produced by that revolution, or that it should be pushed without regard thereto, conformably
to the instructions originally sent us. We trust that your letters on that
subject must be now on their way and we are in impatient expectation
of recieving them.

Whatever we shall learn from you to be the President's intention on
this subject we shall immediately proceed to execute; and we trust you
will readily see that the present system of prolongation which we have
taken on ourselves does not proceed from a desire to exercise our own
will—but to leave time for being more unquestionably informed of that
of the President. We are fully persuaded the line we have thus pursued
will be considered the proper one; and particularly as the greatest inconvenience which could result therefrom, as it appeared to us, was a short
delay, whereas an opposite one might have produced very disagreeable
and perhaps dangerous effects, which both the U.S. and Spain might
have repented of hereafter in vain.

Our letters will have already given you such a statement of affairs
here at that time as to have exhibited this dilemma in a very clear point
of view. Still we beg leave to recapitulate it here, for the greater certainty of its reaching you. This we consider the more important, as generally speaking, the eve of a nation's being drawn into a war being an

auspicious moment for those who are at peace with them, to demand a restitution of their rights, this may therefore be considered in America, the proper time for the U.S. to have urged their claims here.

Our joint commission arrived at Madrid, as we have already had the honor of informing you, on the 1st. of february, almost at the same moment with the news of the catastrophe of the 21st. of January. The probability which had principally existed of this country being brought into an union of measures with England, was now changing daily into certainty—and before the commencement of our conferences was placed beyond doubt. Although Spain thus circumstanced would consider her position in general as a much less eligible one than whilst united with France, yet with respect to us in particular she would consider her present position more favorable than her former one—or in other words, she would consider herself better secured against us, whilst united with England against France already attacked by the most formidable powers of Europe, than whilst united with France whose partiality for us she distrusted, and opposed to England whose concert with us she would have apprehended.

We were persuaded of this both from the nature of the case and from different circumstances which occurred. Our first conference with M. de Gardoqui put this beyond doubt, and shewed unquestionably that it was far from the intention of the cabinet at this time to yield any thing correspondent to our claims, whatever it might have been under the administration of Ct. de Florida Blanca—or whatever assurances unknown to us, they may have formerly given to the President, so as to have induced his sending a commission to treat here.

Whilst we were fully impressed with this conviction, and satisfied that no mode of negotiation which we could adopt would induce this court to come to any terms which we were authorized under your instructions to accept, we saw Spain and England now decidedly placed on the same side by having a common enemy, and then treating of the basis of their future union. It was unquestionable that England would desire this to be as close as possible in order to have Spain the more in her dependence, and to cut off hopes of the revival of the family compact in the case of a counter-revolution in France. It was as unquestionable that Spain keeping still an eye on this event, and being the weaker and more distrustful power, would enter timorously and cautiously into this system.

It could not be doubted that the effects of their distrust with respect to England would be diminished in proportion to their apprehension of danger from any other quarter. Had we then pressed this negotiation and convinced them of our fixed determination not to desist from any part of what we consider as our right (and what they seem now to consider as a commencement of the loss of their American commerce and territorial possessions)—and forced them by this means to give us a positive refusal on a solemn demand[1] having been made by an express commission formed and sent for that purpose, it is impossible in whatever manner we might have recieved it, or whatever reasons we might have given to have persuaded them of the pacific intentions of the U.S. that they should not have supposed it their determination[2] to have resorted to other means of redress. That apprehension acting on them would unavoidably have made them more tractable with respect to England, and would have secured them the protection of that country, as they would have made fewer difficulties about the price to be paid for it.

This kind of alarm in the Spanish cabinet with respect to us would at any time during the war have an influence on their relations with England, different from what we should desire—but it appeared to us that it would be still greater at the moment the two courts were feeling each other's pulse as it were, and agreeing on the arrangements to be entered into against a common enemy, than at any future period. Although we have remained altogether uninformed of the present dispositions of England with respect to the U.S. still we could not help supposing that the present situation of European affairs would appear to that power as by no means favorable to them so far as should relate to their European connexions, or prospect of aid from thence in case of need.

From pushing the negotiation immediately to its close under these circumstances we apprehended the inconveniences abovementioned. On the other hand it appeared to us that a temporizing mode of proceeding presented several advantages.

It enabled us (being fully convinced of the decision of this court without proceeding further) to inform you of that decision and give time for whatever measures might be thought proper to be taken before the views of the U.S. with respect to what they will invariably insist on, are fully and officially known here; which will not be until the breaking off of our conferences, as they may still suppose that we may be induced to recede from a part of what we stated in our first conference as our right. It enabled us also to recieve (before taking steps that might render it too late) further instructions from you grounded on the changes of European affairs, which had been such as to render it highly probable that the President might chuse to adapt thereto those which you had forwarded to us under circumstances so different.

These considerations seemed to us to exact our pursuing the line we have mentioned—and we did not doubt the delay, which we then contemplated, would be amply repaid by those advantages. However disagreeable this mode of prolonging a business of which we already know the issue, has been and still is personally to us, still we do not think ourselves authorized thereby to risk what we consider disadvantageous to the public.

As circumstances have turned out we cannot help considering it unfortunate that an express commission should have been sent to treat here. It seems to us desirable that the U.S. and their claims should have been as much as possible out of the view of this country whilst forming their arrangements with England. That court will certainly excite whatever alarm they can here, with respect to us—and this country may under that influence and the hope of full protection and good treatment from England do many things that she would not be willing to do hereafter when she shall have made trial of her protectress. Between two countries, one characterised by indolence, wealthy possessions, and the desire to preserve them by monopoly—the other, by commercial enterprize and insatiable avidity, it appears to us difficult to suppose that there can long remain confidence and union. Of course we should imagine Spain would be less ready to apply to England for protection against us, at any future period than the present. And at present she will be more or less ready to do it in proportion as she may apprehend more or less from the present conduct of the U.S.

Arrangements between England and Spain have for some time been negotiating, as you have been informed. Nothing has yet transpired of their particulars which can be relied on, or of the progress made in them. It seems certain however that these arrangements are concerting here without the participation of the other powers already leagued and at war also against France. It is believed by some that something conclusive has been settled and was forwarded from hence by a special messenger dispatched by the English Embassador eight days ago. This however is only conjecture among those the most in the way of being informed. We cannot assure you of it; nor can we satisfy ourselves whether in the negotiation on foot, any arrangements have been really proposed, which are eventually to regard the U.S. and their claims with respect to the Mississipi, and territorial limits. You will readily see however that should this country from apprehension with respect to us have been induced to consider such arrangements as essential, they have in their power very tempting means for procuring them.

We have had the honor of informing you in a precedent letter of the particularly hostile dispositions of M. de Gardoqui as to the rights of the U.S. We have found on the contrary from his mode of proceeding in business of every kind, the greatest facility given to the temporizing system we have adopted. Hitherto we have followed the conferences as regularly as his ministerial occupations would admit of; and they have been employed in discussing the general subjects of our commission, saving those of the navigation of the Mississipi and limits. We shall probably not be pressed by him to come forward in a more direct way, not only because from want of order he is always overwhelmed and in arrear of his department, but also because that business affects him much more sensibly and presses him much more than that with us.

We flatter ourselves however that we shall ere long be relieved from this position by the reciept of your letters, which will dictate to us the line to pursue and which we shall follow without deviation and without regard to our own opinion. Were we allowed to consult it, it would be that it would be most advantageous for the U.S. that the joint and express commission with which we are charged, should be recalled without our being obliged to press the negotiation to its end at this time—and that this court should be informed that the continuance of the negotiation was confided to their former standing representative here, or whomever the President should name for that purpose, with proper powers. In this manner it might be suspended without exciting alarm here, and pushed whenever any proper opportunity should present itself, if it should be judged most advisable to wait for that mode of obtaining the rights which we are persuaded the U.S. will never abandon.

In our late conferences with M. de Gardoqui we have resumed our representations with respect to the conduct of the agents of the Spanish government in America and particularly of the person who stiles himself a commissioner of H.M. with the Creek nation. M. de Gardoqui, as we have already had the honor of informing you, opposed his denial of any such conduct of their agents to our affirmation supported by the testimony with which you furnished us, and to which he considered very little authority as due. Since recieving the attestation with respect to Olivier and the copy of the passport he gave we brought forward that circumstance as being clearly authenticated by an act of his own. M. de Gardoqui assured us that he was convinced himself that no such person had been authorized—he added however that he would make enquiry in the foreign department. After having done this he confirmed to us what he had previously said. We proposed that he should give us a disavowal of this commissioner in writing, that we might transmit it officially to the President of the U.S. to which he assented with much willingness. He observed that the proper mode would be for us to write to him on the subject to which he would give us an immediate answer, conformably to what he had expressed to us verbally.

In consequence thereof we wrote to him on the 26th. ulto.—and according to his promise should have recieved his answer without delay. One day of conference has since intervened. In it he told us he had translated our letter and submitted it to H.M. and that he would send us the answer immediately on having recieved his orders thereon; still confirming what he had formerly told us with respect to the disavowal. As yet however we have not recieved it—and from M. de Gardoqui's mode of doing business, we cannot say when we shall, although we shall not cease to press him on his own promise. The answer if commensurate with our letter and conformable to his promise, will contain also an assurance of the orders given to their agents in America, and a promise of their being reminded of His Majesty's intentions that they should strictly adhere thereto.

Such assurances are of little importance in themselves—but this being given or withheld, and particularly the manner in which it is done, may be some indication of the ground on which they consider themselves with respect to England and us. So soon as we shall recieve this answer of whatever nature it may be, we shall not fail to transmit it to you.

The last letter which we have had the honor of recieving from you was of the 3d. of Nov. (the duplicate only came to our hands as mentioned formerly). What we have said will apprize you agreeably to your desire, at least as far as we know, of what may be expected from Spain with respect to their conduct towards our Indian neighbors. Whatever assurances they may give to the contrary, we believe they will endeavour to strengthen them and make them their friends and our enemies, until the territorial and other claims shall be settled—and that that being done, they will be indifferent as to those who remain within our limits. We have the honor to be with the most perfect respect Sir, your most obedient & most humble servants   [W CARMICHAEL]

W: SHORT

PrC (DLC: Short Papers); in Short's hand, with Carmichael's name as signatory supplied from Tr; at foot of first page: "The secretary of State for the United States—Philadelphia." Tr (DNA: RG 46, Senate Records, 3d Cong., 1st sess.); contains minor variations. Tr (Lb in same, Tr). Recorded in SJL as received 9 Sep. 1793. Enclosed in George Washington to TJ, 10 Sep. 1793.

SPANISH COMMISSARIES: Josef de Jaudenes and Josef Ignacio de Viar, the Spanish government's agents in Philadelphia. CATASTROPHE OF THE 21ST OF JANUARY: the execution of Louis XVI. YOUR INSTRUCTIONS: see Report on Negotiations with Spain, 18 Mch. 1792. FURTHER INSTRUCTIONS: a reference to the directions Carmichael and Short hoped to receive from TJ in consequence of the CHANGES OF EURO-PEAN AFFAIRS stemming from British and Spanish involvement in hostilities with France. TJ had anticipated this matter to some extent in his 23 Mch. 1793 letter to Carmichael and Short, but it is clear from their remarks near the end of the above letter that they had not yet received it. The SOMETHING CONCLUSIVE between Spain and Great Britain was an early intimation of the treaty of alliance of 25 May 1793 whereby they joined forces in the war against France (Bemis, *Pinckney's Treaty*, 168-9). THEIR FORMER STANDING REPRESENTATIVE HERE: William Carmichael, who since 1784 had been the United States chargé d'affaires in Madrid (Bemis, *Pinckney's Treaty*, 167).

[1] Preceding four words interlined.
[2] Preceding two words interlined in place of "our intention."

To Edmond Charles Genet

June 6. 93.

Th: Jefferson has the honor to inclose to Mr. Genet the letter &c. he mentioned to him yesterday. The parties are substantial. The samples of wood are arrived in Philadelphia, but not delivered. They shall be sent to Mr. Genet.

RC (ICHi). Not recorded in SJL.

The enclosed LETTER, not found, had been transmitted in William Foushee to TJ, 23 May 1793.

From George Gilmer

DEAR SIR   6 June 1793 Pen Park

Your favor inclosing the paper with Madns. observations, I much thank you for, and had trespassed on you long since, but finding no incident worth observation laid it by till the present moment, when I can inform you of an incident that reflects an evidence of my still retaining some small degree of my former elasticity Lucy having on the 25th. Inst. blessed me with a fine girl and is now perfectly well, but what is this, to the great incidents that are now talked of, tis impossible Demourier should immitate Arnold. I feel as much incited by the events in the french struggle as I used to experience in our own hope they'l be victorious and make no doubt of their terminating all their business in the complete imancipation of human nature. Cousin Lucy begs her best compliments may be acceptable to you. Shall have my Porter in perfection by your arrival. Adieu   GEORGE GILMER

RC (DLC); minimum punctuation supplied; endorsed by TJ as received 19 June 1793 and so recorded in SJL.

TJ's FAVOR was dated 15 Mch. 1793.

From John Garland Jefferson

DEAR SIR   Goochland June 6. 1793.

I have this moment received your favor of May 19. I was induced before the reception to take up a few goods of Mesrs' Shelton & Harris. Their desires that I shoud deal with them, their offers to furnish little sums of cash, for necessaries which require cash, Mr. Sheltons conduct on his disappointment, with respect to the money due for a quarters board, the difficulty of getting to Charlottesville, an expectation that my proposition woud meet with your approbation, from a supposition that it woud be as easy for you to pay here, as there, all conspired to make me take this immature step. But it is taken and cant be revoked! I am sorry for it. I will add to what I have already said, that I had taken up a few things before I heard from you. Of course I then expected to have had the cash, and to have been at liberty to furnish myself where I pleased. I hope my dear Sir, you will pardon the step I have taken, which tho contrary to your wishes, was actuated by the purest intention. And if it is the intention which makes a man guilty, I shall stand acquitted by you. To your candour, and known friendship, I submit with confidence my conduct. I lost in the course of last spring at least a month for the want of books. This to a man in my situation is a loss of importance. I have prevailed on Mr. William Pope to lend me a horse and chair to go in person for them. I expect to sit off to morrow. I will send your letter to Colo. Bell, and apologize to him for not takeing the credit you there gave me. I am my dear Sir, with the most grateful esteem, Your most obliged servant.   JNO G: JEFFERSON

June 19. Since I wrote the above I have been to Monticello. At the time I wrote it, I expected to have sent it to the office directly. I have received some of the books I wanted. Others are not there. It is to be lamented that those who borrow books, think so little of returning them.

RC (ViU: Carr-Cary Papers); at foot of text: "Thomas Jefferson Esqr."; endorsed by TJ as received 27 June 1793 and so recorded in SJL.

According to SJL, John Garland Jefferson wrote a missing letter to TJ of 8 Aug. 1793 from Monticello that was received on 19 Aug. 1793.

From Hans Rodolph Saabÿe

Copenhagen, 6 June 1793. He encloses an abstract of a section of a law, passed since his letter of 21 May, "extending the Priveledge of laying up Goods, without Obligation to pay the duty immediately, imposing on such Goods a Recognition of one ℔ Ct.," that is simultaneously advantageous to the Danish import trade and favorable to Americans trading here, who are thereby relieved of the high duties formerly imposed on them. He hopes this will increase American trade with this port and notes that commodities from America, like most other articles of trade, have been little in demand because of the recent reduction of credit and confidence among merchants. The restoration of peace would much improve commerce. He hopes that America will remain neutral; Denmark's neutrality is advantageous to Danish trade and navigation. Despite the spilling of blood, the combined allied armies have so far failed to achieve their goal of restoring a government contrary to the wishes of the generality of the French nation. May this confusion enable mankind in the future to be governed more on the basis of rational equality and render posterity truly happy.

Dupl (DNA: RG 59, CD); 3 p.; at head of text: "Duplicate"; endorsed by TJ as received 9 Nov. 1793 and so recorded in SJL. Enclosure: "Extract of an act for extending the Priviledge of laying up goods, without Obligation to pay the duty immediately, dated at the Palace of Christiansborg, the 31st. May 1793," abolishing the additional duty on merchandise imported second hand and providing that the privilege of avoiding the immediate payment of duties for laying up certain merchandise, hitherto restricted to those who imported the merchandise first hand in Danish ships, would now be extended to Danish subjects who imported the goods second hand in foreign bottoms, subject to the payment either of a one percent ad valorem duty on goods imported in privileged ships or of the additional duty on unprivileged ships, except with respect to West Indian and American products imported from the West Indies or America in foreign ships, which were to pay only the one percent ad valorem duty regardless of whether they were privileged or unprivileged (Tr in same; in Saabÿe's hand).

TJ submitted this letter and enclosure to the President on 9 Nov. 1793 and received them back the same day (Washington, *Journal*, 250).

To Angelica Schuyler Church

DEAR MADAM   Philadelphia June 7. 1793.

Monsr. de Noailles has been so kind as to deliver me your letter. It fills up the measure of his titles to any services I can render him. It has served to recall to my mind remembrances which are very dear to it, and which often furnish a delicious resort from the dry and oppressive scenes of business. Never was any mortal more tired of these than I am. I thought to have been clear of them some months ago: but circumstances will retain me a little while longer, and then I hope to get back to those scenes for which alone my heart was made. I had understood we were more shortly to have the happiness of seeing you in America. It is now I think the only country of tranquility, and should be the asylum of all those who wish to avoid the scenes which have crushed our friends in Paris. What is become of Me. de Corny? I have never heard of her since I returned to America. Where is Mrs. Cosway? I have heard she was become a mother, but is the new object to absorb all her affections? I think if you do not return to America soon you will be anchored in England by new family connections; for I am sure my dear Kitty is too handsome and too good not to be sought and sought again, till for peace sake she must make somebody happy. Her friend Maria writes to her: and I greet her with sincere attachment. Accept yourself assurances of the same from Dear Madame your affectionate friend & humble servt

TH: JEFFERSON

RC (Peter B. Olney, Old Saybrook, Connecticut, 1950); at foot of text: "Mrs. Church." PrC (MHi). Tr (MHi); 19th-century copy with lacunae.

Mrs. Church's LETTER was dated 17 Feb. 1793.

Memorial from George Hammond

The Undersigned, his Britannic Majesty's Minister Plenipotentiary to the United States, has the honor of acknowledging the receipt of the Secretary of State's two letters of the 15th. of May and of the 5th. of this month.

The Undersigned requests permission to express the satisfaction with which from the general tenor of these communications he has perceived the disposition of this government to adhere to the principles of neutrality so clearly and unequivocally asserted in the President's proclamation. He desires to add that with respect to those objects of his memorials, on which his opinions have been so fortunate as to have obtained the sanction of the executive government of the United States, he entertains the most implicit confidence that the assurances he has received of a determination to prevent a repetition of the grievances, of which he has complained, will be uniformly carried into complete and energetic effect.

Possessing this conviction of the general disposition of this government, the Undersigned cannot but regret that there should remain a most essential point, on which a difference of sentiment appears to subsist between it and himself. The confidence which he expressed in his memorial of the 8th. ulto. that the vessels captured by the two privateers, fitted out at Charleston, would be restored to their owners, arose from a persuasion that the government of the United States would regard—the act of fitting out those privateers in its ports as an insult offered to its sovereignty—and any prizes made by them as an unwarrantable aggression on the commerce carried on between its citizens and the subjects of a friendly power, relying on the protection of this government, and unsuspecting that the means of annoying them would be furnished within the harbours of the United States, or would be sanctioned by any of their officers. The Undersigned did not deem it necessary to enter into any exposition of facts relative to the mode of fitting out, equipping, arming and manning these privateers; as it is a matter of public notoriety at Charleston—that they were purchased, armed and equipped in that port—that houses of rendezvous were opened in that town for the express purpose of inviting American citizens and others to enter on board of them—that with the exception of two or three Frenchmen in each of the privateers, they were in fact manned by American citizens or British subjects, who, it is presumable, had been previously in the employ of American citizens—and, that in proceeding to effectuate their views of depredation, they were suffered to pass the fort near Charleston under a written permission from the Governor of South

[216]

Carolina. There is farther a reasonable ground of presumption that the Privateers themselves are at this moment actually owned by American citizens residing in Charleston.

Under the impression resulting, from his consideration of the principle respecting these privateers, and his knowledge of the facts he has stated, the Undersigned cannot conceal his concern that the principle itself should not have been regarded by the Secretary of State in a similar point of view, and that the facts should have been presented to him under so different an aspect. But even admitting that the facts had been such as they have been represented to the Secretary of State—that the privateers had been "purchased by French citizens with their own money, armed, equipped, and manned by themselves"—the Undersigned is of opinion that no commission whatsoever could justify any individuals, being under the protection of another power, in preparing in a neutral port such means of attack on the subjects of a nation at peace with the Sovereign of that port, whose previous consent and concurrence, or the stipulations of a treaty, alone, could have authorized such a proceeding. The insult and the aggression would therefore not have been essentially[1] varied by that circumstance.

For all these reasons, notwithstanding the deference which he shall ever preserve for the sentiments of this government, the Undersigned conceives himself justified in having entertained a confidence, that the government of the United States would not only have repressed this insult offered to its sovereignty, but also that the aggression on the subjects of the crown of Great Britain would have been repaired by the restitution of the vessels thus captured.

With regard to the extent to which the mischiefs arising from these privateers have been carried, exclusively of the long interruption which, in consequence of them, has occurred in the commerce between the Southern States and Great Britain, the annexed list of prizes will prove that their *actual* depredations have not been confined to a very narrow compass. And there is too much reason to apprehend that their *future* depredations will not be more limited, as it is generally understood that one of the privateers in question (le citoyen Genêt) is at this instant augmenting her force within the port of Philadelphia.

The Undersigned has esteemed it his duty to submit these observations in this form, lest his silence might have been construed into a dereliction of the arguments he had advanced, or of the facts he had alledged. The determination of the executive government of the United States relative to them is of a nature infinitely too delicate and important for him to venture giving an opinion upon it. He must therefore content himself for the present with respectfully assuring the Secretary of State that he will lose no time in communicating it to his Majesty's Ministers in England for their information and final decision.

Philadelphia   GEO. HAMMOND
7th June 1793.

RC (DNA: RG 59, NL); in the hand of Edward Thornton, signed by Hammond; at foot of first page: "Mr Jefferson"; endorsed by TJ as received 8 June 1793 and so recorded in SJL. FC (Lb in PRO: FO 116/3). Tr (same, 5/1). Tr (Lb in DNA: RG 59, NL).

TJ submitted Hammond's memorial to the President on 8 June 1793 (Washington, *Journal*, 165).

[1] Word interlined.

ENCLOSURE

List of British Vessels Captured by French Privateers on the American Coast

[7 June 1793]

List of British vessels captured on the coasts of the United States by the Schooner Privateers, le Citoyen Genêt and the Sans Culottes fitted out at Charleston

By the Schooner Privr. le Citoyen Genêt	Ship William of Glasgow.	Capt. Leggett
	Brige. Active of Bermuda.	Capt. Bassett
By the Schooner Privateer the Sans Culottes.	Brige. Fanny of London.	Capt. Pyle
	Schoonr. John of New Providce.	Capt. Richardson
	Sloop Spry of Do.	Capt. Brown
	Schoonr. Eunice of Do.	Capt. Tucker
	Snow Joseph of Do.	Capt. Prance*
	Bermuda Sloop driven on shore.	

*The life of this person is despaired of in consequence of the wounds he received in the action with the Sans Culottes.

FC (Lb in PRO: FO 116/3); undated. Tr (same, 5/1); undated; with minor variations.

From Henry Lee

Richmond, 7 June 1793. If TJ can give letters of introduction to the bearer, Mr. Livingston, a very worthy man and good citizen who proposes to visit France in order to establish personal and commercial connections, he might give essential help to a truly respectable man who, as a result of the part he took in the late war, sacrificed a very large fortune in Jamaica.

RC (DLC); 2 p.; endorsed by TJ as received 6 July 1793 and so recorded in SJL.

Muscoe Livingston was a sea captain who had served briefly as a second lieutenant in the Continental navy and resided at various times in London, Jamaica, Norfolk, and Essex County, Virginia, where he lived at this time and where his estate was probated in 1798 (WMQ, 1st ser., XIII [1905], 262, 263; Franklin, *Papers*, XXVI, 256; Morris, *Papers*, VI, 23; Syrett, *Hamilton*, XV, 366).

Notes on Conversations with
John Beckley and George Washington

June. 7. 93. Mr. Beckley, who is returned from N. York within a few days, tells me that while he was there Sr. John Temple, Consul genl. of the Northern states for Gr. Br. shewed him a letter from Sr. Gregory Page Turner a member of parliament for a borough in Yorkshire, who he said had been a member for 25 years, and always confidential for the ministers, in which he permitted him to read particular passages of the following purport 'that the government were well apprised of the predominancy of the British interest in the US. That they considered Colo. Hamilton, Mr. King and Mr. W. Smith of S. Carolina as the main[1] supports of that interest, that particularly they considered Colo. Hamilton and not Mr. Hammond as their effective minister here, that if the Antifederal interest [that was his term] at the head of which they considered Mr. Jefferson to be, should prevail, these gentlemen *had secured* an asylum to themselves in England.' Beckley could not understand whether they had secured it *themselves, or whether they were only notified that it was secured to them. So that they understand that they may go on boldly, in their machinations to change the government, and if they should be overset and chuse to withdraw, they will be secure of a pension in England as Arnold Deane &c had. Sr. John read passages of a letter [which he did not put into Beckley's hand as he did the other] from Ld. Grenville saying nearly the same things. This letter mentions to Sr. John that tho' they had divided the Consul-generalship and given the Southern department to Bond, yet he, Sr. John, was to retain his whole salary. [By this it should seem as if, wanting to use Bond, they had covered his employment with this cloak.] Mr. Beckley says that Sr. John Temple is a strong republican.—I had a proof of his intimacy with Sr. John in this circumstance. Sr. John received his new Commission of Consul general for the Northern department, and instead of sending it thro' Mr. Hammond, got Beckley to inclose it to me for his Exequatur. I wrote to Sr. John that it must come thro' Mr. Hammond, inclosing it back to him. He accordingly then sent it to Mr. Hammond.

In conversation with the President to-day, and speaking about Genl. Greene, he said that he and Genl. Greene had always differed in opinion about the manner of using militia. Greene always placed them in his front: himself was of opinion they should always be used as a reserve to improve any advantage, for which purpose they were the *finest fellows* in the world. He said he was on the ground of the battle of Guilford with

[In the margin:] *Impossible as to Hamilton. He was far above that.

a person who was in the action and who explained the whole of it to him. That General Greene's front was behind a fence at the edge of a large feild, thro which the enemy were obliged to pass to get at them; and that in their passage thro this they must have been torn all to peices if troops had been posted there who would have stood their ground; and that the retreat from that position was through a thicket, perfectly secure. Instead of this he posted the N. Carolina militia there, who only gave one fire and fell back, so that the whole benefit of their position was lost. He thinks that the regulars with their field pieces would have hardly let a single man get through that feild.

eod. die. [June 7.] Beckley tells me that he has the following fact from Govr. Clinton. That before the proposition for the present general government i.e. a little before, Hamilton concieved a plan for establishing a monarchical government in the US. He wrote a draught[2] of a circular letter, which was to be sent to about _____ persons, to bring it about. One of these letters in Hamilton's handwriting is now in possession of an old Militia Genl. up the North river, who at that time was thought *orthodox* enough to be entrusted in the execution. This General has given notice to Govr. Clinton that he has this paper, and that he will deliver it into his hands and no one's else. Clinton intends the first interval of leisure to go for it, and he will bring it to Philada. Beckley is a man of perfect truth as to what he affirms of his own knolege, but too credulous as to what he hears from others.[3]

MS (DLC); entirely in TJ's hand; written on same sheet as "Anas" entries for 10 and 12 June 1793; brackets in original; last sentence and note in margin added by TJ in a different ink at a much later date. Recorded in SJPL under 7-12 June 1793: "Notes. Ham. King. W. Smith. Sr Gregory Page Turner. Greene's method of using militia—on plan to usurp govmt." Included in the "Anas."

If John Beckley's record of his conversation with Sir John Temple is accurate, Temple probably overstated the prominence of Sir Gregory Page Turner, who had represented Thirsk, a BOROUGH IN YORKSHIRE, for only eight years and was evidently an administration backbencher of somewhat independent views rather than a ministerial confidante (Lewis Namier and John Brooke, *The House of Commons 1754-1790*, 3 vols. [New York, 1964], III, 244). Grenville's brief official dispatch of 8 Mch. 1793 notifying Temple of his effective demotion resulting from the division of THE

CONSUL-GENERALSHIP (PRO: FO 5/2) did not mention NEARLY THE SAME THINGS as Turner's letter, though the possibility cannot be excluded that Grenville did make such comments in a private missive. For Temple's exchange with TJ relating to his new EXEQUATUR, see TJ to Temple, 13 May 1793, and note.

There is no credible evidence that Alexander Hamilton had ever CONCEIVED A PLAN FOR ESTABLISHING A MONARCHICAL GOVERNMENT IN THE US. or circulated one, in the way recorded here, around the time of the Philadelphia Convention of 1787, when such schemes were in the air. Nevertheless, TJ's record of the story told to Beckley by Governor George Clinton of New York, a longstanding political foe of Hamilton's, is the only extant documentary evidence of the rumor prior to 1804, when the charge resurfaced during that year's bitter New York gubernatorial campaign. According to Clinton's later recollection, around 1787 William Malcom, the OLD MILITIA GENL., showed him an unsigned and unaddressed copy of A CIRCULAR LETTER which had been sent from Connecticut proposing the second son of George III, Frederick Augustus, Prince Bishop of Osnabrück and Duke of York and Albany, as the monarch of a United States transformed into a parliamentary government led by an Anglo-American aristocracy, enlarged to include Canada and Nova Scotia, given part of the British navy, and tied to Britain by a perpetual treaty of offensive and defensive alliance (Louise B. Dunbar, *A Study of Monarchical Tendencies in the United States from 1776 to 1801* [Urbana, Ill., 1922], 76-98; Clinton to Hamilton, 29 Feb., 6 Mch. 1804, Syrett, *Hamilton*, XXVI, 202-3, 209-10).

Clinton's conversation with Beckley was probably prompted by an equally unlikely variation of the story—one involving a clerk in Hamilton's law office allegedly seen preparing for distribution to the southern states in the spring or summer of 1787 a letter received from John Adams endorsing British overtures to the same effect—that had been recently related to the governor by Pierre Van Cortlandt, Jr., a law student of Hamilton's from 1784 to 1786 who was the son of a staunch Republican and later became Clinton's son-in-law (Van Cortlandt to [Clinton?], 27 Feb. 1804, Jacob Judd, ed., *Van Cortlandt Family Papers*, 4 vols. [Tarrytown, N.Y., 1976-81], III, 152-4; Syrett, *Hamilton*, XXVI, 197n). This revelation apparently moved Clinton sometime after his conversation with Beckley to inspect the letter held by Malcom, only to find that it was not in the handwriting of Hamilton or his clerk, but rather was "a Copy of the original Copy only" (Clinton to Van Cortlandt, 7 Mch. 1804, Judd, *Van Cortlandt Family Papers*, III, 160-1).

Despite the lack of trustworthy evidence of Hamilton's personal involvement in this implausible scheme, Clinton and Van Cortlandt continued to tell the story to friends. Hamilton had long been aware that a rumor to this effect was circulating, but he was unable to identify a source for it until 1804, when he denounced the story as a slanderous fabrication and vigorously sought to identify its originator, an effort in which he was only partially successful before his death at the hands of Aaron Burr later that year (same, 142-6, 152-4, 157-8, 160-1, 165; Memorandum of Nathaniel Pendleton, [ca. 25-27 Feb. 1804], Hamilton to Clinton, 27 Feb., 2, 7, 9 Mch. 1804, James Kane to Hamilton, 28 Feb. 1804, Syrett, *Hamilton*, XXVI, 196-202, 208-9, 211-12). It was sometime after this that TJ added his comments about Beckley and Hamilton.

[1] Word interlined in place of "material."
[2] Word written on top of "plan," erased.
[3] Sentence interlined at a later date.

From Benjamin H. Phillips

Curaçao, 7 June 1793. He acknowledges receipt of TJ's 20 Feb. letter with his consular commission and refers to the enclosed certificate for his ensuing conversation with the governor of the island. Last month an armed ship flying the flag of the States General brought into Aruba a Baltimore schooner, Robert Ross master, bound from Hispaniola to St. Thomas, and took from her 18 to 20 slaves and 2 boxes or trunks. The commander of the Dutch vessel claimed that the property was French. Ross reportedly has gone to St. Thomas and upon his return from Hispaniola intends to stop here, where the slaves have been brought. He shall pay attention to the instructions he has received and is grateful to the President for his appointment.

RC (DNA: RG 59, CD); 2 p.; at foot of text: "Thomas Jefferson Esquire"; endorsed by TJ as received 1 July 1793 and so recorded in SJL. Enclosure: Certificate of Petrus Bernardus Van Starckenborgh, secretary of the States General in Curaçao, 4 June 1793, describing a 30 May 1793 meeting between Phillips and Governor Johannes Abrahamszoon de Veer during which the governor stated that he could allow no foreign consul to serve on the island without express permission from the States

General and suggested that the American minister at The Hague request such permission for Phillips (MS in same, in Dutch, in a clerk's hand, signed by Van Starckenborgh; Tr in same, in English). Letter enclosed in Tobias Lear to TJ, 15 July 1793.

TJ submitted this letter to the President on 11 July 1793 (Washington, *Journal*, 191).

From William Short

SIR   Aranjuez June 7 1793.

Since my arrival in Spain I have had the honor of writing to you on the 3d. of feb. and 6th. of March. Nothing has since occurred which seemed to authorize my troubling you, except in my joint communications with Mr. Carmichael. The ordinary business of this mission has been followed by him of course exclusively, as well as his usual correspondence with you. The several state papers and public acts which have appeared here from time to time he has forwarded therewith, as he has informed me by the way of Cadiz and Lisbon.

Our joint letters will have informed you of the progress or rather of the stagnation of the negotiation with which we are jointly charged. This situation of things which it has appeared to us impossible to avoid under present circumstances, is extremely painful to us both, but peculiarly so to me, from the distance which I have been sent for this express object at a considerable expence to the public, and without a probability of rendering them any service whatever. I have not thought myself as yet authorized to relieve myself from this situation by returning to my residence, because that would have been breaking off the conferences which could not have failed in whatever manner it had been done, to have excited here the alarm which we thought it essential to avoid under present circumstances, for the reasons which have been detailed to you in our joint letters. I flatter myself however that this will not long be the case, as I hope we shall soon recieve letters from you written after the President shall have been informed of the change of relations between this country France and England. These are now so different from what they must have appeared to you at the time of your instructions being drawn up, that we have considered it our indispensable duty to leave time for additional ones. Our last advices from you being of Nov. 3: seem not to have contemplated their probability—and indeed could not well have done it, from the unsettled state of political data, at that time. We have since recieved the American gazettes to the 1st: of Jany.—and at that epoch our information from America stops. This ignorance of affairs there adds also to our hesitation here.

[222]

In my last letters I gave you my particular opinion of the situation of this country and the efforts they might find within their power for the present war. There still remains a great deal of zeal and unanimity in all the influential classes with respect to it. Offers continue to be made by all descriptions of persons. It is said that few have been realized, because the King has declined accepting them as not being in want—but in general voluntary contributions must be considered as a precarious resource. Some very great efforts however have certainly been made by individuals both of the laity and clergy. Several of the former have raised considerable bodies of troops at their own expence—and in one respect their zeal has done injury, as they have paid so large bounties and given so considerable pay to their troops, as to have checked the enlisting in the main army, for the bounty and pay there allowed.

Still a very great number of troops have been put on foot—they are divided into three armies—one in Catalonia under the command of M. Ricardos. It is by far the largest and the most active—a considerable part of it has advanced into Roussillon and has gained several advantages over the French troops—the numbers are differently stated—the best accounts state those who have passed the frontier at twenty thousand. It is said they treat the inhabitants well—a great number of villages have sollicited to remain under the King's authority—and several certainly sent to invite M. de Ricardos to pass the frontier to their relief. The probability is that before the arrival of the Spanish troops there were two parties—and that afterwards, the greater number were for the strongest side, and that the rest remained silent, so as to give the appearance of unanimity of which the Spanish government boasts. The second and smallest army, consisting of about 15,000[1] men, is in Aragon under the command of the Prince de Castel franco—it has not yet passed the frontier. The third is commanded by M. Carott—its number uncertain, from its extending over several posts, on the frontier of Biscay. It has made different incursions into France, always with advantage, but has returned after each success. It has been expected for some time that it would proceed and besiege Bayonne—as that of Ricardos has done Bellegarde, which place it is thought can not make a long resistance.

These armies are known to be very illy provided with all the usual articles—either from bad management—or from want of funds—constant complaints have been coming from the generals to the minister of war—who throws the blame on the minister of finance—the want of necessaries, it is said alone prevents the two main armies from penetrating further into France.

This country has also made considerable efforts in the marine department—the list which they have published amounts 50 ships of the line

equipped for sea, of which 8 of 112. guns—37. vessels above 30. guns—
and 49. smaller—making in the whole 136 vessels carrying 5736
guns—and 44,381 men. If this account could be closely examined there
would no doubt be found several puffed articles. Still they have certainly
fitted out a very considerable fleet. They have in the Mediterranean at
sea 25. ships of the line—this fleet lately proceeded to Sardinia—the
French troops on two little islands adjoining to Sardinia, surrendered to
the Spanish admiral, to the number of 1000—with one or two frigates.
The French fleet of 22. sail of the line was expected to sail from Toulon
about three or four weeks ago—all communication with that country
being cut off, except by sea from Italy or England, we know nothing
later from thence. The English fleet it is expected will soon join the
Spanish. It is thought their object will then be to pursue the French fleet
if at sea—or take them if at Toulon, and destroy that port. What will
surprize you is that the Spanish desire this latter event, and would aid
to effect it.

These efforts have been made by Spain without laying new taxes, and
without loans. It is a matter of surprize how these additional expences
could be faced[2] without additional revenue and that with a deficit which
it is supposed existed previous to the war. The only extraordinary
means, which are known, are the offers abovementioned (which certainly could have not have gone a great way towards equalling the extraordinary expences) and an operation made some time ago with which
you were certainly duely informed by Mr. Carmichael, the taking into
the King's possessions the sums which the several commonalties and
chambers of commerce, had in their respective common treasures to
answer their common needs—these sums were considerable, and as the
charges which occur are gradual and much inferior to them, and which
the King is in future to take on himself, it put at his disposition a considerable quantity of disponible cash. This however, was opposed by several commonalties as being a violation of their property, and in some
instances, though I believe few, their opposition was successful. The
general dissatisfaction that this fiscal measure gave, has been stifled by
subsequent events.

In addition to these means some suspect that there has been an abuse
also in adding to the sum of *Vales reales*. This however would be soon
detected, and their current price does not seem to indicate a well
founded suspicion of such an abuse.

The importation of specie from America is also mentioned as a
means—but only the excedent of the present or last year, above the
other years can be taken into that account[3] as this resource made a part
of the ordinary revenue. It seems generally agreed that the late importations both on public and private account[4] have been more than former

ones, and this is corroborated by the statement of coinage in Mexico for the year 1792. which I have procured here, and which I have the honor of inclosing to you.

Should the war continue these extraordinary means must be exhausted and it is generally thought there would be considerable difficulty in levying additional taxes which would then seem indispensable. Several look to this moment as a very trying one for this country, and indeed it has been found to be such for every country whose taxes were already oppressive, and pushed to so great an extent. Attempts will probably be made towards anticipating on the revenue of posterity, in order to meet present wants. Should this country be able to push that system as far proportionally, as some others of Europe have done, they will find it a rich mine. Hitherto they have not been obliged, or not been able from the state of their credit to exploite it to any considerable degree.

On the whole this country, it seems to me, may be considered in a state of probation both with respect to its internal and external affairs: and time (perhaps a short time will suffice) must be the authority to which I must refer you.

I need not mention to you the steps which have been taken to place the supreme administration in the hands of a young favorite, as you will have of course been informed of them—the effects produced by this event are very different, from what was expected, owing in a considerable degree to the character and disposition of the present minister, and the art which was employed by the Queen to bring it about—and still more perhaps to the minds of all being exclusively occupied by the events in France and the war with that country.

During Ct. de Florida Blanca's administration, all those who desired to see his fall, placed their eyes on Ct. Daranda for his successor. They might both be considered as national favorites. The Queen alone perhaps looked to her favorite as a rival for them both. She saw that the step from Ct. de Florida Blanca to a young *Garde du corps* without education, fortune, connexions or any other known recommendation but an handsome person would be too great, and particularly over the head of Ct. Daranda. His ruin was therefore resolved on, at the same time that it was determined that he should be the instrument of the ruin of his rival—this was done by bringing him into the ministry, and preventing him whilst there from taking any measure that could [serve?] any part of the public. As they had begun by excusing Ct. de Florida Blanca's disgrace in favor of Ct. Daranda's promotion—they ended by ill humour against him for having deprived them of a favorite without doing any thing to replace him in their affections. As the public march quick in this line they were soon out of sight of the past services and reputation of Count D'Aranda and saw only the present contemptible role he was made to play. When the public mind was found thus prepared the favorite was brought forward to supplant him and was supported in some degree by the public voice, from opposition or ill will to Count D'Aranda, who is kept as a sitting member in the council, in order to prevent his recovering from his loss of public opinion. As Madrid being the capital, is the most apprehended by the court they have kept themselves and the favorite out of its sight as it were, by residing at the different sitios. The young minister in the mean time by popular manners has gained the affections of the people around him— and by an uncommon degree of prudence, never committing himself on any occasion has acquired a good deal of respect, so that he begins to be really, contrary to what could have ever been expected, a favorite minister with the public. Whether the same caution and prudence will be used when he shall find himself well established in their affections, as have been to acquire them I cannot say—but if that should be the case he may I think promise himself a long administration. He enjoys one advantage also which will be found[5] to give him a considerable advantage over his predecessors. The established usage here of every minister being absolute in his own department has ever impeded the march of administration. Ct. de Florida Blanca in the height of his power only commanded the departments where he had been able to place his favorites—the American department for instance was always independent of him during the life of M. de Galvez. The present minister on the contrary, by being identified as it were with the persons of the Royal family, is raised above envy and would meet with opposition from none of the ministry—and thus the government has acquired a degree of unity and force which it had not before. This unexpected effect of the ministry of a young uninformed man brought so rapidly from the lowest condition to the highest degree of power—and which in other countries would have produced a general outcry on one side, and imprudent insolence on the other, besides the causes above mentioned must depend in some degree also on the Spanish character. The issue cannot be said yet to be fully ascertained, but there seems every reason to believe it will end well for all parties.

Notwithstanding these subjects do not make a part of the business with which I am charged here jointly with Mr. Carmichael, still I have thought it might not be improper to give you my sentiments respecting them, as they appear to me to have necessarily an indirect connexion with it. It is for the same reason I mention the following intelligence which has been lately communicated to me with a good deal of caution though I think in a way that may be relied on.

It is the intention of this government to make New Orleans a free port to all nations with the restriction that vessels in order to be admitted there must first touch on their way at one of two Spanish ports assigned for that purpose—viz. Alicant in the Mediterranean—and a port on the coast of Gallicia on the Atlantic side. A person in the department of the Indies, is now preparing the subject and the ordinance for the purpose by the order of M. de Gardoqui who has that department. It is said this will take place very soon, by which is meant from three to six months. The object is to form an entrepot at New Orleans, by which Spain may supply their American possessions with such goods as they may chuse to admit there—and to encourage the fur trade with the Indians.

It does not appear that the U.S. are contemplated in this arrangement, or at least in a favorable manner—nothing is intended therein to facilitate the coming down the river to N. Orleans—and there does not appear as yet any idea of exempting American vessels going by sea, from touching at one of the Spanish ports abovementioned.

M. de Gardoqui has never given us the most distant hint of this intention of making N. Orleans a free port, and indeed we should have inferred a very contrary disposition from all his conversations with us. Should it be realized on the footing abovementioned it would seem rather to be with an hostile view to the U.S. and in order to enlist in the defense of their possession of N. Orleans, such nations as should be benefited by being thus admitted to it. I shall endeavor to ascertain the progress of this business—and will inform you of such as may be made during my stay here.

There is a circumstance which has been for some time and still is depending between this country and England with which you have undoubtedly been made acquainted by Mr. Pinckney, and which it may not be amiss to repeat here, as it shews a disposition in the parties on which we counted in some degree. When Ld. St. Helens arrived here, he proposed to the minister that the rules with respect to re-captures should be the same between England and Spain, as those inserted in the treaty of commerce between England and France. At that time the English commerce in the Mediterranean was much exposed to the French cruisers—and the ministry here thought it would be a losing agreement for Spain—some delay took place therefore before its acceptation. In the mean time a English vessel was recaptured by a Spanish cruiser—and after some difficulty was either delivered or agreed to be delivered—about the time of this agreement, the rich Register ship with specie and merchandize to the value, it is said of 4,000,000 of dollars was recaptured by a part of the English fleet. The Spaniards are now earnest in reclaiming her. The English, it seems, make difficulties—and affirm that Spain did not agree to give up the English vessel until after the minister got notice of the recapture of the Register ship although unknown to the English Ambassador here. It is doubted much here whether she will be restored and this has created already much ill humour in the administration. How far they will venture to shew it I cannot say—but I do not doubt this country will with time have many reasons to repent of their present position, and many causes of dissatisfaction with their new friends.

I have only now to beg pardon for troubling you with so long a letter, and to assure you of the perfect respect with which I have the honor to be, Sir, your most obedient & most humble servant   W Short

PrC (DLC: Short Papers); one word illegible; at head of text: "No. 125"; at foot of first page: "The Secretary of State, for the United States." Tr (Lb in DNA: RG 59, DD); with variations. Recorded in SJL as received 24 Oct. 1793; an extract, not found, is recorded in SJL as received 9 Sep. 1793. Enclosure not found.

YOUNG FAVORITE: Manuel Godoy Alvarez de Faria, Duque de la Alcudia, the first secretary of Spain. LD. ST. HELENS: Alleyne Fitzherbert, Baron St. Helens, the British ambassador to Spain, 1790-94, was chief negotiator of the recent Anglo-Spanish treaty of alliance (DNB).

TJ submitted this letter to the President on 2 Nov. 1793 and received it back the same day (Washington, *Journal*, 242, 243).

[1] Tr: "ten thousand."
[2] Tr: "forced."
[3] Remainder of sentence interlined.
[4] Preceding six words interlined.
[5] Short here canceled "of public utility."

From John Matthew Bulkeley

St. Petersburg, 8 June 1793. His partnership with Robert Hay expired on 31 Dec. 1792, since which, with the approval and advice of his father and brother, John Bulkeley & Son of Lisbon, and other friends, he has carried on business here himself under the name of John Matthew Bulkeley & Company. Having transacted considerable American business under former firms and gained much experience of the quality of goods best suiting that market, for which line principally he was encouraged to form his new establishment, he offers his services when any business is to be transacted here, promising attentive, honest, punctual service.

RC (DLC); 2 p.; printed circular, with salutation and date by a clerk and signatures by Bulkeley as an individual ("J M Bulkeley") and a firm ("John Matthew Bulkeley Co"); at head of text in clerk's hand: "Honble. Thomas Jefferson Monticello near Charlotte Ville Virginia"; with price current for Russian produce printed on verso; endorsed by TJ as a letter from "Bulkeley & sons" received 2 Dec. 1793 and so recorded in SJL.

From Nathaniel Cutting

Sir   Falmouth, 8th. June, 1793.

I have the honor to acquaint you that I arrived in this Port yesterday, which compleated thirty-four days from the time of my departure from the Delaware. The Ship waits here for orders from London, therefore I intend to set out for that metropolis, by land, to morrow.

At this extreme corner of the Kingdom, I find very little authentic intelligence respecting public affairs. It is reported and believed here, that Dumourier, after all his brilliant exploits under the Banners of the French Republic, has taken the same step that La Fayette did, and is now resident in the Austrian Territories, a deserter from those Colours which he display'd with such eclat in the Netherlands the year past. Some pretend to account for this from the proverbial versatility of his Countrymen, and the implacable resentment of some influential Characters in the Convention whose native rigidity has never admitted the amiable polish of liberality and whose jealous temperatures lead them to suppose their own individual merit depreciated by the virtues or successes of a Competitor.

It seems that the French conducted with so little address or discretion in Brabant or Flanders that they disgusted those whose friendship they ought to have been solicitous to secure; so that instead of extending their glorious career through the States of Holland, as was expected by some[1] in America, they have been obliged precipitately to relinquish all the Territory their rapid successes over-ran in course of the last year; But having once retreated within the proper boundaries of their Realm, they seem to be invincible. Several severe engagements between large Detachments of the combined forces, and the troops of the French Republic are reported to have taken place, in which the English confess the latter were either compleatly victorious, or maintained their ground with all the address of military veterans and all the firmness of men who think it a disgrace to yield to anything less than omnipotence!

By Sea the Republic makes but a despicable figure; and I think it good policy that it does not attempt much in that line. French Privateers and light Cruizers are said to swarm through all the navigable world, and by their predatory warfare distress the Commerce of their Enemies, and of course injure them more essentially, than the same force could do if applied in any other way. I am told that a prodigious number of English merchantships have been captured, and many of them have arrived safe in French Ports notwithstanding the British Fleet proudly exults in its superiority and rides triumphant on the broad Atlantic as well as in the narrow seas. The most it has hitherto effected has been now and then capturing a Privateer, or retaking a Prize. One of each of these descriptions was recently sent into England which are said to be the most valuable that ever fell into the hands of an Enemy. The French Privateer call'd the Dumourier, had captured a Spanish Register Ship, took out of her two hundred and fifty Boxes of Silver, and instead of judiciously shaping different courses for different Ports, they both kept together till they fell in with the British fleet which effectually alter'd their route. The specie and bullion captured as abovemention'd is reported and believed to amount to above one million sterling. This it seems, agreably to the marine Laws of Spain in similar cases, will be wholly condemned as prize to the Re-captors. The share of Lord Hood, as Admiral of the Fleet, is computed at Sixty thousand pounds.

The English at this Port confidently assert that French Cruizers when they meet with any American Vessel laden with Provision, bound to any Port in the Territory of their Enemies, they violate the Laws of Neutrality by obliging her to proceed to some port in France. This I take to be a piece of calumny calculated to mislead our Countrymen and irritate them against a people who, though guilty of many excesses which make humanity shudder, are exerting every nerve in Support of that political freedom in which the Americans have so long gloried!

It is reported here likewise that English Cruizers have also intercepted American [Vessels][2] bound to France with Provisions; but I understand that Government disavows having authorized such wanton violations of the laws of declared neutrality. I sincerely hope that such unwarrantable stretches of power, exercised by rapacious and lawless individuals may not excite any serious altercation between our Government and either of the belligerent [Powers][3] but on the other hand I flatter myself that we shall not pusilanimously crouch to the insolent authority that[4] may presume to insult the American Flag. I have the honor to be, most respectfully, Sir, Your most obedient humble servant

NAT. CUTTING

RC (DNA: RG 59, MLR); slightly torn; addressed: "The Secretary of State, for the United States, Philadelphia"; postmarked; endorsed by TJ as received 1 Aug. 1793 and so recorded in SJL. FC (Lb in MHi: Cutting Papers); in Cutting's hand; contains numerous minor variations.

[1] FC: "many."

[2] Word inadvertently omitted by Cutting supplied from FC.

[3] Word torn away supplied from FC.

[4] Remainder of sentence in FC: "shall presume to insult the Flag of the United States of America!"

From Robert W. Fox

Falmouth, 8 June 1793. He acknowledges TJ's favors of 20 Feb. and 21 Mch. addressed to Edward Fox—mistakenly, he believes, because Robert Morris, who recommended either him or his brother to serve as American consul here, has informed them that the appointment was made, and there is no Edward Fox in Falmouth—and asks for another appointment in his own name. In the meantime he will act as consul if the minister in London does not object. He will abide to the best of his ability by TJ's directions and forward the executed bond after the American minister in London approves it. Since the outbreak of war between England and France a great number of American ships have arrived here and been permitted to leave with their cargoes to wherever their proprietors choose, though lately none has been ordered to France, but many to Spain, where wheat sells for 60/ to 70/ per 8 bushels and flour 42/ to 48/ per barrel. He hopes soon to receive his new appointment and will immediately inform the minister in London of anything important. The government will presumably attend to his representations, as he and his brother are known to several Lords of the Treasury and Admiralty.

RC (DNA: RG 59, CD); 4 p.; addressed: "For The Secretary of State for the United States of America at Philadelphia"; postmarked; endorsed by TJ as received 1 Aug. 1793 and so recorded in SJL. Tr (same); at head of text: "(Copy)"; possibly the text recorded in SJL as received 12 Sep. 1793.

Robert Were Fox (d. 1818), a Quaker shipping agent in Falmouth who was the father of the noted English scientific writer of the same name, was mistakenly nominated and confirmed as the United States consul at that port under the name of Edward Fox in February 1793. He functioned as acting consul until he was renominated and reconfirmed under his own name in May 1794 and served until his death (JEP, I, 129, 130-1, 158, 159, III, 170, 172; DNB; Fox to TJ, 10 Aug., 7 Sep. 1793). For the first of the two letters TJ mistakenly addressed to Edward Fox, see note to TJ to Robert Montgomery, 20 Feb. 1793.

From Edmond Charles Genet

Philadelphie le 8. Juin 1793.

MONSIEUR L'an 2e. de la Republique Française.

J'ai vu avec peine par votre lettre du 5 de ce mois que M. le President des Etats unis persistait à penser qu'une nation en guerre n'avoit pas le droit de donner des Commissions en guerre[1] à ceux de ses vaisseaux qui se trouvaient dans les Ports d'une nation neutre: cette mesure etant selon lui un acte de souveraineté.

Je vous avouë, Monsieur, que cette Opinion me parait contraire aux principes du droit naturel, aux usages des nations, aux liens qui nous unissent et même à la proclamation de Mr. le Président.

Le droit de s'armer, Monsieur, à l'effet de pourvoir à sa deffense et de repousser d'injustes aggressions peut selon moi etre éxercé par une nation en guerre dans un etat[2] neutre à moins que par des traités ou des loix particulières de cet Etat, ce droit ne soit restreint à une seule nation amie ou alliée et interdit éxpréssement aux autres. Ce cas est exactement celui ou nous nous trouvons, les Etats unis, amis des français, leurs alliés et garans de leurs possessions en amerique leur ont permis d'entrer armés[3] et de sejourner dans leurs ports, d'y amener leurs prises, de s'y reparer, de s'y equiper tandis qu'ils ont refusé éxpressement cet avantage à leurs énemis. L'intention des Etats Unis a été de nous faciliter les moyens de protéger éfficacement notre commerce et[4] de deffendre nos possessions en amérique si utiles à notre prosperité commune, et tant que les Etats unis assemblés en congrès n'auront point décidé que cet engagement solemnel ne doit pas être effectué,[5] il n'appartient à personne d'entraver nos opérations et d'en annuller l'effet en empechant ceux de nos marins qui se trouvent dans les Ports d'amérique de se prévaloir des Commissions que le Gouvernement français m'a chargé de leur faire donner[6] pour les autoriser à se deffendre et à[7] remplir s'ils en trouvent l'occasion tous les devoirs de Citoyens[8] contre les ennemis de l'Etat. Au Surplus, Monsieur, dans tous les tems de pareilles Commissions en tems de guerre ont été délivrées à nos navires. Les Officiers de la marine les leur remettaient en france,[9] et les Consuls dans les païs etrangers et c'est en vertu de cet usage, qu'aucune puissance n'a jamais imaginé de regarder comme un acte de souveraineté, que le conseil éxécutif a envoyé ici de semblables commissions.[10]

Cependant, Monsieur, toujours animé du desir de maintenir la bonne harmonie qui regne si heureusement entre nos deux païs j'ai prescrit aux Consuls de n'accorder des lettres[11] qu'aux Capitaines qui s'obligent sous serment et sous caution à respecter le territoire des Etats unis et les opinions politiques de leur President, en attendant que les representans du[12] Souverain les aient confirmées ou rejetées; c'est là tout ce que le Gouvernement americain peut attendre de notre défférence, tout ce qui se passe hors des Eaux des Etats unis n'étant pas de sa compétence.

Il resulte de cette notte, Monsieur, que les Commissions remises en vertu des ordres du conseil exécutif de la République francaise aux vaisseaux français qui se trouvent dans les ports des Etats Unis ne sont qu'une simple autorisation de s'armer,[13] fondée sur le droit naturel et l'usage constant de la france;[14] que ces commissions ont été expediées de tout tems dans de pareilles circonstances; que leur distribution ne peut être considerée que comme un acte d'administration consulaire et non de souveraineté et que toute entrave mise par le Gouvernement des Etats Unis à l'armement des vaisseaux francais serait une atteinte portée aux droits de l'homme sur lesquels reposent l'indépéndance et[15] les loix des Etats Unis, une violation des liens qui unissent les Peuples de france et d'amerique et même une contradiction manifeste dans le sistème de neutralité de M. Le Président; car en effet si nos navires marchands ou autres n'avaient pas la liberté de s'armer dans un moment où les Français resistent seuls à la ligue de tous les tirans contre la Liberté des Peuples, Ils seraient exposés à une ruine certaine en sortant des ports des Etats Unis;[16] ce qui n'est certainement pas l'intention du Peuple americain: Sa voix fraternelle a retenti de toute part autour de moi et ses accens ne sont point équivoques; Ils sont purs comme le coeur de ceux qui les ont exprimés et plus ils ont touché mon ame plus ils doivent interesser au bonheur de l'amerique la nation que je représente; plus je souhaite, Monsieur, que le Gouvernement fœdéral observe autant qu'il est en lui les engagemens publics que les deux peuples ont[17] contractes et que par cette conduite[18] généreuse et prudente, il donne, au moins,[19] au monde l'exemple d'une véritable neutralité qui ne consiste pas à abandonner lachement ses amis dans le moment ou le danger les menace, mais à s'en tenir strictement, si l'on ne peut faire mieux, aux obligations que l'on a contractées envers eux. C'est par de pareils procédés que l'on se rend réspectable à toutes les puissances que l'on conserve ses amis et que l'on merite d'en augmenter le nombre.   (signé) GENET

PrC of Tr (DLC); in the hand of George Taylor, Jr.; at head of text: "Le Ministre de la République Française au secrétaire d'Etat des Etats Unis." Dft (DLC: Genet Papers); at head of text: "⟨Prises et armemens⟩ Note dans laquelle le Citoyen genet défend le droit que les francois ont d'armer dans les ports des Etats unis"; contains numerous emendations and revisions, only the most important of which are noted below. Tr (AMAE: CPEU, XXXVII); with minor variations. Tr (NNC: Gouverneur Morris Papers). PrC of another Tr (PRO: FO 97/1); in Taylor's hand. FC (DLC: Genet Papers); in English. FC (same); in English. FC (same); in English; draft translation of preceding FCs. Tr (DNA: RG 46, Senate Records, 3d Cong., 1st sess.); in English. Recorded in SJL as received on 14 June 1793. Printed with translation in *Message*, 10-11 (App.), 23-4; translation printed in ASP, *Foreign Relations*, I, 151. Enclosed in TJ to Gouverneur Morris, 16 Aug. 1793.

Genet's contention that the United States had authorized the French by treaty to fit out privateers in American ports rested upon the assumption that the specific denial of this right to the enemies of France in Article 22 of the 1778 treaty of amity and commerce constituted an implicit grant of it to the French (Miller, *Treaties*, II, 19-20). See also Thomas, *Neutrality*, 118-37.

[1] In Dft Genet apparently first wrote "⟨de nouvelles Commissions⟩ des lettres de Marque" and then altered it to read as above.

[2] In Dft Genet first wrote "chés une nation" and then altered it to read as above.

[3] Preceding word written in margin of Dft.

[4] In Dft Genet first wrote "a été de nous mettre exclusivement en mesure" and then altered it to read as above.

[5] In Dft Genet first wrote the preceding clause as "et Il n'appartient qu'à ces Etats réunis en Congrès de décider si Cet engagement doit être éffectué." *Message*: "les états assembles en Congrès."

[6] In Dft Genet here canceled "par les Consuls."

[7] Preceding five words interlined in Dft in place of "à s'armer pour se défendre ou pour."

[8] Dft and AMAE Tr: "de bons citoyens."

[9] In Dft Genet here canceled "et dans les colonies."

[10] In Dft Genet wrote "ici les Commissions ⟨en question⟩" in place of "des ⟨lettres de marque⟩ commissions aux differents Consulats dans les Etats unis pour être distribuées aux navires de la nation, mais."

[11] Except for the first two words, the sentence to this point in Dft, ending with "ces lettres," is written in the margin in

place of "d'après mes ordres les Consuls n'en ont accordé Jusqu'a présent."

[12] Preceding three words interlined in Dft in place of "le."

[13] Preceding three words written in margin of Dft.

[14] In Dft Genet here canceled "et d'autres nations de s'armer en guerre."

[15] Preceding three words written in margin of Dft.

[16] In Dft Genet first wrote "⟨non seulement⟩ en sortant des ports ⟨et des eaux⟩ des Etats unis ⟨mais aussi dans⟩ et peut être dans ces ports et dans ces eaux vû leur" and then altered it to read as above.

[17] In Dft Genet here canceled "cimentés de leur sang."

[18] Here in Dft Genet wrote "grande."

[19] Preceding two words written in margin of Dft.

From William Lambert

SIR   Philadelphia, 8th: June, 1793.

The many instances of politeness and indulgence I received from you, during my continuance in your office, demand my sincere acknowledgments. There are some of them, in particular, which conferred the highest obligations, and will ever be remembered with sentiments of gratitude and respect.

I have reason to suppose, that the arrangements which will probably be made in the office of the Clerk of the House of Representatives, at the next Session of Congress will be favorable to me, and I have had the strongest assurances from Mr. Beckley, of his friendship and support. Permit me, Sir, to hope that as far as my conduct may appear to deserve it, your influence will also be employed in my behalf. I have the honor to be, with the most perfect esteem, Sir, Your most Obedient Servant.

WILLIAM LAMBERT

RC (DLC); at foot of text: "The Secretary of State"; endorsed by TJ as received 8 June 1793 and so recorded in SJL.

William Lambert (d. 1834) of Virginia, a skilled mathematician, served in 1788 as a clerk helping to arrange the state's accounts with the United States. He was principal clerk to John Beckley during the latter's service as clerk of the House of Representatives during the first session of the First Congress. TJ employed him as a clerk in the Department of State from November 1790 until the end of September 1792. Thereafter he held various governmental clerkships, often under Beckley at the House though, as with Beckley, his fierce Republicanism temporarily cost him his position in the late 1790s. Restored to their positions after the Republicans gained a majority in the House in 1801, they later quarreled and

Beckley fired Lambert in 1805. Lambert corresponded frequently with TJ during his presidency and retirement about topics in astronomy, especially Lambert's tireless but largely fruitless efforts to improve the calculation of longitude, establish a national observatory, and obtain governmental sanction for the establishment of a point at Washington, D.C., to replace Greenwich, England, as America's prime meridian ([Washington] *Daily National Intelligencer*, 21, 23 Oct. 1834; CVSP, IV, 362, 466; Berkeley, *Beckley*, 57, 223-4, 239, 267-9; Lambert to TJ, 15 Dec. 1804, 31 July 1805, 2 Apr. 1806, 6 July 1825; TJ to Lambert, 22 Dec. 1804, 29 Nov. 1822; Charles O. Paullin, "Early Movements for a National Observatory, 1802-1842," *Records of the Columbia Historical Society*, XXV [1923], 40-3). The date when Lambert's service ended at the Department of State—

given incorrectly as 1793 in Vol. 17: 356n, 358n, and Vol. 24: 367n—is established by salary accounts of the Department of State for the quarters ending 31 Dec. 1792 and 31 Mch. 1793 (MSS in DNA: RG 217, MTA; dated 31 Dec. 1792 and 31 Mch. 1793, respectively; in the hand of George Taylor, Jr., signed by TJ; registered in the Treasury under Nos. 3402 and 3834); and by Lambert to TJ, 27 July 1819.

To John Nicholas, Jr.

DEAR SIR   Philadelphia June 8. 1793.

Your favor from Richmond was duly received, and the advertisement put into Freneau's and Fenno's papers, as these go through most of the states. I changed the direction of the application *to the printers*, and desired each of them to send the applicants to me. It is not in my power to give you any exact information on the subject of the mines, as I was too young at the death of my father to notice such things minutely. I have little news to give you in addition to what you will see in the public papers. We learn from the islands of St. Domingo and Martinique that they are preparing to oppose the English, and that they are disposed and able to repel them if an attack should be attempted. The Indian treaty will, we learn, be a month later than was contemplated. I am longing to be with you in Albemarle, without being able to fix the time. My attachments to that part of the world and it's inhabitants will let me be happy no where else and with no others. Remember me affectionately to all our neighbors and particularly to Mrs. Nicholas. I am Dear Sir your affectionate friend & servt   TH: JEFFERSON

PrC (DLC); at foot of text: "Colo. J. Nicholas."

Nicholas's partially dated FAVOR FROM RICHMOND is printed under 24 May 1793.

To Robert Quarles

SIR   Philadelphia June 8. 1793.

I received, on the 3d. instant your favor of May 19. and immediately transmitted it to the accountant of the war office, and now inclose you his answer. Whatever you shall think proper to decide on this subject, if you will be so good as to inform me by letter, it shall be properly communicated, and brought to such an issue as the laws will justify. I am Sir Your very humble servt   TH: JEFFERSON

PrC (DLC); at foot of text: "Mr. Robert Quarles. Columbia." Tr (DLC); 19th-century copy. Enclosure not found.

The ACCOUNTANT OF THE WAR OFFICE was Joseph Howell, Jr. (Syrett, *Hamilton*, XI, 451n).

To James Sullivan

Sir   Philadelphia June 8 1793.

I was yesterday honored by the receipt of your letter of June 2. on the subject of Mr. Letombe's continuance in the consulship, and am sorry to inform you that an appointment had taken place three days before and the Exequatur had issued. I should with pleasure have handed in your testimony in favor of Mr. Letombe had it not been too late; in which I should have been gratified in rendering a service to him as well as in doing what would have been agreeable to you. I with pleasure avail myself of this, as of every other occasion, of repeating to you assurances of the respect with which I am Sir Your most obedt & most humble servt   TH: JEFFERSON

PrC (DLC); at foot of text: "The honble James Sullivan. Boston." Tr (DLC); 19th-century copy.

From William Thornton

Sir   June 8th: 1793.

In consequence of your Intimation respecting the Mace for Virginia I have drawn one which I submit to your superior Judgment.

The Rattle-snake, Crotalus horridus, is peculiar to America, and though one of the most terrible of his Tribe, is nevertheless endowed with Qualities which make it a striking Emblem of this Government: for,

it is peaceable, and strikes only in necessity or self-defence. It does not, like other Animals, take Advantage; but gives due warning of Danger.

The Bald-Eagle I think is not peculiar to America, [for, if I am not mistaken it is found in Russia] and, if it were, there is nothing in its Appearance characteristic of either power or Dignity: Besides, by adopting it we imitate with *servility* the Devices of several Courts of Europe—they took it from the Romans, and the Romans most probably from the Persians, for, according to Xenophon, they used the Eagle.

The Rattle-snake entwined round one Staff I consider as a proper Mace for the Individual States; round many Staves, for the United States. The Staves being of polished Silver and the Snakes enamelled in proper Colours, would have a noble Appearance. They may be made light, and the Mace of the general Government contain as many Fasces or Staves as there are States in the Union. Plutarch says that Publicola took the Ax from among the Fasces, considering it rather as an Emblem of Terror than of Power.

I think in this Device you will find as much Simplicity yet significance as can be required, nor will a Motto be requisite. An Emblem that requires a Motto, is like a Fable that requires a Moral or Inference.

With this you will receive my Opusculum, entitled Cadmus, of which I request your acceptance. I am, Sir, with much respect and sincere attachment   WILLIAM THORNTON

RC (Vi: Executive Papers); brackets in original; addressed: "Thomas Jefferson Secretary of State of the United States"; endorsed by TJ as received 10 June 1793 and so recorded in SJL. FC (Lb in DLC: Thornton Papers); lacks last sentence and part of complimentary close. Enclosure: William Thornton, *Cadmus: or, a Treatise on the Elements of Written Language, Illustrating, by a philosophical division of Speech, the power of each character, thereby mutually fixing the Orthography and Orthoepy. . . . With an Essay on the mode of teaching the Surd or Deaf, and consequently Dumb, to Speak* (Philadelphia, 1793); at head of title page: "Prize Dissertation, which was honored with the Magellanic Gold Medal, by the American Philosophical Society, January, 1793"; see Sowerby, No. 1126. Other enclosure printed below. Enclosed in TJ to Henry Lee, 28 June 1793.

William Thornton (1759-1828), a native of the British Virgin Islands, was trained as a physician at Edinburgh and Aberdeen and came to the United States in 1786. Although he lacked formal training as an architect, his design for the United States Capitol was chosen earlier in 1793 in a competition sponsored by the federal government, and thereafter he made repeated and only partly successful efforts to force reluctant supervising architects to conform as far as possible to his design. He served as a commissioner of the Federal District from 1794 until the commission was abolished in 1802, at which point he was appointed clerk at the Department of State in charge of patents. An inventor himself and the first individual specifically chosen to superintend patents, Thornton ably filled this post until his death and is credited with saving the office's records and models from destruction when the British burned Washington in 1814. He corresponded regularly with TJ during his presidency and retirement (DAB; TJ to George Washington, 17 July 1793, and note; Daniel Preston, "The Administration and Reform of the U.S. Patent Office, 1790-1836," *Journal of the Early Republic*, v, [1985], 334-51).

TJ must have asked Thornton for ideas for a MACE FOR VIRGINIA after 23 May 1793, when he received Governor Henry Lee's letter on the subject (Lee to TJ, 16 May 1793). Xenophon described the gold eagle as a royal standard used in the army of the PERSIANS in *Anabasis*, 1.10.10-18 (Carleton L. Brownson and others, eds. and trans., *Xenophon*, 7 vols. [Cambridge, Mass., and London, 1914-25; repr. 1968], III, 99). The removal of THE AX FROM AMONG THE FASCES is described in Plutarch's *Publicola*, 10.5-6 (Bernadotte Perrin, ed. and trans., *Plutarch's Lives*, 11 vols. [London and New York, 1914-26], I, 529).

William Thornton's Designs for Maces

MS (Vi: Executive Papers); drawing in Thornton's hand.

To George Washington

June 8. 1793.

Th: Jefferson has the honor to inclose to the President a letter from our bankers at Amsterdam stating a balance due them on the foreign intercourse fund Apr. 2. of 13,255 florins equal to about 5,300 Dollars.—This being communicated for the information of the President, the following explanation is necessary. Independant of the fund on which this balance appears, the bankers had in their hands the 50,000 Doll. for the Algerine negociations. For this reason Th:J. had not thought it proper to call on the Treasury for any part of the 40,000 D. of this year, merely to increase the dead mass in the hands of the bankers. When Capt. Cutting went, with powers to Colo. Humphreys to draw the Algerine money, Th:J. sent by him also to Mr. Pinckney bills for between 17. and 18,000. Doll. These would of course turn the balance in our favor about 12,000 Doll. independantly of the Algerine fund, and before that could be drawn out. This remittance, at the rate of 10,000 D. the quarter, will last to about the middle of July. Th:J. is therefore now looking out for 10,000.D. in good bills, to be remitted to the bankers in time for a fresh supply.

RC (DNA: RG 59, MLR); addressed: "The President of the US."; endorsed by Tobias Lear. PrC (DLC); partially faded and overwritten in a later hand. Tr (Lb in

DNA: RG 59, SDC). Recorded in SJPL. Enclosure: Willink, Van Staphorst & Hubbard to TJ, 4 Apr. 1793.

To James Brown

DEAR SIR   Philadelphia June 9. 93.

I have received your favor of the 3d. and thank you for your kind attentions to the manifold little concerns with which I have plagued you. With respect to my furniture there are several packages which must never be put into a waggon: and these and others must go under peculiar care of being covered against the weather. This would require details of attention which could neither be expected nor given by any body but myself. I conclude therefore to leave them in their present deposit till I come to Virginia myself.—I am glad to hear that Donald & Burton will go on with their own business. You will therefore judge whether to address my tobacco to them or to whom. I am in hopes our merchants will buy up foreign bottoms for the transportation of our produce. Tho' *these* will not be favored in the import duties, as if they were *home-built*, yet they will be entitled to passports, as American property, foreign nations being bound to respect whatever *bonâ fide belongs to us*, some by express treaty, and all by the law of nations. As in this way we may suddenly enlarge our stock of shipping, we shall suffer the less. The government has accordingly instructed the custom house officers to furnish passports to all vessels bonâ fide belonging to Americans, attending rigorously however to prevent fraudulent covers. I am with sincere esteem Dear Sir your friend & servt

TH: JEFFERSON

PrC (DLC); at foot of text: "Mr. Brown." Tr (PRO: FO 95/1); extract consisting of the four sentences immediately preceding complimentary close; on verso of extract of TJ to Nathaniel Anderson, 4 June 1793. Tr (DLC); 19th-century copy with lacunae.

To James Madison

June 9. 1793.

I have to acknolege the receipt of your two favors of May 27. and 29. since the date of my last which was of the 2d. inst.—In that of the 27th. you say 'you must not make your final exit from public life till it will be marked with justifying circumstances which all good citizens will respect, and to which your friends can appeal.'—To my fellow-citizens the debt of service has been fully and faithfully paid. I acknolege that such a debt exists: that a tour of duty, in whatever line he can be most useful to his country, is due from every individual. It is not easy perhaps to say of what length exactly this tour should be. But we may safely say of what length it should not be. Not of our whole life, for instance, for that would be to be born a slave. Not even of a very large portion of it. I have now been in the public service four and twenty years; one half of which has been spent in total occupation with their affairs, and absence from my own. I have served my tour then.—No positive engagement, by word or deed, binds me to their further service.—No commitment of their interests in any enterprize by me requires that I should see them through it.—I am pledged by no act which gives any tribunal a call upon me before I withdraw. Even my enemies do not pretend this. I stand clear then of public right in all points.—My friends I have not committed. No circumstances have attended my passage from office to office, which could lead them, and others through them, into deception as to the time I might remain; and particularly they and all have known with what reluctance I engaged and have continued in the present one, and of my uniform determination to retire from it at an early day. If the public then has no claim on me, and my friends nothing to justify, the decision will rest on my own feelings alone. There has been a time when these were very different from what they are now: when perhaps the esteem of the world was of higher value in my eye than every thing in it. But age, experience, and reflection, preserving to that only it's due value, have set a higher on tranquility. The motion of my blood no longer keeps time with the tumult of the world. It leads me to seek for happiness in the lap and love of my family, in the society of my neighbors and my books, in the wholesome occupations of my farm and my affairs, in an interest or affection in every bud that opens, in every breath that blows around me, in an entire freedom of rest or motion, of thought or incogitancy, owing account to myself alone of my hours and actions. What must be the principle of that calculation which should balance against these the circumstances of my present existence! Worn down with labours from morning till night, and day to day; knowing them as fruitless to others as they are vexatious to myself, committed singly in desperate and eternal contest against a host who are systematically undermining the public liberty and prosperity, even the rare hours of relaxation sacrificed to the society of persons in the same intentions, of whose hatred I am conscious even in those moments of conviviality when the heart wishes most to open itself to the effusions of friendship and confidence, cut off from my family and friends, my affairs abandoned to chaos and derangement, in short giving every thing I love, in exchange for every thing I hate, and all this without a single gratifica-

tion in possession or prospect, in present enjoyment or future wish.—
Indeed my dear friend, duty being out of the question, inclination cuts
off all argument, and so never let there be more between you and me, on
this subject.

I inclose you some papers which have passed on the subject of a new
loan. You will see by them that the paper-Coryphaeus is either un-
daunted, or desperate. I believe that the statement inclosed has secured
a decision against his proposition.—I dined yesterday in a company
where Morris and Bingham were, and happened to set between them.
In the course of a conversation after a dinner Morris made one of his
warm declarations that, after the expiration of his present Senatorial
term, nothing on earth should ever engage him to serve again in any
public capacity. He did this with such solemnity as renders it impossible
he should not be in earnest.—The President is not well. Little lingering
fevers have been hanging about him for a week or ten days, and have
affected his looks most remarkeably. He is also extremely affected by the
attacks made and kept up on him in the public papers. I think he feels
those things more than any person I ever yet met with. I am sincerely
sorry to see them. I remember an observation of yours, made when I
first went to New York, that the satellites and sycophants which surrounded him had wound up the ceremonials of the government to a
pitch of stateliness which nothing but his personal character could have
supported, and which no character after him could ever maintain. It
appears now that even his will be insufficient to justify them in the appeal of the times to common sense as the arbiter of every thing. Naked
he would have been sanctimoniously reverenced. But inveloped in the
rags of royalty, they can hardly be torn off without laceration. It is the
more unfortunate that this attack is planted on popular ground, on the
love of the people to France and it's cause, which is universal.—Genet
mentions freely enough in conversation that France does not wish to
involve us in the war by our guarantee. The information from St. Domingo and Martinique is that those two islands are disposed and able to
resist any attack which Great Britain can make on them by land. A
blockade would be dangerous, could it be maintained in that climate for
any length of time. I delivered to Genet your letter to Roland. As the
latter is out of office, he will direct it to the Minister of the Interior. I
found every syllable of it strictly proper. Your ploughs shall be duly
attended to. Have you ever taken notice of Tull's horse-houghing
plough? I am persuaded that that, where you wish your work to be very
exact, and our great plough where a less degree will suffice, leave us
nothing to wish for from other countries as to ploughs, under our circumstances.—I have not yet received my threshing machine. I fear the

late long and heavy rains must have extended to us, and affected our wheat. Adieu. Your's affectionately.

RC (DLC: Madison Papers); unsigned. PrC (DLC).

The PAPERS . . . ON THE SUBJECT OF A NEW LOAN included TJ's Opinion on a New Foreign Loan, 5 June 1793, and probably George Washington to TJ, 4 June 1793, and enclosure. For Madison's LETTER TO ROLAND, see note to Madison to TJ, 29 May 1793. The HORSE-HOUGHING PLOUGH is described in Jethro Tull, *Horse-Hoeing Husbandry* . . ., 4th ed. (London, 1762), 285-307 and pl. 1; see Sowerby, No. 701.

From James Currie

HBLE. SIR   Richmond June 10th. 1793

I take the opportunity by Judge Irdell to write you this short Epistle, and to apologise in Some measure for the liberty lately taken upon two Occasions: viz of two Short letters of introduction by A Mr. Campbell and a Mr. Maitland to be delivered by their respective bearers and a liberty I am conscious ought seldom or ever to take place but between friends on the most intimate footing. I hope however youll excuse it on the Score of former freindship; I am very anxious and am afraid rather too urgent to hear the fate of my debt against J. Griffin, your having mentioned in a former letter it would come to issue at the April term, I hope it has been terminated at that time and anxiously hope in my favor; before this reaches you, youll probably hear the decision of the fœderal court in respect to the British debts in general and concerning those paid into the Treasury in particular the Only cause tried here has come to no issue the Jury not being able to come to any agreement that, no judgement Writ of Error, or Consent of parties having taken place no Appeal can lay to the Supreme Court to decide and it seems to me the matter is in a worse situation than before the suit was tried at all; our late accounts from France seem unfavorable to the cause of liberty; Dumourier speaks in a State of disgust, and the loss of him must be great to the republican cause; we have had the most flattering prospects of great Crops particularly of Wheat till very lately. The rust is got among the Wheat and many crops I am told are totally destroyed and Others greatly injured by it to the great dissapointment and loss of the Country at large. All your friends in this part of the World are Well. Coll. TMR. has Recovered from his late dangerous disease but it has left both mind and body so Weak he can scarcely be said to be alive. I hope to have the pleasure of seeing you in this state in the Fall enjoying some relaxation from the weighty matters of state. That you may ever be healthy and happy is the fervent wish of Hble Sir Yr most devoted & V. H. Servt.   JAMES CURRIE

RC (DLC); endorsed by TJ as received 17 June 1793 and so recorded in SJL.

Currie's letter of introduction for CAMPBELL has not been found and is not recorded in SJL; that for MAITLAND is dated 3 June 1793. The CAUSE TRIED HERE in the United States Circuit Court was Ware v. Hylton (see note to George Washington to TJ, 1 June 1793). TMR.: Thomas Mann Randolph, Sr.

From Alexander Hamilton

SIR   Treasury Department June 10th 1793.

The Comptroller of the Treasury has reported to me that "On examining the subsisting contracts between the United States and the Government of France and the Farmers General and a comparison thereof with the foreign accounts and documents transmitted to the Treasury the following facts appear.

That, previous to the Treaty of February 1778, the sum of Three Millions of livres had been advanced by the Government of France to the Agents of the United States, under the title of gratuitous assistance, for which no reimbursement was to be made.

That the payments which composed the before mentioned sum of Three millions of Livres are stated in a letter of Mr. Durival to Mr. Grand, dated in 1776, to have been made at the following periods. . . .

One Million delivered by the Royal Treasury the 10th of June 1776, and two other millions advanced also by the Royal Treasury in 1777, on four receipts of the Deputies of Congress of the 17th of January, 3d. of April, 10th of June and 15th of October of the same year.

In the accounts of Mr. Ferdinand Grand, Banker of the United States, the following sums are credited viz—

1777 January 31st	Livres	500,000
" April 28th		500,000
" June 4th		1,000,000
" July 3rd		500,000
" October 10th		500,000
Amounting, in the whole, to Livs		3,000,000

The Farmers General of France claim a large balance from the United States on account of one million of Livres which they contend was advanced in June 1777, in consequence of a special contract with Messrs. Franklin and Deane, to be repaid by the delivery of Tobacco at certain stipulated prices . . . . . and the advance made by the Farmers General is said to be the same money as is credited by Mr. Grand on the 4th of June 1777.

After a careful examination of the foreign accounts, it is found that no more than Three millions of Livres have been credited by any Agents of the United States.

An opinion was entertained by the late Officers of the Treasury, that the sum claimed by the Farmers General, composed a part of the sum supplied as a gratuitous aid by the Government. Subsequent explanations have, however, rendered it probable, that, including the claim of the Farmers General, the sum of four millions of livres were in fact received: it is, however, indispensable, that it should be known to whom the money was paid.

The most direct mode of obtaining this information will be to call for Copies of the receipts mentioned in Mr. Durivals letter of 1786, and, more particularly, a Copy of that said to have been given on the 10th of June 1776" . . . . and, as explanatory of the Transaction, has sent me the documents herewith transmitted.

The most likely conjecture, in my mind, considering the period of the advance and the circumstances of that period is that the unaccounted for Million went into the hands of M. De Beaumarchais. The supplies which he furnished to the United States exceeded his own probable resources, besides the imprudence of having hazarded so much at that stage of our affairs upon our ability to pay—and there were many symtoms at the time of his having been secretly put in motion by the Government.

It is now become urgent that the truth of the case should be known. An account has recently passed the Auditor's Office, admitting, in favor of M. De Beaumarchais, a balance of 422,265 Dollars and 13 Cents— with a reservation only of the question of the Million. If he has received that Million, which has been acknowledged as a free gift from the French Government, it is unjust that he should be able to establish a claim against the United States for supplies which must have been the proceeds of that sum. . . If he has never received the million every days suspension of his claim, after the immense delays heretofore incurred, is a grievous hardship upon him. It concerns, materially, the Interests and more the Justice, the Credit and the Character of the United States, that as speedy a solution, as possible, of the enigma may be obtained.

With a view to this I have the honor to make you the present communication, that you may be pleased to take such steps as shall appear to you the most proper and efficacious, to procure, as speedily as the nature of the case will admit, the requisite explanations. With great respect, I have the honor to be, Sir, Your Mo. Obedt Servant,

ALEXANDER HAMILTON

RC (DLC); in a clerk's hand, signed by Hamilton; ellipses in original; at foot of text: "The Secretary of State"; endorsed by TJ as received 12 June 1793 and so recorded in SJL. Tr (NNC: Gouverneur Morris Papers); in the hand of George Taylor, Jr., and endorsed by him in part: "with documents denominated 'sundry papers relative to the lost Million.'" PrC (DLC). Tr (Lb in DNA: RG 59, DCI). Enclosures: (1) Extract of Benjamin Franklin to Ferdinand Grand, Philadelphia, 11 July 1786, enclosing letters between Franklin and Charles Thomson regarding three million livres acknowledged to have been received before the February 1778 treaty as a "*Don gratuit*" from the King of France, of which only two million are recorded in Grand's accounts, unless the million from the farmers-general is included; stating Franklin's assumption that all funds from the King, whether loans or gifts, passed through Grand's hands and that the money obtained from the farmers-general was distinct from royal aid; expressing wonder that he had signed, and that both he and Grand had examined, a contract acknowledging a gift of three millions when they could only account for two; observing that if the million ostensibly furnished by the farmers-general was a disguised gift from the crown, the farmers-general are in debt to the United States for two cargoes of tobacco shipped on account of that payment; and requesting Grand to get the matter explained so as to clear Franklin of possible charges of not accounting for a million livres received. (2) Jean Durival to Grand, Versailles, 30 Aug. 1786, acknowledging his letter of 28 Aug. 1786 regarding the advance of one million livres from the farmers-general to the United States on 3 June 1777; stating that he has no knowledge of that advance, and that the free gift of three million livres which the King verified by the contract of 25 Feb. 1783 consisted of a one million livre payment from the Royal Treasury on 10 June 1776, and two million livres advanced by the Royal Treasury on receipts from the deputies of Congress dated 17 Jan., 3 Apr., 10 June, and 15 Oct. 1777; and suggesting that for more information on the advance by the farmers-general he confer with Mr. Gérard, whose knowledge extends beyond the payments by the Royal Treasury. (3) Same to same, 5 Sep. 1786, stating that he submitted both of his letters to the Comte de Vergennes, who observed that the royal free gift of three million livres had nothing to do with the one million livres Congress may have received from the farmers-general in 1777, that consequently the receipt he asked about would not satisfy his needs, and that providing a copy of it would be useless. (4) Grand to Franklin, Paris, 9 Sep. 1786, acknowledging his letter covering copies of three letters from Thomson seeking explanation of the million livres not included in Grand's accounts; commenting that he would have found it difficult to prove that he had not pocketed this money had he not applied to Durival, whose enclosed answer shows that one million livres were paid by the Royal Treasury on 10 June 1776; averring that this is the missing million, since he can account for the 1777 payments of two million by the Royal Treasury and one million by the farmers-general; noting that it remains only to determine to whom this missing million was paid, and that he could not have received it, since he was not charged with the business of Congress until January 1777; reporting that he asked Durival for a copy of the receipt for the unexplained million and encloses his answer, and that he has written again but received no answer as yet. (5) Durival to Grand, 10 Sep. 1786, stating that he laid Grand's letter of 9 Sep. before Vergennes, who persists in his view that the receipt of which Grand seeks a copy has no relation to the work he has done for Congress and that he can easily prove this because the payment in question by the Royal Treasury preceded his selection to transact the business of Congress. (6) Postscript from Grand to Franklin, Paris, 12 Sep. 1786, written in hopes that at Lorient it can be joined to his letter of 9 Sep., enclosing No. 5, stating that he cannot understand Vergennes's reserve, especially since if the payment was made the recipient must have kept an account and will in time be known, and wishing him better luck in resolving the mystery in America. (7) Franklin to Charles Thomson, Philadelphia, 25 Jan. 1787, reminding him of a letter he wrote last June on the missing million, advising that an explanation could probably be obtained from Grand or TJ; that, wanting the matter resolved, he had written Grand himself and now encloses Nos. 1-6 (Durival being in charge of French expenditures on foreign affairs), all of which, while proving that the million in question was paid on 10 June 1776, do not indicate to whom, although it could not have been the Commissioners from Congress, who did not meet in France until the end of 1776 or the beginning of 1777, nor Grand, who took charge of their affairs thereafter; conjecturing from the refusal of the minister to provide a copy of the receipt that the lost million was advanced to be spent on America by Beaumarchais and is a *"Mystere du Cabinet,"* that the French were unwilling to admit to having supported America against Britain so early, and that the payment should perhaps be inquired into further only if Beaumarchais asks more of the United States than is just; inquiring if Beaumarchais has dropped his demands or continues to press them; asking to have the enclosures returned but authorizing him to copy them; noting that the million will not affect the account with the King of France since it is stated as a free gift, but that if it passed through the hands of any American agents or ministers, they ought to account for it, and that he does not remember whether Deane arrived in France by 10 June 1776 but thinks from his great lack of money when Franklin joined him there a few months later that it could hardly have been paid to him; and suggesting that TJ might do better than Grand in obtaining the information and should be directed to try if further demands by Hortalez & Company or some other cause make it necessary (Trs in DLC: TJ Papers, 88: 15153-9; Trs in NNC: Gouverneur Morris Papers; Trs in Lb in DNA: RG 59, DCI; printed in Francis Wharton, ed., *The Revolutionary Diplomatic Correspondence of the United States*, 6 vols. [Washington, D.C., 1889], I, 376-9, 380). Also transmitted by Hamilton with this letter or shortly thereafter was the Contract between the American Commissioners to France and the farmers-general, [24 Mch. 1777], by which the former agreed that during 1777 Congress would acquire and deliver to French ports for the use of the farmers-general five million pounds of tobacco in exchange for one million livres tournois payable during the ensuing month and another million when the first shiploads arrived (Tr in NNC: Gouverneur Morris Papers; undated; printed in Franklin, *Papers*, XXIII, 514-17). Enclosed in TJ to Gouverneur Morris, 13 June 1793.

Hamilton's letter, written on the seventeenth anniversary of the payment of what came to be known as "The Lost Million," represented the first effort of the United States government to unravel this obscure episode as part of the Treasury Department's settlement of the accounts of the Continental and Confederation Congresses.

The section of this letter within quotation marks is a reorganized but otherwise almost verbatim extract of a letter to Hamilton of 29 Mch. 1792 from Oliver Wolcott, Jr., the COMPTROLLER OF THE TREASURY (Syrett, *Hamilton*, XI, 210-11).

TJ promptly referred the matter to Gouverneur Morris, the American minister to France (TJ to Morris, 13 June 1793). Six months after TJ left office Morris succeeded in obtaining a copy of the receipt for the payment of the one million livres tournois, which showed that this sum—part of the three million livres in GRATUITOUS ASSISTANCE which France claimed in 1783 to have made to America prior to 1778— had indeed gone INTO THE HANDS OF M. DE BEAUMARCHAIS. Although the other claims of Beaumarchais were finally paid by the Treasury in 1806, seven years after his death, his heirs continued to lobby for payment of the unaccounted "lost million." Nonetheless, thanks to the extremely murky state of the accounts of American agents abroad in the first years after independence, the continuing reluctance of the French government to admit publicly to such an early payment to rebels against a nation with which it was at peace, and the persisting disagreement between the American and French governments and Beaumarchais and his heirs over the implications of this payment, a settlement was not made until 1837, when with American approval his heirs received 800,000 francs in return for relinquishing all other claims on the United States. Even afterwards the rights and wrongs of the case remained controversial (Miller, *Treaties*, II, 119; Syrett, *Hamilton*, XI, 207-9; Morris, *Papers*, V, 321-8; Charles J. Stillé, "Beaumarchais and 'The Lost Million,'" PMHB, XI [1887], 1-36; see also TJ to the Senate and House of Representatives, 6 Feb. 1807). As indicated in Wolcott's letter to Hamilton, the letter from Durival to Grand DATED IN 1776 was actually written on 30 Aug. 1786 (Enclosure No. 2 above).

Preserved among TJ's papers is a record of a conversation set down by Nicholas P. Trist at Monticello on 24 Dec. 1827—possibly in connection with the pending consideration in Congress of the claims of Beaumarchais's heirs for the "lost million"—in which his late grandfather-in-law had given his own views on this tangled affair: "In relation to Beaumarchais's claim Mr. Jefferson once told me (N. P. Trist) that having been a good deal pestered on the subject, while in Paris, he mentioned the circumstance in conversation with Count Vergennes. [I am positive it was to the *french minister*; and almost certain that the *Count* was that minister]. The minister's countenance immediately assumed the expression of great surprise mingled with indignation. 'Hah! Does *he* apply for this money?' broke from his lips. It was altogether in the way of *exclamation*, however and did not lead to any farther conversation on the subject. The whole scene nevertheless satisfied Mr. Jefferson that Beaumarchais's claim had no sort of foundation" (MS in DLC; in Trist's hand; brackets in original).

To Adam Lindsay

SIR   Schuylkill June 10. 1793.

I received a considerable time ago your favor of Feb. 26. The croud of business which follows for some time after the close of Congress, and then my removal from the city into the country which has for a while put my papers out of their place, has prevented my performing earlier the duty of acknoleging it and remitting you for the candles which came safely to hand. I now inclose you a bank post note for 53D–28c equal to £15–19– 8½ with many acknolegements for your kindness.— Letters from our Commissioners to the Indian treaty inform us of their safe arrival at Niagara, but that the treaty would be a month later than had been expected. We have nothing new on the subject of the war. The generosity of the French in declaring to us by their new minister that they do not wish to disturb our prosperity by calling us into the war on account of the guarantee, gives us hopes that we may preserve our neutrality. I do not find it as much known as it ought to be to our merchants that all vessels *owned by Americans*, (no matter where built) are entitled against all nations to pass freely, as well as all other American property in whatever form. The law of nations never considers where a vessel was built, but to whom she belongs. And this is expressly confirmed by our treaties with such nations as have treated with us. Orders are accordingly given to our custom house officers to furnish foreign-built vessels with passports if they are *bonâ fide owned by Americans*. This will not however entitle such vessels to the benefit of low-import duties, that being confined by law to home built vessels. I take the liberty of mentioning this, that it may be known, and our stock of shipping augmented by purchase so as to be equal to the carrying off all our produce. I am with good esteem Sir Your most obedt. servt.

TH: JEFFERSON

Apr. [i.e. June] 12. 93.
P.S. The person whom I had desired to go and procure me a bank post note on the 10th. when I wrote the preceding letter, having failed to do

it till this day, your favor of the 4th. came to hand on the 11th. I am really vexed at the circumstances which occasioned my delaying so long to answer your letter. I repeat assurances of the esteem with which I am Sir your very humble servt.   TH:J.

PrC (DLC); with misdated postscript on separate sheet; at foot of letter: "Mr. Adam Lindsay." Tr (DLC); 19th-century copy; lacks postscript.

From John Nixon

SIR   Monday June 10. 1793

You sent me the Policys, bill of Sale and bill of Lading belonging to Mr. Cruger which I wrote that Gentleman. He writes for more papers, which he apprehends his Brother left with you. Be kind enough to inform me, if you have any more belonging to this business. I am Yr very hl Serv   JOHN NIXON

RC (DNA: RG 76, France, Unbound Records); at foot of text: "Thomas Jefferson Esqr"; endorsed by TJ. Recorded in SJL as received 10 June 1793.

Notes on Ceremonial at New York

June 10. 93. Mr. Brown gives me the following specimen of the phrenzy which prevailed at New York on the opening of the new government. The first public ball which took place after the President's arrival there, Colo. Humphreys, Colo. W. S. Smith, and Mrs. Knox, were to arrange the ceremonials. These arrangements were as follows. A Sopha at the head of the room raised on several steps whereon the Presidt. and Mrs. Washington were to be seated. The gentlemen were to dance in swords. Each one when going to dance was to lead his partner to the foot of the Sopha, make a low obeisance to the Presidt. and his lady, then go and dance, and when done bring his partner again to the foot of the Sopha for new obeisances and then to retire to their chairs. It was to be understood too that gentlemen should be dressed in bags.— Mrs. Knox contrived to come with the President and to follow him and Mrs. Washington to their destination, and she had the design of forcing an invitation from the Presidt. to a seat on the Sopha. She mounted up the steps after them, unbidden, but unfortunately the wicked Sopha was so short that when the Presidt. and Mrs. Washington were seated, there was not room for a 3d. person; she was obliged therefore to descend in the face of the company and to sit where she could. In other respects the ceremony was conducted rigorously according to the arrangements, and the President made to pass an evening which his good sense rendered a very miserable one to him.

MS (DLC); entirely in TJ's hand; written on same sheet as "Anas" entries for 7 and 12 June 1793. Recorded in SJPL under 7-12 June 1793: "[Notes.] ceremonials at N. York." Included in the "Anas."

John BROWN, then of the part of Virginia soon to become Kentucky, was elected to the House of Representatives in the first Congress but did not take his seat until 15 June 1789 (*Annals*, I, 471). Thus he was not in attendance on 7 May 1789 at the FIRST

PUBLIC BALL after George Washington's arrival in New York, and his account is implausible, because on that date MRS. WASHINGTON had not yet reached New York and MRS. KNOX was apparently also absent (Rufus W. Griswold, *The Republican Court: or American Society in the Days of Washington* [New York, 1855], 154-7; W. W. Abbot, Dorothy Twohig, and others, eds., *The Papers of George Washington*, Pres. Ser., 4 vols. [Charlottesville, 1987-], II, 205n).

From Thomas Pinckney

DEAR SIR   London 10 June 1793

Dr. Adair who is going on his private business to Virginia being introduced to me by a Gentleman of my acquaintance here, I avail myself of the opportunity of forwarding to you the model of the threshing machine which I have been so long in getting the mechanic who made it to finish. He has made it upon the improved plan of Mr. Adam's which will execute much more than one I saw first at Mr. Patersons but of course it requires more power. He has with my consent adapted it both to the power of water and of horses; this gives it the appearance of being more complex and has rendered it more expensive, the whole cost now being 13 Guineas, though he at first said he could make a simple one for 5. Every part which in the model is of Brass may be made of wood except the two long fluted Cylinders which in the original is of cast iron, which is necessary on account of the weight as it is by the pressure alone of the upper one that they hold the grain to the threshing wheel—the joint in the end of the upper wheel must be observed—by means of this they thresh even the large horse beans; of wheat the original of this threshes 150 bushels in 8 hours with six horses and 5 Men. 5 bushels is a days work for a labourer to thresh by hand in the same County. The scale is $\frac{1}{2}$ an inch to a foot. Dr. Adair has seen these machines work in Scotland and will be able to give any explanation that may be necessary. With sincere esteem & respect I remain Dear Sir Your most obedient and most humble Servant   THOMAS PINCKNEY

RC (MeHi); at head of text: "Private"; at foot of text: "Mr Jefferson"; endorsed by TJ as received 30 Aug. 1793 and so recorded in SJL. PrC (ScHi: Pinckney Family Papers).

Enclosed in James B. M. Adair to TJ, [ca. 28 Aug. 1793].

This date Benjamin Vaughan wrote a letter to TJ from London announcing that he would send TJ "a little packet" by the first vessel bound for Philadelphia, introducing Dr. James B. M. ADAIR, the "son of Dr. McKittrick (Adair) of Antigua," who was "going to Virginia to pursue a claim," and urging TJ to assist him (RC in MHi; endorsed by TJ as received 12 Jan. 1794 and so recorded in SJL, which indicates that TJ received it from Adair while at Fredericksburg on his return to Monticello).

To Martha Jefferson Randolph

MY DEAR MARTHA   Philadelphia June 10. 93.

I wrote you last on the 26th. of the last month. On the 3d. of the present I received Mr. Randolph's favor of May 22. I sincerely congratulate you on the arrival of the Mocking bird. Learn all the children to venerate it as a superior being in the form of a bird, or as a being which will haunt them if any harm is done to itself or it's eggs. I shall hope that the multiplication of the cedar in the neighborhood, and of trees and shrubs round the house, will attract more of them: for they like to be in the neighborhood of our habitations, if they furnish cover. I learn from Mr. Brown that all my furniture is safely arrived and stored at Rocket's. Maria is here, but too lazy to write. She says in excuse that you do not write to her.—Mrs. Shippen lost her little son Bannister the last week. He died of a dysentery. Our letters from Mr. Bev. Randolph and the other commissioners are that they were safely arrived at Niagara; and that their treaty was likely to be delayed a month longer than was expected. Consequently their return will be later. My sincere affections to Mr. Randolph and kiss dear Anne for me. Yours with constant love

TH: JEFFERSON

RC (NNP); at foot of text: "Mrs. Randolph"; endorsed by Mrs. Randolph. PrC (MHi).

From Elias Vanderhorst

Bristol, 10 June 1793. Since his 10 Apr. letter, having heard nothing from TJ, he adds that by order in council the ports of the kingdom will continue to be open to the importation of foreign corn and flour to the end of Parliament's present session, subject to low duties on wheat and flour. Although this is uncertain, the policy will probably be prolonged thereafter because of the scarcity of corn in this island and most parts of the continent. The government has lately purchased upwards of 7,000 barrels of American flour here and large quantities of it and wheat in other ports where they were available, "no doubt with a double view, not difficult to discover." The prospect for growing corn here is favorable, but it is too early in the season to be certain of the harvest. Manufacturing and commerce grow worse, and the government's offer of aid in the form of Exchequer bill loans is ill calculated to improve matters, since an excess of paper credit has been the main cause of the kingdom's present distressed state. The principal remedy lies in peace, which will open the channels of commerce shut or greatly obstructed by the war. A French privateer from St. Malo, the *Tyger*, Captain Dugue, captured the *Commerce*, Captain Preble, an American ship bound from Charleston to here. Presuming through ignorance or villainy that not all of the property on board the *Commerce* was American, Dugue took her entire cargo of sixteen casks of indigo and seven hogsheads of deer skins, replaced all of her crew but the master and cabin boy with fifteen Frenchmen, and ordered her to Brest. A British frigate retook the *Commerce* on 29 May and two days later she arrived at Spithead. He has taken steps to recover four casks of the indigo, invoiced at £252.16 Carolina money, which had been consigned to him by his friends Smiths, DeSaussure & Darrell of Charleston, joint owners of them with their Georgetown house, John Cogdell & Company, but if they are not successful he trusts that there will be an opportunity to do these Americans justice on TJ's side of the water. He has been unable to conclude the matter mentioned in his last letter at the customhouse here and is convinced the delay is due to the resentment of some customs officials whose fees have been reduced because he has secured the cancellation of "the Custom of *Bonding* Rice, when in their possession (and in the King's Casks) and that of paying a *Debenture* charged when Shipped (tho no duty had been paid on it)." He has written to the board of commissioners and believes this will make it possible for him to obtain the materials needed for the accounts he must send TJ. In view of the need for agents in some outports under his consular jurisdiction, he has appointed Edmund Granger and Samuel Banfill Esqrs. at Exeter, John Hawker Esqr. at Plymouth, George Croker Fox and Robert Were Fox at Falmouth, and Richard Hart Davis Esqr., a Bristol banker, to represent him during his absences. A few days after his commission received royal approval he learned that Auldjo had encroached on his consular jurisdiction by appointing Messrs. Fox of Falmouth to serve as his deputies there as well as in the other Cornwall ports and the Scilly Islands. Auldjo, rejecting his contention that these areas were part of his jurisdiction, suggested that he appeal to TJ for a ruling. But Pinckney, to whom he appealed, decided against Auldjo, who withdrew the appointments. Since the heavy duties of his office cannot be discharged without injury to his private affairs, he hopes Congress will provide a salary adequate to its trouble, expense, and dignity. He encloses a few of the latest newspapers and a state of the market here for American produce. [P.S.] Mr. Fox of Falmouth has just informed him of his appointment as United States consul for that port and district. Since all of the kingdom's specie, if put into the public treasury, would not pay two shillings per pound of the nation's enormous debt, it is astonishing that credit is as good as it is. No one can calculate how long this fabric can last.

RC (DNA: RG 59, CD); 4 p.; addressed: "Thomas Jefferson Esqr Philadelphia"; endorsed by TJ as received 3 Aug. 1793 and so recorded in SJL. Enclosure: Price current of American produce in Bristol, 10 June 1793 (MS in same; in Vanderhorst's hand).

To Edmond Charles Genet

Sir   Philadelphia June 11. 1793.

I had the honor of laying before the President your Memorial of the 22d. of May proposing that the United States should now pay up all the future instalments of their debt to France, on condition that the sum should be invested in produce. The President having fully deliberated on this subject, I have now the honor of inclosing you a Report from the Treasury department, made in consequence thereof, and explaining the circumstances which prevent the US. from acceding to that proposition.

In fact, the instalments, as they are settled by Convention between the two nations, far exceed the ordinary resources of the US. To accomplish them completely and punctually, we are obliged to anticipate the revenues of future times, by loans, to as great an extent as we can prudently attempt. As they are arranged however by the Convention, they give us time for successive and gradual efforts. But to crowd these anticipations all into a single one, and that to be executed in the present instant, would more than hazard that state of credit, the preservation of which can alone enable us to meet the different paiments at the times agreed on. To do even this hitherto, has required, in the operations of borrowing, time, prudence and patience: and these operations are still going on in all the extent they will bear. To press them beyond this, would be to defeat them both now and hereafter. We beg you to be assured, and through you to assure your nation, that among the important reasons which lead us to economise and foster our public credit, a strong one is the desire of preserving to ourselves the means of discharging our debt to them with punctuality and good faith, in the times and sums which have been stipulated between us.—Referring to the inclosed Report for a more particular developement of the obstacles to the proposition, I have the honor to assure you of the sentiments of particular esteem & respect with which I am Sir Your most obedient & most humble servt.   TH: JEFFERSON

RC (AMAE: CPEU, Supplément, xx); at foot of first page: "The Minister Plenipotentiary of France." PrC (DLC). PrC of Tr (DLC); in a clerk's hand. Tr (NNC: Gouverneur Morris Papers). Tr (DNA: RG 46, Senate Records, 3d Cong., 1st sess.). PrC (PRO: FO 97/1). FC (Lb in DNA: RG 59, DL). Tr (AMAE: CPEU, xxxvii); in French. Tr (DLC: Genet Papers); in French; draft translation of preceding Tr. Printed in *Message*, 34. Enclosure: Alexander Hamilton's Report on the American Debt to France, 8 June 1793, Document viii in a group of documents on Jefferson and the American debt to France, at 3 June 1793. Letter enclosed in TJ to George Washington, 12 June 1793, and Washington to TJ, 12 June 1793. Enclosed in TJ to Gouverneur Morris, 13 June and 16 Aug. 1793, and TJ to Thomas Pinckney, 14 June 1793.

Memorial from George Hammond

The Undersigned, his Britannic Majesty's Minister Plenipotentiary to the United States, has the honor of submitting to the Secretary of State the annexed deposition; from which it appears that the British brigantine Catharine, James Drysdale Master bound from Jamaica to the Port of Philadelphia, was on Saturday last the 8th. curt. captured by the French frigate the Embuscade off Hereford at the distance of not more than two miles, or at the utmost two miles and a half from the state of New Jersey.

The Undersigned can entertain no doubt that the executive government of the United States will consider the circumstances of this capture as an aggression on the territory and jurisdiction of the United States, and will consequently pursue such measures as to its wisdom may appear the most efficacious for procuring the immediate restitution of this vessel to its owners as soon as it shall arrive at New York (for which port it is understood to have been sent as prize) or within any other harbour of the United States.

The Undersigned ventures to hope that the annexed deposition will be regarded by the executive government of the United States as evidence sufficient to authenticate the fact of the capture and the circumstances by which it has been accompanied. When he is informed of the actual arrival of the brigantine Catharine, within any port of the United States, he will obtain the corroborating testimony of the master and pilot now on board of that vessel, which testimony he will not fail to transmit without delay to the Secretary of State.

The Undersigned thinks it expedient to add that he has lately received information, on which he can depend, from Charleston, that the brig, the Morning Star, which on the 9th. of last month was condemned as legal prize by Mr. Mangourit the French Consul at that place, was taken by the French frigate the Embuscade (on the 15th. of April) at the distance of not *more than two miles from the bar of Charleston*, and within sight of the town. The Undersigned is taking the proper measures to collect the proof of this fact, which, if substantiated will, added to the capture of the present vessel, and that of the Ship Grange within the bay of Delaware constitute the third instance of similar aggression on the territory and jurisdiction of the United States, that has been committed by the French frigate the Embuscade within the short period of two months.

Philadelphia 11th June 1793   GEO. HAMMOND

RC (DNA: RG 59, NL); in the hand of Edward Thornton, signed by Hammond; at foot of first page: "Mr Jefferson"; endorsed by TJ as received 11 June 1793 and so recorded in SJL. FC (Lb in PRO: FO 116/3); misdated 10 June 1793. Tr (same, 5/1). Tr (same, 115/2); misdated 10 June 1793. Tr (Lb in DNA: RG 59, NL). Enclosure: Deposition of Allen Erskine and four others, Philadelphia, 11 June 1793, wherein four of the deponents, escaped crew members of the *Catharine*, stated that this brigantine of Halifax, James Drysdale master, had been on her way to Philadelphia from Jamaica when she was captured by the *Embuscade*, a French frigate commanded by Citizen Bompard, on 8 June at about 2 P.M., "off Hereford a little to the northward of Cape May And not more than two miles from the Shore of the State of New Jersey," with the pilot James Skillinger on board to guide the brigantine into the Bay and River of Delaware; and wherein the fifth deponent, who had witnessed the capture from a nearby pilot boat, confirmed the testimony of the others, except that in his judgment the *Catharine* was about two-and-a-half miles from the shore when captured (MS in DNA: RG 59, NL, in the hand of Asheton Humphreys, notary public of Philadelphia, signed by deponents; attested by Humphreys; Tr in PRO: FO 5/1; Tr in Lb in DNA: RG 59, DL). Letter and enclosure enclosed in TJ to George Washington, 11 June 1793, Washington to TJ, 11 June 1793, and TJ to Richard Harison, 12 June 1793.

The legal maneuvers stemming from the capture in American territorial waters of the BRITISH BRIGANTINE *Catharine* by the FRENCH FRIGATE *Embuscade* vividly illustrate the difficulties the Washington administration experienced in relying on the federal judiciary to enforce its neutrality policy. In accordance with a decision of the Cabinet, TJ instructed Richard Harison, the federal district attorney in New York, to institute legal proceedings to determine whether in fact the ship had been taken in waters under American jurisdiction (Cabinet Opinions on the *Republican* and the *Catharine*, 12 June 1793; TJ to Harison, 12 June 1793; Washington, *Journal*, 168, 169). In Harison's absence, Robert Troup, a Federalist attorney in New York, filed a libel in the United States District Court of New York on behalf of George Meade and John Dunkin—the administrators of the *Catharine* after the death of her owner, a British subject who had resided in Philadelphia, and his son, the owner of the ship's cargo of Jamaica rum, pimento, and ginger—demanding restoration of the ship and cargo to them on the ground that "they were taken within the territory, and under the protection of the United States." Although the *Catharine*'s captors refused to respond to the libel, Alexandre Maurice d'Hauterive, the French consul in New York, formally protested to the District Court that French consuls in the United States possessed exclusive admiralty jurisdiction over French captures of enemy prizes. District Court Judge James Duane ruled in January 1794 that the Court lacked jurisdiction over cases involving violations of American sovereignty by a foreign nation and that the libellants had to seek restitution from the executive branch, but the following August District Court Judge John Laurance, adhering to the Supreme Court's February 1794 ruling in Glass v. the Sloop Betsey that district courts did have jurisdiction in such cases, ordered the *Catharine* to be restored to the libellants and awarded them costs and damages (Duane, *Decree*, 3, 8, 19-35; Harison to TJ, 20 June, 24 July 1793; note to Lucas Gibbes and Alexander S. Glass to TJ, 8 July 1793; Syrett, *Hamilton*, xv, 11-12; Edward P. Alexander, *A Revolutionary Conservative: James Duane of New York* [New York, 1938], 208-10).

To William Jackson

DEAR SIR   Philadelphia June 11. 1793.

The letter on public business which I took the liberty of troubling you with to Mr. Pinckney was intended to go by the packet. Touching therefore on a particular subject, I mentioned that I should avoid saying more through *that channel of conveyance*. Hearing you were about to go,

I detained the letter and sent it to you. The expression, by this *change of channel*, would convey to Mr. Pinckney ideas as unjust as unintended, which I will pray you to correct by shewing him this letter, which I write in the first moment of recollecting the circumstance. I have the honour to be with great esteem Dear Sir Your most obedt. humble servt   TH: JEFFERSON

PrC (DLC); at foot of text: "Majr. Jackson."

TJ's LETTER to Thomas Pinckney was dated 4 June 1793.

From John Loehmann

Philadelphia, 11 June 1793. He served as an American army surgeon during the Revolution and fell prisoner at Charleston, South Carolina, where the rigors of a long captivity added to what he had undergone during his army service left him without the use of his limbs when he was liberated. Crippled to this day, he is unable to work and lacks any means of support. He and his wife employed their remaining property and effects with the greatest frugality, but that resource is now gone. Having applied for relief several times to Congress both at New York and Philadelphia, traveling for that purpose from Carolina to here, where he has lived some years now, and made every exertion to be placed on the pension list, he procured the necessary certificates but was delayed until the passing of the last act of Congress and is now told he cannot receive the pension unless three freeholders attest to his disability and mode of life for the first two years. Since this is not now in his power, he must rely on the charity of the members of the Cincinnati and other benevolent persons for his subsistence and hopes for relief of his poverty and distress from TJ.

RC (ViW: Tucker-Coleman Collection); 1 p.; addressed: "Thomas Jefferson Esqr Secretary of State"; endorsed by TJ: "Lockman John. Northern liberties near Noah's ark."

Dr. John Loehmann, one of the South Carolinians banished from Charleston by the British, arrived in Philadelphia in December 1781 and thereafter described himself variously as surgeon's mate and "Surgeon in the Hospital for the Southern Department" in the Continental Army while unsuccessfully peppering the Confederation and United States Congresses with requests for a pension between 1783 and 1812. Although he was admitted to the Society of the Cincinnati during his lifetime, he is not listed in the standard historical register of Continental Army officers (Mabel L. Webber, ed., "Josiah Smith's Diary, 1780-1781," *South Carolina Historical and Genealogical Magazine,* XXXIV [1933], 81; JCC, XXIV, 358; JHR, I, 502, 618, II, 56, 250, 649, III, 87, V, 471, VI, 101, 358, VII, 42, 135, 443, VIII, 72, 568; Office of Finance Diary, 5, 23, 28, 29, 30 May, 13 June, 9 July, and 18, 28 Aug. 1783, DLC: Robert Morris Papers; Bryce Metcalf, *Original Members and Other Officers Eligible to the Society of the Cincinnati, 1783-1938* [Strasburg, Va., 1938], 201; Heitman, *Register).*

[255]

To John Nixon

June 11. 93.

Th: Jefferson with his compliments to Mr. Nixon has now the honor to inclose him all the remaining papers of Mr. Cruger which were put into his hands. It is impossible any one can be missing, as they have been constantly in the wrapping in which they are now returned.

PrC (DLC). Tr (ViU: Edgehill-Randolph Papers); 19th-century copy. Enclosures not found.

To William Stokes

June 11. 93.

Th: Jefferson presents his compliments to Mr. Stokes, and begs leave, should he persevere in his proposition of going to France, to give him letters to some of his friends there: tho' he thinks the plan will deserve consideration. He returns many thanks to Mr. Stokes for his inaugural dissertation, and for the flattering notice he has been pleased to prefix, respecting himself and for which he feels himself entirely indebted to Mr. Stokes's partiality. The subject of the dissertation, one of the most interesting in human affairs, is treated in a manner particularly interesting and ingenious.

PrC (DLC); on same sheet as PrC of TJ to William Thornton of this date. Tr (DLC); 19th-century copy; on same sheet as Tr of TJ to Thornton of this date.

William Stokes, a Virginian, received A.B. and M.D. degrees from the University of Pennsylvania in 1791 and 1793, respectively. His INAUGURAL DISSERTATION was dedicated to Dr. William Shippen and TJ (*General Alumni Catalogue of The University of Pennsylvania 1922* [Philadelphia?, 1922], 11, 482; William Stokes, *Tentamen Medicum Inaugurale, quædam de Asphyxia* . . . [Philadelphia, 1793]). See Sowerby, No. 942.

To William Thornton

June 11. 93.

Th: Jefferson, with his compliments to Dr. Thornton returns him many thanks for the device of the Mace; and still more for his dissertation on the elements of language which he had read in manuscript with great satisfaction, but shall do it with more in print.

RC (DLC: Thornton Papers); addressed: "Doctr. Thornton." PrC (DLC); on same sheet as PrC of TJ to William Stokes of this date. Tr (DLC); 19th-century copy; on same sheet as Tr of TJ to Stokes of this date.

From George Washington

June 11th: 1793

The President of the United States sends to the Secretary of State a letter and enclosures which he has just received from the Governor of New York, respecting the detention of an Armed vessel which was about to sail from New York, supposed to be commissioned as a privateer by one of the European belligerent Powers.

The President wishes the Secretary of State to lay these documents before the Heads of the other Departments, *as soon as may be*, and to let the President know what is their opinion, as well as the Secretary's of State, of the measures which should be taken in the case—and what answer should be given to the Governor's letter. If there be a concurrence of opinion as to the Answer which ought to be given to the Governor, the President wishes the Secretary to draft it agreeably thereto.

RC (DLC); in the hand of Tobias Lear; endorsed by TJ as received 11 June 1793. Recorded in SJPL. Enclosures: (1) Master Warden Thomas Randall to George Clinton, New York, 8 June 1793, 9:00 P.M., reporting, in compliance with Clinton's proclamation, that an armed sloop manned by British or American sailors and commissioned as a privateer by one of the belligerent European powers would sail this evening from "Swartwoudt's Wharf at the North-River" unless this was prevented (Tr in DNA: RG 59, LGS, in Clinton's hand; PrC of Tr in DLC, in a clerk's hand; PrC of another Tr in DNA: RG 59, MLR, in a clerk's hand; Tr in Lb in same, DL). (2) Alexandre Maurice d'Hauterive to Clinton, New York, 9 June 1793, protesting as a violation of neutrality the detention of an armed French ship about to sail to assist in the French struggle for liberty and demanding that it be freed (Tr in DNA: RG 59, LGS, in French, in DeWitt Clinton's hand, except for penciled note at head of text by TJ: "this letter singly to be copd & press copd"; PrC of Tr in DLC, in French, in a clerk's hand; PrC of another Tr in DNA: RG 59, MLR, in French, in a clerk's hand; PrC of another Tr in PRO: FO 97/1, in French, in the hand of George Taylor, Jr.; Tr in NNC: Gouverneur Morris Papers, in French; Tr in Lb in DNA: RG 59, DL, in French and English; Tr in same, LGS, English translation in Philip Freneau's hand; Tr in DNA: RG 46, Senate Records, 3d Cong., 1st sess., variant English translation). (3) Clinton to Hauterive, New York, 9 June 1793, stating that in response to a request from the President he had ordered a detachment of militia to detain the armed sloop in question until the President was notified of the facts of the case because the ship reportedly had been manned and equipped in New York to serve as a privateer under a commission from a belligerent European power; and that he would immediately communicate a copy of No. 2 to the President (Tr in DNA: RG 59, LGS, in Clinton's hand; PrC of another Tr in DLC, in a clerk's hand; PrC of another Tr in DNA: RG 59, MLR, in a clerk's hand; Tr in Lb in same, DL). (4) Clinton to Washington, 9 June 1793, stating that, in compliance with the President's request as communicated in a 24 May letter from the Secretary of War, he had ordered a small detachment of militia to detain a sloop armed and manned in New York and about to sail with a privateering commission from a belligerent European power until such time as the President rendered a decision on the case; that, in addition to the information contained in Nos. 1-3, the sloop, formerly known as the *Polly*, had been transferred by its owners, "a Mr. Noble of Hudson and others," to a French citizen residing in New York, was now called the *Republican*, and was commanded by Citizen Orset, a French captain, with what appeared to be a partially French crew; and that to justify his use of the militia he thought it necessary that they be considered as called into service under United States authority (RC in DNA: RG 59, LGS; PrC of Tr in DLC, in a clerk's hand; PrC of another Tr in DNA: RG 59, MLR, in a clerk's hand; Tr in Lb in same, DL).

For the Cabinet's response to the fitting out in New York of the *Republican*, the French privateer that was the subject of the enclosures listed above, see Cabinet Opinions on the *Republican* and the *Catharine*, 12 June 1793.

To George Washington

June 11. 93.

Th: Jefferson has the honor to inclose to the President a memorial from Mr. Hammond. He proposes to ask a meeting with the Secretaries of the treasury and war at 9. aclock tomorrow, in time to write by the post of tomorrow. Should the President think fit that the inclosed should be the subject of deliberation, it may be considered at the same time.

RC (DNA: RG 59, MLR); addressed: "The President of the US."; endorsed by Bartholomew Dandridge, Jr. Tr (Lb in same, SDC). Not recorded in SJL. Enclosure: Memorial from George Hammond, 11 June 1793, and enclosure.

From George Washington

June 11th. [1793]

The President returns Mr. Hammond's memorial and the deposition accompanying it—and desires that they may be laid before the Heads of the Departments tomorrow with the communications from Governor Clinton.

RC (DLC); in the hand of Tobias Lear; partially dated; addressed: "The Secret[. . .]." Recorded in SJPL. For enclosures, see enclosures listed at TJ to Washington, 11 June 1793.

From Thomas Bell

DEAR SIR   June 12th. 1793

It would have given me pleasure to Supplied Mr. J. G. Jefferson with his Summer Supplies but from a letter recived a few days Since from him enclosing yours to me he writes me that previous to yours coming to hand, he had taken up what few goods he wanted from Messrs. Shelton & Haris—he was induced he Says to do so by their being so convenent to him, and their willingness to Supply him as well with goods as what little cash he might Stand in need of. This being the case he writes me Your letter of Credit becomes unecessary.

On Settling a/c. the other day with Colo. Lewes we find that he had Omitted charging you with Some Orders drawn on me which I paid off and charged to him expecting he had charged you. They are now transfered to your debit—which has Swelled your a/c. Some thing more than you had a right to expect. However these matters may rest until you return when they will be more fully explained. I am really Sorry Mr. J. Jefferson had not applied to me for what goods he might have wanted. It is more than probable the payments would have been more Accomodating to you as Corn &c would always Suit me.

As to Our friend Mr. DeRiux's matters I am Truely Sensible how much you are disposed to Serve him. His a/c with me now is about £260—a considerable part of which is assumed. And are now pressing hard for payment. Besides this he Owes Several other Stores &c Small Sums that are pressing upon him. He dropt a hint the other day that induc'd me to believe he has given out the Idea of purchasing land. As there is little probability of Lewes redeeming the place in Town and unless that can be Affected I fear his funds ortherwise will come Short. (And forsooth She thinks She could not live in the country.)

Perhaps there has not been less than 3,000. barrels of flower carried from Milton this Spring. And nearly 500. Hhds. Tobacco Wheat &c. What might we expect If the River was opened farther and more good Mills—but we want a leader.

It is truely a disgrace to our county that we have not Mills—the prospect of Wheat is Greater than ever known in this county—And must give the benefit of Grinding &c to others.

Our Neighbours are all well. Mrs. Gilmer Another fine Daughter and the Doctor Says he is not to Stop yet. I am Sir with respect Your most Ob. Sert.   Tho. Bell

RC (DLC); addressed: "Thomas Jefferson Se. of State Philadelphia"; franked; endorsed by TJ as received from Charlottesville 22 June 1793 and so recorded in SJL.

TJ's letter of credit to Bell was dated 14 Apr. 1793, as was his letter enclosing it to John Garland Jefferson.

Cabinet Opinions on the *Republican* and the *Catharine*

June 12. 1793.

The President having required the opinions of the heads of the three departments on a letter from Governor Clinton of the 9th. inst. stating that he had taken possession of the sloop Polly, now called the Republican, which was arming, equipping and manning[1] by French and other citizens to cruize against some of the belligerent powers, and desiring to know what further was to be done, and they having met and deliberated thereon, are unanimously of opinion, that Governor Clinton be desired to deliver over to the civil power the said vessel and her appurtenances, to be dealt with according[2] to law: and that the Attorney of the US. for the district of New York be desired, to have such proceedings at law instituted as well concerning the said vessel and her appurtenances, as against all the persons citizens or aliens participating in the armament or object thereof as he shall think will be most effectual for punishing the said offenders, and preventing the said vessel and appurtenances from being applied to the destined purpose: and that if he shall be of opinion that no judiciary process will be sufficient to prevent such application of the vessel to the hostile purpose intended that then the Governor be desired to detain her by force till the further advice of the General government can be taken.

The President having also required the same opinions on the Memorial of the British minister of the 11th. inst. on the subject of the British brigantine Catherine captured by the French frigate the Embuscade within the limits of the protection of the US. as is said, and carried into the harbour of New York, they are of opinion unanimously, that the Governor of N. York be desired to seize the said vessel in the first instance, and then deliver her over to the civil power, and that the Attorney of the US. for the district of New York be instructed to institute proceedings at law in the proper court for deciding whether the said capture was made within the limits of the protection of the US. and for delivering her up to her owners if it be so decided: but that if it shall be found that no court may take cognisance of the said question, then the said vessel to be detained by the Governor until the further orders of the General government can be had thereon.   TH: JEFFERSON

H KNOX

ALEXANDER HAMILTON

MS (DLC: Washington Papers); in TJ's hand, signed by TJ, Knox, and Hamilton; endorsed by Tobias Lear. Enclosed in TJ to George Washington, 12 June 1793.

This day TJ submitted this document to the President, who instructed him to write to the federal district attorney of New York in accordance with the Cabinet's recommendations (Washington, *Journal*, 169; see also TJ to Richard Harison, 12 June 1793).

[1] TJ first wrote "arming and equipping" and then altered it to read as above.

[2] Preceding five words written over what appears to be "and all the persons [. . .]."

From George Hammond

Wednesday [12 June 1793]

Mr. Hammond presents his compliments to Mr. Jefferson and has the honor of inclosing to him the deposition of the Pilot on board of the Brig Catharine, which he begs Mr. Jefferson to annex to the other deposition upon the subject of the Brigantine's capture.

RC (DNA: RG 59, NL); partially dated; endorsed by TJ as a letter of 12 June 1793 received 13 June 1793 and so recorded in SJL. Tr (Lb in same). Enclosure: Deposition of James Skillinger, Philadelphia, 12 May [i.e. June] 1793, stating that he boarded the brig *Catharine* on 7 June to pilot her into Philadelphia; that on the 8th the *Catharine* was not more than half a mile from Seven Mile Beach in Cape May County, New Jersey, when between 11:00 and 12:00 A.M. she was hailed in French by the nearby frigate *Embuscade*, which was so close that fifteen minutes later it "fell foul" of the *Catharine* and "carried away her Foretopmast Steering Sail Boom"; that after hailing in French three times, despite his request that it hail in English, the *Embuscade* boarded the *Catharine* about two hours after the first hail when she was between two and two-and-a-half miles from Seven Mile Beach; that he considered the *Catharine* to be in possession of the *Embuscade* from the time of the first hailing; and that after putting him on a pilot boat the *Embuscade* sailed with the *Catharine* toward New York (MS in same, in a clerk's hand, signed by Skillinger and notarized by Asheton Humphreys of Philadelphia; PrC of Tr in DLC, in a clerk's hand; Tr in PRO: FO 5/1; Tr in Lb in DNA: RG 59, DL).

To Richard Harison

SIR   Philadelphia June 12. 1793.

As it was apprehended by the President of the US. that attempts might be made by persons within the US. to arm and equip vessels for the purpose of cruising against some of the powers at this time engaged in war, whereby the peace of the US. might be committed, the Governors of the several states were desired to be on the watch against such enterprizes, and to seize such vessels found within the jurisdiction of their states. In consequence of this the Governor of New York has informed the President that he has seised the sloop Polly, now called the Republican, which he found to be arming, equipping and manning for the purpose of cruising against some of the belligerent powers. The Governor is hereupon desired to turn the said vessel and her appurtenances over to the civil power: and I am to ask the favor of you to take up the business on the part of the US. instituting such proceedings at law against the vessel and her appurtenances as may place her in the custody of the law, and may prevent her being used for purposes of hostility against any of the belligerent powers. But if you shall find that no judiciary process will be adequate to this object, then the Governor

[261]

is desired to detain her by force until further advice can be had from the Executive of the General government.

In the first instance like the present which happened here, the government, desirous of acting with moderation and of animadverting through the channel of the laws on as few persons as possible while it was supposed they might have acted without due information, directed prosecutions against such only as were citizens of the US. But the present being a repetition of offence after due notice that it would be proceeded against, you will be pleased to institute such prosecutions before the proper courts as you shall find most likely to punish according to law all persons, citizens or aliens, who had taken such a part in the enterprize commenced as abovementioned, as may be punishable by law.

It has been suggested by the British Minister here, and evidence indeed produced, whereof I send you a copy, that the British brigantine Catharine has been captured by the French frigate the Embuscade within the limits of the protection of the US. and carried into the harbour of New York. The Governor is hereupon also desired to seize the said brigantine and deliver her up to the civil power: and I am to ask the favor of you to institute proceedings at law in the proper court for deciding whether the said brigantine was taken within the limits of the protection of the US. and for redelivering her to the owners, if it be so decided. But if you shall find that no court will take cognizance of the said question, then the Governor is desired to detain the said brigantine until further orders can be had thereon from the general government.

In both these cases you will be pleased to have a proper communication and concert with the governor for the purpose of receiving the vessel from the custody of the military into that of the civil power, and of reinstating her under the military if the civil power should be found inadequate.

In the latter case of the brigantine Catharine be so good as to procure as speedy a determination as possible, in order to lessen inconveniences to the parties having right. I have the honor to be with great esteem & respect, Sir Your most obedient & most humble servt

TH: JEFFERSON

PrC (DLC); at foot of first page: "The Attorney of the US. for the district of N.Y." PrC of Tr (DLC); in a clerk's hand. FC (Lb in DNA: RG 59, DL). PrC of another Tr (DNA: RG 360, PCC, AL); in a clerk's hand; incomplete; misfiled at December 1790. Enclosures: (1) Enclosures to Memorial from George Hammond, 11 June 1793. (2) Enclosures to George Washington's first letter to TJ, 11 June 1793. Enclosed in TJ to Washington, 12 June 1793, TJ to Gouverneur Morris, 13 June 1793, and TJ to Thomas Pinckney, 14 June 1793.

This day TJ submitted this letter to the President, who immediately returned it with a one-word undated note—"Approved"—beneath which TJ wrote: "June

12. 1793. This was the letter to the Attorney of the district of New York written this day" (RC in DLC; addressed: "Mr. Jefferson"; endorsed by TJ as received 12 June 1793; recorded in SJPL).

On 14 June 1793 TJ wrote a brief letter to Harison enclosing "another deposition lately furnished me by the British minister" on the case of the *Catharine* (PrC in DLC, at foot of text: "Mr. Harrison atty of the US. for the district of N. York"; FC in Lb in DNA: RG 59, DL). The enclosure is listed at George Hammond to TJ, [12 June 1793].

From Josef de Jaudenes and Josef Ignacio de Viar

Sir   Philadelphia. June 12. 1793.

Desiring to convince the President of the US. by proofs that there was no error (as you supposed in your favor of the 5th. inst.) in the information which had been given us relative to the last letter which we had the honor of writing to you, we transmit to you a literal copy of one of the patents given by Govr. Blount in the creation of Great Medals (the original of which is in our hands, and may be exhibited here in this hotel of the king when you shall chuse.)

We also copy literally for you the relation of the Indian Chief Ugulayacabe of what happened to him in his journey to Cumberland, and what obliged him to undertake it. And we can likewise assure you that medals have fallen into the hands of the Governor of N. Orleans of the tenor which we mentioned to you in our former, distributed by Messrs. Antony Foster, James Randolph, and David Smith, Commissioners, sent by the US. to the Choctaws and Chickasaws for the purpose: who, to attach more strongly various chiefs of the said nations gave them the said medals, notwithstanding it must have been known to them that they had them from Spain ever since the year 1784.

We leave to the wise consideration of the President of the US. if after these, and many other steps (which we do not mention at present) taken, some with the open authority of your government, and others perhaps without it, but still by it's officers, the US. can justify easily any complaints whatever which they may make against the Governor of N. Orleans (which we doubt if founded but in presumption or suspicion) even should he have proceeded on the footing of reciprocity.

We do not pretend to impeach the character of Governour Blount nor would we produce evidence against him, if we were not persuaded, that since they declaim so bitterly in these states against the Governor of N. Orleans in words, it is very just that we should vindicate his proceedings, and shew those of Govr. Blount and others, not only in words but palpable facts.

We duly note the other contents of your letter, and repeat assurances of the sincere esteem & respect &c   JAUDENES   VIAR

Tr (DNA: RG 59, NL); entirely in TJ's hand; at head of text: "Translation of a letter from messrs. Viar & Jaudenes to T. Jefferson." PrC (DLC: TJ Papers, 77: 13302); consists of second page only. RC (DNA: RG 59, NL); in Spanish; in Jaudenes's hand, signed by Jaudenes and Viar; endorsed by TJ as received 13 June 1793 and so recorded in SJL. Tr (AHN: Papeles de Estado, legajo 3895); in Spanish; attested by Jaudenes and Viar. Tr (DLC: William Short Papers); in Spanish. PrC (DLC). Tr (Lb in DNA: RG 59, DCI); in Spanish. Tr (DNA: RG 46, Senate Records, 3d Cong., 1st sess.); in English. Tr (Lb in same, TR); in English. Recorded in SJPL. Letter and enclosures enclosed in TJ to William Carmichael and William Short, 30 June 1793.

The LAST LETTER to TJ from the Spanish agents was that of 25 May 1793.

TJ submitted translations of the present letter and its enclosures to the President with a brief covering letter of 14 June 1793 that also included his letter of the same date to Thomas Pinckney (RC in DNA: RG 59, MLR, addressed: "The President of the US.," endorsed by Bartholomew Dandridge, Jr.; Tr in Lb in same, SDC, misdated 19 June 1793; not recorded in SJL). See also Washington, *Journal*, 177.

ENCLOSURES

I

Patent Issued by William Blount

Literal copy of a patent given by Govr. Blount.

No. 6. William Blount governor in and over the territory of the US. of A. South of the river Ohio, and Superintendant of Indian affairs for the Southern district, to all who shall see these presents Greeting.   Know ye that in consideration of the proofs of fidelity and friendship which we have had of the Indian called Ittahoomastuble of the Choctaw nation, maintaining close union with the US., of his valour and consequence with the neighboring nations, and of his good disposition and knowlege to command, desiring to recommend such good qualities, I do appoint him Chief and Grand Medal admonishing him of the value he ought to put thereon, the obligation to govern his people well, and the respect he is to bear the people of the US. venerating the name of the President.   For these reasons we require all citizens of the US. to acknolege him Chief and Grand Medal as aforesaid, the same to the Indians of his nation, that they respect and obey him. Given under my hand and seal in the said territory this 10th. day of Aug. 1792.

by the Governor, signed DANIEL SMITH
signed WM. BLOUNT

Tr (DNA: RG 59, NL); entirely in TJ's hand; at foot of text: "a copy Jaudenes. Viar." PrC (DLC: TJ Papers, 77: 13302). Tr (DNA: RG 59, NL); with first line in Spanish; attested by Jaudenes and Viar. Tr (DLC: Short Papers). PrC (DLC: TJ Papers, 89: 15402). Tr (DNA: RG 46, Senate Records, 3d Cong., 1st sess). Tr (Lb in DNA: RG 59, DCI).

II
Relation of Ugulayacabe

[after November 1792]

Copy of the relation of Ugulayacabe of the occurrencies of his journey to Cumberland.

He said that on his return from visiting his father the Chief of New Orleans, from whence he came with a very handsome present, which had contented and satisfied him much, he met in the road two Americans, who persuaded him pressingly to go to Cumberland, where he would receive (as they told him) a good present. Ugulayacabe answered them, that he had then been to see his father at N. Orleans who had given him whatever he desired, that the Spaniards were his Whites, that he desired no others; after which answer they sollicited him no more. But having arrived at his nation, they went to his cabin, and teased him so much, that he found himself under the necessity of consenting to take the journey to Cumberland, with the design of seeing if it was true that Pyamingo had ceded lands to the Americans, as he had heard say, and if in truth these were solliciting them from the Indians, as they had informed him. That having arrived at Cumberland, they spoke to Governor Blount, who caressed him much, and proposed to him to establish a factory or magazine of trade at Bear creek, which Ugulayacabe refused, because[1] he did not desire any such establishment there nor any where else; that he had the Spaniards for his Whites, that they furnished his nation all the goods they wanted,[2] that he might see by the cloaths he had on, that he wanted for nothing: that on this Govr. Blount looked at him with evil eyes, and said to him 'you have sold your lands well to the Spaniards' to which he replied it was not so, since they had no need of them: that then Govr. Blount asked him if he would assist the Americans if they should have war with the Whites, to which Ugulayacabe answered that he would stand back and let them fight one another, but that he would never permit the Americans to establish themselves further in advance than where they were. That Govr. Blount gave him a great coat, and a hat, a very pretty little one, which he could not get on his head,[3] and so gave it to his son[4] because he was going to be married: that the Americans gave a dozen cart loads of goods to the Indians for the value (as they told him) of 5000. dollars: that he had little ammunition, no axes, mattocks, nor hatchets, some guns, much whiskey, victuals in abundance, meat at pleasure.

Tr (DNA: RG 59, NL); entirely in TJ's hand, with omission and translating errors (see notes below); undated; at head of text: "Translation"; at foot of text: "a copy Jaudenes. Viar." PrC (DLC: TJ Papers, 96: 16469-70). Tr (DNA: RG 59, NL); in Spanish; attested by Jaudenes and Viar. Tr (DLC: Short Papers); in Spanish. PrC (DLC: TJ Papers, 89: 15400-1). Tr (Lb in DNA: RG 59, DCI); in Spanish. Tr (DNA: RG 46, Senate Records, 3d Cong., 1st sess.); English translation in a clerk's hand; at foot of text in TJ's hand: "Department of State to wit. The preceding letters and documents are true copies from those remaining in the office of this department.

Th: Jefferson." TJ's note refers to the enclosures from the Department of State in Washington's 16 Dec. 1793 message to Congress on relations with Spain (ASP, Foreign Relations, I, 247-88). Recorded in SJPL between 16 and 22 May 1793.

Ugulayacabe was a Chickasaw chief considered by Spanish authorities to be friendly to the United States. His relation begins with his return from a November 1792 conference in New Orleans between Baron Francisco Luis Hector de Carondelet, the governor of Louisiana and West Florida, and various Southern Indian leaders, during which Carondelet had sought to form a confederation of Southern tribes under Spanish auspices to serve as a barrier to further American expansion in the Southwest (John W. Caughey, *McGillivray of the Creeks* [Norman, Okla., 1938], 343, 349).

[1] In light of the first Spanish Tr in DNA, the preceding four words should be translated as "to which Ugulayacabe replied that."

[2] TJ here omitted a phrase in the first Spanish Tr in DNA that in translation should read "treating them well and giving them gifts."

[3] In light of the first Spanish Tr in DNA, this passage in translation should read "a very pretty hat, which he refused to put on."

[4] In light of the first Spanish Tr in DNA, the remainder of this clause should be translated as "for him to go hunting."

From Gouverneur Morris

DEAR SIR   Sainport 12 June 1793

This will accompany Duplicates of No. 30 and 31. I have now the Honor to transmit a Copy of the Decision made by the Municipality of Dunkerque on the third Instant respecting the Ship Fame which I receivd last night in a Letter from that Place of the seventh which informs me that the Ship was then sail'd. I have just now written to Mr. Le brun (who by the bye is *en État d'arrestation*) a Letter of Acknowlegement Copy whereof is enclos'd. I did this the more readily because I shall have new Complaints to make in all human Probability for in the best regulated Governments it is difficult to prevent the Violation of the Rights of neutral Powers and much more so where in the Tempests of a Revolution Government resembles more a Weather Cock, marking from whence the Hurricane arises than a tower to resist its Force. Whenever a good Opportunity presents itself I shall take the Liberty to hazard my Opinion on the late *Events* for I cannot yet say *Revolution* because it is not quite determin'd whether that shall be the conventional appellation of what pass'd in the End of May. I am with Esteem and Respect Dr Sir your obedient Servant   GOUV MORRIS

RC (DNA: RG 59, DD); at head of text: "No. 32"; at foot of text: "Thomas Jefferson Esqr Secretary of State"; endorsed by George Taylor, Jr. FC (Lb in DLC: Gouverneur Morris Papers). Tr (DNA: RG 46, Senate Records, 3d Cong., 1st sess.). PrC (DNA: RG 59, MD). Tr (Lb in same, DD). Enclosures: (1) Extract from the Registers of the Municipality of Dunkirk, 3 June 1793, stating that, upon the presentation by Citizen Brown of a 30 May 1793 letter from the minister for foreign affairs to Captain Alexander Frazer of the *Fame* authorizing him to proceed on his voyage, and after a conference with his representative, Citizen Carnot, it was agreed yesterday to lift the embargo on this vessel so that Frazer could leave when he was ready, to void the seizure of the vessel and cargo, and to pay Brown an indemnity of 15,000 livres. (2) Morris to Lebrun, 12 June 1793, expressing satisfaction with his decision to permit the *Fame* to leave Dunkirk with her cargo of brandy and to grant Captain Frazer an indemnification for the delay, promising to communicate this news immediately to the ministers of the United States, and assuring him that the conduct of France would calm the uneasiness which particular facts might have created in the minds of Americans

(Trs in DNA: RG 59, DD, in French; Trs in DNA: RG 46, Senate Records, 3d Cong., 1st sess., in French and English, the latter in the hand of George Taylor, Jr.; PrCs in DNA: RG 59, MD; Trs in Lb in same, DD, in French and English).

THE LATE EVENTS: a reference to the final phase of the struggle for power between the Jacobins and the Girondins, which came to a head on 2 June 1793 when the Jacobins gained control of the National Convention and put under house arrest twenty-nine Girondin deputies and two Girondin ministers, including Lebrun, the minister of foreign affairs (Georges Lefebvre, *The French Revolution*, trans. Elizabeth M. Evanson and others, 2 vols. [New York, 1962-64], II, 40-54).

Notes on Alexander Hamilton and "Veritas"

June 12. Beckley tells me that Klingham has been with him to-day and relates to him the following fact. A certificate of the old Congress had been offered at the treasury and refused payment and so indorsed in red ink as usual. This certificate came to the hands of Francis [the quondam clerk of the treasury, who on account of his being dipped in the infamous case of the Baron Glaub[ec][1] Hamilton had been obliged to dismiss to save appearances, but with an assurance of all future service, and he accordingly got him established in New York]. Francis wrote to Hamilton that such a ticket was offered him but he would not buy it unless he would inform him and give him his certificate that it was good. Hamilton wrote him a most friendly letter and sent him the certificate. He bought the paper and came on here, and got it recognized, whereby he made 2500. Dollars. Klingman saw both the letter and certificate.

Irving a clerk in the treasury, an Irishman is the author of the pieces now coming out under the signature of Veritas, and attacking the President. I have long suspected this detestable game was playing by the fiscal party, to place the Presidt. on their side.

MS (DLC); entirely in TJ's hand; partially dated; brackets in original except where noted; written on same sheet as "Anas" entries for 7 and 10 June 1793. Recorded in SJPL under 7-12 June 1793: "[Notes.] Ham. Klingman. Francis. Glaubeck.—Veritas by Irving." Included in the "Anas."

The story related by John Beckley, the strongly Republican clerk of the House of Representatives, on the basis of the testimony of Jacob Clingman, a clerk of Pennsylvania Representative Frederick A. C. Muhlenberg, reflected the continuing efforts of both men to uncover evidence of Hamiltonian corruption in the Department of the Treasury. Clingman's account was grossly exaggerated, however, for Andrew G. Fraunces, the disgruntled QUONDAM CLERK, was about to appeal to the President, public opinion, and Congress precisely because of Hamilton's refusal to approve his claim to two Board of Treasury warrants issued in 1787 and 1789 (Vol. XVIII, 658-9n; Syrett, *Hamilton*, XIV, 460-71, 476, 528-30; Berkeley, *Beckley*, 92-8). For contrasting accounts of Hamilton's role in the INFAMOUS CASE of Peter William Joseph Ludwig, Baron de Glaubeck, which involved charges of official favoritism to the widow of General Nathanael Greene, see Vol. XVIII, 686-8n; and Syrett, *Hamilton*, XIV, 462-3n).

No other evidence has been found to confirm TJ's assertion that William Irvine, A CLERK in the office of the Comptroller of the Treasury, was VERITAS, the author of four letters to the President, dated 30 May to 10 June 1793, that appeared in the *National Gazette* between 1 and 12 June 1793 (Syrett, *Hamilton*, XIII, 464). These letters

sharply criticized Washington for issuing the Proclamation of Neutrality and warned the American people of the danger of regarding him with almost monarchical reverence. In light of TJ's conviction that the letters were part of a Federalist design to discredit the Republican opposition in the eyes of the President, it is ironic that Edmond Charles Genet mistakenly informed the French government that TJ himself was "Veritas" (Turner, *CFM*, 245).

[1] MS torn; letters supplied from Ford, I, 234.

To George Washington

June 12. 93.

Th: Jefferson has the honor to submit to the President his answer to Mr. Genet on the subject of the French debt. He had prepared it yesterday morning, but unluckily left it at home, which has delayed it a day.

RC (DNA: RG 59, MLR); addressed: "The President of the US."; endorsed by Bartholomew Dandridge, Jr. Tr (Lb in same, SDC). Not recorded in SJL. Enclosure: TJ to Edmond Charles Genet, 11 June 1793.

From George Washington, with Jefferson's Note

June 12t. 1793

The President approves the enclosed and wishes the Secretary to send it as soon as convenient.

[*Note by TJ:*]
This was the letter to Mr. Genet on his proposal respecting the French debt.

RC (DLC); in the hand of Tobias Lear; addressed: "The Secretary of State"; with note by TJ at foot of text; endorsed by TJ as received 12 June 1793. Recorded in SJPL.

To George Washington

June 12. 93.

Th: Jefferson has the honor to inclose to the President some letters received from Mr. T. Digges which contain some interesting information on the subject of our coins.

RC (DNA: RG 59, MLR); addressed: "The Preside[. . .]"; endorsed by Bartholomew Dandridge, Jr. Tr (Lb in same, SDC). Not recorded in SJL. Enclosures: (1) Thomas Digges to TJ, 10 Mch. 1793. (2) Digges to Thomas Pinckney, 21 Mch., 6 Apr. 1793 (enclosed in Pinckney to TJ, 10 Apr. 1793).

George Washington to the Secretaries of State, Treasury, and War

GENTLEMEN [12 June 1793]

As you are about to meet on other business, it is my desire that you would take the enclosed application into consideration. It is not my wish, on one hand, to throw unnecessary obstacles in the way of gratifying the wishes of the applicants. On the other it is incumbent on me to proceed with regularity. Would not the granting of a Patent then, which I believe is always the concluding act, and predicated on the Survey (as an essential[1] document) have too much the appearance of placing the Cart before the Horse. And does not the Law enjoin something on the Attorney General of the U. States previous to the signature of the President? What can be done with propriety I am willing to do. More I ought not to do.

Go: WASHINGTON

RC (DLC); undated; at foot of text: "The Secretaries of State Treasury & War"; addressed: "The Secretary of State &c."; endorsed by TJ as received 12 June 1793. Dft (PWacD: Feinstone Collection, on deposit PPAmP); dated 12 June 1793; contains one significant variation; at foot of text: "To the Secretaries of State Treasury & War"; docketed by Washington. FC (Lb in DNA: RG 59, SDC); dated 12 June 1793; wording follows Dft. Recorded in SJPL.

The ENCLOSED APPLICATION was a letter from John Cleves Symmes to Alexander Hamilton of 8 June 1793. No text of the letter has been found, but the journal of the President, to whom Hamilton sent it on 10 June 1793, described it as a communication "on the subject of the land granted to him & his associates" which "mentions his readiness to have the Acts of Congress relative to the land carried into effect and suggests the proper situation for land for an Academy" (Washington, *Journal*, 166). The laws in question modified Symmes's 1788 contract with the Board of Treasury to buy land in the Northwest Territory (*Annals*, III, 1357, 1373-4).

[1] All other texts: "a necessary."

To George Washington

June 12. 1793.

Th: Jefferson has the honor of inclosing to the President the opinion on the two cases of vessels referred to the heads of the department, and the letter he has prepared in consequence to the Attorney of the district. Genl. Knox will wait on him with his letter to the Governor.— Symmes's case is to be considered of tomorrow, as it required some enquiry.

RC (DNA: RG 59, MLR); addressed: "The Presid[. . .]"; endorsed by Bartholomew Dandridge, Jr. Tr (Lb in same, SDC). Not recorded in SJL. Enclosures: (1) Cabinet Opinions on the *Republican* and the *Catharine*, 12 June 1793. (2) TJ to Richard Harison, 12 June 1793.

In accordance with a presidential instruction of this date, Henry Knox's LETTER TO THE GOVERNOR, which has not been found, was supposed to direct Governor George Clinton of New York to hand over to the civil power for prosecution the *Republican*, a French privateer commissioned in New York City that was currently in the custody of a detachment of the state militia (Washington, *Journal*, 169). For SYMMES'S CASE, see preceding document.

To George Hammond

SIR   Philadelphia June 13. 1793.

Your Memorial of the 11th. instant, stating that the British brigantine Catharine has been taken by the French frigate the Embuscade within 2. or $2\frac{1}{2}$ miles of the shores of the US. was duly laid before the President, and in consequence thereof the Governor of New York, where the brigantine is understood to be arrived, is desired to take possession of her. It being now supposed that the tribunals of the country will take cognisance of these cases, so far as they involve *acts of force committed within the limits of the protection of the US.* instructions are given to the Governor to turn the case over immediately to the civil power, and to the Attorney of the US. for the district of New York to put it into a proper channel for decision. I am therefore to desire you will be so good as to have the parties interested apprised without delay that they are to take measures as in ordinary civil cases for the support of their rights judicially. Should the decision be in favor of the jurisdiction of the court, it will follow that all future similar cases will devolve at once on the individuals interested[1] to be taken care of by themselves, as in other questions of private property provided for by the laws. The Governors of the several states, as the head of their militia, are desired to aid the civil power should it be necessary. This train of things is much more desireable for the Executive, whose functions are not analogous to the questions of law and fact produced by these cases, and whose inter-ference can rarely be proper where that of the Judiciary is so.

The Governor of New York, in consequence of circular instructions issued, having informed the President that he had taken possession of a sloop lately called the Polly, and now the Republican, on evidence that she was armed, equipped and manned in the port of New York to cruize on the enemies of the French republic, he has been desired to turn that case also over to the civil power, and the attorney for the district is instructed to institute proceedings at law before the proper court for preventing the vessel from being applied to the purpose of her destina-tion, and for punishing all the individuals concerned in the enterprize. I have thought it proper to communicate to you this transaction as it shews that the measures taken by the executive to prevent these enter-prizes are likely to be efficacious: the Governors being, in these also, desired to interpose the aid of their militia where the power or position of the offenders are beyond the ordinary means of coercion wherewith the civil authority is provided. It was perhaps to be expected that in the first moments of a foreign war, the minds of most persons here would be unapprised of the laws of their new position: and we have little reason to doubt, from the habits of order which characterize our citi-zens, that a short time will suffice to bring them acquainted with the line they are to pursue, and to lessen the occasions of recurrence to the pub-lic authority. I have the honour to be with sentiments of great esteem & respect Sir, your most obedient & most humble servt.

Th: Jefferson

PrC (DLC); at foot of first page: "The Min. Pleny. of Gr. Britain." FC (DLC); in the hand of George Taylor, Jr. FC (Lb in DNA: RG 59, DL). Tr (Lb in PRO: FO 116/3). Tr (same, 5/1). Recorded in SJPL. Enclosed in George Washington to TJ, 13 June 1793, and TJ to Thomas Pinckney, 14 June 1793.

CIRCULAR INSTRUCTIONS ISSUED: see TJ to Henry Knox, with Proposed Circular to the Governors of the States, 21 May 1793, and note.

[1] Remainder of clause interlined.

From Josef de Jaudenes

Thursday morning [13 June 1793]

Don Joseph de Jaudenes presents his Compliments to Mr. Jefferson, and has the pleasure to inform him, that Messrs. Walls are about dis-patching the Ship Kingston for Cadiz in two, or three days, Mr. Swanwick the Ship Interprize about the same time, Mr. Leamy the [. . .] for Coruña the latter end of next week, and the bigining of the same week he learnet also the Ships Aretusa, and the Amable are to sail for Cadiz, and Ferrol, the owners of these two last vessells he does not know yet.

RC (DLC); partially dated; torn; addressed: "Thomas Jefferson Esqr. &ca. &ca. &ca.";
endorsed by TJ as a letter of 13 June 1793 received that day.

From James Madison

My dear Sir   Orange June 13. 93.

My last was of the 27 May. It inclosed among other things a letter to the French Ministre de l'Interieur, in answer to one inclosing a Decree of the Nat: Assemb. On the propriety of the answer I wished your freest judgment; and as the sending one at all may be rendered by events improper, I must request the favor of you not to forward the letter, if intelligence should confirm such to be the State of things that it would be totally mal-apropos *there*. Provided it be proper there, and consequently proper in itself, I shall not trouble myself about any comments which the publication attending all such things, may produce here. The letter preceding my last as well as the last, contained some other papers which I wish to know have been received.

Your two last favors were of May 27. and June 2. The latter confirms the apostacy of Dumourier, but relieves us from the more alarming account of his being supported in it by the army. Still however much is to be dreaded from the general posture of things. Should they take a turn decidedly wrong, I fear little regard will be paid to the limited object avowed by the Austrian General in his first proclamation. In fact if the plan of Dumourier had succeeded, it is probable that under the clause of the Proclamation relating to an amendment of imperfections in the Constitution of 1791 the *form* of the national sanction would have been obtained, as in the Restoration of Charles II, to whatever establishment military despotism might please to dictate. The only hope of France, next to the success of her own efforts, seems to lie in the number of discordant views of her combined enemies.

I observe that the Newspapers continue to criticise the President's proclamation; and I find that some of the criticisms excite the attention of dispassionate and judicious individuals here. I have heard it remarked by such with some surprise that the P. should have declared the U.S. to be neutral in the unqualified terms used, when we were so notoriously and unequivocally under *eventual engagements* to defend the American possessions of F. I have heard it remarked also that the impartiality enjoined on the people was as little reconciliable with their moral obligations, as the unconditional neutrality proclaimed by the Government is with the express articles of the Treaty. It has been asked also whether the authority[1] of the Executive extended by any part of the Constitution to a declaration of the *Disposition* of the U.S. on the subject of war and peace? I have been mortified that on these points I could offer no bona fide explanations that ought to be satisfactory. On the last point I must own my surprise that such a prerogative should have been exercised. Perhaps I may have not attended to some part of the Constitution with sufficient care, or may have misapprehended its meaning: But, as I have always supposed and still conceive, a proclamation on the subject could not properly go beyond a declaration of the fact that the U.S. were at war or peace, and an enjunction of a suitable conduct on the Citizens. The right to decide the question whether the duty and interest of the U.S. require war or peace under any given circumstances, and whether their disposition be towards the one or the other seems to be essentially and exclusively involved in the right vested in the Legislature, of declaring war in time of peace; and in the P. and S. of making peace in time of war. Did no such view of the subject present itself in the discussions of the Cabinet? I am extremely afraid that the P. may not be sufficiently aware of the snares that may be laid for his good intentions by men whose politics at bottom are very different from his own. An assumption of prerogatives not clearly found in the Constitution and having the appearance of being copied from a Monarchical model, will beget animadversion equally mortifying to him, and disadvantageous to the Government. Whilst animadversions of this sort can be plausibly ascribed to the spirit of party, the force of them may not be felt. But all his real friends will be anxious that his public conduct may bear the strictest scrutiny of future times as well as of the present day: and all such friends of the Constitution will be doubly pained at infractions of it under auspices that may consecrate the evil till it be incurable.

It will not be in my power to take the step with the Friend of our Friend, which you recommend. It is probable too that it would be either unnecessary or without effect. If the complexion of the former be such as is presumed, he will fairly state the Truth and that alone is wanted. If, as I deem not impossible, his complexion be a little different from the general belief, there would be more harm than good in the attempt. The great danger of misconstruing the sentiment of Virginia with regard to Liberty and France is from the heretical tone of conversation in the Towns on the post-road. The voice of the Country is universally and warmly right. If the popular disposition could be collected and carried into effect, a most important use might be made of it in obtaining contributions of the necessaries called for by the danger of famine in France. Unfortunately the disaffection of the Towns which alone could give effect to a plan for the purpose, locks up the public gratitude and beneficence.

Our fine prospects in the Wheat fields have been severely injured by the weather for some time past. A warm and moist Spring had pushed the wheat into rather a luxuriant state. It had got safe into the head however, and with tolerable weather would have ripened into a most exuberant crop. Just as the grain was in a milky state, the weather became wetter than ever, and has continued raining or cloudy almost constantly since. This has brought on a little of the rust, and pretty universally in this quarter a decay of the ear called the Rot. Should the weather be ever so favorable henceforward, a considerable proportion will be lost: and if unfavorable, the loss may be almost entire. We are at this moment both excessively wet and hot. The forwardest wheat is turning fast and may be nearly safe. The generality is not sufficiently advanced to be out of danger of future or beyond the effect of past causes.

The (Kentucky) Coffee Trees in this Neighbourhood are all too young to bear for some years. I will do all I can to get the seed for Bartram from Kentucky as soon as possible. Adieu

RC (DLC: Madison Papers); unsigned; endorsed by TJ as received 22 June 1793 and so recorded in SJL.

May 1793. The FRIEND OF OUR FRIEND was Wilson Cary Nicholas (TJ to Madison, 2 June 1793).

Madison's LAST was actually dated 29

[1] Word written over "Right," erased.

To Gouverneur Morris

DEAR SIR   Philadelphia June 13. 1793.

The insulated state in which France is placed with respect to all the world almost by the present war, has cut off all means of addressing letters to you through other countries. I embrace the present occasion by a private individual going to France directly, to mention that since the date of my last public letter, which was April 24. and which covered the President's proclamation of Apr.   I have received your Nos. 17. to 24. M. de Ternant notified us of his recall on the 17th. of May, and delivered the letter of the Provisory Executive council to that effect. I now inclose you the President's answer to the Council, which you will be pleased to deliver: a copy of it is also inclosed, open, for your information. Mr. Genet delivered his credentials on the same day on which M. de Ternan took his leave, and was received by the President. He found himself immediately immersed in business, the consequence of this war. The incidents to which that gives daily rise, and the questions respecting chiefly France and England, fill the Executive with business, equally delicate, difficult and disagreeable. The course intended to be pursued being that of a strict and impartial neutrality, decisions, rendered by the President rigourously on that principle, dissatisfy both parties, and draw complaints from both. That you may have a proper idea of them, I inclose you copies of several Memorials and letters which have past between the Executive and the ministers of those two countries, which will at the same time develope the principles of the proceedings, and enable you to justify them in your communications should it be necessary. I inclose also the answer given to Mr. Genet on a proposition from him to pay up the whole of the French debt at once. While it will enable you to explain the impracticability of the operation proposed, it may put it in your power to judge of the answers which would be given to any future propositions to that effect, and perhaps to prevent their being brought forward.—The bill lately passed in England prohibiting the business of this country with France from passing through the medium of England is a temporary embarrasment to our commerce, from the unhappy predicament of it's all hanging on the pivot of London. It will be happy for us should it be continued till our merchants may establish connections in the countries in which our produce is consumed and to which it should go directly.

Our Commissioners have proceeded to the treaty with the North Western Indians. They write however that the treaty will be a month later than was expected. This delay should it be extended will endanger our losing the benefit of our preparations for the campaign, and consequently bring on a delicate question whether these shall be relinquished for the result of a treaty in which we never had any confidence? The Creeks have proceeded in their depredations till they assume the appearance of formal war. It scarcely seems possible to avoid it's becoming so. They are so strong, and so far from us as to make very serious addition to our Indian difficulties. It is very probable that some of the circumstances arising out of our affairs with the Indians, or with the belligerent powers of Europe may occasion the convocation of Congress at an earlier day than that to which it's meeting stands at present.

I send you the forms of the passports given here. The one in three columns is that now used: the other having been soon discontinued. It is determined that they shall be given in our own ports only, and to serve but for one voyage. It has also been determined that they shall be given to all vessels bonâ fide owned by American citizens *wholly*, whether built here or not. Our property, whether in the form of vessels, cargoes, or any thing else, has a right to pass the seas untouched by any nation, by the law of nations: and no one has a right to ask where a vessel was built, but where is she owned? To the security which the law of nations gives to such vessels against all nations, are added particular stipulations with three of the belligerent powers. Had it not been in our power to enlarge our national stock of shipping suddenly in the present exigency, a great proportion of our produce must have remained on our hands for want of the means of transportation to market. At this time indeed a great proportion is in that predicament. The most rigorous measures will be taken to prevent any vessel not wholly and bonâ fide owned by American citizens from obtaining our passports. It is much our interest to prevent the competition of other nations from taking from us the benefits we have a right to expect from the neutrality of our flag: and I think we may be very sure that few if any will be fraudulently obtained within our ports.

Tho our spring has been cold and wet, yet the crops of small grain are as promising as they have ever been seen. The Hessian fly however to the North, and the weavil to the South, of the Patowmac, will probably abridge the quantity. Still it seems very doubtful whether we shall not lose more for want of the means of transportation, and have no doubt that the ships of Sweden and Denmark would find full employment here.

We shall endeavor to get your newspapers under the care of Majr. Read the bearer of this letter. I have the honor to be with great respect & esteem Dear Sir your most obedient & most humble servt

TH: JEFFERSON

RC (NNC: Gouverneur Morris Papers); at foot of first page: "Mr. Morris." PrC (DLC). FC (Lb in DNA: RG 59, DCI). Sent with this and the second letter to Morris of this date was a separate list of their enclosures entitled "Contents of the last dispatch sent by Major Reed to Mr. Morris 13. June 1793" (PrC in DLC, in the hand of George Taylor, Jr.; FC in Lb in DNA: RG 59, DCI; Dft in DLC, in Taylor's hand, consisting of preliminary list omitting the newspapers). A note of 14 June 1793 on all three texts of the list records that a letter of Washington to Morris, 13 June 1793 (Fitzpatrick, *Writings*, XXXII, 501-2), was also delivered to Reed on 14 June 1793 before he left Philadelphia. Enclosures (with quotations from PrC of list): (1) "Fennos and Freneau's papers down to this day." (2) *Journal of the House of Representatives of the United States, at the Second Session of the Second Congress* (Philadelphia, 1793). (3) TJ to Morris, Thomas Pinckney, and William Short, 26 Apr. 1793. (4) Memorial from George Hammond, 2 May 1793. (5) Last three Memorials from Hammond, 8 May 1793. (6) Edmund Randolph's Opin-

ion on the *Grange*, 14 May 1793. (7) Enclosures to Washington's first letter to TJ, 14 May 1793. (8) TJ to Jean Baptiste Ternant, 15 May 1793. (9) TJ to Hammond, 15 May, 5 June 1793. (10) TJ to William Rawle, 15 May 1793. (11) Final text of George Washington to the Provisional Executive Council of France, [24 May 1793]. (12) Edmund Randolph's Opinion on the Case of Gideon Henfield, 30 May 1793. (13) TJ to Edmond Charles Genet, 1 June (second letter), 5 and 11 June 1793. (14) Alexander Hamilton's Report on the American Debt to France, 8 June 1793, Document VIII in a group of documents on Jefferson and the American debt to France, at 3 June 1793. (15) Enclosures to Washington's first letter to TJ, 11 June 1793. (16) TJ to Richard Harison, 12 June 1793. (17) "3 forms of different passports issued Marked 1. 2. 3 the later being the one now used" (not found; but see note to TJ to Alexander Hamilton, 8 May 1793). Letter enclosed in Washington to TJ, 13 June 1793.

THE BILL LATELY PASSED IN ENGLAND: see note to Thomas Pinckney to TJ, 5 Apr.

1793. For the letter from OUR COMMISSIONERS advising that most of the NORTH WESTERN tribes could not return from their winter quarters in time to begin treaty negotiations on the Lower Sandusky on 1 June 1793, see Beverly Randolph and Timothy Pickering to Henry Knox, 21 May 1793, ASP, *Indian Affairs*, I, 343. See also George Washington to the Cabinet, 17 Feb. 1793, and enclosure.

To Gouverneur Morris

DEAR SIR   Philadelphia. June 13. 1793.

It has long since been observed that of the three millions of livres given by the court of France to aid us in the commencement of our revolution, one million was unaccounted for by the hands into which it was paid. The date of the paiment is fixed to have been the 10th. of June 1776. but to whom it was paid has never been known. Suspicions are that it was to Beaumarchais; and that with this very money he purchased the supplies furnished us by him, for which large sums have been paid him already, and a further large sum is lately certified to be due to him as the balance of that account. I inclose you a letter from the Secretary of the Treasury on this subject, with all the papers relative to the same which his office can furnish: and as you are on the spot, I must beg the favor of you to make an immediate and thorough[1] investigation of it. No reasons of state can now exist for covering the transaction longer under mystery. I have the honour to be with great & sincere esteem Dear Sir your most obedt. & most humble servt.

TH: JEFFERSON

RC (John Watson Foster Dulles, New York City, 1950); at foot of text: "Mr. Morris." PrC (DLC). FC (Lb in DNA: RG 59, DCI). Enclosures: Alexander Hamilton to TJ, 10 June 1793, and enclosures.

On this day TJ submitted the above letter to Washington with a brief note describing it as "another letter to Mr. Morris, on a sub-ject just now put into his hands" (RC in DNA: RG 59, MLR, addressed: "The President of the US.," endorsed by Bartholomew Dandridge, Jr.; Tr in Lb in same, SDC; not recorded in SJL).

[1] TJ first wrote "make a thorough" before altering the passage to read as above.

From Samuel A. Otis

Philadelphia, 13 June 1793. This morning he received an application from his son Samuel A. Otis to the President asking for the consulship at Saint-Domingue. As the business concerns TJ's department, his support will oblige him and his son, who served his apprenticeship in Cap-Français, knows the country's language and modes of doing business, and is esteemed and generally applied to by Eastern merchants who trade there, to whom, and to any French residents of the Cap, TJ is referred for further information. To escape the intolerable weather he intends to travel to the eastward in a few days and will gladly execute any commission for TJ.

RC (DLC: Washington Papers, Applications for Office); 2 p.; at foot of text: "The Secretary of The department of State"; endorsed by TJ as received 13 June 1793 and so recorded in SJL.

The application was Samuel A. Otis, Jr.,

to George Washington, Cap-Français, May 1793, requesting the consular appointment at Saint-Domingue and noting that he had lived at the Cap for seven years and run a mercantile establishment there for two years (DLC: Washington Papers, Applications for Office).

From Thomas Mann Randolph, Jr.

DEAR SIR   Monticello June 13: 1793.

You will observe by the abstract of my diary that we have had an uncommon proportion of rainy weather this spring; our fields of Wheat and Rye from this will give a smaller and a meaner product than we have hitherto expected from them. The plants, where they were tall and stood close, have "lodged" as the farmers term it and of course cannot perfect the grain; where this has not happened many of the grains in every head appear to me to be of a smaller size than usual, alltho' the plants themselves are much larger than the same soil would produce in an ordinary year. There cannot, well, be too much rain for the Indian Corn, but the Weather has been so cold that it is but little advanced for the season; the last 8 or 10 days however have been so favorable, and it has improved so much in that time, that we expect an abundant récolte. We have not prospered in our gardening this year alltho, for the first time, our exertions have been sufficiently great. Our young vegetables have been separated from the root under ground by grubs, or eaten in the seed-leaf by a very minute tribe of grasshoppers and two species of still more minute volatile insects, or devoured in whole squares when farther advanced by immense swarms of insects resembling a good deal the fire-fly wanting its phosphorus. Having once had some little technical knowledge in Entomology I felt a curiosity to ascertain the families to which these different insects belong but from the insufficiency of Linnaeuses descriptions and the smallness of the subjects I have not been able to satisfy it. The earth is alive with these creatures this summer owing I suppose to their being spared by the frost last winter. Patsy and the little boy are perfectly well. Anna looks badly and does not grow which we with sorrow impute to worms. My Father has recovered his health. Dr. Sir your most sincere & affectionate friend

TH: M. RANDOLPH

May
22. 73. f.
23. 73. cloudy.   71. fair
24. 68. f.   70. c.
25. 65. c.   66. c.
26. 64. r.   66. f.
27. 70. f.   75. f.
28. 72. f.   79. f.
29. 68. rain from the E. 64. r.
30. 63. r.   63. r.
31. 60. r.   65. f.

June.
1. 57. f.   63. f.
2. 58. f.   63. f.
3. 59. f.   . r.
4. 62. r
5. 64. light flying cls. 67. dark.
6. 64. r.   72. r.
7. 69. f.a.r.   73. f.
8. 69. f.a.r.   78. f.
9. 72. f.   83. f.
10. 75. f.   80. r. a shower with light: & th.
11. 76. f.   79.   a slight shower
12. 75. c.   80.   showers.
13. 72. r.   75. f.

RC (MHi); addressed: "Thomas Jefferson, Secretary of State Philada."; franked; endorsed by TJ as received 22 June 1793 and so recorded in SJL.

From William Stokes

Sir   June 13th. 1793

Sensibly impressed with a grateful Sense of the important Service you propose doing me I cannot refrain from returning you my most warm and sincere thanks and acknowledgments for such benevolence.

As soon as I return from Virginia (which I hope will be in 3 or 4 weeks) it is my intention to request the favor of declaring to you the object and views of the present design.

Shou'd they be honor'd with your approbation I shall persue them with redoubled vigor. With the highest Sentiments of Esteem & admiration I have the honor to be your most obt. Hble servt.

Wm Stokes

RC (MHi); addressed: "Thomas Jefferson Esquire Secy. of State &ca"; endorsed by TJ as received 14 June 1793 and so recorded in SJL.

From George Washington

June 13. 1793

The President returns to the Secretary of State, with his approbation, the Answer to Mr. Hammond's Memorial—and the letter to M. Morris which have been submitted to him—and hopes the documents mentioned to be sent to Mr. Morris will be as full as they can be with propriety. The President also suggests the expediency of sending copies of the same to Mr. Pinckney by Majr. Jackson, or some other direct and safe opportunity.

RC (DLC); in the hand of Tobias Lear; endorsed by TJ as received 13 June 1793. Recorded in SJPL. Enclosures: (1) TJ to George Hammond, 13 June 1793. (2) TJ to Gouverneur Morris, 13 June 1793 (first letter).

TJ had submitted "draughts" of the enclosed letters to the President with a brief covering note of this date (RC in DNA: RG 59, MLR, addressed: "The President of the US.," endorsed by Bartholomew Dandridge, Jr.; Tr in Lb in same, SDC; not recorded in SJL). See also Washington, *Journal*, 171.

From George Washington

June 13th: 1793

The President sends to the Secretary of State the Counterpart of An Agreement with the Bank of the U.S. for 800,000 dollars, to have the ratification prepared in the usual way for the President's signature.

RC (DLC); in the hand of Tobias Lear; endorsed by TJ as received 13 June 1793. Recorded in SJPL. Enclosure: Agreement between the Secretary of the Treasury and the Bank of the United States, 31 May 1793, by which the Bank agrees to loan the United States a total of $800,000 in equal installments to be advanced on 1 June, 1

July, 1 Aug., and 1 Sep. 1793, the sums to bear 5 percent interest per annum and be repaid within six months of receipt or earlier at the borrower's discretion (Tr in Lb in DLC: Washington Papers, where it is quoted in full as part of the President's ratification of 17 June 1793; printed in Syrett, *Hamilton*, XIV, 500-1).

From David M. Clarkson

St. Eustatius, 14 June 1793. He encloses the bond for the performance of his consular duties here. The numerous British privateers in these seas bring to their ports for examination all vessels suspected of carrying French property and discharge it when found. Only some of the privateers pay for freight so discharged, and many American vessels are now in British ports discharging the French property they had on board. He hopes TJ will approve his appointment of Robert Clinton to act as deputy consul during his absence in Europe for a few months on private business, as he is certain Clinton will comply with TJ's instructions and support the honor and dignity of the United States.

RC (DNA: RG 59, CD); 1 p.; at foot of text: "The Honorable The Secretary of State for Foreign Affairs"; endorsed by TJ as received 21 Aug. 1793 and so recorded in SJL. Enclosure not found.

From Edmond Charles Genet

MONSIEUR   Philadelphie le 14.[1] Juin 1793. l'an 2e. de la Republique.

Vous[2] verrez par les pieces ci jointes qu'au mépris des traités[3] qui unissent les Français et les Americains, qu'au mépris du droit des nations,[4] des officiers civils et judiciaires des Etats Unis[5] se sont permis d'arrêter à Philadelphie la vente[6] de batimens pris par une goelette française armée[7] et de s'opposer à New York à la sortie[8] d'un vaisseau français muni d'une commission du Conseil Exécutif de la République Française. Je vous prie, Monsieur, d'informer Mr. le President des Etats Unis[9] de ces faits, de l'avertir qu'on s'est servi de son nom pour commettre ces infractions aux loix et aux traités[10] des Etats Unis et de l'engager à devellopper dans les circonstances présentes[11] toute l'autorite[12] que le Peuple des Etats Unis lui a confié pour faire éxécuter ces loix et ces traités. Ne doutant point, Monsieur, de la pureté des sentimens de Mr. le Président, j'espere obtenir incessamment à l'aide de ses bons offices et de son énergie restitution avec dommages et interêts[13] des prises françaises arretées et saisies à Philadelphie par un juge incompétent, d'après un ordre que je dois croire supposé et restitution également avec dommages et interets[14] du batiment[15] arrêté et saisi à New York.

C'est par l'entremise des Ministres publics que doivent se traiter des affaires de la nature de celles qui motivent mes plaintes et mes réclamations; Représentant d'un peuple généreux et confiant avec ses amis,[16] j'ai déja donné des preuves des sentimens qui l'animent, en faisant restituer, sans examen,[17] à la demande du Gouvernement fédéral,[18] le navire anglais le Grange pris par un vaisseau de la République:[19] Je montrerai une égale déférence dans toutes mes demarches,[20] mais en même tems, Monsieur, Je crois etre fondé à attendre de votre Gouvernement tout l'appui dont j'ai besoin pour deffendre, aujourdhui,[21] dans le sein des Etats Unis, les interets, les droits et la dignité de la nation française que des gens dont le tems nous fera justice[22] travaillent secretement à faire méconnoitre.   GENET

PrC of Tr (DLC); in a clerk's hand; at head of text: "Le Citoyen Genet, Ministre de la République française à M. Jefferson Secretaire d'Etat des Etats Unis." Dft (DLC: Genet Papers); at head of text: "⟨Prises et armemens⟩ Plainte du C. genet sur l'arrestation faite à Philadelphie en vertu des ordres du Président d'une prise d'un corsaire de le Repe. armé à Charles Ton et d'un Nouveau Corsaire le Republicain armé à N.Y."; with numerous emendations, only the most important of which are noted below. Tr (AMAE: CPEU, xxxvii). Tr (NNC: Gouverneur Morris Papers). Tr

(PRO: FO 97/1). FC (DLC: Genet Papers); in English. FC (same); in English. FC (same); in English; draft translation of preceding FCs. Tr (DNA: RG 46, 3d Cong., 1st sess.); in English. Recorded in SJL as received 14 June 1793. Enclosures: (1) Affidavit of Pierre Barriere, Philadelphia, 7 June 1793, made before François Dupont, stating that on this day a deputy marshal of the United States District Court of Pennsylvania tried to prevent him as agent ad hoc of the *William* and the *Active*, prizes captured by the *Citoyen Genet*, from selling the *William* and its cargo on the grounds that they were seized by the court; that he nevertheless proceeded with the sale in conformity with Article 17 of the treaty of commerce, but because of the deputy's action was obliged to sell the *William* for less than a fourth of its value and the cargo below its value; that he sold the *Active* for no more than a third of its value because the deputy marshal's interference implied that it was comprehended in the seizure of the *William*; and that he therefore seeks to recover damages from the court, from those who instituted the prosecution, and from all others concerned in it. (2) Alexandre Maurice d'Hauterive to George Clinton, 9 June 1793 (see Enclosure No. 2 listed at George Washington's first letter to TJ, 11 June 1793). (3) Affidavit by Hauterive, New York, 10 June 1793, stating that in consequence of a 9 June requisition made by him on the mayor of New York City and the governor of New York for a replevin of the *Républicain*, owned by Louis Alexis Hocquet de Caritat and commanded by Citizen Orset, the governor replied to him by signed letter that in conformity with a presidential injunction he had ordered a detachment of state militia to detain this vessel until the President was informed of the facts of the case, upon which he delivered to the governor a signed and certified act (PrCs of Trs of Nos. 1 and 3 in DLC, in French, with 8 June 1793 attestations of No. 1 by Dupont and J. B. Lemaire, all in a clerical hand; Trs in NNC: Gouverneur Morris Papers, in French; PrCs of other Trs in PRO: FO 97/1, in French, in the hand of George Taylor, Jr.; Trs in DNA: RG 46, Senate Records, 3d Cong., 1st sess., in English). Letter and enclosures with translations printed in *Message*, 11-13 (App.), 26-8, Enclosure No. 2 being printed in translation only; translations printed in ASP, *Foreign Relations*, I,

152-3. Letter and enclosures enclosed in TJ to Gouverneur Morris, 16 Aug. 1793.

TJ read this letter to the President on 15 June 1793, at which time Washington instructed him to submit it to a Cabinet meeting to be held two days later (Washington, *Journal*, 178). See also Cabinet Opinion on French Privateers, 17 June 1793.

The case of the *William*, the French prize at issue in Philadelphia, is discussed in note to George Hammond to TJ, 5 June 1793. For the case of the *Republican*, the French privateer under detention in New York City, see enclosures to Washington to TJ, 11 June 1793. For the restoration of the GRANGE, see note to Memorial from Hammond, 2 May 1793.

[1] Date altered in Dft, perhaps from "12" or "13."

[2] In Dft Genet began the letter with an unfinished sentence which he canceled: "Le desir de maintenir la bonne harmonie ⟨entre la⟩ et l'amitié entre la nation que j'ai l'honneur de représenter et ⟨celles⟩ les."

[3] In Dft Genet here canceled "et des sentiments."

[4] In Dft Genet here canceled a heavily emended passage that in its final state appears to read "et qu'en simple vertu d'Instructions privées emanées de l'autorité seule du Président des Etats unis Il vient de se passer à Philadelphie et à New York des."

[5] In Dft Genet here canceled "sous la simple autorisation du Président des Etats unis."

[6] In Dft Genet here interlined and then canceled "legale."

[7] Preceding two words interlined in Dft in place of "de la République." In the margin Genet canceled "et de saisir les dites prises ⟨et⟩ contre la capture des quelles le gouvernement federal n'avoit fait aucune réclamation."

[8] Preceding two words substituted in Dft for "l'armement."

[9] In Dft Genet first wrote the sentence to this point as "Je vous demande M. d'obtenir de Mr. le President des Etats unis réparation de cette ⟨double insulte. La punition⟩ violation faite aux traites" and then altered it to read as above.

[10] Preceding five words altered in Dft from "aux lois et aux devoirs les plus sacrés."

¹¹ Preceding five words substituted in Dft for "⟨prendre⟩ ⟨développer⟩ se servir promptement de."

¹² Here in margin of Dft Genet canceled "éxécutive."

¹³ Sentence to this point altered from a canceled passage appended to the preceding sentence that in its final state read "et faire rendre a la nation francoise la Justice et les réparations qui lui sont dues. Je demande restitution des batiments."

¹⁴ Preceding five words written in the margin in Dft.

¹⁵ Remainder of sentence written on a separate page in Dft.

¹⁶ In Dft Genet first wrote "d'un peuple Juste et genereux" and then altered it to read as above.

¹⁷ Preceding two words written in the margin in Dft.

¹⁸ Word interlined in Dft in place of "des Etats unis."

¹⁹ In Dft Genet here canceled "m'en rapportant aveuglément à son amitié pour nous et à son équité."

²⁰ Preceding four words written in the margin in Dft.

²¹ Preceding word written in the margin in Dft.

²² In Dft Genet first wrote "gens que le tems condamnera au mépris" and then altered it to read as above.

From Edmond Charles Genet

MONSIEUR   Philadelphie le 14[1] Juin 1793 l'an 2e: de la République.

Il est dans le caractère des ames élevées, des hommes libres de ne point s'exposer deux fois à un refus. Je vous ai prié de faire connoitre au Président des Etats Unis les besoins urgents de la République Française; je ne vous ai point caché qu'ayant armé les bras de près d'un million de soldats, elle éprouvoit un déficit considérable dans ses reproductions et qu'elle seroit livrée avec ses colonies aux horreurs de la famine, si les Etats Unis ne lui fournissoient point, en deduction de leur dette, une partie des subsistances qui lui manquent; je vous ai[2] offert en vertu de mes pouvoirs[3] de prendre en payement, à défaut d'argent, des billets ou *bons* d'Etat, portant interêt jusqu'aux époques fixées par nos conventions pour le remboursement de votre dette; je vous ai fait sentir les avantages qui résulteroient de cette opération pour les deux pays[4] et pour l'Amérique surtout dans un moment où les grains et farines y abondent. Mais voyant, Monsieur, par la lettre que vous m'avez écrite le 11. Juin et par le rapport du Secrétaire de la Trésorerie qu'aucune de nos propositions n'ont été agréées; sans entrer dans les raisons financieres qui ont motivé ce refus, sans essayer de vous faire sentir qu'il tend à accomplir le système infernal du Roi d'Angleterre et des autres rois[5] ses complices[6] pour faire périr par la famine les Republicains Français avec la liberté, je n'écoute dans le cas présent que la voix de ma patrie et comme[7] ses besoins et ceux de ses Colonies deviennent de jour en jour plus pressants, comme elle m'a chargé d'y pourvoir à quelque prix que ce puisse être, je vous prie, Monsieur, d'informer Mr. le President des Etats Unis qu'étant autorisé à donner au nom de la République Française des délégations aux négocians ou fermiers[8] americains en payement des fournitures qu'ils lui feront, à défaut de nouvelles avances[9] de la part des dits Etats,[10] je désire qu'afin de me mettre en mesure de faire usage de ce pouvoir,[11] il prescrive au[12] Secretaire de la Trésorerie de regler promptement avec moi le compte de la dette des Etats Unis envers la France. L'expédient auquel je vais avoir recours[13] sera vraisemblablement onéreux a la Nation Française; mais puisque le Gouvernement Fédéral croit pouvoir prendre sur lui de nous mettre dans la nécéssité de l'employer sans consulter le Congrès sur une matiere aussi importante, je suis forcé, Monsieur, de suivre mes instructions.

GENET

PrC of Tr (DLC); in a clerk's hand; at head of text: "Le Citoyen Genet, Ministre de la République Française à Mr. Jefferson, Secrétaire d'Etat des Etats Unis." Dft (DLC: Genet Papers); with numerous emendations, only the most important of which have been noted below. Tr (AMAE: CPEU, XXXVII). Tr (NNC: Gouverneur Morris Papers). PrC of another Tr (PRO: FO 97/1); in the hand of George Taylor, Jr. FC (DLC: Genet Papers); in English. Tr (DNA: RG 46, 3d Cong., 1st sess.); in English. Recorded in SJL as received 14 June 1793. Printed with translation in *Message*, 13 (App.), 35-6; translation printed in ASP, *Foreign Relations*, I, 156-7. Enclosed in TJ to Gouverneur Morris, 16 Aug. 1793.

TJ read this letter to the President on 15 June 1793, at which time Washington instructed him to submit it to a Cabinet meeting to be held two days later (Washington, *Journal*, 178). For the Washington administration's rejection of Genet's request for advance payment of the American debt to France, see Editorial Note and documents on Jefferson and the American debt to France, at 3 June 1793.

[1] Date altered from "12" or "13" in Dft.
[2] In Dft Genet here canceled "fait sentir les avantages qui résulteroient pour les deux pays."
[3] Preceding five words written in the margin in Dft.

[4] Remainder of sentence written in the margin in Dft.
[5] In Dft Genet here first wrote "et de ses confreres" and then altered it to read as above.
[6] Clause to this point written in the margin in Dft in place of a heavily revised and canceled passage that in its final state read "ma Confiance dans la pureté des sentiments du gouvernement des Etats unis pour la France et pour la Cause qu'elle défend me rend même industrieux à chercher des motifs pour le trouver fondé; Je rejette avec indignation le soupçon que cette decision put être un des hideux résultats des intrigues et des machinations du Roi d'angleterre et de ses confreres."
[7] Clause to this point written in the margin in Dft in place of "Mais Comme."
[8] Preceding two words written in the margin in Dft.
[9] Preceding two words interlined in Dft in place of "payement."
[10] Preceding clause written in the margin in Dft.
[11] Preceding two words interlined in Dft in place of "ce droit."
[12] Preceding three words interlined in Dft in place of "Je le prie ⟨d'ordonne⟩ de charger le."
[13] Preceding five words written in the margin in Dft.

From George Hammond

SIR   Philadelphia 14th June 1793

I have the honor of acknowledging the receipt of your letter of yesterday.

In conformity to your recommendation I have instructed the parties interested in the British brigantine Catharine to adopt without delay in the district Court of New York the proper legal measures for the support of their rights and for the recovery of their property.

I desire you to be persuaded, Sir, that I entertain a just sense of the very dignified conduct that the Governor of the State of New York has pursued in the transaction which you have been so obliging as to communicate to me, and from which I derive the firmest confidence that the measures taken by the executive government of the United States, to prevent a repetition of enterprizes similar to that which has been thus repressed at New York, will be equally efficacious in other parts of the Union.

My satisfaction upon this occasion is however mingled with considerable regret, in consequence of authentic information which I have recently received, that not only one of the two privateers originally fitted out at Charleston named le Citoyen Genêt has (as I stated in my memorial of the 7th. of this month) augmented its force in the port of Philadelphia; but that the other, named le Sans Culottes, has increased its force also in the port of Baltimore, wherein it now remains in the *avowed* intention of watching the motions of a valuable British Ship now lying in the port of Baltimore, of following it out to sea, and of endeavoring to capture it. The consideration of these circumstances renders it in my opinion an act of indispensable duty in me to require of you, Sir, respectfully whether from the expression in your letter of the 5th. curt.— "that the President has required as a reparation of their breach of respect to the United States that 'these' vessels so armed and equipped shall depart from 'your' ports"—I am to deduce as a necessary inference, that these vessels will not be allowed to return to the dominions of the United States, nor to send into any of their ports any prizes which they may happen to make, in the course of their future depredations on the subjects of the King my master. I have the honor to be with sentiments of the greatest respect, Sir, Your most obedient humble servant,

GEO. HAMMOND

RC (DNA: RG 59, NL); in the hand of Edward Thornton, signed by Hammond; at foot of first page: "Mr Jefferson"; endorsed by TJ as received 15 June 1793 and so recorded in SJL. FC (Lb in PRO: FO 116/3). Tr (same, 5/1). Tr (same, 115/2). Tr (Lb in DNA: RG 59, DL).

TJ submitted this letter to the President on 15 June 1793, at which time Washington instructed him to lay it before the Cabinet at a meeting to be held two days later (Washington, *Journal*, 178). See also Cabinet Opinion on French Privateers, 17 June 1793.

From Richard Harrison

SIR   Auditors Office June 14. 1793.

On looking over the Account which you did me the honor to leave with me a few days since, I am doubtful whether your payments to Col. Humphreys, Mr. Cutting and Mr. Morris (particularly that to the latter) ought to be considered as *Advances on Account*, or as Compensations allowed by the President for services of a *special* nature. If of the latter description, I take the liberty to observe that such a Certificate as the law requires, will be necessary to their admission as *final expenditures*. I have the honor to be, with perfect respect, Sir, Y. obed. hble Servt

R. HARRISON

RC (DLC); at foot of text: "The Honble. Tho. Jefferson Secretary of State"; endorsed by TJ as received 15 June 1793 and so recorded in SJL.

The PAYMENTS and LAW in question are detailed in TJ to George Washington, 3 Nov. 1792, and note.

To Thomas Pinckney

DEAR SIR   Philadelphia. June 14. 1793.

My last letters to you have been of the 7th. of May and 4th. inst. Since the last date yours of Apr. 15. has come to hand. I now inclose you two forms of passports for our vessels, as given here. That in three columns is the form now used; the other having been early laid aside. They will be given in our own ports only, and to serve for the single voyage. These forms will enable you to decide on the genuineness of such as may be produced to you.—I inclose you also several memorials and letters which have passed between the executive and the ministers of France and England. These will develope to you the principles on which we are proceeding between the belligerent powers. The decisions being founded in what is conceived to be rigorous justice, give dissatisfaction to both parties, and produce complaints from both. It is our duty however to persevere in them, and to meet the consequences. You will observe that Mr. Hammond proposes to refer to his court the determination of the President that the prizes taken by the Citoyen Genet could not be given up. The reasons for this are explained in the papers. Mr. Genet had stated that she was manned by French citizens. Mr. Hammond had not stated the contrary, before the decision. Neither produced any proofs. It was therefore supposed that she was manned principally with French citizens. After the decision Mr. Hammond denies the fact, but without producing any proof. I am really unable to say how it was. But I believe it to be certain there were very few Americans.—He says the issuing the commission &c. by Mr. Genet within our territory was an infringement of our sovereignty; therefore the proceeds of it should be given up to Great Britain. The infringement was a matter between France and us. Had we insisted on any penalty or forfeiture by way of satisfaction to our insulted rights, it would have belonged to us, not to a third party. As between Great Britain and us, considering all the circumstances explained in the papers, we deemed we did enough to satisfy her.—We are moreover assured that it is the standing usage of France, perhaps too of other nations in all wars[1] to lodge blank commissions, with all their foreign consuls to be given to every vessel of their nation merchant or armed, without which a merchant vessel would be punished as a pirate were she to take the smallest thing of the enemy that should fall in her way. Indeed the place of the *delivery* of a commission is immaterial. As it may be sent by letter to any one, so it may be delivered by hand to him, any where. The place of *signature by the sovereign* is the material thing. Were that to be done in any other jurisdiction than his own, it might draw the validity of the act into question. I mention these things, because I think it would be proper that after considering them and such other circumstances as appear in the papers or may occur to yourself, you should make it the subject of a conversation with the minister. Perhaps it may give you an opportunity of touching on another subject. Whenever Mr. Hammond applies to our government on any matter whatever, be it ever so new or difficult, if he does not receive his answer in two or three days or a week, we are goaded with new letters on the subject. Sometimes it is the sailing of the packet which is made the pretext for forcing us into premature and undigested determinations. You know best how far your applications meet such early attentions, and whether you may with propriety claim a return of them: you can best judge too of the expediency of an intimation that where dispatch is not reciprocal, it may be expedient and justifiable that delays should be so.

Our Commissioners have set out for the place of treaty with the North Western Indians. They have learnt on their arrival at Niagara that the treaty will be a month later than was expected. Should further procrastination take place, it may wear the appearance of being intended to make us lose the present campaign for which all our preparations are made. We have had little expectations of any favorable result from the treaty: and whether for such a prospect we should give up a campaign, will be a disagreeable question.   The Creeks have proceeded in their depredations and murders till they assume the appearance of unequivocal war. It scarcely seems possible to avoid it's becoming so. It is very possible that our affairs with the Indians or with the belligerent powers of Europe, may occasion the convocation of Congress at an earlier day than that to which it's meeting stands at present.

Though our spring has been cold and wet, yet the crops of small grain are as promising as could be desired. They will suffer however by the Hessian fly to the North and the weavil to the South of the Patowmac.

My letter of the 4th. inst. was written to go by the packet. But hearing before it's departure that Majr. Jackson was to go in a few days by a private vessel, it was committed to him, as is also the present letter. I have the honor to be with great & sincere esteem Dear Sir your most obedt. & most humble servt   TH: JEFFERSON

RC (CtY); at foot of first page: "Mr. Pinckney"; endorsed by William A. Deas. PrC (DLC). FC (Lb in DNA: RG 59, DCI); with subjoined list of enclosures. Recorded in SJL as a letter of 13 June 1793. Enclosures: (1) Enclosures Nos. 1, 4-10, and 12-17 listed at TJ to Gouverneur Morris, 13 June 1793, except that No. 1 is described as "Fenno's paper 104 a 108 Freneau's 61 a 65" and No. 17 as "Forms of three Passports No. 1. 2. 3." (2) TJ to George Hammond, 13 June 1793.

TJ submitted this letter to the President with a brief covering letter of this date (see note to Jaudenes and Viar to TJ, 12 June 1793). Washington immediately returned it with a one-word note—"approved"—beneath which TJ wrote: "This was my letter of June 14. 93. to Mr Pinckney" (RC in DLC: TJ Papers, 88: 15178; undated; addressed: "The Secretary of State"; endorsed by TJ as received 14 June 1793; recorded in SJPL under 13 June 1793). See also Washington, *Journal*, 177.

On this day TJ also wrote a brief letter to Pinckney introducing Major William JACKSON and stating that if Jackson ever needed "your official interference on his behalf you will of course interpose it as well on account of his personal worth, as of his character as an American citizen" (PrC in DLC, at foot of text: "Mr. Pinckney"; Tr in DLC, 19th-century copy). See also TJ to Gouverneur Morris, 1 June 1793, and note.

¹ Preceding three words interlined.

From Thomas Pinckney

DEAR SIR   London 14 June 1793

I have to acknowledge the favor of your private letter accompanying the Presidents correspondence for Mr. Carew the directions concerning which shall be observed. I am happy to hear of the arrival of the Pigou at Philadelphia after a short passage as you will have been informed thereby that one of my papers which had been missing and about which I was extremely sollicitous, had been sent by mistake to Mr. G. Morris who returned it to me from Paris. I think I must have some public dispatches from you in the hands of the Captn. or Passenger of one of the last Ships that arrived who may not yet have reached London as the Session of Congress had finished a considerable time and the laws were printed and the important Proclamation relating to our neutrality has been inserted in the News papers though I had not received it officially. The Packet of News papers sent by the way of Holland are I believe still in the hands of Messrs. Vanstaphorsts who I suppose have not been able to find a conveyance for them.

I expect to be able to send the Copper for the use of the Mint by the return of the George Barclay a more advantageous offer having been made for the supply from hence than from any other place.

The public papers herewith will convey all the intelligence relating to the public state of Europe. It is expected that the parliament of this kingdom will be prorogued in a few days. It is said that the disturbances in Ireland have occasioned the countermanding of two Regiments destined from thence to the West India Islands. The failures of mercantile houses in this Country have not been so numerous lately as they were some time ago, but well informed people here are of opinion that they must again increase in a short period. I remain with sincere respect and esteem Dear Sir Your faithful & obedient Servant

THOMAS PINCKNEY

RC (DNA: RG 59, DD); at foot of text: "The Secretary of State"; endorsed by TJ as received 30 Aug. 1793 and so recorded in SJL. PrC of Tr (ScHi: Pinckney Family Papers); in the hand of William A. Deas, unsigned. Tr (Lb in DNA: RG 59, DD). Enclosed in James B. M. Adair to TJ, [ca. 28 Aug. 1793].

TJ's PRIVATE LETTER to Pinckney was that of 27 Apr. 1793. MR. CAREW: John Carey, who was preparing an edition of George Washington's correspondence with the Continental Congress (see note to Carey to TJ, 30 June 1792).

TJ submitted this letter to the President on 30 Aug. 1793 and received it back the same day (Washington, *Journal*, 235).

From John Clarke

HON'BLE SIR   Richmond June 15th 1793

Having heard nothing respecting my petition for a patent for my Machine for a considerable time, And being Anxious to know the success it has met with, I have once more taken the liberty to address you on that subject and humbly request that you will inform me what State the matter is in, the first time you are at leisure.

I have not yet found a man who will Lease your mill-seat at Monticello, altho' I have conversed with several who appeared much inclined to do it, but they seemed to think three hundred Barrels of Corn or the value of it, too great a Rent. I however think differently and would not advise you to take a smaller Rent, nor lease it for so long a term as twenty years (which you proposed when we conversed on that subject). The generality of the planters of this State, and those on James River in particular, have almost droped the culture of Tobacco, and turn their attention principally to the raising of wheat, the greater part of which is purchased by Merchants who are situated on Navigation for that purpose, who find their interest in having it Manufactured before it is sent down the River as it seldom happens that a Boat-load of wheat is brought a considerable distance down the River, free from injury, which if manufactured could not easily be damaged. This is so often the case that the purchasers get all the wheat manufactured up the Country they Can, and I am positive that if there were a sufficient number of Mills to manufacture all the wheat up the Country, there would be none brought down the River unmanufactured. The Flour business has lately become a consequential one in this State, and Millseats are a spieces of property which increase in value faster than any other that I know of, These are the reasons which lead me to think your Mill-seat inferior to none in any respect whatever. And I do not doubt but in a short time it will command as great a price as any situation I am acquainted with, for neither its local situation with respect to geting wheat nor the power of the Stream to do the business, can be doubted. I am Hon'ble sir Your Cordial Friend and Well-wisher   JOHN CLARKE

RC (DLC); at foot of text: "The Hon'ble Mr Jefferson"; endorsed by TJ as received 25 June 1793 and so recorded in SJL.

From Edmond Charles Genet

MONSIEUR   A Philadelphie le 15. Juin 1793. l'an 2e. de la Républ.

Le Citoyen Hauterive Consul de la République à New-York vient de m'informer qu'il s'est élevé entre lui et le Gouvernement de l'Etat dans lequel il réside à l'occasion de la Frégate l'Embuscade,[1] une discussion sur un point de droit.[2] Il s'agit de savoir si dans un port neutre un vaisseau armé doit laisser une trêve de 24. heures aux batimens ennemis[3] pour en sortir. Le Citoyen Hauterive reçût a ce sujet, relativement au départ du Paquebot Anglais, une requisition formelle du Gouverneur, qui, sans lui dire d'une maniere positive[4] que le Gouvernement local avoit le droit d'empêcher la Fregate de[5] sortir avant l'expiration de la trêve de 24. heures et qu'il useroit de ce droit, le lui donnoit à entendre et paroissoit croire[6] qu'il étoit universel.

Le Citoyen Hauterive, Monsieur, s'est borné à me référer ce fait et à me demander à ce sujet des instructions pour lui et pour le capitaine de la Frégate. Je joins ici une copie de celles que je viens de lui faire passer: Je ne les ai rédigées qu'après le plus mur examen de la question et quoique mon opinion diffère éssentiellement de celle du Gouverneur de New-York je suis persuade que Mr. Le President[7] des Etats Unis, après avoir pris en considération les autorités et les raisonnemens qui m'ont guide pour tracer[8] au Consul de la Republique la marche qu'il devoit suivre fera[9] passer au Gouverneur de New-York des[10] ordres[11] dignes de sa justice[12] et de son impartialité.   GENET

PrC of Tr (DLC); in a clerk's hand; at head of text: "Le Citoyen Genet, Ministre de la République française a Mr. Jefferson Secrétaire d'Etat des Etats Unis." Dft (DLC: Genet Papers); only the most significant emendations are recorded below. Tr (NNC: Gouverneur Morris Papers). PrC of another Tr (PRO: FO 97/1); in the hand of George Taylor, Jr. Tr (DNA: RG 46, Senate Records, 3d Cong., 1st sess.); in English. Recorded in SJL as received 15 June 1793. Enclosure: Genet to Alexandre Maurice d'Hauterive, 15 June 1793, stating that according to various European treaties a belligerent armed vessel in a neutral port was not obliged to allow a twenty-four hour truce to an enemy vessel desiring to leave the port; that Governor Clinton's effort to subject French warships to an indefinite truce in such situations contravened the letter and the spirit of French treaties with the United States; that the United States could only require France to commit no hostilities against her enemies on American territory or in American territorial waters; and that Hauterive should energetically oppose any additional restrictions on French warships (PrC of Tr in DLC, in French, with attestation by Genet, in a clerk's hand; Tr in NNC: Gouverneur Morris Papers, in French; PrC of another Tr in PRO: FO 97/1, in French, in Taylor's hand; Tr in DNA: RG 46, Senate Records, 3d Cong., 1st sess., in English). Letter and enclosure with translations printed in *Message*, 13-14 (App.), 36-8; translations printed in ASP, *Foreign Relations*, I, 157-8. Letter and enclosure enclosed in TJ to Gouverneur Morris, 16 Aug. 1793.

TJ read this letter to the President on 15 June 1793, at which time Washington instructed him to submit it to a Cabinet meeting to be held two days later (Washington, *Journal*, 178). At that time the question of whether a belligerent armed vessel in an American port had to observe the European custom of a twenty-four hour truce with respect to an enemy vessel leaving the same port was apparently one of the points which, according to the President's journal, the Cabinet "referred for further consideration." This subject, which was obviously of

great importance to the success of French privateering efforts against the British, is not mentioned in the official Cabinet minutes of that day or in TJ's subsequent correspondence with Genet, though it was one of the neutrality issues on which the Washington administration unsuccessfully solicited the opinion of the United States Supreme Court in July 1793 (same, 181; Cabinet Opinion on French Privateers, 17 June 1793; Questions for the Supreme Court, [18 July 1793], Document IV of a group of documents on the referral of neutrality questions to the Supreme Court, at 18 July 1793). The administration did not resolve this matter until six months after TJ left office when, in response to George Hammond's insistence that it clarify its position on this controverted issue, Secretary of State Edmund Randolph informed the British minister in a letter of 18 June 1794 that the United States government would observe a somewhat ambiguous variant of the twenty-four hour rule discussed by Genet. Henceforth, he announced on the President's behalf, belligerent warships and privateers would have to wait twenty-four hours before they could pursue enemy warships or enemy merchant ships crossing "beyond the jurisdictional line of the United States on the ocean" and not simply leaving American ports. At the same time, he added, the government would take unspecified measures to nullify any prizes "brought within the power of the United States" that were captured in contravention of this rule (Hyneman, *Neutrality*, 68-70). For European precedents for the twenty-four hour rule, see same, 71-2.

[1] Preceding eight words written in the margin in Dft.

[2] In Dft Genet here canceled "public relativement à la frégatte l'Embuscade qui se trouve à New york."

[3] In Dft Genet wrote "batiments marchands énnemis."

[4] Preceding four words written in the margin in Dft.

[5] In Dft Genet here first wrote "d'empêcher les Vaisseaux de guerre de" and then altered the text to read as above.

[6] Remainder of sentence interlined in

Dft in place of "à l'éxistence et à l'univer-salité de cette loi qu'il regardait comme une disposition generale du droit des gens."

[7] Preceding three words interlined in Dft in place of "le gouvernement."

[8] In Dft Genet first wrote "les faits et les raisonnements d'après les quels J'ai tracé" and then altered it to read as above.

[9] Word interlined in Dft in place of "voudra bien faire."

[10] In Dft Genet here canceled "Instructions."

[11] In Dft Genet here canceled a heavily emended passage that in its final state appears to read "Conformes à nos traités et même aux principes qu'il a lui même recommandé aux Citoyens des Etats unis d'observer."

[12] Remainder of sentence interlined in Dft in place of "éclairée et de sa fidelité à défendre les droits de tous et particulierement ceux des amis et des alliés des Etats unis."

From John Tayloe Griffin

SIR   Wilmington. June 16th. 1793.

You will perhaps think me an interested person who never solicited the honor of a correspondence with you until I had a favor to ask, but I hope my present unfortunate situation will be my excuse.

I wish most earnestly to return to Virga. and fully intended to have accompanied my friend Mr. Randolph, who offered me a seat in his carriage, but was unluckily prevented by the want of money, nor was it in his power to furnish me, not having more than barely sufficient to defray his expences to Richmond, or He woud chearfully have advanced it for me. I have taken the liberty to request the favor of you to supply me with fifty dollrs. and have inclosed You a draft on my Brother Cyrus for that sum, which I know will be duly honored. I am very sensible, I have no right to make this application to you, but trust that with you my situation will pardon it. If it shoud be inconvenient for You to spare the money, your Note to me payable in 60 days will answer me a very good purpose, and the draft will be paid long before the expiration of that time. If you can comply with my request, you will confer a favor which I shall remember with the liveliest sense of gratitude to the latest hour of my life, and it will relieve me from a great load of anxiety and distress.

Was there any possible hazard, I woud not have troubled You on this occasion, but I have some property in the hands of my Brother, and have many valuable friends in Virga. I have the honor to be with much esteem & respect Yr. obt Servt   JOHN T. GRIFFIN

The Bearer, who is very trusty, will wait Your answer.

I shou'd most certainly have done myself the honor to have waited on you in person, but do not think it safe to appear in Phila.

RC (MHi); dateline precedes postscripts; addressed: "The Honble Thomas Jefferson Esq. near Grays-ferry"; endorsed by TJ as received 17 June 1793 and so recorded in SJL. Enclosure not found.

John Tayloe Griffin (b. 1750), a Virginian who studied at the College of William and Mary and the University of Edinburgh, was a physician and unsuccessful merchant. His only other recorded contact with TJ came in 1791 when at James Currie's request TJ energetically but unsuccessfully attempted to help Currie obtain payment of a debt Griffin owed him (WMQ, 1st ser., XIII [1905], 184, XIX [1911], 156, 2d ser., I [1921], 33; Syrett, *Hamilton*, XXIII, 278n; Currie to TJ, 14 Mch., 7, 13 Apr., 25 July 1791; TJ to Currie, 24 Mch., 15 May 1791).

From George Washington

DEAR SIR   Sunday 16th. June 1793.

I should be glad if you would give the enclosed a perusal, and let me know if you think the reasons there given are sufficient to authorise the additional Loan of 3,000,000 of florins applied for by the Secretary of the Treasury in a letter which you have seen.

The answers contained in the Report, shew the points on which I required information from him. In addition to the motives assigned in the Report for borrowing the additional Sum, there are others (if the act of doing it is warranted by law) very cogent in my mind as inducements to the measure—namely—the uncertain result of the Indian Treaty—the invasion of our Southern frontiers—and the peculiarly delicate situation in which we are placed with respect to some of the European[1] Powers—who in spite of all we can do may involve us in a dispute with one or other of them—In which case it might be too late to effect a loan. If the propriety of borrowing on the plan, and for the purposes mentioned in the Report is clear in your Mind the Report may be returned by the bearer. If not any time before nine[2] tomorrow may do. Yours always   GO: WASHINGTON

RC (DLC); at foot of text: "Mr. Jefferson"; endorsed by TJ as received 16 June 1793. Dft (DNA: RG 59, MLR); with one significant variation. FC (Lb in same, SDC); wording generally follows Dft. Recorded in SJPL.

The other VERY COGENT . . . INDUCEMENTS in favor of the new loan proposed by Alexander Hamilton had been advanced in the Treasury Secretary's 15 June 1793 letter to Washington covering the enclosure printed below (Syrett, *Hamilton*, XIV, 550-1).

[1] "Belligerent" interlined in place of this word in Dft.
[2] FC: "noon."

ENCLOSURE

Alexander Hamilton's Report on a New Foreign Loan

The Secretary of the treasury in obedience to the order of the President of the US. of the 6th. inst. respectfully makes the following report.

The statement herewith transmitted, marked A. shews in the Credit side thereof, the amount of the fund arising from foreign loans transferred to the US. amounting to 2,965,643.47 D. and, on the Debt side thereof, the amount of the sums which have been *actually* disbursed, and are *in a course of disbursement* out of that fund for specific purposes, being 2,400,159.19 D.

There of course remains free for and subject to application, according to the laws authorizing the loans, a balance of 565,484.28 D.

To this will be to be added, when ascertained, certain sums of interest subsequent to the year 1790. which will have been included in the payments to France and Spain out of the proceeds of the foreign loans, and which will thereby have been virtually transferred to the US., provision having been made for that object out of domestic funds. The addition however will not be large.

Hence results an answer to the 1st. question stated by the President.

In answer to the 2d. question, the Secretary has the honor to observe that it would be in his opinion expedient for the reason which has governed hitherto, the convenience of which has been fully experienced, namely the *power of applying the fund to the purposes of either law according to circumstances*, that the proposed loan should be made upon the authority of both acts, and not upon the separate authority of either of them.

The following summary answers the 3d. question proposed.

The sum allowed to be borrowed by the two acts of the 4th. and 12th. of Aug. 90. is 14,000,000.D. The whole amount of the loans hitherto made is 19,550,000. Gilders, equal at $36\frac{4}{11}$ ninetieths of a dollar per gilder to 7,898,989 Doll. and 88. Cents. Consequently 'the balance remaining unborrowed of the two sums allowed to be borrowed' is 6,101,010.12 D. which leaves much more than sufficient latitude for a loan of 3,000,000 of florins in addition to that for 2,000,000. already directed, and probably set on foot.

The immediate main object of this further loan would be the purchase of the debt.

The instalments of the debt to France falling due in Sep. and Nov. next, and the interest for a year upon so much of the debt as by the terms of contract would fall due after the present time, amount to 3,335,000. livres, or Dollars 605,302.50 which, *if to be wholly paid* will more than absorb the balance on hand of the foreign fund.

Supposing the application of this balance to that purpose, there would remain to be borrowed for the purpose of purchases of the debt, Dollars 1,715,098.11.

The two millions of guilders already directed to be borrowed and the three millions, the loan of which is proposed to be authorised, would amount together to 2,020,202.02 D. which would exceed the sum requisite for purchases of the debt by 305,103.91 D.

But it is so possible that events may arise which would render it desireable to the US. to increase it's payments to France as in that view alone to make such an excess not inconvenient. Besides that on the 1st. of June 1794. another instalment of the Dutch loans becomes payable, and it is probable if instructions to set on foot the loan should go at this time, the entire payment of the sums subscribed to the loan would not be completed much sooner than June next. Add to this that it is frequently possible to get the periods of payment protracted.

It would have been fortunate in every sense, if the state of the Treasury had permitted the entering the market for purchases, in force; but the detail, which has been given, shews that it could not have been done, under the obstacles which the state of European affairs lately threw in the way of loans, without materially hazarding the credit of the US.

While it is prudent to wait, till it is experimentally ascertained, that these obstacles have been removed by the change of affairs, it is desireable to be provided to the extent of the authority given with means of prosecuting purchases.

It is probable that, for a considerable time to come, the prices of stock will remain at a point which will render purchases extremely advantageous.

The further consideration which has been stated with reference to France and the next instalment of the Dutch loans may not be found unworthy of attention. All which is respectfully submitted.

(signed) ALEXANDER HAMILTON Secy. of the Treasy.

Treasury department. June 15. 1793.

[A]

Dr. State of monies transferred to the US. out of the proceeds of foreign loans.

To this sum expended in purchases of the public debt.	284,901.89
To this sum pd. & to be paid to France for the use of St. Domingo.	726,000.
To this sum pd. & to be pd. to France on acct. of the 3,000,000. of livres promised	544,500.
To this sum paid to France for miscellaneous purposes	49,400.
To this sum paid & to be paid to Foreign officers.	191,316.90
To this sum appropriated to the 1st. instalmt. due to the Bank of the US.	200,000.
To this sum remitted to Europe for paying an instalment due the 1st. of June on the Dutch debt 1,000,000 of guilders @ $36\frac{4}{11}$ 90ths. pr. guilder	404,040.40
	2,400,159.19
Balance subject to future disposition	565,484.28
	2,965,643.47

Cr.

By this sum drawn for by Saml. Meredith Treasurer	2,305,769.13
By this sum applied in Amsterdam to the payment of interest for which provision was made out of domestic funds, & thereby virtually drawn to the US. 1,633,189. guilders 2. stivers @ $36\frac{4}{11}$ 90ths per guildr	659,874.34
	2,965,643.47

Tr (DLC); entirely in TJ's hand; bracketed line supplied. PrC (DLC). Recorded in SJPL: "Hamilton's report on applicn of the loans." Enclosed in TJ to James Madison, 29 June 1793.

For the antecedents, see Opinion on a New Foreign Loan, 5 June 1793, and note.

From Sylvanus Bourne

[*Philadelphia*], *17 June 1793, "Mrs Dunns No 153 markett street."* Having made a contract with Mr. Morris that will enable him to return to Cape François, he urges TJ to consult with the President about resuming his old consular commission or his reappointment to the place, a necessary condition of his present plan; as his former commission bears the endorsement on his reception, perhaps it will more easily facilitate his readmission by the governor there. Since the business in contemplation would suffer by delay, a decision before TJ leaves town would greatly oblige him.

RC (DLC: Washington Papers, Applications for Office); 2 p.; at foot of text: "The Secy of State"; endorsed by TJ as received 17 June 1793 and so recorded in SJL.

Bourne had resigned as United States consul for Saint-Domingue in December 1791 because French authorities on the island refused to recognize his authority (Bourne to TJ, 29 Apr., 30 June, 29 Dec. 1791).

Cabinet Opinion on French Privateers

June 17. 1793

At a meeting of the heads of departments at the President's this day, on summons from him, a letter from Mr. Genet of the 15th. inst. addressed to the Secretary of state on the subject of the seizure of a vessel by the Govr. of New York as having been armed, equipped and manned in that port with a design to cruize on the enemies of France, was read, as also the draught of an answer prepared by the Secretary of state, which was approved.

Read also a letter of June 14. from Mr. Hammond to the Secretary of state, desiring to know whether the French privateers the Citizen Genet and Sans Culottes are to be allowed to return or send their prizes into the ports of thc US. It is the opinion that he be informed that they were required to depart to the dominions of their own sovereign and nothing expressed as to their ulterior proceedings. And that in answer to that part of the same letter which states that the Sans Culottes has increased it's force in the port of Baltimore and remains there in the avowed intention of watching the motions of a valuable ship now lying there, it be answered that we expect the speedy departure of those privateers will[1] obviate the inconveniences apprehended,[2] and that it will be considered[3] whether any practicable arrangements can be adopted to prevent the augmentation of the force of armed vessels.

TH: JEFFERSON
A HAMILTON
H. KNOX

MS (DLC: Washington Papers); in TJ's hand, with emendations, signed by TJ, Hamilton, and Knox; written with Cabinet Opinions on Relations with Spain and Great Britain, 20 June 1793, on a sheet folded to make four pages, with opinions on first two pages and endorsement by Washington on the fourth, the third being blank. FC (DLC); entirely in TJ's hand, with names of signatories and some words abbreviated and one phrase omitted; written on a sheet bearing on verso Cabinet Opinions on Relations with Spain and Great Britain, 20 June 1793. Entry in SJPL: "Notes of a meeting at the Pres's. privateers—prizes." Enclosed in TJ to George Washington, 19 June 1793.

The President met with the Cabinet this day in order to consider the neutrality issues raised in four letters from the French and British ministers that TJ had submitted to him two days before (Edmond Charles Genet to TJ, 14, 15 June 1793; George Hammond to TJ, 14 June 1793; Washington, *Journal*, 178). The letter OF THE 15TH INST. was actually Genet's second letter to

TJ of 14 June 1793. The DRAUGHT OF AN ANSWER approved by the Cabinet was the letter of this date from TJ to Genet that was actually sent to the French minister. For the letter TJ wrote to the British minister pursuant to the Cabinet's directions, see TJ to Hammond, 19 June 1793. In addition to the points it resolved, the Cabinet this day also deferred certain other issues "for further consideration" and postponed consideration of them again when it next met on 20 June 1793 (Washington, *Journal*, 181, 183). For the issues in question, see TJ to Genet, 15 June 1793, and note, and TJ's unsent letter to Genet, 17 June 1793, and note.

[1] TJ here canceled "soon put an end to these questions."

[2] TJ originally ended the sentence at this point before adding the remainder.

[3] TJ first wrote "and that armed vessels will not be permitted," and then canceled the last six words and wrote "the US. will consider" before reworking the passage to read as above.

To Edmond Charles Genet

SIR   Philadelphia June[1] 17. 1793.

I shall now have the honor of answering your letter of the 8th.[2] instant, and so much of that of the 14th. (both of which have been laid before the President) as relates to a vessel armed in the port of new York and about to depart from thence, but stopped by order of the Government; and here I beg leave to premise, that, the case supposed in your letter, of a vessel arming merely for her own defence, and to repel unjust aggressions, is not that in question, nor that on which I mean to answer, because, not having yet happened, as far as is known to the Government, I have no instructions on the subject. The case in question is that of a vessel armed, equipped, and manned, in a part of the united States, for the purpose of committing hostilities on nations at peace with the united States.

As soon as it was perceived that such enterprises would be attempted, orders to prevent them, were dispatched to all the States and ports of the Union. In consequence of these, the Governor of new York, receiving information that a Sloop, heretofore called the Polly, now the Republican, was fitting out, arming, and manning in the port of new

York, for the express, and sole purpose of cruising against certain Nations, with whom we are at peace; that she had taken her guns and ammunition aboard and was on the point of departure, seized the vessel. That the Governor was not mistaken in the previous indications of her object, appears by the subsequent avowal of the citizen Hauterive, consul of France at that port, who, in a letter to the Governor, reclaims her as "Un vaisseau armé en guerre, et pret à mettre à la voile," and describes her object in these expressions "Cet usage etrange de la force publique contre les citoyens d'une nation amie qui se reunissent ici *pour aller defendre leurs freres*," &c. and again "Je requiers, monsieur, l'autorité dont vous etes revetu, pour faire rendre à des François, à des alliés &c. la liberté *de voler au secours de leur patrie*." This transaction being reported to the President, orders were immediately sent to deliver over the vessel, and the persons concerned in the enterprise to the tribunals of the Country, that if the act was of those forbidden by the law, it might be punished, if it was not forbidden, it might be so declared, and all persons apprised of what they might or might not do.

This we have reason to believe is the true state of the case, and it is a repetition of that which was the subject of my letter of the 5th. instant, which animadverted not merely on the single fact of the granting commissions of war, by one nation, within the territory of another; but on the aggregate of the facts: for it states the Opinion of the President to be "That the arming and equipping vessels in the ports of the United States, to cruise against nations with whom they are at peace, was incompatible with the sovereignty of the United States; that it made them instrumental to the annoyance of those nations, and thereby tended to compromit[3] their peace"—and this opinion is still conceived to be not contrary to the principles of natural law, the usage of nations, the engagements which unite the two people, nor the proclamation of the President, as you seem to think.

Surely not a syllable can be found in the last mentioned instrument, permitting the preparation of hostilities in the ports of the united States. It's object was to enjoin on our citizens "a friendly conduct towards all the belligerent powers," but a preparation of hostilities is the reverse of this.

None of the engagements in our treaties stipulate this permission. The XVIIth. article of that of commerce, permits the armed vessels of either party, to enter the ports of the other, and to depart with their prizes freely: but the entry of an armed vessel into a port, is one act; the equipping a vessel in that port, arming her, manning her, is a different one, and not engaged by any article of the Treaty.

You think, Sir, that this opinion is also contrary to the law of nature and usage of nations. We are of opinion it is dictated by that law and usage; and this had been very maturely enquired into before it was adopted as a principle of conduct. But we will not assume the exclusive right of saying what that law and usage is. Let us appeal to enlightened and disinterested Judges. None is more so than Vattel. He says L. 3. §. 104. "Tant qu'un peuple neutre veut jouïr surement de cet état, il doit montrer en toutes choses une exacte impartialité entre ceux qui se font la guerre. Car s'il favorise l'un au prejudice de l'autre, il ne pourra pas se plaindre, quand celui-ci le traitera comme adhérent et associé de son ennemi. Sa neutralité seroit une neutralité frauduleuse, dont personne ne veut être la dupe.—Voyons donc en quoi consiste cette impartialité qu'un peuple neutre doit garder.

Elle se rapporte uniquement à la guerre, et comprend deux choses. 1°. Ne point donner de secours quand on n'y est pas obligé; ne fournir librement ni troupes, ni armes, ni munitions, ni rien de ce qui sert directement à la guerre. Je dis *ne point donner de secours*, et non pas *en donner egalement*; car il seroit absurde qu'un Etat secourût en même tems deux ennemis. Et puis il seroit impossible de le faire avec egalité; les mêmes choses, le même nombre de troupes, la même quantité d'armes, de munitions, &c. fournies en des circonstances differentes, ne forment plus des secours équivalens." &c. If the neutral power may not, consistent with it's neutrality, furnish men to either party, for their aid in war, as little can either enrol them in the neutral territory, by the law of nations. Wolf §. 1174. Says "Puisque le droit de lever des Soldats est un droit de majesté, qui ne peut être violé par une nation etrangere, il n'est pas permis de lever des soldats sur le territoire d'autrui, sans le consentement du maître du territoire." And Vattel, before cited L. 3. §. 15. "Le droit de lever des soldats appartenant uniquement à la nation, ou au souverain, personne ne peut en enroler en pays etranger sans la permission du souverain:—Ceux qui entreprennent d'engager des soldats en pays étranger sans la permission du Souverain, et en general quiconque débauche les sujets d'autrui, viole un des droits les plus sacrés du prince et de la nation. C'est le crime qu'on appelle *plagiat*, ou vol d'homme. Il n'est aucun Etat policé qui ne le punisse très-sévérement." &c. For I chuse to refer you to the passage, rather than follow it thro' all its developments. The testimony of these, and other writers, on the law and usage of nations, with your own just reflections on them, will satisfy you that the united States in prohibiting all the belligerent powers from equipping, arming, and manning vessels of war in their ports, have exercised a right, and a duty with justice, and with great moderation. By our treaties with several of the belligerant powers, which are a part of the laws of our land, we have established a State of peace with them. But without appealing to treaties, we are at peace with them all by the law of nature. For by nature's law, man is at peace with man, till some aggression is committed, which, by the same law, authorizes one to destroy another as his enemy. For our citizens then, to commit murders and depredations on the members of nations at peace with us, to combine to do it, appeared to the Executive, and to those whom they consulted, as much against the laws of the land, as to murder or rob, or combine to murder or rob it's own citizens, and as much to require punishment, if done within their limits, where they have a territorial jurisdiction, or on the high seas, where they have a personal jurisdiction, that is to say, one which reaches their own citizens only, this being an appropriate part of each nation on an element where all have a common jurisdiction. So say our laws as we understand them ourselves. To them the appeal is made. And whether we have construed them well or ill, the constitutional Judges will decide. Till that decision shall be obtained, the Government of the United States must pursue what they think right with firmness, as is their duty. On the first attempt that was made the President was desirous of involving in the censures of the law, as few as might be. Such of the individuals only therefore as were citizens of the United States, were singled out for prosecution. But this second attempt being after full knowledge of what had been done on the first, and indicating a disposition to go on in opposition to the laws, they are to take their course against all persons concerned, whether Citizens, or aliens; the latter, while within our Jurisdiction and enjoying the protection of the laws, being bound to obedience to them, and to avoid disturbances of our peace within, or acts which would commit it without, equally as Citizens are. I have the honor to be, with sentiments of great respect & esteem, Sir, Your most obedient and most humble servant

PrC (DLC); in the hand of George Taylor, Jr., unsigned; with dateline completed in ink by Taylor (see note 1 below) and a clerical correction in ink by TJ; at foot of first page: "M. Genet, minister plenipoy. of the Repub. of France." PrC of Tr (DLC); in a clerk's hand. Tr (NNC: Gouverneur Morris Papers). Tr (DNA: RG 46, Senate Records, 3d Cong., 1st sess.). PrC (PRO: FO 97/1). FC (Lb in DNA: RG 59, DL). Tr (DLC: Genet Papers). Tr (AMAE: CPEU, xxxvii); in French. Tr (DLC: Genet Papers); in French; draft translation of preceding Tr, with revisions and docketing by Genet. Printed in *Message*, 28-30. Enclosed in TJ to Gouverneur Morris, 16 Aug. 1793.

Before sending this letter to Genet, TJ first secured presidential and Cabinet approval of it this day (Cabinet Opinion on French Privateers, 17 June 1793). For the ORDERS ... DISPATCHED TO ALL THE STATES, see TJ to Henry Knox, with Proposed Circular to the Governors of the States, 21 May 1793, and note. The AVOWAL OF THE CITIZEN HAUTERIVE is in Enclosure No. 2 at George Washington to TJ, 11 June 1793.

[1] Remainder of dateline inserted in ink.
[2] PrC: "18th." The Trs in NNC, PRO, AMAE, and the Genet Papers in DLC correctly give the date as "8"; all other texts follow the PrC.
[3] Supplied from TJ to Genet, 5 June 1793. PrC and all other English texts: "commit." French texts: "compromettent."

To Edmond Charles Genet

Sir   Philadelphia June 17th. 1793.

I have received and laid before the President, your letter of the 14th. instant, stating that certain judiciary Officers of the united States, contrary to the law of nations, and to the treaties subsisting between France and the united States, had arrested certain vessels and Cargoes taken by a French armed vessel and brought into this port, and desiring that the authority of the President might be interposed to restore the prizes with damages for their detention.

By the laws of this Country every individual claiming a right to any Article of property, may demand process from a court of Justice, and a decision on the validity of his claim. This is understood to be the case, which is the subject of your letter. Individuals claiming a right to the prizes, have attached them by process from the court of Admiralty, which that Court was not free to deny, because justice is to be denied to no man. If, at the hearing of the cause, it shall be found that it is not cognisable before that court, you may so far rely on it's learning and integrity as to be assured it will so pronounce of itself. In like manner, if, having jurisdiction of the cause, it shall find the right of the claimants to be null, be assured it will pronounce that nullity; and, in either case the property will be restored; but whether with damages or not, the court alone is to decide. It happens in this particular case that the rule of decision will be, not the municipal laws of the United States but the law of nations, and the law maritime, as admitted and practised in all civilized countries; that the same sentence will be pronounced here that would be pronounced in the same case in the Republic of France, or in any other country of Europe; and that if it should be unfavorable to the captors, it will be for reasons understood and acknowledged in your own Country, and for the justice of which we might safely appeal to the Jurists of your own Country. I will add that if the seizure should be found contrary to the treaties subsisting between France and the united States, the Judges will consider these treaties as constituting a conventional Law for the two Nations, controuling all other law, and will decree accordingly.

The functions of the Executive are not competent to the decision of Questions of property between Individuals. These are ascribed to the Judiciary alone, and when either persons or property are taken into their custody, there is no power in this country which can take them out. You will therefore be sensible, Sir, that though the President is not the Organ for doing what is just in the present case, it will be effectually done by those to whom the constitution has ascribed that duty; and be assured that the interests, the rights and the dignity of the French nation will receive within the Bosom of the United States all the support which a friendly nation could desire, and a neutral one yield. I have the honor to be with sentiments great respect and esteem, Sir, Your most obedient and Most humble servant

Dft (DLC); in the hand of George Taylor, Jr., except for "not sent" written at head of text and line drawn lengthwise through the first page by TJ; unsigned; at foot of first page: "M: Genet, minister plenipy. of the Repub. of france." PrC (DLC); with "not sent" added in ink at head of text by TJ; lacks line drawn across first page. Entry in SJPL: "Th:J. to Genet. draught of a letter not sent."

Judging from the date, it seems likely that TJ prepared this letter for this day's meeting of the Cabinet, which the President summoned to consider several communications from the French and British ministers, including Genet's 14 June 1793 letter to the Secretary of State complaining about the detention by the United States District Court of Pennsylvania of the *William* and the *Active*, the English VESSELS AND CARGOES seized by the *Citoyen Genet*. The decision to withhold the letter is not recorded in the official minutes of the Cabinet meeting (Cabinet Opinion on French Privateers, 17 June 1793).

From James Madison

MY DEAR SIR   Orange June 17. 1793

Your favor of the 9th. I received late last night by a messenger from the neighbourhood of Fredg. who returns early this morning. I have therefore not had time to read the papers inclosed in it and even the letter itself but hastily. Its silence as to France is a cordial to the fears we have been kept in by the newspapers and reports here, of hearing every moment of her final catastrophe. If the army had stood by Dumourier's treason, as was the uncontradicted idea for a time, scarce a possibility seemed to remain of any other result. I fell in two days ago with French Strother who was returning circuitously from Richmond. He had seen W.[1] Nicholas on his way, and spoke of him as among the decided friends of the French cause. In general I discovered that his testimony and conviction corroborated the fact that the people of this country, where you can not trace the causes of particular exceptions, are unanimous and explicit in their sympathy with the Revolution. He was in Richmond during the session of the Court of the U.S. and heard the opinions of the Judges on the subject of the British debts. Jay's he says was that the depreciated payments into the Treasury discharged the debtor, but leave the State liable to the Creditor. It would be a hard tax on those who have suffered themselves by the depreciation to bear such a burden. It would be severely felt by those who put money into the Treasury on loan and have received certificates by the scale, and those again further reduced by the modifications of the assumption. I asked S. who told me he was under the same roof with Jay and a good deal in his Society, what language he held on French topics. He never opened his lips, was the answer. In Fredg. on his way to Richmond, he was less reserved. I understood that in a conversation there with M. Page who was full of zeal, on the side of France, his enmity broke out in a very decided tone.

We have had no rain since my last which was of the 13th. The Wheat however has continued to suffer, partly by the rust, but chiefly by the rot. In the lower country the damage is said to be very great. In this quarter I think very saving crops will be made; perhaps as much as would be called a good crop in ordinary years. Several fields I examined yesterday, will I am confident not lose as much by the late bad weather, as they had gained beyond the medium fecundity by the previous influence of the season. I have not heard from Albemarle, but have no reason to doubt that it has as good fare as its neighbour county. The harvest will commence in two or three days here.

My imagination has hunted thro' the whole State without being able to find a single character fitted for the mission to N. O. Young Marshal seems to possess some of the qualifications, but there would be objections of several sorts to him. In general the men of understanding in[2] this Country are either preoccupied or too little acquainted with the world in the sense necessary for such functions. As a mercantile mask would be politic, the difficulty of providing a man here is the greater.

My plows I find have been finished and forwarded. They are not meant so much as innovations here, as models of a proper execution. One of them is the common barr share, the other a plow preferred in the practice of Dr. Logan. I have Tull and have noticed superficially that you allude to. We are not yet ripe for such nice work. In a former letter I asked the favor of you to see to the re-payment of the price, and must still rely on your goodness for that purpose. The price will be made known by Billey. Yrs. always & affy.   J. M. JR.

RC (DLC: Madison Papers); addressed: "*private* Mr. Jefferson Philada."; endorsed by TJ as received 27 June 1793 but recorded in SJL as received a day later.

N. O.: New Orleans.

[1] Madison later interlined "C." here.
[2] Preceding four words interlined in place of "young men of."

Second Opinion on a New Foreign Loan

I cannot see my way clear in the case on which the President has been pleased to desire my opinion, but by recurring to these leading questions.

Of the 7,898,999.86 D. borrowed, or rather of the 7,545,912.D. nett proceeds thereof, how much has been applied to the *payment* of the *foreign*, and *purchase* of the *general* debt?

To the balance thereof, which should be on hand, and the 2. millions of florins now borrowing, is any and what addition necessary *for the same objects* for the years 1793. 1794?

The statement furnished by the Secretary of the Treasury does not answer these questions. It only shews what has been done with somewhat less than 3. millions out of near 8. millions of Dollars which have been borrowed: and in so doing it takes credit for two sums which are not to come out of this fund, and therefore not to be left in the account. They are the following.

1. a sum of 284,901.89 D. expended in purchases of the public debt. In the general Report of the trustees of the Sinking fund, made to Congress the 23d. of Feb. last, and printed, it appears page 29. that the whole amount of monies laid out by them was 1,302,407.64 D from which were to be deducted, as is mentioned in the note there subjoined, the purchases made out of the interest fund (then about 50,000.D. as well as I recollect.) Call the sum paid then 1,252,407.64 D. By the Treasury report pa. 38. (new edition) it appears that the surplus of domestic revenue to the end of 1790. appropriated to this object was 1,374,656.40 D and page 34. that the monies drawn from Europe on account of the foreign loans were not the instrument of these purchases: and in some part, to which I am not able just now to turn, I recollect pretty certainly that it is said these purchases were actually carried to account, as was proper, against the Domestic surplus. Consequently they are not to be allowed in the foreign account also. Or if allowed in this, the sum will then be due from the Surplus account, and so must lessen the sum to be borrowed for the sinking fund, which amounts to the same.

2. The 1st. instalment due to the bank 200,000.D.   Though the first payment of the subscription of the US. to the bank might have been made, in the first instant, out of the foreign monies, to be immediately repaid to them by the money borrowed of the bank, yet this useless formality was avoided, and it was a mere operation of the pen on paper, without the displacement of a single dollar. See Reports pa. 12. And, in any event, the final reimbursement was never to be made out of the foreign fund, which was appropriated solely to the *paiment* of the *foreign*, and *purchase* of the *general* debt. [1]

These two sums therefore of 284,901.89 D. and 200,000.D. are to be added to the balance of 565,484.28 D. subject to future disposition, and will make 1,050,386.17 D. actually here, and still to be applied to the proper appropriation.

However, this account, as before observed, being only of a part of the monies borrowed, no judgment can be formed from it of the expediency of borrowing more: nor should I have stopped to make a criticism on it, but to shew why no such sums, as the two above mentioned, were inserted in the general account sketched for the President June 5. I must add that the miscellaneous sum also of 49,400.D. in this account, is probably covered by some other articles of that, as far as it is chargeable to this fund, because that account under one form or another, takes up all the articles, chargeable on this fund, which had appeared in the printed Reports.

I must therefore proceed to renew my statement of June 5. inserting therein the 1st. instalment of the Dutch loan, 404,040.40 D. payable this month, which not having been mentioned in any of the Reports heretofore published, was not inserted in my statement. I will add a like sum for the year 1794. because I think we should now prepare for the whole of that year.

As the Secretary of the treasury does not seem to contemplate the furnishing any fixed sum for the Sinking fund, I shall leave that article out of the account. The President can easily add to it's result any sum he may decide to have furnished to that fund. The account, so corrected, will stand thus.

	The Trust for loans Dr.			D.	
To Nett amount of loans to June 1. 1792.				7,545,912.	
To loan now going on for 2,000,000 florins				808,080.	D
				8,353,992.	

Cr.

		florins s.		D.	
By charges on remittances to France		10,073–1			
By reimbursement to Spain		680,000.			
By Interest paid to Foreign officers		105,000.		D.	
		795,073–1=		321,239.46	
By Principal paid to Foreign officers				191,316.90	
By amt. of French debt, Principl.		livres			
& Intt. payable to end of 1791.		26,000,000.			
By do.	for 1792.	3,450,000.			
		29,450,000.	= 5,345,171.		
By do.	for 1793.	3,410,000.		618,915.	
By 1st. instalmt. of Dutch debt due	June 1793.			404,040.40	
By Instalment & Interest to France	for 1794.	3,250,000.		569,875.	
By Instalment to Holland	for 1794.			404,040.40	
Balance will then remain in hands of the trust				499,393.84	
				8,353,992.	

So that it appears there would be a balance in the hands of this trust at the close of 1794. of 499,393.84 D. were no monies to be furnished in the mean time to the Sinking fund. But should the President determine to furnish that with the 900,000.D. proposed in my statement of June 5. then a loan would be necessary for about 400,000.D. say in near round numbers 1,000,000. of guilders, in addition to the 2. millions now borrowing. I am, *individually*, of opinion that that sum ought to be furnished to the Sinking fund, and consequently that an additional loan to this extent should be made, considering the subject in a *legal point of view* only.

It remains then to see whether, under *any other point of view*, the loan should be extended still 2. millions further.[2]

The reasons in favor of the extension of the loan are

The apprehension of the extension of our war to other Indian nations, and perhaps to Europe itself:

The disability this might produce to borrow at all: [this is, in my judgment, a weighty consideration]

The possibility that the government of France may become so settled, as that we may hazard the anticipation of payments, and so avoid dead interest.

The reasons against it are

The possibility that France may continue, for some time yet, so unsettled as to render an anticipation of payments hazardous:

The risk of losing the capital borrowed, by a succesful invasion of the country of deposit, if it be left in Europe, or by an extension of the bankruptcies now shaking the most solid houses, and when and where they will end, we know not:

The loss of interest on the dead sum, if the sum itself be safe:

The execution of a power for one object, which was given to be executed but for a very different one:

The commitment of the President, on this account, to events, or to the criticisms of those who, tho' the measure should be perfectly wise, may misjudge it through error or passion:

The apprehension that the head of the department means to provide idle money to be lodged in the banks ready for the corruption of the next legislature, as it is believed the late ones were corrupted by gratifying particular members with vast discounts for objects of[3] speculation.

I confess that the last reasons have most weight with me.

Th: Jefferson
June 17. 1793.

PrC (DLC: TJ Papers, 88: 15207-10); brackets in original. Tr (Martin Weiner, Clifton, New Jersey, 1959); entirely in TJ's hand; contains marginal query (see note 1 below) and omissions and variations, only the most important of which are noted below. PrC (DLC: TJ Papers, 88: 15201-

4); lacks marginal query. Entry in SJPL: "Opn of Th:J. on [Hamilton's report on applicn of the loans]." Enclosed in TJ to James Madison, 29 June 1793.

This is the last document exchanged between TJ and the President respecting Alexander Hamilton's proposal to open a new loan of 3,000,000 florins in Europe (for the antecedents, see Opinion on a New Foreign Loan, 5 June 1793, and note; Washington to TJ, 16 June 1793, and enclosure). With this second opinion from TJ in hand, over the next month Washington sought to clarify with Hamilton the statutory authority behind his proposal and satisfy himself as to the amount to borrow. When, in their correspondence, Washington posed to the Treasury Secretary the substance of TJ's question as to whether the government's first $200,000 reimbursement of its loan from the Bank of the United States was chargeable under the acts of 4 and 12 Aug. 1790 or any other statute, Hamilton pointed to an act of 2 Mch. 1793 stipulating that the payment was to come from the $2,000,000 loan authorized by the act of 12 Aug. 1790, thus demonstrating that the Secretary of State had been mistaken in asserting that the $200,000 reimbursement of the bank WAS NEVER TO BE MADE OUT OF THE FOREIGN FUND, as TJ's subsequent marginal note on a collateral text of his opinion appeared to acknowledge (see note 1 below). The President, however, deferred a final decision until he could obtain the opinion of Attorney General Edmund Randolph, who did not return from a trip to Virginia until around 21 July 1793 (TJ to James Madison, 21 July 1793). Meanwhile, having received news from Hamilton on 19 July 1793 that the American bankers in Holland had renegotiated over a term of ten years repayment of a loan of 1,000,000 florins which came due on 1 June 1793, Washington obtained his concurrence in reducing by half the existing loan of 2,000,000 florins intended in part to repay that debt. Then, instead of the additional 3,000,000 florins which Hamilton had originally wished to borrow, Washington, carefully distinguishing between the two 1790 acts, authorized

Hamilton to borrow the remaining balance of $1,515,098.11 (about 3,787,745 florins) from the $2,000,000 authorized by the 12 Aug. 1790 act for application to the general debt, and 1,000,000 florins under the 4 Aug. 1790 act, to be used to meet the installment on the Dutch loan of 1782 coming due in June 1794 (Syrett, *Hamilton*, XV, 9-10, 21-4, 118, 119, 125-6, 136-8; *Annals*, III, 1452). The President's careful review of Hamilton's proposal, especially his insistence on scrupulously dividing his own authorization into separate parts linked to specific statutes, underscored his intention to exercise stricter financial oversight in the wake of Republican attacks on the Secretary of the Treasury during the 1792-93 session of Congress, but ultimately he authorized a larger loan than Hamilton had originally sought, being more impressed by the need to have money available in case of THE EXTENSION OF OUR WAR against the Western Indians to those in the South than by the Secretary of State's fears that the money might be at risk abroad or used at home for the CORRUPTION OF THE NEXT LEGISLATURE. In the end, however, Hamilton only sought a new foreign loan of 3,000,000 florins (Syrett, *Hamilton*, XV, 230-3).

The date of the REPORT OF THE TRUSTEES OF THE SINKING FUND was actually 25 Feb. 1793 (Commissioners of the Sinking Fund to the Speaker of the House of Representatives, 25 Feb. 1793). The new edition of the TREASURY REPORT was *Communications from the Secretary of the Treasury, to the House of Representatives of the United States. Printed agreeably to a Resolution of the House, of the 2d of March 1793* (Philadelphia, [1793]).

[1] Here in margin of Tr TJ wrote: "but see act 1793. c.69. [and?] qu?"
[2] Preceding sentence omitted from Tr.
[3] Preceding two words interlined.

To Thomas Mann Randolph, Jr.

June 17. 93.

All well, but not a moment to write.   TH:J.

RC (DLC); addressed: "Thomas M. Randolph junr. esq. at Monticello near Charlottesville"; franked and postmarked. Not recorded in SJL.

From Hilary Baker

18th. June 1793

Messrs. Armand Gabriel Francois Paparel la Boissier at present of Philadelphia Gentleman a Native of Cape Francois in St. Domingo—and Jean Louis Du Cret also at present of Philada. Gentleman a Native of the Province of Lorain in France have this day taken the Oath of Allegiance to the State of Pennsylva. before me.   HILARY BAKER

RC (DNA: RG 59, Certificates of Naturalization and Proofs of Citizenship); at foot of text: "Honble. Thomas Jefferson Esqr. Secretary of the United States No. 307 High Street."

Hilary Baker (ca. 1750-98), a Philadelphia alderman and future mayor (PMHB, X [1886], 450), wrote a similar letter to TJ on 12 July 1793 stating that the Philadelphia merchants Francis Adrian Thibault, Joseph Hilary Carbonnel, James Chossan, Peter Castels, and John Baptist Reliau had appeared before him on that day and taken the oath of allegiance to Pennsylvania (RC in DNA: RG 59, Certificates of Naturalization and Proofs of Citizenship; at foot of text: "Honble. Thomas Jefferson Esqr."; with a check mark before each name). Baker's letters were essential preliminaries to the issuance of wartime passports to French emigrants. For the importance of proofs of citizenship in disputed prize cases, see TJ to Clement Biddle, 28 June 1793.

Agreement with Samuel Biddle

It is agreed between Mr. Samuel Biddle and myself that he shall overlook certain parts of my affairs in Virginia as explained in a letter to him of Dec. 12. 1792. for which I am to pay him one hundred and twenty dollars a year. His wages are to begin the 1st. day of September next, and he is to proceed to Virginia about the middle of October.

TH: JEFFERSON
Philadelphia June 18. 1793

He is to carry his bedding. I promised to provide him half a dozen flag chairs, a table, pot &c the carpenters to fix up little conveniencies for him. To find him a horse, 5 or 600 wt. of pork, or rather mutton &c equivalent.

PrC (MHi); entirely in TJ's hand; with text below dateline possibly added in ink.

From Edmond Charles Genet

MONSIEUR   Philadelphie le 18. Juin 1793. l'an 2e. de la République.

J'ai pris connoissance[1] de la correspondance qui a eu lieu entre vous et mon prédécesseur relativement[2] à des demandes de fonds qu'il a faites au Gouvernement fédéral pour acquitter certaines traites des adminis-

trateurs de St. Domingue et procurer des vivres à cette Colonie.[3] Je
rends hommage, Monsieur, à la justesse des observations que vous avez
transmises au citoyen Ternant au sujet de cette demande[4] arrachée a sa
circonspection par les pressantes instances des administrateurs de St.
Domingue. Je conçois que cette requisition a du infiniment embarrasser
votre Gouvernment et sous ce rapport Je sens toutes les obligations que
nous lui avons d'avoir, comme vous l'avez exprimé vous même, moins
consulté en y adhérant la prudence que l'amitié. Vous avez remarqué
avec raison,[5] Monsieur, que le décrêt qui affectoit aux besoins des Colonies 4. millions a prendre sur la dette des Etats Unis envers la France,
n'étant point parvenu[6] au Gouvernment fédéral[7] revêtu des formes officielles d'usage, ne devoit point avoir une application aussi positive, aussi
determinée que celle que les commissaires et les administrateurs de
Saint Domingue lui ont donnée, et qu'il etoit vraisemblable que le Ministère français[8] avoit eu recours pour subvenir aux besoins de cette
Colonie à des opérations d'une autre nature que celles qui avoient eu
lieu. En effet, Monsieur, les traites pour l'acquittement desquelles les
commissaires de Saint Domingue pressés par des circonstances
impérieuses[9] ont en quelque sorte obligé le Citoyen Ternant à vous
demander des fonds n'ont été autorisées ni par la Convention Nationale
ni par le Conseil Éxécutif[10] et Je dois même vous dire qu'il m'a été
prescrit[11] de ne payer sur les fonds mis à ma disposition que celles
de ces traites qui auroient été acceptées[12] par le Consul Laforest en vertu
des ordres de mon prédécesseur. Mais en arrivant ici J'ai été instruit que
ce Consul[13] avoit recu du Ministre Plénipotentiaire[14] l'ordre d'enregis-
trer[15] toutes les traites emises par les administrateurs de Saint Domingue et de les payer sur les nouveaux fonds que le Gouvernement
fédéral avoit accordés[16] provisoirement, sur la base du décret du 26.
Juin, quoiqu'il ne lui fut point notifié officiellement. Je n'ai pas cru,
Monsieur, devoir arrêter subitement le payement de ces traites, dans
l'espérance que le mode de remboursement de votre dette[17] que vous
avez mis à ma réquisition sous les yeux du Président des Etats Unis
seroit adopté par lui, et me donneroit les moyens, 1°. de faire honneur
aux traites enregistrées par ordre de mon prédécesseur et dont le payement[18] avoit été ordonné par lui; 2e. de pourvoir en même tems aux
besoins urgens de la France et de ses Colonies.[19] Mais ayant été trompé
dans mon attente par des motifs qu'il ne m'appartient pas d'examiner, Je
me vois privé[20] de l'avantage de concilier tous les interets et contraint de
n'obéir qu'à l'empire des circonstances qui me prescrivent[21] de suspendre le payement des traites coloniales et d'employer les fonds destinés à
leur acquittement à des achats de vivres pour la France et pour ses Colonies. Cette disposition, Monsieur, ne doit allarmer ni les porteurs des
traites enrégistrées ni ceux des autres[22] traites émises et non enrégistrées

des administrateurs de Saint Domingue et des autres Colonies de la Republique française. La Nation remplira certainement envers eux les engagemens contractés[23] par ses agens. Je sais qu'elle a destiné des fonds particuliers à cet objet; Je sais aussi que les Colonies ont fait des contributions[24] en denrées pour remplir leurs obligations et pourvoir elles mêmes à une partie de leurs besoins et c'est d'après ces notions que Je me suis determiné a faire insérer dans les papiers publics l'avis ci joint dont le but est de calmer les inquiétudes des porteurs des traites que Je suis obligé d'écarter, et d'encourager les citoyens des Etats Unis à continuer de[25] porter des secours a leurs freres les Républicains français des Antilles, dont le sors dépend de cet acte de générosité sans lequel[26] les Colonies francaises pourroient se trouver reduites par la famine a passer sous une Gouvernement dont les principes commerciaux ne seroient assurément[27] pas aussi avantageux aux Etats Unis que ceux qu'une politique[28] eclairée et un attachement sans bornes pour le peuple americain nous ont fait embrasser.   GENET

PrC of Tr (DLC); in a clerk's hand; at head of text: "Le citoyen Genet, Ministre de la République française a Mr. Jefferson, Secrétaire d'Etat des Etats Unis." Dft (DLC: Genet Papers); dated 19 June 1793; at foot of text in another hand: "voyez les Gazettes pour l'avis"; contains numerous emendations, only the most significant being recorded below. Tr (NNC: Gouverneur Morris Papers). PrC of another Tr (PRO: FO 97/1); in the hand of George Taylor, Jr. Tr (DNA: RG 46, Senate Records, 3d Cong., 1st sess.); English translation in a clerk's hand, with corrections by TJ. Recorded in SJL as a letter of 18 June 1793 received that date. Printed with translation in *Message*, 14-15 (App.), 38-9; translation printed in ASP, *Foreign Relations*, I, 158. Enclosed in TJ to Gouverneur Morris, 16 Aug. 1793.

In this letter Genet announced that henceforth he would use advances on the American debt to France solely to purchase supplies in the United States for France and her colonies, and thus was suspending payment on the TRAITES or bills of exchange drawn by French officials at Saint-Domingue on the French minister and the French consul general in Philadelphia for supplies shipped to the island directly by American citizens. His action followed the Washington administration's refusal to advance payment of the entire American debt to France, which the Girondin ministry that

appointed him had anticipated would be the main source of financial support for his diplomatic mission and the purchase of provisions for France and its colonies (see Editorial Note and documents on Jefferson and the American debt to France, at 3 June 1793; TJ to Genet, 11 June 1793).

The bills in question, currently amounting to about $93,000, were held by fifteen individuals or mercantile firms, most of whom were American and located in Philadelphia. Of the total, $45,000 worth had been registered with Antoine René Charles Mathurin de La Forest, the French consul general in Philadelphia until Genet's arrival in Philadelphia in the middle of May 1793, and were scheduled for payment in July 1793 (George Hammond to Lord Grenville, 7 July 1793, PRO: FO 5/1, giving the value of the bills based on information received from Alexander Hamilton; Syrett, *Hamilton*, XVII, 537-8, listing the holders of the bills; Hardie, *Phila. Dir.*; Turner, *CFM*, 217, 233; Ammon, *Genet Mission*, 44, 71, 80-6).

TJ submitted Genet's letter to the President and the Cabinet on 22 June 1793. "Tho' from the tendency of this proposition an answer was embarrassing," the Cabinet that day agreed to insist that the French minister discharge the bills and, if he refused, to pay the holders of the bills registered with La Forest from "other monies" in the Treasury (Washington, *Journal*, 187). TJ communicated the thrust of the Cabinet's decision to Genet in a letter of 23 June 1793 drafted by Alexander Hamilton. When Genet continued to refuse payment, the Cabinet met on 5 July in the absence of Washington and Attorney General Edmund Randolph and approved Hamilton's recommendation to authorize payment of all the suspended bills out of the September 1793 installment on the debt to France (Notes of a Cabinet Meeting and on Conversations with Edmond Charles Genet, 5 July 1793; Syrett, *Hamilton*, xv, 29-30, 437, xvii, 537-8). The Editors have found no evidence that Genet ever published his enclosed announcement to the American people.

[1] Preceding four words written in the margin of Dft in place of "Les differentes occupations qui ont absorbé toute mon attention depuis que Je suis à Philadelphie ne m'avoient point encore permis ⟨de vous entretenir d⟩ de prendre."

[2] Sentence from this point to "traites" written in the margin of Dft in place of "aux traites qui ont été faites par."

[3] In Dft Genet here canceled: "⟨Je viens de remplir ce devoir, M, et Je m'empresse de rendre⟩ et Je voudrais rendre."

[4] Remainder of sentence written in the margin of Dft in place of "que les pressantes instances de nos Commissaires nationaux ont arrachées à sa circonspection," a passage Genet had substituted in the margin for "⟨et Vous avés⟩ Elles sont parfaitement d'accord avec mes instructions."

[5] Preceding three words interlined in Dft in place of "parfaitement senti."

[6] In Dft Genet here canceled "officiellement."

[7] In Dft Genet first wrote the remainder of this clause in the margin as "dans les formes officielles que deux grandes puissances doivent observer" before revising it to read as above.

[8] Preceding three words written in the margin of Dft in place of "la ⟨Métropole⟩ france."

[9] Preceding five words written in the margin in Dft.

[10] In Dft Genet here canceled "et bien loin de les ⟨sanctionner⟩ accepter."

[11] Word interlined in Dft in place of a passage that in its final state read "défendu d'en compter aucune que celles que mon predecesseur avoit admises Jusqu'au No. ."

[12] Remainder of sentence written in Dft in place of "par mon predecesseur Jusqu'au No. ."

[13] In place of the preceding three words, Dft in its final state reads "que l'on avoit passe ce nombre et que le cidevant Consul laforest."

[14] Preceding three words written in the margin in Dft.

[15] Here in Dft Genet canceled "et de payer presque." Sentence from this point to "Saint Domingue" written in the margin in Dft of place of "les traites ⟨coloniales⟩ de St. domingue Jusques et Compris le No. à l'effet d'être acquittées sur les nouveaux fonds Jusqu'à la Concurrence à peu de choses près des 4 mons."

[16] Slightly variant version of remainder of sentence written in the margin of Dft in place of "et qui devoient absorber la presque totalité des [. . .]. ⟨l'ordre⟩ La réquisition du Citoyen Ternant étant officielle a."

[17] In Dft Genet wrote "pour la totalité de votre dette" in the margin before altering it to read as above.

[18] Preceding ten words written in the margin or interlined in Dft in place of "revêtues [. . .]."

[19] In Dft Genet first wrote "besoins ultérieurs des Colonies française et à ceux de la Mét" and then altered it to read as above.

[20] Word interlined in Dft in place of "dans la nécessité."

[21] In Dft Genet first wrote: "et de ne Considerer que celui du moment lequel me prescrit" and then altered it to read as above.

[22] Word interlined in Dft in place of "nouvelles."

[23] Sentence to this point altered in Dft from "La fidelité de la nation à remplir ses engagements est un sur garant."

[24] Word interlined in Dft in place of "Collectes."

[25] In Dft Genet first wrote "et de soutenir le Zêle de ceux des Citoyens des Etats unis qui" and then altered it to read as above.

[26] In Dft Genet first wrote "generosité et de politique" and then altered it to read as above.

[27] Word interlined in Dft.

[28] In Dft Genet here canceled "et une philosophie."

Edmond Charles Genet's Notice to the Citizens of the United States

Citizen Genet Minister Plenipotentiary of the french Républic to the citizens of the United States.

Whereas several american citizens who have furnished provisions to the Colonies of the French Republic in the West Indies, have received bills drawn by the administrators of the respective colonies on citizen Laforest late Consul Général of the Républic in the United States and lately on myself in payment for such supplies, I inform them, that these draughts will certainly be paid the national convention having appropriated large sums for that object. But as I am not as yet authorized to discharge them, I can only in the mean while advise the holders of such bills which have not yet been registered by Citizen Laforest to have them recorded in the office of Citizen Dupont Consul of the french Republic at Philadelphia in order to ascertain the dates of their presentation; at the same time, I cannot too much encourage the citizens of the United States to continue to assist with unremitting exertions their republican brethren of the french West Indies, whose existence, from the liberal principles adopted by the national Convention with regard to the Colonies of the french Républic must essentially contribute to the prosperity of the United States. The american citizens may rest assured that the most efficacious measures have been taken as well in France as in the Colonies to protect their property in all the Ports of the Republic, and to ensure to them a prompt payment for their supplies in cash or in merchandize, and at the same time to secure to them the enjoyment of those favors which the national Convention has lately granted to the citizens of the United States which assimilate them, in respect to commercial advantages, to the citizens of France.

Philadelphia June 17th: 1793, the second year of the French Republic.

PrC of Tr (DLC); in a clerk's hand. Tr (NNC: Gouverneur Morris Papers). PrC of another Tr (PRO: FO 97/1); in a clerk's hand. Tr (DNA: RG 46, Senate Records, 3d Cong., 1st sess.). Printed in *Message*, 39. Enclosed in TJ to Gouverneur Morris, 16 Aug. 1793.

To John Tayloe Griffin

SIR   June 18. 1793.

I received last night your favor from Wilmington and am sorry it is utterly out of my power to furnish what you desire. A very great disappointment in a remittance from Richmond has not only disabled me for the present, but placed me under difficulties which will continue for some time, and consequently render it as impossible to make a future as a present engagement. I am endeavoring to persuade your messenger to wait for Mr. Morris's answer which he says cannot be had till tomorrow. He objected he had not money to bear his expences if he staid. I have offered him what he said would suffice, but I do not know whether he will be prevailed on. I inclose your note and have the honor to be Sir your most obedt servt   TH: JEFFERSON

PrC (MHi); at foot of text: "Dr. J. Griffin."

From Josef de Jaudenes and Josef Ignacio de Viar

SIR   Philadelphia. June 18. 1793.

Since our last letter which we had the honor of sending you we are newly informed of different acts practised by Govr. Blount which not only are contrary to the treaty itself which the US. concluded with the Creeks, and which your government wishes to maintain, but which manifest views very distinct from those pacific and friendly ones towards our nation and those Indians, of which the US. have so repeatedly assured us.

We will state some of the undeniable ones, and which merit great attention.

The 1st. article of the treaty between the US. and the Creeks promises to maintain perpetual peace and friendship, between both the contracting parties and the 14th. article promises to carry into full execution what is stipulated in the treaty by both parties, with good faith and sincerity.

Permit us to ask now, does it denote good faith, or prove sincerity to incite the Chickasaws to commence war against the Creeks with the palpable views, that they, being less numerous than the Creeks, may be under the necessity to ask the protection of Governor Blount and his troops, and so give him then a good occasion of asking in recompence from the Chickasaws lands to form an establishment at the place called the Ecores Amargos,[1] and have a source whence[2] to incommode and intercept the communication between New Orleans and the establishments of Spain at the Illinois and New Madrid, practised with barks, which, by the eddy formed there by the river Missisipi, must pass within pistol shot of a point which commands the river at that place.

With this object, and proceeding to the said place, a son of Genl. Robertson's passed by New Madrid the 7th. of May, and about that time had already past several Americans to the same post.

Does it argue good faith or sincerity towards the Creeks to succour the Chickasaw nation with a portion of corn, that they might with the more convenience pursue the war, which the son of Genl. Robertson carried with him? and moreover a piece of artillery the use of which the Indians never knew, and always feared?

[313]

The Governor of New Madrid saw all this with his own eyes, and it was confirmed by many Indians of the Chickasaw nation, who went with the same young man, Mr. Robertson, who confessed that Congress had ordered this cannon to be given them at present, a declaration which indicates that it is also contemplated to furnish them more.

In the 11th. article of the treaty between the US. and the Creeks, these last oblige themselves to give information to the citizens of the former, of every design which they shall know or suspect to be formed in any of the neighboring tribes or by any person whatever against the peace and interests of the US.

Is it good reciprocity, sincerity, or good faith, on the part of these not only not to inform the Creeks of the disposition of the Chickasaws against them, but that the said states should be the principal and inciting cause.

Let us pass under silence a thousand just reflections on the impropriety of the US. meddling with the affairs of nations who are by treaties solemn and ratified, allied with Spain, and let us leave to the superior penetration of the President of the US. to decide if the repeated and positive assurances which we have given to these states in the name of the king our master, of the firm disposition and desire to preserve the strictest friendship with the US. and to exert himself in effecting a continuance of the same on the part of the Indian nations under his royal protection: if the different proofs which we have produced of what has been practiced by the governors of Louisiana and St. Augustine, and the recent one which we have the honor to inclose, merit such a return as that which is experienced on the part of the US.

You may vindicate the government of the US. (in those cases which want equal evidence with that which we have produced in some others and which admits no reply) by insinuating again that steps of such a nature, if they have been taken, is without the authority or knolege of the government. Let us suppose it in the article which admits of it, and let us pass on to the other.

Does it admit excuse that the US. after such repeated complaints on our part, founded on palpable facts, and documents which cannot be refuted, against the persons employed to manage the business of the Indians, should not have availed themselves of efficacious means to prevent the disorders in question? To the justice of the President of the US. we leave the answer.

Are the steps which the government of the US. has taken (evident from the proofs which we have presented before) less prejudicial than those which their subalterns have put in practice without the authority of the government as you affirm? We are persuaded they are not.

Recapitulating all the proceedings of the US. and of their agents with respect to our nation, and the various nations of Indians, our allies, and comparing them with those of the king our master and his agents, we foresee with no small sensibility, that the continuation of the peace, good harmony and perfect friendship which have so happily prevailed till now between our nation and the US. is very problematical for the future, unless the US. shall take more convenient measures, and of greater energy than those adopted for a long time past.

These same considerations urge us to desire you to inform the President of the US. of the contents of this letter, and to intreat him earnestly on our part to use all his power and influence to hinder the fatal consequences, to which in the contrary event, the US. stand indubitably exposed, an event which cannot but be sensible to two nations whose reciprocal interests evidently require that they should remain united, in friendship and good faith.

So we wish that it may be, and in the mean time we repeat assurances of the sincere esteem & respect &c.   JAUDENES   VIAR

Tr (DLC); entirely in TJ's hand, with a translating error (see note 2 below); at head of text: "Translation." RC (DNA: RG 59, NL); in Spanish; in a clerk's hand, signed by Jaudenes and Viar; at foot of text: "Señor Don Thomas Jefferson. &ca."; endorsed by TJ as received 19 June 1793 and so recorded in SJL. Tr (AHN: Papeles de Estado, legajo 3895); in Spanish; attested by Jaudenes and Viar. Tr (DLC: William Short Papers); in Spanish. PrC (DLC). Tr (Lb in DNA: RG 59, DCI); in Spanish. Tr (CtY); in English; misdated 18 June 1792. PrC (MoSHi: Bixby Collection). Tr (DNA: RG 46, Senate Records, 3d Cong., 1st sess.); in English. Tr (Lb in same, TR); in English. Recorded in SJPL. Letter and enclosure enclosed in TJ to William Carmichael and William Short, 30 June 1793, and TJ to Thomas Pinckney, 11 Sep. 1793.

The TREATY BETWEEN THE US. AND THE CREEKS was the 1790 Treaty of New York (ASP, Indian Affairs, I, 81-2). Despite the claim by the Spanish agents that William Blount, the governor of the Southwest Territory, urged the Chickasaws TO COMMENCE WAR AGAINST THE CREEKS, it was actually the Chickasaws, reacting to the murder of a Chickasaw hunter in February 1793 by Creeks anxious to prevent a rapprochement between the Chickasaws and the

United States, who successfully appealed to Blount, General James Robertson, the leader of a settlement at Cumberland that was also the object of Creek attacks, the President, and the Secretary of War, among others, for arms and ammunition to make war on the Creeks (Arrell M. Gibson, The Chickasaws [Norman, Okla., 1971], 83-8). In addition to supplying the Chickasaws with A PORTION OF CORN, the United States also did the same for the Creeks, in consequence of a severe drought that devastated the crops of both tribes in 1792 (ASP, Indian Affairs, I, 443; Randolph C. Downes, "Creek-American Relations, 1790-1795," JSH, VIII [1942], 360).

TJ submitted this letter to a meeting of the President and the Cabinet on 20 June, when it was read and found to be "exceptionable both in its matter & manner" (Washington, Journal, 183). For the outcome of the meeting, see Cabinet Opinions on Relations with Spain and Great Britain, 20 June 1793, and note.

[1] Above this word TJ wrote its translation, "bitter," an interlineation that appears in all other English texts.

[2] TJ having misread "fuente" for "fuerte" in the RC, the preceding four words should actually be translated as "raise a fortress with which."

Cherokee Nation to Baron de Carondelet

Translation from a Spanish translation of a paper written by the Cherokee nation to the Governor of New Orleans.

Full of respect and gratitude, the Cherokee nation united, has heard with satisfaction the message by the persons you sent, and gives you expressive thanks for the great generosity with which you offer to assist them with all the means which depend on your power. A general meeting of the Indians is convoking for this effect, and what the warrior Bloody fellow and the other chiefs have expressed to you on the oppression which we suffer is the same which the nation represents.

It complains bitterly of the ungenerous method with which the Americans have appropriated to themselves their dwelling lands. The first treaty which was held after the war with Gr. Britain was at Seneca, and was called the treaty of Hopewell. In this treaty the whites obtained concessions from the Indians, tho' not by general consent of the nation, because it is certain that the lands were settled before their consent was asked. The passion of the Americans for establishing themselves on the lands of the Indians is too well known to you to need explanation: in a word, since the Americans, by the fraudulent means, used among them have usurped the lands of the Indians, the nation universally reclaims and insists to preserve it's antient limits, on which they agreed with the British nation. They pray you to employ all your force to obtain from his majesty (if it be possible) this favor; and if it cannot be obtained, they insist that the settlement at Cumberland alone shall be removed at all events. Without this, nothing will satisfy the Cherokees and Talapuches.

Cumberland was settled towards the conclusion of the last war by a certain Robertson and some companions of his, who, concealing their journey and designs, took possession by force of those lands. Perhaps the Americans will make it appear that they possess these by free and lawful treaties. But it is not so; and all the nation declares on the contrary that neither the last treaty nor the former were explained to the Indians, and they only knew their contents on their return to their nation.

Robertson and his companions are the real and true cause, that so much blood has been spilt; and the confusion which has subsisted and still subsists is owing entirely to this settlement, and while it remains in this place, there is no hope of a solid peace. This settlement taken away, the Cherokee nation declares, that it does not desire to be an enemy to the Americans: it declares moreover that it does not entertain this sollicitude from caprice or pique: that they never questioned the legality of their former treaties, because under the British government they were treated with justice and humanity.

The nation moreover informs you that they all will preserve in remembrance your words, and will give attention to your friendly councils, do nothing (if possible) against them. But if on the other side necessity compels them to take the feild, they pray you will not impute it to their fault, because force alone will be the cause, which places them under such an extremity, which they would avoid, if possible. The Creeks pass daily in great numbers through this nation which prays you to induce them to keep themselves quiet till the issue of the negociation about their lands is known.   Given in the Cherokee nation by me and at the particular desire of the chiefs and warriors thereof, this 5th. of April 1793. Bloody fellow. his mark—Glass. his mark—Charles of Chuck-

amogga. his mark.—Walter Hunter. cásique of Chickamogga. his mark.—
Spiller of Lookout mountn. his mark.—Richard Justice.—Badger's mother
warriors—Guillermo Shewrey his mark—in name of all the rest of the nation.—
Señor Baron de Carondelet.

Tr (DLC); in TJ's hand; at foot of text: "A copy. Jaudenes.—Viar." Tr (DNA: RG 59, NL); in Spanish; attested by Jaudenes and Viar. Tr (DLC: William Short Papers); in Spanish. PrC (DLC). Tr (Lb in DNA: RG 59, DCI); in Spanish. Tr (CtY); in English. PrC (MoSHi: Bixby Collection). Recorded in SJPL between 16 and 22 May 1793.

Notice for Rental of Mill Seat

To be rented

A Mill seat, near Charlottesville, in Albemarle county Virginia, at
the head of the navigation of the Rivanna river, being the North branch
of James river. The water for the mill is taken out of the river about
three quarters of a mile above the seat of the mill house, where a natural
ledge of rocks crosses the river, and requires only two or three sluices,
of a few feet wide, to be filled with loose stones, to turn any proportion
of the river through the canal. The fall of water is 20 feet, or perhaps a
few inches more. The country round about is very healthy, fertile, and
producing a wheat of the best quality, weighing from 60. to 63.℔. The
common price of it is from 5/ to 6/3 the bushel Pensylvania currency.
There is not a single merchant mill on that river, nor within many miles
of it. It is about 70. miles from Richmond, to which there is batteau
navigation, except in the dry parts of the year, and good roads leading
to the same place.

There was formerly a toll mill at the place, which has been discontinued in order to enlarge and lengthen[1] the canal so as to do without a
dam. The canal will accordingly be finished this summer, and the seat
will be rented then for 1500. bushels of Indian corn a year, worth there
generally a quarter of a Dollar the bushel. The former mill brought in
about two thirds of that quantity in toll, and a pair of stones appropriated to grind for the neighbors now since the increase of population, it
is supposed would pay the whole rent. The millhouse and works may be
built either by the owner, or tenant, as shall be desired, proper allowances being made to the builder, and a lease of almost any length may be
had.   TH: JEFFERSON
June 18. 1793.

PrC (DLC); entirely in TJ's hand.

[1] Preceding two words interlined.

TJ's decision to seek a tenant for his MILL SEAT was premature, since his CANAL was finished in 1803 (Betts, *Farm Book*, 343).

To John Spurrier

Sir   Philadelphia June 18. 1793.

The bearer hereof, Mr. Biddle, is a person whom I have employed as a manager of my farms in Virginia. As I have a mill-seat there for which I wish to find a tenant, I have given him a description of it, and desired him to make some enquiry about Brandywine to see if any body there is disposed to take such a place. As he as well as myself is a stranger there, I take the liberty of desiring him to call on you, in hopes you will be so kind as to advise him how to go to work to look out for a tenant. I have for some time intended to come to Brandywine myself, and still think to do it, if you can give me any hopes of finding a tenant there for my mill seat. I should wish to take up my head quarters with you, if you still have a public house as you had when I had the pleasure of seeing you at Philadelphia. I should also like to know whether we may hope to see your book published. Your advice to the bearer will oblige Sir Your humble servt   Th: Jefferson

PrC (MHi); at foot of text: "Mr. John Spuryear."

John Spurrier described himself as "an old experienced farmer, late of the county of Herts, in Great Britain: and now of Brandywine Hundred," New Castle County, Delaware, on the title page of his book, *The Practical Farmer: being a New and Compendious System of Husbandry, adapted to the different soils and climates of America* (Wilmington, 1793). See Sowerby, No. 702. TJ subscribed to five copies of the work, which Spurrier dedicated to him "as well on account of your being a promoter of every degree of useful knowledge, as by your judicious conduct in public and private life: setting an example worthy of imitation."

From Etienne Clavière

Paris le 19 Juin 1793 L'an deux de la republ.

Je vous adresse, monsieur, un jeune homme infiniment recommandable, fils d'un des plus anciens amis et compatriote. Il aura l'avantage de vous remettre la presente. Ses Superieurs l'envoyent dans l'amerique libre pour y fonder un établissement de commerce destiné à correspondre avec toutes les parties du monde connu. Né et elevé à Geneve, il a les mœurs republicaines autant par raison que par habitude; il aime le travail et il est capable de conduire des affaires très étendues. Ses Parens Sont à la tête de très grands établissemens; et celui que le Citoyen Jaques Odier, c'est le nom du jeune homme, formera dans une de vos villes, fera partie de ces établissemens.

Je vous propose donc, monsieur, de recevoir le Citoyen Odier, comme un homme utile aux developemens commerciaux, qui doivent augmenter de plus en plus la consistance et la prosperité des Etats unis. Il ne S'agit point ici d'un particulier qui S'éloigne d'Europe pour tenter la fortune; mais d'un commercant qui apartient à une societé puissante, laquelle étend Ses vues et Ses relations a mesure que ses moyens prennent de l'accroissement. Vous avez trop de lumieres, vous êtes un trop bon Citoyen, pour ne pas Sentir que ces Sortes de missionnaires en valent bien d'autres, qu'ils méritent, Surtout, d'être acceuillis avec fraternité, et que leurs premiers pas doivent être protégés et encouragés jusques à ce que la connoissance du pays, leur ait donné le moyen de s'y Soutenir Sous la protection des Loix, par leurs propres forces.

L'interest patriotique auquel je m'adresse n'empêche pas, monsieur, que je ne recommande le jeune homme à votre bienveillance personnelle; et que je ne réclame pour lui, vos bons offices, au nom du souvenir amical que vous avez bien voulu conserver de moi. Je vous aurai une obligation toute particuliere des Services que vous aurez la bonté de lui rendre, et je les Sollicite avec d'autant plus de confiance, que le Citoyen Odier vous prouvera bientot qu'il en est digne.

Il vous aprendra que depuis deux jours je ne suis plus ministre. Nous Sommes encore dans le fort de tous les mouvemens qu'il est aise de concevoir chez une Nation nombreuse, puissante, vive et très neuve dans la Carrière de la liberté: toutes les passions Sont au combat. Puisse le triomphe rester à celles qui vous ont mis irrévocablement dans l'état social le plus propre au bonheur. Agréez mes vœux pour tout ce qui peut étendre et affermir le votre. CLAVIERE

P.S. Je vous prie de vouloir bien recommander le C. Odier à Monsieur hamilton Secretaire d'Etat au département des finances, en me rapellant à Son Souvenir.

RC (DLC); mistakenly endorsed by TJ as received 10 June, but correctly recorded in SJL as received 10 Dec. 1793 "by Mr. Odier."

This was the last letter written to TJ by Clavière, who had been deposed as French finance minister two days before by the overthrow of the Girondin government in Paris and was under house arrest. He committed suicide in December 1793 while awaiting trial at the hands of the Jacobins (Scott and Rothaus, *Historical Dictionary*, I, 191-2).

From Bartholomew Dandridge, Jr.

United States 19 June 1793.

By direction of the President of the UStates Bw. Dandridge has the honor to enclose to the Secretary of State, two pardons—one for Hezekiah Usher, the other for Geo. Dunbar Usher, in order to have the Ud. States seal affixed to them; and to request that the Secretary will wait on the President tomorrow morning at *nine* o'Clock, to take into consideration certain matters which were postponed on Monday.

RC (DLC); at foot of text: "The Secy. of State"; endorsed by TJ as a letter from George Washington received 19 June 1793. Dft (DNA: RG 59, MLR). FC (Lb in same, SDC). Entry in SJPL: "B.D. for G.W. to Th:J.—pardons." Enclosures not found.

Bartholomew Dandridge, Jr. (d. 1802), the son of Martha Washington's brother Bartholomew, served as one of the President's secretaries from 1791 until Washington left office. He subsequently saw service as secretary to the American legations at The Hague and London before going into business in New York City. In 1800 he was appointed United States consul to the southern district of Saint-Domingue, and as President TJ gave him the post of commercial agent at Port Republican on the same island (WMQ, 1st ser., V [1897], 36, VI [1898], 251; Freeman, *Washington*, VI, 362-3n, VII, 96, 444-5; JEP, I, 357, 402, 405, 406, 407).

The Ushers had been penalized for customs violations in Rhode Island (Washington, *Journal*, 183).

To Edmond Charles Genet

SIR   Philadelphia June 19. 1793.

According to the desire expressed in your letter of the 14th. instant, the President will give the instructions necessary for the settlement of the instalments of principal and interest still due from the US. to France. This is an act equally just and desireable for both parties: and though it had not been imagined that the materials for doing it were to be had here at this moment, yet we shall be pleased to find that they may. In the mean time, what is further to be done, will doubtless be the subject of further reflection and enquiry with you: and particularly the operation proposed in your letter will be viewed under all it's aspects. Among these we think it will present itself as a measure too questionable both in principle and practicability, too deeply interesting to the credit of the US. and too unpromising in it's result to France, to be found eligible to yourself. Finally we rest secure that what is of mutual concern, will not be done but with mutual concert. I have the honor to be with great respect & esteem, Sir, Your most obedient & most humble servt.

TH: JEFFERSON

RC (AMAE: CPEU, Supplément, xx); at foot of text: "The Minister Plen. of France." PrC (DLC). PrC of Tr (DLC); in a clerk's hand. Tr (NNC: Gouverneur Morris Papers). Tr (DNA: RG 46, Senate Records, 3d Cong., 1st sess.). PrC (PRO: FO 97/1). FC (Lb in DNA: RG 59, DL). Tr (AMAE: CPEU, XXXVIII); in French. Tr (DLC: Genet Papers); in French; draft translation of preceding Tr with one revision by Genet. Recorded in SJPL. Printed in *Message*, 36. Enclosed in TJ to Alexander Hamilton and Henry Knox, 19 June 1793, and TJ to Gouverneur Morris, 16 Aug. 1793.

TJ first secured approval for this letter from the Secretary of the Treasury and the Secretary of War—the only other Cabinet members in Philadelphia at this time—before submitting it to the President this day (TJ to Hamilton and Knox, 19 June 1793; Washington, *Journal*, 183).

To Alexander Hamilton and
Henry Knox, with their Approvals

June 19. 1793.

Th: Jefferson has the honor to inclose to the Secretaries of the Treasury and war, draughts of two letters of this day's date to the Ministers of France and England. He confesses himself not satisfied with the latter altogether, as it has somewhat of the appearance of evasion. The gentlemen will be pleased to propose any alterations either may desire, handing the letters round to him to be finally submitted to the President.

Approved A HAMILTON
approved H KNOX

RC (DLC); entirely in TJ's hand, except for subjoined notations and signatures by Hamilton and Knox; addressed: "The Secretaries [. . .]." PrC (DLC); lacks notations and signatures. Tr (DLC); 19th-century copy of letter only. Entry in SJPL: "H. & K.'s approbn of lres to Min. of France & Engld." Enclosures: (1) TJ to Edmond Charles Genet, 19 June 1793. (2) TJ to George Hammond, 19 June 1793 (first letter).

To George Hammond

SIR   Philadelphia. June 19. 1793.

In answer to your letter of the 14th. inst. I have the honor to inform you that the French privateers therein mentioned were required to depart to the dominions of their own sovereign, and nothing particularly expressed as to their ulterior movements; that it is expected that the speedy departure of those vessels will obviate the inconveniencies apprehended in your letter; and that it will be considered whether any practicable arrangements can be adopted to prevent the augmentation of the force of the armed vessels of any of the belligerent powers within our ports by means which we have a right to controul. I have the honour to be with great respect Sir your most obedient & most humble servt

TH: JEFFERSON

PrC (DLC); at foot of text: "The Minister Plenipoteny. of Gr. Britain." FC (Lb in DNA: RG 59, DL). Tr (Lb in PRO: FO 116/3). Tr (same, 5/1). Recorded in SJPL. Enclosed in TJ to Alexander Hamilton and Henry Knox, 19 June 1793.

TJ drafted this letter at the behest of the President and the Cabinet and secured approval of it from Alexander Hamilton and Henry Knox—the only other Cabinet members in Philadelphia at this time—before submitting it to Washington on this day (Cabinet Opinion on French Privateers, 17 June 1793; TJ to Hamilton and Knox, 19 June 1793; Washington, *Journal*, 183).

To George Hammond

Sir   Philadelphia June 19. 1793.

I had the honour to address you a letter on the 29th. of May was twelvemonth on the articles still unexecuted of the treaty of peace between the two nations. The subject was extensive and important, and therefore rendered a certain degree of delay in the reply, to be expected. But it has now become such as naturally to generate disquietude. The interest we have in the Western posts, the blood and treasure which their detention costs us daily, cannot but produce a corresponding anxiety[1] on our part. Permit me therefore to ask when I may expect the honour of a reply to my letter, and to assure you of the sentiments of respect with which I have the honor to be Sir your most obedient & most humble servt   Th: Jefferson

PrC (DLC); at foot of text: "The Minister pleny. of Gr. Britain." Tr (DNA: RG 46, Senate Records, 3d Cong., 1st sess.). FC (Lb in DNA: RG 59, DL). Tr (Lb in PRO: FO 116/3). Tr (same, 5/1). Printed in *Message*, 105. Enclosed in TJ to George Washington, 19 June 1793.

TJ dispatched this letter to the British minister only after it was approved by the President and the Cabinet on the following day (Cabinet Opinion on Relations with Spain and Great Britain, 20 June 1793). See also note to TJ to Hammond, 29 May 1792.

[1] Word interlined in ink in place of "impatience."

From George Hammond

Sir   Philadelphia 19 June 1793

In acknowledging the receipt of your letter of this date, I cannot avoid expressing to you my concern at your not having deemed it expedient to return a definite answer to the questions, which I had the honor of submitting to you in my letter of the 14th. curt., and which appeared to me extremely plain and obvious in their import.

As an individual, I am not interested in any measures which the United States may pursue for the purpose of vindicating their own dignity; the apprehensions therefore that I had formed on the subject of the privateers, to which I have so frequently been obliged to allude, are in no manner dissipated by the information that "*as a reparation of their breach of respect to the United States*," they have been required to proceed to the dominions of another sovereign: But as the Minister of the Crown of Great Britain in this country, it is essential for me to learn whether these two vessels, of which the executive government of the United States conceives itself authorized to require the departure from its ports, will be subsequently allowed to return to them; or to send into them any captures which they may happen to make in the course of their future depredations on the subjects of the power which I have the honor to represent. I am with the greatest respect, Sir, Your most obedient humble servant, GEO. HAMMOND

RC (DNA: RG 59, NL); in Edward Thornton's hand, signed by Hammond; at foot of first page: "Mr Jefferson"; endorsed by TJ as received 20 June 1793 and so recorded in SJL. FC (Lb in PRO: FO 116/3). Tr (same, 115/2). Tr (same, 5/1). Tr (Lb in DNA: RG 59, NL).

TJ submitted this letter to the President on 20 June 1793 and received instructions from him to "give such an answer as he & the other heads of Departments should think

proper, if it was necessary to give any at all" (Washington, *Journal*, 184). Two days later the President and the Cabinet formally considered Hammond's letter and decided that it was "sufficient to say, that the Government were too much employed to go into a discussion of hypothetical questions; but would be always ready to meet & decide with justice, cases as they actually arose" (same, 186). See also TJ to Hammond, 25 June 1793.

To William Hylton

DEAR SIR   Philadelphia June 19. 1793.

I duly received your favor of May 25. and the specimens of the oak leaves, which I immediately sent to Mr. Genet. The blocks of the wood could not be found out till the day before[1] yesterday. They are also sent to the same gentleman, with whom I shall with pleasure render you any services in my power. I have the honor to be Sir Your most obedt. & most humble servt.   TH: JEFFERSON

PrC (DLC); at foot of text: "Mr. W. Hylton." Tr (DLC); 19th-century copy.

This day TJ wrote a letter to William Foushee which acknowledged his letter of 23 May 1793 but was otherwise nearly identical to the one above (PrC in DLC; at foot of text: "Dr. Foushee"); and another to

Daniel L. Hylton of the same purport except for its acknowledgment of Hylton's letter of 21 [i.e. 24] May 1793 (PrC in DLC, at foot of text: "Mr. D. L. Hylton"; Tr in DLC, 19th-century copy).

[1] Preceding three words interlined.

From James Madison

DEAR SIR   Orange June 19. 1793.

The date of my last was the 17th. It acknowledged yours of the 9th. instant. Our harvest commenced today. It will turn out I think far beyond expectation. On one of two little farms I own, which I have just surveyed, the crop is not sensibly injured by either the rot or the rust, and will yield 30 or 40 perCet. more than would be a good crop in ordinary years. This farm is on the Mountain Soil. The other is on a vein of limestone and will be less productive, having suffered a little both from the rot and the rust. My father's and brother's crops will not be inferior to mine. From these samples, and those of the neighbourhood generally as far as I am informed, the alarm which has of late prevailed is greater than the calamity. I have not heard from the neighbourhood of Monticello, but can not doubt that its situation ensures it an equal fortune with the similar one here. The weather at present is extremely favorable for the harvest, being dry. It is the reverse however for the laborers, being excessively hot. The Thermometer at this moment (4 oC. p. m.) is up at 96°.

Every Gazette I see (excerpt that of the U.S.) exhibits a spirit of criticism[1] on the anglified complexion charged in the Executive politics. I regret extremely the position into which the P. has been thrown. The unpopular cause of Anglomany is openly laying claim to him. His enemies masking themselves under the popular cause of France are playing off the most tremendous batteries on him. The proclamation was in truth a most unfortunate error. It wounds the National honor, by seeming to disregard the stipulated duties to France. It wounds the popular feelings by a seeming indifference to the cause of liberty. And it seems to violate the forms and spirit of the Constitution, by making the executive Magistrate the organ of the disposition the duty and the interest of the Nation in relation to war and peace, subjects appropriated to other departments of the Government. It is mortifying to the real friends of the P. that his fame and his influence should have been unnecessarily made to depend in any degree on political events in a foreign quarter of the Globe: and particularly so that he should have any thing to apprehend from the success of liberty in another country, since he owes his pre-eminence to the success of it in his own. If France triumphs the ill-fated proclamation will be a mill-stone, which would sink any other character, and will force a struggle even on his.

Your plan is much approved and will be adopted by my brother. I find I was misunderstood in my enquiry as to the proper width of the Portico: I did not mean the proportion it ought to bear to the side of the House to which it is attached: but the interval between the columns and the side of the House; or the distance which the Pediment ought to project. If there be any fixt rule on this subject, I will thank you to intimate it in your next. Yrs. always & affey.

RC (DLC: Madison Papers); unsigned; endorsed by TJ as received 29 June 1793 and so recorded in SJL; with TJ's notes for the postscript to his 29 June 1793 reply penciled at foot of text: "Pacificus
      Commrs. Rept.
      Portico."

[1] Madison first wrote "the spirit of criticism which prevails" before altering it to read as above.

From Thomas Mann Randolph, Jr.

DEAR SIR   Monticello June 19: 1793.

Your favor of 19. ult: with Pollies of the same date only reached us last night. My letters I am convinced must not unfrequently be as slow in geting to you: how this happens, sometimes, I have just discovered, and will take care to prevent it from that cause in future. Our postmaster closes the mail for Richmond at no certain hour, alltho, he has given out, that it will be dispatched allways early, on Friday morning: the mail-carrier, where he comes into Charlottesville early in the day on Tuesday, makes such progress on the rout to Staunton that, when he is inclined to push his horse he can be ready to take the letters soon in the day on Thursday: the postmaster, improperly I think, gives them to him and we miss the post, thursday being our writing day. To remedy this, we have resolved to write hereafter on Wednesday, alltho' this is not so convenient, as we sometimes do not get our letters from Charlottesville till the evening of that day.

The horse I purchased for you will be sufficiently robust I believe after the rest he is now taking for any service. His limbs are all perfectly sound and strongly made and he is only 7 years old at which age it is not probable his constitution should be injured beyond repair. He has never appeared fatigued nor has he ever lost his appetite but he was afflicted with what is called the "thumps"[1] the first journey he performed after he came into my hands and this I know is rather the effect of temporary debility than constitutional weakness. He is of a color rather brighter than Remus, with a small spot of White in the face, his tail of the natural length and very fine; he is something higher than either of your horses and I think much handsomer; his carriage uncommonly elegant. He is very gentle; enough so for Patsy to ride him without the least apprehension. We have driven him frequently in the chariot.[2] Should you wish, rather to replace Tarquin than match your present pair, I can procure for you one, which I conceive to be equal to any that has been raised in Virginia, since Tarquin, and can procure him on good terms too, for this horse would be taken in part payment I believe; indeed, if this should not suit you I can part with him without loss to a person who knows him better than myself. The horse I speak of is of a bad color, sorrel with much white, but has no other fault. He is extremely tall, more than 16 hands, I believe, and is not 5 years old. I could have bought him, when I saw the owner of him last, for 80 or 85£. payable some time hence. I think Tarquin may be disposed of well in Virginia.

All the timber you ordered, except the joists of 31 feet, is lying hewn and ready for the saw. I was not anxious to have it sawed immediately, knowing, that it would cut better dry, that the pieces would be less apt to warp, and that at any time we could cut it faster than we could bring it in. The Stuff for window frames was ready to be worked up in October last. Among the trees which were felled last winter there were not as many as would make both the long triangular sleepers and the joists of 31 ft. I gave the former the preference. The picking and hewing this timber so as to leave only the heart has consumed much more time than I had any idea of. The Wheels you ordered were executed but in such a manner that they are not worth shoing. Davy can use the Wheelrights tools but has no rule in working: he cannot make a wheel with all the felloes in the same plane. They all go to the harvest in a day or two: when that is finished I shall set them to work on the canal. Yours most affectionately   TH: M. RANDOLPH

We are all well. Patsy visited Mrs. Monroe yesterday, and expects her here tomorrow.

          Diary.

June

14. 68. f.	73. clouds
15. 67. f.	
16. 73. c.	
17. 72. c.	81. f.
18. 79. light clouds.	85.
19. 81. f.	86. f.

RC (MHi); endorsed by TJ as received 29 June 1793 and so recorded in SJL.

[1] Closing quotation mark supplied.
[2] Sentence interlined.

Report on the Proceedings of the Southwest Territory

The Secretary of State having received from the Secretary of the territory of the US. South of the Ohio a report of the[1] proceedings of that government from Sep. 1. 1792. to the 16th. of Feb. 1793.

Reports to the President of the US.

That they do not contain any thing necessary for him to act on: unless, as it is suggested by Mr. Smith, it should be necessary to lay before Congress the act of their legislature of Nov. 20. 1792. That tho' the Secretary of state knows of no law or circumstance which requires this to be done, yet he thinks it will be safe to consult the Attorney General of the US. whether there be any such law, before any conclusion taken.   TH: JEFFERSON
June 19. 1793.

RC (DNA: RG 59, MLR); endorsed by Bartholomew Dandridge, Jr. PrC (DLC). Tr (Lb in DNA: RG 59, SDC). Enclosures: (1) Journal of the Proceedings of Governor William Blount of the Southwest Territory, 10 Sep. 1792-16 Feb. 1793 (Tr in DNA: RG 59, SWT, in the hand of Daniel Smith; Tr in Lb in DNA: RG 76, Yazoo Land Claims; printed in *Terr. Papers*, IV, 451-3). (2) Act of the Governor and Judges of the Southwest Territory, 20 Nov. 1792, authorizing the county courts to levy poll and land taxes, beginning 1 Jan. 1793, to be used to erect and maintain courthouses and prisons, pay jurors, and defray contingent county expenses (Tr in DNA: RG 59, SWT, in Smith's hand; printed in *Terr. Papers*, IV, 218-19). Recorded in SJPL: "Report on proceedings of S. W. Territory." See also Washington, *Journal*, 183.

In his letter transmitting the enclosures to TJ, Daniel Smith, THE SECRETARY of the Southwest Territory, indicated that he had placed THE ACT of 20 Nov. 1792 "on a separate sheet because it is to have the approbation of Congress" (Smith to TJ, Knoxville, 1 Mch. 1793, RC in DNA: RG 59, SWT, at foot of text: "Thos. Jefferson Esquire Secretary of State," endorsed by TJ as received 15 June 1793 and so recorded in SJL; Tr in Lb in DNA: RG 76, Yazoo Land Claims; printed in *Terr. Papers*, IV, 240). While the Northwest Ordinance of 1787 did not require that Congress consent to laws passed by the territoral governor and judges, it did specify that such acts were to be reported to Congress, which had a right to negative them (*Terr. Papers*, II, 42-3, IV, 18). See also Edmund Randolph to TJ, 25 July 1793.

[1] TJ here canceled "executive."

To George Washington

June 19. 1793.

The decision of the case of the British debts which was expected to have taken place at Richmond, being now deferred, Th: Jefferson has the honor of submitting to the President the draught of a letter to Mr. Hammond, asking an answer on the subject of the treaty of peace.

RC (DNA: RG 59, MLR); addressed: "The President of the US."; endorsed by Bartholomew Dandridge, Jr. PrC (DLC). Tr (Lb in DNA: RG 59, SDC). Recorded in SJPL. Enclosure: TJ to George Hammond, 19 June 1793.

For the DECISION in question, see note to Washington to TJ, 1 June 1793.

To George Washington

June 19. 1793.

Th: Jefferson has the honor to return to the President the minutes of the 17th. inst. The letters then agreed on are sent to the Secretaries of the Treasury and war for their corrections, and will then be handed to the President.

He sends him also a letter from the Attorney of Kentuckey for his information, and because the subject of it belongs to another department.

RC (DNA: RG 59, MLR); addressed: "The President of the US."; endorsed by Bartholomew Dandridge, Jr. Tr (Lb in same, SDC). Not recorded in SJL. Enclosure: Cabinet Opinion on French Privateers, 17 June 1793. For the other enclosure, see below.

THE LETTERS THEN AGREED ON: enclosures listed at TJ to Alexander Hamilton and Henry Knox, 19 June 1793. Concerning the 7 May 1793 letter to TJ from George Nicholas, the newly appointed United States District ATTORNEY OF KENTUCKEY, see TJ to Nicholas, 15 July 1793, and note.

Cabinet Opinion on Relations with Spain and Great Britain

June 20. 1793.

At a meeting this day of the heads of departments at the President's on summons from him, a letter from Messrs. Viar and Jaudenes dated June 18. and addressed to the Secretary of state, was read: whereupon it is the opinion that a full detail of the proceedings of the US. with respect to the Southern Indians, and the Spaniards be prepared, and a justification as to the particular matters charged in the said letter, that this be sent with all the necessary documents to our Commissioners at the court of Madrid with instructions to them to communicate the same to the court of Madrid, leaving to them a discretion to change expressions in it which to them may appear likely to give offence in the circumstances under which things may be at the time of their receiving it, and that a copy be sent to Mr. Pinckney for his information, and to make such use of the matter it contains as to him shall seem expedient: that an answer be written to Messrs. Viar and Jaudenes, informing them that we shall convey our sentiments on the subject to their court through our commissioners at Madrid, and letting them see that we are not insensible of the stile and manner of their communications.

A draught of a letter from the Secretary of state to Mr. Hammond asking when an answer to his letter of May 29. 1792. might be expected, was read and approved.

TH: JEFFERSON
A HAMILTON
H. KNOX

MS (DLC: Washington Papers); in TJ's hand, signed by TJ, Hamilton, and Knox; written on verso of a sheet bearing Cabinet Opinion on French Privateers, 17 June 1793. FC (DLC); entirely in TJ's hand, with names of signatories and some words abbreviated; written on verso of a sheet bearing Cabinet Opinion on French Privateers, 17 June 1793. Entry in SJPL: "[Notes of a meeting at the Pres's.] on Viar & Jaudenes's lre—on Th:J's to Hammond."

For the NOTIFICATION TO OUR COMMISSIONERS, see TJ to William Carmichael and William Short, 30 June 1793, and enclosures listed there. A COPY was sent in TJ to Thomas Pinckney, 11 Sep. 1793. TJ's ANSWER TO VIAR AND JAUDENES is dated 11 July 1793. His letter to MR. HAMMOND is printed above under 19 June 1793.

From George Hammond

SIR Philadelphia 20 June 1793

I have duly received your letter of yesterday.

In a written communication which I had the honor of addressing to you on the 2nd. of June 1792, and also in a conversation which I had with you on the following day, I assured you that I should lose no time in conveying to the King's Ministers in England your representation dated the 29th. of May: And it was in fact forwarded to them in the course of some few days afterwards.

On the receipt of that paper, I was informed by his Majesty's principal Secretary of State that it would be taken into immediate consideration, and that, after it had been thoroughly examined, I should receive some farther instructions relative to it. The transmission of those instructions, which I daily expect, has I presume hitherto been delayed in consequence of the very interesting events which since the receipt of it have occurred in Europe, and which have been of a nature so pressing and important as probably to have attracted the whole attentions of his Majesty's ministers and thus to have diverted it from objects that are more remote, and that may perhaps have been regarded as somewhat less urgent. Whenever I shall learn his Majesty's pleasure on the subject of your representation, you may depend, Sir, on speedily receiving my reply, to the preparation of which but little time will be requisite on my part, as, in consequence of my exertions for the purpose, I have already collected, in this country, the evidence necessary to substantiate most of the principal facts advanced in my statement of the 5th. of March, to which that representation was intended as an answer.

There is one passage in your letter of yesterday, Sir, of which it becomes me to take some notice. The passage I allude to is that wherein you mention "the blood and treasure which the detention of the Western posts costs the United States daily." I cannot easily conjecture the motives in which this declaration has originated. After the evidence that this government has repeatedly received of the strict neutrality observed by the King's governors of Canada during the present contest between the United States and the Indians, and of the disposition of those officers to facilitate as far as may be in their power any negociations for peace, I will not for a moment imagine that the expression I have cited was intended to convey the insinuation of their having pursued a different conduct, or that it had any reference to those assertions, which have been lately disseminated with more than usual industry though the public prints in this country, that the Western posts have been used by the government of Canada as the medium of supplying military stores to the Indians now engaged in war with the United States.

I can assure you, Sir, that if the delay on the part of my country in the execution of certain articles of the treaty of peace is such as to create disquietude in this government, I also experience similar impressions with respect to those articles which have hitherto not been carried into effect by the United States: As I am perpetually receiving complaints from the British creditors and their agents in this country of their inability to procure legal redress in *any* of the Courts of Law in one or two of the Southern States, in which states the greatest part of the debt remaining due to the subjects of Great Britain still continues to exist in the same condition as that in which it was at the conclusion of the war. I have the honor to be with great respect, Sir, Your most obedient Servant   GEO. HAMMOND

RC (DNA: RG 59, NL); in the hand of Edward Thornton, signed by Hammond; at foot of first page: "Mr Jefferson"; endorsed by TJ as received 21 June 1793 and so recorded in SJL. FC (Lb in PRO: FO 116/3). Tr (same, 5/1). Tr (Lb in DNA: RG 59, NL). Tr (DNA: RG 46, Senate Records, 3d Cong., 1st sess.). Printed in *Message*, 105-6.

TJ submitted this letter to the President on 21 June 1793, and on the following day Washington and the Cabinet formally considered it and decided, with respect to Hammond's comments on British retention of the Western posts, "to refer him to the former communication on the subject for the sentiments of the Government thereon adding that the conduct of the Indians was a *natural* consequence of our not occupying these Posts" (Washington, *Journal*, 186, which misdates Hammond's letter). For TJ's response to the British minister on this point, which was carefully revised in light of Alexander Hamilton's review of the draft, see TJ to Hammond, 25 June 1793.

For Hammond's CONVERSATION with TJ ON THE FOLLOWING DAY, see Notes of a Conversation with George Hammond, printed under 4 June 1792, and note.

From Richard Harison

SIR   Albany 20th: June 1793.

Your Letter of the 12th. Instant was delivered to me this Morning upon my Return from a View with the Commissioners appointed by the Legislature of the State to ascertain the contested Boundaries of some ancient Patents.

My Duty to my Clients, and the important Nature of their Business, render it impossible for me to depart from hence until the Hearing is concluded, which I expect will happen in the Course of a few Days. In the mean Time my Friends Messrs. Troup and Hoffman will attend to the public Business in New York on my Behalf, and will pursue every legal Measure in their Power which the Executive may direct, and the Honor and Interest of the Nation require at this important Crisis.

I have judged it prudent to inform Judge Duane who is now at Schenectady of the Expectations of Government with Respect to the Brigantine Catharine, that he may convene a District Court to try the Legality of the Capture; and I shall lose no Time in repairing to New York as soon as may be possible, that I may in Person evince my Zeal to promote the public Welfare and my Respect for the Instructions with which I have been honored. I am, Sir, Your most obedt Servt.

RICH: HARISON

RC (DNA: RG 59, MLR); at foot of text: "Honble. Thos. Jefferson Esqr."; endorsed by TJ and George Taylor, Jr., as received 27 June 1793, but recorded in SJL as received the following day.

For the problem of the CONTESTED BOUNDARIES, see Syrett, *Hamilton*, XV, 12. On 17 June 1793 Robert TROUP, a New York attorney, wrote a missing letter to TJ on behalf of District Attorney Harison "giving an accot. of what had been done with the privateer Liberty & the prize Ship Catharine." According to SJL, TJ received the letter on 20 June 1793; he submitted it to the President on the same day (Washington, *Journal*, 184). See also note to Memorial from George Hammond, 11 June 1793.

From David Humphreys

SIR   Lisbon June 20th. 1793.

My last was of the 19th. of May. Since which time no vessel has sailed from this Port for the U.S.

I have anxiously expected Captain Cutting by every Packet from England, and particularly by that which arrived the day before yesterday. But there is no intelligence of him. Had he fortunately arrived at this instant, we might have obtained a Swedish or Danish vessel for our purpose. Those occasions being lost, I know not when we may find another.

The communication with France by the ordinary Post continuing still to be cut off, we receive little intelligence but by accidental arrivals or the British Packet. Without relying on all the particulars we obtain through these channels, we collect however that the French fight desperately in every quarter, that the allied forces make little progress and gain no advantages but at the expence of blood, that great confusions prevail in Paris, and that large bodies of Counter-Revolutionists are in arms in different Provinces. The enclosed English Gazette is the last we have and may give you some details.

The American vessel which carried from hence for Havre M. D'Arbot (whom I mentioned was intended as French Minister to this Court) has been taken and sent to Guernsey. The Cargo was French Property.

No war has yet taken place between this Country and France. The Portuguese fleet sailed a few days ago: the destination unknown. A Camp consisting of eight Regiments is formed between this and Centra.

Mr. Freire, when he left Lisbon some time ago for London, informed me he should go within a few months to America.

Mr. Church has not arrived. Of course the vessel which was chartered here to go for him a very long time since, must have been embargoed at Bourdeaux, or employed on some other service. For we had news of its arrival there. With sentiments of sincere & great esteem & respect I have the honour to be Sir Your most obedient & Most humble Servant   D. HUMPHREYS

RC (DNA: RG 59, DD); at head of text: "(No. 74)"; at foot of text: "The Secretary of State &c. &c. &c."; endorsed by TJ as received 9 Aug. 1793 and so recorded in SJL. Tr (Lb in same).

TJ submitted this letter to the President on 10 Aug. 1793 and received it back from him the same day (Washington, *Journal*, 218).

From Thomas Pinckney

DEAR SIR   London 20th June 1793

Since my letter of the 14th. of June which goes by the same conveyance with this I have received your several favors of the 15th. 16th. and 20th. of March, of the 12th. of April and the 7th. of May. The letter you mention to have written on the 26th. of April is not yet arrived. This I presume covers the Presidents Proclamation relating to our neutrality which I shall be glad to receive officially.

I have presented the Bills drawn on London for acceptance and sent that on Liverpool to our Consul there. I am to send for the Bills offered for acceptance today and hope to inform you in time for this conveyance that they have been honored.

When I had written thus-far Mr. Leslie called upon me with the dispatches you intrusted to his care. I have only time to say that the contents of all your favors shall be duly attended to:[1] but I have no hope that this government will accede to that principle of the armed neutrality that free ships shall make free goods since Russia, Denmark, and Sweden do not insist upon it for the present war.

Mr. Cutting purposes proceeding to Lisbon with the first proper conveyance. I purpose writing by him to Colo. Humphreys. Amsterdam appears now to be in a state of security I shall therefore of course place the funds you have sent to me in the hands of our Bankers at that place.

Mr. Deas is returned from the City. The Bills drawn by Robert Gilmer & Co. on Strachan and McKenzie are accepted, that drawn by Willing Morris & Swanwick on John & Francis Baring for £3000 is noted for non acceptance. The person with whom Mr. Deas spoke at the house of Messrs. Barings however said he wished to speak with me on that and some other business for which purpose he would call on me

soon and that he did not know but that the Bill tho' noted for non acceptance might be paid. I have the honor to be with sincere regard & great
respect Dear Sir Your most faithful & obedt. Servant

THOMAS PINCKNEY

RC (DNA: RG 59, DD); written partly in code, with interlinear decipherment in the hand of George Taylor, Jr. (see note 1 below); at foot of text: "The Secretary of State"; endorsed by TJ as received 30 Aug. 1793 and so recorded in SJL. PrC (ScHi: Pinckney Family Papers). Tr (Lb in DNA: RG 59, DD); entirely *en clair*. Enclosed in James B. M. Adair to TJ, [ca. 28 Aug. 1793].

TJ submitted this letter to the President on 30 Aug. 1793 and received it back the same day (Washington, *Journal*, 235).

The Editors here rectify two oversights with respect to the numbering of codes which appeared in Volumes 24 and 25 of this series. The cipher used for the first time

in Thomas Barclay to TJ, 27 Dec. 1792, should have been designated as Code No. 14, and the cipher used for the first time in TJ to Thomas Pinckney, 1 Jan. 1793, should have been designated as Code No. 15. Pinckney also used Code No. 15 in his letters to TJ of 19 Mch. and 5, 10, and 27 Apr. 1793, before switching to Code No. 16 in the letter printed here. The Editors have been unable to reconstruct significant portions of these codes.

[1] Remainder of paragraph written in code, the text being supplied from Taylor's decipherment and verified by the Editors using their partial reconstruction of this code, which is designated in TJ Editorial Files as Code No. 16.

From George Washington

SIR   June 20th. 1793.

I leave it to you, and the heads of the other two Departments to say what, or whether any answer should be given to the B. Minister's letter of the 19th. It would seem as if neither he, nor the Spanish Commissioners were to be satisfied with any thing this Government can do. But on the contrary, are resolved to drive matters to extremity. Yours

GO: WASHINGTON

I send the enclosed to be signed.

RC (DLC); addressed: "The Secretary of State"; endorsed by TJ as received 21 June 1793. Dft (DNA: RG 59, MLR); lacks postscript. FC (Lb in same, SDC); lacks postscript. Recorded in SJPL.

THE ENCLOSED may have been the Cabinet Opinion on Relations with Spain and Great Britain, 20 June 1793.

Petition from Eli Whitney

To the Honourable Thomas Jefferson Esquire
Secretary of State for the United States of America:

The Petition of Eli Whitney of the County of Worcester and Commonwealth of Massachusetts, humbly sheweth: That having invented a Machine for the Purpose of ginning Cotton, he is desirous of obtaining an
exclusive Property in the same.

Concerning which invention, your Petitioner alledges as follows
(viz) first.

That it is entirely new and constructed in a different manner and upon
different principles from any other Cotton Ginn or Machine heretofore
known or used for that purpose.

2d. That with this Ginn, if turned with horses or by water, two persons will clean as much cotton in one Day, as a Hundred persons could
cleane in the same time with the ginns now in common use.

3d. That the Cotton which is cleansed in his Ginn contains fewer
broken seeds and impurities, and is said to be more valuable than Cotton, which is cleaned in the usual way.

Your Petitioner, therefore, Prays your Honour to Grant him the said
Whitney a Patent for the said Invention or Improvement: and that your
Honour cause Letters Patent to be made out, in the Name of the United
States, granting to him your said petitioner, his hiers Administrators
and Assigns, for the term of fourteen Years, the full and exclusive right
and liberty of making, constructing using and vending to others to be
used, the said Invention or improvement.

Philadelphia   ELI WHITNEY
20th June 1793

FC (CtY: Eli Whitney Papers); in Whitney's hand; at foot of text: "Copy."

Eli Whitney (1765-1825), a 1792 Yale
graduate, invented the cotton gin and was a
pioneer in the use of interchangable parts in
the manufacture of firearms. Owing to delays in preparing the model of the machine,
the patent was not issued to Whitney until
14 Mch. 1794, though it had an effective
date of 6 Nov. 1793, the day TJ received
the supporting descriptions and drawing.
Under the terms of Whitney's copartner-
ship agreement with Phineas Miller, signed
on 21 June 1794, the firm of Miller & Whitney struggled precariously for years to overcome competition from infringing machines, difficulties enforcing their claims in
court and obtaining credit, and initial hesitation by British spinners to purchase
ginned cotton. However, late in the four-
teen-year life of the patent Miller & Whitney
succeeded in effecting sales of licensing
agreements to the states of South Carolina,
North Carolina, and Tennessee and in obtaining legal awards for damages in Georgia
which enabled the firm to benefit from the
patent and turn a modest profit overall
(Whitney to TJ, 15 Oct. 1793; TJ to Whitney, 16 Nov. 1793; D. A. Tompkins, Cotton and Cotton Oil [Charlotte, N.C., 1901],
461-2; Mirsky and Nevins, Eli Whitney, 72-
9, 92-127, 147-76, 286-8, 307-9; DAB).

Memorial from George Hammond

The Undersigned, his Britannic Majesty's Minister plenipotentiary to the United States, has the honor of representing to the Secretary of State that the suit (the particulars of which he stated in his letter of the 5th. curt.) instituted in the federal district Court of Pennsylvania by the owners of the British Ship William of Glasgow captured by the Schooner le Citoyen Genêt, has been this day terminated by the declaration of the Judge that his court had no jurisdiction in questions of that nature.

The owners of this vessel having failed in their endeavors to obtain legal redress, in consequence of the incompetence of the Court to afford it, it becomes the duty of the Undersigned to submit to the Secretary of State the annexed protest of the Master and part of the crew of the Ship William, and the affidavit of the pilot who was on board of it at the time of the capture.

From these papers it is manifest that the British Ship William was taken (according to the protest of the Master at the distance of two miles from the shore of the territory of the United States and according to the deposition of the pilot at the distance of not more than five miles at the utmost from it) within the territory and jurisdiction of the United States. The Undersigned therefore entertains no doubt that the executive government of the United States will consider the circumstances of this capture as an aggression on its sovereignty, and will consequently pursue such measures as to its wisdom may appear the most efficacious for procuring the immediate restoration to its rightful owners of the British Ship William thus illegally taken, and now lying as a prize in the port of this city.

Philadelphia   GEO. HAMMOND
21 June 1793.

RC (DNA: RG 59, NL); in Edward Thornton's hand, signed by Hammond; at foot of first page: "Mr Jefferson"; endorsed by TJ as received 22 June 1793 and so recorded in SJL; with later notations by TJ, the last line being in a different ink:
"Ship William.
taken by the Citoyen Genet. proscribed before ⟨Aug. 7.⟩
within limits."
FC (Lb in PRO: FO 116/3). Tr (same, 115/2). Tr (same, 5/1). Enclosures: (1) Deposition of James Legget, John Whiteside, James Ramsay, and James Manson, being respectively master, chief mate, second mate, and boatswain of the William, Philadelphia, 18 May 1793, protesting that at 4 P.M. on 3 May 1793, while on a voyage from Bremen to Maryland and "being then about two miles off the Light house at Cape Henry in five fathom water and as near the shore as the pilot on board judged it proper to go," the William was fired upon and captured by the privateer Citoyen Genet, commanded by Pierre Johanene from Charleston, and declaring that the William was sent, under a prize master and seven men from the captor, to Philadelphia, where the deponents, having previously been transferred to the privateer, arrived on 14 May 1793 and were set on shore alternately one by one until being united this day. (2) Deposition of Benedict Wheatley, St. Marys County, Maryland, 18 May 1793, stating that on 3 May 1793, an

hour after he had been taken aboard the *William* as pilot and brought the ship within the mouth of Chesapeake Bay no more than "five miles at the utmost" off the lighthouse on Cape Henry, it was fired upon and taken as a prize by the schooner "Cincanatus," a privateer with four guns commissioned at Charleston by the French ambassador, that its captain was said to be French and the seven or eight members of its crew of about fifty men who boarded the *William* appeared to be American or English, and that the captors said they were not authorized to take prizes less than nine miles from land (PrCs of Trs in DLC: TJ Papers, 89: 15355-7, 15369-71, with notarization of Asheton Humphreys of Philadelphia, dated 23 May 1793, subjoined to No. 1, and attestations of St. Marys County Justice of the Peace Mordecai Jones and County Court Clerk Timothy Bowes, dated respectively 18 and 20 May 1793, subjoined to No. 2, all

in a clerk's hand; PrCs of other Trs in same, 15365-7, 15358-9, in clerical hands; Trs in NNC: Gouverneur Morris Papers; Trs in DNA: RG 46, Senate Records, 3d Cong., 1st sess.; PrCs in PRO: FO 97/1; Trs in Lb in DNA: RG 59, DL). See also Memorandum to George Washington, [11-13 July 1793].

TJ submitted Hammond's letter to the President on 22 June 1793 and evidently received his sanction of the step he had immediately taken, upon receiving it earlier that day, to prevent the captors of the *William* from disposing of the vessel before the Washington administration could act on the British minister's complaint about its capture in American territorial waters (see TJ to Henry Knox, 22 June 1793; Washington, *Journal*, 187). For the antecedents, see Hammond to TJ, 5 June 1793, and note.

Petition and Memorial from Peter Lemaigre

To Thomas Jefferson Esquire Secretary of State for the United States of America

The Petition and Memorial of Peter LeMaigre Merchant residing in the City of Philadelphia and A Citizen of the United States.

Respectfully sheweth

That your Memorialist being a Native of France came into the United States in the Year 1779 and settled in the City of Philadelphia as a Merchant and in the same Year took the Oaths of Allegiance to the State of Pennsylvania before one of the Justices of the said State in Manner and Form prescribed by the Laws of the said State and that from that time he hath continued to reside and is married and hath a Family in the said City of Philadelphia and hath carried on an extensive Trade here as a Citizen of the United States being well known and during the said Term fully recognized as such. That in the last Spring George Makepeace a Native and Citizen of the State of Massachusetts residing in and carrying on Trade as a Merchant in the Town of Boston and who had been in Correspondence with your Memorialist for some time before being Owner of the Snow *Sucky* an American built Vessel duly registered as such in the Name of the said Makepeace as sole Owner and which had lately arrived in this Port of Philadelphia from the West Indies consigned to your Memorialist did by his Letters and Power of

Attorney authorized your Memorialist to sell or employ the said Snow *Suckey* and that not finding an Opportunity to sell her at the limited Price your Memorialist did employ the said Snow on Freight in a Voyage for Port au Prince and the said Snow then remaining the sole Property of the said Makepeace your Memorialist on the Removal of the former Captain put her under the Command of Anthony Andaulle a Native of France but who had arrived in the United States in the Year   and had continued to sail out of this Port and in the Year   took the Oaths of Allegiance to the State of Pennsylvania before a Justice of said State according to the Directions of the Laws of said State and who hath since continued to own or command different Vessels under the American Flag and hath been recognized as a Citizen of the United States during that time at the Custom House in Philadelphia And that your Memorialist did load on board the said Snow at this Port of Philadelphia 484 Barrels of Flour five Tierces of Hams 25 Barrels of Biscuit 26 Firkins of Hogs Lard six thousand feet of Pine boards 2000 Staves two Cases containing Saddles and Bridles and one Case containing Hatts the whole of which were the sole Property of your Memorialist and that no Subject of the present belligerent Powers or any other Power whatsoever had any Property Share or Interest therein that he also loaded on board the said Vessel 50 barrels of Flour 4 Tierces of Hams 3 Barrels of Pork 25 small Barrels of Biscuits and 22 Firkins of Hogs Lard under the Mark P.R for account of John Baptist Pellessier a Passenger who embarked in the said Vessel also two Boxes and one Barrel of Merchandizes marked VD shipped on Freight by JB Drouillard consigned to Castaing Charleslegnay & Co. and also 170 Barrels of Flour 11 Barrels of Gammon two Tierces of Gammons 10 Barrels of Biscuit the whole marked A of the private Adventure of the said Captn. Andaulle 5 Cases of Queens Ware marked *Herbert* one Barrel of Beef marked *Belin* And having also for Passengers on board twelve Passengers and two Negroes together with the said Pellesier the said Snow set Sail from this Port of Philadelphia on or about the 11th. Day of April last bound for Port au Prince being furnished with her American Register and clearance from the Collector of the Customs for the Port of Philadelphia as an American Vessel And that the said Vessel having the said Cargo and Passengers on board and proceeding on her Voyage for Port au Prince was on the eighth Day of May last about 8 O'Clock in the Evening about 2 Leagues Distance from the Grange he was met by an english Privateer Brigantine who fired a Cannon at him and four others successively afterwards and the said Andaulle having no dread of said Privateer as he knew that the United States were not at War and supposing the said Brig would examine him or had Occasion for Provisions or Water he hove too and the said Privateer which he found to be the Brig Maria of Kingston in Jamaica commanded by Captain   McIver sent her boat on board and examined the said Andaulles Papers and forcibly took Possession of the said Snow notwithstanding the Remonstrances of said Andaulle shewing the Injustice of his Conduct and stating that he could have eluded the said Privateer but for his Confidence in his neutrality And that the said Privateer continued to keep the said Snow in Custody having taken part of her Crew out and put a part of the Privateers people on board (until 9 O'Clock) in the Morning of the next Day when the said Privateer discovering a Brigantine also American which they found to be the *Hannah* Capn. Ross from North Carolina bound to Cape Francois the said Privateer sent her boat on board this Vessel to examine her and finally sent on board from the said Snow to the said Brig Hannah the said Passengers (except one Negro Woman who they kept) and ordered the said Captain Andaulle to go on board the said Brig Hannah which he refused to do declaring that it was his Duty and he would pursue the Fate of his Vessel as his Voyage was just and his papers clear and legal and that he would not leave his Vessel unless compelled to it which Orders being imperiously persisted in by the Captain of said Privateer who wished to take Advantage of his Absence and to corrupt the Mate and Crew the said Andaulle was compelled to leave his said Snow and go on board the said Brig Hannah yielding to Force and Necessity And that the said Snow and Cargo being unjustly and forcibly taken and detained by the said english Privateer and as they declared with a View of being sent as a Prize to Jamaica that the said Captain Andaulle and Passengers of said Snow proceeded in the said Brigantine Hannah to Cape Francois where they arrived on the 12th. Day of May last and the said Captain there entered his Protest in due form to which and the other Documents herewith handed in support of the Facts herein set forth your Memorialist begs leave to refer And that the said Captn. Andaulle having taken his Passage at Cape Francois for this port of Philadelphia in Order to inform your Memorialist of his Capture arrived here on Friday last And your Memorialist relying on the Justice of the Government of the United States to support her Citizens in the free Exercise of their Commerce according to their Rights as a neutral Power And to support the Individuals against the unjust Capture and Detention of their Vessels and Cargo humbly submits his Case to your Consideration as well on behalf of himself as Agent for and authorized by and on the part of the said George Makepeace of Boston the Owner of the said Snow Suckey and prays that you will take the said Case into your immediate Consideration and enable your Memorialist by your powerful Aid to obtain Redress either by Application to the British Minister here or by furnishing him with such Letters and Authorities to his Agent who he may send to

Jamaica to support their Claim to said Vessel and Cargo as to you in your Wisdom shall seem just and meet.

Philadelphia   P LEMAIGRE
21st. May [June] 1793

RC (DNA: RG 76, British Spoliations); in a clerk's hand, signed by Lemaigre; misdated; endorsed by TJ as received 22 June 1793 and so recorded in SJL. PrC of Tr (same, Great Britain, Unbound Records); in a clerk's hand; misdated. Enclosures: (1) Declaration of Anthony Andaulle to the Cap-Français Municipality, 12 May 1793, describing the capture of the *Suckey* by the *Maria* in substantially the same terms as above. (2) Declaration of Andaulle to the Cap-Français Admiralty, 13 May 1793, of the same import. (3) Declaration of Jean Lasmartres, Pierre Lesponne, and Jean Baptiste Pellissier to same, 14 May 1793, vouching, as passengers on the *Suckey*, for the truth of the facts set forth in No. 2 by Andaulle, who was still at Cap-Français (Trs in same, British Spoliations, with copies of 21 May 1793 attestations by the Cap-Français Admiralty subjoined to Nos. 2 and 3, all three being certified by Peter Le Barbier Du Plessis in Philadelphia on 19 June 1793

as exact translations from the French; Trs of Nos. 2 and 3 in same, Great Britain, Unbound Records, certified by Du Plessis).

Peter Lemaigre, a Philadelphia merchant primarily involved in trade with Saint-Domingue, was located at 77 North Water Street (Hardie, *Phila. Dir.*, 83).

Internal evidence strongly suggests that Lemaigre actually wrote this petition a month later than the given date. Although according to Lemaigre Captain Andaulle arrived in Philadelphia ON FRIDAY LAST— 17 May if the inscribed date is accepted— Andaulle was still in Saint-Domingue as late as 14 May, and he could not have reached Philadelphia in such a short period of time. Consequently, Lemaigre must have written the petition on 21 June 1793, the day before TJ received it—a hypothesis also borne out by Lemaigre's reference to Andaulle's arrival at Cap-Français ON THE 12TH: DAY OF MAY LAST.

From Edmond Charles Genet

MONSIEUR   A Philadelphie le 22. Juin 1793. l'an 2e de la Republique.

Les discussions sont courtes quand on saisit les affaires par leurs véritables principes. Expliquons nous en Republicains; ne nous abaissons pas au niveau de l'ancienne politique par des subtilités diplomatiques; soyons aussi francs dans nos ouvertures, dans nos declarations, que le sont nos deux Nations dans leurs affections et par cette marche simple et loyale allons au but par la voie la plus courte.

Tous les raisonnemens renfermés, Monsieur, dans la lettre que vous m'avez fait l'honneur de m'écrire le 17. de ce mois sont extremement ingenieux; mais je vous dirai sans détour qu'ils portent sur une base que je ne puis admettre. Vous opposez à mes plaintes, à mes justes réclamations sur des points de droit les opinions privées ou publiques de Mr. le President des Etats Unis, et cette égide ne vous paroissant pas suffisante, vous mettez en avant des aphorismes de Vatel pour justifier ou éxcuser des infractions faites à des traités positifs. Monsieur, cette conduite n'est point parallelle a la notre. En arrivant parmi vous, j'ai dit avec candeur que la Nation française chérissant plus les interets des

Etats Unis que les siens, ne s'occupoit que de leur bonheur, au milieu des dangers qui l'entourent, et qu'au lieu de les presser de remplir envers elle toutes les obligations qui leur sont imposées par nos pactes, par la reconnoissance et par une politique prévoyante, elle venoit d'accorder de nouvelles faveurs à leur commerce, de partager avec eux les benéfices de sa navigation, de leur ouvrir tous ses ports dans les deux mondes et de les assimiler en un mot à ses propres citoyens.

Des procédés aussi désinteressés, aussi amicals auroient du rendre le Gouvernement fédéral, Monsieur, industrieux à chercher au moins tous les moyens de nous servir autant que les circonstances le lui auroient permis; mais au lieu d'attendre que le Congrès eut pris en considération les importans objets qui devroient deja l'occuper, qu'il eut jugé si la guerre de la liberté, si le destin de la France et de ses Colonies etoient pour l'Amérique des objets indifférens, qu'il eut décidé s'il etoit de l'interêt des Etats Unis de profiter ou non de la position où les laisse la magnanimité française, on s'est empressé, poussé par je ne sais quelle influence, de suivre une autre marche. On a multiplié devant moi les difficultes et les entraves. Nos traités n'ont été interprétés que d'une maniere défavorable; des ordres arbitraires ont dirigé contre nous l'action des tribunaux; enfin si j'en excepte ma réception diplomatique, je n'ai rencontré dans les négociations dont j'ai été chargé que des dégouts et des obstacles.

Ce n'est point ainsi que le peuple américain veut que nous soyons traités; il ne m'est pas permis d'en douter et j'aime à croire que des démarches de cette nature n'ont point été concues dans le coeur du Général Washington, de ce héros célebre de la liberté; je ne puis les attribuer qu'a des impressions étrangeres, dont le tems et sa vérité triompheront. Je vous prie en conséquence, Monsieur, de mettre sous les yeux de ce premier Magistrat de Votre République les deux protestations ci jointes qui viennent de m'être addressées par les consuls de la République française à New-York et à Philadelphie; vous y verrez que ces officiers se plaignent qu'on a saisi dans ces deux ports, par les ordres de Mr. le Président les prises françaises dont le jugement appartiens exclusivement aux tribunaux consulaires. J'attends de l'equité du Gouvernement fédéral, Monsieur, le prompt redressement de ces irregularités et j'ose esperer aussi que Mr. le Président voudra bien examiner de nouveau l'affaire du navire le *Republicain* de New-York et considérer qu'abstraction faite du droit que nous avons d'armer en course, aucune des éxpressions dont s'est servi le Consul Hauterive pour réclamer la levée de la saisie qui en a été faite ne prouve que ce batiment ait été armé pour cet objet; le citoyen Hauterive a fait entendre clairement au contraire qu'il a été armé par des français, dans un moment où le plus saint des devoirs est pour eux de voler de toutes les parties de la terre au

Edmond Charles Genet

George Washington

Alexander Hamilton

Henry Knox

Edmund Randolph

First Page of Edmond Charles Genet's Draft Letter to
Jefferson on a New Commercial Treaty

very great and good friends & allies. Purtill —

The citizen Ternant has delivered to me the letter wherein you inform me that yielding to his desire to serve his country in the military line, you had determined to recall him from his mission as your minister plenipotentiary to the US. his conduct during the time of his residence in this country has been such as to meet my entire approbation & esteem; and it is with great pleasure I render him the justice of this testimony. in whatever line of service you may hereafter think proper to employ him, I have no doubt he will so conduct himself as to merit well of his country and to obtain it's favor and protection.

I assure you with a sincere participation, of the great friendships and constant friendships which these US. bear to the French nation, of the interest they feel in whatever concerns their happiness & prosperity, and of their wishes for a perpetual fraternity with them. and I pray god to have them & you, very great & good friends and allies, in his holy keeping.

Written at Philadelphia this 24 day of May in the year of our lord 1793 & of the independence of the US. the 17th.

signed Go. Washington
By the President
Th. Jefferson

To the Provisory Executive council of the republic of France.

14941

Jefferson's Draft of George Washington's Letter to the
Provisional Executive Council of France

Sir 6¼   Philadelphie June 28. 1793.

The bearer hereof mr Michaux is a citizen of the French republic, who has resided several years in the U.S. as the conductor of a botanical establishment belonging to the French nation. he is a man of science and merit, & goes to Kentuckey in pursuit of objects of Natural history & botany, to enrich the literary acquirements of the two republics. I take the liberty of making this gentleman known to you, and of recommending him to your notice, your counsels & good offices, so far as they may respect both his person & pursuits. I am persuaded your further knolege of him will justify any services you may render him, and the liberty I take of making him known to you. it will the more require justification, as I have not the honour of being personally known to you. but this circumstance has not prevented my entertaining for you those sentiments of esteem & respect which your own character is entitled to inspire, and of which I beg permission to assure you: being with respect your Excellency's

       most obedt

         & most humble servt

           Th: Jefferson

15334 H. E. Govr. Shelby

Jefferson's Draft Letter to Governor Isaac Shelby
Introducing André Michaux

Seventh Page of Jefferson's Draft Letter to Gouverneur Morris Requesting the Recall of Edmond Charles Genet

Les Français Libres

à leurs freres de la

LOUISIANE.

by Genet.

L'an 2d de la République Françoise.

Title Page of Edmond Charles Genet's Address to the French People of Louisiana

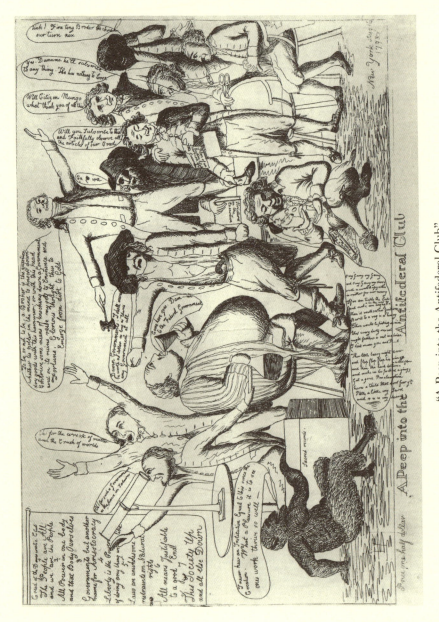

"A Peep into the Antifederal Club"

secours de leur patrie et de remplir envers elle les devoirs aux quels les américains seroient également tenus, si nous n'avions point le desir de laisser à leur sagesse et à leur honneur l'arbitrage de leur conduite. Il est incontestable que le traité de commerce, article XXII. autorise expressement nos armemens dans les ports des Etats Unis et interdit cette faculté à toute nation ennemie; au surplus cet acte même ne forme qu'une partie de nos pactes conventionnels et c'est dans leur ensemble que l'on doit envisager des contrats d'alliance et de commerce faits simultanément, si l'on veut en saisir le sens et interpreter fidelement les intentions des peuples qui les ont cimentés et des hommes de génie qui les ont dictés. Si vous ne pouvez point proteger notre commerce et nos colonies, qui contribueront beaucoup plus à l'avenir à votre prospérité qu'a la notre, au moins n'arretez pas le civisme de nos propres citoyens, ne les exposes point à une perte certaine en les forçant à sortir sans armes de vos ports et ne punissez point les braves individus de votre nation qui se rangent d'eux mêmes sous nos bannieres, sachant tres bien qu'aucune loi des Etats Unis ne donne au Gouvernement le triste pouvoir d'arrêter leur zêle par des actes de rigueur. Les américains sont libres; ils ne sont point attachés à la glebe comme les esclaves de Russie; ils peuvent changer d'état quand bon leur semble, et en acceptant dans ce moment ci le secours de leurs bras accoutumés à terrasser les tirans, nous ne commettons point le plagiat dont vous parlez. Le véritable vol, le véritable crime seroit d'enchaîner le courage de ces bons citoyens, de ces amis sincères de la plus belle des causes.

J'ignore, Monsieur, quels sont les juges constitutionnels auxquels le Gouvernement fédéral paroit avoir le projet de renvoyer l'examen des différentes questions de droit public qui se sont élevés entre nous, mais il me semble que ces juges ne peuvent etre considérés que comme conseils, attendu qu'aucun tribunal particulier n'a le droit ni le pouvoir de s'interposer entre deux nations, dont les seuls arbitres, quand elles ont un desir sincère de vivre fraternellement et amicalement ensemble, ne peuvent etre, dans l'etat actuel des sociétés humaines que la bonne foi et la raison. Agreez, Monsieur, l'expression de mon estime et de mes sentimens respectueux. GENET

PrC of Tr (DLC); in a clerk's hand, with several corrections in ink by TJ; at head of text: "Le citoyen Genet, Ministre Plenipotentiaire de la Republique française à Monsieur Jefferson Secrétaire d'Etat des Etats Unis." Tr (AMAE: CPEU, xxxvii). Tr (NNC: Gouverneur Morris Papers). PrC of another Tr (PRO: FO 97/1); in the hand of George Taylor, Jr. FC (DLC: Genet Papers); in English. FC (same); in English; with marginal corrections. FC (same); in English; draft translation of preceding FCs. Tr (DNA: RG 46, Senate Records, 3d Cong., 1st sess.); in English. Recorded in SJL as received 26 June 1793. Enclosures: (1) Protest of Alexandre Maurice d'Hauterive, New York, 21 June 1793, declaring that the United States District Court of New York had no jurisdiction over the case of the *Catharine*, the French government having recently authorized its consulates to act as courts of admiralty with exclusive jurisdiction over cases involving French prizes, that the court's intervention is proscribed by the treaties between France and the United States, and that he refuses to recognize the validity of the District Court's decisions in this matter (PrC of Tr in DLC, in French, in a clerk's hand, with two corrections in ink by TJ, and notation at foot of text by clerk: "Certifié Conforme à l'original"; Tr in AMAE: CPEU, xxxvii; Tr in NNC: Gouverneur Morris Papers; PrC of another Tr in PRO: FO 97/1, in Taylor's hand; Tr in DLC, in English, dated 24 June 1793, in a clerk's hand except for note at foot of text: "I certify the foregoing to be a true copy of the original translation filed in my office. Robt Troup Clerk of the District"). (2) Protest of François Dupont, Philadelphia, 22 June 1793, condemning the placement of a guard on the *William* by the United States government as an outrage against the rights of the French nation, especially after the United States District Court of Pennsylvania had disclaimed jurisdiction over cases involving the legality of French prizes, and asserting that no nation could interfere with France's efforts to defend itself against its enemies, that the government's action denied the principle expressed in Article 17 of the treaty of commerce between France and the United States, and that it would be liable for damages and interest for preventing the purchasers from obtaining possession of the ship (PrC of Tr in DLC, in French, in a clerk's hand; Tr in AMAE: CPEU, xxxvii; Tr in NNC: Gouverneur Morris Papers; PrC of another Tr in PRO:

FO 97/1, in Taylor's hand). Letter and enclosures with translations printed in *Message*, 15-18 (App.), 30-4; translations printed in ASP, *Foreign Relations*, I, 153-4, 155-6. Letter and enclosures enclosed in Tobias Lear to TJ, 15 July 1793, and TJ to Gouverneur Morris, 16 Aug. 1793. Letter enclosed in TJ to Edmund Randolph, with Jefferson's Note, [23 July 1793].

This letter—with its express opposition to key elements of the Washington administration's neutrality policy, its serious misunderstanding of the constitutional relationship between the President and Congress in the conduct of foreign affairs, and its insinuation that Washington was ill-disposed to the French cause—further exacerbated Genet's relations with the executive branch. Alexander Hamilton and Henry Knox, to whom TJ obviously showed it during the President's absence in Virginia, denounced it as "the most offensive paper, perhaps, that ever was offered by a foreign Minister to a friendly power, with which he resided," and warned Washington that it was part of a settled French design "*to endeavour to controul the Government itself, by creating, if possible, a scism between it and the people* and inlisting them on the side of France, in opposition to their own constitutional authorities" (Syrett, *Hamilton*, xv, 75). TJ submitted the letter and its enclosures to the President on 13 July 1793 (Washington, *Journal*, 195). For the sequel, see TJ to Genet, [ca. 16 July 1793], and note.

To Henry Knox

Dr Sir   Philadelphia June 22. 1793.

I have this moment received a letter from Mr. Hammond informing me that the court of Admiralty having determined against it's own jurisdiction in the case of the ship William, he applies to the Executive to detain her, as having been taken within the limits of our protection. As this detention can only be by the Military, I take the liberty of submitting to you whether the Governor should not be desired to take possession of the vessel, if she be liberated by the officer of the court. This being within your department, I have made free to write to you directly without passing thro' the President, as he is much engaged, and it is a plain case, and may require immediate interposition. I have the honor to be with great respect & esteem, Dr. Sir Your most obedt. & most humble servt   TH: JEFFERSON

PrC (DLC); at foot of text: "The Secretary at War." FC (Lb in DNA: RG 59, DL).

George Washington to the Commissioners of Accounts for the States

GENTLEMEN   [22 June 1793][1]

Having considered the two questions referred to me in your letters of yesterday, I am of opinion that the Report of your proceedings may be made to the President of the US. and that your books and papers will be most properly deposited in the Treasury department. You will therefore be pleased to deliver them to the order of the Secretary of the Treasury.[2]

Dft (DNA: RG 59, MLR); in TJ's hand, undated, with additions by Washington and Bartholomew Dandridge, Jr. (see notes below); at foot of text in Dandridge's hand: "Wm. Irvine Jno. Kean & W: Langdon Comers."; endorsed by Dandridge as a letter of 22 June 1793.

The two LETTERS of 21 June 1793 from the Commissioners to the President posed the questions answered here (DNA: RG 59, MLR; see also Fitzpatrick, *Writings*, XXXII, 508). The President and the Cabinet agreed to the substance of this response in a meeting on 22 June 1793 (Washington, *Journal*, 187). The letter as sent by Washington under this date followed the emended draft (Fitzpatrick, *Writings*, XXXII, 509).

On 29 June 1793 the Commissioners sent TJ their REPORT of that date in a brief covering letter asking him to transmit it to the President (RC in DNA: RG 59, MLR; in a clerk's hand, signed by Irvine, Kean, and Langdon; at foot of text: "The Secretary of State"; endorsed by TJ as received 29 June 1793 and so recorded in SJL). The report announced the final settlement of state accounts with the United States for the cost of the Revolutionary War, listing seven creditor states and six debtor states, Virginia being among the latter (MS in RG 53, Records of the Bureau of the Public Debt, signed by Irvine, Kean, and Langdon, and subjoined to minutes of the Commissioners' meeting of 27 June 1793; Tr in Lb in DLC: Washington Papers; printed in ASP, *Miscellaneous*, I, 69). TJ listed the balances due to the creditor states and owed by the debtor states on a sheet for his own files (MS in DLC; entirely in TJ's hand, with subtotals for each group added in pencil; recorded in SJPL: "balances of the several states as settld by the Commrs."). For the commissioners' work, see E. James Ferguson, *The Power of the Purse: A History of American Public Finance, 1776-1790* (Chapel Hill, 1961), 332-3.

[1] Washington here added "Phila. June 22d 1793."

[2] After Washington initialed the text below this sentence, Dandridge subsequently wrote the following words over the initials: "Should there be any thing in this business, requiring, in your opinions, my further agency, I shall be ready at any time to give the necessary attention thereto either personally or in writing. Go:W."

To Edmond Charles Genet

SIR   Philadelphia June 23. 1793.

I have the honor to inform you that in consequence of the general orders given by the President, a privateer fitted out by English subjects within the state of Georgia to cruize against the citizens of France has been seized by the Governor of Georgia, and such legal prosecutions are ordered as the case will justify. I beg you to be assured that the government will use the utmost vigilance to see that the laws which forbid these enterprises are carried into strict execution. I have the honor to be with great & sincere esteem, Sir, Your most obedt. & most humble servt   TH: JEFFERSON

PrC (DLC); at foot of text: "The Minister Plenipotentiary of France." PrC of Tr (DLC); in a clerk's hand. Tr (NNC: Gouverneur Morris Papers). Tr (DNA: RG 46, Senate Records, 3d Cong., 1st sess.). PrC (PRO: FO 97/1). FC (Lb in DNA: RG 59, DL). Tr (DLC: Genet Papers). Tr (same); in French; docketed by Genet. Printed in *Message*, 40. Enclosed in TJ to Gouverneur Morris, 16 Aug. 1793.

TJ wrote this letter two days after submitting to the President a letter from the GOVERNOR OF GEORGIA on the seizure of a British privateer in that state (Washington, *Journal*, 185; Edward Telfair to TJ, 1 June 1793).

To Edmond Charles Genet

SIR   Philadelphia. June 23.[1] 1793.

In answer to your letter of the 18th. instant, on the subject of the bills drawn by the administration of St. Domingo in favor of certain citizens of the US.[2] I am instructed[3] to inform you that the funds therein mentioned have[4] been so clearly[5] understood on all hands to be specifically appropriated for the payment of the bills which were recognised by the former agents of France here, as to be incapable of being diverted, without disappointing the just expectations of our citizens, holders of those bills.

Indeed the government has been so much a party in countenancing[6] those expectations, as, in such an event, to lie under an obligation, in point of propriety, to satisfy the parties themselves,[7] to the extent of the balance which yet remains to be advanced.[8] I have the honor to be with great & sincere esteem[9] Sir Your most obedient & most humble servt

TH: JEFFERSON

RC (AMAE: CPEU, Supplément, xx); at foot of text: "The Minister Plenipy. of France." PrC (DLC). Dft (DLC); in Alexander Hamilton's hand, except for salutation, dateline, one interlined phrase, complimentary close, initials, and name of addressee by TJ; at foot of text in TJ's hand: "The Minister Plenipy. of the republic of

France"; only the most significant variations are noted below; recorded in SJPL. PrC of Tr (DLC); in a clerk's hand. Tr (NNC: Gouverneur Morris Papers). Tr (DNA: RG 46, Senate Records, 3d Cong., 1st sess.). PrC (PRO: FO 97/1). FC (Lb in DNA: RG 59, DL). Printed in *Message*, 39-40. Enclosed in TJ to Gouverneur Morris, 16 Aug. 1793.

The President and the Cabinet agreed to "an answer" to Genet's letter OF THE 18TH. INSTANT during a meeting on 22 June 1793 (Washington, *Journal*, 187). For the antecedents, see note to Genet to TJ, 18 June 1793.

[1] Digits reworked in Dft from what appears to be "19."

[2] Clause to this point represented in Dft by "——— : ———."

[3] Dft here reads: "by the President."

[4] Dft: "fund in question has."

[5] Preceding two words interlined in Dft.

[6] Word interlined in Dft in place of "giving."

[7] Preceding four words interlined in Dft by TJ in place of "*see that the parties are satisfied*," which Hamilton had substituted for "make itself the payments."

[8] Remainder of Dft in TJ's hand.

[9] Dft: "with great respect & esteem."

To La Forest

Sir   Philadelphia. June 23. 1793.

In the evening of the day on which I had the honor of seeing you last, I had that of seeing Mr. Genet also. I explained to him what had past, and asked him what kind of letter, on the subject of your situation, would remove the scruples about his instructions: and after some further conference he concluded by saying he would not trouble our government with any interference in it, but would undertake to accomodate you in some manner adequate to the necessities of your situation. Sincerely desirous that this should be done, I am happy at the same time that it may be done without our government's intermeddling where it did not seem to be regular and perhaps not respectful to the French government. I wish you with great sincerity a happy return and welcome reception in your own country, and that the fidelity of your services here may ensure you an approbation of them there. I have the honor to be with great esteem Sir your most obedt & most humble servt

TH: JEFFERSON

PrC (DLC); at foot of text: "M. la Forest." Tr (DLC); 19th-century copy.

La Forest was about to return to France after losing his position as consul general to the United States as a result of a reorganization of the French consular service in America by the Provisional Executive Council

(Frédéric Masson, *Le Département des Affaires Étrangères pendant la Révolution, 1787-1804* [Paris, 1877], 407-8; Edmond Charles Genet's first letter to TJ, 22 May 1793, and note). La Forest had written a letter to TJ on 20 June 1793, which was recorded in SJL as received 21 June 1793, but has not been found.

To James Madison

Dear Sir June 23. 1793.

My last was of the 17th. if I may reckon a single line any thing. Yours of the 13th. came to hand yesterday.—The proclamation as first proposed was to have been a declaration of neutrality. It was opposed on these grounds 1. that a declaration of neutrality was a declaration there should be no war, to which the Executive was not competent. 2. that it would be better to hold back the declaration of neutrality, as a thing worth something to the powers at war, that they would bid for it, and we might reasonably ask as a price, the *broadest privileges* of neutral nations. The 1st. objection was so far respected as to avoid inserting the term *neutrality*, and the drawing the instrument was left to E.R. That there should be a proclamation was passed unanimously with the approbation or the acquiescence of all parties. Indeed it was not expedient to oppose it altogether, lest it should prejudice what was the next question, the boldest and greatest that ever was hazarded, and which would have called for extremities, had it prevailed.—Spain is unquestionably picking a quarrel with us. A series of letters from her commissioners here prove it. We are sending a courier to Madrid. The inevitableness of war with the Creeks, and the probability, I might say the certainty of it with Spain (for there is not one of us who doubts it,) will certainly occasion your convocation. At what time I cannot exactly say. But you should be prepared for this important change in the state of things.— The President is got pretty well again. He sets off this day to Mount Vernon, and will be absent a fortnight. The death of his manager, hourly expected, of a consumption, is the call. He will consequently be absent on the 4th. of July. He travels in a Phaeton and pair. Doctr. Logan sends you the inclosed pamphlet. Adieu. Your's affectionately.

RC (DLC: Madison Papers); unsigned; addressed: "Mr. Madison." PrC (DLC). Enclosure: [George Logan], *Letters addressed to the Yeomanry of the United States, containing some Observations on Funding and Bank Systems: By an American Farmer* (Philadelphia, 1793).

TJ's letter of THE 17TH is not recorded in SJL and has not been found, but see Madison to TJ, 29 June 1793. Spain's COMMISSIONERS HERE: Josef Ignacio de Viar and Josef de Jaudenes. George Washington's MANAGER: Anthony Whiting (Freeman, *Washington*, VII, 95-6).

From William Short

Dear Sir Aranjuez June 23 1793

The last private letter which I have had the happiness of recieving from you was of the 3d. of Jany. with a postscript of the 15th. I answered it on the 5th. of April (having previously acknowleged its reciept in my two letters of the 2d. of April) so minutely and went into such lengthy details and in so long, prolix and tedious a letter, that I have not had courage to take up my pen on the same subject since that time, although it was my intention. I know not whether I should have prevailed on myself to do it even now if it were not for the uncertainty of letter conveyance by sea in these times—and if I had not experienced the danger of depending on single conveyances at all times.

Being deterred from copying my letter of April the 5th. by its length[1] I will comprize its substance as to the delay of the payments to France in as small a compass as possible to save trouble both to you and myself.

At the end of the year 91. when the loan was agreed for at Amsterdam, there was not only no cash on hand applicable to France, but there was a deficit of about 300,000 florins to make up the $2\frac{1}{2}$ millions which the Sec. of the treasury had directed to be held appropriated to his draughts, by his letter of May 24. 91. This was of course to be taken from the first money which came in. On the 1st. of Febry. 92. there became due 330,000 florins for interest and premium on preceding loans—and on the 1st. of March 125,000 for interest. To face these demands the sums arising on the loan were first to be applied before any part could be disponible towards the French payments. The loan commenced the 1st. of Jany.—was for three million of florins, and to be paid at the rate of 500,000 florins a month for six months—that is to say the undertakers were not obliged to pay sooner though they had a right to do it if they should find it to their interest. It was probable they would pay somewhat more than the 500,000 florins a month, but we had no right to count on it. Had the Secretary therefore drawn for the money which he had appropriated to his draughts, the bankers would have been obliged to have advanced a part of the sum necessary on the 1st. of Febry.

Under this view of the subject I could have no difficulty when I left Amsterdam in the beginning of Jany. to direct them to make no further payments to France until further orders. It then appeared there could be no money disponible until towards the end of Febry. about which time the undertakers would make their payments for that month—and even then the sum could be but small. Before the expiration of that time I recieved intelligence of the President having named another person to reside in Paris—and as he was in London I expected daily his arrival there.[2]

Previous to making any further payment to France it was necessary or at least highly proper to settle the rate of depreciation—a former letter from the Sec. of the treasury had authorized me to do this—but after knowing that the President had placed his confidence in another[3] it would have been a piece of indelicacy which I hope would not be expected from me, to have hastened to have taken this on myself[4] by taking advantage of my being on the spot. Besides in the President's instructions to the Sec. of the treasury of which he sent me a copy, he is directed to employ the Minister for the time being at Paris for arrangements with respect to the French debt—and the settling of the depreciation I considered as a very delicate arrangement.

Thus you will see that before there was any cash at my disposition to be applied to the French payment I was placed in a situation which forbad my making payments even if there had been cash; and thus far at least I hope I shall be exempted from blame as to any delay.

Besides this you will be so good as to observe another circumstance which existed at the time of my leaving Amsterdam in Jany. and which would have induced me also to have delayed the immediate application to the French payment of the sums coming in gradually on the loan— and that was that the minister of marine had made a report to the national assembly in favor of applying the American debt to the purchase[5] of succours for their islands. This appeared so advantageous for the U.S. that I was disposed to contribute all I could to it—and as it was expected that the assembly would soon approve the report, it became advisable to hold back such small sums as might be disponible when the assembly should have passed the decree—as the payment once made[6] would be less likely to be applied in the U.S.[7]—and the suspending the payments for that reason, M. Morris informed me was the wish of the Minister of Marine.

Contrary to expectation this decree was postponed being passed from day to day—and before it was passed I recieved from Mr. Morris who was in London, an account of the President having nominated him for Paris. As yet there was no money disponible—but if there had been I certainly should have left the mode of applying the cash to the succours of S. Domingo, to Mr. Morris now become the agent of the U.S. since before his becoming so, or being any way employed by them (at least as far as I knew) he had been active in concerting the measure with the minister of marine. I say I should have left it to him unless some circumstance should render the delay prejudicial.

His arrival in Paris as you know was postponed for a long time after his nomination. In the mean time the decree was passed—and the minister of marine pressing me to concert with him the means of execution, observing it would not admit of delay, I consented to go so far as to engage that the sum of 800,000 dollars should be at the disposition of France in the treasury of the U.S. in America, leaving the number of livres for which they should have credit as the value of these dollars (or in other words the depreciation) to be settled between the two governments. I immediately gave notice thereof to the Sec. of the treasury that he might draw therefore on the bankers in Amsterdam, intending that that amount in proportion as it came in from the loan then on foot should be held appropriated to that purpose. A day or two after I had another meeting with the minister of marine to settle the business finally when some doubts being suggested to him by one of his clerks[8] as to the extent of the decree, and some difficulties having arisen between him and the commissaries of the treasury, he chose to suspend the business until he could obtain from the assembly an explanatory decree. This he expected and indeed was sure would take place in a few days. I was then sure also that M. Morris would arrive in a few days, and proposed to him that the business should be settled between them two, as that could be the cause of no delay, to which he consented and thus we parted. I immediately gave the Sec. of the treasury notice of this suspension—and on Mr. Morris's arrival at Paris I gave immediate notice thereof also to the Minister of marine—and from that time naturally considered the business as no longer in my hands, being then on my departure for the Hague.

Before I set out I recieved a letter from the Sec. of the Treasury which shewed he had occasion for a greater sum for domestic purposes, and desiring me accordingly to open a loan for that purpose. I communicated This to Mr. Morris and it was agreed between us that it would be proper to hold the loan already made, appropriated to that purpose (not knowing then how soon another might be obtained) and in case the minister of marine should apply to him for the execution of my promise, that he should be told the long delay he had made use of had rendered it necessary for the money to be otherwise applied.

I mentioned that of the cash in the hands of the bankers, $2\frac{1}{2}$ million of florins were kept appropriated to the Secr'ys. draughts in consequence of his orders given before the opening of the loan in Jany. 92.—this appropriation was out of the six millions loaned in Septr. 91. On the 30th. of Nov. 91. he wrote me that he should draw for no more than the million he had already announced to have drawn for—this left $1\frac{1}{2}$ million more disponible—one of the copies of this letter has never yet come to my hands—the other went to the Hague and was detained as I informed you in Mr. Dumas's hands until my arrival there in June 92.—and of course was of no avail as I had in the mean time recieved his directions to open another loan for domestic purposes.

A few days before I left Paris I learned from the commissioners that they had succeeded in opening a second loan at 4 per ct. for 3 millions of florins. This again left the cash in hand free to be applied to France, as the loan just opened and which would be coming in gradually might answer the draughts of the Sec. of the Treasury.

Thus matters stood when I left Paris on the 2d. of June. Mr. Morris and myself both considered at that time, all arrangements with France with respect to the debt as being his appanage: And the being relieved from that delicate part of the money arrangement, I considered some consolation for the manner in which I had been kept in Paris for so long and painful a period of uncertainty, hope, and finally mortification. I mentioned to him the delay which had already taken place as to the settlement of the depreciation and pressed him to take up that business immediately, which he seemed fully determined to do, mentioning two causes which might occasion a short delay, namely his having not yet been presented to the King, and a paragraph in a letter from you, which seemed to indicate that the depreciation was to be thrown on France, and of which he hoped soon to have a further explanation.

In whatever manner the cash on hand was applied towards the French debt, whether by bills of exchange as before, to the national treasury, or by the way of succours to the French islands—a previous arrangement became necessary in order to settle the depreciation, or rate at which the florins or dollars should be credited in livres, and as this arrangement was considered by me as belonging to M. Morris, no payment of course could be ordered by me until I recieved from him the account of his having done this. All I could do was to press him to lose no time—and this I did both before and after my departure from Paris, as much and with as much importunity as it was possible to do. In this manner we separated as I have frequently informed the Sec. of the treasury and particularly in my letter to him of June 28. and Aug. 6. 92. and of which letters he acknowleged the receipt before he gave the information to Congress which you mention, of Mr. Morris's having nothing to do with these payments, and throwing all the blame of the delay on me. (I wish if practicable you would be so good as to take the trouble of reading my letters to him written during the year 1792.)

It was not until Aug. 17th. (after I had been informed of the King's suspension) that I recieved the letter of the Sec. of the Treasury informing me it was the President's intention that the payments to France were to remain as before in my hands. Until then every circumstance both of reason and propriety implied its belonging in part at least to Mr. Morris—and the Prests. original instructions with respect to employing me to make loans—and the Minister of the U.S. at Paris for the time being with respect to all arrangements as to this debt, were express on this subject. After recieving the Secy.'s letter it was impossible as you will see to have done any thing (the government being changed) however I might have been disposed to have done it. Yet it would have been impossible not to have considered it somewhat cruel that a mark of confidence of that kind, in appearance so much more[9] flattering for me than for Mr. Morris should[10] have produced for me the[11] ungrateful favor of being employed only in the most odious and delicate parts of a business, while another was placed in the more lucrative and honorable post of Min. Plenipotentiary—this dangerous business being subtracted from the charge of the Paris mission (to which it was originally destined)[12] as soon as it was Mr. Morris who was to fill it.

At length M. Morris made an arrangement with the commissaries of the treasury, and in consequence thereof directed me to order the bankers to pay to the French agents 1,625,000 florins. It was not said whether he had settled the depreciation—but as I considered that affair belonging to him, I should have had the money immediately paid had it not been for the then existing circumstances, namely the Kings suspension—the entry of the Duke of Brunswic in France, and every human probability of his getting to Paris, or at least of the then existing government being overturned. Prudence as I thought exacted of me to require a saving clause in the reciept to be given by the bankers of France at Amsterdam—they took time to consider of it and at length refused to give it. Finding Mr. Morris in favor of the payment being made as the contract had been entered into prior to the suspension—and averse that so large sums, as had then come in from the loans,[13] should remain on hand at a dead interest, I yielded my opinion and directed the payment to be made without the clause in the receipt. This was done on the 4th. of Sept.—the delay was therefore from the 17th. of Aug. to that date; and this delay the only one which can in any manner be attributed to me, I think the critical and embarassing situation in which I was placed, will justify. I then thought and still think that neither I or any other agent of our government, directed to pay to the King had a right to pay to the then ministry until directed to do so by our government; and I was happy to find by the letters of the Sec. of the treasury written as soon as he had received news of the revolution of the 10th. of Aug. that both the Prest. and himself desired that there might be a suspension of further payments—and this before he had recieved[14] information of my having done so.[15] This I think may be considered[16] as a full approbation of the delay my scruples had occasioned from Aug. 17. to Sep. 4.

My letters to the Sec. of the treasury above alluded to will shew what was the conduct of Mr. Morris in this affair, who after these difficulties arose, wrote me I think in Sept.[17] that on looking over his papers he had found that this business was committed wholly and of course exclusively to me, and that therefore he was determined to meddle no further with it—notwithstanding by the steps he had taken he had put the business as it were out of my reach at least as to the 1,625,000 florins—conducting himself with that kind of prudence which might enable him to claim credit for whatever might turn out well, and avoid being considered the author, by people in general of what might have a different issue.

Thus I have given a full state of what passed, and on that simple state leave you to judge how far it was candid to throw on me a blame where my repeated letters then in the hands of the Sec. of the treasury, had shewn him, and might have shewn the public that the business was considered both by Mr. Morris and myself as having passed into his hands. I will add nothing more to this long letter than to assure you of the sentiments with which I shall ever remain my dear Sir,[18] your unalterable[19] friend & servant   W. SHORT

RC (DLC); at head of text: "*Private*"; at foot of first page: "Mr. Jefferson—Monticello"; endorsed by TJ as received 8 Nov. 1793 and so recorded in SJL. PrC (DLC); endorsed by TJ: "Duplicate." Dft (PHi: Gilpin Collection); at head of text: "⟨*Copy*⟩"; only the most significant variations are recorded below.

ANOTHER PERSON TO RESIDE IN PARIS: a reference to Gouverneur Morris's appointment in January 1792 as United States minister to France, a position Short himself had coveted. The FORMER LETTER FROM THE SEC. OF THE TREASURY to Short on adjusting for the depreciation of assignats in payments on the American debt to France, dated 2 Sep. 1791, is in Syrett, *Hamilton*, IX, 158-62.

For the PRESIDENT'S INSTRUCTIONS TO THE SEC. OF THE TREASURY of 28 Aug. 1790 directing him to contract up to $14,000,000 in loans for the payment of the foreign debt and the redemption of the domestic debt, see same, VI, 579-80. The 19 Dec. 1791 REPORT TO THE NATIONAL ASSEMBLY by Minister of Marine Antoine François, Marquis Bertrand de Molleville, recommending that payments on the American debt to France be used to purchase supplies for the relief of Saint-Domingue, which was undergoing a massive slave revolt, is in *Archives Parlementaires*, 1st ser., XXXVI, 253-6. The DECREE . . . PASSED by the Legislative Assembly on 28 Mch. 1792 authorized the Minister of Marine to expend 6,000,000 livres on the relief of Saint-Domingue, and a subsequent decree passed by it on 26 June 1792 specifically empowered the same official to obtain two-thirds of this sum from the American debt to France

(same, XL, 578, XLV, 593-5). Short IMMEDIATELY GAVE NOTICE in a 22 Apr. 1792 letter to Alexander Hamilton of his preliminary agreement with Minister of Marine Jean de Lacoste under the terms of the first decree to use $800,000 of the American debt to France for the purchase of supplies in the United States for Saint-Domingue (Syrett, *Hamilton*, XI, 326-7). Three days later he wrote another letter to Hamilton giving NOTICE OF the SUSPENSION of this agreement (same, 333).

The 21 Mch. 1792 LETTER FROM THE SEC. OF THE TREASURY authorizing Short to borrow 3,000,000 florins for the redemption of the domestic debt is in same, 165. Hamilton's ORDERS GIVEN BEFORE THE OPENING OF THE LOAN IN JANY. 92 were contained in a 24 May 1791 letter to Short (same, VIII, 356). The LETTER from TJ to Morris WHICH SEEMED TO INDICATE THAT THE DEPRECIATION WAS TO BE THROWN ON FRANCE was that of 10 Mch. 1792. The 14 June 1792 LETTER OF THE SEC. OF THE TREASURY informing Short that he was still responsible for the payment of the American debt to France, despite Morris's appointment as minister to that country, is in same, XI, 519-20. Hamilton informed Short in letters of 1 and 16 Oct. 1792 that there was to be a SUSPENSION OF FURTHER PAYMENTS on the American debt to France in consequence of the overthrow of Louis XVI (same, XII, 513-14, 576-7). See also TJ to Gouverneur Morris, 15 Oct. 1792, and note.

[1] Dft: "huge length."
[2] In Dft Short here canceled "(not being informed until after of the delay which took place in the Senate)."

[3] Short here canceled "(or even knowing that." In Dft he canceled "it would be (or even knowing that he was about to fix his choice which I did not know at the time of recieving the Secrys. letter)."

[4] Remainder of sentence interlined here and in Dft in place of "until that choice should be known."

[5] Dft here reads: "in the U.S."

[6] Dft here reads: "into the French treasury."

[7] Remainder of sentence added in Dft sometime after Short wrote the rest of the text.

[8] Preceding five words interlined; they are written in the margin in Dft.

[9] Preceding two words interlined in Dft.

[10] Short here canceled "only." He retained it in Dft, where sentence to this point is interlined in place of "—although it was impossible, notwithstanding an apparently so flattering mark of confidence, not

to consider it somewhat cruel that it should only."

[11] Dft here reads: "sterile and."

[12] Parenthetical phrase interlined in Dft without parentheses.

[13] Preceding clause interlined in Dft.

[14] Short here canceled "my letters."

[15] In Dft Short first wrote "and this before he knew I had done so" and later altered it to read "before he received information done so" without completing the revision.

[16] In Dft Short first wrote "This I might consider" and then altered it to read as above.

[17] Preceding four words interlined in Dft.

[18] In Dft Short here canceled an emended passage which reads "whatever pain, anxiety mortification ⟨and⟩ humiliation ⟨I⟩[. . .] neglect I may be exposed to."

[19] Word interlined in Dft.

From George Washington

DEAR SIR   Philadelphia June 23d. 1793.

If you should have leizure between this and my return, to furnish me with your thoughts on Mr. Arthur Youngs queries (Transmitted to you some time ago) It would enable me to solve his questions soon afterwards. Yours always and sincerely   GO: WASHINGTON

RC (NNP); at foot of text: "Mr. Jefferson"; endorsed by TJ as received 24 June 1793.

For Young's QUERIES, see enclosure to Washington to TJ, 13 May 1793.

Petition from Abijah Babcock

Philadelphia, 24 June 1793. Requests a patent for a machine he has invented "for propelling Boats or Vessels and Carriages, and working Mills, which he conceives will be found of great use in Navigation, and saving of labour in the branches to which it is applied."

Tr (DP: Scientific Library, Propulsion of Vessels, 1791-1810); 1 p.; with Enclosure No. 1 subjoined; at head of text: "To Thomas Jefferson Esqr. Secretary of State"; with accompanying notation by Nicholas King that he copied the petition and enclosures in 1811 from the originals in the Patent Office of the Department of State; and another notation in the margin by Robert Schuyler indicating that he had received these texts "from the Heirs of Robert Fulton in 1841." Enclosures: (1) Babcock's "Explanation of the Springe Machine, which may be made of any given size," Philadelphia, 24 June 1793, describing his method of using springs to impart motion to rag wheels, spur wheels, wallowers, and a spiral wheel (Tr in same; witnessed by State Department clerks George Pfeiffer and Jacob Blackwell; with Babcock's subjoined deposition that he invented the machine sworn before Philadelphia alderman Hilary Baker, 24 June 1793). (2) Three drawings of Babcock's invention, with explanatory key (Tr in same; undated).

Babcock received a patent for his invention on 2 Dec. 1793 (*List of Patents*, 8).

From Tench Coxe

[24 June 1793]

Mr. Coxe has the honor to inform Mr. Jefferson, that the House of Pragers are not drawing at this time. They expect advices of Shipments from Virginia in which event they will draw. Mr. Jacob G. Koch a dutch house is drawing at 3/– or $\frac{36}{90}$ of a dollar ℔ Guilder, but tho Mr. Coxe does not doubt his goodness, he cannot say he knows enough to induce a decided recommendation. Mr. Vaughan expresses himself to the same effect concerning Mr. K[och. He] has not procured [. . . .][1]

RC (DLC); foot of text torn away, with possible loss of dateline; endorsed by TJ as a letter of 24 June 1793 received the same day and so recorded in SJL.

[1] One or more lines missing.

From Grand & Cie.

MONSIEUR   Paris le 24e Juin 1793

Le paquet par lequel nous avons l'honneur de vous addresser les duplicats de nos lettres du 25e. May dernier étant dejà cacheté, nous avons celui de joindre ici une copie des Titres à l'appui du Compte des Etatsunis, pareille à celle que nous avons eu l'honneur d'envoyer à Monsieur Hamilton. Nous n'avions pas eu l'idée de joindre cette copie à notre premier paquet, nous le faisons aujourdhui pour le cas où ces nottes pourroient, Monsieur, vous être de quelqu'utilité. Nous avons l'honneur d'être avec beaucoup de respect Monsieur vos très humbles & très obeissans Serviteurs   GRAND & CO

RC (DLC); at foot of first page: "Son Excellence Monsieur Thomas Jefferson Sécrétaire d'Etat Au Département des Affaires Etrangères à Philadelphie"; endorsed by TJ as received 9 Nov. 1793 and so recorded in SJL. Enclosure: "Copie de divers Mandats de Son Excellence Monsieur Ths. Jefferson pour compte des Etats-Unis," n.d., consisting of two sets of orders drawn by TJ and others on Grand & Cie. for account of the United States, one of eight orders covering the period 21 Aug. 1787-3 Dec. 1789 and another of ninety orders covering the period 20 Aug. 1784-4 Aug. 1787 (MS in DLC: TJ Papers, 32: 5412-19; in clerical hands). Enclosed in Alexandre Maurice d'Hauterive to TJ, 13 Oct. 1793.

From Alexander Hamilton

Sir   Treasury Department June 24 1793.

I have the honor to inform you that the Collectors have been furnished with all the Sea letters that have been received from Your Department, And that a demand exists at several of the Custom Houses for more. With great respect, I have the honor to be, Sir, your Obedt Servt.

A HAMILTON

RC (NNP); in a clerk's hand, signed by Hamilton; at foot of text: "The Secretary of State"; endorsed by TJ as received 24 June 1793 and so recorded in SJL.

To Samuel A. Otis

Sir   Philadelphia June 24. 1793.

I received several days ago your favor proposing the appointment of your son to the Consulship of St. Domingo, but the press of business has hitherto prevented my answering it: You know that Mr. Bourne was lately our Consul there. He has sollicited that the appointment may be revived. But this cannot be done till the meeting of Senate. He thinks it possible that in the mean time he may change his views. Should he not, I rather presume the President will think his former possession of the office and some disadvantages into which it led him, as giving him a better title than any other person. Your application shall be laid in time before the President, and should Mr. Bourne decline, I have no doubt the titles of your son will be duly respected. I am with much esteem, Sir Your most obedt. humble servt   TH: JEFFERSON

PrC (DLC); at foot of text: "Mr. Saml. A. Otis." Tr (DLC); 19th-century copy.

Otis's reply of 8 July 1793, recorded in SJL as received from Boston on 15 July 1793, has not been found.

To Thomas Mann Randolph, Jr.

Dear Sir   Philadelphia June 24. 1793.

I have to acknolege your two favors of May 31. and June 13. I was so much pressed the last week on the post-day that it was impossible for me to write. The President is at this time gone to Mount Vernon, for a few days only. Maria has the mumps in the city, so that she has not been with me for a week past. She has it favorably. The person engaged for me as a manager, came up from Elkton to see me the last week. He is not yet certain on the subject of tenants, his brother, who had decided to go as one, having met an advantageous situation at home, and his cousin, whom I formerly wrote you was gone to see place,[1] having been intercepted by another offer. He still thinks he shall get some, and is to let me know definitively by the last of August. The time of the tenant's removing in Maryland is not till March. This man is about 30. years of age, of not a very bright appearance, but seems as if he would be docile, so that I hope to get my own outlines followed by him. He agrees in condemning Indian corn and hogs, and in preferring the potatoe and clover to every other means of feeding all kinds of stock, even horses. If he does not get tenants for my lands on the East side of the river I shall perhaps propose to Clarkson to go there, unless I could find a person more kind to the labourers and with a smaller family. In the mean time it would be better he should know nothing of my arrangements, unless indeed he were to have an offer elsewhere, which I would not chuse he should lose.—The late accounts from France give us hopes that DuMourier's desertion has had no other effect than to derange that army a while, whilst it shews the unshaken republicanism of the army and people. Their internal insurrections do not wear the face they were made to assume. They seem to have been confined chiefly to Britanny, where the noblesse was more numerous than the people, and turned against the revolution from the moment of suppressing titles. There was a considerable insurrection there before I left France. The French have been guilty of great errors in their conduct towards other nations, not only in insulting uselessly all crowned heads but endeavoring to force liberty on their neighbors in their own form.[2] They seem to be correcting themselves in the latter point. The war between them and England embarrasses our government daily and immensely. The predilection of our citizens for France renders it very difficult to suppress their attempts to cruize against the English on the ocean, and to do justice to the latter in cases where they are entitled to it.—I begin to be uneasy at not receiving my threshing machine. It cannot now be in time for this harvest. My fear is that it may have been in some vessel which is captured. I condole with you on the misfortunes of your garden. From a feeling of self interest I would propose a great provision of Celery plants to be made. My love to my dear Martha, and am Dear Sir most affectionately Yours

Th: Jefferson

RC (DLC); addressed: "Thomas M. Randolph junr. esq. Monticello." PrC (DLC). Tr (ViU: Edgehill-Randolph Papers); 19th-century copy.

The PERSON ENGAGED FOR ME AS A MANAGER: Samuel Biddle.

[1] Thus in manuscript.
[2] Preceding four words interlined.

To Paul Bentalou

S<small>IR</small>   Philadelphia June 25. 1793.

I have duly received your favor of the 18th. inst. Many objections lie to the issuing of passes by foreign agents to our vessels. In the case of a foreign Consul at Boston who officiously undertook to do it, the thing was forbidden. Were some of our vessels to have these passes, the want of them might subject others to doubts and obstacles in their voyages. The permission to grant these passes might lead to the most dangerous abuses, and the passports which we grant to our own vessels are perfectly sufficient. No instance, has occurred, as far as we know, of our passports having been disrespected. The vessels of ours, taken hitherto, were such as had left our states before a knowlege of the war had reached us, and consequently before we had begun to issue passports. I am Sir Your very humble servt   T<small>H</small>: J<small>EFFERSON</small>

PrC (DLC); at foot of text: "Mr. Paul Bentaloo. Baltimore." FC (Lb in DNA: RG 59, DL). Recorded in SJL as a letter of 24 June 1793.

Bentalou's FAVOR OF THE 18TH INST., recorded in SJL as received from Baltimore on 21 June 1793, has not been found.

From the Commissioners of the Federal District

S<small>IR</small>   George Town 25th. June 1793

Majr. Ellicott has returned to us, at this meeting a new map of the Territory of Columbia which as well as the old one we have committed to Mr. Lears care for you. We are Sir Your Most Obdt. Servts.

T<small>H</small> J<small>OHNSON</small>
D<small>D</small> S<small>TUART</small>
D<small>ANL</small>. C<small>ARROLL</small>

FC (DNA: RG 42, DCLB); at head of text: "Commrs. *to* Mr. Jefferson."

Andrew Ellicott's NEW MAP of the Federal District, apparently the basis for a 1794 copperplate engraving, is evidently the topographical manuscript reproduced and discussed in Ralph E. Ehrenberg, "Mapping the Nation's Capital: The Surveyor's Office, 1791-1818," *Quarterly Journal of the Library of Congress*, XXXVI (1979), 280, 282-4. For the OLD ONE, not found, see TJ to the Commissioners, 15 Jan. 1793, and note; and TJ to George Washington, 18 Feb. 1793, and note.

To Edmond Charles Genet

Sir   Philadelphia June 25th. 1793.

In the absence of the President of the united States, I have consulted with the Secretaries of the Treasury and War, on the subject of the Ship William,[1] and generally of vessels suggested to be taken within the limits of the protection of the united States, by the armed vessels of your nation, concerning which I had the honor of a conversation with you yesterday, and we are so well assured of the President's way of thinking in these cases, that we undertake to say it will be more agreeable to him that such vessels should be[2] detained under the orders of yourself or of the Consuls of France in the several ports, until the Government of the united States shall be able to inquire into and decide on the fact. If this arrangement should be agreeable to you, and you will be pleased to give the proper orders to the several Consuls of your nation, the Governors of the several States will be immediately[3] instructed to desire the Consul of the port to detain vessels on whose behalf such suggestion shall be made, until the government shall decide on their case. It may sometimes, perhaps, happen that such vessels are brought into ports where there is no Consul of your nation resident, nor within any convenient distance. In that case the Governors would have to proceed to the act of detention themselves, at least until a consul may be called in. I have the honor to be, with much respect Sir, Your most obedient and most humble servant

                                Th: Jefferson

PrC (DLC); in the hand of George Taylor, Jr., signed by TJ; at foot of text: "The minister plenipoy. from the Republic of France." Dft (DLC); entirely in TJ's hand; only the most important emendations are noted below. PrC of Tr (DLC); in a clerk's hand, with a correction in ink; at foot of text: "Copy." Tr (NNC: Gouverneur Morris Papers). Tr (DNA: RG 46, Senate Records, 3d Cong., 1st sess.). PrC (PRO: FO 97/1). FC (Lb in DNA: RG 59, DL). Tr (DLC: Genet Papers). Tr (same); in French; initialed by Genet. Tr (same); in French; draft translation of preceding Tr; docketed by Genet. Tr (AMAE: CPEU, xxxvII); in French. Recorded in SJPL. Printed in *Message*, 43. Enclosed in Memorandum to George Washington, [11-13 July 1793], Tobias Lear to TJ, 15 July 1793, and TJ to Gouverneur Morris, 16 Aug. 1793; draft enclosed in TJ to Alexander Hamilton and Henry Knox, 25 June 1793.

[1] Here in Dft TJ canceled "of" and wrote the ensuing passage "and generally . . . concerning" in the margin.

[2] In Dft TJ here canceled "held in the."

[3] In Dft TJ here canceled "desired to."

From Edmond Charles Genet

Philadelphia le 25 Janvier [Juin] 1793.

MONSIEUR

L'an 2e. de la Republique fse.

J'apprends avec infinement de plaisir par votre lettre du 23 de ce mois[1] que le Gouvernement[2] de la Georgie à fait arreter un Corsaire armé dans cet etat pour croiser contre les francais et que les armateurs de ce batiment seront poursuivis. Il est a souhaiter, Monsieur, que la même surveillance et la même fermete soient déployées dans tous les Etats de l'union,[3] car vous verres par les rapports ci Joints des Consuls de la Republique à Charleston, a Baltimore,[4] à Philadelphie et a New York que beaucoup de batimens ennemis s'y sont armes, y sont entrés, armés y sont restés et en sont sortis armes[5] au mepris de nos traités tandis que l'on poursuivait avec acharnement[6] en vertu des instructions de Mr. Le President des Etats unis tous les armateurs[7] francais[8] qui ont cru pouvoir se mettre en état de deffense[9] dans les ports de leurs alliés[10] pour en sortir sans danger[11] et remplir d'ailleurs selon les circonstances, leur devoir de Citoyen contre les ennemis de l'etat. Agreés Monsieur mon estime et mon respect.   GENET

PrC of Tr (DLC); misdated; in a clerk's hand; at head of text: "Le Citoyen Genet Ministre plenipotentiaire de la Republique française a Mr. Jefferson Secretaire d'Etat des Etats Unis." Dft (DLC: Genet Papers); at head of text: "Remerciements du Cit genet à Mr. Jefferson et informations relatives à d'autres armements faits par les Anglois"; lacks complimentary close; with variations and emendations, only the most important of which are noted below. Tr (AMAE: CPEU, XXXVII); with variations. Tr (NNC: Gouverneur Morris Papers); misdated 25 Jan. 1793, with corrective note by George Taylor, Jr. PrC of another Tr (PRO: FO 97/1); in Taylor's hand; misdated 25 Jan. 1793. FC (DLC: Genet Papers); in English. FC (same); in English. Tr (DNA: RG 46, Senate Records, 3d Cong., 1st sess.); in English; misdated 25 Jan. 1793, with corrective note by TJ. Recorded in SJL as a letter of 25 June 1793 received 26 June 1793. Printed with translation in *Message*, 18 (App.), 40; translation printed in ASP, *Foreign Relations*, I, 159. Enclosed in Memorandum to George Washington, [11-13 July 1793], Tobias Lear to TJ, 15 July 1793, and TJ to Gouverneur Morris, 16 Aug. 1793.

[1] Sentence to this point interlined in Dft in place of "Je suis on ne peut pas plus sensible à l'avis que vous m'avés donné."

[2] AMAE Tr: "Gouverneur."

[3] AMAE Tr: "de l'amérique."

[4] Preceding two words written in the margin of Dft, but omitted in AMAE Tr.

[5] Dft and AMAE Tr: "s'y sont armés y sont entrés armés et y ont resté armés." *Message*: "s'y sont armés, y sont entre armés, y sont restés, et en sont sortis armés."

[6] In Dft Genet here canceled "dans les mêmes ports."

[7] Word interlined in Dft in place of "batimens."

[8] Sentence from this point to "alliés" written in the margin of Dft in place of a heavily emended passage that in its final state appears to read "qui se sont mis en état de se défendre et de sortir sans danger et que armés quoi."

[9] Preceding nine words interlined in Dft in place of "qui s'y sont armés ⟨quoique les traités les y auto⟩ en guerre."

[10] In Dft Genet here canceled "et pour se proteger [. . .]."

[11] Preceding five words not in Dft.

E N C L O S U R E

Extracts from French Consular Reports, with Genet's Observations

Philadelphie le 25 Juin 1793. L'an 2e. de la République française.
Extraits des rapports des Consuls et Vice Consuls de la Republique française
a Charleston, a Baltimore a Philadelphie et a New York au Citoyen Genet.

Charleston du 24. Mai au 6. Juin.

Un batiment Bermudien a achete 4 Canons dans ce port pour proteger son retour.

Un batiment Hollandais entré dans ce port sans Canons en est sorti avec 14. Des batimens anglais s'y sont également armés.[1]

Baltimore du 21. Juin.

Un batiment anglais nommé le Trusty Capitaine Hale a été publiquement armé en Course[2] dans ce port par le Sr. Hirland de cette ville. Le vice Consul en a porté plainte aux Gouverneur et au procureur generaux de l'Etat de Maryland.

Philadelphia le 21. Juin 1793.

Il est sorti de ce port le 20.[3] un batiment Bermudien appartenant a des sujets du roi d'angleterre, lequel etait monté de 12. Canons[4] achetés en cette ville. Il etait sorti quelques Jours avant un batiment anglais armé de 4 Canons. Le Consul n'en a été informe qu'a la datte de son rapport.

New York le 18. Juin.

La lettre de marque anglaise le Swallow commandée par le Capitaine Lion armée de 8. Canons montée de 20 hommes au moins et paroissant du port de 150. tonneaux est mouillée dans ce port depuis un espace de tems qui ne permet pas de croire que ce batiment y ait été Jetté[5] en détresse quoique l'art. 1[7].[6] du traité de commerce entre la france et l'amerique, exclue formellement des ports de l'une et de l'autre les batimens ennemis qui auraient fait des prises et que tous corsaire anglais qui entre etant autorisé par le Gouvernement anglais[7] a prendre, bruler et detruire nos batimens: Il reste toujours indécis si tel batiment armé de cette nation qui entre a éxécuté ou non de pareils ordres. Le Consul Hauterive a porté ces observations au Gouverneur de l'etat de New York et lui a fait sentir que tout vaisseau armé en guerre et appartenant à nos ennemis etant sujet à l'exclusion portée par nos loix conventionelles devait etre obligé de sortir du port de New York.

Il est parvenu à la Connoissance du Citoyen Genet, par des voïes indirectes d'autres rapports; qu'il s'est fait par les ennemis de la République française plusieurs[8] autres armemens dans les ports Americains et que ces vaisseaux[9] on pris à leur bord sans aucune opposition un grand nombre de Torys sujets des Etats unis, tandis que quelques bons whigs amis de la france qui on pris parti pour elle sur ses vaisseaux ont été saisis et[10] Jettés dans des cachots d'ou le Citoyen n'a encore pu les arracher que sous caution.

PrC of Tr (DLC); in a clerk's hand; at foot of text: "Certifié conforme aux rapports que m'ont été faits. Le ministre plénipotentiaire de la République Française." Dft (DLC: Genet Papers); undated; only the most important emendations have been noted below. Tr (AMAE: CPEU, xxxvii); with variations. Tr (NNC: Gouverneur Morris Papers). PrC of another Tr (PRO: FO 97/1); in the hand of George Taylor, Jr.

FC (DLC: Genet Papers); in English. FC (same); in English. Tr (DNA: RG 46, Senate Records, 3d Cong., 1st sess.); in English; with corrections by TJ. Printed with translation in *Message*, 18 (App.), 40-1; translation printed in ASP, *Foreign Relations*, I, 159. Enclosed in TJ to Gouverneur Morris, 16 Aug. 1793.

[1] Dft: "Un vaisseau hollandais et plusieurs Anglois se sont également armés." AMAE Tr follows Dft, substituting "s'y sont" for "se sont." In Dft Genet here canceled "Le Consul s'en est plaint."

[2] Preceding two words interlined in Dft.
[3] Supplied from Dft. PrC of Tr: "2e." *Message*: "2."
[4] In Dft Genet here canceled "Il n'en avoit que quatre lorsqu'."
[5] *Message*: "amené."
[6] Supplied from Dft.
[7] AMAE Tr: "de son Pays."
[8] Word interlined in Dft in place of "un grand nombre d'."
[9] Preceding two words altered in Dft from "les vaisseaux anglois."
[10] Preceding two words interlined in Dft.

To Alexander Hamilton and Henry Knox, with their Replies

June. 25. 1793.

Th: Jefferson has the honor to submit to the correction and approbation of the Secretaries of the Treasury and War, the inclosed draughts of letters to the French minister on the subject of the ship William and others in her situation, and to Mr. Hammond and Mr. Pinckney on the subject of the Snow Suckey.

[*Replies by Alexander Hamilton and Henry Knox:*]

The letters to Mr. Hammond and Mr. Pinckney appear to me proper, according to the facts stated in them.

The object of that to Mr. Genet also appears to me desireable; but I am not wholly without scruple as to the proposition going from the UStates.   A HAMILTON

Approved H KNOX

RC (DLC); addressed: "The Secretaries of the Treasury & War"; with replies by Hamilton and Knox at foot of text. PrC (DLC); lacks replies. Tr (DLC); 19th-century copy; lacks replies. Recorded in SJPL.

Enclosures: (1) Draft of TJ to Edmond Charles Genet, 25 June 1793. (2) Draft of TJ to George Hammond, 26 June 1793. (3) Draft of TJ to Thomas Pinckney, 26 June 1793.

To George Hammond

SIR   Philadelphia June 25th. 1793.

In a letter of Feb. 2d. 1792. I had the honor of conveying to you[1] the President's sentiments on the assurances you had then been pleased to give of the strict neutrality of your Government between us and the Indians in our neighborhood. You do[2] to that testimony but the Justice[3]

which it merits, in not allowing yourself, for a moment, to infer from the passage, in my letter of the 19th. instant, quoted in your's of the 20th., a meaning which would be disrespectful to your nation.—Were the Western posts in our possession, it cannot be doubted but there would be an end to the murders daily committed by the Indians[4] on our North Western frontier, and to a great part of the expense of our armaments in that Quarter. Those inconveniencies, therefore, are connected, as consequences, with the Detension of our Posts; to convey which Idea alone, was the intention of the expressions to which you refer.[5] I have the honor to be, respectfully, Sir, Your most obedient and most humble Servant   TH: JEFFERSON

PrC (DLC); in the hand of George Taylor, Jr., signed by TJ; at foot of text: "The minister Plenipotentiary of Great Britain." Dft (DLC: TJ Papers, 89: 15419); in TJ's hand, with note in margin by Alexander Hamilton (see note 5 below); undated and unaddressed. FC (Lb in DNA: RG 59, DL). Tr (Lb in PRO: FO 116/3). Tr (same. 5/1). Enclosed in second Memorandum to George Washington, [11 July 1793], and Tobias Lear to TJ, 15 July 1793.

[1] In Dft TJ here canceled "assurances."
[2] Word interlined in Dft in place of "pay."
[3] Word interlined in Dft in place of "respect."

[4] Preceding three words interlined in Dft.
[5] Preceding sentence adopted verbatim by TJ from a marginal note written by Alexander Hamilton in the Dft. There TJ had written: "My expression therefore was scrupulously exact that the detention of those posts is the cause of these murders and expences, and I thank you sincerely for the justice you have done me in not imagining a meaning as foreign from the direct import of the words, as from my mind in using them." Hamilton bracketed this sentence and next to it wrote "Instead of the Passage between [   ]" and the substitute TJ adopted.

To George Hammond

SIR   Philadelphia June 25th. 1793.

I have the honor of your's of the 19th. instant. In mine of the same date, I had that of stating to you the matter of fact of the President's requisition to the privateers in question. The development of it's terms, and the inferences from them[1] will, it is conceived, be most properly referred to the occasion which shall call for them. Such occasion may never happen; but, if it does, the[2] disposition which has been manifested, is a security that, that will be done, which shall be right. I have the honor to be, respectfully, Sir, Your most obedient and most humble servant,   TH: JEFFERSON

PrC (DLC); in the hand of George Taylor, Jr., signed by TJ; at foot of text: "The minister Plenipotentiary of Great Britain." Dft (DLC: TJ Papers, 89: 15418); in TJ's hand, with notations in margin by Alexander Hamilton (see notes below); undated and unaddressed. FC (Lb in DNA: RG 59, DL). Tr (Lb in PRO: FO 116/3). Tr (same,

5/1). Enclosed in second Memorandum to George Washington, [11 July 1793], and Tobias Lear to TJ, 15 July 1793.

¹ In Dft TJ here wrote "are open to all, or may be left." Alexander Hamilton

bracketed this passage and wrote the next eight words opposite it in the margin.

² In Dft TJ here wrote "President's justice." Alexander Hamilton bracketed these words and wrote the next five words opposite them in the margin.

To Zebulon Hollingsworth

SIR   Philadelphia June 25. 1793.

The Secretary at war has delivered me your letter of the 20th. inst. to him, which concerning the civil (not military) proceedings against Hooper it becomes my duty to answer. It is the President's desire that in the arrest and other proceedings all the respect may be shewn to the French nation which may not be inconsistent with the security of the criminal, and the substantial prosecution of him. But the prosecution is to be effectually taken care of, and the party brought to the punishment which the laws of his country may have prescribed. The issue will shew whether these have left unprovided for so great a case as that of an individual undertaking to dispose of the lives and fortunes of his fellow citizens, by committing them to war. It is unnecessary for me to observe to you, Sir, that in this country the person and dwelling of a public minister, are alone exempted from arrest, and that the pretence is without foundation which would extend that exemption to a foreign officer or foreign vessel. I have the honor to be with great respect Sir Your most obedt. humble servt   TH: JEFFERSON

PrC (DLC); at foot of text: "Mr. Zebulon Hollingsworth. Baltimore." Tr (DLC); 19th-century copy.

Zebulon Hollingsworth (1762-1824) was the United States district attorney for Maryland. In 1806 he became associate judge of Maryland's sixth district court, which embraced Baltimore and Harford counties (JEP, I, 125, 126; Joseph A. Stewart, *Descendants of Valentine Hollingsworth*,

Sr. [Louisville, 1925], 27-8; Edward C. Papenfuse and others, *A Biographical Dictionary of the Maryland Legislature, 1635-1789*, 2 vols. [Baltimore, 1979-85], I, 448; Carl N. Everstine, *The General Assembly of Maryland 1776-1850* [Charlottesville, 1982], 275-6, 366-7).

Hollingsworth's LETTER OF THE 20TH. to Henry Knox has not been found. For the case of Captain John HOOPER, see William Vans Murray to TJ, 9 May 1793.

From Gouverneur Morris

DEAR SIR   Sainport 25 June 1793

This will I expect accompany my last No. 32 of the twelfth Instant no Opportunity having offered since it was written. I do myself the Honor to enclose herein the Copy of what I wrote on the nineteenth Instant to

Monsieur Le Brun respecting an atrocious Violation of our Flag and respecting a very extraordinary Step taken by the Convention in the repeal on Motion of a Member, of the Decree by which our Ships were exempted from the Seizure to which those of others were expos'd. I was inform'd that the Object of the Decree I complain of was to effect the Confiscation of a large Cargo belonging to Citizens of the State of South Carolina, and which has been sometime since acquitted at Havre, but an Appeal made from the Decision of the Court, tho' grounded on the clearest Principles. The Captors then declar'd that they would obtain a Decree for the Confiscation by Means of their Friends in the Convention, and Sometime afterwards that of the ninth of May appear'd, in which a retrospective Clause cover'd precisely the Object they had in View. Such a Coincidence of Circumstances was somewhat remarkable however I made no Allusion to it in my first Application which (as you will have seen) produc'd the desir'd Effect, being the Decree of the twenty third of May. The interested Parties as soon as this Decree was pass'd went to work (as I was afterwards inform'd) and by Force of Money (as my Informant says) procur'd the Decree of the twenty eighth. Certain it is that the former was not sent on to be enregister'd untill after the latter had pass'd, and then both were immediately forwarded together. It did not become me to give Ear to calumnious Suggestions, nor yet could I be totally deaf to a Matter of such general Importance to the United States. You will perceive in the Close of my Letter to Mr. Lebrun some general Observation which may render the corrupted Members (if such there be) a little more cautious. I shall also enclose herewith a Copy of Mr. Lebrun's Answer of the twenty first Instant to mine of the nineteenth. I had directed Mr. Coffyn the Agent at Dunkerque to cause a Prosecution to be commenced against the Murderer of our Fellow Citizen.

In a Letter written long since I mention'd to you[1] Sir that I was in Quest of Monsieur Merlino. I have since found him and convers'd with him. He is immensely rich but seems to have been the Father of his own Fortune, amass'd (as Fortunes frequently are) without rendering the Possessor respectable. If I can judge from his Countenance, the Enquiry was set on Foot in the Hope of negative Answers, and the Affirmative is of Course not pleasing. Certain it is that he shew'd no Inclination to spare to the Necessities of his Nephews a Part of his own Abundance, but this is the less reprehensible in that he treats himself no better than his needy Relatives.

Your Favor of the twentieth of April reach'd me two Days ago and now I have those of the eighth of that Month and[2] twelfth and fifteenth of March. To the Contents of the last mention'd Letter I shall pay all due Attention whenever Opportunities can be found or made for the

Purpose.[3] I am happy to find by what you say in the Begining of
yours of the twelfth of March, that your Sentiments accord so entirely
with those which I had the Honor to express in mine of the twenty
second of August, and that the Conduct which I had thought it proper
to pursue is thereby justified. My Correspondence with Mr. Short will
have shewn you Sir that I have been very far from questioning the Principles which you state; And I perfectly agree that there is little Difficulty
or Embarrassment in the application of clear Principles, when the Facts
are clear. But while Events are doubtful the Feebleness of human Fore-
sight may I hope be pardon'd for Hesitating where Things of vast Moment depend on Steps to be immediately taken. A Man of no little Eminence in the late Revolutions and who has since left France urg'd me
much to go away, shortly after the tenth of August. As I had not (and
have not) any Reason to question, either on my own Account or on that
of my Country, the Sincerity of his advice I could only examine the
Ground of his Judgment, which has always been esteemed a good one.
We differed in Opinion but this Sentiment he express'd strongly. "In
your Case, said he, I would go to England or Holland and from thence
state the existing Facts, and ask my Court to decide at once on my Conduct, without waiting for future Events." As it was clear from hence
that his Reflections turn'd principally on my personal Situation, I told
him that my Conduct would be influenced by Considerations totally
different, and therefore conceiving it most conducive to the Interests of
the United States I should stay.

In the present Moment you will observe, Sir, by the public Papers,
that a Majority of the Departments declare themselves against the Authority of the present Convention, after the Arrestment of their Fellow
Members, just as in the Month of June last a similar Majority declar'd
their Execration of the Attempts on Louis the sixteenth; but who will
venture to tell us what August is to produce? No small Part of France
is in open War with the Rest, and wherever the Insurgents arrive it
appears that the whole Country is friendly to them; so that if[4] one were
to Judge by what passes in that quarter, France would be nearly unanimous in the ReEstablishment of Royalty should they come on in Force
to Paris. Then the establish'd Principle of Administration would undoubtedly be, that all which has been done within the last Year was an
abominable Usurpation &ca. &ca.; And without questioning our Principles of Government, they might dissent from the Application of them
by a subtle Distinction between the Voice of a Nation and what would
then be call'd the Voice of a Faction. Under Circumstances of this Sort
I am particularly happy to have receiv'd your Orders, which I shall
implicitly obey. Accept I pray you my sincere Thanks for having given
them so opportunely.

I will apply to the Minister for the orders you wish respecting Payments to our Citizens, and make no Doubt that they will be transmitted. And indeed I should suppose that if, without such orders, the Payments were made by the Treasury of the United States, the Government of this Country (let whatever Government may be established) would allow the Justice of a Deduction to the Amount from what we owe. It is possible that we may hereafter have occasion to insist on that Principle, among other Reasons, because of the Plundering of our Ships, of which Complaints are daily made to me, and which the present⁵ Government of this Country is too feeble to prevent. Doubtless there are many Things of the Sort which do not come to my Knowlege, for in some Cases the Masters and Crews being taken out of the American Ships and put on Board of the Privateers, are carried very far from where their Vessels arrive, and put on Shore where Chance directs or Circumstances permit, and as many of the Privateers are taken by British Cruizers, some of Our Citizens may find their way to England, and some to the British Colonies and foreign Possessions.

I am very happy to find that it has been in the Will and in the Power of the United States to make Advances for the Colony of St. Domingo, and also to send Supplies of Bread to this Country. On the twenty seventh of September, I mention'd to you the Plan of Speculation on Drafts to have been made on the United States could my Concurrence have been procur'd. Events have shewn that this Speculation would have been a good one to the Parties who would have gain'd (and the french Nation of Course have lost) about fifty thousand Pounds Sterling in less than Eighty thousand. I was inform'd at that Time that the disappointed Parties would attempt to have me recall'd, and some more tractable Character sent, who would have the Good Sense to take Care of his own Interest. Well Sir nine Months have elapsed, and now if I were capable of such Things I think it would be no difficult Matter to have some of them hang'd: indeed it is highly probable that they will experience a Fate of that Sort. It is a Year ago, that a Person who mix'd in Tumults to see what was doing told me of a Sans Culotte who belowing against poor Monsieur de la fayette, when Petion appeard chang'd at once his Note to Vive Petion, and then turning round to one of his scurvy Companions "Vois tu! C'est notre Ami n'est ce pas? Eh bien il passera comme les autres." And lo! the Prophecy is fulfill'd: and I this Instant learn that Petion, confin'd to his Room, as a Traitor or Conspirator, has fled on the twenty fourth of June 1793 from those whom he sent on the twentieth of June 1792 to assault the King in the Tuileries. In short you will find in the List of those who were ordered by their Brethren to be arrested, the Names of those who have proclaim'd themselves to be the prime Movers of the Revolution of the tenth of August, and Fathers of the Republic.

I am hurt and vexed at the Delay of my Letters. By what you say of the advices you had receiv'd on the eighth of April mine down to the thirteenth of February ought to have reach'd you by that Time, and indeed notwithstanding the Length of Winter Passages there was Room enough for their Arrival. But the Mischeif arises from the Ports where Vessels are put up as to Sail on one Day named, and some four or five Weeks after we learn that they are still detain'd. I have not yet receivd the Plans of the fœderal Town which you was so kind as to send, which I am sorry for because if there is any Part markd out for Sale in Europe I think in the present critical Moment Purchasers would be found. By the Bye I think a Plan might be formd for Purchasing Land and Building Houses there by Way of Actions, but I shall not dwell thereon at present and will write more fully about it when I receive the Plans and Letter accompanying them.

By the first very good Conveyance which may offer I will send out the Dies you order, at present I have none such, and only Time to write by the Person who takes this with him and who is to sail from Havre for New York. I would rather give them in Charge to some one who is himself going over, for great Neglects happen in the Ports as I know by frequent Experience.

Mr. Pinkney has doubtless inform'd you long since that Mr. Droz declin'd going out to America. There was some Misunderstanding on the Subject between him and Mr. Short, which he entered into a long History of and desir'd me to communicate it to you for whom he exprest the utmost Deference and Respect. As I found it impossible to get him into the Service of the United States which was the main Object, I thought it unnecessary to trouble you with a long Chapter of little Sorenesses, which were I could clearly see the Effect of prudential Caution in Mr. Short on the irritable Delicacy of the Artist. I am sorry however for the Thing, because the Conversation I had with him and the Enquiries I made lead me to beleive that he would have been a very faithful able and useful officer.

The Assurances you give in your Letter of the twentieth of April that our fellow Citizens are dispos'd to preserve an exact Neutrality gives me sincere Pleasure, as you will find from what I took the Liberty to say on that Subject in former Letters. I fear that the frequent Violations of our Neutrality by the Privateers fitted out in the french Ports may provoke a Change of Sentiment. I labor incessantly to keep Things quiet in that Regard, and I think it likely that some of my Countrymen may think me too much attach'd to France, because I do not enter into the Violence of their Resentments for which there is (as you will see) more Ground than I chuse to acknowlege to them. How long the War may last I know not, but this I know that it is very much our Interest not to be drawn into it. The new Constitution, upon which at present I shall make no Remarks but send you a Copy, may if adopted with Enthusiasm be the Means of lengthening out the Struggle, in which Case France (or rather the ruling Party in France) might triumph over all opposition. Otherwise it would seem (humanly speaking) that if there be a perfect Accord between the different Powers without, and the Royalists within, this Campaign must put an End to the whole Affair. Yet who can answer for the Contingencies of War and the Fluctuations of opinion? With perfect Esteem & Respect I am Sir your obedient Servant   GOUV MORRIS

RC (DNA: RG 59, DD); at head of text: "No: 33"; at foot of first page: "Thomas Jefferson Esqr. Secretary of State"; endorsed by TJ as received 30 Nov. 1793 and so recorded in SJL; with penciled comments by TJ (see notes 1 and 3 below) and passages later marked in pencil, possibly by Edmund Randolph, for omission in Tr submitted to Senate. FC (Lb in DLC: Gouverneur Morris Papers). Tr (Lb in DNA: RG 59, DD). Tr (DNA: RG 46, Senate Records, 3d Cong., 1st sess.); copy made by State Department early in 1794, with blanks left for omissions. PrC (DNA: RG 59, MD); more complete text containing two pages not corresponding to Tr. Enclosures: (1) Morris to Lebrun, 19 June 1793, complaining about the 6 June 1793 capture near Dunkirk by the privateer *Vrai Patriote* and the *Argus*, a lugger belonging to the French Republic, of the American vessel *Little Cherub*, bound from Le Havre (where it had dropped off thirty French passengers driven off by the Spanish government) to Hamburg with a passport from the Provisional Executive Council; protesting the harsh treatment meted out to the captain and crew, who offered no resistance, and the unprovoked murder of its mate, whose brains were blown out by one of the French captors; requesting an inquiry into the affair and, if true, punishment of the murderer by death; and protesting the provisional repeal by the National Convention on 28 May 1793 of the 23 May exemption of American shipping from its 9 May decree, thus reviving a situation contrary to the treaty of commerce with France that must be settled definitively, not only because the fate of a very rich cargo depends upon it, but also to prevent similar instances of the corruption of the public interest by private cupidity. (2) Lebrun to Morris, 21 June 1793, enclosing his report to the Committee of Public Safety, which also reflects the views of the Provisional Executive Council; declaring that the afflicting outrage aboard the *Little Cherub*, if true, would not pass with impunity; and assuring that the Republic would act to prevent violations of the neutrality of its friends and allies. (3) Lebrun's Report to the Committee of Public Safety, n.d., urging that the murder of the mate of the *Little Cherub*, if true, be severely punished for the interest, honor, and justice of the French Republic, and that its captain be fully indemnified for this injury as well as for the delay he has suffered; insisting on a prompt decision on Morris's complaints because, apart from the fraternal connections between the two countries, the United States is more and more the granary of France and its colonies and has courageously recognized the republic formally despite the menaces of Great Britain; and arguing that American ships should enjoy in full the neutral rights guaranteed them by Article 16 of the 1778 treaty of commerce, as long as that neutrality assures supplies for the French Republic and its colonies (Trs in DNA: RG 59, DD, in French and English; Trs in Lb in same, in French and English; Trs in DNA: RG 46, Senate Records, 3d Cong., 1st sess., in French, with English translations in the hand of George Taylor, Jr.; PrCs in DNA: RG 59, MD; English texts printed in ASP, *Foreign Relations*, I, 367-8). (4) *Acte constitutionnel, précédé de la Déclaration des droits de l'homme et du cito-*

yen. Présenté au peuple français par la Convention nationale, le 24 Juin 1793, l'an deuxième de la république (Paris, 1793). Enclosed in TJ to George Washington, 30 Nov. 1793.

For the DECREE BY WHICH OUR SHIPS WERE EXEMPTED, as well as the related decrees mentioned by Morris, see notes to Morris to TJ, 20 May, 1 June 1793. LETTER WRITTEN LONG SINCE: see Morris to TJ, 21 Dec. 1792. A MAN OF NO LITTLE EMINENCE: Jean Antoine Louis LeBègue de Presle, Chevalier Duportail, a veteran of the Continental Army who served as French Minister of War, 1790-91, and fled France shortly after the overthrow of the monarchy in August 1792, ultimately settling on a farm in the United States (Scott and Rot-

haus, *Historical Dictionary*, I, 340-1; Morris, *Diary*, II, 491). Jerome PETION de Villeneuve, a former Jacobin who was mayor of Paris at the time of the storming of the Tuileries in June 1792, had recently fled Paris to escape a Jacobin proscription based upon his alleged involvement in General Dumouriez's defection to the Austrians (Scott and Rothaus, *Historical Dictionary*, II, 758-9).

[1] Above the rest of this sentence, TJ penciled "Query Who is Mr. Merlino?"
[2] Preceding five words interlined.
[3] At this point TJ interlined in pencil "to wit, relative to La Fayette."
[4] Above these three words an unidentified hand penciled "Quære."
[5] Word interlined.

From Jedidiah Morse

Charlestown, 25 June 1793. In conformity to the copyright law, he encloses for deposit in the office of the Secretary of State a copy of *The American Universal Geography*, of which he is author and proprietor.

RC (DNA: RG 59, MLR); 1 p.; addressed: "Thomas Jefferson Esqr. Secretary of State Philadelphia"; endorsed by George Taylor, Jr., as received 1 July 1793.

Jedidiah Morse (1761-1826), a Yale graduate who served as Congregational minister at Charlestown, Massachusetts,

1789-1819, was a staunch conservative in religion and politics and a prolific author whose popular works on geography were the first on that subject published in America. TJ acquired a later edition of the enclosed work, which first appeared in 1789 as *The American Geography* (DAB; Sowerby, No. 3963).

Memorial from Nicholas Cruger and Others

To Thomas Jefferson Esquire Secretary for the Department of Foreign Affairs for the United States

The Memorial of Nicholas Cruger of the City of New York Merchant, Andrew Burke of same place Mariner And Jacob & Philip Mark, John Alsop, Thomas Randall, Paschal N. Smith, William Laight, Richard Yates & George Pollock, Daniel Cotton, William Minturn, Minturn & Champlin, James Scott & Co., Gulian Verplanck, George Ludlow, Samuel Ward & Brothers, John P. Mumford & Co.,

Gouverneur & Kemble, John McVickar, Shedden Patrick & Co., James Cockroft, John DeWint, Carlile Pollock, Charles Smith & Co., Robert Dale, Daniel Ludlow & Co., Le Roy & Bayard, Henry Sadler and Theophylact Bache & Charles Mc.Evers Junr. all of the said City of New York Merchants.

Sheweth

THAT your Memorialists Nicholas Cruger and Andrew Burke are the Owners of a certain Schooner or Vessel called the YORK which Vessel sailed from this Port of New York on the 27th. day of the month of November last past (being then armed with eleven Blunderbusses, Six Muskets, twelve Cutlasses and four Pistols for a Defence against the Spaniards if they should find it necessary and commanded by the said Andrew Burke) having on board sundry Merchandizes and One thousand Weight of Gunpowder bound upon a Voyage to the Islands of St. Thomas and Curracoa, there to ship an additional number of Men compleat their Cargo and from thence to proceed on a trading Voyage to the Coast of Campeachy on the Spanish Main in the Bay of Mexico.

That the said Vessel sailed on the said 27th: day of November on her said Voyage and arrived at St. Thomas's the twelfth day of December following where they shipped one Man and sailed again the seventeenth day of said Month for Curracoa where they arrived the twenty first day of same month and having shipped eight hands including Domingo Campo his Spanish Trader and sundry Articles of Merchandize he left the said Island of Curracoa and arrived on the Coast of Campeachy on the 14th. day of the Month of January following.

That Your Memorialist Andrew Burke found it impossible to trade on the Coast of Campeachy at that Period, the Country being in very great Confusion and disorder, owing as he understood to the Governor of that Place having been assassinated. That the said Schooner York having suffered much by bad weather on the Voyage proved leaky and was also very short of Water and Provisions which rendered it absolutely necessary for the preservation of the Lives of Your Memorialist Andrew Burke and his Crew and the benefit of all concerned in the said Vessel and her Cargo that they should go to some Port immediately to get the necessary Supplies and Repairs.

That your Memorialist Andrew Burke from thence sailed first for the Island of Mohairs in hopes of procuring Water which they stood most in need of, but after two days ineffectual search at the said last Island, he left it with the said Vessel intending then to make the best of his Way for the Island of St. Domingo. That on the twenty first day of said last month being off Savannah La Mar in the Island of Jamaica and having only one Gallon of Water on board that was drinkable, Your Memorialist Andrew Burke put into that Port to get a Supply. That the Govern-

ment of that Island not permitting American Vessels to stay there he
was only allowed to remain till next morning during which time he
supplied himself with some water and making his Protest sailed from
thence at the appointed hour and proceeded for Port au Prince confiding in the Treaties subsisting between France and the United States of
America and not doubting that he should there meet with every Assistance and be allowed to make the necessary Repairs and procure the
Supplies he wanted for the said Vessel.

That Your Memorialist Andrew Burke arrived at Port au Prince on
the third day of February following and immediately brought the said
Schooner too under the Guns of the Fort and along side of a Vessel of
War belonging to the French Republic and he went directly on board
the said Vessel with all his Papers consisting of his Register, Invoices of
his Cargo, Protest made at Jamaica &ca. intending to state the Condition of the said Schooner York and to demand Permission to get the
necessary Supplies. That there was not any person on board the said
Vessel who understood English and therefore he returned to the said
Schooner York on board of which he found some Custom House Officers to whom he reported his Cargo and his Reasons for putting into
that Port.

That the said Officers seized the said Vessel in Defiance of the Treaties existing between that Government and the United States and notwithstanding his fair and open Conduct and the Distress they were in
upon a pretence that the Powder and Arms she had on board might be
intended for the use of the Negroes who had revolted.

That your Memorialist Andrew Burke made use of every Exertion in
his Power to procure the Release of the said Schooner York and her
Cargo And the Court of Admiralty at Port au Prince (after hearing his
Reasons, inspecting his Papers which he delivered to them for that Purpose and causing the said Vessel and her Stores to be examined) adjudged that the said Schooner York and her Cargo should be released
from the Seizure but at the same time Your Memorialist was not suffered to depart nor even to take charge of his Vessel and he was obliged
to pay all Costs and Expences. And Afterwards another Suit was instituted against him and he was compelled to wait a Decision from the
Government Council which Decision reversed the Sentence of the
Court of Admiralty and the said Schooner York and her Cargo were
finally condemned And Your Memorialist Andrew Burke was also sen-
tenced to pay a fine of One thousand Livres or suffer Imprisonment
which Judgement was given altogether on Suspicion and without Your
Memorialist having been guilty of any one Act to authorize such a Suspicion. That he applied to have this cruel and unjust Sentence set aside
but without Effect and he was forced to pay the Fine. That he also

requested to have his Papers returned to him particularly his Protest made at Jamaica which was likewise refused when finding he could not obtain any Satisfaction or Redress he left that Place.

That your Memorialists Nicholas Cruger and Andrew Burke in support and confirmation of the truth of the foregoing Relation have transmitted to you the following Vouchers and Documents Vizt.

Bill of Sale (No. 1) Bill of Lading (No. 2) Disbursements at New York (No: 3) Invoice of Cargo at New York (No: 4) Invoice of Cargo at St. Thomas' and Curracoa, Capt. Burks disbursements and Account Current (No. 5, 6, 7, 8, 9) Capt. Burk and his Mates Protest at New York (No. 10) Affidavits Capt. Burk, his Mate and Mr. Westphal to prove the injustice of the Condemnation (No. 11) And also all the original French Documents of the proceedings at Port au Prince as well on the part of Capt. Burk as by the Government there[1]

by which it will appear that Your Memorialists Nicholas Cruger and Andrew Burke have at this present time sustained an actual Loss by the Seizure of the said Vessel and her Cargo to the Amount of Five thousand Six hundred and twenty nine pounds four shillings and six pence or Fourteen thousand and seventy three spanish milled dollars, Six[2] Cents, as appears by General Account No. 12 Also transmitted with the foregoing Papers. That is to say the said Nicholas Cruger the Sum of Three thousand Seven hundred and fifty two pounds, sixteen shillings and four pence and the said Andrew Burke the Sum of One thousand eight hundred and seventy Six pounds eight shillings and two pence exclusive of the Damages suffered by the Detention of their Property which is very considerable particularly to your Memorialist Andrew Burke who is by this means thrown entirely out of Employment with a large Family to maintain.

That your Memorialists Jacob & Philip Mark, John Alsop, Thomas Randall, Paschal N. Smith, William Laight, Richard Yates & George Pollock, Daniel Cotton, William Minturn, Minturn & Champlin, James Scott & Co., Gulian Verplanck, George Ludlow, Samuel Ward & Brothers, John P. Mumford & Co., Gouverneur & Kemble, John McVickar, Shedden Patrick & Co., James Cockcroft, John DeWint, Carlile Pollock, Charles Smith & Co., Robert Dale, Daniel Ludlow & Co., Le Roy & Bayard, Henry Sadler and Theophylact Bache & Charles McEvers Junr. are Underwriters on the said Schooner York and her Cargo to the Amount of Three thousand five hundred pounds as will appear by authenticated Copies of the Policies also transmitted to you marked with the Letters A and B—whereby they may ultimately be obliged to pay the said Sum of Three thousand five hundred pounds to the said Nicholas Cruger provided due restitution is not made by the Government of the French Republic to the said Nicholas Cruger and

Andrew Burke for the Seizure and Condemnation of the said Vessel and her Cargo.

Your Memorialists beg leave further to represent that this Seizure and Condemnation appear to them contrary to every principle of Justice and Equity violating the nineteenth Article of the Treaty of Amity and Commerce entered into between the United States of America and his Most Christian Majesty and Destroying the Friendship and Confidence that has so happily subsisted hitherto between the Citizens of the two Republics. That it is evident from the Proofs transmitted to you that the said Cargo was bought for and intended to be disposed of on the Coast of Campeachy And that the said Andrew Burke was reduced to the necessity of putting into Port au Prince to procure Water and Provisions and repair the said Vessel; That there is not the smallest Spark of Evidence adduced to shew that the said Andrew Burke made any Attempt to dispose of his Powder and Arms or any other Part of his Cargo at the said last Port On the contrary from the small Quantity he had on board and his bringing the said Schooner too under the Guns of the Fort and along side of the Ship of War it is strongly to be presumed he could not possibly have any View or Intention of the Kind imputed to him.

That your Memorialists are willing to believe that this unjust Seizure and Condemnation arose from the general Confusion which prevailed at that Period in the Government at Port au Prince owing to the Insurrection of the Negroes and to the differences subsisting amongst the People on political Subjects As also to the said Andrew Burke and his Interpreter not sufficiently comprehending each other and that upon a fuller Investigation of the Merits of this Cause Your Memorialists will receive ample Satisfaction.

And therefore upon all these Considerations and a full Confidence in the propriety and justness of their demand Your Memorialists pray that you will be pleased to make such Representations or Remonstrances to the Government of the French Republic as shall enable them to obtain their just Rights as Citizens of America and a Restitution of the said Schooner York and her Cargo with all damages and Expences now incurred or which may hereafter be incurred Or some other sufficient Compensation for the Injury done to them as Owners and Underwriters of the said Schooner York and her Cargo by the Seizure and Condemnation of the said Vessel and her Cargo And as in Duty bound they shall ever pray &ca.

New York June 26th. A D 1793

WM LAIGHT	NICH. CRUGER
J MARK & Co.	ANDREW BURKE
THEOPHYLACT BACHE &	DANL LUDLOW & CO
CHARLES MCEVERS JUN	CHARLES SMITH & CO.

R Yates & G. Pollock

John Mc.Vickar

Danl. Cotton

Gouverneur & Kemble

J: P: Mumford & Co

James Cockcroft

John DeWint
  by his atty
Peter C. DeWint

Saml. Ward & Brothers

John Alsop

Sheddin Patrick & Co.

Robert Dale

Henry Sadler

Gulian Verplanck

Thos. Randall

Paschal N. Smith

Carlile Pollock

James Scott

Minturn & Champlin

William Minturn

Le Roy & Bayard

George Ludlow

RC (DNA: RG 123, United States Court of Claims, French Spoliation Case Files, Case No. 3356); in a clerk's hand, signed by those listed above; filed with notarization of 26 June 1793 by John Wilkes of New York City and certification of 29 June 1793 in French by Alexandre Maurice d'Hauterive, the French consul at New York. PrC of Tr (DNA: RG 76, France, Unbound Records); in a clerk's hand. Enclosures not found. Enclosed in TJ to Edmond Charles Genet, 12 July 1793.

Nicholas Cruger (1743-1801), the scion of a New York mercantile family and a close friend of Alexander Hamilton, had been a merchant in New York City since 1785. For twenty years before that Cruger was a merchant in St. Croix, where from about 1768 to 1772 Hamilton served as his clerk (Mitchell, *Hamilton*, I, 21-4).

[1] "And . . . there" interlined.
[2] Remainder of sentence interlined.

From Edmond Charles Genet

Monsieur   a Philadelphie le 26. Juin 1793. l'an 2e. de la Republique

La lettre que vous m'avez fait l'honneur de m'écrire depuis le départ de Mr. le Président des Etats unis renferme des dispositions dignes de votre sagesse et des sentimens qui vous caracterisent. L'arrangement que vous proposez, Monsieur, nous convient à tous égards; je le communiquerai aux Consuls et Vice Consuls de la République, et, en leur recommandant de s'y conformer, je joindrai aux instructions que je leur ai déja données sur le fait des prises de nouvelles regles dont l'éxécution[1] rigide prouvera au gouvernement fédéral que[2] nous regardons comme le premier de nos devoirs[3] de respecter tous les droits de souveraineté[4] des Etats Unis, de ne rien entreprendre qui puisse leur etre désagreable et de reunir tous nos efforts pour perpétuer et resserer de plus en plus les liens qui unissent si heureusement nos deux Républiques.   Genet

PrC of Tr (DLC); in a clerk's hand; at head of text: "Le Citoyen Genet Ministre Plenipotentiaire de la Republique Francaise à Monsieur Jefferson, Secrétaire d'Etat des Etats unis." Dft (DLC: Genet Papers); at

head of text: "Reponse du C. genet à la note de Mr. Jefferson du 25. Juin"; only the most significant emendations have been noted below. Tr (AMAE: CPEU, xxxvii); with minor variations. Tr (NNC: Gouverneur

Morris Papers). PrC of another Tr (PRO: FO 97/1); in the hand of George Taylor, Jr. FC (DLC: Genet Papers); in English. FC (same); in English. FC (same); in English; draft translation of preceding FCs. Tr (DNA: RG 46, Senate Records, 3d Cong., 1st sess.); in English. Recorded in SJL as received 26 June 1793. Printed with translation in *Message*, 19 (App.), 43; translation printed in ASP, *Foreign Relations*, I, 160-1. Enclosed in Memorandum to George Washington, [11-13 July 1793], Tobias Lear to TJ, 15 July 1793, and TJ to Gouverneur Morris, 16 Aug. 1793.

LA LETTRE: TJ to Genet, 25 June 1793. On this day TJ discussed with the French minister aspects of the war he anticipated between the United States and Spain and its British ally. According to Genet's rough notes of their conversation, "Il craint la guerre, la croit inévitable. Il pense que l'amerique n'a que deux moyens d'agir contre nos énnemis c'est de tomber sur leur Commerce et sur la nouvelle orleans et le Canada. La nouvelle Orleans est mieux disposée que le Canada. Dans la première on manque de vivres et d'argent, dans le Canada Il y a plus d'argent. L'éxpédition des americains pendant la guerre n'a manqué que parceque les Americains n'y ont porté comme nous dans la Belgique que du papier. Il pense que les Etats unis ne peuvent point se mêler ostensiblement de l'affaire du Mississipi ayant entamé des négociations avec l'Espagne dont Il faut attendre le résultat. Mais que les Kentukois peuvent toujours aller s'en emparer quitte à le rendre si l'Espagne consent à accorder la navigation. [*In the margin:* et nos freres que deviendroient Ils?] Il convient que cette éxpédition seroit très facile.

"Je l'ai éxcité à faire tout ce qui dépend de lui pour que les Et. U. se mettent au moins en Etat de défense" (MS in NjP: Andre DeCoppet Collection; in Genet's hand; at head of text: "Entretient avec M. Jefferson le 26. Juin"; minimum punctuation supplied).

[1] Preceding three words interlined in Dft in place of "qui prouve."

[2] Word interlined in Dft in place of "si notre devoir nous préscrit."

[3] Remainder through "heureusement nos" written in the margin of Dft in place of "de ne rien négliger pour conserver la bonne harmonie qui regne si heureusement entre nos."

[4] Preceding two words interlined in Dft.

To George Hammond

SIR   Philadelphia June 26. 1793.

The Government here has received complaint that the Snow Suckey, belonging to George Makepeace, a citizen of the United States, with her Cargo, belonging chiefly to Peter Le Maigre, and wholly to citizens of the United States, and not at all of the character of contraband,[1] commanded by Anthony Andaulle a citizen also of the United States, and bound from the Port of Philadelphia to Port au Prince, was, on her way thither, on the 8 of May last, taken by an english Privateer Brig, called the Maria, of Kingston in the Island of Jamaica, commanded by a Captain Mc.Iver, who immediately put the Captain of the said Snow on board a vessel, accidentally met with at sea, in order to deprive her of her proper patron and defender. The persons interested propose immediately to send an Agent, properly authorized, in quest of their Vessel and Cargo. They mean to go in the first place to Jamaica. I have the honor to enclose you copies of their papers establishing the facts, and to ask the aid of your letters, either open or closed, directed to such persons in authority in Jamaica, or elsewhere, as you may think proper, recommending to their patronage, the person and proceedings of the said Agent, so far as shall be just, for the recovery of the property taken. And as doubtless the laws of the place will have provided for the punishment of the offenders, I trust that your Government will make a point of bringing them to justice, if the Case should really prove to be as it is represented, in order to ensure[2] to the commerce and navigation of peaceable Nations that freedom from interruption to which they are entitled.

Your interposition cannot but be the more effectual in the present case, as the principal Owner of the Cargo is a long-established[3] and well-known-merchant of reputation, of this place, and it would be easy for you to Satisfy yourself in the most perfect manner of the property of the Vessel and Cargo.

The distance, and consequent delay, which would attend the sending of this complaint to the Government[4] of England, and the probable escape of the persons and property, if so much time were given for it, has induced me to presume on your concurrence in this more speedy method of pursuit. I have the honor to be, with much respect Sir, Your most obedient and Most humble servant   TH: JEFFERSON

PrC (DNA: RG 76, British Spoliations); in the hand of George Taylor, Jr., signed by TJ; at foot of first page: "The Minister Plenipoy. of Great Britain." Dft (DLC); entirely in TJ's hand, unsigned; only the most significant emendations have been noted below. Tr (DNA: RG 59, Notes to Foreign Missions); in Taylor's hand. PrC (DLC). FC (Lb in DNA: RG 59, DL). Tr (Lb in PRO: FO 116/3). Tr (same, 5/1). Recorded in SJPL. Enclosures: (1) Deposition of Peter Lemaigre, Philadelphia, 20 June 1793, stating that, though a native of France, he came to the United States in 1779, when he settled in Philadelphia as a merchant and swore an oath of allegiance to Pennsylvania, and has ever since considered himself an American citizen and owned vessels under American papers; restating the substance of his petition and memorial to TJ, printed under 21 June 1793, concerning the cargo and capture of the snow *Suckey* on the way to Port-au-Prince by the British privateer *Maria*, but adding that he had been authorized by its owner, George Makepeace, to sell it for £1,000; and declaring that there was no "secret or covert trust" by which the vessel and the said part of the cargo were held for the use of a citizen or subject of the belligerent powers. (2) Deposition of Anthony Andaulle, Philadelphia, 20 June 1793, stating that, though a French

native, he had come to the United States in 1784 and since regarded himself as a citizen of it, taking an oath of allegiance to the United States in 1789; that during these years he had commanded many American merchant vessels and been recognized as a United States citizen by customs officials in Philadelphia and elsewhere; and that having been placed in command of the *Suckey* by Lemaigre he had received on board sundry goods from him and also loaded a cargo belonging solely to himself and not held "in covert or in Trust" for anyone else, especially subjects of a belligerent power; and relating details of the subsequent capture of the *Suckey* by the *Maria* (Trs in DNA: RG 76, British Spoliations, certified by Philadelphia notary public Clement Biddle; Trs in Lb in DNA: RG 59, DL). Letter and enclosures enclosed in TJ to Thomas Pinckney, 26 June 1793; letter enclosed in second Memorandum to George Washington, [11 July 1793], and Tobias Lear to TJ, 15 July 1793. The following documents pertaining to this case were apparently sent to TJ with the above enclosures in Clement Biddle's missing 26 June 1793 letter (see TJ to Biddle, 28 June 1793, and note), but were not submitted to Hammond: (1) George Makepeace to Lemaigre, Boston, 2 Mch. 1793, enclosing his power of attorney authorizing Lemaigre to sell the *Suckey*, and stating that he wished to obtain about £1,000 for the ship and had also ordered his son, who had gone to Port-au-Prince, to sell it (Tr in DNA: RG 76, British Spoliations, with subjoined power of attorney, bearing Biddle's 26 June 1793 certification; Tr in same, Great Britain, Unbound Records). (2) Three bills of lading for the *Suckey*, two for Lemaigre and one for J. B. Drouillard, Philadelphia, 9-10 Apr. 1793 (Trs in British Spoliations; consisting of printed forms with blanks filled in; with Biddle's 26 June 1793 certification on verso of Drouillard's bill). (3) Proof of Citizenship of Anthony Andaulle, 28 Nov. 1789, consisting of certification by Philadelphia alderman Joseph Swift that on this date Andaulle had subscribed before him the oath of allegiance and fidelity to the United States (Tr in same; certified by Biddle on 20 June 1793). (4) Proof of Citizenship of Peter Lemaigre, 21 June 1793, consisting of Biddle's certification that he had verified the original record of Lemaigre's oath of allegiance to Pennsylvania on 10 Dec. 1779, which made him "from said Date a Citizen of said United States" (Dupl in same; in a clerk's hand signed by Biddle; at foot of text: "Duplicate").

This letter, sent with the approval of the Cabinet during the President's absence, sought redress for the first British violation of American neutrality to come to TJ's attention (TJ to George Washington, 25 July 1793). It soon led to a conversation with Hammond in which the British minister officially informed TJ for the first time of his government's policy toward neutral shipping during the war with France. Hammond described the discussion to the British foreign minister as follows: "In a conversation, which I had with Mr. Jefferson on the subject of this last mentioned letter, he informed me that the particulars, referred to in it, would be transmitted to Mr. Pinckney, and that that Gentleman would be farther instructed to submit to his Majestys ministers some general propositions, relative to the security of the uninterrupted navigation of American vessels. From this I took occasion to reply that, having given information generally to the merchants of the conduct which the King's government intended to pursue with respect to neutral vessels, I had not deemed it expedient to make any formal communication to him upon this point; as I imagined that such a proceeding on my part, might probably have been construed into an unnecessary anticipation of a discussion, which might with greater propriety have been expected to have originated with himself. But as he had now stated the subject, I would inform him briefly that I was authorized to declare—that in the prosecution of the present war, into which she had been forced by the unprovoked aggression of France, Great Britain had determined to pursue that conduct towards the vessels of neutral powers, which she had invariably observed in all preceding wars—that she would seize the property of her enemies wherever she could find it, and would not suffer neutral ships to cover and protect it— that she would take such articles as came under the denomination of *contraband de guerre*, though they might be the property of citizens of a neutral power—and that she would not allow neutral vessels to enter into a port which was besieged or blocked up by her ships of war. Mr. Jefferson's answer to this declaration was so moderate and lukewarm, as to incline me to believe that in reality he coincides with Mr. Hamilton in the sentiments, which I have ascribed to that Gentleman in my dispatch No. 14, and that any propositions of a contrary tendency, which Mr. Pinckney may be instructed to offer are not meant to be seriously enforced" (Hammond to Lord Grenville, 7 July 1793, PRO, FO 5/1). Hammond's statement to TJ was based upon the description of British policy on neutral shipping contained in a 12 Mch. 1793 dispatch from Grenville that reached Hammond about two months later (same to same, 17 May 1793, same; Mayo, *British Ministers*, 36-40).

In response to TJ's request for the AID OF YOUR LETTERS, Hammond informed Grenville that he intended to write a letter on behalf of the agent of the owners of the *Suckey* to Governor Adam Williamson of Jamaica "briefly stating the object of his voyage to Jamaica and recommending him generally to such protection and favor as his case may appear to deserve" (Hammond to Grenville, 7 July 1793, PRO: FO 5/1).

[1] Preceding nine words interlined in Dft.
[2] Word interlined in Dft in place of "give."
[3] Next three words interlined in Dft.
[4] Word written in Dft over "court of," erased.

To George Hammond

June 26. 93.

Th: Jefferson presents his compliments to Mr. Hammond and would be glad to be informed if there is any other testimony than that he sent him relative to the place of capture of the Ship William? He has heard that some one saw it from the shore whose testimony might be had. It is desireable that all the evidence possible should be produced.

PrC (DLC). Tr (DLC); 19th-century copy. Enclosed in Tobias Lear to TJ, 15 July 1793.

TJ submitted this letter to the President on 13 July 1793 (Washington, *Journal*, 196).

Memorial from George Hammond

The Undersigned, his Britannic Majesty's Minister Plenipotentiary to the United States, has the honor of submitting to the Secretary of State the annexed deposition of Michael Pile, late Master of the British brigantine Fanny and the protest of the said Michael Pile and part of the crew of the abovementioned vessel.

From these papers it appears that on the 8th. of May last the British brigantine Fanny was captured by the Schooner le Sans Culottes J. B. A. Fery Commander at the distance of four or five miles from Cape Henry in the state of Virginia, and consequently within the territory and jurisdiction of the United States. Upon this principle the Undersigned presumes to hope that the executive government of the United States will consider this act as an aggression on its sovereignty and will pursue such measures as it may deem the most efficacious for procuring the restitution of the British brigantine Fanny, now lying as a prize in the harbour of Philadelphia, to its rightful owners.

The Undersigned esteems it his duty to add that the evidence of the facts of this capture is necessarily not so complete as the testimony which he has had the honor of adducing in former similar instances—in consequence of the unwarrantable conduct of the person commanding le Sans Culottes, who in opposition to the common usages of war forced the crew from the vessel he had taken, and set them on shore in a neutral country, viz. at Lynhaven in the state of Virginia, not far distant from the place where the vessel was captured. The greatest part of these unfortunate individuals thus deprived of their property were compelled to recur to some immediate means of gaining a subsistance, and were thence of necessity incapacitated from proceeding to this city, for the purpose of offering, in defence of their rights and in the endeavor to recover their property, their testimony; the prevention of which it is more than probable has been the motive that instigated the oppressive and unjustifiable treatment they have experienced. For these reasons the Undersigned cannot but indulge the persuasion that the Secretary of State, so far from allowing these circumstances to invalidate the evidence submitted to him will consider them as additional acts of aggression on the part of the person commanding le Sans Culottes, and as additional inducements to afford every degree of redress which the case may appear to deserve.

Philadelphia   GEO. HAMMOND
26 June 1793.

RC (DNA: RG 59, NL); in the hand of Edward Thornton, signed by Hammond; at foot of first page: "Mr Jefferson"; endorsed by TJ as received 27 June 1793 and so recorded in SJL, which describes it as a document of that date; with later notation by TJ: "Brig Fanny.
taken, by the Sans culottes. proscribed before June 5. i.e. May 8."
FC (Lb in PRO: FO 116/3). Tr (same, 115/2). Tr (same, 5/1). Tr (Lb in DNA: RG 59, NL). Enclosures: (1) Deposition of Michael Pile, David MacIntosh, and John MacCattie, Norfolk, 13 May 1793, stating, as master, mate, and sailor of the *Fanny* respectively, that after leaving Lucia, Jamaica, on 14 Apr. 1793 bound for Baltimore with a cargo of rum and sugar the *Fanny* was hailed on 7 May by a schooner about seven leagues off Cape Henry and told there was a pilot on board for the Chesapeake; that on the following day it was captured in eight fathoms of water "four or five miles" off Cape Henry by the same schooner, which turned out to be the *Sans Culotte*, a French privateer with four guns and two swivels and a crew of forty-five men commanded by J. B. A. Ferey; and that after being detained aboard the privateer for three days the deponents were set ashore at Lynnhaven Bay in Virginia (Tr in DNA: RG 59, NL, with deponents' protest of 13 May 1793 against the privateer and its crew

for all losses incurred by any one interested in the *Fanny* and its cargo appended by Norfolk notary public John Nivison, and certification of 14 May 1793 by John Hamilton, British consul in Norfolk, all in Thornton's hand; PrC of Tr in DLC, in the hand of George Taylor, Jr.; Tr in NNC: Gouverneur Morris Papers; Tr in DNA: RG 46, Senate Records, 3d Cong., 1st sess.; PrC in PRO: FO 97/1; Tr in Lb in DNA: RG 59, NL). (2) Deposition of Michael Pile, Philadelphia, 24 June 1793, reiterating the substance of No. 1 and adding that the *Fanny* was a London ship; that the *Sans Culottes* had been commissioned a privateer by the French consul in Charleston; that the captors had sent the *Fanny* to Philadelphia; and that the deponent had come there alone to reclaim the ship and cargo because lack of friends and money had forced his officers and crew to sign on with other vessels in Virginia (MS in DNA: RG 59, NL, in the hand of Phineas Bond, signed by Pile, attested by Philadelphia alderman John Barclay; PrC of Tr in DLC, in Taylor's hand; PrC of another Tr in DLC, in a clerk's hand; Tr in NNC: Gouverneur Morris Papers; Tr in DNA: RG 46, Senate Records, 3d Cong., 1st sess.; PrC in PRO: FO 97/1; Tr in Lb in DNA: RG 59, DL; Tr in Lb in same, NL; Tr in PRO: FO 5/1). Enclosed in Memorandum to George Washington, [11-13 July 1793].

To Thomas Pinckney

SIR   Philadelphia, June 26th. 1793

I enclose you a copy of a letter I have written to Mr. Hammond, and of the papers accompanying it, on the subject of the Snow Suckey, and her cargo belonging to citizens of the United States, captured by an

English privateer, and carried, as is supposed, into Jamaica. I will ask you to obtain, without delay,[1] orders from the British Government to proper persons in[2] their Colonies, to have justice rendered immediately to the complainants and due punishment inflicted on the offenders, if the case shall be as has been stated. I think it would be proper also to make this the occasion of obtaining from that Government, general orders to their West India colonies, to watch, with vigilance, over[3] violations of this kind, which, probably[4] will be multiplied on us, and of which those Colonies will be the receptacle. I have the honor to be, with much respect & esteem Sir, Your most obedient and most humble servant

TH: JEFFERSON

PrC (DLC); in the hand of George Taylor, Jr., signed by TJ; at foot of text: "Mr. Pinckney." Dft (DLC); entirely in TJ's hand. FC (Lb in DNA: RG 59, DCI). Recorded in SJPL. Enclosures: TJ to George Hammond, 26 June 1793, and enclosures.

[1] In Dft TJ here canceled "proper."
[2] In Dft TJ here canceled "Jamaica."
[3] In Dft TJ here canceled "irregularities in the."
[4] In Dft TJ first wrote "of which we shall probably experience many" and then altered it to read as above.

From Martha Jefferson Randolph

DEAR PAPA   Monticello June 26, 1793

We recieved your 3 Last letters yesterday which by the carelessness of the post master in Richmond have been detained many weeks, indeed their negligence is intolerable, we have just heard of some of Mr. Randolphs Letters to you that have gone on to Lexington in kentucke. Those that we do get, come so irregularly without any regard to their dates that it is impossible to follow your directions with any degree of punctuality. Mr. Randolph thinks it would be most adviseable to have all your furniture brought by water as it is not only much more oeconomical but also safer. I have a terible account to give you of your cyder. Of 140 bottles that were put away you will hardly find 12. It flew in such a manner as to render it dangerous going near them. Those that were carelessly corked forced their corks the rest burst the bottles amongst which the havoc is incredible. The servants cloaths are not arrived nor have we been able to hear any thing about them. I am going on with such spirit in the garden that I think I shall conquer my *oponents* the *insects* yet, tho Hither to they have been as indifadigable in cutting up as I have been in planting. I have added to your accasia which is at Least 2 feet high 2 lemmon trees and have the promiss of an egg plant from Mr. Derieux. My dear little Anna daily more and more entertaining she is very observing and very talkative of course charming in the eyes of a mother. The dear Little boy tho not in perfect health is very well for one that is cutting teeth. *You* will easily concieve how great the satisfaction is I derive from the company of my sweet Little babes tho none but those who have experienced it can. I have allways forgot to mention Petit in any of my Letters. My negligence hurt his feelings I know, as it is not my design to do so you would oblige me infinitely by delivering some message to him *de ma part*. Adieu my dear Papa. Believe me with tender affection yours M RANDOLPH

RC (MHi); endorsed by TJ as received 8 July 1793 and so recorded in SJL.

To William Rawle

SIR   June 26. 1793.

It being left to the Executive to determine the case of the ship William, I will beg the favor of your information whether the parties had provided evidence on both sides as to the distance of the capture from the shore, and whether a copy of it could be furnished us? We shall thank you also for the authorities (a citation of them I mean) quoted on both sides to prove what is the distance to which a state may extend it's protection. I am with much esteem, Sir, Your most obedt. humble servt.   TH: JEFFERSON

RC (PHi: Rawle Papers); addressed: "Mr. Rawle." Not recorded in SJL.

Rawle evidently responded in a letter of 26 June 1793, recorded in SJL as received the same day, but not found.

From George Hammond

Thursday Morng [27 June 1793]

The British Minister presents his compliments to the Secretary of State and has the honor of informing him that he has just learnt that the person who has the care of the Light House on Cape Henry was a witness of the capture of the Ship William. The necessary steps are taken for procuring the deposition of this person on this subject without delay.

RC (DNA: RG 59, NL); partially dated; endorsed by TJ as a letter of 27 June 1793 received 29 June 1793. Tr (Lb in same).

From James Monroe

DEAR SIR   Albemarle June 27. 1793.

I have been favored with yours of the 4th. and shall observe the instruction respecting the fund in the hands of Mr. Pope by directing its immediate application to Mr. Barrett.

In my last I made some observations evincing the propriety and policy of our neutrality in the present European war, but as that sentiment appears to be general, I refer to it now only as a proof that it is likewise mine. It leaves me more at liberty to comment on the conduct of the Executive since, which I do the more freely as I do not know what part you have borne in it. The measure I particularly refer to is the proclamation declaring this neutrality, with the reply to the address of some merchants of Phila. and the order for the prosecution of two marines who had embarked in a privateer licensed by the French minister. I must confess I had considerd the proclamation at first as only an admonition to the people to mind their own business, and not interfere in the controversy; and in this view altho' I could not perceive the necessity of the measure, yet I was inclined to deem it harmless. As the executive magistrate, the competent authority having not otherwise declared, the President might, if he was distrustful of his constituents, endeavor to restrain them within the limits such authority had prescribed, or rather allowed; if indeed there exists in the government, a right to inhibit the citizens of the States from taking commissions from either of the powers at war and fighting in their service. I did not suppose it was intended as a matter of right to declare what should be the conduct of these States in relation to that controversy, but the reply to the merchants and the prosecution above mentioned seem to denote the contrary, and to shew that the President meant it as such. Upon this construction I deem it both unconstitutional and impolitick.

I cannot conceive upon what principle the right is claimed. I think the position incontrovertible that if he possesses the right to say we shall be neutral, he might say we should not be. The power in both instances must be in the same hands, for if the Executive could say we should be neutral, how could the legislature, that we should war. In truth a right to declare our neutrality, as a distinct authority, cannot exist, for that is only the natural state of things, when the positive power of declaring war is not exerted; and this belongs to the legislature only. Any interference therefore with it, by the Executive, must be unconstitutional and improper.

As little can in my opinion be said in favor of its policy. Tis possible G. B. might wish to keep us neutral: if such were her disposition it became her interest to cultivate our friendship, by surrendering the posts &ca. Whilst our conduct was in suspense that anxiety would be increased; but by this precipitate declaration the point has been given up. And for what object? What do we gain by it? We committed no offence untill we should violate the laws of neutrality, and no power could compel us to say what part we would take in the controversy, by holding aloof on that head none could be dissatisfied except France in case she should claim the guarantee. Declarations of neutrality I believe generally succeed applications for them, or the contrary course. Had France applied for our aid, or had Britain that we would not aid her, then in either case, such notification would have been regular. But a declaration like ours is I suspect without precedent. It loses the merit of having not refused France, or of accomodating Britain. It gives us no claim upon either court. France indeed it outrages, for it denies her claim of guarantee, or yeilding it up, the merit of the concession. And Britain it assures of an accomodation where she may wish it, without even the trouble of asking for it.

Again, why prosecute our citizens, for taking commissions in the French service? against what law have they offended, or upon what principle are they charged? The mere acceptance of the commission cannot be deemed criminal, and the act of hostility upon the British vessel was without the jurisdiction of these States, as I presume upon the high seas—and the doctrine is well established that no offence can be committed against the laws of any society beyond the limits within which they operate: for instance that an offence, such as murder or the like, committed in France can not be punished here; and if upon the sea, the principle is the same, unless the party be a pirate, and in that case amenable to the admiralty tribunals of every country. The subsequent act of bringing the vessel into port here, does not I suppose constitute the ground for prosecution, more than if these men had carried, or aided in carrying her, to the Island of St. croix or elsewhere and returned here, for if it does the purchasers or mariners afterwards hired, to take care of her, are equally criminal. This I take to be the doctrine of the common law—Tis certainly the basis upon which seperate and independent societies are erected. Nor has it been enlarged by any act of the legislature that I know of; tho' indeed I have not the acts with me. So far upon the idea that the French commission gives no seperate rights or[1] immunities, to one of our citizens, otherwise than if he had none. But does it give none, and of which he may avail himself against the opposit power, and even against his own country? If taken can he be treated as a pirate? The laws and usages of Nations are otherwise. Can we be made answerable for his conduct? If we had hired him to France or Britain, as the Swiss in particular do, we could not be. As a volunteer then we certainly are not.

I do not absolutely deny the right of a society to restrain its members from the commission of certain enormities, beyond the limits of its own jurisdiction, under such penalties as it may impose—tho' according to my present view of the subject, but few if any benefits can be derived from it, and some objections occur. The local tribunal will always be sufficient for his punishment if apprehended, and if he escapes, yet the power disposed may surrender him to justice. This I should think enough either for the suppression of vice, or national security. But to give our laws cognizance of offences committed in other countries, must be deemed not only sanguinary as it respects our citizens, but a derogation of the sovereignties, in which they may be. The offence for instance, by a fiction of the law must be considered as committed here. May we demand then and rescue him from their courts to be punished here, or shall he be twice punished for the same offence? Nor am I an advocate for privateering; on the contrary could wish the practice suppressed—but presume such reformation should be brought about by conventions throughout the world, and not the desultory operations of any one nation. But by taking the laws as they are, I cannot perceive wherein they have offended, or upon what principle the prosecution can be supported. In this position I think myself founded in relation to foreign authorities, for there where the doctrine of allegiance binds the subject in perpetual obedience to his sovereign, it has never been otherwise construed or applied, than to prohibit the right of expatriation and of course, the taking up arms against his native country. To fight in the service of one Prince against another was never denied I believe to any one. I suspect it was never asked unless the party were already in the service of his own. But with us, will not the rights of citizenship be construed more freely? will that of expatriation be denied? and may not the mere act of accepting a commission in a foreign service be deemed such if the party pleases? In this state there is a law to authorize it, but that law is drawn in such cautious terms, as to leave the point as it stood before, upon foreign authorities, improved by the principles of our revolution, and was intended not to abrogate any rights[2] but to make sure, what had been doubted.

But admitting it to be an offence and punishable by our Laws, why prosecute these people untill formally demanded by that court, in case she had a right to demand it? Is it that we affect an extraordinary degree of refinement and political purity? The parties at war will not I apprehend ascribe it to that motive. Nations more generally shelter their citizens from punishment when due and demanded than otherwise. But to commence it ourselves, unauthorized, as I believe, and pursue it with such rigor will be ascribed to some other. If we so seriously abhorred vice, and were disposed to banish it from our country, has no other instance of enormity presented itself worthy reprehension?

I have but little hope of a fortunate issue from the negotiation in spain, for I observe that it is conducted on the part of that court by Gardoqui a subtile and malignant little wretch, highly incensed against us for defeating him on that point here, and he well knows the support he received upon that occasion from a party still high in office and all powerful in the present administration. The association of Carml. too will I fear prove a Clog on it, for tis possible he might deem a rapid success as a feather to his colleague taken from himself. And with Britain my expectation is on the same level, for our conduct to her since the adoption of the present government, as more fully shewn by this declaration of neutrality, and the acceptance of her patronage (for such I presume to be the case by our comrs. taking the rout of Niagara) to obtain our peace with the Indians, must convince them of our subservience to their views, or how extremely impotent and contemptible we are. We forced that nation to abandon those very Indians in her treaty with us, and now when opposed to them alone, divided too on their part, and strengthened on ours by alliances with several tribes, we accept, if not solicit, her aid to make our peace with those whom they had sacrific'd. Either this nation must be among the most unprincipled, or she will endeavor to compensate her allies at our expense. To expect the contrary, unless we have the fullest assurance of her perfidy, must shew the weakness of our councils. I trust that our humiliation has attained its lowest point, when we are capable of placing ourselves in a situation so degrading and shameful. But the solidity of our credit with the brokers at Amsterdam is a medicine of sufficient virtue to heal every wound that can be given to the national honor and reputation. Excuse this letter which has exceeded the bounds I had contemplated, and be assured of the sincerity with which I am your affectionate friend & servt.

JAS. MONROE

RC (DLC); endorsed by TJ as received 8 July 1793 and so recorded in SJL.

[1] Monroe here canceled "authorities."
[2] Preceding two words interlined.

To Francis Walker

DEAR SIR   Philadelphia June 27. 1793.

I received two days ago your favor of May 31. on the subject of Mr. Underwood and immediately put the papers of recommendation into the hands of Genl. Knox, satisfying him of the respectability of the persons subscribing the recommendation. He will do for Mr. Underwood whatever and whenever justice will permit.—I think it very possible that Congress may be called together something earlier than the day now fixed for their meeting, which I mention that you may calculate your own movements accordingly. We have nothing new more than you will see in the public papers. My best and most affectionate respects are tendered to your father, and assurances to yourself of the esteem of Dr. Sir Your most obedt. humble servt.   TH: JEFFERSON

PrC (DLC); at foot of text: "Mr. Francis Walker." Tr (DLC); 19th-century copy.

To Thomas Bell

DEAR SIR   Philadelphia June 28. 1793

I am favored with yours of June 12.—Mr. Jefferson my relation had detained the letter to you till he could write back to me and inform me of the difficulty of getting to Charlottesville, and how much more convenient it would be to him to take his goods in Goochld. My business made me late in answering him, and I then repeated my request to him to apply to you, as I observe that from a want of circulation, the smallest *money* engagements are serious things, and therefore to be made only where *commodities* of some sort will be taken. Before the receipt of my letter his necessities had obliged him to supply himself.—I am really sorry to learn that Mr. Derieux has so much anticipated his resources. If this aid is all expended before hand, and he is left with his Charlottesville house on his hands, he will get through the world with difficulty. Mr. Vaughan tells me he will make him his last remittance in a few days.—I am glad to learn the Doctr. has given such proofs of energy. I wish I could hear of Mr. Lewis's perfect reestablishment also. Be so good as to present my sincere affections to both families.—I am striving to get a tenant for my mill, in which case she will be built as a merchant mill. I offer her to the Brandywine people for 20. years. My chief object is to fix a market for my own grain at home. I am with great & sincere esteem Dr Sir your friend & servt   TH: JEFFERSON

PrC (DLC); at foot of text: Colo. Thos. Bell." Tr (DLC); 19th-century copy with lacuna.

THE DOCTR.: George Gilmer.

To Clement Biddle

SIR   Philadelphia June 28. 1793.

I have written to the British Minister here on the case of Mr. Lemaigre. He has this day called on me and promised that he will furnish the Agent of Mr. Le Maigre with a letter to the Governor of Jamaica, recommending his case to his attention and justice. In addition to this I can only furnish the agent with a passport naming his general business. Mr. Lemaigre cannot arm his Agent with too much testimony of the citizenship of all the parties. I am with great esteem Sir Your most obedt. servt.   TH: JEFFERSON

PrC (DLC); at foot of text: "Colo. Clemt. Biddle." FC (Lb in DNA: RG 59, DL); misdated 23 June 1793.

TJ was probably responding to a missing letter from Biddle of 26 June 1793, recorded in SJL as received the same day, which presumably enclosed documents detailing Peter Lemaigre's complaint, some of which TJ passed on to George Hammond, THE BRITISH MINISTER HERE, in a letter also dated 26 June 1793.

To John Clarke

SIR   Philadelphia June 28. 1793.

Mr. Taylor wrote you a letter on the 10th. inst. (which you probably received a day or two after your's of the 15th. and) which would inform you of what was necessary to be done by you to prosecute the claim to your discovery under the new law. I can add nothing more on the subject, but that as far as the choice of arbitrators shall be left to me, I shall endeavor to select from the Philosophical society, members of integrity and other proper qualifications for the enquiry. I am with esteem Sir Your very humble servt   TH: JEFFERSON

PrC (DLC); at foot of text: "Mr. John Clarke." Tr (DLC); 19th-century copy.

From Joseph Fenwick

SIR   Bordeaux 28 June 1793.

I have none of your favours to reply to. This covers a Bond Executed by me for the performance of the Consular Functions.

The uncertainty of the Intercourse with America from this Country during the War, will deprive me of writing to you as often as I shou'd otherwise do—and the little respect English Privateers shew to letters, requires Circumspection in all remarks from hence.

The Neutrality of America, and her Flagg has been generally respected by all the Belligerent Powers in Europe, tho' their Cruizers commit many depredations, as You will see by the Protests and Judgement herewith sent: and I must observe that, altho' the French commit many Errors in deciding on the Validity of Vessels Papers on the High Seas, they respect infinitely more, the Rights of Men, and Nations, preserve decency, and moderation in their proceedings, respect the Sanctity of letters and Seals, and are more ready and disposed to do Justice, and repair Injuries than the English or Spaniards, particularly the English Cruizers, who have in many instances added insult to Injustice, as you will See by the Papers inclosed. The Brig Sally Captain Storch of Salem, bound from Havre to Bordeaux and Alexandria, was taken and brought in here by a French Armed Vessel. The Court of Admiralty on the verification of her Papers and my application, immediately restor'd to the Captain the Vessel and Cargo, free of Injury and Costs. I inclose you the Judgement.

Another Brig from Same place, the Nancy Captain Barker has been carried into Bayonne, and I have reason to expect equal Justice will be Shewn her. The National Convention decreed the 9th. May, that their Armed Ships might Stop all Neutral Vessels bound to an Enemys Port, and take out any part of their Cargoes that was not Neutral Property. On immediate Representations made to them, they excepted the American Flag the 23d: of same month.

The Political Situation of this Country appears precarious—the most wise cannot See how things will end. American produce and Ships are very much demanded at the Rates below. Exchange on London about 3d. Stg. per Livre. I have the honor to be Sir your most obt: hble St

JOSEPH FENWICK

Flour 100^{tt} pr: barrel
Wheat 18^{tt} a 20^{tt} pr: Amn: bushel
W: Oil 80^{tt} p$\frac{0}{0}$ Rice 60^{tt} a 65^{tt} p$\frac{0}{0}$
Tobacco 120^{tt} a 150^{tt} p$\frac{0}{0}$

= dollars pr: tons, of 4 Wine Hheads =

Freights—To the W: Indies 35 a 38—and 10 p$\frac{0}{0}$ primage & Avarage
To America   24 a 32   do.   do.
To the Cape of Good Hope & Isle of France and back, 80 a 84 dollars & 10 p$\frac{0}{0}$—Up the channel £3 a £5 Stg and 10 p$\frac{0}{0}$

RC (DNA: RG 59, CD); in a clerk's hand, signed by Fenwick; at foot of first page: "Thomas Jefferson Esqr. Minister of State—Philadelphia"; endorsed by TJ as received 7 Sep. 1793 and so recorded in SJL. Dupl (same); in a clerk's hand, signed by Fenwick; endorsed by TJ as received 11 Sep. 1793. Tripl (same); in a clerk's hand, signed by Fenwick; endorsed by TJ as received 24 Oct. 1793 and so recorded in SJL. Enclosures: (1) Fenwick's consular bond, 1 May 1793, for $2,000 (MS in same; in a clerk's hand, signed by Fenwick). (2) Public Instrument of Protest, Bordeaux, 15 June 1793, wherein Joseph Strout, master, Pierce Troy, mate, and William Scott, seaman of the Sally, a brig from Salem, protest against the capture of this vessel, while bound from Le Havre to Bordeaux with a cargo of dry goods and ballast, seven leagues from Cordovan on 12 June 1793 by the Espoir, a French aviso brig of war commanded by Captain Lamille, and her subsequent detention in Bordeaux; subjoined to which is a 20 June statement wherein Strout, Troy, and Scott declare that upon inspecting the Sally after its release by the Court of Commerce of Bordeaux after eight days of detention they found damages to her amounting to £64.10 sterling (Tr in same; filed with Dupl; certified by Fenwick as having been sworn before him in the United States consular chancery in Bordeaux). (3) Judgment of the Tribunal of Commerce and Admiralty in Bordeaux, 19 June 1793, ordering the restoration of the Sally and her cargo to Captain Strout (Tr in same, in French, with subjoined statement in English by Fenwick certifying its authenticity, 2 July 1793; Tr in same, in French, with subjoined statement in English by Fenwick certifying its authenticity, 5 July 1793). (4) Public Instrument of Protest, 22 June 1793, wherein Henry Hockett, master,

John Heming, mate, and John Fletcher, seaman, of the *Prosperity*, a ship which arrived in Bordeaux on 21 June with a cargo of flour from Baltimore, complain of damages the *Prosperity* sustained from the privateer *Ann* of Liverpool, Captain James Hannagan, which on 2 June put twelve French prisoners aboard her; from the privateer *Achilles* of Weymouth, Captain William le Cheminant, which on 8 June took from her two barrels of superfine flour for ten dollars and one barrel of ships bread for nothing; from the privateer *Favorite*, Captain Bradley, which on 8 and 9 June opened her letters, detained her captain and crew, ransacked her cargo, and put four more French prisoners aboard her; from the privateer *Sudden Death*, Captain Baxter, and the ship *Duke William* of Liverpool, the former of which on 11 June took from her two barrels of superfine flour for nine dollars; and from the privateer *Hopewell* of Liverpool, Captain John McGhir, which on 13 June took from her two barrels of superfine flour and two barrels of ship flour for an order on Liverpool merchant John Thomas (Tr in same; filed with Dupl; certified by Fenwick as having been sworn before him in the United States consular chancery in Bordeaux).

On this date, or on 2 Aug. or 24 Sep. 1793, Fenwick wrote the following letter to TJ: "I had the honor of writing you this day by the Poly Capt. Chandler. I now add a few papers that have since come to hand—which I beg the favor of you to send Mr. Mason after reading them also the inclosed packet which I have taken the liberty to put under your cover for security. The Captains refuse letters frequently" (RC in DNA: RG 59, CD; undated; at foot of text: "Thomas Jefferson Esquire Secretary of State Philadela."; endorsed by TJ as received 24 Oct. 1793; enclosures not found). According to SJL, on 24 Oct. 1793 TJ received letters from Fenwick written on all three dates, but there is no way to determine on which of them he wrote this letter.

To George Gilmer

DEAR DOCTOR   Philadelphia June 28. 1793

I give you sincere joy on the physical energies of which you have lately (or rather Mrs. Gilmer for you) produced such a living proof. I hope they will be repeated for years to come. Dumourier was known to be a scoundrel in grain. I mentioned this from the beginning of his being placed at the head of the armies: but his victories at length silenced me. His apostasy has now proved that an unprincipled man, let his other fitnesses be what they will, ought never to be employed. It has proved too that the French army, as well as nation, can not be shaken in their republicanism. DuMourier's popularity put it to as severe a proof as could be offered. Their steadiness to their principles ensures the issue of their revolution against every effort but by the way of famine. Should that take place the effect would be incalculable, because our machine, unsupported by food, is no longer under the controul of reason. This crisis however is now nearly over as their harvest is by this time beginning. As far as the last accounts come down, they were retiring to within their own limits, where their assignats would do for money (except at Mentz). England too is issuing her paper, not founded, like the assignats, on land, but on pawns of thread, ribbons, buckles &c. They will soon learn the science of depreciation, and their whole paper system vanish into the nothing on which it is bottomed. My affectionate respects to Mrs. Gilmer & am Dear Doctor Your's sincerely

Th: Jefferson

PrC (DLC); at foot of text: "Doctr. Gilmer."

To Thomas Greenleaf

Sir   Philadelphia, Jan. [June] 28. 1793.

I received in due time your favor of May 5. and the Volume of your papers which I had desired and now inclose you the price as stated in your letter towit 6D–16c. with thanks for your attention to the request, and am Sir your most obedt servt   Th: Jefferson

PrC (DLC); misdated; at foot of text: "Mr. Greenleaf." Tr (DLC); 19th-century copy misdated 28 Jan. 1793. Recorded under 28 June 1793 in SJL.

To John Hancock

Sir   Philadelphia June 28. 1793.

Mr. Duplaine, Consul of France for Boston, will of course have presented you his Exequatur and would also of course receive from you those attentions which his office entitles him to. But Mr. Genet, minister from the same nation here, desirous that the affairs of the two nations should be conducted with that cordiality which animates the two nations, and which would be promoted by the personal and mutual esteem of it's agents, has desired me to present Mr. Duplaine to you according to his personal merit as well as his formal authority. I have not the pleasure of a personal acquaintance with Mr. Duplaine, but he bore the reputation here of a man of worth, and a very sincere republican. I am sure that both of these qualifications will be titles for your esteem, and that on that ground I may safely recommend him to your attentions and good offices, and especially to that concert in his official proceedings which will render the exercise of them agreeable to himself and useful to both countries. I have the honour to be with sentiments of the highest esteem & respect Your Excellency's Most obedt & most humble servt

Th: Jefferson

PrC (DLC); at foot of text: "H.E. Govr. Hancock." Tr (DLC); 19th-century copy.

To Henry Lee

Dear Sir   Philadelphia June 28. 1793.

I should much sooner have answered your favor of the 15th. of May on the subject of a Mace, by sending you the inclosed design of Dr. Thornton, whose taste and imagination are both good: but that I have not myself been satisfied with the introduction of the rattlesnake into the design. There is in Man as well as brutes, an antipathy to the snake, which renders it a disgusting object wherever it is presented. I would myself rather adopt the Roman staves and axe, trite as it is; or perhaps a sword, sheathed in a roll of parchment (that is to say an imitation in metal of a roll of parchment) written over, in the raised Gothic letters of the law, with that part of the constitution which establishes the house of representatives, for that house, or the Senate, for the Senate. However if you have the same disgust for the snake, I am sure you will yourself imagine some better substitute: or perhaps you will find that disgust overbalanced by stronger considerations in favor of the emblem. I have the honour to be with great esteem & respect Dear Sir Your most obedt & most humble servt   Th: Jefferson

RC (Vi: Executive Papers); at foot of text: "H. E. Govr. Lee of Virginia"; endorsed by Lee. PrC (DLC). Tr (DLC); 19th-century copy. Enclosure: William Thornton to TJ, 8 June 1793, and enclosure.

Lee's favor of the 15th was actually dated 16 May 1793.

From Henry Lee

Sir   Richmond June 28th. 1793.

I beg leave to transmit to you the enclosed copy of a letter from Colonel Newton.

The President will if he thinks proper direct measures to avert the apprehended evil.

To the general Government I conceive belongs the right to act on the subject.

The law in this Commonwealth relative thereto contemplates the Agency of the officers of the Customs who are now responsible only to the General Government and therefore could not be used by state Authority, if the same was constitutionally admissible. I have the honor to be Sir with perfect respect your ob: Ser.   Henry Lee

RC (DLC); in a clerk's hand except for complimentary close and signature; endorsed by TJ as received 5 July 1793 and so recorded in SJL. FC (Vi: Executive Letter Book). Enclosure: Thomas Newton, Jr., to Lee, Norfolk, 16 June 1793, reporting that a form of plague has broken out in the Windward Islands; quoting in full the 8 June 1793 proclamation of South Carolina Governor William Moultrie just received from Charleston stating that he has credible information to this effect and, to prevent the pestilence from being introduced into the state, enjoining all pilots boarding vessels coming from Grenada and the other islands to remain below deck for examination with their crews by physicians of the port; advising that he has other but less reliable ac- counts of the same purport; and relating that the British fleet was in Barbardos on 28 May but had not attacked Martinique (Tr in DLC). Enclosed in second Memorandum to George Washington, [11 July 1793], and Tobias Lear to TJ, 15 July 1793.

For the 1783 LAW IN THIS COMMONWEALTH RELATIVE to quarantine, see Hening, XI, 329-31.

To James Monroe

DEAR SIR   Philadelphia June 28. 1793.

I have to acknolege your favor of May 28. I believe that through all America there has been but a single sentiment on the subject of peace and war, which was in favor of the former. The Executive here has cherished it with equal and unanimous desire. We have differed perhaps as to the tone of conduct exactly adapted to the securing it. We have as yet no indications of the intentions or even the wishes of the British government. I rather believe they mean to hold themselves up, and be led by events. In the mean while Spain is so evidently *picking a quarrel* with us, that we see a war absolutely inevitable with her. We are making a last effort to avoid it, but our cabinet is without any division in their expectations of the result. This may not be known before the last of October, earlier than which I think you will meet. You should therefore calculate your domestic measures on this change of position. If France, collected within her own limits, shall maintain her ground there steadily, as I think she will (barring the effects of famine which no one can calculate) and if the bankruptcies of England proceed to the length of an universal crush of their paper, which I also think they will, she will leave Spain the bag to hold. She is emitting assignats also, that is to say Exchequer bills to the amount of 5. millions English or 125. millions French: and these are not founded on land as the French assignats are, but on pins, thread, buckles, hops and whatever else you will pawn in the exchequer of double the estimated value. But we all know that 5. millions of such stuff forced for sale at once on the market of London where there will be neither cash nor credit, will not pay storage. This paper must rest then ultimately on the credit of the nation as the rest of their public paper does, and will sink with that. If either this takes place, or the confederacy is unsuccesful, we may be clear of war with England.—With respect to the increase of our shipping, our merchants have no need, you know, of a permission to buy up foreign bottoms. There is no law prohibiting it. And when bought, they are American property and as such entitled to pass freely by our treaties with some nations, and by the law of nations with all. Such accordingly, by a determination of the Executive will receive American passports. They will not be entitled indeed to import goods on the low duties of *home built* vessels, the laws having confined that privilege to these only. We have taken every possible method to guard against fraudulent conveyances, which, if we can augment our shipping to the extent of our own carriage, it would not be our interest to cover.

I inclose you a note from Freneau explaining the interruption of your papers.—I do not augur well of the mode of conduct of the new French minister. I fear he will enlarge the circle of those disaffected to his country. I am doing every thing in my power to moderate the impetuosity of his movements, and to destroy the dangerous opinion, which has been excited in him, that the people of the US. will disavow the acts of their government, and that he has an appeal from the Executive to Congress, and from both to the people.—Affairs with the Creeks seem to present war there as inevitable. But it will await for you. We have no news from the Northern commissioners, but of the delay likely to be attempted by the Indians. But as we never expected peace from the negociation, I think no delay will be admitted which may defeat our preparations for a campaign. Crops here are likely to be good, tho' the beginning of the harvest has been a little wet.—I forget whether I informed you that I had chosen a house for you, and was determined in the choice by the Southern aspect of the back buildings, the only circumstance of difference between the two presented to my choice. Give my best love to Mrs. Monroe, & be assured of the affectionate esteem of Dr. Sir your friend & servt   TH: JEFFERSON

RC (NN: Presidential Papers); at foot of first page: "Colo. Monroe." PrC (DLC). Enclosure not found.

A DETERMINATION OF THE EXECUTIVE: see Opinion on Ship Passports, 3 May 1793, and note.

To Isaac Shelby

SIR   Philadelphia June 28. 1793

The bearer hereof Mr. Michaud is a citizen of the French republic who has resided several years in the US. as the Conductor of a botanical establishment belonging to the French[1] nation. He is a man of science and merit, and goes to Kentuckey in pursuit of objects of Natural history and botany, to augment[2] the literary acquirements of the two republicks. Mr. Genet the Minister of France here, having expressed to me[3] his esteem for Mr. Michaud and good opinion of him, and his wish that he should be made known to you, I take the liberty of recommending him to your notice, your counsels, and good offices.[4] His character here persuades me they will be worthily bestowed on him, and that your[5] further knowlege of him will justify[6] the liberty I take of making him known to you. This will the more need[7] justification, as I have not the honor of being personally known to you myself.[8] This[9] circumstance however has not prevented my entertaining for you those sentiments of esteem and respect which your[10] character is entitled to inspire, and which I beg leave to tender you, with sincere assurances of attachment and regard from[11] Your Excellency's Most obedt & most humble servt

PrC (DLC); incorporating some revisions made to Dft on 5 July 1793; at foot of text: "H.E. Governr. Shelby." Dft (DLC); variant text with penciled emendations added on 5 July 1793. PrC (DLC); lacks penciled emendations. Tr (DLC); 19th-century copy of final PrC. Recorded in SJPL.

Although this letter to the governor of Kentucky appears to be nothing more than a routine introduction for the French botanist André Michaux—who with TJ's encouragement had accepted a commission from the American Philosophical Society in April 1793 to undertake a search for a western water route to the Pacific—it was also a subtle exercise in calculated ambiguity stemming from two conflicting forces that converged late in June and early in July 1793 with potentially explosive implications. On the one hand, TJ's conviction that the intrigues of Spanish officials in Louisiana with the Southern Indians were threatening to provoke a war between Spain and the United States predisposed him to look with qualified and unofficial favor on a plan by the French minister, Edmond Charles Genet, to employ Michaux as an agent to help carry out a Girondin-inspired project to liberate Louisiana from Spanish rule using a force of American and Indian volunteers to be raised in Kentucky under the command of the Revolutionary War hero George Rogers Clark. On the other hand, even though the plan might help the United States vindicate its right to navigate the Mississippi, Genet's increasingly open defiance of American neutrality inclined TJ to

distance himself from the obstreperous French minister (Editorial Note on Jefferson and André Michaux's proposed western expedition, at 22 Jan. 1793; TJ to James Monroe, 28 June 1793; TJ to William Carmichael and William Short, 30 June 1793). In balancing these scientific and political concerns, TJ went as far as he could in his letter to Shelby to encourage Genet's plans without endorsing his proposed expedition against Louisiana.

Despite identical datelines inscribed on the original and final versions of this letter, TJ prepared them a week apart—the former on 28 June and the latter on 5 July 1793 (Notes of Cabinet Meeting and Conversations with Edmond Charles Genet, 5 July 1793). TJ's retention of the original date when revising the letter on 5 July has led some historians to conclude that he prepared the final version before Genet revealed his plans for the Louisiana expedition (Malone, *Jefferson*, III, 105-7; Peterson, *Jefferson*, 496-8). While there is reason to question whether TJ was aware of the connection between Michaux's mission to Kentucky and the projected invasion of Louisiana when he wrote the original version of the letter, there can be no doubt that he knew of Genet's plans for the expedition when he prepared the final version.

A few months earlier the Secretary of State had learned that France was contemplating an expedition under Francisco de Miranda to seize New Orleans and liberate the Spanish colonies south of it (Notes on Conversations with William Stephens Smith and George Washington, 20 Feb. 1793). Despite the abundant confirmation he received in May and early June of Genet's unwillingness to respect American neutrality, there is no indication that TJ received any communication from the French minister about his western plans until after the middle of June 1793, when in accordance with his secret instructions Genet began to prepare in earnest for a coordinated land and sea attack on Louisiana. Appointing Michaux as his agent to facilitate matters in Kentucky, Genet asked TJ ca. 21 June to issue an exequatur for a commission naming him French consul in that state, and by the 24th he had prevailed upon Senator John Brown of Kentucky to write letters to Clark and Shelby introducing Michaux. Genet later reported that he had approached Brown on TJ's recommendation after informing the Secretary of State about the proposed assault on Louisiana, but his dispatches home cannot always be accepted at face value, as Dumas Malone observed in connection with this episode. Moreover, Genet's notes of a conversation with TJ on 26 June about an expedition against Louisiana remain ambiguous. In any event, although TJ rejected Genet's request for an exequatur for Michaux, either at this meeting or at one held on the following day, he acceded to his appeal for a letter to Governor Shelby introducing Michaux (Editorial Note on André Michaux's proposed western expedition, at 22 Jan. 1793; C. S. Sargent, "Portions of the Journal of André Michaux, Botanist, written during his Travels in the United States and Canada, 1785 to 1796," APS, *Proceedings*, XXVI [1889], 90-1; Notes of Cabinet Meeting and Conversations with Edmond Charles Genet, 5 July 1793; AHA, *Annual Report*, 1896, I, 982-3; Genet to the Minister of Foreign Affairs, 25 July 1793, Turner, *CFM*, 220-2; note to Genet to TJ, 26 June 1793; Malone, *Jefferson*, III, 107).

Whatever the degree of TJ's knowledge of the true nature of Michaux's Kentucky mission on 28 June 1793, the Secretary of State was fully aware of it a week later after Genet unofficially disclosed his plan in considerable detail and asked him to revise his letter to the governor. Retaining the original date in his final version, TJ emphasized at Genet's request that the botanist enjoyed the French minister's confidence—a comment Senator Brown had earlier included in his letter to Shelby—but toned down his

original broad endorsement of Michaux's activities (see notes 4 and 6 below). It is possible that TJ kept the earlier date in order to preserve plausible deniability of his knowledge of Michaux's plans, and indeed some years later he was to stress that he had introduced Michaux as a botanist (Notes on Conversations with Hugh Henry Brackenridge and Benjamin Rush, 27 Mch. 1800). In any event, although TJ warned Genet on 5 July not to enlist Americans in this enterprise, almost two months elapsed before a formal complaint by Spain's diplomatic agents in Philadelphia compelled him to inform the President of the French minister's plan to overthrow Spanish rule in Louisiana—a serious omission considering the diplomatic consequences that might have ensued from an attack launched from American territory on part of the Spanish empire. The Secretary of State soon after instructed Shelby to take all necessary steps to thwart Genet's plan, but there is no evidence that TJ ever disclosed his unofficial knowledge of the French minister's scheme to the President or the Cabinet (Josef Ignacio de Viar and Josef de Jaudenes to TJ, 27 Aug. 1793, and enclosure; TJ to Shelby, 29 Aug., 6 Nov. 1793). For the collapse of Michaux's mission to Kentucky and the projected French invasion of Louisiana in the aftermath of the fall of the Girondins in France, see Editorial Note on Jefferson and André Michaux's proposed western expedition, at 22 Jan. 1793.

[1] Word interlined in pencil in Dft.

[2] Dft: "enrich."

[3] Preceding two words not in Dft.

[4] In Dft TJ originally wrote "I take the liberty of making this gentleman known to you, and of recommending him to your notice, your counsels and good offices, as they may respect both his person and pursuits." He subsequently revised the entire sentence in pencil to read "Mr. Genet the Min. of Fr. here having expressed his esteem for and confidence in Mr. Michaud and his wish that he should be made known to you, I take the liberty of recommending him to your notice, your counsels and good offices."

[5] Sentence to this point interlined in pencil in Dft in place of "I am persuaded your."

[6] Here in Dft TJ bracketed "any services

you may render him, and" for deletion in pencil.

⁷ In Dft TJ first wrote "It will the more require" before altering the passage in pencil to read as above.

⁸ Word interlined in pencil in Dft.

⁹ Sentence to this point in Dft reads: "But this."

¹⁰ Here in Dft TJ marked "own" for deletion in pencil.

¹¹ In Dft TJ originally wrote "and of which I beg permission to assure you; being with great respect" before revising the passage in pencil to read as above.

To George Washington

DEAR SIR   Philadelphia June 28. 1793.

I should have taken time ere this to have considered the observations of Mr. Young, could I at this place have done it in such a way as would satisfy either him or myself. When I wrote the notes of the last year, I had never before thought of calculating what were the profits of a capital invested in Virginia agriculture. Yet that appeared to be what Mr. Young most desired. Lest therefore no other of those, whom you consulted for him, should attempt such a calculation, I did it. But being at such a distance from the country of which I wrote, and having been absent from that, and from the subject in consideration, many years, I could only, for my facts, recur to my own recollection, weakened by time and very different applications, and I had no means here of correcting my facts. I therefore hazarded the calculation rather as an essay of the mode of calculating the profits of a Virginia estate, than as an operation which was to be ultimately relied on. When I went last to Virginia, I put the press-copy of those notes into the hands of the most skilful and succesful farmer in the part of the country of which I wrote. He omitted to return them to me which adds another impediment to my resuming the subject here. But indeed if I had them, I could only present the same facts, with some corrections and some justifications of the principles of calculation. This would not, and ought not to satisfy Mr. Young. When I return home I shall have time and opportunity of answering Mr. Young's enquiries fully. I will first establish the facts as adapted to the present times, and not to those to which I was obliged to recur by recollection, and I will make the calculation on rigorous principles. The delay necessary for this will I hope be compensated, by giving something which no endeavors on my part shall be wanting to make worthy of confidence. In the mean time Mr. Young must not pronounce too hastily on the impossibility of an annual production of £750. worth of wheat coupled with a cattle product of £125. My object was to state the produce of a *good* farm, under *good* husbandry as practised in my part of the country. Manure does not enter into this, because we can buy an

acre of new land cheaper than we can manure an old one. *Good* husbandry with us consists in abandoning Indian corn, and tobacco, tending small grain, some red clover, fallowing, and endeavoring to have,
while the lands are at rest, a spontaneous cover of white clover. I do not
present this as a culture judicious in itself, but as *good* in comparison
with what most people there pursue. Mr. Young has never had an opportunity of seeing how slowly the fertility of the *original soil* is exhausted, with moderate management of it. I can affirm that the James
river low grounds with the cultivation of small grain will never be exhausted: because we know that under that cultivation we must now and
then take them down with Indian corn, or they become, as they were
originally, too rich to bring wheat. The highlands where I live have
been cultivated about 60. years. The culture was tobacco and Indian
corn as long as they would bring enough to pay the labour. Then they
were turned out. After 4. or 5. years rest[1] they would bring good corn
again and in double that time perhaps good tobacco. Then they would
be exhausted by a second series of tobacco and corn. Latterly we have
begun to cultivate small grain: and excluding Indian corn, and fallowing, such of them as were originally good, soon rise up to 15. or 20.
bushels the acre. We allow that every labourer will manage 10. acres of
wheat, except at harvest.—I have no doubt but the coupling cattle and
sheep[2] with this would prodigiously improve the produce. This improvement Mr. Young will be better able to calculate than any body
else. I am so well satisfied of it myself, that having engaged a good
farmer from the head of Elk (the style of farming there you know well)
I mean in a farm of about 500. acres of cleared land and with a dozen
laborers to try the plan of wheat, rye, potatoes, clover, with a mixture of
some[3] Indian corn with the potatoes, and to push the number of sheep.
This last hint I have taken from Mr. Young's letters which you have
been so kind as to communicate to me. I had never before considered
with due attention the profit from that animal. I shall not be able to put
the farm into that form exactly the ensuing autumn, but against another
I hope I shall, and I shall attend with precision to the measures of the
ground and of the product, which may perhaps give you something
hereafter to communicate to Mr. Young which may gratify him. But I
will furnish the ensuing winter what was desired in Mr. Young's letter
of Jan. 17. 93. I have the honor to be with great & sincere esteem Dear
Sir, your most obedt. humble servt   TH: JEFFERSON

RC (DLC: Washington Papers); at foot
of first page: "The President of the US."; endorsed by Washington. PrC (DLC). Enclosed in second Memorandum to George
Washington, [11 July 1793].

NOTES OF THE LAST YEAR: Notes on
Arthur Young's Letter to George Washington, 18 June 1792. For extracts from MR.
YOUNG'S LETTER OF JAN. 17. 93, see enclosure to Washington to TJ, 13 May 1793.

The present letter to Washington was subsequently published in Young, *Letters from His Excellency General Washington, to Arthur Young, Esq. F. R. S.* (London, 1801), 136-40.

[1] Word interlined.
[2] Preceding two words interlined.
[3] Word interlined.

To Phineas Bond

SIR   Philadelphia June 29. 1793.

I have this moment received your favor of yesterday informing me that you have appointed Edward Thornton to be your vice Consul at Baltimore and desiring that measures may be taken to have him received. The only measure to be taken is to furnish Mr. Thornton with the President's Exaquatur, which is in the nature of an Inspeximus, reciting that Mr. Thornton's 'commission has been produced to him.' This of course renders it requisite that the Commission should be presented to the President. It is also necessary to retain a copy in my office, to be entered among the records. This has been the course with all Consular and Viceconsular commissions. I must therefore trouble you, Sir, for Mr. Thornton's commission when the President returns, and the Exaquatur can then be issued. I have the honor to be Sir Your most obedt servt   TH: JEFFERSON

PrC (DLC); at foot of text: "Mr. Bond." FC (Lb in DNA: RG 59, DL).

On 28 June 1793 Bond, the British consul general for the middle and southern states, had written a letter to TJ announcing the appointment of Edward Thornton, George Hammond's secretary, as his vice-consul in Maryland to reside in Baltimore, and trusting that the United States government would receive him as such (RC in NFC; addressed: "Mr: Jefferson"; endorsed by TJ as received 29 June 1793 and so recorded in SJL). The President received Thornton's vice-consular commission from the Department of State on 12 July 1793, whereupon he issued an exequatur for Thornton and sent it to TJ for countersignature (Exequatur for Thornton, 12 July 1793, FC in DNA: RG 59, Exequaturs). See also Washington, *Journal*, 194.

To Edmond Charles Genet

SIR   Philadelphia June 29. 1793.

The persons who reclaimed the Ship William, as taken within the limits of the protection of the united States, having thought proper to carry their claim first into the Courts of Admiralty, there was no power in this Country which could take the vessel out of the custody of that Court, till it should decide itself whether it had jurisdiction or not of the cause; having now decided that it has not jurisdiction, the same Complaint is lodged with the Executive.

I have the honor to enclose you the testimony whereon the Complaint is founded. Should this satisfy you that it is just, you will be so good as to give orders to the Consul of France at this port to take the vessel into his Custody and deliver her to the owners. Should it be overweighed in your judgment by any contradictory evidence, which you have, or may acquire, I will ask the favor of a communication of that evidence, and that the Consul retain the Vessel in his custody until the Executive of the united States consider and decide finally on the Subject. I have the honor to be with much respect Sir, Your most obedient and most humble servant   Th: Jefferson

PrC (DLC); in the hand of George Taylor, Jr., signed by TJ; at foot of text: "The minister plenipoy. of France." PrC of Tr (DLC); in a clerk's hand. Tr (NNC: Gouverneur Morris Papers). Tr (DNA: RG 46, Senate Records, 3d Cong., 1st sess.). PrC (PRO: FO 97/1). FC (Lb in DNA: RG 59, DL). For enclosures, see enclosures listed at Memorial from George Hammond, 21 June 1793. Letter and enclosures printed in *Message*, 44-6. Enclosed in Memorandum to George Washington, [11-13 July 1793], and TJ to Gouverneur Morris, 16 Aug. 1793.

To Edmond Charles Genet

Sir   Philadelphia June 29th. 1793.

A complaint is lodged with the Executive of the united States that the Sans Culottes, an armed privateer of France, did on the 18th. of may last capture the British brigantine Fanny within the limits of the protection of the united States, and sent the said Brig as a prize into this port, where she is now lying.

I have the honor to enclose you the testimony whereon the complaint is founded. Should this satisfy you that it is just, you will be so good as to give orders to the Consul of France at this port to take the vessel into his custody and deliver her to the owners. Should it be over-weighed in your judgment by any contradictory evidence, which you have, or may acquire, I will ask the favor of a communication of that evidence and that the Consul retain the vessel in his custody until the Executive of the united States shall consider and decide finally on the subject. I have the honor to be with much respect Sir, Your most obedient and most humble servant   Th: Jefferson

PrC (DLC); in the hand of George Taylor, Jr., signed by TJ; at foot of text: "The Minister plenipoy of France." PrC of Tr (DLC); in a clerk's hand. Tr (NNC: Gouverneur Morris Papers). Tr (DNA: RG 46, Senate Records, 3d Cong., 1st sess.). PrC (PRO: FO 97/1). FC (Lb in DNA: RG 59, DL). For enclosures, see enclosures listed at Memorial from George Hammond, 26 June 1793. Letter and enclosures printed in *Message*, 46-8. Enclosed in Memorandum to George Washington, [11-13 July 1793], and TJ to Gouverneur Morris, 16 Aug. 1793.

From Edmond Charles Genet

M.   Philadelphie le 29. Juin 1793. l'an 2e. de la R.

J'ai eu l'honneur de vous remettre dans ma premiere conference offi-cielle avec vous le seul éxemplaire que J'eusse entre mes mains de l'éxposé de la Conduite de la nation françoise envers le peuple Anglois et des motifs qui ont amené la rupture entre la République françoise et le Roi d'angleterre. Je viens de recevoir d'autres éxemplaires de ce re-cueil publié par ordre de la Convention nationale et Je m'empresse de vous les faire passer en vous priant d'avoir la Complaisance de les dis-tribuer aux differents membres de l'Exécutif des Etats unis. Je vous adresse également ci Joint M., quelques éxemplaires du plan de Cons-titution présenté à la Convention nationale par le comité de Constitution et un recueil de pieces Interessantes relatives au Jugement de Louis capet[1] dernier Roi des françois.

Dft (DLC: Genet Papers); at head of text: "Le C. Genet à M. Jefferson." Tr (AMAE: CPEU, xxxvii). FC (DLC: Ge-net Papers); in English. Enclosures: (1) [National Convention], *Exposé de la con-duite de la nation française envers le peuple anglais* . . . (Paris, 1793). (2) [Marquis de Condorcet], *Plan de constitution présenté à la convention nationale, les 15 & 16 février 1793, l'an II de la République* (Paris, 1793). See Sowerby, No. 2675. Other enclosures not found.

[1] Preceding three words altered from "du."

To James Madison

June 29. 1793.

I wrote you on the 23d. and yesterday I received yours of the 17th. which was the more welcome as it acknoleged mine of the 9th. about the safety of which I was anxious. I now risk some other papers, the sequel of those conveyed in that. The result I know not. We are sending a courier to Madrid to make a last effort for the preservation of honorable peace. The affairs of France are recovering their solidity: and from the steadiness of the people on the defection of so popular and capital a commander as Dumourier, we have a proof that nothing can shake their republicanism. Hunger is to be excepted; but the silence of the late papers on that head and the near approach of harvest makes us hope they will weather that rock. I do not find that there has been serious insurrection but in Brittany, and there, the noblesse having been as numerous as the people, and indeed being almost the people, the counterrevolutionary spirit has been known always to have existed since the night in which titles were suppressed. The English are trying to stop the torrent of bankruptcies by an emission of 5. millions of Exchequer bills, to be loaned on the pawn-broking plan: consequently much inferior to the assignats of France. But that paper will sink to an immediate level with their other public paper, and consequently can only complete the ruin of those who take it from government at par, and on a pledge of pins, buckles &c. of double value, which will not sell so as to pay storage in a country where there is no specie, and now we may say no paper of confidence. Every letter which comes expresses a firm belief that the whole paper system will now vanish into that nothing on which it is bottomed. For even the public faith is nothing, as the mass of paper bottomed on it is known to be beyond it's possible redemption. I hope this will be a wholesome lesson to our future legislature. The war between France and England has brought forward the Republicans and Monocrats in every state so openly, that their relative numbers are perfectly visible. It appears that the latter are as nothing. H. is endeavoring to engage a house in town for the next year. He is in the country for the summer.

As I must ere long put my general plan of farming into the hands of my Elkton manager, I have lately endeavored to establish a proper succession of crops for a farm of red highland of about 500. acres of open land fit for culture. In all successions of crops, the feilds must be supposed equal, each feild to go through the same succession, and each year's crop be the same. On these data, the laws of combination pronounce that the number of feilds and number of years constituting a compleat rotation, must be always equal. If you cultivate three equal feilds only, your rotation will be of 3. years, 5. feilds, 5 years &c. I propose 8. feilds of 60. acres each, and of course an 8. years rotation, in the following succession. 1st. year, wheat and fall fallow. 2d. peas with Indn. corn thinly planted. 3d. wheat and fall fallow. 4th. potatoes with Indn. corn thinly planted. 5th. rye or barly[1] and fall fallow. 6th. 7th. and 8th. red clover. The following diagram will shew the system better; the initials of every article only being written in each square or feild, to wit cl. for clover

co.   corn
f.   fallow
pe.   peas
po.   potatoes
r.   rye
w.   wheat.

	1st year	2d	3d	4th	5th	6th	7th	8th
A	wf	pe co.	wf	po. co.	rf	cl.	cl.	cl.
B	pe. co.	wf.	po. co.	rf.	cl.	cl.	cl.	wf.
C	wf	po. co.	rf.	cl.	cl.	cl.	wf.	pe. co.
D	po. co.	rf.	cl.	cl.	cl.	wf.	pe. co.	wf.
E.	rf.	cl.	cl.	cl.	wf.	pe. co.	wf.	po. co.
F	cl.	cl.	cl.	wf.	pe. co.	wf.	po. co.	rf.
G	cl.	cl.	wf.	pe. co.	wf.	po. co.	rf.	cl.
H.	cl.	wf	pe. co.	wf	po. co.	rf.	cl.	cl.

This gives 2. feilds of wheat   120. acres
          1.   of rye or barly[2]   60
          1.   of peas & corn   60
          1.   of potatoes & corn   60.
          1. of the 1st. year's clover   60
          1.   2d.   do   60
          1.   3d.   do.   60
                                               480.
Also 2.[3] eighths of your farm are cleansing⎫
     3. eighths   fallowing⎬ every year.
     3. eighths   resting⎭
     8.

Bye articles as follow.
Oats and flax, a few acres only wanting. To be with the new sown clover.
Hemp, turneps, pumpkins, in the new clearings.
Artichokes in a perpetual feild.
Orchard grass in the hill sides too steep for the plough. Qu?
Lucerne, St. foin, cotton, in appropriate feilds.
Buckwheat to be ploughed into the washed lands.
When a 9th. feild shall be added by new clearings, add it to the rotation as a feild at absolute rest or spring fallowed.[4]
So of a 10th. &c.[5]
As you are now immersed in farming and among farming people, pray consider this plan for me, well, and give me your observations fully and

freely as soon as you can. I mean to ask the same from the President, and also from my son in law. Cattle to be raised in proportion to the provision made for them, also what number of labourers and horses will be necessary? Errors are so much more easy to avoid than to correct afterwards, that I am anxious to be well advised before I begin. Adieu, Yours affectionately.

P.S. June 30. Since writing the above yours of June 19. is received. A Portico may be from 5. to 10. diameters of the column deep, or projected from the building. If of more than 5. diameters there must be a column in the middle of each flank, since it must never be more than 5. diameters from center to center of column. The portico of the Maison quarrée is 3 intercolonnations deep. I never saw as much to a private house.—The Commissioners (Irvine &c.) yesterday delivered in their books and accounts, so that that business is closed. The result not yet known.   In Fenno's paper of yesterday you will see a peice signed pacificus in defence of the proclamation. You will readily know the pen. I know it the more readily because it is an amplification only of the topics urged in discussing the question when first proposed. The right of the *Executive* to declare that we are *not bound to execute the guarantee* was then advanced by him and denied by me. No other opinion expressed on it. In this paper he repeats it, and even considers the proclamation as such a declaration. But if any body intended it as such (except himself) they did not then say so.—The passage beginning with the words 'the answer to this is &c.'[6] is precisely the answer he gave at the time to my objection that the Executive had no authority to issue a declaration of neutrality, nor to do more than declare the actual state of things to be that of peace.—'For until the new government is acknoleged the treaties &c. are of course suspended.' This also is the sum of his arguments the same day on the great question which followed that of the Proclamation, to wit Whether the Executive might not, and ought not to declare the treaties suspended? The real milk and water-views[7] of the Proclamation appeared to me to have been truly given in a piece published in the papers soon after, and which I knew to be E.R.'s from it's exact coincidence with what he had expressed. Upon the whole, my objections to the competence of the Executive to declare neutrality (that being understood to respect the future) were supposed to be got over by avoiding the use of that term. The declaration of the *disposition* of the US. can hardly be called illegal, tho' it was certainly officious and improper. The truth of the fact[8] lent it some cover. My objections to the impolicy of a premature declaration were answered by such arguments as timidity would readily suggest. I now think it extremely possible that Hammond might have been instructed to have asked it, and to offer *the broadest neutral privileges*, as the price, which was exactly the price I wanted that we should contend for.—But is it not a miserable thing that the three heresies I have above quoted from this paper, should pass unnoticed and unanswered, as they certainly will? For none but mere bunglers and brawlers have for some time past taken the trouble to answer any thing.—The Probationary odes [written by S.G.T. in Virga.] are saddled on poor Freneau, who is bloodily attacked about them.

RC (DLC: Madison Papers); unsigned; brackets in original. PrC (DLC); upper left corner of third page torn away; lacks several additions to RC (see notes 3, 4, and 7 below). Tr (DLC); 19th-century copy of final two pages only, with gaps. Enclosures: (1) Alexander Hamilton's Report on a New Foreign Loan, 15 June 1793 (enclosed in George Washington to TJ, 16 June 1793). (2) Second Opinion on a New Foreign Loan, 17 June 1793.

THE COMMISSIONERS: the Commissioners of Accounts for the States. Hamilton's first essay as PACIFICUS defending the Proclamation of Neutrality is printed in Syrett, *Hamilton*, XV, 33-43. For more on the Cabinet debate over the Proclamation and the French treaties, see Cabinet Opinion on Washington's Questions on Neutrality and the Alliance with France, [19 Apr. 1793]; and Editorial Note on Jefferson's opinion on the treaties with France, at 28 Apr. 1793. The MILK AND WATER justification of the Proclamation which TJ attributed to Attorney General Edmund Randolph, an ascription the Editors have been unable to corroborate, was probably the one in an unsigned

article beginning "When foreign nations engage in war" in *Dunlap's American Daily Advertiser*, 29 Apr. 1793. St. George Tucker's PROBATIONARY ODES attacking the alleged corruptions of the Hamiltonian financial system were printed under the pseudonym "Jonathan Pindar" between 1 June and 31 Aug. 1793 in the *National Gazette*. In 1796 they constituted the first part of a published edition which TJ acquired (Sowerby, No. 4511; see also William S. Prince, ed., *The Poems of St. George Tucker of Williamsburg, 1752-1827* [New York, 1977], 16-22, 82).

[1] Preceding two words interlined, but lacking in PrC.
[2] Preceding two words added, but lacking in PrC.
[3] Digit reworked from "3."
[4] Preceding sentence interlined.
[5] Preceding sentence interlined, but lacking in PrC.
[6] Closing quotation mark supplied.
[7] TJ first wrote "real views" before revising the passage to read as above.
[8] TJ here canceled "perhaps."

From James Madison

My dear Sir   June 29. 93.

Your last was of the 17th. inst: and covered *one* paper of the 12th. The weather has been very unfavorable for saving our crops of wheat. It has been from the commencement of the harvest either rainy, cloudy, or hot and damp. I still hope however our crops will be respectable. I have not been able to learn how Albemarle has fared. I have no reason to apprehend that you have more to complain of than we have. The present appearance of the weather is rather favorable. A few days more will put the wheat out of its reach.

My last was of the 19th. I have since seen several of the Natl. Gazettes which continue to teem with animadversions on the Proclamation. My opinion of it was expressed in my last. I foresee that a communication of it will make a part of the Speech to the next Congs. and that it will bring on some embarrassments. Much will depend on events in Europe; and it is to be regretted that the popularity of the President, or the policy of our Government should ever be staked on such contingencies. I observe that our vessels are frequently and insolently seized and searched for French Goods. Is not this complained of by our own people as a breach of the *Modern* law of nations; and whilst British Goods are protected by the Neutrality of our bottoms, will not remonstrances come from France on the subject? The present conveyance to Fredg. being made known at this instant only, I am obliged to conclude in haste with assurances of the affection with which I remain Dear Sir Yrs. sincerely   J. M. Jr

RC (DLC: Madison Papers); endorsed by TJ as received 8 July 1793 and so recorded in SJL.

From James Simpson

Gibraltar, 29 June 1793. Having last written on 1 June, he now has just enough time to advise by way of the American brig *Bacchus*, recently released from detention by a Spanish privateer in Algeciras, that the army Muley Suliman sent from Rabat to the province of Shauia has been totally routed by a superior force opposed to its proceeding southward, in consequence of which Suliman returned to Mequinez with no hope for the present of "succeeding[1] to the general command of that unhappy Empire."

RC (DNA: RG 59, CD); 2 p.; at foot of first page: "Thomas Jefferson Esqr &ca"; endorsed by TJ as received 17 Aug. 1793 and so recorded in SJL. Tr (same); in a clerk's hand; at head of text: "Copy."

TJ submitted this letter to the President on 19 Aug. 1793, and Washington returned it to him the same day (Washington, *Journal*, 225).

[1] "Speedily Succeeding" in Tr.

To William Carmichael
and William Short

Gentlemen   June 30. 1793.

I have received from Messrs. Viar and Jaudenes the representatives of Spain at this place, a letter, which, whether considered in itself, or as the sequel of several others, conveys to us very disagreeable prospects of the temper and views of their court[1] towards us. If this letter is a faithful expression of that temper, we presume it to be the effect of egregious misrepresentations by their agents in America. [2] Revising our own dispositions and proceedings towards that power, we can find in them nothing but those of peace and friendship for them; and conscious that this will be apparent from a true statement of facts, I shall proceed to give you such a one to be communicated to the court of Madrid. If they find it very different from that conveyed to them by others, they may think it prudent to doubt, and to take and to give time for mutual enquiry and explanation. I shall proceed to give you this statement, beginning it from an early period.

At the commencement of the late war, the US. laid it down as a rule of their conduct to engage the Indian tribes within their neighborhood to remain strictly neutral. They accordingly strongly pressed it on them, urging that it was a family quarrel with which they had nothing to do, and in which we wished them to take no part: and we strengthened these recommendations by doing them every act of friendship and good neighborhood which circumstances left in our power. With some these sollicitations prevailed: but the greater part of them suffered themselves to be drawn into the war against us. They waged it in their usual cruel manner, murdering and scalping men, women and children indiscriminately, burning their houses, and desolating the country. They put us to vast expence, as well by the constant force [3] we were obliged to keep up in that quarter, as by expeditions of considerable magnitude which we were under the necessity of sending into their country from time to time.

Peace being at length concluded with England, we had it also to conclude with them. They had made war on us without the least provocation or pretence of injury, they had added greatly to the cost of that war; they had [4] insulted our feelings by their savage cruelties, they were by our arms completely subdued and humbled. Under all these circumstances we had a right to demand substantial satisfaction and indemnification. We used that right however with real moderation. Their limits with us under the former government were generally ill-defined, questionable, and the frequent [5] cause of war. Sincerely desirous of living in their peace, of cultivating it by every act of justice and friendship, and of rendering them better neighbors by introducing among them some of the most useful arts, it was necessary to begin by a precise definition of boundary. Accordingly at the treaties held with them, our mutual boundaries were settled; and notwithstanding our just right to concessions adequate to the circumstances of the case, we required such only as were inconsiderable: and for even these, in order that we might place them in a state of perfect conciliation, we paid them a valuable consideration and granted them annuities in money which have been regularly paid, and were equal to the prices for which they have usually sold their lands. [6] Sensible as they were of the wrong they had done, they expected to make some indemnification, and were for the most part satisfied with the mode and measure of it. [7] In one or two instances where a dissatisfaction was observed to remain as to the boundaries agreed on, or doubts were entertained [8] of the authority of those with whom they were agreed, the US. invited the parties to new treaties, and rectified what appeared to be susceptible of it. This was particularly the case with the Creeks. They complained of an inconvenient cession of lands on their part, and by persons not duly representing their nation. They were therefore desired to appoint a proper deputation to revise their treaty and that there might be no danger of any unfair practices they were invited to come to the seat of the general government, and to treat with that directly. They accordingly came. A considerable proportion of what had been ceded was, on the revision, yielded back to them, and nothing required in lieu of it: [9] and tho' they would have been better satisfied to have had the whole restored, [10] yet they had obtained enough to satisfy them well. Their nation too would have been satisfied, for they were conscious of their aggression and of the moderation of the indemnity with which we had been contented. But at that time came among them an adventurer of the name of Bowles, who acting from an impulse with which we are unacquainted, flattered them with the hope of some foreign interference, which should undo what had been done, and force us to consider the naked grant of their peace as a sufficient satisfaction for their having made war on us. Of this adventurer the Spanish government rid us: but not of his principles, his practices, and his excitements against us. These were more than continued by the officers commanding at [11] New Orleans, and Pensacola, and by agents employed by them and bearing their commission. Their proceedings have been the subject of former letters to you, and proofs of these proceedings have been sent to you. These with others now sent establish the facts that they called assemblies of the Southern Indians, openly persuaded them to disavow their treaties and the limits therein established, promised to support them with all the powers which depended on them, assured them of the protection of their sovereign, gave them arms in great quantities for the avowed purpose of committing hostilities on us, and promised them future supplies to their utmost need. The Chickasaws, the most steady and faithful friends of these states, have remained unshaken by these practices. So also have the Choctaws [12] for the most part. The Cherokees have been teazed into some expressions of discontent, delivered only to the Spanish governors, or their agents; while to us they have continued to speak the language of peace and friendship. One part of the nation only, settled at Chuckamogga, and mixed with banditti and outcasts from the Shawanese and other tribes, acknoleging controul from none, and never in a state of peace, have readily engaged in the hostilities against us to which they were encouraged. But what was much more important, great numbers of the Creeks, chiefly their young men, have yeilded to these incitements, and have now, for more than a twelve-month, been committing murders and desolations on our frontiers. Really desirous of living in peace with them, we have redoubled our efforts to produce the same disposition in them. We have borne with their aggressions, forbidden all returns of hostility against them, tied up the hands of our people insomuch that few instances of retaliation have occurred even from our suffering citizens, we have multiplied our gratifications to them, fed them when starving from the produce of our own feilds and labour. No longer ago than the last winter, when they had no other resource against famine, and must have perished in great numbers, we carried into their country and distributed among them gratuitously 10,000 bushels of corn; and that too at the very time when their young men were daily committing murders on helpless women and children on our frontiers. And tho' these depredations now involve more considerable parts of the nation, we are still[13] demanding the punishment of the guilty individuals[14] and shall be contented with it.   These acts of neighborly kindness and support on our part have not been confined to the Creeks, tho' extended to them in much the greatest degree. Like wants among the Chickasaws had induced us to send to them also, at first[15] 500. bushels of corn, and afterwards 1500. more. Our language to all the tribes of Indians has constantly been to live in peace with one another, and in a most especial manner we have used our endeavors with those in the neighborhood of the Spanish colonies to be peaceable towards those colonies. I sent you on a former occasion[16] the copy of a letter from the Secretary at War to Mr. Seagrove, one of our Agents with the Indians in that quarter, merely to convey to you the general Tenor of the conduct marked out for those Agents: and desired you, in placing before the Eyes of the Spanish ministry, the very contrary conduct observed by their agents here, to invite them to a reciprocity of good offices with our Indian neighbors, each for the other, and to make our common peace, the common object of both nations. I can protest that such has hitherto been the candid and zealous endeavors of this Government; that if it's Agents have in any instance acted in another way, it has been equally unknown and unauthorized by us,[17] and that were even probable proofs of it produced, there[18] would be no hesitation to mark them with the disapprobation of the Government. We expected the same friendly condescension from the Court of Spain, in furnishing you with proofs of the practices of the Governor de

Carondelet in particular; practices avowed by him and attempted to be justified in his letter.[19]

In this state of things, in such dispositions towards Spain, and towards the Indians, in such a course of proceedings, with respect to them, and while negotiations were instituted at Madrid for arranging these and all other matters which might affect our friendship and good understanding, we received from Messrs. de Viar and Jaudenes their letter of May 25th. which was the subject of mine of May 31st. to you; and now again we have received that of the 18th. instant, a copy of which is enclosed. This letter charges us, and in the most disrespectful Style with

1. exciting the Chickasaws to war on the Creeks:
2. furnishing them with provisions and arms:
3. aiming at the occupation of a post at the Ecores amargas:
4. giving medals and marks of distinction to several Indians:
5. meddling with the affairs of such as are allies of Spain:
6. not using efficacious means to prevent these proceedings.

I shall make short observations on these charges.

1. Were the 1st. true, it would not be unjustifiable. The Creeks have now a second time commenced against us a wanton and unprovoked war, and the present one in the face of a recent Treaty, and of the most friendly and charitable Offices on our part. There would be nothing out of the common course of proceeding then, for us to engage allies, if we needed any for their punishment. But we neither need, nor have sought them. The fact itself is utterly false, and we defy the world to produce a single proof of it. The declaration of war by the Chickasaws, as we are informed, was a very sudden thing, produced by the murder of some of their people by a party of Creeks, and produced so instantaneously as to give nobody time to interfere either to promote or prevent a rupture. We had, on the contrary most particularly exhorted that nation to preserve peace, because in truth we have a most particular friendship for them. This will be evident from a copy of the message of the President to them, among the papers now enclosed.[20]

2d. The Gift of provisions was but an act of that friendship to them, when in the same distress, which had induced us to give five times as much to the less friendly nation of the Creeks.—But we have given arms to them. We believe it is the practice of every white nation to give arms to the neighboring Indians. The agents of Spain have done it abundantly, and we suppose not out of their own pockets, and this for purposes of avowed hostility on us, and they have been[21] liberal in promises of further supplies. We have given a few arms to a very friendly Tribe, not to make war on Spain, but to defend themselves from the atrocities

[409]

of a vastly more numerous and powerful people, and one, which by a series of unprovoked and even unrepelled attacks on us, is obliging us to look towards war as the only means left of curbing their insolence.

3. We are aiming, as is pretended, at an establishment on the Missisippi, at the Ecores amargas. Considering the measures of this nature with which Spain is going on, having, since her proposition to treat with us on the subject, established posts at the Walnut hills[22] and other places for 200 miles upwards,[23] it would not have been wonderful if we had taken countervailing[24] measures. But the truth is, we have not done it. We wished to give a fair chance to the negotiation going on, and thought it but common candour to leave things in statu quo, to make no innovation, pending the negotiation. In this spirit we forbid and deterred even by military force a large association of our Citizens, under the name of the Yazoo companies, which had formed to settle themselves at those very walnut hills, which Spain has since occupied.[25] And so far are we from meditating the particular establishment so boldly charged in this letter, that we know not what place is meant by the Ecores amargas. This charge then is false also.

4. Giving medals and marks of distinction to the Indian Chiefs. This is but blindly hinted at in this letter, but was more pointedly complained of in the former. This has been an antient Custom from time immemorial. The medals are considered as complimentary things, as marks of friendship to those who come to see us, or who[26] do us good offices,[27] conciliatory of their good will towards us, and not designed to produce a contrary disposition towards others. They confer no power,[28] and seem to have taken their origin in the European practice of giving medals or other marks of friendship to the negotiators of treaties, and other diplomatic Characters, or visitors of distinction. The British government, while it prevailed here, practised the giving Medals, Gorgets, and Bracelets to the Savages invariably. We have continued it, and we did imagine, without pretending to know, that Spain also did it.[29]

5. We meddle with the affairs of Indians in alliance with Spain. We are perfectly at a loss to know what this means. The Indians on our frontier have treaties both with Spain and us. We have endeavored to cultivate their friendship, to merit it by presents, charities and exhortations to peace with their neighbors, and particularly with the subjects of Spain. We have carried on some little commerce with them, merely to supply their wants. Spain too has made them presents, traded with them, kept agents among them, though their country is[30] within the limits established as ours at the general peace.[31] However Spain has chosen to have it understood that she has some claim to some parts of that Country, and that it must be one of the subjects of our present negotiations. Out of respect for her then, we have considered her pre-

tensions to the Country; though it was impossible to believe them serious,[32] as colouring pretensions to a concern with those Indians on the same Ground with our own, and we were willing to let them go on till a treaty should set things to rights between us.

6. Another article of complaint, is that we have not used efficacious means to suppress these practices. But if the charge is false, or the practice justifiable, no suppression is necessary.

And lastly, these Gentlemen say that on a view of these proceedings of the United States with respect to Spain and the Indians their allies, they foresee that our peace with Spain is very problematical in future. The principal object of the letter being *our* supposed excitements of the Chickasaws against the Creeks, and *their* protection of the latter, are we to understand from this that if we arm to repel the attacks of the Creeks, on ourselves,[33] it will disturb our peace with Spain? That if we will not fold our arms and let them butcher us without resistance, Spain will consider it as a cause of war? This is, indeed, so serious an intimation that the President has thought it could no longer be treated with subordinate Characters, but that his sentiments should be conveyed to the Government of Spain itself, through you.

We love and we value peace: we know it's blessings from experience. We abhor the follies of war, and are not untried in it's distresses and calamities. Unmeddling with the affairs of other nations, we had hoped that our distance and our dispositions would have left us free in the example and indulgence of peace with all the world. We had, with sincere and particular dispositions courted and cultivated the friendship of Spain. We have made to it great sacrifices of time and interest, and were[34] disposed to believe she would see her interests also in a perfect[35] coalition and good understanding with us. Cherishing still the same sentiments, we have chosen, in the present instance, to ascribe the intimations in this letter to the particular character of the writers, displayed in the peculiarity of the style of their communications; and, therefore, we have removed the cause from them to their sovereign, in whose justice and love of peace we have Confidence. If we are disappointed in this appeal, if we are to be forced into a contrary order of things, our Mind is made up. We shall meet it with firmness. The necessity of our position, will supercede all appeal to calculation, now as it has done heretofore. We confide in our own strength, without boasting of it; we respect that of others, without fearing it. If we cannot otherwise prevail on the Creeks to discontinue their depredations, we will attack them in force.[36] If Spain chuses to consider our self-defence against savage-butchery as a cause of war to her, we must meet her also[37] in war, with regret, but without fear; and we shall be happier to the last moment to repair with her to the tribunal of peace and reason.

The President charges you to communicate the contents of this letter to the Court of Madrid, with all the temperance and delicacy, which the dignity and character of that Court, render proper; but with all the firmness and selfrespect, which befit a nation conscious of it's rectitude, and settled in it's purpose.[38] I have the honour to be with sentiments of the most perfect esteem & respect, Gentlemen, your most obedient and most humble servant

TH: JEFFERSON

RC (DLC: Short Papers); incomplete text in the hand of George Taylor, Jr., with complimentary close, signature, and one or two clerical corrections by TJ; endorsed by Short; estimated first four missing pages supplied from Dft (see note 16 below). Dft (DLC); written by TJ ca. 20-22 June 1793 and revised by him at various times down to 30 June 1793; contains numerous emendations, only the most important being noted below. Tr (CtY); in Taylor's hand; at foot of first page: "To Messrs. Carmichael & Short." PrC (DLC). Tr (DNA: RG 46, Senate Records, 3d Cong., 1st sess.). Tr (Lb in same, TR). FC (Lb in DNA: RG 59, DCI). Recorded in SJPL. Sent with this letter was a separate list of the enclosures described below entitled "Documents accompanying the letter from the Secy. of State of this day, to Messrs. Carmichael & Short," dated 30 June 1793 (MS in DLC: Short Papers, in Taylor's hand, with a line drawn above the last two entries, the second of which is canceled, and bearing a later note at foot of text pertaining to the other: "this latter enclosed in a letter of 12th. July 1793. written in cypher"; PrC in DLC, lacking cancellation of last entry and note at foot of text, but containing later marginal note by Taylor in ink: "these were the sub. of a partr. ler."; FC in Lb in DNA: RG 59, DCI, consisting of unrevised list). The last two entries in question were documents TJ received on 2 July 1793 from Edmond Charles Genet pertaining to the opposition of the French government under Louis XVI to American claims to a right of navigation on the Mississippi: "Note sur les principes de l'Espagne relativement à la Navigation du Missisipi" and "Extrait des instructions données au Cte. de Moustier le 30. 7bre. 1787." After the President, and possibly the Cabinet, considered them on 11 and 12 July 1793, TJ sent only the first one to the American commissioners in Spain (enclosure to TJ's first Memorandum to George Washington, [11 July 1793]; TJ to Carmichael and Short, 12 July 1793; Washington, *Journal*, 191, 194). Enclosures: (1) Josef de Jaudenes and Josef Ignacio de Viar to TJ, 12 and 18 June 1793, and enclosures. (2) John Sullivan to William Brown, Charleston, 24 Sep. 1787, urging Brown to take up land on the Tennessee river in the state of Franklin, as "we will be speedily in possession of New Orleans," to keep this letter secret, and to reply immediately about his intentions; with subjoined 6 Nov. 1787 attestation by Robert and Gouverneur Morris. (3) Extract of Governor William Blount to Henry Knox, 28 July 1791, enclosing a dependable report by Captain David Smith of Nashville stating that on 22 May 1791 he observed Spaniards under Governor Gayoso's direction building a fort at Walnut Hills. (4) Extract of Timothy Barnard to Creek Indian Agent James Seagrove, Flints River, 13 July 1792, stating that the Cusseta king accepted his account of Bowles, that the Spanish planned to meet at Pensacola and Mobile with the Cherokees, Chickasaws, Choctaws, and Creeks to arm them against Americans, and that despite his efforts to plant doubts about Spanish motives, the Cusseta king asserted that he planned to meet with the Spanish because matters with Georgia could not be settled until toward fall. (5) Extract of Knox to Brigadier General Josiah Harmar, War Office, 16 Oct. 1787, stating that, in consequence of the publication of a letter of 1 Mch. last from John Sullivan to Don Diego de Gardoqui, Congress was ordering Harmar to seize and confine Sullivan if he came into federal territory and to report this to Knox when it happened for Congress's information and orders. (6) Extract of same to same, 14 Nov. 1787, enclosing a copy of No. 2 and ordering Harmar to prevent any attacks on New Orleans by western settlers as suggested therein. (7) Extract of same to same, 19 Dec. 1787, stating that although a person from Franklin has assured him that there is no plan to attack New Orleans as suggested in No. 2, Harmar should still be on the alert to prevent one, and that western settlers may rely on protection from the union for their legal pursuits. (8) Extract of same to same, 24 Apr. 1788, stating that Harmar had done well to visit Monsieur Cruzat, the Spanish commandant at St. Louis, that he should strive to convince all Spanish officers of American good will toward Spain, and that there seemed to be no foundation to the intelligence about Sullivan's design on New Orleans, though Harmar should observe the congressional resolves about arresting Sullivan in federal territory. (9) Extract of Knox's Instructions to Captain Henry Burbeck, 8 Apr. 1790, enjoining him to maintain good relations with the nearby Spanish garrison. (10) Extract of Knox to Seagrove, 29 Apr. 1792, enjoining him to maintain good relations with the Spanish government and interest along the southern border, and to inform the Spanish of any other desperado like Bowles or of any hostile Indian designs against them. (11) Extract of Knox's Instructions to Major Henry Gaither, 11 Aug. 1792, ordering all officers on the St. Marys river to respect the Spanish officers and government. (12) Extract of Knox's Instructions to Major General Arthur St. Clair, 21 Mch. 1791, discussing two proclamations designed to prevent Dr. James O'Fallon from raising troops in Kentucky to settle Indian lands purchased by private companies from the state of Georgia in violation of United States treaties, and stating that if this approach failed the federal government was considering the use of military force to deter O'Fallon. (13) Extract of The Turkey to Governor Blount, Turkey Town, 2 Sep. 1792, stating that only the five lower towns of the Cherokees on Big river were determined to go to war with the United States on 8 Sep. 1792, that these towns had been armed by the Spanish, and that even though the Spanish insisted that these arms were to be kept in reserve and not used for war, they were to blame for this situation. (14) Extract of John Thompson to same, Turkey Town, 2 Sep. 1792, stating that the five lower towns of the Cherokees planned to go to war on 8 Sep., that Blount could rely on the Creeks to do their part, and that the Spanish were blameworthy for arming the hostiles, even if they did claim that they gave them the weapons to keep in reserve and not to make war. (15) Extract of Cherokee Indian Agent Leonard D. Shaw to same, 29 Aug. 1792, stating that on 24 Aug. the Creeks killed Mr. Ramsay and a person just arrived from Charleston, that the day before the Creeks came close to killing Moses Price, even though he was accompanied by the Kingfisher and his wife, that it is the Creeks' "open and avowed intention" to kill every white man they meet, and that all this is attributable to the arming of the Indians by the Spanish. (16) Extract of Information from the Cherokee Red Bird, enclosed in a 15 Sep. 1792 letter of Governor Blount, stating that John Watts had brought home with him from Pensacola seven horseloads of ammunition and accoutrements to equip 200 horsemen, that Watts had been appointed to command the Creeks and Cherokees called to war, and that a Creek council had accepted Watts's appointment. (17) Extract of Ben James to Governor Blount, Choctaw Nation, 30 June 1792, stating that every white man among the Choctaws must be dependent on the Spanish government, and that Alexander McGillivray's current visit to New Orleans was good neither for the United States nor the Choctaws. (18) Extract of Information from the Hanging Maw, enclosed in a 7 Oct. 1792 letter of Governor Blount, stating that, based upon information from the reliable half-breed John Boggs, the Creeks were on their way to attack the Cumberland settlement in the Mero District, that they were joined by 100 to 200 Cherokees, among them John Watts, who had been armed by the Spanish, that Richard Findleston and a Frenchman had passed from Pensacola to Cumberland to obtain intelligence of that country, and that the five lower towns of the Cherokees were expelling those wanting peace and welcoming migrants from the upper towns who favor war. (19) Extract of Mr. Wallace's Report, 15 Dec. 1792, enclosed in a 16 Dec. 1792 letter of Governor Blount, stating that he delivered Blount's message to the Cherokee towns of Chilhowee and Tallassee warning them to refrain from violence against nearby whites, that the head man of Chilhowee pleaded his inability to prevent the Creeks and the lower towns of the Cherokees from passing through his towns to kill frontiersmen and steal their horses, that Watts had 1,600 men ready to fight in the lower towns, and that the Spanish had offered land and weapons to the head man's town, even to boys under twelve. (20) Extract of a Conference of Governor Blount, John Sevier, and others with the Cherokees, Knoxville, 26 Dec. 1792, in which the Hanging Maw described how Governor Arturo O'Neill at Pensacola had shown the Hare magazines of ammunition for the Indians, saying they would have plenty and that the Americans, "great rogues," would give them very little for a high price. (21) Extract of Information given to Governor Blount by James Carey, United States interpreter in the Cherokee nation, Knoxville, 3 Nov. 1792, transmitted in Blount to Knox, 8 Nov. 1792, stating that in May 1792 John Watts had received a letter from Mr. Panton, written at the home of Mr. McDonald, inviting Watts and the Bloody Fellow in Governor O'Neill's name to bring ten packhorses to Pensacola to carry weapons to the Cherokees; that in the same letter Panton also promised to supply goods to the Cherokees; that with McDonald acting as interpreter Panton invited the Little Turkey to Pensacola for the same reason, offered to supply his people with goods much cheaper than before, and assured him that the Creeks had agreed to allow the Spanish to erect a fort at the Alabama fork a mile below McGillivray's house to store arms and ammunition for the protection of the Creeks and Cherokees; that Watts and the Bloody Fellow visited McDonald, who wrote two letters to O'Neill, one highly recommending Watts and his uncle Talteeske and the other (in the name and at the request of the Bloody Fellow) announcing that the Bloody Fellow, having decided to break with the United States and align with Spain, wanted Watts to return with arms and ammunition from Pensacola and would later visit O'Neill with the Little Turkey and some other chiefs; that Panton dissuaded the Bloody Fellow from appearing before a Cherokee council to report on his negotiations with the federal government in Philadelphia; that at this same June council Spanish influence led the Little Turkey to demand a boundary with the United States at the ridge between the Cumberland and Green rivers; that after his return from Pensacola late in August Watts informed the Cherokees of O'Neill's promise to arm the Indians in the middle of October at Pensacola with matériel sent by the King of Spain, of O'Neill's assurances that Spain had no interest in acquiring Indian lands, of

O'Neill's argument that it was a propitious time for the Southern Indians to strike while the United States was at war with the Western Indians, and of O'Neill's announcement that Spain was going to build a fort at the Alabama forks with Creek consent and would build a magazine for the Cherokees at Wills Town; and that in consequence of Watts's overtures the Creeks had decided to send some warriors to Pensacola to acquire arms and others to James Seagrove at Rock Landing to obtain as many presents as possible until the Creeks were ready for war. (22) Extract of James Seagrove to George Washington, Rock Landing, 5 July 1792, stating that the account of the Spanish officer mentioned in No. 23—a Frenchman named Captain Olivier who had been appointed by Baron de Carondelet to succeed McGillivray, with his support, as Spanish agent to the Creeks—was untrustworthy; that during McGillivray's current visit to New Orleans Olivier forbade the Creeks to run a boundary line with Georgia and sell land to, or have anything to do with, the United States, furnished them with goods and ammunition, and urged them to treat with the Spanish at Pensacola; that the Creeks believed the Spanish would seek permission at the Pensacola conference to build forts and establish garrisons in their lands; that the Spanish are playing a double game with William Augustus Bowles in regard to the United States, having treated him leniently and dispatched him to Spain; that McGillivray is unfaithful to the United States and has probably withdrawn to the Spanish so that Olivier can lead active Creek opposition to it; and that McGillivray's evasions with Seagrove and the Secretary of War about carrying out the Treaty of New York apparently resulted from the influence of his Spanish and English friends, and not from Indian opposition to it. (23) Alexander McGillivray to Seagrove, Upper Creeks, Little Tallassee, 18 May 1792, stating that his efforts to carry out the Treaty of New York were frustrated by the appearance among the Creeks of Bowles, who before his arrest by the Spanish promised British aid and encouraged a majority of the towns to oppose ceding more than the east side of the Oconee river to Georgia, of Indians from New Orleans, and of a Spanish officer who tells the Creeks that he is under orders to prevent them from running a line or dealing with the Americans and who invites them to a meeting at Pensacola in September; that the Indians are distracted, being tampered with on every side, and he is "in the situation of a Keeper of Bedlam and nearly fit for an Inhabitant"; that Randall has been sent to the Cusseta chiefs with a talk urging them to run the line, though their compliance is doubtful; and that to avoid a horrid war the Indians should not be asked for more land cessions at present. (24) Extract of Seagrove to Washington, 27 July 1792, stating that the Spanish were conspiring to involve the four Southern Indian nations in a war with the United States, and enclosing the sworn testimony of James Leonard, a respectable citizen of Massachusetts new to this country, attesting to the new perfidy of Spain and the unfaithfulness of McGillivray. (25) Message from Knox to the Chickasaws, 27 Apr. 1793, stating that the President was aware of their great need for arms, ammunition, and corn; that the President commended the way of peace to them; and that the United States was about to negotiate for peace with the hostile Western Indians but was ready to go to war with them if negotiations failed (PrCs of Trs in DLC: TJ Papers, 89: 15410-14, 96: 16505-16, 16532-40, 16517-31, 16541-2, in various clerical hands, with attestations by John Stagg, Jr., chief clerk of the War Department; Trs in Lb in DNA: RG 59, DCI). Enclosed in TJ to Thomas Pinckney, 11 Sep. 1793.

TJ's letter reflected the growing crisis in Spanish-American relations resulting from the efforts of Francisco Luis Hector, Baron de Carondelet, the governor of Louisiana and West Florida, to halt further American expansion in the southwest through the formation of a confederation of Southern Indian tribes under Spanish auspices (Bemis, *Pinckney's Treaty*, 174-85; and Whitaker, *Frontier*, 153-6, 163-70). It was specifically occasioned by a letter of 18 June 1793 from the agents of the Spanish government in Philadelphia warning of the possibility of war between Spain and the United States because of allegedly hostile American interference with these tribes. In response to this communication, the President and the Cabinet met two days later, when the agents' letter was read and the Cabinet decided that TJ should prepare a full statement of American relations with the Southern Indians and the Spanish for Carmichael and Short to transmit to the Spanish court. Meeting again on 22 June, they approved "with some alterations" the text of such a statement, presumably the draft of the letter above (as well as TJ's brief reply to the Spanish representatives of 11 July). Thereafter, judging from its 30 June 1793 dateline, TJ evidently continued to work on the draft until it was ready for his chief clerk to copy on that date. TJ waited for the President to return to Philadelphia from Mount Vernon on 11 July before entrusting the dispatch and its enclosures on the following day to a special messenger to Madrid, but there is no evidence that he showed the final text of the letter to Washington or the Cabinet (Jaudenes and Viar to TJ, 18 June 1793; Cabinet Opinion on Relations with Spain and Great Britain, 20 June 1793; TJ to Viar and Jaudenes, 11 July 1793; TJ to James Blake, 12 July 1793; Washington, *Journal*, 183, 186-7, 190-1, 194-6). For the reception of TJ's letter in Spain, see Bemis, *Pinckney's Treaty*, 187-90.

The 1790 Treaty of New York was the agreement the Creeks negotiated at the SEAT OF THE GENERAL GOVERNMENT (ASP, *Indian Affairs*, I, 81-2). In conjunction with his efforts to create an independent Creek-Cherokee state under his leadership and in alliance with Great Britain, the flamboyant ADVENTURER William Augustus BOWLES, a loyalist from Maryland and a half-pay British officer who became a Creek chief after the American Revolution, had incited tribal opposition to this treaty during his stay among the Creeks in 1791-92. Although Bowles was not an official agent of the British government, unofficially his enterprise enjoyed the support of Lord Grenville, the British foreign minister, and Lord Dunmore, the royal governor of the Bahamas. Early in 1792 Bowles was arrested by Spanish officials in Florida, who feared that his projected Indian state threatened Spain's position in the region. Despite his subsequent efforts to convince Carondelet and Luis de Las Casas, the governor of Cuba, that his plan was actually consistent with Spanish interest in creating an Indian buffer between the United States and their American empire, soon thereafter Bowles was sent to Spain, where he was currently being held as a political prisoner (Coker and Watson,

Indian Traders, 148-56; J. Leitch Wright, Jr., *William Augustus Bowles: Director General of the Creek Nation* [Athens, Ga., 1967], 3-18, 27-8, 37-8, 52-80).

TJ's letter to Carmichael and Short of 14 Oct. 1792 was the FORMER OCCASION when he informed them of Henry Knox's instruction to Creek Indian agent James SEA-GROVE to preserve peace between these Indians and the Spanish, though at that time he did not actually enclose a copy of Knox's letter to this effect. ECORES AMARGAS: Ecores à Margot, or Chickasaw Bluffs, a site on the Mississippi river at modern-day Memphis, Tennessee, that Carondelet himself was actually planning to fortify in order to prevent American settlement in the area and on which he had a fort erected in 1795 to foil the settlement plans of one of the Yazoo land speculation companies (Whitaker, *Spanish-American Frontier*, 214-16; Coker and Watson, *Indian Traders*, 171-2, 175, 181). For the Washington administration's opposition to the South Carolina Yazoo Company—the LARGE ASSOCIATION OF OUR CITIZENS which sought to create an independent state in Choctaw country on the basis of a land grant from Georgia and with Spanish support—see John C. Parish, "The Intrigues of Doctor James O'Fallon," MVHR, XVII (1930), 238-56. The Spanish CLAIM TO SOME PARTS OF THAT COUNTRY is discussed in Bemis, *Pinckney's Treaty*, 41-5.

¹ Tr in CtY: "conduct."
² TJ continued this sentence as follows: "desirous perhaps for their own purposes of bringing on scenes in which they may have a chance to gather up something." He subsequently bracketed this passage and wrote next to it in the margin "separate letter." The passage is not in the other texts.
³ Word interlined in place of "guards."
⁴ TJ here canceled "distressed."
⁵ TJ here canceled "subjec."
⁶ Preceding sentence written in margin in place of the following passage: "Some we were obliged to require. Sufficiently distressed for the means of raising and paying souldiers during the war, one of the resources to which we had been obliged to recur was the engaging to them grants of land at the close of the war. It was necessary to enable ourselves to comply with this engagement: and it being one item only in the long account of damages which

the wanton injustice of our Indian neighbors had done us, it was but a temperate measure of satisfaction to exact from them this part of the expences which they had brought on us. They were generally." Before striking this passage, TJ wrote in the margin near the end of it notes for the sentence he substituted: "qu. and even for this valuable consideration and annual sum given them."
⁷ TJ first wrote "They were generally sensible of the wrong they had done, expected to make some indemnification, and were for the most part satisfied with the measure ⟨and mode of indemnification⟩ required" and then altered it to read as above.
⁸ TJ initially wrote the sentence to this point as "In one or two instances where there remained a dissatisfaction with the boundaries agreed on, or doubts" before altering it to read as above.
⁹ TJ first wrote "Great alterations in their favor were made in the limits; a considerable cession was given back to them in one quarter, in lieu of a very small one in another" and then altered it to read as above.
¹⁰ Preceding three words interlined in place of "it back for nothing."
¹¹ Preceding three words interlined in place of "Governors of." Next to this line TJ wrote in the margin "commandt."
¹² Remainder of sentence interlined.
¹³ TJ here canceled "only peaceably," above which he interlined and then canceled "acting on the defensive and in an amicable manner."
¹⁴ Remainder of sentence interlined. Next to it in the margin TJ wrote "to be corrected."
¹⁵ Word lacking in Tr in CtY.
¹⁶ Text to this point supplied from Dft.
¹⁷ In Dft TJ first wrote the remainder of this sentence as "and that were proofs produced against them which could satisfy the mind of the government there would be no hesitation to withdraw them from the charges committed to them" before altering it to read as above.
¹⁸ In Dft TJ wrote in the margin next to this word, which begins a line, "would be properly noticed."
¹⁹ In Dft TJ here canceled "We judged from our own dispositions that indulgence towards a particular officer would never be weighed a moment in the scale against the peace and friendship of a neighbor nation."

[20] Preceding sentence inserted in Dft by TJ sometime after the next paragraph was written. Before adding the sentence he had written in the margin "here refer to message &c."

[21] In Dft TJ first wrote "Spain has done ⟨to⟩ it extravagantly, for purposes of avowed hostility on us, and has been still more" before altering it to read as above.

[22] Next to the preceding five words in Dft TJ, apparently in this order, wrote "qu?" in the margin and above it "O Fallon's design to establish at the Walnut hills."

[23] Word interlined in Dft in place of "above."

[24] Word interlined in Dft in place of "corresponding."

[25] Preceding sentence written in the margin of Dft.

[26] In Dft TJ here canceled "otherwise."

[27] Remainder of sentence interlined in Dft.

[28] In Dft TJ here canceled "for we pretend to none over ⟨an independent⟩ a nation of independent government."

[29] In Dft TJ wrote "qu." in the margin next to this sentence.

[30] Preceding four words interlined in Dft in place of "the only circumstance which could render this proceeding offensive from them to us was that they have done it to Indians residing."

[31] In Dft TJ here canceled "and it has been generally understood among the white nations of America that they are to have nothing to do with the Indians within each others limits." Next to this passage he wrote in the margin "guard this expression."

[32] In Dft TJ first wrote "which we did not think serious" and then altered it to read as above.

[33] Preceding two words interlined in Dft.

[34] Remainder of this sentence and first five words of the following sentence interlined in Dft in place of "still disposed to sacrifice whatever justice and honor would permit."

[35] In Dft TJ here canceled "friendship and."

[36] In Dft TJ here canceled "Probably we shall be forced to it within a very short time."

[37] Word interlined in Dft.

[38] In Dft TJ here wrote "and you will give us the earliest communications of what we may expect." He subsequently bracketed the clause and wrote next to it in the margin "to be in separate letter."

To Edmond Charles Genet

Sɪʀ   Philadelphia June 30. 1793

I have to acknolege the receipt of your favor of the 25th. inst. on the subject of vessels belonging to the enemies of France which have procured arms within our ports for their defence. Those from Charleston and Philadelphia have gone off before it was known to the government, and the former indeed in the first moments of the war, and before preventive[1] measures could be taken in so distant a port.   The day after my receipt of your letter the communications now inclosed from the governor of Maryland came to hand, and prevented our interference on the subject of the Trusty Capt. Hale, a vessel loaded with flour and lumber and bound to Barbadoes. You will perceive by these papers that the governor of Maryland had got information that she was buying guns, and had given orders for the examination of the fact, but that she got off before the officer could get on board, having[2] cleared out three or four days before. It appears that she was of 300. tuns burthen and had mounted 4. small guns.   The case of the Swallow is different from any which has yet been presented to the President. It shall be submitted to him on his return; and no doubt will meet his earliest attention and decision. I have the honor to be with sentiments of the most perfect esteem & respect Sir your most obedt. & most humble servt.

TH: JEFFERSON

PrC (DLC); at foot of text: "The M. P. of France." Tr (NNC: Gouverneur Morris Papers). Tr (DNA: RG 46, Senate Records, 3d Cong., 1st sess.). PrC (PRO: FO 97/1). FC (Lb in DNA: RG 59, DL). Tr (DLC: Genet Papers). Tr (AMAE: CPEU, XXXVII); in French. Tr (DLC: Genet Papers); in French; draft translation of preceding Tr; docketed by Genet. Enclosures: (1) Extract of Thomas Sim Lee to Henry Knox, In Council, Annapolis, 22 June 1793, stating that Nos. 2-3 will explain the first case calling for action since receipt of Knox's communication on the outfitting of fighting vessels in their jurisdiction and will show that the ship escaped because of the unintended application of the officer to Mr. Ireland for the information desired, and promising to be better prepared in the future for similar occurrences expected at the same port. (2) Lee to the Baltimore Customs Collector, 20 June 1793, ordering him to investigate immediately the arming, loading, manning, and destination of the British ship consigned to Mr. Ireland in Baltimore, and whether the twelve pieces of ordnance it was reportedly mounting were intended for offensive or defensive purposes, so that the Council could decide whether to prevent its departure under the Proclamation of Neutrality until the President was acquainted with the circum-

stances. (3) Daniel Delozier, Deputy Customs Collector, to Lee, Baltimore, 21 June 1793, stating that in the absence of the collector and on the presumption that the ship in question was the *Trusty*, John Hall master, which arrived from Barbados on 1 Mch. and cleared for there on 17 June with a cargo of flour and lumber, he learned from Mr. Ireland that it mounted four small guns, came with a crew of twenty and had no more than seventeen when cleared, and was upwards of 300 tons; and that because of a vague report differing from this account he decided to examine the ship itself, only to find it already under sail (PrCs of Trs in DLC: TJ Papers, in a clerk's hand; Trs in NNC: Gouverneur Morris Papers; Trs in DNA: RG 46, Senate Records, 3d Cong., 1st sess.; PrCs in PRO: FO 97/1; Trs in Lb in DNA: RG 59, DL; Trs in DLC: Genet Papers, except for No. 1; Trs in same, in French, except for No. 1). Letter and enclosures printed in *Message*, 41-3. Letter and enclosures enclosed in Memorandum to George Washington, [11-13 July 1793], Tobias Lear to TJ, 15 July 1793, and TJ to Gouverneur Morris, 16 Aug. 1793.

[1] Word interlined.
[2] Manuscript: "have." All other texts: "having."

From William Lyall and Others

SIR   Cross Mill Printfield 30th June 1793

We must begin our letter with apologizing for presuming to write to one so elevated in life, by holding so high and Honorable office in such a great State. It being on a subject that however interesting we may think it is to us as individuals, is but of small importance to You, but the many testifications to the world of the worthy Presidents and the other Legislators fatherly care of the prosperity and happiness of their Subjects, and their eagerness to establish and encourage every branch of Manufacture in America, has induced us to throw aside every obstacle, and make bold to intrude, as the only way we could think of to obtain sure information respecting the state and progress of the particular branch of Manufacture which we profess. Sir the under signed persons have served a regular apprenticeship of seven Years to the different Branches necessary to carry on the Callico Printing Business, and hearing that altho it has hitherto made but little progress in America, that Government was now encouraging Gentlemen to enter partnership for to Establish it, and that they were building houses and making out grounds for that purpose, but was at a loss for people bred to the Business to carry it on. As we are all willing to engage if encouragement was given, we have used every endeavour to find if the report was true, by applying to people in business who have Correspondence in America, but they either could not give us that satisfaction or rather was not willing as most of them dissuaded us from leaving our own Country, being apprehensive of us carrying away the art of our Manufacture. And being sensable that on account of the complex nature of our business that it cannot be established to any extent in any country untill it is well advance in other trade and Manufactures we think it would be a risk to come over on mere report as we could be of little service to ourselvs and families if we did not find employment at our own Business and of Consequence incumberers of Society. Being also altogether at a loss how to direct to any person carrying it on, or about to do so we are under the necessity of adopting this method which we hope Sir You will pardon, and are hopefull if there is any Company stands in need of such as us you will be so good as take the trouble to give them information where to apply. Sir most of us have been employed at a printing Manufactary that sends goods into the Market equal in point of Quality to any in this Country. And we also can say that hitherto we have been sober Industrous members of Society, which several respectable people will attest, we therefore are in no doubt but we will give satisfaction to our employers.

Sir It is necessary to give the reasons which makes us desirous of leaving our own Country. It is because we have for along time been liable to be engaged in that Monster War, for we are no sooner out of one dispute and bustle of preparation for Wars with some or other of our nighbours, but we are into another, which nevers fails to do much mischief to a Nation that abounds so much in trade and Manufacture and of Consequence throws many usefull members of Society out of employment which this unpopular contest we are presently engaged in evidences in a too conspicuous manner, and we have reason to belive that such circumstances will be the Case while a reformation of the abuses that has creept into our Constitution is not obtained—for while that is not obtained, so long must we continue a dupe to the humour and Caprice of the Minister of the day. Sir these are the reasons which has caused many thousands with ourselves be desirous of removing to a Country [whose?] present purity of Constitution and Situation renders it in all Human probability much more free from such disastrous circumstances.

Sir we again Humbly request that if You know the Business to be in such a State as to requier operators and consistant with the Rank You hold in the State to take notice of this, please cause them direct to William Lyall Callico Printer Crossmill Printfield Care of Messrs. McDonald & McAlpin Merchants Trongate Glasgow which will be much Esteem'd by Sir Your most obedient and very Humble Servants

WILLIAM LYALL—Printer and Colour maker

JOHN BOWMAN   Drawer & Print Cutter

ALEXR BOWMAN   Cutter

JOHN BAIRD   Printer

JAMES DUNLOP   Printer

WILLIAM GARDNER   Printer

JAMES LYLE   Printer

PETER SYM   Printer

JAMES BRUCE   Printer

JAMES PEACOCK   Printer

WILLIAM PEACOCK   Printer

JAMES SCOT   Printer

WILLIAM BARRY   Dyer

JAMES ROBERTSON   Bleacher

NB These profess the branch we call Block Printing but we can also have Engravers and Copper plate Printers.   W L

RC (DNA: RG 59, MLR); in Lyall's hand except for other signatures; torn at seal; addressed: "Mr Jefferson Secretary of State for Foreign affairs to the United States of America"; noted by Lyall as carried by "Mr John Craig passanger in the Ship Almy from Greenock to New York"; franked; postmarked at New York 14 Sep. 1793; endorsed by Benjamin Bankson as received 16 Sep. 1793; endorsed by TJ as received 2 Oct. 1793 and so recorded in SJL. Enclosed in Bankson to TJ, 23 Sep. 1793.

From Michael Morphy

Málaga, 30 June 1793. On the 20th he received by the schooner *Fredericksburg Packet* of Philadelphia, Atkinson Anderson master, TJ's letter of 2 Mch., the consular commission for him granted by the President and Senate, and related laws, which with the 26 Aug. 1790 circular to consuls and vice-consuls will serve as his standing instructions. He thanks the President, Senate, and TJ for his appointment and promises to use his residence of forty years in Spain to the advantage of American trade and navigation. He forwarded his commission on the 25th to William Carmichael in order to obtain a royal exequatur, as without it no consul can act officially in the seaports. He is pleased by the strict neutrality of the United States during the present European war and hopes that it will redound to her commercial advantage. To the east of Málaga, however, there is great danger from the Algerine rovers hovering off the Spanish coast, two of which captured the schooner *Lark* of Marblehead, John Pattin master, on 9 May while bound for here from Cartagena with a few barrels of beef and 1,000 dollars on board. The master and crew escaped, but a small American naval force is needed in the Mediterranean to bring about a speedy settlement with the states on the African coast. The Portuguese squadron stationed at Gibraltar protects ships of powers at war with the Algerines. Despite the lack of a commercial treaty between the United States and Spain, American vessels and subjects receive the same treatment in ports on this continent as those of favored powers, a situation he will strive to maintain. The trade of nations at war with France suffers, but the contest is expected to end soon because of defeats of the French, divisions among them, and the growing strength of the royalist party. He encloses a list of the forces under the command of Lord Hood, whose fleet left Gibraltar for the Mediterranean on 27 June to join the Spanish fleet of 26 ships of the line and several frigates, armed vessels, and gunboats, though for what purpose only time will tell. The King of Sardinia awaits their arrival to commence operations with his army, and the Spanish armies make progress in France near the frontier and apparently will soon be masters of all Roussillon. He hopes Congress will establish special dues on trade to compensate consuls for their expenses in maintaining the dignity of their offices, especially in Spain. He requests a copy of the navigation act passed by the last session of Congress allowing consuls to own vessels under American colors, as well as any other act proper for his office, and asks TJ to number his letters. He wishes to know if the report on trade he must submit to TJ's department every six months is to include the quality of goods only or the contents. If the latter, masters of vessels should sign a report of their homeward cargoes before him for presentation at the customs house, for it seems useless to delay in conveying this information.

RC (DNA: RG 59, CD); 4 p.; at head of text: "No. 1"; at foot of first page: "Thomas Jefferson Esqr. &ca. &ca."; endorsed by TJ as received 6 Sep. 1793 and so recorded in SJL. Enclosure: "A correct List of Ships and Vessels under the Command of Vice Adml. Lord Hood in the Mediterranean," with subjoined list of "Junior Flag Officers of the Fleet," n.d. (MS in same; in Morphy's hand).

Michael Morphy, described by the Philadelphia merchant John Leamy as "a Gentle-

man of the strictest honor and integrity," was a merchant in Málaga who for a decade had acted as a voluntary agent for American ships trading with that Spanish port. He applied for the American consulship there as early as November 1791 and was appointed on 2 Mch. 1793, with the support of Leamy and the Spanish agent Josef Ignacio de Viar (Morphy to Congress, 11 Nov. 1791, and Leamy to TJ, 27 Feb. 1793, in DLC: Washington Papers, Applications for Office; Memorandum on Consular Appointments, 1 Mch. 1793, and note).

To Thomas Mann Randolph, Jr.

Dear Sir   Philadelphia June 30. 1793.

I received yesterday your favor of the 19th. I have perceived at times that a week has been lost by the post. The following is a list of the dates and receipts of your letters of May and June, where there is one instance of 12. days in coming and another of 19. The exact time is 8. or 9. Your letter of May 8. arrived May 18. being 10. days

16.	25	9.
22.	June 3.	12.
31.	19.	19.
June 13.	22	9.
19.	29.	10.

My last letter to you was on the subject of my farm. This will be so also. The approach of the season of preparation for another year, has rendered it necessary for me to consider for some time past what is to be the plan of farming I am to take up, and to give to my new manager for his government. I will suppose my farm at Monticello to furnish 500. acres of land open, and capable of producing. In all successions of crops, the fields must be supposed equal, each feild to go through the same succession, and each year's crop to be the same. These fundamentals being laid down, the laws of combinations decide inflexibly that the number of feilds, and number of years constituting the compleat rotation must be always equal. If your rotation is of 3. years, you must have 3. feilds, if of 5. years 5. feilds &c. I propose to adopt the following rotation. 1st. year, wheat and fall-fallow. 2d. peas with Indian corn thinly interspersed. 3d. wheat and fall fallow. 4th. potatoes with Indian corn thinly interspersed. 5th. rye, or[1] barley and a fall fallow. 6th. 7th. 8th. red clover. This occupying 8. years, will require 8. feilds, which of course will be of 60. acres each.

The following diagram will shew the system better, the initals of every article only being written in each square or feild. To wit.

cl.	for clover
co.	corn
f.	fallow
pe.	peas
po.	potatoes
r.	rye or barley
w.	wheat.

field	1st. year	2d year	3d. year	4th. year	5th. year	6th. year	7th. year	8th. year
A.	w.f.	pe. co.	w.f.	po. co.	r.f.	cl.	cl.	cl.
B.	pe. co.	w.f.	po. co.	r.f.	cl.	cl.	cl.	w.f.
C.	w.f.	po. co.	r.f.	cl.	cl.	cl.	w.f.	pe. co.
D.	po. co.	r.f.	cl.	cl.	cl.	w.f.	pe. co.	w.f.
E.	r.f.	cl.	cl.	cl.	w.f.	pe. co.	w.f.	po. co.
F.	cl.	cl.	cl.	w.f.	pe. co.	w.f.	po. co.	r.f.
G.	cl.	cl.	w.f.	pe. co.	w.f.	po. co.	r.f.	cl.
H.	cl.	w.f.	pe. co.	w.f.	po. co.	r.f.	cl.	cl.

this gives

2. fields of wheat	120. acres.
1. rye or barley	60.
1. peas & corn	60
1. potatoes & corn	60
1. of 1st. year's clover	60
1. of 2d. do.	60
1. of 3d. do.	60
	480.

thus also
2 eighths of the farm   are cleansing
3. eighths   fallowing } every year.
3. eighths   resting
8.

The following bye-articles.

Oats and flax. A few acres only wanting. To be with the new sown clover.

Hemp, turneps, pumpkins. In the new clearings.

Artichokes in a perpetual feild.

Orchard grass in the hill sides too steep for the plough. Qu?

Lucerne, St. foin in appropriate feilds.

Buckwheat to be ploughed into worn lands.

When a 9th. feild shall be added by new clearings, insert it in the rotation, as a feild of absolute rest, or pasture, or fallow. So of a 10th. feild &c.

Such a farm will well maintain 150. cattle, which properly attended to will make manure enough for one feild every year.

I suppose 5. ploughs and pair of horses, will do the business of such a farm, as in the throngest season, which is that of seeding and fallowing, there will be 6. feilds (say 360. acres) to plough. I have troubled you with these details with a view to trouble you further to give me your observations fully and freely on all the particulars. I am too little familiar with the practice of farming to rely with confidence on my own judgment, and in engaging in a plan of rotation it is material to set out right, as it is so much easier to correct a mis-combination before it is begun, than after one is embarked in it. I am asking the observations of 2. or 3. other friends in like manner, and on recieving the whole, shall proceed to fix my rotation permanently, and put it into the hands of my manager. The produce of an acre of peas, *in drills*, (because it is to cleanse the grounds) I am unacquainted with. Also what number of constant hands will suffice for such a farm, supposing them men and women in equal numbers? I presume that oxen may be substituted for half the horses. I will ask as early an answer to this as you can give satisfactorily.

Maria is with me to-day, just recovering from her mumps. The feeble state of her general health has made her feel this disease more than I had at first expected. Bless the little ones for me, and remember me to my dear Martha. I am most sincerely & affectionately my dear Sir Your's &c   TH: JEFFERSON

P.S. I shall not have occasion for a successor to Tarquin. In keeping 4. good carriage-horses, one is sure to have some one which will do for the saddle, at least for a person who does not go journies on horse-back.

RC (DLC); at foot of first page: "Mr. Randolph."

THRONGEST: busiest.

[1] Word written over "and f," erased.

From George Washington

DEAR SIR   Mount Vernon June 30th: 1793.

The enclosed letter from the Governor of New York, covering a communication to him from the Consul of the French Republic at that place, respecting the continuance of a British Letter of Marque in the Harbour of New York—reached my hands by the post of last evening; and I now transmit it to you, that it may be taken into consideration by yourself and the other Heads of the Departments, as soon as may be after this letter gets to your hands. If you should be unanimous in Your opinions as to the measures which ought to be pursued by the Government, in the case now communicated[1]—You, or the Secretary of War (to whose department it belongs)[2] will transmit, in my name,[3] the result of your deliberations on the subject, to the Governor of New York for his information—and to be communicated by him to the French Consul at that place. But in case there should be a difference of sentiment among the Gentlemen on the matter, I must request that the several opinions may be sent to me for my consideration—and the Governor of New York informed, that a decision will be had in the case as soon as I return to the seat of Government; which I expect will be about the tenth of next month—notwithstanding the death of my Manager and the consequent derangement of my concerns would make my presence here for a longer time, at this important season, almost indispensable: But I know the urgency and delicacy of our public affairs at present will not permit me to be longer absent, I must therefore submit with the best grace I can to the loss and inconvenience which my private affairs will sustain from the want of my personal[4] attention,[5] or that of a confidential Character, the obtaining of which I have no prospect at present. With very great regard, I am, Dear Sir, Your Affecte & Obedt Servt.

G WASHINGTON

RC (DLC); in Tobias Lear's hand, signed by Washington; at foot of text: "The Secretary of State"; endorsed by TJ as received 5 July 1793 and so recorded in SJL. Dft (DNA: RG 59, MLR); in Lear's hand, with emendations by Washington (see notes below). FC (Lb in same, SDC). Recorded in SJPL. Enclosures: (1) George Clinton to Washington, New York, 22 June 1793, transmitting No. 2 concerning the brig *Swallow*, a British privateer, and a copy of a report to him on the ship's arrival. (2) Alexandre Maurice d'Hauterive to Clinton, New York, 18 June 1793, protesting that the *Swallow*, an English privateer commanded by Captain Lyon, armed with eight cannon and manned by at least twenty men, had stayed in New York harbor too long to be considered a distressed vessel under Articles 17 and 22 of the 1778 treaty of amity and commerce between the United States and France, which effectively closed American ports to privateers of nations at war with France except under strictly defined conditions of distress (RCs in DLC; with No. 2 written in French; recorded in SJPL under 30 June 1793).

[1] In Dft Lear here canceled "I request."
[2] Preceding ten words interlined in Dft by Washington.
[3] Preceding three words interlined in Dft by Washington.
[4] Word interlined in Dft by Lear.
[5] Remainder of sentence written in Dft by Washington.

From George Washington

DEAR SIR   Mount Vernon June 30th: 1793.

You will find by the enclosed letter from the Commissioners that Mr. Hallet reports unfavorably of Doctor Thornton's Plan "on the great points of practicability, time and expence": And that I am referred "to Mr. Blodget, Hoben and Hallet, whose verbal information will be better than any we can give you"—on which to form ultimate Instructions.

Mr. Blodget I met at Baltimore in the moment I was about to leave it—consequently I had little conversation with him on the subject referred; but Mr. Hallet is of opinion that the execution of Doctor Thornton's Plan (independent of the cost, which would far exceed our means—and the time allowed for the accomplishment of the buildings) is impracticable; or if practicable, would not in some parts answer the ends proposed. Mr: Hoben seemed to concur in this opinion; and Mr. Blodget, as far as I could come at his sentiments, in the short time I was with him, approved the alterations in it which have been proposed by Mr. Hallet.

It is unlucky that this investigation of Doctor Thornton's plan, and estimate of the cost had not preceded the adoption of it; but[1] knowing the impatience of the Carrollsburg interest and the anxiety of the Public to see both buildings progressing—and supposing the plan to be correct, it was adjudged best to avoid delay. It is better, however,[2] to correct the error, though late,[3] than to proceed in a ruinous measure,[4]—in the adoption of which I do not hesitate to confess I[5] was governed by the beauty of the exterior and the distribution of the apartments—declaring then, as I do now, that I had no knowledge in the rules or[6] principles of Architecture—and was equally unable to count the cost. But if there be such material defects as are represented—and such immense time and cost to complete the building—it would be folly in the extreme to proceed on the plan which has been adopted. It has appeared to me proper, however, before it is laid aside, and Justice and respect to Doctor Thornton requires, that the objections should be made known to him, and an opportunity afforded to explain and obviate them if he can.

For this reason, and because Mr. Blodget is in Philadelphia, and it might not be convenient for Doctor Thornton to leave it; I have requested Mr. Hallet and Mr. Hoben to repair without delay to Philadelphia, with all the plans and documents which are necessary to elucidate this subject—and do pray you to get all the parties herein named[7] together, and after hearing the objections and explainations report your opinion on the case and the plan which ought to be executed. Nothing can be done to the foundation until a final decision is had—and this decision ought not to be delayed one moment that can be avoided; because time is wasting fast—because the public expectation is alive—and because the dæmon of Jealousy may be at work in the lower[8] Town when one building is seen to progress rapidly—and a plan for the other not yet decided on. Whether it be practicable (even at an expence) to call in the aid of any other scientific Character in Philadelphia to assist in deciding this point—or whether there be any there—is more than I can tell. Your own knowledge of this, and judgment will decide. The case is important. A Plan must be adopted—and good or bad it must be entered upon. With very great regard, I am, Dear Sir, Your Affectte. & Obedt. Servt.

Go: WASHINGTON

RC (DLC); in Tobias Lear's hand, signed by Washington; at foot of text: "The Secretary of State"; endorsed by TJ as received 7 July 1793. Dft (DLC: Washington Papers); in Washington's hand except for abbreviated complimentary close and name of addressee in Lear's hand; contains emendations and variations in wording and punctuation, only the most important of which are noted below; docketed by Bartholomew Dandridge, Jr. FC (Lb in same); wording follows Dft. Recorded in SJPL. Enclosure: Commissioners of the Federal District to Washington, Georgetown, 23 June 1793, enclosing and discussing a letter from Andrew Ellicott proposing changes in the southern branch of the canal; relating that at their request Stephen Hallet has studied William Thornton's plan for the Capitol, reported unfavorably on it, and prepared a simplified and abridged plan which they have not had time to consider but which is evidently favored by Samuel Blodget, Jr., James Hoban, and Collen Williamson, from the first two of whom and Hallet verbal information superior to their own can be obtained, and asking for his instructions; advising that the bridge probably cannot be saved owing to the "very ticklish state" of the center arch, that even if Leonard Harbaugh keeps the span from falling its proportion and beauty are gone, and that if it collapses a temporary one must be erected; and stating that they expect Washington to come here soon to decide about the canal and the Capitol (FC in DNA: RG 42, DCLB). Enclosed in TJ to William Thornton, 8 July 1793.

Washington enclosed this letter in one of 1 July 1793 to Stephen Hallet and James Hoban requesting them to REPAIR WITHOUT DELAY TO PHILADELPHIA (Fitzpatrick, *Washington*, XXXIII, 1-2).

[1] Remainder of sentence inserted in margin of Dft.
[2] Preceding four words interlined in Dft in place of "it is never too late to [alter?]."
[3] Preceding two words interlined in Dft in place of "at any time."
[4] Word interlined in Dft in place of "plan."
[5] Preceding six words interlined in Dft.
[6] Preceding two words interlined in Dft.
[7] Preceding two words interlined in Dft.
[8] Here in Dft "interest" is canceled.

From David Humphreys

Lisbon, 1 July 1793. In compliance with the instruction in TJ's letter of 15 Mch. 1791 he encloses a state of his accounts with the United States and vouchers for the past year. He was surprised to learn a few days ago that Mace and Lucas, the British consuls in Barbary mentioned in his 8 Feb. letter, were still at Gibraltar. Both seemed anxious to avoid delay, and Mace especially assured him of his urgent need to return to Algiers on public business. If Captain Cutting (from whom he has not yet received intelligence) had arrived by an early passage, they might have gone at the same time as the British consuls, who will supposedly leave as soon as Lord Hood arrives momentarily to convoy them. He has heard nothing from the American captives in Algiers since transmitting information about them. The *Lark*, a Marblehead schooner commanded by Captain Patten, was lately captured by an Algerine cruiser off Cape Gata; the crew escaped and is at Gibraltar. He did not see Montgomery of Alicante when he passed by here a few days ago on his way to England. Moroccan affairs are far from settled, as indicated by an extract of a late letter from Simpson giving news from Tangier of the defeat of some of Muley Suliman's troops by inhabitants of the midland provinces, thus blasting his hopes of suddenly winning sole dominion over Morocco. He expects shortly to have an opportunity of writing by way of New York and hopes then to be able to announce Cutting's arrival. P.S. 4 July. The Minister of Marine here has learned that Lord Hood has arrived at Gibraltar and that as soon as he is joined by part of his fleet watering at Cádiz he will proceed up the Mediterranean with 21 ships of the line and a similar number of frigates and other armed vessels, so that something important there might be expected. The Portuguese fleet, mentioned in his last letter as having sailed for an unknown destination, encountered a storm that forced several ships to return for refitting. A misunderstanding between the Minister of Marine and some of the commanders has led to the resignation of the admiral and two captains of great families. The fleet left again two days ago for England after some British naval officers previously sent for arrived to serve under another Portuguese admiral. There is no interesting news about belligerent military operations, and by the last advices Valenciennes and Conde were untaken.

RC (DNA: RG 59, DD); 4 p.; at head of text: "(No. 75)"; at foot of third page: "The Secretary of State"; endorsed by TJ as received 20 Dec. 1793 and so recorded in SJL. Tr (Lb in same). Enclosure not found.

To George Logan

July 1. 1793.

Th: Jefferson presents his friendly compliments to Dr. Logan. Having engaged a good farmer to go and put one of his plantations in Virginia into a regular course of farming, and being about to give him his plan, he takes the liberty of submitting it to Dr. Logan, in whose experience and judgment he has great confidence. He begs him to favor him with his observations on it, freely and as fully in writing as his leisure will permit. He is himself but a tyro in agriculture, and it being of great importance to set out right in plans *de longue haleine*, he hopes it will be his excuse with Dr. Logan for the trouble he gives him.   What number of constant labourers (men and women in equal number) would such a farm require?—If sheep, instead of cattle, should be made the principal object, what number of sheep are equivalent to a given number of cattle old and young, for making manure? Th:J. is desirous of substituting sheep for cattle to as great an extent as a true calculation of interest will admit.—Mr. Young's writings are so voluminous one cannot think of buying the whole. Which of them must one buy, in order to have every thing useful which he has written? For it is apprehended that many of his volumes are mere repetitions of what is to be found in the others.

PrC (DLC). Not recorded in SJL.

The enclosed PLAN of Jefferson's proposed crop rotation was probably identical to the one given in his letters of 29 June 1793 to James Madison and of 30 June 1793 to Thomas Mann Randolph, Jr., and may in fact have been the missing PrC of the latter.

From William Short

SIR   Madrid July. 1. 1793.

The court having determined to transfer its residence from Aranjuez to this place I preceded it four days ago with the members of the corps diplomatique.

I had the honor of writing to you last on the 7th. of June—that letter was sent by a person going from hence to England, who was to forward it from Lisbon or England as he should find best—together with a joint letter from Mr. Carmichael and myself. As copies of these letters were sent also by the same conveyance from hence I flatter myself you will have recieved them in due time.

In my last I had the honor of mentioning to you the information I had recieved with respect to the intention of this government as to N. Orleans. An ordinance on the subject has been since printed in date the 9th. of June—this is the date of its being passed—its impression is later—and though now printed it will not be published perhaps for some time, according to what I am told is the usage here. A copy has been lent me on the condition of my returning it immediately. Not having time to translate it at full length, I have extracted from it the most important parts, which I here inclose to you.

I mentioned to you in my letter of the 7th. of June, that one of the objects of this plan was to supply the Spanish possessions from N. Orleans with such goods as they might chuse to admit. I find however I was misinformed in this, as one of the articles of the ordinance prohibits communication between N. Orleans and their other American possessions. I am well assured now that the plan has been adopted at the earnest sollicitation of the inhabitants of Louisiana and the Floridas, and will no doubt give them very high satisfaction—the ground of their demand is their being for the present deprived of their commerce with France.

The ordinance is stated to be a temporary one, and it is said it is to continue only until the Minister shall have matured and brought forward a new and general system of commerce, on which he has been for some time meditating. I hardly expect however this will take place very soon, nor do I know of what nature it is to be. Such as it may be you will of course be informed of it by your agent at this place.

The Spanish arms continue to be successful against the French and particularly in Roussillon, where they direct their principal efforts. The French seem to have entirely neglected their southern frontier. The mode of their declaring war against this country and of preparing for it, shewed a contempt for their enemy which the event has by no means warranted. The exertions of this country have been really great and made with a degree of facility that have astonished most people. As yet no new tax has been laid—no new loan made—public credit supports itself at a favorable point—and the minister seems confident of the public resources continuing commensurate with the public demands.

I find opinions however varying on this subject, and that among some much better acquainted with the country from their long residence here than I can be. They say that the commencement of war expenses has ever presented the same facility from the system of anticipation used with the various contracting companies who supply every thing on credit, though at an onerous rate. There may be a good deal and no doubt there is something in this. Still it seems equally certain that the resources of this country, even under its present mode of administration, are far from being as contemptible as they were supposed to be in France.

I avoid troubling you with a repetition of the common occurrences here, as you will be informed of them by Mr. Carmichael—and particularly what relates to the stoppage of several of our vessels, under the idea of their having French property on board. This subject not being comprehended within our joint instructions Mr. Carmichael treats of it of course separately with the Minister of foreign affairs.

Since my last letter in which I mentioned to you our ignorance of every thing which had taken place in America (having recieved nothing later than your letter of Nov. 3. 1792.—and the newspapers down to Jan. 1. 1793.) we have remained in the same state, except the recieving the President's proclamation of April last which Colo. Humphreys was so good as to copy from a newspaper which had fallen into his hands, and to forward to us.

Our letters will have informed you of our embarassment on this account which I can now only confirm to you—as well as the assurances of the perfect respect & attachment with which I have the honor to be sir your most obedient & most humble servant   W Short

PrC (DLC: Short Papers); at head of text: "*No. 126*"; at foot of first page: "The Secretary of State, for the United States—Philadelphia." Tr (Lb in DNA: RG 59, DD). Tr (DNA: RG 46, Senate Records, 3d Cong., 1st sess.); consists of extract of first five paragraphs. Tr (Lb in same, TR); consists of extract of first five paragraphs. Recorded in SJL as received 2 Dec. 1793. Enclosure: "Extract of an Ordinance for regulating provisionally the commerce of Louisiana & the Floridas," 9 June 1793, defining the terms under which, as a result of the wartime disruption of their commerce with France, the inhabitants of these provinces could trade freely in Europe and America with all friendly nations that had commercial treaties with Spain (Tr in Lb in DNA: RG 59, DD; Tr in DNA: RG 46, Senate Records, 3d Cong., 1st sess.; printed in ASP, *Foreign Relations*, I, 273).

PRESIDENT'S PROCLAMATION: the Proclamation of Neutrality of 22 Apr. 1793 (Fitzpatrick, *Writings*, XXXII, 430-1).

TJ submitted this letter and its enclosure to the President on 3 Dec. 1793 (Washington, *Journal*, 263).

From Willink, Van Staphorst & Hubbard

SIR   Amsterdam 1 July 1793.

Since our last Respects of 4 April, We are honored with your esteemed favors of 20 March and 12 April through Thos. Pinckney Esqr. who advised us to have received from you bills of Exchange to the amount of £4000. Stg. of which

£3,000. Dft of Willing Morris & Swanwick on John & Francis Baring & Co. of London has been protested for non acceptance, but hope has been given it will be paid.

400. Do. of Walter Stewart on Joseph Birch of Liverpool has been protested for non acceptance.

150. ⎫
200. ⎬ Do. of Robert Gilmor & Co. on James Srackan [Strachan]
250. ⎭ & James Mackenzie in London have been accepted.

£4,000. Stg. That we have requested Mr. Pinckney to endorse to our order, and afterwards to deliver unto our Correspondents in London subject to our disposal.

We shall attend to do the needfull with these Bills, returning unto You with protests such as will be finally refused payment, and crediting the Department of State for those that will be paid.

In the mean time, to comply with Your standing directions, we inclose You the account current of the Department of State with us, up to the 30th. June, the Balance whereof due unto us, Cy. ƒ36,795.17. We transfer unto the Debit of a New Account: Against which will be placed the produce of the aforegoing Remittance made by You to Mr. Pinckney.

Mr. Pinckney writes us in advising the fate of your remittances, "I doubt not however you will take such measures as will prevent the public service from suffering in case these Bills should not be paid when due, as I know the purpose for which Colo: Humphreys is Authorized to draw is of considerable importance." Upon which point We shall tranquillize him perfectly, by to morrow's post, in full confidence you will not leave the account for the department of State with us, in long Sufferance.

We likewise send You the State of the Separate appropriations You have made of Funds in our hands, lest they may be requisite to enable You to make up Your annual accounts, the Completion of which we shall punctually furnish.

Should You make us any further remittances in Bills upon England, We beg of You to forward them to our Friends Messrs. John Henry Cazenove Nephew & Co. of London, desiring them to procure the acceptance thereof, and to hold them subject to our disposal; by which means the period of their payment and the risque will be the sooner expired. They are nevertheless to be indorsed by You to us.

The Crisis this Country has been in by the invasion of the French being now over, the Correspondence with us may be continued in the usual direct manner. We are respectfully Sir! Your most obedient humble Servants WILHEM & JAN WILLINK

N. & J. VAN STAPHORST & HUBBARD

Dupl (DLC); in the hand of Van Staphorst & Hubbard, signed by both firms; at head of text: "(Duplicate)"; at foot of text: "Thos. Jefferson Esqr."; endorsed by TJ as received 2 Oct. 1793 and so recorded in SJL. Enclosures: Account of the Department of State with Willink, Van Staphorst & Hubbard, 1 July 1793, with entries for 2 Apr.-1 July 1793 and subjoined statement of appropriations made between 27 Aug. 1792 and 15 Mch. 1793 in pursuance of TJ's letter to them of 3 July 1792 (MS in DLC, in a clerk's hand, signed by Willink, Van Staphorst & Hubbard; PrC of Tr in DLC, in a clerk's hand; PrC of another Tr in DLC, in a clerk's hand; Tr, Mrs. Francis H. Smith, University of Virginia, 1946, 19th-century copy). Enclosed in Benjamin Bankson to TJ, 23 Sep. 1793.

From Richard Söderström

[3 July 1793]

The Swedish Sloop Betsey, Willm. Johnston Master, from and belonging to St: Bartholome, Being duely Registered and documented by the Governour of said Island, and owned by Messrs. Houseman & Mashiler, Swedish Burgers and Subjects of said mentioned Island, Said Vessell also loaded with Sugar and Rum partly for the said owners, and partly for two passengers Accounts, and Bills of ladings Signed for Baltimor—This Vessell was taken possession of by a franch privatire last Wednesday, In sight of land, the Pilot having been on board some hours previous, and in whose Care she than was, Sent in to Baltimor and their arrived safe last Saturday morning.

RC (DNA: RG 59, NFC); undated, unsigned, and unaddressed; endorsed by TJ as a letter from Söderström received 3 July 1793.

The case of the SLOOP BETSEY is discussed in note to Lucas Gibbes and Alexander S. Glass to TJ, 8 July 1793.

According to SJL, on 8 July 1793 TJ received a letter of that date from Söderström, the Swedish consul in Philadelphia, that has not been found. With it Söderström undoubtedly enclosed copies of two documents concerning the capture of the *Betsey* by the *Citoyen Genet*, which had taken place on LAST WEDNESDAY, 26 June 1793: a letter from Söderström to Edmond Charles Genet of 6 July 1793 affirming that the *Betsey* and part of its cargo were Swedish-owned, and expressing the hope that "from Respect to the Laws of Nations and the Rights of Newtral Powers" the ship and cargo would be delivered to John Hollins of Baltimore, the consignee; and Genet's reply of 8 July 1793, in which he promised to examine the report on this case expected shortly from the French vice-consul in Baltimore, to whose tribunal the matter had been brought, and to make a decision conformable to the generous principles of the French nation, the law of nations, the rights of neutrals, and his high esteem for the Swedes, whose kindness, virtue, and valor he had experienced since his youth (Trs in DNA: RG 59, NFC; the first in Söderström's hand, the second in French).

From George Washington

July 3d: 1793

The President Sends to the Secretary of State the enclosed letter from Mr. Chiappe, which has been forwarded by Mr. Simpson at Gibralter. If, upon translating this letter, there should be found in it any thing important to be communicated to the President—the Secretary will do it when the President arrives in Philadelphia.

The President proposes to set out from this place on sunday next.

RC (DLC); in Tobias Lear's hand; endorsed by TJ as received 8 July 1793. Recorded in SJPL. Enclosures: (1) Francisco Chiappe to Washington, Rabat, 20 Mch. 1793, acknowledging his letter of 8 Nov. 1791 and TJ's of 13 May 1791, and reminding him that since then he has sent news through Barclay at Gibraltar; complaining that he has received neither an official American title nor an annual salary and advising that Barclay agrees that his claim is just and will write to Washington on the subject; stating that he deserved some distinction for his good offices, which had saved the United States from war several times, and that an early reply would bode well for continued American tranquility; and reporting that the kingdom continues on the same footing, with Muley Suliman at Mequinez and Muley Ischem at Morocco (RC in DLC: Washington Papers, in Italian, endorsed by Lear as received 30 June 1793; Dupl in DNA: RG 59, MLR, at head of text: "*Duplicato*"; recorded in SJL as received 8 July 1793). (2) James Simpson to Washington, Gibraltar, 30 Apr. 1793, transmitting No. 1 (RC in DNA: RG 59, CD; endorsed by TJ as received 8 July 1793 and so recorded in SJL). See second Memorandum to Washington, [11 July 1793]; and Lear to TJ, 15 July 1793.

From James Maury

Liverpool, 4 July 1793. There has been no material change since the price current of 3 June enclosed in his last letter. He will pay special attention to the orders about the American flag in TJ's 21 Mch. letter. His brother Fontaine informs him the bond has been effected. On 23 June the *Aerial* of Philadelphia, Stephen Decatur master, was seized and brought here by the Liverpool privateer *Union* while on its way from St. Thomas to Bordeaux with 24 French passengers and sundry merchandise, enough of which the captors claim is French property to justify the capture. The usual proceedings have just begun, and Decatur has left for London. On 1 July the *George*, Captain Latouche, bound from Baltimore to Le Havre with a cargo of flour, was brought here after being captured on 21 June by the Liverpool privateer *Ann*, recaptured by the French, and then taken by another Liverpool privateer. He encloses an 8 June paper just published.

RC (DNA: RG 59, CD); 2 p.; at foot of text: "The Secretary of State to the United States Philadelphia"; endorsed by TJ as received 9 Sep. 1793 and so recorded in SJL. Enclosure: Additional Instructions from George III to the commanders of British warships and privateers , 8 June 1793 (Tr in same; see Enclosure No. 1 listed at Thomas Pinckney to TJ, 5 July 1793). Another text of this letter and its enclosure, recorded in SJL as received 28 Aug. 1793 but not found, was enclosed in TJ to George Washington, and Washington to TJ, both 30 Aug. 1793.

From John M. Pintard

Madeira, 4 July 1793. He has received TJ's 3 Jan. reply to his letter of 5 Oct. and is pleased to learn that the subject of consular fees at Madeira and Lisbon had already been brought to TJ's attention and that it is planned to submit information thereon with the consular act to the Attorney General for an opinion. In response to TJ's request for information, he advises that these fees would not be given to someone else if the consul refused them because they are paid for services rendered by a consul and no one else could claim them. His letter of 5 Nov. informed TJ that these fees were received for actual services the Portuguese government imposes on the consul. In those countries where the consul has no services to perform, fees would burden commerce, "but where a man works he ought to be paid for his labour." The duties of his office require the constant attendance of himself or his vice-consul, and the attendant writing requires an extra clerk. If he charged two dollars for every declaration or other act made before him by captains, he is confident his fees would exceed those he now takes, a matter more fully described in a declaration signed by American shipmasters who were here last September. He hopes to hear from TJ on this subject. He encloses a copy of the passports that in conformity with Article 25 of the commercial treaty with France he has given to all vessels belonging to the United States which have sailed from here since the French declaration of war and wishes to know whether he should continue to give them to vessels arriving from the United States without a presidential passport or whether he should endorse on the back of them the time of entry and clearance of the vessels from here. Since the death of the French consul here, French prisoners have applied to him several times to appear "as the Consul of an Ally of their Nation," but he has avoided doing anything publicly until receiving TJ's opinion, though he has assisted them with advice and got some liberated.

Tr (DNA: RG 59, CD); 3 p.; at head of text: "The Honble. Thos Jefferson Esqr"; at foot of text: "(Copy)"; conjoined to Pintard to TJ, 23 July 1793. Recorded in SJL as received 15 Aug. 1793. Enclosure not found.

A 5 Nov. 1792 letter from Pintard not being recorded in SJL, the reference is presumably to his letter of 5 Oct. 1792 (see TJ to Pintard, 3 Jan. 1793, and note). Pintard apparently enclosed the declaration of American shipmasters in Madeira in an 11 Sep. 1792 letter to TJ, recorded in SJL as received 23 Oct. 1792 but not found.

From James Simpson

Gibraltar, 4 July 1793. He encloses a copy of his 29 June dispatch to TJ sent by the brig *Bacchus* of Philadelphia, since which there has been no interesting news from Barbary. Seeing no likelihood of a speedy accommodation between the pretenders to the Moroccan throne, Spain has sought to demonstrate her neutrality by lately sending one consul to reside in Safi under Muley Ischem's dominion and another to Tangier under Muley Suliman. Last Sunday a Turkish bashaw, lately governor of the Crimea, arrived in Leghorn on his way to Muley Suliman's court, some say to act as the Grand Segnior's mediator between the two brothers and others for private business. The row boats from Oran that continue to infest the hithermost parts of the Mediterranean make navigation above Málaga very unsafe for unarmed vessels with American colors. The Moorish cruisers all lay totally neglected; none of the larger ones will ever be fit for sea again, and the smaller galleys are little better. Lord Hood sailed from here for the Mediterranean on 27 June with twenty sail of the line and about the same number of frigates and smaller vessels, joined by Don Juan de Lángara from Cádiz, besides the Cartagena fleet, with five three-deckers and three 70-gun ships. Other than deterring the ships at Toulon, the object of this grand fleet is publicly unknown.

RC (DNA: RG 59, CD); 3 p.; at foot of first page: "The Honble Thomas Jefferson Esqr &ca. &ca."; endorsed by TJ as received 12 Sep. 1793 and so recorded in SJL. A Dupl recorded in SJL as received 2 Dec. 1793 has not been found.

TJ submitted this letter to the President on 10 Dec. 1793, and Washington returned it to him the same day (Washington, *Journal*, 265).

From Elias Vanderhorst

Plymouth, 4 July 1793. He takes this opportunity by the American ship *Amsterdam Packet*, Captain Weeks, bound for New York from London, to advise that two ships owned by United States citizens have been brought here and detained on the pretense that all or part of their cargoes are French property. The *Eliza*, Captain Worsley, bound from the Isle of France to Dunkirk and Ostend, was captured by the *Liberty*, a privateer from London, where Worsley now is and where the ship and cargo, it appears, will soon be released with the payment of damages for detention. The *Jay*, Captain Thomas Durry, bound from New York to Le Havre, was captured by the royal armed brig *Orestes*, Lord Augustus Fitzroy, who left again on another cruise immediately thereafter. The failure to libel the *Jay*, which has been in port for twenty days, suggests that the captors have little hope of securing the condemnation of any part of the cargo and that the chief object is to prevent the provisions aboard her from reaching France, wherefore he expects the government to pay for the whole cargo and to make satisfaction to all concerned in the ship and cargo. As mentioned in a previous letter, he had intended to continue in office John Hawker, the vice-consul appointed by Thomas Auldjo for this port, but he assumed that his consular authority here had lapsed after learning that Robert Were Fox had been appointed vice-consul for Falmouth, which includes Plymouth. Informed last night, however, by Thomas Were Fox that, on Pinckney's advice, his brother could not serve because his commission was made out by mistake to Edward Fox, he has resumed his consular authority here and hopes that allowances will be made for his lack of experience with the many new and untried matters in public affairs. For further particulars on this and other matters, he refers TJ to the bearer, Dr. Adair, who during a short stay here proved to be a well-informed gentleman and a friend to America and mankind. He encloses a hasty but true declaration by Captain Durry. Three days ago he received TJ's 21 Mch. letter with the accompanying laws of the last congressional session and will reply more fully to his instructions at a more convenient time.

RC (DNA: RG 59, CD); 3 p.; at foot of text: "The Secretary of State, Philadelphia"; endorsed by TJ as received 30 Aug. 1793 and so recorded in SJL. Enclosure: Memorandum of Information sworn by Thomas Durry, Plymouth, 4 July 1793, stating that on 17 May 1793 the *Jay* left New York under his command bound for Le Havre with a cargo consisting of 217 barrels of flour and 1,000 barrels of beef and pork shipped by Samuel Ward & Brothers, flour, ox hides, and furs variously shipped by Hugh Stocker, the ship's owner, William Seton, and Daniel Ludlow & Company, and a bag containing 177¾ dollars shipped by Greenleaf & Company; that his papers indicated that the shipment by Ward & Brothers was to be delivered to the mayor of Le Havre or to Delamotte, the American consul there; that on 12 June a ship posing as an armed French brig stopped the *Jay* 19 leagues off Lizard Point and, seeing from his papers and declarations that his cargo was French property bound for Le Havre, revealed itself to be H.M.S. *Orestes*, Lord Augustus Fitzroy commander, and took it into Plymouth as a prize on 14 June; that except for the second mate and carpenter (who escaped and later admitted they were not native Americans) his entire crew were impressed into the Royal Navy despite their sworn affidavits that they were citizens of the United States, though since then they have admitted, "probably from Improper

Influence," that they were British subjects and have been identified as such by witnesses who knew them or were similarly prevailed upon; that Vanderhorst was unable to secure their release and was denied access to the ship's papers; that the High Court of Admiralty has appointed commissioners to investigate the claim of Fitzroy and his agents that the *Jay* and its cargo were lawful prizes because most of the cargo was the property of French citizens; that he has deposed on oath to the commissioners that both ship and cargo belonged to citizens of the United States, while conceding that the cargo would probably have become French property after delivery; and that there is reason to believe from this case and others like it that British warships are under orders to bring into British ports American vessels carrying provisions to France, "as even the Cargoes of those Ships which being thus loaded have call'd at different Ports for Orders have been detain'd and Purchas'd by the British Governmt. on the Lowest possible Terms" (MS in same; in a clerk's hand, signed by Durry and attested by Vanderhorst). Enclosed in James B. M. Adair to TJ, [ca. 28 Aug. 1793].

From George Washington

DEAR SIR   Mount Vernon July 4th: 1793.

I send, for the information and[1] consideration of the Heads of the Departments, a letter which I received by the post of Yesterday from the Governor of North Carolina, stating the measures which he has taken relative to a privateer fitted out from South Carolina under a French Commission, and which had arrived, with a prize, in the Port of Wilmington in North Carolina.

I intend setting out for Philadelphia on Sunday next; but do not expect to reach that place till Thursday, as I shall be detained in George Town[2] the remainder of the day on which I leave this. With very great regard, I am, Dear Sir, Your Affecte. & Obedt. Servt.

Go: WASHINGTON

RC (DLC); in Tobias Lear's hand, signed by Washington; at foot of text: "The Secretary of State"; endorsed by TJ as received 10 July 1793. Dft (DNA: RG 59, MLR); in Lear's hand; only the most important emendations being noted below. FC (Lb in same, SDC); wording follows Dft. Recorded in SJPL. Enclosure: Richard Dobbs Spaight to Washington, New Bern, 24 June 1793, reporting that three days earlier he learned that a schooner of Wilmington, North Carolina, fitted out as a French privateer in South Carolina took a British vessel and now lies with it in Wilmington; that in conformity with instructions from the Secretary of War of 23 and 24 May he sent an express ordering the commanders of militia in New Hanover and Brunswick counties to seize both vessels pending further instructions from the President and that he also wrote the port's collector, Colonel Read, instructing him, if consistent with his duty, to direct Captain Cook of the revenue cutter to assist the militia; that the schooner in question, the *Hector*, Captain Almsted, sailed to Charleston in May to get a French commission, left that port on 7 June as an American ship bound for the West Indies but sent back its American papers when it crossed the bar and went into Georgetown, South Carolina, where it mounted guns it may have carried there from Charleston; that it then left Georgetown, captured an English vessel bound to that port, and went with it to Wilmington; that the commission and bill of sale to the French captain to whom it was to be delivered at sea are both dated 1 June even though it left Charleston under American papers six days later; that Colonel Brown gave him this information and the enclosed copy of the ship's commission; that while the militia can follow War Department instructions to detain privateers outfitted in the state's ports, it needs naval support to suppress privateering in the surrounding waters; and that, if properly equipped and manned and periodically stationed at Ocracoke and Cape Fear, the revenue cutter might prove useful against small privateers (FC in Nc-Ar: Governor's Letterbooks).

[1] Preceding two words interlined in Dft.
[2] In Dft Lear here canceled "'till Monday Morning."

From Alexander Hamilton

July 5: [1793]

Mr. Hamilton presents his Compliments to the Secretary of State—requests to be informed, if it will be convenient to him to meet the Secretary at War and Mr. H. to day at twelve oClock. If it will, they will be at that hour at Mr. Jefferson's office.

RC (DLC); partially dated; endorsed by TJ as received 5 July 1793 and so recorded in SJL.

Notes of Cabinet Meeting and Conversations with Edmond Charles Genet

July 5. 1793. A meeting desired by A.H. at my office.   Himself, Knox and my self met accordingly.

He said that according to what had been agreed on in presence of the President, in consequence of Mr. Genet's declining to pay the 45,000 D. at his command in the treasury to the holders of the St. Domingo bills, we had agreed to pay the holders out of other monies to that amount: that he found however that these bills would amount to 90,000D. and the question was whether he should assume the 90,000.

to be paid out of the September instalment. This he said would enable the[1] holders to get discounts at the banks, would therefore be equal to ready money, and save them from bankruptcy.

Unanimously agreed to.

We also agreed to a letter written by Genl. Knox to Govr. Mifflin to have a particular enquiry made whether the Little Sarah is arming &c. or not.

I read letter from the Presidt. about the Swallow letter of Mark at N. York, complained of by the French Consul. Agreed as the case was new, to let it wait for the Presidt.

I read also Govr. Lee's letter about the Govr. of S.C.'s proclamation respecting pestilential disease in W. Indies. We are all of opinion the evidence is too slight for interference and doubt the power to interfere. Therefore let it lie.

===

Mr. Genet called on me and read to me very rapidly instructions he had prepared for Michaud who is going to Kentuckey, an address to the inhabitants of Louisiana, and another to those of Canada. In these papers it appears that besides encouraging those inhabitants to insurrection, he speaks of two generals at Kentuckey who have proposed to him to go and take N. Orleans if he will furnish the expence about £3000. sterl. He declines advancing it, but promises that sum ultimately for their expences, proposes that officers shall be commissioned by himself in[2] Kentuckey and Louisiana, that they shall rendezvous *out of the territories of the US*: suppose in Louisiana, and there making up a battalion to be called the   of inhabitants of Louisiana and Kentuckey and getting what Indns. they could, to undertake the expedition against N. Orleans, and then Louisiana to be established into an independant state connected in commerce with France and the US. That two frigates shall go into the river Missisipi and cooperate against N. Orleans.[3]—The address to Canada, was to encourage them to shake off English yoke, to call Indians to their assistance, and to assure them of the friendly dispositions of their neighbors of the US.

He said he communicated these things to me, not as Secy. of state, but as Mr. Jeff. I told him that his enticing officers and souldiers from Kentuckey to go against Spain, was really putting a halter about their necks, for that they would assuredly be hung, if they commd. hostilities against a nation at peace with the US. That leaving out that article I did not care what insurrections should be excited in Louisiana.

He had, about a fortnight ago sent me a commission for Michaud as Consul of France at Kentuckey, and desired an Exequatur. I told him this could not be given, that it was only in the *ports* of the US. they were entitled to Consuls, and that if France should have a consul at Kentuckey Engld. and Spain would soon demand the same, and we should have all our interior country filled with foreign agents. He acquiesced, and asked me to return the commission and his note, which I did. But he desired that I would give Michaud a letter of introduction for Govr. Shelby. I sent him one a day or two after. He now observes to me that in that letter I speak of him only as a person of botanical and natural pursuits, but that he wished the Govr. to view him as something more, as a French citizen possessing his confidence. I took back the letter, and wrote another. See both.[4]

MS (DLC); entirely in TJ's hand, with last two words probably added at a later date (see note 4 below). Recorded in SJPL: "Ntes. paimt of French bills—Little Sarah—Swallow. Genet's instrns to Michaux—address to Canada & Louisiana." Included in the "Anas."

The antecedents to the Cabinet discussion of the French minister's refusal to pay THE HOLDERS OF THE ST. DOMINGO BILLS are given in Edmond Charles Genet to TJ, 18 June 1793, and note. The LETTER WRITTEN BY GENL. KNOX TO GOVR. MIFFLIN has not been found (but see note to Cabinet Opinions on the *Little Sarah*, 8 July 1793). The LETTER FROM THE PRESIDT. was dated 30 June 1793; that from GOVR. LEE was dated 28 June 1793. Genet's INSTRUCTIONS to André Michaux are given in AHA, *Annual Report*, 1896, p. 990-5. His anonymously-published addresses to THE INHABITANTS OF LOUISIANA and OF CANADA are printed as enclosures to Josef Ignacio de Viar and Josef de Jaudenes to TJ, 27 Aug. 1793, and Genet to TJ, [30 Oct. 1793], respectively. TWO GENERALS AT KENTUCKEY: George

Rogers Clark and Benjamin Logan. Fortuitously for Genet, who was already under instructions to promote an EXPEDITION AGAINST N. ORLEANS, Clark had written him in February 1793 offering to lead such a venture (AHA, *Annual Report*, 1896, p. 960, 961-2, 967-74, 991). Michaux's COMMISSION as French CONSUL at Kentucky and Genet's accompanying NOTE to TJ are not mentioned in SJL and have not been found. The LETTER OF INTRODUCTION for Michaux was TJ to Isaac Shelby, 28 June 1793.

Genet subsequently gave a variant account of TJ's reaction to his plans—one that was evidently based on talks the French minister had with him on 26 June and 5 July 1793 (Genet to the Minister of Foreign Affairs, 25 July 1793, Turner, *CFM*, 221; note to Genet to TJ, 26 June 1793). See also Malone, *Jefferson*, III, 104-9).

[1] MS: "to."
[2] Preceding three words interlined in place of "at."
[3] Preceding sentence interlined.
[4] Preceding two words written in a different ink, probably at a later date.

From Thomas Pinckney

DEAR SIR   London 5th. July 1793

The inclosed copy of additional Instructions to the Commanders of British men of War and Privateers will shew the farther embarrassment to which our commerce will be subjected in the present War. These instructions though dated the eighth of June were not finally issued to the Admiralty till the 28th. Lord Grenville justifies them from the authority of the writers on the law of nations particularly 2d. Vattell. 72. 73 and urges that by the doctrine there laid down they have not gone so far as they would have been justified in proceeding considering the prospect they have of reducing their enemy by such means, the instructions not extending to all kinds of provisions, nor to confiscation of those kinds that are mentioned. That the existing circumstances justifying them in considering grain as among contraband articles they come within the Proclamation issued by the President. That the French Government are in fact the only importers of grain into that country. That the measure was so guarded by directing the property to be paid for together with the freight that the owners could suffer no loss, a liberal price being always allowed in these cases, and he was hopeful the matter would be so conducted as to give satisfaction to the parties concerned. I urged every argument that suggested itself to me in support of the neutral rights which I contended were injured in this instance, pointed to inconveniencies that would attend the execution of the instructions and urged that the case put by Vattell of a well grounded hope of reducing the enemy by famine did not exist provisions being now cheaper in the Ports of France than in those of England. Ld. G. on being asked said Spain would pursue the same line of conduct and upon it being objected that even their late Convention with Russia did not extend to this object, he answered that though it was not expressly mentioned it was fully understood by both parties to be within the intention of it. At the close of the conversation I told him I should transmit these instructions to you accompanied by his reasons in their justification. *Although I thought it right to say all I could in support of the neutral rights, yet I am of opinion, that if they pay a liberal price the measure will be beneficial to our Grain trade, by opening their ports to us here when corn is under the act of parliament price, and if they extend it to the West Indies, giving our cargoes there, admission in our own bottoms.* [1] Lord Grenville spoke in high terms of approbation of the Answer to Mr. Hammond's memorials which he received by the Packet. [2] I have presented to the Austrian and Prussian Ministers here as well as to the Secretary of State copies of the Presidents Proclamation accompanied by the inclosed note. I forward by this opportunity copies of two conventions entered into between this country and Russia and another with Sardinia. *I am informed another treaty either is or will soon be compleated with Austria, by which Great Britain will be fully embarked in all the plans of the combined Crowns. My letter of the 22d. April gave notice of the intentions of this Cabinet to enter into such measures, and all their conduct since seems consonant thereto. France, I am well informed would have given them* [3] *Carte blanche to detach them from the Confederacy, but they refused to treat. Several regiments are under orders to embark from Ireland, I have no certainty of their destination, they are said to be for the Continent of Europe, but have been hitherto detained by the internal disturbances which have not totally subsided.* A Treaty has been entered into between the King of Great Britain and the Prince of Hesse Cassel for the hire of 8000 Hessian Troops to serve in any part of Europe. The Swedish Minister at the Hague has imparted to that Court the intention of their Government to send convoys for the protection of their trade and I believe the same notification has been made here though it is not yet published. Mr. Cutting has not yet been able to procure a neutral Vessel to go to Lisbon his present idea therefore is to embark in a British Vessel which will sail soon under convoy for that Port. I have the honor to be with the utmost respect Dear Sir Your most faithful & obedient Servant

THOMAS PINCKNEY

RC (DNA: RG 59, DD); written partly in code (see note 1 below); at foot of text: "The Secretary of State"; endorsed by TJ as received 12 Sep. 1793 and so recorded in SJL. PrC (ScHi: Pinckney Family Papers). Dupl (DNA: RG 59, Duplicate Diplomatic Dispatches); in the hand of William A. Deas; written partly in code; at head of text: "(Duplicate)"; filed with decipherment of second coded passage in an unidentified hand. Tr (same, DD); in Benjamin Bankson's hand; entirely *en clair*, with deciphered passages underscored; endorsed by TJ: "Pinckney Thos. copy of his lre of July 5.93." Tr (Lb in same); entirely *en clair*, deciphered sections being in brackets and containing a minor anomaly. Tr (DNA: RG 46, Senate Records, 3d Cong., 1st sess.); extract consisting of text to note 2 below except for intervening coded sentence. Enclosures: (1) Additional instructions of George III to the commanders of British warships and privateers, 8 June 1793, authorizing them to stop and send into British ports all vessels carrying corn, flour, or meal to any French port or any port occupied by French armies, the vessels to be released either after the British government purchased these provisions with an allowance for freight or after the Court of Admiralty approved security given by their masters that they would deliver these provisions to the ports of any country at peace with Britain; to seize for condemnation all ships, regardless of their cargo, attempting to enter a blockaded port, except for Danish and Swedish ships, which were to be prevented from entering such a port on their first attempt but seized for condemnation on their second attempt; and to

warn away ships at sea headed for blockaded ports that had left their home ports before the declaration of the blockade had been advertised in them and to seize them for condemnation if thereafter they tried to enter blockaded ports, as well as all other ships that either left ports after the advertisement of a blockade or received notice of it during their voyage (Tr in DNA: RG 59, DD, in Deas's hand, with "These are of Mr. Banksons" penciled at head of text and "2 copies to be made of these" penciled on verso by TJ; Tr in DNA: RG 46, Senate Records, 3d Cong., 1st sess.; Tr in Lb in DNA: RG 59, DD). (2) Pinckney to Lord Grenville, 21 June 1793, enclosing copies of the Proclamation of Neutrality and TJ's 23 Apr. 1793 letter to foreign ministers in the United States as proof of the desire of the United States to preserve peace and friendship with all the belligerent powers and relying that they will in return extend a scrupulous protection to all American citizens, one that will be exactly reciprocated in similar cases (Tr in DNA: RG 59, DD, in Deas's hand; Tr in Lb in same). (3) Pinckney to the Austrian Envoy Extraordinary and Minister Plenipotentiary in London, 22 June 1793, of the same import as No. 2 (Tr in same, in Deas's hand, with his note on verso: "a similar Note addressed, To the Envoy Extraordinary and Minister Plenipotentiary of his Prussian Majesty"). (4) Extract from the Anglo-Russian Convention of 25 Mch. 1793, consisting of Article 3, by which the signatories bound themselves to shut their ports to French ships, to prevent the exportation from their ports to France of military and naval supplies and

foodstuffs, and to do all in their power to injure French commerce; and Article 4, by
which they bound themselves to prevent
neutral powers from directly or indirectly
lending their protection to French commerce or property at sea or in French ports;
with subjoined description of the Anglo-
Sardinian Treaty of 25 Apr. 1793, by which
Sardinia promises to maintain an army of
50,000 to defend itself and act against the
common enemy, and by which Britain
agrees to send a fleet to the Mediterranean,
furnish Sardinia with a subsidy of £240,000
payable quarterly in advance, and restore all
territory taken during the war (Tr in same;
in Deas's hand; with penciled note by TJ at
head of text: "these are of Mr. Banksons").
Letter and Enclosure No. 1 printed in *Message*, 109-12. Enclosed in TJ to George
Washington, 15 Sep. 1793.

Enclosure No. 1 was grounded on the
British order in council of 8 June 1793,
which contravened the American government's insistence on the principle that free
ships made free goods (Bemis, *Jay's Treaty*,
206-14; Charles R. Ritcheson, *Aftermath of
Revolution: British Policy Toward the United
States, 1783-1795* [Dallas, 1969], 278-83).

The passage in 2D. VATTELL. 72. 73, which
deals with the obligation of a sovereign to
prevent his subjects from injuring the citizens of another nation, provided no justification for the British policy of confiscating
certain provisions bound for French ports in
neutral vessels. As he made clear in another
context, Lord Grenville meant to invoke
book 3, section 112-13, which argued that
such confiscation was justifiable when there
was a hope of reducing an enemy by famine
(for a translation, see Emmerich de Vattel,
*The Law of Nations, or, Principles of the Law
of Nature, Applied to the Conduct and Affairs
of Nations and Sovereigns* [London, 1797],
162, 336-8; Mayo, *British Ministers*, 40-1).
ANSWER TO MR. HAMMOND'S MEMORIALS:
see TJ to George Hammond, 15 May 1793.

[1] This and the subsequent passage in
italics are written in code, the text being
supplied from the decipherment in the first
Tr, except as noted below, and verified in
part by the Editors using partially reconstructed Code No. 16.

[2] Tr in DNA: RG 46 ends here.

[3] Here "a" is erroneously inserted in the
first two Trs.

From Benjamin Peirce

SIR   Newport July 6th 1793

Mr. B. Bourn has communicated to me your desire to be informed of
the commercial transactions between the United States of America and
Denmark, and the embarrasments it is subject too for want of a commercial treaty. Tobacco, rice, and Indigo, with all other articles of
American produce admissible in the ports of Denmark for consumption
are liable to an exaction of 50 ⅌ Ct. upon the Duties of the like goods
imported in English, Dutch, or the Ships of any Nation in treaty with
Denmark, (which is call'd the Aliens duty). For your information have
inclosed a Copy of the Customhouse charges against a Cargo of rice and
tobacco exactly as they would Stand against an English and American
Ship, from which you will discover that the extra duty in an American
bottom amounts the Customary Peace freight.

Suppose Mr. Saabye the American Consul at Copenhagen who is
one of the most Intelligent merchants in Europe has furnished you with
an account of the american goods landed in that port in the Year 1792,
from which you will discover the advantage the English, Dutch &c have

over the Americans in carrying our own produce to market. This difficulty of the duty of aliens would be removed the moment a treaty is Signed, and as the Danes at present appear to be the most rational Nation in Europe and much attached to the American flag, I think we may expect to have the priveledges of the most favored nations in a commercial treaty, if it was managed with address. Any further information I shall freely communicate. I am, sir, with respect Your Obedient Hble Servant   BEN PEIRCE

PS. The Exports of St. Petersburg for 1792 is inclosed.

RC (DLC); with dateline above postscript; endorsed by TJ as received 29 July 1793 and so recorded in SJL. Enclosures: (1) Notes on Danish duties on tobacco and rice, n.d., comparing customs duties on 126 hogsheads of tobacco and 306 tierces of rice imported on a ship "in treaty with Denmark" with those imported on an American ship, "which gives about £230 Sterling in favor of our rivals in a Single passage to Europe" (MS in DLC: TJ Papers, 236: 42320; in Peirce's hand). (2) Account of goods exported by British and American

ships from St. Petersburg for 1792 (undated broadside in same, 80: 13888-9).

Benjamin Peirce of Rhode Island, master of a merchant ship in the Danish trade, in which he had been active since 1785, provided the above information in connection with the Report on Commerce that TJ finally presented to Congress on 16 Dec. 1793 (note to Report on Appointment of Consul at Copenhagen, 10 Jan. 1792; Benjamin Bourne to TJ, 22 July 1793, and note).

From J. Wheatcroft

SR   Havre 6th. July 1793.

My last packet of papers Address'd to you was so unlucky as to be left behind, I have forwarded those with the remainder of the series to the present time, if you have not the leisure some of your Friends may like to go over the transactions of France for the last 6 months, a Faction of dissorginators have now got the lead with us but it is hoped the reign will not be long. I am wth sincere esteem Your most Obdt. Hme. Servt
                                                    J WHEATCROFT SENR.

RC (DLC); addressed: "Thos. Jefferson Esqr Philadelphia"; endorsed by TJ as received 10 Sep. 1793 and so recorded in SJL.

Wheatcroft wrote another letter to TJ on 29 Aug. 1793 that is recorded in SJL as received 11 Nov. 1793 but has not been found.

To James Madison

DEAR SIR   July 7. 1793.

I wrote you on the 30th. ult. and shall be uneasy till I have heard you have received it. I have no letter from you this week. You will perceive by the inclosed papers that they are to be discontinued in their present form and a daily paper published in their stead, *if subscribers enough can be obtained*. I fear they cannot, for nobody here scarcely has ever taken his paper. You will see in these Colo. H's 2d. and 3d. pacificus. Nobody answers him, and his doctrine will therefore be taken for confessed. For god's sake, my dear Sir, take up your pen, select the most striking heresies, and cut him to peices in the face of the public. There is nobody else who can and will enter the lists with him.—Never, in my opinion, was so calamitous an appointment made, as that of the present minister of F. here. Hotheaded, all imagination, no judgment, passionate, disrespectful and even indecent towards the P. in his written as well as verbal communications, talking of appeals from him to Congress, from them to the people, urging the most unseasonable and groundless propositions, and in the most dictatorial style &c. &c. &c. If ever it should be necessary to lay his communications before Congress or the public, they will excite universal indignation. He renders my position immensely difficult. He does me justice personally, and, giving him time to vent himself and then cool, I am on a footing to advise him freely, and he respects it. But he breaks out[1] again on the very first occasion, so as to shew that he is incapable of correcting himself. To complete our misfortune we have no channel of our own through which we can correct the irritating representations he may make. Adieu. Yours affectionately.

RC (DLC: Madison Papers); unsigned. PrC (DLC); bottom corner torn away, with loss of several words. Tr (MHi); 19th-century copy.

TJ's letter to Madison of 29 June 1793 had a postscript added on the 30th. John Fenno's proposal to turn his *Gazette of the United States* into a daily paper first appeared in the 3 July 1793 issue. The newspaper became a daily when it resumed publication with a slightly altered title on 11 Dec. 1793 after a hiatus caused by the yellow fever epidemic (Brigham, *American Newspapers*, ii, 912). The 2d. and 3d. pacificus essays by Alexander Hamilton defending the Proclamation of Neutrality were published in the *Gazette of the United States* on 3 and 6 July 1793 (Syrett, *Hamilton*, xv, 55-63, 65-9). no channel of our own: a reference to the unpopularity with the French government of Gouverneur Morris, the American minister to that country.

[1] TJ wrote "will break out" before altering the phrase to read as above.

From Thomas Mifflin

Sir   Phil: 7 July 1793.

In consequence of the request contained in a letter from the Secretary at War, I instituted an enquiry, respecting the equipment of the Little Sarah, as an armed vessel, in this Port; and as she will probably sail this day, I am anxious to receive a communication from the officers of the

Federal Government on the Subject. I have dispatched a messenger to Genl. Knox, requesting an interview; and I have inclosed the Report of the Master Warden, which you will be pleased to return. I am, with great esteem, Sir, Yr. most obedt Serv.   THO MIFFLIN

RC (DLC: Henry A. Willard Collection); in a clerk's hand, signed by Mifflin; at foot of text: "To Thomas Jefferson Esqr Secretary of State"; endorsed by TJ as received 7 July 1793 and so recorded in SJL. Enclosed in first Memorandum to George Washington, [11 July 1793], and Tobias Lear to TJ, 15 July 1793.

For the LETTER FROM THE SECRETARY OF WAR that prompted the report enclosed by Mifflin, see Notes of Cabinet Meeting and Conversations with Edmond Charles Genet, 5 July 1793. The case of the *Little Sarah* and the context of the report are discussed in Cabinet Opinions on the *Little Sarah*, 8 July 1793, and note.

ENCLOSURE

Nathaniel Falconer to Thomas Mifflin

SIR   Wardens Office Philadelphia 6th. July 1793
  In obedience to your Excellencys Letter of the 5th. Instant; I beg Leave to make the following report on the Little Brig Sarah.
  From the Best Information I can obtain; When She Sailed from this Port she had four Iron Cannon Mounted, and a number of wooden; and She returned into this port a Prize to the Frigat L'Ambuscaid in the Same Situation.
  Her present Situation, as to Military Equipment is 14 Iron Cannon and Six Swivels now mounted. The Crew is to consist (including Officers, Men and Boys) of One Hundred and Twenty but there is at present very few of her Crew on Board; The officer on Board says he does not Know of any American having entered. There seem's to be plenty of French Sailors about the wharves.
  The Captains Uniform is Blue turned up with read.
  This is the Best Information I can obtain at Present. I am your Excellencyes Most obedt. Humble Servant   NATHL FALCONER Master warden
                                                of the port

RC (PHarH: Executive Correspondence); in a clerk's hand, signed by Falconer; addressed: "His Excellency Thomas Mifflin Governor of the State of Pennsylvania"; with undated notation, possibly by Mifflin: "Enquire whether the Guns are French Property."

To Martha Jefferson Randolph

MY DEAR DAUGHTER   Philadelphia July 7. 1793.
  My head has been so full of farming since I have found it necessary to prepare a plan for my manager, that I could not resist the addressing my last weekly letters to Mr. Randolph and boring him with my plans.— Maria writes to you to-day. She is getting into tolerable health, tho' not good. She passes two or three days in the week with me, under the trees, for I never go into the house but at the hour of bed. I never before

knew the full value of trees. My house is entirely embosomed in high plane trees, with good grass below, and under them I breakfast, dine, write, read and receive my company. What would I not give that the trees planted nearest round the house at Monticello were full grown.— Can you make a provision of endive plants for the winter? Of celery I take for granted it may be done. But endive in great abundance would be a most valuable addition. I shall be in time for preparing covered places to transplant it to. Present me affectionately to Mr. Randolph and to the friends you have with you, and kiss the dear children for me. Adieu my dear. Yours with unceasing affection   TH: JEFFERSON

RC (NNP); at foot of text: "Mrs. Randolph"; endorsed by Mrs. Randolph. PrC (DLC). Tr (ViU: Edgehill-Randolph Papers); 19th-century copy.

Cabinet Opinions on the *Little Sarah*

At a meeting at the State house of the city of Philadelphia July 8. 1793.

Present the Secretary of state, the Secretary of the Treasury, the Secretary at War.

It appears that a brigantine called the Little Sarah[1] has been fitted out at the port of Philadelphia, with fourteen cannon, and all other equipments indicating that she is intended as a Privateer[2] to cruise under the authority of France, and that she is now lying in the river Delaware at some place between this city and Mud-island; that a conversation has been had between the Secretary of state and the Minister Plenipotentiary of France, in which conversation the Minister refused to give any explicit assurance that the brigantine[3] would continue until the arrival of the President and his decision in the case, but made declarations respecting her[4] not being ready to sail within the time of the expected return of the President from which the Secretary of state infers with confidence that she will not sail till the President[5] will have an opportunity of considering and determining the case.—That in the course of the conversation the Minister declared that the additional guns which had been taken in by the Little Sarah were French property, but the Governor of Pensylvania declared that he has good ground to believe that two[6] of her cannon were purchased here of citizens of Philadelphia.[7] The Governor of Pensylvania asks advice what steps, under the circumstances he shall pursue?

The Secretary of the Treasury and the Secretary of war[8] are of opinion that it is expedient that immediate measures should be taken provisionally for establishing a battery on Mud island, under cover of a party of militia, with direction that if the brig Sarah should attempt to depart before the pleasure of the President shall be known concerning her,[9] military coercion be employed to arrest and prevent her progress.

ALEXANDER HAMILTON
H KNOX

The Secretary of state dissents from this opinion.

TH: JEFFERSON[10]

MS (DLC: Washington Papers); in TJ's hand, being copied from Hamilton's Dft, and signed by Hamilton, Knox, and TJ; with marginal note by TJ (see note 2 below); endorsed by Tobias Lear. PrC (DLC); lacks signatures of Hamilton and Knox. Dft (DLC: Hamilton Papers); variant text in Hamilton's hand with addition by Knox and note by TJ (see notes 2 and 8 below), signed by TJ only; includes additional paragraphs (see note 10 below). Tr (DLC); variant text in the hand of Bartholomew Dandridge, Jr.; conjoined to Tr of Dissenting Opinion on the Little Sarah, 8 July 1793. Entry in SJPL: "Ons of heads of deptmts. on Little Sarah." Included in the "Anas." Enclosed in Hamilton to TJ, 10 July 1793, and TJ to George Washington, [11 July 1793].

The case of the Little Sarah, a British merchant ship captured by the French frigate Embuscade and taken as a prize to Philadelphia, brought to a head the growing tensions between Edmond Charles Genet and the Washington administration and led the President and the Cabinet to seek his recall by the French government. At stake in this dispute was Genet's open defiance of the federal government's clearly enunciated ban on the arming of belligerent privateers in American ports. Convinced from the first that France's treaty of commerce with the United States gave it the right to fit out privateers in American ports, in this case Genet also defied the ban because he planned to dispatch the Little Sarah (renamed the Petite Démocrate) and the Embuscade to New Orleans in order to provide naval support for an expeditionary force that he hoped to raise in Kentucky and Louisiana as part of a Girondin plan to liberate Louisiana from Spanish rule (TJ to Jean Baptiste Ternant, 15 May 1793; TJ to Genet, 5 June 1793; Genet to TJ, 22 June

1793; note to TJ to Isaac Shelby, 28 June 1793; Turner, CFM, 223).

The Little Sarah affair first came to the Washington administration's attention on 22 June 1793, when Governor Thomas Mifflin of Pennsylvania transmitted to the President a report by Master Warden Nathaniel Falconer suggesting that the Little Sarah was being fitted out as a French privateer in the nation's capital. Washington submitted this report to the Cabinet on the same day, in consequence of which Secretary of War Henry Knox requested Mifflin to inform the President promptly of changes made to the ship since its arrival. Two days later Mifflin sent Washington another report by Falconer mentioning a number of minor alterations made to the Little Sarah thus far and indicating that the ship's armament had actually been reduced since its arrival because of the transfer of two of its four iron cannon to the Citoyen Genet. These documents did not reach Washington before he left Philadelphia on 24 June 1793 for a visit to Mount Vernon, and the Cabinet neither forwarded them to him nor returned a reply to Mifflin. Uncertain now whether the case of the Little Sarah was covered by Knox's 24 May 1793 circular to the state governors ordering them to prevent belligerent privateers from fitting out in American ports, Mifflin took no further action (Falconer to Mifflin, 22, 24 June 1793, PHarH: Executive Correspondence; Mifflin to Washington, 22 June, 8 July 1793, same; Pa. Archs., 9th ser., I, 598, 599; Washington, Journal, 187).

This period of American inaction came to an end on 5 July when Alexander Hamilton met with TJ and Knox and notified them that preparations for fitting out the Little Sarah as a privateer were already well advanced. In response to a new request by Knox for further information that grew out of this meeting, Mifflin submitted to the

Secretary of War on the following day a report by Falconer on the arming of the *Little Sarah* and asked for an opinion from the federal government on "the propriety of detaining her" (for the report, see enclosure to Mifflin to TJ, 7 July 1793). Before the Cabinet could respond, however, the crisis worsened on the evening of 6 July when Alexander J. Dallas, the strongly Republican secretary of the Commonwealth of Pennsylvania, received word that the *Little Sarah* would sail from port the next morning. Informed of this news by Dallas, Mifflin resolved to call out a detachment of militia to prevent the ship from leaving Philadelphia. In an effort to avert hostilities, Mifflin agreed to a suggestion by Dallas that the secretary first meet with Genet in order to persuade him to keep the *Little Sarah* in port until the President had an opportunity to decide whether arming the vessel violated American neutrality. But Dallas's dramatic meeting with Genet about an hour before midnight on the 6th only aggravated the situation. In addition to defending his right to fit out the *Little Sarah* as a privateer and criticizing the federal government for being hostile to the French Republic, Genet refused to delay the ship's sailing until Washington returned to Philadelphia, promised to repel force with force if Mifflin employed the militia, and threatened to appeal from the President to the American people in order to vindicate his actions. In the face of Genet's defiance, Mifflin called into service a unit of militia without specifying their mission and sought guidance from TJ and Knox on what the federal government wanted him to do about the *Little Sarah*. At this point TJ prevented a possibly violent confrontation by meeting with Genet on 7 July and extracting from him a highly equivocal statement about the readiness of the *Little Sarah* that the Secretary of State chose to regard as an assurance that the ship would not sail until after the President had returned to Philadelphia and examined the case. As a result, Mifflin the same day disbanded the militiamen who had gathered in response to his call (Notes of Cabinet Meeting and Conversations with Edmond Charles Genet, 5 July 1793; Memorandum of a Conversation with Edmond Charles Genet, 10 July 1793; Mifflin to Washington, 8 July 1793, PHarH: Executive Correspondence; *Pa. Archs.*, 9th ser., I, 614;

Dallas to the Public, 7 Dec. 1793, *General Advertiser*, 10 Dec. 1793).

It was against this background that the three Cabinet members then in Philadelphia met this day and expressed the discordant views on the *Little Sarah* case recorded in the document printed above. But, even as Mifflin began preparations immediately after this meeting to carry out the deterrent strategy advocated by Hamilton and Knox, Genet himself rendered moot the divergence of opinion in the Cabinet by having the *Little Sarah* moved to Chester, Pennsylvania, just south of Philadelphia and below the proposed fortifications on Mud Island. The ship was still there on 11 July when Washington arrived in Philadelphia and ordered the Cabinet to confer with him the next day about Genet's latest challenge to American neutrality (Genet to TJ, 9 July 1793; Washington to TJ, 11 July 1793; *Pa. Archs.*, 9th ser., I, 617-22; Washington, *Journal*, 191).

The summoning of the Cabinet to reconsider the *Little Sarah* affair gave TJ a final opportunity to mitigate the severity of Genet's defiance. In advance of the Cabinet meeting of 12 July 1793, TJ obtained an assurance from Genet that the *Little Sarah* would not go to sea until the President had reached a decision on the case (TJ to Washington, [11 July 1793]). At the meeting itself the Cabinet decided to request Genet to keep the *Little Sarah* and some other French prizes from sailing until the executive had obtained counsel from the justices of the Supreme Court on a number of questions relating to American neutrality. Among other things, these questions involved the permissibility of arming French privateers with French cannon and manning them with French nationals, two of the circumstances Genet had adduced to justify his actions with respect to the *Little Sarah*. At the same time Hamilton and Knox also urged that the United States ask France to recall Genet, but as TJ disagreed and Washington expressed no view the Cabinet came to no decision on this matter (Cabinet Opinion on Consulting the Supreme Court, 12 July 1793; TJ to Edmond Charles Genet and George Hammond, 12 July 1793; Notes on Neutrality Questions, 13 July 1793).

Genet himself dashed whatever hope TJ may have had of lessening the French minister's offense in the eyes of the President and the Cabinet. About two days after TJ communicated to him the substance of the Cabinet's deliberations, Genet dispatched the *Little Sarah* to prey on enemy shipping in the Atlantic in violation of his pledge to TJ that the ship would remain in place until the President had decided the case. Genet thus abandoned his original plan to send the *Little Sarah* to New Orleans because he now hoped to enlist the more formidable support of a French fleet recently arrived off the American coast from Saint-Domingue for his projected invasion of Louisiana (Turner, *CFM*, 223; Woodfin, "Citizen Genet," 614-15). But in taking this action Genet tipped the balance of opinion among the President and his closest advisors in favor of seeking the increasingly obstreperous French minister's recall (see Editorial Note on the recall of Edmond Charles Genet, at 16 Aug. 1793).

[1] In Dft Hamilton first wrote "It appeared, that an armed Brigantine called the Sarah" and then altered it to read as above.

[2] TJ drew a box around the preceding three words and in another box in the margin wrote "omit these words." When copying Hamilton's Dft, he boxed the same words in that text and keyed them with a cross to a note he wrote at the foot of the first page: "omit the words 'as a privateer.' " The words are omitted in the Tr.

[3] Word interlined in Dft by Hamilton in place of "Sarah."

[4] In Dft Hamilton here canceled "state of preparation."

[5] In Dft Hamilton here canceled "returns."

[6] In Dft Hamilton here wrote "that ⟨at least three⟩ ⟨three⟩ at least two."

[7] Preceding sentence written in the margin of Dft by Hamilton.

[8] Preceding four words inserted in Dft by Knox in a space left blank by Hamilton.

[9] Preceding eleven words interlined in Dft by Hamilton in place of "she be fired upon the [. . .]."

[10] The Dft contains these additional paragraphs by Hamilton:

"⟨It being first⟩

Information having also been received that ⟨there were⟩ part of the Crew of the Sarah are citizens of the UStates ⟨on board the Sarah as part of her crew⟩; as can be testified by Charles Biddle of this City.

⟨It is the opinion⟩

The abovementioned heads of Departments agree that this information shall be communicated to the Atty. of the District in order that pursuant to his former instruction he may take measures for apprehending and bringing them to Trial."

Dissenting Opinion on the *Little Sarah*

I am against the preceding opinion of the Secretaries of the Treasury and War, for ordering a battery to be erected on Mud-island, and firing on the Little Sarah, an armed vessel of the Republic of France.

Because I am satisfied from what passed between Mr. Genet and myself at our personal interview yesterday, that the vessel will not be ordered to sail till the return of the President, which, by a letter of this day's post, we may certainly expect within eight and forty hours from this time.

Because the erecting a battery and mounting guns to prevent her passage, might cause a departure not now intended, and produce the fact it is meant to prevent.

Because were such battery and guns now in readiness and to fire on her, in the present ardent state of her crew just in the moment of leaving port, it is morally certain that bloody consequences would follow. No one could say how many lives would be lost on both sides, and all experience has shewn that, blood once seriously spilled, between nation and nation, the contest is continued by subordinate agents, and the door of peace is shut. At this moment too we expect in the river 20. of[1] their ships of war, with a fleet of from 100. to 150. of their private vessels, which will arrive at the scene of blood in time to continue it, if not to partake in it.

Because the actual commencement of hostilities, against a nation, for such this act may be,[2] is an act of too serious consequence to our countrymen to be brought on their heads by subordinate officers, not chosen by them, nor cloathed with their confidence; and too presumptuous on the part of those officers, when the chief magistrate, into whose hands the citizens have committed their safety, is within eight and forty hours of his arrival here, and may have an opportunity of judging for himself and them, whether the buying and carrying away two cannon, (for according to information, the rest are the nation's own property) is sufficient cause of war between Americans and Frenchmen.

Because should the vessel, contrary to expectation, depart before the President's arrival, the adverse Powers may be told the truth of the case, that she went off contrary to what we had a right to expect, that we shall be justifiable in future cases to measure our confidence accordingly, that for the present we shall demand satisfaction from France, which, with the proofs of good faith we have already given, ought to satisfy them. Above all, Great Britain ought not to complain: for, since the date of the order forbidding that any of the belligerent powers should equip themselves in our ports[3] with our arms, these two cannon are all that have escaped the vigilance of our officers on the part of their enemies, while their vessels have carried off more than ten times the number, without any impediment: and if the suggestion be true (and as yet it is but suggestion) that there are 15. or 20. Americans on board the Little Sarah, who have gone with their own consent, it is equally true that more than ten times that number of Americans are at this moment on board English ships of war, who have been taken forcibly from our Merchant vessels, at sea or in port, wherever met with, and compelled to bear arms against the friends of their country. And is it less a breach of our neutrality towards France to suffer England to strengthen herself with our force, than towards England to suffer France to do so? And are we equally ready and disposed to sink the British vessels in our ports by way of reprisal for this notorious and avowed practice?

Because it is inconsistent for a nation which has been patiently bearing for ten years the grossest insults and injuries from their late enemies, to rise at a feather against their friends and benefactors; and that too in a moment when circumstances have kindled the most ardent affections of the two people towards each other; when the little subjects of displeasure[4] which have arisen are the acts of a particular individual, not yet important enough to have been carried to his government as causes of complaint; are such as nations of moderation and justice settle by negociation, not making war their first step; are such as that government would correct at a word, if we may judge from the late unequivocal[5] demonstrations of their friendship towards us; and are very slight shades of the acts committed against us by England, which we have been endeavoring to rectify by negociation, and on which they have never condescended to give any answer to our Minister.

Because I would not gratify the combination of kings with the spectacle of the two only republics on earth destroying each other for two cannon; nor would I, for infinitely greater cause, add this country to that combination, turn the scale of contest, and let it be from our hands that the hopes of man receive their last stab.

It has been observed that a general order has been already given to stop by force vessels arming contrary to rule in our ports, in which I concurred. I did so; because it was highly presumeable that the destination of such a vessel would be discovered in some early stage, when there would be few persons on board, these not yet disposed nor prepared to resist, and a small party of militia put aboard would stop the procedure, without a marked infraction of the peace. But it is a much more serious thing, when a vessel has her full complement of men, (here said to be 120.) with every preparation and probably with dispositions to go through with their enterprize. A serious engagement is then a certain consequence. Besides, an act of force, committed by an officer in a distant port, under general orders, given long ago, to take effect on all cases, and with less[6] latitude of discretion in him, would be a much more negociable case, than a recent order, given by the general government itself, (for that is the character we are to assume) on the spot, in the very moment, pointed at this special case, possessing full discretion, and not using it. This would be a stubborn transaction, not admitting those justifications and explanations which might avert a war, or admitting such only as would be entirely humiliating to the officers giving the order, and to the government itself.

On the whole, respect to the chief magistrate, respect to our country men, their lives, interests and affections, respect to a most friendly nation who, if we give them the opportunity, will answer our wrongs by correcting[7] and not by repeating them, respect to the most sacred cause that ever man was engaged in, poising maturely the evils which may flow from the commitment of an act which it would be in the power and probably in the temper of subordinate agents to make an act of continued war, and those which may flow from an eight and forty hours suspension of the act, are motives with me[8] for suspending it eight and forty hours, even should we thereby lose the opportunity of committing it altogether. Th: Jefferson

July 8.[9] 1793.

MS (DLC: Washington Papers); entirely in TJ's hand; endorsed by Tobias Lear. Dft (DLC: Hamilton Papers); in TJ's hand; with altered date; endorsed by Hamilton. PrC (DLC); with alterations in ink. Tr (DLC); in the hand of Bartholomew Dandridge, Jr.; subjoined to Tr of Cabinet Opinions on the *Little Sarah*, 8 July 1793. Entry in SJPL: "T:J.'s opn on the [*Little Sarah*]." Included in the "Anas." Enclosed in first Memorandum to George Washington, [11 July 1793].

THE PRECEDING OPINION: Cabinet Opinions on the *Little Sarah*, 8 July 1793. Alexander Hamilton and Henry Knox elaborated on their opinion in a joint statement of reasons that Hamilton drafted for the President this day and TJ submitted to Washington three days later (TJ to Washington, [11 July 1793]). The LETTER OF THIS DAY'S POST from which TJ expected the arrival of the President within 48 hours was Washington to TJ, 3 July 1793. The ORDER FORBIDDING the fitting out of belligerent privateers in American ports was contained in a 24 May 1793 circular letter from Knox to the state governors (see note to TJ to Henry Knox, with Proposed Circular to the Governors of the States, 21 May 1793). In addi-

tion, TJ had twice informed the British and French ministers in Philadelphia of the government's opposition to this practice (TJ to George Hammond, 15 May, 5 June 1793; TJ to Jean Baptiste Ternant, 15 May 1793; TJ to Edmond Charles Genet, 5 June 1793).

[1] In Dft TJ interlined "twenty" in place of "a squadron." He interlined the word in ink on PrC.

[2] Preceding clause interlined in Dft and in ink on PrC.

[3] Preceding three words interlined in Dft and in ink on PrC.

[4] Word interlined in Dft, and in ink on PrC, in place of "complaint."

[5] Word interlined in Dft.

[6] Word interlined here and in Dft, as well as in ink on PrC, in place of "very little."

[7] Preceding thirteen words interlined in Dft, and in ink on PrC, in place of what appears to be "disposed if we give the opportunity to transact any negociations."

[8] Preceding four words interlined here and in Dft, as well as in ink on PrC, in place of "I am."

[9] Date reworded from "9" in Dft and in ink on PrC.

From Edmond Charles Genet

Monsieur

Philadelphie le 8 Juillet 1793.
l'an 2e. de le République francaise.

Le navire français armé en guerre le Vainqueur de la Bastille de construction américaine et portant ci devant le nom d'Hector est sorti de Charleston muni d'une commission française et de son ancien régistre américain que son commandant Hervieux a renvoyé à la Douane après avoir franchi la barre de ce port.

Cette conduite qui n'est condamnable que par sa timidité[1] a porté la Douane de Charleston à réquérir le Gouvernement de la Caroline du Sud de le faire arrêter et par une suite de cette procédure le Vainqueur de la Bastille à été saisi à Wilmington avec une prise qu'il y avait conduite. Les loix des Etats Unis ne prononcent de peine dans le cas présent que lorsqu'il y a eu intention de se soustraire aux droits imposés par les Etats, et comme il est prouvé par la commission en guerre et par les instructions dont le capitaine Hervieux est porteur qu'il n'est sorti du Port de Charleston que pour résister autant qu'il est en lui aux injustes attaques de nos ennemis, devoir que tous les traités[2] l'autorisent à remplir, qu'aucune loi des Etats Unis et que par conséquent aucun ordre de l'Executif de ces États ne peut lui interdire je vous prie, Monsieur, de demander au Gouvernement fédéral la liberté du Capitaine Hervieux et de tout son équipage du Vainqueur de la Bastille ci-devant l'Hector, et de sa prise actuellement détenue dans le Port de Wilmington dans la Caroline du Nord.   GENET

PrC of Tr (DLC); in a clerk's hand; at head of text: "Le Ministre de la République française près les Etats Unis à Monsieur Jefferson Secretaire d'Etat des Etats Unis." Dft (NHi: Genet Family Papers); slightly variant text in a clerk's hand, with several revisions by Genet; at head of text in Genet's hand: "Note par laquelle le C. Genet demande que le Vainqueur de la Bastille Corsaire armé à Charleston et arrêté à Wilmington soit relaché." Tr (AMAE: CPEU, XXXVII); with minor variations. Tr (NNC: Gouverneur Morris Papers). PrC of another Tr (PRO: FO 97/1); in the hand of George Taylor, Jr. FC (DLC: Genet Papers); in English. FC (same); in English. FC (same); in English; draft translation of preceding FCs. Tr (DNA: RG 46, Senate Records, 3d Cong., 1st sess.); in English. Recorded in SJL as received 9 July 1793. Printed with translation in *Message*, 19 (App.), 48; translation printed in ASP, *Foreign Relations*, I, 163. Enclosed in Memorandum to George Washington, [11-13 July 1793], and TJ to Gouverneur Morris, 16 Aug. 1793.

[1] Preceding eight words interlined in Dft by Genet in place of "inconsequente."
[2] Dft: "que nos traités."

From Lucas Gibbes and Alexander S. Glass

Philadelphia 8th: July 1793.

Lucas Gibbs and A: S: Glass In part Owners of the Cargo of the Sloop Betsy lately Captured by a French Privatier called Citizen Genet, Captn. Johannes and brought into Baltimore; as well for themselves as on behalf of the owners of the Said Sloop and of the Residue of the Cargo beg to declare and Show that Houseman & Mashiler & Mason & Hordman of the Island St: Bartholomew Subjects to the King of Sweden are the true and real Owners of the Said Sloop. That the said Sloop has been duly registerd agreeable to the Laws of Sweden, and furnished with all such papers and Documents from the Governor and other officers of St: Bartholomew as are usual and proper. They therefor conceive that the said Sloop and Cargo ought not to have been captured by the

Said French Privatier and humbly pray that you will cause them to be delivered to Mr: John Hollins of Baltimore to whom they are consigned.   LUCAS GIBBES

ALEXANDER S. GLASS

RC (DNA: RG 59, NFC); in Richard Söderström's hand, signed by Gibbes and Glass; at head of text: "To the Honble. Thos: Jefferson Secretary of State for the United States of America."

The capture by the French privateer *Citoyen Genet* of the *Betsey*, a Swedish merchant ship owned by Swedish subjects on St. Barthélemy carrying a cargo belonging in part to them, in part to Lucas Gibbes and other Swedish subjects on that island, and in part to Alexander S. Glass of New York, led to a landmark decision by the United States Supreme Court respecting the enforcement of American neutrality. Eight days after signing this letter Glass brought suit before the United States District Court of Maryland for the restitution of the ship and cargo, which had in the meantime been condemned as lawful prize by the French vice-consul in Baltimore, on the ground that both were neutral property. After the District Court decided in August 1793 that it had no jurisdiction in the case, Glass sought to obtain redress from the executive branch of government, only to be advised that the executive could not intervene until after all legal appeals had been exhausted. Glass thereupon appealed to the United States Circuit Court of Maryland, which in November 1793 sustained the District Court's denial of jurisdiction. Upon further appeal, however, the Supreme Court in February 1794 ruled that the case was within the District Court's plenary admiralty jurisdiction and therefore remanded it to the lower court for a final decision. At the same time the Supreme Court also ruled that French consuls had no right to exercise admiralty jurisdiction in the United States. Thus in this decision the Supreme Court eliminated the doubts that many district courts had entertained about their jurisdiction over cases involving French captures of merchant ships belonging to citizens of foreign nations at peace with the United States, while rejecting the claim to admiralty authority that French consuls in the United States had routinely invoked in support of their pretensions to exclusive jurisdiction over such cases (Richard Söderström to TJ, [3 July 1793], and note, and 16 Nov. 1793; TJ to Söderström, 10 Sep., 20 Nov. 1793; TJ to Glass, 10 Sep. 1793; TJ to Henry Knox, 10 Sep. 1793; Knox to TJ, 11 Sep. 1793; Memorial from Alexander S. Glass and Others, 12 Nov. 1793, and enclosure; Glass to Edmund Randolph, 23 May 1794, DNA: RG 76, France, Unbound Records; James Brown Scott, ed., *Prize Cases Decided in the United States Supreme Court, 1789-1918*, 3 vols. [Oxford, 1923], I, 9-19; Goebel, *Supreme Court*, 760-5).

From Thomas Pinckney

DEAR SIR   London 8th[1] July 1793

I wrote to you by the way of Falmouth on the 5th. of this month and sent a copy of that letter by this opportunity since closing this last I received from Mr. Johnson the inclosed Protest stating the misconduct of the commander of a French Frigate. Mr. Johnson was particularly requested to forward it to our Government or I would have sent it directly to Mr. Morris at Paris. As enquiries concerning the event will probably be made in the same channel you will oblige me by enabling me to answer them. With great respect I am Dear Sir Your faithful & obedt Servt.   THOMAS PINCKNEY

RC (DNA: RG 59, DD); at foot of text: "Mr Jefferson"; endorsed by TJ as received 10 Nov. 1793 and so recorded in SJL. PrC (ScHi: Pinckney Family Papers). Tr (Lb in DNA: RG 59, DD). Enclosure: Deposition of Thomas Hickling, acting American consul at St. Michael, 28 May 1793, stating— on the basis of the testimony of Keyran Welsh, master of the *Maria*, and his passengers Dom Vincente Cano, former governor of the Grand Canary Island, Lieutenant Dom Gracia Manrigo of the Spanish navy, Cano's wife, and a maidservant—that on 19 May the *Maria*, a brigantine owned by Ebenezar Stocker of Newburyport and bound from Tenerife to Cádiz with a cargo wholly belonging to Stocker and Welsh, was captured on the high seas by the French frigate *Medie*, Captain Minbielle; that after the French had taken part of the ship's cargo, plundered everything belonging to its captain, crew, and passengers to the value of more than 10,000 dollars, and were taking it into the nearest French port, the *Maria* was retaken on 25 May by the *Ned*, a privateer from Liverpool commanded by George Makwell, and brought to St. Michael two days later; and that Welsh requested him on behalf of all concerned to accept his protest against the piratical actions of the *Medie* with a view to obtaining compensation (MS in same, in a clerk's hand, signed by Hickling, with subjoined 31 May 1793 certification by five merchants of Ponta Delgada; Tr in same). For other texts of the enclosure, see note to David Humphreys to TJ, 20 July 1793.

¹ Digit reworked from "7."

To William Thornton

July 8. 1793.

Th: Jefferson presents his compliments to Dr. Thornton and incloses him a letter he has received from the President, with some observations of Mr. Hallet, the object of which the papers themselves will explain to Dr. Thornton. Th:J. has not yet seen any of the persons mentioned in the letter. He will be happy to receive Dr. Thornton's observations in any way which shall be least troublesome to himself. The President seems to wish as quick a procedure on the subject as possible. He prays him to return the President's letter.

RC (NHi: Miscellaneous Manuscripts). Not recorded in SJL. Enclosure: George Washington to TJ, 30 June 1793. Other enclosure not found.

From James Wood

Sir   In Council 8th. July 1793.

I do myself the honor of enclosing you the Copy of a Letter Just Received by express, from the Mayor of the Borough of Norfolk, with the Proceedings of the Court of Aldermen On the Subject of it. To Afford a Temporary Relief to the Distressed emigrants, the Executive have Directed two thousand Dollars to be immediately Advanced, which is to be Applied Agreeably to the direction of the Common-hall; and the Board have Approved the proceedings of the Court, in Accommodating the sick and wounded with the use of the Marine Hospital. I have the honor to be with great Respect Sir Yr. Mo Obt. Servt.

JAMES WOOD

RC (DLC); endorsed by TJ as received 13 July 1793 and so recorded in SJL. FC (Vi: Executive Letterbook). Probably the letter recorded in SJPL under 12 July 1793: "Govr. of Virga's lre on arrival of French in distress from the Cape." Enclosures: (1) Robert Taylor, Mayor of Norfolk, to Governor Henry Lee, 6 July 1793, stating that by order of the Norfolk Court of Aldermen he was enclosing a paper about the French 74-gun ship *Jupiter*, which had arrived in Hampton Roads seeking permission to land 400 sick and wounded from that and other ships; that on 20 June a force of whites had lost a battle with blacks and mulattoes near Cap-Français; that a day later that town was destroyed by fire and from ten to twelve thousand of the inhabitants massacred; that those who escaped boarded a French fleet of 150 vessels that will arrive any moment in Hampton Roads, their first port since Cap-Français, lacking money or clothes and seeking succor; that the directors of the Marine Hospital have agreed to accommodate the sick and wounded there, although it is unfinished, but desire authorization, since it is a public building; that he is directed to furnish these unfortunates with every necessary but that if all the distressed individuals land here the sum he can apply will be only a trifle, wherefore he asks the executive to supply him with the necessary orders on this business; and that in the meantime every possible attention will be paid to the refugees by the inhabitants, who feel for their misfortunes (Tr in DLC; in Archibald Blair's hand and attested by him). (2) Minutes of Court of Aldermen of Norfolk Borough, 6 July 1793, giving its unanimous opinion, based on information received from the mayor of the French request to land refugees from Cap-Français, that the inhabitants would do everything in their power to relieve them and that the mayor should ask the president and directors of the Marine Hospital for permission to shelter the sick and wounded there, seek assistance from the county's civil and military authorities in providing relief, report by express to the governor about the borough's actions and request guidance on how to proceed, and meanwhile furnish the sufferers with whatever immediate relief was necessary (Tr in DLC; attested by Alexander Moseley). Enclosed in Tobias Lear to TJ, 15 July 1793.

TJ submitted this letter to the President on 13 July 1793 (Washington, *Journal*, 196).

From Edmond Charles Genet

MONSIEUR

Philadelphie le 9. Juillet 1793.
l'an 2e. de la Republique française

Vous m'avéz demandé des details sur le Brigantin La Petite Democrate ci devant La Petite Sarah qui se trouve actuellement armé et pret a sortir de la Delaware les voici. Ce batiment, Monsieur, de propriété anglaise armé par nos ennemis de 4 canons de plusieurs pierriers et d'autres armes a été pris par la Fregatte de la Republique francaise l'Embuscade et envoyé a Philadelphie. Sa construction etant élégante et solide, son corps doublé en cuivre sa marche superieure, son greement et sa mature en bon état J'ai jugé d'apres le rapport du capitaine de L'Embuscade et d'autres marins eclairés que l'acquisition de ce vaisseau serait avantageuse à la marine de la République et cette considération jointe au désir que j'avais de procurer de l'emploi a un assés grand nombre de marins français qui se trouvaient ici exposés aux dangers qui accompagnent souvent le desoeuvrement et la misere, m'a determiné à le prendre pour le compte de l'Etat.

Je l'ai fait aussitot reparer J'ai fait completter son armement avec des canons qui se trouvaient à bord de 4 vaisseaux français, J'en ai confié le commandement au Citoyen Amiot, enseigne non entretenu de la République et Je le ferai appareiller muni d'une commission du conseil exécutif et de mes instuctions particulieres aussitot qu'il sera pret. Je dois me borner, Monsieur, a vous presenter ces faits qui ne sont susceptibles d'aucune discussion de ma part et qui ne peuvent donner lieu à aucune difficulté de celle de votre gouvernement. Quand les traités parlent les agens des nations ne peuvent qu'obeir. Agréez, Monsieur, mon estime et mon respect.   GENET

PrC of Tr (DLC); in a clerk's hand; at head of text: "Le Citoyen Genet Ministre plenipotenre. de la Republique française à Monsieur Jefferson secretaire d'etat." Tr (AMAE: CPEU, xxxvII); with minor variations. Tr (NNC: Gouverneur Morris Papers). PrC of another Tr (PRO: FO 97/1); in the hand of George Taylor, Jr. FC (DLC: Genet Papers); in English. FC (same); in English. FC (same); in English; draft translation of preceding FCs. Tr (DNA: RG 46, Senate Records, 3d Cong., 1st sess.); in English. Recorded in SJL as received 9 July 1793. Printed with translation in *Message*, 19 (App.), 49; translation printed in ASP, *Foreign Relations*, I, 163. Enclosed in first Memorandum to George Washington, [11 July 1793], Tobias Lear to TJ, 15 July 1793, and TJ to Gouverneur Morris, 16 Aug. 1793.

From Edmond Charles Genet

Philadelphie le 9. Juillet 1793.
MONSIEUR   L'an 2e. de la Republique francaise.

Le Consul de la Republique Francaise dans cet etat a réquis depuis quatre jours le Gouverneur de la Pennsylvanie de faire sortir du Port de Philadelphie le Corsaire Anglais le Jane armé de 16 canons qui y est entré le quatre de ce mois sans avoir aucun signe de détresse.

Le Gouverneur lui à répondu qu'il ne pouvait prendre aucune décision à cet égard pendant l'absence de monsieur le President des Etats unis. Quoique cette reponse, Monsieur, soit accompagnée d'expressions très obligeantes et tres amicales, je crois devoir vous observer que d'après les dispositions de l'article XXII de notre traité d'amitié et de commerce il n'est nullement nécessaire d'attendre la décision de Mr. Le President pour le faire partir ce Corsaire n'etant point entré ici en relâche forcée, ayant eu tout le tems pour y prendre beaucoup plus de vivres qu'il ne lui en faut pour se rendre au port le plus voisin de la Puissance dont il tient sa commission, et d'après différens rapports que je viens de recevoir, augmentant son armement. Les traités etant considérés par le peuple Américain comme ses loix les plus sacrées tous les

Gouvernemens locaux des Etats Unis sont tenus de les connaitre, et tous les magistrats obligés de les faire éxécuter sans délai. Je vous prie en conséquence, monsieur, de présenter ces considérations au Gouverneur de la Pennsylvanie et de le déterminer à remplir contre le Corsaire le Jane les devoirs qui lui sont imposés par nos traités.

GENET

PrC of Tr (DLC); in a clerk's hand; at head of text: "(Copy)" and "Le Citoyen Genet Ministre Plenipotentiaire de la Republique francaise à Monsieur Jefferson Secrétaire d'etat des Etats Unis." Dft (NHi: Genet Family Papers); slightly variant text in a clerk's hand, with minor revisions and docketing by Genet. Tr (AMAE: CPEU, xxxvii); with minor variations. Tr (NNC: Gouverneur Morris Papers). PrC of another Tr (PRO: FO 97/1); in the hand of George Taylor, Jr. FC (DLC: Genet Papers); in English. FC (same); in English. FC (same); in English; draft translation of preceding FCs. Tr (DNA: RG 46, Senate Records, 3d Cong., 1st sess.); in English. Recorded in SJL as received 9 July 1793. Printed with translation in *Message*, 20 (App.), 49; translation printed in ASP, *Foreign Relations*, I, 163. Enclosed in Memorandum to George Washington, [11-13 July 1793], and TJ to Gouverneur Morris, 16 Aug. 1793.

From Edmond Charles Genet

MONSIEUR   Philadelphie le 9. Juillet 1793. l'an 2e. de la Republique.

J'ai deja eu plusieurs fois l'honneur de vous entretenir du traitement révoltant que les vaisseaux de guerre anglais faisaient essuyer dans toutes les mers aux batimens américains. Je vous ai instruit des visites sévères aux quelles ils les assujettissoient et des saisies qu'ils se permettoient de faire, à leur bord et sous la protection du Pavillon des Etats Unis, des personnes et des propriétés des citoyens français.

Les rapports de tous les navigateurs attestent la vérité de ces faits, et les plaintes ci jointes en présentent de nouvelles preuves. Je vous prie, Monsieur, de les porter à la connoissance de M. le Président des Etats Unis et d'avoir la complaisance de me faire savoir les mesures qu'il a prises ou celles qu'il se propose de prendre pour faire respecter par nos ennemis le pavillon des Etats Unis autant que nous le respectons nous mêmes, et pour faire rendre à nos concitoyens les propriétés dont ils ont été dépouillés injustement.

Je dois vous observer, Monsieur, que comme les anglais continue-ront vraisemblablement à enlever impunement nos citoyens et leurs propriétés a bord de nos[1] vaisseaux, sans s'embarrasser des principes philosophiques proclamés par le Président des Etats Unis, les engagemens que nous avons contractés avec vous nous mettant dans la position la plus desavantageuse vis-a-vis de nos ennemis, en nous privant de la faculté[2] d'user en tout point à leur égard du droit de représailles,[3] il est urgent autant pour votre interêt que pour le notre que nous convenions de prendre promptement d'autres mesures. J'attends incessamment, Monsieur une réponse positive du Gouvernement fédéral[4] sur cet objet, et j'espere qu'elle sera conforme à la dignite et a la justice du Peuple Américain, qui ne doit point exiger, s'il est hors d'Etat aujourd'hui[5] d'en imposer aux anglais qu'il a vaincus autrefois,[6] que nous nous exposions et que nous l'exposions lui même plus longtems par une débonnaireté déplacée aux insultes de cette nation vis-a-vis de la quelle[7] les procédés genereux[8] ne conduisent en Général qu'a de nouveaux outrages. Agreez, Monsieur, mon respect & mon estime.

GENET

PrC of Tr (DLC); in a clerk's hand; at head of text: "Le Citoyen Genet, Ministre de la République Française près les Etats Unis, à Monsieur Jefferson, Secretaire d'Etat des Etats Unis." Dft (DLC: Genet Papers); variant text in a clerk's hand, with revisions, complimentary close, and signature by Genet. Tr (AMAE: CPEU, xxxvii). Tr (NNC: Gouverneur Morris Papers). PrC of another Tr (PRO: FO 97/1); in the hand of George Taylor, Jr. FC (DLC: Genet Papers); in English; with abbreviated complimentary close and signature by Genet. Tr (DNA: RG 46, Senate Records, 3d Cong., 1st sess.); in English. Recorded in SJL as received 9 July 1793. Enclosures: (1) Declaration of Silvat Ducamp to Jean Baptiste Lemaire, Chancellor of the French consulate in Philadelphia, 27 June 1793, stating that on 9 May he left St. Lucia bound for Philadelphia aboard the American brigantine *Columbia*, Captain John Green of that city, with a cargo of sugar, cotton, coffee, handkerchiefs, and cash, worth in all 21,909 livres, the first three of which were to be sold in Philadelphia on account of Jean Mercié of Bordeaux and others; that regardless of her flag four days later the *Columbia* was captured by the brigantine *Fanny*, an English privateer commanded by Captain Bloomsberry of St. Vincent, and brought to Basseterre in St. Christopher, where six or seven other American vessels had been brought by force; and that he protested the seizure of his merchandise by the admiralty court there. (2) Declaration of Pierre Nouvel, Chouquet de Savareau, Gaston de Nogère, and G. Bautier, 7 June 1793, stating that on 21 May they left Jérémie, Saint-Domingue, bound for Baltimore aboard the American galiot *Regulator*, Captain Simon White, with a cargo of coffee, cotton, and slaves; that four days later the *Regulator* and three other American ships were stopped and searched by the *Joseph and Mary*, an English privateer from Kingston, Jamaica, commanded by Captain David Harris and owned by Allen & White; and that after ransacking their personal effects, seizing Captain White's money, and cutting open many coffee bags, the privateer took the slaves and allowed the *Regulator* to proceed on its voyage (PrCs of Trs in DLC, with attestation of No. 1 by François Dupont and certifications of both by Genet, all in a clerk's hand; Trs in NNC: Gouverneur Morris Papers; PrCs of other Trs in PRO: FO 97/1, in Taylor's hand; Trs in DNA: RG 46, Senate Records, 3d Cong., 1st sess., in English). Letter and enclosures with translations printed in *Message*, 20-2 (App.), 50-3; translation of letter printed in *Correspondence*, 23; letter printed in *Correspondance*, 29-30; translations printed in ASP, *Foreign Relations*, I, 164-5). Letter and enclosures enclosed in Memorandum to George Washington, [11-13 July 1793], Tobias Lear to TJ, 15 July 1793, and TJ to Gouverneur Morris, 16 Aug. 1793; letter enclosed in TJ to Edmund Randloph, with Jefferson's Note, [23 July 1793].

[1] Dft, AMAE Tr, and *Correspondance*: "vos."

[2] Preceding six words interlined in Dft by Genet in place of "et que par vos interêt."

[3] Remainder of sentence interlined in Dft by Genet.

[4] Preceding three words interlined in Dft by Genet.

[5] Word written in the margin in Dft by Genet.

[6] Preceding seven words interlined in

Dft by Genet in place of "à la marine anglaise."
⁷ In Dft the clerk first wrote "aux insultes de ces Suppôts d'un gouvernement vis

à vis du quel" and then Genet altered it to
read as above.
⁸ Dft, AMAE Tr, and *Correspondance*:
"modérés."

From Henry Cooper

St. Croix, 10 July 1793. He wrote to TJ on 1 May and received his 21 May
circular, but will not be able to provide the information expected in his 26 Aug.
1790 request for a semiannual report on American trade with this island. Most
American imports here are subject to a 10 percent duty without the privilege of
exporting part of the value thereof in sugar. Few American products fall into the
category of permission articles, which are subject to a 5 percent duty with the
privilege of exporting half the value thereof in sugar. Rum can be exported
freely. It will therefore be apparent to TJ how those entries and clearances are
made and that they do not accord with the reports made at American customhouses. If it will be useful, he will endeavor to send an abstract of these matters
from the customhouse books here every six or twelve months. He doubts that
the government here, which is jealous of all foreign trade, would allow him to
hold the regular office necessary to obtain the information requested about
American vessels entering and clearing the island. He will pay attention to the
other points mentioned by TJ and by the next conveyance send the required
bond. Late accounts from Denmark confirm the opinion here that it will not
become involved in the war. This year's crop is very abundant, and prospects
for next year's are very favorable.

RC (DNA: RG 59, CD); 2 p.; at foot of text: "The Secretary of State for the United
States of America"; endorsed by TJ as received 5 Aug. 1793 and so recorded in SJL.

From Alexander Hamilton

July 10 [1793]

The Secretary of the Treasury presents his Compliments to the Secretary of State. He has signed the Counterpart; but for the present leaves
in the words as a privateer to consider jointly of some substitute the kind
of vessel not being wholly indifferent and there being a doubt whether
the general words would be descriptive enough.

The letter supposed to have been received from the Commissioner of
loans cannot be found. Yet the impression is so strong of one of the
import mentioned to Mr. Jefferson having been received . . . that the
reality of it is scarcely doubted. This inference too is confirmed by the
circumstance that *no answer* to the letter to the Commissioner appears
on *file* and it is utterly unlikely that it should have remained so long
unanswered. A Duplicate will go by tomorrow's Post. It is regretted
that the Doubt cannot *now* be cleared up.

RC (DLC); partially dated; ellipsis in original; endorsed by TJ as received 11 July 1793, but recorded in SJL as received the day before.

The COUNTERPART was the fair copy of Cabinet Opinions on the *Little Sarah*, 8 July 1793; see the note to that document for the dispute over the words AS A PRIVATEER. For the misplaced letter from the COMMISSIONER OF LOANS for Virginia, see Enclosure No. 1 listed at Hamilton to TJ, 26 July 1793.

Memorial from George Hammond

The undersigned, his Britannic Majesty's Minister plenipotentiary to the United States, has the honor of submitting to the Secretary of state the annexed depositions, relative to the capture, by the armed Schooner, fitted out at Charleston, named le Citoyen Genêt, of the British Brigantine, the Prince William Henry from Baltimore to Barbadoes, and of the British brigantine the lovely Lass belonging to Barbadoes, both of which, together with the Schooner that took them, are arrived in the Port of Baltimore.

The undersigned, deeming it unnecessary to place any stress on the aggravating circumstances specified in these depositions—of the evident concert subsisting between the Pilots of Chesapeak bay and the person commanding the schooner, and of the unwarrantable proceeding of the latter in firing into the Prince William Henry, after her colours had been ordered to be struck &c—esteems it sufficient for him to confine himself to the mere fact of the capture of these vessels: For, after the formal assurance he has received of the President's having required the schooners, le Citoyen Genêt and le sans culotte "to depart to the dominions of" another "sovereign" and after the "expectation" expressed in the Secretary of states letter to him of the 19th. ulto. that "the speedy departure of those vessels will obviate the inconveniences apprehended" by the undersigned—he must presume, (until he is informed of a contrary determination on the subject) that the executive government of the United states will pursue the most efficacious measures for procuring the immediate restitution of the vessels thus captured to their respective owners.

GEO: HAMMOND

Philadelphia 10th July 1793.

RC (DNA: RG 59, NL); at foot of first page: "Mr Jefferson"; endorsed by TJ as received 10 July 1793 and so recorded in SJL; with later note by TJ:
 "Brigs Lovely Lass
   Prince Wm. Henry
 taken by the Citoyen Genet proscribed
  before Aug. 7."
FC (Lb in PRO: FO 116/3). Tr (same, 5/1).

Tr (same, 115/2). Tr (Lb in DNA: RG 59, NL). Enclosures: (1) Deposition of James Mitchell, master of the *Prince William Henry*, Baltimore, 6 July 1793, declaring that after this British brigantine departed from Baltimore for Barbados on 18 June and while detained at New Point Comfort until 26 June by contrary winds, various pilots informed him that an English schooner privateer from Halifax was lying off the capes; that on the basis of these assurances he cleared the capes on 28 June and was sailing about eight leagues off Cape Henry when the *Prince William Henry* was attacked and captured by a French privateer which turned out to be the *Citoyen Genet*, Captain Johanene, which fired on his ship even after he agreed to surrender it, wounding one of his seamen; that immediately after the capture the rest of the crew "except a negro boy" was sent to Baltimore on the *Prince William Henry*, and three days later he, his mate, and a seaman were released and put aboard a pilot boat off the capes; that upon arriving in Baltimore on 5 July he learned that the prize master of his ship was born in North Carolina; and that because about a fourth of the privateer's crew spoke English, they were either English or American. (2) Deposition of Thomas Gibbes Williamson, master of the *Lovely Lass*, Baltimore, 7 July 1793, stating that this Bar-

badian brigantine sailed from Hampton Roads on the morning of 4 July with the ship *Trusty* and the brigantine *Cornwallis*; that leaving the Cheseapeake near Cape Henry and encountering an armed schooner flying French colors and supposed to be the *Citoyen Genet*, the *Trusty* dropped anchor and the unarmed *Lovely Lass* made for the southern shore, fearing it would be the first to be attacked; that the privateer captured the *Lovely Lass* at anchor in six fathoms of water six or seven miles from land; that the privateer's captain declared he would have considered the *Lovely Lass* to be a lawful prize had it been only half a mile from land; and that after the *Trusty* and the *Cornwallis* evaded capture, the privateer brought the *Lovely Lass* to Baltimore on 6 July (MSS in DNA: RG 59, NL, both in the hand of Edward Thornton, signed by Mitchell and Williamson, respectively, attested by Baltimore justice of the peace Gros Almon, and endorsed by TJ; Trs in Lb in same).

James Hoban's Observations on William Thornton's Design for the Capitol

Observations

On drawings delivered by Doctor Thornton, for a Capitol to be built in the City of Washington.

1st. The extent of bearing of the Repository Ceiling, and the Ceiling of the Halls.

2nd. The intercolumnations.

3rd. The entrances.

4th. Darkness and irregularity.

5   the Staircases.

[6] Inconveniences to the Members.

7   Impractability of the Gallerys.

8   Disagreement between the ornamental and necessary points of the internal structure——&c.

July 10th. 1793   JAMES HOBAN

MS (DLC); entirely in Hoban's hand; torn at seal; endorsed by TJ as received in July, but recorded in SJL as received 10 July 1793. Enclosed in Tobias Lear to TJ, 15 July 1793.

James Hoban (ca. 1762-1831), architect and builder, was a native of Ireland who moved to Philadelphia after the Revolution, lived for several years in South Carolina, and in 1792 settled and spent the rest of his life at the District of Columbia. In that year he won the competition for the design of the President's House sponsored by the Commissioners of the Federal District, and later he supervised both its construction and its rebuilding after the British burned it in 1814 (DAB).

TJ submitted Hoban's communication to the President on 13 July 1793. These and other criticisms of William Thornton's prize-winning design for the Capitol soon led to its modification (Washington, *Journal*, 195; Washington to TJ, 30 June 1793, and note; TJ to Washington, 17 July 1793, and note).

From Robert Leslie

SIR   London July 10th 1793

I Arrived here on sunday 9th. of June, with my family all in good health. I Delivered the letter you honoured me with to Mr. Pinkney, a few days after who politely offered me any service in his power, Mr. Cutting is gone to Irland, I have found several Gentlemen here who have been very attentive, and seem desirous of forwarding my designs, tho I have not yet been able to put any of them in execution, being engaged in purching an asortmen of watchs to send over, the repeating watch, you was pleased to order for Miss Jefferson, shal be sent by the first spring ship, I am very anxious to hear how your great Clock gowes, and also your timepiece, if either or boath do not gow right, if you will be so obliging as to let me know it I will send you others from this place, as I can have them mad much better here, and if there is any thing else I can serve you in, I hope you will let me know it, for I shall certainly have no grater pleasure than in serving you to the best of my abilites, please to inform me wheather I shall in the spring direct to you in Philadelphia or Virginia, if you should favour me with a line at any time, please to leave it with Mr. Price my Partner, to be forwarded to me, as It will be but a few week before I move from the place I am now at, and do not know what part the Town I shall gow to. Pleas to except of my Sincerest thanks for the favours you have done me, and belive me always your very humble Servent   ROBERT LESLIE

RC (DLC); endorsed by TJ as received 24 Oct. 1793 and so recorded in SJL.

THE LETTER: TJ to Thomas Pinckney, 24 Apr. 1793.

Memorandum of a Conversation with Edmond Charles Genet

July 10. 1793. The Secretary of the Treasury having communicated to Genl. Knox and myself that he had been informed that the Little Sarah

had much augmented her arms, and was greatly advanced in her preparations, we concurred in opinion that the Govr. should be desired to
have a reexamination of the fact. It was done and a Report made that she
had entered the port with only 4. guns, and now had 14. &c. The next
day, being Sunday the 7th. inst. I received a Letter from the Govr. by
express informing me he understood she would sail that day. I went
instantly to town. He told me he had received the intelligence the night
before and had sent Mr. Dallas at midnight to Mr. Genet. Mr. Dallas
told me that on his proposing the subject of detaining the vessel he flew
into a great passion, talked extravagantly and concluded by refusing to
order the vessel to stay. As the Govr. had sent for Genl. Knox also, I
told him I would in the mean time go to Mr. Genet and speak with him
on the Subject. I went.

On his coming into the room I told him I called on the subject of the
Little Sarah, that our information was that she was armed contrary to
the decision of the President which had been communicated to him, and
that she would sail that day and I requested that he would detain her till
we could enquire into the fact and lay it before the President who would
be here on Wednesday. He took up the subject instantly in a very high
tone, and went into an immense feild of declamation and complaint. I
found it necessary to let him go on, and in fact could do no otherwise, for
the few efforts which I made to take some part in the conversation were
quite ineffectual. It is impossible for me to state the particulars of what
he said. Such of the general topics as I can now recollect were these; he
charged us with having violated the treaties between the two nations,
and so went into the cases which had before been subjects of discussion,
complained that we suffered our flag to be insulted and disregarded by
the English, that they stopped all our vessels took out of them whatever
they suspected to be French property, that they had taken all the provisions he had embarked in American vessels for the colonies, that if we
were not able to protect their vessels in our ports nor their property on
the high seas, we ought to permit them to protect it themselves, that
they on the contrary paid the highest respect to our flag, that tho it was
notorious that most of the cargoes sent from America were British property, yet being in American vessels, or pretended American vessels,
they never touched it, and thus had no chance of retaliating on their
enemies; that he had been thwarted, and opposed in every thing he had
had to do with the government, that he found himself in so disagreeable
a situation that he sometimes thought of packing up and going away, as
he found he could not be useful to his nation in any thing; he dwelt on
the friendly propositions he brought from his nation, on the instructions
and dispositions with which he came to do whatever would gratify us;
that to such propositions such a return ought not to have been made by

the Executive without consulting Congress, and that on the return of the President he would certainly press him to convene the Congress. He had by this time got into a more moderate tone, and I stopped him at the subject of calling Congress, explained our constitution to him, as having divided the the functions of government among three different authorities, the Executive, Legislative and Judiciary, each of which were supreme in all questions belonging to their department and independent of the others: that all the questions which had arisen between him and us belonged to the Executive department, and if Congress were sitting could not be carried to them, nor would they take notice of them. He asked if they were not the sovereign? I told him No, they were sovereign in making laws only, the Executive was sovereign in executing them, and the Judiciary in construing them where they related to their department. But says he, at least, Congress are bound to see that the treaties are observed. I told him No, there were very few cases indeed arising out of treaties which they could take notice of; that the President is to see that treaties are observed. And if he decides against the treaty, to whom is a nation to appeal? I told him the constitution had made the President the last appeal. He made me a bow, and said that indeed he would not make me his compliments on such a constitution, expressed the utmost astonishment at it, and seemed never before to have had such an idea. He was now come into perfect good humour and coolness, in which state he may be spoken with with the greatest freedom. I observed to him the impropriety of his conduct in persevering in measures contrary to the will of the government and that too within it's limits wherein they had unquestionably a right to be obeyed. But, says he, I have a right to expound the treaty on our side. Certainly, says I, each party has an equal right to expound their treaties: you, as the agent of your nation, have a right to bring forward your exposition, to support it by reasons, to insist on it, to be answered with the reasons for our exposition where it is contrary: but when, after hearing and considering your reasons, the highest authority in the nation has decided, it is your duty to say you think the decision wrong, that you cannot take upon yourself to admit it, and will represent it to your government to do as they think proper; but in the meantime you ought to acquiesce in it, and to do nothing within our limits contrary to it.[1] He was silent as to this, and I thought was sensible it was right. I brought him to the point of the Little Sarah, and pressed his detention of her till the President's return. Why detain her said he?—Because, said I, she is reported to be armed with guns acquired here. He said the guns were all of French property, and surely we did not pretend to controul them in the disposal of their own property, that he could name to me the French vessels from whom he had taken every gun. I told him I would be obliged to him for any evidence of that fact with which he would furnish me, and repeated my request to detain the vessel. He was embarrassed, and unwilling, he said he should not be justifiable in detaining her. I told him it would be considered as a very serious offence indeed if she should go away, that the government was determined on the point, and thinking it right, would go through with it. After some hesitation he said he could not make any promise, it would be out of his duty, but that he was very happy in being able to inform me that the vessel was not in readiness and therefore could not sail that day. I asked him if I might rely that she would not be ready to sail before the return of the President? He then spoke of her unreadiness indefinitely as to time, said she had many things to do yet, and would not be ready for some time, he did not know when. And whenever I tried to fix it to the President's return, he gave the same answer that she would not be ready for some time, but with the look and gesture which shewed he meant I should understand she would not be gone before that. But says he she is to change her position and to fall down the river to-day but she will not depart yet. What, says I, will she fall down to the lower end of the town? I do not know exactly where says he, but some where there for the convenience of getting ready some things, but let me beseech you, says he, not to permit any attempt to put men on board her. She is filled with high spirited patriots, and they will unquestionably resist; and there is no occasion, for I tell you she will not be ready to depart for some time. I told him then I would take it for granted she would not be ready before the President's return, that in the mean time we[2] would have enquiries made into the facts, and would thank him for information on the subject, and that I would take care that the case should be laid before the President the day after his return. He promised to give me a state of facts the next day.[3]—I then returned to the Governor, told him what had passed, and that I was satisfied that tho the vessel was to fall some where down the river, she would not sail. He thereupon ordered the militia to be dismissed. On repeating to him and Mr. Dallas what Mr. Genet had said, we found that it agreed in many particulars with what he had said to Mr. Dallas: but Mr. Dallas mentioned some things which he had not said to me, and particularly his declaration[4] that he would appeal from the President to the people.[5] He did in some part of his declamation to me[6] drop the idea of publishing a narrative or statement of transactions, but he did not on that, nor ever did on any other occasion in my presence, use disrespectful expressions of the President. He from a very early period shewed that he believed there existed here an English party, and ascribed to their misinformations industry[7] and maneuvres some of the decisions of the Executive. He is not reserved on this subject. He complains of the partiality of the information of those employed by the government, who never let a single movement of a French vessel pass unnoticed, nor ever

inform of an English one arming, or not till it is too late to stop her.—
The next day, Monday, I met the Secretaries of the Treasury and War,
in the Governor's office. They proposed our ordering a battery to be
erected on Mud island immediately, guns to be mounted, to fire at the
vessel, and even to sink her if she should attempt to pass. I refused to
concur in the order, for reasons assigned in another paper. The vessel
was then at Gloucester point. Whether any intimation of this proposition got out or not, I do not know, but she very soon after fell down to
Chester. On a suggestion that there were 15. or 20. Americans on
board, we desired Mr. Rawle to take measures to prosecute them. See
his answer both as to the fact and the law.   TH: JEFFERSON

MS (DNA: RG 59, MLR); entirely in
TJ's hand; endorsed by Tobias Lear. PrC
(DLC). FC (DLC); entirely in TJ's hand
and signed by him, with many words written in abbreviated form; at foot of text:
"copd. frm. ye orignl. in ye hands of ye
Presidt. endorsed by the Pres. 'Minutes of
a conversn between the Secy. of sta. & mr
Genet. July 1793.' " Tr (Lb in DNA: RG
59, SDC). Entry in SJPL: "Notes on conversn with Genet on the [Little Sarah]." Included in the "Anas." Enclosed in first
Memorandum to George Washington, [11
July 1793].

    TJ had communicated the DECISION OF
THE PRESIDENT forbidding the fitting out of
belligerent privateers in American ports in
his letter to Genet of 5 June 1793. For the
subsequent political controversy over Genet's threat to APPEAL FROM THE PRESIDENT
TO THE PEOPLE, see Malone, *Jefferson*, III,

135-44. For TJ's refusal TO CONCUR IN THE
ORDER proposed by Alexander Hamilton
and Henry Knox, see Cabinet Opinions on
the *Little Sarah*, 8 July 1793. ANOTHER
PAPER: Dissenting Opinion on the *Little
Sarah*, 8 July 1793. The ANSWER of Wil-
liam Rawle, the federal district attorney for
Pennsylvania, was contained in a letter to
TJ of 9 July 1793, recorded in SJL as re-
ceived the same day but not found.

¹ TJ here canceled "He appeared to."
² Word interlined in place of "I."
³ Preceding sentence interlined.
⁴ Preceding two words interlined.
⁵ Preceding sentence bracketed in pencil
by an unidentified hand, possibly the President's. See Washington to TJ, 11 July
1793.
⁶ Preceding two words added in the
margin.
⁷ Word interlined.

From Alexander J. Dallas

SIR   Sec: Office, Philad. 11. July 1793.
    The Governor being absent upon Public business, I take the liberty
of inclosing for your information a representation, made by the Father
and Master of an Apprentice boy, named George Allison, who, it
seems, has entered on board the Little Democrat (formerly the Little
Sarah) a French armed vessel. I am, with great respect & esteem, Sir,
Yr. most obed Serv   A. J. DALLAS
                                      Secy of the Com. of Pennsa

    Dft (PHarH: Executive Correspon-
dence); at foot of text: "To Thos. Jefferson
Esqr. Secretary of State." FC (same, Secretary's Letterbooks). Mistakenly recorded in

SJL as received 10 July 1793. Enclosure
not found.

    Alexander James Dallas (1759-1817),

who immigrated to Philadelphia from Jamaica in 1783 and became a lawyer, was Secretary of the Commonwealth of Pennsylvania from 1791 to 1801. This staunch Republican played a key role in welcoming Edmond Charles Genet to Philadelphia in May, helped to organize the Democratic Society of Pennsylvania in the weeks following, and earlier in July acted as a gubernatorial emissary to the French minister in the affair of the *Little Sarah*. Appointed United States Attorney for the Eastern District of Pennsylvania by TJ in 1801, Dallas held this office until 1814 and then served as Secretary of the Treasury under Madison until 1816 (DAB; note to Cabinet Opinions on the *Little Sarah*, 8 July 1793).

To Edmond Charles Genet

SIR   Philadelphia July 11. 1793.

The bearer hereof Mr. John Nicholson has applied to me on the subject of an apprentice of his, named George Allison, about 17. years of age, who has absconded from him and has been recieved on board the Little Democrat, where he now is. As the condition of the young man renders him in some degree the property of Mr. Nicholson, and that as well as his age leave him not free to take such a step without consent, I am persuaded you will be so good as to give orders to have him delivered to Mr. Nicholson who will give any evidence you require of the truth of the facts. Permit me to ask the same with respect to another apprentice in the same circumstances, bound to another person, who has authorised him to act for him, as being well acquainted with all the circumstances relating to it. I have not the name either of the master or apprentice in the latter case, but he will furnish them. I have the honor to be with great respect & esteem Sir your most obedt. humble servt

TH: JEFFERSON

PrC (DLC); at foot of text: "The Min. Plen. of the republic of France." FC (Lb in DNA: RG 59, DL). Tr (DLC: Genet Papers); with an undated note from Genet to François Dupont, the French consul in Philadelphia, subjoined in a clerk's hand, ordering him to comply promptly with TJ's request for the return of the two apprentices.

Genet replied to both this and another letter from TJ of 12 July 1793 in a letter of the latter date that is recorded in SJL as received 15 July 1793 but has not been found.

Memorandum from Stephen Hallet

Methode usité a paris pour la Preparation et l'employ du Plâtre
1° La Pierre se Brule sur la Carriere par un feu Constant de 12 a 18 heures selon quelle est plus ou moins dure.
2° elle est ensuite Battue et reduite en poudre et Se transporte au Batiment dans des Sacs: la on le passe dans une Claye ou Pannier, le plus

Gros et le moins Cuit qui reste dans le pannier est battu de nouveau pour être employé Comme mortier pour hourder les murs et autres gros ouvrages: le plus fin qui est aussi le plus Cuit est reservé pour les plafonds, languettes de Cheminées; enduis Profiles et autres legers ouvrages.

3° on le Gache plus Serre pour les Gros ouvrages et plus Clair pour les legers, mais la quantité d'eau varie Comme la quotité du Platre, en sorte qu'il n'y a point regle Constante et que la proportion ne peut Se determiner que par la pratique.

Nota les Sculpteurs ou Mouleurs de sculpture Choisissent leur platre en pierre les plus Cuittes quils pulverisent quand ils sont pret a l'employer et le Gachent très Clair: S. HALLET
11 Juillet 1793.

MS (DLC); entirely in Hallet's hand; endorsed by TJ: "Plaister of Paris."

From George Hammond

SIR   Philadelphia 11th July 1793
In the conversation which I had with you yesterday, you were pleased to inform me that a complaint had been addressed to the President on the subject of the British letter of marque-ship Jane, William Morgan Commander, having augmented her force within the port of Philadelphia.

Notwithstanding the loose and general manner, in which this intimation was expressed to me, and my conviction that the facts were not such as I presumed they had been represented, I entertained too great a respect for this government to suffer such a circumstance to remain unnoticed and unexplained. I therefore went myself to observe the vessel in question, and have obtained from her commander a declaration relative to the mode and extent of her force and equipment on her arrival here—to the object of her voyage hither—and to the repairs, which have been, or are intended to be, made in her, antecedently to her departure. This declaration, which I have the honor of inclosing, Captain Morgan is willing to confirm by his oath, and to annex to it, if required, a certificate, from the carpenter employed, of the specific nature of the repairs which this vessel is undergoing.

The readiness I have evinced to anticipate a complaint of this kind, that has not yet been formally communicated to me, will I trust be regarded as a manifestation on my part that I will not countenance or protect any British subjects in any proceedings, which may be considered as disrespectful to the sovereignty of the United states, or as infringements on that neutrality, which the executive government of this country has professed to adopt, and has recommended to its citizens rigidly to observe, in the contest subsisting between France and the other belligerent powers. I have the honor to be, with sentiments of great respect Sir, your most obedient humble Servant,

GEO. HAMMOND

RC (DNA: RG 59, NL); endorsed by TJ as received 12 July 1793 and so recorded in SJL. FC (Lb in PRO: FO 116/3). Tr (same, 5/1). Tr (Lb in DNA: RG 59, NL). Enclosure: William Morgan to Hammond, 11 July 1793, stating, in his capacity as commander of the *Jane*, a letter of marque ship commissioned by the lieutenant governor of Jamaica, that he had brought this vessel to Philadelphia for the sole purpose of loading a cargo of flour for shipment to Jamaica, that he is making no alteration to his 16-gun ship to prepare it for war or increase its strength, that he did not need or plan to purchase ad-ditional military stores or ammunition, and that he had no plans for privateering on the voyage to Jamaica (RC in DNA: RG 59, NL; Tr in Lb in same). Enclosed in Tobias Lear to TJ, 15 July 1793.

TJ submitted this letter and its enclosure to the President on 13 July 1793 (Washington, *Journal*, 195). For a discussion of the Washington administration's subsequent efforts to ensure that the *Jane* did not take on additional armaments in Philadelphia, see Syrett, *Hamilton*, xv, 88n.

From Thomas Mann Randolph, Jr.

DEAR SIR   Monticello July 11. 1793.

We received your favors of June 24. and 30. on the 9. inst. at night. We are extremely happy to learn that Maria has got well over the mumps.

I send you now the scheme of cultivation which I formed last year and am adopting at Edgehill.[1] An indisposition, and the preparation for a journey to Richmond prevent my accompanying it with any comment at present.[2] You will observe that it differs from yours in four principal points. First there are two distinct systems, intended to be[3] coexistent. 2d. the years of rest are not successive. 3d. white clover is substituted for red; (a consequence of the 2d.) 4th. one field undergoes a summer fallow. I shall endeavor in my next to give my reasons for these. The system for small fields I think you will adopt. The other and yours I myself am ballancing. Besides the division of my farm which this scheme will require I have set aside a well-watered valley for a standing meadow. It is necessary to break up meadow grounds once in 5 or 6 years, and on the 5th. or 6th. part of mine[4] I rely for Hemp and flax which, with us, thrive no where so well as in the flat grounds on our little streams. You will see that they are not included in the rotation. Lucerne and St. Foin are too long-lived for it. The fields marked pasture I suppose to have nothing in them that is not spontaneous, but there I mean to introduce the white-clover generally as soon as possible by sowing it in Autumn with[5] the grain. The red-clover you observe I prefer sowing with the Barley in Autumn. This may not be necessary in every soil but in ours I am convinced it will do better then than in the Spring. I suppose it to be intended alltogether for the Scythe. I am Dr. Sir your most sincerely affectionate friend.   TH: M. RANDOLPH

P.S. Patsy and her little ones are well.

[*On verso of address cover:*]

	1st.	2d.	3d.	4th.	5th.	6th.	7th.	8th.	years.
No. 1	Corn & Peas	Wheat	Fallow	Wheat	Pasture	Corn & Potatoes	Rye	Pasture	
2	Wheat	Fallow	Wheat	Pasture	Corn & Potatoes	Rye	Past.	Corn & Peas.	
3	Fallow	Wheat	Past.	Corn & Potatoes	Rye	Past.	Corn & Peas	Wheat	
4	Wheat	Pasture	Corn & Potatoes	Rye	Past.	Corn & Peas	Wheat	Fall:	Fields of 60 acres.
5	Pasture	Corn & Potatoes	Rye	Past.	Corn & Peas	Wheat	Fall.	Wheat	
6	Corn & Potatoes	Rye	Past.	Corn & Peas	Wheat	Fall:	Wheat	Past:	
7	Rye	Past.	Corn & Peas	Wheat	Fall:	Wheat	Past.	Corn and Potatoes	
8	Pasture	Corn & Peas	Wheat	Fallow	Wheat	Past:	Corn & Potatoes	Rye.	

	1st	2d	3d	4th	5th	6th	year.
No. 1	Pumpkins	Barley	Clover	Clover	Turnips	Oats	
2	Barley	Clover	Clover	Turnips	Oats	Pumpkins	
3	Clover	Clover	Turnips	Oats	Pumpk.	Barley	Fields of
4	Clover	Turnips	Oats	Pump.	Barley	Clover	10 acres.
5	Turnips	Oats	Pump.	Barley	Clover	Clover	
6	Oats	Pump.	Barley	Clover	Clover	Turnips	

RC (MHi); addressed: "Thomas Jefferson, Secretary of State, Philada."; with crop rotation tables on verso of address cover; note by Randolph below address: "Lodged at the Post-office in Charlottesville on the eleventh July"; endorsed by TJ as received 20 July 1793 and so recorded in SJL. FC (DLC); variant text written on verso of address cover of unidentified letter to Randolph with grid for first table on recto, first row only being filled in; postscript torn away and second table lacking; other important variations noted below; at head of text: "A Copy."

[1] FC: "last year for Edgehill and am now adopting."
[2] Preceding two words omitted from FC.
[3] Preceding three words interlined; they are omitted from FC.
[4] Preceding two words interlined.
[5] FC: "after."

To William Short

DEAR SIR   Philadelphia July 11. 1793.

Your *two* favors dated Aranjuez, Apr. 2. (Private) have been duly received. Your letter of Dec. 18. inclosing one open to Mr. Brown had been before received, and his forwarded, but no answer come to hand when I heard of the failure of Donald & Burton. I was told it in the street, and went instantly to the Treasury office and entered a caveat against the transfer of your property by the best general description I could. I wrote to Mr. Brown by the same post which carried him the news of the failure, as also the caveat. I likewise wrote to Mr. Skipwith to beg he would go down to Richmond and use his personal influence with Brown to get your property out of his hands. I have never got an answer from him, but I inclose you an extract from Brown's dated Apr. 15. As the letter he therein promised did not come, I wrote again. You have inclosed an extract from his second answer June 3. In the mean time yours of Apr. 2. came, covering a power of attorney to me. I went with this instrument to the Treasury, to shew that I was authorised to enquire after your property. No trace of it could be found here. However one of the officers very soon after informed me that in consequence of the caveat I had first entered, a letter had come from the deputy in Richmond informing them that that property was all transferred to your name. I have waited till the last moment by the present opportunity to have the letter found: but the researches for it have been fruitless, tho' their recollection of having recieved such a letter seems perfect. They have written to Richmond a second time for information, but this will not be in time to send you now. In the mean while you may be assured of two facts. 1. that putting together this recollection of the letter, and Brown's information of June 3. it is quite certain that all your property now stands in your own name. 2. that the American effects of Donald & Burton will pay every American creditor, preferred as they are by our laws to all others. I do not know whether it might not be practicable to save, under this privilege, what you had in Donald's hands in London, if we had evidence of it. I shall leave this place the 1st. day of October, that ending the quarter at which the accounts of my department are settled, no more to return. I will employ some broker (they are most to be relied on) to recieve your interest quarterly and invest it, when prices are proper, in new paper, till you direct what shall be done with it. We are beginning in Virginia to think of tenanting our lands, and I believe it will be practicable at a rent of 5. per cent on the value. It will still however be a troublesome revenue, but an increasing capital. Never did mortal long so much for an object as I do for the 1st. of October. No conjecture can be formed who will be my successor. It is not in my power to say a word about your future destiny, not a word having been said to me on the subject since what I first communicated to you. I presume that will take place. Direct all your future public letters to 'the Secretary of state for the US.' I inclose you a letter from your brother, which will doubtless give you your family news. I recollect no death nor other article of private intelligence which can interest you, and a throng of business obliges me here to conclude with the assurances of the sincere esteem & constant attachment of Dear Sir your affectionate friend & servt   TH: JEFFERSON

RC (ViW); at head of text: "Private"; at foot of first page: "Mr. Short"; endorsed by Short as received 27 Sep. 1793. PrC (DLC). Tr (ViU: Edgehill-Randolph Papers); incomplete 19th-century copy. Enclosures: Extracts of James Brown to TJ, 15 Apr., 3 June 1793. Other enclosure not found.

To Josef Ignacio de Viar and Josef de Jaudenes

GENTLEMEN   Philadelphia. July 11.[1] 1793.

Your letter of the 8th. of June[2] has been duly recieved and laid before the President of the US. The matter it contains is of so serious a complexion that he chuses to treat of it with your government directly. To them therefore his sentiments thereon will be communicated, through the channel of our commissioners at Madrid, with a firm reliance on the justice and friendship of his Catholic majesty. In doing this it will be impossible not to manifest the impression which the style as well as matter of your communications make on the government of the US. I have the honor to be with due respect & esteem Gentlemen Your most obedt. servt.   TH: JEFFERSON

Tr (CtY); in TJ's hand; at foot of text: "Messrs. Viar & Jaudenes." PrC of Dft (DLC); entirely in TJ's hand; with date altered, probably from 23 June 1793. Tr (DLC: William Short Papers); entirely in TJ's hand and initialed by him. PrC (DLC); with address added in ink by George Taylor, Jr. Tr (DNA: RG 46, Senate Records, 3d Cong., 1st sess.). Tr (Lb in same, TR). FC (Lb in DNA: RG 59, DL). Tr (AGI: Papeles de Cuba, legajo 88). Tr (AHN: Papeles de Estado, legajo 3895); in Spanish; attested by Jaudenes. Entry in SJPL: "Th.J. to Viar & Jaudenes. ye actual lre, of which June 23 is the draught." Enclosed in first Memorandum to George Washington, [11 July 1793], TJ to William Carmichael and William Short, 16 July 1793, and TJ to Thomas Pinckney, 11 Sep. 1793.

The LETTER OF THE 8TH. OF JUNE was actually the letter from Jaudenes and Viar of 18 June 1793. The initial draft of this reply to them, couched "simply & in a few words," was approved by the Cabinet "with some alterations" on 22 June 1793, but has not been found. The revised draft, which was probably dated 23 June 1793 in view of the entry for it under that date in SJPL, and presumably a draft of one of TJ's letters of 25 June 1793 to George Hammond, may have been the documents approved by Alexander Hamilton and Henry Knox in a missing item recorded in SJPL under 24 June 1793 as "H. & K. approbn of lres to Hammond & V. & J." (Washington, *Journal*, 186-7; note to TJ to William Carmichael and William Short, 30 June 1793).

[1] Month and day reworked in ink from earlier date, probably 23 June, in PrC of Dft.

[2] Preceding two words interlined in ink in place of "instant" in PrC of Dft.

To Josef Ignacio de Viar and Josef de Jaudenes

July 11th. 1793.

The Secretary of State presents his Compliments to Messrs. Viar and Jaudenes, and informs them that the government of the United States having occasion to send public dispatches to their Commissioners plenipotentiary at the Court of Madrid, James Blake, a Citizen of the United States is employed as their Courier to be the Bearer of them. He is to embark on board the Ship   bound from this port[1] to Cadiz in Spain, and the Secretary of State asks from the Commissioners of Spain their Passport for the said Courier, in such form as may protect his person and dispatches from harm and search both by Sea and Land. The Secretary of State offers to have conveyed by the same person any dispatches they may chuse to transmit by him to the country he is going to. He departs the 13th. instant.

FC (Lb in DNA: RG 59, DL). Tr (DNA: RG 46, Senate Records, 3d Cong., 1st sess.). Tr (Lb in same, TR). Enclosed in Tobias Lear to TJ, 15 July 1793.

TJ submitted this letter to the President on 13 July 1793 (Washington *Journal*, 196).

[1] Preceding three words interlined; they are omitted in Trs.

From Josef Ignacio de Viar and Josef de Jaudenes

Sir   Philadelphia. July 11. 1793.

Rumors have been circulating for some days among the people, giving to understand that there prevails on the part of the King our master, and of ourselves, some design of interrupting the friendship and good correspondence which so happily subsists between the two nations, on the subject of the Indians.

We have heard without noticing this hitherto, endeavoring to convince those who have spoken to us on the subject, with such reasons as justice and our understanding have suggested. But a peice having been published in the gazette of Mr. Bache of this morning, the contents of which cannot but produce great disgust against his Majesty and those whom we have the honor to represent, it appears to us indispensable to desire you to be so good as to inform the Presidt. of the US. thereof on his return that he may be pleased to take, in justification, those measures which he may judge most proper to remove from the public the impression of so unfounded a charge with which they calumniate the King and ourselves.

You well know, Sir, that in all our communications we have had the honor to assure the US. of the pacific and sincere disposition of his majesty towards them, and the Indians their neighbors, and that the K's orders to us and all the governors of his possessions on the frontiers have been of the same nature, and you know also that whatever information we have given to the US. on the turbulent disposition of the Indians towards the US. and of the conduct of their Agents on the frontiers, have and could have no other object than to induce the US. to use all possible means on their part to prevent the dissentions now in fermentation, our government promising to continue doing the same, as it has proved to have done hitherto.

You are equally possessed of the different evident proofs which we have had the honor of producing to the US. by which it is discovered clearly that the Agents of the government of the US. have not proceeded conformably to the principles of friendship, good correspondence and sincerity which you have repeatedly assured us is the object of the US.

The principal object in all our communications has been, and is, to obtain from the US. a cessation of acts which may be construed in a sense neither pacific nor friendly, while a negociation is depending between the two nations, pledging ourselves solemnly that the same shall be done by the king's governors on the frontier.

The reciprocal tranquility and interest of the two nations require that the minds of the inhabitants should not be irritated on either side; and in a government of the nature of that of the US. the opinion of the people is of the greatest importance.

This consideration urges us to intreat the Presidt. of the US. to be pleased to assure the public, in such way as he thinks most convenient and satisfactory, that the disposition of the K. our master, as well as of his representatives, neither has been, nor is, to foment discord between the two nations, nor with the Indians, but on the contrary to establish the most solid and reciprocal friendship and advantageous correspondence, and that on all occasions they have given unquestionable proofs of it, the discord observed at present flowing solely from misintelligence, or a defect of rigorous observance of the orders of their superiors by the Agents of this government on the frontiers: assuring you that if any of the Agents of the K. has contravened the orders of H.M. (of which we have no proof but quite the reverse) and the US. shall produce to the K. due proof of the fact, we have no doubt they will obtain the most complete satisfaction, they doing the same on their part.

We are firmly persuaded that the Presidt. of the US. with his superior understanding will adopt the most proper and efficacious remedies which this inveterate ill requires, until the negociation depending shall present a radical cure. We have the honor to repeat our regard to you, & to subscribe ourselves with the greatest esteem & respect Sir your mo. ob. & mo. hble servts

JOSEPH IGNACIO DE VIAR   JOSEPH DE JAUDENES

Tr (DLC); in TJ's hand; at head of text: "Translation. ⟨of a letter⟩"; at foot of text: "To Mr. Jefferson &c." PrC (MoSHi: Bixby Collection). RC (DNA: RG 59, NL); in Spanish; in Viar's hand, signed by Viar and Jaudenes; endorsed by TJ as received 11 July 1793, but erroneously recorded in SJL as received 10 July 1793. Tr (AHN: Papeles de Estado, legajo 3895); in Spanish; attested by Jaudenes and Viar. Tr (AGI: Papeles de Cuba, legajo 88); in Spanish; in Viar's hand; attested by Viar and Jaudenes. Tr (DLC: William Short Papers); in Spanish. PrC (DLC); at head of text in ink in TJ's hand: "here was inserted the letter of Th:J of July 11. to Messrs. Viar & Jaudenes, among the dispatches made up for Messrs. Carmichael & Short." Tr (CtY); in Spanish. PrC (DLC). Tr (Lb in DNA: RG 59, DCI); in Spanish. Tr (DNA: RG 46, Senate Records, 3d Cong., 1st sess.); in English. Tr (Lb in same, TR); in English. Re-

corded in SJPL. Enclosed in TJ to William Carmichael and William Short, 16 July 1793, and TJ to Thomas Pinckney, 11 Sep. 1793.

The Spanish agents were prompted to write this letter by the appearance of an item in the Philadelphia *General Advertiser* of this date under the heading of "From a Correspondent" alleging that the "Spanish-American government" had incited hostilities by the Creeks and other Southern Indians against the United States, that Viar and Jaudenes had suggested to the federal executive that the Spanish court would support the Creeks if the United States failed to comply with certain unspecified Creek demands, and that Spanish policy in this respect was part of a settled design by the European coalition opposing the French Revolution to destroy liberty in France and America.

Memorandum to George Washington

[11 July 1793]

Papers requiring the President's instant attention.

Th:J's letter to Viar and Jaudenes.
Genet's communications relative to } the Courier goes on Saturday.
  Spain

Little Sarah. the Governor's letter of June 24. and Warden's 1st. report.
    the Governor's letter of July 7.
  x Th:J's conversation with Genet.

x Th:J's opinion against firing on the Little Sarah.
  Rawle's letter. July 9.
  Genet's letter. July 9.

MS (DNA: RG 59, MLR); undated; entirely in TJ's hand, except for two marks in a different ink, probably made by Tobias Lear, next to items retained by Washington; endorsed by Lear: "Memo. of letters & papers deld. to the President by the Secy of State 9th July 1793." Tr (DLC: Washington Papers, Journal of the Proceedings of the President); entered under 11 July 1793. Not recorded in SJL.

Despite Tobias Lear's endorsement, TJ almost certainly wrote this and the following memorandum on 11 July 1793—the date of the first document listed here—when he submitted the papers enclosed in them to the President, who had just returned from Mount Vernon. After reading the documents covered by this first memorandum, Washington ordered the Cabinet to consult with him the following day (Washington, *Journal*, 190-1).

LETTER TO VIAR AND JAUDENES: TJ's first letter to them of 11 July 1793. GENET'S COMMUNICATIONS: see enclosures printed below. For the substance of Governor Thomas Mifflin's LETTER OF JUNE 24 to the President and the WARDEN'S 1ST. REPORT, see note to Cabinet Opinions on the *Little Sarah*, 8 July 1793. TJ's memorandum of his CONVERSATION WITH GENET is dated 10 July 1793; see that document and note for the context of the missing letter from William Rawle. OPINION . . . ON THE LITTLE SARAH: Dissenting Opinion on the *Little Sarah*, 8 July 1793.

ENCLOSURES

Papers on Spain Received from Edmond Charles Genet

I

Note on the principles of Spain relative to the navigation of the Missisipi.

There must be in the records of the Secretary of state of the US. a letter from Vergennes to Mr. Jay dated the 6th. Sep. 1782, with a Memoir of that Minister of foreign affairs, the object of which was to engage the US. not to think of the navigation of the Missisipi, and to leave things on the footing which existed then, which exists yet, and which probably will exist a long time if the US. do not take energetic measures to change it. This step of the Minister of foreign affairs was taken at the instigation of Spain, whose invariable principles are contained in the extract, here subjoined, from a Report of Montmorin to Vergennes.[1]

'The Cabinet of Madrid, Monsr. le Comte, thinks it has the greatest interest not to open the Missisipi to the Americans, and to disgust them from making establishments on that river, as they would not delay to possess themselves of the commerce of New Orleans and Mexico, whatever impediments should be opposed to their progress, and that they would become neighbors the more dangerous for Spain, as even in their present weakness they conceive vast projects for the conquest of the Western shore of the Missisipi.'[2]

Montmorin adds 'that Spain is decided to make the savages a barrier between her possessions and those of the Americans, that it would oppose if necessary, other obstacles to their progress, and that his M.C.M. could not give to his Catholic Majesty a greater proof of his attachment, than in employing his influence in the US. to divert their views from the navigation of the Missisipi.'

The court of France conformed itself constantly to this insinuation, as is proved by the instructions which it gave to all it's Ministers with Congress.

Tr (DNA: RG 59, NL); undated; in TJ's hand, with his notation at head of text subsuming all three documents: "Translation of papers communicated to Th: Jefferson by Mr. Genet July 2. 1793"; written on recto of a sheet containing No. II on verso. PrC (DLC: TJ Papers, 90: 15441); with penciled notes by TJ (see notes below); part related to Montmorin overwritten in a later hand. Dft (DLC: Genet Papers); in French; in Genet's hand. Tr (DLC: William Short Papers); in French. Tr (CtY); in French; endorsed by Thomas Pinckney. PrC (DLC: TJ Papers, 90: 15483-4). Tr (Lb in DNA: RG 59, DCI); in French. Tr (Lb in same, SDC); in English. Tr (DNA: RG 46, Senate Records, 3d Cong., 1st sess.); in English; lacks one paragraph (see note 1 below). Enclosed in TJ to William Carmichael and William Short, 12 July 1793, TJ to Genet, 23 July 1793, and TJ to Thomas Pinckney, 11 Sep. 1793.

In order to demonstrate that the French Republic was a more suitable ally for the United States than the recently overthrown Bourbon monarchy, the Provisional Executive Council provided Genet with extracts from various diplomatic documents purporting to show that the government of Louis XVI had consistently acted contrary to vital American interests (Turner, *CFM*, 202-3). Genet made some of these extracts available to TJ on 2 July 1793, evidently to further his efforts to obtain American acquiescence in French plans to liberate Canada and Louisiana (Notes of a Cabinet Meeting and on Conversations with Edmond Charles Genet, 5 July 1793). The LETTER FROM VERGENNES and the MEMOIR by him, which were designed to secure for Spain complete control of the Mississippi south of the Ohio and thus to deny the American claim to a right to navigate that vital waterway, were actually written by Joseph Matthias Gérard de Rayneval, undersecretary to the Comte de Vergennes, then French minister of foreign affairs (Richard B. Morris and Ene Sirvet, eds., *John Jay, The Winning of the Peace: Unpublished Papers, 1780-1784* [New York, 1980], 329-33).

[1] In the PrC TJ later penciled lengthwise in the margin next to this paragraph "this part not to be copd.," so as to ensure its omission in the Tr submitted to the Senate.

[2] In the PrC TJ later interlined in pencil above the first two lines of this paragraph "Extract of lre from M. de Montmorin Ambassador of France at Madrid to M. de Vergennes Minister of Foreign affairs," which served almost verbatim as the heading for the Tr submitted to the Senate.

II

Proofs of the Machievelism of the Cabinet of Versailles.

Extract of a letter of M. de Vergennes to the Chargé des affaires of France with the US.

Versailles. July 21. 1783.

'The future existence of the Congress presents important questions to discuss, and I foresee that it will be some time before they will be decided. I think as you do, that the preservation of the Congress would suit us; but what perhaps suits us better is that the US. should not acquire the political consistence of which they are susceptible: because every thing convinces me that their views and their affections will be very versatile, and that we cannot count on them, if ever there happen to us new discussions with England.'

Note. This opinion has been entirely adopted since, and has served as the basis of the instructions given in 1787. to M. de Moustier.

Tr (DNA: RG 59, NL); undated; translation in TJ's hand; written on verso of No. I. PrC (DLC: TJ Papers, 96: 16467). Tr (same, 9: 1511); in French; in a clerk's hand. Tr (Lb in DNA: RG 59, SDC); in English. Recorded in SJPL between 26 and 28 June 1793 as "Vergennes' lre on the Congress. July 1. 83." Enclosed in TJ to Edmond Charles Genet, 23 July 1793.

Vergennes in fact wrote this letter to the Chevalier de La Luzerne, the French minister to the United States at the time, and not to the secretary who frequently acted as his CHARGÉ DES AFFAIRES, François Barbé Marbois (Samuel F. Bemis, "The Rayneval Memoranda of 1782 on Western Boundaries and Some Comments on the French Historian Doniol," American Antiquarian Society, *Proceedings*, XLVII [1937], 89; E. Wilson Lyon, *The Man Who Sold Louisiana: The Career of Francois Barbé-Marbois* [Norman, Okla., 1942], 24).

III

Extract from the Instructions given to the Ct. de Moustier Sep. 30. 1787.

'The Ct. de Moustier will have seen in the correspondence of the Sr. Otto that the Americans are occupied with a new constitution. This object interests but weakly the politicks of the king. His Majesty thinks, on the one hand, that these deliberations will not succeed, on account of the diversity of affections, of principles, and of interests of the different provinces, on the other hand, that it suits France that the US. should remain in their present state, because if they should acquire the consistence of which they are susceptible, they would soon acquire a force or a power which they would be very ready to abuse. Notwithstanding this last reflexion, the Minister of the king will take care to observe a conduct the most passive, neither to shew himself for, nor against, the new arrangements on which they are occupied, and when he shall be forced to speak, he will only express the wishes of the king, and his own personal wishes, for the prosperity of the US.'

Tr (DNA: RG 59, NL); translation in TJ's hand. PrC (DLC: TJ Papers, 33: 5714). Tr (same, 5715); in French; in a clerk's hand; at head of text: "Preuves du Machiavelisme et de la duplicité du Cabinet de Versailles." PrC (MoSHi: Bixby Collection); with penciled note at head of text in unidentified hand: "Jaudens Mr." Tr (Lb in DNA: RG 59, SDC); in English. Recorded in SJPL between 26 and 28 June 1793: "Instrns to Du Moustier. Sep. 30. 1787."

Elénore François Elie, Comte de MOUS-TIER, was French minister to the United States, 1787-91, and Louis Guillaume OTTO was French chargé d'affaires in the United States, 1785-88 and 1789-91.

Memorandum to George Washington

[11 July 1793]

To be read at the President's leisure.

Governr. H. Lee's letter. June 28. concerning supposed pestilential disease in W.I.

The Suckey. Th:J's letter June 26. to Mr. Hammond.

Th:J. to Mr. Hammond. June 25. on insinuation concerning Western posts.

do.   to do.   do.   developement of order about privateers arming.

Philips's letter June 7. cannot be received as Consul at Curaçoa.

Chiappe's letter Mar. 20. Th:J. will read it to the President.

Simpson's do. Apr. 30.

Th:J.s letter to the President. on Mr. Young's queries.

MS (DNA: RG 59, MLR); undated; entirely in TJ's hand. Tr (DLC: Washington Papers, Journal of the Proceedings of the President); entered under 11 July 1793. Not recorded in SJL.

For the dating of this memorandum, see note to TJ's first memorandum to the President of this date. Francisco CHIAPPE's and James SIMPSON's letters to the President were enclosed in Washington to TJ, 3 July 1793. LETTER TO THE PRESIDENT: TJ to Washington, 28 June 1793.

Memorandum to George Washington

[11-13 July 1793]

Th:J. has the papers in the following cases which require as early consideration as the President can well give them.

Vainqueur de la Bastille. Genet's letter July 8. and Govr. of Carolina's June 24.

Le Citoyen Genet and prizes. Hammond's letter July 10.[1]

Genet's letter June 26. covering protests of the Consuls against interference of the Admiralty courts, and expressing very improper principles.

Th:J's letter to Genet. June 25. } arrangement that prizes reclaimed
Genet's answer. June 26. } may remain in hands of Consuls, till decision.

Ship William—reclaimed.
     Hammond's letter June 21.
     Th:J. to Genet. June 29.

Brig Fanny—reclaimed.
     Hammond's letter. June 26.
     Th:J. to Genet. June 29.

Brig Swallow. Papers from the President. } two British letters of
Ship Jane. Governor's letter and papers. July 5. } Marque. required to
          Genet's letter to Th:J. July 9. } be ordered away.

Genet's letter to Th:J. June 25.

Governr. of Maryland's letter and papers. June 20. the Trusty. Th:J's letter to Genct. June 30.

this is a complaint of enemy ships armed in the ports of the US.

———

Genet's letter. July 9. complaining of

Vexatious usage of French passengers on an American vessel, by a British privateer

French property taken out of an American vessel by a British privateer.

MS (DNA: RG 59, MLR); undated; entirely in TJ's hand; endorsed by Tobias Lear: "Memo. of papers submitted to the Presidt. by the Secy of State July 9th: 1793." Not recorded in SJL.

Although TJ did not actually submit some of the documents listed in this memorandum until 13 July 1793, Tobias Lear's endorsement notwithstanding, he probably began it two days earlier, as it mentions no documents written or received later than 10 July 1793 (Washington, *Journal*, 195). THE LETTER FROM EDMOND CHARLES GENET OF JUNE 26. COVERING PROTESTS OF THE CONSULS is printed under 25 June 1793. For the papers relating to the BRIG SWALLOW, see Washington to TJ, 30 June 1793, and note. The papers concerning the SHIP JANE were: Governor Thomas Mifflin of Pennsylvania to Washington, 5 July 1793, in which, citing Articles 17 and 22 of the 1778 treaty of commerce with

France, he expressed his disagreement with the contention of François Dupont, the French consul in Philadelphia, that the *Jane*, an armed British vessel which had recently arrived at Mud Island in the Delaware, should not be allowed to enter Philadelphia harbor (Tr in PHarH: Governor's Letterbooks); Dupont to Mifflin, 5 July 1793, arguing that the *Jane* should not be allowed to enter Philadelphia harbor or obtain provisions there (Tr in same, Executive Correspondence); Mifflin to Dupont, 5 July 1793, voicing his disagreement with the consul over the *Jane* and notifying him that he was referring the case to the President (Tr in same, Governor's Letterbooks); and a report on the *Jane* by Nathaniel Falconer, Master Warden of Philadelphia, 5 July 1793, which has not been found. See *Pa. Archs.*, 9th ser., I, 611.

[1] Preceding three lines interlined.

From George Washington

SIR   Philadelphia July 11th. 1793.

Before[1] I had read the Papers put into my hands by you, requiring "instant attention" and[2] a messenger could reach your Office, you had left town.

What is to be done in the case of the Little Sarah, now at Chester? Is the Minister of the French Republic to set the Acts of this Government at defiance—*with impunity*? and then threaten the Executive with an appeal to the People. What must the World think of such conduct, and of the Government of the U. States in submitting to it?

These are serious questions. Circumstances press for decision—and as you have had time to consider them (upon me they have come unex-

pected) I wish to receive your opinion upon them—even before tomorrow—for the Vessel may then be gone.   Go: WASHINGTON

RC (DLC); endorsed by TJ as received 11 July 1793. Dft (InU: M. A. I. Blair Papers). FC (Lb in DNA: RG 59, SDC); wording follows Dft. Recorded in SJPL.

For the PAPERS in question, see TJ's first memorandum to Washington printed under this date.

[1] "After" interlined in place of "Before" in Dft.
[2] Here in Dft "before" is interlined.

To George Washington

[11 July 1793]

Th: Jefferson presents his respects to the President. He had expected that the Secretaries of the Treasury and War would have given to the President immediately the statement of facts in the case of the Little Sarah, as drawn by the former and agreed to, as also their Reasons: but Colo. Hamilton having informed Th:J. that he has not been able to prepare copies, Th:J. sends the President the copies they had given him, which being prefixed to his opinion will make the case complete, as it is proper the President should see both sides of it at once.

Th:J. has had a fever the two last nights which has held him till the morning. Something of the same is now coming on him. But nothing but absolute inability will prevent his being in town early tomorrow morning.

Th:J. had written the above before he had the honor of the President's note on the subject of this vessel. He has received assurance from Mr. Genet to-day that she will not be gone before the President's decision. Th:J. is himself of opinion that whatever is aboard of her of arms, ammunition or men contrary to the rules heretofore laid down by the President, ought to be withdrawn. On this subject he will have the honor of conferring with the President, or any others, whenever he pleases.

RC (DNA: RG 59, MLR); undated; addressed: "The President of the US."; endorsed by Tobias Lear in part as "recd July 11th: 1793." PrC (DLC: TJ Papers, 89: 15420). Tr (Lb in DNA: RG 59, SDC); dated 11 July 1793. Recorded in SJPL.

Enclosures: (1) Cabinet Opinions on the Little Sarah, 8 July 1793. (2) Reasons for the Opinion of Alexander Hamilton and Henry Knox on the Little Sarah, 8 July 1793 (Syrett, Hamilton, xv, 74-9).

To James Blake

Sir

You will proceed with all diligence in the Ship[1]   bound to Cadiz,[2] in Spain, with the dispatches committed to you for Messrs. Carmichael and Short, Commissioners Plenipotentiary of the United States of America, at Madrid. When arrived at your port of destination, or any other to which you may by accident be forced, proceed directly to Madrid by such conveyance as will best reconcile safety, reasonable dispatch and due Economy. You will be furnished with proper passports from the Commissioners of Spain residing here and from myself, to ensure to yourself, as the Courier of this Government, and the dispatches of which you are the Bearer, that protection from harm, and freedom from search or impediment, which you will be entitled to by the law of nations, from a friendly nation. When arrived at Madrid deliver your dispatches into the Hands of the Commissioners themselves, and no other. Await there, their Orders, and return to this place with their answers, in such way as will again best combine safety, dispatch and Economy. Keep an exact account of your disbursements, letting them be perfectly reasonable, according to the character in which you go; providing vouchers for such Articles as will admit of it, and proving the residue on oath.

Over and above these reasonable expenses, you will be allowed at the rate of 500[3] dollars a Year, for your time and trouble.

(L.S.) Given under my hand and the Seal of the Department of State this twelfth day of July 1793.

PrC (DLC); in the hand of George Taylor, Jr., with insertions by him in ink; unsigned; at head of text: "To Mr. James Blake." Tr (DNA: RG 46, Senate Records, 3d Cong., 1st sess.). Tr (Lb in same, TR). FC (Lb in DNA: RG 59, DL). Enclosed in Tobias Lear to TJ, 15 July 1793.

James Blake, a resident of Philadelphia, had recently applied unsuccessfully for a clerkship in the Department of State (see George Meade to TJ, [25 Mch. 1793], and note). DISPATCHES COMMITTED TO YOU: TJ to William Carmichael and William Short, 31 May, 30 June, and 12 July 1793, and enclosures. In connection with his mission, TJ this day made out a draft on the Bank of the United States directing it to pay Blake $800 and and to "charge the same to the department of state as for public service" (FC in DLC; in TJ's hand and signed by him, with Blake's signature at foot of text).

TJ submitted this document to the President on 13 July 1793 (Washington, *Journal*, 196).

[1] Word inserted in ink.
[2] Word inserted in ink.
[3] Digits inserted in ink.

Passport for James Blake

To all to whom these presents shall come. GREETING:

THE Bearer hereof James Blake, a citizen of the United States of America, being sent in the character of a Courier, to carry public dispatches of the Government of the said United States to their Commissioners Plenipotentiary at Madrid, and embarking for that purpose on board the Ship   at Philadelphia, bound for   in Spain, THESE ARE TO PRAY all persons, public and private, subjects or citizens of France, Spain, Great Britain, the United Netherlands, Portugal, and all other Countries with whom the said United States are in Peace and Friendship, meeting the said James Blake by Sea or Land, to permit him to pass, according to his destination, without hindrance or delay, but on the contrary giving to him every hospitable and friendly aid and dispatch, as these United States will do for their citizens or subjects in the like Case.

 GIVEN under my Hand and the Seal of the Department of State of the United States aforesaid, the twelfth day of July, 1793, and of the Independence of the United States of America, the Eighteenth.

PrC (DLC); in the hand of George Taylor, Jr., unsigned. FC (Lb in DNA: RG 59, DL); with TJ as signatory. Enclosed in Tobias Lear to TJ, 15 July 1793.

TJ submitted this document to the President on 13 July 1793 (Washington, *Journal*, 196).

Cabinet Opinion on Consulting the Supreme Court

July 12. 1793. At a meeting of the heads of the departments at the President's on summons from him, and on consideration of various representations[1] from the Ministers Plenipotentiary of France and Great Britain on the subject of vessels arming and arriving in our ports, and of prizes it is their opinion that letters be written to the said Ministers informing them that the Executive of the US., desirous of having done what shall be strictly conformeable to the[2] treaties of the US. and the laws respecting the said cases has determined to refer the questions arising therein to persons learned in the laws: that as this reference will occasion some delay, it is expected that in the mean time the Little Sarah or Little Democrat the Ship Jane[3] and the ship William in the Delaware, the Citoyen Genet and her prizes the brigs Lovely Lass and Prince William Henry, and the brig Fanny in the Chesapeake do not depart till the further order of the President.

That letters be addressed to the Judges of the Supreme court of the US. requesting their attendance at this place on Thursday the 18th. instant to give their advice on[4] certain matters of public concern which will be referred to them by the President.

That the Governor be desired to have the ship Jane attended to with vigilance, and if she be found augmenting her force and about to depart, that he cause her to be stopped.

TH: JEFFERSON
ALEXANDER HAMILTON
H KNOX

MS (DLC: Washington Papers); in TJ's hand, signed by TJ, Alexander Hamilton, and Henry Knox; endorsed by Tobias Lear. FC (DLC); entirely in TJ's hand; at head of text: "Copy of a minute given to the President." Entry in SJPL: "Report of opns of heads of deptmts. on consulting the judges."

Letters to the MINISTERS and JUDGES: TJ to Edmond Charles Genet and George Hammond, 12 July 1793, and Circular to the Justices of the Supreme Court, 12 July 1793. A day later Governor Thomas Mif-flin issued instructions to the Warden of the Port of Philadelphia to HAVE THE SHIP JANE ATTENDED TO (Pa. Archs., 9th ser., I, 621).

[1] Word interlined in place of "cases of complaint."

[2] TJ here canceled "laws and."

[3] TJ first wrote "and the Ship Jane be not permitted to depart" before altering the passage to read as above.

[4] Preceding four words interlined in place of "take into consideration."

To William Carmichael and William Short

GENTLEMEN   Philadelphia July 12. 1793.

Since writing my letter of 30 ult.[1] I have received the inclosed paper containing extracts from letters of M. de Montmorin to his court while[2] he was their Ambassador at Madrid. Without pretending to say that they contain the genuine views of Spain towards us, it must be acknoleged that had[3] their views been such, their proceedings would have been exactly what they have been. I have thought it material to add this paper to those[4] I have sent you as it may contribute towards your understanding the proceedings of the Spanish Cabinet.

It is thought extremely important[5] and indeed necessary that Mr. Blake, the bearer of these dispatches should be here by the middle[6] of December, when Congress will[7] be in session. Of course he should leave Madrid by the middle[8] of October. You will therefore be pleased to press your negociations forward so as to be able by that date to give us at least[9] a certain opinion of what you believe will be their[10] issue: a great object in sending this courier being[11] to fix a term to those[12] incertainties which have now existed for 10. years, Spain in the mean time advancing her posts into our country and meditating, as it is[13] believed to take new posts. You will be pleased to remain at Madrid till further orders, whatever be the prospect of issue to your negociations. If it be unfavorable you will allege as the cause of your stay that you expect ulterior instructions.[14] I have the honour to be with much respect Gentlemen, your mo ob & mo hum servant   TH: JEFFERSON

Dft (DLC); unsigned; *en clair* text in TJ's hand, except for additions by George Taylor, Jr.; at foot of text in Taylor's hand: "Messrs. Carmichael & Short"; complimentary close and signature supplied from RC; endorsed by TJ: "to be put into cypher." RC (DLC: Short Papers); in Taylor's hand, signed by TJ; in code except for salutation, day and year in dateline, and several words in text and complimentary close, with interlined decipherment in Short's hand; contains encoding errors. PrC (DLC); unsigned. FC (Lb in DNA: RG 59, DCI); entirely *en clair*. The Editors have verified the Dft against the encoded RC and Short's interlinear decipherment using partially reconstructed Code No. 10, anomalies being recorded below.

EXTRACTS FROM LETTERS OF M. DE MONTMORIN: see Enclosure I to first Memorandum to George Washington, [11 July 1793].

[1] Date added by George Taylor, Jr.
[2] Word encoded as "rec" and so deciphered by Short in RC.
[3] Word encoded as "Spain" and so deciphered by Short in RC.
[4] Word encoded as "to" and left undeciphered by Short in RC.
[5] Word omitted in RC.
[6] Word interlined in place of "beginning."
[7] Word undeciphered by Short in RC.
[8] Word interlined in place of canceled and illegible digit.
[9] Word omitted in RC.
[10] Word encoded as "the" and so deciphered by Short in RC.
[11] Word encoded as "be which" and so deciphered by Short in RC.
[12] Word interlined in place of "our."
[13] Word omitted in RC.
[14] Remainder of text, including Short's decipherment of encoded words in complimentary close, supplied from RC.

To Edmond Charles Genet

SIR   Philadelphia July 12. 1793.

I take the liberty of inclosing to you the Memorial of Nicholas Cruger and others, citizens of the US. owners and underwriters of the schooner the York. They set forth that their vessel had been sent on a voyage to the Spanish coast in the bay of Mexico, with a cargo assorted to that market, and armed as usual in such cases; that on their return, being distressed for water and other necessaries, they put into Port au Prince, where they were seized, and libelled before the court of admiralty, were cleared by that court, but afterwards condemned by the Governour and council, upon mere suspicion as they suggest, and without foundation. The separate packet which accompanies this letter contains their evidence, and seems really to support their suggestions, and to countenance what they alledge that the condemnation is to be ascribed to the troubles then existing in the island, or to other circumstances not explained. The object of the present letter is to ask your patronage of their case so far as to obtain a re-examination of their case on full evidence before the proper authority, and the restitution of their property if it shall be found that injustice has been done them; this being consistent with the practice of friendly nations in such cases. Mr. Cruger proposes to have the honour of waiting on you himself. I have that of assuring you of the esteem & respect of Sir your most obedt. humble servt

TH: JEFFERSON

RC (NjP); at foot of text: "The Min. Plen. of France." PrC (DLC). FC (Lb in DNA: RG 59, DL). Enclosure: Memorial from Nicholas Cruger and Others, 26 June 1793. Other enclosures not found.

Genet's response to this letter has not been found (see note to TJ to Genet, 11 July 1793).

To Edmond Charles Genet and George Hammond

SIR   Philadelphia July 12. 1793

The President of the US. desirous of having done what shall be strictly conformeable to the treaties of the US. and the laws respecting the several representations received from yourself and the Minister Plenipotentiary of Great Britain[1] on the subject of vessels arming or arriving within our ports, and of prizes, has determined to refer the questions arising thereon to persons learned in the laws. As this reference will occasion some delay, he will expect from both parties that in the mean time the Little Sarah or Little Democrat, the ships Jane and William in the Delaware, the Citoyen Genet and her two prizes the Lovely lass and Prince William Henry and the brig Fanny in the Chesapeake do not depart until his ultimate determination shall be made known. You may be assured, Sir, that the delay will be as short as possible, and the object of it being to obtain the best advice possible on the sense of the laws and treaties respecting the several cases, I am persuaded you will think the delay well compensated. I have the honor to be with sentiments of the most perfect esteem & respect Sir Your most obedient & most humble servt

TH: JEFFERSON

PrC (DLC); in TJ's hand; at foot of first page in the hand of George Taylor, Jr.: "The Minister of France." PrC of Tr (DLC); in a clerk's hand; at foot of text: "(Copy)." Tr (NNC: Gouverneur Morris Papers); addressed: "The Minister of France." Tr (DNA: RG 46, Senate Records, 3d Cong., 1st sess.); addressed: "The Minister of France." PrC (PRO: FO 97/1). FC (Lb in DNA: RG 59, DL); at head of text: "The Minister Plenipo. of France"; at foot of text: "The same to the Minister plenipo. of Great Britain." Tr (DLC: Genet Papers). Tr (same); in French. Tr (same); in French; draft translation of preceding Tr; docketed by Genet. Tr (AMAE: CPEU, XXXVII); in French. Tr (Lb in PRO: FO 116/3); addressed: "The Minister Pleny of Great Britain." Tr (same, 5/1). Tr (MdHi: Scharf Collection); addressed: "The Minister Plenipy of Gt Britain." Printed in *Message*, 50. Enclosed in Tobias Lear to TJ, 15

July 1793; letter to Genet enclosed in TJ to Gouverneur Morris, 16 Aug. 1793.

TJ submitted texts of his letters to Genet and Hammond to the President on 13 July 1793 (Washington, *Journal*, 196).

On this day TJ received from Richard Söderström, the Swedish consul in Philadelphia, a translation of a 25 Mch. 1793 letter to Söderström from Fredrik Sparre, the grand chancellor of Sweden, informing him that Swedish ships were exempted from the recent French trade embargo, that Sweden intended to maintain her current neutrality, and that this should enable him to allay any

apprehensions that might arise in America "as to the safety of the Swedish flag" (Tr in DNA: RG 59, NFC; in Söderström's hand, with his subjoined attestation of 11 July 1793; endorsed by TJ as an 11 July 1793 letter from Söderström received 12 July 1793 and so recorded in SJL). TJ submitted this document to the President on 13 July 1793, and Washington returned it two days later (Washington, *Journal*, 195; Tobias Lear to TJ, 15 July 1793).

[1] Preceding two words in the texts addressed to Hammond read "of France."

Circular to the Justices of the Supreme Court

SIR   Philadelphia, July 12th. 1793.

The President of the United States, being desirous of asking the advice of the Judges of the Supreme Court of the United States, on certain matters of great public concern, requests your attendance at this place on Thursday the 18th. instant. It is on his particular charge that I have the honor of informing you of this. I have that of being with sentiments of great respect and esteem, Sir, Your most obedient and most humble servant   TH: JEFFERSON

PrC (DLC); in the hand of George Taylor, Jr., signed by TJ; at foot of text: "Chief Justice Jay." RC (NN: Ford Collection); in Taylor's hand, signed by TJ; at foot of text: "Judge Iredell"; endorsed by Iredell in part: "Ansd." PrC of another RC (DLC); in Taylor's hand, signed by TJ; at foot of text: "Judge Paterson." FC (Lb in DNA: RG 59, DL); at head of text: "Chief Justice Jay"; at foot of text: "The same to Judge Paterson."

For the issues on which the ADVICE OF THE JUDGES was sought, see Questions for

the Supreme Court, [18 July 1793], Document IV in Editorial Note and group of documents on the referral of neutrality questions to the Supreme Court, at 18 July 1793. TJ submitted the texts for Jay and Paterson to Washington on 13 July 1793, and the President returned them two days later (Washington, *Journal*, 196, 198). Although the endorsement of Justice James Iredell indicates that he answered this letter, no written response has been found and none is recorded in SJL.

To William Short

[ca. 12 July 1793]

Th: Jefferson in writing to Mr. Short forgot to mention that the present occasion by Mr. Blake will be a happy one to receive from him the

Letters of Fernand Cortez published by the Archbishop of Mexico (afterwards Toledo) as mentioned in 3d. Borgoyne's travels 303. which he so much wishes to get. If Mr. Short will send it by Mr. Blake and note the price it shall be added to the first investment to be made by his brother here. Better to send it unbound.

RC (ViW); undated; addressed: "Mr. Short." Not recorded in SJL.

This letter was apparently written about the same time as TJ's letter of 12 July 1793

to James Blake. For the LETTERS OF FERNAND CORTEZ and BORGOYNE'S TRAVELS, see note to TJ to David Humphreys, 11 Apr. 1791.

From William Thornton

SIR   [ca. 12 July 1793]

After the Receipt of your[1] Communication, accompanied by the five Manuscript Volumes in folio by Mr: Hallet, I hasten to attempt[2] that Satisfaction which is required relative to the Objections made against the Plan which I had the honor of submiting to the Commissioners.

I will first endeavour to remove the most material Objection, which respects the Time requisite to the perfection of the Work.

It has been said that I thought it would not probably[3] be finished in thirty Years. I did not hear whether it was said in a qualified or unqualified manner. I do not remember that I made the Observation however if I did it must only have had relation to the ornamental Parts, and it matters not whether they be finished in ten or forty Years provided they are not incorporated in the Building; but I have always said, and do now repeat it, that the Building might be made ready for the *reception of Congress* in the time specified for their removal thither. It is but of small magnitude when compared to[4] many-private Edifices of Individuals in other parts of the World. I am aware, however, that the Americans ought not to feel prone[5] to imitate foreign nations—except where such imitation is peculiarly adapted to their Government and local habits. Yet, when we consider the Building in contemplation, that it is designed for the accommodation[6] of 15 States (and[7] others in addition here after)[8] that it is a work which ought to endure for many ages[9] it can hardly, I should suppose, be thought either too large or too expensive. The Condition of America is every day improving—her population encreasing and her riches accumulating. This is, perhaps, not the case elsewhere—for countries long settled are generally stationary[10] or upon the decline. But to return to the time necessary for the Completion of a building upon the plan I had the honour to exhibit, and to prove that under due exertions, nothing is to be feared on that score let me call your recollection to a fact. The Escurial of Spain, that enormous and expensive Pile, was finished in about 6 years. Doubtless a multitude of hands were employed to effect so great a work in so short a time. But, it was only expending those monies in 6 years which a less number of hands would have absorbed in a longer term.

To you, Sir, it cannot be necessary to repeat, What writers tell us— that[11] the Escurial contains 14000 Windows—11,000[12] Doors— 1800 pillars 17 cloisters or piazzas and 22 Courts.

In answer, to Mr. Hallet's objection as to the great[13] length of time supposed to be requisite for completing a capitol after my plan, permit me to say, it has been brought forward as an assertion only, when candour required facts to have been adduced in proof.

I conceive that, under present circumstances, any number of workmen may be procured from Europe. Those might be employed in completing the capitol or so much of it as would give the desired accomodation to Congress within the term limited. The remaining parts might afterwards be finished at leisure. And those workmen would[14] be found useful in carrying on future works both public and private[15] in the City of Washington. Whether the funds of the Commissrs. will allow them to engage so many men on[16] the parts first needful in the capitol, within a short term of years, is a consideration[17] for them to determine. There can be no doubt but the value of the lots will take an important rise whenever the public buildings[18] shall appear to be in *active* prosecution. The confidence of the people will then it is presumable, be established. And it is certainly a convenience, circumstances considered, that the first or basement story of the plan I submitted is that part of the work which requires the least expence—the expence part of the columns and decorations standing high up on the principal floor.[19]

I will now make a few observations upon the objections which Mr. Hallet has brought forward. Not having before me either his Sections (which point out the supposed defects in my plan)[20] or the plan itself I cannot be so particular here as I could wish.[21]

Mr. Hallet has founded His calculations upon the dearest materials— as if such were absolutely requisite. When I mentioned Marble for the Columns &c. it did not preclude the propriety[22] of employing free stone. Of course candour seems to require, that the calculation of the expence of marble, should have been accompanied with another of free stone.

The lengthy remarks he has thrown together upon the necessity of placing the base of the dome *perpendicularly* on the Columns—have been condensed into a formidable objection. But would it not have been well, at the same time in Mr. Hallet to have observed that this was a mere inaccuracy in the draft, which no *skilful* workman could think himself necessitated to follow in the execution. He might and *ought* to have said that those columns could be drawn a little nearer towards the center of the dome so as to give the perpendicularity required—and this without deranging in the least the disposition of the building.

The Intercolumniation of the portico is objected.[23] The Ancients had five proportions, (viz) the Picnostyle containing $1\frac{1}{2}$ Diameter; the Sistyle 2 Diameters; the Eustyle $2\frac{1}{4}$ Dia:; the Diastyle 3 Diam:; and the Aræostyle 4 Diameters. The Eustyle is reasoned the most elegant in general, but deviations are allowed according to circumstances, and I have designedly increased the intercolumniations in the present case[24] to give a better proportion to the Arcade—which otherwise would have appeared too narrow for the elevation. Should however this immaterial[25] objection be insisted on, it is not difficult to obviate it. The Arcade (not being absolutely necessary) can be turned into a[26] wall, pierced with windows and a door. The End openings to remain for Carriages—for Mr. Hallet must suffer me to insist in my turn, upon the utility of such a convenience, even in a *"Republic"*—where would be the crime if a person can afford to keep a carriage alighting dry from it to enter the house. The poorest and most stern[27] republican would not willingly[28] be drenched with rain, if he could procure the means to keep himself dry. And foreign Ministers would think such a provision a real accomodation.

If the arcade should be changed for[29] a wall, then the Columns of the portico might be drawn nearer to one another, so as to produce a more received proportion in the intercolumniation. In this case, however, some little alteration in the disposition of the adjoining parts will be necessary. Upon the whole, I would prefer the portico, as it stands.

The Senate Chamber is the next scene of objection. In Mr. Hallet's Section the coving of the cieling passed through the upper windows. This,[30] I grant, is a real defect in my plan, and which doubtless I should have perceived and remedied myself, if time had permitted me to make a section. I should, in that case, have mentioned in the Explanation of the plan, that those windows should be omitted at *both* ends of the building [for, in fact, none there are needful] and their places filled up with ornamental Tablets. It is to be observed here, that in my Explanation accompanying the plan, a sky light was recommended to be added to the Senate Chamber, as without it, the 3 lower windows would be insufficient. I am sorry I cannot concede to[31] Mr. Hallet's other objections[32] to the Senate Chamber. He has I think,[33] unnecessarily, not to say unhandsomely, availed himself again of a trifling inaccuracy in the plan.[34] In laying down the 2 columns on each side of this Apartment it seems the diameter of them was made too large. From this, it appears that Mr. Hallet has traced out the Shafts and Capitals, giving to the former a correspondent diameter and[35] consequently Car-

rying the Columns to an impracticable height. As Columns in this particular situation need not be regulated by the intercolumniation—the
Elevation of the architrave here[36] whatever it may be, is the obvious and
natural point at which the capital must stop.[37]

If these 4 columns are included In the calculation of the expence they
must have added to the error because they were intended to be of wood.

Objections are brought against the Conference room and the Colonade before it. With respect to the first I can only say at present, that my
intentions have in some measure been misapprehended. It is not possible for me to answer particularly, without an inspection of the plans. I
dare say however, that if there are defects here, they[38] can be remedied
with ease.[39] The Windows here require but a thought to correct them—
which I am ready to explain verbally[40] on revising my plan.[41]

In regard to the measurements below Mr. Hallet is mistaken. This I
will also shew.

As to the Colonade of the Conference room, the intercolumniations of
which seem to become an objection—because it is surmized, the stones
for the architrave over each intercolumniation[42] would be too ponderous
to be raised—I answer, that it would require a small expence of genius
only[43] to raise stones of much greater magnitude.[44] The same observation will apply to the architrave over the double[45] columns at each end
of the Portico. Mr. Hallet will recollect that the lofty[46] Colonade of the
Louvre is composed of double pillars—and consequently has very wide
intercolumniations. Let me ask him,[47] how were the stones raised there?

If the difficulty should still be[48] insisted on, there is still an easy way
of oversetting it—by cutting the Stones of the architrave each into 2 or
3 pieces perpendicularly lengthwise.

Fault is found with the semicircular projections at the ends, as losing
their effect or appearing disproportionate on a front of such extent. I
would ask, whether in a front of any less[49] length having such projections, if seen out of the *proper* point of view, the like effect would not
happen? These projections[50] will be most properly viewed from the
ends. There they are ornamental, and useful. The double pilasters
which they admit have, in my opinion, a bold and beautiful effect.[51]
They correspond in a happy manner with the double pillars seen over
the Carriage way of the portico on one side and those[52] of the Colonade
on the other—producing a grand and striking part of the composition
which I should be very sorry to part with. Besides in an insulated building every front should exhibit the same or similar elegance of stile.

Some particular parts are said to want light—such as the stairs leading from the Arcade of the Colonade and the[53] passages through the
Basement. In the former, it is conceived the objection is not valid, light
enough coming in from the arcade:[54] which may be increased[55] by small
circular windows looking into the colonade—and which I ought to

have[56] noticed in my Explanation[57]—if it is not already done. With respect to the passages, I conceived a Sufficiency of light for a basement story, would come thro windows over the doors of the apartments,[58] and the open doors of the ends of the passages. If, however, upon farther consideration this should appear doubtful, we have only to break an open arched aperture in the bases supporting the two projecting pillars on each side of the Colonade[59]—and of course leaving out the niches[60] which are placed there in the[61] plan—tho' I can not believe either this alteration or Mr. Hallet's lamps to be at all necessary.[62]

As to the waste room or space in the Basement Story, I have only to say, That the Capitol will require extensive cellar room for Fuel, public Stores &c.—and the inside walls may be all of the common foundation stone.

The want of unity between the Ornaments and the Order, forms another objection in Mr. Hallet's report. I trust he will permit me in this instance[63] to prefer the authorities of the best books.

Thus, Sir, I have given[64] a few short observations in answer to the voluminous objections which have been brought forward. I believe they embrace all or more than all that required to be answered. I could, however, have been much more particular if the plans had been in my possession—and if Mr. Hallet's Report had been written in[65] a more legible hand. I have the honour to be with Great respect, Sir Your obedt. hble Sert.

The Water Closets objected to in the upper Story may, if deemed improperly placed, be substituted by those below.[66]

Dft (DLC: Thornton Papers, 7: 1329-32, 1325); unsigned and undated; heavily emended text consisting of eight numbered pages on four sheets of one kind of paper and a ninth numbered page on a different type of paper with postscript on verso, the last sheet and many of the revisions being in a different ink; only the most significant emendations are recorded below; brackets in original. Enclosed in TJ to George Washington, 12 July 1793.

YOUR COMMUNICATION: TJ to Thornton, 8 July 1793. This reply represents Thornton's initial response to the critique of his prize-winning design for the United States Capitol that Stephen Hallet, the frustrated runner-up in the competition who was now supervising the construction of the edifice, had prepared at the direction of the Commissioners of the Federal District. Because Hallet's FIVE MANUSCRIPT VOLUMES IN FOLIO and Thornton's original PLAN are lost, the letter provides the best contemporary evidence of what Thornton originally proposed and of the shortcomings identified by Hallet. For the resolution of the architectural issues surrounding the Capitol, see TJ to George Washington, 17 July 1793, and note. A missing letter from Thornton to TJ of 14 July 1793 was recorded in SJL as received on 15 July 1793.

[1] Thornton here canceled "kind."

[2] Word interlined in place of "give."

[3] Word interlined.

[4] Remainder of sentence interlined in place of "the private Palaces of ⟨Individuals⟩ Private Persons in Europe."

[5] Word interlined in place of "themselves bound."

[6] Thornton here canceled "of the ⟨People⟩ Representation."

[7] Thornton here canceled "probably."

[8] Thornton here canceled "and."

[9] Preceding twelve words interlined.

¹⁰ Thornton first wrote "for in all old countries the Nations are either stationary" and then altered the phrase to read as above.

¹¹ Thornton first wrote "to observe that" before altering the passage to read as above.

¹² Number reworked from "14,000."

¹³ Word interlined.

¹⁴ Word, followed by "⟨possibly⟩ ⟨afterwards⟩," interlined in place of "might probably."

¹⁵ Preceding four words interlined.

¹⁶ Preceding five words interlined in place of "defray the expence of."

¹⁷ Thornton here canceled "that ⟨of which I am⟩ ⟨was⟩ does not belong to me to judge of."

¹⁸ Thornton here canceled "are in forwardness."

¹⁹ Thornton first wrote "all the columns and decorations of weight standing on that" before altering the passage to read as above.

²⁰ Closing parenthesis supplied.

²¹ Sentence written lengthwise in margin.

²² Word interlined in place of "possibility."

²³ Word interlined in place of "stated as a matter of fact. Mr. Hallet says, the Italian and French [Schools] allow both. I would answer [. . .]."

²⁴ Preceding fourteen words written lengthwise in margin in place of what appears to be "My intercolumniation I designedly made rather wider than the [most?] approved. And my reasons for it were these 1st. [. . .]."

²⁵ Word interlined.

²⁶ Thornton here canceled "solid."

²⁷ Word interlined in place of "rigid [. . .]."

²⁸ Preceding two words interlined in place of "never wish to."

²⁹ Thornton first wrote what appears to be "If I have said the arcade, may be turned into" and then altered the phrase to read as above.

³⁰ Thornton here canceled "indeed, could be called a defect."

³¹ Thornton here interlined and canceled "one of."

³² Thornton first wrote "Hallet's next objection" before altering the phrase to read as above.

³³ Preceding two words interlined in place of "very."

³⁴ Thornton here canceled "which ⟨he⟩ his Section has tortured into an aspect that must ⟨confound⟩ frighten any persons viewing it and would threaten the whole ⟨building⟩ fabric with instant dissolution in the eyes of those unable to trace the thing back to its source."

³⁵ Preceding eight words interlined in place of "and."

³⁶ Preceding two words interlined in place of "⟨room⟩ part they support gives the proportion of their diameter."

³⁷ Thornton here canceled "and the shaft derives a diameter."

³⁸ Thornton here canceled "may be open to ready correction—remedies are not."

³⁹ Thornton wrote "without difficulty" before altering the phrase to read as above.

⁴⁰ Thornton here canceled "at once."

⁴¹ Sentence written lengthwise in the margin.

⁴² Preceding three words interlined.

⁴³ Thornton here canceled "⟨to⟩ laid out in a proper Mechanical Apparatus."

⁴⁴ Thornton here canceled "I ⟨presume⟩ do not remember the dimensions of the Colonade of the Louvre—but its intercolumniation [will I think be?]."

⁴⁵ Word interlined.

⁴⁶ Word interlined.

⁴⁷ Word interlined.

⁴⁸ Dft: "should ⟨be⟩ still to be."

⁴⁹ Word interlined.

⁵⁰ Thornton here canceled "are for the decoration."

⁵¹ Thornton here canceled "⟨corresponding⟩ Besides I conceive them absolutely necessary towards a correspondence with."

⁵² Thornton here canceled "on the end."

⁵³ Remainder of sentence interlined in place of "wide part of the passages before the Apartment appropriated for select committees of both houses to meet in."

⁵⁴ Thornton here canceled "and colonade ⟨in the⟩ the latter will draw its light."

⁵⁵ Word interlined in place of what appears to be "assured."

⁵⁶ Preceding four words interlined in place of "if I mistake not, were."

⁵⁷ Remainder of sentence interlined.

⁵⁸ Remainder of sentence interlined.

⁵⁹ Word interlined in place of "portico."

⁶⁰ Word written in the margin in place of "statues."

⁶¹ Thornton here canceled "⟨plan⟩ Elevation."

⁶² Eighth numbered page ends here. At the top of the ninth page Thornton can-

celed "I do not recollect that there was much, if any, lost Space in the basement Story—⟨I believe that in a building of such magnitude the Cellars must⟩ there must be extensive Cellar⟨s⟩ room for ⟨various⟩ Fuel, ⟨&ca.⟩ ⟨and⟩ public Stores &c—and as to."

[63] Preceding three words interlined.

[64] Word interlined in place of "hastily thrown together."

[65] Thornton here canceled "an English hand."

[66] Sentence preceded by a canceled sentence of substantially the same import.

From Josef Ignacio de Viar and Josef de Jaudenes

July 12th. 1793.

His Catholic Majesty's Commissioners present their Compliments to the Secretary of State, and have the honor to transmit herein the Passport requested from them.

The Commissioners are extreamly obliged to the Secretary of State for his polite offer in haveing their dispatches conveyed by the same person, and with pleasure would embrace so favourable opportunity, had they not fixed to forward them by a Spanish Gentleman who will sail about the same time.

RC (DNA: RG 59, NL); in Jaudenes's hand; endorsed by TJ as received 13 July 1793 and so recorded in SJL. Enclosure: Passport for James Blake, 12 July 1793, in which Jaudenes and Viar request Spanish naval commanders, merchants, and government officials to grant him safe passage as an official courier of the United States government (PrC of Tr in DLC, in Spanish, in a clerk's hand; Tr in Lb in DNA: RG 59, DL, in Spanish).

To George Washington

July 12. 1793.

Th: Jefferson has the honor to send to the President Dr. Thornton's answer to Mr. Hallet's objections this moment received, and which he has not had time to read. Perhaps the President may think it worth while to communicate them to Mr. Hobens and see what he thinks of them, for which reason he sends them to the President in the instant of recieving them.

RC (DNA: RG 59, MLR); endorsed by Tobias Lear. Tr (Lb in same, SDC). Not recorded in SJL. Enclosure: William Thornton to TJ, [ca. 12 July 1793].

From Gaetano Drago di Domenico

Genoa, 13 July 1793. All intercourse between France and Great Britain having ended late in February, he encloses via a friend in London a copy of the 25 Mch. letter he sent by way of France and entreats TJ's support for the object of it. Since writing that letter the price of wheat here has risen to 86 shillings British sterling per quarter because of heavy French demand. Several convoys of 20 to 30 merchant ships loaded with corn sailed from here and Leghorn to Marseilles before this practice was halted by the late appearance off this harbor of a Spanish fleet of 24 ships of the line and 9 frigates. A French frigate and 12 trading vessels with corn for France sequestered in this port by the fleet are just leaving after learning that it has left this coast. It is not unlikely this French convoy will encounter the British Mediterranean fleet because the division commanded by Admiral Hood reportedly arrived at Gibraltar on 19 June; joined to the 22 sail of the line, besides frigates, of Vice Admiral Gell, Cosby, and Hotham, as well as the Spanish fleet, this will constitute a force more formidable than any the French can mount in these seas. He hears that the French are readying with the utmost dispatch the 20 ships of the line and 13 frigates they have at Toulon. While the French find it difficult to penetrate into Piedmont on the Nice side, they have captured several camps and advanced posts from the "Austro Piedmentese" and driven them back to "Savigio and Monte Ravs," though they have suffered severe losses in three unsuccessful attacks on the latter place, which like the former is deemed invulnerable. With 40,000 men there now and reinforcements daily arriving, the French do not seem to be abandoning their project. The King of Sardinia, much embarrassed by the present state of things, has scarcely enough revenue to meet his expenditures; although reportedly the Court of St. James has lately sent him a large sum of money, his fear of a French advance into Piedmont has led him to send his archives to Mantua. It is reported that news about the Spanish and British fleets has led the King of Naples to join the coalition against France. It is further presumed that the belligerent powers are trying to win the accession of Tuscany. Thankfully the Genoese republic remains neutral, with almost all of its troops sent to the frontier and with the town itself under the control of its greatest noblemen, genteel families, and people of property.

RC (DLC: Washington Papers, Applications for Office); 3 p.; addressed: "The Honorable Thomas Jefferson Minister of State of the Thirteen United Provinces of N. America Philadelphia"; endorsed by TJ as a letter of 25 Mch. 1793 received 24 Oct. 1793 and so recorded in SJL. Enclosure: Tripl of Drago di Domenico to TJ, 11 Mch. 1793 (dated 25 Mch. 1793).

From George Hammond

Sɪʀ   Philadelphia 13 July 1793 11 oClock AM

I have received your letter dated yesterday, and I cannot conceal from you my surprize at the requisition contained in it—that the President expects from me, as one of two parties specified, that none of the vessels you have enumerated shall "depart until his ultimate determination" respecting them "shall be made known." I have no wit of controul over any of them: Indeed, *one alone excepted*, they are all either vessels of force, fitted out, armed and equipped in the ports of the United states, for the purpose of committing hostilities on the subjects of Great Britain, or British property captured, by one of those vessels so fitted out, armed and equipped, and by another of a similar description, le sans culottes, which you have omitted, and which continues, as I am assured, to augment its force in the port of Baltimore.

The *single* exception I have made refers to the British letter of marque ship, Jane, with respect to your mention of which, I should feel nearly as much surprize, as at the other subjects of your communication, were I not convinced that the letter, which I transmitted to you yesterday morning at half past ten o'Clock, cannot have been laid before the President, previously to your writing to me: For I should, in that case, have flattered myself that the evidence I have adduced and the corroborating testimony I have offered to adduce, relative to that vessel, would have been sufficiently satisfactory to have exempted it from being included in the enumeration which you have been pleased to communicate to me. I have the honor to be, with sentiments of great respect Sir, your most obedient humble Servant,   GEO: HAMMOND

RC (DNA: RG 59, NL); at foot of first page: "Mr Jefferson"; with marginal notation by TJ: "[g]eneral order for detention of vessels"; endorsed by TJ as received 13 July 1793 and so recorded in SJL. FC (Lb in PRO: FO 116/3). Tr (same, 5/1). Tr (Lb in DNA: RG 59, NL). Enclosed in Tobias Lear to TJ, 15 July 1793.

TJ submitted this letter to the President on 13 July 1793 (Washington, *Journal*, 196).

From Josef de Jaudenes and Josef Ignacio de Viar

SIR   Philadelphia July 13. 1793.

It is with great sensibility we observe that the office which we had the honor to send you on the 18th. of June last has given any kind of disgust to the government of the US. as we perceive by your favor of the 11th. inst.

We assure you particularly, with the purest truth, that if any warmth is observed in it, it has no other object than to give all possible energy to the reason which we are persuaded is on our side, and that we are very far from having the least desire of offending the government of the US. nor of shewing the least want of respect but the most cordial affection to their most worthy President and to your own merit.

Be pleased, Sir, to present this to the President of the US. and to receive yourself this sincere assurance of our true esteem and indubitable attachment to the US. and the very worthy heads of it's government, while we remain firmly convinced that the K. our master will not fail to prove the justice, friendship and generosity which characterize him, and which he has always manifested to the US. We have the honor to subscribe ourselves with the most profound respect & sincere esteem Sir your mo. ob. & mo. hble servts.

JOSEPH DE JAUDENES   JOSEPH IGNATIUS DE VIAR

Tr (DLC); in TJ's hand; at head of text: "Translation"; at foot of text: "Mr. Jefferson &c." PrC (MoSHi: Bixby Collection). RC (DNA: RG 59, NL); in Spanish; in a clerk's hand, signed by Jaudenes and Viar. Tr (AHN: Papeles de Estado, legajo 3895); in Spanish; in Jaudenes's hand and attested by him. Tr (AGI: Papeles de Cuba, legajo 88); in Spanish; in Viar's hand; attested by Viar and Jaudenes. Tr (DLC: William Short Papers); in Spanish. PrC (DLC). Tr (Lb in DNA: RG 59, DCI); in Spanish. Tr (DNA: RG 46, Senate Records, 3d Cong., 1st sess.); in English. Tr (Lb in same, TR); in English. Recorded in SJL as an "apology" received 13 July 1793. Recorded in SJPL. Enclosed in TJ to William Carmichael and William Short, 16 July 1793, and TJ to Thomas Pinckney, 11 Sep. 1793.

Notes on Neutrality Questions

A recapitulation of questions whereon we have given opinions.

Does the treaty with France leave us free to prohibit her from arming vessels in our ports? Th:J. H. K. and R. unanimous it does.

As the treaty obliges us to prohibit the enemies of France from arming in our ports, and leaves us free to prohibit France, do not the laws of Neutrality oblige us to prohibit her. Same persons unanimous they do.

How far may a prohibition now declared, be retrospective to the vessels armed in Charlestown before the prohibition, towit the Citoyen Genet and Sans Culottes, and what is to be done with their prizes? Th:J. it cannot be retrospective at all; they may sell their prizes, and continue to act freely as other armed vessels of France. H. and K. the prizes ought to be given up to the English, and the privateers suppressed. R. they are free to sell their prizes and the privateers should be ordered away, not to return here till they shall have been to the dominions of their own sovereign and thereby purged the illegality of their origin. This last opinion was adopted by the President.

Our citizens who have joined in these hostilities against nations at peace with the US. are they punisheable? E.R. gave an official opinion they were. Th:J. H. and K. joined in the opinion. All thought it our duty to have prosecutions instituted against them, that the laws might pronounce on their case. In the 1st. instance two only were prosecuted, merely to try the question and to satisfy the complaint of the British Min. and because it was thought they might have offended unwittingly. But a subsequent armament of a vessel at New York taking place with full knolege of this prosecution, all the persons engaged in it, citizens and foreigners, were ordered to be prosecuted.

May the prohibition extend to the means of the party arming, or are they only prohibited from using our means for the annoyance of their enemy. Th:J. of opinion they are free to use their own means, i.e. to mount their own guns &c. H. and K. of opinion they are not to put even their own implements or means into a posture of annoyance. The President has as yet not decided this.

May an armed vessel arriving here[1] be prohibited to employ their own citizens found here, as seamen or marines? Th:J. they cannot be prohibited to recruit their own citizens. H and Knox they may and ought to be prohibited. No decision yet by the President.

It appears to me the President wishes the Little Sarah had been stopped by military coercion, that is, by firing on her. Yet I do not believe he would have ordered himself had he been here, tho he would be glad we had ordered it.

The US. being a ship building nation may they sell ships prepared for war to both parties? Th:J. They may sell such ships in their ports to both parties, or carry them for sale to the dominions of both parties. E.R. of opinion they could not sell them here, and that if they attempted to carry them to the dominions of the parties for sale, they might be seized by the way as *contraband*. H. of same opinion, except that he did not consider them as seizable for contraband, but as the property of a power making itself a party in the war by an aid of such a nature, and consequently that it would be a breach of neutrality.

H. moves that the government of France be desired to recall Mr. Genet, Knox adds and that he be in the mean time suspended from his functions. Th:J. proposes that his correspondence be communicated to his government with friendly observations. Presidt. silent.

[*In the margin:*]
This is committed to writing the morning of the 13th. of July. i.e. the whole page.

MS (DLC); entirely in TJ's hand, with note containing date added lengthwise in margin; written on recto of a sheet containing on verso "Anas" entries for 15 and 21 July 1793. PrC (DLC); partly torn. Recorded in SJPL under 13-21 July 1793:

"Opns of heads of dep. on various questions of neutrality." Included in the "Anas."

TJ undoubtedly composed these notes in preparation for carrying out the decision made by the Cabinet the preceding day to request the advice of the Supreme Court on certain neutrality issues that had arisen in the wake of the issuance of the Proclamation of Neutrality on 22 Apr. 1793 (see Cabinet Opinion on Consulting the Supreme Court, 12 July 1793). Since Attorney General Edmund Randolph was then in Virginia, the views ascribed to him by TJ were those he had expressed at earlier Cabinet meetings or in formal written opinions.

BEFORE THE PROHIBITION: that is, before TJ officially announced this ban in his 5 June 1793 letter to Edmond Charles Genet. E.R. GAVE AN OFFICIAL OPINION: see Edmund Randolph's Opinion on the Case of Gideon Henfield, 30 May 1793. COMPLAINT OF THE BRITISH MIN.: George Hammond's fourth Memorial to TJ of 8 May 1793. A SUBSEQUENT ARMAMENT: see TJ to Richard Harison, 12 June 1793.

[1] Preceding five words interlined in place of "they."

To Thomas Carstairs

Sunday July 14. 1793.

Th: Jefferson will be obliged to Mr. Carstairs if he can be at his office tomorrow exactly at 10. aclock in the morning to go with him to the President's with the drawings &c.

RC (Mrs. L. Carstairs Pierce, Wayne, Pennsylvania, 1946). Not recorded in SJL.

Thomas Carstairs (1759-1830) was a Scottish carpenter, draftsman, and architect who immigrated before February 1784 to Philadelphia, where he built the house TJ had earlier rented from Thomas Leiper. TJ subsequently employed him in small carpentry jobs, consulted him in the summer of 1793 in connection with the construction of the United States Capitol, and later sought his advice on the appropriate wages for craftsmen building the University of Virginia (Sandra L. Tatman and Roger W. Moss, *Biographical Dictionary of Philadelphia Architects: 1700-1930* [Boston, 1985], 131-2; Charles E. Peterson to the Editors, 13 Oct. 1988, TJ Editorial Files; TJ to Leiper, 4 Aug. 1790, 19 May 1791; MB, 6 Apr., 19 Dec. 1791, 7 Jan., 3 July, 17 Dec. 1793, 1 Jan. 1794; TJ to George Washington, 17 July 1793; TJ to Carstairs, 1 Nov. 1817, 16 Jan. 1818, 13 Jan. 1824; Carstairs to TJ, 26 Jan. 1818).

To James Madison

July[1] 14. 93.

I wrote you on the 7th. since which yours of the 29th. of June is received acknoledging mine to the 17th. of June. I am anxious to know as early as possible the *safe* delivery of my letters to you. I am not able to say any thing more about the convening of Congress at an earlier day than the regular one. I have lately suspected some disinclination to it. But the grounds are slight. I must see you and be with you some days before it meets. Whether here or at Monticello must[2] depend on the time of it's meeting. But we shall have warning enough to arrange the particulars. I am excessively afraid that an open rupture will take place between the French min. and us. I think there has been something to blame on both sides, but much more on his. He is so evidently in the wrong that those are pressing for an appeal to the people, who never looked towards that tribunal before. They know too well that the whole game is played into their hands, and that there is right enough on both sides to marshal each nation with it's own agents, and consequently against one another, and consequently also us with England. I have written a long letter to-day to Munroe, and must therefore be shorter with you. Adieu. Your's affectionately.

RC (DLC: Madison Papers); unsigned. PrC (DLC). Tr (ViU: Edgehill-Randolph Papers); 19th-century copy.

[1] To the left of the dateline TJ wrote, then erased, "Dear."
[2] Word written over "will," erased.

To James Monroe

Dear Sir   Philadelphia July 14. 1793.

Your favor of June 27. has been duly received. You have most perfectly seised the *original* idea of the proclamation. When first proposed as a declaration of neutrality it was opposed 1. because the Executive had no power to declare neutrality, 2. as such a declaration would be premature and would lose us the benefits for which it might be bestowed. It was urged that there was a strong impression in the minds of many that they were free to join in the hostilities on the side of France, others were unapprised of the danger they would be exposed to in carrying contraband goods &c. It was therefore agreed that a Proclamation should issue, declaring that we were in a state of peace with all the parties, admonishing the people to do nothing contravening it, and putting them on their guard as to contraband. On this ground it was accepted or acquiesced in by all, and E.R. who drew it brought to me the draught to let me see there was no such word as *neutrality* in it. Circumstances forbid other verbal criticisms. The public however soon took it up as a declaration of neutrality, and it came to be considered at length as such.—The arming privateers in Charleston, with our means entirely, and partly our citizens, was complained of in a memorial from Mr. Hammond. In our consultation it was agreed we were by treaty *bound* to prohibit the enemies of France from arming in our ports, and were *free* to prohibit France also, and that by the laws of neutrality we were bound to permit or forbid the same things to both, as far as our treaties would permit. All therefore were forbidden to arm within our ports, and the vessels armed before the prohibition were on the advice of a majority ordered to leave our ports. With respect to our citizens who had[1] joined in hostilities against a nation with whom we were at peace, the subject was thus viewed. Treaties are laws. By the treaty with England we are in a state of peace with her. He who breaks that peace, if within our jurisdiction, breaks the laws, and is punisheable by them. And if he is punisheable he ought to be punished, because no citizen should be free to commit his country to war. Some vessels were taken within our bays. There foreigners as well as natives are liable to punishment. Some were committed in the high seas. There, as the sea is a common jurisdiction to all nations, and divided *by persons*, each having a right to the jurisdiction over their own citizens only, our citizens only were punisheable by us. But they were so, because within our jurisdiction. Had they gone into a *foreign land* and committed a hostility they would have been clearly out of our jurisdiction and unpunishable by the existing laws. As the armament in Charlestown had taken place before our citizens might have reflected on the case, only two were prosecuted, merely to satisfy the complaint made and to serve as a warning to others. But others having attempted to arm another vessel in New York after this was known, all the persons concerned in the latter case, foreign as well as native, were directed to be prosecuted. The Atty. Genl. gave an official opinion that the act was against law, it coincided with all our private opinions, and the lawyers of this state, New York and Maryland who were applied to, were unanimously of the same opinion. Lately Mr. Rawle, Atty. of the US. for this district, on a conference with the District judge, Peters, supposes the law more doubtful. New acts therefore of the same kind are left unprosecuted till the question is determined by the proper court, which will be during the present week. If they declare the act no offence against the laws, the Executive will have acquitted itself, towards the nation attacked by their citizens, by having submitted them to the sentence of the laws of their country, and towards those laws, by an appeal to them in a case which interested the country and which was at least doubtful. I confess I think myself that the case is punisheable, and that, if found otherwise Congress ought to make it so, or we shall be made parties in every maritime war in which the piratical spirit of the banditti in our ports can engage.—I will write you what the judicial determination is.—Our prospects with Spain appear to me, from circumstances taking place on this side the Atlantic, absolutely desperate. Measures are taken to know if they are equally so on the other side, and before the close of the year that question will be closed, and your next meeting must probably prepare for the new order of things.—I fear the disgust of France is inevitable. We shall be to blame in part. But the new Minister much more so. His conduct is indefensible by the most furious Jacobin. I only wish our countrymen may distinguish between him and his nation, and if the case should ever be laid before them, may not suffer their affection to the nation to be diminished. H. sensible of the advantage they have got, is urging a full appeal by the government to the people. Such an explosion would manifestly endanger a dissolution of the friendship between the two nations, and ought therefore to be deprecated by every friend to our liberty, and none but an enemy to it would wish to avail himself of the indiscretions of an individual to compromit two nations esteeming each other ardently. It will prove that the agents of the two people are either great bunglers or great rascals when they cannot preserve that peace which is the universal wish of both.—The situation of the St. Domingo fugitives (aristocrats as they are) calls aloud for pity and charity. Never was so deep a tragedy presented to the feelings of man.[2] I deny the power of the general government to apply money to such a purpose[3] but I deny it with a bleeding heart. It belongs to the state governments. Pray urge ours to be liberal. The[4] Executive should hazard themselves more[5] on such an occasion, and the legislative when it meets ought to approve and extend it. It will have a great effect in doing away the impression[6] of other disobligations towards France.—I become daily more and more convinced that all the West India islands will remain in the hands of the people of colour, and a total expulsion of the whites sooner or later take place. It is high time we should foresee the bloody scenes which our children certainly, and possibly ourselves (South of Patowmac) have to wade through, and try to avert them.—We have no news from the continent of Europe later than the 1st. of May.—My love to Mrs. Monroe. Tell her they are paving the street before your new house. Adieu. Yours affectionately.

PrC (DLC); unsigned; at foot of first page: "Colo. Monroe."

The MEMORIAL FROM MR. HAMMOND, the decision to prosecute the effort to arm AN-OTHER VESSEL IN NEW YORK, and the OFFI-CIAL OPINION of the Attorney General are identified in note to TJ's Notes on Neutrality Questions, 13 July 1793.

[1] TJ here canceled "commi."
[2] Sentence interlined.
[3] Remainder of sentence interlined.
[4] TJ here canceled "assembly."
[5] Word interlined.
[6] Word interlined in place of "effect."

To Thomas Mann Randolph, Jr.

DEAR SIR   Philadelphia July 14. 1793.

I received yesterday your favor of the 4th. inst. and will immediately have Mr. Peyton's name placed among the candidates for the superintendancy of the magazines at Columbia. It will be not amiss to observe however that if there be a keeper at present and he chuses to remain, he would not be deprived without evident ill conduct. As I observe that through the negligence of the posts my letters are sometimes long on the way, I will take the present early moment to ask that the horse you have been so good as to procure for me may be sent on to George town the 1st. day of September, that is to say to leave Monticello that day. Either Jupiter or Tom Shackleford would I think be the best hand, to come with him. His route should be by Mr. Madison's, Orange C.H. Porter's mill, Stevensburg, Herring's, Norman's ford, Slate run church, Colchester, Georgetown; and his stages would be Mr. Madison's, Herring's, Colchester, and George Town putting up at Shuter's tavern there. I will send off Tarquin so as to arrive there the same day to wit the 4th.[1] to be exchanged by the riders, Tarquin to go on to Monticello, and the carriage horse come on here and have time to recruit for the journey back. Each messenger to be instructed to wait at George town till the other arrives, as accidents may happen on both sides, and it is indeed very possible that Tarquin may be able to go but short journies daily. Clarkson should furnish the messenger about 9. days expences, allowing liberal feeding for the horse. The expences at George town I will provide for from hence.—You will have heard, before you recieve this, of the massacre of about one half the inhabitants of Port au Prince, and the flight of the other half, who are arrived or about to arrive in the Chesapeake. A similar massacre has taken place in Martinique, and I think it cannot be doubted but that sooner or later all the whites will be expelled from all the West India islands. What is to take place in our Southern states will depend on the timely wisdom and liberality of their legislatures. Perhaps the measures they ought to begin to think of may be facilitated by having so near an asylum established. We have no news from the continent of Europe later than the beginning of May. We have reason to presume that French affairs are going on firmly. My best affections to my dear Martha. Present me also to the friends you may have with you, & beleive me to be my dear Sir with the sincerest attachment, and greatest impatience to be with you Your's &c   TH: JEFFERSON

RC (DLC); at foot of first page: "Mr. Randolph." PrC (DLC). Tr (DLC); 19th-century copy. Randolph's missing FAVOR OF THE 4TH. INST. was recorded in SJL as received from Monticello on 13 July 1793.

[1] Preceding four words interlined.

To Josef Ignacio de Viar and Josef de Jaudenes

GENTLEMEN   Philadelphia July 14. 1793.

I have laid before the President your letters of the 11th. and 13th. instant. Your residence in the United States has given you an opportunity of becoming acquainted with the extreme freedom of the Press in those States. Considering it's great importance to the public liberty, and the difficulty of subjecting it to very precise rules, the laws have thought it less mischievous to give greater scope to it's freedom, than to the restraint of it. The President has therefore no authority to prevent publications of the nature of those you complain of in your favor of the 11th. I can only assure you that the Government of the United States has no part in them, and that all it's expressions of respect towards his Catholic Majesty, public and private, have been as uniform, as their desire to cultivate his friendship has been sincere.

With respect to the letters I have had the honor of receiving from you for some time past, it must be candidly acknowledged that their complexion was thought remarkable, as to the matters they brought forward as well as the style of expressing them. A succession of complaints, some founded on small things taken up as great ones, some on suggestions contrary to our knowledge of things, yet treated as if true on very inconclusive evidence, and presented to view as rendering our peace very problematical, indicated a determination to find cause for breaking that peace. The President thought it was high time to come to an eclaircissement with your government directly, and has taken the measure of sending a Courier to Madrid for this purpose. This of course transfers all explanation of the past to another place. But the President is well pleased to hope from your letters of the 11th. and 13th. that all perhaps had not been meant which had been understood from your former Correspondence, and will be still more pleased to find these and all other difficulties between the two Countries settled in such a way as to ensure their future friendship. I beg you to accept assurances of my particular esteem, and of the real respect with which I have the honor to be, Gentlemen Your most obedient and most humble Servant.

PrC (DLC); in a clerk's hand, unsigned; at foot of first page: "Messrs. de Viar & Jaudenes." FC (Lb in DNA: RG 59, DL). Tr (DLC: William Short Papers). PrC (DLC). Tr (CtY). PrC (DLC). Tr (DNA: RG 46, Senate Records, 3d Cong., 1st sess.). Tr (Lb in same, TR). Tr (AGI: Papeles de Cuba, legajo 88). Tr (AHN: Papeles de Estado, legajo 3895); in Spanish; attested by Viar and Jaudenes. Recorded in SJPL under 13 July 1793. Enclosed in TJ to William Carmichael and William Short, 16 July 1793, and TJ to Thomas Pinckney, 11 Sep. 1793.

From Tobias Lear

July 15th: 1793.

In obedience to the President's commands T. Lear has the honor to return to the Secretary of State the following letters and papers which have been put into the President's hands by the Secretary. viz.

Genet's communications relative to Spain
Letter from Govr. of Pennsyv. dated 24th. June and Warden's report.
Do.   from Do.   7th. July.
Copy of Mr. Rawle's letter 9th. July
Genet's letter 9 July.
Govr. of Virga. letter 28th. June.
Secy.'s letter to Mr. Hammond 26th. June
Do.   to Do.   25 June
Do.   to Do.   25 Do.
Philips' letter 7th. June
Chiappe letter 20th. March.
Simpson's do. 30th. Apl.
Genet's letter 22d. June
Do.   Do.   25 do.
Do.   Do.   26 do.
Do.   Do.   9 July.
Hoben's Notes on Capitol.
B. Minister's letter 11th. July
Sodderstrom's letter 11 July
Lt. Govr. Wood's letter 8 July with enclosures.
B. Minister's letter 13 July.
Secy.'s letter to M. P. of France 30th. June
Copy of a letter from Govr. of Maryland to the Collector of Baltimore
    20th. June
Do. of   Do. from Collectr. to the Govr. 21 June
Extract of a letter from Govr. of Maryld. to Secy. of War. 22d. June.
Secy.'s letter to M. P. of France 12 July
Do.   Do.   to B. Minister   Do.
Do. Note to Mess. Viar and Jaudennes 11th. July.
Instructions to Mr. James Blake 12 July.
Passport   for   Do.   Do.
Secy.'s letter to Chief Justice Jay   Do.
Do.   Do. to Judge Patterson   Do.
Do.   Do. to M. P. of France   25 June
Do.   Do. to B. Minister   26 Do.

RC (DLC); endorsed by TJ as a letter from George Washington received 15 July 1793.

James Hoban's NOTES on the CAPITOL are dated 10 July 1793. For the exchange between Governor Thomas Sim Lee of Maryland and the COLLECTOR OF BALTIMORE and the EXTRACT from Lee to Secretary of War

Henry Knox, see note to TJ to Genet, 30 June 1793. The letters to CHIEF JUSTICE John Jay and JUDGE William Paterson were texts of the Circular to the Justices of the Supreme Court, 12 July 1793. Other documents in this list are identified in TJ's three memorandums to Washington printed under 11 July 1793, and notes.

To George Nicholas

SIR   Philadelphia July 15.[1] 1793.

Your letter of May 7. was received and duly laid before the President of the US. On enquiry into the circumstances which you mention as producing difficulty in the district of Kentucky, in order to see what could be done, he found that a letter had been written by the Commissioner of the revenue to the collector which would relieve much of that difficulty, at least as much of it as there is legal authority to relieve. I have the honor to inclose you a copy[2] of that letter, and it is hoped that it will lessen so much the number of disagreeable cases which would present themselves in the exercise of the office proposed to you, as to place it nearly on the footing you desired; and therefore that we may consider your objections so far removed as that you accept the appointment. It will give me pleasure to be authorised by a letter from yourself to inform the President that you do. I have the honor to be Sir Your most obedient & most humble servt.   TH: JEFFERSON

RC (NNP); at foot of text: "George Nicholas esq."; alterations in punctuation by a later hand have been ignored. PrC (DLC). FC (Lb in DNA: RG 59, DL); with marginal note identifying enclosure (see note 2 below). Enclosure: Extract of Tench Coxe, Commissioner of the Revenue, to Thomas Marshall, Inspector of the Revenue for Survey No. 7 at Buckpond, Kentucky, Treasury Department Revenue Office, 13 Mch. 1793, stating that he had conferred with the Secretary of the Treasury about the discontent and questions that have arisen about duties on spirits and stills which may have accrued after the Excise Act was passed but before officers were appointed or knowledge of the law became widely dispersed; that the similar problem which arose when the impost and tonnage duties were first collected was resolved with

the decision that duties were owed only after customhouses were organized and not from the date the acts were passed; and that prudence and judgment called for analogous leniency as the excise duties came into effect, though such clemency was not to extend beyond the first year of the act's operation (PrC of Tr in DLC; in a clerk's hand; attested at foot of text as extracted on 10 July 1793).

Nicholas's LETTER OF MAY 7, recorded in SJL as received from Kentucky on 15 June 1793, has not been found, but in it he must have declined his recent appointment as United States district attorney for Kentucky because of concern about the difficulty and unpopularity involved in enforcing the excise laws. Nicholas evidently remained adamant in his missing letter to

TJ of 25 Aug. 1793, recorded in SJL as received from Kentucky on 2 Oct. 1793, for a successor was appointed later that year (note to William Murray to TJ, 7 Dec. 1792).

[1] Month and date written over "May 7," erased.

[2] Marginal note keyed to this word in FC: "Vide Letter of Tench Coxe Esqr. to T. Marshal Inspector of Revenue. Buckpond. Kentucky. dated March 13th. 1793. on file."

Notes of a Cabinet Meeting

July 15. Th:J. H. and K. met at the President's. Govr. Mifflin had appld. to Knox for the loan of 4. cannon to mount at Mud Isd. informed him he should station a guard of 35. militia there, and asked what arrangement for rations the general government had taken. Knox told him nothing could be done as to rations and he should ask the Presidt. for the cannon. In the mean time he permitted him to put the Cannon on board a boat, ready to send off as soon as permission was obtained. The Presidt. declared his own opinion *first* and fully that when the orders were given to the governors to stop vessels arming &c. in our ports even by military force, he took for granted the Govrs. would use such diligence as to detect those projects in embryo and stop them when no force was requisite or a very small party of militia would suffice: that here was a demand from the Governr. of Pensva. to lend 4. cannon under pretext of executing orders of general government, that if this was granted we should be immediately appld. to by every other governor, and that not for one place only, but several, and our cannon should be dispersed all over US. That for this reason we had refused the same request to the Govrs. of S.C. Virga., and RI. That if they erected batteries, they must establish men for them, and would come on us for this too, he did not think the Executive had a power to establish permanent guards, he had never looked to any thing permanent when the orders were given to the governors, but only an occasional call on small parties of militia in the moments requiring it. These sentiments were so entirely my own, that I did little more than combat on the same grounds the opinions of H. and K. The latter said he would be ready to lend an equal number to every governor to carry into effect orders of such importance: and H. that he would be ready to lend them in cases where they happened to be as near the place where they were to be mounted.

Hamilton submitted the purchase of a large quantity of salt petre, which would outrun the funds destined to objects of that class by Congress. We were unanimous we ought to venture on it, and to the procuring supplies of military stores in the present circumstance, and take on us the responsibility to Congress, before whom it should be laid. The President was fully of the same opinion.

In the above case of the cannon the President gave no final order while I remained, but I saw that he was so impressed with the disagreeableness of taking them out of the boat again, that he would yield. He spoke sharply to Knox for having put them in that position without consulting him, and declared that, but for that circumstance he would not have hesitated one moment to refuse them.

MS (DLC); entirely in TJ's hand; partially dated; written with "Anas" entry for 21 July 1793 on verso of sheet containing "Anas" entry for 13 July 1793. Included in the "Anas."

The President summoned this Cabinet meeting to consider the appeal this day by Governor Thomas Mifflin of Pennsylvania to Secretary of War Henry Knox for cannon to fortify Mud Island in the Delaware River and for ammunition and other supplies for the militia ordered there as a result of the *Little Sarah* case. According to the account of this meeting in the presidential journal, the Cabinet came to no decision on this matter even after TJ was obliged to leave (*Pa. Archs.*, 9th ser., I, 622; Washington, *Journal*, 199, 200n).

To George Washington

July 15. 93.

Th: Jefferson with his respects to the President returns him Montmorin's letter, which he thought he would wish to keep, and sends him a letter from Govr. Chittenden, open as he received it. Also the letter from Algiers in which there is nothing new but their present marine force in the last page but one.[1]

RC (DNA: RG 59, MLR); with final sentence written a day later (see note 1 below); addressed: "The President of the US."; endorsed by Tobias Lear. Tr (Lb in same, SDC). Not recorded in SJL.

MONTMORIN'S LETTER: see Enclosure I to first Memorandum to Washington, [11 July 1793]. The letter from Governor Thomas CHITTENDEN of Vermont has not been found. The LETTER FROM ALGIERS, transmitted to TJ by Washington on 16 July 1793, was addressed to Congressman Jonathan Trumbull, Jr., of Connecticut, by the American captives there (Washington, *Journal*, 200). Writing to the President in a letter of 8 July 1793 from Lebanon, Connecticut, Trumbull had forwarded it among certain "inclosed papers" respecting the captives that he deemed "of such a nature that I think it my duty to transmit them to the supreme Executive of the Union" (DNA: RG 59, MLR). None of the papers have been found.

[1] Sentence added on 16 July 1793 when the President transmitted to TJ the enclosure mentioned therein.

To William Carmichael

Sɪʀ   Philadelphia July 16. 1793

The present opportunity is so favorable for obtaining answers to the several particular cases, relative to individuals, which had been committed to your care at Madrid before I came into office, and also those of the same nature since, that I must ask the favor of you to give, by the return of Mr. Blake, a particular statement of what has been done in each case, addressing your letter 'to the Secretary of state of the US' as I shall retire from the office before his return. While in it, I have had the honor of receiving from you but a single letter, which was sent by Colo. Humphreys on his leaving Madrid. The case of the Dover Cutter, which has for so long a time been the subject of so many letters, is still the subject of constant sollicitation and enquiry here. I have the honor to be with great esteem Sir Your most obedient & most humble servt

Tʜ: Jᴇꜰꜰᴇʀsᴏɴ

PrC (DLC); at foot of text: "Mr. Carmichael." FC (Lb in DNA: RG 59, DCI).

Since becoming Secretary of State TJ had actually received two letters from Carmichael—one of 24 Jan. 1791 and the other of 19 Aug. 1791. For the ᴄᴀsᴇ ᴏꜰ ᴛʜᴇ ᴅᴏᴠᴇʀ ᴄᴜᴛᴛᴇʀ, see TJ to Carmichael, 11 Apr. 1791, and note.

To William Carmichael and William Short

Gᴇɴᴛʟᴇᴍᴇɴ   Philadelphia July 16. 1793.

Mr. Blake's departure being, by the unreadiness of the vessel, put off till this day gives me an opportunity of inclosing you the last letters which have passed between the Chargés des affaires of Spain and myself, and which probably close this subject of correspondence here. I have the honor to be with great respect & esteem Gentlemen Your most obedt. & most humble servt   Tʜ: Jᴇꜰꜰᴇʀsᴏɴ

RC (DLC: Short Papers); at foot of text: "Messrs. Carmichael & Short." PrC (DLC). FC (Lb in DNA: RG 59, DCI). Enclosures: (1) TJ to Josef Ignacio de Viar and Josef de Jaudenes, 11, 14 July 1793. (2) Viar and Jaudenes to TJ, 11, 13 July 1793.

To Edmond Charles Genet

Sɪʀ   [ca. 16 July 1793]

Your letter of June 22. received during the absence of the President, could not be laid before him till his return, and then has been of necessity postponed to matters which pressed more in point of time. In point of importance nothing could more require attention than the doctrines laid down in the Protests of [1] the Consuls of France at New York and Philadelphia, sanctioned by the cover of your letter, and which by setting up rival and independant authorities in every country, tend to destroy every where government at home and peace abroad. These Consuls assert that the limits of the Consular jurisdiction depend *solely* on the foreign government for which it acts, which may extend or restrain it at will: that the government of France has recently given to their foreign [2] consulates jurisdiction of prizes at sea, and thus completely constituted them courts of admiralty: that no authority on earth has the right to interpose between the French nation and it's enemies: (speaking of a case arising within our jurisdiction) that if a privateer of that nation commits a hostility within the jurisdiction of the US. neither the Executive nor Judiciary of the country has a right to punish the aggressors, nor make restitution to the injured party, but must appeal for that to the minister of the nation.

These principles are so diametrically opposite to what we conceive to be the common rights of nations, and to the particular laws of our own which the Executive are bound to see preserved, that it becomes it's duty to declare in opposition to them,

That a [3] nation has of natural right entire and exclusive jurisdiction over the territory it occupies: that if it cedes any portion of that jurisdiction to judges appointed by another nation, it's limits depend on the instrument of cession: that the Consular Convention between France and the US. has given no power to either party to establish complete courts of admiralty within the territory of the other, nor to exercise jurisdiction therein in the particular questions of Prize or not Prize: that every nation on earth has a right to preserve peace, to punish acts in breach of it, and to restore property taken by force, within it's own limits; that it is bound in duty to do this, and does not depend for it on an appeal to any other person or power: that every foreign vessel, armed or unarmed, private or public, entering our jurisdiction, enters it either as a friend or an enemy; if as an enemy indeed, their acts cannot be punished by the laws of the land (but our peace with all the world puts a hostile entrance out of the question). If as a friend, then they are entitled to the protection of those laws, bound at the same time to obey them, and amenable to them if they do not: ('dans les cas ou les citoyens respectifs auront commis quelque crime ou infraction de la tranquilité publique, ils seront justiciables des juges du païs' is the language of the Consular convention between our two nations [4] in affirmance of that of the rights of nations). Whether the cognisance thereof has been given to the Judiciary or the Executive organs, depends on the laws and constitution of the country. One of our subordinate[5] tribunals has been of opinion it is not given to them. Another, perhaps may be of a contrary opinion. An appeal to the court of last resort will decide that finally. If the Judiciary has it not, the Executive, by it's general commission to have the laws executed will be charged with the duty, *solely* and *exclusively* of all others. Till such final decision, by the court of last resort, complainants are free to appeal to either organ.

These are the principles which we hold claimable of right by every nation: they are those by which we are bound to govern ourselves, and in contradiction to which no person within our limits will be permitted to act: and if you will be so good as to admonish the Consuls of France accordingly it may prevent them from infringing laws to which the 2d. article of the Convention has made them expressly amenable.

While these Consular gentlemen treat in so high a tone the presumption of our tribunals for having merely considered Whether by the laws they ought to take cognisance of a question, the proceedings of the Executive have been equally unfortunate in your estimation. You are pleased to consider us as bringing forward diplomatic subleties, and the aphorisms of Vattel, to justify infractions of positive treaties. I shall agree with you that reason is the only rightful umpire between nation and nation. It's dictates constitute the true law of nature and nations. These have been the subject of investigation with many writers, some of whom have succeeded in delineating them so much in unison with the general judgment of men, that their evidence is appealed to with very great respect. I need not repeat *to you* the names of Grotius, Puffendorf, Bynkershoeck, Wolf, Vattel and others. Nor shall I pretend that their conclusions are always incontrovertible. But they are so much respected as to put on those who deny them the burthen of demonstrating their error by a sounder logic. It is far from being evident that the happiness of mankind would be advanced by abandoning suddenly those rules of conduct which by a general consent they have sanctioned with the appellation of the Law of nations, and to which they profess a common acquiescence. Their umpirage must be bad indeed if not better than that of the sword: or, if they are only to be exchanged for others, where are those others to be found, and where the authority which shall establish them? The President, in deciding the cases which have arisen within our limits between your nation and it's enemies, has respected those rules of nations to which all the parties have hitherto professed respect. In renouncing this test of reason and right you have doubtless been governed by a different one; and that those who act by different rules, should differ in their result is not wonderful. This will account for the obstacles which you complain of having experienced in some of the matters you have been pleased to propose here; and, with the inability of our treasury to pay monies not yet demandeable, will, I believe, make up the sum of those obstacles. We can assure you, Sir, with the purest truth, that none of them have arisen from unfavorable dispositions of our country towards yours. These are friendly and sincere, placing the happiness of your nation among the first of it's wishes, and prompting to do for you whatever justice to others will admit, and our means enable us to do: and we should deem it a great calamity indeed were any circumstances to give our friends a different opinion. But we hope it to be impossible, and have so much confidence in their justice and the solidity of the principles by which we have been governed, as to trust they will see in their observance new motives of confidence and esteem.

You seem to be of opinion that the President has decided some cases which should have awaited the decision of Congress. When you shall have had time to become better acquainted with the constitution of the US. you will become sensible that this question can only arise between him and the legislature: that the Executive is the sole organ of our communications with foreign governments; that the Agents of those governments are not authorized to judge what cases are to be decided by this or that department; but to consider the declarations of the President conclusive as to them, and sufficient evidence that the proper department has pronounced on the case.

You have so often in your letters quoted the will of the citizens of the US. as something well known on these particular questions, and different from that of the President, that it is[6] apprehended you may have been led into errors on that subject by individuals neither qualified to collect, nor authorized to pronounce it. You will more faithfully collect it from the same instrument, the constitution, wherein they have declared *their will* to be that the person whom they freely chuse as their President shall administer the Executive offices of their government as he shall think wisest and best in every particular case; that the persons whom they shall freely chuse as their legislature shall make the laws as they shall think wisest and best. In these they repose their confidence. Through these organs they express *their will* in every particular case, and not through individuals whom they have never seen, nor known, nor nominated for the declaration of their will, and who might use that respectable cover for purposes very distinct from the interests of those about whom they presume to misinform you.[7]

Dft (DLC: TJ Papers, 92: 15830-1, 15833); undated and unfinished, but composed ca. 16 July 1793; entirely in TJ's hand, with "Not sent" written at head of text at a later date; at foot of first page: "Mr. Genet"; with additional paragraph written on separate sheet (same, 15832) on or after 23 July 1793 (see below); note penciled by Edmund Randolph on verso of fol. 15833, but actually intended for TJ to Genet, 24 July 1793: "In all respects [tenable and accurate.]." Recorded in SJPL under 22 July 1793: "Th:J. to Genet. draught of a lre not sent." Enclosed in TJ to George Washington, 16 July 1793, and TJ to Edmund Randolph, with Jefferson's Note, [23 July 1793].

The antecedents of this unsent letter are discussed in note to Genet to TJ, 22 June 1793. After pondering TJ's draft on 23 July 1793, the Cabinet referred the matter to Attorney General Edmund Randolph for an opinion, which has not been found. In response to a suggestion made at the meeting by Henry Knox, TJ wrote on a separate sheet an additional paragraph admonishing the French minister for the offensive tone in which he spoke of the President in his letters (see note 7 below). The President and the Cabinet ultimately decided to make no reply to Genet, but instead to request his recall by the French government (Washington, *Journal*, 206; TJ to Randolph, with Jefferson's Note, [23 July 1793]; Notes of Cabinet Meeting on Edmond Charles Genet, 23 July, 1, 2 Aug. 1793; Editorial Note and documents on the recall of Edmond Charles Genet, at 16 Aug. 1793).

The 1788 CONSULAR CONVENTION between France and the United States is in Miller, *Treaties*, II, 228-41. For the decision of ONE OF OUR SUBORDINATE TRIBUNALS on American admiralty jurisdiction over belligerents, see note to George Hammond to TJ, 5 June 1793. For the result of an appeal in a different case to the COURT OF LAST RESORT—the Supreme Court of the United States—concerning both American and French admiralty jurisdiction in the United States, see note to Lucas Gibbes and Alexander S. Glass to TJ, 8 July 1793. See also Thomas, *Neutrality*, 206-19.

[1] Preceding four words interlined in place of "by."
[2] Word interlined.
[3] Word interlined in place of "every."
[4] TJ first wrote "of our Consular convention" before revising it to read as above.
[5] TJ here canceled "courts."
[6] TJ here canceled "fear."
[7] TJ wrote the following paragraph on a separate sheet after the Cabinet meeting of 23 July 1793 and later added "Not inserted" above it: "The terms in which you permit yourself, in this and some other of your letters, to speak of the President of the US. and the influence and impressions you venture to ascribe to him, are calculated to excite sentiments which need no explanation. On what grounds of truth they are hazarded, how to reconcile them to decorum, to the respect due to the person and character of our chief magistrate, and to the nation over which he presides and that too from the representative of a friendly people, are questions left to your maturer reflection."

To George Washington

July 16. 1793.

Th: Jefferson has the honor to submit to the President the rough draught of an answer to Mr. Genet's letter of June 22. It is left unclosed, in case any other matters should be thought proper to be added. Otherwise he would propose to close it with reiterations of friendship to his nation.

RC (DNA: RG 59, MLR); addressed: "The President of the US."; endorsed by Tobias Lear. Tr (Lb in same, SDC). Not recorded in SJL. Enclosure: see preceding document.

From John Clarke

Hon'ble Sir   Richmond July 17th 1793.

I recieved yesterday your favor of the 28th. of June, for which I humbly thank you. Being unacquainted in Philadelphia, I was at a loss to know who I should get to be my arbitrator, but was happy to find by your letter that you intend to select (for arbitrators) men of integrity and other proper qualifications for deciding who is best entitled to the patent contended for. I was also happy to find, in the latter part of the ninth Section of the new Law, that "where there shall be more than two interfereing applications and the parties applying shall not all unite in appointing three Arbitrators, it shall be in the power of the Secretary of State to appoint three arbitrators for the purpose." As there are more than two interfereing applications in the present case, I anxiously wish and request that you will appoint the arbitrator or arbitrators, required. I recieved Mr. Taylor's letter of the 10th. of June, a few days before your last came to hand, and shall endeavour to comply with the requisitions mentioned therein, he informs me that you have fixed on the last Monday in the present month for makeing the reference to arbitration, And that the Arbitrators and evidences of the parties must be at 12 Oclock on that day at the office of the Secretary of State in Philadelphia. I feared at first that he meaned that the evidences were to appear in person, but on opening his former letter to me upon the same subject, he says "procure and send under cover to the Secretary of State in season, such written Testimony either by oath or otherwise, as you may think worthy of consideration, and useful to substantiate the originality of the invention on your part." I therefore trust that you do not require, that the evidences shall appear in person, but by deposition &c. as it would be exceedingly inconvenient and expensive to me. I have already sent my petition to you for a patent for my invention, and descriptions of it signed by Myself and attested by two witnesses, according to the new Law. These papers I expect you recieved some time ago; for fear that those sent before have miscarried, I here inclose Mr. James Merrideth's deposition, And my own Memorial. Mr. Merrideth's deposition is accompanied by two Certificates of his integrity and good Character, from gentlemen who have known him from his Childhood Viz; The certificates of The Hon'ble Robert Goode, one of the council of this state, And the certificate of The Hon'ble William Fleming one of the Judges of the Court of appeals. Mr. David Ross's Narrative was sent to you some ago, but fearing that it miscarried I would now send another, but his being a considerable distance from this place now prevents my doing it. He is daily expected to return. If he should time enough[1] I shall have another Narrative sent to you immediately. I have sent you here inclosed Bank Notes for the Thirty Dollars required by Law. I hope and request that you will have all the papers (if you think them necessary) that I have sent you heretofore, or such of them as you think proper, produced at the trial. Having omited no requisition that I know of, I conclude with a firm reliance on your haveing Strict Justice done. I am Hon'ble Sir Your most Obedient and most Humble Servant

JOHN CLARKE

RC (DLC); at foot of text: "To The Honorable Mr Jefferson"; endorsed by TJ as received "with 30.D. inclosed" on 25 July 1793, but recorded in SJL as received a day earlier. Enclosures not found.

For the NEW LAW on patents enacted on 21 Feb. 1793, see *Annals*, III, 1431-5. Missing letters to TJ by William Hay, writing from Richmond on 29 July 1793, and by John Wilson, dated 2 Aug. 1793, were recorded as received 3 Aug. 1793 in SJL, which indicates that they were written "[for Clarke &   ]."

[1] Thus in manuscript.

From Tench Coxe

July 17. 1793.

Mr. Coxe has the honor to inclose to Mr. Jefferson one of the most striking productions he has ever read. The Author fled from the place in which it was written and has become an inhabitant of the U.S. Mr. Coxe has promised to return it carefully.

He is very sorry to inform Mr. Jefferson that the Pragers are not drawing nor can he find any Bills on Holland. He had some communication[1] with Mr. Vaughan, who observed that he stated the same things to Mr. Jefferson, as he represented to Mr. C.

RC (DLC); endorsed by TJ. Enclosure not found.

[1] Word interlined in place of "conversation."

To Henry Lee

SIR   Philadelphia July 17. 1793.

I was honored in due time with your favor of June 16. on the subject of an infectious disease supposed to be prevailing in the Windward islands, and the precautions necessary to be taken on our part. The absence of the President prevented it's being immediately laid before him. That has been now done, and it is thought that no provision on the subject has been made by the laws of the general government which would enable the President to interfere. I have the honor to be with great esteem & respect Your Excellency's Most obedt & most humble servt

TH: JEFFERSON

RC (RPAB); addressed: "His Excellency Governor Lee Richmond"; franked and stamped. PrC (DLC). FC (Lb in DNA: RG 59, DL).

Lee's FAVOR was actually dated 28 June 1793; it contained an enclosure dated JUNE 16.

To Stephen Sayre

SIR   Philadelphia July 17. 1793.

I have duly received your favor of the 13th. on the same subject with one written to the President, and I have the honor to inform you that the circumstances of the case not leaving room for the appointment therein proposed, the offer of service you are pleased to make cannot be made use of. I have the honor to be Sir Your most obedt. humble servt

TH: JEFFERSON

PrC (DLC); at foot of text: "Mr. Stephen Sayre." FC (Lb in DNA: RG 59, DL).

Sayre's letter of 13 July 1793, recorded in SJL as received 15 July 1793, has not been found. In a letter of the same date to the President, Sayre had requested an appointment as a diplomatic agent to negotiate the release of the American captives in Algiers and the conclusion of a commercial treaty with that country (Sayre to George Washington, 13 July 1793, DLC: Washington Papers, Applications for Office). David Humphreys had already been entrusted with a similar agency (TJ to Humphreys, 21 Mch. 1793).

To George Washington

SIR   Philadelphia July 17. 1793.

According to the desire expressed in your letter of June 30. I called together Doctr. Thornton, Mr. Hallet, Mr. Hoben, and a judicious undertaker of this place, Mr. Carstairs, chosen by Dr. Thornton as a competent judge of the objections made to his plan of the Capitol for the City of Washington. These objections were proposed and discussed on a view of the plans: the most material were the following.

1. The intercolonnations of the western and central peristyles are too wide for the support of their architraves of Stone: so are those of the doors in the wings.

2. The colonnade passing through the middle of the Conference room has an ill effect to the eye, and will obstruct the view of the members: and if taken away, the cieling is too wide to support itself.

3. The floor of the central peristyle is too wide to support itself.

4. The stairways on each side of the Conference room want head-room.

5. The windows are in some important instances masked by the Galleries.

6. Many parts of the building want light and air in a degree which renders them unfit for their purposes. This is remarkably the case with

some of the most important apartments, to wit, the chambers of the Executive and the Senate, the anti-chambers of the Senate and Representatives, the Stair-ways &c. Other objections were made which were surmountable, but those preceding were thought not so, without an alteration of the plan.

This alteration has in fact been made by Mr. Hallet in the plan drawn by him, wherein he has preserved the most valuable ideas of the original and rendered them susceptible of execution; so that it is considered as Dr. Thornton's plan reduced into practicable form. The persons consulted agreed that in this reformed plan the objections before stated were entirely remedied; and that it is on the whole a work of great merit. But they were unanimously of opinion that in removing one of the objections, that is to say, the want of light and air to the Executive and Senate Chambers, a very capital beauty in the original plan, to wit, the Portico of the Eastern front, was suppressed, and ought to be restored; as the recess proposed in the middle of that front instead of the Portico projecting from it, would probably have an extreme ill effect. They supposed that by advancing the Executive chamber, with the two rooms on it's flanks, into a line with the Eastern front, or a little projecting or receding from it, the Portico might be re-established, and a valuable passage be gained in the center of the edifice, lighted from above, and serving as a common disengagement to the four capital apartments, and that nothing would be sacrificed by this but an unimportant proportion of light and air to the Senate and Representatives rooms; otherwise abundantly lighted and aired.

The arrangement of the windows in front on different levels was disapproved, and a reformation of that circumstance was thought desirable though not essential.

It was further their opinion that the reformed plan would not cost more than half what the original one would.

I need not repeat to you the opinions of Colo. Williams an undertaker also produced by Dr. Thornton, who on seeing the plans and hearing the objections proposed, thought some of them removeable, others not so, and on the whole that the reformed plan was the best. This past in your presence, and with a declaration at the same time from Col. Williams that he wished no stress to be laid on opinions so suddenly given. But he called on me the day after, told me he had considered and conferred with Dr. Thornton on the objections, and thought all of them could be removed but the want of light and air in some cases. He gave me general ideas of the ways in which he would remove the other objections, but his method of spanning the intercolonnations with secret arches of brick, and supporting the floors by an interlocked framing appeared to me totally inadequate; that of unmasking the windows by lowering the Galleries was only substituting one deformity for another, and a conjectural expression how head-room might be gained in the Stairways shewed he had not studied them.

I have employed Mr. Carstairs to calculate the cost of the whole masonry of the building, according to the Philadelphia prices, because the cost of the walls of a building furnishes always a tolerable conjecture of the cost of the whole, and because I thought that a statement in detail of the Philadelphia prices of materials and work might be of some value to the Commissioners. I have the honor to be with the most perfect esteem and respect, Sir Your most obedient & most humble Servant.

Th: Jefferson

RC (DNA: RG 59, MLR); in a clerk's hand, signed by TJ; at foot of text: "The President of the United States"; endorsed by Bartholomew Dandridge, Jr. PrC (DLC); unsigned. Tr (Lb in DNA: RG 59, SDC). Tr (DNA: RG 42, PBG); at head of text: "Copy." Tr (same, DCLB). Recorded in SJPL.

The conference on the design of the United States Capitol described in this letter took place on 15 July 1793 after the President again called for a meeting of the interested parties. Immediately after the meeting Washington and TJ agreed that Stephen Hallet's modification of William Thornton's award-winning plan was the preferred design and that work should begin as soon as alterations were made to it (Washington, Journal, 198-9, 202; Thornton to TJ, [ca. 12 July 1793]; Tobias Lear to Thornton, 13 July 1793, DLC: Thornton Papers; TJ to Thomas Carstairs, 14 July 1793). Whether the modified design was DR. THORNTON'S PLAN REDUCED INTO PRACTICABLE FORM, as Thornton also considered it, or departed fundamentally from it, as Hallet maintained, has long been debated by architectural historians, but there is general agreement that the compromise merged the form of Thornton's exterior design with Hallet's modifications. The President enclosed a copy of TJ's letter when he wrote the Commissioners of the Federal District on 25 July 1793 notifying them of

this decision (Fitzpatrick, Writings, xxxiii, 29-30). TJ subsequently sent the Commissioners an estimate of the COST OF THE WHOLE MASONRY prepared by Thomas Carstairs, and the cornerstone of the Capitol was laid on 18 Sep. 1793 in a ceremony attended by the President in masonic regalia (TJ to the Commissioners of the Federal District, 15 Aug. 1793, and enclosure; Charles H. Callahan, Washington: The Man and The Mason [Alexandria, 1913], 289-93 and plate facing 310). Hallet was dismissed as superintendent of construction by the Commissioners in 1794 when he persisted in deviating from the accepted plan. For a comparison of the adopted design with reconstructed elements of Thornton's lost plan which argues that TJ may have stressed similarities between them only to "preserve appearances," see Fiske Kimball and Wells Bennett, "William Thornton and the Design of the United States Capitol," Art Studies: Medieval, Renaissance and Modern, I (1923), 76-92, esp. 87-8; for a more recent supporting assessment which indicates that "Thornton's elevations were married to Hallet's revised plan," see Pamela Scott, "Stephen Hallet's Designs for the United States Capitol," Winterthur Portfolio, xxvii (1992), 145-70, esp. 150, 166. Both studies reproduce related drawings of the Capitol, among them Hallet's conference design (Kimball and Bennett, pl. 72, facing p. 88; Scott, fig. 9, p. 151).

To James Wood

Philadelphia July 17. 1793.

I am honored with your favor of the 8th. instant and have laid the same before the President of the US. The case of the refugees from St. Domingo is really deplorable, and calls with a loud voice for charitable succours: but it is a case wherein the general government has not been authorised to furnish them. It is therefore hoped that the particular states will come in with liberality to the relief of the sufferers, and the temporary relief furnished by the Executive of Virginia cannot fail to meet with general approbation. I have the honor to be with great respect & esteem, Sir Your most obedt & most humble servt

TH: JEFFERSON

RC (RPAB); addressed: "Lieutt. Governor Wood Richmond"; franked and stamped. PrC (DLC). Tr (DLC); 19th-century copy.

To the Justices of the Supreme Court

GENTLEMEN Philadelphia July 18. 1793.

The war which has taken place among the powers of Europe produces frequent transactions within our ports and limits, on which questions arise of considerable difficulty, and of greater importance to the peace of the US. These questions depend for their solution on the construction of our treaties, on the laws of nature and nations, and on the laws of the land; and are often[1] presented under circumstances which do not give a cognisance of them to the tribunals of the country. Yet their decision is so little analagous to the ordinary functions of the Executive, as to occasion much embarrasment and difficulty to them. The President would therefore be much relieved if he found himself free to refer questions of this description to the opinions of the Judges of the supreme court of the US. whose knolege of the subject would secure us against errors dangerous to the peace of the US. and their authority ensure the respect of all parties.—He has therefore asked the attendance of such of the judges as could be collected in time for the occasion, to know, in the first place, their opinion, Whether the public may, with propriety, be availed of their advice on these questions? and if they may, to present, for their advice, the abstract questions which have already occurred, or may soon occur, from which they will themselves strike out such as any circumstances might, in their opinion, forbid them to pronounce on.[2] I have the honor to be with sentiments of the most perfect respect Gentlemen Your most obedt & most humble servt

TH: JEFFERSON

RC (NNC: John Jay Papers); at foot of first page: "The Chief Justice, & Judges of the Supreme court of the US."; endorsed by Jay. PrC (DLC); first page only, with abbreviated complimentary close added in ink (see note 2 below). FC (Lb in DNA: RG 59, DL).

[1] Word interlined.
[2] PrC ends here, with "I have the honor to be &c" added at foot of text in ink.

From James Madison

Dear Sir   July 18. 1793

The season of harvest having suspended all intercourse with Fredg. your favor of the 7th. inst: has but just been received. That of the 29th. Ult: came to hand at the same time. The preceding one of the 23d. would have been acknowledged before but for the cause above mentioned. The present is the first opportunity and like several others leaves me but a moment to prepare for it.

I have read over the subject which you recommend to my attention. It excites equally surprise and indignation, and ought certainly to be taken notice of by some one who can do it justice. In my present disposition which is perfectly alienated from such things, and in my present situation which deprives me of some material facts and many important lights, the task would be in bad hands if I were otherwise better qualified for it. I am in hopes of finding that some one else has undertaken it. In the mean time I will feel my own pulse, and if nothing appears, may possibly try to supply the omission. Return my thanks to Docr. Logan for the pamphlet and also for the plows arrived at Fredg., tho' by a singular succession of errors and accidents lie still on the road between this and that. Your acct. of G——[1] is dreadful. He must be brought right if possible. His folly will otherwise do mischief which no wisdom can repair. Is there no one thro' whom he can be *effectually* counselled. D. L. F:[2] is said to be able, and if himself rightly disposed as I have understood him to be, might perhaps be of great use. The result of the Harvest is perhaps less favorable than I once supposed. I hope however the crop of wheat as to quantity at least will be tolerable. Of the quality I have great apprehensions. The season for getting it in was as bad as was possible. Every other article of our cultivation is prosperous, and will help to make amends, if the rest of the year be favorable. The corn is particularly luxurient in all quarters. Yrs. always & affy

RC (DLC: Madison Papers); unsigned; endorsed by TJ as received 29 July 1793 and so recorded in SJL.

The subject which excited surprise and indignation was Alexander Hamilton's "Pacificus" essays in defense of the Proclamation of Neutrality (TJ to Madison, 7 July 1793). d. l. f: Antoine René Charles Mathurin de La Forest, the French consul general who was returning to France as a result of the consular reorganization

carried out by Edmond Charles Genet and
was thus no longer a possible moderating
influence on the French minister (TJ to La
Forest, 23 June 1793, and note).

¹ At a later date Madison expanded the
abbreviation to "Genet."
² At a later date Madison expanded the
abbreviation to "De La Forest."

Notes on James Cole Mountflorence
and on Federalist Intrigues

July 18. 93. At a meeting at the Presid's Genl. Knox tells us Govr.
Blount (now in town) has informed him that when Mt.florence was in
France, certain members of the Execve. council enquired of him what
were the dispositions of Cumbld. settlemt. &c. towards Spain?
Mt.florce. told them unfriendly. They then offered him a commission to
embody troops there, to give him a quantity of blank commissions to be
filled up by him making officers of the republic of France those who
should command, and undertaking to pay the expences. Mt.florce. desired his name might not be used. Blount added that Mt.florce. while in
France pretended to be a great friend to their revolution tho an enemy
to it in his heart.

———

eod. die. Lear calls on me. I told him that Irvine, an Irishman, and a
writer in the Treasury, who on a former occasion had given the most
decisive proofs of his devotion to his principal, was the author of the
peices signed Veritas: and I wished he could get at some of Irvine's
acquaintances and inform himself of the fact, as the person who told me
of it would not permit the name of his informer to be mentioned. [Note
Beckley told me of it, and he had it from Swaine the printer to whom the
peices were delivered.] That I had long before suspected this excessive
foul play in that party, of writing themselves in the character of the most
exaggerated democrats, and incorporating with it a great deal of abuse
on the President to make him believe it was that party who were his
enemies, and so throw him entirely into the scale of monocrats. Lear
said he no longer ago than yesterday expressed to the President his
suspicions of the artifices of that party to work on him. He mentioned
the following fact as a proof of their writing in the character of their
adversaries. To wit. The day after the little incident of Ricket's¹ toasting
'the man of the people' [see the gazettes] Mrs. Washington was at Mrs.
Powel's, who mentioned to her that when the toast was given there was
a good deal of disapprobation appeared in the audience, and that many
put on their hats and went out: on enquiry he had not found the fact
true, and yet it was put into   's paper, and written under the
character of a republican, tho he is satisfied it is altogether a slander of
the monocrats. He mentioned this to the Presidt. but he did not mention

to him the following fact, which he knows, that in N. York the last summer when the parties of Jay and Clinton were running so high, it was an agreed point with the former, that if any circumstances should ever bring it to a question whether to drop Hamilton or the President the[2] had decided to drop the Presidt. He said that lately one of the loudest pretended friends to the government damned it, and said it was good for nothing that it could not support itself, and it was time to put it down and set up a better, and yet the same person in speaking to the Presidt. puffed of that party as the only friends to the government. He said he really feared that by their artifices and industry they would aggravate the Presidt. so much against the Republicans as to separate him from the body of the people. I told him what the same cabals had decided to do if the Presidt. had refused his assent to the bank bill, also what Brockhurst Livingston said to   that Hamilton's life was much more precious to the community than the Presid's.

MS (DLC); entirely in TJ's hand; second entry written in different ink; brackets in original. Entry in SJPL: "Notes. Mountflorence. French Exve council.—Blount.— Irvine a treasury clerk the writer of Veritas.—artifices practisd on Presidt." Included in the "Anas."

For James Cole Mountflorence's reaction to the French Revolution, see his letter to TJ, 1 Feb. 1793, and enclosure. The LITTLE INCIDENT occurred on 13 July 1793, when George and Martha Washington attended the circus of John Bill Ricketts, who honored the President by offering a toast to "*The Man of the People!*" Both *The Federal Gazette and Philadelphia Daily Advertiser*, 15 July 1793, and *Dunlap's American Daily Advertiser*, 16 July 1793, reported that the audience greeted Ricketts's encomium with loud applause, but in the 17 July 1793 issue of the *National Gazette*, the pseudonymous "Philogenet" assumed THE CHARACTER OF A REPUBLICAN to argue that the toast had been followed by "the vain and unsuccessful attempts of a few to raise an huzza." TJ may have told Lear that in February 1791 Northern Federalist CABALS HAD DECIDED that if Washington REFUSED HIS ASSENT TO THE BANK BILL, they would retaliate by scuttling an act which would satisfy the President's strong desire that Alexandria be included in the Federal District (Editorial Note on locating the Federal District, in Vol. 19: 29-40; Kenneth R. Bowling, "The Bank Bill, the Capital City and President Washington," *Capitol Studies*, I [1972], 59-71).

[1] TJ here canceled "drinking."
[2] Thus in MS.

The Referral of Neutrality Questions to the Supreme Court

I. ALEXANDER HAMILTON'S QUESTIONS FOR THE SUPREME COURT,
[CA. 18 JULY 1793]

II. THOMAS JEFFERSON'S QUESTIONS FOR THE SUPREME COURT,
[CA. 18 JULY 1793]

III. HENRY KNOX'S QUESTIONS FOR THE SUPREME COURT,
[CA. 18 JULY 1793]

IV. QUESTIONS FOR THE SUPREME COURT, [18 JULY 1793]

V. THOMAS JEFFERSON TO GEORGE WASHINGTON, 18 JULY 1793

EDITORIAL NOTE

The number and complexity of questions about what constituted neutral behavior by the United States with respect to the warring nations of Europe grew rapidly in the summer of 1793 in the face of Edmond Charles Genet's persistent challenges to American neutrality policy. With its energies increasingly tied up in the resolution of proliferating appeals by foreign diplomats, especially British minister George Hammond, and by its own citizens, for intervention against alleged French violators of American neutrality, the federal executive resolved to appeal to the Supreme Court for guidance in correctly interpreting existing treaties and the law of nations and in eliminating any ambiguities in the positions set forth in the Proclamation of Neutrality and Jefferson's 15 May 1793 letters to Hammond and Jean Baptiste Ternant, Genet's predecessor as minister of France. Jefferson and his formidable rival at the Treasury Department united to draft a set of questions stating the full range of knotty issues on which the government's stance was or could be expected to be disputed by the belligerent powers. When the justices declined to intervene, obliging the Washington administration to enforce neutrality without their guidance, the Court set an important negative precedent.

Beginning early in May 1793, when Hammond presented the Secretary of State with a series of complaints against hostile acts committed on behalf of France by Americans and French nationals which compromised American neutrality, the Washington administration had been repeatedly called upon to resolve disputes which hinged on the correct interpretation of the law of nations and of American treaties with France. Hitherto the President had decided each question piecemeal after discussion in the Cabinet, and in May he had been advised by Alexander Hamilton that the judiciary was not competent to determine a question concerning the restoration of prizes because such a matter must be "settled by reasons of state, not rules of law" (Memorials from Hammond, 2, 8 May 1793; Hamilton to Washington, 15 May 1793, Syrett, *Hamilton*, xiv, 459). However, in the immediate aftermath of the crisis over the arming of the *Little Sarah* as a French privateer, in which Genet's refusal to obey the administration's ban on fitting out such ships in American ports nearly led to the outbreak of hostilities, Washington and the three Cabinet members then in Philadelphia met on 12 July and unanimously decided to summon the justices of the Supreme Court to the capital on 18 July in order to seek their legal advice on the obligations of the United States as a neutral power. Jefferson immediately dispatched the summonses and notified the British and French ministers that seven vessels whose status had been disputed would be detained until the judges could be consulted (note to Cabinet Opinions on the *Little Sarah*, 8 July 1793; Cabinet Opinion on Consulting the Supreme Court, 12 July 1793; Washington, *Journal*, 194; Circular to the Justices of the Supreme Court, 12 July 1793; TJ to Genet and Hammond, 12 July 1793).

The decision to seek formal legal guidance from the Supreme Court was based on Anglo-American precedents. In England, the monarch and House of Lords were entitled to obtain opinions from the judges of the highest courts, and the Massachusetts and New Hampshire constitutions echoed English practice by giving the governor or legislature recourse to the state supreme court for advisory opinions. Although a similar provision had been proposed but not adopted at the 1787 Federal Convention, Chief Justice Jay had himself supplied Washington with a legal opinion during the 1790 Nootka Sound war crisis and until as late as April 1793 advised Washington and Hamilton on other legal and political matters (James B. Thayer, *Legal Essays* [Boston, 1908], 42-54; Opinion of the Chief Justice, 28 Aug. 1790, in Vol. 17: 134-7; Jay to Washington, 23 Sep. 1791, DLC: Washington Papers; Jay to Hamilton, 28 Nov. 1790, 8 Sep. 1792, 11 Apr. 1793, Syrett, *Hamilton*, VII, 166-7, XII, 334-5, XIV, 307-10). The neutrality questions posed by the Washington administration, however, were addressed to the entire Court.

Although Jefferson began the work of preparing questions for the justices on 13 July 1793 by digesting the issues already debated within the administration, the Cabinet deferred final discussion and preparation of the document for the Court in the hope that Attorney General Edmund Randolph would return from a trip to Virginia in time to participate. He had not arrived by the evening of 17 July, when Chief Justice John Jay asked the President when the object of the summons would be made known to the members of the Court. Washington was obliged to admit that nothing was ready as yet, and early the next morning he asked the Secretary of State to prepare a general statement for the judges, so that they could begin considering the preliminary question of whether they could with propriety give legal advice to the executive. Jefferson immediately complied (Notes on Neutrality Questions, 13 July 1793; Washington to TJ, 18 July 1793; TJ to the Justices of the Supreme Court, 18 July 1793).

The Cabinet convened on the same day to consider specific questions for the justices drafted by Hamilton, Jefferson, and Secretary of War Henry Knox (Washington, *Journal*, 203). The Treasury Secretary's list (Document I below) was probably considered first, perhaps because it was the most detailed and made the greatest effort to address all of the subtle legal points involved. Of the twenty-two questions Hamilton submitted, the Cabinet rejected only the final one, but he had emended his draft so heavily that Jefferson later experienced considerable difficulty in deciphering his interlineations when making a fair copy of the questions approved by the Cabinet (see Document V below). The Cabinet approved seven of Jefferson's fourteen questions (Document II below), the next six having been rendered redundant by analogous questions in Hamilton's draft. Jefferson's final question, about the extent of the President's authority, which the Treasury Secretary had not posed, presumably failed of adoption because Hamilton and Knox had fewer doubts about the limits of executive authority. Since the substance of all the points Knox raised had already been covered by Hamilton and Jefferson, none of his formulations (Document III below) were used. After Jefferson submitted a fair copy of the approved questions (Document IV below), together with the Hamilton and Knox drafts, in a covering letter to Washington (Document V below), he added at the President's request a final question asking whether armed vessels could pursue enemy merchantmen as soon as they left American ports, a query evidently prompted by Genet's earlier missive on the subject (Genet to TJ, 15 June 1793).

On 19 July 1793 Washington instructed Jefferson to submit the questions to the justices (Washington, *Journal*, 204). Having received verbal assurances from the Secretary of State on the same day that an answer to his letter of 18 July was not urgently required, the four justices then in Philadelphia advised Washington and Jefferson on 20 July that they were prepared to respond to the general question of their willingness to advise the government on legal questions but would prefer to postpone answering until their absent colleagues arrived (TJ to Washington, 19 July 1793; Justices of the Supreme Court to TJ, 20 July 1793, and enclosure). Jefferson drafted the President's response agreeing to such a postponement, but apparently becoming convinced that the Court would decline to intervene, the Cabinet completed a set of neutrality rules on 3 Aug. 1793 before the justices could respond (Washington to the Justices of the Supreme Court, [22 July 1793]; TJ to Washington, 22 July 1793; Notes of Cabinet Meeting on Neutrality, 29 July 1793; Rules on Neutrality, 3 Aug. 1793). Five days later the Court concluded that it would be improper to answer the executive's questions. In a letter to Washington signed by every justice except William Cushing, the jurists explained that "The Lines of Separation drawn by the Constitution between the three Departments of Government— their being in certain Respects checks on each other—and our being Judges of a Court in the last Resort—are Considerations which afford strong Arguments against the Propriety of our extrajudicially deciding the questions alluded to; especially as the Power given by the Constitution to the President of calling on the Heads of Departments for opinions, seems to have been *purposely* as well as expressly limited to *executive* Departments" (Justices of the Supreme Court to Washington, 8 Aug. 1793, DNA: RG 59, MLR). Disappointed by this response, Jefferson suggested to Randolph that a bill be drafted to create a body to advise the executive on neutrality matters. Unhappy with Randolph's counterproposal that this responsibility be annexed to the Attorney General's office, Jefferson evidently let the matter drop (TJ to James Madison, 11 Aug. 1793).

Compilation of the questions for the Supreme Court no doubt helped the Cabinet develop a more coherent and unified vision of the legal problems associated with maintaining neutrality and thus served as a useful prelude to the administration's promulgation of new regulations. The scope and complexity of the issues, however, were guaranteed to make the justices ponder the constitutional precedent they would be setting if they rendered an advisory opinion. The Washington administration's exercise ultimately proved self-defeating when it came to eliciting a response from the Court, whose refusal set a time-honored precedent against official advisory opinions by federal jurists (Thomas, *Neutrality*, 146-50; Charles Warren, "The First Decade of the Supreme Court of the United States," *University of Chicago Law Review*, VII [1940], 645-8; Charles G. Haines, *The Role of the Supreme Court in American Government and Politics 1789-1835* [Berkeley and Los Angeles, 1944], 143-5).

I. Alexander Hamilton's Questions
for the Supreme Court

[ca. 18 July 1793]

Agreed ×

I   Do the Treaties[1] between the United States and France[2] give to France or her Citizens[3] a *right*, when at War with a Power with whom the UStates are at peace, to fit out originally, in and from the[4] Ports of the UStates, vessels armed for War,[5] with or without commission?

Agreed

II   If they[6] give such a *right* Does it extend to all manner of armed vessels or to particular kinds only? If the latter, to what kinds does it extend?

Agreed

III   Do they give to France or her Citizens,[7] in the case supposed, a right to refit or arm anew vessels, which before their coming within any port of the UStates were armed for war—with or without commission?

Agreed

IV   If they give such a right; does it extend to all manner of armed vessels or to particular kinds only? If the latter, to what kinds does it extend? Does it include an *augmentation* of force, or does it only extend to replacing the vessel in *statu quo*?

Agreed

V   Does[8] the XXII Article of the Treaty of Commerce in the case supposed,[9] extend to Vessels armed for War, on account of the *Government* of a Power at War with [France],[10] or to Merchant-armed vessels belonging to the subjects or citizens of that Power (viz.) of the description of those which by the English are called Letter of Marque-Ships by the French "Batiments armé en marchandize et en guerre"?

Agreed

VI   Do the Treaties aforesaid prohibit the UStates from permitting in the case supposed, the armed vessels belonging to a Power at War with France—or to the citizens or subjects of such Power to come within the ports of the UStates there to remain as long as they may think fit except in the case of their coming in with Prizes made of the subjects or property of France?

Agreed

VII   Do they prohibit the UStates from permitting in the case supposed, vessels armed on account of the Government of a Power at War with France or vessels armed for merchandize and war, with or without Commission on account of the subjects or citizens of such Power or any vessels other

[527]

than those commonly called Privateers[11] to sell freely whatsoever they may bring into the Ports of the UStates and freely to purchase in and carry from the ports of the U States goods merchandize and commodities; except as excepted in the last question?

VIII   Do they oblige the United States to permit France in the case supposed to sell in their ports the prizes which she

Agreed

or her citizens may have made of [12] any Power at War with her, the Citizens or subjects of such Power; or exempt from the payment of the usual duties, on ships and merchandize, the prizes so made, in the case of their being to be sold within the Ports of the UStates?

IX   Do those Treaties particularly the Consular[13] Convention[14] authorize France *as of right* to erect Courts

Agreed

within the Jurisdiction of the UStates for the trial and condemnation of Prizes made by armed vessels in her service?

Agreed

X   Do the laws and usages of Nations authorize her as of right to erect such Courts for such purpose?

XI   Do the laws of neutrality considered relatively to the

Agreed

Treaties of the UStates with Foreign Powers or Independently of those Treaties permit the UStates, in the case supposed, to allow to France or her citizens,[15] the privilege of fitting out *originally* in and from the Ports of the UStates[16] vessels armed and Commissioned for War[17] either on account of the Government or of private persons or both?

XII   Do those laws permit the UStates to extend the like privilege to a Power at War with France?

XII   Do the laws of Neutrality considered as aforesaid

Agreed

permit the UStates in the case supposed to allow to France or her Citizens the privilege of refitting or arming anew vessels which before their coming within the UStates were armed and commissioned for war. May such privilege include an *augmentation* of the force of such vessels?[18]

XIII   Do those laws permit the UStates to extend the like privilege to a Power at War with France?

XIV   Do those laws, in the case supposed, permit Mer-

Agreed
XIV

chant vessels of either of the powers at War to arm in the Ports of the UStates, without being commissioned? May this privilege be rightfully[19] refused?

XV   Does it make any difference in point of principle, whether a vessel be armed for War or the force of an armed

Agreed the
XV

vessel be augmented in the ports of the UStates, with *means* procured in the UStates or with *means* brought into them, by the party[20] who shall so arm or augment the force of such Vessel? If the first be unlawful is the last lawful?[21]

Agreed.
XVI

XVI   Do the laws of neutrality considered as aforesaid authorise the U States to permit to France her subjects or Citizens the sale within their Ports[22] of Prizes made of the subjects or property of a power at War with France before they have been carried into some Port[23] of France and there condemned,[24] refusing the like privilege to her enemy?

Agreed

XVII Do those Laws authorise the UStates to permit to France the erection of Courts within their territory and jurisdiction for the trial and condemnation of Prizes; refusing that privilege to a Power at War with France?

Agreed

XVIII If any armed vessel of a foreign[25] power at War with another, with whom the UStates are at Peace, shall make prize of the subjects or property of its enemy within the territory or jurisdiction of the UStates—have not the UStates a right to cause restitution of such prize? Are they bound or not by the principles of neutrality so to do, if such prize shall be within their power?

Agreed

XIX   To what distance, by the laws and[26] usages of Nations, may the UStates exercise the right of prohibiting the hostilities of foreign Powers at War with each other[27]— within rivers, bays and arms of the sea,[28] and upon the sea along the Coasts of the UStates?

Agreed

XX   Have Vessels armed for War under commission from a foreign Power[29] a right, without the consent of the UStates, to engage within their jurisdiction seamen or soldiers for the service of[30] such vessels being[31] Citizens of that Power or of another foreign Power[32]—or Citizens of the UStates?

XXI   Is it lawful for the Citizens of such Power or citizens of the States so to engage being within the jurisdiction of the UStates?

Dft (DLC: Washington Papers); undated and heavily emended text entirely in Hamilton's hand prepared for Cabinet meeting of 18 July 1793, only the most significant revisions being recorded below; two questions added in the margin and remainder renumbered (see note 21 below), with numbering error at question XII resulting in total of 22 questions; marginal notations of assent and a few minor revisions added at Cabinet meeting; bracketed passages torn away supplied from Document iv below. Enclosed in Document v below.

The TREATIES BETWEEN THE UNITED STATES AND FRANCE were the treaties of alliance and commerce of 1778 and the consular convention of 1788 (Miller, *Treaties*, ii, 3-47, 228-44). The XXII ARTICLE OF THE TREATY OF COMMERCE provided that privateers of nations at war with France or the United States could not be fitted out in the ports of the other or sell their prizes there, and could purchase only enough supplies to get to the nearest port of their own country (same, 19-20).

[1] Hamilton here canceled "of alliance and of Amity and Commerce."

[2] Hamilton here canceled "both or either of them."

[3] Preceding three words interlined, with last word substituted for "subjects or."

[4] Preceding eight words interlined in place of "to equip armed vessels in the."

[5] Preceding four words interlined in place of "armed vessels, either on account of the Government or of private persons or both [. . .]."

[6] Word interlined in place of "⟨they⟩ those Treaties or either of them." Hamilton made similar substitutions in questions III-IV and VI-VIII; see also notes 8 and 13 below.

[7] Hamilton first wrote "France, her Citizens or subjects," before altering the phrase to read as above. He made similar substitutions in questions VIII, XI, and in the second question XII.

[8] Hamilton initially began this question with "Do the Treaties or either of them prohibit."

[9] Preceding four words interlined. Hamilton made similar insertions in questions VI and XI.

[10] Hamilton here canceled "one of the contracting parties, the other being at Peace with such Power."

[11] Preceding nine words added in the margin.

[12] Hamilton here canceled "her enemies."

[13] Preceding five words interlined in place of "those Treaties or either of them ⟨either⟩ or the Laws."

[14] Hamilton here canceled "made with France   or the laws and."

[15] Preceding three words interlined in place of "the privilege in the case supposed."

[16] Preceding eight words interlined.

[17] Hamilton here canceled "or armed and not commissioned for war &ca."

[18] Hamilton here canceled "What is to be un."

[19] Word interlined.

[20] Hamilton first wrote "with the means of the UStates or with the means of the [. . .] party" before altering the phrase to read as above.

[21] Hamilton added this and the preceding question in the left margin, positioning question XIV below question XV, and then renumbered the remaining questions. He subsequently recorded Cabinet assent to the right of them.

[22] Preceding three words interlined.

[23] Word interlined in place of "Court."

[24] Preceding thirteen words interlined.

[25] Preceding five words interlined.

[26] Hamilton here canceled "jurisdiction."

[27] Preceding fifteen words interlined in place of "claim jurisdiction."

[28] Hamilton originally wrote "rivers, within bays and such arms of the sea, as make flow between" before altering the phrase to read as above.

[29] Preceding six words interlined in place of "and commissioned."

[30] Preceding ten words interlined in place of "seamen for manning."

[31] Word interlined in place of "within the U States whether ⟨the?⟩."

[32] Hamilton first wrote "Citizens of the Power to which they belong" before altering the phrase to read as above.

II. Thomas Jefferson's Questions for the Supreme Court

[ca. 18 July 1793]

√ 1. ⟨*Are we free, by the treaty, to prohibit France from arming vessels within our ports to cruize on her enemies?*⟩

2. If we are free to prohibit her, are we, by the laws of neutrality, bound to prohibit her?

agreed.   3. What are the articles, by name, to be prohibited to both
              or either party?

            4. May[1] the prohibition extend to the use of *their own means*
              e.g. mounting their own guns, transferring guns from
              one of their own vessels to another &c.

            5. May they receive[2] on board their armed vessels their own
              sailors and citizens found within our ports?
              May they receive other foreigners?

agreed   6. To what extent does the *reparation*, permitted in the
                    [3] article, go?

agreed   7. What may be done as to[4] vessels armed in our ports be-
              fore the President's proclamation?[5] and what as to the
              prizes they made before and after?

            8. A trading vessel belonging to the enemies of France,
              coming here for the purposes of commerce, but armed,
              and having a letter of marque authorising her to cruize
              &c. as usual, are we obliged by the   article to order
              such a vessel out of our ports?

            9. What landlocked waters, and what extent from the sea-
              shore, may be deemed within the limits of our protection
              so as to render captures within them unlawful?

agreed.   10 May we within our own ports[6] sell ships to both parties
              prepared merely for merchandize?   agreed   pierced for
              guns?[7]

agreed   11. May we carry either or both kinds to the ports of the bel-
              ligerent powers for sale?

agreed   12. Is the principle that free bottoms make free goods, and
              enemy bottoms make enemy goods, to be considered as
              now an established part of the law of nations?

agreed   13 If it is not, are nations with whom we have no treaties
              authorized by the law of nations to take out of our vessels
              enemy passengers, not being soldiers, and their bag-
              gage?[8]

            14. Which of the above prohibitable things are within the
              competence of the President to prohibit?

Dft (DLC: TJ Papers, 96: 16463); un-   18 July 1793; entirely in TJ's hand, with
dated, but prepared for Cabinet meeting of   canceled   question   restored;   numbering

added after addition of two questions in margin (see note 8 below); marginal notations of assent added at Cabinet meeting; endorsed by TJ: "Questions."

BY THE TREATY: a reference to Article 22 of the 1778 treaty of commerce with France (see note to Document I above). REPARATION: Article 19 of the treaty of commerce provided that French or American warships or merchant vessels forced into the other nation's ports by weather or enemies must "be permitted to refresh and provide themselves at reasonable Rates with victuals and all things needful for the sustenence of their Persons or reparation of their Ships and conveniency of their Voyage" (Miller, *Treaties*, II, 17-18). The PRESIDENT'S PROCLAMATION was the 22 Apr. 1793 Proclamation of Neutrality (Fitzpatrick, *Writings*, XXXII, 430-1). Article 17 of the treaty of commerce denied shelter or refuge in American ports to foreign warships or privateers which captured French vessels, citizens, or property and required that all proper means be vigorously used to send OUT OF OUR PORTS as soon as possible those that had been forced to enter under defined emergency conditions (Miller, *Treaties*, II, 16-17).

[1] Word interlined in place of "Should."
[2] Word interlined in place of "take."
[3] TJ completed the blank in question 23 of Document IV below.
[4] TJ here canceled "priva."
[5] Preceding two words interlined in place of "prohibition."
[6] Preceding four words interlined.
[7] Preceding three words substituted for "for war [but?]."
[8] TJ wrote this and the preceding question in the margin before numbering the questions.

III. Henry Knox's Questions for the Supreme Court

[ca. 18 July 1793]

First What distance on the sea Coast may be established, consistently with the usage and laws of nations as *the limits of the protection of the* UStates. May all rivers and all[1] bays which are enclosed such as New York[2] the Delaware Chesapeak, and the sounds of North Carolina and Long Island,[3] be considered as within such protection? A cannon shot may be projected about 4 Miles.

second Do the treaties with france authorize the creating[4] fitting out in our ports, commissioning, and manning Vessells of War, by that power to cruise against the Vessells of any of the other belligerent powers, which are at peace with the US.

3d Is such a practice if not stipulated by treaty consistent with the duty of a neutral Nation provided the Vessell, cannon Arms, and all other means of Equipment workmen included belong *entirely* to the republic or to[5] Citizens of france?

4th Is such a practice to be tolerated in our ports provided the means and workmen are *partly* procured of our citizens, and partly, from the french.

5th May any of the Vessells of france which shall come into our ports armed be permitted to *augment* their military force of

[532]

Guns Men &c., either belonging to that Nation or to the US.?[6]

6th   May merchant Vessells belonging to any of the powers at War with france Arm themselves in our ports, provided such armament is intended merely for their own defence on their passage to the ports of their destination.

7   May armed[7] Vessells termed letters of Marque belonging to any powers at War with france come into our ports and be permitted to take a load of merchandize or otherwise to remain during their pleasure.

8.   May ships of War either public or private belonging to any of the powers at War with france be permitted to come into our ports and there remain during pleasure provided they do not bring any prizes with Them captured from france.

9.   May prizes taken by french Vessells and sent into our ports, be there sold, under any process of trial and condemnation of the Consuls of france.

10.   May any of our Citizens, enter on board the Vessells of any of the belligerent powers which may be in our ports with impunity?

11.   May foreign mariners[8] usually sailing from our ports, or who may be there, enter on board of the Armed Vessells of any of the belligerent parties, although such Mariners were formerly the subjects of the power on board of Whose Vessell they may enter.

12.[9]

Dft (DLC: Washington Papers); undated, but prepared for Cabinet meeting of 18 July 1793; entirely in Knox's hand; with question added in the margin (see note 6 below); endorsed by Tobias Lear: "Questions proposed to the Judges of the Supreme Court for their Opinion—18 July 1793." Tr (DLC: TJ Papers, 96: 16464); in a clerk's hand. PrC (same, 16465-6). Enclosed in Document v below.

[1] Preceding three words interlined.
[2] Preceding two words interlined.
[3] Preceding three words interlined.
[4] Word interlined.
[5] Preceding four words interlined.
[6] Knox added this question lengthwise in the margin and renumbered the next two questions.
[7] Word interlined in place of "letters of."
[8] Knox first wrote "foreigners" before altering it to read as above.
[9] Knox here canceled "May a foreign nat."

IV. Questions for the Supreme Court

[18 July 1793]

1. Do the treaties between the US. and France give to France or her citizens a *right*, when at war with a power with whom the US. are at peace, to fit out originally in and from the ports of the US, vessels armed for war, with or without commission?[1]

2. If they give such a *right*, does it extend to all manner of armed vessels, or to particular kinds only? If the latter, to what kinds does it extend?

3. Do they give to France, or her citizens, in the case supposed, a right to refit, or arm anew vessels, which before their coming within any port of the US. were armed for war, with or without commission?

4. If they give such a right, does it extend to all manner of armed vessels, or to particular kinds only? If the latter, to what kinds does it extend? Does it include an *augmentation* of force, or does it only extend to replacing the vessel in statu quo?

5. Does the 22d. article of the Treaty of commerce, in the case supposed, extend to vessels, armed for war on account of the *government* of a power at war with France, or to merchant armed vessels belonging to the subjects or citizens of that power (viz.) of the description of those which, by the English, are called Letters of marque Ships, by the French 'batiments armés en marchandize et en guerre'?

6. Do the treaties aforesaid prohibit the US. from permitting in the case supposed, the armed vessels belonging to a power at war with France, or to the citizens or subjects of such power to come within the ports of the US. there to remain as long as they may think fit, except in the case of their coming in with prizes made of the subjects or property of France?

7. Do they prohibit the US. from permitting in the case supposed vessels armed on account of the government of a power at war with France, or vessels armed for merchandize and war, with or without commission on account of the subjects or citizens of such power, or any vessels other than those commonly called privateers, to sell freely whatsoever they may bring into the ports of the US. and freely to purchase in and carry from the ports of the US. goods, merchandize and commodities, except as excepted in the last question?

8. Do they oblige the US. to permit France, in the case supposed, to sell in their ports the prizes which she or her citizens may have made of any power at war with her, the citizens or subjects of such power; or exempt from the payment of the usual duties, on ships and merchandize,

the prizes so made, in the case of their being to be sold within the ports of the US?

9. Do those treaties, particularly the Consular convention, authorize France, as of right, to erect courts within the jurisdiction of the US. for the trial and condemnation of prizes made by armed vessels in her service?

10. Do the laws and usages of nations authorize her, as of right, to erect such courts for such purpose?

11. Do the laws of Neutrality, considered relatively to the treaties of the US. with foreign powers, or independantly of those treaties permit the US. in the case supposed, to allow to France, or her citizens the privilege of fitting out *originally*, in and from the ports of the US. vessels armed and commissioned for war, either on account of the government, or of private persons, or both?

12. Do those laws permit the US. to extend the like privilege to a power at war with France?

13. Do the laws of Neutrality, considered as aforesaid, permit the US. in the case supposed, to allow to France or her citizens, the privilege of refitting, or arming anew, vessels which before their coming within the US. were armed and commissioned for war? May such privilege include an *augmentation* of the force of such vessels?[2]

14. Do those laws permit the US. to extend the like privilege to a power at war with France?

15. Do those laws, in the case supposed, permit merchant vessels of either of the powers at war, to arm in the ports of the US. without being commissioned? May this privilege be rightfully refused?

16. Does it make any difference in point of principle, whether a vessel be armed for war, or the force of an armed vessel be augmented, in the ports of the US. with *means* procured in the US. or with means brought into them by the party who shall so arm or augment the force of such vessel? If the first be unlawful, is the last lawful?

17. Do the laws of neutrality, considered as aforesaid, authorize the US. to permit to France, her subjects or citizens, the sale within their ports of prizes made of the subjects or property of a power at war with France, before they have been carried into some port of France and there condemned, refusing the like privilege to her enemy?

18. Do those laws authorize the US. to permit to France the erection of courts within their territory and jurisdiction, for the trial and condemnation of prizes, refusing that privilege to a power at war with France?

19. If any armed vessel of a foreign power at war with another, with whom the US. are at peace, shall make prize of the subjects or property of it's enemy within the territory or jurisdiction of the US. have not the

US. a right to cause restitution of such prize? Are they bound or not by the principles of neutrality so to do, if such prize shall be within their power?

20. To what distance, by the laws and usages of nations, may the US. exercise the right of prohibiting the hostilities of foreign powers at war with each other, within rivers, bays, and arms of the sea, and upon the sea along the coasts of the US?

21. Have vessels armed for war under commission from a foreign power, a right, without the consent of the US. to engage, within their jurisdiction, seamen or souldiers, for the service of such vessels, being citizens of that power, or of another foreign power, or citizens of the US?

22. What are the articles, by name, to be prohibited to both or either party?[3]

23. To what extent does the *reparation* permitted in the 19. Article of the treaty with France, go?[4]

24. What may be done as to vessels armed in our ports before the President's proclamation? and what as to the prizes they made *before* and *after*?

25. May we, within our own ports, sell ships to both parties, prepared merely for merchandize? May they be pierced for guns?

26. May we carry either or both kinds to the ports of the belligerent powers for sale?

27. Is the principle that free bottoms make free goods, and enemy bottoms make enemy goods, to be considered as now an established part of the law of nations?

28. If it is not, are nations with whom we have no treaties, authorized by the law of Nations to take out of our vessels enemy passengers, not being souldiers, and their baggage?

29. May an armed vessel belonging to any of the belligerent powers follow *immediately* merchant-vessels, enemies, departing from our ports, for the purpose of making prizes of them?—If not, how long ought the former to remain after the latter has sailed? And what shall be considered as the place of departure, from which the time is to be counted? And how are the facts to be ascertained?[5]

MS (DLC: Washington Papers); entirely in TJ's hand; undated, but prepared immediately following Cabinet meeting of 18 July 1793; with questions 1-21 by Alexander Hamilton taken from Document I above, questions 22-28 by TJ taken from Document II above, and final question added at the President's behest after PrC was made; endorsed by Tobias Lear: "Questions proposed to be submitted to the Chief Justice & Judges of the Sup. Court of U.S. July 1793." PrC (DLC: TJ Papers, 90: 15550-4); with three marginal notations (see notes 1, 3, and 5 below) and final question added by TJ in ink; at head of text by TJ in ink: "Questions to be proposd to the Judges." Tr (MHi: Knox Papers); in the hand of a State Department clerk; undated. PrC (DLC: TJ Papers, 61: 10619-22); at foot of text by TJ in ink: "the first 21. questions by A.H. 22. to 28. by Th:J. 29. [by the Presidt.?]." Tr (DLC: Washington Papers); in Lear's hand; undated, but endorsed by Lear in part: "July 1793." Tr (DLC: Hamilton Papers); in the hand of Daniel Brent; undated. Recorded in SJPL under 18 July: "Queries for [the judges]." Enclosed in Document v below; TJ to Washington, 31 July 1793; and TJ to James Madison, 3 Aug. 1793.

[1] In the margin of the PrC next to this question TJ added "A.H." in ink to indicate Hamilton's authorship of questions 1-21.

[2] Preceding sentence interlined.

[3] In the margin of the PrC next to this question TJ added "T.J." in ink to indicate his authorship of questions 22-28.

[4] Word written over "extend," erased.

[5] TJ added this question after the PrC was made. In the PrC he added the question in ink, writing "Presidt." in the margin to indicate Washington's responsibility for it.

V. Thomas Jefferson to George Washington

July 18. 1793.

Th: Jefferson has the honor to inclose to the President a copy of the questions to be proposed to the judges, which he has endeavored to make with exactness, but cannot be sure he may not have mistaken some of the interlineations of the original. He has added at the end those from his own paper which were agreed to. They are the numbers 22. &c. to the end.

He incloses also the rough draughts of Colo. Hamilton and Genl. Knox; the former may serve to correct any errors of copying which he may have committed.

RC (DNA: RG 59, MLR); addressed: "The Presiden[. . .]"; endorsed by Tobias Lear. Tr (Lb in same, SDC). Not recorded in SJL. Enclosures: Documents I, III, and IV, the last prior to the addition of the final question.

From George Washington

DEAR SIR   Philadelphia July 18th. 1793.

The Chief Justice and Judge Paterson are in Town. The former called upon me yesterday evening to know at what time he should receive my communications. I was embarrassed—but declared the truth, that by waiting for the Attorney General, the business which it was proposed to lay before them, was not fully prepared.

I shall expect to see you by Nine; and as the Judges will have to decide whether the business which, it is proposed to ask their opinion upon is, in their judgment, of such a nature as that they can comply, it might save time if you were to draft some thing (before you come) that will bring the question properly before them. I am always & sincerely Yours   Go: Washington

P.S. As the Attorney General is not present—quere, would a verbal communication, and explanation of the wishes of Government, made to them by you be better than by letter?

RC (DLC); endorsed by TJ as received 18 July 1793. Recorded in SJPL.

From John Clarke

Hon'ble Sir   Richmond July 19th 1793

    As I am uncertain whether or not you will require of me a power of attorney in Appointing Arbitrators, I have Sent one, with a blank for the name of the person you please to appoint. I rather suppose it will be unnecessary, for According to the latter part of the ninth section of the new Law, if the parties do not all unite in Chooseing three Arbitrators, The power rests with you to appoint three Arbitrators for the purpose And I sincerely hope you will appoint them. If the inclosed power of Attorney is unnecessary it may be destroyed. I am Honble Sir Your most Humble Servant   John Clarke

RC (DLC); at foot of text: "The Hon'ble Mr Jefferson"; endorsed by TJ as received 25 July 1793 but recorded in SJL as received a day later. Enclosure: Power of Attorney of John Clarke of Powhatan County, Virginia, 19 July 1793, authorizing the appointment of an arbitrator "to decide a matter of Controversy between my self and two Other Men Concerning the invention of An improvement in the art of building and Constructing of Mills by means of Valves or hinged buckets" (MS in DLC; in an unidentified hand, signed by Clarke and witnessed by William Pasteur, Lew Jones, and Robert Watkins).

Letters from Clarke to TJ of 14 Dec. 1793, received from Richmond on 23 Dec. 1793, and of 12 Mch. 1794, received 2 May 1794, as well as a letter from TJ to Clarke of 6 May 1795, are recorded in SJL but have not been found.

From J. P. P. Derieux

Charlottesville, 19 July 1793. He wrote on 25 May thanking TJ for the seeds and acknowledging his letter of 10 Mch. He fears that his letter may have miscarried and so repeats his request that TJ advise him of the progress of the sale and propose to Vaughan that his merchandise which is perishable or selling slowly be exchanged for coarse dry goods such as brown cloth which would easily be sold here or in Richmond, especially now when all kinds of merchandise have increased in price. If luxury items sell as well as other goods, as is common in large cities, Vaughan might not object to giving him an advantage that is not detrimental to himself. He is anxious to conclude this sale only because his creditors show their impatience daily. Neither he nor Gamble has learned more of his bill of exchange for 5,000 livres, which prompts him to ask TJ to forward the enclosed letter to Fenwick, as well as another to Madame Bellanger, about whom he is very worried because he has had no news since hers of 29 Dec. He has written her by various routes but supposes that they are less reliable than TJ's and that the letters did not reach her. He asks TJ to send an order for £7.17.0, deductible from the sale of his merchandise and payable in produce from Monticello, to Peter Mark, to whom he owes that amount. Mark asked him to obtain this favor, which would provide him with bread for his family. [*P.S.*] Since Madame Derieux has totally adopted the good method of making Virginia cloth for their family, he asks TJ to buy him a bale of good spinning cotton from the proceeds of his merchandise, if the shipping cost would not bring it above the selling price in Richmond.

RC (MHi); 4 p.; in French; at foot of first page: "Mr Jefferson"; endorsed by TJ as received 29 July 1793 and so recorded in SJL. Enclosures not found.

From George Hough

Concord, District of New Hampshire, 19 July 1793. He encloses a copy of *The Female Guide*, which he claims the right to as proprietor and has deposited in the clerk's office of this district, for deposit in the office of the Secretary of State, agreeably to act of Congress.

RC (DNA: RG 59, MLR); 1 p.; addressed: "Honble. Thomas Jefferson, Esquire, Secretary of State, Philadelphia"; endorsed by George Taylor, Jr., as received "with a Book" on 5 Aug. 1793. Enclosure: John Cosens Ogden, *The Female Guide: or, Thoughts on the Education of that Sex. Accommodated to The State of Society, Manners, and Government, in the United States* (Concord, 1793), which Hough printed.

George Hough (1757-1830), a native of Connecticut, was a printer and newspaper publisher in Windsor, Vermont, and subsequently in Concord, where he was also the postmaster, 1793-1802, and member of the state House of Representatives, 1815-16 (James O. Lyford, ed., *History of Concord, New Hampshire,* 2 vols. [Concord, 1903], II, 1017-19, 1357, 1362).

From John Parish

Hamburg, 19 July 1793. On 6 July he received TJ's 20 Feb. and 21 Mch. letters, the first with his consular commission from the President. Four days later he presented his credentials to the presiding Burgomaster, who that day submitted them to the Senate, which received them favorably. He encloses translations of the usual form of acceptance they instructed their secretary to draft and the covering letter from the Syndic. He will observe the laws of the United States TJ sent him and encloses his consular bond with two respectable securities duly executed. The European war still rages. France is attacked in every quarter and her troops fight obstinately. Condé has reportedly fallen and it is doubtful that Valenciennes and Mainz can hold out much longer, but the allies will not penetrate far into France because of their financial exhaustion. Complete anarchy reigns there under the current rulers, the livre is reduced to

2d., and without a favorable turn assignats "will be without a Course." The general opinion seems to be that the war cannot last much longer, but meanwhile it offers ample employment to American ships, who are engaged as soon as they arrive and can get almost any freight their captains ask. He has ordered them not to load any contraband in order to ensure the neutral rights they now enjoy and has imposed mandatory inspection of the registers of captains entering here under American colors as the only method to detect foreign usurpation of the flag. Although the French took a number of Hamburg ships with valuable cargoes after the city, acting on the order of the Diet of Ratisbon, reluctantly requested the departure of the French minister Le Hoc, they allow them to pass unmolested for the present. The shipment of all kinds of grain to France is forbidden here, and the English bring up any vessel they find, friend or foe, carrying any sort of grain or provisions to France. Captain Caleb Earl, master of the *Brothers* of Philadelphia, was captured on 23 Mch. while carrying wheat to Brest and brought to Portsmouth, where he was detained until 9 June. His cargo was unloaded and his ship was returned here in ballast without payment of freight or demurrage. Johnson, the consul in London, will presumably obtain satisfaction for this. He encloses a report of all American ships entering this port between January and the end of June. Although he could not obtain information on vessels which arrived and cleared prior to the receipt of his appointment, the ship registers now being produced will enable him to send more complete reports every six months.

RC (DNA: RG 59, CD); 4 p.; in a clerk's hand, signed by Parish; at foot of text: "To The Right Honorable The Secretary of State for the United States of America at Philadelphia"; endorsed by TJ as received 24 Oct. 1793 and so recorded in SJL. Enclosures: (1) Warrant of the Burgomasters and Senate of Hamburg, 12 July 1793, recognizing Parish's consular commission and noting Parish's declaration that notwithstanding this capacity he would remain a citizen of Hamburg. (2) Sieveking, Syndic of Hamburg, to Parish, 13 July 1793, returning Parish's consular commission, transmitting No. 1, and expressing his wishes for good relations and expanded trade with the United States (Trs in same; at head of each text: "Translation of the German Original"). Other enclosures not found, but see note below.

On 23 July 1793 Parish wrote a brief note to TJ enclosing duplicates of the above letter and its enclosures, the originals of which were "to go by the August Packet from Falmouth" (RC in DNA: RG 59, CD; in a clerk's hand, signed by Parish; addressed: "The Right Honorable The Secretary of State for the United States of America at Philadelphia"; endorsed by TJ as received 19 Nov. 1793 and so recorded in SJL). With this letter came a copy of his consular bond, dated 20 July 1793 and bearing the names of John Gabe and Claus Hy. Sonntag as his securities (Tr in same; at head of text: "Copy").

From Thomas Mann Randolph, Jr.

DEAR SIR   Richmond July 19: 1793.

I have just been with Mr. Browns Clerks to make enquiry concerning the package of the Servants Cloaths which you sent last fall. He is not in town himself: from them I can learn nothing more than I have hitherto received. They do not remember that it came to them. Your furniture &c. is safely deposited in a lumber-house at Rockets. Mr.

Browns Clerks inform me that you have ordered a part of it to be left there till your arrival in Virginia and they do not know the particular articles. The waggons I think, from my experience, are not to be trusted with any thing of value. The boats are more certain and as expeditious. Patsy and the little ones were perfectly well on the 14th. I have been laboring under a severe dystentery myself some days, but find it better from the journey. Your most sincere & affectionate friend.

TH: M. RANDOLPH

RC (MHi); endorsed by TJ as received 26 July 1793 and so recorded in SJL.

To George Washington

July 19. 93.

Th: Jefferson with his respects to the President has the honor to inform him that Judges Jay and Wilson called on him just now and asked whether the letter of yesterday pressed for an answer. They were told the cases would await their time, and were asked when they thought an answer might be expected: they said they supposed in a day or two.

RC (DNA: RG 59, MLR); addressed: "The President of the US."; endorsed by Tobias Lear. Tr (Lb in same, SDC). Not recorded in SJL.

From David Humphreys

SIR   Lisbon July 20th. 1793.

Since my last, which was dated the first of July, I have had the honour to receive yours of the 26th. of April, covering the Presidents Proclamation of the 22nd. of the same Month, and other communications on the subject of it. Hitherto hostilities have not taken place between this Country and France. Should they commence (which is not very improbable) I shall take care to comply with your Instructions.

I mentioned in a Postscript to my last, that the Portuguese fleet had sailed for England. I have now to advise you, that six Regiments of Infantry and some Companies of Grenadiers are under orders to embark for Spain (probably for Bilboa) under the command of General Forbes, a Scotch officer in this service with whom I am particularly acquainted. This last arrangement was made, unexpectedly to the Public, upon the arrival of a Courier from Madrid a few days since; and, as some intelligent officers surmise, in consequence of a check the Spaniards have received on their frontiers. But for the authenticity of this I am not able to answer.

[541]

My last letter, which was forwarded by a vessel to Virginia, contained my accounts with the Public for the year past.

Mr. Church arrived here with his family from Bourdeaux about ten days ago. He brings no news, except that great confusions and insurrections exist in the Departments. Santerre, who was sent with the national Guards from Paris to quell the Insurrection, had been totally defeated. In the part of the Country from which Mr. Church could receive genuine intelligence, Marat and the predominant faction were generally execrated. Notwithstanding all these tumults and threatening circumstances, every article of Provisions was plenty and cheap; and the armies on the frontiers fought invincibly. It is a phænomenon in political as in natural history, that, while the heart is mortally sick, the members should be more vigorous than usual.

In order to leave no possible precaution omitted which might tend to prevent the flag of the U.S. from being insulted, and the property of their Citizens from being violated by any of the belligerent Powers, Mr. Church and I have thought proper that all vessels of the U.S. sailing from Portugal should be furnished with Passports, in the English, French, and Dutch languages, signed by me, and countersigned by him. I have the honour to transmit the form we have made use of. It will be difficult to calculate the vast advantages which must result to the U.S. from their neutrality; and especially, if neutral bottoms can be made to protect all property which is not usually considered as Counterband.

A short time since, I received from the Island of St. Michael's the original Protest of the Captain of a vessel belonging to the U.S. against the Captain of a French national Frigate, of which the enclosed is a copy. The original I sent (under a flying seal) to Mr. Pinckney in London, that he might forward it to our Minister in France, whenever occasion should occur, in order that the said Minister should make such use of it as should be deemed expedient for obtaining immediate reparation for the outrages committed on a Citizen of the U.S. by the Captn. of a French national Frigate, on the high Seas. With sentiments of perfect respect & esteem I have the honour to be, Sir, Your most obedt & most hble Servt   D. HUMPHREYS

P.S. Although three Packets have arrived from England since my last, I have no news of Captn. Cutting. The 29th. of last month Valenciennes and Condè were not taken. Lord Hood sailed from Gibralter the 27th. ulto.

RC (DNA: RG 59, DD); at head of text: "(No. 76.)"; at foot of text: "The Secretary of State &c. &c. &c."; endorsed by TJ as received 9 Sep. 1793 and so recorded in SJL.

Tr (Lb in same). Enclosure: Deposition of Thomas Hickling, 28 May 1793 (Tr in same, in a clerk's hand, with 20 July 1793 attestation by Humphreys; Tr in Lb in same). For a summary and other texts of the enclosure, see note to Thomas Pinckney to TJ, 8 July 1793. Other enclosure not found.

From the Justices of the Supreme Court

SIR   Philadelphia 20 July 1793

The enclosed Letter from us to the President being on the Subject of the one which by his Direction you did us the Honor to write on the 18th. Instant; we think it most proper and regular that it should pass to him thro' your Hands; and for that purpose commit it to your Care. We have the Honor to be Sir your most obt. & hble Servts.

JOHN JAY
JAMES WILSON
JA. IREDELL
WM. PATERSON

RC (DNA: RG 59, MLR); in Jay's hand, signed by Jay, Wilson, Iredell, and Paterson; at foot of text: "The Honb. Ths. Jefferson Esqr Secy. of State"; endorsed by TJ as received 20 July 1793 and so recorded in SJL. Dft (NNC: Jay Papers); written entirely in Jay's hand on other side of sheet bearing Dft of enclosure.

ENCLOSURE

The Justices of the Supreme Court to George Washington

SIR   Philadelphia 20 July 1793

We have taken into Consideration the Letter written to us by your Direction,[1] on the 18th. Instant, by the Secretary of State.

The Question "whether the public may with propriety be availed of the advice of the Judges, on the Questions alluded to?" appears to us to be of much[2] Difficulty as well as Importance—as it affects the judicial Department, we feel a Reluctance to decide it, without the Advice and participation of our absent Brethren.[3]

The occasion which induced our being convened, is doubtless urgent: of the *Degree* of that Urgency we cannot judge, and consequently cannot propose that the answer to this Question be postponed, untill the Sitting of the Sup. Court.

We are not only disposed but desirous to promote[4] the welfare of our Country, in every way that may consist with our official Duties. We are pleased Sir! with every opportunity of manifesting our Respect for you, and are[5] sollicitous to do whatever may be in our power[6] to render your administration as easy and agreable to yourself as it is to our Country.

If Circumstances should forbid further Delay, we[7] will immediately[8] resume the Consideration of the Question, and decide it. We have the Honor to be with perfect Respect Sir your most obedient & most h'ble Servants

JOHN JAY
JAMES WILSON
JA. IREDELL
WM. PATERSON

RC (DNA: RG 59, MLR); in Jay's hand, signed by Jay, Wilson, Iredell, and Paterson; at foot of text: "The President of the United States"; endorsed by Tobias Lear. Dft (NNC: Jay Papers); written entirely in Jay's hand on other side of sheet containing Dft of covering letter; only the most important emendations are noted below. Enclosed in Washington to TJ, 20 July 1793.

[1] Preceding three words interlined in Dft.

[2] In Dft Jay here canceled "Magnitu."

[3] Here in Dft Jay canceled a new line starting the next paragraph: "We are persuaded that from our being convened."

[4] Preceding two words interlined in Dft in place of "being instrumental to."

[5] Word added in Dft in place of "we personally regret every ⟨Restrict⟩ obstacle which may restrain us from."

[6] Preceding three words interlined in Dft in place of "proper."

[7] In Dft Jay here canceled "wish to receive some of the Questions."

[8] Word interlined in Dft.

From George Washington

Philadelphia, July 20th: 1793

The President sends to the Secy. of State a letter from the Chief Justice and the Judges of the Supreme Court on the subject which has been laid before them—and requests, that if the Secretary should be of opinion that an answer ought to be given to this letter, he will prepare one agreeably to what was suggested yesterday.

RC (DLC); in Tobias Lear's hand; endorsed by TJ as received 22 July 1793. Recorded in SJPL. Enclosure: enclosure to Justices of the Supreme Court to TJ, 20 July 1793.

From Francis Eppes

DR SIR   Eppington July 21st. 1793

I am sorry its not yet in my power to remit any part of your proportion of the Debt due from A. Cary's Estate tho' flater myself it will not be long before it will be in my power to do something for you as Mr. Page gives me very flatering promises. You may assure your self the moment the money gets into my hands it shall be remited. Your note inclosing Polly's letter to her Aunt came to hand a few days ago, this serves as a cover to the answer. I am with every wish for the health of you both Dr Sir Your Friend   FRANS. EPPES

RC (ViU: Edgehill-Randolph Papers); endorsed by TJ as received 30 July 1793 and so recorded in SJL. Enclosure not found.

TJ's NOTE INCLOSING POLLY'S LETTER is not recorded in SJL and has not been found. A missing letter from Eppes to TJ of 27 June 1793 is recorded in SJL as received from Eppington on 5 July 1793.

To James Madison

July 21. 93.

I wrote you on the 14th. since which I have no letter from you. It appears that two considerable engagements took place between France and the combined armies on the 1st. and 8th. of May. In the former the French have had rather the worst of it, as may be concluded by their loss of cannon and loss of ground. In the latter they have had rather the best: as is proved by their remaining on the ground, and their throwing relief into Condé which had been the object of both battles. The French attacked in both. They have sent commissioners to England to sound for peace. Genl. Felix Wimpfen is one. There is a strong belief that the bankruptcies and demolition of manufactures through the three kingdoms will induce the English to accede to peace.—E. R. is returned. The affair of the loan has been kept suspended, and is now submitted to him. He brings very flattering information of the loyalty of the people of Virginia to the general government, and thinks the whole indisposition there is directed against the Secretary of the Treasury *personally*, not against his measures. On the whole he has quieted uneasiness here.—I have never been able to get a sight of Billy till yesterday. He has promised to bring me the bill of your ploughs which shall be paid. Adieu. Your's affectionately.

RC (DLC: Madison Papers); unsigned. PrC (DLC).

Note on Edmond Charles Genet and Alexander Hamilton

July 21. 93. At Dr. Logan's to-day Genet told us that Colo. Hamilton had never in a single instance addressed a letter to him as the Minister of *the republic of France*, but always as the minister of France.

MS (DLC); entirely in TJ's hand; written with "Anas" entry for 15 July 1793 on verso of sheet containing "Anas" entry for 13 July 1793. Included in the "Anas."

To Martha Jefferson Randolph

Th:J. TO HIS DEAR DAUGHTER   Philadelphia July 21. 1793.

We had peaches and Indian corn the 12th. instant. When do they begin with you this year?—Can you lay up a good stock of seed-peas for the ensuing summer? We will try this winter to cover our garden with a heavy coat of manure. When earth is rich it bids defiance to droughts, yeilds in abundance and of the best quality. I suspect that the insects which have harassed you have been encouraged by the feebleness of your plants, and that has been produced by the lean state of the soil.— We will attack them another year with joint efforts.—We learn that France has sent commissioners to England to treat of peace, and imagine it cannot be unacceptable to the latter, in the present state of general bankruptcy and demolition of their manufactures. Upon the whole the affairs of France, notwithstanding their difficulties external and internal, appear solid and safe. Present me to all my neighbors; kiss the little ones for me, and my warmest affections to yourself and Mr. Randolph.

RC (NNP). PrC (MHi). Tr (ViU: Edgehill-Randolph Papers); 19th-century copy.

To John Vaughan

July 21. 93.

Th: Jefferson presents his compliments to Mr. Vaughan, and finding that the Pragers do not draw at present, he must endeavor to procure any other good bills on London or Amsterdam to a smaller amount for the present moment. If Mr. Vaughan can recommend him any (say to amount of 5000.D.) the drawers having property here to secure us, and not dealing in paper,[1] he will oblige Th:J.

Can Mr. Vaughan close the business of Mr. Derieux?

RC (PPAmP); addressed: "Mr. Vaughan"; endorsed by Vaughan as received 22 July 1793; with unrelated notes of later date. Not recorded in SJL.

[1] Preceding six words interlined.

From Benjamin Bourne

SIR   Providence 22d. July 1793

I do myself the honor to forward herewith inclosed some information relative to the commerce between the United States and Denmark. Capt. Pearce, who furnishes it has commanded a Vessel several

Voyages in that Trade and is in great repute for his veracity and Intelligence. In the hope that this information may conduce to place our commerce with Denmark on a more favorable footing I remain very respectfully your obedt. Servt.   B. BOURN

RC (DLC); at foot of text: "Thos. Jefferson Esqr."; endorsed by TJ as received 29 July 1793 and so recorded in SJL.

Benjamin Bourne (1755-1808), a Harvard graduate, Revolutionary War veteran, and state legislator, represented Rhode Island in the House of Representatives from 1790 to 1796, and served as a United States District Court judge in that state from 1796 to February 1801, when he accepted an appointment from John Adams as a judge of the new First Circuit Court (DAB; *Biog. Dir. Cong.*; JEP, I, 217, 381, 383).

Bourne probably enclosed Benjamin Peirce's 6 July 1793 letter to TJ, judging from the fact that TJ received both letters on the same day. He may also have enclosed another document in which Peirce listed colonial Danish import, tonnage, and anchorage duties and port charges (all of which were paid equally by Danish subjects and American citizens and none of which were levied on imports from Denmark), identified contraband items, and noted that "All goods paying 5 ⅌Ct. duty is intitled to a *permission* for Exporting Sugars: the Value of which is equall to the Duty" (MS in DLC: TJ Papers, 236: 42319; in Peirce's hand; undated, but with the reference to contraband suggesting a date of composition after February 1793).

Two other documents pertaining to American trade with Denmark were evidently enclosed in a 10 Dec. 1793 letter from South Carolina Representative William L. Smith, recorded in SJL as received that date but not found. The first was an 11 July 1793 letter to Smith from Nathaniel Russell, a Charleston merchant, reminding him of their conversation about a commercial treaty with Denmark, enclosing a letter he had received from John J. Clark pointing out the advantages of such an agreement to the United States, and urging Smith to use his influence to bring one about (RC in DLC; addressed: "The Honble. William Smith Esqr."). The second was Clark's letter to Russell, written at Wilmington, North Carolina, on 20 Mch. 1793, stating that a commercial treaty with Denmark was especially necessary for the southern states because without it rice and tobacco were subject to the "duty of Aliens, which is one third more than Nations pay that are in treaty with them"; that in practice Americans paid 50 percent more in duties on a hogshead of tobacco and a cask of rice than citizens of nations having commercial treaties with Denmark; that in 1792 1,000 hogsheads of tobacco and 4,800 casks of rice were sold in Copenhagen, all imported on American ships; that members of the Danish court and merchants in Copenhagen believe that Congress should take the initiative in making a treaty with the Danish court, it being older than Congress and the Danish king having expressed his support for such an agreement; and that Smith should press for action at the next meeting of Congress or apply immediately to the President or the Secretary of State so that during recess orders might be given to the American minister in London to negotiate a treaty with the Danish ambassador there (RC in DLC; addressed: "Nathaniel Russell Esqr Merchant Charleston").

Memorial from George Hammond

The undersigned, his Britannick Majesty's Minister plenipotentiary to the United States, has the honor of representing to the Secretary of state, that he has received authentic information, that the brig (formerly the little Sarah, captured by the French frigate Ambuscade and now named) the Democrat has left this port, and was seen on the morning of Friday last, the 19th. curt., in the act of chasing and bringing to a large ship, at the distance of about seven leagues to the southward of the Capes of Delaware.

The undersigned will content himself for the present, with merely asserting his knowledge, of this fact, and likewise of the circumstance of this vessel having been fitted out, armed, commissioned and manned, (with a crew as it is said amounting to about one hundred and twenty in number) in the port of Philadelphia; for the purpose of committing depredations on the property of the subjects, of the King his master, and of the other powers, now engaged in war with the present rulers of France.

In addition to this statement, the undersigned esteems it his duty to express his conviction, that these measures have been pursued not only without the approbation, but even without the privity, of the federal executive government. In fact he could not reconcile a contrary course of conduct on its part, with the assurances which the Secretary of state was pleased to make to him in his communication of the 15th. of May— "that the practice of commissioning, equipping and manning vessels in the ports of the United States, to cruize on any of the belligerent parties, was entirely disapproved, and that the government would take effectual measures to prevent a repetition of it"—or with the declaration contained in the Secretary of State's letter to him of the 12th. of this month that "the President expected" that several vessels specified, of which the little Sarah or Democrat was the first mentioned, "should not be allowed to depart until his ultimate determination" respecting them "should be made known."

Philadelphia 22 July 1793   GEO. HAMMOND

RC (DNA: RG 59, NL); in a clerk's hand, signed by Hammond; at foot of first page: "Mr Jefferson"; endorsed by TJ as received 22 July 1793 and so recorded in SJL. FC (Lb in PRO: FO 116/3). Tr (same, 5/1). Tr (Lb in DNA: RG 59, NL).

From James Madison

DEAR SIR   July 22.[1] 1793

My last was on the 18th. and acknowledged yours of the 30th. ult: and 7th. inst: I had not then time to mention that W.N.[2] passed an evening with me on his way home from his brother's where he had met E.R.[3] on his return to Pha. From his conversation, his sentiments are right and firm on the French Revoln. and in other respects I discovered no symptoms of heresy. He spoke particularly and emphatically of the unquestionable unanimity of the Country in favor of the cause of F. I have no doubt that he held this language to every one, and consequently that the impressions depending on him have been rightly made. I could not but infer from all that he said with regard to E. R. that he considered the sentiments of him on French affairs as similar to his own, and to such as were expressed by myself. Some allowance however in all such conversations must be made for the politeness or policy of respecting the known sentiments of the party to which they are addressed or communicated. He had seen the first part of H's publication and spoke of it as from that quarter. He expressed some surprise at the doctrines and cabinet efforts of the Author as he had learnt them from E.R. and seemed unable to account for some things without suspecting H. of a secret design to commit and sacrifice the Pt. His ideas on this subject must have grown out of the language of E. R. if not actually copied from it. I have read over with some attention the *printed* papers you inclosed, and have made notes towards a discussion of the subject. I find myself however under some difficulties first from my not knowing how far concessions have been made on particular points behind the Curtain, 2dly. from my not knowing how far the P. considers himself as actually committed with respect to some doctrines, 3dly. from the want of some lights from the Law of Nations as applicable to the construction of the Treaty, 4th. from my ignorance of some material facts—such as whether any call was made by G.B. or any other Belligerent power for the intentions of the U.S. prior to the Proclamation—whether F. was heard on the subject of her constructions and pretensions under the Treaty—whether the Ex. had before them any authentic documents or entered into any discussions, on the question whether the war between F. and G.B. is offensive or defensive &c: I do not mean that all such information ought to be brought into the controversy, tho' some of it is necessary and some more might be used to advantage. But all or most of it seems proper in order to avoid vulnerable assertions or suppositions which might give occasion to triumphant replies. If an answer to the publication be undertaken, it ought to be both a solid, and a prudent one. None but intelligent readers will enter into such a controversy, and to their minds it ought principally to be accomodated. If you can lay your hands on the Explanatory publication of the real object of the Proclamation referred to in your last, or the preceding one, send it to me. The one I had is no longer in my hands. I expect to day to receive your letter next in date to the 7th.

RC (DLC: Madison Papers); unsigned; endorsed by TJ as received 1 Aug. 1793 and so recorded in SJL.

TJ's letter OF THE 30TH. ULT: the postscript to TJ's letter of 29 June 1793. H's PUBLICATION: the first "Pacificus" essay

by Alexander Hamilton (see note to TJ to Madison, 29 June 1793).

[1] Date reworked from "18."

[2] At a later date Madison here interlined "W. C. Nicholas."

[3] At a later date Madison here interlined "Ed: Randolph."

To George Washington

July 22. 93.

Th: Jefferson with his respects to the President has the honor of inclosing him some letters just received also the draught of a letter to the Judges.

RC (DNA: RG 59, MLR); endorsed by Tobias Lear. Tr (Lb in same, SDC). Not recorded in SJL. Enclosures: (1) William Carmichael and William Short to TJ, 18 Apr., 5 May 1793. (2) David Humphreys to TJ, 29 May 1793. (3) Washington to the Justices of the Supreme Court, [22 July 1793].

This letter and its enclosures reached the President on 23 July 1793 (Washington, *Journal*, 205-6).

George Washington to the Justices of the Supreme Court

GENTLEMEN   [22 July 1793][1]

The circumstances which had induced me to ask your counsel on certain legal questions interesting to the public, exist now as they did then: but I by no means press a decision whereon you wish the advice and participation of your absent brethren. Whenever therefore their presence shall enable you to give it with more satisfaction to yourselves, I shall accept it with pleasure.[2]

Dft (DNA: RG 59, MLR); undated; in TJ's hand, with date, complimentary close, and names of addressees added by Tobias Lear as noted below; at foot of text in Lear's hand: "John Jay Chief Justice James Wilson James Iredell William Paterson Associate Judges of the Sup. Court of the U.S."; endorsed by Lear. PrC (DLC); entirely in TJ's hand, with date added in ink as noted below. Recorded in SJPL under 22 July 1793. Enclosed in TJ to Washington, 22 July 1793. For the letter as sent by

Washington under the date of 23 July 1793, which varies only in punctuation from the emended Dft, see Fitzpatrick, *Writings*, XXXIII, 28.

[1] At head of text Lear added "Philada. July 23d: 1793." At foot of text in PrC TJ added "July 22. 93." in ink.
[2] Lear here added "With sentiments of high respect I am Gentlemen Your most Ob. St."

From George Washington

United States 22d. July 1793.

The President of the U. States requests the attendance of the Secretary of State at his House tomorrow morning at *Nine* o'Clock.

RC (DLC); in the hand of Bartholomew Dandridge, Jr.; endorsed by TJ as received 22 July 1793. Recorded in SJPL.

From Tench Coxe

July 23d. 1793

Mr. Coxe has the honor to inform Mr. Jefferson that Mr. John Wilcocks of this city has a few hundred pounds Stg. to sell, in bills on London, at 175 PCt: or five PCt. premium. His Bills are considered as very safe. No other Person is drawing, except Mr. Nicholson, that Mr. Coxe has heard of. Mr. J. has been already informed of Mr. N's bills.

Mr. Coxe has the honor to send Mr. Jefferson two Volumes of the Bee, containing several papers in continuance of the pamphlet by the same hand. The Writer intends to republish and enlarge them.

RC (DLC); with dateline above postscript; endorsed by TJ as received 24 July 1793.

Neither the specific volumes of *The Bee, or Literary Weekly Intelligencer* (Sowerby, No. 4927), nor the PAMPHLET and its WRITER have been identified.

To Edmond Charles Genet

July 23. 1793.

Th: Jefferson has the honor of inclosing to Mr. Genet the communications of M. de Vergennes and M. de Montmorin which he was so kind as to put into his hand. He begs pardon for having made an endorsement on them in a moment when he had forgotten that they were to be returned.

PrC (DLC). FC (Lb in DNA: RG 59, DL). For the enclosures, see enclosures I and II printed at first Memorandum to George Washington, [11 July 1793].

From James Monroe

DEAR SIR   Richmond July 23. 1793.

I came here yesterday upon some business in the office of the Ct. of chancery, and shall return to morrow. I shall see Barrett to day and give him a line to Mr. Pope for the adjustment of his claim.

Mr. Lewis and Divers have valued Thenia and children but have not furnished me the statement. They will on my return. I am likewise in your debt for the Encyclopedia. Be so obliging as state in your next the amount and I will include the whole in the same bond. Tis impossible to adjust the transaction in a manner more agreeable to me and therefore hope it will likewise be so to you.

The information contained in your last of the prospect of a war with

Spain is truly alarming—but I still hope it may be avoided—as it embarks us of course in the general war of Europe and puts our fortunes afloat on the event. The unanimity of our Executive[1] councils on the subject begets strange suspicions with me. By the proclamation so far as it had a right, we are seperated from France. The progress of the war then is not intended to be in great harmony with that nation, as for the support of publick liberty. We shall however be at war with Spain upon a private quarrel of our own—for instance for the Missisippi, and which I hear has been lately guaranteed by Britain to that power—but the guarantee has not been published and perhaps not intended to be. The commencement in the object and parties to the war, contains as little hostility to Britain and monarchy as possible; the odium of it too with the present Indian war—will be placed to account of the western country, already unpopular enough throughout the continent. Britain it is obvious will prescribe the terms of the peace and what these may be, in the unsettled state of the world with respect to government the disposition of many with respect to the western country[2] and torn to peices as we are, by a malignant monarchy faction is altogether incertain. Besides upon what principle can it be accounted for, that the certificate party lose the support of Hamilton upon this occasion furnished them upon all others? The certificates are in the dust if we are involved in a war, and he has shewn he could bear any kind of indignity from the Bh. Ct. The whole is misterious to me. I fear the party, finding its affairs desperate and that by fair discussion before the publick it will be crushed and that the publick credit partly[3] by the mismanagement of the public finances, and partly by the present war whose effect is felt, are disposed to precipitate us into some dreadful catastrophe[4] which may end we know not where. The circumstance of a Sph. war is of all others the happiest expedient for them. They have shewn themselves the patrons and advocates for peace by the proclamation—a war, and for the Missisippi or southern boundaries will not be theirs—its odium will fall elsewhere.

I am (against every invitation to war) an advocate for peace. The insults of Spn. Britain or any other of the combined powers, I deem no more worthy our notice as a nation, than those of a lunatic to a man in health—for I consider them as desperate and raving mad. To expose ourselves to their fury if we can get out of their way would be as imprudent in the former as the latter case. To preserve peace will no doubt be difficult but by accomplishing it, we shew our wisdom and magnanimity—we secure to our people the enjoyment of a dignified repose, by indulging which they will be prosperous and happy.

There is no sacrifice I would not be willing to make for the sake of France and her cause—but I think by this course we advance her interest—and I am persuaded she must so understand it. In the mean time, whatever the principles of neutrality would allow of should be granted her.

I observe a curious publication signed "pacificus" written no doubt by Mr. H. The principles it contains are really novel. The President he says may of himself annull any treaty or part of a treaty he thinks fit, as the Organ of communication with foreign powers—that he has done so by the proclamation—in respect to the guarantee, which he has declared void, and the other two articles he has permitted to remain in force. It contains other doctrines equally exceptionable—but which I have not time at present to notice nor you I presume to read. With great sincerity I am yr. affectionate friend & servant   JAS. MONROE

I received Mr. Freneau's note excusing the omission about his paper[5] respecting which I return an answer. Is it not surprising the pamphlet entitled "an examination &ca." has not reached this—I never could obtain a view of it till the other day a copy was presented me for perusal.

RC (DLC); endorsed by TJ as received 30 July 1793 and so recorded in SJL. Enclosure not found.

For the PAMPHLET, see note to Notes on Stockholders in Congress, 23 Mch. 1793.

[1] Word interlined.
[2] Preceding ten words interlined.
[3] Word interlined.
[4] Remainder of sentence interlined.
[5] Preceding six words interlined.

Notes of Cabinet Meeting on Edmond Charles Genet

July 23. 1793. A meeting at the Pr's of the 3 heads of departments and E.R.

Genet had told me about a fortnight ago that he had come here with instructions to let all his contracts to the lowest bidder of sufficient ability, that he had been privately admonished however at the same time by some individuals who had been in America that, if he meant to succeed, he must put his contracts into the hands of Rob. Morris &c. who were all-powerful in the government. That he paid little regard to this, and pursuing rigorously the plan of his instructions he had failed, as I knew, meeting to every proposition for obtaining money, the decided opposition of the Secy. of the Treasury.—Knowing as I did how decidedly the Sy. of the Tr. had been against every the smallest *advance* beyond what was actually exigible, and even for a day, I[1] was attentive to him. He continued, that he had now found out that if he would put the contract into the hands of Mr. Hamilton's friends[2] he could get money. That he had already been in treaty with Cuningham & Nesbit, had agreed with them on terms mutually acceptable tho' not as good as in the way pointed out in his instructions, and that Mr. Hamilton had also agreed, tho' it was not yet in writing. I could not help saying 'are you sure Colo. H. is agreed. I think it impossible.' I am sure says he, and you shall see. Accordingly at this meeting Colo. H. proposes to[3] agree to pay the[4] orders of Mr. Genet to the amount of the instalments of this year[5] that is to say, to note at the treasury those orders as presented, and to say to the persons that such a sum will be paid at the day of the instalment and he presented a letter ready cut and dry for the purpose. The Presidt. came into it at once, on account of the distresses of the refugees from St. Domingo, for whom some of it was to be used. Knox asked no other question than whether it was convenient to the treasury. I agreed to it on my old grounds, that I had no objections to an advance. E.R. alone was afraid, and insisted the Secy. of the Try. should present a written paper to each holder of a bill letting them see that we would pay for the *government of France on such a day* such a sum, so that if a counter-revolution should take place between this and the day (to wit, some day in Sep. and another in Nov.) in time to be known here, we should not be held to pay to the holder but to the new government. Hamilt. agreed to arrange this with E.R. which in private he will easily do.

At this meeting (E.R. being called away on business) I proposed an answer to Genet's letter of July 9. on French property taken by the English in American bottoms, which was agreed to in toto—Also an answer to his letter of June 14. covering protests of Consuls about Admiralty courts arresting their prizes. To this it was thought some additions were necessary, and particularly Knox proposed some notice should be taken of the expressions towards the Presidt. personally. So it was referred to another day.

The Presidt. mentioned that we must shortly determine what was to be done with Mr. Genet, that in his own opinion his whole correspondence should be sent to G. Morr' with a temperate but strong representation of his conduct, drawing a clear line between him and his nation, expressing our friendship to the latter, but insisting on the recall of Genet, and in the mean time that we should desire him either to withdraw or cease his functions. Hamilton hereon made a long speech exhorting the Presidt. to firmness, representing that we were now in a crisis whereon the continuance of the government or it's overthrow by a faction depended, that we were still in time to give the tone to the public mind by laying the whole proceedings before them, and that this should be done in addition to what he had proposed. That as yet the great body of the people could be kept on the right side by proper explanations, but that if we let the incendiaries go on, they would soon have taken side with them.—Knox told some little stories to aggravate the

Pr. To wit, that Mr. King had told him, that a lady had told him, that she had heard a gentleman say that the Pr. was as great a tyrant as any of them and that it would soon be time to chase him out of the city—that Mr. Stagg lately from N. York had told him that the St. Tammany society now had meetings to the number of 500. persons, and that Consul Hauterive appeared to be very intimate with them.

The President also desired us to reflect on the question of calling Congress.

Hamilton and Knox told the President they had extorted from Beach a confession that Pascal (one of the Secretaries of Genet) sent him the queries inserted in his paper 2 or 3 days ago and to one of[6] which the Visct. Noailles gave the lie in the paper of to-day. He said Talon had never been but twice to his house, which was to public dinners, and that he had dined once with Talon, in a large company.

MS (DLC); entirely in TJ's hand, with one alteration possibly made at a later date (see note 2 below). Entry in SJPL: "Notes. Genet's informn of Ham's favor to Cuningham & Nesbit. remarkable. free ships free goods—arrest of prizes.—Genet's dismissn.—on calling Congress.—Talon." Included in the "Anas."

On 19 July 1793 Edmond Charles Genet requested from Alexander Hamilton authorization to draw upon the American debt to France in order to supply the "urgent wants" of a French fleet of about 15 warships and 120 merchant vessels that had first reached Norfolk on 7 July 1793 and later stopped off at various American ports with about 10,000 REFUGEES from the great Saint-Domingue slave revolt. This exodus had been triggered in June after the struggle for power between Thomas François Galbaud, the colony's governor recently appointed by the Provisional Executive Council, and Léger Félicité Sonthonax and Etienne Polverel, the civil commissioners appointed in 1792 by the Legislative Assembly, led to armed conflict between their respective supporters, resulting in a victory for the latter marked by the burning of the town of Cap-Français and a grant of freedom by the commissioners to all rebellious slaves who fought for the Republic against foreign and domestic enemies on the island. Most of the merchantmen sailed to Baltimore, while most of the warships anchored in New York harbor from early August to early October 1793, during which time Genet made a se-

ries of ultimately unsuccessful efforts to enlist the fleet in his projected expeditions against Canada and Louisiana (Genet to Hamilton, 19 July 1793, Syrett, *Hamilton*, xv, 116-17; Ammon, *Genet Mission*, 111, 120-5; Childs, *French Refugee Life*, 15; Ott, *Haitian Revolution*, 69-72; Stein, *Sonthonax*, 63-77; DeConde, *Entangling Alliance*, 271-6). Five days later—in the LETTER READY CUT AND DRY that the Cabinet approved this day—Hamilton informed Genet that he could use for this purpose the September and November 1793 installments on the debt to France, subject to the deduction from the former of over 94,000 dollars to compensate holders in the United States of unpaid bills drawn on the government of Saint-Domingue (Hamilton to Genet, 24 July 1793, Syrett, *Hamilton*, xv, 124; note to Genet to TJ, 18 June 1793).

TJ's ANSWER to Genet's LETTER OF JUNE 14 was in fact his draft reply to Genet's letter of 22 June 1793 (see TJ to Genet, [ca. 16 July 1793]; Washington, *Journal*, 206).

BEACH: Benjamin Franklin Bache, printer of the *General Advertiser*. In the 20 July 1793 issue "A Correspondent" suggested that Alexander Hamilton was unfit to be Secretary of the Treasury because he consorted with an unnamed man who had allegedly purloined money provided him by Louis XVI to bribe members of the French National Convention and that Henry Knox was unfit to be Secretary of War because he had allegedly allowed an unnamed former French general officer to exult to him that Saint-Domingue was ruined. The Vicomte de NOAILLES denied that he was the officer in question in a brief note published in the same newspaper three days later.

¹ TJ here canceled "could not help saying these."
² TJ first wrote "of Mr. Hamilton" and then altered it to read as above, possibly at a later date.
³ TJ here canceled "pay up the instal."
⁴ TJ here canceled "mer."
⁵ TJ first wrote "next instalments" and then altered it to read as above.
⁶ Preceding two words interlined.

From John M. Pintard

Madeira, 23 July 1793. The foregoing is a copy of his 4 July letter, since which a vessel arrived here that left Lisbon on the 9th, at which time there was no news of war between France and Portugal. Although lacking official news of such a war, a few weeks ago the governor detained here a French Indiaman bound from Mauritius to Toulon that had put into Porto Santo upon hearing that England and Spain were at war with France, imprisoned the captain, crew, and passengers, and lodged the cargo in the customhouse here. Several English ships, however, brought news that such a war had been reported when they left England, and a British frigate arrived in May with a Portuguese brig that had been captured by a French privateer from Nantes, the Dutch property aboard on its way to Holland from Oporto being assigned by the prize master as the reason for the seizure. In response to a plea by the Indiaman's captain, he requested the governor to release the ship, crew, passengers, and cargo, but the governor refused until instructions arrived from Lisbon; as a result, he has agreed to act as attorney for the captain and the ship's owners, and since the cargo is worth £80,000 sterling he should earn a very handsome commission if the ship is released. This arrangement earned the wrath of the intendant of the customhouse, whose father-in-law is a Portuguese merchant who used to transact most French business here; certain of war, they ignored the Indiaman until after word came from Lisbon that France was not at war with Portugal, when they offered their services and were declined. As a result, under the intendant's influence, the governor doubled the guard on the French, forbidding any communication with them, and has refused until he hears from Lisbon to grant clearance papers for a ship he had chartered for Bordeaux, being convinced by the intendant that the ship, for which he is paying £65 sterling a month, was chartered by the Frenchmen to bring news of their imprisonment to Bordeaux, even though he actually chartered it to take advantage of news from Joseph Fenwick about the high freights that American ships could fetch there. He has written to Humphreys about this and wishes to know if the governor should pay him demurrage for the ship. He also wishes to know if he can serve as French consul here while holding his American consular office. If he can, he asks TJ to recommend him to Genet. The lack of news from Lisbon about the combined armies suggests that they have received a check. He encloses a statement by the French captain and his officers, which they ask to be shown to Genet, and a list of ships for the last six months.

RC (DNA: RG 59, CD); 6 p.; endorsed by TJ as received 9 Sep. 1793 and so recorded in SJL; subjoined to Pintard to TJ, 4 July 1793. Enclosure: Statement of Captain J. J. B. Feraud and three other officers, Funchal, Madeira, 19 July 1793, protesting the detention since 26 June of the *Commerçant* and its passengers, crew, and cargo by the governor of Madeira, despite earlier assurances from the commandant of Porto Santo that France and Portugal were then at peace; suggesting that Pintard, who volunteered his services to them, be appointed French consul at Madeira; and criticizing the governor's rejection of Pintard's effort to secure the release of the ship and its officers, crew, passengers, and cargo even after the arrival on 13 July of a vessel from Lisbon confirming the absence of war between France and Portugal (MS in same; in French; in a clerk's hand, signed by the four officers). Other enclosure not found.

To Edmund Randolph, with Jefferson's Note

TH: JEFFERSON TO E.R. [23 July 1793]

I inclose you a letter of Genet's of July 9. and the draught of an answer to it, which is approved by the other gentlemen but we wish your sentiments on it, and as soon as possible as it is pressing.—The other of June 22. is only under deliberation, and sent to you for your information and consideration against we meet again.

[*Note by TJ:*]

July 23. 93.

E.R. returned this note and the two answers. On that to the letter of June 22. he had indorsed with a pencil 'In all respects tenable and accurate.' Which was meant however for the other.

RC (DLC); undated; with note by TJ at foot of text. Recorded in SJPL between 23 and 25 July 1793. Enclosures: (1) Edmond Charles Genet's third letter to TJ, 9 July 1793. (2) Drafts of TJ to Genet, [ca. 16] and 24 July 1793.

Although he did not date the note itself, TJ clearly wrote it and received it back on 23 July 1793, the same day the President and the Cabinet met and considered the two enclosed letters to the French minister, a meeting from which Randolph was called away to attend to other business (Washington, *Journal*, 206; Notes of Cabinet Meeting on Edmond Charles Genet, 23 July 1793).

To Edmond Charles Genet

SIR Philadelphia July 24. 1793.

Your favor of the 9th. instant covering[1] the information of Silvat Ducamp, Pierre Nouvel, Chouquet de Savarence, Gaston de Nogeré and G. Beustier, that being on their passage from the French West Indies to the United States, on board merchant vessels of the United States with slaves and merchandize of their property, these vessels were stopped by British armed vessels and their property taken out as lawful prize.

I believe it cannot be doubted but that, by the general law of nations, the goods of a friend found in the vessel of an enemy are free, and the goods of an enemy found in the vessel of a friend are lawful prize. Upon this principle, I presume, the British armed vessels have taken the property of French Citizens found in our vessels in the cases abovementioned, and I confess I should be at a loss on what principle to reclaim it. It is true that sundry nations, desirous of avoiding the inconveniencies of having their vessels stopped at sea, ransacked, carried into port and detained, under pretence of having enemy goods aboard, have, in many instances, introduced by their special treaties, another principle between them, that enemy bottoms shall make enemy goods, and friendly bottoms friendly goods; a principle much less embarrassing to commerce, and equal to all parties in point of gain and loss: but this is altogether the effect of particular treaty, controuling in special cases the general principle of the law of nations, and therefore taking effect between such nations only as have so agreed to controul it. England has generally determined to adhere to the rigorous principle, having in no instance, as far as I recollect, agreed to the modification of letting the property of the goods follow that of the vessel, except in the single one of her treaty with France. We have adopted this modification in our treaties with France, the United Netherlands, and Prussia: and therefore as to them, our vessels cover the goods of their enemies, and we lose our goods when in the vessels of their enemies. Accordingly you will be pleased to recollect that in the late case of Holland & Mackie, citizens of the United States who had laden a cargo of flour on board a British vessel which was taken by the French Frigate the Ambuscade and brought into this port, when I reclaimed the cargo, it was only on the ground that they were ignorant of the declaration of war when it was shipped. You observed, however, that the 14th. Article of our treaty had provided that ignorance should not be pleaded beyond two months after the declaration of war, which term had elapsed in this case by some few days, and finding that to be the truth, though their real ignorance of the declaration was equally true, I declined the reclamation, as it never was in my view to reclaim the cargo, nor apparently in yours to offer to restore it, by questioning the rule established in our treaty that enemy bottoms make enemy goods. With England, Spain, Portugal, and Austria, we have no treaties: therefore we have nothing to oppose to their acting according to the general law of nations, that enemy goods are lawful prize though found in the bottom of a friend. Nor do I see that France can suffer on the whole. For though she loses her goods in our vessels when found therein by England, Spain, Portugal, or Austria, yet she gains our goods when found in the vessels of England, Spain, Portugal, Austria, the United Netherlands, or Prussia: and I believe I may safely affirm that we have more goods afloat in the vessels of these six nations than France has afloat in our vessels: and consequently that

France is the gainer and we the loser by the principle of our treaty. Indeed we are losers in every direction of that principle, for when it works in our favor, it is to save the goods of our friends, when it works against us, it is to lose our own, and we shall continue to lose while the rule is only partially established. When we shall have established it with all Nations we shall be in a condition neither to gain nor lose, but shall be less exposed to vexatious searches at sea. To this condition we are endeavoring to advance, but as it depends on the will of other nations as well as our own, we can only obtain it when they shall be ready to concur.

I cannot therefore but flatter myself that on revising the cases of Ducamp and others, you will perceive that their losses result from the state of war which has permitted their enemies to take their goods tho' found in our vessels; and consequently from circumstances over which we have no controul.

The rudeness to their persons practised by their enemies is certainly not favorable to the character of the latter. We feel for it as much as for the extension of it to our own Citizens their companions, and find in it a motive the more for requiring measures to be taken which may prevent repetitions of it. I have the honor to be with great respect and esteem, Sir Your most obedient & most humble Servant.

PrC (DLC); in a clerk's hand, unsigned; at foot of first page: "The Minister Pleny. of the Republic of France." PrC of Tr (DLC); in a clerk's hand, with a correction by TJ (see note 1 below); at foot of text: "(Copy)." Tr (NNC: Gouverneur Morris Papers). Tr (DNA: RG 46, Senate Records, 3d Cong., 1st sess.). PrC (PRO: FO 97/1). FC (Lb in DNA: RG 59, DL). Tr (AMAE: CPEU, xxxviii); in French. Printed in *Message*, 55-6; printed in *Correspondence*, 25-6, and in French in *Correspondance*, 30-1, without first paragraph. Enclosed in TJ to Gouverneur Morris, 16 Aug. 1793; draft enclosed in TJ to Edmund Randolph, with Jefferson's Note, [23 July 1793], and Randolph to TJ, 25 July 1793.

On the previous day TJ had submitted a draft of this letter to a meeting of the President and the Cabinet. For their approval, see Washington, *Journal*, 206; Notes of Cabinet Meeting on Edmond Charles Genet, 23 July 1793; TJ to Randolph, with Jefferson's Note, [23 July 1793]; and Randolph to TJ, [ca. 24], 25 July 1793.

HER TREATY WITH FRANCE: see Article 20 of the 1786 commercial treaty between France and Great Britain (Clive Parry, ed., *The Consolidated Treaty Series*, 231 vols. [Dobbs Ferry, N.Y., 1969-81], L, 83). For the relevant articles of OUR TREATIES WITH FRANCE, THE UNITED NETHERLANDS, AND PRUSSIA, see Miller, *Treaties*, II, 20-1, 68-70, 170-1.

It was possibly in connection with this letter, or his letter of 16 Aug. 1793 to Gouverneur Morris, that TJ compiled brief notes on European treaties on the subjects of "Contraband," "free ⟨bottoms⟩ ships make free goods," and "enemy bottoms make enemy goods" (MS in MHi; entirely in TJ's hand; undated; bearing on verso TJ's undated notes on John Carey, ed., *The System of Short-hand, practised by Mr. Thomas Lloyd, in taking down the Debates of Congress . . .* [Philadelphia, 1793]; see Sowerby, No. 1133).

[1] Word altered in ink by TJ to "covered" in PrC of Tr. Tr in DNA and *Message*: "covered."

From Richard Harison

SIR   New York. 24th. July 1793

I had the Honor of writing to you on the Receipt of your Letter of the 12th. June from Albany, and soon after upon my return to this place found, that although the Facts respecting the sloop Polly were generally known, yet no sufficient Testimony had been procured to serve as the foundation of Criminal Proceedings: I have since endeavoured to discover, and procure, the proper Evidence, but hitherto without success, and am apprehensive from the Guarded silence, and Caution, of those concerned in the Transaction, that it will be impossible to bring forward any Proof strong Enough to Justify the Commencement or Prosecution of a suit.

Colonel Troup had in my absence filed a Libel in the district Court of new York praying Restitution of the Brig Catharine and her Cargo as taken within the Territorial Limits and protection of the united States. This measure was calculated to bring forward the question as to the authority of the national Judiciary in matters of this nature, and to settle the Rights of the parties If that authority was admitted. Accordingly the vessel was taken into the Custody of the marshall, and monitions Issued for all Parties Interested to make their respective Claims. Soon after these proceedings had taken place, The Consul of France thought proper to exhibit a Protest against them, which was received by the Clerk, and upon Judge Duanes Coming to Town was by his order Translated and considered as a plea to the Jurisdiction of his Court. A Copy of the Protest as Translated will be found inclosed In order to be laid before the Executive if it should be considered as proper to do so.

In consequence of the Judges order respecting the Protest, It became necessary to shew that the district Court was authorised to take Cognizance of the Cause, and this Point was argued at large by Colonel Troup and myself on the part of the Libellants, no Counsel appearing either for the Captors, or to maintain the Doctrines contained in the Consular Protest. In my opinion, It was originally intended to have manifested a supercilious neglect for the Proceedings, and authority of the Court, In confidence that the Decision of Judge Peters upon a similar occasion, would be considered as decisive. But since the argument, other Ideas appear to have prevailed, and a Gentleman of the Law who disclaims to be employed Either by the Consul, or by Citizen Bompart; has nevertheless applied to be heard on behalf of some persons who (he says) are interested in the Capture.

Judge Duane having determined to indulge the applicant with a Hearing, and to give him some days to prepare for it, and I being under the necessity of Leaving Town in a day or two and solicitous to be present at the argument, That I might reply with propriety, in a Case so Interesting in itself, and in which Government had thought proper to interfere, It became necessary to adjourn the Farther Consideration of the Cause until my return from Albany.

This delay I hope will not be attended with any material inconvenience to the parties interested, Especially as on the behalf of the Libellants we are disposed to consent that the property in Contest may be sold and the proceeds await the determination of the Court. During my absence Colonel Troup will transact all my Official Business, and will I am persuaded pay the Highest attention, to Every Command with which You may Honor him. I remain with the utmost Respect Sir Your most obedient & most Humble Servant   RICH: HARISON

Atty D. N. Y.

RC (DLC); in a clerk's hand, signed by Harison; at foot of text by Harison: "Honble Thos. Jefferson Esqr."; endorsed by TJ as received 26 July 1793 and so recorded in SJL. For the enclosure, see Enclosure No. 1 listed at Edmond Charles Genet to TJ, 22 June 1793.

A GENTLEMAN OF THE LAW: Brockholst Livingston, a New York Republican attorney (Duane, *Decree*, 4).

From Edmund Randolph

[ca. 24 July 1793]

Mr. J. rightly supposed, that the approbation of E.R. was by mistake written upon the answer to the letter of the 22d. of June, instead of that of July. The latter is the only one, which attracted my particular attention; as the other seemed to be a subject of future deliberation. The propriety of the addition intended to accommodate Genl. K. depends upon the measures to be pursued in regard to Mr. Genet. If no movement is to be made towards his removal, by inclosing his offensive correspondence to the Executive council of France, or some other step, I should think, that the paragraph proposed is well suited to call him to his senses. If, however, something farther is to be done, I should be inclined to reserve every communication of sensibility to his indecorums, until it was[1] absolutely decided to take some decisive measure, to which your reply might be adjusted.

As to the letter at large, if to be sent now[2] I cannot find room for criticism; unless it may be better to strike out the word *complete*, as connected with admiralty. For how can France in right establish an admiralty, under any modification?

Perhaps too the latitude of power eventually assigned to the President, at the bottom of the second page, is capable of some reduction. But

I question, whether the letter ought not to be delayed. For if Genet is to be recalled, the subject ought in all respects to be prepared for the eyes of the world.[3]

Mr. Fisher of Va. eats ham with me to-day between 2 and 3—Will you come down.

RC (DLC: TJ Papers, 91: 15617); undated. Recorded in SJPL under 1 Aug. 1793.

Despite TJ's entry in SJPL, internal evidence suggests that this document was written between TJ's 23 July 1793 letter to Randolph and Randolph's 25 July 1793 letter to TJ. The ANSWER TO THE LETTER OF THE 22D. OF JUNE was the draft of TJ's unsent letter to Edmond Charles Genet, [ca. 16 July 1793], for which TJ prepared an ADDITION INTENDED TO ACCOMMODATE Henry Knox. THAT OF JULY: TJ to Genet, 24 July 1793.

[1] Randolph here canceled "complete."
[2] Preceding five words interlined.
[3] Preceding two sentences inserted after Randolph wrote the next paragraph.

From Josef Ignacio de Viar and Josef de Jaudenes

Wednesday morning [24 July 1793]

Don Joseph de Viar, and Don Joseph de Jaudenes present their Compliments to Mr. Jefferson, and would wish to know what time he will have a little leisure tomorrow morning, that they may call on him upon some business.

RC (DNA: RG 59, NL); in Jaudenes's hand; partially dated; endorsed by TJ as received 25 July 1793.

On the following day Viar and Jaudenes met with TJ and formally complained to him "of sundry pieces published in the Newspapers of Philada. tending to set the King of Spain in an unfavorable light; & to raise a belief that the Spanish Nation is inimical to this Country." In order to resolve this problem they submitted to TJ a proposed statement, to be issued in the name of the President, in which Washington was to inform the American people that he had been requested by the two Spanish agents to convey their official assurances that their government continued to desire peaceful relations with the United States and hoped to consolidate them in the negotiations underway at Madrid (MS in DNA: RG 59, NL, in Viar's hand; undated; endorsed by TJ as received 25 July 1793). On the same day TJ informed Washington about this complaint, but apparently not about the proposed presidential statement, and promised to convey to Viar and Jaudenes Washington's observation that in regard to the offending newspaper articles "there appeared no means of preventing publications of that kind, unless they should take such a course as to require legal interference & that the Commrs. must impute it to the freedom of the press & not consider it as a thing particularly countenanced by the Government" (Washington, *Journal*, 207; see also Viar and Jaudenes to TJ, 11 July 1793, and note).

From Tench Coxe

July 25th. 1793

Mr. Coxe has the honor to inform Mr. Jefferson that Mr. Nicholson is not in Town, and is not expected to be at home before Friday Evening.

Mr. Kingston was to have given information by 1, oClock this day concerning £1000 Stg. but has not yet done it. This was the Cause of Mr. Coxe's omitting the present Note till this hour.

RC (DLC); endorsed by TJ as received 25 July 1793.

From Edmond Charles Genet

MONSIEUR A Philadelphie le 25 Juillet 1793. l'an 2e. de la R. F.

Je recois tous les jours de nouvelles plaintes sur[1] les insultes que les Anglais se plaisent à faire essuyer[2] au pavillon des Etats Unis;[3] les pieces cijointes vous prouveront que la souveraineté de votre pays est impunement violée non pas par l'exercice légitime que nous avons voulu faire[4] de quelques droits que les traités nous accordent, mais par la spoliation, le pillage, le mauvais traitement exercés[5] par nos ennemis au mepris de vos loix et à l'ombre même des signes de votre souveraineté. Sur toutes les mers une piraterie audacieuse poursuit jusque dans vos vaisseaux les propriétés françaises et même celles des americains, quand elles sont destinées pour nos ports;[6] vos droits politiques ne sont comptes pour rien. En vain les principes de neutralité établissent ils que les vaisseaux amis rendent les propriétés amies; En vain le President des Etats Unis cherche-t'il par sa proclamation à réclamer l'observation de[7] cette maxime;[8] En vain le desir de conserver la paix fait-il sacrifier les interets de la France à cet interet du moment;[9] En vain la soif des richesses[10] l'emporte telle sur l'honneur dans la balance politique de l'Amerique.

Tous ces ménagemens, toute cette condescendance, toute cette humilité n'aboutissent à rien; Nos ennemis en rient[11] et les francais trop confiant sont punis pour avoir cru que la Nation américaine[12] avoit un pavillon, qu'elle avoit quelque égard pour ses loix, quelque conviction[13] de ses forces et qu'elle tenoit au sentiment de sa dignité. Il ne m'est pas possible, Monsieur, de vous peindre toute ma sensibilité sur ce scandale[14] qui tend à la diminution de votre commerce, à l'oppression du notre[15] et à l'abaissement à l'avilissement des Républiques.[16] C'est aux américains à faire entendre sur ces outrages leur généreuse indignation[17] et Je dois me borner à vous[18] demander une seconde fois de me faire connoitre les mesures que vous avez prises pour obtenir la restitution des propriétés qui ont été enlevées à mes concitoyens sous la protection de votre pavillon. C'est de notre Gouvernement qu'ils ont appris que les américains etoient nos alliés, que la Nation Américaine etoit souveraine et qu'elle sauroit [19] se faire respecter. C'est donc sous la sanction [20] même de la Nation Française qu'ils ont confié leurs biens et leurs personnes à la sauvegarde du pavillon Américain, et c'est sur elle qu'ils se reposent du soin de faire valoir leurs droits. Mais si nos concitoyens ont été trompés, si vous n'etes point en état de soutenir la souveraineté de votre peuple, parlez, nous l'avons garantie quand nous etions esclaves, nous saurons la rendre redoutable étant devenus libres. [21] Agrées, Monsieur, mon estime & mon respect   GENET

PrC of Tr (DLC); in a clerk's hand; at head of text: "Le Citoyen Genet, Ministre de la République francaise à Mr. Jefferson, Secrétaire d'Etat des Etats Unis." Dft (DLC: Genet Papers); heavily emended text in Genet's hand, with several revisions by a clerk; only the most significant emendations are recorded below. Tr (AMAE: CPEU, xxxviii); misdated 29 July 1793; certified by Genet. Tr (NNC: Gouverneur Morris Papers); misdated 23 July 1793. PrC of another Tr (PRO: FO 97/1); in a clerk's hand; misdated 23 July 1793. FC (DLC: Genet Papers); in English; with abbreviated complimentary close and signature by Genet. Tr (DNA: RG 46, Senate Records, 3d Cong., 1st sess.); in English. Recorded in SJL as a letter of 25 July 1793 received 26 July 1793. Enclosure: Declaration of M. La Roussie to François Dupont, Philadelphia, 18 July 1793, stating that he was a Bordeaux merchant who left St. Marc on 12 June 1793 aboard the American brigantine *Governor Pinckney*, Captain D. Jenkins, belonging to Mr. Therick of Charleston; that two days later a privateer from St. Vincent stoppped the ship before Môle St. Nicolas and brought it to New Providence on the sole pretext that it was carrying French passengers, but not before first plundering some of his personal property; that after remaining at New Providence for eleven days at a daily cost of a quarter of a dollar they were freed because of a shortage of provisions on the island; and that Captain Jenkins, whom along with others he supposes were won over by the British, declared the complainant's cargo of coffee, cotton, and sugar to be French property (PrC of Tr in DLC, in French, with attestations by Dupont and Binet Oster and certification by Genet, all in a clerk's hand; Tr in NNC: Gouverneur Morris Papers, in French; PrC of another Tr in PRO: FO 97/1, in French,

in a clerk's hand; Tr in DNA: RG 46, Senate Records, 3d Cong., 1st sess., in English). Other enclosures not found, but see note below. Letter and enclosure with translations printed in *Message*, 22-3 (App.), 53-4; translation of letter printed in *Correspondence*, 24; letter printed in *Correspondance*, 32; translation printed in ASP, *Foreign Relations*, I, 165-6. Letter and enclosure enclosed in TJ to Gouverneur Morris, 16 Aug. 1793.

TJ read this letter to the President on 27 July 1793, which led Washington to describe it as "another insulting letter, written in French, from the French Minister, respecting the treatment of french property on board American vessels, by the British privateers" (Washington, *Journal*, 210).

Although it is not clear how he did so, according to the manuscript list of enclosures cited in note to TJ's 16 Aug. 1793 letter to Gouverneur Morris, Genet sent two other documents about British depredations on American shipping. In the first, the Philadelphia mercantile firm of Conyngham, Nesbit & Company reported in a 26 July 1793 letter to Genet that the ship *Sally*, Captain Griffith, which they had loaded with flour for a voyage from Baltimore to Le Havre, had just returned to Baltimore with news that it had been captured by a privateer and taken to Guernsey or Jersey, and that the *Columbia* of Baltimore had been captured by the same privateer while carrying the French minister driven from Portugal. In the second, a declaration made in the chancery of the French consulate in New York on 30 July 1793, Morles, Sarrazin, Guel le Sieur, Bouithon, and Lamarque stated that, having left Cayemite on 2 June 1793 bound for New York aboard the American brig *Ranger*, Captain Perkins, they were captured and brought to Nassau on New Providence by an English privateer armed by M. Moz, a merchant there; that they would not have exposed their fortunes had they not believed in the inviolability of treaties of neutrality, which should guarantee property on neutral vessels; and that notwithstanding this the privateer plundered 230,000 pounds of coffee they owned with four other passengers on the pretext of a proclamation by Washington that the property of subjects of belligerent powers could be lawfully taken from American ships (PrCs of Trs in DLC, the second in French, with certifications in French by Genet, all in a clerk's hand; Trs in NNC: Gouverneur Morris Papers, the second in French; PrC of first, and PrC of another Tr of second in French, in PRO: FO 97/1, in the hands of a clerk and George Taylor, Jr.; Trs in DNA: RG 46, Senate Records, 3d Cong., 1st sess., in English; both enclosures printed, the second with translation, in *Message*, 23 (App.), 55; text of first and translation of second printed in ASP, *Foreign Relations*, I, 166).

[1] In Dft Genet here canceled "sur le mépris avec le q."

[2] In Dft Genet first wrote "dont les Anglois couvrent tous les Jours" before altering the passage to read as above.

[3] In Dft Genet here canceled "Ces faits consignés dans."

[4] In Dft Genet here canceled "comme quelques uns ont ⟨voulu⟩ osé le dire."

[5] Here in margin of Dft Genet canceled "contre vous," for which he substituted the next three words.

[6] Preceding twelve words written in the margin of Dft by a clerk.

[7] Preceding three words interlined in Dft.

[8] In Dft Genet wrote the remainder of this paragraph and the first sentence of the next paragraph through "rien" in the margin.

[9] In Dft Genet first wrote "En vain sacrifie-t-il nos Interêts pour complaire à nos rivaux et acheter ⟨leur⟩ un Interêt du moment" and then altered it to read as above.

[10] Preceding four words interlined in Dft in place of "la fortune de quelques particuliers."

[11] In Dft Genet first wrote "⟨Les françois sont punis⟩ Nos énnemis en rient et pretendent au contraire comme vous le verrés, M., par une des lettres du Cit. hauterive que cette même proclamation les autorise à

⟨exercer leur brigandage⟩ agir comme ils le font, Ils enlevent ⟨les personnes⟩ nos concitoyens mêmes comme Je vous l'ai deja dit à bord de vos vaisseaux." Genet then canceled all but "Nos énnemis en rient" before adding, then canceling, "en attendent des succès, mieux des." "Nos ennemis en rient" omitted in *Correspondance*.

[12] Preceding three words interlined in Dft in place of "vous."

[13] Word interlined in Dft in place of "sentiment."

[14] Here in the margin of Dft Genet canceled "non comme françois mais comme le représentant de vos seuls alliés."

[15] Remainder of the sentence interlined or written in the margin in Dft.

[16] Word reworked from "Republicains" in Dft.

[17] Here in the margin of Dft Genet canceled "⟨et a⟩ c'est à eux à reclamer la garantie q."

[18] Remainder of the sentence interlined and written in the margin of Dft by Genet and a clerk in place of the following canceled passage: "requerir au nom de quelques malheureux qui spoliés ⟨sur vos⟩ sous la protection de votre pavillon en infraction de vos lois et de vos traités pensent que c'est aux conservateurs de ces lois qu'ils ont le droit de demander si vous êtes en mesure de requerir par les voies diplomatiques la restitution de leurs biens. C'est aux agens de la République qu'ils adressent d'abord leur reclamation parce que."

[19] *Message* and *Correspondance*: "savait."

[20] Word interlined in Dft in place of "garantie."

[21] Preceding sentence written in the margin of Dft in place of a canceled passage which in its final state read: "Sans doute la restitution retombera en derniere analyse sur les ravisseurs; mais en attendant la Justice finale dont les succès de nos armes accelerent de Jour en Jour le développement les dangers du commerce et les besoins des malheureux demandent des mesures promtes et des déterminations expéditives pour prévenir de nouvelles déprédations veritablement humiliantes pour la nation Americaine, et qui me font un devoir de vous déclarer M. que la nation françoise toujours fidele à remplir ses engagements est prête à soutenir la souveraineté du peuple Americain qu'elle a garantie et que nos énnemis communs méconnoissent dans les vues les plus perfides."

From Parry Hall

25 July. 93.

Parry Hall incloses a Proof Sheet of the Notes on Virginia; which, with the gratest Respect, and a high sense of Obligation, he lays before the Honble. Mr. Jefferson.

RC (MHi); addressed: "Honble. Mr. Jefferson"; endorsed by TJ as received 25 July 1793.

Despite printing a PROOF SHEET, which has not been found, Hall went no further in republishing TJ's NOTES ON VIRGINIA (Benjamin Rush to TJ, 28 Mch. 1793, and note).

Petition and Remonstrance from Peter Lemaigre

To his Excellency Thomas Jefferson Secretary of State for the United States of America

The Petition and Remonstrance of Peter Lemaigre of the City of Philadelphia Merchant and a Citizen of the United States.

Respectfully Sheweth

That your Petitioner has before exhibited Proofs to you in the Case of the Snow Suckey that he has been for upwards of Thirteen Years a Citizen of the United States residing and exercising Business as a Merchant in the City of Philadelphia. That your Petitioner having been largely interested in Trade to the Island of St. Domingo had very considerable Sums of Money due to him there which he was desirous to withdraw from thence and not only directed his Property there to be shipped as well in his own Vessels which he hath from time to time sent to the said Island as in such other American Vessels as would receive Freight for this Port of Philadelphia, That your Petitioner having already stated to you the Capture and Detention of the said Snow Sucky Captain Andaule which was taken and sent into Jamaica by a British Privateer and for the reclaiming of which he is waiting for further Proofs of the Property of the Vessel from Boston, is sorry that he is reduced to the Necessity of again coming forward, humbly to represent the further Capture and Detention of his Property by British Privateers. That your Petitioner being sole Owner of the Brig or Vessel called the Molly whereof Bernard Razer is or was Commander fitted her out and loaded her at this Port of Philadelphia in the Month of May last with a Cargo of flour and other Articles for his own Account for Port Au Prince in the Island of St. Domingo and that the said Vessel having arrived at Port au Prince there delivered her Cargo here loaden and received on board a full Cargo of the produce of said Island and four thousand eight hundred Dollars in Specie wholly for Account of your Petitioner and set Sail therewith (bound for this Port of Philadelphia). That Your Petitioner hath received a Letter from Captain Bernard Razer the Commander of his said Brig Molly dated at new Providence the 9th. Day of this present Month informing him that his said Vessel and Cargo were captured and sent into said Island of New Providence with a full Cargo and that they had taken from him 4,800 Dollars in Cash the Property of your Petitioner, that they had unbent his Sails for a Trial of his Vessel and Cargo and that he could not inform what would be the Consequence as they bribe the Sailors get them drunk and ship them on board their Privateers, leaving some Vessels but one or two Hands and sending them into Port—that the said Captain Razer's Letter of which Copy is herewith handed you also informs your Petitioner that a great Number of other Vessels belonging to other Ports in these States several of which have Property on board for your Petitioner, have also been captured by the British and carried into the said Island of New Providence. That your Petitioner is deprived of the Means of making his Claims for the Recovery of his Property by the violent and unjust Measures made use of by the said British Cruisers and must with other Merchants concerned in Trade to the French Islands be involved in Ruin unless some Measures are taken as well to recover the Property thus forcibly and unjustly taken and detained as to secure their Vessels and Cargoes from like Capture and Detention, therefore your Petitioner relying on the Wisdom and Justice of the general Government respectfully submits his Case to your Consideration and prays that you will grant him such Relief herein as to you in your Wisdom shall seem meet.

Philadelphia   P. LeMaigre
July 25. 1793.

RC (DNA: RG 76, British Spoliations); in a clerk's hand, signed by Lemaigre; endorsed by TJ as received 25 July 1793 and so recorded in SJL. PrC of Tr (DLC); in the hand of George Taylor, Jr. Tr (Lb in DNA: RG 59, DL). Enclosure: Bernard Raser to Lemaigre, New Providence, 9 July 1793, of the same import as described above, but adding the names of four Philadelphia ships detained in New Providence: the schooner *Commerce*, Captain Foulk; the brig *Hannah*, Captain Connell; the sloop *Eliza*, Captain Davidson; and the schooner *Linnet*, Captain Vallingtine (Tr in DNA: RG 76, Great Britain, Unbound Records; PrC of another Tr in DLC, in Taylor's hand; Tr in Lb in DNA: RG 59, DL). Petition and enclosure enclosed in TJ to George Hammond, 8 Aug. 1793; petition enclosed in TJ to George Washington, 25 July 1793, and Washington to TJ, 26 July 1793.

For the PROOFS . . . IN THE CASE OF THE SNOW SUCKEY, see the documents listed at Petition and Memorial from Lemaigre to TJ, 21 [June] 1793, and TJ to George Hammond, 26 June 1793.

From Edmund Randolph

E. R. to Mr. J.   July 25. 1793.

We have been at cross purposes about the inclosed letter of July 24. 1793. in answer to Mr. Genets of the 9th. I am much mistaken, if my note intimated a doubt of its propriety. I certainly always approved it. My remarks as to delay[1] were applicable to the answer to the inflammatory memorial;[2] to which General Knox suggested an addition. Is that some word[3] omitted in the first sentence of the inclosed?

I have lost my copy of the laws of Congress, at the session commencing in 1792. Look at the index of the laws of last session, under the head of territory; and you will find, that a limitation act has been disapproved by congress. Perhaps the necessity of laying the act before them will appear from the laws, which I miss. But I confess, that it does not strike my eye in the act concerning the Southern territory, the ordinance[4] establishing the Northern territory, nor the cession of No. Carolina. I will examine further.

RC (DNA: RG 59, Letters from and Opinions of the Attorney General); endorsed by TJ as received 26 July 1793. Enclosure: TJ to Edmond Charles Genet, 24 July 1793.

My NOTE: Randolph to TJ, [ca. 24 July 1793]. ANSWER TO THE INFLAMMATORY MEMORIAL: TJ to Edmond Charles Genet, [ca. 16 July 1793]. In May 1792 Congress disapproved a LIMITATION ACT, passed by the governor and judges of the Northwest Territory in 1788, which set specific time limits for commencing certain civil ac-

tions and prosecuting certain crimes (*Annals*, III, 1396; Theodore C. Pease, ed., *The Laws of the Northwest Territory, 1788-1800*, Illinois State Historical Library, *Collections*, XVII [1925], 25-6). See also Report on the Proceedings of the Southwest Territory, 19 June 1793.

[1] Preceding three words interlined.
[2] Word interlined in place of "letter."
[3] Thus in manuscript.
[4] Word interlined in place of "resolution."

To George Washington

                                 July 25. 1793.

Th: Jefferson has the honor to inclose to the President a second complaint of Peter Le Maigre a merchant of this city, for a second vessel taken from him by the British. In the former case, which happened during the absence of the President, it was unanimously agreed by the heads of the departments that it would be proper to communicate the case to Mr. Hammond, and desire his interference.

RC (DNA: RG 59, MLR); addressed: "The President of the US."; endorsed by Tobias Lear as a letter of 22 July 1793. Tr (Lb in same, SDC); misdated 22 July 1793. Not recorded in SJL. Enclosure: Petition

and Remonstrance from Peter Lemaigre, 25 July 1793.

For the FORMER CASE, see note to TJ to George Hammond, 26 June 1793.

From George Washington

Sir   Philadelphia July 25th: 1793.

A letter from Colo. S. Smith (of Baltimore) to the Secretary of the Treasury, giving information of the conduct of the Privateers—Citizen Genet and Sans Culottes—is sent for your perusal: after which it may be returned; because contained therein, is a matter which respects the Treasury Department solely.

As the letter of the Minister from the Republic of France, dated the 22d. of June, lyes yet to be answered; and as the Official conduct of that Gentleman—relatively to the Affairs of the Government—will have to undergo a very serious consideration (so soon as the Special Court at which the Attorney General is now engaged will allow him to attend with convenience) in order to decide upon measures proper to be taken thereupon: It is my desire that all the letters to, and from that Minister may be ready to be laid before me, the heads of Departments and the Attorney General—with whom I shall advise on the occasion—together with the minutes of such Official Oral communications as you may have held with him on the subjects of those letters &ca. And as the Memorials from the British Minister, and answers thereto, are materially connected therewith, it will be proper, I conceive, to have these ready also.

Go: Washington

RC (DLC); at foot of text: "The Secretary of State"; endorsed by TJ as received 25 July 1793. Dft (DNA: RG 59, MLR). FC (Lb in same, SDC). Recorded in SJPL. Enclosure not found.

The President might have requested the information about Edmond Charles Genet called for in the second paragraph of this letter in response to Attorney General Edmund Randolph's advice that he "add to the instruction, to be given to Mr. Jefferson concerning Mr. Genet's conduct, that he should state the verbal conversations with him, which respected the granting of commissions within the U.S., and the order, that the privateers, so commissioned, should quit the ports of the U.S." (Randolph to Washington, [24 July 1793], DLC: Washington Papers).

THE SPECIAL COURT: the special session of the United States Circuit Court of Pennsylvania that was currently trying the case of Gideon Henfield (see note to Memorial from Edmond Charles Genet, 27 May 1793).

To John Bringhurst

July 26. 1793.

Th: Jefferson is to receive at the bank of the US. on the 1st. day of October, 875. Dollars, towit, a quarter's salary. It would be very convenient to him to anticipate 600.D. of that sum now, that is to say 300.D. to take up his note at the bank of N. A. due from Tuesday to Friday next, and 300.D. for current purposes of Aug. and September. He will ask the favor of Mr. Bringhurst to endorse a note of that amount to the bank of the US.—Having no money connections in Philadelphia, he applies on this occasion to Mr. Bringhurst, because he stands secured by the state of their particular accounts tho' this note is not to enter into them, but to be paid by Th:J. out of the money which the bank will have in their own hands as before mentioned.

PrC (DLC).

John Bringhurst (1764-1800) was a Philadelphia hardware merchant at 26 High Street in 1791 and a "fancy-goods" merchant at 12 South Third Street in 1793, when he aided TJ in a number of financial transactions. A Quaker disowned for bankruptcy by the Philadelphia Monthly Meeting in July 1794, he later moved to Wilmington, Delaware, and in 1797 visited TJ at Monticello. He was living with a brother in Philadelphia when TJ visited him on his deathbed (Josiah G. Leach, *History of the Bringhurst Family* . . . [Philadelphia, 1901], 32, 38; Clement Biddle, *The Philadelphia Directory* [Philadelphia, 1791], 14; Hardie, *Phila. Dir.*, 15; Harwood A. Johnson and Diana Edwards, "Ornamental Wedgwood wares in Philadelphia in 1793," *Antiques*, cxlv [1994], 166-73; Bringhurst to TJ, [ca. 11 Sep. 1793]; MB, 5 Jan. 1794, 10 Sep. 1797, and note; James Madison to TJ, 31 Jan., 21 Feb. 1796, 2 Aug. 1797).

Bringhurst endorsed TJ's note for $600 to the Bank of North America on 30 July 1793, having previously endorsed TJ's $300 NOTE AT THE BANK on 30 May 1793 (MB, 30 May, 30 July 1793). TJ's letter of 28 May 1793 to John Kean, cashier of the Bank of the United States, seeking instructions on how to obtain a discount for this amount is not recorded in SJL and has not been found (*Catalogue of the Interesting and Valuable Collection of Autograph Letters . . . of the late John Dillon, Esq. . . . Sold by Auction, by Messrs. Sotheby, Wilkinson & Hodge* . . . [London, 1869], Lot 566).

To Edward Dowse

Dear Sir   Philadelphia July 26. 1793.

I received a few days ago, by the way of Charleston, your favor dated at Ostend Mar. 4. wherein you mention your expectation of being at Boston in two months. At the same time came the two boxes of china mentioned in your letter. I am extremely sensible of your friendly attention in this business, and of the thanks I owe you for it. It has happened that being placed, on my return to America, in a situation which obliged me to go to housekeeping at once, without even waiting for the furniture I had left at Paris in expectation of returning there, I was under a necessity of purchasing a pretty large stock of china here. Afterwards I received that which I had left at Paris, so as to have become doublestocked, when this third supply arrives. You had been so good as to insist on furnishing it at it's simple cost and charges, a kindness I had no right to expect. I am happy therefore to be in a situation to leave you free to dispose of it to others at the profit which is the just reward of the merchant's toil and risk, and peculiarly due to you after so long a voyage. I mention however my state of supply merely to place you at your ease in doing what shall be to your best advantage. For should no purchaser be found for it, I hold myself certainly bound to keep you clear of all loss, in a case where nothing but favor was intended to me. The boxes are here, unopened, and shall be delivered in that state to your order. If at this time, in any future voyage, or on any future occasion I can be useful to you, I shall be so with sincere pleasure, having, in the course of our short acquaintance at Cowes, seen the best ground for esteeming your principles and talents, and being with sincere esteem, Dear Sir Your most obedt. humble servt   TH: JEFFERSON

PrC (DLC); at foot of text: "Mr. Edward Dowse. Boston."

From Alexander Hamilton

July 26th 1793.

Mr. Hamilton presents his Compliments to Mr. Jefferson And has the honor of sending him, herewith, the Copies of two letters from the Commissioner of Loans for Virginia on the subject of Mr. Short's Stock.

RC (DLC: William Short Papers); in a clerk's hand; endorsed by TJ as received 27 July 1793 and so recorded in SJL. Enclosures: (1) John Hopkins to Hamilton, 29 Apr. 1793, reporting that stock held in James Brown's name in trust for William Short has been transferred to Short as Brown requested this day, answering the object of TJ's letter to Hamilton of 19 Apr. (2) Hopkins to Hamilton, 16 July 1793, enclosing a duplicate of No. 1, reporting that Short's holdings of stock now consist of $15,008 in 6 percent assumed debt, $11,256 in 3 percent assumed debt, $7,504 in deferred debt, and $1,093 in 6 percent public debt, and indicating that no transfers of this stock had taken place while Brown held it in trust (Trs in same; conjoined; printed in Syrett, *Hamilton*, XIV, 356, XV, 99-100).

Memorandum of Conversations with Edmond Charles Genet

Note given to the Presidt. [1]

Mr. Genet's declaration to the President at his reception, that France did not wish to engage the US. in the present war by the clause of guarantee, but left her free to pursue her own happiness in peace, has been repeated to myself in conversation, and to others, and even in a public answer, so as to place it beyond question.

Some days after the reception of Mr. Genet (which was May 17.) I went to his house on business. The Atty. Genl. went with me to pay his first visit. After he withdrew, Mr. Genet told me Mr. Ternant had delivered him my letter of May 15. on the 4. memorials of Mr. Hammond: he said something first of the case of the Grange, and then of the vessels armed[2] at Charleston. He said that on his arrival there he was surrounded suddenly by Frenchmen full of zeal for their country, pressing for authority to arm with their own means for it's assistance, that they would fit out their own vessels, provide every thing, man them, and only ask a commission from him: that he asked the opinion of Govr. Moultrie on the subject, who said he knew no law to the contrary, but begged that whatever was to be done, might be done without consulting him, that he must know nothing of it &c. That hereupon he gave commissions to the vessels: that he was of opinion he was justified not only by the opinions at Charleston but by our treaties. I told him the President had taken full advice on the subject, had very maturely considered it, and had come to the decision expressed in my letter. He said he hoped the President had not so absolutely decided it, but that he would hear what was to be said against it. I told him I had no doubt but that the President, out of respect to him and to his country, would receive whatever he should have to urge on the subject, and would reconsider it with candour. He said he would make it his business to write me a letter on the subject, that he thought the arming the privateers was justifiable. But that if the President should finally decide otherwise, tho' he could not think it would be right, yet he must submit: for that assuredly his instructions were to do whatever would be agreeable to us. He shewed indeed by his countenance, his manner and words that such an acquiescence would be with reluctance; but I was and am persuaded he then meant it.

Mr. Genet called at my office on Tuesday was sennight or fortnight (say July 16th. or 9th.) but I think it was Tuesday was sennight, and know it was on a Tuesday because he went from thence to the President's. He was summing up to me the strength of the French naval force now arrived. I took that occasion to observe to him that having such great means in his hands, I thought he ought not to hesitate in abandoning to the orders of the government the little pickeroons which had been armed here unauthorised by them, and which occasioned so much embarrasment and uneasiness, that certainly their good dispositions must be worth more than the trifling services these little vessels could render. He immediately declared that having such a force in his hands he had abandoned every idea of further armament in our ports, that these small objects were now beneath his notice and he had accordingly written to the Consuls to stop every thing further of that kind: but that as to those which had been fitted out before, their honour would not permit them to give them up, but he wished an oblivion of every thing which had past, and that in future the measure so disagreeable to the government should not be pursued, tho he thought it clearly justified by the treaty. I told him the government was of a different opinion, that both parties indeed had equal right to construe the treaty, that consequently he had done his duty in remonstrating against our construction, but that since the government remained finally persuaded of the solidity of it's own construction, and had a right to act accordingly within their own limits, it was now his duty, as a diplomatic man to state the matter to his government, to ask and await their orders, and in the mean time to acquiesce, and by no means to proceed in opposition within our limits.—It was at the same time he informed me that he had sent out the Little Democrat to obtain intelligence of the state of the coast, and whether it was safe for the fleet to proceed round from Norfolk to New York. [3]

July 26. 1793.

MS (DLC); entirely in TJ's hand, with first line and final sentence added at a later date (see notes 1 and 3 below). PrC (DLC); lacks first line and final sentence. Entry in SJPL: "Notes of a conversn with Genet. given to the Presidt." Included in the "Anas."

TJ prepared these notes for the President in response to his request for information about the Secretary of State's dealings with Edmond Charles Genet (see Washington to TJ, 25 July 1793). It is not known, however, when TJ submitted these notes or when Washington returned them.

CLAUSE OF GUARANTEE: Article 11 of the 1778 treaty of alliance with France obliged the United States to guarantee forever "the present Possessions of the Crown of france in America as well as those which it may acquire by the future Treaty of peace" (Miller, *Treaties*, II, 39). Before Genet arrived in Philadelphia TJ and other Cabinet officials were concerned that France might invoke this clause to request American assistance in defending the French West Indies during

the current European war (see Editorial Note on Jefferson's opinion on the treaties with France, at 28 Apr. 1793).

Despite Genet's insistence that he commissioned privateers at Charleston, South Carolina, merely because of the importunities of FRENCHMEN FULL OF ZEAL FOR THEIR COUNTRY and the OPINION OF GOVR. MOULTRIE, he had actually left France with explicit instructions from the Provisional Executive Council to commission privateers in the United States as part of the French Republic's war effort (Turner, *CFM*, 207-9, 211). The letter to TJ in which Genet contended that ARMING THE PRIVATEERS WAS JUSTIFIABLE was dated 27 May 1793. For the FRENCH NAVAL FORCE NOW ARRIVED, see Notes of Cabinet Meeting on Edmond Charles Genet, 23 July 1793, and note.

[1] Line written in a different ink at a later date and lacking in PrC.

[2] TJ here canceled "in our ports."

[3] Sentence written in a different ink at a later date and lacking in PrC.

From Van Staphorst & Hubbard

Sir   Amsterdam 26 July 1793.

We have the pleasure to advise You the Receipt of Your esteemed favor of 18 March of last Year, forwarded by You in the Brigg Sion which foundered at Sea: We have advised Mr. Short, that as He has had duplicates of the dispatches by this Vessel, We shall hold them by us, untill his Return from Spain, unless He should direct us how otherwise to dispose of them.

Felicitating you that the Fate of these papers, about which Mr. Short entertained much anxiety, is now ascertained to his wishes, We are respectfully Sir! Your most obedient humble Servants

N & J. Van Staphorst & Hubbard

RC (DNA: RG 59, Accounting Records, Letters from Amsterdam Bankers); in a clerk's hand, signed by the firm; at foot of text: "Thomas Jefferson Esqr."; endorsed by TJ as received 24 Oct. 1793 and so recorded in SJL. Dupl (DLC); in a clerk's hand, signed by the firm; at head of text: "Origl. pr. Snow Mary Nath. Goodwin, Via Newyork (Duplicate)."

For TJ's 18 Mch. 1792 letter to Van Staphorst & Hubbard and the DISPATCHES relating to William Carmichael and William Short's dealings with the Spanish government, see note to Report on Negotiations with Spain, 18 Mch. 1792.

From George Washington

July 26th: 1793

The President returns to the Secretary of State the Letter from Peter Le Maigre, complaining of a second vessel having been taken from him by the British. If any thing more effectual than was done in the former case can be done in this, the President would wish it; but if there appear no other measures which can be taken with propriety, the President thinks the same steps should be followed as in the former case.

RC (DLC); in Tobias Lear's hand; endorsed by TJ as received 26 July 1793. Recorded in SJPL. Enclosure: Petition and Remonstrance from Peter Lemaigre, 25 July 1793.

To Delamotte

Sir   Philadelphia July 27. 1793.

The bearer hereof, Mr. Livingston, goes to France with a view of settling some commercial correspondences. I have not the pleasure of being acquainted with him myself, but he is recommended to me by Governor Lee of Virginia, as a worthy and respectable citizen, and as such I take the liberty of presenting him to you, and asking for him that information and advice which may be useful to him in the line of his pursuits. I have the honor to be with great esteem Sir Your most obedt. humble servt

Th: Jefferson

PrC (DLC); at foot of text: "M. La Motte." Tr (ViU: Edgehill-Randolph Papers); 19th-century copy.

TJ wrote an identical letter of the same date to Joseph Fenwick at Bordeaux (PrC in DLC, at foot of text: "Mr. Fenwick"; Tr in ViU: Edgehill-Randolph Papers, 19th-century copy).

To James Madison

July 28. 93

Your last was of June 29. acknoledging mine of the 17th. Since that I wrote you June 23. 29. July 1. 7. 14. and 22.—I have only time to mention the death of Roger Sherman. Adieu.

PrC (DLC); unsigned; conjoined to PrC of other letter to Madison of this date. Tr (ViU: Edgehill-Randolph Papers); incomplete 19th-century copy; conjoined to Tr of other letter to Madison of this date. Only one of the two letters of this date to Madison is recorded in SJL. After letterpressing the sheet on which he wrote them, TJ evidently cut it in two and sent the missives separately, this first note probably covering the newspaper mentioned in the second.

TJ's letter of JULY 1. to Madison is recorded in SJL but has not been found.

To James Madison

July 28. 93

Your last received was of June 29. which acknoleged a scrip of mine of June 17. Consequently my subsequent letters of June 23. 29. July 1. 7. 14. and 22. are unacknoleged, and give me so much anxiety lest some infidelity should be practised on the road, that I am afraid to do any thing more than warn you of it, if it should be so. I will send this through Mr. Maury, and the newspaper as usual through Mr. Blair. If there is any thing wrong this may get to you.—Roger Sherman is dead. Adieu.

PrC (DLC); unsigned; subjoined to PrC of other letter to Madison of this date. Tr (ViU: Edgehill-Randolph Papers); 19th-century copy; subjoined to Tr of other letter to Madison of this date.

From Benjamin H. Phillips

Curaçao, 28 July 1793. Since writing on 8 June by the brig *John*, he has received and attended to TJ's letter of 21 Mch. by the schooner *Ceres*. The *Fury*, a brig registered in Philadelphia that arrived here from Grenada with slaves, sailed under United States colors for Hispaniola before he received his consular commission, its captain and its owners, Peter W. Marrenner and Domingo Costino, not being citizens according to secretarial papers. Almost two hundred soldiers arrived here lately, and a brig left St. Eustatius for here about two weeks ago, but on account of very rapid currents probably "fell to Leeward loaded Cannon &c." The home government intends to make this place strong and to rely on British forces to defend St. Eustatius and St. Martin.

RC (DNA: RG 59, CD); 1 p.; in a clerk's hand, with complimentary close and signature by Phillips; at head of text: "Thomas Jefferson Esqr."; endorsed by TJ as received 16 Aug. 1793 and so recorded in SJL.

Phillips's last letter to TJ was actually dated 7 June 1793. TJ submitted the present letter to the President on 19 Aug. 1793 and received it back the same day (Washington, *Journal*, 225).

On 8 Aug. 1793 Phillips wrote a brief letter to TJ from Curaçao stating that he had sent his 28 July dispatch by the sloop *Driver*, Captain Samuel Tibbalds, via New York, and that he was now enclosing a certificate by the fiscal on the island proving the identity of the *Fury*'s true owners (RC in DNA: RG 59, CD; at foot of text: "Thomas Jefferson Esqr."; endorsed by TJ as received 31 Aug. 1793 and so recorded in SJL). The enclosed certificate by Theodore

Van Teylingen, Attorney General of the Netherlands and member of the Curaçao Council or Raad Fiscal, dated 8 Aug. 1793, stated that, after some initial hesitation because a French subject named M. Bastard had claimed a one-third ownership in the American ship *Fury* and he could not allow Dutch subjects to enter into French employ, he complied with the request of Captain Peter William Kerrener on 20 Apr. 1793 to note down some hands who were going with him to Saint-Domingue on the ship, as appears by the attached muster roll, after learning from Kerrener that he and Domingo Contini & Company were the sole owners (MS in same; in a clerk's hand, signed by Van Teylingen; with attested copy in Dutch of the 20 Apr. 1793 muster roll).

To Thomas Mann Randolph, Jr.

DEAR SIR   Philadelphia July 28. 1793.

I have to acknolege your two favors of the 11th. and 19th. inst. The miscarriage of the servants clothes has happened, I presume, from the stupidity of the person here who carried them to the vessel, and (the captain being absent) delivered them to a saylor and took his receipt. The vessel has never come to this port again since I began to suspect the roguery.—I desired Mr. Brown to let all my furniture remain in the warehouse till I should come to Virginia, as I knew there would not be water in our river, before that, sufficient for navigation. I think to have the whole carried by water, if it can be guarded from rain.—I am availing myself of the time I have to remain here, to satisfy myself by enquiry from the best farmers of all the circumstances which may decide on the best rotation of crops; for I take that to be the most important of all the questions a farmer has to decide. I get more information on this subject from Dr. Logan than from all others put together. He is the best farmer in Pensylva. both in theory and practice, having pursued it many years experimentally, and with great attention. He thinks that the whole improvement in the modern agriculture of England consists in the substitution of red clover instead of unproductive fallows. He says that a rotation which takes in 3. years of red clover instead of 3. years of fallow or rest, whether successive or interspersed, leaves the land much heartier at the close of the rotation; that there is no doubt of this fact, the difference being palpable. He thinks it much best to sow it alone after harvest, for then it is in it's prime the next year, whereas if sown in the spring it can neither be cut nor pastured that year. He takes generally but the spring cutting, which yeilds him 2. tons to the acre, and pastures the rest of the year. It is the red cover alone[1] which has enabled the English farmer to raise and maintain cattle enough to make a coat of dung a regular part of his rotation. I had at first declined the introduction of red clover into my rotation because it lengthens it so much: but I have determined now to take it in, because I see it the source of such wonderful richness round this place. And for a Virginia table it will certainly give unbounded plenty of meats, milk, butter, horse-food, instead of being eternally on the scramble for them as we are in Virginia for the want of winter and summer food. Dr. Logan considers a green-dressing of buckwheat as equal to a coat of 10. loads of dung to the acre. (20 loads to the acre is what he thinks a good coat.) And as it is but 5. weeks from the sowing to it's being fit to plough in, it may be well introduced after a harvest of small grain, if your next crop is only to be put in in the spring. After a great deal of consultation therefore with him, we have arranged my rotation thus. 1st. year. a crop of Wheat. Then a green-dressing of buck wheat. | 2d. peas and corn mixed. | 3d. wheat, and after it a green dressing of buck wheat, and, in the succeeding winter put on what dung you have. | 4th. potatoes and corn mixed. | 5th. rye and after it sow red clover. | 6th. cut the 1st. crop of clover and pasture the 2d. | 7th. pasture the 1st. crop, and cut the 2d. This change gives spring pasture and eases the mowing.[2] | 8th. pasture. | Or expressed more shortly

1.	2.	3.	4.	5.	6.	7.	8.
w.|bw.	pe. co.	w.|bw. d	po. co.	r.|cl.	cl.pa.	pa.cl.	pa.

He observes that if it were not for the want of the 8th. year's pasture, the rotation might close the 7th. year, and would then be clear of weeds and produce the heaviest crop of wheat possible: but he thinks the rotation will need the pasture of the 8th. year, and that this will introduce so many weeds as to render an extra ploughing requisite. Supposing the fields of 60. acres each, this rotation gives you 9 times 60. acres, say 540. acres to plough between harvest and the end of seed-time, which I think may be done by 6. ploughs with a pair of oxen each, especially if 4. waggon horses are kept and called in to the aid of the ploughs a part of the fall.   The President thinks that when corn and potatoes are mixed (in drills 8.f. apart, and the stalks of corn 8.f. apart in the drill) that as much is made from each as the same number of plants would yeild if alone. Logan reckons 300. bushels of potatoes to the acre an average crop, and 2. bushels of potatoes to yeild as much nutriment as one of corn. He allows a bushel of potatoes a day to a fattening ox, and a peck a day to a work horse, mixing a handful of bran, or rye-meal with each to give it flavor.—He considers the above rotation to be the best possible, where you are confined to the articles there mentioned, and that the land will improve very much under it. He has promised however to study it still more fully for me, so that something further may be yet done to it. The winter-spewing of our land may prevent sowing the clover in the fall of the 5th. year. Dr. Logan is making some experiments to determine what number of sheep are equivalent to a given number of cattle as to the articles of dung, food etc. I am at loss what standing force will be sufficient for such a rotation. Taking gangs of half men and half women, as with us, I guess we must allow a hand for every 5. acres content of each feild, say 12. hands if the feilds are of 60. acres each.—You see how much my mind is gone over to the business of a farmer, for I never know when to finish, if once I begin on the subject. My love to my dear Martha. I am uneasy at the situation in which your letter from Richmond mentions you to be. A dysentery, a journey, and the heats of July are three as ill assorted things as could come together. I hope your next will inform me you are at Monticello and recovered. Accept my sincerest affections & Adieu   Th:J.

RC (DLC); endorsed by Randolph as received 6 Aug. 1793. PrC (DLC).

[1] Word interlined.
[2] Preceding four words interlined.

From George Washington

Sunday 28 July 1793.

The President of the United States will be glad to see the Secretary of State tomorrow morning at Nine o'Clock.

RC (DLC); in the hand of Bartholomew Dandridge, Jr.; endorsed by TJ as received 28 July 1793. Recorded in SJPL.

From Bartholomew Dandridge, Jr.

Monday 29 July 1793.

It is requested as a favor of The Secretary of State to attend, as Pall bearer, the Funeral of Mrs. Lear, this afternoon at five o'Clock. The procession will move from the House of the President US.

RC (DLC); unsigned; endorsed by TJ as a letter from Tobias Lear received 29 July 1793.

Notes of Cabinet Meeting on Neutrality

July 29. 1793. At a meeting at the President's on account of the British letter of marque[1] ship Jane, said to have put up wasteboards, to have pierced 2 port holes and mounted 2 cannon (which she brought in) on new carriages which she did not bring in, and consequently having 16. instead of 14. guns mounted,[2] it was agreed that a letter of marque, or vessel armé en guerre et en marchandise is not a privateer, and therefore not to be ordered out of our ports. It was agreed by Ham. Kn. and myself that the case of such a vessel does not depend on the treaties, but on the law of nations. E.R. thought as she had a mixed character of merchant vessel and privateer she might be considered under the treaty, but this being overruled the following paper was written.

'Rules proposed by Attorney General.

agreed 1. That all equipments purely for the accomodation of vessels, as merchantmen, be admitted.

agreed 2. That all equipments, doubtful in their nature, and applicable equally to commerce or war, be admitted, as producing too many minutiae.

agreed 3. That all equipments, solely adapted to military objects, be prohibited.

Rules proposed by the Secretary of the Treasury.

agreed 1. That the original arming and equipping of vessels for military service offensive or defensive[3] in the ports of the US. be considered as[4] prohibited to all.

negatived. the Secy. of the Treasy. only holding the opinion. 2. That vessels which were armed before their coming into our ports, shall not be permitted to augment these[5] military equipments in the ports of the US. but may repair or replace[6] any military equipments which they had when they began their voyage for the US. That this however shall be with the exception of privateers of the parties opposed to France, who shall not refit or repair.

agreed 3. That for convenience, vessels armed and commissioned before they come into our ports may engage their own citizens, not being inhabitants of the US.

I subjoined the following

I concur in the rules proposed by the Atty. Genl. as far as respects materials or means of annoyance furnished by us. And I should be for an additional rule that as to means or materials brought into this country and belonging to themselves they are free to use them.

Th J.'

⟨*Knox agreed to the rules of the A. Genl. in toto, consequently they were established by the vote of three. Ham. proposed to put questions on all the propositions separately, and he took the paper and put questions on the 3. of the Atty. Genl. which were agreed. He was going on with questions on his own propositions without asking us distinctly but by a sort of a look and a nod, and noting in the margin. I observed I did not understand that opinion, that we had agreed to the Atty. Gen's propositions, he said it was to take a question on each distinctly. Knox observed that as we understood these rules to extend only to cases out of the treaty we had better express it. I agreed and proposed to add some such words as these 'excepting always where the treaties shall have otherwise provided.' Hamilton broke loose at this and pretended it was meant they should go to all cases. All of us bore testimony against this and that he himself had shewn that the present case was out of the treaties. He said he would rather specify the exceptions expressly, than leave them on the general terms I proposed; so it was agreed to take till tomorrow to examine the treaties and specify the exceptions if it could be done.—While this was passing E.R. took the paper in his hand and read Ham's marginal notes, as above, and seeing that he had written 'agreed' opposite to his own (Ham's) 1st. proposition, he observed to Knox so that I overheard him that that had not been agreed, which was the truth. To his 3d. proposition we had all agreed in conversation, but it had not been agreed to add it to the rules.—It was pretty evident from Ham's warmth, embarrassment, eagerness, that he wanted to slip in something which might cover cases we had not in contemplation.*⟩

A question then arose whether we should expressly say that these articles were meant[7] to extend to cases out of the treaty. It was referred to the next day.

MS (DLC); entirely in TJ's hand, with the part consisting of "the following paper" incorporated verbatim from Dft with original numbering of rules and one copying error (see note 5 below); written on the first side of two sheets containing "Anas" entries for 30 July and 1, 2, 3, and 6 Aug. 1793. Dft (DLC: Alexander Hamilton Papers); consists on recto of "Rules proposed by Attorney General" in Edmund Randolph's hand and "Rules proposed by the Secretary of the Treasury" in Hamilton's hand, with headers, marginalia, and renumbering of rules into one sequence by Hamilton after rejection of his second rule; verso consists of concurring statement in TJ's hand. Entry in SJPL: "Opns of heads of dep. on several points of Neutrality." Included in the "Anas."

For the background of the rules on equipping belligerent vessels in American ports, which the Cabinet considered this day and approved in final form on 3 Aug. 1793, see Thomas, *Neutrality*, 143-53.

[1] Preceding three words interlined.
[2] TJ here canceled "the Attorney gene."
[3] Preceding six words interlined by Hamilton in Dft.
[4] Preceding two words interlined by Hamilton in Dft.
[5] Hamilton wrote "their" in Dft.
[6] Preceding two words interlined by Hamilton in Dft.
[7] Word interlined in place of "not."

Notes on Treaties and Neutrality

[29-30 July 1793]

Homologous[1] articles of the treaties.

17.F.   Enemy vessels having made[2] prizes shall have no shelter. If forced by weather, to retire as soon as possible.[3]

18.F. 16.D. 9.P.   shipwrecked vessels shall have all friendly assistance.—P. expressly to *repair*.

19.F. 17.D. 18.P.   ships public and of war or private and of merchants forced through stress of weather, pursuit of pirates, or enemies or any other urgent necessity permitted to provide themselves with all things needful for reparation of their ships.—P. extends this to all[4] vessels.

22.F.   enemies not to fit their privateers, to sell what they have taken, or to exchange ships or merchandize.

   22.D. 19.P.   salvo of art. 9. 10. 17. 22. of treaty with France.—P. salvo of 17th.

'but it is not meant that these rules shall contravene, as of right they cannot, the provisions of the treaties of the US, and particularly the 17th. 18th. 19th. and 22d. articles of that with France, the 16th. 17th. and 22d. of that with the UN. and the 9th. 18th. and 19th. of that with Prussia.'

MS (DLC: TJ Papers, 91: 15616); entirely in TJ's hand; undated, but probably set down on 29 or 30 July 1793, with summary statement written on latter date and one word of the heading added at a later date (see note 1 below). MS (DLC: Alexander Hamilton Papers); entirely in TJ's hand; undated; consists of final summary statement only. Recorded in SJPL under 1 Aug. 1793: "homologous articles of treaties."

TJ evidently wrote these notes in two stages between 29 July 1793, when the Cabinet decided that an investigation was needed of the relationship between existing American treaty obligations and a proposed set of neutrality rules on equipping belligerent vessels in American ports, and 30 July 1793, when the Cabinet considered a preliminary statement of these obligations drafted while it met by Alexander Hamilton and Edmund Randolph (Notes of Cabinet Meeting on Neutrality, 29, 30 July 1793; Washington, *Journal*, 210). The different ink of the summary statement and the extra space above it suggest that TJ set down the list of treaty obligations before the Cabinet met on 30 July and added the statement in response to the document Hamilton and Randolph prepared during that meeting, later making a copy of the latter for Hamilton's use. For the articles cited by TJ from the treaties of amity and commerce with France, the Netherlands, and Prussia, see Miller, *Treaties*, ii, 16-18, 19-20, 73-4, 78, 168, 174-5.

[1] Word interlined in a different ink at a later date in place of "Commensurate."
[2] Preceding two words interlined in place of "with their."
[3] Sentence added.
[4] TJ here canceled "articles."

From Henry Remsen

Dr. Sir   New York July 29th. 1793

I have the honor to inform you now, that Capt. Dennis commanding the revenue cutter belonging to this port, returned from Sandy Hook last evening, and brought with him a challenge to Capt. Bompard of the Ambuscade—from Capt. Courtenay of the Boston, a british frigate of 32 guns. The Ambuscade on her return from her last cruise, needed a top mast and some other repairs, which are readiness[1] to be put to her; but she was not to have sailed, as I understood from one of the Officers yesterday morning, 'till about ten days hence. However it is to be presumed they will hasten the necessary repairs, and accept the challenge, as the honor of the Republic of France is in a manner involved, the challenge being noted on the Coffee house books, which has given it the greatest publicity. A great majority of us here, wish and expect the Ambuscade success in the event of an engagement.

I mean to write again respecting the silver ink stand you directed me to purchase for you, and also the final determination of Schneider the fresco painter, when Mr. Taylor returns to Philadelphia; and in the mean time, subscribe myself with the greatest respect & esteem, Dr. Sir Your most obt. & h'ble servt   Henry Remsen

PS. We have no late arrivals either from Europe or the West Indies, except a brig from Ireland in ten weeks with 300 passengers, who are destined to go on a settlement in the North western parts of this State.

RC (DLC); at foot of text: "Thomas Jef-   [1] Thus in manuscript.
ferson Esqr."; endorsed by TJ as received
30 July 1793 and so recorded in SJL.

George Washington to the Cabinet

Gentlemen   Phila 29th July 1793.

It will not be amiss, I conceive, at the meeting you are about to have to day, to reconsider[1] the expediency of directing the Custom house Officers to be attentive to the Arming or equipping Vessels—either for offensive or defensive War in the several Ports to which they belong—and make Report thereof to the Governor, or some other proper Officer.

Unless this, or some other *effectual* mode is adopted to check this evil in the first stage of its growth, the Executive of the United States will be incessantly harrassed with complaints on this head, and probably when it may be difficult to afford a remedy.   Go: Washington

RC (DLC); at head of text: "To—The heads of the Departments and the Attorney General"; endorsed by TJ as received 30 July 1793. FC (Lb in DNA: RG 59, SDC); with one variation (see note 1 below). Recorded in SJPL.

There is no record of the Cabinet having considered the President's suggestion about CUSTOM HOUSE OFFICERS during its meeting of this date, but Alexander Hamilton did incorporate it into his 4 Aug. 1793 circular letter to federal customs collectors on the enforcement of the rules on American neutrality that grew out of this Cabinet meeting (Notes of Cabinet Meeting on Neutrality, 29 July 1793; Rules on Neutrality, 3 Aug. 1793; Syrett, *Hamilton*, xv, 178-81). For the previous controversy on this subject, see Notes on Alexander Hamilton and the Enforcement of Neutrality, 6 May 1793, and note.

[1] FC: "consider."

From Enoch Edwards

London July 30. 1793

The Day I did myself the Honor to take my Leave of you in Philadelphia—I engaged to write to you—and I should have done so before now but the Fact is that so little can be said from hence that will give a true State of the politicks of Europe (owing to the extreem Torrent that has for some time past prevailed here on the Side of Royalty) that I have scarce thought it worth while to give you any trouble. But this is altering and that very fast too, and the People are cooling down and beginning to abate of their Fervancy in Favor of the Throne, and are now thinking a little for themselves. The present War is growing very fast[1] excessively unpopular—and the Ministry have received a Check by the Account of the numeraus Acquittals in the Prosecutions for Libels from different Counties. It is thought now that no more Verdicts will be found. The Manufactures, are generally speaking, nearly stoped from Buisness—and the Rage for Emigration to America, is beyond every thing you can concieve of—all the Vessells here are crouded and they have refused hundreds who are ready to embark and distressed to find they cannot get away.

When I left you I intended you may recollect to go immediately to Paris. I should have done so, but unfortunately Mrs: Edwards got a fall in geting out of a Carriage from Falmouth to London—which has entirely confined Her ever since we have been here. As soon as ever she recovers, and she now mends very fast We immediately go over where I will reside all next Winter. I am satisfied as to the safety of the Place. Valenciennes is not taken nor do I believe it will be at least in time for them to make any Head this fall—and from every thing that appears I believe that the combined Powers are as far from making a Conquest of France or Republicanism as they were before England joined that cruel Confederacy.

In fact England is very sick of this War and I am mistaken if it is not oblidged to make a Peace. The States general we are sure intend to do it as soon as ever they can. The King of Prussia does nothing till lately[2] but stay about home cuting up Poland, and the Emperor I hope will have an Account to settle before long with the Turk. In short at present there is very little Idea here of ever conquering them by any other Means than dividing the present Factions which have prevailed.

I send you a Number of News-Papers. They will I believe give as good a Complection of Matters[3] as can be obtained.

It is reported here that you intend to resign the Office you hold, and there are not a few who wish it may be true, because they wish that no Person of genuine Republicanism should be in Office in any Country— but I contradict it and I hope I am telling the Truth. I find where I did not expect it that many have a very imperfect Account of our Government—our Principles our Men, and our Measures. But I also find We have many well wishers in this Country.

If you do me the Favor to let Me know you have received this, I will write you again from France. A Letter directed to Me to the Care of Frederick Pigou Merchant London—or to Mr: Pinkney will come safe to hand. I am with very great Respect & Esteem your obedt Srt

ENO: EDWARDS

RC (DLC); endorsed by TJ as received 18 Nov. 1793 and so recorded in SJL.

[1] Word interlined.
[2] Preceding two words interlined.
[3] Edwards here canceled "here."

Memorial from George Hammond

The undersigned, his Britannic Majesty's Minister plenipotentiary to the United States, has the honor of representing to the Secretary of state that, on Saturday last the 27th. curt., the snow Jane of Dublin, bound from Antigua to Baltimore, was sent into this port as a prize to the armed schooner le Citoyen Genet, fitted out at Charleston.

The master and crew of this vessel being detained prisoners on board of the privateer (for the purpose, as is presumable, of suppressing their evidence) it is impossible for the undersigned to ascertain with precision, either the date of its capture, or the situation in which it was at the time. He nevertheless conceives himself fully justified in asserting his belief that, from the statement of the fact in the public prints of yesterday, it must have been taken subsequently to the late departure of the armed schooner le Citoyen Genet from Baltimore.

This deficiency of proof is however the less to be regretted in the present case, since, from the circumstances of it, the undersigned cannot but regard an accurate exposition of the particulars of the capture as totally unnecessary. For—after the assurance which on the 5th. of June, he received from the executive government of this country, that this privateer had been required to depart from the ports of the United States, and after the explicit declaration of the Secretary of state on the 12th. of this month that "the President expected that this privateer le Citoyen Genet" which, in contravention of this requisition, had returned to one of the ports of the United States (Baltimore) "should not depart from it until his ultimate determination respecting it should be made known"—the Undersigned trusts he may conclude that the unauthorized return and departure of the schooner le Citoyen Genet to and from the port of Baltimore, (wherein it remained so long only, as it could augment the complement of its crew to seventy men) and its subsequent capture of the snow Jane of Dublin, will be considered as insults on the sovereignty of the United states so flagrant, and as aggressions on the commerce of Great Britain so unwarrantable as to incline the federal executive government to enforce the immediate restoration of the snow Jane, thus taken, to its rightful owners, who are subjects of the sovereign, whom the undersigned has the honor to represent.

GEO. HAMMOND

Philadelphia 30th July 1793.

RC (DNA: RG 59, NL); at foot of first page: "Mr Jefferson"; endorsed by TJ as received 30 July 1793 and so recorded in SJL. FC (Lb in PRO: FO 116/3). Tr (same, 5/1). Tr (Lb in DNA: RG 59, NL).

TJ submitted this memorial to the President on this day (Washington, *Journal*, 211). See also Cabinet Opinions on Privateers and Prizes, 5 Aug. 1793; and TJ to Hammond, 7 Aug. 1793.

From James Madison

DEAR SIR   July 30. 1793

My last was of the 22d. inst: I have since received yours covering the paper now returned, that covering the report of the Comsrs. of Accts. between the U.S. and the particular States, and that of the 21st. inst: The intermediate one of the 14th. was left by mistake in a secure place by the person who was to bring it up from Fredg., and is not yet arrived. The delay has been inconvenient as it deprives me of part of the publication which I wish to see in all its parts before I formed a regular view of any. As I intimated in my last I have forced myself into the task of a reply. I can truly say I find it the most grating one I ever experienced; and the more so as I feel at every step I take the want of counsel on some points of delicacy as well as of information as to sundry matters of fact.[1] I shall be still more sensible of the latter want when I get to the attack on French proceedings, and perhaps to the last topic proposed by the writer, if I ever do get to it. As yet I have but roughly and partially gone over the first; and being obliged to proceed in Scraps of time, with a distaste to the subject, and a distressing lassitude from the excessive and continued heat of the season, I can not say when I shall finish even that. One thing that particularly vexes me is that I foreknow from the prolixity and pertinacity of the writer, that the business will not be terminated by a single fire, and of course that I must return to the charge in order to prevent a triumph without a victory.

Do you know what is the idea of France with regard to the defensive quality of the Guarantee; and of the criterion between offensive and defensive war which I find differently defined by different jurists; also what are the ideas of the P. on these points. I could lay my course with more advantage thro' some other parts of the subject if I could also know how far he considers the Proclamation as expressing a neutrality in the sense given to that term, or how far he approves the vindication of it on that ground.

I am sorry to find the journey to Virga. from which useful lessons were hoped, ending in a confirmation of errors. I can only account for it by supposing the public sentiment to have been collected from tainted sources which ought to have suggested to a cautious and unbiassed mind the danger of confiding in them. The body of the people are unquestionably attached to the Union, and friendly to the Constitution:[2] but that they have no dissatisfaction at the measures and spirit of the Government, I consider as notoriously untrue. I am the more surprised at the misconception of our Friend as the two latest sources consulted, the two brothers I mean, are understood to be both of them, rightly[3] disposed as well as correctly informed.

I have got my plows at last. They are fine ones and much admired. Repeat my thanks to Dr. Logan if you have an opportunity and think of it. The *patent plow* is worth your looking at if you should visit his farm. You will See your theory of a mouldboard more nearly realised than in any other instance, and with the advantage of having the iron wing, which in common bar shares or in great lies useless under the wood, turned up into the sweep of the Board and relieving it from the brunt of the friction. By fixing the Colter, which is detached, to the point of the share, it will I think be nearly compleat. I propose to have one so constructed. The detached form may answer best in old clea[r?] ground; but will not stand the shocks of our rough and rooty land, especially in the hands of our ploughmen.

Little wheat having been yet tried in bread I can not say how the quality will turn out. The more I see and hear of it, the more I fear it will be worse than was at first supposed. The Corn suffers now for want of rain, but appearances as to that article are on the whole very flattering. The worst effect of the dry weather, at present felt, is the extreme hardness of the earth which makes plowing, particularly in fallow land, but barely possible. So many heavy rains on ground wet for six months, succeeded by the present hot spell, has almost beat it and baked it into Brick.

RC (DLC: Madison Papers); unsigned; one word illegible; endorsed by TJ as received 9 Aug. 1793 and so recorded in SJL.

Neither of the two letters from TJ which Madison acknowledges here without date have been found, and neither is recorded in SJL, unless one is the missing letter of 1 July 1793 (see note to TJ to Madison, 28 July 1793). For TJ's transcription of the 29 June 1793 REPORT OF THE COMSRS., see note to George Washington to the Commis-

sioners of Accounts for the States, [22 June 1793]. The PUBLICATION Madison wanted TO SEE IN ALL ITS PARTS was Alexander Hamilton's "Pacificus" essays. OUR FRIEND: Edmund Randolph. TWO BROTHERS: John and Wilson Cary Nicholas.

[1] Madison first wrote "material facts" before altering the phrase to read as above.
[2] Word interlined in place of "Govt."
[3] Word interlined in place of "well."

From Michael Morphy

Málaga, 30 July 1793. Having written on 30 June by the American schooner *Fredericksburg Packet*, Captain Anderson, bound for Philadelphia, he confirms his report about the interference of the African states with American ships trading in the Mediterranean, especially eastward of this port. Since Spain gave up the port and fortress of Oran on the coast of Mascara to the Moors, small privateers fitted out there have preyed upon the powers at war with them and particularly American ships, none of which venture to pass Málaga for fear of enslavement, thereby depriving them of the benefits of carrying American products to where they are most wanted. The schooner *Madison*, James Parrock from Philadelphia, with flour and tobacco for Marseilles, and the brigantine *Fox*, Robert Millen from New York, with wheat for Barcelona, have had to stop and sell their cargoes here. In the absence of measures ensuring free navigation for Americans in this part of the world, the only remedy is for the United States to send an armed force to repel the barbarians and protect its trade. American and British seamen abroad commit great abuses by changing their allegiance as it suits them when brought before consuls of these powers or magistrates of countries they are in to settle their disputes. He recently found means to quiet the majority of the crew of the *Neptune* of Boston, who quarreled with their captain, Edward Preble, and falsely called themselves British subjects in an effort to serve aboard an English man-of-war here. To prevent similar incidents, those who serve on American ships should be enrolled on a separate document before they leave port on a foreign voyage in which "every man Should Sign and declare his Vassalage of the Country he belongs to," as it is difficult for masters to replace mariners in foreign ports. In addition to the Spanish fleet under Admiral Borja mentioned in his last and the British fleet under Lord Hood that had gone up the Mediterranean, Admiral Lángara with seven heavy ships from Cádiz and Admiral Gravina with four from Coruña have since followed them. There is no account here of any junction between British and Spanish naval forces or their plans of operations. Borja's fleet was lately forced to return to Cartagena in order to land 4,000 sick men. Hood, who passed Barcelona on the 18th while heading eastward, is expected to sail to Corsica in order to aid General Paoli, who has arrived there with a British commission and is now at the head of thousands of Corsicans in the back and mountain settlements waiting for the arrival of British naval forces to begin hostilities with the French army there. Since it is generally believed that the projected plans against France will not be achieved during this campaign, another one may cause some changes among the belligerent powers, especially those who cannot support heavy war expenses. The Prussian and Austrian armies cause great distress and slaughter to the enemy, but evidently gain no ground in French territory. In the face of a few provincial troops the Spanish have been more successful in Roussillon and need only conquer Perpignan to be masters of the province.

RC (DNA: RG 59, CD); 4 p.; at head of text: "No. 2"; at foot of first page: "Honble Thomas Jefferson, &ca &ca."; endorsed by TJ as received 2 Dec. 1793 and so recorded in SJL.

Notes of Cabinet Meeting on Neutrality

July 30. Met at my office. I proposed to add to the rules a proviso that they should not be understood to contravene, as of right they could not, the provisions of the   article of our treaty with France, the   of that with the U. N. or the   of that with Prussia. Before Ham. and Kn. came into the room E.R. declared himself for a general reference, or a verbal quotation of the words of the treaties, and against all comments or substitutions of new words. When they arrived, Ham. proposed a reference to the articles of the treaty by a description of the cases in shorter terms, which he proposed as equivalent to those of the treaty. E.R. said plumply and without one word of preface that he had been for a general reference to the treaties, but if the special descriptions would give more satisfaction, he would agree to it. So he and Hamilton drew their chairs together and made up the form: but it was agreed to be put off for more mature digestion.

MS (DLC); partially dated; written entirely in TJ's hand on first and second sides of two sheets containing "Anas" entries for 29 July and 1, 2, 3, and 6 Aug. 1793. Possibly recorded in SJPL between 29 July and 1 Aug. 1793 as "Rules to be establd." Included in the "Anas."

For the PROVISIONS in question, see Notes on Treaties and Neutrality, [29-30 July 1793]. The FORM prepared by Alexander Hamilton and Edmund Randolph (Syrett, *Hamilton*, XV, 141-2) contained most of the provisions listed by TJ. For the Cabinet's final disposition of this issue, see rules 3, 4, 6, and 7 of Rules on Neutrality, 3 Aug. 1793.

From Edward Church

Lisbon, 31 July 1793. He and his family arrived here by an expensive chartered vessel on 8 July after a long wait in Bordeaux. In order to comply with the request in TJ's 26 Aug. 1790 letter for an account of American ships entering and clearing ports in his district, he must be furnished with their registers. Although this practice is customary with consuls of other nations, there is no American law or authority requiring American captains to deposit their registers in his consular office, a circumstance of which recalcitrant captains can easily take advantage. Two captains here deny him their registers, not because they are masked or sailing under false colors—a frequent practice arising from the consuls' lack of power that greatly injures American citizens and produces serious mischief in the present crisis—nor because they wish to conceal something or are refractory, but only because of bad advice, for one confessed that he had been advised by his merchant or consignee to "throw his Ship on my hands" rather than comply. He has therefore thought it prudent not to demand this ship's register and hopes TJ will pardon this departure from orders. The head of an immensely rich English house here, which has almost monopolized American trade for more than twenty years, watches him with "an envious jealous Eye," fearing that he will obtain a small share of this commerce, and has complained about his charging two dollars for the consular seal and encouraged captains to do likewise, even though the resultant annual income is much less than a tithe of the income of the British consul here and significantly less than what the consuls of other nations receive. Since leaving America after his first consular appointment he has already expended more than the present consular fees would produce in ten years, and he is also informed that it will cost more than twenty johannes in fees to pass his patent through the various offices from the Secretary of State downward. He hopes that the duties and authority of American consuls will be more particularly defined so that they can maintain with "becoming dignity" the character and station that public officers in a foreign country need to discharge their responsibilities successfully. He will obey all of TJ's commands to the best of his ability and wishes to know if the last Congress passed any laws relating to commerce or consuls. P.S. Since arriving in Lisbon he received TJ's 14 Nov. 1792 letter.

RC (DNA: RG 59, CD); 4 p.; at foot of text: "Honble. Thos. Jefferson Esqr. Secretary of State for the United States of America Or—if retired—To his Successor in the Office"; endorsed by TJ as received 2 Dec. 1793 and so recorded in SJL. Another text of this letter, received on 25 Nov. 1793 according to SJL but not found, was enclosed in Church to TJ, 22 Sep. 1793.

From Tench Coxe, with Jefferson's Note

July 31. 1793

Mr. Coxe has the honor to inform Mr. Jefferson that he has purchased of Mr. John Wilcocks a bill on London at 174 ⅌Ct. to the amount of

5000 Drs. Mr. Wilcocks wishes for the Cash this day and will give Mr. Coxe the bills by the time Mr. Jefferson can send a check on the Bank.

[*Note by TJ:*]
gave instantly an order on the bank for 5000. D. payable to John Wilcocks or bearer. Tʜ J.

RC (DLC); with TJ's undated note subjoined; endorsed by TJ as received 31 July 1793 and so recorded in SJL.

TJ's ORDER of this date was drawn on the Bank of the United States "on account of the department of state" (FC in DLC; entirely in TJ's hand).

From Tench Coxe

Wednesday July 31. 1793

Mr. Coxe has the honor to enclose to Mr. Jefferson a bill of Mr. John Wilcocks for £1077.11.9 Stg. which, at 174 ℔Ct., amounts to 5000 Drs.

Mr. Vaughan this day informed Mr. Coxe that he was negociating for 50,000 Drs. in Bills on London to be delivered on the 18th. of Augt., which he said he should procure on much more favorable terms than 74 ℔Ct.—but he did not say how low. He added that 5000 Drs. could be secured for Mr. Jefferson, if he could be authorized tomorrow to [. . . .] [1]

RC (DLC); frayed at foot of text; with dateline above postscript; endorsed by TJ as received 1 Aug. 1793 and so recorded in SJL. Enclosure: Bill of exchange of John Wilcocks for £1,077.11.9 on Messrs. Edward MacCulloch & Company of London

payable to Thomas Pinckney, 31 July 1793 (printed form, signed by Wilcocks, with blanks filled in, in DLC; consisting of fourth set of exchange).

[1] Estimated one or two lines missing.

From Jean B. Desdoity

Mᴏɴsɪᴇᴜʀ   New york 31. Juillet 1793.

J'ai L'honneur de vous remettre ci-joint une Lettre de Messrs. Grand & Cie. de Paris, par laquelle Ils ont la bonté de me recommander à votre bienveillance et à vos bons offices dans ce Continent. J'aurois été bien flatté que mes occupations m'eussent permis d'aller moi même vous présenter cette Lettre et vous offrir L'hommage de mon respect; mais plusieurs affaires qui exigent ma présence dans cette ville m'empêchent d'avoir cette douce Satisfaction et m'obligent de différer de quelques Semaines le plaisir que J'aurai à vous présenter mes très humbles devoirs.

Il y a un an Passé que je Suis établi dans Cette ville et L'importance de mes affaires exigeroit que je fusse naturalisé *Citoyen Americain*. On m'a assuré que je ne pourrai pas l'être avant deux années de Séjour. Cependant, Monsieur, Si par Votre intervention Il étoit possible d'abréger Le delai que j'ai encore a attendre, Je vous en aurois une éternelle obligation, et vous me renderiez le plus grand Service. Je me Soumettrai volontiers à toutes les formalités usitées et telles qu'on exige en pareil cas. Permettez moi, Monsieur, de Solliciter Votre bienveillance en cette occasion et être persuadé que ma reconnoissance égalera dans tous les tems les Sentimens de respect et de considération avec les quels je Suis Monsieur Votre très humble & très obeissant Serviteur

DESDOITY

RC (DLC); at foot of first page: "his Excellency Ths. Jefferson, Philadelphie"; endorsed by TJ as received 2 Aug. 1793 and so recorded in SJL. Enclosure: Grand & Cie to TJ, 1 May 1793.

Jean B. Desdoity, who subsequently anglicized his forename, was a French emigrant who established himself as a merchant at 50 Maiden Lane in New York City (William Duncan, *The New-York Directory and Register* . . . [New York, 1793], 41; William Duncan, *The New-York Directory, and Register* . . . [New York, 1795], 62).

From Thomas Mann Randolph, Jr.

DEAR SIR   Monticello July 31: 1793.

I prepare now to give you some reasons according to promise for my preference of the plan of cultivation I transmitted you 3 weeks since to the one you did me the honor to consult me on.

The system of small fields in my plan, is nothing more than an extension of method beyond what you thought requisite in farming. The crops of this rotation, alltho of small value comparatively, are yet worth a methodical treatment on the following principle, if on no other. From the diversity of constitution in plants, some are injured while others are benefited, in the same stage of growth, by great heats or colds, by excessive moisture or drought. The weather every day in the year, must be the most favorable that can be, for some particular crop. Again, there are few plants which have exactly the same length of life, or which flourish exactly in the same season: Hence by a judicious arrangement the operations of sowing their seeds and gathering their fruits may be carried on without interference. The cultivation of a great variety of kinds will ensure plenty. A perpetual seed time will make a perpetual harvest. Thus many plants are worthy of regular cultivation, which are of no value in the market, and cannot in consequence be introduced into the great system with propriety, as the equality of the fields is indispensable. Peas and Potatoes are of this Class and ought not to keep their place among the Corns, if they are not greatly serviceable in preventing the washing of the land. Your plan gives 3 successive years of rest in every 8, to each field, mine the same number at intervals. For the preference I give the latter I have two or three reasons. Three years of rest successive to land full of the roots of trees, must occasion considerable trouble in grubing and cleaning up to prepare for a crop, at the end of that time. Our mountain land is so extremely prone to throw out the tulip-tree, the Locust, the Mulberry, and the Sasifrass, that after one year of rest, if it be not exhausted, a great deal of grubing is requisite. After three, the labor of cleaning would be immense. The soil is so compact, and so much the worse allways for being trodden, that a field after being grazed 3 years, would probably yield a trifling crop at first if it did not get the very best tillage. These objections would be obviated by sowing the land with Red Clover, and shuting it up for the Scythe, which would keep down the young trees, but I question whether this could be done readily to such an extent. Supposing it determined that the years of rest should be successive; I think it would be better to sow the white clover than the red, unless the force on the farm be sufficient to prepare 60 acres annually for the Scythe. The red clover is liable to be extirpated by the bite and treading of animals; the white bears grazing extremely well. The red clover would require to be sown annually in one of the fields of the farm; the white when once established would perpetuate itself; let it be eaten as closely as possible it perfects its seed in so short a time, that it will allways keep the earth well stocked, and will spring again the moment the field is out of cultivation. The red clover indeed, affords a much greater quantity of food, and I believe will bear much better the want of rain, which is an immense advantage with us. This is best on a small farm under exact management, the other does better for large fields and a loose agriculture. With respect to the summer fallow I know it is thought injudicious to expose land bare, to the summer sun, but it will never be bare I think, there will allways be a coat of weeds to shelter it, and there is a considerable advantage in this, that it will divide the business of breaking up the ground, between Autumn and Spring. The field, which is to go from rest immediately into Wheat in my plan, may receive the first ploughing in Spring. Those which are to bear Corn with Peas and Potatoes, must be broken up as soon as the seed time is over. If I understand your system, one of the fields destined for Wheat will be ploughed the first time, between Harvest and seed-time, and will be sown immediately after. Would not this be inconvenient, as that season is rendered the busiest in the year by our apprehensions of the Weevil? Wheat after Red clover would not succeed I fear, unless a fallow intervene, to give the clover[1] roots time to rot. This may be remedied at once, if a remedy be found requisite, by sowing the clover on the Rye. Six months may be thus gained in the age of the clover, and in consequence a fallow of six months or 12 even[2] may precede the Wheat. If sown in the fall it will give one, perhaps two, crops of hay the next Summer, after the Rye is taken off, and 2 or 3 each summer following for 2 years; after which it will be worth little. I saw a field of clover ready for the Scythe a fortnight ago which had been sown upon Barley last fall. When sown in the Spring, it never I believe, yields a tolerable crop of hay that summer. I am, Dear Sir, yours most affectionately

Th: M. Randolph

P.S. Patsy and the children are well.

RC (MHi); endorsed by TJ as received 10 Aug. 1793 and so recorded in SJL.

[1] Word interlined.
[2] Preceding two words and digits interlined.

To George Washington

Dear Sir   Philadelphia July 31. 1793.

When you did me the honor of appointing me to the office I now hold, I engaged in it without a view of continuing any length of time, and I pretty early concluded on the close of the first four years of our republic as a proper period for withdrawing; which, I had the honor of communicating to you. When the period however arrived circumstances had arisen, which, in the opinion of some of my friends, rendered it proper to postpone my purpose for a while. These circumstances have now ceased in such a degree as to leave me free to think again of a day on which I may withdraw, without it's exciting disadvantageous opinions or conjectures of any kind. The close of the present quarter seems to be a convenient period; because the quarterly accounts of the domestic department are then settled of course, and by that time also I may hope to recieve from abroad the materials for bringing up the foreign account to the end of it's third year. At the close therefore of the ensuing month of September, I shall beg leave to retire to scenes of greater tranquility, from those which I am every day more and more convinced that neither my talents, tone of mind, nor time of life fit me. I have thought it my duty to mention the matter thus early, that there may be time for the arrival of a successor, from any part of the union, from which you may think proper to call one. That you may find one more able to lighten the burthen of your labors, I most sincerely wish; for no man living more sincerely wishes that your administration could be rendered as pleasant to yourself, as it is useful and necessary to our country, nor feels for you a more rational or cordial attachment and respect than Dear Sir Your most obedient & most humble servt. Tн: Jefferson

RC (DNA: RG 59, MLR); addressed: "The President of the US."; endorsed by Tobias Lear. PrC (DLC). Tr (Lb in DNA: RG 59, SDC).

To George Washington

July 31. 93.

Th: Jefferson has the honor to return to the President the copy of questions which had been destined for the judges.

RC (DNA: RG 59, MLR); addressed: "The President of the US."; endorsed by Tobias Lear. Tr (Lb in same, SDC). Not recorded in SJL. Enclosure: Questions for the Supreme Court, [18 July 1793], Document IV of a group of documents on the referral of neutrality questions to the Supreme Court, at 18 July 1793.

From George Washington

Dear Sir   Philadelphia July 31st. 1793.

As there are several matters which must remain in a suspended state—perhaps not very conveniently—until a decision is had upon the conduct of the Minister of the French Republic—and as the Attorney General will, more than probably, be engaged at the Supreme Court next week—It is my wish, under these circumstances, to enter upon the consideration of the letters of that Minister to morrow, at 9 'Oclock; I therefore desire you will be here at that hour; and bring with you[1] his letters, your answers, and such other papers as are connected with the subject.

As the consideration of this business may require sometime, I should be glad if you and the other Gentlemen would take a family[2] dinner with me at 4 'Oclock. No other company is, or will be envited. Sincerely & affectly. I remain—Yrs.   Go: Washington

RC (DLC); endorsed by TJ as received 31 July 1793. Dft (DNA: RG 59, MLR); undated; with part of complimentary close and signature or initials clipped. FC (Lb in same, SDC); wording follows Dft. Recorded in SJPL.

[1] Dft here reads "all."
[2] Word underscored in Dft.

From Fulwar Skipwith

SIR   Fort Republic Mque   July 1793

Many details of the disaster which have befallen this devoted Island have doubtless reached you e'er this—and in no one can any great exaggeration have been made of the waste and horrors mutually committed by the two contending parties. The Royalists, however, are entirely driven from the Island with the British armament at their heels. Whether they will repeat their visit or not after the hurricane months, depend I immagine upon the intermediate events of Europe, and should then the success of British arms induce them to hazard a second siege, I am of opinion, that they will find the conquest of the Island Still more difficult. Should even the situation of the mother Country be so wretched as to preclude every hope of protection or assistance, the Island will be more tenable than strangers suppose. The colored people, aided by about two thousand of select slaves, are well armed, and desperately determined. Besides seven months provision of flour, their chief attention is turned to the cultivation of farine manioc. Indeed Men of all descriptions seem to be prepared to die at their posts.

With such dispositions and such means, the Island, notwithstanding is left in a most deplorable state. Murders, Massacres and Burning have been exercised in their most unbounded fury—the plantations saved from total ruin are abandoned by their proprietors—the Negros, consequently, 'tho not in actual insurrection, are all in a state of disobedience; and all civil law[s?] suspended. I am with most other men, in a commercial line, a sufferer, and in the present position of things seeing little prospect of redress, I contemplate soon to make my final adieu to this unhappy Island.

Many Vessels of the United States I am informed continue to be carried into the neighbouring British ports under suspicion of having french property on board. Having no communication with those Islands, I am ignorant of the degree of vexation, to which they may be subject. I have however put the American flag as much on their guard as has been in my power. With great Respect I have the honor to remain Sir Your mo ob and mo Hum Servant   FULWAR SKIPWITH

The decree of the National Assembly for admitting of Vessels of the United States into their colonial Ports upon the same footing with their own has not been yet officially received in this Island. The inclosed is a statement of the Duties which continue to be inflicted on all kinds of Merchandize brought in and carried out by American Vessels.

RC (DNA: RG 59, CD); partially dated; margin frayed; endorsed by TJ as received 24 Aug. 1793 and so recorded in SJL. Enclosure: Statement of duties imposed in

Martinique on imported and exported goods carried in foreign vessels, with observations, St. Pierre, 14 May 1793 (Tr in same; in French; with copy of certification of same date by d'Augui).

For the repulse in June 1793 of an attempted conquest of Martinique by a British expeditionary force led by Admiral Alan Gardner, an enterprise encouraged and supported by French royalist planters on the island, see Henry Lémery, *La Révolution Française à la Martinique* (Paris, 1936), 223-46. DECREE OF THE NATIONAL ASSEMBLY: see note to Joseph Fenwick to TJ, 25 Feb. 1793.

TJ submitted this letter to the President on 24 Aug. 1793, and Washington returned it the same day (Washington, *Journal*, 230).

From Samuel Biddle

SIR   Back Creek Augt 1 1793

I take this Opportunity of Informing you that I have been enquiring after people to Move to your lands but Cannot find any Inclin'd to Move this fall but says theyl go and See it in the fall. There are three or four has promised me to go. I stopt at Brandywine and Mr. Spurier Inform'd me that he should use his Influence in your favour and that he Should See you in A short time. I expect to be at Brandywine Shortley, so no more from sir Yr. Most Obt Hble Servt.   SAML. BIDDLE

RC (DLC); endorsed by TJ as received 6 Aug. 1793 and so recorded in SJL.

To George Hammond

SIR   Philadelphia August 1st. 1793.

I have this day laid before the President of the United States the enclosed papers, which you put into my hands before your departure for New York, and it is his opinion that if the vessel the Republican, therein mentioned as having been sent into New York, be a prize made on the Citizens of France, she ought not to be detained, but to be ordered to retire as soon as possible: And that if she be not a prize there is no ground for ordering her away. In the former case a reasonable delay will doubtless be admitted on account of the circumstance of her hands having been sent away. I have the honor to be with great respect, Sir Your most obedient and Most humble Servant.

PrC (DLC); in a clerk's hand, unsigned; at foot of text: "The Minister Plenipotentiary of Great Britain." FC (Lb in DNA: RG 59, DL). Tr (Lb in PRO: FO 116/3). Tr (same, 5/1). Enclosures: (1) Governor George Clinton to Sir John Temple, New York, 29 July 1793, stating that, having been asked by the French consul on the basis of Article 17 of the commercial treaty with France to interpose in the case of the English frigate which sent the French privateer *Republican* into this port, he intends to report on this matter to the President and wishes to know if Temple will engage to keep the *Re-*

publican and her officers and crew in port until the President's instructions arrive, in which case he will not need to take any other measure to detain her. (2) Temple to Clinton, 29 July 1793, stating that, as it would be very inconvenient for the commander and sailors of the tender belonging to the ship *Boston* that arrived here today to remain in port until the President's answer is received, the commander of the schooner will deliver it tomorrow to any person or persons authorized by Clinton to take custody of it. (3) Clinton to Temple, 30 July 1793, requesting him to order the schooner to proceed to sea without delay, since it is a tender rather than a prize of the *Boston* and

the commercial treaty with France only requires armed enemy vessels driven into American ports by the stress of weather to depart as soon as possible (PrCs of Trs in DLC, in a clerk's hand; Trs in Lb in DNA: RG 59, DL). Hammond evidently enclosed these papers in a letter of 31 July 1793 recorded in SJL as received that day but not found.

The President's OPINION was based on Article 17 of the 1778 commercial treaty with France (see note to Document II of a group of documents on the referral of neutrality questions to the Supreme Court, at 18 July 1793).

From John Harriott

RIGHT HONBLE: SIR   Baltimore Augst: 1. 1793

Landing last Night at Baltimore, after a tedious Passage of ten Weeks, I take the earliest opportunity of sending the accompanying Letters and Parcells, with the care of which, I have been much honored by Mr. Pinckney. Mr. Pinckney having likewise favored me with a Line of Introduction, I shall be proud of an opportunity of delivering it in Person, whenever it may offer. At present I am disagreably confin'd by lameness. And finding Baltimore no ways suitable to fix my Family in, while I make excursions in the different States to find Land likely to answer my purpose for Agriculture, I am at an uncertainty where I shall remove to for the present with my Family, whether the Neighborhood of New York, Rhode Island, or directly up into the back Country.

I have long had a predilection for this Country and Government. I have now cast the Die with a bold Hand (being sensible of the risque with so large a family) and must trust the Event to Providence. I have the Honor to subscribe myself Right Honble: Sir Your Devoted & faithful Hble Servt: JOHN HARRIOTT

RC (MHi); endorsed by TJ as received 3 Aug. 1793 and so recorded in SJL. Enclosures: Thomas Pinckney to TJ, 11, 15 May 1793, the latter not found (see note to TJ to Pinckney, 22 Aug. 1793).

John Harriott (1745-1817), a native of the county of Essex, England, had a colorful career which included travel to the West Indies and the Levant while serving in the Royal Navy, visits to America as a ship's

mate on merchant vessels, a wound incurred while leading sepoys in battle in India, and the reclamation from the sea of an island in Essex, which he farmed until a disastrous fire led him to immigrate to the United States. In this and a subsequent stay he tried farming near Newport, Rhode Island, and on Long Island, but in 1796 he moved back to England permanently, where he patented several inventions and in 1798 helped found the Thames River police, which he served as resident magistrate until just prior to his death (DNB; John Harriott, *Struggles Through Life*, 2d ed., 2 vols. [London, 1808], esp. II, 10, 90, 158-64, 190-1; Harriott to TJ, 4 Oct. 1793).

Thomas Pinckney's LINE OF INTRODUCTION of 11 May 1793 is summarized in note to Pinckney's other letter to TJ of that date.

Notes of Cabinet Meeting on Edmond Charles Genet

Aug. 1. Met at the President's to consider what was to be done with Mr. Genet. All his correspondence with me was read over. The following propositions were made. 1. that a full statement of Mr. Genet's conduct be made in a letter to G. Morris, and be sent with his correspondence, to be communicated to the Exec. council of France, the letter to be so prepared as to serve for the form of communication to the council. Agreed unanimously. 2. that in that letter his recall be required. Agreed by all, tho' I expressed a preference of expressing that desire with great delicacy. The others were for peremptory terms. 3. to send him off. This was proposed by Knox, but rejected by every other. 4. to write a letter to Mr. Genet, the same in substance with that written to G.M. and let him know we had applied for his recall. I was against this, because I thought it would render him extremely active in his plans, and endanger confusion. But I was overruled by the other three gentlemen and the Presidt. 5. that a publication of the whole correspondence, and statement of the proceedings should be made by way of appeal to the people. Hamilton made a jury speech of $\frac{3}{4}$ of an hour as inflammatory and declamatory as if he had been speaking to a jury. E.R. opposed it. I chose to leave the contest between them. Adjourned to next day.

MS (DLC); partially dated; written entirely in TJ's hand on the second side of two sheets containing "Anas" entries for 29 and 30 July and 2, 3, and 6 Aug. 1793. Recorded in SJPL under 1 Aug. 1793 with

"Anas" entries for 2, 3, and 6 Aug. 1793: "Notes. Consultn at Pres's.—Genet.—appeal to people—privateers & prizes. call of Congress.—engagemt of Ambuscade & Boston." Included in the "Anas."

From Thomas Pinckney

MY DEAR SIR   London 1st. August 1793

I was hopeful you would have received the Copper for the mint by this conveyance but the Contractors have already carried a small quantity down to the Wharff and I have no doubt they will put 20,000 wt. which will be near half the quantity our funds can purchase on board of the Pigou Captn. Loxley who will sail in a few days.

I have to acknowledge the receipt of your favors by Majr. Jackson the contents of which shall be attended to and a more particular answer than I can now give to some parts of them shall be sent by the Pigou. No alteration in our affairs here render it necessary to enter into any details & I remain with the utmost respect Dear Sir Your most faithful & obedt Servant

THOMAS PINCKNEY

RC (DNA: RG 59, DD); at foot of text: "The Secretary of State"; endorsed by TJ as received 24 Oct. 1793 and so recorded in SJL. Tr (Lb in same).

On 2 Nov. 1793 TJ submitted this letter to the President, who returned it the same day (Washington, *Journal*, 242).

From Henry Remsen

DR. SIR   New York August 1st. 1793

You may recollect that you desired me to purchase and send you a small silver inkstand when I was last in Philada. On my return here I found that Berry & Rogers had sold all of their's, and that there was not one at any other shop in town. I concluded therefore to wait 'till spring before I wrote to you on the subject, when Mr. Rogers assured me he should receive a supply. He did accordingly receive a few, but as they were much larger both in length and diameter, of higher price, a different shape and destitute of a pen, I judged such a one would not answer. A few days since I accidentally met with just such a one as you had before, and have now the pleasure to enclose it. I am thus particularly, Sir, lest my silence may have been attributed to inattention.

Schneider informs me, after having duly considered what you wrote respecting his going to Virginia, that he cannot take less than two dollars per day while actually employed, that is, from his arrival and readiness to begin to work until his discharge, and one dollar per day for his travelling expences in going and returning. He is now engaged in painting, in dry fresco, a large room for the reception and deposit of the curiosities belonging to the Tammanial society, and receives that pay. I have seen his work, and it looks well. From what I could learn, he appears to prefer this as his residence, as he frequently is employed by the Theatre in scene painting.

The Ambuscade sailed yesterday morning for Sandy Hook. She got under way and attempted it the day before, but the wind being directly ahead and blowing strong, and the pilot declining then to take charge of her, she was obliged to come to anchor. Unfortunately one of her lieutenants with a boats crew, who were out reconnoitering the English frigate, approached too near to her and were taken. The enclosed paper, into which the inkstand is wrapped, contains our latest advices from

Europe. I have the Honor to be with great respect & esteem Dr. Sir Your most obt. & h'ble servt.   HENRY REMSEN

PS. A report prevails, brought to town by a man from Long island, that there was a considerable firing this morning early which lasted about 50 minutes. We hope the Ambuscade has been successful, if it was only to repress the pride and vanity of some of our anglo-americans.

PS—August 1st. 6 O'Clock. P: M: By a pilot boat just come up we have the following particulars, which are generally credited and which I believe may be relied on. About 5 O'Clock this morning the Ambuscade and Boston met 10 leagues distant from Sandy Hook, and without exchanging a single word began to engage. The Ambuscade fired the first broadside, and having the wind in the beginning preserved it the whole time. She attempted twice to board her antagonist, but failed from the tempestuousness of the wind, and each time was raked. About 8 O'Clock a:m: the English frigate put before the wind, and sailed off, and the French, as soon as could repair her damages a little, crouded all her sails in pursuit. During the engagement each ship had her colours shot down. The Ambuscade lost her main yard arm, and her fore sail was much torn by the shot. The Boston lost her main top mast with all its appendages, and immediately after clearing herself of them made off. Captains of Vessels say if the Ambuscade has overtaken her before another mast could be erected, she must be made a prize. I hope you will pardon my freedom, Sir, in giving you this detail. It interests us much here; and I thought it might not be altogether unacceptable, at least from it's novelty, as many people among us, who feel an interest in the success of the efforts now making by the French, have not yet got over the foolish prejudice of supposing, that an English armed vessel will of course take any other of equal force with which she may engage.

RC (DLC); addressed: "Thomas Jefferson Esqr. Secy of State Philadelphia"; endorsed by TJ as received 3 Aug. 1793 and so recorded in SJL.

From Phineas Bond

SIR   Chestnut Street 2d. Augt. 1793.

In the Absence of his Majesty's Minister pleny: I have the Honor to inclose You a Copy of the Affidavit of Donald Stewart Master of the Brigantine Jane of Dublin taken and sent into the Port of Philadelphia by the Privateer Schooner sans Culotte commanded by Capt. Johanene.

As some Communications have already been made to You on this Subject by his Majesty's Minr:—it is sufficient for me to observe that the Affidavit fully ascertains the Capture by the Schooner sans Culotte.

And I flatter myself the particular Circumstances of this Case will justify me in the Hope that Measures will be taken to detain this Vessel and her Cargo until the Determination of the Government of the United States upon the Legality of the Capture can be obtained. With Sentiments of perfect respect, I have the Honor to be Sir Your very faithful & most obdt. Servt: P. BOND

RC (DNA: RG 59, NL); at foot of text: "Secretary of State"; with notes on verso by TJ: "⟨brig⟩ Jane of Dublin taken by the Citizen Genet. proscribed. before Aug. 7."; endorsed by TJ as received 3 Aug. 1793 and so recorded in SJL. Tr (Lb in same). Enclosure: Deposition of Donald Stewart, Philadelphia, 1 Aug. 1793, stating, as master of the brigantine *Jane* of Dublin, that on 24 July 1793, seventeen days after leaving Antigua bound for Norfolk, Virginia, with 65 puncheons of rum and 20 barrels of limes, his ship was captured by the French privateer *Citoyen Genet*, Captain Johanene, "5 Leagues from Cape Henry . . . being then within Sight of the Land, and having been so for about half an Hour, and in 8 fathom Water"; that after all but one boy in the crew and one passenger were transferred to the

privateer a prize master and four men brought his ship to Philadelphia, where it now was; that he, his mate, and three of his men were put on the sloop *Laura* of Rhode Island and reached Baltimore on 30 July; that, while on board the privateer, he learned from Captain Johanene that he had lately been to Baltimore to careen and had sailed from Hampton Road the evening before the capture, observed that the privateer was never farther than ten leagues from land, and overheard some of its officers say that it mostly cruised off the Virginia capes (Tr in same, in Bond's hand and sworn before him; Tr in Lb in same).

As indicated by the enclosure, the PRIVATEER SCHOONER in question was actually the *Citoyen Genet*.

From Joseph Fenwick

Bordeaux, 2 Aug. 1793. Indisposition obliging him to leave Bordeaux for what he hopes will be no longer than two months, he has left his consular procuration with Jonathan Jones, a Pennsylvania native and gentleman well known here and in America for his worth, integrity, and attachment to the welfare of the United States, and hopes his absence will produce neither reproach nor inconvenience.

RC (DNA: RG 59, CD); 1 p.; at foot of text: "The Honorable Secretary of State of the U.S. Philadelphia"; endorsed by TJ as received 24 Oct. 1793 and so recorded in

SJL. Also received that day, according to SJL, was a letter from Fenwick to TJ of 24 Sep. 1793 that has not been found.

Notes of Cabinet Meeting on Edmond Charles Genet

Aug. 2. Met again. Hamilton spoke again $\frac{3}{4}$ of an hour. I answered on these topics. OBJECT of the appeal.—The Democratic society—this the great circumstance of alarm; afrd. it would extend it's connections over continent. Chiefly meant for the local object of the ensuing election of governor. If left alone would die away after that is over. If opposed, if proscribed, would give it importance and vigor, would give it a new object, and multitudes would join it merely to assert the right of voluntary associations.—That the measure was calculated to make the Pres. assume the station of the head of a party instead of the head of the nation.—PLAN of the appeal. To consist of FACTS and the DECISIONS of the Pres.—As to facts we are agreed. But as to the decisions there has been great differences of opinion among us. Sometimes as many opinions as persons. This proves there will be ground to attack the decisions—Genet will appeal also. Will become contest between Pres. and Genet.—Anonymous writers.—Will be same difference of opinion in PUBLIC, as in our Cabinet.—Will be same difference in CONGRESS, for must be laid before them.—Would therefore work very unpleasantly at HOME.—How could it work ABROAD?—France. Unkind. After such proofs of her friendship, should rely on that friendship and her justice. Why appeal to the world? Friendly nations always negotiate little differences in private—never appeal to the world, but when they appeal to the sword.—Confedcy. of Pilnitz was to overthrow government of France. The interference of France to disturb other governments and excite insurrections was a measure of reprisal. Yet these princes have been able to make it believed to be the system of France. Col. Ham. supposes Mr. Gen's proceedings here are in pursuance of that system. And we are to declare it to the world and to add our testimony to this base calumny of the princes. What a triumph to them to be backed by our testimony. What a fatal stroke at the cause of liberty.—ET TU BRUTE!—We indispose the Fr. government, and they will retract their offer of the treaty of commerce. The President manifestly inclined to the appeal to the people.[1] He said that Mr. Morris, taking a family dinner with him the other day went largely and of his own accord into this subject, advised this appeal and promised if the Presidt. adopted it that he would support it himself, and engage for all his connections.—The Presidt. repeated this twice, and with an air of importance.—Now Mr. Morris has no family connections. He engaged then for his political friends.—This shews that the President has not confidence enough in the virtue and good sense of mankind to confide in a government [bottomed on][2] them, and thinks other props necessary. Knox in a foolish incoherent sort of a speech introduced the Pasquinade lately printed, called the funeral of George W—n and James W—n, king and judge &c. where the President was placed on a Guillotin. The Presidt. was much inflamed, got into one of those passions when he cannot command himself. Run on much on the personal abuse which had been bestowed on him. Defied any man on earth to produce one single act of his since he had been in the government which was not done on the purest motives.

That he had never repented but once the having slipped the moment of resigning his office, and that was every moment since. That *by god* he had rather be in his grave than in his present situation. That he had rather be on his farm than to be made *emperor of the world* and yet that they were charging him with wanting to be a king. That that *rascal Freneau* sent him 3. of his papers every day, as if he thought he would become the distributor of his papers, that he could see in this nothing but an impudent design to insult him. He ended in this high tone. There was a pause. Some difficulty in resuming our question—it was however after a little while presented again, and he said there seemed to be no necessity for deciding it now: the[3] propositions before agreed on might be put into a train of execution, and perhaps events would shew whether the appeal would be necessary or not. He desired we would meet at my office the next day to consider what should be done with the vessels armed in our ports by Mr. Genet and their prizes.

MS (DLC); partially dated; written entirely in TJ's hand on the second and third sides of two sheets containing "Anas" entries for 29 and 30 July and 1, 3, and 6 Aug. 1793; with addition in margin (see note 1 below); two words torn away. Included in the "Anas."

THE APPEAL: Alexander Hamilton's proposal that the Washington administration publish its reasons for requesting the French government to recall Edmond Charles Genet (see Notes of Cabinet Meeting on Edmond Charles Genet, 1 Aug. 1793). THE DEMOCRATIC SOCIETY of Pennsylvania, founded by Philadelphia Republicans after Genet's arrival in May 1793 to support the French Revolution and preserve American republicanism from perceived Federalist corruption, inspired the establishment of almost forty other similar popular societies

in the United States during the next five years (Eugene P. Link, *Democratic-Republican Societies, 1790-1800* [New York, 1942], 10-16). CONFEDCY. OF PILNITZ: a reference to the 27 Aug. 1791 Declaration of Pillnitz wherein Emperor Leopold II and King Frederick William II of Prussia asserted that the situation of Louis XVI after his abortive flight to Varennes was a matter of concern to all European sovereigns and invited other European powers to join them in restoring effective monarchical government in France (Scott and Rothaus, *Historical Dictionary*, I, 300-1).

[1] TJ inserted an asterisk above this word to serve as a key to the next five sentences, which he wrote lengthwise in the margin.

[2] MS torn; words supplied from Ford, I, 254n.

[3] TJ here canceled "other."

Cabinet Opinion on Prizes and Privateers

That the Minister of the French Republic[1] be informed that the President considers[2] the UStates as bound pursuant to positive assurances,[3] given in conformity to the laws of neutrality,[4] to effectuate the restoration of, or to make compensation for,[5] prizes which shall have been made of any of the parties at war with France subsequent to the fifth day of June last by privateers fitted out of their ports.

That it is consequently expected, that he will cause[6] restitution to be made of all prizes[7] taken and brought into our Ports subsequent to the abovementioned day by such privateers; in defect of which The President considers it as incumbent[8] upon the UStates to indemnify the Owners of those prizes . . . the indemnification to be reimbursed by the French Nation.[9]

That[10] besides taking efficacious measures to prevent the future fitting out of Privateers in the Ports of The UStates, they will not give asylum therein to any which shall have been at any time so fitted out,[11] and will cause restitution[12] of all such prizes as shall be hereafter brought within their Ports by any of the said Privateers.

That instructions be sent to the respective Governors in conformity to the above communication.[13]

The foregoing having been duely considered and being now unanimously approved they are submitted to The President of The United States. August 3. 1793.

TH: JEFFERSON
ALEXANDER HAMILTON
H KNOX
EDM: RANDOLPH

MS (DLC: Washington Papers); in Hamilton's hand, signed by TJ, Hamilton, Knox, and Randolph; fourth paragraph added as a result of Cabinet discussion (see note 13 below); ellipsis in original; endorsed by Tobias Lear. Dft (DLC: Hamilton Papers); undated; entirely in Hamilton's hand, unsigned; consists of heavily emended variant text of first three paragraphs only, the most significant emendations being noted below. PrC of Tr (DLC); in the hand of George Taylor, Jr.; at foot of text: "(Copy)." PrC of Tr (DLC: Washington Papers); in Taylor's hand; at foot of text: "(Copy)"; on verso in ink: "Rules." Recorded in SJPL under date torn away: "Opn of heads of dep. on compensn for prizes after June 5."

This document consists of the Cabinet's response to the diplomatic problems arising from Edmond Charles Genet's defiance of the decision, announced in TJ's letter to the French minister of THE FIFTH DAY OF JUNE LAST, that all privateers commissioned by him in the United States were thenceforth to depart from American ports. Internal evidence in the draft suggests that Alexander Hamilton probably presented it in unrevised form to the Cabinet this day as a basis

for discussion, and that he amended it while the Cabinet met, one of the key alterations deriving from TJ's opposition to his proposed use of military force to secure restoration of the prizes brought into American ports by such privateers after 5 June 1793 (see note 11 below). At the behest of the Cabinet Hamilton also added the fourth paragraph to his fair copy of the opinion (see note 13 below). TJ submitted the signed document to the President on this day (Washington, *Journal*, 213; Notes of Cabinet Meeting on Neutrality, 3 Aug. 1793; Washington to TJ, 4 Aug. 1793).

[1] Dft: "Mr. Genet."

[2] Preceding three words interlined here and in Dft.

[3] In Dft Hamilton first wrote "the UStates consider themselves bound in conformity to their assurances to the Minister of Great Britain" before altering the passage to read as above.

[4] Dft here reads: "founded on the principles of the neutrality they have declared."

[5] Preceding three words interlined in Dft in place of "make indemnification ⟨indemnify⟩ for all."

[6] Here in Dft Hamilton interlined "immediate."

[7] Remainder of clause in Dft: "heretofore made by such privateers."

[8] In Dft Hamilton first wrote "⟨they shall proceed to⟩ it will ⟨become the duty of the⟩ in the opinion of the President be incumbent" before altering the passage to read as above.

[9] Clause interlined in Dft in place of "and will charge the amount of such indemnification against the debt which they owe to France."

[10] Remainder of clause in Dft interlined by Hamilton in slightly variant form.

[11] In Dft Hamilton here canceled "within ⟨such Ports⟩ the same. And if any shall hereafter come in they will employ ⟨military force⟩ such means as shall be necessary and effectual to suppress or expel them." For the source of this alteration, see Notes of Cabinet Meeting on Neutrality, 3 Aug. 1793.

[12] In Dft Hamilton here canceled "by the like means."

[13] Hamilton inserted this paragraph after writing the next one or after the signatures were affixed. For the source of this addition, see Notes of Cabinet Meeting on Neutrality, 3 Aug. 1793.

From Enoch Edwards

DEAR SIR   August 3rd. 1793 London

By the William Penn I wrote you a Letter and inclosed you a Number of News-Papers—to the Care of our Friend Doctor Rush—but as I suppose this Letter may reach You before that Ship arrives, I embrace the Oportunity to inform You that Valenciennes is now actually taken by the combined Armies. The Letter I then wrote to you expresses a Doubt of its being taken at all—it was written the Evening before the News arrived—next Day the Penn sailed—and will carry that Intelligence to You.

Thank God there is no Event in a good Cause that does not afford a Scource for Consolation in adverse Fortune. We now think here that it will be for the better, as it may and probably will unite those jarring Interests which have hitherto splitt up and divided France. If they can only be brought to coallece so far as to oppose the *common Enemies*—for they all seem to be Republicans in one Shape or other—the present Crusade against Liberty would be ineffectual.

This is a very excellent Place to give a Man a real Love for Republicanism—so much so that it would be worth while for the Gouverment of the United States to pay the Expences of all its Aristocrats—over to this Country, and let them be eye Witness's to the truely deplorable Situation of the fallen and insulted[1] Majesty of Liberty. I sincerely believe unless the Decrees of Heaven forbid the Conversion that it would now even make a Proselyte of Publicola himself. But though as I mention in my last Liberty is begining again to raise her affrighted head, like on the american Cent,[2] yet the breath that displays the Breast in which it is contained—is oblidged to lie rather low and softly—tho' there is plenty to be seen every where that sufficiently evinces discontent.

[605]

The Rage for Emigration from this Country exceeds every thing you can conceive of, whole Congregations of Independents, and other Dissenters are now geting ready to embark for America.

If you will do me the Honour to exchange the Information from the different Countries—it will be made a good Use of here and entitle you to my Exercions to give You the best I can. I am very respectfully, with great Esteem Your obedt. srv.   ENO: EDWARDS

RC (DLC); addressed: "Thomas Jefferson Esqr: Philadelphia"; endorsed by TJ as received 24 Oct. 1793 and so recorded in SJL.

PUBLICOLA: John Quincy Adams's *nom de plume* in a series of eleven newspaper es-

says which attacked Thomas Paine's *Rights of Man* in 1791 (see Vol. 20: 280-6).

[1] Preceding two words interlined.
[2] Preceding seven words interlined.

To James Madison

Aug. 3. 93.

Yours of July 18. and 22. are received and have relieved my anxieties about mine of June 27. 30. and July 7. Those of July 14. 21. and 28. I hope soon to have acknoleged. We have decided unanimously to *require*[1] the *recall of Genet. He will sink the republican* interest if they do not *abandon him. Hamilton pressed eagerly an appeal*[2] to the *people.* It's consequences you will readily seize, but *I hope we shall prevent it* tho the *President is inclined* to it.—The *loan* is agreed to to the full extent on *E.R.'s advice*[3] splitting off a *few dollars* to give himself the airs of *independance.*

I will send you the little peice written by him on *the proclamation* if I can find it. I will here note your several requisitions in your letter of July 22. 1. what concessions have been made on particular points behind the curtain. I think it is better you should not know them. 2. how far *the President*[4] considers himself as committed with respect to some doctrines. He is certainly uneasy at those grasped at by *Pacificus* and as *the author* is universally known and I believe indeed denied not even by himself, it is foreseen that the vulnerable points, well struck, stab the party vitally.—3. lights from the law of nations on the constructions of treaties. Vattel has been most generally the guide, Bynkershoeck often quoted, Wolf sometimes. 4. no call was made by any *power* previous to the *proclamation. Genet* has been fully heard on his most unfounded pretensions under *the treaty.* His ignorance of every thing written on the subject is astonishing. I think he has never read a book of any sort in that branch of science. The question whether the war between France and Gr. Br. is offensive or defensive *has not been*[5] *particularly discussed.*

Hamilton has insisted it was offensive by the former. I will send you the French collection of papers on that subject.—A paper inclosed will lead you to inform yourself on questions which may come into discussion perhaps at the next session of Congress. They were prepared *for the judges who however will not agree*[6] I believe *to give opinions. I informed*[7] *the President by letter three* days ago that *I should resign* the last day of *September*. Consequently *I shall see you* the middle of *october*. Adieu.

RC (DLC: Madison Papers); unsigned; partly in code (see note 1 below), with interlinear decipherment inserted much later in first paragraph by an unidentified hand and in second paragraph by William C. Rives. PrC (DLC); with interlinear decipherment in ink by TJ. Tr (MHi); 19th-century copy; with interlinear decipherment following PrC. Enclosure: Questions for the Supreme Court, [18 July 1793], Document IV at Editorial Note and documents on the referral of neutrality questions to the Supreme Court, at 18 July 1793.

TJ's letters to Madison OF JUNE 27. 30. were actually dated 23 and 29 June 1793, although the latter contained a 30 June postscript. For the new foreign LOAN, approval of which had been deferred pending the ADVICE of Attorney General Edmund Randolph, see TJ's opinions of 5 and 17 June 1793, and notes. Randolph's LITTLE PEICE is described in note to TJ to Madison, 29 June 1793.

[1] This and subsequent words in italics are written in code, the text being supplied, except as noted, from TJ's decipherment in PrC and verified by the Editors against Code No. 9 (see also TJ to Madison, 18 Aug. 1793, and note). TJ mistakenly deciphered this word as "request."

[2] TJ mistakenly encoded the last letter of this word as "145," the cipher used for either "i" or "j."

[3] Word deciphered by the Editors; in PrC TJ mistakenly deciphered it as "opinion."

[4] Preceding two words deciphered by the Editors; TJ did not decipher them in PrC.

[5] Preceding three words mistakenly deciphered by TJ in PrC as "was never."

[6] Word mistakenly placed after "I believe" in TJ's decipherment in PrC.

[7] TJ wrote "I in" *en clair* before erasing it and beginning the sentence in code.

Notes of Cabinet Meeting on Neutrality

Aug. 3. We met. The rules being now reduced on one paper I considered them, and not[1] finding any thing against the treaties as far as I could see, they were agreed to and signed by us all.—We proceeded to consider what should be done as to the French privateers armed in our ports, and their prizes taken since they were ordered away. Randolph recapitulated his old opinion. Hamilton proposed to suppress the privateers by military coercion[2] and deliver the prizes to their owners. I proposed to require from Mr. Genet a delivery of the prizes to their owners, otherwise that, in consequence of the assurances we had given the British minister, we should be bound to pay for them and must take credit for it with France, and to inform him that we would allow no further asylum in our ports to the said privateers. [These were the Citoyen

Genet, Sans culottes, Vainqueur de la Bastille and petite Democrate. The two last had been armed subsequent to the prohibition.] My proposition was agreed to with an addition that the Governor's should be notified that the privateers were no longer to be permitted to stay in our ports.

The President wrote to take our opinions Whether Congress should be called. Knox pronounced at once against it. Randolph was against it. Hamilton said his judgment was against it, but that if any two were for it or against it, he would join them to make a majority. I was for it. We agreed to give separate opinions to the Presidt.—Knox said we should have had fine work if Congress had been sitting these two last months. The fool thus let out the secret. Hamilton endeavored to patch up the indiscretion of this blabber, by saying 'he did not know; he rather thought they would have strengthened the Executive arm.' It is evidence they[3] do not wish to lengthen the session of the *next Congress*, and probably they particularly wish it should not meet till Genet is gone.—At this meeting I received a letter from Mr. Remsen at N.Y. informing me of the event of the combat between the Ambuscade and the Boston. Knox broke out into the most unqualified abuse of Capt. Courtnay. Hamilton, with less fury, but with the deepest vexation, loaded him with censures. Both shewed the most unequivocal mortification at the event.

MS (DLC); partially dated; written entirely in TJ's hand on the third side of two sheets containing "Anas" entries for 29 and 30 July and 1, 2, and 6 Aug. 1793; brackets in original. Included in the "Anas."

RULES: Rules on Neutrality, 3 Aug. 1793. For the measures proposed to deal with FRENCH PRIVATEERS ARMED IN OUR PORTS, see Cabinet Opinion on Prizes and Privateers, 3 Aug. 1793.

[1] TJ here canceled "being able to."
[2] Preceding two words interlined in place of "force."
[3] TJ here canceled "fear."

Rules on Neutrality

1.[1] The original arming and equipping of vessels in the ports of the United States by any of the belligerent parties, for military service offensive or defensive, is deemed unlawful.

2. Equipments of merchant vessels[2] by either of the belligerent parties in the ports of the United States, purely for the accommodation of them as such, is deemed lawful.

3. Equipments in the ports of the United States[3] of vessels of war in the immediate[4] service of the Government of any of the belligerent parties, which if done to other vessels would be of a[5] doubtful nature, as being applicable either to commerce or war, are deemed lawful; except those which shall have made prize of the subjects, people, or property of

France coming with their prizes into the Ports of the United States pursuant to the seventeenth Article of our Treaty of Amity and commerce with France.

4. Equipments in the Ports of the united States,[6] by any of the parties at war with France,[7] of vessels fitted for Merchandize and war, whether with or without Commissions, which are doubtful in their nature as being applicable either to commerce or war, are deemed lawful; except those which shall have made prize, &c.[8]

5. Equipments[9] of any of the vessels of France, in the Ports of the United States, which are doubtful in their nature, as being applicable to commerce or war, are deemed lawful.

6. Equipments of every kind in the Ports of the United States, of privateers of the Powers at war with France, are deemed unlawful.

7. Equipments[10] of vessels in the Ports of the United States, which are of a nature solely adapted to war,[11] are deemed unlawful; except those stranded or[12] wrecked, as mentioned in the eighteenth Article of our Treaty with France, the sixteenth of our Treaty with the United Netherlands, the ninth of our Treaty with Prussia, and except those[13] mentioned in the nineteenth Article of our Treaty with France, the seventeenth of our Treaty with the United Netherlands, the eighteenth of our Treaty with Prussia.

8. Vessels of either of the parties not armed, or armed previous to their coming into the ports of the United States, which shall not have infringed any of the foregoing rules, may lawfully engage or inlist therein[14] their own Subjects or[15] Citizens, not being inhabitants of the United States; except privateers of the Powers at War with France, and except those vessels which shall have made prize, &c.[16]

August 3. 1793

The foregoing rules having been considered by us at several meetings, and being now unanimously approved, they are submitted to the President of the United States.

TH: JEFFERSON
ALEXANDER HAMILTON
H. KNOX
EDM: RANDOLPH

MS (DLC: Washington Papers); in the hand of George Taylor, Jr., signed by TJ, Hamilton, Knox, and Randolph, with date and final paragraph in Randolph's hand; endorsed by Tobias Lear. PrC (DLC); undated and unsigned; lacks final paragraph. Dft (DLC: TJ Papers, 91: 15625); undated; in Hamilton's hand, with some revisions subsequently made by him in a darker ink and a marginal note by Randolph (see note 6 below), only the most important alterations being recorded below. PrC of Tr (DLC: Washington Papers); in Taylor's hand. Recorded in SJPL under 1 Aug. 1793: "Hamilton's rough draught of rules.—fair copy."

Designed to address problems that had arisen at various times after the issuance of the Proclamation of Neutrality, these rules emerged from a series of Cabinet meetings that began on 29 July 1793. On that day the

Cabinet approved five of six general neutrality rules proposed by Edmund Randolph and Alexander Hamilton, and on the following day it agreed in principle to a proposal by TJ to include mention of the treaty provisions that formed exceptions to them (Notes of Cabinet Meeting on Neutrality, 29, 30 July 1793). On the basis of these decisions, Hamilton produced a draft consisting of eight rules that he later amended, partly in response to suggestions made by members of the Cabinet. On instructions from the President, the Cabinet met this day and approved a text of the rules made from Hamilton's revised draft by George Taylor, Jr., TJ's chief clerk, to which Randolph added a final paragraph. TJ submitted the signed document to the President, who approved it on 4 Aug. 1793. Hamilton enclosed the rules in a circular letter to United States customs collectors dated 4 Aug. 1793, but not before it was approved by the Cabinet, including one important modification suggested by TJ, and received the President's sanction on 9 Aug. 1793 (Tr in DLC; entirely in a clerk's hand, unsigned, with clerk's note in margin recording suggestions made by TJ; at foot of text in clerk's hand: "Approved H Knox" and "approved with the alteration of armed vessel for Privateer Th: Jefferson"; recorded in SJPL; variant text printed in Syrett, *Hamilton*, xv, 178-81, alterations made in response to TJ's suggestion being described on 179n, and another modification, in a different text, agreed to and signed by Knox, TJ, and Randolph being recorded on 180n). Washington also approved that same day a circular letter of 7 Aug. 1793 from Knox to the state governors informing them of the rules (Notes of Cabinet Meeting on Neutrality, 3 Aug. 1793; Washington to TJ, 4 Aug. 1793; and Washington, *Journal*, 212, 213, 216, 218n).

[1] Dft begins in Hamilton's hand: "At a Meeting of the Secretary of State The Secretary of the Treasury The Secretary at War and the Attorney General at the   The following rules were   agreed to."

[2] Remainder of clause interlined by Hamilton in Dft.

[3] Preceding seven words interlined by Hamilton in Dft.

[4] Word interlined by Hamilton in Dft.

[5] Preceding nine words interlined in a darker ink by Hamilton in Dft in place of "are of a."

[6] In Dft Hamilton originally wrote the next two clauses as "of vessels armed for Merchandize and War" before revising the passage as above.

[7] Preceding four words interlined in Dft by Hamilton in a darker ink after revising the passage described in the preceding note. He made this change in response to a note Edmund Randolph wrote in the margin next to this rule: "qu: if not better to say something here to distinguish vessels of France; altho' taken up in the next article."

[8] In Dft Hamilton here canceled his original fifth rule, which he later used in slightly variant form as rule 6.

[9] Remainder of clause interlined by Hamilton in Dft.

[10] "All" canceled by Hamilton with darker ink before this word in Dft.

[11] Preceding word altered by Hamilton in Dft from "warlike purposes."

[12] Word interlined by Hamilton in a darker ink in Dft in place of "and."

[13] In Dft Hamilton here canceled with darker ink "putting into the Ports of the UStates through stress of weather pursuit of pirates or [enemies] or other urgent necessity or accident as."

[14] Word interlined by Hamilton in Dft.

[15] Preceding two words interlined by Hamilton in a darker ink in Dft.

[16] On a small sheet filed with the Dft, Hamilton wrote "The following rules were proposed but not agreed to." These rules have not been identified.

George Washington to the Cabinet

GENTLEMEN   Philadelphia August 3d 1793

Fresh occurrences, but communicated through private channels, make it indispensable that the general principles which have already been the Subject of discussion, should be fixed and made known for the government of all concerned as soon as they can be, with propriety.

To fix rules on substantial and impartial ground, conformably to treaties and the Laws of Nations, is extremely desirable.

The Verdict of the late Jury in the case of Henfield, and the decision of yesterday respecting the French Minister, added to the situation of Indian affairs and the *general* complexion of public matters, induce me to ask your advice whether it be proper—or not—to convene the Legislature at an earlier period than that at which it is to meet, by Law? And if it be thought advisable, at what time?   Go: WASHINGTON

RC (DLC); at head of text: "To—The heads of Departments and Attorney-General"; endorsed by TJ as received 3 Aug. 1793. FC (Lb in DNA: RG 59, SDC); with minor variations. Recorded in SJPL under date torn away.

To Edmond Charles Genet

SIR   Philadelphia Aug. 4. 1793.

In consequence of your letter of the 2d. inst. reclaiming the French Vessel the Republican, as being captured within the limits of the protection of the US. I have desired of the British minister that she may be detained till enquiry can be made into the fact. In the mean time I must ask the favor of you to furnish me with the depositions or other competent testimony of the fact, that the detention, if improper, may not be inconveniently extended.

Due attention has been paid to the British vessel the Jane which was the subject of your letter of July 9. It was found on enquiry that she was not a privateer, but a Merchant vessel which had for many years been engaged in the commerce between the US. and West Indies. She brought a cargo here, and took away a cargo. She was armed when she arrived: but having mounted some additional guns here, opened some new port-holes, and procured some new carriages, she was compelled to dismount the additional guns, stop her new port-holes, and to land her new-carriages before she was permitted to depart. I have the honor to be with great respect & esteem Sir your most obedient & most humble servt   TH: JEFFERSON

PrC (DLC); at foot of text: "The Min. Pleny. of The republic of France." FC (Lb in DNA: RG 59, DL).

Genet's LETTER OF THE 2D. INST., recorded in SJL as received 3 Aug. 1793, has not been found.

From Edmond Charles Genet

MONSIEUR   Philadelphie le 4 Aout 1793 l'an 2e de la République

Je m'empresse de vous dénoncer des hommes qui abusent de l'azile qu'ils ont trouvé dans les Etats Unis pour former de nouveaux complots contre leur Patrie. Ces hommes Sont ceux qui ont attiré à la Colonie de St. Domingue tous les maux qui l'accablent aujourdhui par leur opiniâtre resistance aux Loix par leurs passions, par leurs préjugés. Des avis certains m'ont appris qu'ils forment dans ce moment ci l'odieux projet de Se rassembler sur le territoire même des E.U. pour aller Soutenir ceux de leurs complices qui osent encore lutter contre les autorités constituées par la République Française pour maintenir l'ordre et la tranquillité à St. Domingue.

L'intéret de la France et de l'Amérique, Monsieur, exige et que le gouvernement fédéral prenne les mesures les plus pressantes pour decouvrir la trame de cette nouvelle conspiration et en prevenir les funestes effets et je Suis persuadé qu'en portant à Sa connaissance les faits que je vous dénonce cet objet sera rempli.

Dft (DLC: Genet Papers); in a clerk's hand, unsigned, with minor revision by Genet; above salutation: "Le Citoyen Genet à Mr jefferson Sec. d'Etat des E.U." Tr (AMAE: CPEU, xxxix); docketed and signed by Genet. Recorded in SJL as received 5 Aug. 1793.

On 6 Aug. 1793 Secretary of War Henry Knox, to whom Genet's letter was submitted either by TJ or the President, wrote a letter instructing Governor Thomas Sim Lee of Maryland to investigate the French minister's allegation that Saint-Domingue refugees in Baltimore were planning a military expedition against the French island.

Acting governor James Brice subsequently informed Knox that an investigation of this matter by Maryland councillor John Kilty, including a consultation with F. Moissonnier, the French vice-consul at Baltimore, revealed that there was no basis for the charge (W. H. Browne and others, eds., *Archives of Maryland*, 72 vols. [Baltimore, 1883-1972], LXXII, 345; Brice to Knox, 23 Aug. 1793, MdAA: Letter Books of Governor and Council). For a description of Genet's general concerns about the alleged designs of the royalist refugees from the Saint-Domingue slave revolt, see Childs, *French Refugee Life*, 165-75.

To George Hammond

SIR   Philadelphia Aug. 4. 1793.

Since I had the honor of addressing you on the 1st. instant on the subject of the Republican sent into New York by the Boston frigate as her tender, I have received a letter from the Minister of France alledging that the Boston captured the Republican within the limits of the protection of the US. Should this be agreeable to the fact in your own judgment, I would request her delivery to her owners; but should you have, or be able to procure evidence to the contrary I will ask the favor of a communication of that evidence, and that the British Consul retain the vessel in his custody until the Executive of the US. shall consider and decide finally on the subject. I have the honor to be with great respect Sir, Your most obedt. & most humble servt   TH: JEFFERSON

PrC (DLC); at foot of text: "The Min. Pleny. of Gr. Br." FC (Lb in DNA: RG 59, DL). Enclosed in TJ to Sir John Temple, 4 Aug. 1793.

From David Humphreys

Lisbon, 4 Aug. 1793. Three vessels arrived here a few days ago from St. Michael with distinguished Moors, whom he visited with Church and Dohrman to offer assistance after receiving an account of them, via the American captain of one of these ships, in a letter from Thomas Hickling, acting consul at St. Michael, whose Portuguese patent he encloses. The Moors consisted of two widows of the old Emperor Sidi Muhammad, one of the late Emperor Muley Yezid, two wives and eleven concubines of Muley Absulem (the blind prince visited by Lamprière and reported to have been the old emperor's favorite), some young princes and princesses, and many attendants, all under the care of a Director of Finances, Mahomet Squierz, a sensible old man who was grateful for himself and on behalf of the royal family for their visit and attention (the first the Moors had received here), as well as for Hickling's services to them, of which they have given a written declaration under the royal seal. Squierz, who dined with him the first day, expressed in their absence a strong wish to be useful to the United States. The civilities they showed him cannot be prejudicial to the United States, given the confidence he enjoys by virtue of the party entrusted to him and the old emperor having employed him in confidential and foreign negotiations. After some delay the Portuguese court now overwhelms the Moors with honors and accommodations, and many paragraphs about them appear in the Lisbon gazettes. A few days ago they debarked under a royal salute in the queen's barge, attended on shore by a multitude of people and the Prince of Brazil, and were taken in six state carriages by an escort of horse and foot guards to the royal palace of the Necessidades. He believes that this is "the first entire Moorish Harem that ever came to Europe," and this treatment, since the expulsion of the Moors from Portugal, is as singular a circumstance. The motives and incidents of their intended voyage from Santa Cruz to Salé are accurately reported in the 27 July Lisbon Gazette. To prove their rank the Moors have brought the original of the last treaty between Morocco and Portugal. Other accounts of the voyage indicate that Muley Absulem, the governor on the Atlantic coasts under his brother Muley Ischem, has defected to the party of his brother Muley Suliman and arrived safely from Santa Cruz at Fez, whence it seems pretty certain the Moorish royal family has received letters from him. Accounts by the last post from Gibraltar state that there is no appearance of any settlement of the Moroccan succession, that no nation is treating with either of the pretenders, and that Ischem still resides at Morocco while Suliman has returned to Mequinez from Rabat, whence a force of about 10,000 men sent by him to the southward was beaten back with heavy losses by the people of the middle province. An officer he knows has just arrived from Gibraltar with a report that a rich and distinguished basha from Tripoli has gone to Morocco via Gibraltar to negotiate an accommodation between the two brothers. He encloses a copy of a letter he lately received on this subject from de la Mar in Amsterdam, the self-styled envoy extraordinary from the Moroccan court, but the Dutch minister here states positively that no person has been recognized at The Hague in that character. Sharpe, who delivered that letter, complains of the great inconvenience encountered by United States ships trading with Santa Cruz, Mogador, and other places for want of someone to dispatch them and especially to give them bills of health, a problem he promised him to bring to the executive's attention through TJ. By the last letters from Gibraltar it appears that nothing has been heard for a long time of the American prisoners in Algiers, that surprisingly Mace is still at Gibraltar, Lord Hood having refused to provide a ship for him because of the plague in Algiers, that Algerine cruisers are at sea, and that some row boats from Oran are near Gibraltar, the Portuguese fleet alone keeping them in the Mediterranean. Two boats had been at Tetuán, according to the officer from Gibraltar, and another source reports that some American ships destined up the Mediterranean had consequently unloaded at Málaga. He has had no news of Cutting by the packet that arrived since his last letter and fears some accident has befallen him. By the last mail he learned that Condé was taken but not Valenciennes. English papers report that the Provisional Executive Council has declared in consequence of a National Convention decree that, except for military stores, no enemy property on United States ships is liable to capture. The new constitution was agreed to in Paris and offered to the primary assemblies for discussion and acceptance on the 10th. P.S. He wishes the President to know that Hickling, formerly of Boston and now a wealthy merchant and Swedish consul at St. Michael, is generally represented as a very respectable man who has rendered services to and deserves well of the United States. The Portuguese court has given a great promotion to the principal judge at St. Michael for his services there to the Moorish princesses. He encloses an authentic declaration in Hickling's favor.

RC (DNA: RG 59, DD); 8 p.; at head of text: "(No. 77.)"; above postscript: "The Secretary of State &c. &c. &c."; endorsed by TJ as received 2 Dec. 1793 and so recorded in SJL. Tr (Lb in same). Enclosures: (1) Declaration by Dr. João Manoel Pereira da Costa Silveira, Ponta Delgada, 4 Oct. 1784, accepting on behalf of the king of Portugal the application of Thomas Hickling, an American-born merchant working with an established mercantile firm here, to serve as provisional consul for the United States on St. Michael, with Hickling's oath of 6 Oct. 1784 to discharge the duties of this office well and faithfully (Tr in same, in Portuguese, certified 28 June 1793 and signed by Hickling; Tr in same, in Hickling's hand; Tr in Lb in same). (2) Declaration of Mahomet Squerz, Ponta Delgada, 27 June 1793, stating, in his capacity as Inspector of the Treasury and Conductor of the Royal Family of the Prince of Morocco, Muley Absulem Suliman, that he was deeply grateful for Hickling's offer in the name of the United States to do everything in his power to assist him and his royal charges

(Tr in same, in Portuguese, signed by Hickling; Tr in same, in Hickling's hand; Tr in Lb in same). (3) Masohed de la Mar to Humphreys, Amsterdam, 1 July 1793, stating, in his capacity as envoy extraordinary of the Moroccan court, that he has been instructed by dispatches from Emperor Muley Ischem sent through William Sharpe to inform Congress, in consideration of the treaty with Morocco and the recognition by European nations of the throne he has occupied for two years, that the Emperor wishes to continue the friendship that existed under his father and seeks approval of his appointment of Sharpe, an American from Wilmington, Delaware, who has long lived on the Barbary coast and is now a resident merchant at Safi, to act as consul for the United States (Tr in same, in Humphreys's hand; Tr in Lb in same).

TJ submitted this letter to the President on 3 Dec. 1793, and Washington returned it the same day (Washington, Journal, 263, 264).

Opinion on Convening Congress

The President having been pleased to propose, for consideration, the question Whether it be proper or not to convene the legislature at an earlier period than that at which it is to meet by law? and at what time? I am of opinion it will be proper.

1. Because the protection of our Southern frontiers seems to render indispensable a war with the Creeks, which cannot be declared, nor provided for but by the legislature, nor prudently undertaken by the Executive on account of the consequences it may involve with respect to Spain.

2. Because several legislative provisions are wanting to enable the government to steer steadily through the difficulties daily produced by the war of Europe, and to prevent our being involved in it by the incidents and perplexities to which it is constantly giving birth.

3. Because should we be involved in it, which is every day possible, however anxiously we endeavor to avoid it, the legislature meeting a month earlier will place them a month forwarder in their provisions for that state of things.

I think the 1st. Monday in November would be a proper time for convening them, because, while it would gain a month in making provisions to prevent or prepare for war, it leaves such a space of time for their assembling, as will avoid exciting alarm either at home or abroad.

Th: Jefferson
Aug. 4. 1793.

MS (DLC: Washington Papers); entirely in TJ's hand; addressed: "The President of the US."; endorsed by Washington. PrC (DLC). Recorded in SJPL under date torn away: "Th:J's opn on calling Congress."

Article II, section 3, of the United States Constitution provided that the President could convene one or both houses of Congress "on extraordinary Occasions." Although Washington had favored convening Congress AT AN EARLIER PERIOD, he accepted the opposing counsel of Alexander Hamilton, Henry Knox, and Edmund Randolph, all of whom argued that there was no pressing need for an earlier meeting of Congress, that in any case Congress could be assembled only a month sooner than scheduled, and that any advantages in time gained would be outweighed by the public alarm foreseeable if the President were to exercise this power (Notes of Cabinet Decisions, 6 Aug. 1793; Hamilton to Washington, 5 Aug. 1793, Syrett, *Hamilton*, xv, 194-5; Knox to Washington, 5 Aug. 1793, Randolph to Washington, [5 Aug. 1793], DLC: Washington Papers).

From Edmund Randolph

E. Randolph to Mr. Jefferson   Philadelphia August 4. 1793.

I can never believe, that the impeachment of Mr. G. should be drawn from any other sources, than his written and verbal communications with you. That he is the president of a particular society; that his secretary may have written inflammatory queries, &c may be reasons, privately operating to the demand of his recal, I shall not absolutely deny; because foreign ministers may give causes of displeasure, and render themselves unacceptable for intercourse by acts, which may not however be strong enough to become articles of formal accusation. But[1] they will not satisfy the American mind; which constitutes the soul of our government.

In the letter therefore, to be written to him, the people, to whom the whole of the affair will sooner or later be exposed, ought to be kept in view: and it ought not to be forgotten, that Mr. G. has some zealous partizans, and the French nation too many, to suffer subtleties or caprices to justify the harsh measure.

I do not conceive it to be any part, of what you have requested of me, or in any degree necessary, to suggest the outlines of those remarks, which ought to precede the charges. It is only for me, to assign the reasons, upon which I grounded my opinion for a recal.

1. His assurances, that no other commissions should be granted to privateers within the U.S.; and the repetition notwithstanding.

2. The continuance of the consuls within his controul and knowledge, to exercise the functions of the admiralty; his declarations to the contrary notwithstanding.

3. His sending off the Little Democrat, against the wishes of the government, expressed to him.

4. His reprehensible language concerning, and addressed to, the Executive; discarding however, all ambiguities.

5. His undertaking to reclaim those citizens of the U.S., who had been prosecuted for entering on board of French privateers.

RC (DLC). Recorded in SJPL.

This letter was intended to assist TJ in preparing the letters to Gouverneur Morris and Edmond Charles Genet on the Washington administration's request for the French minister's recall that the Cabinet had agreed on at a meeting held three days before (Notes of Cabinet Meeting on Edmond Charles Genet, 1 Aug. 1793; TJ to Morris, 16 Aug. 1793; TJ to Genet, [7 Sep. 1793]). Genet was PRESIDENT of the Société Française des Amis de la Liberté et de l'Égalité, an organization of Frenchmen in Philadelphia dedicated to supporting the French Revolution and monitoring the activities of royalist refugees from Saint-Domingue (Childs, *French Refugee Life*, 146-8, 166-7). INFLAMMATORY QUERIES: see Notes of Cabinet Meeting on Edmond Charles Genet, 23 July 1793, and note.

[1] Word interlined in place of "At any rate."

To Martha Jefferson Randolph

My dear Martha   Philadelphia Aug. 4. 1793.

I inclose you two of Petit's receipts. The orthography will amuse you, while the matter of them may be useful. The last of the two is really valuable, as the beans preserved in that manner, are as firm, fresh, and green, as when gathered.—Mr. D. Randolph is at Philadelphia, and well. He delivered me your watch, which I will have ready to send by him. He proposes to set out for Monticello in 8. or 10. days. Present my best respects to Mrs. Randolph and my regrets at my absence during the favor of her visit. I hope to be more fortunate another time.—We have had a remarkeable death here which I will mention for example sake. Mrs. Lear, wife of the gentleman who is secretary to the President, by eating green plumbs and apples brought on a mortification of the bowels which carried her off in six days. She was 23. years old, and of as fine healthy a constitution as I ever knew. Tell Anne this story, and kiss her for me, in presenting one of the inclosed caricatures. I put up several as Mrs. Randolph may have some of her family to whom they may give a moment's pleasure. My best affections are with Mr. Randolph and yourself. Adieu my dear.

RC (NNP); unsigned; at foot of text: "Mrs. Randolph." PrC (MHi). First enclosure printed below; other enclosures not found.

ENCLOSURE

Recipes of Adrien Petit

Pour faire des peches à l'eau-de-vie.

Il faut essuyer les peches pour oter le duvet. Ensuite les piquer avec une fourchette dans 5. à 6. endroits. Vous faites bouiller de l'eau. Quand elle bout, vous jettez vos peches pour les blanchir, seulement. Laissez faire un bouillon. Ensuite vous les retirez, et mettez tout-de suite à l'eau froid. Vous les retirez de l'eau pour les egoutter. Vous faites clarifier du sucre et les laissez bouillir, pour retirer l'eau vous verrez quand il sera assez bouilli en trempant le doigt dedans, et frottez les deux doigts. Si vous sentez que vos doigts tiennent ensemble, c'est qu'il est assez. Vous le laissez refroidir. Quand il est froid, vous y mettez les peches pour les y laisser 24. heures. Ensuite vous faites bouiller votre sucre un seconde fois, en y ajoutant une *pinte d'eau de vie. Ne laissez pas le sucre sur le feu. Vous vous brouillerez la figure, si vous ne prenez pas cette precaution. Vous laissez refroidir le sucre. Ensuite vous remettez les peches. Le lendemain vous faites bouillir votre sucre, jusqu'a ce que vous voyez qu'il soit gras à vos doigts. Vous le retirez pour verser encore la quantité d'eau de vie qu'il faut. Vous y mettrez vos peches pour les faire bouillir un bouillon ou deux. Vous les retirez du feu pour les laisser refroidir. Quand elles sont froides, vous les mettez dans

* an American pint.

des bouteilles à large goulot, tout doucement. Vous passez le syrop au travers d'une serviette, et le versez sur les peches. Vous bouchez bien vos bouteilles et le tout est fini.

Pesez vos peches. Sur 4. livres de peches un livre de sucre et un pinte d'eau de vie.

To preserve haricots vers for winter use.

Take a tight barrel, with one head out, and set it up an-end. Let your snaps be green but their moisture dried out a little. Lay in a layer of salt and a layer of beans alternately, each about a finger thick, and finish with a layer of salt. Lay the loose head on them and weight it pretty well down with stones.

About 2 bushels of beans will serve a family the winter.

Tr (DLC: TJ Papers, 234: 41870-1); entirely in TJ's hand; undated; endorsed by TJ: "preserves." For a loose English translation of the first recipe, see Marie Kimball, *Thomas Jefferson's Cook Book* (Charlottesville, 1976), 38.

To Sir John Temple

SIR   Philadelphia Aug. 4. 1793.

I put the inclosed letter under cover to you on the presumption that Mr. Hammond is with you. Should he be returned to this place, you will be so good as to send it to him by post. In that case I take the liberty of desiring you to retain the Republican till you hear from Mr. Hammond on the subject; the purport of the inclosed letter being to inform him that the Minister of France has reclaimed the Republican, as taken by the Boston frigate within the limits of the protection of the US. and to ask the favor of him to furnish what evidence he can on the question, for the consideration of the President. I have the honor to be with great respect & esteem, Sir your most obedt. & most humble servt

TH: JEFFERSON

PrC (DLC); at foot of text: "Sr. John Temple." FC (Lb in DNA: RG 59, DL). Tr (PRO: FO 5/2). Enclosure: TJ to George Hammond, 4 Aug. 1793.

From George Washington

SIR   Phila. Augt. 4th. 1793.

If the heads of Departments and the Attorney General, who have prepared the eight rules which you handed to me yesterday, are well satisfied that they are not repugnant to treaties, or to the Laws of Nations; and moreover, are the best we can adopt to maintain Neutrality; I not only give them my approbation, but desire they may be made known without delay for the information of all concerned.

The same expression will do for the other paper, which has been subscribed as above, and submitted to my consideration for restoring, or making restitution of Prizes under the circumstances therein mentioned.

It is proper you should be informed that the Minster of France intends to leave this City for New York tomorrow; and not amiss, perhaps, to know that in mentioning the seasonable aid of hands which the Ambuscade received from the French Indiaman, the day preceeding her meeting the Boston, he added that Seamen would no longer be wanting, as he had *now* 1500 at his command. This being the case (altho' the allusion was to the Subject he was then speaking upon) some of these Men may be employed in the equipment of other Privateers than those *now* in existence; as the right of fitting out such, *in our Ports* is asserted in unequivocal terms.

Was the propriety of convening the Legislature at an earlier day than that on which it is to assemble by Law, considered yesterday? The late decree of the National Convention of France—dated the 9th. of May—authorising their Ships of War and Armed Vessels to stop any Neutral Vessels loaded in whole, or part with Provisions, and send them into their Ports, adds another motive for the adoption of this measure.

Go: Washington

RC (DLC); at head of text: "To the Secretary of State"; endorsed by TJ as received 4 Aug. 1793. PrC (DNA: RG 59, MLR). FC (Lb in same, SDC); with a minor variation. Recorded in SJPL with date torn away.

EIGHT RULES: Rules on Neutrality, 3 Aug. 1793. OTHER PAPER: Cabinet Opinion on Prizes and Privateers, 3 Aug. 1793. 1500 AT HIS COMMAND: a reference to the seamen in the French fleet from Saint-Domingue that had recently arrived in New York and that over the next two months Genet sought unsuccessfully to integrate into his plans for French expeditions against Canada and Louisiana (Ammon, *Genet Mission*, 120-6).

To George Washington

Sunday Aug. 4. 93.

Th: Jefferson presents his respects to the President and will pay due attention to his letter of this day. The question of convening the legislature was considered and as our opinions differed, we agreed to give them separately which will be done tomorrow. We are to meet at 10, aclock tomorrow to apply the rules, now approved by the President, to the several memorials and complaints as yet undecided, the result of which will be submitted to the President.

RC (DLC: Washington Papers); addressed: "The President of the US."; endorsed by Washington. Not recorded in SJL.

Cabinet Opinions on Privateers and Prizes

At a meeting of the heads of departments and the Attorney general at the Secretary of state's office Aug. 5. 1793.

The case of the Swallow letter of marque at New York, desired to be sent out of our ports, as being a privateer. It is the opinion that there is no ground to make any order on the subject.

The Polly or Republican, in the hands of the Marshal at New York, on a charge of having been armed in our ports to cruize against nations at peace with the US. It is the opinion there is no ground to make any new order in this case.

The Little Democrat, the Vanqueur de la Bastille, the Citoyen Genet, and the Sans Culottes. A letter to be written to Mr. Genet as was determined on the 3d. instant, and an instruction in conformity therewith be given to the governors. Mr. Hammond to be informed thereof and to be assured the government will effectuate their former resolution on this subject. [1]

The Lovely Lass, the Prince William Henry, and the Jane of Dublin, prizes to the Citoyen Genet. Mr. Genet to be [2] written to as was agreed on the 3d. inst.

The brig Fanny and Ship William reclaimed as taken within the limits of our protection. As it is expected that the court of Admiralty may very shortly reconsider whether it will take cognisance of these cases, it is thought better to [3] take no new measure therein for the present.

The Schooner fitting out at Boston as mentioned in a letter of Mr. Gore to Mr. Lear. The Governor of Massachusetts to be written to to suppress her.

Mr. Delaney's letter of the 24th. of July on the question whether duties are to be paid on prize goods landed for sale. It is the opinion the duties are to be paid.

A letter from Mr. Genet of the 4th. of Aug. informing the Secretary of state that certain inhabitants lately arrived from St. Domingo are combining to form a military expedition from the territory of the US. against the constituted authorities of the said island. It is the opinion that the Governor of Maryland be informed thereof (because in a verbal communication to the Secretary of state Mr. Genet had named Baltimore as the place where the combination was forming) and that he be desired to take measures to prevent the same.

Th: Jefferson
Alexander Hamilton
H Knox

The Secretary of State and Attorney General are of opinion that Mr. Hammond be informed that measures are taking to procure restoration of the prizes the *Lovely Lass the Prince William Henry* and the *Jane of Dublin*, and in case that cannot be effected that Government will take the subject into further consideration.[4]

The Secretaries of the Treasury and of War are of opinion that Mr. Hammond be informed that measures are taking to effect the restoration of the prizes The *Lovely Lass*, The *Prince William Henry* and the *Jane of Dublin*; that in case this shall not be effected The President considers it as incumbent upon the UStates to make compensation for those Prizes; and that prizes in similar circumstances which shall be hereafter brought into the Ports of the UStates will be restored.[5]

MS (DLC: Washington Papers); with first nine paragraphs in TJ's hand, signed by TJ, Hamilton, and Knox, and last two paragraphs in Hamilton's hand; endorsed by Tobias Lear. PrC (DLC). Dft (DLC: TJ Papers, 92: 15839); undated; consists of variant texts of next to last paragraph in Randolph's hand and of last paragraph in Hamilton's hand (see notes 4 and 5 below). Entry in SJPL: "Opns of heads of dep.— Swallow &c." Draft recorded in SJPL under 24 Aug. 1793: "Notes of E.R. and A.H. as to informn to Hammond.—Th:J's do." Included in the "Anas."

The CASE OF THE SWALLOW is discussed in the enclosure to Edmond Charles Genet to TJ, 25 June 1793. For the government's previous actions with respect to the POLLY OR REPUBLICAN, see Cabinet Opinions on the *Republican* and the *Catharine*, 12 June 1793. The letters to GENET and HAMMOND are printed below under 7 Aug. 1793, the difference of opinion in the Cabinet over the content of the latter being decided by the President in favor of Hamilton and Knox (see TJ to Washington, [ca. 18-19 Aug. 1793]). For the circular letter TO THE GOVERNORS subsequently prepared by Henry Knox in conformity with the Cabinet's opinion, see Washington, *Journal*, 216. There is no evidence that the United States District Court of Pennsylvania reconsidered its decisions that it lacked jurisdiction over the cases of the BRIG FANNY AND SHIP WILLIAM (see note to Hammond to TJ, 5 June 1793). According to his later account, Christopher GORE, the United States District Attorney in Massachusetts, had reported the fitting out in Boston of the French privateer *Roland* in missing letters

to Tobias Lear of 4 and 6 Aug. 1793, but clearly the one considered by the Cabinet must have been written even earlier (Gore to Lear, 24 Aug. 1793, DNA: RG 59, MLR). For Knox's letter instructing Governor John Hancock TO SUPPRESS HER, see Washington, *Journal*, 216-17. The LETTER OF THE 24TH. OF JULY from Sharp Delany, the customs collector in Philadelphia, to Alexander Hamilton has not been found, but see same, 208. For Knox's letter to Governor Thomas Sim Lee on the INHABITANTS LATELY ARRIVED FROM ST. DOMINGO, see same, 217.

TJ submitted this document to the President this day (Washington, *Journal*, 214).

[1] Sentence interlined.
[2] TJ here canceled "informed th."
[3] TJ here canceled "let."
[4] In Dft Randolph wrote this paragraph as follows: "To inform Mr. Hammond, that measures are to procure restoration of the vessels; and in case, that cannot be effected, that government will take the subject into farther consideration."
[5] In Dft Hamilton wrote this paragraph as follows: "That Mr. Hammond be informed that ⟨Government are⟩ measures are taking to effect the restoration of the Prizes The Lovely Lass the Prince William Henry and the Jane of Dublin ⟨and⟩ that in case this shall not be effected The President considers it as incumbent upon the UStates to make compensation for those prizes; and that ⟨that for the fut⟩ ⟨in future⟩ ⟨will in future cause⟩ measures will be taken for the immediate restitution of such Prizes as shall hereafter brought into the UStates in ⟨a⟩ similar ⟨predicament⟩ circumstances."

To Jean B. Desdoity

[Dear Sir]   Aug. 5. 1793.[1]

[. . .][2] favor of [. . .][3] Grand & Co. of Paris. I am always glad to recieve their commands, and shall with chearfulness testify it in rendering you any service I can. In the particular case on which you are pleased to consult me, I will observe that[4] though the law of the United states requires a residence of two years to make a citizen, yet some of the states admit a citizen on shorter residence, perhaps some of them without any residence at all. If you will therefore give yourself the trouble of enquiring into the rules of citizenship established by the different states, you will probably find some of them adapted to your situation and views, and if you can make yourself a citizen of any one state, you are thereby a citizen of every one. There is no other way of hastening your attainment of that character, as there is no power in this country to dispense with the laws. I have the honor to be with due respect, Sir Your most obedt. humble servt.   TH: JEFFERSON

PrC (DLC); with dateline added in ink, possibly at a later date, and salutation and most of first line of text badly faded; at foot of text: "M. Desdoity. mercht. New York."

Desdoity's FAVOR was dated 31 July 1793.

[1] Dateline added in ink by TJ, with "Aug." written over "July."

[2] Estimated three or four words illegible.

[3] Estimated four or five words illegible.

[4] TJ here canceled "the different states."

To John Harriott

[Dear Sir]   [Philadelphia] Aug. 5. 1793.

I have duly received your [. . .][1] [pack]ages from Mr. Pinckney for your care of which I return you my thanks. Your object being to settle yourself in this country, you have certainly taken the wisest course, that of going yourself to see the different parts of it, and chuse for yourself. This choice, in order to make it a happy one, depending on the circumstances of climate, soil, cheapness of land, state of society &c. adapted to the views of the person, none but himself can make it. You mention doubts between New York, Rhode-island, and the back country. There are circumstances which would render it worth your while to look also a little way Southwardly. From my knoledge of the different parts of the middle states I would advise you to visit the country lying along the little mountains about 20. or 25. miles below the blue ridge in Virginia, crossing the Patowmac about Leesburg, passing South Westwardly by the Red house Fauquier court house, Culpepper court house and along the South West mountains. There is no healthier nor finer climate in

America, the winters do not eat up the summers, as is the case North-wardly, the soil of the richest and best adapted to farming, and having been kept in the hands of tobacco makers, remains still ill in it's appear-ance, consequently cheap, but capable of becoming excessively rich, and in a very short time, in the hands of a farmer. I take the liberty of men-tioning this, because I know that particular circumstances lead the views of uninformed strangers in a direction[2] which does not give them a fair choice to suit their views and interests: and I have thought I could not serve you better than by apprising you of it. I have the honor to be Sir Your most obedt. humble servt.   TH: JEFFERSON

PrC (DLC); salutation, dateline, and part of first line of text badly faded, with dateline partly overwritten in ink by TJ; at foot of text: "Mr. John Harriot. Baltimore."

[1] Estimated four words illegible.
[2] TJ here canceled "not always the."

From James Madison

Augst. 5[1] 93

At the date of my last which was on thursday last, yours of the 14. had not arrived. I have since received it. That of the 28th. is also just handed me. A review of mine will shew you that all yours from June 23 forward have now been acknowledged. Your account of the ticklish sit-uation with respect to Genet in the 14th. is truly distressing. His folly would almost beget suspicions of the worst sort. The consequences you point out in case matters come to an extremity are so certain and obvi-ous[2] that it is hardly conceivable he can be blind to them. Some-thing must be done if possible to get him into a better train. I find by the paper of the 27. that P. has entered and I suppose closed his last topic. I think it a feeble defence of one important point I am striking at: viz. the making a declaration *in his sense of it*, before the arrival of Genet. I argue that the Act does not import a decision against the Casus foederis from the manifest impropriety of doing so on the ground that F. was the aggressor in *every* war, without at least[3] waiting for evidence as to the question of fact who made the first attack admiting for the sake of argu-ment that to be the criterion. A difficulty has occurred which will retard my remarks more than I expected. They must be prepared for the *same Gazette*, consequently copied into another hand. I am laying a plan for having it done here, but it cannot be done as quickly as I wish. The drouth begins to be severe and alarming for the corn. In a hurry yrs. always

RC (DLC: Madison Papers); unsigned; endorsed by TJ as received 13 Aug. 1793 and so recorded in SJL.

THURSDAY LAST was 1 Aug. 1793, a date for which no letter has been found to TJ from Madison, who was probably alluding to his letter of 30 July 1793. F.: France. On 27 July 1793 Alexander Hamilton's seventh and last "Pacificus" essay defending the Proclamation of Neutrality appeared in the *Gazette of the United States*, the SAME GAZETTE which on 24 Aug. began printing the responses Madison penned as "Helvid-ius" (Syrett, *Hamilton*, xv, 130-5; Madison, *Papers*, xv, 66-73).

[1] Digit reworked from "6."
[2] Preceding two words interlined.
[3] Preceding two words interlined.

To Edmund Randolph

DEAR SIR   Philadelphia Aug. 5. 1793.

Having determined to retire from my office before the term of paiment of the inclosed bill and so informed the President, it is indispensable for me to wind up all my money concerns as fast as I can, in which operation I am actually engaged. This circumstance renders it impossible for me to enter into any new engagement here, my first object now being to see myself cleared out, and neither owing nor answerable for a single shilling here. My anxiety to get into this situation will I hope excuse my declining the endorsement of the inclosed note, which would be utterly against the plan I am proceeding on for my perfect liberation from this place. I sincerely feel for the embarrasments of the accident you mention, and wish I could have aided in lessening them, being with sincere esteem Dr Sir Your friend & servt   TH: JEFFERSON

PrC (DLC); at foot of text: "Mr. Randolph." Enclosure not found.

From Abraham Runnels & Son

SIR   Philadelphia Markett Street No. 222 5th. Augst. 1793

The Peculiar disagreableness of the business I am at present entangled in and the Extraordinary chain of Circumstances attending it equally injurious to me and offensive to the Neutrality of this Country, obliges me to seek refuge through your Medium from that Power which dispenses equal justice to all.

I beg leave to refer you to the Accompanying Documents for the Particulars of a Capture made (by a French Privateer the Sans Culottes Captn: Mollinery) of an American Vessell, loaden by my Firm at St. Bartholomew a Neutral Port, and bound to another Neutral Port; The Brig and Property are still in possession of the Captors, and who have hitherto shewn no Disposition to restore either. I find myself Honor'd with Liberal Protection from His Swedish Majesty's Consul and have exerted all the Measures which he Conceived either Prudent or Necessary to preserve my Right of Recovery of Such Damages as shall be

Adjudged to have arisen from the unlawfull Capture and Detention of my Property, which has now lasted so long, that Common regard to my Interest Compells me Sir to take a Liberty with you, which nothing but that and the Exigency of the Case could Authorize. It is not for me Sir to Suggest what measures may have now become necessary to Procure Restitution of my Property as well as proper Indemnification for the Disadvantages which have necessarily Accrued from the Detention, but I shall take pains to Represent to you, with that Candor and Integrity upon which only the Interests of my Cause, and the Magnitude it is of to this Country rests, every Circumstance that does in any Wise relate to it, and for that Purpose give me leave Sir to pray you to Appoint me an Hour when it shall Suit you that I may have the Honor of a Personal Interview. In the Interim Mr. Soderstroom was kind enough to say he would sue a Conversation with you and open some few of the Particulars of this business to you.

I shall Consider myself favoured by your interference in the Business which with due defference I conceive to be indispensably Necessary to the obtaining a Decission, as it has long since been under the Investigation of the French Minister and Consul, whose delay is by no means Consistent, with my Interest, as every part of the Cargo of the Vessell Captured, is Perishable. I have the Honor to be with all Possible respect & the most Distinguished Consideration Sir your most obedient & very Humble Svt   A RUNNELS & SON

RC (DNA: RG 59, MLR); at foot of first page: "The Honorable Jefferson Esqr: Secretary of State &c &c &c"; endorsed by TJ as received 6 Aug. 1793 and so recorded in SJL; with note by TJ:

"brig Betsey
taken by Sans Culottes of Marseilles
Swedish property
redress in courts?
turned over to War deptmt."

Enclosure: Protest of Abraham Runnels, Philadelphia, 24 July 1793, stating, as a Swedish subject and a partner in the mercantile firm of P. H. & Abraham Runnels on St. Barthélemy, that in late April or early May 1793 he and his partner chartered the brigantine *Betsy*, William Clark master, owned by John Hollingsworth & Company of Philadelphia, to carry from that island to Hamburg a cargo of sugar, coffee, and other articles wholly owned by the two partners; that after being properly cleared the *Betsy*, on which he was a passenger and supercargo, embarked from St. Barthélemy on 28 May and was captured on 15 June "in or about the Latitude of 36 d: No., and Longitude 45 d. West," by the French privateer *Sans Culottes* of Marseilles, but lately from Nantes, flying Spanish colors and commanded by Captain Joseph Mulrinez; and that after taking possession of the ship and its cargo, Mulrinez identified his vessel, announced that France was at war with Sweden, and forcibly transferred him and his servant to the privateer, which arrived in Philadelphia on 23 July, shortly after the *Betsy*; with subjoined statement of Clement Biddle, notary public, protesting the seizure and detention of the *Betsy*, its cargo, and Runnels and his servant, and seeking damages on behalf of Runnels from all those involved because their actions were "Contrary to the Rights of Neutrality and to the Law and Rights and Customs of Nations" (Tr in DNA, RG 76, France, Unbound Records; with statement at foot of text signed by Biddle). Other enclosures not found.

From Vanuxem & Lombairt

Philadelphia August 5. 1793.

James Vanuxem and Herman Jh. Lombairt, both Cityzens of the United states partners in Trade under the firm of Vanuxem & Lombairt (their Certificates of Cityzenship are dated, of the former in the year 1778, and 1784 of the Latter). They find themselves in a situation of Claiming the Protection of their Country and humbly submit their claims on seven hogsheads of Coffee which they have on board the American Brig Called the *Defiance* James Nowell master, which vessel has been taken and Carried into the Island of Jamaica on suspicion of having property on board belonging to Cityzens of the french republik.

Their seven Hogsheads of Coffee were Shipped on board said Brig Defiance by Dennis Cottineau of Port au Prince under the mark Z M No. 1 a 7. and Mr. Cottineau advised Messrs. Zollickoffer & Messonnier (Vanuxem & Lombairt's Correspondants in Baltimore) that this shipment was made for account and risk of V & L. In consequence of which Mr. Messonnier caused the Insurance to be made and advised them that the same was Compleated.

The Proofs that these Seven Hogsheads are Vanuxem & Lombairt's Property, are first, The Bill of Loading

2ly. The invoice

3ly. The Policy of Insurance, and

4ly. Their account Current with D. Cottineau, Certified by John L. Clark their Book Keeper; for the amount of which seven Hogsheads of Coffee he has been duly Creditted with and that the Balance as it appears in said account is Still in their favour.

The foregoing vauchers Vanuxem & Lombairt submit to the Executive Counsil of the United states of America; praying, that Honorable Body to take the facts above related into it's most serious consideration, that they may obtain Justice in their Claim.

VANUXEM & LOMBAIRT

RC (DNA: RG 76, British Spoliations); at foot of text: "The Honble. Ths. Jefferson secretary of state"; endorsed by TJ as received 5 Aug. 1793 and so recorded in SJL. Enclosure: Denis Cottineau in account with Vanuxem & Lombairt, 28 July 1793, of the same import as described above, showing a balance of £45.3.5 Pennsylvania currency due to the firm (MS in same; in the hand of John L. Clark, with his attestation of 3 Aug. 1793 notarized by Peter S. Du Ponceau). Other enclosures not found.

Vanuxem & Lombairt was a mercantile firm located at 73 South Water Street in Philadelphia (Hardie, *Phila. Dir.*, 149).

ZOLLICKOFFER: John Conrad Zollicoffer of Baltimore, who wrote letters to TJ of 27 May 1793, recorded in SJL as received 31 May 1793, and 16 May 1796, recorded in SJL as received 27 May 1796, neither of which has been found.

Notes of Cabinet Decisions

Aug. 6. The President concurs with Ham. and Kn. in notifying Mr. Hammond what we propose to do as to restitution of the prizes made by the Citoyen Genet &c. or compensation, because says he if you notify it to[1] the party to whom it will give displeasure, we should do it to that also which will feel satisfaction from it.

He said he should have been for calling Congress himself, but he found the other gentlemen were against it.

MS (DLC); partially dated; written entirely in TJ's hand on the fourth side of two sheets containing "Anas" entries for 29 and 30 July and 1, 2, and 3 Aug. 1793. Included in the "Anas."

These notes evidently record the results of a meeting with THE PRESIDENT that took place on 5 Aug. 1793 (see TJ to Washington, [ca. 18-19 Aug. 1793]). WHAT WE PROPOSE TO DO: see Cabinet Opinions on Privateers and Prizes, 5 Aug. 1793.

[1] TJ here canceled "Genet, you."

Notes of a Conversation with George Washington

Aug. 6. 1793. The President calls on me at my house in the country, and introduces my letter of July 31. announcing that I should resign at the close of the next month. He again expressed his repentance at not having resigned himself, and how much it was increased by seeing that he was to be deserted by those on whose aid he had counted: that he did not know where he should look to find characters to fill up the offices, that mere talents did not suffice for the departmt. of state, but it required a person conversant in foreign affairs, perhaps acquainted with foreign courts, that without this the best talents would be awkward and at a loss. He told me that Colo. Hamilton had 3. or 4. weeks ago written to him, informing him that private as well as public reasons had brought him to the determination to retire, and that he should do it towards the close of the next session. He said he had often before intimated dispositions to resign, but never as decisively before: that he supposed he had fixed on the latter part of the next session to give an opportunity to Congress to examine into his conduct: that our going out at times so different increased his difficulty, for if he had both places to fill at one he might consult both the particular talents and geographical situation of our successors. He expressed great apprehensions at the fermentation which seemed to be working in the minds of the public, that many descriptions of persons, actuated by different causes[1] appeared to be

[627]

uniting, what it would end in he knew not, a new Congress was to assemble, more numerous, perhaps of a different spirit: the first expressions of their sentiments would be important: if I would only stay to the end of that it would relieve him considerably.

I expressed to him my excessive repugnance to public life, the particular uneasiness of my situation in this place where the laws of society oblige me to move always exactly in the circle which I know to bear me peculiar hatred, that is to say the wealthy Aristocrats, the Merchants[2] connected closely with England, the new created paper fortunes that thus surrounded, my words were caught, multiplied, misconstrued, and even fabricated and spread abroad to my injury, that he saw also that there was such an opposition of views between myself and another part of the administration as to render it peculiarly unpleasing, and to destroy the necessary harmony. Without knowing the views of what is called the Republican part,[3] here, or having any communication with them, I could undertake to assure him from my intimacy with that party in the late Congress, that there was not a view in the Republican party as spread over the US. which went to the frame of the government, that I believed the next Congress would attempt nothing material but to render their own body independant, that that party were firm in their dispositions to support the government: that the maneuvres of Mr. Genet might produce some little embarrasment, but that he would be abandoned by the Republicans the moment they knew the nature of his conduct, and on the whole no crisis existed which threatened any thing.

He said he believed the views of the Republican party were perfectly pure, but when men put a machine into motion it is impossible for them to stop it exactly where they would chuse or to say where it will stop. That the constitution we have is an excellent one if we can keep it where it is, that it was indeed supposed there was a party disposed to change it into a monarchical form, but that he could conscientiously declare there was not a man in the US. who would set his face more decidedly against it than himself.—Here I interrupted him by saying 'no rational man in the US. suspects you of any other disposition, but there does not pass a week in which we cannot prove declns. dropping from the monarchical party that our government is good for nothing, it is a milk and water thing which cannot support itself, we must knock it down and set up something of more energy.'[4]—He said if that was the case he thought it a proof of their insanity, for that the republican spirit of the Union was so manifest and so solid that it was astonishing how any one could expect to move them.

He returned to the difficulty of naming my successor, he said Mr. Madison would be his first choice, but he had always expressed to him such a decision against public office that he could not expect he would undertake it. Mr. Jay would prefer his present office. He said that Mr. Jay had a great opinion of the talents of Mr. King, that there was also Mr. Smith of S. Carola. E. Rutledge &c.:[5] but he observed that name whom he would some objections would be made, some would be called speculators, some one thing, some another, and he asked me to mention any characters occurring to me. I asked him if Govr. Johnson of Maryld. had occurred to him? He said he had, that he was a man of great good sense, an honest man, and he believed clear of speculations, but this says he is an instance of what I was observing, with all these qualifications, Govr. Johnson, from a want of familiarity with foreign affairs, would be in them like a fish out of water, every thing would be new to him, and he awkward in every thing. I confessed to him that I had considered Johnson rather as fit for the Treasury department. Yes, says he, for that he would be the fittest appointment that could be made; he is a man acquainted with figures, and having as good a knolege of the resources of this country as any man. I asked him if Chancr. Livingston had occurred to him? He said Yes, but he was from N. York, and to appoint him while Hamilton was in and before it should be known he was going out, would excite a newspaper conflagration, as the ultimate arrangement would not be known. He said Mc.lurg had occurred to him as a man of first rate abilities, but it is said that he is a speculator. He asked me what sort of a man Wolcot was. I told him I knew nothing of him my self; I had heard him characterised as a cunning man. I asked him whether some person could not take my office par interim, till he should make an appointment? as Mr. Randolph for instance. Yes, says he, but there you would raise the expectation of keeping it, and I do not know that he is fit for it nor[6] what is thought of Mr. Randolph. I avoided[7] noticing the last observation, and he put the question to me directly. I then told him that I went into society so little as to be unable to answer it: I knew that the embarrasments in his private affairs had obliged him to use expedients which had injured him with the merchants and shop-keepers and affected his character of independance: that these embarrasments were serious, and not likely to cease soon. He said if I would only stay in till the end of another quarter (the last of Dec.) it would get us through the difficulties of this year, and he was satisfied that the affairs of Europe would be settled with this campaign, for that either France would be overwhelmed by it, or the confederacy would give up the contest. By that time too Congress will have manifested it's character and views.—I told him that I had set my private affairs in motion in a line which had powerfully called for my presence the last spring, and that they had suffered immensely from my not going home; that I had now calculated them to my return in the fall, and to fail in going then would be the loss of another year, and prejudicial beyond measure. I asked him whether he could not name Govr. Johnson to my office, under an express arrangement that at the close of the session he should take that of the treasury. He said that men never chose to descend: that being once in a higher department he would not like to go into a lower one. He asked me whether I could not arrange my affairs by going home. I told him I did not think the publick business would admit of it, that there was never a day now[8] in which the absence of the Secretary of state would not be inconvenient to the public.[9] And he concluded by desiring that I would take 2. or 3. days to consider whether I could not stay in till the end of another quarter, for that like a man going to the gallows he was willing to put it off as long as he could: but if I persisted, he must then look about him and make up his mind to do the best he could: and so he took leave.

MS (DLC); entirely in TJ's hand. PrC (DLC: Madison Papers). Entry in SJPL: "Notes of conversn with Pres. on my re-signing.—successor." Included in the "Anas." Enclosed in TJ's second letter to James Madison, 11 Aug. 1793.

Alexander Hamilton had expressed his DETERMINATION TO RETIRE in a letter to Washington dated 21 June 1793 (Syrett, *Hamilton*, xv, 13).

[1] TJ here canceled "were."
[2] TJ here canceled "trading."
[3] Word altered from "party."
[4] Closing quotation mark supplied.
[5] Preceding three words interlined.
[6] Word interlined in place of a period.
[7] TJ here canceled "answering the question."
[8] Word interlined.
[9] Preceding two sentences added in a box at foot of text and keyed by TJ for inclusion here.

From Sir John Temple

SIR   New York 6th. August 1793

I have had the honor to receive your letter of the 4th. enclosing one for Mr. Hammond which I send to him by this mornings post to Philadelphia. He left this on Saturday and will no doubt have inform'd you that the Republican sail'd from this Port, permitted so to do by the Governor, on the 2d. Instant. I have the honor to be with great Respect, Sir Your most Obedient, and, most Humble Servant   J TEMPLE

Tr (PRO: FO 5/2); at foot of text: "Thomas Jefferson Esqr Secretary of State &c &c." Recorded in SJL as received 8 Aug. 1793.

From Clement Biddle

SIR   walnut Street 7 August 1793

Mr. LeMaigre and Mr: L. Crousillat having determined to send a pilot boat to Jamaica with the proofs of their property in the Vessels belonging to them and which have been captured and sent into that

Island by British privateers, they request the favour of You to furnish them with such Letters as you may think proper as well from yourself as from the British Minister to forward their Claims, as the Vessel will be ready to sail tomorrow. I am with great respect Your mo: Obedt. Very humble Servt CLEMENT BIDDLE

RC (DNA: RG 76, British Spoliations); endorsed by TJ as received 7 Aug. 1793 and so recorded in SJL.

A letter from Biddle of 1 Aug. 1793, recorded in SJL as received on that date, has not been found.

To Nicholas Collin

August 7. 1793.

Th: Jefferson presents his compliments to Dr. Colin and asks the favor of him to act as an Arbitrator with Mr. Patterson and Mr. Boardley in the case of three interfering applications for a Patent for the discovery of a wheel with vertical valves to be turned by any moving fluid in which it is immersed. The parties will attend the Arbitrators at any time and place they may appoint: and as the models and papers are all at the Secretary of State's office, Th: J. supposes it might be agreeable to the Gentlemen to meet there—if not they shall be attended wherever they please. He asks the favor of Dr. Colin to inform him whether he may insert his name in the appointment.

RC (RSAS: Collin Papers); in a clerk's hand. Not recorded in SJL.

The government of Sweden sent Nicholas Collin (1746-1831) to America in 1769 as a missionary of the Swedish Lutheran Church. From 1770 to 1786 he served the congregation at Raccoon, now Swedesboro, New Jersey, after which he officiated as rector of three churches in and near Philadelphia until his death. Active in the American Philosophical Society, he shared with TJ an interest in natural history, meteorology, and philology (Amandus Johnson, *The Journal and Biography of Nicholas Collin, 1746-1831* [Philadelphia, 1936]).

THE THREE INTERFERING APPLICATIONS were those of Daniel Stansbury, Apollos Kinsley, and John Clarke, with Clarke ultimately receiving the disputed patent on 31 Dec. 1793. This was the first case to trigger a provision in the 21 Feb. 1793 patent law mandating the use of ARBITRATORS to resolve conflicting claims (*List of Patents*, 8; *Annals*, III, 1434).

Petition and Memorial from Lewis Crousillat

To Thomas Jefferson Esquire Secretary of State for the United States of America.

The Petition and Memorial of Lewis Crousillat of the City of Philadelphia Merchant
Respectfully Sheweth.

That your Memorialist Came to this Country from France in the year One Thousand seven hundred and eighty one and settled in the city of Philadelphia where he hath continued to reside and carry on Business as a Merchant and Owner of Vessels under American passports—that in the same year 1781 he took the oath of Allegiance to the State of Pennsylvania before a Justice of the peace of the City of Philadelphia aforesaid, but that having lost his certificate, and not recollecting the name of the Justice before whom he had taken the said oath, he did again on the 26th. Day of January in the year 1792 take and subscribe the oath to support the Constitution of the United States before Joseph Swift Esquire one of the Aldermen for the City of Philadelphia, and that being a Citizen of the United States of America he is Owner of different Vessels and Cargoes and that particularly he is sole owner of the Schooner Flora whereof Thomas Arnold is Master which said vessel being cheifly loaded for account of your memorialists at the Island of St. Domingo and proceeding on her voyage for this port of Philadelphia, was as he is informed by Letter from said Captain Arnold, on the 16th. day of June last captured by a British Privateer who kept the said Captain for ten days prisoner on board the said privateer, and sent the said vessel as a prize to Kingston in the Island of Jamaica giving for reason that there was French Property on board (which was the case) although the principal part of the Cargo was the property of your memorialist, and that they had taken from his said vessel a considerable sum of Money belonging to your memorialist. And detained the said vessel to the great loss and damage of your memorialist, And that he is also informed that the Brig Sophia whereof George Price is Master, which is the sole property of your memorialist, and also the principal part of the Cargo on board was also on her voyage from the said Island of St. Domingo for this port of Philadelphia Captured by the same British privateer and sent into the said port of Kingston in Jamaica, and there detained and libelled in the Admiralty Court of said Island—that Your Memorialist with other persons has determined to send a Pilot Boat to Kingston with proper documents to prosecute his claims to the said vessels and Cargoes and he humbly submits his case to your consideration that such measures may be pursued for Obtaining Justice as to you in your Wisdom shall seem meet. And Your Memorialist shall pray &ca.

Philadelphia   L Crousillat
August 7th. 1793

RC (DNA: RG 59, MLR); in a clerk's hand, signed by Crousillat. PrC of Tr (DLC); in the hand of Benjamin Bankson. Tr (Lb in DNA: RG 59, DL). Enclosures: (1) Deposition of John Taylor and John Duffield, Philadelphia, 17 July 1793, swearing that for upwards of seven years Crousillat had been a resident merchant of Philadelphia and was considered a citizen of Pennsylvania. (2) Deposition of Crousillat, Philadelphia, 26 July 1793, swearing that he had resided in Philadelphia for almost thirteen years, during which time he had been absent for less than two years; that in December 1781 he had taken the oath of allegiance to Pennsylvania and had since considered himself a citizen or subject of the United States; and that in January 1792 he took the oath of allegiance again before Alderman Joseph Swift of Philadelphia, being unable to locate the books of the judge before whom he took it originally (Trs in DNA: RG 59, MLR, consisting of No. 1, being in part a printed form with blanks filled in, attested by notary public Clement Biddle, and No. 2, subjoined, with Biddle's 7 Aug. 1793 certification of Crousillat's sec-

ond oath of citizenship; PrCs of Trs in DLC, in Bankson's hand; Trs in Lb in DNA: RG 59, DL, lacking certification on second enclosure). Petition and enclosures enclosed in TJ's first letter to George Hammond, 8 Aug. 1793.

Lewis Crousillat, a French-born merchant who was heavily involved in trade with his native land, resided at 30 North Eighth Street in Philadelphia (Hardie, *Phila. Dir.*, 30; Abraham Ritter, *Philadelphia and her Merchants* . . . [Philadelphia, 1860], 71).

To Edmond Charles Genet

SIR   Philadelphia August 7th. 1793.

In a letter of June 5th. I had the honor to inform you that the President, after reconsidering at your request the case of vessels armed within our ports to commit hostilities on nations at peace with the united States, had finally determined that it could not be admitted, and desired that all those which had been so armed should depart from our ports. It being understood afterwards, that these vessels either still remained in our ports or had only left them to cruize on our coasts, and return again with their prizes, and that another vessel, the Little Democrat had been since armed at Philadelphia, it was desired in my letter of the 12th. of July, that such vessels with their prizes should be detained till a determination should be had of what was to be done under these circumstances. In disregard, however, of this desire the Little Democrat went out immediately on a cruize.

I have it now in charge to inform you that the President considers the united States as bound, pursuant to positive assurances, given in conformity to the laws of neutrality, to effectuate the restoration of, or to make compensation for prizes, which shall have been made of any of the parties at war with France subsequent to the fifth day of June last, by privateers fitted out of our ports.

That it is consequently expected, that you will cause restitution to be made of all prizes taken and brought into our Ports subsequent to the abovementioned day by such privateers, in defect of which the President considers it as incumbent upon the United States to[1] indemnify the Owners of those prizes—the indemnification to be reimbursed by the French nation.

That besides taking efficacious measures to prevent the future fitting out of Privateers in the Ports of the united States, they will not give asylum therein to any which shall have been at any time so fitted out, and will cause restitution of all such prizes as shall be hereafter brought within their Ports by any of the said Privateers.

It would have been but proper respect to the authority of the country had that been consulted before these armaments were undertaken. It would have been satisfactory, however, if their sense of them, when declared, had been duly acquiesced in. Reparation of the injury to which the United States have been made so involuntarily instrumental, is all which now remains, and in this your compliance cannot but be expected.

In consequence of the information given in your letter of the 4th. instant, that certain citizens of St. Domingo, lately arrived in the United States, were associating for the purpose of undertaking a military expedition from the territory of the United States against that Island, the Governor of maryland, within which State the expedition is understood to be preparing, is instructed to take effectual measures to prevent the same. I have the honor to be, with great respect, Sir, Your most obedient and most humble servant   TH: JEFFERSON

PrC (DLC); in the hand of George Taylor, Jr., signed by TJ; at foot of first page: "The minister Plenipy. of the Repc. of France"; with paragraphs 2-4 drawn almost verbatim from Cabinet Opinion on Prizes and Privateers, 3 Aug. 1793. PrC of Tr (DLC); in a clerk's hand. Tr (NNC: Gouverneur Morris Papers). Tr (DNA: RG 46, Senate Records, 3d Cong., 1st sess.). PrC (PRO: FO 97/1). FC (Lb in DNA: RG 59, DL). Tr (DLC: Genet Papers); certified by Bournonville. Tr (same). Tr (DLC: John Trumbull Letterbook). Tr (AMAE: CPEU, XXXIX); in French; docketed and certified by Genet. Tr (DLC: Genet Papers); in French; draft translation of preceding Tr. Printed in *Message*, 57. Enclosed in TJ to George Washington, 7 Aug. 1793, and TJ to Gouverneur Morris, 16 Aug. 1793.

[1] Remainder of paragraph underscored and followed by a series of exclamation points in first Tr in Genet Papers.

To George Hammond

SIR   Philadelphia, 7th. August 1793.

A constant expectation of carrying into full effect the declaration of the President, against permitting the armament of vessels within the Ports of the united States, to cruize on nations with which they are at Peace, has hitherto prevented my giving you a final answer on the subject of such vessels and their prizes. Measures to this effect are still taking, and particularly for excluding from all further asylum in our ports, the vessels so armed, and for the restoration of the Prizes the Lovely Lass, the Prince William Henry and the Jane of Dublin taken by them: and I am authorized in the mean time to assure you, that should the measures for restoration fail in their affect, the President considers it as incumbent on the United States to make compensation for the vessels. I have the honor to be, with great respect Sir, Your most obedient and most humble Servant   TH: JEFFERSON

PrC (DLC); in the hand of George Taylor, Jr., signed by TJ; at foot of text: "The minister Plenipotentiary of Great Britain." FC (Lb in DNA: RG 59, DL). Tr (Lb in PRO: FO 116/3). Tr (same, 5/1). Tr (DLC: John Trumbull Letterbook). Enclosed in TJ to George Washington, 7 Aug. 1793.

For the difference of opinion in the Cabinet over the wording of this letter, see Cabinet Opinions on Privateers and Prizes, 5 Aug. 1793, and note.

From Gouverneur Morris

DEAR SIR   Sain Port 7. August 1793

Enclos'd herewith you will find my Account up to the first of the last month. I did not send it sooner because I wish'd to comprize therein those of the Consulates none of which are come forward. I shall therefore write to them on the Subject. You will observe that I charge therein 24^{tt} given to an American Sea Officer. He appear'd to be, and really was, in very great distress, so that I could not avoid giving what I conceiv'd needful to carry him to the nearest Seaport. He has since applied to me again repeatedly but he has been refus'd all farther aid. You will find also a Charge for engraving passports. This became necessary because from the Time of my arrival, or very shortly after it, the Difficulties in the way of travelling were so great that people with all formalities required by Law could scarcely get along, And among the Municipalities a handsome Piece of Paper with a seal to it had much more Effect than the ministerial Signatures. If however either or both of these Charges be deem'd improper Let them be recharg'd to me. I sent out more Pamphlets than those I have brought to account, because when an Opportunity offer'd I put up not only those I had procured for your Office, but all others which were at Hand, and which having been originally purchased for my own Information I did not think it proper to charge them to the United States.

I also enclose herein a Table of the Value of the Assignats compared with Specie for one year ending with last June. During the Month of July they may be stated at about 20 per % But upon that Value as well as on those contain'd in the Table it is necessary to observe First that the Fluctuations of Exchange are great, so that to determine with precision the Value requires Information which I beleive it is impossible to acquire. For instance Louis d'ors have sometimes borne a premium of above 5 per % compared with Silver, and other Times have gone at Par.

Nay this Change has taken place from one Day to another, and on the same day there has been a difference of above 5 per % in the price of Specie. It would be necessary therefore to know at which of two such different prices the greatest Sum was negotiated, and also in other cases whether the principal Negotiations were in Gold or Silver. At first sight indeed it might be supposed that the metal of highest price was the one principally bought, but I am assured that this rule did not hold good: and as for the Reason why it did not hold, we must seek in the Trick of the Day, or the Lie of the Day. Sometimes also in the Searchings and Plunderings. But secondly, This Table however accurate it might be, would not I conceive form a proper Standard on which to proceed in our Custom Houses; because the Value of Comodities has been by no means dependent on that of the assignats. The prices have considerably encreased but not proportionately; and the particular encrease depends on the article, so that a History of each would be necessary. Bread (altho Supplies have constantly been brought from abroad) has been kept very nearly to the old Standard. Flesh is more than double, Vegetables four five or six Times as dear as formerly. Merchandizes for export have not risen in Proportion, Wines and Brandies were getting up rapidly, but the War damped them. They took afterwards a great Rise from the Demand of the Armies so that the low Burgundies got up to the price of the High almost. I am not enough acquainted with the Subject to go into the needful Details, and only say thus much to shew that Merchandizes did not depend for Price on the same Principles with the precious metals, since these last were purchased by the Nation for its Armies; by the Emigrants for their Support; and by People in general as a Ressource in the moment when Paper should be decried. Lastly; the Price of Specie did not go on regular Principles of Apportionment or Comparison with the mass of Paper. In the months of May and June 1792 it rose because the old Ministers having purchased large Sums of Specie, their Successors found that they could dispense with immediate Supplies. In July August and September, Notwithstanding the political Events it was kept tolerably steady by Stock jobbing manoeuvres back'd with the sums in the Treasury, and also by the fear of plunder after the tenth of August: for many were plundered during the *Visites domiciliares* and it was given out by Authority that Specie would be taken by force and Paper given in Exchange. The benefits which those at the Center of these Operations expected to derive were prevented by the great and unlook'd for Success of the french Arms in October and November. In the End of that last Month, and in the Beginning of December, the Proportion was about 73. per Cent being higher than is stated in the Table, because in November the Exchange was lower in the Beginning and in December at the End of the month, wherefore the

Average of each is diminished. In the month of December the Trial of the King, the Probability that he would be put to Death, the Consequences naturally resulting from that Catastrophe, the certainty of another and more serious Campaign, the Situation of the Armies, and in fine the abundance of the Assignats, when the Cold Weather forc'd back presumptuous Hope into the Region of austere Reflection brought down the Exchange to about 60 per %. In January it was tolerably steady at about 58 And in February at about 56. The paper during this Period went on its natural Course of gentle Decay. In the Beginning of March it was still at about 56 but the Successes of the Enemy shortly after reduced it to 48. In the Beginning of April it was brought down to about 44 so that in one month's Time it lost about $\frac{1}{5}$ of its Value. From that time it went on gradually again being about 42 at the End of April, and then rapidly so as to be at about 30 in the End of June consequently the Degradation monthly for those two months was about $\frac{1}{6}$ each. But in July it took a terrible Plunge viz from 30 to 20 being $\frac{1}{3}$ of the value taken off in a few days. This was owing in Part to a view of public affairs both foreign and domestic and partly to Stock Jobbing manœuvres carried on by Authority with a view to ruin the Stock Jobbers. These manoeuvres had in Part their Effect for having forced the Exchange below its natural Level it rose towards the End of the month and of Course those who speculated on a farther fall were taken in. The prime movers did indeed expect a wonderful rise from taking out of Circulation about 1700,000,000^{tt} on which the Kings Head is impress'd, but this Stroke was broken by the necessity of confining it to one Half the Sum, being the large Assignats, because the small ones dispersed in the Hands of the Sans Culottes might have deprived the Government of the Support of its Friends. But besides this the Stroke was in itself a bad one because it injures the Paper more by destroying its Credit than it benefits what remains by lessening the mass even could the mass be thereby lessened which it is not for all the Effect is to give a different Direction to the proscribed paper in those Districts which respect the Decree. Many people persist in believing that the Assignats with that condemn'd Impression are better than the others and even that their value is encreas'd by the Decree which drawing a Line of division between them leaves the *future Government* at Liberty to annul the Circulation now favored with an Appearance of Justice. You will observe that Men calculate upon the Dissolution of the present System as on a Datum, altho the Period in which it is to arrive is considered as uncertain. It is far from impossible that they reckon without their Host but the Opinion is as important as the thing in Respect to a Species of money whose Value depends on Opinion. Another Circumstance which should have been taken into Consideration and which was not duly weighed is that the Value of the mass of Paper depends on the Course in the Capital and there the new Assignats must be rather more plentiful than the old; of Course destroying the old cannot do much good to the new and besides the holders of the Old as well as the New being in Effect the great money Dealers they can by their united efforts apportion the value to each as they please and their common Interest will excite a common Action. And they have over the Government an Advantage which no power of Legislation can compensate because they act with the paper in Circulation and the Government with that which goes to encrease the Circulation and which of Course lessens the Value they wish to encrease. From all this I conclude that the Paper must go on perishing Day by Day and like other consumptive Patients be alike weakened by the Doctor and the Disease. On the whole Sir, to return to your original Object, I beleive the safest way in America and the most equitable would be to value Articles imported from this Country at the Prices of 1788. I am with Respect and Esteem Dr. Sir Your Obedient Servant

GOUV MORRIS

P.S. I will continue to send you the State of Depreciation according to your Orders and exactly as I can.

Dupl (DNA: RG 59, DD); in a clerk's hand, signed by Morris; at head of text: "No. 34 *Duplicate*"; at foot of first page: "Thomas Jefferson Esqr. Secretary of State"; endorsed by Edmund Randolph as received 19 Mch. 1794. FC (Lb in DLC: Gouverneur Morris Papers). Tr (Lb in DNA: RG 59, DD). Enclosures: (1) Morris's account with the United States, 1 Aug. 1793. (2) Table showing the specie value of French paper money from June 1792 to June 1793 (Trs in same). Enclosed in Morris to TJ, 22 Sep. 1793.

TJ submitted the missing recipient's copy of this letter to the President on 11 Nov. 1793, the date he received it according to SJL, and Washington returned it the same day (Washington, *Journal*, 251).

To Benjamin Rush

Aug. 7. 93.

Th: Jefferson presents his compliments to Dr. Rush and will be happy if he can take a dinner with him in the country with a small party of friends on Friday at three aclock.—He presumes Dr. Rush knows that his house is on this side the river 3, or 400 yds. below Grey's ferry.

RC (J. William Middendorf, Jr., Baltimore, 1949); addressed: "Dr. Rush." Not recorded in SJL.

To George Washington

Aug. 7. 93.

Th: Jefferson has the honor to inclose to the President the draught of a letter to Mr. Genet, in pursuance of the opinion of Saturday last approved by the President.

RC (DNA: RG 59, MLR); addressed: "The President of the US."; endorsed by Tobias Lear. Tr (Lb in same, SDC). Not recorded in SJL. Enclosure: TJ to Edmond Charles Genet, 7 Aug. 1793.

THE OPINION OF SATURDAY LAST: see Cabinet Opinion on Prizes and Privateers, 3 Aug. 1793.

The President this day returned the enclosed letter to TJ with a one-word note—"approved"—beneath which TJ wrote "this was the letter of Aug. 7. to Genet" (RC in DLC: TJ Papers, 91: 15667; undated; addressed: "The Secretary of State"; endorsed by TJ as received 7 Aug. 1793; recorded in SJPL under 7 Aug. 1793).

To George Washington

Aug. 7. 93.

Th: Jefferson has the honor to inclose the draught of a letter to Mr. Hammond. If the President approves it, he will send it to Mr. Hammond's immediately, as tomorrow's post is the last one which will be in time for the Packet.

RC (DNA: RG 59, MLR); addressed: "The President of the US."; endorsed by Tobias Lear. Tr (Lb in same, SDC). Not recorded in SJL. Enclosure: TJ to George Hammond, 7 Aug. 1793.

The President approved the enclosed letter this day (Washington, *Journal*, 215).

To George Hammond

SIR   Philadelphia Augt. 8. 1793.

I have to trouble you in the following cases of captures of American vessels by British privateers, and to ask your intervention therein. The first is, that of M. le Maigre, a citizen of this State, on whose behalf I had on a former occasion to apply to you on the capture of the Snow Suckey, his property. He has lately had also a Brig called the Molly commanded by Captain Bernard Razer, laden on his own account at Port au Prince and bound to this port, taken and carried into New Providence by a British privateer.

The next is of Mr. Crousillet, also a citizen and merchant of this State, whose schooner, called the Flora, commanded by Thos. Arnold, loaded at St. Domingo, chiefly on his own account and proceeding to this port; as also the Brig Sophia, George Price commander, the property of the said Crousillet, loaded likewise at St. Domingo for this port, chiefly on his own account, were taken by a British privateer and sent into Kingston in Jamaica as you will more particularly be informed by the enclosed copies of papers, the originals of which are deposited in my office.

Mr. Crousillet proposing to send off a pilot boat instantly to Jamaica to recover his property, I have the honor to request your interposition with the proper authority to have justice done him and of being with great respect Sir, Your most obedient and most humble Servant

Th: Jefferson

PrC (DLC); in the hand of George Taylor, Jr., signed by TJ; at foot of text: "The Minister Plenipotentiary of Gr. Britain." FC (Lb in DNA: RG 59, DL). Enclosures: (1) Petition and Remonstrance from Peter Lemaigre, 25 July 1793, and enclosure. (2) Petition and Memorial from Lewis Crousillat, 7 Aug. 1793, and enclosures.

From George Hammond

Sir   Philadelphia 8 August 1793

I have had the honor of receiving your letter of yesterday; and I desire you to be assured that I entertain a proper sense of the principles of Justice, which have dictated the President's determination, of "excluding from all further asylum in the ports of the United States the vessels that have been armed therein, to cruize on nations with which the United States are at peace," and of effecting the restitution of, or of making a compensation for, the particular prizes, that are specified in your communication.

But all these prizes having been made by one privateer alone, le Citoyen Genet, I hope, Sir, you will not esteem me too importunate, if I request to be informed whether the armed Schooner, le Sans Culottes, fitted out at the same time, and place, as was le Citoyen Genet, and the privateers, le petit Democrat, le Vainqueur de la Bastille, and l'anti-George, all of which have been fitted out clandestinely, and subsequently to the President's proclamation (the first at Philadelphia the second in the port of Charleston and the third at Savannah in Georgia) are not to be included in a predicament similar to that of le Citoyen Genet—of exclusion from the ports of the United States, and of restitution of any British vessels, which they may have already taken, or may hereafter happen to capture. I have the honor to be with sentiments of the greatest respect Sir Your most obedient humble Servant

Geo. Hammond

RC (DNA: RG 59, NL); at foot of first page: "Mr Jefferson"; endorsed by TJ as received 8 Aug. 1793 and so recorded in SJL. FC (Lb in PRO: FO 116/3). Tr (same, 5/1).

Tr (Lb in DNA: RG 59, NL). Enclosed in TJ to George Washington, and Washington to TJ, both 8 Aug. 1793.

To George Hammond

Sir   Philadelphia Aug. 8. 1793.

I have just received your favor of this morning and am authorized to assure you that the denial of asylum in our ports, was not meant to be confined to the Citoyen Genet, but to extend to all vessels armed in our ports. I had no information before of the Anti-George, named in your letter. But if she is in the same predicament, she will be subject to the same rule. I have the honor to be with great respect Sir your most obedt & most humble servt   Th: Jefferson

PrC (DLC); at foot of text: "Mr. Hammond M. P. of Gr. Br." FC (Lb in DNA: RG 59, DL). Tr (Lb in PRO: FO 116/3). Tr (same, 5/1). Enclosed in TJ to George Washington, and Washington to TJ, both 8 Aug. 1793.

From Andrew Porter

Dr Sr   Phila. Augst. 8th 1793

An Indented Servant-Man of mine run away, and was taken up coming on Shore from the french Frigate, with the enclosed Letter.

Altho' I am again in possession of my property, yet I Judged it necessary, that the Officers of Government should be enformed, of the easy Access our Indented servants have to enter on Board their Vessels of War. I am with every Sentiment of Respect & Esteem Dr Sr. Your Obedt Humble Servt.   Andrew Porter

RC (DNA: RG 76, France, Miscellaneous Claims); at foot of text: "Thomas Jefferson Esqr."; endorsed by TJ as received 8 Aug. 1793 and so recorded in SJL. Enclosure not found.

Andrew Porter (1743-1813), a Pennsylvania schoolmaster, surveyor, and agriculturalist, who served as a Continental marine and artillery officer during the Revolutionary War and as a state militia general from 1800 until his death, was currently a farmer in Norriton Township, Pennsylvania (William A. Porter, "A Sketch of the Life of General Andrew Porter," PMHB, IV [1880], 261-6, 297).

To George Washington

Aug. 8. 93.

Th: Jefferson has the honor to inclose to the President a letter just received from Mr. Hammond, and the answer he proposes to give to it.

RC (DNA: RG 59, MLR); addressed: "The President of the US."; endorsed by Tobias Lear. Tr (Lb in same, SDC). Not recorded in SJL. Enclosures: George Hammond to TJ, and TJ to Hammond, both 8 Aug. 1793.

From George Washington

SIR   8th. Augt. 1793.

The answer to Mr. Hammonds letter is conformable to the measures which have been advised—and of course is approved.

Go: WASHINGTON

RC (DLC); addressed: "The Secretary of State"; endorsed by TJ as received 8 Aug. 1793. Recorded in SJPL. Enclosures: George Hammond to TJ, and TJ to Hammond, both 8 Aug. 1793.

To Clement Biddle

SIR   Philadelphia Aug. 9. 1793.

I yesterday wrote to Mr. Hammond, Minister Plenipotentiary of Great Britain, inclosing copies of the papers in the cases of Mr. Lemaigre and Mr. Crousillet, and asking his interposition with the proper authorities in New Providence and Jamaica to obtain justice for them in the cases which were the subjects of their memorials. It will be proper for them to apply to Mr. Hammond for his letters. I am with great esteem Sir Your most obedt humble servt   TH: JEFFERSON

PrC (DLC); at foot of text: "Colo. Clement Biddle." FC (Lb in DNA: RG 59, DL).

A letter from TJ to Biddle of 25 Sep. 1794, recorded in SJL, has not been found.

From George Hammond

SIR   Philadelphia 9 August 1793

I have had the honor of receiving your letter of yesterday, and though the circumstances of Mr. Crousillat's complaints are not quite of so exceptionable a nature as those alleged in Mr. Lemaigre's former statement, relative to the Suckey, I shall nevertheless willingly give to any

Agent, whom Mr. Crousillat may appoint, a letter for the Governor of Jamaica, similar to that which I gave to Mr. Lemaigre. I am with great respect Sir Your most obedient humble Servant   GEO. HAMMOND

RC (DNA: RG 59, NL); at foot of text: "Mr Jefferson"; endorsed by TJ as received 9 Aug. 1793 and so recorded in SJL. Tr (Lb in same).

From Arthur St. Clair

SIR   Cincinnati County of Hamilton Augt. 9th. 1793

I have had the honor to receive your Letter of the 19th. of April together with the ten Volumes of the Acts passed at the 2d. Session of the second Congress, which shall be distributed in such manner as to render an acquaintance with them as general as possible.

In my progress to this Place[1] Having halted at Marietta to see the Magistrates and enquire a little into the State of that Settlement, and an Opportunity to Pittsburgh presenting at the Moment, on the 25 of July I issued a Proclamation for the meeting of the Legislature of the Territory on the first of September at this Place, and took the Liberty to enclose a Copy of it to you, with a request that you would cause copies to be sent to the Judges Symmes and Turner, neither of whom I knew where to find, but it was probable their residence might be known to You. I am very sensible Sir, this was a Liberty that demands an Apology, and I was sensible of the impropriety at the time and nothing would have induced me to take it but the uncertainty as to the places where they were to be found, and the expence that would have attended the sending an Express, if one could have been obtained, which would have been difficult. Be assured Sir, unless it should be a very pressing Case indeed I shall not take it again.

I have the pleasure[2] to inform you that the difficulties which existed with respect to the Court of Common Pleas for this County are accommodated in a manner that gives Satisfaction, and any irregularities that have happened in their proceedings will, I hope be helped by the Legislature. At the same time the Dignity of the Government has not been committed, nor the just and necessary prerogative of the Governor weakened.[3] The particulars have been communicated to the Attorney General and I have at the same time made some Observations upon some of the Laws passed here at the last Session of the Legislature, and may possibly make some more, but I realy do not know whether it is to him or to you that the Laws of this Territory are referred for consideration; tho it should seem of course that they be referred to him. This may be considered as a work of supererogation in me—but Sir the Circumstances of different parts of this Territory are extremely dissimilar, and it is very difficult to adapt general Laws[4] to those various Circumstances, and the Operation of the Laws falling more immediately within the observation of the Governor than of any Person at the Seat of Government, tho infinitely better-qualified to judge of them in the Abstract, I have presumed that it would not be deemed an intrusion[5] and should it be to you they are referred, and you will permit me any Observations which I may think necessary, shall be addressed to you. With Sentiments of the greatest Esteem and respect I have the honor to be Sir Your most obedient and most humble Servant

Dft (O, on deposit OHi: St. Clair Papers); unsigned; below complimentary close: "The honorable Thomas Jefferson"; endorsed by St. Clair. Recorded in SJL as received 12 Sep. 1793.

In his LETTER OF THE 19TH. OF APRIL 1793 to the governors of the Northwest and Southwest Territories, TJ according to law transmitted TEN copies of both the published acts passed at the second session of the Second Congress and a separate index to the laws of both sessions of this Congress (FC in Lb in DNA: RG 59, DL; at head of text: "Governors St. Clair & Blount"; not recorded in SJL). Even though its official date was 25 July 1793, the PROCLAMATION undoubtedly was enclosed in St. Clair to TJ, 24 July 1793, recorded in SJL as received from "Muskingham" on 10 Aug. 1793 but not found (see TJ to John Cleves Symmes, 11 Aug. 1793; Terr. Papers, III, 412-13). The DIFFICULTIES with THE COURT OF COMMON PLEAS consisted of a dispute over the tenure of its judges. The possible IRREGULARITIES were committed when

the judges refused to accept commissions running during the governor's pleasure and continued to exercise their duties under the old ones, which were granted during good behavior but which St. Clair contended had been superseded. In a 9 May 1793 letter to Edmund Randolph communicating THE PARTICULARS, St. Clair also expressed his intention henceforth to submit his observations on territorial acts awaiting congressional review to THE ATTORNEY GENERAL (William Henry Smith, The St. Clair Papers: The Life and Public Services of Arthur St. Clair, 2 vols. [Cincinnati, 1882], II, 312-16). See also TJ to St. Clair, 13 Sep. 1793.

[1] Sentence to this point added.
[2] Word interlined in place of "Satisfaction."
[3] Sentence written lengthwise in the margin.
[4] Manuscript: "Law general Laws."
[5] Sentence to this point added at foot of text and remainder of clause interlined in place of "if I have been mistaken on this point."

From James Simpson

Gibraltar, 9 Aug. 1793. He encloses a copy of the letter he wrote on 4 July by way of Charleston. Since then Muley Suliman has remained at Fez, where he is rumored to be gathering another army to make another attempt on Morocco. The two consuls mentioned in his last as having been sent by Spain to Safi and Tangier have not in fact assumed the consular character or brought presents to the pretenders in whose dominion they are. They intimated that their purpose was to protect Spanish trading vessels and assured the respective princes that Spain would send an ambassador as soon as the succession was firmly established. Weeks ago Muley Suliman directed that one of his ships at Larache be fitted out to carry some sheriffs of Taroudant who were with him to Santa Cruz, but because none was seaworthy save for a frigate coppered at Cádiz in Muley Yezid's reign that would cost 2,000 dollars to repair, a ship will be chartered to carry them—a situation that supports his previous opinion on the general condition of Moorish cruisers. Despite the plague raging at Algiers, two Dutch frigates have gone there to make peace with the Regency. On 21 July Lord Hood's fleet was damaged in a violent gale, especially the 74-gun *Berwick*, which lost her bowsprit and three topmasts. By last report the fleet was off Toulon and had only captured a sloop of war and a privateer.

RC (DNA: RG 59, CD); 4 p.; at foot of first page: "The Honble Thomas Jefferson Esqr &c &c &c"; endorsed by TJ as received 2 Dec. 1793 and so recorded in SJL.

TJ submitted this letter to the President on 10 Dec. 1793, and Washington returned it the same day, his journal noting that it contained "Nothing of importance" (Washington, *Journal*, 265).

To Vanuxem & Lombairt

Aug. 9. 1793.

Th: Jefferson presents his compliments to Messrs. Vanuxem & Lombart, and will be glad to see either of them at his office about 12. aclock of any day which shall best suit them, on the subject of their application of the 5th. instant.

PrC (DLC). FC (Lb in DNA: RG 59, DL).

From Robert Clinton

St. Eustatius, 10 Aug. 1793. Clarkson having deputed him to act as consul during the President's pleasure, and his absence, and several American citizens having applied to him for consular acts, he has thought it prudent, because of the interim governor's refusal to recognize Clarkson as consul or to look at Clarkson's deputation, to evince a respect for the laws of Holland and guard against suits by disappointed applicants by obtaining the enclosed opinion of an eminent Dutch lawyer and former fiscal affirming the propriety of his exercising his consular office as far as it relates to facilitating the business of American citizens with the United States and with each other. He also encloses a copy of the certificate that in a few instances he has issued at the request of masters of American vessels who have taken on freight here for Europe and have not had an opportunity to apply for sea passes in the United States since the maritime war began, and of another that, in order to ensure their safe navigation, he has issued to American vessels with proper sea passes that have discharged their cargoes and loaded West Indian produce for Europe not mentioned in those passes. *14 Aug.* Since writing the above he granted the application of Captain Frederick William Callahan of the brigantine *Julius Pringle* of Charleston for the second kind of certificate, affixing it with his seal to Callahan's pass. Interim governor Joannes Runnels removed the certificate from the pass, summoned and then rebuked him "in Language of Gross abuse and invective" for acting as consul, ordered him in the presence of his second in command, Jacobus DeWindt, not to do so in any way, declared that he would prosecute him for having received the oaths of American citizens relating to their affairs and granted them certificates, and detained as evidence against him his certificate to Callahan. The brigantine left without the certificate, and on the 12th he refused to comply with a subaltern militia officer's summons to do duty as a private.

RC (DNA: RG 59, CD); 3 p.; in a clerk's hand, signed by Clinton; at foot of text: "The Honourable Secretary of State for the United States of America"; endorsed by TJ as received 2 Dec. 1793 and so recorded in SJL. Enclosures: (1) Certificate for masters of American ships lacking passports from the United States (printed form in same; in English and French). (2) Certificate for masters of ships with passports (Tr in same). (3) Clinton to J. L. Ter Hoeven, 19 July 1793, stating that Governor Runnels had not recognized David M. Clarkson's consular commission from the President or Clinton's deputy consular commission from Clarkson, that Runnels had not expressly prohibited the exercise of consular functions with respect to Americans, and that several Americans had applied for the performance of consular acts to fulfill American laws and treaties and safeguard their navigation and fortunes, offering to depose under oath as to the facts relating to these acts; and asking whether therefore it would be a violation of Dutch laws for him to perform those parts of his consular office required by American law and to administer oaths to Americans in St. Eustatius (Tr in same; signed by Clinton). (4) Opinion of Ter Hoeven, 22 July 1793, stating that without violating Dutch laws Clinton could perform such parts of his office as passing acts and administering oaths, but only for American citizens voluntarily requesting them; that these acts and oaths could not be used as evidence in St. Eustatius or any other Dutch country as long as the consul was not acknowledged by the rulers of this place and his functions were regulated by Article 21 of the 1782 commercial treaty between the Netherlands and the United States; and that upon request by the United States, the States General could from the plenitude of its power declare all acts and oaths before the consul to be good from the beginning of his appointment (Tr in same; at head of text: "Translation of the Opinion as approved by Mr. Terhoeven").

From Robert W. Fox

Falmouth, 10 Aug. 1793. He wrote on 8 June to request a new consular commission from the President in place of the one mistakenly made out to Edward Fox. He encloses a somewhat incomplete list of American ships that arrived here. He has consistently interceded to procure the release of American sailors impressed here as British subjects; he has been successful in some late cases and hopes to retrieve one man still detained on a king's ship. After the American ship *Portland*, Captain Robinson, was captured while on its way to Le Havre with flour, beef, and pork and brought here by the privateer *Thought*, he demanded the return of the ship and cargo to Robinson and protested against the captain of the privateer for damages. Since then an order has been issued to land the cargo and pay the freight from the cargo's net proceeds, "the full amount of which is to be paid in the Commons." His firm has been asked to inspect the cargo in order to report on its quality, in which case he apprehends the government will take it to their account and the net proceeds will be paid to the court pending the issue of the trial. He has rendered every assistance to and informed Thomas Pinckney of the American ship *Active*, Captain Blair, which was captured and brought here by the same privateer while bound from Philadelphia to Nantes with a cargo of sugar, coffee, cotton, tobacco, etc. Nothing has been determined about the fate of this ship and cargo, but the necessary steps have been taken at London to protect both. There is little political news here except for the arrival of a warship from Lord Howe's fleet whose officers report that the British fleet drove the French into Brest. "American produce is rather low in England," wheat and flour are dear in Lisbon and Barcelona, and it has fallen much in Cádiz because of large importations directly from the United States and London. [P.S.] The return of the French fleet to Brest is uncertain because both fleets parted at night after having been in sight of each other.

RC (DNA: RG 59, CD); 4 p.; in a clerk's hand, with signature and postscript by Fox; at foot of text: "Thomas Jefferson Esqr."; endorsed by TJ as received 24 Oct. 1793 and so recorded in SJL. Enclosure not found.

According to SJL, Fox wrote a missing letter to TJ from Falmouth on 12 Aug. 1793 that was received on 24 Oct. 1793. Although the President's journal records that TJ submitted this letter to him on 2 Nov. 1793 and received it back the same day, the entry seems to describe the 10 Aug. letter (Washington, *Journal*, 242, 244n).

From Willink, Van Staphorst & Hubbard

SIR   Amsterdam 10 August 1793.

The extreme uncertainty of the effects the present War in Europe may have upon the tranquillity and prosperity of this Country, and the fears We entertain on the subject, induce us to wish to become Citizens of the United States, so as at all events, to secure to ourselves under your Government, the invaluable priviledges of true Liberty and protection of property: And We are the more eager to obtain our Naturalisation from Congress, to open the field to the settlement in your Country, of some of our Children or successors, who We flatter ourselves, will be disposed to second our views in this respect, for the promotion of their happiness.

Not doubting, but that the enlightened patriotic Congress of the United States, will chearfully grant our request, which will acquire for members of the community, persons of our means and who are already deeply interested in the general Welfare of America, We have authorized M. Samuel Sterett of Philadelphia, to apply in our names by petition or in any other proper manner for the naturalisation or Right of Citizenship in the United States, of,
Wilhem Willink
Jan Willink
Nicolaas van Staphorst
Jacob van Staphorst
and Nicolaas Hubbard,
and should it be possible for their Descendants also.

We take the liberty to inclose this letter under his cover, desiring him to deliver it unto You Sir, and to ask your advice about the measures he had best pursue: In furnishing him which, You will infinitely oblige us, and if you will add thereunto Your efficacious recommendation, where such may be needful and effectual, We shall consider your aid in procuring us this our favorite object, as a strong proof of the approbation of our services for the United States during a long space of years, and hold it a truly pleasing because an honorable Reward for them. We are respectfully Sir! Your most obedient humble Servants

WILHEM & JAN WILLINK
N & J. VAN STAPHORST & HUBBARD

RC (DLC); in the hand of Van Staphorst & Hubbard, signed by the two firms; at foot of text: "Thos. Jefferson Esqr."; endorsed by TJ as received 2 Jan. 1794 and so recorded in SJL.

From James Wood

SIR   In Council 10th. August 1793.

I do myself the honor of enclosing the Copy of a letter from John Hamilton, esqr. British Consul at Norfolk. The communications contained in Mr. Hamilton's letter have been transmitted by direction of the Executive, to the Commandants of the Militia of the Borough of Norfolk, and the Counties of Nansemond and Norfolk. I have the honor to be, with sentiments of respect and esteem, &c.   JAMES WOOD

FC (Vi: Executive Letterbook); at head of text: "To the Secretary of State." Recorded in SJL as received 17 Aug. 1793. Enclosure: Hamilton to the Governor of Virginia, 8 Aug. 1793, communicating information he has received that Captain John Cooper of Suffolk is about to sail with a ship carrying eighteen guns fitted out there along with a smaller vessel as a tender, which he regards as a direct violation of the Proclamation of Neutrality, so that the governor can act to prevent any infringement of neutrality that might ensue (printed in CVSP, VI, 475).

Wood's circular letter TO THE COMMANDANTS OF THE MILITIA in the relevant jurisdictions was also dated 10 Aug. 1793 (Vi: Executive Letterbook).

To Henry Knox

Aug. 11. 1793.

Th: Jefferson presents his compliments to General Knox, and being entirely uninformed where Judge Symes should be directed to in Jersey he asks the favor of General Knox to put his direction on the inclosed, and his advice how it may be conveyed.—He has reflected on the proposition for publishing the rules of Aug. 3. and thinks the inserting them in the newspapers with some such preface as the inclosed would be as effectual as any other and as little exceptionable on the whole. It will be taken for granted, in this way, that the copy has been furnished by some of the subordinate officers to whom it has been sent.

PrC (DLC). Tr (ViU: Edgehill-Randolph Papers); 19th-century copy. Enclosure: TJ to John Cleves Symmes, 11 Aug. 1793. Other enclosure not found.

The neutrality RULES approved by the Cabinet on 3 Aug. 1793 were first published in the 14 Aug. 1793 issue of *The Federal Gazette and Philadelphia Daily Adver-* *tiser* under the heading of "Rules adopted by the President of the United States." It is not known to what extent this heading corresponded with TJ's missing PREFACE. In addition, the rules were preceded by a text of Alexander Hamilton's 4 Aug. 1793 circular letter to United States customs collectors on their enforcement (Syrett, *Hamilton*, xv, 178-81).

To James Madison

DEAR SIR   Aug. 11. 1793.

I wrote you last on the 3d. inst. Your's of July 30. came to hand yesterday. Besides the present which goes by post, I write you another to-day to go by Mr. D. Randolph who sets out the day after tomorrow for Monticello, but whether by the direct route or viâ Richmond is not yet decided. I shall desire that letter to be sent to you by express from Monticello. I have not been able to lay my hands on the newspaper which gave a short but true view of the intention of the proclamation. However having occasion to state it in a paper which I am preparing, I have done it in the following terms, and I give you the very words from the paper, because just as I had finished so far, *the President*[1] called on me, I read it to him, he said it presented fairly his view of the matter, he recalled to my mind that I had, at the time, opposed it's being made a declaration of neutrality on the ground that the Executive was not the competent authority for that, and therefore that it was agreed the instrument should be drawn with great care. My statement is in these words. 'On the declaration of war between France and England, the US. being at peace with both, their situation was so new and unexperienced by themselves that their citizens were not, in the first instant, sensible of the new duties resulting therefrom, and of the laws it would impose *even on their dispositions* towards the belligerent powers. Some of them imagined (and chiefly their transient sea-faring citizens) that they were free to indulge those dispositions, to take side with either party, and enrich themselves by depredations on the commerce of the other, and were meditating enterprizes of this nature, as was said. In this state of the public mind, and before it should take an erroneous direction difficult to be set right, and dangerous to themselves and their country, the President thought it expedient, by way of Proclamation, to remind our fellow citizens that we were in a state of peace with all the belligerent powers, that in that state it was our duty neither to aid nor injure any, to exhort and warn them against acts which might contravene this duty, and particularly those of positive hostility, for the punishment of which the laws would be appealed to, and to[2] put them on their guard also as to the risks they would run if they should attempt to carry articles of contraband to any.'————'Very soon afterwards we learnt that he was undertaking to authorize the fitting and arming vessels in that port, enlisting men, foreigners and citizens, and giving them commissions to cruize and commit hostilities against nations at peace with us, that these vessels were taking and bringing prizes into our ports, that the Consuls of France were assuming to hold courts of Admiralty on them, to try, condemn and authorize their sale as legal prize, and all this before Mr. ———— had[3] presented himself or his credentials to the President, before he was received by him, without his consent or consultation, and directly in contravention of the state of peace existing and declared to exist in the Pres's proclamation, and which it was incumbent on him to preserve till the constitutional authority should otherwise declare. These proceedings became immediately, as was naturally to be expected, the subject of complaint by the representative here of that power against whom they would chiefly operate &c.' This was the sense of the proclamation in the view of the draughtsman and of the two signers, but H. had other views. The instrument was badly drawn, and made the P. go out of his line to declare things which, tho' true, it was not exactly his province to declare. The instrument was communicated to me after it was drawn, but I was busy, and only run an eye over it to see that it was not made a declaration of neutrality, and gave it back again, without, I believe, changing a tittle.

Pacificus has now changed his signature to 'No Jacobin.' Three papers under this signature have been published in Dunlap. I suppose they will get into Fenno. They are commentaries on the laws of nations, and on the different parts of our treaty with France. As yet they have presented no very important heresy.—Congress will not meet till the legal day. It was referred to a meeting at my office to consider and advise on it. I was for calling them. Kn. against it. H. said his judgment was against it, but he would join any two who should concur so as to make a majority either way. R. was pointedly against it. We agreed to give our opinions separately, and tho' the P. was in his own judgment for calling them, he acquiesced in the majority.—I pass on to the other letter: so Adieu. Your's affectionately.

RC (DLC: Madison Papers); unsigned; with two words in code (see note 1 below). PrC (DLC).

The PAPER which TJ read to George Washington and from which he quoted here was an early draft of TJ to Gouverneur Morris, 16 Aug. 1793. Edmond Charles Genet was the man UNDERTAKING to undermine American neutrality. The DRAUGHTS-MAN of the Proclamation of Neutrality was Edmund Randolph, and the President and TJ were its TWO SIGNERS. The first three of Alexander Hamilton's nine pseudonymous "No Jacobin" essays appeared in *Dunlap's American Daily Advertiser* on 31 July and 5 and 8 Aug. 1793 (Syrett, *Hamilton*, xv, 145-51, 184-91, 203-7).

[1] The preceding two words are written in code, the decipherment being supplied by the Editors using TJ's key to Code No. 9.

[2] TJ here canceled "inform them also."

[3] Preceding rule and word written over "Genet," erased.

To James Madison

DEAR SIR   Philadelphia Aug. 11. 1793.

I write a second letter to-day, because going by a private conveyance I can venture in it a paper which never could have been hazarded by the post. Timely information of it's contents (which must be sacredly kept to yourself unless you have an opportunity of communicating them to Monroe) may enable you to shape your plan for the state of things which is actually to take place. It would be the moment for dividing the Treasury between two equal chiefs of the Customs, and Internal taxes, if the Senate were not so unsound. A declaration of the true sense of the Constn. on the question of the bank, will suffice to divorce that from the government, tho' made by a single house. Censures on censurable things clearly confessed in the reports &c.—With respect to the Proclamation, as the facts it declared were true, and the desire of neutrality is universal, it would place the republicans in a very unfavorable point of view with the people to be cavilling about small points of propriety; and would betray a wish to find fault with the President in an instance where he will be approved by the great body of the people who consider the substance of the measure only, and not the smaller criticisms to which it is liable. The conduct of Genet too is transpiring and exciting the indignation it is calculated to excite. The towns are beginning generally to make known their disapprobation of any such opposition to their government by a foreigner, are declaring their firm adherence to their President, and the Proclamation is made the groundwork of these declarations. In N. York, while Genet was there, the vote of a full meeting of all classes was 9. out of 10. against him, i.e. for the Proclamation. We are told that the cortege which was collected to recieve him (except the committee) consisted only of boys and negroes. All the towns Northwardly are about to express their adherence to the proclamation and chiefly with a view to[1] manifest their disapprobation of G's conduct.[2] Philadelphia, so enthusiastic for him, before his proceedings were known, is going over from him entirely, and if it's popular[3] leaders have not the good sense to go over with them, they will go without them, and be thus transferred to the other party.—So in Congress, I believe that it will be true wisdom in the Republican party to approve unequivocally of a state of neutrality, to avoid little cavils about who should declare it, to abandon G. entirely, with expressions of strong friendship and adherence to his nation and confidence that he has acted against their sense. In this way we shall keep the people on our side by keeping ourselves in the right.—I have been myself under a cruel dilemma with him. I adhered to him as long as I could have a hope of getting him right, because I knew what weight we should derive to our scale by keeping in it the love of the people for the French cause and nation, and how important it was to ward off from that cause and nation[4] any just grounds of alienation. Finding at length that the man was absolutely incorrigible, I saw the necessity of quitting a wreck which could not but sink all who should cling to it.—It is determined to insist on his recall, and I am preparing a statement of his conduct to be laid before the Executive council. Hamilton and Knox have pressed an appeal to the people with an eagerness I never before saw in them. They made the establishment of the democratic society here the ground for sounding an alarm that this society (which they considered as the *antifederal and discontented faction*) was put into motion by Mr. G. and would by their corresponding societies in all the state draw the mass of the people, by dint of misinformation, into their vortex and overset the government. The Pres. was strongly impressed by this picture, drawn by H. in three speeches of $\frac{3}{4}$ of an hour length each. I opposed it totally, told the President plainly in their presence, that the intention was to dismount him[5] from being the head[6] of the nation, and make him the head of a party: that this would be the effect of making him in an appeal to the people declare war against the Republican party. R. according to his half-way system between wrong and right urged the *putting off* the appeal. The Pr. came into his idea;[7] or rather concluded that the question on it might be put off indefinitely to be governed by events. If the demonstrations of popular adherence to him become as general and warm as I believe they will, I think he will never again bring on the question: if there is any appearance of their supporting Genet, he will probably make the appeal.—I can by this confidential conveyance speak more freely of R. He is the poorest Cameleon I ever saw having no colour of his own, and reflecting that nearest him. When he is with me he is a whig, when with H. he is a tory, when with the P. he is what he thinks will please him. The last is his strongest hue, tho' the *2d. tinges him very strongly. The first is what I think he would prefer in his heart if he were in the woods where he could see nobody, or in a society of *all*

*When he is with people whom he thinks he can guide, he says without reserve that the party in opposition to the fiscal system, are antifederal, and endeavoring to overturn the constitution. These people name you as having apostatised from your antient federalism, and my self as having never been of that sentiment. I say *they* name us, because my information is not expressly that R. named us so to them.

whigs. You will remark an expression in the inclosed paper with respect to him. It has in some degree lessened my apprehensions of the estimation in which the Pr. held him. Still it is not the less true that his opinion always makes the majority, and that the President acquiesces *always* in the majority; consequently that the government is now solely directed by him. As he is not yet openly thrown off by the whig party, it gives to the public a false security that fair play is given to the whiggism of the Pr. by an equal division of whig and tory among his counsellors. I have kept on terms of strict friendship with him hitherto, that I might make some good out of him, and because he has really some good private qualities. But he is in a station infinitely too important for his understanding, his firmness, or his circumstances.—I mentioned to you that we had convened the judges to consult them on the questions which have arisen on the law of nations. They declined being consulted. In England you know such questions are referred regularly to the judge of Admiralty. I asked E.R. if we could not prepare a bill for Congress to appoint a board or some other body of advice for the Executive on such questions. He said he should propose to annex it to his office. In plain language this would be to make him the sole arbiter of the line of conduct for the US. towards foreign nations.—You ask the sense of France with regard to the defensive quality of the guarantee. I know it no otherwise than from Genet. His doctrine is that without waiting to be called on, without waiting till the islands were attacked[8] the moment France was engaged in war, it was our duty to fly to arms as a nation, and the duty of every one to do it as an individual. He insisted much on Henfeild's counsel (who were engaged and paid by him) defending Henfeild on this ground. But they had more sense. Adieu. Your's affectionately

TH: JEFFERSON

P.S. The Pres. is extremely anxious to know your sentiments on the Proclamation. He has asked me several times. I tell him you are so absorbed in farming that you write to me always about ploughs, rotations &c.

RC (DLC: Madison Papers); at foot of first page: "Mr. Madison"; footnote and postscript written lengthwise in margin. PrC (DLC). Tr (DLC); 19th-century copy. Enclosure: Notes of a Conversation with George Washington, 6 Aug. 1793.

For the STATEMENT of the CONDUCT of French Minister Edmond Charles Genet, see TJ to Gouverneur Morris, 16 Aug. 1793. The JUDGES of the United States Supreme Court DECLINED BEING CONSULTED on 8 Aug. 1793 (see Editorial Note on the referral of neutrality questions to the Supreme Court, at 18 July 1793). Gideon HENFEILD'S COUNSEL: Peter S. Du Ponceau, Jared Ingersoll, and Jonathan Dickinson Sergeant (see note to TJ to Genet, 27 May 1793).

It was probably with this letter that TJ sent Madison a copy of his letter of this date to George Washington and an unsigned paragraph from the *Federal Gazette and Philadelphia Daily Advertiser* of 30 July 1793 commenting on the acquittal of Gideon Henfield by a jury in the United States

Circuit Court of Pennsylvania, the author of which TJ identified as Edmund Randolph: "It must not be supposed, that because on the indictment against *Gideon Henfield*, there was a verdict of acquittal; it is therefore lawful for any citizen of the United States to enter on board French privateers, and commit hostilities against the subjects of Great-Britain. On the contrary, the court, with whom the law rests, most explicitly and unanimously declared that such conduct is in violation of our treaty with his Britannic majesty, and that the treaty is not only a law, the breach of which is criminal and punishable, but by the constitution, it is the *supreme law of the land*, more solemn, more obligatory than an act of Congress itself. The jury have acquitted *Gideon Henfield*—but as the law is so undeniably clear and explicit, it may be presumed—it must be presumed, that it was owing to some deficiency in point of fact, or some *equitable* circumstances attending this case, which are the points of consideration for the jury. I do not mean to argue the case over again—To me it is clear, a conviction should have taken place, although I would most heartily have wished a remission of the punishment. I mean merely to let it be understood that this verdict does not by any means amount to a decision, that it is not unlawful to enlist on board French privateers" (newspaper clipping in DLC: Madison Papers; headed "For the Federal Gazette"; at foot of text in TJ's hand: "by E.R.").

[1] TJ here canceled "declare."
[2] TJ here canceled "Even," which he had written over "I think," erased.
[3] Preceding two words interlined in place of "their."
[4] Preceding four words interlined in place of "them."
[5] TJ here canceled "as the."
[6] Word written over "lead," erased.
[7] TJ here canceled "so far."
[8] Preceding seven words interlined.

From James Madison

DEAR SIR   Augst. 11. 93

Yours of Aug: 3. has just come to hand. All the preceding have been acknowledged. I am extremely mortified in looking for the Key to the Cypher, to find that I left it in Philada. You must therefore repeat any thing that may be of use still to be known, particularly any thing that may relate to the time of your leaving Phila. which I wish to know as long as possible before it takes place. The task on which you have put me, must be abridged so as not to go beyond that period. You will see that the first topic is not yet compleated. I hope the 2d. and 3. to wit the meaning of the Treaty and the obligations of gratitude will be less essential. The former is particularly delicate; and tho' I think it may be put in a light that would reflect ignominy on the author of P. yet I had rather not meddle with the subject if it could be avoided. I can not say when I shall be able to take up those two parts of the job. Just as I was embarking on the general subject I received from the reputed Author of Franklyn a large pamphlet written by him against the fiscal system, particularly the Bank; which I could not but attend to. It is put on a footing that requires me to communicate personally with Monroe, whom I ought to have seen before this, as the publication of the work is to be contrived for the Author. It really has merit always for its ingenuity generally for its solidity, and is enriched with many fine strokes of imagination, and a continued vein of pleasantry and keen satire, that will sting deeply.[1] I have received a letter from the Author wishing to hear from me. I must therefore take a ride as far as Charlottesville as soon as I make out the next packet for you, and suspend the residue of the business till I return. I shall endeavor in my absence[2] to fulfil a promise to Wilson Nicholas which will lengthen the suspension. I forward to F____[3] a copy of the little thing of Ld. Ch: the last sentence is struck out as not necessary, and which may perhaps wound too indiscriminately certain characters, not at present interested in supporting public corruptions. The drouth has done irreparable injury to the Corn in many parts of the Country. It has been interrupted within a few days past, by a pretty extensive rain. We shared in it here but scantily. I understand that at Charlottesville which had been favored with several preceding ones, it was plentiful. Be good eno' to contrive an excuse to Mr. R. at Monto: for my not forwarding the Gazettes latterly: if you have not already thought of it. I know not how to apologize myself—and shall feel some awkwardness, as I shall not carry them when I go into his neighborhood.

[*On separate sheet:*]

The paper for J. F. could not otherwise get to him than with your aid. You must therefore take the trouble of having it handed into the post office whence the penny post will take it, unless you can do it at some shorter hand. I wish you to look over what is said critically, and if you think there be any thing of importance wrong, or that may do more harm than good, that you will either erase it, where that will not break the sense, or arrest the whole till I can make the correction. Delay I know is bad; but vulnerable parts that would be siezed for victories and triumphs would be worse. I beg you also to attend particularly to three passages slightly marked with a pencil, the first, the declaration of the principles and sentiments of the author—2d. begining with "Writers such as Locke and Montesqeue"[4] &c—to the pencil mark in the ¶. 3 the quotation from the Federalist. If you think the first had better be omitted it can come out without leaving the least gap—so can the 2d. My doubts as to that proceed from the danger of turning the controversy too much into the wilderness of Books. I use Montesqeue also from memory, tho I believe without inaccuracy. The 3d. can also come out without affecting the peice, and I wish you to erase it if you think the most scrupulous delicacy, conjecturing the author, could disapprove it. One No. more or 2 short Nos. will close the first topic and supersede the last. They will be sent as soon as finished and copied. These would have been sent somewhat sooner, but for the delay caused by the last circumstance.

RC (DLC: Madison Papers); unsigned; endorsed by TJ as received 17 Aug. 1793 and so recorded in SJL; filed with undated continuation on separate sheet, probably a wrapper for first two "Helvidius" essays, both parts possibly having been dispatched on 12 Aug. 1793 (see Madison to TJ, 20 Aug. 1793). Enclosures: (1) Drafts of Madison's first two "Helvidius" essays refuting the defense of the Proclamation of Neutrality by "Pacificus" (printed in Madison, *Papers*, xv, 66-73, 80-7). (2) [Madison] to John Fenno, consisting of undated covering letter to first enclosure (same, 73n). Other enclosure discussed below.

John Taylor of Caroline was the RE-PUTED AUTHOR of six essays which appeared under the pseudonym "Franklin" in the *National Gazette* between 16 Feb. and 20 Mch. 1793. The pieces accused the Secretary of the Treasury of shady financial practices perpetrated with the aim of subverting the Constitution and replacing a republican with a monarchical government. The LARGE PAMPHLET was a draft of *An Enquiry into the Principles and Tendency of certain Public Measures* (Philadelphia, 1794), an anonymously-issued work in which Taylor again warned of the corrupting and anti-republican tendencies of Hamilton's FISCAL SYSTEM (Sowerby, No. 3175; Shalhope, *Taylor*, 218, 219). Taylor's letters to Madison enclosing the draft and WISHING TO HEAR FROM ME are dated 20 June and 5 Aug. 1793 (Madison, *Papers*, xv, 34-6, 52). The draft subsequently went to TJ, who helped to edit it (James Monroe to TJ, 21 Aug. 1793; TJ to Madison, 1, 8 Sep. 1793).

The COPY OF THE LITTLE THING intended for Philip Freneau, editor of the *National Gazette*—an extract from a 22 Nov. 1770 speech in the House of Lords by William Pitt, Earl of Chatham—has not been found, but apparently TJ and Madison had already exchanged a text which TJ evidently made at some point and which included THE LAST SENTENCE that Madison STRUCK OUT. This fuller extract reads: "There is a set of men, my Lords, in the city of London, who are known to live in riot and Luxury, upon the plunder of the ignorant, the innocent and the helpless, upon that part of the community, which stands most in need of, and best deserves the care and protection of the legislature. To me, my Lords, whether they be miserable jobbers of Change-alley, or the lofty Asiatic plunderers of Leaden-Hall street, they are equally detestable. I care but little whether a man walks on foot, or is drawn by eight horses, or six horses; if his luxury be supported by the plunder of his country, I despise and abhor him. My Lords, while I had the honour of serving his Majesty, I never ventured to look at the treasury, but from a distance; it is a business I am unfit for, and to which I never could have submitted. The little I know of it, has not served to raise my opinion of what is vulgarly called the monied interest: I mean that *bloodsucker*, that *muckworm*, which calls itself *the friend of government*, which pretends to serve this or that administration, and may be purchased on the same terms by any administration. Under this description I include the whole race of commissaries, jobbers, contractors, clothiers and remitters" (Tr in DLC: Madison Papers, undated, almost certainly in TJ's disguised hand, with "Extract from Ld. Chatham's Speech in the debate on the Falkland's Islands" at head of text; PrC in DLC: TJ Papers, 91: 15631). See also TJ to Madison, 18 Aug. 1793; and [William Cobbett, ed.], *The Parliamentary History of England, from the earliest period to the year 1803*, 36 vols. [London, 1806-20], xvi, 1091-1108, esp. 1106-7).

J. F.: John Fenno, editor of the *Gazette of the United States*. TJ must have decided against deleting any of the THREE PASSAGES SLIGHTLY MARKED WITH A PENCIL, since they are all in the first "Helvidius" essay as it appeared in the *Gazette of the United States* on 24 and 28 Aug. 1793 (Madison, *Papers*, xv, 66-7, 68, 72-3).

[1] Madison here canceled "I must set out if possible."
[2] Preceding three words interlined.
[3] Rule partly written over "kln."
[4] Closing quotation mark supplied.

To Thomas Mann Randolph, Jr.

DEAR SIR   Philadelphia Aug. 11. 1793.

Your favor of July 31. came to hand yesterday. I wish this may get to you in time to ask the favor of you to instruct Tom Shackleford or Jupiter, or whoever brings the horse to Georgetown to ride a mule and lead the horse. He will by that means come the fresher, and the sooner recover for the journey back. Besides, there is a person here who I think will purchase Tarquin; in which case the mule will be necessary for the return of the messenger.—Biddle, my new manager, writes me from Elkton, that the persons who had it in contemplation to go and tenant my lands, will not engage till they go to see them, which they will do in the fall. I must therefore take measures for going on with their culture myself the next year: and as I have engaged Biddle for Monticello, I must get you to announce it to Clarkson, and offer him the plantations over the river, on the terms given him for Monticello. This removal may be rendered palateable to him by being told it is the effect of my resolution to put Monticello into a farm on the plan of this country, with which he will know he is unacquainted. If he determines to quit altogether, and you can find any good overlooker for the plantations I must trouble you to engage one on any terms (not involving the payment of *money*) which you may think adviseable. I must also trouble you to direct such sowings of small grain on both sides the river as you shall think best, and in good season, which overseers, about to remove, are apt to put off. If Clarkson goes to Shadwell, he will of course see to the sowings on that side himself. Biddle will be at Monticello about the middle of October.

Your reasons for a rotation of bye-articles in a set of small feilds are perfectly sound. Nothing is more prudent than to vary articles of culture in order to have something to meet the varying seasons of the year.— My letter of the 28th. will have informed you of some alterations proposed in my rotation. The difference between your's and mine is the 3. years of clover (by which term I always mean *red* clover) instead of 3. years of rest or fallow; and this depends on the great problem of the clover husbandry. I did not at first propose to adopt it, because it lengthens the rotation so much. But further reflection, and observation here on it's great and palpable advantages, determined me to attempt it. My not explaining that by the term clover I always meant the *red*, left a just opening for the objection that three years of clover would produce a strong and troublesome growth of bushes. Every year, in my rotation, carries either the plough or the scythe through every feild; except the 8th. year, and I have considerable hopes I can lop off that year from the rotation altogether by other resources for pasture.—One difficulty you suggest is a very great one indeed, that I shall have too much ploughing in the fall, considering how busy a season our apprehensions of the weavil make that. I found considerable hopes on the threshing machine expected, as 4. horses suffice to work that, and I had proposed to work my ploughs with oxen. Should that machine fail, more horses must be kept for treading wheat in the proper season, and to be employed in waggoning at other times. Or the raising horses for sale[1] must be gone into so as to derive assistance in treading a year or two before they are sold. Still these are but conjectural remedies for the difficulty, which are by no means certain in their effect.—On revising my letter of the 28th. ult. I find I have illy expressed the President's method of mixing corn and potatoes. He puts them in alternate drills, 4f. apart, so that the rows of corn are 8.f. apart, and a single stalk every 18.I. or 2.f. in the row. Judge Peters, an excellent farmer in this neighborhood, tells me he has taken this method from the President, and has generally made 40. bush. of corn and 120. bush. of potatoes to the acre, strictly measured. I propose the mixture because unless this or some other mode of cultivating corn can be found which may prevent it's ravages in our land, I should decline it's culture altogether. Still our habits in favor of that plant render it eligible to try to reconcile the saving our lands with some degree of corn-culture. Perhaps your idea of dressing our grounds absolutely flat, without hills or ridges, may be adopted for the corn, potatoes, and peas. Mr. D. Randolph discorages me as to the last article by the difficulty of gathering them. I recieve encoragement from him in the article of manure, of which he tells me he makes from 7. to 10. loads for every head of cattle. This corroborates Dr. Logan's experiment according to which 150. cattle will manure 60. acres a year. However should we fall short in this, I rely on supplying it by green dressings of buckwheat.

Mr. D. Randolph is well. He is gone at present to Trenton. He proposes setting out for Monticello the day after tomorrow. Whether directly or viâ Presquisle is not yet decided. Present my best respects to Mrs. Randolph, and my love to my daughter. Her watch is repaired and will be sent by Mr. Randolph. I am with constant and sincere attachment Dear Sir Your's affectionately   Th: Jefferson

RC (DLC); at foot of first page: "Mr. Randolph"; endorsed by Randolph as received 20 Aug. 1793. PrC (DLC).

[1] Preceding two words interlined.

To Thomas Mann Randolph, Jr.

DEAR SIR   Philadelphia Aug. 11. 1793.

The inclosed letter to Mr. Madison is extremely confidential. Should it arrive before they set off with my horse, it may be sent by that opportunity; otherwise I will thank you to send a messenger express with it. Having written to you to-day by post I shall only add assurances of the sincere esteem of Dear Sir Your's affectionately   TH: JEFFERSON

RC (DLC); addressed: "Thomas M. Randolph junr. esq. Monticello favored by mr D. Randolph"; endorsed by Randolph as received 30 Aug. 1793. PrC (DLC). Tr

(ViU: Edgehill-Randolph Papers); 19th-century copy. Enclosure: TJ to James Madison, 11 Aug. 1793 (second letter).

To John Cleves Symmes

SIR   Philadelphia Aug. 11. 1793.

Governor Sinclair has inclosed me a Proclamation dated July 24. and summoning the legislature of the North-Western territory to meet at Cincinnati on the 1st. day of September, of which he desired me to notify yourself and Judge Turner. It is out of my power to do it as to the latter, as I do not know where he is. I have the honor to be with great respect, Sir Your most obedt. humble servt   TH: JEFFERSON

PrC (DLC); at foot of text: "honble Judge Symes." FC (Lb in DNA: RG 59, DL).

For the PROCLAMATION, whose official date was 25 July 1793, see Arthur St. Clair to TJ, 9 Aug. 1793, and note. A missing letter from Symmes to TJ of 6 Sep. 1793 is recorded in SJL as received from Elizabethtown on 7 Sep. 1793.

To George Washington

Aug. 11. 1793.

Th: Jefferson with his respects to the President, begs leave to express in writing more exactly what he meant to have said yesterday. A journey home in the autumn is of a necessity which he cannot controul after the arrangements he has made, and, when there, it would be his extreme wish to remain. But if his continuance in office to the last of December, as intimated by the President, would, by bringing the two appointments nearer together, enable him to marshal them more beneficially to the public, and more to his own satisfaction, either motive will suffice to induce Th:J. to continue till that time. He submits it therefore to the President's judgment, which he will be glad to receive when convenient, as the arrangements he had taken may require some change.

RC (DNA: RG 59, MLR); addressed: "The President of the US."; endorsed by Tobias Lear. PrC (DLC). PrC of same RC (DLC: Madison Papers). Tr (Lb in DNA: RG 59, SDC). Probably enclosed in TJ to James Madison, 11 Aug. 1793 (second letter).

From Tobias Lear

August 12th: 1793

By the President's Command T. Lear has the honor to transmit to the Secretary of State the Report of the Proceedings in the Executive Departmt. of Governmt. in the Territory of the U.S. North West of the Ohio, for six months, ending the 30th. of June last—which the President wishes the Secretary to examine at his leisure and report to him anything that may be found therein requiring the Agency of the President.   TOBIAS LEAR

RC (DLC); endorsed by TJ as a letter from George Washington received on 14 Aug. 1793. Recorded in SJPL under date of receipt as "proceedings of Exve of N.W. territory." Enclosure: Journal of Executive Proceedings in the Northwest Territory, 2 Jan.-18 June 1793 (MS in DNA: RG 59, NWT, in the hand of Winthrop Sargent; printed in *Terr. Papers*, III, 390-411). See also Washington, *Journal*, 218.

From George Washington

DEAR SIR   Philadelphia Augt. 12th. 1793.

I clearly understood you on Saturday. And, of what I conceive to be two evils, must prefer the least—that is—to dispense with your temporary absence in Autumn (in order to retain you in Office 'till January) rather than part with you altogether at the close of September.

It would be an ardent wish of mine, that your continuance in Office (even at the expence of some sacrifice of inclination) could have been through the whole of the[1] ensuing Session of Congress, for many—very many weighty[2] reasons which present themselves to my mind: one of which, and not the least is, that in my judgment, the affairs of this Country as they relate to foreign Powers—Indian disturbances—and internal policy—will have taken a more decisive, and I hope agreeable form, than they now bear, before that time—When perhaps, other public Servants might also indulge[3] in retirement. If this cannot be, my next wish is, that your absence from the Seat of Government in Autumn, may be as short as you conveniently can make it. With much truth & regard I am—Yr. Obedt. & Affecte. Servt   GO: WASHINGTON

RC (DLC); at foot of text: "Mr. Jefferson"; endorsed by TJ as received 12 Aug. 1793. Dft (PP: Jay Treaty Papers, William M. Elkins Collection); endorsed by Washington. FC (Lb in DNA: RG 59, SDC). Recorded in SJPL.

[1] Preceding three words interlined in Dft.
[2] Preceding three words interlined in Dft.
[3] In Dft Washington wrote "might be indulged" before altering the phrase to read as above.

From Archibald Campbell

Dr Sir   Baltimore Augt. 13th 1793

The enclosed letter came under cover to me by a late arrival here from Bordeaux—and accompanied a bill of Lading for 14 Cases of wine Shipt for you by my friends Messrs. Fenwick Mason & Coy. who write me to take your direction where to forward the wine after arrival here. If you have an invoice of its cost—you will please Send it me—or a copy thereof—in order to have the necessary entry made at the Naval office and the duties settled thereon.

I have already got liberty to have the wine put into Store. I remain with much respect sir Your obdt. hble servt   Archd Campbell

The freight is payable here.

RC (MHi); endorsed by TJ as received 16 Aug. 1793 and so recorded in SJL. Enclosure: Fenwick, Mason & Company to TJ, 16 May 1793.

Archibald Campbell (ca. 1747-1805), a Baltimore merchant and director of the Bank of Maryland, had a dwelling, countinghouse, and warehouse on South Gay Street in 1796 (Robert Barnes, *Marriages and Deaths from Baltimore Newspapers, 1796-1816* [Baltimore, 1978], 49; Hamilton Owens, *Baltimore on the Chesapeake* [Garden City, N.Y., 1941], 141; William Thompson and James L. Walker, *The Baltimore Town and Fell's Point Directory...* [Baltimore, 1796], 12).

From Alexander Hamilton

Tuesday Aug 13th 1793

The Secretary of the Treasury proposes to the Secretary of State a Meeting of the Trustees of the Sinking Fund at the Office of the Secy. of State[1] the day after tomorrow twelve oClock. If convenient to him he will please to give notice accordingly to The Atty. General. If the Sy. of the Treasury hears nothing to the contrary he will attend of course.

RC (DLC); endorsed by TJ as received 13 Aug. 1793.

[1] Hamilton originally wrote "at his Office tomorrow" and then altered the phrase to read as above.

From Gouverneur Morris

Enclos'd herein you will find Copies of my Letters of the 27 and 28 June 4. 21. and 24 July and 6 August to the Minister of foreign Affairs with Copies of his Letters to me of the 3. 19. 29 and 30 July. From these you will perceive that my Application for an Order to the Minister of France in America to pay out of the Funds to be furnished by the United States the Drafts made on his Predecessor from S. Domingo produc'd the desir'd Effect. Some subsequent Circumstances have induc'd me to beleive that under that Cover an Attempt will be made to pay the Bills drawn on Europe in favor of french Citizens. I have certified Signatures which seem'd to be calculated for that Purpose but as I presume that Measures will be taken of a cautionary Nature I shall not pretend to suggest any.

You will perceive Sir in this Correspondence one of the many Violations of our Flag in the Case of the little Cherub which being attended with Circumstances of peculiar Atrocity call'd for more pointed Animadversion. The Conduct of the Government on the Occasion was perfectly proper. The Person who committed the Murder has however been acquitted on the Testimony of his Companions in direct Contradiction to that of the American Master and Crew. The Case of the Ship is still depending and I know not what will be the Event. It now appears that a Part of the Cargo on Board of her was for Account of flemish Merchants and to be delivered at Ostende. But more of this presently. I must however take the Liberty of recommending to the Notice of Government Francis Coffyn of Dunkerque an old Deputy of Mr. Barclay while he was Consul General. On Many Occasions and especially in the Affair of the little Cherub he has behav'd with much Sense Spirit and Industry. The Conduct of such Business is by no Means pleasant neither is it without some personal Danger for in the present Situation of this Country the Laws are but little respected and it would seem as if pompous Declarations of the Rights of Man were reiterated only to render the daily Violation of them more shocking.

You will see Sir in my Letter of the fourth of July a Clause asking the Liberty of an American Citizen. In my Application on that Subject I have been very cautious fearing that I might be deceiv'd by british Seamen and consequently that our Countrymen might afterwards be without Redress; As in such Case the Government here would throw all the Complaints aside as being unfounded. Among others who have ask'd the Protection of the United States are some Nantucket Whale Men. And at first their Requests were so artfully made that I was near being the Dupe. I have however declin'd all Interference in their Favor telling them that when they embark'd under a foreign and rival Flag they forfeited by their own Act the Protection afforded by that of the United States and must console themselves in their present Situation by the Privileges which they formerly enjoyed and which tempted them to engage in the british Service. This is the general Idea I have held out but differently modified according to the various Circumstances which Individuals have brought forward. These People are a Sort of Citizens of the World and wherever they went were the most pernicious Enemies to their native Country because every where they solicited either the Exclusion of or else heavy Duties on the produce of our Fisheries. At present those who were settled at Dunkerque have I am told engagd in privateering. Probably if the War lasts the whole Hive may settle again within the Territory of the United States and the more they endure in the mean Time the sooner will they adopt that salutary Determination.

The Decree respecting neutral Bottoms so far as it respects the Vessels of the United States has you will see been bandied about in a Shameful Manner. I am told from Havre that it is by the Force of Money that the Determinations which violate our Rights have been obtain'd and in comparing Dates Events and Circumstances this Idea seems to be but too well supported. I will make no Comments on the facts because my opinions are of no Consequence. The true State of them will result from the enclos'd Pieces and the United States will judge thereon. I am with sincere Esteem Dr Sir your obedient Servt.

GOUV MORRIS

RC (DNA: RG 59, DD); at head of text: "No. 35."; at foot of first page: "Thomas Jefferson Esqre Secretary of State"; endorsed by Edmund Randolph as received 23 Feb. 1794. FC (Lb in DLC: Gouverneur Morris Papers). Tr (DNA: RG 46, Senate Records, 3d Cong., 1st sess.). PrC (DNA: RG 59, MD). Tr (Lb in same, DD). Enclosures: (1) Morris to François Louis Michel Chemin Deforgues, 27 June 1793, stating that, having demonstrated its attachment to the French nation by advancing 4,000,000 livres for the succor of Saint-Domingue in response to the request of Jean Baptiste Ternant and on the basis of a decree of the National Assembly, and by advancing 3,000,000 livres to purchase provisions for France in response to another demand of Ternant, the United States government wished the French Republic to instruct its minister in Philadelphia to apply part of the funds he is to receive from the United States

Treasury to pay bills issued to American merchants by the administration of Saint-Domingue for the purchase or seizure of their cargoes. (2) Deforgues to Morris, Paris, 3 July 1793, stating that he was about to instruct Edmond Charles Genet to reimburse American merchants as requested by Morris; that Genet had already been instructed to inform the President of French gratitude for American aid to Saint-Domingue; and that he was enclosing decrees of the National Convention expressing indignation about the violence committed aboard the *Little Cherub* and exempting United States vessels from the decree of 9 May. (3) Decree of the National Convention, 1 July 1793, directing that the minister of justice institute an immediate investigation of the murder at Dunkirk on 6 June of the mate of the *Little Cherub*, and of the conduct of the captains and crews of the *Vrai Patriote* and *Argus* toward the captain and crew of the *Little Cherub*, and transmit the result to the Convention without delay; that the *Little Cherub* be released and that the minister of marine ascertain the indemnities due to the ship for delay and spoliation and to the family of the murdered mate; and that Deforgues communicate this decree to Morris and Genet. (4) Decree of the National Convention, 1 July 1793, exempting United States vessels from the decree of 9 May 1793 in conformity with Article 16 of the commercial treaty of 1778. (5) Morris to Deforgues, 28 June 1793, stating that he and the United States government reciprocated the recently nominated foreign minister's sentiments of friendship; that the 9 and 28 May 1793 decrees of the National Convention threatened American trade by setting a precedent of commercial restrictions for England and the enemies of France to follow and by inspiring French privateers to commit illegal outrages as long as they were permitted to bring into French ports, far from their intended destinations, American ships carrying foodstuffs to countries at war with France; and that damages were due for the brigantine *Patty*, commanded by Captain Pease, owned by New York merchants, and carrying a cargo of flour addressed to the mayor of St. Valéry, which was forced by a French fleet in May to enter Cherbourg, where the municipality made Pease unload his cargo and where his ship was so badly damaged by being run aground that it could not proceed on an intended voyage to Gothenburg. (6) Deforgues to Morris, 29 July 1793, stating that he had received no response from Cherbourg to his inquiries about damages to the *Patty*, but that since Morris had informed him that one of its owners was pursuing this matter directly with the minister of the interior, this minister would undoubtedly do justice to the owner if his claim was well founded. (7) Morris to Deforgues, 4 July 1793, expressing satisfaction with Nos. 2, 3, and 4; requesting the liberation of Thomas Toby, a United States citizen who had been returning to America aboard an English ship cast away on the French coast and was being detained as an Englishman in the hospital of Boulogne-sur-Mer; and hoping that the order demanded in the enclosed letter from Messrs. Le Couteulx of Rouen could be expedited. (8) Deforgues to Morris, 19 July 1793, enclosing an extract from the register of the Provisional Executive Council on the case of Captain John Brice of the *Juno* of Philadelphia as a new proof of the French Republic's friendship for American citizens. (9) Extract from the Register of the Provisional Executive Council, 14 July 1793, stating that although Captain Brice was blameworthy and not entitled to an indemnity because of his refusal to make known the *Juno*'s colors when it was stopped on 17 May 1793 by the frigate *Capricieuse*, Citizen Savari, in the interests of fair treatment for the citizen of an ally of the French Republic Brice was to be paid a sum equivalent in value to articles allegedly taken from the *Juno* after it was brought to the Island of Aix, a subsequent examination having shown that its papers were regular. (10) Morris to Deforgues, 21 July 1793, stating that he was grateful for Nos. 8 and 9 and would send an account of them home; and that since No. 5 one of the owners of the *Patty* had come to Paris to seek justice from the minister of the interior after being informed by the municipality of Cherbourg that their conduct toward the *Patty* had been dictated by that minister and that damages and expenses must be sought from him. (11) Morris to Deforgues, 24 July 1793, stating that he hoped the French Republic would do justice in the case described in an extract of a 20 July letter from Le Havre alleging that efforts to secure the restitution of the *Laurens*, Captain White, and its cargo on the basis of a 1 July 1793 decree of the National Convention after four months of detention were being frustrated by the owners of the privateer which captured them, whose attorney had persuaded the district tribunal to postpone judgment in this case until 31 July by citing a letter from Paris by one of the owners maintaining that certain members of the Convention would induce it to pass a new decree modifying that of 1 July. (12) Deforgues to Morris, 30 July 1793, stating that he and the minister of marine would immediately act on the case of the *Laurens* and meet Morris's demand about Captain White if he had conformed to the laws on transporting warlike stores and other objects prohibited in wartime (Trs, in French, in DNA: RG 59, DD; Trs, in French and English, in DNA: RG 46, Senate Records, 3d Cong., 1st sess.; PrCs in DNA: RG 59, MD; Trs, in French and English, in Lb in same, DD; printed in ASP, *Foreign Relations*, I, 369-72).

DECREE RESPECTING NEUTRAL BOTTOMS: the 27 July 1793 decree of the National Convention, which revoked the exemption described in Enclosure No. 4 above (*Archives Parlementaires*, 1st ser., LXIX, 582; see note to Morris to TJ, 20 May 1793).

From Edmund Randolph

[ca. 13 Aug. 1793]

A Man has 3500 £ P.C. to pay in instalments of 500£ each beginning 1. Oct: 1795, and continuing for six years without interest. What sum in hand is equal?

RC (DLC: TJ Papers, 93: 16019); unsigned, undated, and unaddressed note written on a small scrap; date conjectured from endorsement inadvertently inscribed by TJ on his reply.

P.C.: Pennsylvania currency.

To Edmund Randolph

[ca. 13 Aug. 1793]

Suppose interest at 6 pr. Cent, the arrangement to commence Oct. 1. 1793.

£			£
67.567	with 8. years interest	=	100.
70.422	7	=	100
73.529	6	=	100
76.923	5	=	100
80.645	4	=	100
84.745	3	=	100
89.285	2	=	100
543.116			700
× by 5			× by 5
2715.58			3500

FC (DLC: TJ Papers, 93: 16018); in TJ's hand, unsigned, undated, and unaddressed; endorsed by TJ as a letter from Edmund Randolph received 13 Aug. 1793, an endorsement intended for the preceding document. Not recorded in SJL.

To George Washington

August 13. 1793

Thomas Jefferson presents his compliments to the President. The report of the Commissioners of public accounts was delivered to Mr. Taylor to be filed away. He was called to new York on Saturday by the illness of his child, and Mr. Blackwell has been searching some time for it without being able to find it. He will continue to search, and when found it shall be sent to the President.

Tr (Lb in DNA: RG 59, SDC); at head of text: "The President of the United States." Not recorded in SJL.

For THE REPORT, see Washington to the Commissioners of Accounts for the States, [22 June 1793], and note. On 15 July 1793 the President sent it to TJ to be copied for presentation to Congress and FILED AWAY in his office, but on this day he sent for it "in order to send it to the Office of the Secretary of the Treasury where it should be lodged conformably to an implication of a law passed on the 5th. Augt. 1790" (Washington, *Journal*, 198, 219; see also *Annals*, II, 2357-9). On 19 Aug. 1793 the document was located and transmitted to Tobias Lear (George Taylor, Jr., to Lear, 19 Aug. 1793, RC in DNA: RG 59, MLR, endorsed by Lear; Tr in Lb in same, SDC). Lear sent it to Hamilton the same day (Syrett, *Hamilton*, XV, 252-3).

From Tobias Lear

Augt 14th. 1793

By the President's command T. Lear has the honor to transmit to the Secretary of State the enclosed letters and papers from the Judge of the District of Rhode Island relating to the Ship Catharine. After the Secretary shall have considered the enclosed documents the President wishes his opinion of the measures which should be taken on the subject.

RC (DLC); endorsed by TJ as a letter from George Washington received 15 Aug. 1793. Recorded in SJPL under 15 Aug. 1793. Enclosures: (1) Judge Henry Marchant to Washington, Newport, 3 Aug. 1793, stating that on 31 July, a day after the *Catharine*, Captain William James Davis master, an armed British merchant ship bound from Jamaica to New Brunswick, anchored here, some of its passengers who appeared to be gentlemen told two local gentlemen that during its voyage this ship had boarded an American sloop and plundered it of considerable property; that after taking the deposition of one of these passengers, Richard Birch, he consulted about it with the United States district attorney, who advised him to have Davis served with a warrant for piracy; that Davis had evaded service of this warrant by sailing away despite being fired upon by the fort; and that the President's thoughts on this matter were needed (RC in DNA: RG 59, MLR; endorsed by George Taylor, Jr.). (2) Marchant's warrant to the marshal or deputy marshal of the District of Rhode Island, 31 July 1793, authorizing the arrest of Captain Davis on a charge of piracy for stopping an unnamed American sloop off Cape Hatteras on or about 20 July and plundering it of three or four large bags of money and other American property to the value of $2,000; with a subjoined note of 1 Aug. 1793 by Deputy Marshal Jabez Champlin stating that Davis was not in the district. (3) Deposition of Richard Birch, Newport, 31 July

1793, describing, as a British passenger aboard the *Catharine*, the stopping and plundering of the American sloop; adding that Davis had left untouched a cargo of coffee belonging to the American captain and that the money he took had belonged to the sloop's French passengers; and noting that on 26 July Davis had admitted to an officer from the British frigate *Boston* that the money was French property and had given him a large bag of it for the commander, Captain Courtenay, who was related to Davis, while retaining about $2,000 for delivery to the proper authorities in New Brunswick or elsewhere. (4) Deposition of Dr. John Harris, Newport, 1 Aug. 1793, containing an account, as a passenger aboard the *Catharine*, of its encounter with the American sloop similar in import to that of No. 3, but adding that Davis planned to share some of the $2,000 with his crew; with an addendum of 3 Aug. 1793 stating that Davis had not followed advice to take out a commission before leaving Jamaica and that the master of the American sloop was Captain Mackay. (5) Deposition of Mary Fitch, Newport, 1 Aug. 1793, containing an account, as a passenger aboard the *Catharine*, of its encounter with the American sloop similar in import to those of Nos. 3 and 4, but adding that Davis had de-livered $850 of the plundered money to the *Boston*. (6) Deposition of Joseph Fitch, Newport, 2 Aug. 1793, containing an account, as a passenger aboard the *Catharine*, of its encounter with the American sloop similar in import to that of No. 5 (Trs in same; certified by Marchant). (7) Manifest of the cargo and passengers' baggage aboard the *Catharine*, Newport, 31 July 1793. (8) Customs certificate, Kingston, Jamaica, 21 June 1793, stating that the *Catharine*, a registered, armed British ship with a cargo of rum, fruit, and a coach bound for New Brunswick, had given bond of £2,000 to land its cargo at no European port north of Cape Finisterre except in Great Britain. (9) Clearance form for the *Catharine*, 21 June 1793 (Trs in same; certified by United States Customs Collector William Ellery). (10) Marchant to Washington, 3 Aug. 1793, stating that several hours after swearing out his deposition Birch returned to him with the British vice consul Mr. Moore; that both complained Birch had not been legally summoned before being put under oath; but that after he explained why the summons had not been served Birch signed a slightly altered version of the deposition and Moore indicated that Davis would appear before Marchant and give his side of the story (RC in same).

From Thomas Mann Randolph, Jr.

DEAR SIR   Monticello Aug: 14: 1793

I have set George and his company to work in the canal according to your desire: Jupiter is with them and is constantly employed in blowing the rock at the upper end which it was their first business to lay bare for him. Part of the timber intended for the house has been brought up, and the remainder will be in place before the middle of next month. The two houses for the servants I am sorry to say are not yet built, the men having been so much deceived in the quantity of timber requisite for the stables, as to have none left for the former when the latter were finished and, then the sap had begun to ascend. I shall have them built as soon as the fall of the leaves commences, and this I fear will be full early enough for the accomodation of the Scotchmen, of whom I could hear nothing when I was in Richmond.

We have had a very long drought, which has injured the Indian Corn greatly. The crop will be less by a 4th. or perhaps a 3d. than was expected some weeks ago. It has probably been of service in checking the Weevil, which appeared very early, but has scarcely increased fast enough to give alarm.

One of the Italians whom Mazzei brought over, Giovannini, applied to me lately for a farm of 30 or 40 acres on Edgehill which he says he can cultivate and yet devote at least three days a week to a garden. He is an excellent gardener and one of the most sober, industrious men I ever knew. I mention this to you, thinking that you might perhaps be inclined to take him on those terms yourself. If you do not I shall take him without hezitation as I know he can cultivate a garden of considerable size well and have half the week to spare.

The family is in very good health; our guests are allso. Your most sincere & aff. friend   Th M Randolph

RC (MHi); endorsed by TJ as received 26 Aug. 1793 and so recorded in SJL.

From George Washington

Wednesday Eveng 14 Augt. 1793

The President wishes the Heads of the Departments to meet at his house tomorrow at *ten* o'clock.

RC (DLC); in the hand of Tobias Lear; endorsed by TJ as received 14 Aug. 1793. Recorded in SJPL.

For a brief description of this Cabinet meeting, see Cabinet Opinions on Edmond Charles Genet, 23 Aug. 1793.

From William Carmichael and William Short

Sir   Madrid Aug. 15: 1793

In our last letter of the 6th. of June we had the honor of informing you of our having written a letter to Mr. Gardoqui on the 26th: of May, agreeably to his desire and in consequence of his promise to give us an immediate answer, to be transmitted officially to the President of the U.S.

That answer though promised to us daily at every interview, was daily postponed until the court began to prepare for their departure from Aranjuez, on account of its being necessary as he informed us, to concert the answer for form sake with the foreign department. From that time we were assured we should have it on their arrival at Madrid—And then as is done with all business, it was delayed for some time on account of papers not being unpacked. After this he came to what is considered the last step in the procrastinating routine—viz. to desire us to write to him again on the subject, observing that that would enable him to push the foreign department.

In consequence thereof we wrote to him our letter of July the 15th. On the 5th. of August we recieved his answer which was dated the 1st. of the same month probably by mistake, as it must have got to our hands in an hour after coming from his. On the 11th. we replied thereto previously to his leaving this place for St. Ildefonso on the 13th. We do ourselves the honor to inclose you copies of these several pieces Nos. 1. 2. 3. and 4. As we consider it proper to send them by duplicate we hope you will excuse one of the copies being from the press.

They will render any comment on our part unnecessary; except as to Mr. Gardoqui's answer being so different from what we had expected. The only external cause to which we could have attributed it would have been what we mentioned in the last page of our letter of June the 6th. There are some circumstances however which induce us to believe that the ground there mentioned is not at present as agreeable here as it was expected it would be. Although this ground may become more favorable yet from what has hitherto taken place we should rather imagine now that the difference between Mr. Gardoqui's written and his verbal answer, may have proceeded from his having been in an error himself at first as to this commissary, and having been confirmed in it also perhaps from his first enquiry from the Minister of foreign affairs. For it appears to us at least as likely that this minister should be ignorant of the existence of that commissary as M. de Gardoqui, who is in correspondence with the Spanish agents in America, and who from the time of his being named to treat with us here would naturally have been informing himself in all these subjects. And he acknowleges in his letter his having told us of his own ignorance of a commissary having been employed with the Indians.

Our letters will have informed you of the conduct we had determined to pursue with respect to the negotiation with which we are jointly charged and of our reasons therefore. It appeared to us at that time unquestionable that you would do us the honor to write to us immediately on your being informed of the circumstances therein alluded to. And from our idea of the time you would have received that information from the persons there mentioned it seemed to us certain we might expect your letter before any considerable lapse of time: We have gone on with some degree of impatience and anxiety under this expectation until now, and although we have not had the honor of recieving from you the orders expected, yet we had been so firmly persuaded that you would have thought it necessary to have written to us after the circumstances abovementioned, although it should have been merely to have expressed that they had occasioned no change in the President's intentions, that we continued to impute our not hearing from you rather to the accidents of the sea than your not having written.

After so long a delay we have begun to be less easy about your opinion as to the propriety of the line we have adopted, although our own sentiments on that subject remain the same with those we have hitherto expressed to you. Being persuaded however that whilst the court resided here it would be impossible for the minister to enter seriously on the business, we have considered it best not to bring it forward before their being settled at St. Ildefonso, as this will still give us a further opportunity of previously hearing from you. They arrived at that place on the 13th. and we are now about to follow them. From the considerations abovementioned and our present view of circumstances we have determined whilst there to proceed to the discussion if we should have recieved no letter from you. We should add however that we have no reason whatever to suppose the result will be different from what we have formerly announced to you.

We have thought it proper to give you this previous notice of our intention and we shall do ourselves the honor of writing to you immediately on any step being taken in consequence thereof.

This letter will be sent by post and will carry you assurances of the profound respect with which we have the honor to be, sir, your most obedient & most humble servants.

[Wm. Carmichael]
W Short

PS. The last letter we have had the honor of recieving [from][1] you was dated Nov. 3. 1792. Your circular of April 26. has been recieved by each of us.

PrC (DLC: Short Papers); in Short's hand, with Carmichael's name as signatory supplied from Tr; at foot of first page: "The secretary of State for the United States—Philadelphia." Tr (DNA: RG 46, Senate Records, 3d Cong., 1st sess.); lacks postscript. Tr (Lb in same, TR); lacks postscript. Recorded in SJL as received 4 Nov. 1793, where TJ, confusing it with Enclosure No. 1 listed below, mistakenly identified it as a letter of 26 May 1793. Enclosures: (1) Carmichael and Short to Don Diego de Gardoqui, Aranjuez, 26 May 1793, stating that they hoped he would soon make it possible for them to inform the President officially of his assurances to them that Olivier was not authorized by the Spanish court to serve as a commissioner to the Creeks, that measures would be taken to discontinue this abuse of the king's name, and that some Spanish agents, particularly Baron de Carondelet, had acted contrary to orders in inciting Indian animosity toward the United States; and that they wished him to join with them in working out arrangements whereby Spain and the United States could dispose the Indians in their territories or on their frontiers to the arts of peace and civilization (PrC in DLC: Short Papers, in Short's hand, unsigned; printed in ASP, Foreign Relations, I, 274-5). (2) Same to same, Madrid, 15 July 1793, stating that, having been frequently assured by him in conversation that a formal response to No. 1 was being delayed only by form, they hoped that they would soon be able to transmit officially to the President his assurances that Spain discountenanced the efforts of its agents in America to excite the Indians against the United States (PrC in DLC: Short Papers, in Short's hand, unsigned; Tr in DNA: RG 46, Senate Records, 3d Cong., 1st sess.; printed in ASP, *Foreign Relations*, I, 275). (3) Gardoqui to Carmichael and Short, 1 Aug. 1793, stating that he did not remember assuring them that Spain had not authorized Olivier or any other person to serve as agent or commissary to the Creeks; that it was the commissaries of the United States and particularly Seagrove who had misrepresented the measures of the Spanish agents and the governor of Florida with the Creeks, who by treaty in 1784 had acknowledged the king of Spain as their only sovereign and protector; that this treaty entitled the governor of West Florida to appoint an agent to reside among the Creeks in order to keep them at peace and to counter Seagrove's efforts to break their alliance with Spain; that last year Spanish agents had prevented the Creeks from going to war with Georgia in order to recover lands the state had usurped from them, as TJ himself must know by virtue of information he received from the Spanish chargé, including an extract of a 24 Sep. 1792 letter from the governor of Louisiana; that, as he had repeatedly stated to President Washington, the demarcation of boundaries was necessary to remove one of the principal causes of complaint between Spain and the United States; and that in the meantime the king had given and would give the strictest orders to his agents to preserve harmony with the United States (RC in DLC: Short Papers, in Spanish; Tr in DNA: RG 46, Senate Records, 3d Cong., 1st sess., in English; printed in ASP, *Foreign Relations*, I, 275-6). (4) Carmichael and Short to Gardoqui, 11 Aug. 1793, stating that prior to their writing No. 1 he had in fact verbally assured them that Olivier had received no authorization from Spain to act

as agent to the Creek Indians; that the 1784 treaty, which they had never seen, could only apply under international law to Indians inhabiting Spanish dominions, as otherwise it would be subversive of social order and government; that the United States had confined its own treaty with the Creeks, which was immediately made public and a copy of which they had given to him, to those living in American territory; that Seagrove had a standing instruction to prevent the Creeks from committing hostilities against Spain's dominions, which the United States government would have enforced against any effort by Seagrove or any other agent to contravene it; that Georgia had purchased by virtue of the Creek treaty with the United States the Indian lands it was alleged to have usurped and the United States was disposed to mark the boundary established by that treaty; that TJ had informed them that the Creeks had actually attacked the United States instead of being restrained from doing so by Spanish agents; and that their government still expected Spain to prevent its agents and particularly Baron de Carondelet from arming the Indians and inciting them to make war on the United States (PrC in DLC: Short Papers, in Short's hand and signed by him; Tr in DNA: RG 46, Senate Records, 3d Cong., 1st. sess.; printed in ASP, *Foreign Relations*, I, 276-7). Letter and enclosures enclosed in TJ to George Washington, 5 Nov. 1793.

THIS COMMISSARY: Pedro Olivier, the Spanish agent to the Creeks appointed early in 1792 by Baron de Carondelet, governor of Louisiana and West Florida (see TJ to Josef Ignacio de Viar and Josef de Jaudenes, 9 July 1792, and note).

[1] Word supplied.

To the Commissioners of the Federal District

GENTLEMEN   Philadelphia Aug. 15. 1793.

By this day's post I have the honour to return the drawings of the Capitol which had been left here in order to have an estimate made; I send also that estimate, together with the rates of the different work, as made by a skilful workman here. The sum total it is supposed will enable you to form some idea of the whole cost of your building, as there is a tolerably well-known proportion between the cost of the walls of a building, and it's whole cost; and the rates will serve as information perhaps in contracts which you may have to make hereafter. I have the honor to be with great respect Gentlemen, Your most obedt & most humble servt   TH: JEFFERSON

PrC (DLC); at foot of text: "The Commissioners of Washington." FC (Lb in DNA: RG 59, DL); misdated 13 Aug. 1793. Tr (DNA: RG 42, DCLB).

ENCLOSURE

Thomas Carstairs's Estimate of the Cost of Masonry for the Capitol

[ca. 15 Aug. 1793]

At the request of the President of the United States, and the Honble. Thomas Jefferson, the subscriber has measured and estimated the cut stone and Ruble work of a Capitol as seen in the plan and one elevation hereto annexed at the Philadelphia rates, viz. [1]

Cut Stone round building[2] including $24\frac{3}{4}$

Columns and 2. pelestars[3]	£⁴37278.13.0
Setting Do. & building rough Stone work	14705. 0.0
Rough Stone Lime & Sand for building	12571.17.6
	64,555.10.6
or $	172,148.$\frac{6}{100}$

THOMAS CARSTAIRS

The above estimate is as follows[5]

Rusticated Stone at 5/. per foot.
Plain Cut Stone at 4/. per foot.
Building in rough Stone work at 6/. per perch.
Stone lime & Sand   at 11/3. per perch.
    N.B. The cost for Carriage for Virginia Stone from thence to Philadelphia at 20d. per foot.   T. C.

PrC of Tr (DLC: TJ Papers, 91: 15720); in a clerk's hand; undated. Tr (Lb in DNA: RG 59, DL). Tr (DLC: TJ Papers, 232: 41559); entirely in TJ's hand; at head of text: "Carstairs' estimate of the Capitol at the Philadelphia prices"; lacks two sentences and contains an additional calculation in pencil; endorsed by TJ: "building."

For the provenance of this estimate and the enclosed PLAN, see TJ to George Washington, 17 July 1793, and note. The ELEVATION may be that reproduced in Pamela Scott, "Stephen Hallet's Designs for the United States Capitol," *Winterthur Portfolio*, XXVII (1992), 150. Washington also transmitted a copy of the estimate to the Commissioners later in the month (Fitzpatrick, *Writings*, XXXIII, 74-5).

[1] Text to this point lacking in Tr in DLC.
[2] Tr in DLC: "round the building."
[3] Tr in DLC: "pilasters."
[4] Tr in DLC: "£ Pensva. curry."
[5] This line and preceding signature omitted in Tr in DLC.

From David Humphreys

Lisbon, 15 Aug. 1793. Expecting no other opportunity to occur for some time, he forwards the gazettes. Although this is the campaign season, he has nothing remarkable to communicate. No packet has arrived since his last letter, he has heard nothing of Captain Cutting, and the Moorish princesses have sailed for Tangier under convoy of a warship. The Portuguese troops mentioned in his 20 July letter are slowly preparing to go to Spain with no fixed time for embarkation. The Spanish have certainly received a considerable check, though Short does not mention it in his 6 Aug. letter just received. The vessel carrying this letter is about to descend to Belem, but if a packet or anything important arrives before the ship ultimately departs he will forward it by boat to the captain.

RC (DNA: RG 59, DD); 2 p.; at head of text: "(No. 78.)"; at foot of text: "The Secretary of State &c. &c. &c."; endorsed by TJ as received 24 Oct. 1793 and so recorded in SJL. Tr (Lb in same).

TJ submitted this letter to the President on 2 Nov. 1793, and Washington returned it the same day, noting that it contained "Nothing of importance" (Washington, *Journal*, 243).

From Thomas Pinckney

DEAR SIR   London 15 Augt. 1793

The frequent interruptions our vessels experience especially in navigating the European seas induce me to address you in cypher.[1] I have had several conversations with Lord Grenville, but do not find that this government will at all relax in the measures they have adopted toward the neutral nations. I have urged every thing in my power in opposition to the policy as well as the right of these measures, and have assured him that they will be considered by our government as infringements of the neutral rights. As I cannot speak from authority on the subject, I have not said what measures we shall adopt in consequence—altho' I have strongly insisted on the detriment to the Commercial interests of this country which must necessarily ensue from the various impediments opposed to a free intercourse, as well as from the ill will they will excite. I may perhaps estimate too highly the blessings of peace in general and the advantages of our Neutral situation, notwithstanding all the deductions to be made on account of the conduct of this Country. But it appears to me that if the United States should deem it necessary to go beyond the line of remonstrance on this occasion, prudence will dictate that our opposition should be confined to commercial regulations;[2] not knowing however what sentiments may prevail on your side of the Atlantic, I thought it my duty to enquire of the Danish and Swedish Envoys what support might be expected in Europe from stronger measures. They both tell me that they do not insist upon the principle of free

Ships making free goods, or the other stipulations of the armed neutrality of the last war, and that they shall be very happy if they can obtain the performance of the express Treaties they have with this country, which has by no means been the case hitherto. Sweden says she will send convoys with her merchantmen, Denmark thinks this is an impolitic measure, for unless they are convoyed by an adequate force, it may, without materially benefitting, only serve to involve them in actual hostilities. The opinions of both in short are, that the neutral powers are not strong enough to cause their rights to be respected. You will see in the public papers a curious *diplomatique morceau* of Lord Hervey the British Minister at the Court of Florence, which will illustrate this subject. I enquired of Lord Grenville the reason of the distinction made in favor of the Danish and Swedish vessels going to blockaded ports. Upon his replying that it was in consequence of their treaties, I told him that although from circumstances of which he was apprized, we had no commercial treaty with them, yet I considered the commercial advantages derived by G. Britain from the U.S. to be superior to what they received from either of those powers, and therefore, tho' not strictly bound by treaty I should conceive it politic in them to give us equal advantages. He said no difference was made but in that article which was more a matter of form than of real utility. If I were to judge from my ideas of the interests of this nation, and from the sentiments I hear expressed by the majority of the people with whom I converse, I should conceive the present campaign would terminate the war—but judging, as I take the safer rule to be, by the characters and views of those who direct their Councils, I think the war will be persisted in until inability to support the expence will force its termination, and happily for mankind that period does not appear to be far distant. The information which was expected from Consul Bond and which was the reason assigned for postponing arrangements concerning the impressment of our seamen is not yet arrived. Perhaps you may be able to expedite that business, if the whole be not calculated merely to avoid meeting a discussion which may terminate either in a fair arrangement or an avowal of principles which, however repugnant to our rights they think necessary for the prosperity of their Marine. I find from official conversations here that the pretence of infractions on our part still prevent the full effect of the treaty of peace—that a variety of objections to the statement of facts as [3] offered by you are brought forward, and that the indecision of the Virginia case is strongly relied upon. Our mint will receive by this opportunity a considerable part of the copper contracted for—by the next Vessels, (which will sail in a short time) I hope to send the remainder. With the utmost respect & sincere regard I remain Dear Sir Your faithful & obedient Servant.   THOMAS PINCKNEY

RC (DNA: RG 59, DD); written partly in code (see note 1 below); at foot of text: "The Secretary of State"; with penciled note by TJ below endorsement: "to be decyphered"; endorsed by TJ as received 1 Nov. 1793 and so recorded in SJL. PrC (same, MD); at head of text in ink: "Duplicate"; endorsed by Edmund Randolph. Tr (same, DD); in the hand of Benjamin Bankson; entirely *en clair*; with penciled copying directions by George Taylor, Jr. Tr (Lb in same); entirely *en clair*, with coded section in brackets containing several anomalies. Tr (DNA: RG 46, Senate Records, 3d Cong., 1st sess.); *en clair* extract described in note 2 below, with complimentary close, signature, and inside address subjoined. Printed in *Message*, 112.

For the measures the British government had adopted TOWARD THE NEUTRAL NATIONS, see Pinckney to TJ, 5 July 1793, and note. The OTHER STIPULATIONS espoused by the League of ARMED NEUTRALITY are discussed in Jonathan R. Dull, *A Diplomatic History of the American Revolution* (New Haven, 1985), 129-30. DIPLOMATIQUE MORCEAU: a reference to the effort by John Augustus, Lord Hervey, the British minister at Florence, in view of the imminent arrival in the Mediterranean of a combined British and Spanish naval force in May 1793, to coerce the Grand Duke of Tuscany into abandoning the neutral stance he had assumed during the current European war, by writing a threatening letter to the Duke's secretary of state in which he asserted that in the final analysis the allied powers would determine whether or not Tuscany remained neutral and then by circulating it to the other foreign ministers in Florence with a covering letter in which he attributed Tuscany's neutral course solely to the secretary's malign influence (*The London Packet; Or, New Lloyd's Evening Post*, 22-24 July 1793). For the DISTINCTION MADE IN FAVOR OF THE DANISH AND SWEDISH VESSELS, see Enclosure No. 1 listed at Pinckney to TJ, 5 July 1793. STATEMENT OF FACTS: see TJ to George Hammond, 29 May 1792. VIRGINIA CASE: see note to George Washington to TJ, 1 June 1793.

TJ submitted a deciphered text of this letter to the President on 9 Nov. 1793, and Washington returned it the same day (Washington, *Journal*, 249, 250).

[1] Except for the last sentence, complimentary close, and signature, the remainder is written in code, the decipherment being supplied from the first Tr and verified in part by the Editors using partially reconstructed Code No. 16.

[2] Extract in RG 46 Tr ends here.

[3] Word omitted in first two Trs.

From David Meade Randolph

DEAR SIR   Philadelphia 15: August 1793

I am disappointed not receiving a letter to-day—if you shall have had one from Monticellow, I shall thank you to mention any Thing relative to my family, which may have been communicated to you. I shall set out to-morrow, by the Stage for Virginia. Shou'd any letters be directed to your care, I shall be thankful to have them returned to the Richmond Post Office where I shall find them, as I shall be detained there necessarily several days in order to equip for the expedition to Monticellow. I am Sir, with every sentiment of personal regard your most Obet. Sert.

D M RANDOLPH

RC (DLC); endorsed by TJ as received 15 Aug. 1793 and so recorded in SJL.

To George Washington

Sir   Philadelphia Aug. 15. 1793.

Mr. Albion Coxe, engaged in England by Mr. Pinckney as Assayer of the mint, has not yet completely qualified himself by giving security as required by law; in the mean time he has been of necessity[1] employed at the mint in his proper capacity, and of course is entitled to paiment for his services. The Director of the mint asks instruction on this subject, and I should be of opinion he might pay him for his services at the rate allowed by law, for the time he has been employed by him, and out of the general fund from which he pays his other workmen. This is submitted to your approbation.

The Director also informs me that much silver is brought to him to be exchanged for coin, but not having the coin ready the silver is carried away again. He is of opinion that if the Treasurer was directed to deliver him 1000. Dollars to be coined into dismes and half-dismes, and to be permitted to lie in the mint till wanted for the Treasury, it would serve him in the mean time as a stock for exchange, and enable him to take in the parcels of silver offered as beforementioned. He would by this means throw small silver into circulation and greatly relieve[2] the demand for copper coinage. I have the honor to be with great respect & attachment, Sir, Your most obedt. & most humble servt   Th: Jefferson

RC (DNA: RG 59, MLR); addressed: "The President of the US."; endorsed by Tobias Lear. PrC (DLC). Tr (Lb in DNA: RG 59, SDC). Recorded in SJPL.

[1] Preceding two words interlined.
[2] Word interlined in place of "ease."

From George Washington, with Jefferson's Note

Sir   Phila. Augt. 15th. 1793.

The Captn. of Marines on Board the Ambuscade has just put the enclosed into my hands. He was sent he says on purpose to do it—and waits only for an answer. Give it I pray you such an one as it ought to receive.[1] Yours

Almost dark   Go: Washington

[Note by TJ:]
This was Genet's letter of Aug. 13. addressed to the Presidt.

RC (DLC); at foot of text: "The Secy of State"; with TJ's note at foot of text; endorsed by TJ as received 15 Aug. 1793. Dft (DNA: RG 59, MLR); lacks time of day.

FC (Lb in same, SDC); wording follows Dft. Recorded in SJPL.

[1] Here in Dft Washington canceled "The Officer lodges at the F. Ministers."

ENCLOSURE

Edmond Charles Genet to George Washington

New York le 13 aoust 1793.
l'an 2. de la république française.

MONSIEUR

Chargé de deffendre dans cette partie du monde les intérets et les droits du peuple français, comme vous l'etes vous même de maintenir ceux du peuple americain, J'ai juré à mon païs et Je me suis promis à moi même qu'aucune convenance privée qu'aucun motif qui serait etranger au bien général ne m'arreterait dans la marche que Je me suis tracée. J'ai mis dans ma conduite cette energie et cette franchise qui doivent former le caractere d'un vrai républicain. C'est à vous seul, par l'entremise de votre ministre des affaires etrangeres, que J'ai porté mes plaintes contre les principes que vous avés adoptés et contre les decisions qui en ont été les suittes: c'est à vous que J'ai dit que loin d'etre sensible a nos généreux procedés,[1] aux nouveaux avantages que nous offrions au commerce des Etats Unis, à toutes les marques que nous leur donnions de notre amitie veritable et desinteressée, le Gouvernement federal sacrifioit nos interets a ceux de nos ennemis par la maniere dont il interpretait nos traités; c'est à vous que J'ai exposé sans detour que cette conduite ne me paraissait pas conforme aux intentions du peuple américain, a son desir d'observer fidelement ses pactes, à son amour pour la cause de la liberté à la quelle sont attachés son existence et son bonheur et plusieurs Jugemens rendus par vos propres tribunaux,[2] plusieurs voeux exprimés par vos concitoyens prouvent que Je pouvais sans crime avoir une semblable pensée. Maintenant certaines personnes dirigées par des vues que le tems nous devoilera ne pouvant attaquer mes principes s'attachent à ma personne et dans l'espoir de me faire perdre l'estime que le public accorde au Delegué des republicains[3] français publient avec une affectation marquée[4] que Je vous ai insulté[5] que Je vous ai menacé d'un appel au peuple comme s'il etait vraisemblable que vous vous laissassiés impunement manquer de respect, comme si l'idée meme d'un appel,[6] qu'un magistrat du peuple vraiment digne des fonctions dont il est revetu doit toujours desirer ardemment[7] etait pour vous le comble de l'offense. Il est essentiel, Monsieur, que ces sombres calomnies soient dissipées par la vérité et la publicité. J'ose donc attendre de votre probité une déclaration qui atteste que Je ne vous ai jamais parlé d'un appel au peuple, qu'il est faux que des opinions politiques differentes des vôtres m'ayent jamais porte a oublier ce que Je dois a votre caractere,[8] à l'imposante renommée que vous aves acquise en combattant pour la liberté,[9] contre un tiran que vous aves vaincu. La publicité de cette declaration, Monsieur, sera la seule réponse que Je ferai a ces hommes de parti qui[10] melent toujours des individus aux questions d'etat,[11] qui ne sont pour eux que des mots de ralliement et que souvent par cette raison ils n'osent traitter que sous le voile méprisable de l'anonime. Quant a moi, Monsieur, J'ai toujours dit tout haut ce que Je pensais et signé ce que J'écrivais et si d'autres personnes ont cru servir mes vues en entrant pour moi dans la lice de vos paragraphistes et de vos polemistes ils se sont bien trompés.

Une bonne cause n'a pas besoin d'avocats. Le temps et la vérité seuls doivent la faire triompher et la notre triomphera en dépit de nos implacables ennemis et de la froideur de quelques uns de nos anciens amis. GENET

P.S. Je charge de cette lettre Monsieur un officer de l'Embuscade qui attendra votre réponse.

PrC of Tr (DLC); in a clerk's hand; above salutation: "Le citoyen Genet Ministre plenipotentiaire de la république française au General Washington President des Etats Unis"; with several clerical errors silently corrected. Dft (DLC: Genet Papers); in a clerk's hand, signed by Genet, with revisions by him, the most important being recorded below. Tr (AMAE: CPEU, xxxviii); with one significant omission (see note 5 below) and several minor variations; certified by Genet. Tr (NNC: Gouverneur Morris Papers). PrC of another Tr (PRO: FO 97/1); in the hand of George Taylor, Jr. Enclosed in TJ to Gouverneur Morris, 16 Aug. 1793.

Genet wrote this letter to the President as part of his effort to rebut the charge made by Chief Justice John Jay and New York Senator Rufus King in a 12 Aug. 1793 letter published the same day in the New York *Diary; or, Loudon's Register*, that the French minister "had said he would Appeal to the People from certain decisions of the President." After receiving TJ's response of 16 Aug. 1793, Genet promptly published both letters in the 21 Aug. 1793 issue of that newspaper, his letter to the President following the draft with only minor variations and being accompanied by a translation. The letters were quickly and widely reprinted. For a discussion of the controversy generated by this Federalist effort to discredit the French minister in the eyes of the American people, which stemmed from remarks Genet made to Alexander J. Dallas

and TJ during the *Little Sarah* affair in July 1793, see Syrett, *Hamilton*, xv, 233-9.

[1] Remainder of clause through "ceux" inserted in Dft by Genet in place of "nos interets etaient sacrifiés à ceux."
[2] In Dft Genet here interlined "par vos Jurés."
[3] In Dft Genet here interlined and canceled "des democrates."
[4] Sentence to this point in Dft altered by Genet from "Maintenant on publie de toute part."
[5] Preceding five words not in AMAE Tr.
[6] In Dft the clerk first wrote "comme si vous ne savies pas vous faire respecter, comme si vous pouvies craindre un appel," which Genet then altered to read as above.
[7] Remainder of sentence added in Dft by Genet.
[8] Preceding three words followed by "et" interlined in Dft by Genet.
[9] Remainder of sentence interlined by Genet in Dft, the last word there being "terrassé," in place of "a votre Caractere et au mien."
[10] Word interlined in Dft by Genet in place of "dont ⟨le genre etroit⟩ les conceptions etroites ne pouvant s'elever à la hauteur des principes."
[11] Remainder of text, including postscript, inserted in Dft by Genet in place of "qu'ils n'osent Traitter qu'en se couvrant du voile meprisable de l'anonime. Agrées, Monsieur, mon profond respect." Genet left the complimentary close uncanceled.

From Willink, Van Staphorst
& Hubbard

SIR   Amsterdam 15 August 1793

Confirming what We had the honor to write you the 1 Ulto. with the
Account Current of the Department of State up to 30 June, We have
now the pleasure to advise you, the Acceptance of

£3000.   Draft of Willing Morris & Swanwick on John & Francis Bar-
         ing & Cy. of London,

  400.   Ditto of Walter Stewart on Joseph Birch of Liverpool.

£3400.   Which had been noted on their first presentation for Non-
Acceptance. We are respectfully Sir Your most obedient and very humble Servants   WILHEM & JAN WILLINK
                        N & J. VAN STAPHORST & HUBBARD

Dupl (DLC); in the hand of Van Staphorst & Hubbard, signed by the two firms; at foot
of text: "Thos. Jefferson Esqr."; endorsed by TJ as "Duplicate." According to SJL, TJ
received the missing RC on 4 Nov. 1793.

From Enoch Edwards

DEAR SIR   London Augt: 16. 1793

Since I have been in London I have written you two Letters—One by
the Wm: Penn the other by the Way of New York. I hope this third will
entitle Me to an Answer. I have mentioned to you the Rage that exists
here for Emigration to our Country. I have by some Means or other,
without any Steps taken on my own Part to procure it, become more
known than I had any Right to expect in this Country—so much so that
I am written to from [1] many Parts of the Kingdom respecting the Situation of our Country. I have sen't over several original Letters (I received
many of them from Men I had no Knowledge of and situated above two
hundred Miles apart) to my Friend Charles Biddle to be kept for Me,
and have desired him to let You peruse them. I wish you very much to
take the Trouble of casting your Eyes over them, they will give you
some Idea of what Spirit prevails here.

Mr. Richards the writer of several of them is an eminent Dissenting
Clergyman and one of the most accurate Historians I am told in this
Country.

Doctor Priestly has had several Interviews with Me—two of his Sons
embarks in the Pigou and he follows them as soon as possible to America (to use his own Words) as an Asylum. He is a very amiable Man of

a mild and humble Deportment and has suffered as you know for no other Crime than because he is the Friend of his fellow Creatures.

I received a Letter from Sr: John St: Clair and inclose you at his Request a Copy. I shall answer what I can of it—but if you can assist Me, I shall thank you. As to the Gypsum I can only relate my own Experience of it, and my observations—any Answers you can make to this, by what you can collect will be verry acceptable.

The Buffaloe Clover I have only heor'd of it growing at Kentucky— and seen the Leaves. Perhaps you know something in particular of this.

I have nothing more extraordinary to inform you of now. Indeed I write more to give a Testimony of my Esteem for you, than for any other Purpose. I am very respectfully your obedt: Sert

ENO: EDWARDS

P.S. A Letter directed either to Mr. Pinckney, or to Mr: Frederick Pigou, Merchant London will come safe to Me.

I cannot conceive what this Country means by their Hostillities commited against Us at Sea—unless it is to go to War and check the Current of Emigration, as they did that of Liberty when they waged it with France.

RC (DLC); with dateline above postscript; addressed: "Mr: Jefferson"; endorsed by TJ as received 18 Nov. 1793 and so recorded in SJL.

[1] Edwards here canceled "all."

ENCLOSURE

Sir John Sinclair to Enoch Edwards

SIR   Whitehall 13th. Augst. 1793

The conversation I had the pleasure of holding with you a few days ago, having given rise to a variety of reflections which may be of service to Great Britain and America, I think it right to take this mode of submitting them to your consideration.

In the first place, I think it might be of considerable utility were you to draw up for our Board, in the order of printed queries, a general view of the Agriculture of Pensylvania, with which you seem to be particularly well acquainted, and would annex to it an account of any practices in your Husbandry, which are likely to be of service to this Country. So far as I could judge from our conversation together the other day, *under the latter head* the following points deserve more particular attention.

1 Upland Water Meadows

The watering of Land is but very partially attended to in Great Britain, principally in the counties of Wilts Dorset and Devon, and there only flat lands are thus treated. The introducing the same practice into hilly districts, is an object of great importance to many parts of these Kingdoms, and when we have the pleasure of meeting in Scotland, I hope that we shall have a trial made of it that will sufficiently prove it's peculiar importance to that part of the Island.

2d. An Account of your Drill Husbandry and Drills

There are many soils in which Drill Husbandry can be adopted to advantage, though I scarcely think that it can ever become an universal practice. It is of great importance, however, that the machines for Drilling should be as simple, and as perfect as possible, and as you seem to think, that the American Drills are rather on a better Construction than ours, on that head information would be desireable.

3d. Gypsum.

Any additional evidence respecting the advantage of Gypsum, would also be of consequence, as the efficacy of that manure, is still disbelieved in this Country. Perhaps, you will be able to point out the proper Soil for trying it, the proper Season of the year for putting it on, and the sort that is most likely to answer.

4 Timothy Grass

The acount you give of this grass, of the Quantity of hay it produces, of its growing so well in low cold grounds, and of it's remaining so long productive, are circumstances which seem to render this plant entitled to the farther attention of the Farmers of this Country, at least in particular districts, and you will be able to point out in what soils and places, it is the most likely to be successfull.

5 Buffaloe Clover

I think the new plant you mention found at Kentucky, called Buffaloe Clover, is well entitled to a trial in this country, and may be safely recommended for that purpose, particularly if it would produce a great quantity of hay (which is probable from the largeness of its leaf) and wou'd grow in wet and boggy places. Perhaps also it may stand frost better than the common clovers.

6 Spring Houses

The description you give of what are called in America *Spring houses*, for Dairies, I consider to be not only a matter of luxury, but of real use, which may be [of][1] service in many of our Districts, where Dairies are kept on a great Scale. Full descriptions of them, with drawings, therefore, I should be glad to have, also an account of your mode of making Butter in America, in which the English and Irish differ so much, the first using cream alone, the second churning *all the milk*. To the superiority of the latter practice, the greater excellence of the Irish Butter is attributed. Your churns also seem to be on a better construction than ours.

7 Making hay

Your process of making hay in America, particularly of Clover, seems to be worthy the attention of British Agriculturists. I shou'd beg therefore to trouble you for an accurate description of it. The superior greenness of your hay, sufficiently proves the advantages of the plan you have adopted.

8 Salting Coarse Hay

You mentioned to me, a practice in America, of Salting coarse hay, which made it be devoured by the Cattle with greater Avidity, which I think might be recommended to our ffarmers here.

There are probably other points which will naturally occur to you in the course of your Tour through this Country.

I am also of opinion that such a paper should contain any hints, which may occur to you, respecting the best mode of making the Agriculture of America and that of Great Britain usefull to one another. I certainly do not think that American corn ought to be admitted, except in times of great scarcity. It is dangerous depending upon a foreign and distant country for bread. It is absurd to suffer American Wheat to be imported into Liverpool, and British wheat at the same time exported, *with a high bounty* from Norfolk, and from the account of Middlesex here with sent, you will see, that so small an addition to our Land in Tillage, as 15,000 acres would Supply us with all the Wheat we want. But there are other articles, the produce of the Soil, by supplying which, the Agriculture of America, might be of essential service to that of Great Britain.

1st: Clover Seed

From your accounts, it would appear that the Clover of America, is infinitely more productive than that of England, I should think therefore, that the importation of American clover seed, ought to be tried, for though in time it would degenerate, yet the first crops would probably be equal to yours, and Good Husbandmen never think, at present, of taking more than one crop of that grass. It would be worth while, therefore, to ascertain the price of your clover seed, how it stands the frost and whether it can bear a little wet, or even drowning. There is a small tax at present upon the importation of foreign Clover seed, which upon a proper representation, from The Board of Agriculture, would probably be taken of. The consumption of this article is every day encreasing, and if it could be had cheap would be very great. In Scotland They mix Rye grass with their Clover, the seed of which, it would also be desireable to have from the same quarter.

2 Rape and Flax Seeds

I should imagine that any quantity of rape and flax seeds, might be raised in America, and that the consumption of these articles, in this Country, might *be immense.* It is found, that there is no method of ffattening Cattle and Sheep, so quickly as by these seeds. Some give the Seeds merely bruised, without expressing the oil, others express the oil and only give the cake to their Cattle. A Practice is now beginning to be introduced for making use of oil cake, as a top dressing, or manure, so that in ffact, there is hardly any limit to the consumption of these Articles, in this country, could they be had on reasonable terms.

3. Sun Flower Seed

This is an article of less importance, but at the same time if its oil is equal to that of Olives the consumption might be of some moment.

I have already written a longer letter than I intended, but at the same time being a warm Friend to a good understanding between America and Great Britain, I am thence led to make a few additional observations respecting the articles, which I think, might be the basis of a very important commercial intercourse between the two Countries, and beneficial to both, independent of the Articles now imported as Tobacco, Rice &c.

1 Hemp

I have often wondered that Hemp was not more attended to in America, instead of which, I believe that since the Declaration of Independancy, and even since the conclusion of the late war, many American Vessels have been loaded at Petersburgh with that article.

I have now the pleasure of hearing from you, that in some Districts of America, they have already begun to raise hemp in considerable quantities, and are getting mills to prepare it for Market, I think it is impossible for you to raise this article under greater disadvantages than Russia—The Districts where it grows in that Country, being from 12, to 1500 miles from the Sea. I am perswaded, that in many parts of America, your Soil and Climate, is as well calculated for hemp, as that of the Ukraine, and you will not probably think it a difficult matter, to supply great Britain with that Article, when I can assure you, that to raise hemp for the consumption of this Country, does not require, above 70,000 acres, of which our Navy requires 12,000 acres in time of peace and 20,000 in time of war. I have not yet learned whether your hemp, is as good as the Russian. What grows in England is greatly superior. If the East India hemp thrives with,[2] as I am told it is likely to do, it may be productive of very important consequences.

2 Flax

I believe that this is an article already imported, but if a proper commercial treaty were entered into between the two Countries, I have no doubt that it might be greatly encreased. I understand, however, that the Flax produced in some Provinces of America, is of a very inferior quality, and better callculated for Sail cloths, than for fine linnen. The superior richness of your Soil may occasion the coarseness of the fibre.

3 Iron

We are certainly getting fforwards in Manufacturing Malleable iron, by pit coal, but its quality, I apprehend, is not equal to that made with Charcoal; and as considerable quantities of this article, must still be imported, I see no reason, why it should not, on fair and equal terms, be got from America, as well as from other Countries.

4 Timber

It is incredible the quantities of timber annually imported into Great Brittain, and as it is an article of sure sale, and of immense consumption, I think it a pity that America should not have a Share in that branch of our Commerce. By the means of your Navigable rivers, you certainly may have immense logs, from the interior parts of your Country, which is the best mode of transporting timber here, both the freight and duty being proportionably cheaper.

5 Bark &c

I think it probable that Bark is an article, which we shall be glad to have from America. Also hides, if you cou'd spare them, and Tallow. It would be difficult at the same time to enter into a competition with the Russians in regard to tallow, as they have Sheep in such abundance, that they kill the Animal for the sake of it's fat merely.

6 Fruits

It occurs to me that the fruits of America, notwithstanding the greatness of the distance, might be imported here to advantage, particularly into the Northern parts of the Kingdom where nature is not favourable to productions of that sort. In the Southern States, Oranges might certainly be had in great quantities, the consumption of which is immense. The mere duty on Oranges and Lemons amounts to from 12,000 to 15,000 per Annum.

7 Wax and Honey

These are articles, which undoubtedly might be raised to any extent in America, and which in this country must always be in demand.

On the whole, I have no doubt, if these points were properly canvassed, that the two Countries would speedily come to an understanding together, that a Treaty of Commerce beneficial to both, might speedily be formed, and that every remnant of prejudice and zealousy would soon be completely done away. Were we cordially to co-operate together, for our mutual benefit, there is, I think every reason to believe, that those who speak the language of England,

Sir

might soon attain as much power abroad and happiness at home, as any wise nation can aspire to. I have the honour to be, Sir Your obedient, and ffaithfull humble Servant

Tr (DLC).

Earlier this year Sinclair had been the leading spirit in the founding of the BOARD of Agriculture and Internal Improvement, and became the first president after it was chartered on 26 Aug. (DNB; Rosalind Mitchison, *Agricultural Sir John: The Life of Sir John Sinclair of Ulbster, 1754-1835* [London, 1962], 137-49). As its first project, the board initiated agricultural surveys of each British county and in this connection it published thirty-five PRINTED QUERIES, as well as Sinclair's estimate that tilling an additional 15,000 acres of land would end British grain exports, in the enclosed AC-COUNT OF MIDDLESEX: Thomas Baird, *General View of the Agriculture of the County of Middlesex* (London, 1793), 1-2, 45; see Sowerby, No. 762.

[1] Word supplied.
[2] Thus in manuscript.

To Edmond Charles Genet

Sir   Philadelphia Aug. 16. 1793.

The President of the US. has received the letter which you addressed to him from New York on the 13th. instant, and I am desired to observe to you that it is not the established course for the diplomatic characters residing here to have any direct correspondence with him. The Secretary of state is the organ thro' which their communications should pass.

The President does not concieve it to be within the line of propriety or duty for him to bear evidence against a declaration which, whether made to him or others, is perhaps immaterial. He therefore declines interfering in the case. I have the honor to be with great respect, Sir, Your most obedt. & most humble servt   TH: JEFFERSON

RC (DLC: Genet Papers); at foot of text: "The Minister Plenipotentiary of the republic of France." PrC (DLC). PrC of Tr (DLC); in the hand of George Taylor, Jr. PrC of another Tr (NNC: Gouverneur Morris Papers); in a clerk's hand. PrC of another Tr (PRO: FO 97/1); in Taylor's hand. FC (Lb in DNA: RG 59, DL). Tr (DLC: Genet Papers); in French. Tr (AMAE: CPEU, XXXVIII); in French. Enclosed in TJ to Gouverneur Morris, 16 Aug. 1793.

For the LETTER in question, and its publication with this response from TJ, see enclosure to George Washington to TJ, 15 Aug. 1793, and note.

The Recall of
Edmond Charles Genet

EDITORIAL NOTE

The decision to demand Edmond Charles Genet's recall less than three months after his arrival in Philadelphia as the French Republic's first minister to the United States resulted from the irrepressible conflict between the Washington administration's insistence on maintaining strict American neutrality during the War of the First Coalition and Genet's mandate from his Girondin superiors to enlist American support for the French cause by all means short of formal belligerency—a clash exacerbated by the French minister's impetuosity and the crosscurrents of American party politics.

The Girondin leaders who defined the objectives of Genet's mission—the orator and publicist Brissot de Warville, the foreign minister Lebrun, and the finance minister Clavière—conceived of it as an integral part of the French Republic's growing challenge to the old regime in Europe. Genet's appointment under Brissot's influence in November 1792 to succeed Louis XVI's last minister to the United States, Jean Baptiste Ternant, was one sign of the beginning of a more radical phase in France's war with Austria and Prussia. Over the next few months, with Girondins in the forefront, the National Convention embarked on a crusade to spread revolutionary republicanism through Europe that brought Great Britain, the Netherlands, Spain, and a number of lesser European powers into the Austro-Prussian coalition against France starting early in 1793 (Claude Perroud, ed., *J.-P. Brissot: Correspondance et Papiers* [Paris, 1911], 380; Woodfin, "Citizen Genet," 60-72; T. C. W. Blanning, *The Origins of the French Revolutionary Wars* [London and New York, 1986], 99-112, 135-49).

Genet was dispatched to the United States in anticipation of the war with Great Britain and Spain to which the Girondins realized their policies were leading. In the event of hostilities with these two powers, which would give the current European conflict a new maritime dimension, the Girondins were confident that France could count on the support of her sister republic across the Atlantic. Since the United States lacked a navy and its small army was hard-pressed to deal with hostile Indians in the Northwest Territory, the Girondins realized that the United States could best serve the French cause as a neutral supplier of provisions to France and her West Indian colonies. But, while counting on the United States to fulfill this function, the Girondins also hoped that it would help to offset the expected British and Spanish war effort in Europe by supporting French plans to subvert British and Spanish imperial power in America (Turner, *CFM*, 201; "Rapport sur la Mission du Citoyen Genet," [Jan. 1793], AMAE: CPEU, xxxvii; "Observations sur les reproches fait au

[685]

Citoyen Genet," same, endorsed in a different hand as written "mai 1793," but actually composed shortly after the French government received the American demand for Genet's recall on 8 Oct. 1793).

Girondin hopes that the United States would join with France in helping to expand what they called the "Empire de la Liberté" were clearly enunciated in the instructions from the Ministry of Foreign Affairs and the Ministry of Public Contributions that Genet carried with him when he sailed for America in mid-February 1793. Drafted under the influence of Brissot, Lebrun, Clavière, and perhaps Genet himself, and approved by the Provisional Executive Council on 4 and 17 January 1793—two weeks before the National Convention declared war on Great Britain and the Netherlands and approximately seven weeks before it declared war on Spain—the instructions directed Genet to achieve a high degree of American cooperation with the French war effort. They envisioned the prompt payment in advance of about two-thirds of the estimated $4,400,000 still outstanding on America's Revolutionary War debt to France, as calculated by the French government, and the purchase with this money of arms and food supplies in the United States for the French Republic and its colonies in the West Indies. They offered the United States a comprehensive new commercial treaty under which the citizens of both nations would enjoy the benefits of mutual naturalization in trade. They anticipated the use of the United States as a base for French privateering by insisting on strict compliance with articles in the 1778 commercial treaty obliging the United States to prevent the enemies of France from fitting out privateers or selling prizes in American ports, while assuming a more dubious right under that treaty to fit out French privateers in these ports. Finally, the instructions authorized Genet—with or without official American approval—to use United States territory as a base of operations for French efforts to liberate Canada from Great Britain and Louisiana from Spain, for which he was empowered to enlist American citizens and Indians alike in French service. To secure American support for these ambitious designs, the instructions held out to the United States the prospect of enjoying along its western borders the presence of a Louisiana freed from Spanish rule, obtaining the right to navigate the Mississippi currently denied it by Spain, and possibly acquiring Canada. Although Genet was not instructed to ask the United States to honor its obligation under the 1778 treaty of alliance to help defend the French West Indies against enemy attack, he was otherwise expected to obtain a level of American support for the French war effort that almost certainly would have embroiled the nation in hostilities with the British and Spanish empires (Enclosures Nos. 1 and 3 listed at Genet's third letter to TJ, 22 May 1793; Genet to TJ, 23 May 1793, and note; Turner, *CFM*, 202-11; Aulard, *Recueil*, I, 393-4, 397-9, 478; Woodfin, "Citizen Genet," 73-9; F. A. Aulard, "La Dette Américaine envers la France," *Revue de Paris*, XXX [1925], 537).

Genet's instructions were based upon a serious misunderstanding of the federal Constitution that was destined further to bedevil his mission. By designating Genet as minister to the "Congrès des Etats Unis de l'Amérique Septentrionale" and directing him to negotiate the proposed commercial treaty with the "Ministres du Congrès," the instructions signified that the Girondins failed to appreciate the dramatic structural changes in the American government brought about by the transition from the Articles of Confederation to the Constitution of 1787. As Genet demonstrated again and again during his ministry in America, he and his Girondin superiors both assumed that under the Constitution, as under the Articles, the President was merely the agent of Congress and that therefore even in foreign policy his decisions were provisional until ratified by the national legislature (Turner, *CFM*, 202, 203-4; Memorandum of a Conversation with Edmond Charles Genet, 10 July 1793; Genet to TJ, 18 Sep. 1793).

Genet's zealous adherence to his instructions quickly brought him into open conflict with the Washington administration's decision to follow a policy of strict neutrality toward the warring European nations. Soon after Genet arrived in Philadelphia on 16 May 1793, he learned through one of Jefferson's last letters to Ternant that the federal government condemned as violations of American neutrality the fitting out of French privateers in American ports, the enlistment of American citizens in French service, and the exercise of admiralty jurisdiction by French consuls—activities the new French minister had begun, before the issuance of the Proclamation of Neutrality, during his stay in Charleston, where he had first arrived on 8 April 1793. Although this news was offset to some extent by the federal government's adherence to its treaty obligations to allow other French privateers and warships to bring their prizes into American ports, while forbidding the enemies of France to arm privateers or bring prizes within the jurisdiction of the United States, Genet was dealt a quick succession of other staggering blows during his first month in Philadelphia. The Washington administration decided on 20 May to order all French privateers fitted out in the United States to depart from American ports, thus threatening further to weaken France's maritime efforts against its enemies. Contrary to Jefferson's wishes, the President and the Cabinet studiously avoided taking any action on the overtures for a new commercial treaty with France that Genet made three days later, thus frustrating Girondin hopes for drawing the two republics closer together in a common struggle against the forces of monarchy. And on 11 June Jefferson informed Genet of the government's rejection of the minister's request for a substantial advance payment on the American debt to France, thereby depriving him of the one monetary resource on which the Girondins had counted both to finance his mission and to purchase arms and food supplies in the United States for the beleaguered French Republic and its West Indian colonies (Memorials from George Hammond, 8 May 1793; TJ to Ternant, 15 May 1793; Notes on the *Citoyen Genet* and its Prizes, 20 May 1793; Genet to TJ, 22, 23 May 1793; TJ to Madison, 27 May 1793; TJ to Genet, 5, 11 June 1793; TJ to Washington, 6 June 1793, Document v of a group of documents on Jefferson and the American debt to France, at 3 June 1793; Notes of Cabinet Meeting on a Commercial Treaty with France, 23 Aug. 1793; *Archives Parlementaires*, 1st ser., LIX, 18-19).

As Girondin dreams of a close partnership between the two republics foundered on the imperatives of American neutrality, Genet, imbued with a zeal for revolutionary republicanism, began as early as May 1793 to challenge the administration's neutrality policy and seek to mobilize popular support for greater American assistance to the French war effort. Accordingly he defiantly insisted to Jefferson that France was entitled by treaty, by natural right, or by international law to fit out privateers in the United States, to enlist Americans in French service, and to exercise consular admiralty jurisdiction in American ports, while refusing to accede to American demands that he halt these practices. He denied the President's authority to decide neutrality issues without congressional approval and claimed an ultimate right to appeal from the executive and the legislature to the American people. He insinuated that Washington had succumbed to British influence in formulating American neutrality—a perception shaped in part by Jefferson's private revelations to him of pro-British sentiment in the Cabinet—and charged that the United States ignored British seizures of French goods on American ships. He openly aligned himself with the Republican opposition in Philadelphia, attending various Republican civic feasts, patronizing the Democratic Society of Pennsylvania, assuming the presidency of the Société Française des Amis de la Liberté et de l'Egalité in the national capital, and agitating for an early session of Congress to reconsider neutrality policy. More circumspectly, he proceeded with ultimately abortive plans—which he communicated unofficially to Jefferson—to use the United States as a base for French efforts to subvert British and Spanish rule in Canada and Louisiana. Genet's defiance of the Washington administration came to a head during the first half of July 1793 when, in undisguised contempt of the federal government's ban on this practice, he had the British prize *Little Sarah* fitted out as a French privateer in Philadelphia, ignored a request by Jefferson to keep the ship in port until Washington returned from Mount Vernon and examined the case, and threatened to appeal from the President to the American people for vindication of his actions (Genet to TJ, 27 May, 8, 14, 22 June, 9, 25 July, 18 Sep. 1793; Notes of Cabinet Meeting and Conversations with Edmond Charles Genet, 5 July 1793; TJ to Madison, 7 July 1793; Cabinet Opinions on the *Little Sarah*, 8 July 1793, and note; Turner, *CFM*, 216-17, 221, 245; "Rapport du Citoyen Genet . . . sur son Voyage et sa Réception populaire dans les Etats Unis de l'Amérique," [14 July 1793], AMAE: CPEU, XXXVIII; Woodfin, "Citizen Genet," 231-9, 304-11).

Genet's flagrant show of disrespect for federal authority during the *Little Sarah* affair led the Washington administration to consider asking the French government to recall its minister. The President and the Cabinet resolved the issue during a series of meetings in July and August 1793 for which Jefferson's confidential memorandums in what later became the "Anas" provide the most detailed record. At a Cabinet meeting on 12 July 1793, when the *Little Sarah* still had not put out to sea, Alexander Hamilton, who wished to take advantage of Genet's defiance of American neutrality to distance the United States from France and weaken the rising Republican party, urged that the government ask France to recall Genet. Henry Knox, who shared Hamilton's objectives, advocated that it also forbid him to act as minister while this request was pending. Jefferson, who wished to preserve friendly relations with France and avoid any political damage to Genet's Republican supporters, countered by suggesting that the government communicate his correspondence with the French minister to the French government with friendly observations, possibly in the hope that Genet would then be instructed to respect American neutrality. But shortly after the Cabinet adjourned without reaching a decision on any of these proposals, Genet irreversibly tipped the balance of opinion in favor of his recall by sending the *Little Sarah* out to sea before Washington could determine its status within the framework of American neutrality (Notes on Neutrality Questions, 13 July 1793).

This latest act of defiance shifted the Cabinet's focus of attention from the wisdom of requesting Genet's recall to the manner of bringing it about. On 23 July Washington informed the Cabinet that he favored the recall of Genet as well as the preservation of friendly relations with France. The President, who still viewed the French alliance as a cornerstone of American diplomacy, then proposed that the government send to Gouverneur Morris, for submission to the proper authorities in Paris, Genet's entire correspondence with Jefferson and a strong representation setting forth Genet's transgressions against American neutrality and, with expressions of friendship for the French nation, insisting on the appointment of a new minister. He also suggested that in the meantime the American government demand that Genet either leave the United States or suspend his diplomatic mission. While approving all of Washington's proposals, Hamilton strongly urged that the government also "lay the whole proceedings" with "proper explanations" before the American people in order to prevent Genet and his American supporters from capitalizing upon popular sympathy for the French cause and undermining the nation's confidence in the Washington administration. Although Knox seconded Hamilton's criticisms of Genet's American partisans while Jefferson remained uncharacteristically silent, the Cabinet adjourned without reaching a decision on the issue of recall, evidently because Edmund Randolph had left the meeting to attend to other business, probably the trial of Gideon Henfield (see note to Memorial from Genet, 27 May 1793). Two days later the President directed Jefferson to prepare his correspondence and a record of his official conversations with Genet, together with relevant portions of his correspondence with British minister George Hammond, for review by the Cabinet. After Jefferson's correspondence with Genet was read on 1 August with Randolph present, the Cabinet unanimously agreed to transmit it to the Provisional Executive Council along with a letter to Morris describing the French minister's conduct and demanding his recall. Jefferson suggested that he phrase this demand delicately, but the other members of the Cabinet insisted that he do so peremptorily. The Cabinet then rejected a proposal by Knox to expel Genet from the United States, a course that had once been supported by Washington and Hamilton. Instead the President and the rest of the Cabinet decided to notify Genet of the application for his recall, despite Jefferson's warning that this would make the French minister "extremely active in his plans and engender confusion" (Notes of Cabinet Meeting on Edmond Charles Genet, 23 July, 1 Aug. 1793; Washington to TJ, 25 July 1793, and note; Cabinet Opinions on Edmond Charles Genet, 23 Aug. 1793).

The general agreement in the Cabinet over the manner of demanding Genet's recall quickly gave way to a conflict over a renewed effort by Hamilton to discredit the French Republic and its Republican supporters in America. With Jefferson and Randolph on one side and Knox and Washington on the other, the Cabinet spent much of its time on 1 and 2 August debating a proposal by Hamilton for a public statement to the American people emphasizing that Genet's challenge to American neutrality and his alignment with the Republican opposition were parts of a systematic French revolutionary strategy of stirring up popular discontent in order to subvert governments opposed to France. Aware that the proposed statement might jeopardize popular support for the French Revolution and the Republican party, Jefferson, with the backing of Randolph, who valued the French alliance as the sheet anchor of American diplomacy and was keenly sensitive to the political implications of the overwhelming popular support the French Revolution enjoyed in America, argued that the proposed appeal would deeply divide the American people and precipitate a diplomatic crisis with France. Although Knox and Washington supported Hamilton, in the end the President decided to wait until events showed whether such a statement was imperative. Soon thereafter, spurred on by Hamilton-inspired revelations about Genet's threat to appeal from the President to the people, Washington began to receive numerous popular addresses criticizing the French minister's defiance of him and expressing wholehearted support for his administration's neutrality policy. Reassured that Genet's efforts to mobilize popular opinion against him had failed, Washington decided that Hamilton's proposed public statement was unnecessary (Notes of Cabinet Meeting on Edmond Charles Genet, 1, 2 Aug. 1793; TJ to Madison, 3, 11, 18 Aug. 1793; Hamilton to Rufus King, [23-24 Aug. 1793], Syrett, *Hamilton*, xv, 267; Opinion of Randolph, 6 May 1793, DLC: Washington Papers; Ammon, *Genet Mission*, 102-3, 113-19, 132-46).

Having helped to thwart Hamilton's proposed statement, Jefferson turned to the task of drafting the letter to Morris demanding Genet's recall. Hamilton and Randolph both advised Jefferson to emphasize Genet's challenge to American neutrality and disrespect for constituted authority, but Hamilton went further and urged Jefferson also to stress Genet's interference in domestic politics (Document I below). Responding to his own imperatives, and mindful of the President's preference for a statement distinguishing between the French nation and its agent, Jefferson produced a masterful letter written in the spirit of the advice offered by Randolph, who, taking note of the many American supporters of the French Revolution, insisted that the justification for demanding Genet's recall must be based solely on his official communications to the executive in order to "satisfy the American mind; which constitutes the soul of our government" (Randolph to TJ, 4 Aug. 1793).

Working on the project between 6 and 15 August, Jefferson drafted the letter with an eye to two audiences—the French government, to which it would be submitted in the first instance, and the American public, to whom he assumed it would eventually be disclosed, as indeed it was after Washington transmitted it to Congress early in December 1793 as part of a larger body of evidence justifying the French minister's recall that was published later the same month, together with a selection of Jefferson's correspondence with Hammond and Thomas Pinckney concerning British violations of the Treaty of Paris and American neutral rights (TJ's first letter to Madison, 11 Aug. 1793; TJ to Washington, [ca. 18-19 Aug. 1793]; *Message*). While justifying the demand for Genet's recall on the grounds of his repeated opposition to American neutrality and disrespect for the office and person of the President, Jefferson crafted the letter so as to absolve France of any responsibility for this behavior and to avoid a diplomatic crisis with that nation, attributing Genet's improprieties instead to his own willfullness and making no mention of his domestic political entanglements apart from the French minister's insistence that the President was bound to consult with Congress in formulating American neutrality (Document IV below).

Jefferson's draft was reviewed unofficially by Washington and officially by the President and the Cabinet. On 6 August Washington met with Jefferson and approved his defense of the Proclamation of Neutrality in a first and now missing draft of the letter. On 15 and 20 August the President and the Cabinet carefully reviewed the existing draft, and perhaps in preparation for the first of these meetings Jefferson wrote a brief analysis of the letter to facilitate its presentation to his colleagues (Document III below). Possibly in response to the Cabinet's initial review, Jefferson considered but decided against inserting criticism of Genet's assumed right to appeal from the President to the American people, though he did incorporate language clarifying some parts of his rebuttal of Genet's assertions of a right to fit out French privateers in American ports, enlist American citizens in French service, and subject French prizes to the exclusive admiralty jurisdiction of French consuls (TJ's first letter to Madison, 11 Aug. 1793; Documents II and IV below, especially notes 13-15, 22, and 27-30 to the latter). But with American public opinion now beginning to swing against Genet, the main source of contention turned upon a few phrases in the draft that might be construed as slighting the nations at war with France, especially one in which Jefferson had written that any serious conflict between the French and American republics would produce the spectacle of "liberty warring on herself." Hamilton and Knox called for the deletion of these phrases lest they offend the allies, and the same concern drove Randolph to urge the elimination as well of any expressions of friendship for France—an extreme proposal that won no other support and illustrated those frequent oscillations in the Cabinet that Jefferson found so maddening in Randolph. Although Washington supported Jefferson's resistance to these proposed changes, in the end the President agreed to abide by the majority decision of the Cabinet, which determined on 20 August to leave out the offending phrases (Document IV below and notes 12, 36-40, 42-5 thereto; TJ to Madison, 18 Aug. 1793; Notes of Cabinet Meeting on Edmond Charles Genet, 20 Aug. 1793).

Though Jefferson complained bitterly about these deletions, the core of the final text was substantially the same as his draft—a stern demand for Genet's recall accompanied by warm expressions of American friendship for France and an almost complete absence of any mention of Genet's embroilment in domestic politics. "It was," as Dumas Malone observed, "one of the ablest and most skillful of all his diplomatic papers." Meeting on 23 August, the President and the Cabinet decided to backdate the letter to 16 August, so as to correspond with the date of the last enclosure, and approved another letter from Jefferson to Morris expressing American willingness to negotiate a new commercial treaty with a more suitable French minister. Several days later Jefferson dispatched these letters and supporting documents to France by an express vessel. With the Cabinet's approval, Jefferson waited almost two weeks before notifying Genet of this action, so as to make it impossible for the French minister to have this critical missive intercepted before it reached France (Notes of Cabinet Meeting on a Commercial Treaty with France, 23 Aug. 1793; TJ to Washington, 22 Aug. 1793; Cabinet Opinions on Edmond Charles Genet, 23 Aug. 1793; TJ to Gouverneur Morris, [23] Aug. 1793; TJ to Delamotte, 26 Aug. 1793; TJ to Genet, [7 Sep. 1793], and note; Malone, *Jefferson*, III, 126, 128).

Jefferson's letter of recall and its supporting documentation had a dramatic impact on the Jacobin leaders in Paris who had ousted the Girondins from power in June 1793. Since then the Jacobins had been increasingly critical of Genet's failure to obtain much-needed American provisions for France and distressed by his open conflict with the Washington administration, even to the point of considering a proposal in September 1793 to send a two-man commission to the United States to assist him in resolving both problems. At the same time, they also became more and more convinced that the Girondin party that had dispatched Genet to America had been engaged in a long-standing conspiracy to destroy French republican liberty and unity, a belief that led to the presentation to the National Convention a few days before Jefferson's letter arrived in Paris of an omnibus indictment charging forty-one Girondin leaders with various counts of treason to the revolutionary cause and the subsequent public trial and execution of a number of them. With its graphic portrayal of Genet's strong resistance to American neutrality and its hints about the secret springs of

Genet's actions, Jefferson's letter to Morris convinced the preternaturally suspicious Jacobins that Genet was a key part of the alleged Girondin counterrevolutionary plot. Thus, when Morris presented the demand for Genet's recall on 8 October to Deforgues, the Jacobin foreign minister promptly assured him that France would recall Genet, and two days later, after reading Jefferson's letter and documentation, further promised that the French government would punish Genet for his criminal conduct in America. A day later the Jacobin-dominated Committee of Public Safety officially confirmed Genet's recall and decided to replace him with a four-man commission that was directed to disavow the "conduite criminelle de Genet et de ses complices" and ship him back to France for punishment. In the following month, in order to justify Genet's recall to the French people, the Committee of Public Safety portrayed him, through an officially authorized pamphlet by the Jacobin publicist Ducher and a report to the National Convention by the Jacobin leader Robespierre, as a participant in a Girondin plot to alienate the United States from France through a deliberately overzealous challenge to American neutrality (Thomas Paine to Bertrand Barère, 13 Sep. 1793, AMAE: CPEU, xxxviii; "Remarques sur les Etats-unis," 13 Sep. 1793, same; Morris to TJ, 10, 19 Oct. 1793; Morris to Washington, 19 Oct., 12 Nov. 1793, DLC: Washington Papers; Turner, *CFM*, 228-31, 283-6, 308-9, 313-14; G. J. A. Ducher, *Les Deux Hémisphères* [Paris, 1793], passim; *Moniteur*, 12, 18 Nov. 1793; *Archives Parlementaires*, 1st ser., LXXIX, 380; Aulard, *Recueil*, VII, 359-60; M. J. Sydenham, *The Girondins* [London, 1961], 21-8; Paul Mantoux, "Le Comité de Salut public et la mission de Genet aux États-Unis," *Revue d'Histoire Moderne et Contemporaine*, XIII [1909-10], 5-29). It is supremely ironic that Jefferson's letter of recall achieved his primary objective of averting a diplomatic crisis with France at the cost of convicting Genet in the minds of his Jacobin superiors as an agent of counterrevolution—the very last offense of which he stood accused in American eyes.

Fortunately for the disgraced French minister, the magnanimity of the President enabled him to escape the likely fate that awaited him at the hands of Jacobin revolutionary justice in Paris. When the French commissioners finally reached Philadelphia late in February 1794, seven weeks after Jefferson's retirement as Secretary of State, his successor Edmund Randolph assured them in Washington's name that the United States government considered Genet's dismissal to be sufficient atonement for his transgressions and refused to comply with their demands for his arrest (Randolph to Washington, 21, 23 Feb. 1794, DLC: Washington Papers). Genet thereupon took up political asylum in the United States, married Cornelia Tappen Clinton, a daughter of Governor George Clinton of New York, in November 1794, and settled comfortably into the life of a gentleman farmer and amateur scientist in that state, where he died in 1834.

I. Alexander Hamilton's Outline for the Letter of Recall

[ca. 2 Aug. 1793]

I Discussion of the points in controversy

I fitting out privateers—1 as it stands on the general law of Nations—
2 upon the Treaties

Right of ⎰ ☞   Inlistment of our Citizens as connected with it
[. . .] ⎱   with reference to his *observations*.[1]

II Exercise of consular Jurisdiction—

   I   as it stands on general law of Nations

   II   Upon treaties

   III Upon the principles of France herself—see *Valin*

History of his conduct in regard to these points—

   I   Impropriety of what was done at Charlestown before he had come to the seat of Government had known its sentiments &c

   II   The expectations he gave in conversations—in writing that he would not repeat the fitting of Privateers,[2] and would prevent improper exercise of consular jurisdiction

   III His contraventions of these expectations citing the different instances as to *fitting out privateers* and condemning prizes—

   IV—Attempting to justify them as matters of right—

Enforce the Idea that if his constructions were right his course was wrong—

Ought not have persisted in doing what was contrary to the opinion of the Government, but ought to have referred the matter to National discussion &c &c—

   V   Impropriety of his having *reclaimed* our own offending citizens *as matter of right*—

   V   Disregard of the intimation of the Government with respect to Privateers *Citizens Genet* and *Sans Culottes*

cite the *particulars*—

   VII Disregard of sense of Government in regard to Little Democrat

Stating particulars—

   VIII Offensive stile of his Communications [. . .] instances with *summary comments*

   IX In connection with the last the excessive pretensions of the Vice Consuls disrespectfuly urged and patronised by him by transmitting and upholding their communications.

Improprieties of conduct in other respects—
I His being President of a political society—Society of Friends
of Liberty and Equality
II His declaration to Mr. Dallas that he would appeal from the
President to the People.
General observation on the inference to be drawn from such
circumstances. An inference fortified by the conduct of his Secretary Mr. Pascal stating it with proper remarks on the impropriety of a privileged person pursuing such a course

MS (DLC: TJ Papers, 91: 15627-8); undated; entirely in Hamilton's hand except
for later note at head of text by TJ: "Hamilton's plan of remonstrance against Genet,
when it was concluded to write to Gou-
vernr. Morris, as was afterwards done Aug.
16. 93. Aug. 2. 93."; two words torn away.
Recorded in SJPL between 26 and 29 July
1793: "Hamilton's plan of remonstrance agt
the conduct of Genet."

The presence of this document among
TJ's papers and his notation, recorded
above, both suggest that Hamilton submitted it to TJ on 2 Aug. 1793 in order to assist
him in writing Document IV below in accordance with the Cabinet's decision of the preceding day to ask for the French minister's
recall (Notes of Cabinet Meeting on Edmond Charles Genet, 1 Aug. 1793). Hamilton prepared other notes for TJ's letter to

Morris at about this time, but there is no evidence that he made them available to TJ
(Syrett, *Hamilton*, xv, 166).

HIS OBSERVATIONS: see Genet to TJ, 27
May, 1 June 1793. The work by René
Josué VALIN was probably his *Traité des
prises, ou Principes de la jurisprudence
françoise concernant les prises qui se font sur
mer . . .*, 2 vols. (La Rochelle and Paris,
1763). INTIMATION OF THE GOVERNMENT:
see TJ to Genet, 5 June 1793. DECLARA-
TION TO MR. DALLAS: see Memorandum of a
Conversation with Edmond Charles Genet,
10 July 1793. CONDUCT OF . . . MR. PASCAL:
see Notes of Cabinet Meeting on Edmond
Charles Genet, 23 July 1793, and note.

[1] This and preceding line interlined.
[2] Preceding four words interlined in different ink.

II. Proposed Addition to the Letter of Recall

[ca. 15-20 Aug. 1793]

not inserted[1]
At other times he would correct the decisions of the President by what
he calls the will of the people. 'It is not thus says he that the people of
America wish &c.
As if the will of the people had been pronounced on the several abstract
questions of the Law of Nations and construction of treaties to which his
proceedings have given rise: and as if that will had been communicated
to him.—By the constitution of the US. it is not by their own will,
collectively or individually expressed,[2] that the citizens have chosen to
have their government administered, or their laws made. They know

too well the impossibility of collecting all the inhabitants of a territory of a million of square miles to direct every movement of the government. They determined therefore to exercise one great act of their will, from time to time, sufficient of itself to keep all others in due order, that is, to name the persons to whom they would confide the administration of their government and framing[3] of their laws. To them they trust to do what is right in every case, reserving to themselves only a general and periodical appeal, the effect of which is, not to correct past wrongs,[4] but to prevent the future by removing the wrong-doer. He therefore who proposes to take their will in matters of detail, proposes what he knows to be[5] impracticable, and means to impose, for the general will, that of a few. He proposes too what is against the constitution. With this appeal however to the will of the people, Mr. Genet threatens the President, forgetting the decorum due, by the usage of nations, from foreign ministers to the government with which they are permitted to reside; forgetting that the Executive is the organ of the nation for corresponding with foreign powers and foreign ministers, and the only one to whom it is lawful for him to apply. And to cover his departure from order, he says that a worthy magistrate should desire this appeal. A worthy magistrate will never fear that appeal, constitutionally made, nor permit it to be made unconstitutionally. He will not permit, under this pretext, the public tranquility to be disturbed by a foreign agent, his fellow-citizens[6] to be divided against each other by his intrigues and practices, to be arranged under the banners of this or that foreign nation, and to be thrown into anarchy under the treacherous pretext of referring questions to their will. A wise magistrate will read in the history of an unfortunate state in Europe, the baneful effects of foreign influence, and will resist the first attempts to renew those scenes in the country committed to his charge, as the most atrocious of all hostilities. These practices to subvert our government have not been authorized by the French nation, however Mr. Genet would countenance the imputation by his proceedings. We did not need the evidence of the decree of

Dft (DLC: TJ Papers, 92: 15834); unfinished addition to Dft of Document IV written entirely in TJ's hand on two sheets, the bottom half of the second being blank; undated, but probably written between 15 and 20 Aug. 1793.

Internal evidence suggests that this addition was intended to strengthen the section in the draft of Document IV dealing with Edmond Charles Genet's criticisms of the President, but its provenance and date cannot be more precisely established. The most likely explanation is that TJ drafted it sometime between the Cabinet's initial review of the draft letter on 15 Aug. and its approval of the final text on 20 Aug. 1793 (see Notes of Cabinet Meeting on Edmond Charles Genet, 20 Aug. 1793; Cabinet Opinions on Edmond Charles Genet, 23 Aug. 1793). Whether or not TJ began the addition at the behest of the Cabinet, he left it unfinished and does not seem to have submitted it to his colleagues for their approval, as he did with

several other alterations that were incorporated into the draft.

¹ This line added in a different ink.
² Word interlined.

³ Word interlined in place of "making."
⁴ Word interlined in place of "errors."
⁵ TJ here canceled "impossible."
⁶ Altered from "our citizens."

III. Analysis of the Letter of Recall

[ca. 15-20 Aug. 1793]

Analysis of the letter.

Object of the Proclamation.

Genet's arrival at Charleston, and conduct till his arrival at Philadelphia
his subsequent conduct and correspondence reduced under the following heads.

1. his right to arm in our ports, enlist our citizens, reclaim against their
punishment.

2. the right of the Consuls to hold courts of Admiralty.

    courts of the US. to try questions of Prize or not
    prize.

   of the US. to protect vessels in their waters and on their
   coasts.

3. requisition to drive away letters of Marque, as Privateers.

4. claim to sell prize goods *duty free*.

5. complaint that French goods are taken by the English out of American bottoms.

6. his assuming *to act* in opposition to the declared will of the government within their territory.

Observations

   on his dictating what subjects are proper for Congress, when
   they should be called &c.

   his disrespectful expressions of the President—of the nation.

Proofs of our friendly dispositions—particular instances.

his recall urged—and speedily

MS (DLC: TJ Papers, 92: 15836); entirely in TJ's hand; undated.

Internal evidence suggests that TJ prepared this analysis after writing a text of
Document IV below, though it is not clear
whether he did so after completing the draft
which was considered by the Cabinet on 15
Aug. or the draft as finally revised and approved by the Cabinet on 20 Aug. 1793
(Cabinet Opinions on Edmond Charles
Genet, 23 Aug. 1793). Although the purpose of the analysis remains uncertain, it
seems more likely that TJ wrote it to assist
him in presenting the draft to the Cabinet on
the 15th.

IV. Thomas Jefferson to
Gouverneur Morris

SIR   Philadelphia August 16th:[1] 1793.

In my letter of June 13th. I enclosed to you the copies of several letters, which had passed between Mr. Ternant, Mr. Genet, and myself, on the occurrences to which the present war had given rise within our ports. The object of this communication was to enable you to explain the principles on which our government was conducting itself towards the belligerent parties; principles which might not in all cases be satisfactory to all, but were meant to be just and impartial to all. Mr. Genet had been then but a little time with us; and but a little more was necessary to develop in him a character and conduct, so unexpected, and so extraordinary, as to place us in the most distressing dilemma, between our regard for his nation, which is constant and sincere, and a regard for our Laws, the authority of which must be maintained; for the peace of our Country, which the Executive Magistrate is charged to preserve; for it's honor, offended in the person of that Magistrate; and for it's character grossly traduced in the conversations and letters of this Gentleman. In the course of these transactions, it has been a great comfort to us to believe that none of them were within the intentions or expectations of his employers. These had been too recently expressed, in acts which nothing could discolour, in the letters of the Executive Council, in the letter and decrees of the national Assembly, and in the general demeanor of the nation towards us, to ascribe to them things of so contrary a character. Our first duty, therefore, was to draw a strong line between their intentions, and the proceedings of their Minister; our second, to lay those proceedings faithfully before them.

On the declaration of war between France and England, the United States being at peace with both, their situation was so new and unexperienced by themselves, that their citizens were not, in the first instant, sensible of the new duties resulting therefrom, and of the restraints[2] it would impose even *on their dispositions* towards the belligerent powers. Some of them imagined (and chiefly their transient Sea-faring citizens) that they were free to indulge those dispositions, to take side with either party, and enrich themselves by depredations on the commerce of the other, and were meditating enterprises of this nature, as there was reason to believe.[3] In this state of the public mind, and before it should take an erroneous direction, difficult to be set right, and dangerous to themselves and their country, the President thought it expedient, through the channel of a Proclamation, to remind our fellow-citizens that we were in a state of peace with all the belligerent powers, that in that state, it was our duty neither to aid nor injure any, to exhort and warn them against acts which might contravene this duty, and particularly those of positive hostility, for the punishment of which the laws would be appealed to; and to put them on their guard also as to the risks they would run, if they should attempt to carry articles of contraband to any. This proclamation, ordered on the 19th.[4] and signed the 22d. day of April, was sent to you in my letter of the 26th. of the same month.

On the day of it's publication, we received through the channel of the newspapers the first intimation that Mr. Genet had arrived on the 8th. of the month at Charleston in the Character of minister plenipotentiary from his nation to the united States, and soon after, that he had sent on to Philadelphia the vessel in which he came, and would himself perform the Journey by land.[5] His landing at one of the most distant ports[6] of the Union from his points both of departure and destination, was calculated to excite attention: and very soon afterwards we learnt that he was undertaking to authorize the fitting and arming vessels in that port, enlisting men, foreigners and citizens, and giving them Commissions to cruize and commit hostilities on nations at peace with us, that these vessels were taking and bringing prizes into our ports, that the consuls of France were assuming to hold Courts of Admiralty on them, to try, condemn, and authorize their sale as legal prize, and all this before Mr. Genet had presented himself, or his Credentials to the President, before he was received by him, without his consent or consultation, and directly in contravention of the state of peace existing, and declared to exist in the President's proclamation, and incumbent on him to preserve till the constitutional authority should otherwise declare. These proceedings became immediately, as was naturally to be expected, the subject of complaint by the representative here of that power against whom they would chiefly operate. The British minister presented several memorials thereon, to which we gave the answer of May 15. heretofore enclosed to you, corresponding in substance with a letter of the same date written to Mr. Ternant, the minister of France then residing here, a copy of which I send herewith. On the next day Mr. Genet reached this place, about five or six weeks[7] after he had arrived at Charleston, and might have been at Philadelphia, if he had steered for it directly. He was immediately presented to the President, and received by him as the minister of the Republic; and as the conduct before stated seemed to bespeak a design of forcing us into the war, without allowing us the exercise of any free will in the case, nothing could be more assuaging than his assurances to the President at his reception, which he repeated to me afterwards in conversation, and in public to the citizens of Philadelphia in answer to an address from them, that, on account of our remote situation and other circumstances, France did not expect that we should become a party to the war, but wished to see us pursue our prosperity and happiness in peace. In a conversation a few days after, Mr. Genet told me that M. de Ternant had delivered him my letter of May 15. He spoke something of the case of the Grange, and then of the armament at Charleston, explained the circumstances which led him to it before he had been received by the government, and consulted it's will, expressed a hope that the President had not so absolutely decided against the measure, but that he would hear what was to be said in support of it; that he would write me a letter on the subject, in which he thought he could justify it under our Treaty; but that if the President should finally determine otherwise, he must submit: for that assuredly his instructions were to do what would be agreeable to us. He accordingly wrote the letter of May 27. The President took the case again into consideration, and found nothing in that letter which could shake the grounds of his former decision. My letter of June 5th. notifying this to him, his of June 8th. and 14th. mine of the 17th. and his again of the 22d. will shew what further passed on this subject, and that he was far from retaining his disposition to acquiesce in the ultimate will of the President.—It would be tedious to pursue this and our subsequent correspondencies through all their details. Referring, therefore, for these to the letters themselves, which shall accompany this, I will present a summary view only of the points of difference which have arisen, and the Grounds on which they rest.

1. Mr: Genet asserts his right of arming in our ports, and of enlisting our citizens, and that we have no right to restrain him or punish them. Examining this question under the law of nations, founded on the general sense and usage of mankind, we have produced proofs, from the most enlightened and approved writers on the subject, that a neutral nation must, in all things relating to the war, observe an exact impartiality towards the parties; that favors to one to the prejudice of the other would import a fraudulent neutrality, of which no nation would be the dupe; that no succour should be given to either, unless stipulated by Treaty, in men, arms, or any thing else directly serving for war; that the right of raising troops being one of the rights of sovereignty, and consequently appertaining exclusively to the nation itself, no foreign power or person can levy men, within it's territory, without it's consent; and he who does, may be rightfully and severely punished; that if the United States have a right to refuse the permission to arm vessels and raise men within their ports and territories, they are bound by the laws of neutrality to exercise that right, and to prohibit such armaments and enlistments. To these principles of the law of Nations Mr. Genet answers by calling them 'diplomatic subtleties,' and 'aphorisms of Vattel and others.'[8] But something more than this is necessary to disprove them:

Lets. June 8. 22. 1. May 27.

June 17. Vattel L.3.§.104.

Wolf. 1174. Vat. 3.§.15.

and till they are disproved, we hold it certain that the law of Nations and the rules of neutrality forbid our permitting either party to arm in our ports.

June 22. 8.   But Mr. Genet says that the 22d. article of our treaty allows him *expressly* to arm in our ports. Why has he not quoted the very words of that article *expressly* allowing it? For that would have put an end to all further question. The words of the article are 'It shall not be lawful for any foreign privateers not belonging to subjects of the most christian King, nor Citizens of the said United States, who have Commissions from any prince or state in enmity with either nation, to fit their Ships in the ports of either the one or the other of the aforesaid parties.' Translate this from the general terms in which it here stands into the special case produced by the present war. 'Privateers not belonging to France or the United States and having Commissions from the enemies of one of them,' are in the present state of things 'British, Dutch and Spanish[9] privateers.' Substituting these then for the equivalent terms, it will stand thus. 'It shall not be lawful for British, Dutch, or Spanish privateers to fit their ships in the ports of the United States.' Is this an *express* permission to France to do it? Does the negative to the enemies of France, and silence as to France herself, imply an affirmative to France? Certainly not: it leaves the question, as to France open and free to be decided according to circumstances. And if the parties had meant an affirmative stipulation, they would have provided for it expressly; they would never have left so important a point to be inferred from mere[10] silence, or implication. Suppose they had desired to stipulate a refusal to their enemies, but nothing as to themselves: what form of expression would they have used? Certainly the one they have used: an express stipulation as to their enemies, and silence as to themselves. And such an intention corresponds not only with the words, but with the circumstances of[11] the times. It was of value to each party to exclude it's enemies from arming in the ports of the other, and could in no case embarrass them. They therefore stipulated so far mutually. But each might be embarrassed by permitting the other to arm in it's ports. They therefore would not stipulate to permit that. Let us go back to the state of things in France when this treaty was made, and we shall find several cases wherein France could not[12] have permitted us to arm in her ports. Suppose a war between these States and Spain. We know that, by the Treaties between France and Spain, the former could not permit the enemies of the latter to arm in her ports. It was honest in her, therefore, not to deceive us by such a stipulation. Suppose a war between these States and Great Britain. By the treaties between France and Great Britain, in force at the signature of ours, we could not have been permitted to arm in the ports of France. She could not then have meant in this article to give us such a right. She has manifested the same sense of it again in her subsequent Treaty with England, made eight Years after the date of ours, stipulating in the 16th. article of it, as in[13] our 22d. that foreign privateers, *not being subjects of either crown* should not arm against either, in the ports of the other. If this had amounted to an affirmative stipulation[14] that the subjects of the other crown might arm in her ports *against us*, it would have been in direct contradiction to her 22d. Article with us. So that to give to these negative stipulations, an affirmative effect, is to render them inconsistent with each other, and with good faith: to give them only their negative and natural effect, is to reconcile them to one another, and to good faith, and is clearly to adopt the sense in which France herself has expounded them. We may justly conclude then, that[15] the article only obliges us to refuse this right, in the present case, to Great Britain, and the other enemies of France. It does not go on to give it to France, either expressly, or by implication. We may then refuse it. And since we are bound by treaty to refuse it to the one party, and are free to refuse it to the other, we are bound by the laws of neutrality to refuse it to that other. The aiding either party then with vessels, arms, or men, being unlawful by the Law of nations, and not rendered lawful by the treaty, it is made a question whether our citizens, joining in these unlawful enterprises may be punished? The united States being in a state of peace with most of the belligerent powers by treaty, and with all of them by the laws of nature, murders and robberies committed by our citizens within our territory, or on the high seas,[16] on those with whom we are so at peace, are punishable, equally as if committed on our own inhabitants.[17] If I might venture to reason a little formally, without being charged with running into 'subtleties and aphorisms,' I would say that if one citizen has a right to go to war of his own Authority, every citizen has the same. If every citizen has that right, then the nation (which is composed of all it's Citizens) has a right to go to war, by the authority of it's individual Citizens. But this is not true, either on the general principles of Society, or by our Constitution, which gives[18] that power to Congress alone, and not to the Citizens individually. Then the first position was not true; and no citizen has a right to go to war of his own authority: and for what he does without right, he ought to be punished.—Indeed nothing can be more obviously absurd than to say that all the citizens may be at war, and yet the nation at peace.[19] It has been pretended, indeed, that the engagement of a citizen in an enterprise of this nature,[20] was a divestment of the character of citizen, and a transfer of jurisdiction over him to another Sovereign. Our citizens are certainly free to divest themselves of that character, by emigration, and other acts manifesting their intention, and may then become the subjects of another power, and free to do whatever the subjects of that power may do. But the laws do not admit that the bare Commission of a crime amounts of itself to a divestment of the character of citizen, and withdraws the criminal from their coercion. They would never prescribe an illegal act among the legal modes by which a citizen might disfranchise himself; nor render treason, for instance, [21] innocent by giving it the force of a dissolution of the obligations of the criminal to his Country. [22] Accordingly, in the case of Henfield, a citizen of these States, charged with having engaged in the port of Charleston in an enterprise against nations at peace with us, and with having joined in the actual Commission of Hostilities, the Attorney General of the united States, in an official Opinion declared that [23] the act with which he was charged, was punishable by law. The same thing has been unanimously declared by two of the Circuit Courts of the United States, as you will see in the charges of Chief Justice Jay, delivered at Richmond, and Judge Wilson, delivered at Philadelphia, both of which are herewith sent. Yet Mr. Genet in the moment he lands at Charleston, is able to tell the Governor, and continues to affirm in his correspondence here, that no law of the united States authorizes their government to restrain either it's own Citizens, or the foreigners inhabiting it's territory, from warring against the enemies of France. It is true, indeed, that, in the case of Henfield, the Jury which tried, absolved him. But it appeared on the trial that the crime was not knowingly and wilfully committed; that Henfield was ignorant of the unlawfulness of his undertaking; that in the moment he was apprised of it, he shewed real contrition; that he had rendered meritorious services during the late war, and declared he would live and die an American. The Jury, therefore, [24] in absolving him, did no more than the constitutional authority might have done, had they found him guilty: the Constitution having provided for the pardon of offences in certain cases, and there being no case where it could have been more proper than where no offence was contemplated. Henfield, therefore, was still an American Citizen, and Mr. Genet's reclamation of him was as unauthorized as the first enlistment of him. [25]

2. Another doctrine advanced by Mr. Genet is, That our Courts can take no cognisance of questions whether vessels, *held by theirs*, as prizes, are lawful prizes or not; that this jurisdiction belongs exclusively to their Consulates here, which have been lately erected by the national assembly into complete Courts of Admiralty.

Let us consider first what is the extent of the Jurisdiction which the Consulates of France may rightfully exercise here. Every nation has of natural right, entirely and exclusively, all the jurisdiction which may be rightfully exercised in the territory it occupies. If it cedes any portion of that jurisdiction to Judges appointed by another Nation, the limits of their power must depend on the instrument of cession. The United

States and France, have, by their Consular Convention, given mutually to their Consuls jurisdiction in certain cases specially enumerated. But that Convention gives to neither the power of establishing complete Courts of Admiralty within the territory of the other, nor even of deciding the particular question of Prize, or not prize. The Consulates of France then cannot take judicial cognisance of those questions here. Of this opinion Mr. Genet was, when he wrote his letter of May 27. wherein he promises to correct the Error of the Consul at Charleston, of whom, in my letter of the 15th. I had complained, as arrogating to himself that jurisdiction; though in his subsequent letters he has thought proper to embark in the errors of his Consuls.

June 14. 22.

But the United States, at the same time do not pretend any right to try the validity of captures[26] made *on the high seas*, by France, or any other nation, over it's enemies. These questions belong, of common usage, to the Sovereign of the Captor, and whenever it is necessary to determine them, resort must be had to his Courts. This is the case provided for in the 17th. Article of the Treaty, which says that such prizes shall not be arrested, nor cognisance taken of the validity thereof; a stipulation much insisted on by Mr. Genet and the Consuls, and which we never thought of infringing or questioning. As the validity of captures then, made *on the high seas* by France over it's enemies, cannot be tried within the United States by their Consuls, so neither can it by our own Courts. Nor is this the question between us, though we have been misled into it.

The real Question is Whether the United States have not a right to protect vessels within their waters, and on their Coasts? The Grange was taken within the Delaware, between the shores of Jersey and of the Delaware State, and several miles above it's mouth. The seizing her was a flagrant violation of the jurisdiction of the United States. Mr. Genet, however, instead of apologizing, takes great merit in his letters for giving her up.—The William is said to have been taken within two miles of the Shores of the united States. When the admiralty declined cognisance of the case, she was delivered to the French Consul, according to my letter of June 25th., to be kept till the Executive of the united States should examine into the case; and Mr. Genet was desired by my letter of June 29th. to have them furnished with the evidence, on behalf of the captors, as to the place of capture. Yet to this day it has never been done. The Brig Fanny was alleged to be taken within five miles from our shore. The Catharine within two miles and a half. It is an essential attribute of the jurisdiction of every Country to preserve peace, to punish acts in breach of it, and to restore property taken by force within it's limits. Were the armed vessel of any nation to cut away one of our own from the wharves of Philadelphia, and to chuse to call it a prize, would this exclude us from the right of redressing the wrong? Were it the vessel of another nation, are we not equally bound to protect it, while within our limits? Were it seized in any other waters, or on the shores of the united States, the right of redressing is still the same: and humble indeed would be our condition, were we obliged to depend for that on the will of a foreign Consul, or on negotiation with diplomatic Agents. Accordingly this right of protection, within it's waters, and to a reasonable distance on it's coasts, has been acknowledged by every nation, and denied to none: and if the property seized be yet within their power, it is their right and duty to redress the wrong themselves.—France herself has asserted the right in herself and recognised it in us, in the 6th. Article of our treaty, where we mutually stipulate that we will, *by all the means in our power*, (not by negotiation) protect and defend each others vessels and effects, in our ports or roads, or on the seas near our Countries, and recover and restore the same to the right owners. The United Netherlands, Prussia and Sweden, have recognised it also in treaties with us; and indeed it is a standing formule, inserted in almost all the Treaties of all nations, and proving the principle to be acknowledged by all nations.

How, and by what Organ of the government, whether Judiciary or Executive, it shall be redressed, is not yet perfectly settled with us. One of the subordinate Courts of Admiralty has been of opinion, in the first instance, in the case of the ship William, that it does not belong to the Judiciary. Another perhaps may be of a contrary Opinion. The question is still sub judice, and an appeal to the Court of last resort will decide it finally. If finally, the judiciary [27] shall declare that it does not belong to the *Civil* authority, it then results to the Executive, charged with the direction of the *military* Force of the union, and the conduct of it's affairs with foreign nations. But this is a mere question of internal arrangement between the different Departments of the Government, depending on the particular diction of the laws and Constitution; and it can in no wise concern a foreign nation to which department these have delegated it.

3. Mr. Genet, in his letter of July 9. requires that the Ship Jane, which he calls an English privateer, shall be immediately ordered to depart; and, to justify this, he appeals to the 22d. Article of our treaty, which provides that it shall not be lawful for any foreign *privateer* to fit their Ships in our ports, to sell *what they have taken*, or purchase victuals, &c. The Ship Jane is an English merchant vessel, which has been many years employed in the Commerce between Jamaica and these States. She brought here a cargo of produce from that Island, and was to take away a cargo of flour. Knowing of the war when she left Jamaica, and that our coast was lined with small French privateers, she armed for her defence, and took one of those Commissions usually

called letters of marque. She arrived here safely without having had any rencounter of any sort. Can it be necessary to say that a merchant vessel is not a privateer? That though she has arms to defend herself in time of war, in the course of her regular commerce, this no more makes her a privateer, than a Husbandman following his plough, in time of war, with a Knife or pistol in his pocket, is thereby made a Soldier? The occupation of a privateer is attack and plunder, that of a merchant-vessel is commerce and self-preservation. The article excludes the former from our ports, and from selling *what she has taken*, that is, what she has acquired by war, to shew it did not mean the merchant-vessel and what she had acquired by commerce. Were the merchant-vessels coming for our produce forbidden to have any arms for their defence, every Adventurer who has a boat, or money enough to buy one, would make her a privateer; our Coasts would swarm with them, foreign vessels must cease to come, our Commerce must be suppressed, our produce remain on our hands, or at least that great portion of it which we have not vessels to carry away, our ploughs must be laid aside and agriculture suspended. This is a sacrifice no treaty could ever contemplate, and which we are not disposed to make out of mere complaisance to a false definition of the term *privateer*.—Finding that the Jane had purchased new carriages to mount two or three additional Guns, which she had brought in her hold, and that she had opened additional port-holes for them, the carriages were ordered to be relanded, the additional port holes stopped, and her means of defence reduced to be exactly the same at her departure, as at her arrival. This was done on the general principle of allowing no party to arm within our ports.

4. The 17th. Article of our Treaty leaves armed vessels free to *conduct* whithersoever they please, the Ships and goods taken from their enemies without paying any duty, and to depart and be conducted freely to the places expressed in their Commissions, which the Captain shall be obliged to shew. It is evident that this Article does not contemplate a freedom *to sell their prizes* here: but on the contrary *a departure* to some other place, always to be expressed in their Commission, where their validity is to be finally adjudged. In such case it would be as unreasonable to demand Duties on the goods they had taken from an enemy, as it would be on the cargo of a merchant vessel touching in our ports for refreshment or advices. And against this the Article provides. But[28] the armed vessels of France have been also admitted[29] to land and sell their prize goods here for consumption; in which case it is as reasonable they should pay duties, as the goods of a merchantman landed and sold for consumption. They have, however, demanded, and as a matter of right, to sell them free of duty, a right, they say, given by this Article of the Treaty, though the Article does not give the right to sell at all. Where

a Treaty does not give the principal right of selling, the additional one of selling duty free cannot be given: and the laws in admitting[30] the principal right of selling, may with-hold the additional one of selling duty free. It must be observed that our revenues are raised almost wholly on imported goods. Suppose prize goods enough should be brought in to supply our whole consumption. According to their construction we are to lose our whole revenue. I put the extreme case to evince more extremely the unreasonableness of the claim. Partial supplies would affect the revenue but partially. They would lessen the evil, but not the error, of the construction: and I believe we may say with truth that neither party had it in contemplation, when penning this Article, to abandon any part of it's revenue for the encouragement of the Sea-robbers of the other.

5. Another source of complaint with Mr. Genet has been that the English take French goods out of american vessels, which he says is against the Law of nations, and ought to be prevented by us. On the contrary we suppose it to have been long an established principle of the Law of nations that the Goods of a friend are free in an enemy's vessel, and an enemy's goods lawful prize in the vessel of a friend. The inconvenience of this principle, which subjects merchant-vessels to be stopped at Sea, searched, ransacked, led out of their course, has induced several nations latterly to stipulate against it by treaty, and to substitute another in it's stead, that free bottoms shall make free goods and enemy bottoms, enemy goods; a rule equal to the other in point of loss and gain, but less oppressive to commerce. As far as it has been introduced, it depends on the treaties stipulating it, and forms exceptions in special cases to the general operation of the law of nations. We have introduced it into our treaties with France, Holland, and Prussia; and French goods found by the two latter nations in American bottoms are not made prize of. It is our wish to establish it with other nations. But this requires their consent also, is a work of time, and in the mean while they have a right to act on the general principle, without giving to us, or to France, cause of complaint. Nor do I see that France can lose by it on the whole. For though she loses *her* goods when found in our vessels by the nations with whom we have no treaties, yet she gains *our* goods, when found in the vessels of the same, and all other nations: and we believe the latter mass to be greater than the former.—It is to be lamented, indeed, that the general principle has operated so cruelly in the dreadful calamity which has lately happened in St. Domingo. The miserable fugitives, who, to save their lives, had taken asylum in our vessels, with such valuable and portable things as could be gathered in the moment, out of the ashes of their houses, and wrecks of their fortunes, have been plundered of these remains by the licensed Sea-rovers of their enemies. This

has swelled, on this occasion, the disadvantages of the general principle that 'an enemy's goods are free prize in the vessels of a friend.' But it is one of those deplorable and unforeseen calamities to which they expose themselves who enter into a state of war, furnishing to us an awful lesson to avoid it by justice and moderation, and not a cause or encouragement to expose our own towns to the same burnings and butcheries, nor of complaint because we do not.

6. In a case like the present, where the missionary of one government construes differently from that to which he is sent the treaties and laws which are to form a common rule of action for both, it would be unjust in either to claim an exclusive right of construction. Each nation has an equal right to expound the meaning of their common rules; and reason and usage has established, in such cases, a convenient and well understood train of proceeding. It is the right and duty of the foreign missionary to urge his own constructions, to support them with reasons which may convince, and in terms of decency and respect which may reconcile, the government of the country to concurrence. It is the duty of that government to listen to his reasonings with attention and candor, and to yield to them when just. But if it shall still appear to them that reason and right are on their side, it follows of necessity that, exercising the sovereign powers of the country, they have a right to proceed on their own constructions and conclusions as to whatever is to be done within their limits. The minister then refers the case to his own government, asks new instructions, and in the meantime acquiesces in the authority of the country. His government examines his constructions, abandons them, if wrong, insists on them, if right, and the case then becomes a matter of negotiation between the two nations. Mr. Genet, however, assumes a new and[31] a bolder line of conduct. After deciding for himself ultimately, and without respect to the authority of the country, he proceeds to do what even his sovereign could not authorize,[32] to put himself, within the country, on a line with it's government, act as co-sovereign of the territory, arms vessels, levies men, gives commissions of war, independently of them, and in direct opposition to their orders and efforts. When the government forbids their citizens to arm and engage in the war, he undertakes to arm and engage them. When they forbid vessels to be fitted in their ports for cruising on nations with whom they are at peace, he commissions them to fit and cruise. When they forbid an unceded jurisdiction to be exercised within their territory by foreign agents, he undertakes to uphold that exercise and to avow it openly. The Privateers Citoyen Genet and Sans Culottes, having been fitted out at Charleston (though without the permission of the government, yet before it was forbidden) the President only required they might leave our ports, and did not interfere with their prizes. Instead, however, of

their quitting our ports, the Sans Culottes remains still, strengthening and equipping herself, and the Citoyen Genet went out only to cruise on our coast, and to brave the authority of the country by returning into port again with her prizes. Though in the letter of June 5. the final determination of the President was communicated that no future armaments in our ports should be permitted, the Vainqueur de la Bastille was afterwards equipped and commissioned in Charleston, the Anti-George in Savannah, the Caramagnole in Delaware,[33] a Schooner and a Sloop[34] in Boston, and the Polly or Republican was attempted to be equipped in New York, and was the subject of reclamation by Mr. Genet, in a style which certainly did not look like relinquishing the practice. The Little Sarah or Little Democrat was armed, equipped and manned, in the Port of Philadelphia, under the very eye of the government, and as if meant to insult it. Having fallen down the River, and being evidently on the point of departure for a cruize, Mr. Genet was desired, in my letter of July 12. on the part of the President, to detain her till some inquiry and determination on the case should be had. Yet within three or four days after, she was sent out by orders from Mr. Genet himself, and is at this time cruising on our coasts, as appears by the protest of the master of one of our vessels maltreated by her.

The government thus insulted and set at defiance by Mr. Genet, committed in it's duties and engagements to others, determined still to see in these proceedings but the character of the individual; and not to believe, and it does not believe, that they are by instructions from his employers. They had assured the British minister here that the vessels already armed in their ports should be obliged to leave them, and that no more should be armed in them. Yet more had been armed, and those before armed, had either not gone away, or gone only to return with new prizes. They now informed him that the order for departure should be enforced, and the prizes made contrary to it should be restored or compensated. The same thing was notified to Mr. Genet in my letter of Aug. 7. and, that he might not conclude the promise of compensation to be of no concern to him, and go on in his courses, he was reminded that it would be a fair article of account against his nation.

Mr. Genet, not content with using our force, whether we will or not, in the military line, against nations with whom we are at peace, undertakes also to direct the civil government; and particularly, for the Executive and Legislative bodies, to pronounce what powers may, or may not, be exercised by the one or the other. Thus in his letter of June 8th. he promises to respect the political Opinions of the President, *till the Representatives shall have confirmed or rejected them*: as if the President had undertaken to decide what belonged to the decision of Congress. In his letter of June 14. he says more openly that the President ought not to have taken on himself to decide on the subject of the letter, but that it was of importance enough to have consulted Congress thereon: and in that of June 22d. he tells the President in direct terms that Congress ought already to have been occupied on certain questions, which he had been too hasty in deciding: thus making himself, and not the President, the judge of the Powers ascribed by the Constitution to the Executive, and dictating to him the occasion when he should exercise the power of convening Congress at an earlier day than their own act had prescribed.

On the following expressions no commentary shall be made.

'Les principes philosophiques proclamées par le President.'[35]   July 9.

'Les opinions privées ou publiques de M. le President, et cette egide ne paroissant pas suffisante.'   June 22.

'Le gouvernement federal s'est empressé, poussé par je ne sçais quelle influence.'   June 22.

'Je ne puis attribuer des demarches de cette nature qu'à des impressions etrangeres dont le tems et la verité triompheront.'   June 22.

'On poursuit avec acharnement en vertu des instructions de M. le President, les Armateurs Français.'   June 25.

'Ce refus tend à accomplir le systeme infernal du roi d'angleterre, et des autres rois ses accomplices, pour faire perir par la famine les Republicains Français avec la Liberté.'   June 14.

'La lache abandon de ses amis.'   June 8.

'En vain le desir de conserver la paix fait-il sacrifier les interêts de la France à cet interêt du moment; en vain la soif des richesses l'emportet-elle sur l'honneur dans la balance politique de l'amérique, tous ces menagemens, toute cette condescendance, toute cette humilité n'aboutissent à rien: nos ennemis en rient, et les Français trop confiants sont punis pour avoir cru que la nation Americaine avoit un pavillon, qu'elle avoit quelque egard pour ses loix, quelque conviction de ses forces, et qu'elle tenoit au sentiment de sa dignité. Il ne m'est pas possible de peindre toute ma sensibilité sur ce scandale qui tend à la diminution de votre commerce, à l'oppression du notre, et à l'abaissement, à l'avilissement des republiques.—Si nos concitoyens ont été trompés, si vous n'etes point en etat de soutenir la Souveraineté de votre peuple, parlez; nous l'avons garantie quand nous etions esclaves, nous saurons la rendre redoutable etant devenus libres.'—We draw a veil over the sensations which these expressions excite. No words can render them: but they will not escape the sensibility of a friendly and magnanimous nation, who will do us justice. We see in them neither the portrait of ourselves, nor the pencil of our friends; but an attempt to embroil both; to add still another nation to the enemies of his country, and to draw on both a reproach, which it is hoped will never stain the history of either.[36] The written proofs,[37] of which Mr. Genet was himself the Bearer, were too unequivocal to leave a doubt that the French nation are[38] constant in their friendship to[39] us. The resolves of their national convention, the   July 25.

letters of their Executive council attest this truth in terms which[40] render it necessary to seek, in some other hypothesis, the solution of Mr. Genet's machinations against our peace and friendship.

Conscious, on our part, of the same friendly and sincere dispositions, we can with truth affirm, both for our nation and government, that we have never omitted a reasonable occasion of manifesting them. For I will not consider as of that character opportunities of sallying forth from our ports to way-lay, rob, and murder defenceless merchants and others, who have done us no injury, and who were coming to trade with us in the confidence of our peace and amity. The violation of all the laws of order and morality which bind mankind together would be an unacceptable[41] offering to a just nation. Recurring then, only to recent things, after so afflicting a libel, we recollect with satisfaction that in the course of two years, by unceasing exertions, we paid up seven years arrearages and instalments of our debt to France, which the inefficiency of our first form of Government had suffered to be accumulating: that pressing on still to the entire fulfilment of our engagements, we have facilitated to Mr. Genet the effect of the instalments of the present year, to enable him to send relief to his fellow-citizens in France, threatened with Famine: that in the first moment of the insurrection which threatened the Colony of St. Domingo,[42] we stepped forward to their relief with arms and money, taking freely on ourselves the risk of an unauthorized aid, when delay would have been denial: that we have received according to our best abilities, the wretched fugitives from the catastrophe of the principal town of that Colony,[43] who, escaping from the swords and flames of civil war, threw themselves on us naked and houseless, without food or friends, money or other means, their faculties lost and absorbed in the depth of their distresses: that the exclusive admission[44] to sell here the prizes made by France on her enemies, in the present war, tho' unstipulated in our treaties, and unfounded in her own practice, or in that of other nations, as we believe; the spirit manifested by the late Grand Jury, in their proceedings against those who had aided the enemies of France with arms and implements of war;[45] the expressions of attachment to his nation, with which Mr. Genet was welcomed on his arrival and journey from South to North, and our long forbearance under his gross usurpations and outrages of the laws and authority of our country,[46] do not bespeak the partialities intimated in his letters. And for these things he rewards us by endeavors to excite discord and distrust, between our citizens and those whom they have entrusted with their government, between the different branches of our government, between our nation and his. But none of these Things, we hope, will be found in his power. That friendship, which dictates to us to bear with his conduct yet awhile, lest the interests of his nation here should suffer injury,[47] will hasten them to replace an agent, whose Dispositions are such a misrepresentation of theirs, and whose continuance here is inconsistent with order, peace, respect, and that friendly correspondence, which we hope will ever subsist between the two nations. His government will see too that the case is pressing; that it is impossible for two sovereign and independent authorities to be going on within our territory, at the same time, without collision. They will foresee that if Mr. Genet perseveres in his proceedings, the consequences would be so [48] hazardous to us, the example so humiliating and pernicious, that we may be forced even to suspend his functions before a successor can arrive to continue them. If our citizens have not already been shedding each others blood, it is not owing to the moderation of Mr. Genet, but to the forbearance of the Government. It is well known that if the authority of the laws had been resorted to, to stop the Little Democrat, it's officers and agents were to have been resisted by the crew of the vessel consisting partly of American citizens. Such events are too serious, too possible, to be left to hazard, or to what is worse than hazard, the will of an agent whose designs are so mysterious.—Lay the case then immediately before his government. Accompany it with assurances, which cannot be stronger than true, that our friendship for the nation [49] is constant and unabating; that, faithful to our treaties, we have fulfilled them in every point to the best of our understanding; that, if in any thing, however, we have construed them amiss, we are ready to enter into candid explanations, and to do whatever we can be convinced is right; that in opposing the extravagancies of an agent, whose character they seem not sufficiently to have known we have been urged by motives of duty to ourselves, and justice to others, which cannot but be approved by those who are just themselves; and finally, that, after independence and self-government, [50] there is nothing we more sincerely wish, than perpetual Friendship with them. [51] I have the honor to be with great respect & esteem Dear Sir your most obedt & most humble servt

Th: Jefferson

RC (NNC: Gouverneur Morris Papers); in the hand of George Taylor, Jr., with complimentary close and signature by TJ; at foot of first page: "Mr. Morris, minister plenipoy. of the U.S. to the repub. of France"; endorsed by Morris. Dft (DLC); entirely in TJ's hand, and initialed by him, except as noted below; consists of fair copy made sometime between 11 and 15 Aug. 1793 from an earlier, possibly partial, draft begun 6 Aug. 1793—as indicated by TJ's letter to the President printed under 18 Aug. 1793—and surviving only in the form of slightly variant extracts from the second and third paragraphs quoted in TJ's first letter to James Madison of 11 Aug. 1793;

bears three different sets of emendations reflected in the same number of inks on the holograph: those that are common to the Dft and its PrC and therefore were presumably made prior to the submission of the Dft to the Cabinet on 15 Aug. 1793 (see notes 10-11, 19, 26, 31, 41, and 48 below); those that are unique to the Dft and were presumably made between 15 Aug. 1793, when TJ first submitted it to the Cabinet, and 20 Aug. 1793, when the Cabinet considered it again (see notes 2, 13-15, 17-18, 20-23, 27-30, 32-34, and 51 below); and those that are unique to the Dft and were made as a result of the 20 Aug. 1793 Cabinet meeting (see notes 4, 6, 9, 12, 16, 24-25, 36-40, 42-47, and 49-50 below); complimentary close and initials added by TJ sometime after 15 Aug. 1793; dateline added by Taylor on or after 21 Aug. 1793, the date being reworked to 16 Aug. by him on 23 Aug. (see note 1 below); notations added by Taylor on or after 7 Sep. 1793: (at foot of first page) "Mr. Morris" and (at foot of text) "Note. a copy of the preceding letter was sent enclosed by the Secy. of State, to M. Genet"; with several proposed alterations written by TJ on separate sheets (see notes 15, 22, 27-30 below and Document II above). PrC (DLC: Madison Papers); undated; added in ink at foot of first page by TJ: "Mr. Gouvr. Morris"; lacks dateline, complimentary close, initials, note at foot of text, and most of the emendations in Dft. Tr (DNA: RG 46, Senate Records, 3d Cong., 1st sess.); with same note at foot of text as in Dft. FC (Lb in DNA: RG 59, DCI); with same note at foot of text as in Dft. Tr (NjP: Andre DeCoppet Collection); at head of text: "Duplicate. Copy." Tr (DLC: Genet Papers); in French. Morris also received with this letter a list of the enclosures that was prepared before the dispatch was backdated to 16 Aug. 1793 and is entitled "Contents of the Dispatch of August 22d. 1793, from the Secretary of State to M. Morris. minister plenipotentiary to the Republic of France" (MS in NNC: Morris Papers, in Taylor's hand; PrC in DLC: TJ Papers, 92: 15770-2; Dft in same, 90: 15559, consisting of preliminary list in TJ's hand; recorded in SJPL under 23 [July] 1793). Enclosures (with quotation from MS in Taylor's hand): (1) TJ to Jean Baptiste Ternant, 15 May 1793. (2) Edmond Charles Genet to TJ, 27 May, 1, 8 June 1793. (3) Genet to TJ, 14 June 1793 (two letters), and enclosures to first letter. (4) Genet to TJ, 15, 18, 22, 25 June 1793, and their enclosures. (5) Genet to TJ, 26 June, 8 July 1793. (6) Genet to TJ, 9 July 1793 (three letters), and enclosures to third letter. (7) Genet to TJ, 25 July 1793, and documents described there. (8) TJ to Genet, 1 June (second letter), 5, 11, 17, 19, 23 (two letters), 25, 29 June 1793 (two letters). (9) TJ to Genet, 30 June 1793, and enclosures. (10) TJ to Genet and George Hammond, 12 July 1793. (11) TJ to Genet, 24 July, 7, 16 Aug. 1793. (12) Edmund Randolph's Opinion on the Case of Gideon Henfield, 30 May 1793. (13) Alexander Hamilton's Report on the American Debt to France, 8 June 1793, Document VIII in a group of documents on Jefferson

and the American debt to France, at 3 June 1793. (14) Enclosures to Memorials from George Hammond, 21, 26 June 1793 (see also notes to TJ's 29 June 1793 letters to Genet). (15) Protest of Samuel Derby, master of the *Peggy*, Philadelphia, 12 Aug. 1793, stating that, after leaving Martinique on 20 July bound for Philadelphia, this American brig from Salem, Massachusetts, laden with an American cargo, was stopped between 21 and 31 July by H.M.S. *Culloden*, Captain Thomas Ritchie, the British privateer *Nancy*, and a Spanish privateer, all of which allowed it to proceed after examining its papers; that on 8 Aug., having taken on a pilot thirty miles south of Cape Henlopen to guide it to Philadelphia, the *Peggy* was boarded by a party of Americans and Frenchmen from the privateer *Petite Démocrate*, Captain Amiot, one of whom, Conway, had commanded a Salem privateer during the Revolutionary War; that although he was required to go aboard the *Petite Démocrate*, Amiot could find nothing suspicious about his papers; that during his absence and afterward the boarding party caused damage to the *Peggy* and its cargo, opened two trunks belonging to Fulwar Skipwith, consul at Martinique, and read the papers it contained, and treated the officers and crew abusively; that he was given a certificate by Boucherot, the leader of the party, requesting Genet to make up the damages for opening Skipwith's trunks; and that he reached Philadelphia on 10 Aug. and seeks compensation from all the privateers, as well as their officers and crews, responsible for detaining and damaging the *Peggy* (Tr in NNC: Morris Papers, with copies of subjoined supporting deposition by John Batton, mate, and attestation by notary public Jacob R. Howell; PrC of another Tr in DLC, in a clerk's hand; PrC of another Tr in PRO: FO 97/1, in a clerk's hand). (16) Genet to George Washington, 13 Aug. 1793 (see enclosure to Washington to TJ, 15 Aug. 1793). (17) "Newspapers Freneau's 65 a 86 inclusive Fenno's 108 a 129 do." For the enclosures inadvertently omitted from this letter, see TJ to Morris, 26 Aug. 1793, and note. Printed in *Message*, 57-68. Enclosed in TJ to Genet, [7 Sep. 1793], and TJ to Morris, 11 Sep. 1793; PrC of Dft enclosed in TJ to Madison, 18 Aug. 1793.

ON THE DAY OF IT'S PUBLICATION: news of Edmond Charles Genet's arrival at Charleston had reached Philadelphia at least a day before the President approved the Proclamation of Neutrality on 22 Apr. 1793 (see TJ to Thomas Mann Randolph, Jr., 21 Apr. 1793). THE CASE OF THE GRANGE: see Memorial from George Hammond, 2 May 1793, and note. TJ's interpretation of the 29 July 1793 verdict of the jury of the Circuit Court of Pennsylvania in the CASE OF HENFIELD was later bolstered by an interview Edmund Randolph had with an unnamed juror in the case. The day after the Cabinet reviewed TJ's letter to Morris on 20 Aug. 1793, the Attorney General submitted the following report to the President: "Recollecting an expression in the letter, which was considered yesterday, respecting the motives of the jury in acquitting Henfield, I made a particular enquiry this morning. I find, that the leading man among them expressed himself thus: 'People must not suppose, that because Henfield was acquitted, every person in his situation would be. On the contrary, his declaration, that he would never have inlisted, had he known it to be against General Washington's opinion, was the reason of my voting for his acquittal'" (Randolph to Washington, 21 Aug. 1793, DLC: Washington Papers). For the circumstances under which THE ADMIRALTY DECLINED COGNISANCE OF THE CASE of the *William*, see note to Hammond to TJ, 5 June 1793.

TJ submitted the "draught" of this letter to the President for his approval on 21 Aug. 1793 (Washington, *Journal*, 228).

[1] Reworked in Dft by Taylor from "21."
[2] Word interlined in Dft in place of "laws." Emendation not in PrC or in an earlier draft quoted in TJ's first letter to James Madison, 11 Aug. 1793.
[3] Clause reads "as was said" in earlier draft quoted in TJ's first letter to James Madison, 11 Aug. 1793.
[4] Altered in Dft from "20th." Emendation not in PrC.
[5] Next to the opening line of this sentence in Dft TJ wrote in the margin "see papers of Apr. 22."
[6] Altered in Dft from "the port the most distant of any in." Emendation not in PrC.
[7] Opposite the sentence to this point in Dft TJ wrote in the margin "see Public papers of May 16.17."
[8] Opposite these quotations in Dft TJ wrote in the margin "June 22."
[9] Altered in Dft from "British and

Dutch" here, and again several lines below. Emendations not in PrC.
[10] Word interlined in Dft.
[11] In Dft TJ here canceled "the times one of the parties at least at."
[12] Clause to this point altered in Dft from "and we may imagine several cases wherein it would have been extremely inconvenient to France to." Emendation not in PrC.
[13] Preceding two words interlined in Dft in place of "in the same words with," in accordance with the suggestion of Alexander Hamilton recorded in note 15 below.
[14] Phrase altered in Dft from "a stipulation" in the passage described in the following note.
[15] Sentence to this point and preceding five sentences interlined or written in the margin in Dft in place of "It might have been extremely dangerous for France to permit us to arm in her ports. She reserved the right of refusing it therefore, by not agreeing the contrary; and the reserve and non-agreement were reciprocal to both parties." At this point TJ had previously penciled "qu. see treaties" in the margin. Emendation not in PrC.

TJ had previously written this substitute passage on a separate sheet under the heading "Alteration proposed in the letter to G. Morris, in consequence of an examination of the treaties between France and Great Britain" and submitted it to Alexander Hamilton and Edmund Randolph. Beneath TJ's text Hamilton wrote:

Submitted "*essentially* in the same words with our 22." { "not *being subjects* of either crown" said to be in the same words with our 22 Article. The words of our Article are "not *apartenant*" *not belonging* &c. The *sense* is the same but not the *words*.

Approved with this remark which merely regards accuracy of expression.

Beneath Hamilton's response Randolph wrote: "I am content either way" (MS in DLC: TJ Papers, 92: 15837-8, undated text entirely in TJ's hand, except for notes and signatures at foot of text by Hamilton and Randolph, probably written and approved sometime between 15 and 20 Aug. 1793, and filed with detatched, but apparently related, sheet bearing TJ's undated notations: "The Secretary of the Treasury & Attorney general of the US." and "the Secy. at war has seen & approved"; PrC in DLC: Madison Papers, torn in part and lacking notations by Hamilton and Randolph).

[16] Preceding six words interlined in Dft in place of "jurisdiction." Emendation not in PrC.

[17] In Dft TJ here canceled the following sentence: "I say *within our jurisdiction*; that is to say, within our territory or by our citizens on the high sea; for the jurisdiction of that element being common to all nations, the country of the criminal decides the jurisdiction." Emendation not in PrC.

[18] Sentence to this point altered in Dft from "But this is not true, because the Constitution gives." Emendation not in PrC.

[19] Preceding five sentences written in the margin in Dft—an emendation that is also in PrC with the exception described in the preceding note.

[20] Clause altered in Dft from "that Henfeild's engagement in the enterprize." Emendation not in PrC.

[21] Preceding two words interlined in Dft in place of "or murder." Emendation not in PrC. TJ had made the same alteration in the sentence as he had first written it in the document described in the following note.

[22] Preceding sentence written in the margin of Dft. Emendation not in PrC.

TJ made this alteration, as well as those recorded in notes 27-30 below, in accordance with a series of revisions that he had previously written on a separate sheet and submitted to Alexander Hamilton and Henry Knox (MS in DLC: TJ Papers, 92: 15835, entirely in TJ's hand, except for subjoined notation of approval in Knox's hand signed by him and Hamilton; undated, but probably written by TJ on 16 Aug. 1793 in consequence of the Cabinet meeting of the preceding day; entitled at head of text "Corrections for the letter to Gouvr. Morris. proposed, for the passages, left open for correction yesterday," words two through six being interlined by TJ in a different ink).

[23] Sentence to this point in Dft interlined in place of "Accordingly the Atty. General of the US. in an official opinion in the case of Henfeild, who was reclaimed by Mr. Genet, declared that." Emendation not in PrC.

[24] Word interlined in Dft in place of "yeilded to these tender circumstances, and." Emendation not in PrC.

[25] In Dft TJ first ended the sentence with "as his first enlistment" before altering the conclusion to read as above.

[26] Word interlined in Dft in place of "prizes."

[27] In accordance with the document described in note 22 above, remainder of sentence written in the margin of Dft in place of "disclaim the power, then it results to the Executive, as charged with the general duty of seeing the laws executed." Emendation not in PrC.

[28] In accordance with the document described in note 22 above, in Dft TJ here canceled "by a special indulgence." Emendation not in PrC.

[29] Preceding two words interlined in Dft in place of "permitted," in accordance with the document described in note 22 above, where the first word is lacking. Emendation not in PrC.

[30] In Dft TJ first wrote "the indulgence of the country, in allowing," and later, in accordance with the document described in note 22 above, altered it to read as above. Emendation not in PrC.

[31] Preceding three words interlined in Dft.

[32] Preceding three words altered in Dft from "would not undertake." Emendation not in PrC.

[33] Word inserted in blank space left in Dft. Emendation not in PrC.

[34] Preceding three words interlined in Dft. Emendation not in PrC.

[35] Closing quotation mark supplied.

[36] In Dft TJ here canceled "that of liberty warring on herself" (see Notes of Cabinet Meeting on Edmond Charles Genet, 20 Aug. 1793). Emendation not in PrC.

[37] In Dft TJ here canceled "of friendship." Emendation not in PrC.

[38] In Dft TJ here canceled "firm and." Emendation not in PrC.

[39] Preceding two words interlined in Dft in place of "affections towards." Emendation not in PrC.

[40] In Dft TJ here canceled "cannot be mistaken, and." Emendation not in PrC.

[41] Altered in Dft from "acceptable."

[42] In Dft TJ first wrote "danger which threatened, and still threatens the colonies of France," and then altered it to read as above. Emendation not in PrC.

[43] In Dft TJ first wrote "from the late

catastrophe of St. Domingo" and later altered it to read as above. Emendation not in PrC.

[44] Word interlined in Dft in place of "permission." Emendation not in PrC.

[45] Preceding clause interlined in Dft in place of "who found two bills against those who had aided France with arms, and against those who had aided her enemies." Emendation not in PrC.

[46] Remainder of sentence in Dft altered from "bespeak partialities the reverse of what he would represent them." Emendation not in PrC.

[47] In Dft TJ here canceled "under their present urgencies." Emendation not in PrC.

[48] Word interlined in Dft in place of "too."

[49] Altered in Dft from "for them." Emendation not in PrC.

[50] Altered in Dft from "after our independance." Emendation not in PrC.

[51] Remainder of text in Dft written by TJ in a different ink after 15 Aug. 1793.

From Joseph Barnes

Sir   London Augt. 17th 1793

This will be presented to you by Mr. Cooper, of Manchester, who is concerned in one of the principal Cotton Manufactury's in that place, And, who, from his great efforts in Society, And in writing in favor of the Specific rights And General Liberty of Mankind, has become so Offensive to the present Spirit of the British Government, that he can No Longer in Safety reside in this Country; he therefore goes to Seek an Asylum in the United States.

As I esteem you, Sir, Our great Patron of Republicanism, And of Virtue, 'tis with peculiar pleasure I give this Letter to you, Your Patronage to him will follow of course, So far as you May find him worthy thereof, And I am Sure he will wish it No farther. With grateful esteem I am Sir Yours most respectfully   JOSEPH BARNES

P.S. The Book Which Mr. Cooper has written and Published, I have been well informed, contains the essentials of Mr. Paine's Rights of men, in excellent Language and great demonstration. He is a friend of Doctor Priestley's and of Mr. Walker, of Manchester.   J. B.

RC (DLC); above postscript: "Mr Jefferson"; endorsed by TJ as received 5 Dec. 1793 and so recorded in SJL.

After an exploratory visit heralded by this letter, Thomas COOPER moved his family to the United States permanently in 1794 and six years later began an extensive correspondence with TJ (DAB; Dumas

Malone, *The Public Life of Thomas Cooper 1783-1839* [New Haven, 1926]). The BOOK by him was *A Reply to Mr. Burke's invective against Mr. Cooper, and Mr. Watt, in the House of Commons, on the 30th of April, 1792* (London, 1792). Cooper presented two copies of it to TJ (Sowerby, Nos. 2803, 2827).

From Joseph Barnes

S<small>IR</small>   London Augt. 17th 1793

This will be presented to you by Mr. Priestley, Son of the celebrated Doctor Priestley, who goes to the United States to Seek an Asylum for his father, And, who, previous to Making a purchase, Means to visit all those parts of the States which he conceives an object, in order to enable him to determine on the Most eligible place to reside.

I am happy in giving him this Letter to you, not only, from a knowledge of your being the Most competent to advise, but from a full Sense of the pleasure you will receive in giving, And he in receiving your advice on the Object of his Mission. With the highest esteem I am Sir yours most respectfully   J<small>OSEPH</small> B<small>ARNES</small>

P.S. I have not as yet got the afairs of my deceased friend Mr. Rumsey, So arranged, as to give you that Specific information I Wish; however, I find that Messrs. Parker & Rogers have Acknowledged from under their hands, the Practical effect of all Mr. Rumsey's Machines Stipulated (except the Steam Vessel, the experiments with which are Not finished) to be fully up to contract, And of course the Stipulated Sums due on the Same; but, Not having yet Settled with the Gentlemen in question, I know not what prospect there is of obtaining the Money So due.

'Tis Some time Since I had the pleasure of an interview with Mr. Pinckney, Who received me with much ease And attention; And, who, on my Suggestion, very obligingly promised to write to France for the requisite information relative to Mr. Rumsey's objects in that country—and added that he Should be happy to Serve me when ever in his power.

J. B.

RC (DLC); above postscript: "Mr T. Jefferson"; endorsed by TJ as received 1 Dec. 1793 and so recorded in SJL.

The S<small>ON</small> and namesake of the <small>CELE-BRATED</small> scientist and Unitarian theologian best known for his discovery of oxygen, Joseph Priestley, Jr., soon began buying land for a projected haven for refugees of English political persecution near North-umberland, Pennsylvania. Although plans for the settlement proved abortive, his father took up residence in Northumberland shortly after arriving in America in June 1794 (Thomas Cooper, *Some Information respecting America* [London, 1794], 24n; Mary C. Park, *Joseph Priestley and the Problem of Pantisocracy* [Philadelphia, 1947], 15-18, 34, 51; <small>DAB</small>).

From Pierce Butler

DEAR SIR   Saturday Morning [17 Aug. 1793]

Permitt me to ask You to run Your Eye over the enclosed; and to tell me if the Post mention'd therein is likely to be Establishd. Tho' the present are not the times for me, or a person of my political sentiments, to be under personal Obligations, Yet it is a duty I owe to the State I represent not to let the Applications of any of it's Citizens sink with me. I shall make them known, whenever they are forwarded to me, in such a way as neither to subject myself to Any Mortification by Refusal, nor to A personal Obligation by granting them. I have the honor to be with Sentiments of sincere Regard and Esteem Dear Sir Yr. Most Obedt. Servt: P BUTLER

RC (DLC); partially dated; addressed: "Honble Mr. Jefferson"; endorsed by TJ as received 17 Aug. 1793 and so recorded in SJL. Enclosure not found.

A letter from Butler to TJ of 1 Mch. 1793, recorded in SJL as received 5 Mch. 1793, has not been found.

George Wythe to Thomas Jefferson and Edmund Randolph

GENTLEMEN   Richmond 17th of august, 1793.

The citizens of Richmond wish you, or one of you, if the other be absent, to present to the president their address which is inclosed with This. I am your friend   G. WYTHE

RC (DLC); addressed: "Thomas Jefferson secretary of state and Edmund Randolph, attorney general, Philadelphia." Enclosure: Inhabitants of Richmond and vicinity to George Washington, Richmond, 17 Aug. 1793, expressing approval of American neutrality policy generally, and of the "propriety, justice, and wisdom" of the Proclamation of Neutrality in particular, and pledging their best efforts to restrain any citizen from violating the peace (RC in DLC: Washington Papers, in a clerk's hand, signed by Wythe "by desire and on behalf of the Meeting," addressed "To, The President of the United States," and endorsed by Bartholomew Dandridge, Jr.; Tr in Lb in same; printed in Marshall, *Papers*, II, 198-200).

With the advent of the neutrality crisis, Federalists opened a campaign to capture public opinion by holding and publicizing the proceedings of a series of mass meetings. Initially these gatherings merely expressed strong approval of the Proclamation of Neutrality, but after French minister Edmond Charles Genet's threat to appeal Washington's handling of foreign policy to the American people became common knowledge earlier this month, Alexander Hamilton and other Federalist leaders orchestrated the adoption of resolutions combining support for the President's neutrality policy with attacks on Genet at rallies in New York, New Jersey, Delaware, and Maryland. As a direct challenge in the Republican heartland, however, the RICHMOND meeting was the most important and the most extensively publicized. Although the widely respected jurist Wythe, TJ's mentor and friend, was astutely chosen to chair the meeting, the rising Federalist attorney John Marshall composed both the ADDRESS and a series of reso- lutions also approved by the Richmond meeting which praised the Proclamation of Neutrality and warned against the interfer- ence of foreign diplomats in American inter- nal affairs lest it "lead to the introduction of foreign gold and foreign armies, with their fatal consequences, dismemberment and partition" (Harry Ammon, "The Genet Mission and the Development of American Political Parties," JAH, LII [1966], 725-41; Marshall, *Papers*, II, 196-7). For the Repub- lican response, see James Madison to TJ, 27 Aug. 1793, and note, and 2 Sep. 1793, and note and enclosure.

To Archibald Campbell

SIR   Philadelphia Aug. 18. 1793.

I have received your favor of the 13th. inst. and am obliged to you for your attention to my little affair of the wine. I must beg the favor of you to send it to Richmond to Colo. Robert Gamble merchant to whom I write on the subject by this post. I must trouble you either to draw on me here for the freight, payable at 3. days sight, or let me know the amount and I will remit it to you in a post bill, whichever will best suit you, including therein the freight to Richmond, if you please, because I had rather pay it here than there. I will thank you to send it by the first safe conveyance *to Richmond*, and not to any other place from which it will be to be reshipped for Richmond. As I go to Virginia soon, I should wish it to be arrived in time at my own house.

Mr. Fenwick has sent me no particular invoice, but an account only in which, among other articles, this occupies one line, to wit. $\frac{T!}{T}$ 14 cases of 36. bottles each is 504. bottles Medoc (bottles included) 1008.^{tt} The exchange at the foot of the account is 15d. sterl. for 3.^{tt} and 4/6 sterl. the dollar. Not knowing how the duty is paid, whether on the wine and bottles together or separately I give you their statement separately thus.

	tt	
504. bottles of Medoc, bottle included,	1008.	
bottles & bottling, corks &c	252.	
cost of wine exclusive of bottles	756	at the above exchange is 70. Dollars.

If I can be informed of the amount of the duty I will send the necessary obligation for it to Baltimore or give it here, as the collector pleases. Repeating my thanks for your trouble & attention, I am Sir Your most obedt & most humble servt   TH: JEFFERSON

PrC (DLC); at foot of text: "Mr. Archi- bald Campbell."

The ACCOUNT, which is missing, was en- closed in Fenwick, Mason & Company to TJ, 16 May 1793.

To J. P. P. Derieux

Dear Sir   Philadelphia Aug. 18. 1793.

I am mortified at not having written to you ere this, but if you could follow me from morning to night and from Sunday to Saturday you would agree that I am excusable in not writing when I have nothing essential to communicate. The truth is that for some time past Mr. Vaughan has promised to have your affair wound up and the balance remitted in cash. I was to have had it the week before last, last week, this week, but I have it not yet. But I believe you may count on it in a week or two. I know nothing of the sum, nor did he, as the business has remained in D'Homassel's hands. The moment I receive his note, it shall be forwarded. My friendly respects to Me. De Rieux & am Dear Sir Your friend & servt   Th: Jefferson

PrC (DLC: TJ Papers, 91: 15748); at foot of text: "M. De Rieux." Tr (ViU: Edgehill-Randolph Papers); 19th-century copy.

To Robert Gamble

Dear Sir   Philadelphia Aug. 18. 1793.

Having just received information from Mr. Archibald Campbell merchant of Baltimore of the arrival there of 14. cases of claret for me, I have taken the liberty of desiring him to forward it to Richmond to your address, he drawing on me here for the freight to Richmond. I take this liberty because you will best know of the conveyances up to Monticello, to which place I would pray you to send it by the first *safe* conveyance. I had meant also to take the liberty of addressing to you from this place some stores, of which I shall have occasion on a visit I shall make to Monticello, soon after the stores will go from hence. Consequently shall have to pray your forwarding them also as speedily as can be done *safely* as I know it is not every waggoner who merits to be trusted. After asking your excuse for the freedom of this trouble, I conclude with assurances of the esteem & respect of Dear Sir Your most obedt humble Servt   Th: Jefferson

PrC (DLC); at foot of text: "Colo. Robert Gamble." Tr (ViU: Edgehill-Randolph Papers); 19th-century copy; misdated 8 Aug. 1793.

To James Madison

DEAR SIR   Aug. 18. 93.

My last was of the 11th. since which yours of the 5th. and 11th. are received. I am mortified at your not having your cypher. I now send the key of the numbers in mine of the 3d. This with my letter of the 11th. by post and another of the same date by Davy Randolph who will be at Monticello the last week of this month will put you in possession of the state of things to that date. The paper I now inclose will fill up chinks and needs not a word of explanation. To these I must add that orders are given to drive out of our ports the privateers which have been armed in them before the 5th. of June, by gentler means if it can be done, and if not, by the ultima ratio: and we are seising the prizes brought in since Aug. 7. to restore them to their owners. For those between June 5. and Aug. 7. we engage restitution or compensation. The inclosed paper will explain these distinctions of date, and justify the proceedings.—I return you the little thing of Ld. Chath's because, for particular reasons, were it now to appear it would be imputed to me, and because it will have more effect if published after the meeting of Congress.—I rejoice at the resurrection of Franklin. There was a charming thing from the same pen (I conjecture) on the subject of instrumentality lately published by Freneau from the Virga. papers.—The addresses in support of the proclamation are becoming universal, and as universal a rising in support of the President against Genet. Observe that the inclosed paper has been only read in cabinet for the 1st. time as yet. On that reading H. objected to expressions implying a censure on other nations ('the war of liberty on herself &c.'). He thought expressions of friendship to France suited the occasion. But R. protested against every expression of friendship to that nation lest they should offend the other party, and intimated that he should move to eradicate them all. It will pretty effectually tear up the instrument if he succeeds. Nous verrons. Adieu.—P.S. You are free to shew the inclosed to Colo. Monroe. If the appeal which I have mentioned to you, should be pushed, I think that by way of compromise, I shall propose that instead of that, the whole correspondence be laid before Congress, merely as a matter of information. What would you think of this?

RC (DLC: Madison Papers); unsigned; with postscript added in a different ink. PrC (DLC). Tr (MHi); 19th-century copy with gaps and errors. Enclosures: (1) Partial Key to Code No. 9, consisting of ninety-nine ciphers and their equivalents in two columns, with a note written lengthwise between them: "many numbers are inserted which were not in the letter, merely to baffle all attempts to make out what was in it" (MS in DLC: Madison Papers, entirely in TJ's hand; PrC in DLC: TJ Papers, 91: 15747; Tr in MHi, 19th-century copy). Despite TJ's notation, all but nine of the ciphers were used in his 3 Aug. 1793 letter to Madison. (2) PrC of Dft of TJ to Gouverneur Morris, 16 Aug. 1793.

For the ORDERS to DRIVE OUT privateers armed in American ports, see Alexander Hamilton's 4 Aug. 1793 circular to the collectors of the customs (described in note to Rules on Neutrality, 3 Aug. 1793) and Henry Knox's 16 Aug. 1793 circular to the state governors (Washington, *Journal*, 221). LITTLE THING OF LD. CHATH'S: see note to Madison to TJ, 11 Aug. 1793.

On 3 Aug. 1793 the *National Gazette* reprinted an essay by "Turn-Coat" from the 22 July 1793 Richmond *Virginia Gazette* which attacked the fiscal policy of the Secretary of the Treasury by satirically praising his use of the term INSTRUMENTALITY in reports to Congress in February 1793 to explain why he did not apply to the redemption of the public debt certain funds borrowed in Europe for that purpose, a subject on which TJ had himself criticized Hamilton (Syrett, *Hamilton*, XIV, 32, 94; Editorial Note on Jefferson's questions and observations on the application of France, at 12 Feb. 1793).

To Martha Jefferson Randolph

MY DEAR MARTHA   Philadelphia Aug. 18. 93.

Maria and I are scoring off the weeks which separate us from you. They wear off slowly, but time is sure tho' slow. Mr. D. Randolph left us three days ago. He went by the way of Presquisle and consequently will not enrapture Mrs. Randolph till the latter end of the month. I wrote to Mr. Randolph sometime ago to desire he would send off Tom Shackleford or Jupiter or any body else on the 1st. of September with the horse he has been so kind as to procure for me to meet at George town (at Shuter's tavern) a servant whom I shall send from hence on the same day with Tarquin, to exchange them, Tarquin to go to Monticello and the other come here to aid me in my journey. The messenger to ride a mule and lead the horse. I mention these things now, lest my letter should have miscarried. I received information yesterday of 500 bottles of wine arrived for me at Baltimore. I desired them to be sent to Richmond to Colo. Gamble to be forwarded to Monticello. They will be followed the next week with some things from hence. Should any waggons of the neighborhood be going down they might enquire for them. With the things sent from hence will go clothes for the servants to replace those sent last winter, which I did not conclude to be irrecoverably lost till Mr. Randolph's last letter. My blessings to your little ones, love to you all, and friendly how d-ye's to my good neighbors. Adieu. Your's affectionately   TH: JEFFERSON

RC (NNP); at foot of text: "Mrs. Randolph"; endorsed by Mrs. Randolph. PrC (MHi). Tr (ViU: Edgehill-Randolph Papers); 19th-century copy.

To George Washington

[ca. 18-19 Aug. 1793]

Th: Jefferson on examination of the subject finds that the resolution for restoring or compensating prizes taken by the proscribed vessels was agreed to by the heads of departments and Atty. Genl. on the 5th. There was a difference of opinion how far it should be communicated to Mr. Hammond; the President was pleased to call at the office of Th:J. and to decide in favor of a full communication, on the same day (between 2. and 3. aclock he believes). Th:J. on considering the subject, found it would require caution of expression in both letters, that is, to Mr. Genet and Mr. Hammond. He took therefore till the next day to prepare the draughts. The President called on him in the country the next morning (the 6th.) and after his departure, Th:J. went on with the beginning of the letter to Mr. Gouvr. Morris, which he had begun, and had read a part of to the President. He was therefore later than usual in going to town. When he arrived there he sent the two draughts of letters to Genet and Hammond for the President's approbation. Whether they did not come back to his office till he had left town, or whether they could not be copied in time, he does not recollect; but he finds the press copy of the letter to Mr. Genet, in Mr. Taylor's hand writing, dated Aug. 7.

RC (DNA: RG 59, MLR); undated; addressed: "The President of the US."; endorsed by Tobias Lear in part: "without date—But must have been written about the 18 or 19 Augt 1793." Tr (Lb in same, SDC). Not recorded in SJL.

This letter may be related to the arrival in Philadelphia on 14 Aug. 1793 of the *Hope*, a British sloop from Antigua, and the *Alodia*, an American sloop under Spanish registry from New Orleans. Both ships had been captured by French privateers commissioned by Edmond Charles Genet in the United States and thus fell within the purview of the Cabinet decision ON THE 5TH.

concerning the restoration of such prizes. The President himself only learned officially of their arrival on 17 Aug. 1793, which might account for the conjectural dates Tobias Lear assigned to TJ's letter (Washington, *Journal*, 222, 223n; Cabinet Opinions on Privateers and Prizes, 5 Aug. 1793). Both prizes were restored to their owners (*Dunlap's American Daily Advertiser*, 19 Aug. 1793; *Counter Case*, 610-11).

The final version of the LETTER TO MR. GOUVR. MORRIS was dated 16 Aug. 1793; TJ described reading A PART OF an early draft of it to the President in his first letter to James Madison of 11 Aug. 1793.

From Angelica Schuyler Church

Down Place august 19. 1793

Your letter my dear Sir arrives in time to encourage me to solicit your friendship for a friend of yours and mine, as well as to thank you for your attention to my recommendation. How changed are the fortunes and situations of those we loved at Paris! and whose Welfare were dear to us; La Fayette is in prison at Magdebourg; and enclosed is the extract of a letter he has been so fortunate as to find means of conveying to a friend and relation, who has sought an Asylum in this country; His Love of Liberty has rendered him culpable in the eyes of a Despot: and you Sir cannot read the recital of his sufferings without tears.

General Washington's interference is the only hope left to him and his family;

Madame de Corney is a widow with a very limitted fortune, and retired to Rouen; Mrs. Cosway gone into a convent at Genoa: Monsieur de Condorcet under accusation, but fortunately escaped or concealed in France, Custine *a l'abbaye* a sacrifice for the fall of Valenciennes. And the Queen of France at the conciergerie, and taking her Tryal, Marat assasinated by the *Republicaine* Cordét, who suffered Death with the fortitude and tranquillity of Innocence; I hope soon to remove from the vicinity of such horrors; and retire to America, where I shall look forward with impatience to bring Catherine to her friend Maria, and to renew the assurances of my friendship and to express the satisfaction I receive from Your friendly letter: ANGELICA CHURCH

RC (DLC); at foot of text: "Thomas Jefferson Esq"; endorsed by TJ as received 7 Nov. 1793 and so recorded in SJL.

ENCLOSURE

Lafayette to the Princesse d'Hénin

Magdebourg ce 15 Mars. [1793]

Imaginé vous une ouverture pratiqué dans le rempart de La Citadelle et entouré d'une haute et forte palissade; c'est par la qu'en ouvrant successivement quatre portes, dont chacun armée de chaines, Cadenats, et Bars de fers, on parvient non sans peine et sans bruit jusques a mon cachot, large de trois pieds, et long de cinq et demi; il est Lugubre, humide, et m'offre pour tout ornemens, deux vers françois qui riment par *souffrir* et *Mourir*. Le mur du coté du fossé, se moisée, et celui du devant laisse voir le jour, mais non pas *le soleil*, par une petite fenetre grillét; deux sentinelles dont la vüe plonge dans mon souterrain, mais en dehors de la palissade, pour quils ne parlent pas, des observateurs etrangeres a la guarde; et puis tous ce qu il y a de murs, de rempart, de fossés, et des gardes, en dehors, et dedans de la citadelle de Magdebourg.

La Bruante ouverture de mes quatre portes se renouvelle le matin pour introduire mon domestique; a diner pour manger en presence du commandeur de le Citadelle et de celui de la garde, et le soir pour ramener mon domestique en prison, et apres avoir refermé sur moi toutes les clefs, le commandeur les emporte dans le logement ou depuis notre arrivée le Roi lui ordonné de coucher.

J'ai des livres dont on ote les feüilles blanc, mais point des nouvelles, point des gazettes, point de communication, ni encre, ni plumes, ni papier, ni crayon, c'est *par miracle* que je possede cette feüille, et je vous ecrit avec un curedens.—

Ma santé se deteriore journellement: ma constitution physique a presque autant de besoin de liberté, que ma constitution morale; le peu d'air qui m'arrive en sejournant dans le souterrain, detruise ma poitrine, la fievre sans mele souvent, point d'exercise, peu de sommeil; je *ne me plains plus*, et sais par experience qu'il est au moins inutile de le faire savoir; mais je m'obstine a vivre, et mes amis peuvent compter sur la reunion de tous les sentimens que ma porte a la conservation de moi meme, quoique d'apres ma situation, et le progress de mes souffrances, je ne puisse pas repondre longtems de leur efficacité, peutetre me vaut il mieux les affliger d'avance, que de les surprendre aussi triestement.

Tr (DLC: TJ Papers, 86: 14837-8); extract in the hand of Angelica Schuyler Church; partially dated; at foot of text: "Copied from a letter recived by the Princess d'henin which letter has been sent by Mr. Church, to the President of the united States."

From George Hammond

SIR   Philadelphia 19th August 1793

As the several points, which have been for the last four months under constant discussion between this government and myself, have involved in them questions of the highest national importance to our respective countries, and demanded an immediate investigation and decision; I have been unwilling to mix with them any other matters, not immediately connected with them, or of a distinct and subordinate nature. For this reason, I have deemed it expedient to suspend until this time the observations that I have always intended to submit to you, on your letter of the 18th of April on the case of Mr. Pagan, and on the communications from the Attorney General which it inclosed. I trust Sir that you will have esteemed this delay justified by the considerations above stated, and will not have construed it into a dereliction, either of the Arguments I have formerly alleged, or of the principles I have advanced, upon this subject.

It is not my intention to repeat the several circumstances I have stated in my different communications, in regard—to Mr. Pagan's long and rigorous confinement—to the impropriety of the Judges of the supreme judicial court of Massachusets ever taking cognizance of this question—or to the conduct of those Judges in *still persisting* in their neglect to file their reasons in this cause, according to their solemn assurance of the 27th. of June 1791, which assurance induced the committee of the general court of Massachusets, that had been appointed to enquire into this business, to proceed no farther in it. These facts having been already sufficiently explained, I shall confine myself to the actual situation of the case, as presented in your letter, and in that of the Attorney General.

The observations of the Attorney General may be considered under two points of view—the mode of Mr. Pagan's application to the Supreme federal Court—and the principles, which the Attorney General imagines would have influenced the decision of the Judges, had the writ of error been granted, and the merits of the question submitted to their deliberation.

In regard to the application itself to the Supreme federal Court, I must premise that that measure did not originate in Mr. Pagan or his advisers, but was adopted solely in conformity to a suggestion of yours and of the Attorney General, prescribing this preliminary course of proceeding, as necessary to be pursued, before it could be incumbent on the executive government of the United States to take the subject into its consideration. As to the manner in which the application was enforced—the abilities and integrity of the Lawyer employed by Mr. Pagan are too well known, to excite any suspicion of his neglecting any arguments, which could have promoted the cause of his client. The decision of the Court therefore is the sole circumstance to which it is proper to advert. This was conclusive and fatal to all Mr. Pagan's expectations of obtaining judicial redress. Since the *unanimous* refusal of the Judges to grant the writ of error incontestibly evinced their sense of this case not being of a nature to be susceptible of relief by process of law.

With respect to the Attorney General's opinion, that had the question been fairly brought before the Supreme federal Court "the very merits are against Mr. Pagan"—This opinion is founded *solely* on the difference of the construction of the armistice, by the government of Great Britain, and by that of the United States. It is not necessary to the present question to endeavour to ascertain which interpretation is the most accurate: But I must assert unequivocally that, in neither country, has a Court of Law any right to re-judge the validity of a prize legally condemned by the proper authority in the other. If a citizen of the United States imagines that he has just reason to complain of the principle that may have been established in the British Courts of Admiralty there are means of appeal open to him, or the whole question may fairly become a matter of negociation between the two sovereigns. But by these modes only, can the citizen or subject of either country seek redress. For if it once be admitted that the courts of law in the country, to which the property captured originally belonged, can take cognizance of the validity of its condemnation, by the proper tribunals of the country of the subjects making the capture, the system established for ages upon this point would be subverted, and such a source of litigation opened as it would be almost impossible to repress. In the case of the Silesia loan, the contrary position has been asserted with so much force and perspicuity, as to leave no doubt of its legality as well as of its reasonableness—

"Prize or not prize must be determined by Courts of Admiralty, belonging to the power, whose subjects make the capture." In the propriety of the reasoning contained in the passage, extracted by the Attorney General from the same performance—that "the law of nations founded upon justice, equity, convenience and the reason of the thing, and confirmed by long usage, does not allow of reprisals, except in case of violent injuries, directed and supported by the state, and *justice absolutely denied, in re minime dubia, by all the tribunals, and afterwards by the prince*"—I perfectly acquiesce as applicable to the case of Mr. Pagan: And I therefore venture to hope that the executive government of the United States (in this instance the Prince) will alter its determination, expressed, Sir, in your letter of the 18th. of April, and, as Mr. Pagan has been declared not susceptible of obtaining relief by process of law, will extend to him such redress as to its wisdom and justice shall appear adequate and satisfactory.

Before I conclude, I must intreat you, Sir, to favor me with an answer, as early as convenient: Since Mr. Pagan is naturally become more and more impatient to learn the *final* decision of this government, and since his health, which has already suffered considerably, may sustain still greater injury by the farther continuance of his imprisonment. I have the honor to be with sentiments of great respect Sir your most obedient humble Servant   GEO. HAMMOND

RC (DNA: RG 59, NL); in a clerk's hand, signed by Hammond; at foot of first page: "Mr Jefferson"; endorsed by TJ as received 19 Aug. 1793 and so recorded in SJL. FC (Lb in PRO: FO 116/3); misdated 15 Aug. 1793. Tr (same, 5/1); misdated 15 Aug. 1793. Tr (Lb in DNA: RG 59, NL).

For a discussion of the dispute between Thomas Pagan and Stephen Hooper, see note to Hammond to TJ, 26 Nov. 1791.

From Richard Söderström

SIR   Philadelphia 19. Augt: 1793.

It is my Duty to represent that the Swedish Schooner Jane commanded by Benjn. Stanners and owned by Richard Barden, Burghers of the Island of St. Bartholomew and Subjects of the King of Sweden lately loaded in Philadelphia by Mr: Robt: Ralston with Lumber, Flour, Bees wax and Sugar the Property of the Said Ralston was in her Voyage from hence to Fayal on Saturday last Captured about 5. Leagues from Land by a privateer called the Petit Democrat un lawfully fitted out in the Port of Philadelphia, and has been brought in to the Said Port where she now Rides. That the Said Privateer took out of the Said

Schooner, three Negro Slaves the Property of the Said Barden and two White Sailors of what Nation I know not. Under these Circumstances I trust there will be an immediate order for the Restoration of the Vessell and Cargo—and I have the Honor to remain with Respect Sir Your most Obd: Hble. Servt   RICHD: SÖDERSTRÖM

His Swed: Majs: Consul in America

RC (DNA: RG 59, NFC); at foot of text: "To the Honble. Thos: Jefferson Secret: of State for the united States of America Philadelphia"; endorsed by TJ as received 19 Aug. 1793 and so recorded in SJL.

From George Washington

SIR   August 19th: 1793

I send, for the consideration and opinion of the Heads of the Departments and the Attorney General of the U.S. a communication from the Governor of Pennsylvania respecting the Privateer Citizen Genet—together with Copies of two letters from the French Consul to the Governor on the same subject, and a Report of two persons who had examined the Aforesaid Privateer by the Governor's order. [1]

The Gentlemen will decide whether the circumstances reported respecting the unfitness of the said Privateer to proceed to sea, are such as would make it proper to depart from the rules already adopted, and[2] allow a longer time for her to prepare to depart than is granted by the Governor—or whether the orders given by him on this head shall be executed.

It will be seen that this Subject requires dispatch—and the Secretary of War will inform the Governor of the result of your deliberations on this subject as soon as it is given.   GO: WASHINGTON

RC (DLC); in Tobias Lear's hand, signed by Washington; at foot of text: "The Secretary of State"; endorsed by TJ as received 19 Aug. 1793. Dft (DNA: RG 59, MLR); entirely in Lear's hand; with two significant variations noted below. FC (Lb in same, SDC); wording follows Dft. Recorded in SJPL. Enclosures: (1) Thomas Mifflin to Washington, Philadelphia, 19 Aug. 1793, stating that he is enclosing copies of Nos. 2 and 4, which he received in consequence of a letter he wrote to Dupont and communicated to Henry Knox on the 17th, and a copy of No. 3, which was prompted by the need to investigate allegations about the *Citoyen Genet*'s want of provisions, leakage,

and poor rigging prior to ordering the ship peremptorily to depart; and that though No. 3 will give the President a chance to exercise any discretion he thinks proper, he himself does not think that it would be consistent with the instructions of 16 Aug. to grant the ship the eight-day indulgence requested by Dupont and therefore will order it this morning to leave port within twenty-four hours while allowing it to take on provisions (FC in PHarH: Governor's Letterbook). (2) François Dupont to Mifflin, 17 Aug. 1793, stating that since the *Citoyen Genet* was without provisions and leaking, and its sails were torn up, he wishes the governor to ask the President to allow the ship to stay eight days in Philadelphia for repairs; and that he is astonished at the guards who have seized French ships, a practice that stands in sharp contrast to the favorable treatment the National Convention's 9 May decree has extended to American ships vis-a-vis those of other neutral nations. (3) William Allen and John Justice to Mifflin, 17 Aug. 1793, stating that, having investigated the *Citoyen Genet* at his request, they find it to be so unseaworthy by virtue of battle damage that even the crew refuses to remain on it. (4) Dupont to Mifflin, 19 Aug. 1793, stating that, since the *Citoyen Genet* had been properly commissioned as a French privateer in Charleston and departed before the Proclamation of Neutrality became known there, and in view of French treaty rights and the poor condition of the ship, he hopes the President will allow it the time needed to make itself seaworthy in Philadelphia; that even without a treaty armed ships cannot be refused such a favor; and that he is not authorized to comply with his request to alter the ship but has transmitted it to the owners (RCs in same, Executive Correspondence; Nos. 2 and 4 in French).

Under the terms of a 16 Aug. 1793 circular letter from Henry Knox, the *Citoyen Genet* was one of five French privateers fitted out in the United States to which state governors were enjoined to deny asylum in American ports (Knox to Mifflin, 16 Aug. 1793, PHarH: Executive Correspondence; Washington, *Journal*, 221). The Cabinet agreed this day that the Secretary of War

should inform Governor Mifflin that the President was willing to allow the *Citoyen Genet* to make itself seaworthy in Philadelphia, but only if it transformed itself from an armed privateer to an unarmed merchant ship, a decision of which Knox promptly informed Mifflin in a letter written by TJ's chief clerk, George Taylor, Jr. (Knox to Mifflin, 19 Aug. 1793, PHarH: Executive Correspondence; Washington, *Journal*, 224). Mifflin immediately notified Dupont, the French consul in Philadelphia, of Washington's offer, but before the *Citoyen Genet* could take advantage of it, the ship was attached by order of the United States District Court of Pennsylvania, apparently in response to a complaint by the owner or agent of one of the privateer's prizes. Its privateering career was thus ended temporarily, though once the attachment was lifted it left port and resumed operations (Mifflin to Dupont, 19, 20 Aug. 1793, to the Captain of the *Citoyen Genet*, 20 Aug. 1793, to the Commander of Fort Mifflin, 20 Aug. 1793, and to Washington, 20, 21 Aug. 1793, in PHarH: Governor's Letterbook; TJ to Edmond Charles Genet, 16 Sep. 1793; George Hammond to Lord Grenville, 17 Sep. 1793, PRO: FO 5/1; Syrett, *Hamilton*, xv, 372-3; Woodfin, "Citizen Genet," 607-8).

[1] Dft here adds "which were enclosed in the Governors letter to me."

[2] Preceding seven words interlined in Dft.

From Zebulon Hollingsworth

SIR   Baltimore Augt. 20th. 1793

I have the honour to enclose you a communication from the Collector of the Customs of the Port of Baltimore. As I have not yet received any instructions from the Executive of the United States on this subject I request you to lay this letter before the President. I am with very sincere respect your obedt servt   (signed) Z HOLLINGSWORTH

Tr (MdAA); at foot of text: "Honble Thomas Jefferson"; certified by John Stagg, Jr., Chief Clerk of the War Office, 22 Aug. 1793. Enclosure: Daniel Delozier to

Hollingsworth, Collector's Office, Baltimore, 19 Aug. 1793, reporting, pursuant to general instructions received from the Secretary of the Treasury, that the brigantine

Maxwell of Kirkcudbright, Thomas Milrae commander, has been captured and sent into Baltimore by the schooner *Sans Cu-* *lotte*, a privateer fitted out in Charleston (Tr in same; certified by Stagg). Enclosed in TJ to Henry Knox, 22 Aug. 1793.

From James Madison

DEAR SIR   Aug: 20. 93

Your favor of the 11th. came to hand the day before yesterday. I am just setting off to Monroe's and hope to prevent the trouble of an express from Monticello with the letter referred to in it. I have already acquainted you with the immediate object of this visit. I have just received a line from him expressing a particular desire to communicate with me, and reminding me that he sets off the last of this month for the Courts, and of course will be occupied for some days before with preparations. This hurries me: and has forced me to hurry what will be inclosed herewith, particularly the last No. V which required particular care in the execution. I shall be obliged to leave that and the greater part of the other Nos. to be transcribed sealed up[1] and forwarded in my absence. It is certain therefore that many little errors will take place. As I can not let them be detained till I return, I must pray you to make such corrections as will not betray your hand. In pointing and *erasures* not breaking the sense, there will be no difficulty. I have already requested you to make free with the latter. You will find more quotations from the Fedt. Dark them out if you think the most squeamish Critic could object to them. In No. 5. I suggest to your attention a long preliminary remark into which I suffered myself to be led before I was aware of the prolixity. As the piece is full long without it, it had probably better be lopped off. The propriety of the two last paragraphs claims your particular criticism. I would not have hazarded them without the prospect of your revisal,[2] and if proper, your erasure. That which regards Spain &c. may contain unsound reasoning, or be too delicate to be touched in a Newspaper. The propriety of the last, as to the President's answers to addresses, depends[3] on the truth of the fact, of which you can judge. I am not sure that I have seen all the answers. My last was of the 12th. and covered the 2 first Nos. of H—s:[4] I am assured that it was put into the post office on tuesday evening. It ought therefore to have reached you on Saturday last. As an opportunity to Fredg.[5] may happen before more than the 3d. No. may be transcribed, it is possible, that this may be accompanied by that alone.

The drouth has been dreadful to the Corn. There has been no rain making any sensible impression for seven weeks, of the hottest weather of the hottest year remembered: and at the very period critical to that crop. Yesterday afternoon we had a small shower—and more seemed to be passing around us. No weather however can now possibly add 5 perCt. to the prospect. There can not be more than half crops made generally and much less in many places. Yrs. affy

RC (DLC: Madison Papers); unsigned; addressed: "*private* Mr. Jefferson Philadelphia"; endorsed by TJ as received 30 Aug. 1793 and so recorded in SJL.

INCLOSED HEREWITH were probably drafts of the third and fourth "Helvidius" essays (Madison, *Papers*, xv, 95-103, 106-10). NO. V was not enclosed in this letter, but it reached TJ by 8 Sep. 1793. No letter from

Madison to TJ OF THE 12TH. has been found or is recorded in SJL, but see his letter of the preceding day.

[1] Preceding two words interlined.
[2] Remainder of sentence interlined.
[3] Madison here canceled "chiefly."
[4] At a later date Madison interlined "Helvidius" above this abbreviation.
[5] Preceding two words interlined.

Notes of Cabinet Meeting on Edmond Charles Genet

Aug. 20. We met at the President's to examine by paragraphs the draught of a letter I had prepared to Gouverneur Morris, on the conduct of Mr. Genet. There was no difference of opinion on any part of it, except on this expression. 'An attempt to embroil both, to add still another nation to the enemies of his country, and to draw on both a reproach, which it is hoped will never stain the history of either, that of *liberty warring on herself*.' H. moved to strike out these words 'that of liberty warring on herself.' He urged generally that it would give offence to the combined powers, that it amounted to a declaration that they were warring on liberty, that we were not called on to declare that the cause of France was that of liberty, that he had at first been with them with all his heart, but that he had long since left them, and was not for encoraging the idea here that[1] the cause of France was the cause of liberty in general, or could have either connection or influence in our affairs.—Knox according to custom jumped plump into all his opinions.—The Pr. with a good deal of positiveness declared in favor of the expression, that he considered the pursuit of France to be that of liberty, however they might sometimes fail of the best means of obtaining it, that he had never at any time entertained a doubt of their ultimate success, if they hung well together, and that as to their dissensions there were such contradictory accounts given that no one could tell what to believe.—I observed that it had been supposed among us all along that the present letter might become public; that we had therefore 3 parties to attend to. 1. France, 2. her enemies, 3. the people of the US. That as to the enemies of France it ought not to offend them, because the passage objected to only spoke of an attempt to make the US., *a free nation*, war on France, *a free nation*, which would be liberty warring on herself[2] and therefore a true fact. That as to France, we were taking so harsh a measure (desiring her to recall her minister) that a precedent for it could scarcely be found, that we knew that minister would represent to his government that our Executive was hostile to liberty, leaning to monarchy, and would endeavor to parry the charges on himself, by rendering suspicious the source from which they flowed: that therefore it was essential to satisfy France not only of our friendship[3] to her, but our attachment to the general cause of liberty, and to hers in particular. That as to the people of the US. we knew there were suspicions abroad that the Executive in some of it's parts were tainted with a hankering after monarchy, an indisposition towards liberty and towards the French cause; and that it was important by an explicit declaration to remove these suspicions and restore the confidence of the people in their government. R. opposed the passage on nearly the same ground with H. He added that he thought it had been agreed that this correspondence should contain no expressions which could give offence to either party.—I replied that it had been my opinion in the beginning of the correspondence that while we were censuring the conduct of the French minister, we should make the most cordial declarations of friendship to them: that in the first letter or two of the correspondence I had inserted expressions of that kind but that himself and the other two gentlemen had struck them out: that I thereupon conformed to their opinions in my subsequent letters, and had carefully avoided the insertion of a single term of friendship to the French nation, and the letters were as dry and husky as if written between the generals of two enemy nations. That on the present occasion however it had been agreed that such expressions ought to be inserted in the letter now under consideration, and I had accordingly charged it pretty well with them. That I had further thought it essential to satisfy the French and our own citizens of the light in which we viewed their cause, and of our fellow feeling for the general cause of liberty, and had ventured only four words on that subject, that there was not from beginning to end of the letter one other expression or word in favor of liberty, and I should think it singular at least if the single passage of that character should be struck out.—The President again spoke. He came into the idea that attention was due to the two parties who had been mentioned France and US. That as to the former, thinking it certain their affairs would issue in a government of some sort, of considerable freedom, it was the only[4] nation with whom our relations could be counted on: that as to the US. there could be no doubt of their universal attachment to the cause of France, and of the solidity of their republicanism. He declared his strong attachment to the expression, but finally left it to us to accomodate. It was struck out of course, and the expressions of affection in the context were a good deal taken down.

MS (DLC); entirely in TJ's hand; partially dated, with month torn away and faded word supplied from PrC. PrC (DLC: James Madison Papers). Entry in SJPL: "Notes of meeting on Th:J's lre to G. Morris respecting Genet." Included in the "Anas." Presumably enclosed in TJ to James Madison, 25 Aug. 1793.

DRAUGHT OF A LETTER: see TJ to Gouverneur Morris, 16 Aug. 1793.

[1] TJ here canceled "our."
[2] Remainder of sentence interlined.
[3] Word interlined in place of "attachment."
[4] Word interlined.

From William Short

SIR
St. Ildefonso Aug. 20. 1793

This letter is merely to inclose you a copy of the convention between this country and England. For what reason I know not an uncommon degree of secrecy has been observed with respect to it, even since its being signed. And as yet very few persons even of the corps diplomatique have had a sight of it, or have even known with certainty, whether any such convention was really signed; although it has been suspected by most of them that something had been concluded on between the two countries.

Although it is probable it will be published in England and thus get to you sooner by that route still I have thought it proper by way of precaution to send you the copy which the departure of the post has barely allowed me time to take. I shall by the next post forward it to you by duplicate.

It would seem that the usual language of such pieces, had been abolished, as it was signed I believe only in Spanish and English. I have only seen it in the former. It was communicated to me as a mark of particular friendship and confidence, by a person whose name I am not at liberty to mention, and which of course would be useless. I have the honor to be most respectfully sir, your most obedient & most humble servt.

W SHORT

PrC (DLC: Short Papers); at head of text: "*No. 127*"; at foot of text: "The Secretary of State for the U.S. Philadelphia." Tr (DNA: RG 46, Senate Records, 3d Cong., 1st sess.). Tr (Lb in same, TR). Tr (Lb in DNA: RG 59, DD). Recorded in SJL as received 4 Nov. 1793. Enclosure: Convention of Aranjuez between Great Britain and Spain, 25 May 1793 (Tr in Lb in DNA: RG 59, DD, English translation; Tr in DNA: RG 46, Senate Records, 3d Cong., 1st sess.; printed in ASP, *Foreign Relations*, I, 277). Letter and enclosure enclosed in TJ to George Washington, 5 Nov. 1793.

To Richard Söderström

Philadelphia August 20. 1793.

I duly received your letter of yesterday stating that the schooner Jane belonging to subjects of his Swedish Majesty, had been taken on the high seas by the Petit Democrat a french armed vessel, and was brought into this Port, and desiring an order for her restitution. In the conversation I had the honor of having with you on the same subject you seemed to expect this might be done under the rule for restitution lately established by the President: but that rule was that prises taken from either of the belligerent parties by vessels which had been clandestinely armed by the other in our ports should be restored. But Sweden not being of the powers at War, you will immediately perceive that the rule does not apply to her.

The transaction in question having taken place between nations at peace with each other its discussion belongs to the judiciary department. The Court of Admiralty has full power to give all the redress which by the law of Nations may be given in such cases. To that Court therefore I recommend to you to apply; assuring you at the same time that the Executive of the United States will on its part be careful to extend to the vessels and subjects of his Swedish Majesty while in their Ports the full protection of their laws, and will with real satisfaction embrace every occasion of proving their desire to cultivate the friendship of his Swedish Majesty and to render to his subjects all the good offices which friendly nations owe to each other. I have the honor to be with great esteem Sir Your most obedt. and most humble servt.

Th: Jefferson

PrC (DLC); in a clerk's hand, except for signature by TJ and note at foot of text by George Taylor, Jr.: "The consul of Sweden." FC (Lb in DNA: RG 59, DL).

From George Buchanan

Hon'd Sir   Balte August 21 1793

I hope I have not taken too great a liberty in Dedicating the enclosed to you, the subject I know corresponds with your principles, and the civilities which I had the honor of receiving from you while in Paris, not being obliterated from my memory, enduced me to it. And should it meet with your approbation it will add much to my satisfaction.

I have sent the President a Copy, accompanyed with a letter, offering myself a Candidate for the office vacated by the death of Col. Balard of this Town—and great would be my obligation Sir, if I could pray your assistance in obtaining the request; and trusting that you will immediately make intercession for me before it is too late, suffer me to subscribe myself your very humble servant & Friend   GEO BUCHANAN

RC (DLC); endorsed by TJ as received 26 Aug. 1793 and so recorded in SJL. Enclosure: George Buchanan, *An Oration upon the Moral and Political Evil of Slavery. Delivered at a public Meeting of the Maryland Society, for promoting the Abolition of Slavery, And the Relief of Free Negroes, and others unlawfully held in Bondage. Baltimore, July 4th, 1791* (Baltimore, 1793). See Sowerby, No. 2816.

The dedication of THE ENCLOSED lauded TJ as one "whose Patriotism, since the American Revolution, has been uniformly marked, by a sincere, steady and active Attachment to the Interest of his Country; and whose literary Abilities have distinguished him amongst the first of Statesmen and Philosophers." Buchanan's LETTER to George Washington also bore this date (DLC: Washington Papers, Applications for Office). Robert Ballard was inspector of the port of Baltimore when his death VACATED the office (JEP, I, 104, 111). Buchanan was not appointed.

From Tobias Lear

August 21st: 1793

By the President's command T. Lear has the honor to inform the Secretary of State, that the President has intended several times, when he has seen the Secretary latterly, to have mentioned his opinion respecting Mr. Albion Coxe's wages; but some other subject being introduced put it out of his mind. He now informs the Secretary, that it is his opinion, that Mr. Coxe should be paid wages for the time he has been employed in the Mint, and so long as he shall continue to be so employed ('till he shall have qualified himself) equal to the Salary allowed by law for the Assayer.

The President likewise informs the Secretary, that the sum of one thousand dollars will be furnished from the Treasury Department to commence a coinage at the Mint—and if any agency of the President is necessary for drawing the said sum from the Treasury he will thank the Secretary to mention to him in what way it is necessary that he may do it accordingly.

The President has understood that Mr. Voight the Chief Coiner, has not yet qualified himself, by giving security agreeably to the law. If this be the case, the President wishes the Secretary to consider how far it would be proper to permit a coinage to be commenced.

TOBIAS LEAR

234 Sea Letters or Passports signed by the President are sent to the Office of the Secretary of State by the bearer hereof—and three large packets—one Addressed to the Consul of France—one to the Director

of the Ports at Martinique—and one to the Director of the Ports at the Cape—which came under cover to the President from the Post Office.

RC (DLC); with dateline above postscript; endorsed by TJ as a letter from George Washington. PrC (DNA: RG 59, MLR); endorsed by Lear. FC (Lb in same, SDC). Recorded in SJPL.

From James Monroe

DEAR SIR   Alb: Augt 21. 1793.

On my return from Richmond I was favored with yours of the 14. of July. I should have answered it sooner had I not been prevented by some peculair engagements. At present I should be more full upon some points but that the favor of Mr. Madisons company likewise prevents it. Upon one point I think it necessary to say a few words. You suggest that some indiscretions of Mr. Genet have given an advantage to his adversaries they seem disposed to avail themselves of by an appeal to the people—which you fear in the heat of parties and the probable preponderance of the opposit interest may injure his country. Of one fact I am well assured that in case of such an appeal, the people of this State in deciding on the merits of the controversy, would pardon the errors of the French minister, whilst they would consider those of the administration as inveterate and malignant vices. They would consider his as the effect of the[1] intemperate zeal of an honest heart active in the support of the best of causes, whilst they would deem those of his antagonists, as the effect of unsound hearts and wicked heads planning the ruin of that cause.

A variety of considerations incline me to believe that a crisis is rapidly approaching that will produce some great change in our affairs. I consider[2] this gentleman as an important instrument in bringing on that crisis. The publick mind will not be governed by light or trivial incidents but will take the measures of 4 or 5 years together as the data or rule to decide by—and if upon the whole the measures of the administration partake more of evil than good, let the incident which matures the crisis be what it may, they will condemn it. This is not suggested as a mere matter of surmise. I know the principle to be at work and I am well satisfied it will produce fruit in the course of a short time.

The French historians will record the conduct of this country towards theirs. They will note that of individuals also. Those who shall take any part which the world and posterity may not approve, be them who they may, will be handed down in their proper colours.

I understand from Mr. Madison that you have already received some[3] intimation of the paper enclosed. I have therefore only to request that you will be so kind as forward it to the gentleman to whom it is addressed.

Mr. Randolph and Mr. Jeffn. dined with us to day—his family are well. I am dear sir very affectionately yr. frnd. & servt.

JAS. MONROE

RC (DLC); endorsed by TJ as received 31 Aug. 1793 and so recorded in SJL.

The PAPER ENCLOSED was the draft of a pamphlet by John Taylor of Caroline (see James Madison to TJ, 11 Aug. 1793, and note). The GENTLEMAN TO WHOM IT IS ADDRESSED was probably Philip Freneau, who published extracts from the work in the

National Gazette without Taylor's permission before it appeared in pamphlet form (Taylor to Madison, 25 Sep. 1793, Madison, *Papers*, XV, 123; Shalhope, *Taylor*, 219).

[1] Preceding three words interlined.
[2] Monroe here canceled "the efforts of."
[3] Preceding three words interlined.

From Edward Telfair

SIR   State House Augusta 21st August 1793

Citizen M. A. B. Mangourit Consul of the French Republic at Charleston has made a demand, in the name of his Nation, of a certain Captain Reviers and his two Lieutenants, as will more fully appear by the copy of his letter to me which is herewith transmitted for the purpose of being laid before the President of the United States: As I concieve the purport of this letter to be of the highest political concern I shall await with impatience a reply. I have the honor to be Sir Your Mo Hble Servt

EDWD. TELFAIR

RC (DNA: RG 59, LGS); at foot of text: "Sy of the United States"; endorsed by TJ as received 6 Sep. 1793 and so recorded in SJL. FC (G-Ar: Journal of Proceedings of the Executive Department). Enclosure: Mangourit to Telfair, Charleston, 25 July 1793, quoting in full, and protesting the rejection of, a 15 July 1793 memorial of John Brickell, French Vice-Consul at Savannah, to United States District Judge Nathaniel Pendleton demanding in the name of the French Republic the immediate release from custody of Captain Joseph Riviere of the *Anti-George*, who held a French commission from Mangourit; stating that Riviere had not violated any American law, but rather had been imprisoned for being useful to his country in conformity with the spirit of the treaty of alliance, and that his arrest was "an Act of tyranny, and the more culpa-ble, because it is committed in a land of freedom"; that the governor should beware of "the insidious machinations which the English faction make use of in Georgia" to turn Americans against that eternal alliance and undermine their gratitude to France, and which are reflected in the maxims of the ambitious English nobility and stockjobbing mercantile class; that ingratitude to France would reflect a fatal lack of virtue in the United States and lead it, like Carthage, to perish in the midst of opulence; that if the armed men who seized the shipwrecked Riviere and his crew on 13 July lacked legal authority, they might have been "hired by England to make war on the French" in the United States; that it is admitted at Charleston that American tribunals lack jurisdiction over enemy prizes captured by French vessels; that the Wilmington court has admitted that it cannot detain any Frenchmen, as evidenced by its release of the captain of the French privateer *Vainqueur de la Bastille* when an English captain whose vessel he had taken at sea made a deceitful effort to have him tried; and requesting the immediate release of Riviere and his lieutenants, Hunt and Seymour, if their arrest was indeed founded solely on "the false basis of their being part of a French Privateer," and reparation for the insult given to France (Tr in DNA: RG 59, LGS; English translation from the French by John Peter Vanheddeghem, with his 19 Aug. 1793 certification witnessed by Augusta Mayor John Milton).

The *Anti-George*, one of the privateers commissioned in Charleston by French minister Edmond Charles Genet, took no prizes before it was shipwrecked around 10 July 1793. Its captain, Joseph Riviere, and HIS TWO LIEUTENANTS, Jeffrey Hunt and Richard Seymour, were arrested on suspicion of having violated American neutrality but acquitted in November 1793 (Melvin H. Jackson, "The Consular Privateers; an account of French Privateering in American waters, April to August, 1793," *American Neptune*, XXII [1962], 97-8). See also TJ to Telfair, 9 Sep. 1793.

To George Washington

Aug. 21. 93.

Th: Jefferson has the honor to inclose to the President a letter from Mr. Seagrove.

When he shall[1] have considered of the questions of wages to Albion Coxe (till he shall have qualified himself to draw his regular salary) and the ordering a coinage of 1000 Dollars in small silver for the Treasury, he will be so good as to communicate his determinations.

RC (DNA: RG 59, MLR); addressed: "The President of the US."; endorsed by Tobias Lear. Tr (Lb in same, SDC). Not recorded in SJL.

The enclosure was probably a LETTER from Creek Indian agent James SEAGROVE of 20 July 1793, recorded in SJL as received from St. Marys on 20 Aug. 1793 but not found. An earlier letter from Seagrove to TJ of 3 Apr. 1793, recorded in SJL as received from St. Marys on 30 July 1793 but

not found, evidently enclosed "an application to him from the Spanish Govr. of East Florida, respecting slaves which were detained by the citizens of Georgia" as well as "his answer, & a copy of his letter to the Governor of Georgia on the subject" (Washington, *Journal*, 211). TJ mistakenly listed both letters in SJL under the name of John Seagrove.

[1] TJ wrote "If he should" before altering the phrase to read as above.

To Delamotte

DEAR SIR   Philadelphia. Aug. 22. 1793.

I shall at present not acknolege the receipt of your letters, except that of Jan. 15. because the present is intended to be merely on so much of the subject of that as relates to my books which it mentions you had received from Mr. Froullé. I had desired you to draw on Donald &

Burton for the amount, to whom I wrote and received an assurance they would pay your draught. They stopped payment some time in March, and I have never been able to learn whether you had drawn on them before that period or not. If you had, I rest assured your bill was paid, because they paid some other orders given at the same time, and presented early. If you had not drawn before that period, it would not be in their power to answer it. In that case I will beg the favor of you to draw on me here in favor of any body you please, or to let me know the amount and I will remit it immediately. If the books are not yet come away it is probable there are some more volumes of the Encyclopedie come out which I would be glad to receive with them. I shall go to Virginia to remain at the close of this year. If no opportunity offers for that state, be so good as to send them here to the care of Mr. John Vaughan, merchant of this place. Should the vessel which carries this letter, return here direct (as I believe she will) she will find me still here. I am with great esteem Dear Sir Your most obedt. servt

TH: JEFFERSON

PrC (DLC); at foot of text: "Mr. La Motte." Tr (ViU: Edgehill-Randolph Papers); 19th-century copy. Recorded in SJL as sent "by express vessel."

To Alexander Donald

MY DEAR SIR   Philadelphia Aug. 22. 1793.

I have yet to acknolege your favors of Mar. 10. and Apr. 4. Just before their receipt I had heard of the calamity which had befallen you and which has since befallen so many on your side the water. I heard it with poignant distress, for however it may be with others, I find that my earliest affections are my strongest. I have delayed answering your letter because I wished to be able to say something to you about my tobacco. But it is still out of my power to do it with certainty. I have occasion here for 6. or 800. Dollars, and have been expecting to receive it under an execution I have for between 4. and 5000 dollars, ever since February last. I still expect it, and if I get only so much, my tobacco will be free for me to dispose of, and tho' I had not intended to ship it myself (because I can always get a guinea for it here) yet I will certainly do it, and under the address you recommend. I understood from Mr. Brown that my last year's crop was still unshipped some time ago. I shall leave this place the 1st. day of January to re-establish myself at Monticello. I shall certainly there render you any services which may be in my power: and shall have more leisure to attend to my friendships. I am with very great & sincere affection Dear Sir Your friend & servt

TH: JEFFERSON

P.S. The books from Ireland and those by Mr. Marshal are come safely to hand.

PrC (DLC); unaddressed. Tr (ViU: Edgehill-Randolph Papers); 19th-century copy. Recorded in SJL as sent "by Mr Vaughan."

To Joseph Fenwick

SIR   Philadelphia Aug. 22. 1793.

I have just received your favor of May 16. and at the same time learnt the arrival of my wine at Baltimore, from which place I have ordered it to Virginia, whither I shall follow it finally at the close of the year. I thank you for your attention to the commission, and your bill on me shall be honored, it being more convenient to me to pay it here than remit. I had avoided writing to you because I was quite uncertain whether you had drawn on Donald & Burton. Commissions which I gave at the same time to others, and were drawn immediately were paid, but I knew that if you had postponed it, it would be too late. Under this uncertainty I did not know whether to remit to you or not. As it is, it is in the way which suits me best. I shall probably trouble you annually, and would be obliged to you to inform me of the different places and channels of payment which may suit you, that I may always[1] adopt that which is most convenient at the time. I am with great esteem Sir Your most obedt. servt   TH: JEFFERSON

PrC (DLC); at foot of text: "Mr. Fenwick." Tr (ViU: Edgehill-Randolph Papers); 19th-century copy. Recorded in SJL as sent "by express vessel."

The FAVOR OF MAY 16 was from Fenwick, Mason & Company.

[1] Word interlined.

To Henry Knox

DR SIR   Philadelphia Aug. 22. 1793.

I have just received information that the ship Ann and Susan belonging to William Nelson & Co. citizens of New York with about 400 passengers on board, bound from Ireland to Philadelphia has been taken by the French armed vessel the Little Democrat and is brought into Newcastle in the state of Delaware. This capture was made on the 19th. inst. and consequently is within the rule which provided for restitution of the vessels which should be taken by those armed in our ports: and the act of restitution placing the case under your department, I have the honour to inclose you the original affidavit ascertaining the facts, and recommended that the captain shall wait on you to give you any further information you may desire. I have the honor to be with great respect & esteem Dr Sir Your most obedt servt TH: JEFFERSON

PrC (DLC); at foot of text: "The Secretary at War." FC (Lb in DNA: RG 59, DL). Enclosure: Deposition of George Duplex, 22 Aug. 1793, affirming, as master of the *Ann & Susan* of New York, that on 19 or 20 Aug., while on a voyage from Londonderry to Philadelphia, his ship was captured four leagues from Cape Henlopen by the French privateer *Petite Démocrate* and is now detained by its officers as a prize at New Castle, Delaware (PrC of Tr in DLC, with notarization by Jacob R. Howell, all in the hand of George Taylor, Jr.; Tr in Lb in DNA: RG 59, DL).

To Henry Knox

DR Sir   Philadelphia Aug. 22. 1793.

I have just received a letter from Mr. Hollingsworth attorney of the district of Maryland with information that the Sans Culottes, fitted out at Charleston had taken and sent into Baltimore the Brigantine Maxwell of Kirkcudbright, commanded by Thomas Milrae. As the date of the information renders it probable that the case comes within the rule of restitution, I take the liberty of inclosing to you the original letters which have come to my hands, as belonging to your department. I have the honor to be with great esteem & respect Dr. Sir Your most obedt. servt   TH: JEFFERSON

PrC (DLC); at foot of text: "The Secretary at War." FC (Lb in DNA: RG 59, DL). Enclosure: Zebulon Hollingsworth to TJ, 20 Aug. 1793, and enclosure.

To James McHenry, Robert Gilmor, and Samuel Sterett

GENTLEMEN   Philadelphia Aug. 22. 1793.

I recieved yesterday your favor of the 18th. and called to-day on Mr. Hammond. He said he could not give a passport of any kind which would be an absolute protection to either the French passengers or their baggage, but that he would give a letter of recommendation to all commanders of ships and others exhorting them to permit the passengers and what might be properly called their baggage to pass freely; but even this could be only on condition that there was no merchandize on board the ships: and he seemed to be apprized that these ships were loaded with merchandize of the islands. If you think such a letter of recommendation on such a condition may be useful, and will be so good as to write me accordingly, it shall be sent by return of post. I have the honour to be Gentlemen Your most obedient servt   TH: JEFFERSON

PrC (DLC); at foot of text: "Messrs. Mc.Henry, Gilmer & Sterritt." Tr (ViU: Edgehill-Randolph Papers); 19th-century copy; left margin torn away.

The addressees served on a committee to raise funds for the relief of the large contingent of refugees from the slave insurrection in the French colony of Saint-Domingue which arrived in Baltimore on 9 July 1793 (J. Thomas Scharf, *History of Baltimore City and County* . . . [Philadelphia, 1881], 82-3). In SJL TJ recorded the missing FAVOR OF THE 18TH. as a letter from Gilmor and Sterett received from Baltimore on 21 Aug. 1793.

From James Madison

DEAR SIR   At Col. M— [22 Aug. 1793]

I left home the day before yesterday which was the date of my last. It was to be accompanied by 2. and perhaps tho' not probably 3 additional Nos. of H–l–vd–s. The last towit No. 5. contained two paragraphs the one relating to the accession of S. and P. to the war against F. the other to the answer's of the P. to the addresses on his proclamation, which I particularly requested you to revise, and if improper, to erase. The whole piece was more hurried than it ought to have been, and these paragraphs penned in the instant of my setting out which had been delayed as late as would leave eno' of the day for the journey. I mention this as the only apology for the gross error of fact committed with respect to the term neutrality, which it is asserted the P. has not used in any of his answers. I find on looking into them here, that he used it in the first of all to the Merchants of Philada. and in one other out of three which I have examined. I must make my conditional request therefore an absolute one as to that passage. If he should forbear the use of the term in all his answers subsequent to the perversion of it by Pacificus, it will strengthen the argument used; but that must be a future and contingent consideration. Mr. D. R. was not arrived yesterday. The[1] family here well—so also at M. as you will no doubt learn from the Spot itself. Adieu. Yrs. Affy

RC (DLC: Madison Papers); undated and unsigned; endorsed by TJ as a letter of "abt Aug. 22. 93." received 2 Sep. 1793 and so recorded in SJL.

S. AND P.: Spain and Portugal. Portugal did not enter the war against France until September 1793, and then only as an auxiliary ally of Great Britain promising to adhere to existing defensive treaties (John Ehrman, *The Younger Pitt: The Reluctant Transition* [London, 1983], 278, 280). In reply to a supportive address from THE MERCHANTS OF PHILADA. in May, the President had asserted that his Proclamation of Neutrality would help to ensure "a strict neutrality" (Fitzpatrick, *Writings*, XXXII, 460-1). D. R.: David Meade Randolph. THE SPOT: Monticello.

[1] Preceding two words written over "at Monticello yest," erased.

To Thomas Pinckney

DEAR SIR   Philadelphia Aug. 22. 1793.

My last letters to you were of the 13. and 26th. of June, since which I have received yours of Apr. 27. May 2. 11. and 15.

The object of the present being merely to cover a bill of five thousand dollars, say one thousand and seventy seven pounds, eleven shillings and nine pence sterling drawn by Mr. Wilcocks on Edward Mc.Culloch & Co. of London at 60. days sight, for the use of our diplomatic gentlemen in Europe, I will pray you to negotiate it, and apply it to it's purpose as desired on a former occasion. The impossibility of getting bills on Amsterdam has obliged me to make this remittance to London. I shall not cease my endeavors to procure them on Amsterdam, and keep our foreign fund in it's antient deposit there. Being advised that my letter will go more safely if it contains nothing but this matter of business, I shall here conclude with assurances of the esteem & respect with which I am Dear Sir your most obedt. servt   TH: JEFFERSON

PrC (DLC); at foot of text: "Mr. Pinckney." FC (Lb in DNA: RG 59, DCI). Mistakenly recorded in SJL under 20 Aug. 1793. Enclosure not found, but see those listed at TJ to Pinckney, 11 and 14 Sep. 1793.

Pinckney's 15 May 1793 letter to TJ, enclosed in John Harriott's 1 Aug. letter and recorded in SJL as received 3 Aug. 1793, has not been found.

To Thomas Pinckney

Philadelphia Aug. 22. 93.

Th: Jefferson with his compliments to Mr. Pinckney asks the favor of him to have the inclosed delivered to *Mr. Donald himself.*—Several circumstances have postponed Th:J's departure to the end of the present year, when he will leave this place. He is anxious to hear of his threshing machine from Mr. Pinckney.—He does not write to him on public matters till he can meet with a confidential conveyance. But the newspapers will go by this.

PrC (DLC). Tr (ViU: Edgehill-Randolph Papers); 19th-century copy dated "Aug.   1793." Mistakenly recorded in SJL under 20 Aug. 1793. Enclosure: TJ to Alexander Donald, 22 Aug. 1793.

To George Washington

Aug. 22. 1793.

Th: Jefferson has the honor to inclose to the President the letter of the National assembly to him of Dec. 22. 92. It's most distinct object seems to have been to thank the U.S. for their succours to St. Domingo. It glances blindly however at commercial arrangements, and on the 19th. of Feb. the same assembly passed the decree putting our commerce in their dominions on the footing of natives[1] and directing their Executive council to treat with us on the subject. On this the following questions arise.

1. Would the President chuse to answer the letter, acknoleging it's receipt, thanking them in turn for the favors to our commerce, and promising to consult the constitutional powers (the Senate) on the subject of the treaty proposed?

2. Would he rather chuse to make no reply to the letter, but that Mr. Morris be instructed to negociate a renewal of Mr. Genet's powers to treat, to his successor?

3. or would he chuse that nothing be said on the subject to any body?

If the President would in his judgment be for a treaty on the principles of the decree, or any modification of them, the 1st. or 2d. measure will be to be adopted.

If he is against a treaty on those principles or any modification of them, the 3d. measure seems to be the proper one.

RC (DNA: RG 59, MLR); endorsed by Bartholomew Dandridge, Jr. PrC (DLC). Tr (Lb in DNA: RG 59, SDC). Not recorded in SJL. Enclosure: President of the National Convention of France to Washington, 22 Dec. 1792 (see note to Edmond Charles Genet to TJ, 16 May 1793).

For the President's approval of the second of the alternatives offered by TJ, see Notes of Cabinet Meeting on a Commercial Treaty with France, 23 Aug. 1793.

[1] Remainder of sentence interlined.

From James Anderson

Nantes, 23 Aug. 1793. Last night he arrived here from Paris, from which he traveled as cheaply as possible, and has been appointed consul for this port by Fenwick pending TJ's approval, which he earnestly solicits in the event Carnes does not return to France. Nearly a year ago he wrote to TJ, upon Major Mountflorence's recommendation, soliciting the appointment at Le Havre, which he understands has gone to Cutting. He then mentioned that TJ and the President might learn of his character from Bingham and many other Philadelphia gentlemen. He trusts that his lack of acquaintance with the South Carolina congressional delegation will not militate against his solicitation. In order to counteract the continuing increase in the price of all articles, the National Convention has forbidden the exportation of wines, brandies, sugar, coffee, tallow, leather, and all articles needed for life's support and comfort. This decree has adversely affected two American vessels, one because of freight and the other because of a cargo of wine, brandy, etc. which the captain says was purchased before the decree was passed. As soon as he receives his commission from Fenwick and is accepted as an American agent, he will meet the commissaries the Convention has sent to enforce the decree. The garrison here, supplemented by neighboring troops and 15,000 men from the Mainz garrison who arrived this week in the Vendée, will suffice to protect this city from the nearby rebels.

RC (DLC); 3 p.; at foot of text: "The Hon'ble Mr. Jefferson"; endorsed by TJ as received 12 Nov. 1793 and so recorded in SJL. Dupl (DNA: RG 59, CD); endorsed by Edmund Randolph as received 17 Feb. 1794.

For the outcome of Anderson's quest for a consular APPOINTMENT, see note to Anderson to TJ, 28 Sep. 1792.

To Benjamin Smith Barton

Aug. 23. 93.

Th: Jefferson presents his friendly compliments to Dr. Barton, and being now in the act of sending off his books to Virginia, takes the liberty of asking from Dr. Barton the volumes lent him.—Th:J. has been for some time settled on the banks of the Schuylkill near Gray's ferry, where he would always be very happy to see Dr. Barton, should his rides or walks lead him that way. His absence from town has scarcely given him an opportunity of seeing any body in it.

RC (PHi: Barton Correspondence); addressed: "Dr. Barton"; endorsed by Barton as received 26 Aug. 1793. Not recorded in SJL.

From Phineas Bond

SIR   Chesnut Street—23d. Augt. 1793.

I beg Leave to inform You, I have directed Capt. Stewart, of the Brigantine Jane of Dublin, captured by the Privateer, Citizen Genet, Captain Johanene, to prepare an Estimate of the Value of his Vessel— her Cargo, Apparel and Furniture.

I shall consider it as a particular Favor, if You will be pleased to point out the Mode of Valuation, which the Government of the United States will require, to ascertain the Amount of the Damage, occasioned by this Capture, and by the subsequent Sale of this Vessel &c: As I shall give Instructions to have that Mode strictly complied with, in this and every other Case under similar Circumstances as far as it may be practicable.

With Sentiments of perfect Respect, I have the Honor to be, Sir, Yr very faithful & most obt. Servt.   P. Bond

RC (DNA: RG 59, NFC); at foot of text: "Secretary of State"; endorsed by TJ as received 23 Aug. 1793 and so recorded in SJL. Enclosed in George Washington to TJ, 24 Aug. 1793.

TJ submitted this letter to the President on 24 Aug. 1793 (Washington, *Journal*, 230).

Cabinet Opinions on
Edmond Charles Genet

At meetings of the heads of departments and the Attorney General at the President's on the 1st. and 2d. of Aug. 1793.   On a review of the whole of Mr. Genet's correspondence and conduct, it was unanimously agreed that a letter should be written to the Minister of the US. at Paris, stating the same to him, resuming the points of difference which had arisen between the government of the US. and Mr. Genet,[1] assigning the reasons for the opinions of the former, and desiring the recall of the latter:[2] and that this letter with those which have passed between Mr. Genet and the Secretary of state, and other necessary documents, shall be laid by Mr. Morris before the Executive of the French government.

At a meeting of the same at the President's Aug. 15. the rough draught of the said letter having been prepared by the Secretary of state was read for consideration, and it was agreed that the Secretary of the treasury should take measures for obtaining a vessel either by hire or purchase, to be sent to France express, with the dispatches when ready.

At a meeting of the same at the President's Aug. 20. the said letter was read and corrected by paragraphs and finally agreed to.

At a meeting of the same at the President's[3] Aug. 23. it was agreed that the preceeding letter should bear the date of the last document which is to accompany it, to wit, Aug. 16. and the draught of[4] a second letter to our Minister at Paris was read and unanimously approved, and to bear date this day.—Stated and signed this 23d. day of Aug. 1793.

Th: Jefferson
Alexander Hamilton
H Knox
Edm: Randolph

MS (DLC: Washington Papers); in TJ's hand, signed by TJ, Hamilton, Knox, and Randolph; probably made ca. 26 Aug. 1793 and sent to the President on that date; endorsed by Washington. PrC (DLC); signed

only by TJ. Dft (DLC); entirely in TJ's hand, unsigned; with marginal notes: (by Hamilton) "Approved. It does not appear necessary to be more particular with regard to the Express boat. A Hamilton" and (by

Knox) "agreed to H Knox." PrC (DLC); lacks marginal notes. Entry in SJPL: "Opns of heads of dep. on proceedgs. agt Genet." Enclosed in TJ to Washington, 26 Aug. 1793; draft enclosed in TJ to the Cabinet, 24 Aug. 1793.

[1] In Dft TJ here canceled "and."
[2] Preceding seven words interlined in Dft.
[3] Preceding three words interlined in Dft.
[4] Preceding three words interlined in Dft.

From Robert Gamble

DEAR SIR   Richmond August 23rd. 1793

I have your favor of the 18th. Current informing you have directed to my Care some Cases of Claret That has arived at Baltimore for you in order That they be forwarded to Montecello.

It is in my power by the return Waggons from my Staunton Store, to send your goods to the Care of Colo. Bell in Charlotsville, and I will be Careful When The goods *come*—to deliver Them to Such Waggoners *only* That I can best Confide in.

Should I be absent from Richmond I will leave instructions with my young Man, Who will pay the same attention to your interest as if I was here.

I had like to have suffered very Materially by retaining Flour in consequence of some expectations Mr. Genet gave me that I would be employed by him to purchase for the French Republic in this part of the State. I continued Collecting till I had upward of 5,000 Barrels in my store Houses my self and refused good offers for it. As it was begining to sour I had to part with it to great disadvantage, and part That I shipped to Europe I have no hopes of saving myself.

The Season since Harvest, has been uncomonly dry. On your Estate and the Neighbouring Plantations good Crops of Corn Will be raised—but the upper part of Albemarle—orange, Louisia, Prince Edward, Buckingham &c.—I am well assured, from Creditable persons That little or no Corn will [be][1] made. The Wheat turned out, very indifferent. However, in other parts of the State Corn is very Luxuriant.

We have information to Night from Norfolk that a frigate Said to be *the Concord* has Captured three Vessels off our Capes, and was seen with them going up the Bay supposing to Baltimore—one is the Ship Jupiter Loaded by Donaldson & Stott of Suffolk with 4,000 Barrels of Naval Stores.

You will see by the Resolutions forwarded a few days ago from this place—That the Citizens are alarmed at a report that the American Government has been insulted by Mr. Genet. The flame will Spread. However I hope Prudence will always Guide the great Bulk of the people—And That Foreigners will in future be cautious How they Speak of our beloved president; or the supreme Exccutive of America—be their instructions What they may from their Nation.

Our trade is suffering irreparably—by the infernal Robbers under Character of Privaters—industry is Checked—the Honest individuals who Adventure, on the Ocean, is Ruined—And such Proceedings can be of little Avail to the Nations at War. Our Tobacco to the great injury of the Planter and Merchant lays in the ware houses—our Flour Spoiling—And shall a Nation be ruined for the emolument of a set of Vagabonds and Miscreants Who infest our Coasts. We are as true friends to the french revolution as the French are them selves—or any people can be—But a tame submission to the unreasonable injuries Sustained, by this privateering business, cannot much longer be expected. I am with regard & Esteem Your mo. ob Hum st   Ro. GAMBLE

RC (DLC); addressed: "Honble. Thomas Jefferson Esqr Secretary of State Philadelphia"; endorsed by TJ as received 30 Aug. 1793 and so recorded in SJL.

For the Richmond RESOLUTIONS, see note to George Wythe to TJ and Edmund Randolph, 17 Aug. 1793.

[1] Word supplied.

To Gouverneur Morris

DEAR SIR   Philadelphia, August 22d. [23] 1793.

The letter of the 16th. instant, with it's documents accompanying this, will sufficiently inform you of the transactions which have taken place between Mr. Genet, the Minister of France, and the government here, and of the painful necessity they have brought on, of desiring his recall. The letter has been prepared in the view of being itself, with it's documents, laid before the Executive of the French Government.[1] You will, therefore, be pleased to lay it before them, doing everything which can be done on your part, to procure it a friendly and dispassionate reception and consideration. The President would, indeed, think it greatly unfortunate, were they to take it in any other light; and therefore charges you very particularly with the care of presenting[2] this proceeding in the most soothing view, and as the result of an unavoidable necessity on his part.[3]

Mr. Genet, soon after his arrival communicated the decree of the National Convention of Feb. 15. 1793. authorizing their Executive to propose a Treaty with us on liberal principles, such as might strengthen the bonds of good will, which unite the two Nations; and informed us in a letter of May 23rd.[4] that he was authorized to treat accordingly. The Senate being then in recess, and not to meet again till the fall, I apprised Mr. Genet that the participation in matters of Treaty given by the Constitution to that Branch of our Government, would of course delay any definitive answer to his friendly proposition. As he was sensible of this circumstance, [5] the matter has been understood to lie over till the meeting of Senate. You will be pleased, therefore, to explain to the Executive of France this delay, which has prevented as yet our formal accession to their proposition to treat, to assure them that the President will meet them, with the most friendly dispositions, on the grounds of treaty proposed by the National Convention, as soon as he can do it in the forms of the Constitution, and you will of course suggest for this purpose, that the powers of Mr. Genet be renewed to his Successor.

Since my last, which was of the 13th. of June, your Nos. 25. 26. 27. of March 26. April 4. and 5. have been received. The public papers, sent herewith, will give you the current news of the Country. I have the honor to be, with great respect and Esteem, Dear Sir, Your most obedient and most humble Servant   TH: JEFFERSON

RC (NNC: Gouverneur Morris Papers); in the hand of George Taylor, Jr., signed by TJ; at foot of first page: "M. Morris"; endorsed by Morris. PrC (DLC); with date altered by Taylor to "23d." in accordance with a decision by the Cabinet (see notes below), a change he neglected to make on the RC. Dft (DLC); dated 22 Aug. 1793; unsigned; lacks second paragraph (see note 3 below). Dft (DLC: TJ Papers, 91: 15769); undated; consists of second paragraph in TJ's hand; with marginal notes: (by Alexander Hamilton) "approved A Hamilton" and (by Henry Knox) "Approved H Knox"; at head of text: "[clause proposed for the letter of Aug. 2⟨2⟩3 to Mr Morris. the principal letter is proposed to be dated Aug. 16. the date of the latest documt.]." Tr (DNA: RG 46, Senate Records, 3d Cong., 1st sess.). FC (Lb in DNA: RG 59, DCI). Recorded in SJL under 23 Aug. 1793 as sent "by express vessel"; one or both drafts recorded in SJPL under 22 Aug. 1793. Printed in *Message*, 68-9. Dft of second paragraph enclosed in TJ to George Washington, 24 Aug. 1793; missing Dupl enclosed in TJ to Morris, 11 Sep. 1793.

This letter represents TJ's last effort as Secretary of State to achieve the new commercial treaty with France that he had long sought in order to reduce American economic dependence on Great Britain (see Edmond Charles Genet to TJ, 23 May 1793, and note). For the steps by which TJ secured presidential and Cabinet approval of the present letter, which the Cabinet decided to date 23 Aug. 1793, see TJ to George Washington, 22 and 24 Aug. 1793; Cabinet Opinions on Edmond Charles Genet, 23 Aug. 1793; and Notes of Cabinet Meeting on a Commercial Treaty with France, 23 Aug. 1793. In November 1793 the French government authorized the commissioners appointed to succeed Genet to negotiate a new trade treaty with the United States, but TJ had retired from office and returned to Monticello by the time they arrived in Philadelphia in February 1794, and there is no evidence that they took up this subject with the American government (Turner, *CFM*, 293; ASP, *Foreign Relations*, I, 568).

The National Convention's DECREE was actually dated 19 Feb. 1793 (Joseph Fenwick to TJ, 25 Feb. 1793, and note).

[1] In first Dft TJ first wrote "Executive of France" and then altered it to read as above.

[2] Word interlined in first Dft.

[3] Below this line in first Dft TJ wrote "[here is to come in another paragraph.]."

[4] Preceding five words and digits interlined in second Dft.

[5] Word replaced by "delay" in second Dft.

Notes of Cabinet Meeting on a Commercial Treaty with France

Aug. 23. 93. In consequence of my note of yesterday to the Presidt. a meeting was called this day at his house to determine what should be done with the proposition of France to treat. The importance of the matter was admitted, and being of so old a date as May 22d. we might be accused of neglecting the interests of the US. to have left it so long unanswered, and it could not be doubted Mr. Genet would avail himself of this inattention. The Presidt. declared it had not been inattention, that it had been the subject of conversation often at our meetings, and the delay had proceeded from the difficulty of the thing. If the struggles of France should end in the old despotism the formation of such a treaty with the present government would be a matter of offence: if it should end in any kind of free government he should be very unwilling by inattention to their advances to give offence and lose the opportunity of procuring terms so advantageous to our country. He was therefore for writing to Mr. Morris to get the powers of Mr. Genet renewed to his successor. [As he had expressed this opinion to me the afternoon before I had prepared the draught of a letter accordingly.] But how to explain the delay?—The Secy. of the Treasury[1] observed on the letter of the Natl. Convention, that as it did not seem to require an answer, and the matters it contained would occasion embarrassment if answered he should be against answering it. That he should be for writing to Mr. Morris mentioning our readiness to treat with them and suggesting a renewal of Mr. Genet's powers to his successor, but not in as strong terms as I had done in my draught of the letter, not as a thing anxiously wished for by us, lest it should suggest to them the asking a price: and he was for my writing to Mr. Genet *now* an answer to his letter of May 22. referring to the meeting of the Senate the entering on the treaty. Knox concurred with him. The Attorney Genl. also, except that he was against suggesting the renewal of Mr. Genet's powers, because that would amount to a declaration that we would treat with that government, would commit us to lay the subject before the Senate, and his principle had ever been to do no act, not unavoidably necessary, which in the event of a counterrevolution might offend the future governing powers of that country.—I stated to them that having observed from our conversations that the propositions to treat might not be acceded to immediately I had endeavored to prepare Mr. Genet for it by taking occasion in conversations to apprise him of the controul over treaties which our constitution had given to the Senate, that tho' this was indirectly done (because not having been authorised to say any thing official on the subject, I did not venture to commit myself directly) yet on some subsequent conversation, I found it had struck him exactly as I had wished, for speaking on some other matter, he mentioned incidentally his propositions to treat, and said 'however as I know now that you cannot take up that subject till the meeting of Senate, I shall say no more about it now,' and so proceeded with his other subject, which I do not now recollect. I said I thought it possible by recalling the substance of [2] these conversations to Mr. Genet in a letter to be written now, I might add that the Executive had at length come to a conclusion that on account of the importance of the matter, they would await the meeting of the Senate. But I pressed strongly the urging Mr. Morris to procure a renewal of Genet's powers that we might not lose the chance of obtaining so advantageous a treaty. E. R. had argued against our acceding to it because it was too advantageous, so much so that they would certainly break it, and it might become the cause of war. I answered that it would be easy in the course of the negotiation to cure it of it's inequality by giving some compensation: but I had no fear of their revoking it, that the islanders themselves were too much interested in the concessions ever to suffer them to be revoked, that the best thinkers in France had long been of opinion that it would be for the interest of the mother country to let the colonies obtain subsistence wherever they could cheapest, that I was [3] confident the present struggles in France would end in a free government of some sort, and that such a government would consider itself as growing out of the present one and respect it's treaties.—The Presidt. recurred to the awkwardness of writing a letter now to Mr. Genet in answer to his of May 22d. That it would be certainly construed as merely done with a design of exculpation of ourselves, and he would thence inculpate us.—The more we reflected on this the more the justice of this observation struck us. H. and myself came into it. Knox still for the letter. R. half for it, half against it, according to custom. It was at length agreed I should state the substance of my verbal [4] observations to Mr. Genet, in a letter to Mr. Morris, and let them be considered as the answer intended, for being from the Secy. of state they might be considered as official tho' not in writing.

It is evident that taking this ground for their future justification to France and to the US. they were sensible they had censurably neglected these overtures of treaty. For not only what I had said to Mr. Genet was without authority from them, but was never communicated to them till this day. To rest the justification of delay on answers given it is true in time, but of which they had no knolege till now, is an ostensible justification only.

MS (DLC); entirely in TJ's hand; brackets in original. Entry in SJPL: "Note of meetg. of heads of dep. on treating with France." Included in the "Anas."

On the PROPOSITION OF FRANCE TO TREAT for a new commercial treaty with the United States, see note to Edmond Charles Genet to TJ, 23 May 1793, not MAY 22D. For the DRAUGHT OF A LETTER, see TJ to Gouverneur Morris, 23 Aug. 1793, and note. LETTER OF THE NATL. CONVENTION: see enclosure listed at TJ to George Washington, 22 Aug. 1793.

[1] TJ here canceled "came into the proposition for."
[2] Preceding three words interlined.
[3] TJ here canceled "sure."
[4] TJ here canceled "assurances."

From James Simpson

Gibraltar, 23 Aug. 1793. He encloses a copy of the dispatch he addressed to TJ on 9 Aug. by the *Sophia* for Philadelphia. Last week he opened cases no. 7-10 and 12 that Barclay left in his charge in order to air the contents, which conformed exactly to the inventory he and Humphreys found among Barclay's papers. Most of the goods are in good condition, though some have been damaged by water or mildew, and all will benefit from the airing. In the absence of a neutral vessel to take to Santa Cruz the Sheriffs mentioned in his last letter, orders have been given to fit out the copper-bottomed frigate at Larache for that purpose. Though there has been no interesting news from Morocco of late, he quotes an extract from a 13 Aug. letter from his reliable friend, the Swedish consul general at Tangier, stating that since the defeat of Muley Suliman's army nothing worthy of attention has occurred; that His Majesty remained quietly at Fez with no probability of attacking the Shauians again as soon as his friends wished us to believe; that it will be years before the Empire has one government; that European commerce consequently has nothing to fear from the once terrible Salletin cruisers; that the half galleys are fast decaying on the sand; and that there is no prospect of the frigates leaving the Larache and Salé Rivers because of silting. There has been no news from Algiers since his last. Yesterday a 74-gun ship and a frigate arrived in eight days from Lord Hood's fleet still cruising off Toulon. Prince Augustus Frederick came in the frigate and will go to England in a day or two.

RC (DNA: RG 59, CD); 4 p.; at foot of first page "The Honble Thomas Jefferson Esqr"; endorsed by TJ as received 24 Oct. 1793 and so recorded in SJL.

TJ submitted this letter to the President on 2 Nov. 1793, and Washington returned it the same day after noting in his journal that it contained "Nothing of importance" (Washington, *Journal*, 243).

From George Washington

Friday. 23d Augt. [1793]

The President requests Mr. Jefferson would bring with him the French Minister's letter, communicating his powers to enter upon a New, and liberal Commercial Treaty.

RC (DLC); partially dated; addressed: "Mr. Jeffer[son]"; endorsed by TJ as received 23 Aug. 1793. Recorded in SJPL.

FRENCH MINISTER'S LETTER: Edmond Charles Genet to TJ, 23 May 1793.

To the Cabinet

Aug. 24. 93.

Th: Jefferson submits to the Secretaries of the treasury and War and the Atty. Genl. some sketches of Notes to be signed for the President. As they are done from memory only, they will be pleased to insert whatever more their memories suggest as material. Particularly, the final conclusion as to the express-vessel will be to be inserted, which is most accurately known to the Secry. of the Treasury. When completed, a fair copy shall be made and sent for signature.

RC (DLC); addressed: "The Secretaries of the Treasury and War, & the Attorney Genl. of the US."; evidently returned to TJ with the enclosure. Recorded in SJPL. Enclosure: Draft of Cabinet Opinions on Edmond Charles Genet, 23 Aug. 1793.

To George Hammond

Aug. 24. 1793.

Th: Jefferson presents his compliments to Mr. Hammond and incloses him a copy of a commission of a Mr. Moore to be Vice-Consul of Gr. Britain for the state of Rhode-island, on which an Exequatur is asked. As it has been our practice hitherto, where there is a Minister from the same nation, to issue Exequaturs only on his authentication of the Commission, Th: Jefferson takes the liberty of asking it in the present case.

PrC (DLC). FC (Lb in DNA: RG 59, DL). Enclosure: Commission to Thomas William Moore as British vice-consul in Rhode Island, issued by Thomas Mac-Donogh, British consul for New England in Boston, 8 May 1793 (Tr in DNA: RG 360, PCC).

The President signed an exequatur recognizing Moore's vice-consular commission on 7 Dec. 1793 (Exequatur for Moore, 5 Dec. 1793, FC in DNA: RG 59, Exequaturs, with TJ as countersignatory). See also Washington, *Journal*, 264.

From Joshua Johnson

London, 24 Aug. 1793. He has received TJ's favors of 14 Nov. and 21 Mch. and regrets his intention to retire. Because of the great hardships and inconveniences to which he knew American seamen and commerce would be subjected by the war in Europe that took place prior to receipt of the second letter, he decided to remain in office until he learned the President's pleasure about his resignation, and thus to comply with the law he executed with sureties a bond drawn up by Pinckney and lodged it in his hands. He wishes he could say Americans were virtuous enough to avoid temptation, but he understands that several ships have usurped the American colors in India and proceeded under them to Europe. He has rejected with the contempt they deserved the many applications made to him to approve similar violations here. Although he adheres to his opinion about the compensation he should receive, for the present he will trust that the public's generosity will eventually indemnify him for his sacrifices of time and money. He has rendered an account of his disbursements to Pinckney, who has undoubtedly transmitted it to TJ; as it contains many charges not provided by law, he presumes it must be laid before Congress for approval and payment. He will regularly account to Pinckney for his conduct and asks TJ to correct his errors. He encloses copies of his letters to Philip Stephens, secretary of the Lords of the Admiralty, which have neither been answered nor resulted in the liberation of our fellow citizens, and a list of American ships captured and brought into different British ports by British warships and privateers, many loaded with perishable commodities which may become a total loss to the proprietors because of sentencing delays by the court of admiralty. Added to the detention and expenses of seeking restoration, this may utterly ruin the innocent owners and has made French citizens so fearful of venturing their property in our vessels as neutrals that their value has diminished nearly 100 percent. Representations about the injustice of such treatment have failed to produce any good effect, and he fears that the ministry's blind pride and obstinacy will force Congress to retaliate. In several cases passengers on American ships bound from France to St. Thomas have been jailed and pillaged even of their trinkets contrary to humanity and the law of nations. Captains and owners of privateers have tempted American captains and crews to swear their cargoes were French property, and have fired on the *George*, Captain Latouche of Baltimore, and the *Carolina Packet*, Captain White of Charleston. In Pinckney's absence, he encloses at his request the bill of lading and invoice of the copper for the Mint shipped on the *Pigou*, Captain Loxley. He asks TJ to make his devotions to the President, whose confidence and good opinion he highly esteems, and to assure him that he will be proud if his conduct continues to merit the approval of TJ and the President.

RC (DNA: RG 59, CD); 3 p.; in a clerk's hand, signed by Johnson; above salutation: "Thomas Jefferson Esqr." Dft (same). Recorded in SJL as received 1 Nov. 1793. Enclosures: (1) Johnson to Philip Stephens, 8 July 1793, stating that in consequence of the enclosed proofs of American citizenship he hoped the Lords of the Admiralty would order the immediate release of four impressed seamen—Benjamin Johnston, a black from the *Belvedere* of New York now on H.M.S. *Assistance*, John Barry of the *Pigou* of Philadelphia, and William Moxley and John Packwood of the *Bellona* of Alexandria on the *Dido*; and that John Eason now on the *Dido* would also be released because of the oath attesting to his American citizenship sworn before the Lord Mayor of London by Captain Gardner of the *Republican* of Baltimore. (2) Same to same, 17 July 1793, stating that the absence of a reply to No. 1 indicated that the government was determined to impress Americans "con-

trary to the Customs of Nations, and good Faith"; that if this were so, he wished to know immediately so that he could refrain from future applications; and that as he now understood Barry to be aboard the *Enterprize* "off the Tower" there would be no difficulty in getting him if his protection and certificate were returned. (3) Same to same, 24 July 1793, demanding on the strength of the enclosed proofs the discharge of George Treadwell, unlawfully impressed in Plymouth from the American ship *Cato*, Captain Wardrobe, by an officer of H.M.S. *Adamant*, William Bentinck commander, and of Patrick Molloy, an American citizen now on the "Guard Ship at the Nore" (Trs in same; Trs in same, DD). Other enclosures not found.

TJ submitted this letter to the President on 2 Nov. 1793, and Washington returned it the same day (Washington, *Journal*, 243).

To George Washington

24 August 1793

Thomas Jefferson with his respects to the President incloses a draught of the clause for the letter to Mr. Morris for his consideration.

Tr (Lb in DNA: RG 59, SDC). Not recorded in SJL. Enclosure: Draft of the second paragraph of TJ to Gouverneur Morris, [23] Aug. 1793.

From George Washington, with Jefferson's Note

August 24th: 1793

The President wishes the Secretary of State to let him know what measures, in his opinion, will be proper to be taken on the subject stated by the British Consul Genl.

[*Note by TJ:*]
Bond's letter of Aug. 23.

RC (DLC); in Tobias Lear's hand, with note at foot of text by TJ; addressed: "The Secretary of [State]"; endorsed by TJ as a letter from Washington received 26 Aug. 1793. Recorded in SJPL under 26 Aug. 1793. Enclosure: Phineas Bond to TJ, 23 Aug. 1793.

From George Washington

August 24th: 1793

The President sends to the Secretary of State two letters which he has received from Baltimore, written by persons from St. Domingo.

The President has no knowledge of the writer of the letter in English; but he wishes the Secretary of State to consider it, and if he thinks the circumstances therein mentioned deserve attention, the Secretary will communicate to the President such answer thereto as he may think proper to be given.

If in perusing the letter written in French, the Secretary meets any thing requiring the particular notice of the President, he will be so good as to point it out.

RC (DLC); in Tobias Lear's hand; endorsed by TJ as a letter from Washington received 26 Aug. 1793. Recorded in SJPL. Enclosure: Thomas Millet to Washington, Baltimore, 20 Aug. 1793, stating, in preference to his original plan to publish a warn- ing, that it was dangerous to have the French fleet from Saint-Domingue dispersed in several harbors and having so many unguarded merchant ships in Chesapeake Bay; that in "the great conspiracy of the Kings against the new french republic"

England is more interested in advancing its commercial interest than in restoring the French monarchy, as might be inferred by the devastation wrought in the French West Indies by Polverel, Sonthonax, and their counterrevolutionary collaborators under the influence of English policy and the aristocratic party in the National Convention and perhaps the Provisional Executive Council; that the recent conflagration in Saint-Domingue was the culmination of a deep-laid plan by the English ministry and the French aristocratic party to force the French fleet to flee to the United States, a plot that his involvement during the last three years in Saint-Domingue assemblies and his experience with the Legislative Assembly in Paris will enable him to prove, his efforts to expose it having resulted in his proscription, arrest, and incarceration by Polverel and Sonthonax; that, in return for ignoring its treaty obligation to guarantee French possessions in the West Indies, England and Spain will allow the United States to receive the French merchant ships in the Chesapeake that they plan to seize; that if these seizures take place, England will keep a naval squadron off the American coasts and from them invade Ohio, Canada, and at least the southern states, if not cause a general insurrection in the United States "already so well prepared by some persons of public capacity"; that he plans to go to New York and accompany the unfairly maligned General Galbaud to France, where the latter will report to the National Convention on the various intrigues he has de-scribed, though Genet will be reluctant to allow Galbaud to return to France in his company because the general's report will injure the aristocratic party there; that in October 1790 he conversed in Paris with Sir Hugh Elliot, William Pitt's personal friend, who had gone there to talk with some Saint-Domingue deputy or assemblyman; and that he stands ready to meet with the President on his way to New York (RC in DNA: RG 59, MLR; in halting and rambling English; endorsed by Lear as received 24 Aug. 1793; docketed by Bartholomew Dandridge, Jr.).

Millet, of whom Washington had NO KNOWLEDGE, had served as president of the Colonial Assembly which met briefly at St. Marc in Saint-Domingue in 1790 before adjourning and sending eighty-five delegates to the National Assembly in France to make its case against the *grands blancs* party. He subsequently appeared as one of the accusers of Léger Félicité Sonthonax and Etienne Polverel, two of the three commissioners appointed by the Legislative Assembly in 1792 to help suppress the slave revolt in Saint-Domingue, when a commission appointed by the National Convention considered charges of aiding and abetting the revolt leveled against them by refugee planters in 1795 (Ott, *Haitian Revolution*, 33-5; Stein, *Sonthonax*, 114-20). M. Lentilhon was the author of the LETTER WRITTEN IN FRENCH, which has not been found but is described in TJ to James McHenry, 26 Aug. 1793.

From David Humphreys

Lisbon, 25 Aug. 1793. He avails himself of the unanticipated sailing of a vessel for the United States to note that he has received, by the packet arrived since his last letter, a letter from the bankers of the United States in Amsterdam stating that they had TJ's orders to hold at his disposal the residue of ƒ117,600 from the fund of ƒ123,750 they had received last year for Pinckney's account. As a result he can now make preparatory inquiries and obtain the money in dollars when necessary. He has heard nothing of Cutting. Marat has been assassinated by a young woman and great confusions prevail in the French interior. Valenciennes and Mainz have fallen, the Spanish have suffered a minor defeat at Perpignan, and Portuguese troops are still preparing to sail to Spain. On orders of the Prince, the Duke of Cadaval, the nearest legitimate male heir to the crown, has been arrested and confined to Belem Castle because of a severe beating he and his servants administered at his house to some police officers in search of contraband goods. Quiet prevails here, with the Court still amusing the populace with public diversions for the Princess's birth.

RC (DNA: RG 59, DD); 2 p.; at head of text: "(No. 79.)"; at foot of text: "The Secretary of State &c. &c. &c."; endorsed by TJ as received 9 Nov. 1793 and so recorded in SJL. Tr (Lb in same).

TJ submitted this letter to the President on 9 Nov. 1793, and Washington returned it the same day (Washington, *Journal*, 250).

To James Madison

Aug. 25. 93.

You will percieve by the inclosed papers that Genet has thrown down the gauntlet to the President by the publication of his letter and my answer, and is himself forcing that appeal to the people, and risking that disgust, which I had so much wished should have been avoided. The indications from different parts of the continent are already sufficient to shew that the mass of the republican interest has no hesitation to disapprove of this intermeddling by a foreigner, and the more readily as his object was evidently, contrary to his professions, to force us into the war. I am not certain whether some of the more furious republicans may not schismatise with him.

The following arrangements are established.

Sep. 10. the Pr. sets out for Mt. Vernon, and will be here again the 30th. Oct. 5th. or a little sooner I set out to be absent 6. weeks, by agreement. Consequently I shall be here again about Nov. 17. to remain to Dec. 31. I break up my house the last of Septemb. Shall leave my carriage and horses in Virginia and return in the stage, not to have the embarrasment of ploughing them through the mud in January. I shall take private lodgings on my return.—Billy who is just going on a nautical expedition to Charleston, called on me yesterday to desire I would send you the inclosed account which he said was necessary for you to debit those for whom the articles were. Adieu.

RC (DLC: Madison Papers); unaddressed and unsigned. PrC (DLC). Tr (DLC); fragmentary 19th-century copy lacking first paragraph. Enclosed account not found.

The INCLOSED PAPERS probably included *Dunlap's American Daily Advertiser* and the *Gazette of the United States* for 24 Aug. 1793, each of which reprinted French minister Edmond Charles Genet's LETTER to George Washington of 13 Aug. 1793 (see enclosure to Washington to TJ, 15 Aug. 1793) and MY ANSWER (TJ to Genet, 16 Aug. 1793).

To Thomas Mann Randolph, Jr.

DEAR SIR   Philadelphia Aug. 25. 1793.

In my letter of July 14. I asked the favor of you to send off the horse you had been so kind as to procure for me, on the 1st. of Sep. to meet Tarquin at Georgetown, who is to be sent from hence, there the riders to exchange horses, Tarquin to be carried to Monticello, and the other brought here. I have since that received your letter of July 31. and Maria has received one of Aug. 8. neither of which indicate whether mine of July 14. had got to hand. I have however in subsequent letters repeated the same thing, so that I hope some of them have been recieved, and therefore shall send off Tarquin so as to be at Georgetown on the 4th. of Sep. there to await the arrival of the other horse.—The President sets out for Mt. Vernon the 10th. of Sep. and returns the 30th. I shall be able to leave this place a few days after. I am busily engaged in packing my books, and shall then pack and send off the rest of my furniture, and quit my house for private lodgings, reserving nothing but a portmanteau of clothes. I begin to apprehend I shall be obliged to take a flying trip here about the meeting of Congress, in order to wind up completely. If I do it will be short and by the stage, to avoid ploughing my own horses here and back through mud. My love to my dear Martha, and best affections to your friends with you. Adieu my dear Sir. Your's affectionately   TH: JEFFERSON

RC (DLC); at foot of text: "M. Randolph esq."; endorsed by Randolph as received 3 Sep. 1793. PrC (MHi). Tr (ViU: Edgehill-Randolph Papers); 19th-century copy.

From James Simpson

Gibraltar, 25 Aug. 1793. Having already written by this opportunity, he only mentions that the Portuguese consul was advised from Málaga that some days ago an American schooner, name and destination unknown, was captured off Vélez-Málaga by three Algerine cruisers, but that the crew had escaped and arrived at that port. Two of the cruisers were the small galleys he mentioned from Oran and the third appears to be the American schooner he noted on 1 June as having been taken off Cape Gata and now armed. Since the same use will be made of the one now taken, American commanders destined for the Mediterranean should be alerted so that they will not be deceived by the rigging of those new cruisers.

RC (DNA: RG 59, CD); 2 p.; at foot of first page: "The Honble Thomas Jefferson Esqr"; endorsed by TJ as received 24 Oct. 1793 and so recorded in SJL. TJ submitted this letter to the President on 2 Nov. 1793, and Washington returned it the same day (Washington, *Journal*, 243).

From Joseph Yznardi, Jr.

Boston, 25 Aug. 1793. Intending to embark for Cádiz by the first opportunity, he asks for TJ's commands. He will proceed immediately to Madrid to have his appointment acknowledged by the king and on 1 Jan. he will begin to pay strict attention to TJ's letter of instructions. To end Algerine depredations on American trade and bring about a peace so much desired by merchants he offers, if TJ deems it proper to recommend to the President, to go to Algiers free of charge to the United States with a recommendation from the Spanish court which he can procure "by interest"; if TJ thinks this impractical or disapproves, he should say nothing about it. Yesterday he received letters from Spain stating that a Spanish privateer had taken and brought to the port of Algeciras near Cádiz the American brig *Bacchus*, Captain Roger Robbins of Baltimore, bound from France to Spain, on the pretext that its cargo was French. His father has attended to this matter "in my name" and will follow Carmichael's instructions. He asks for information about the quantity and quality of wine he will have the pleasure of sending TJ upon arrival and wishes to know if he can be of any other service. P.S. He offers to take charge of any dispatches for Madrid or any other part of Spain.

RC (MHi); 3 p.; at foot of text: "Thomas Jefferson Esqr. Secretary of State &c.";
endorsed by TJ as received 6 Sep. 1793 and so recorded in SJL.

To William Channing

SIR   Philadelphia, August 26th. 1793.

I inclose you copies of two letters from Judge Marchant to the President of the United States, and of sundry depositions taken by him, from which there is reason to believe that the Marshal of that district has been guilty of a very unjustifiable negligence, if not a connivance, in suffering the escape of a certain William James Davis, against whom he was charged with criminal process. It is the desire of the President that you should make inquiry into the circumstances of the fact, and if you find sufficient ground for legal prosecution against the Marshal, that you institute and pursue it to effect; and that you be pleased to send here a full statement of the Truth of the Case, as it shall appear from the Evidence of both sides. I am, with great respect, Sir, Your most obedient and most humble servant

PrC (DLC); in the hand of George Taylor, Jr., unsigned; at foot of text: "Mr. Wm. Channing Attorney of the US. for the district of Rhode Island." Tr (DNA: RG 59, MLR); at foot of text: "Copy." FC (Lb in same, DL). Recorded in SJL under 29 Aug. 1793. For the enclosures, see the list at Tobias Lear to TJ, 14 Aug. 1793.

To Delamotte

SIR   Philadelphia Aug. 26. 93.

The sloop Hannah, Capt. Curvan goes on public account to Havre to carry public dispatches for Mr. Morris our minister at Paris. The Captain[1] is to go with those dispatches himself to Paris. I take the liberty of mentioning this to you to ensure to them your particular aid and patronage should it be needed. Tho every precaution has been used to furnish them with every thing or the means within themselves of procuring it, yet should any unforeseen accident call for repairs or other expences of an unexpected nature, if you will be so good as to furnish them, your draught shall be paid at the treasury of the US. at sight, or the amount remitted instantly on receiving your account. I am with great esteem Sir your most obedt. servt   TH: JEFFERSON

PrC (DLC); at foot of text: "M. de la Motte." FC (Lb in DNA: RG 59, DCI). Recorded in SJL as sent "by the express sloop Hannah. Curven."

[1] Word interlined in place of "Mate Mr. Little."

From Alexander Hamilton

Monday Aug 26 [1793]

Mr. Hamilton presents his Compliments to Mr. Jefferson informs him that he has abandonned the intention of sending Mr. Little on being satisfied[1] that the business may as well be confided to the Capt. of the Sloop.

The Sloops name is the Hannah.
The Capts. William Culver.

The letter for our Consul at Havre is all that is now wanting to complete.

RC (DLC); partially dated; with apparently unrelated notes penciled by an unidentified hand on verso; endorsed by TJ as received 26 Aug. 1793.

[1] Preceding two words interlined in place of "feeling."

To James McHenry

SIR   Philadelphia Aug. 26. 1793.

The inclosed paper came to the President from one of the unhappy fugitives of St. Domingo, of the name of Lentilhon, now at Baltimore. He represents himself as 63. years of age, labouring under a fever, uncomfortably lodged, wanting linen, outer clothes, and other necessaries, for the approaching winter, and his passage to France in the Spring. Without doubting that the[1] assistance of the committee at Baltimore for taking care of these unhappy people has been extended to this person in proportion to their funds, and the equal wants of his unfortunate companions in misery, yet as to them alone the matters contained in the paper can be referred, I take the liberty of doing it through you. I have the honor to be Dear Sir Your most obedt. servt   TH: JEFFERSON

PrC (DLC); at foot of text: "Doctr. Mc.Henry." Tr (ViU: Edgehill-Randolph Papers); 19th-century copy. Enclosure not found. Enclosed in TJ to George Washington, 26 Aug. 1793.

[1] Word interlined in place of "your."

To Gouverneur Morris

DEAR SIR   Philadelphia Aug. 26. 1793.

The inclosed papers should have been annexed to the documents of my letter of Aug. 16. but were omitted by inadvertence. They are therefore now inclosed to you separately. I have the honor to be with great esteem & respect Dr Sir your most obedt. servt.   TH: JEFFERSON

Mr. Genet's answer to the address of the citizens of Philada.
do. lately to do. at New York.
     The above contain his declaration that France did not wish to see us engaged in the war.
Judge Jay's Charge delivered at Richmd.
Judge Wilson's do. at Philadelphia.

RC (DLC); at foot of text: "G. Morris esq."; endorsed by Morris. PrC (DLC). FC (Lb in DNA: RG 59, DCI). Recorded in SJL as "inclosing printed documents." Enclosures: (1) Edmond Charles Genet's extemporaneous response to the address of the citizens of Philadelphia, 17 May 1793, thanking them for their warm welcome and assuring them, on account of America's remoteness and other circumstances, that France did not expect the United States to become a party in the war, although it hoped that "her citizens will be treated as brothers in danger and distress" (report printed in National Gazette, 22 May 1793). (2) Genet's answer to the address of the citizens of New York, [8] Aug. 1793, thanking them for their cordial welcome, expressing official French wishes that the United States will continue to remain at peace, calling for strict observation of American treaty obligations, and criticizing the Proclamation of Neutrality (printed in same, 14 Aug. 1793). (3) Chief Justice John Jay's charge to the grand jury of the United States Circuit Court of Virginia on the subject of neutrality, 22 May 1793 (printed in Dunlap's American Daily Advertiser, 26 July 1793). (4) Justice James Wilson's charge to the grand jury of the United States Circuit Court of Pennsylvania in the case of United States v. Gideon Henfield, 22 July 1793 (printed in same, 25 July 1793).

To Thomas Pinckney

Sir   Philadelphia August 26. 1793.

You will perceive by the enclosed affidavits that an act of piracy has been committed by a certain William James Davis, master of the English merchant vessel the Catharine on board an american Sloop called the Rainbow. He afterwards came with his vessel into Newport in Rhode Island, but having some intimation that process of piracy was issuing against him, he slipt his cable in the night and went off, carrying with him the Baggage of his passengers and leaving his papers at the Custom house. You are desired to endeavor through the medium of our Consuls and their agents in the Ports of Great Britain and Ireland to have a good look-out kept, and in case of the arrival of the said Davis within their Districts to have him arrested and prosecuted for piracy. His own crew will be the most likely to furnish Evidence of the fact, or that of the British Schooner the Olive branch, commanded by Capt. Ayscough, whose affidavit, voluntarily given in here, I inclose you; I am authorized to add that the expenses of prosecution will be allowed by the United States. I have the honor to be, with much esteem, Sir, Your most obedient and most humble servant   Th: Jefferson

RC (CSmH); in the hand of George Taylor, Jr., signed by TJ; at foot of text: "Mr. Pinckney." PrC (DLC); unsigned. FC (Lb in DNA: RG 59, DCI). Recorded in SJL under 29 Aug. 1793. Enclosure: Deposition of Captain Richard Ayscough, New York, 28 July 1793, stating, in his capacity as master of the British schooner *Olive Branch*, that he left Kingston bound for New York on 29 June and while in the Gulf of Florida fell in with the British ship *Catharine*, Captain Davis, bound from Jamaica to St. Andrews, Nova Scotia, but intending to land passengers at Sandy Hook; that off Cape Hatteras they encountered the American sloop *Rainbow*, which first Davis and then he boarded and on which they found French ladies and gentlemen on their way to Philadelphia to escape the massacres at Cap-Français; that despite Davis's statement to him that the *Catharine* lacked letters of marque or a commission from the British government and notwithstanding Davis's warning to his men to respect property, he witnessed the transfer of what appeared to be a bag of money from the *Rain-* bow to the boat that had brought Davis to the American ship; that he ascertained from the victims that 16,600 dollars belonging to M. Berniaud and 4,950 dollars and four silver watches belonging to Berniaud's nephew had been taken aboard the *Catharine*; that when he expressed disapproval of this to Davis some of Davis's officers reviled him; and that thereafter they went their separate ways, with the *Olive Branch* proceeding to New York and the *Catharine* sailing in a northeasterly direction as if headed for Montauk Point (MS in DNA: RG 59, MLR; in a clerk's hand, signed by Ayscough and attested by Mayor Richard Varick; with notes at foot of text by Taylor: "sent a Copy to Mr. Pinckney by Mr. West" and [with reference to the enclosures included in Tobias Lear to TJ, 14 Aug. 1793] "press copies of no. 1-9 and copies of Judge Marchants two letters for the district atty. of Rh. Island. Sent in a letter to him of 26 Augt. 1793. No. 3 a 9 & ascough's deposition for Mr. Pinckney"). For the other enclosures, see Enclosures Nos. 3-9 listed at Tobias Lear to TJ, 14 Aug. 1793.

To Thayer, Bartlet & Company

Gentlemen   Philadelphia Aug 26. 1793

I have to acknolege the receipt of your favor of July 5. and of the two boxes of China, and Mr. Dowse's letter. From the length of time (4. years) since Mr. Dowse had been so kind as to undertake to bring me a service of China, he apprehended I must have given up the expectation of it and supplied myself, and therefore in his letter desired me to consult my own convenience only, as it was equal to him to keep it. The fact was as Mr. Dowse had expected, that I had abandoned the expectation of this and supplied myself fully. I have so written him accordingly to Boston where he desired me to lodge a letter for him. He writes me word that the China cost, first price, £79–19–4 lawful money. You will therefore be so good as to consider this parcel as still making part of his cargo, and subject here to his order, which I have expected to recieve, as according to his letter he should have been at Boston by this time. It shall in like manner be subject to any order you shall please to give. I have the honor to be Gentlemen Your most obedt. servt.

Th: Jefferson

RC (Charles S. Boesen, New York, 1948); at foot of text: "Messrs. Thayer Bartlet & co. Charleston." PrC (DLC). Tr (ViU: Edgehill-Randolph Papers); 19th-century copy.

Thayer, Bartlet & Company was a mercantile firm at 31 East Bay Street in Charleston, South Carolina (Jacob Milligan, *The Charleston Directory; and Revenue System of the United States* [Charleston, 1790], 38). The company's FAVOR OF JULY 5, recorded in SJL as received from Charleston on 15 July 1793, has not been found. Edward DOWSE'S LETTER was dated 4 Mch. 1793.

To George Washington

Aug. 26. 93.

Th: Jefferson has the honor to inclose to the President Minutes of what passed on the subject of the letter to Mr. Genet. Also the draught of a letter to the Merchants. Both papers have been twice sent to the Atty. General's, but he is not in town nor will be till tomorrow.

RC (DLC: Washington Papers); addressed: "The Preside[. . .]"; endorsed by Washington. Not recorded in SJL. Enclosures: (1) Cabinet Opinions on Edmond Charles Genet, 23 Aug. 1793. (2) Circular to American Merchants, 27 Aug. 1793.

In a letter of this date Tobias Lear returned the DRAUGHT of the circular TO THE MERCHANTS with the President's "entire approbation" (RC in DLC; addressed: "The Secretary [. . .]"; endorsed by TJ as a letter from Washington received 27 Aug. 1793; recorded in SJPL).

To George Washington

Aug. 26. 93.

Th: Jefferson has the honor to return to the President the memoir of M. Lentilhon, with a letter to Dr. Mc.Henry adapted to his case.

Of the letter of M. Millet he can make very little. It is rendered difficult of comprehension by the bad English in which it is written: and still more by the imperfect and indigested views of the writer. He sees no distinct object in it but to get the President to invite him to come to Philadelphia, which he would make the foundation of some other application. It seems also to be an attempt to draw the President into their incomprehensible party disputes. He is of opinion it would be better to give no answer to the letter.

RC (DNA: RG 59, MLR); endorsed by Bartholomew Dandridge, Jr. PrC (DLC). Tr (Lb in DNA: RG 59, SDC). Recorded in SJPL. Enclosure: TJ to James Mc-Henry, 26 Aug. 1793. Other enclosure not found.

For the LETTER OF M. MILLET, see Washington to TJ, 24 Aug. 1793, and note.

To Benjamin Smith Barton

Schuylkill Aug. 27. 93.

Th: Jefferson begs the favor of Dr. Barton's company to dinner with a small party of friends on Friday the 30th. at 3. aclock.

RC (PHi: Barton Correspondence); addressed: "Dr. Barton." Not recorded in SJL.

From Tench Coxe

Augt. 27th. 1793

Mr. Coxe has the honor to inclose to Mr. Jefferson the paper under this cover with a request that it may be returned when he shall have read or caused it to be transcribed. The Name of the writer Mr. C. will have the honor to communicate *orally*.

RC (DLC); addressed: "The Secretary of State"; endorsed by TJ: "Florida West." Recorded in SJPL.

ENCLOSURE

Unknown to Tench Coxe or Daniel W. Coxe?

DEAR SIR   June 7. 1793.

The information you requested concerning the Province of West Florida I find myself unable to give correctly having never committed any remarks to paper, and must rely entirely to memory for what I mention concerning it—it will however serve you as a clue to obtain better information.

When west Florida was ceded to Great Britain it comprehended the territory situated between East Florida on the one side, and the Missisippi on the other, excepting the Island of New Orleans (whose boundaries were formed by the Lakes Maurepas, Pontchartrain and River Ybberville) and from the sea to the 31st. degree of North Latitude, of which Pensacola was the Capital. If we except a small portion of good land on the River Tombecbe, which with the Alibamon form by their junction the Mobille River, and that which is contiguous to the Missisippi; the remainder of the Province was a sandy desert unfit for cultivation, and inadequate to the views of Government which were to form a barrier there to defend their other Colonies. Governor Johnston having represented this, the King in Council (I think in 1766) *by Proclamation* extended the bounds of the Province to the north as far as the River Yazou, which falls into the Missisippi about 100 miles above the Natches, thereby adding to it a beautiful extent of Country fit for every purpose of agriculture. Georgia and west Florida being what were then called Royal Provinces, *it was said*, the King's prerogative entitled him to add to or diminish their boundaries as he thought best and what was then added to the latter was taken from the former. In consequence of this, grants of land were made, Forts built, and magistrates appointed through that Country by the Government of West Florida, whose jurisdiction was continued in it till the year 1779, when the Natches was taken by Governor Galvez. In the succeeding years of 80 and 81, Mobille and Pensacola fell into his hands, and by this means he completed the conquest of the Province, which he took possession of conformable to the Capitulation of Pensacola from the Yazou to the sea. In this State things continued till the peace, when probably the English and Spanish Commissioners, being equally ignorant of the boundaries of the Province, when it was ceded to Spain never specified them in the treaty they made, thinking that these matters were so well known, as to require no investigation. The Americans better informed, knowing that the tract of Country which lies between the Yazou and the 31st. degree of North latitude, and which formed the best part of West Florida, had formerly belonged to Georgia and for reasons which suited themselves concealing their knowledge of the Kings *Proclamation* which extended the frontier of the one, at the expense of the other, took care to reduce the Province to its original size and by treaty got ceded to them, all which lay northward of the first grant.

Here the British Commissioners committed an unpardonable blunder, they first ceded to Spain the Province which her arms had conquered and then disposed of the best part of it to another power. From this the question in dispute arises, who has the best title to it? In favor of Spain there is conquest as well as Cession, and if the King had really the power of curtailing and extending royal Provinces they having possession of it, and that possession being confirmed by treaty, they seem to me to have a fair claim. Should this power of his Britannic Majesty be an usurpation on the rights of his subjects, the case will be different, for the territory must then be looked upon to have belonged to Georgia, and

[764]

unjustly withheld from it, by the Government of Pensacola. Spain, when she acknowledged the Independence of the States, must virtually have acknowledged all their just claims, and this would have been one.

Had I more time I would endeavor to add something more on the subject, you may think what has been already done is tiresome enough. I shall not, however, conclude this letter without informing you, in order to give you a more perfect idea of our imports and exports, that the duties of last year amounted to 90,000 dollars, the expense of collecting which is about 12000. You who are well acquainted with the custom House arithmetic can easily guess at the real sum which should have been paid, and which from late specimens, I have seen, I really think should have been double the amount. I remain sincerely yours.

A Note by the person to whom the above letter was addressed

From the above statement of duties collected in Louisiana *on the Exports and Imports*, I should conclude that the value of them must be at least 3,000,000 Dollars, or perhaps nearer to 4,000,000. Dollars.

PrC of Tr (DLC); in a clerk's hand. Entry in SJPL: "a letter on Florida & Georgia.—boundaries."

Internal evidence suggests that this letter was written from New Orleans. It was probably addressed either to Tench Coxe or to his brother Daniel W. Coxe, a Philadelphia merchant who had established business connections in New Orleans during a 1791 visit (Jacob E. Cooke, *Tench Coxe and the Early Republic* [Chapel Hill, 1978], 334-6). The boundary of West Florida was extended TO THE NORTH AS FAR AS THE RIVER YAZOU by a royal commission to Governor George Johnstone in 1764, not by a royal PROCLAMATION in 1766 (Clarence E. Carter, "Some Aspects of British Administration in West Florida," MVHR, I [1914], 365-6).

To George Hammond

Aug. 27. 93.

Th: Jefferson has the honour to inform Mr. Hammond, that on examination of the proceedings of his office he finds the usage to be to produce the original of the Consular commissions to the President: and for this reason that if the office be called on by a court of justice on any question relative to the Consul, a certificate in the nature of an Inspeximus is sent them, which supposes there has been an actual inspection of the original.

PrC (DLC). FC (Lb in DNA: RG 59, DL).

From Adam Lindsay

DEAR SIR   Norfolk 27th. August 1793

I received your letter with a post note to the full amount due me. I should have acknowledged it before this but was in hopes of giving you some intelligence from England as different Vessels were to sail from London for this port about the 1st. July.

Last evening came into Hampton Roads the Orian British Ship of 74 Guns from the West Indies she is part of a fleet of 3 Sail of the Line and five frigates come to Clear our Coast of Privateers one of which (the Sans Culottes) she has Captured and has with her. Should any thing particular happen shall do myself the pleasure to inform you. I Remain Dr. Sir Yr. very Hbl. Servt.   ADAM LINDSAY

RC (DLC); endorsed by TJ. Recorded in SJL as received 4 Sep. 1793.

TJ's LETTER WITH A POST NOTE was dated 10 June 1793.

From James Madison

DEAR SIR   Aug: 27. 1793

I wrote you a few lines by the last post from this place just to apprize you of my movement to it. I have since seen the Richmond and the Philada. papers containing, the latter the certificate of Jay and King and the publications relating to the subject of it, the former [1] the proceedings at Richmond dictated no doubt by the Cabal at Philada. It is painful to observe the success of the management for putting Wythe at the head of them. I understand however that a considerable revolution has taken place in his political sentiments under the influence of some disgusts he has received from the State Legislature. By what has appeared I discover that a determination had been formed to drag before the public the indiscretions of Genèt; and turn them and the popularity of the P. to the purposes driven at. Some impression will be made here of course. A plan is evidently laid in Richd. to render it extensive. If an early and well digested effort for calling out the real sense of the people be not made, there is room to apprehend they may in many places be misled. This has employed the conversation of _____ and myself. We shall endeavor at some means of repelling the danger; particularly by setting on foot expressions of the public mind in important Counties, and under the auspices of respectable names. I have written with this view to Caroline, and have suggested a proper train of ideas, and a wish that Mr. P. would patronise the measure. Such an example would have great effect. Even if it should not be followed it would be considered as an authentic specimen of the *Country* temper; and would put other places on their guard against the snares that may be laid for them. The want of opportunities, and our ignorance of trust worthy characters will circumscribe our efforts in this way to a very narrow compass. The rains for several days have delayed my trip to the Gentleman named in my last. Unless tomorrow should be a favorable day, I shall be obliged to decline it altogether. In two or three days I shall be in a situation to receive and answer your letters as usual. That by Mr. DR. has not yet reached me.

RC (DLC: Madison Papers); unsigned; endorsed by TJ as received 9 Sep. 1793 and so recorded in SJL.

For THE CERTIFICATE OF JAY AND KING, see note to enclosure to George Washington to TJ, 15 Aug. 1793. Concerning THE PROCEEDINGS AT RICHMOND, see George Wythe to TJ and Edmund Randolph, 17 Aug. 1793, and note. Wythe's DISGUSTS were probably triggered by a November 1792 act by which the Virginia LEGISLATURE lengthened the interval during which appeals could be made from his High Court of Chancery to the Court of Appeals, which had reg-ularly begun to overturn his rulings owing, Wythe believed, to the personal animus of Edmund Pendleton, its senior judge (Hening, XIII, 421; Imogene E. Brown, *American Aristides: A Biography of George Wythe* [Rutherford, N.J., 1981], 257-62). The person with whom Madison was in CONVERSATION was James Monroe. MR. P.: Edmund Pendleton. DR.: David Meade Randolph.

[1] Word interlined by Madison in place of "latter," apparently at a later date, to correct a slip of the pen.

Circular to American Merchants

GENTLEMEN   Philadelphia August 27th: 1793.

Complaint having been made to the Government of the United States of some instances of unjustifiable vexation and spoliation committed on our merchant vessels by the privateers of the Powers at War, and it being possible that other instances may have happened of which no information has been given to the Government, I have it in charge from the President to assure the merchants of the United States, concerned in foreign commerce or navigation, that due attention will be paid to any injuries they may suffer on the high seas, or in foreign countries, contrary to the law of Nations, or to existing treaties; and that on their forwarding hither well authenticated evidence of the same proper proceedings will be adopted for their relief: the just and friendly dispositions of the several belligerent Powers afford well founded expectation that they will not hesitate to take effectual measures for restraining their armed vessels from committing aggressions and vexations on our citizens or their property.

There being no particular portion or description of the mercantile body pointed out by the laws for receiving communications of this nature, I take the liberty of addressing it to the merchants of New-York for the State of New York,[1] and of requesting that thro' them it may be made known to all those of their state whom it may concern. Information will be freely received either from the individuals aggrieved, or from any associations of merchants who will be pleased to take the trouble of giving it in a case so interesting to themselves and their country. I have the honor to be with great respect, Gentlemen, Your most obedt. servt.   TH: JEFFERSON

RC (CtY: Woolsey Family Papers); in a clerk's hand, signed by TJ. PrC to Charleston merchants (DLC); in a clerk's hand, with dateline and signature by TJ; at head of text in ink in the hand of George Taylor, Jr.: "copy this only once." PrC to Savannah merchants (DLC); in a clerk's hand, with dateline and signature by TJ; at head of text in ink by Taylor: "Duplte." PrC to Boston merchants (DLC: TJ Papers, 92: 15809); in a clerk's hand; undated and unsigned. PrC to Portsmouth merchants (same, 15807); in a clerk's hand; undated and unsigned. FC (Lb in DNA: RG 59, DL); follows Charleston text; at head of text: "To———." Enclosed in TJ's first letter to George Washington, 26 Aug. 1793. The following list identifies recipients of this circular and those to whom it was entrusted by the covering letters recorded below:

New Hampshire.	Portsmouth. John Langdon.	
Massachusetts.	Boston. Messrs. Russel Jones, Higgenson & Parsons	Thos. Russel
Rhode Island.	Providence. Messrs. Brown, Franks, Clarke, & Nightengale.	John Brown
Connecticut.	Hartford. Jeremiah Wadsworth.	
New York	New York. The Chamber of commerce	Constable
New Jersey.	Elizabethtown. Laurence, Dayton & Co. & Wm. Shute.	Mr. Laurence
Pennsylvania.	Philadelphia. Nixon, Fitzsimmons, Wilcocks, Swanwick, Nesbitt, Crawford, Ball, Gurney, Vanuxem, Miller, Waln, Stewart, Ralston.	
Delaware.	Wilmington. Jacob Broom	
Maryland.	Baltimore Messrs. Mc.Henry Gilmer & Sterrett.	Mr. Mc.Henry
Virginia.	Richmond The mayor of the City of Richmond.	
North Carolina.	Newbern. Messrs. Turner, Mc.Kinly, Sheppard, Mc.Carthy, Davis & Guion	Mr. Turner mercht. Newbern N. Carolina
South Carolina.	Charleston. The Chamber of commerce.	delivd. to Mr. Butler
Georgia.	Savannah. Messrs. Wayne, Cuningham, Mc.Readie & Hill	do. to Mr. Butler

(PrC in DLC: TJ Papers, 92: 15812, in a clerk's hand, undated; FC in Lb in DNA: RG 59, DL). The covering letters were of two types. In those sent to individuals, one of which was dated 27 Aug. 1793, TJ wrote: "I take the liberty of putting under cover to you the inclosed letter, and of asking the communication of it according to its superscription" (RC in Ct, in a clerk's hand, signed and franked by TJ, and addressed by George Taylor, Jr.: "The Honorable Jeremiah Wadsworth Merchant Hartford Connecticut"; PrC of another RC in DLC: TJ Papers, 92: 15810, in a clerk's hand, undated and unsigned; FC in Lb in DNA: RG 59, DL, undated, addressed "To ———"). In those sent to groups TJ wrote: "I take the liberty of requesting you to communicate the inclosed to the merchants of   " (PrC in DLC: TJ Papers, 92: 15811, in a clerk's hand, undated and unsigned; FC in Lb in DNA: RG 59, DL, undated, addressed "To ———").

This initiative to gather evidence of depredations on American shipping by the European belligerent powers was probably triggered by the merchants of Philadelphia, who met in mid-August 1793 and appointed a standing committee of thirteen "to collect information respecting the capture or detention of vessels belonging to the citizens of the United States by the cruisers of the nations at war, and to lay the same before the President of the United States, with such representations as they may think necessary." The thirteen names initially chosen match the Pennsylvania recipients of the circular given in the list above (*Dunlap's American Daily Advertiser*, 13, 15 Aug. 1793; William F. Keller, "American Politics and the Genet Mission, 1793-1794" [Ph.D. diss., University of Pittsburgh, 1951], 306-7).

A draft of this letter was evidently "prepared by the Heads of Depmts." prior to TJ's submission of it on 26 Aug. 1793 to the President, who returned it with his approval the same day (Washington, *Journal*, 231).

TJ received a brief acknowledgement of this circular in a letter of 31 Aug. 1793 from James Constable at New York, promising to present it to the next meeting of the Chamber of Commerce of that city and advising that the addressee, his brother William, "has been in Europe since the Year 1791, from whence he will return early next Spring" (RC in DNA: RG 59, MLR; mistakenly endorsed by TJ as a letter from John Constable received 3 Sep. 1793 and so recorded in SJL). The following missing letters probably also acknowledged receipt

of the circular: Jacob Broom to TJ, Wilmington, 31 Aug. 1793, recorded in SJL as received 2 Sep. 1793; Thomas Russell to TJ, Boston, 15 Sep. 1793, recorded in SJL as received 2 Oct. 1793; and Russell "and others" to TJ, Boston, 15 Sep. 1793, recorded in SJL as received 2 Oct. 1793.

One method by which the merchants MADE KNOWN TJ's letter was through publication in local newspapers (see, for example, the *New-York Journal, & Patriotic Register*, 7 Sep. 1793, where the circular is mistakenly dated 17 Sep. 1793; the Hartford *American Mercury*, 9 Sep. 1793; and the Portsmouth *New Hampshire Gazette*, 24 Sep. 1793). The Richmond merchants had the circular and TJ's covering letter to the mayor printed for separate distribution (broadside in DLC: John Tyler Papers, filed with covering letter from John Barret, Benjamin Harrison, and J. Aaron to unnamed addressee, Richmond, 6 Sep. 1793).

[1] Relevant city and state substituted in other texts.

From James Cole Mountflorence

SIR   New York the 27th. August 1793

On Sunday next the 1st. September, I will sail for Amsterdam in the American Ship Cheeseman, from whence I will repair immediately to Paris. Should you wish to transmit any Communication to Mr. Short at the Hague or Mr. Morris at Paris, or to any other Person, I will most chearfully take charge of your Dispatches, and would take the greatest Care of them; In case the Vessel be visited by any armed Vessel of the Powers at War, if you think proper, I would Keep your Dispatches in my Pocket, and throw them into the Sea rather than they should be open, agreeable to the Orders you would be pleased to give to me to that Effect.

The Cheeseman is a fast sailing Vessel, and I hope to have a quick Passage; Should you think proper to give me any Orders, by Post, I must take the Liberty of repeating that the Vessel is to sail from here on Sunday next. I have the Honor to be Sir Yr most Obedt & most humble Servt.

Js. C. MOUNTFLORENCE

No. 15 Duke Street New York

RC (ViW: Tucker-Coleman Collection); endorsed by TJ as received 30 Aug. 1793 and so recorded in SJL.

From Thomas Pinckney

DEAR SIR   London 27th. August 1793

I send herewith the case of Mr. Phillip Wilson as stated by me to Lord Grenville and by him referred to the Lords of the Treasury: Some time after my first application on this subject Lord Grenville told me that on the report of Sir Willm. Scott the Kings Advocate General he had referr'd the matter to the Treasury as a compassionate case; I told him I considered it as a case of justice, but if compensation were made to Mr. Wilson for his loss it was immaterial what motives were assigned as the inducement. After repeated applications and an interview with Mr. Long the Secretary of the Treasury, that Gentleman made an offer to Mr. Wilson of £2000 on the score of compassion. Mr. Wilson considering this as by no means an adequate compensation, I sent in the representation herewith making the claim of Justice. This has been again referr'd to the Treasury and I am told is under consideration, in the mean time the poor man with a large family is in the utmost distress. I urged to Mr. Long the propriety of making some allowance to Mr. Wilson as his case appeared to the board to have merits in one point of view, but was answered that the Lords of the Treasury did not think proper to give any thing to Mr. Wilson 'till a final decision of his claim. As no law authorizes our Executive to advance any support to persons in Mr. Wilson's situation I have recommended as the only measure that could afford him any relief to petition the Legislature and forwarded to you by the last opportunity his petition: how far they may consider Mr. Wilson's claim on Great Britain as founded in justice and if so whether they will think themselves bound either to afford him some support or to take such measures to obtain a speedy redress for him as may be attended with unpleasant circumstances remains for their consideration.

I wish that at the same time it might be considered whether any provision should be made for sending home citizens of the United States who happen to be here in indigent circumstances. The only persons for whom any provision is made is for seamen and that at the expence of the Masters and owners of Vessels, on which account it is frequently eluded; and with respect to other paupers particularly women who happen to be here in distress they are sent by the magistrates to the minister or Consul and remain a tax upon them and such American Citizens as chance to be here and whose humanity induces them to contribute to their support. I have the honor to be with the utmost respect Dear Sir Your most faithful and obedient Servant   THOMAS PINCKNEY

PrC (ScHi: Pinckney Family Papers); in the hand of William A. Deas, signed by Pinckney; at foot of text: "The Secry. of State." Tr (Lb in DNA: RG 59, DD). Recorded in SJL as received 4 Nov. 1793. Enclosure: Pinckney to Lord Grenville, 8 June 1793, requesting compensation for Philip Wilson—who was reduced to penury when his ship *Mentor* was driven on shore and destroyed by H.M.S. *Centurion* and H.M.S. *Vulture* near Cape Henlopen in 39° latitude north on 1 Apr. 1783—on the grounds that this action took place in violation of the terms for the cessation of hostilities set forth in the preliminary peace treaties between Great Britain and the United States in November 1782 and Great Britain and France in January 1783, that the Court of Admiralty's dismissal of Wilson's suit against the *Centurion's* captain was presumably based on the principle expressed by Vattel that the captain had acted in ignorance of the cessation of hostilities, even though Vattel maintained that restitution was due in such cases, that the opinions of a committee of the Privy Council and Advocate General Sir William Scott both agreed that Wilson was entitled to compensation, and that all the circumstances of the case require the British government to make good the damages suffered by Wilson because of its failure to give timely notice to its military commander in America of the terms for ceasing hostilities (Tr in same; with penciled marginal note at foot of text: "The Original not found"). Letter and enclosure enclosed in TJ to George Washington, 5 Nov. 1793.

· For a detailed discussion of the CASE OF MR. PHILLIP WILSON, see note to TJ to Thomas McKean, 23 Dec. 1790.

From Josef Ignacio de Viar and Josef de Jaudenes

Mui Señor nuestro   Philadelphia 27. de Agosto de 1793.

A mediados del mes proximo pasado llegò à nuestra Noticia, que en una Sociedad de Franceses Jacobines establecida privadamente en esta Ciudad, se havìa Resuelto formar una Carta, ê imprimir porcion de exemplares de ella Reservadamente, y dirijirlos con algun Emisario à la Luisiana para su circulacion, con el fin de Revolver Aquella Provincia, y hacerla independiente del Dominio del Rey nuestro Amo.

A consequencia hicimos las investigaciones Necesarias con la precaucion, que Requeria el caso, y por fruto de ellas, pudimos lograr una de las Circulares impresas la misma que tenemos la honrra de pasar à Manos de V. S. adjunta.

Lo hèmos dilatado tanto tiempo con la esperanza de averiguar su autor primitivo, y el Impresor de los exemplares, pero no haviendonos sido posible sacar en limpio bastante para afirmar estos puntos, no nos parece prudente Retardar Mas el Representar al Presidente de los Estados Unidos contra la Sociedad, autor de la Carta, è Impresor de los Exemplares, para que sirviendose dàr aquellas providencias que tubiese por mas acertadas à fin de descubrirlos, se les castigue conforme prescrivan las Leyes, y segun merece el delito de trazar, fomentar, è imprimir en un Pais Neutral, y Amigo de España, proyectos que se dirixen sin Reboso à Revolver y separar del Govierno una de sus Posesiones.

Al mismo tiempo se hace indispensable, (en vista de uno de los Capitulos de dicha Circular en que el Autor promete, que los Habitantes del

Oeste de estos Estados asistiràn, y protexeràn à los de la Luisiana, siempre que pongan en planta la Revolucion) que pidamos à V. S. nos Mani-
fieste, si semejante oferta hà sido hecha con Conocimiento del Govierno
de V. S., y sino, no dudamos que este tomarà igualmente las medidas
para castigar el atrevimiento del Proponente en comprometer con tanta
liberalidad à los Estados Unidos sin autoridad.

Suplicamos à V. S. informe al Presidente de los Estados unidos de
todo el Contenido de esta Carta, y que se sìrba comunicarnos lo que
Resolviese. Nos Repetimos à la obediencia de V. S. con el mas Respe-
tuoso afecto, y verdadera estimacion con que nos Subscrivinos. Señor.
Los mas obedtes, y mas humildes Servidores. Q. B. L. M.

JOSEF IGNACIO DE VIAR   JOSEF DE JAUDENES

EDITORS' TRANSLATION

OUR VERY DEAR SIR   Philadelphia 27 August 1793
In the middle of the last month there came to our attention the fact that in a
society of French Jacobins privately established in this city it had been decided
to compose a letter and secretly to print a certain number of copies of it, and to
send it with some emissary to Louisiana for its circulation, for the purpose of
stirring up that province and making it independent from the dominion of the
King our Master.

Consequently, we have made the necessary investigations, with the precautions required by the case, and as a result of these, we managed to get our hands
on one of the printed circulars, the very one we have the honor to transmit to
your hands herewith.

We have delayed so long because we hoped to find out who the original
author was, as well as the printer of the copies, but it has not been possible for
us to clarify this matter sufficiently to make any firm statement on these questions, so we have not thought it prudent to delay any longer in making a representation to the President of the United States against the society that is the
author of the letter and the printer of the copies, so that he may avail himself of
such measures as he might regard most effective for discovering them, and they
may be punished in accordance with the prescriptions of the law, and as is
appropriate for the crime of plotting, fomenting, and printing in a country that
is both neutral and a friend of Spain, projects that quite openly have as their
object the stirring up of one of her possessions and separating it from the government.

At the same time, it is indispensable (in view of one of the chapters of said
circular in which the author promises that the inhabitants of the western part
of these States will assist and protect the people of Lousiana whenever they
start the revolution) that we ask you to tell us whether such an offer has been
made with the knowledge of your government, and if not, we do not doubt that
your government will properly take measures to punish the daring of the
man who has proposed, without any authority, to involve the United States so
generously.

We beg you to inform the President of the United States of the entire contents
of this letter, and that he be so kind as to communicate his decision to us. We

assure you again of our obedience and most respectful regard and true esteem, with which we subscribe ourselves Sir, Your most obedient and humble Servants. Respectfully yours,   JOSEF IGNACIO DE VIAR   JOSEF DE JAUDENES

RC (DNA: RG 59, NL); in Viar's hand, signed by Viar and Jaudenes; at foot of text: "Sr. Don Thomas Jefferson"; endorsed by TJ as received 27 Aug. 1793 and so recorded in SJL. Tr (AHN: Papeles de Estado, legajo 3895 bis); attested by Jaudenes and Viar.

SOCIEDAD DE FRANCESES JACOBINES: see note to Edmund Randolph to TJ, 4 Aug. 1793.

TJ submitted this letter to the President on 29 Aug. 1793 (Washington, *Journal*, 234).

ENCLOSURE

Edmond Charles Genet's Address to Louisiana

Les Français Libres à leurs freres de la LOUISIANE.

Le moment est arrivé ou le despotisme doit disparoitre de la terre. La France devenuë libre, constitueé en république, après avoir fait connoitre aux hommes leurs droits, après avoir remporté des victoires signalées sur leurs nombreux ennemis, non contente des succès dont elle recueillerait seule le prix, annonce à tous les peuples quelle est prète à faciliter par son puissant appui les efforts de ceux qui voudront suivre son vertueux exemple.

Français de la Louisiane vous aimés encore votre ancienne patrie, cet attachement est inné dans vos cœurs, La nation Française connoit vos sentimens. Elle est indignée de voir en vous des victimes de ses anciens tirans et elle a le pouvoir de vous venger. Un roi parjure, des ministres prevaricateurs, des courtisans vils et orgueilleux qui s'engraissaient des sueurs et du sang du peuple ont été punis de leurs attentats. Le peuple Français rassasié d'outrages, irrité des injustices aux quelles il avait été en butte, s'est levé contre les oppresseurs et ils ont disparu devant lui comme la poussiere devant un vent impétueux.

Votre heure est enfin arrivée, Français de la Louisiane; profités de cette grande leçon. Il est tems que vous cessiés d'etre esclaves d'un gouvernement auquel vous avés été indignement vendus; Il est tems que vous ne soyés plus conduits comme des troupeaux par des hommes qui sont nécessairement vos ennemis, par des hommes qui d'un seul mot peuvent vous faire dépouiller de ce que vous possedés de plus précieux, votre liberté, vos propriétés.

Le despotisme Espagnol a surpassé en atrocité, en stupidité tous les despotismes connus. Ce gouvernement qui a rendu le nom Espagnol éxécrable sur tout le continent de l'Amerique n'y a t'il pas marqué tous ses pas par des barbaries? n'est ce pas sous le masque hypocrite de la réligion qu'il a ordonné ou permis le massacre de plus de 20 millions d'hommes? n'est ce pas pour assouvir son insatiable avidité qu'il a dépeuplé, appauvri, dégradé des nations entieres, qu'il vous a accablé et qu'il vous accable sans cesse de persécutions?

Et quel a été le fruit de tant de crimes? la nullité, le deshonneur, la misere de la nation Espagnole en Europe, l'abrutissement, l'esclavage et la mort d'un nombre infini d'habitans en Amérique.

Lorsque les sauvages veuillent cueillir des fruits ils coupent l'arbre au pied, voila le tableau du despotisme.

En effet peu importe à la tirannie le sort des nations, tout doit être sacrifié a des jouissances passageres, tout doit flechir sous sa volonté.

Français de la Louisiane, les injustices que vous avés éprouvées ne vous ont que trop convaincus de ces tristes vérités et vos malheurs ont, sans doute, gravé dans vos ames le sentiment profond d'une honorable vengeance.

Comparés à votre situation celle de vos amis, de vos voisins les Américains libres. Voyés la province du Kentuckey privée de debouchés, soumise injustement a des entraves qui gênent son commerce et cependant par l'influence seule d'un gouvernement libre croissant avec rapidité *et présageant déja une prosperité qui fait trembler le gouvernement Espagnol.*

Arretés vous à ces derniers mots, ils sont le secret de tous les gouvernemens despotiques, ils dévoilent leurs abominables intentions. Les hommes etaient nés pour s'aimer, s'unir, être heureux, et ils le seraient si ceux qui se disent les images de Dieu sur la terre, si les rois ne cherchoient a les diviser, et a s'opposer a leur félicité.

La population du Kentuckey est l'ouvrage de quelques années; votre colonie mieux située, mais privée de la liberté décroit chaque jour.

Les Americains libres, après avoir passé leur tems à cultiver leurs propriétés, a augmenter leur industrie, sont assurés de jouir paisiblement du fruit de leurs travaux, de leur activité; tout ce que vous possedés, depend du caprice d'un Viceroi presque toujours injuste, avide ou vindicatif.

Voila les maux que peut prévenir une ferme résolution, avec du courage, de l'énergie vous pouvés en un instant changer votre sort: malheur à vous si vous en manquiés pour une pareille entreprise car le titre de Français devenu desormais l'objet de la haine de tous les rois et de leurs complices, rendroit vos chaines plus pesantes et vous exposeroit à des véxations inouies.

Vous frémissés d'indignation, vous sentés en vous le desir de meriter le titre glorieux d'hommes libres; mais la crainte d'échouer, la crainte de ne pas etre soutenus amortit votre zêle: Et bien apprenés que vos freres les François qui ont attaqué avec succés le gouvernement Espagnol en Europe paroitront bientôt sur vos côtes avec des forces navales que les Républicains des Pais de l'Ouest sont prêts a descendre la Belle Riviere et le Mississipi accompagnés d'un grand nombre de Républicains Français pour voler a votre secours sous les bannieres de la France et de la Liberté et que tout vous garantit le succès le plus complet: Montrés vous donc, habitans de la Louisiane; prouvés que le despotisme ne vous a point abrutis, que vous avés conservé dans votre cœur la valeur, le courage et l'intrépidité Francoise, que vous êtes dignes d'etre libres et indépendants, car ce n'est pas a notre empire, mais a celui de la liberté que nous voulons vous réunir: devenus les maitres de vos actions, vous pourrés adopter une Constitution Republicaine et soutenus par la France tant que votre foiblesse ne vous permettra pas de pouvoir vous defendre vous même, vous pourrés vous unir volontairement a elle et a vos voisins des Etats Unis vous pourrés cimenter avec les deux republiques une alliance dans laquelle se confondront d'apres les bases les plus liberales tous nos interets politiques et commerciaux. Votre patrie retirera les plus grands avantages de cette heureuse revolution et votre gloire égalera le bonheur dont vous jouirés ainsi que vos enfants. Point de foiblesse, point de pusillanimité, de la hardiesse, de la resolution, et *ça ira.*

Audaces Fortuna juvat.

Text reprinted from [Edmond Charles Genet], *Les Français Libres à leurs freres de la Louisiane* [Philadelphia, 1793] (DLC: Rare Book and Special Collections Division); written by TJ on title page: "by Genet" (see illustration). See Sowerby, No. 3244. Two other copies, unannotated by TJ, are in DLC: TJ Papers, 96: 16543-50.

From James B. M. Adair

Sir   [ca. 28 Aug. 1793]

I have the honour to inform you, that I have just arrived here in the Ship Amsterdam Packet, after a passage of 68 days from London. Mr. Pinckney did me the honour to entrust to my care several packets addressed to you, two of which you will receive by this post, and I also send by the Coach two parcels of Newspapers, from Mr. Pinckney, and one, of which I wish to request his Excellency the President's acceptance, but which, as it contains a few of the latest Newspapers, I thought might be so interesting to you, Sir, that I might take the liberty to inclose them under your address. May I hope you will have the goodness to pardon this liberty, and the further kindness to transmit them to his Excellency, unless he shall previously have received later intelligence.

Contrary winds obliged us to touch at Plymouth, where, I found, the Ship Jay of New York, Thos. Durry Commander, was detained, having been carried in by the Orestes brig of war belonging to his Britannic Majesty, under pretence that She was laden with provisions, the property of French Citizens.

The attachment I have conceived for the United States of America, of which I have not, however, the happiness to be a Citizen, led me to con[cert?] with Mr. Vanderhorst, their Consul at Bristol a letter from whom accompanies this[1] who happened then to be at Plymouth, in acquiring every possible information with respect to the pretences for this detention. I have the honour to transmit herewith the result of our investigation, in the form of an Affidavit, drawn up by me from Captn. Durry's information, and attested by him before the Consul.

Should you be of opinion, Sir, that by repairing immediately to Philadelphia, I can give any further useful information on the subject, I shall set out immediately on receiving your commands. At any rate, I propose to be very soon there, and I do not recollect, that any thing material is omitted in the Affidavit.

I shall have the honour to bring with me a box addressed to you, Sir, (of which the key is inclosed in a letter from Mr. Pinckney, which, on recollection I have thought right to transmit herewith) containing the model of a threshing mill. I have accidentally discovered that the person who made it, and who seems an ingenious Millwright, came on board the same Ship with myself as a Steerage passenger, with a view to settle in America. Should you, Sir, or any of your friends, have immediate employ for a person of that description, if you will have the goodness to let me know, I shall bring him with me to Philadelphia. I have taken the liberty to mention this, as it occurred to me, that you might wish the mill to be executed. If you direct me, Sir, I shall send the model immediately that you may be enabled to form some idea of his abilities.

I shall have the honour with your leave, Sir, to deliver to you personally letters of introduction from Professor Stewart of Edinburgh, and from Mr. Vaughan M.P. of London. I have the honour to be, with the highest respect, Sir Your most obedient Servant   JAMES M. ADAIR

I shall request you will do me the honour to address to me, if necessary To the care of Charles Wilkes Esqr. New York.

P.S. Having this morning called on Mr. Saml. Ward, he desired I would leave the affidavit above referred to with him, and told me he meant by this post to inclose it, Sir, to you. I therefore refer to his letter.

RC (DLC); undated; illegible word conjectured; at foot of text: "Thomas Jefferson Esqr. &c. &c."; endorsed by TJ as received 30 Aug. 1793 and so recorded in SJL as written from New York. Enclosures: (1) Thomas Pinckney to TJ, 10, 14, 20 June 1793. (2) Elias Vanderhorst to TJ, 4 July 1793, and enclosure.

James Barter Makittrick Adair, the recipient of a medical degree from the University of Edinburgh in 1789, had come to America to pursue a claim in Virginia (Adair, *Dissertatio Medica Inauguralis, de Hæmorrhoea Petechiali* . . . [Edinburgh,

1789]; Thomas Pinckney to TJ, 10 June 1793, and note). His father James Makittrick Adair (1728-1802), a native Scot who took the name of Adair ca. 1783, practiced medicine in Antigua and England and wrote a number of medical treatises, two of which TJ acquired in 1787 (DNB; TJ to John Stockdale, 1 July 1787; Sowerby, Nos. 910, 911).

According to SJL Adair delivered his missing letter OF INTRODUCTION of 7 June 1793 from Dugald STEWART to TJ at Fredericksburg on 12 Jan. 1794.

[1] Preceding six words interlined.

From Thomas Pinckney

DEAR SIR   London 28th. August 1793

Having in my former communications related the conduct of this Government to the neutral powers with the reasons assigned by Lord Grenville for this conduct which reasons as far as they concern enemy's property on board of neutral Vessels his lordship informed me he had directed Mr. Hammond to represent fully to our Government I have only to add that from subsequent conversations there does not appear any probability of the British Government relinquishing this point. These measures are attended for the present with greater inconvenience and consequent irritation to our citizens on account of the Court of Admiralty having as yet given no decision on the freight, demurrage &c. to be allowed to the Vessels brought in. On this subject I have made repeated applications (for although I am convinced of the respect due to the proceedings of the Judiciary of every nation, yet if in any case a delay of justice may be deemed equivalent to a denial it certainly may in the case of Vessels circumstanced as many of ours are) and the Court of Admiralty having adjourned to the 4th. of September without any decision on these points I reiterated my representation to the Secretary of State, who appeared to be surprized at the farther procrastination and I am from circumstances inclined to think that he will endeavor to accelerate this business at the time to which the Court stands adjourned.

As I thought it right that the evidence of our opposition to the measures pursued here should not rest merely on official conversations I took an opportunity of bringing forward the discussion in writing so far at least as to amount to an authentic document of our claim with some of the reasons in support of it, at the same time that I endeavor'd so to guard it, as to leave our Government unembarrassed in any line they might think proper to pursue. I enclose a copy of what passed on this subject.[1] [. . .][2] regiments are to embark in a short [time?] on a [secret?] expedition. They are to be commanded by Sir Charles Grey with Generals Stuart and [Dunda]s under him. Their destination is generally thought to be for the West Indies. You will observe in the news papers the Note delivered by the Russian Minister to the Court of Sweden from whence it appears that though they pursue the same line of conduct to the neutral powers they ground their conduct on a different principle, from what this country assigns as the reason for theirs. Thirty cases containing 9 tons, 11 hundred weight and 16 pounds of sheet copper for the Mint, price (including expences) £1230.1s Stg. were sent by the Pigou the remainder will follow shortly. I hope the quality and price will in some measure compensate the delay that attended the conclusion of this contract. I have deferred forwarding my account for want of those of the Consuls. I shall however wait no longer for them than till the sailing of the next Vessels. I transmit herewith a letter received from Mr. Digges & remain with sentiments of sincere respect Dear Sir Your faithful & obedient Servant

THOMAS PINCKNEY

RC (DNA: RG 59, DD); written partly in code (see note 1 below); at foot of text: "The Secretary of State"; with penciled note by TJ beneath last four words preceding coded section: "copy so far only"; endorsed by TJ as received 4 Nov. 1793 and so recorded in SJL. PrC (ScHi: Pinckney Family Papers). Tr (Lb in DNA: RG 59, DD); lacks coded section. Tr (DNA: RG 46, Senate Records, 3d Cong., 1st sess.); extract consisting of everything preceding coded section. Enclosures: (1) Pinckney to Lord Grenville, 22 July 1793, stating that in conformity to Grenville's desire he was enclosing a memorandum on the American ship *Eliza* and a note on two other vessels, which together covered only a small part of the American ships brought into various British ports; that it was unnecessary to add to what he had personally mentioned to him on this subject; and that he relied on Grenville to prevent any needless aggravation of the inconveniences arising from what the United States government will assuredly regard as infringements of neutral rights. (2) Grenville to Pinckney, 31 July 1793, stating that he had directed inquiries to be made into the cases of the ships mentioned by Pinckney, but apprehends that they were currently insusceptible to government interference because they were all being legally adjudicated; that he would always strive to prevent as far as possible any inconveniences to American citizens resulting from the war in which the European maritime powers were engaged; that the steps taken by Britain, so far from being violations of neutral rights, were more favorable on that subject than the law of nations as established by the most modern and approved writers; and that the rule laid down here was particularly attentive to American commerce in the instance he had previously pointed out—an allusion, Pinckney explained in a subjoined note, "to Rice not being included in the prohibition." (3) Pinckney to Grenville, [13 Aug. 1793], stating, in response to No. 2, that the United States regarded as violations of neutral rights those measures "which contravene the principle that free ships make free goods, and which prevent certain articles of Provision the Produce of the United States from being carried in their own Vessels to the unblockaded Ports of France"; that whatever doubts may once have existed, this principle had been accepted by a considerable majority of European maritime powers during the past twenty years, as witnessed by their practice in the last years of the Revolutionary War, the stipulations made in their treaties with the United States, and Britain's own commercial treaty with France; that Britain benefitted as much from trade with the United States as with France; that it was contrary to reason for a neutral country to be debarred from intercourse with either of two contending belligerent powers in cases not immediately related to military operations; that belligerents had no right to seize enemy property in neutral territory (a doctrine adopted by the United States government in effecting the release of the *Grange*); that this principle also applied to neutral ships, as evidenced by the American practice during the late war of freeing British cargoes captured on such ships; that most of the same arguments applied with equal force to the practice of intercepting and bringing into British ports American provision ships bound for France; that the existence of lower prices in France than in Britain for the prohibited articles meant that the British could not adduce a well founded hope of reducing the French to famine as a legitimate justification for their blockade; that for lack of security American

seamen brought into British ports as a result of this practice were exposed to hazards they otherwise would have avoided; that the blockade adversely affected America's principal export, grain, and deprived Americans of needed French imports; that it subjected Americans to unusually harsh treatment by their British captors, made them susceptible to bribery, and threatened to disrupt friendly relations between the two countries; and that although he could easily offer other arguments, he would conclude by stressing that the United States sought no exemptions to which it was not entitled by reason and that it stood ready to reciprocate for any attentions to its commerce (Trs in DNA: RG 59, DD, at head of texts: "(Copy)"; Trs in Lb in same; Trs in DNA: RG 46, Senate Records, 3d Cong., 1st sess.; with date of No. 3 supplied from PrC in ScHi: Pinckney Family Papers). Other enclosures printed below. Letter and Enclosures 1-3 printed in *Message*, 112-15. Letter and enclosures enclosed in TJ to George Washington, 5 Nov. 1793.

REASONS ASSIGNED BY LORD GRENVILLE: see Mayo, *British Ministers*, 40-2. The NOTE of 30 July 1793 from Notbeck, the Russian chargé d'affaires in Stockholm, to Fredrik Sparre, the grand chancellor of Sweden, announced that in consequence of an agreement with Great Britain, Catherine the Great was sending a fleet of 25 ships of the line and some frigates to cruise in the "North and East seas" in order to cut off French trading ships and provide protection against French privateers. The commander of this fleet was authorized to capture all French ships, regardless of the flag they flew, and to compel neutral vessels bound to France either to turn back or to enter a neutral port. In justification of these measures, Notbeck denied that Catherine was departing from her well-known support of the maritime rights of neutral nations in wartime and cited "the usurpers of the Government in France," who "after having subverted all order, after having imbrued their murderous hands in the blood of their King, have declared themselves, by a solemn decree, the friends and protectors of all those who should commit the same horrors and excesses against their own Government in other States; and they have not only promised them succours and every assistance, but even attacked, by force of arms, most of the adjacent Powers" (*London Chronicle*, 29-31 Aug. 1793). In contrast, the British government justified its own blockade of France on the ground that depriving an enemy nation of provisions was a legitimate means of forcing it to agree to reasonable peace terms (Mayo, *British Ministers*, 41).

On 31 Aug. 1793 Pinckney wrote a brief letter to TJ stating that, at the request of "Baron de Raigersfeld Secretary to the Imperial Mission at this Court," he was introducing Mr. and Mrs. William Payne Georges, "who purpose passing the winter in America," so that through his good offices "they will meet with that reception in our Society to which they are intitled by their own merits as well as by the very respectable recommendation of the Baron" (RC in DLC; at foot of text: "Mr. Jefferson"; endorsed in part by TJ as "private"; recorded in SJL as received 9 Dec. 1793).

[1] The next three sentences are written in code, the text being deciphered in part by the Editors using partially reconstructed Code No. 16.

[2] Undeciphered code 497.

E N C L O S U R E S

I

Thomas Digges to Thomas Pinckney

SIR   Tamworth Augt 13th 1793

Since I was favour'd by Your reply to my Communications from Birmingham relative to the coinage of Dollars &ca. &ca. (which I still am apprehensive are meant to be passd in the United States) I have not had an occasion to intrude upon You, nor as yet been able to get as far as London from the requisite attention it behoov'd me to pay to some moveing Farming Families and the getting forward a Young Bull and some Heifers of the improv'd Midland kind of Cattle to my farms at Warburton and Bladensburgh near the City of Washington.

I have been here for a few days on my way from Colebrook Dale to set some Lands on Lease to Farmers of respectability who have fixd to settle in America, and shall proceed tomorrow for Daventry on alike business and thence into Suffolk and Norfolk on a visit to Mr. Arr. Young and Mr. Coke of Holcomb. I am thus explicit in order to give you an oppertunity of communicating any commands you may wish to make to me for the further discovery or enquiry into what appears to me a serious attempt to counterfeit the publick paper of the United States. At any rate I should be oblig'd by a line from You to know if this gets to hand and my direction for some days will be *at the Post office Daventry*.

In a large Company on Sunday last, when the American Funds and paper was much the subject of Enquiry from me, I was informd by Mr. Harding a Banker and Mr. Heath a Merchant both of this place, that there had been a Man or two from America attempting to induce the Paper makers of this neighbourhood to make them Paper with the water marks of several of the United States. In consequence I yesterday waited on Mr. Robt. Bage of the Elford Paper Mill near Lichfield, and Messrs. W. J. and I. Fowler of the Alder Mills near Tamworth, and took theirs and their workmens memorandums as copyd on the other side.

They are all very respectable and worthy men, and of course upon suspecting an intended fraud rejected the order for the Paper. Messrs. Fowlers are Quakers and I recognized a former acquaintance with Mr. Bage who is of very liberal political sentiments, always an advocate for America, and an Author and publishd Barham Downs, Mount Heneth, The fair Sirian, Man as He is, &ca. &ca.

On my mentioning that I should inform You of their Communications They have promisd to give You any further discoveries which they may make, and will answer any Enquiries or requests you may make to them.

The inclosd is the sort of Paper the person chose for the work at Messrs. Fowlers; But the pattern or first attempt was made at Mr. Bage's mill on a thinner paper *unsizd* and rather lighter colourd 'tho of equal dimentions and when sized would become nearly as thick—a pattern of which is also sent.

Altho the two men came at different periods, they were likely connected or of the same party. They never gave their names and probably would have had fictitious ones. They are most likely Birmingham Artists in this vile tho common practice (as I have before informd You) of Coining and adulterating the monies and forging the paper of other Countries. It is not likely they can be now traced, but the parties to whom they applyd for the paper have promisd to do all they can towards further discoveries, and I have written to two men in Birmingham who may stand a chance to get further information among the makers of those *particular* sort of Letters which make the water marks, some of whom, I make no doubt, have or will soon Employ their genius towards counterfeiting the now circulating new five pound notes of the Bank. I am with great Regard Sir yr obt. Hbe. Servant   Thos. Digges

Pray what American Paper can such Forgeries effect?

RC (DNA: RG 59, DD); at foot of text: "⟨*Mr Jefferson*⟩." Tr (Lb in same).

MEMORANDUMS AS COPYD ON THE OTHER SIDE: see Enclosure II below.

II

Thomas Digges's Memorandums on Counterfeiting

At Mr Bages Mill—Elford nr. Lichfield mondy. 12th of Augt. [1793]
With Mr. B., his Foreman and 3 workmen.
In Feby. last, near the end of Feby., a Man applyd at the mill to get a Ream or two of paper made, of so common a sort that Mr. B. sayd it might be bought in any shop; But on very strong solicitations the men was orderd to get ready the stuf for it the next morning. He then said nothing of a water mark. The next morning, and before Mr. Bage was up, He brought the water mark (to *the description within*) and fixd it upon the wire frame. A sample was made at which He seemd much pleasd and said it would do with proper-sized Paper. On the Men informing Mr. Bage, he stopd the making more than one sheet or two, and thinks both sheets were destroyd and that the man went without the sample rather vexd and agitated at Mr. Bs. seeming suspicions. He had a file with him to make the Edges of the letters *finer* where required, and said He was to divide Each sheet into nine parts Each part with a seperate state name (they recollected only New Jersey, New York, Pensylvania and Connecticut) said there were more. The Letters were made of a whitish hard metal like pewter to look at, all in one frame with the spaces between Each letter open. He staid a night or two at John Bubbs the sign of the Crown in the village of Elford after the refusal of the order—at night sent for one of the foremen, pressd him hard to do it unknown to His master—said He would reward Him with half the money he

possessd which was then but 40/–. Then told the man He had many other marks to get done in Water Colour. (Mr. Bage cannot answer for the man being bribed or not.)

He was a tall thin young man about 24 years or 25 dark complexion and hair—dark Cloaths—Boots and Breeches rather bad or shabby—seemd sickly, and came a Cross road from Birmingham. Said he came from New York and that his Brother was a Governor in the Island of St. Johns at which place He said He got the Letters from a stationer with an order to get the papers made when He came to England—said He landed and had been sometime in Liverpool.

Same day went to Messrs. Fowlers mill a few miles from Mr. Bage's who was good Enough to attend me.

Mr. J. Fowler Jur., and the foreman to whom application was first made for the Paper, said—In *Sepr.* last or thereabouts a man lookd at and applyd for some Cartridge Paper (see sort, size, &ca. on seperate memorandum). He was middle sized aged about 40—tied Black Hair—Genteel well dressd man and came on a well Equipd handsome horse to the Castle Inn in Tamworth. On second application at the Mill He said He wanted to put water marks in the paper to be made and that He wishd to work at it a day or two himself—wishd to set his marks himself. Messrs. Fowlers were suspicious of Him from his manner and the mention of water marks and saying it was for Exportation and He would pay *any* price demanded &ca.—said He wanted a frame to set the marks in and then to get back the marks. He did by perswasion get one of the moulds or frames to the Castle Inn which was carryd to Him by the foreman but recoverd back by Mr. Fowler Senr. going to fetch it when He heard what had passd. The man and Him had not quite fixd in the water mark Letters when Mr. Fowler got it away. They saw the marks but could not say of what State whether N. Jersey or N. York &ca. He had plenty of money and offerd to treat the Foreman—was high and vexd when the frame was taken from Him—said you Englishmen are of the most sharp and suspicious natures. He appeard to have ridden over from Birmingham only 10 or 12 miles off.

Mr. Bage and Messrs. Fowlers say that no Capital paper makers will do such suspicious work, But that there are small and lesser mills who take such orders, and doubt not but their workmen are open to such Bribes as was offerd.

Could get no item of His name or abode.

MS (DNA: RG 59, DD); in Digges's hand; partially dated. Tr (Lb in same). Enclosed in No. 1 above.

Edmund Fanning was GOVERNOR IN THE ISLAND OF ST. JOHNS—later Prince Edward Island—at this time (David P. Henige, *Colonial Governors from the Fifteenth Century to the Present* [Madison, 1970], 161). SEPERATE MEMORANDUM: see Enclosure III below.

III

Thomas Digges's Memorandum on Counterfeiting

This was the Sort of Paper chosen by the Man who wishd to get the water Mark (nearly as below) made in the paper—(see Memorandum).

The paper is about 22 Incs. by 20—call'd cartrige Cap

The following is the size and shape of the letter as given me by one of the Men at Mr. Robt. Bage's Mill in his presence

---

NEW JERSEY

He told them the paper was to have nine different water marks on each sheet. He had other water marks of New York, Pensylvania &ca. but only shewd the workmen this one, which was fixd to the Frame as a trial and he approvd the sample at Mr. Bage's Mill. At the other mill of Messrs. Fowler & Co. the marks were not fixd and no sample was taken, as they rejected his offer.

MS (DNA: RG 59, DD); undated; written by Digges on a sample of "the sort of Paper the person chose for the work at Messrs. Fowlers" (see Enclosure I above); filed with another specimen of paper bearing notation on verso: "Mr Bage's."

MEMORANDUM: see Enclosure II above.

To Edmund Randolph

DR SIR   Philadelphia Aug. 28. 1793.

I have the honor to inclose you the papers of Messrs. Wilson Potts & Easton, merchants of Alexandria, complaining that their brig the Jesse has been taken by a French privateer called the Sans pareil, carried into Charleston, and there condemned by the French Consul and sold. The object of their application is to obtain national interference for redress. But this measure is always slow, rarely effectual, and never proper if the laws of the land give redress. If therefore the laws would give relief to the parties against the vessel and cargo, if still within the US. or against the Captors if here, or the purchasers, or the French Consul, it would be better so to advise the parties, than to take any public measure. Upon this point I take the liberty of asking your opinion, and am with great esteem & respect Dr. Sir Your friend & servt   TH: JEFFERSON

PrC (DLC); at foot of text: "The Atty Genl. of the US." FC (Lb in DNA: RG 59, DL). Enclosures not found.

On 27 Aug. 1793 the President sent TJ "a Letter & Sundry enclosures" received from Wilson, Potts & Easton of Alexandria, Virginia, relating to the capture of the British merchantman *Jessie* by the SANS PAREIL, a French privateer commissioned at Saint-Domingue and commanded by Captain Jean Bouteille, "for his consideration of the steps necessary to be taken" (Washington, *Journal*, 232-3). In a brief covering note of this day TJ enclosed to the President the draft of this letter to the Attorney General in order to "explain his views of the best way of proceeding in that case" (RC in DNA: RG 59, MLR, addressed "The Preside[. . .]," endorsed by Bartholomew Dandridge, Jr.; Tr in Lb in same, SDC; not recorded in SJL). Washington returned the draft on the same day with a brief covering note expressing his approval of it (RC in DLC; in the hand of Tobias Lear; addressed: "The Secret[. . .]"; endorsed by TJ as a letter from Washington received 28 Aug. 1793). For further information on this capture, see Melvin H. Jackson, *Privateers in Charleston, 1793-1796* (Washington, D.C., 1969), 14-15, 16n, 138-9.

From Delamotte

Le Havre, 29 Aug. 1793. He received TJ's 21 Mch. letter on 10 June and will continue the efforts already made in accordance with it to prevent foreign ships from flying the American flag. By the first ship he will send the security of which TJ sent him a model, having overcome the difficulty of finding people to make this commitment by offering a counter-guarantee and mortgage on his property. He encloses a state of American ships frequenting this port for the first six months of the year, but fears that the future will not be as favorable for the United States flag. The English, harassing it even more than France's ill-advised corsairs did, seize all American ships bringing colonial provisions to France and take all French letters on them even though they acknowledge they may not do so. By such determined conduct, he fears, England will not allow the United States to remain neutral. He is pleased that Nathaniel Cutting has been named consul of this department, and when Cutting returns from Lisbon, where he is now thought to be, he will hand over his functions to him and resume them only when Cutting is away.

RC (DNA: RG 59, CD); 2 p.; in French; at foot of first page: "Mr. Ths. Jefferson Secretaire d'Etat à Philadelphie"; endorsed by TJ as received 11 Nov. 1793 and so recorded in SJL. Enclosure not found.

According to SJL, Delamotte also wrote TJ a private letter on this date that was received on 11 Nov. 1793 but has not been found.

From Edward Dowse

SIR   Boston 29th. August 1793

I am just arrived from Europe, and the letter which your Excellency, did me the honour to write, is now before me.

I was under some hesitation whether I ought to have, sent you the China, after having delay'd it so long, and in which time it was natural to suppose you would supply yourself elswhere. But I assure you Sir, your returning it, will not be of the least disadvantage to me; on the contrary, a benefit. You will therefore be pleased to deliver it to the order of Messrs. Mc.Call & Plumsted who will repay you whatever expences of Freight or other Charges you may have been at.

I return you many thanks for the obliging expressions of your Letter, and remain with respectful attachment, Sir, Your most Obedient & Most humble Servant   EDWARD DOWSE

P.S. Will you be pleased to order the inclosed Letters to be left at the Post Office—and oblige Sir, Your most respectful & Obt. Servant

E. DOWSE

RC (MHi); opposite signature: "His Excely. Thos. Jefferson Esqr:"; at foot of text: "Govr. Jefferson Secy—&c"; endorsed by TJ as received 6 Sep. 1793 and so recorded in SJL.

From Robert Gilmor and Samuel Sterett

SIR   Baltimore 29. August 1793

We received Your letter of the 22d. inst. and took the earliest opportunity of communicating it to the Agent of the two Ships destined for France. He assures us that it is not designed to load Merchandize of any sort or description on board of them, nor do we solicit protection for any thing, except the Vessels, the Passengers and what may be properly called their Baggage. If more is found on board, it will, with the Ship and Passengers, be subject to the treatment which the Law of Nations permits. Motives of pity and humanity alone have induced us to interfere in this Business. The situation of the proposed Passengers is truly deplorable and the greater part of the little Baggage we are solicitous to protect to them is perhaps the fruit of the bounty and generosity of our own Citizens. If the British Minister cannot grant an absolute protection, we are authorized to say a recommendatory letter of the Nature he proposed, will be thankfully received. It would be an agreeable circumstance if the Resident from the United Netherlands and the Spanish Commissioners would grant similar letters or passports. With great respect we have the honor to be Sir, Your humb. Servts.

ROBT GILMOR
SAMUEL STERETT

RC (DNA: RG 59, MLR); in Sterett's hand, signed by Gilmor and Sterett; addressed: "Thomas Jefferson Esqr. Secretary of State Philadelphia"; franked and postmarked; endorsed by TJ as received 31 Aug. 1793 and so recorded in SJL.

From Thomas Mann Randolph, Jr.

DEAR SIR   Monticello Aug: 29: 1793.

We received two packets from you on the 20. inst. one of July 21. and another of Aug: 11. The former thro' the negligence of the post-master somewhere, was sent to Kentucké. Some accident of this kind has happened probably to your last, as it did not come to Charlottesville in the mail.

Your friend Mr. Madison has spent several days in our neighbourhood: he did us the honor of a visit on Friday last: his health I fancy is uncommonly good at present as he looks much better than usual. Colo. Monroe and his family are allso well. Mrs. Monroe has received a near fright, from a set of *borrowed* horses again, which ran off with her and Eliza between Charlottesville and their house but were stoped before any mischief was done. This alarm and the unruliness of Colo.

Monroes which have got some way so spoiled that they will not move the carriage from the door, deprive us of the pleasure of seeing her at Monticello, which we greatly regret.

Clarkson has not begun to sow wheat yet; the weevil increased so fast that he found it necessary to get out the whole crop before he employed the horses in any other way. He begins however on Monday on this side of the river: on the other it will take ten days yet to defeat the weevil. I shall pay the most pointed attention to your requests and shall have much pleasure in doing so.

Patsy bids me say to you, in addition to assurances of her love, that you must excuse her not writing as she is obliged to devote all her time to her guests at present. We join in declaring affection for Maria. The little ones are well. Believe me to be dear Sir your most affectionate friend   Th: M. Randolph

RC (ViU: Edgehill-Randolph Papers); endorsed by TJ as received 9 Sep. 1793 and so recorded in SJL.

To Isaac Shelby

Sir   Philadelphia Augt. 29th.[1] 1793.

The Commissioners of Spain residing here have complained to the President of the United States that certain persons at this place are taking measures to excite the Inhabitants of Kentucky to join in an enterprise against the Spanish Dominions on the Missisippi; and in evidence of it have produced the printed address now enclosed. I have it, therefore in charge from the President to desire you to be particularly attentive to any attempts of this kind among the citizens of Kentucky, and if you shall have reason to believe any such enterprise meditated, that you put them on their guard against the consequences, as all acts of hostility committed by them on nations at peace with the United States, are forbidden by the laws, and will expose them to punishment: and that in every event you take those legal measures which shall be necessary to prevent any such enterprise. In addition to considerations respecting the peace of the general Union, the special interests of the State of Kentucky would be particularly committed as nothing could be more inauspicious to them than such a movement at the very moment when those interests are under negotiation between Spain and the United States. I have the honor to be, with great respect and Esteem, Sir, Your most obedient, and most humble servant   Th: Jefferson

PrC (DLC); in the hand of George Taylor, Jr., signed by TJ; with part of dateline added in ink (see note 1 below); at foot of text: "His Excellency The Govr. of Kentucky." Tr (DNA: RG 46, Senate Records, 3d Cong., 1st sess.). Tr (Lb in same, TR).

FC (Lb in DNA: RG 59, DL). For the enclosure, see enclosure to Josef Ignacio de Viar and Josef de Jaudenes to TJ, 27 Aug. 1793.

TJ submitted this letter to the President this day, and Washington approved it the same day (Washington, *Journal*, 234).

[1] Day added in ink in space left blank in original.

To Josef Ignacio de Viar and Josef de Jaudenes

GENTLEMEN   Philadelphia Aug. 29. 1793.

I have laid before the President of the US. the letter of the 27th. inst. which you did me the honor to write, and the printed paper it inclosed; and I am authorised to assure you that the President will use all the powers with which he is invested to prevent any enterprize of the kind proposed in that paper to the citizens of the US. and in general to prevent their concurrence in any hostilities by sea or by land against the subjects of Spain, or it's territories.

The printed paper is accordingly forwarded to the Governor of Kentuckey, with instructions to pay strict attention to any endeavors which may be used among the citizens of that state to excite them to join in the enterprize therein proposed or any other, and to use all the means in his power to prevent it. I have the honor to be with great respect & esteem, Gentlemen Your most obedt. servt   THE: JEFFERSON

PrC (DLC); at foot of text: "The Commissioners of Spain." FC (Lb in DNA: RG 59, DL). Tr (AHN: Papeles de Estado, legajo 3895); in Spanish; in Viar's hand, attested by Viar and Jaudenes. Tr (AGI: Santo Domingo, legajo 2561); in Spanish.

TJ submitted this letter to the President this day, and Washington approved it the same day (Washington, *Journal*, 234).

From Samuel Ward, with Jefferson's Note

SIR   New York 29 Augt 1793

I forward the enclosed at the desire of Mr. Adair—the Jays Cargo was shipd by Saml. Ward & Brothers—and was at their risk till its arrival in France.

I will take the earliest opportunity of laying the particulars of this shipment before you. I am Sir your most obedt sert   SAM WARD

[*Note by TJ:*]

The affidavit inclosed in this letter was sent to Mr. Pinckney. There is a duplicate of it in Mr. Vanderhorst's letter of July 4. 93.

RC (DNA: RG 59, MLR); addressed: "The Secretary of State Philadelphia"; franked and postmarked; with note by TJ at foot of text written no earlier than 1 Sep. 1793 (see note below); endorsed by TJ as received 30 Aug. 1793 and so recorded in SJL. For enclosure, see note to Elias Vanderhorst to TJ, 4 July 1793.

SENT TO MR. PINCKNEY: see TJ to Thomas Pinckney, 1 Sep. 1793.

From James Wood

SIR   In Council August 29th. 1793.

By a letter just received from Colonel Newton Commandant of the Norfolk Militia, the Executive are notified of the Arrival in Hampton Road, of a British ship of 74 Guns, with her Prize the Sans Culotte. The enclosed is a Copy of Colonel Newton's letter and an Application from the British-Consul, that the ship be permitted to Water and take in Provisions. The Board have declined giving any instructions to Colonel Newton, doubts having arisen, whether the Case of the Sans Culotte from the peculiar situation in which she stands would come within the meaning of the 17th. Article of the Commercial Treaty with France. I have the honor to be with greatest respect &c.   JAMES WOOD

FC (Vi: Executive Letterbook); at head of text: "To the Secretary of State." Recorded in SJL as received 6 Sep. 1793. Enclosures: (1) Thomas Newton, Jr., to the Governor of Virginia, Norfolk, [27] Aug. 1793, reporting that the British ship *Orion* of 74 guns has arrived at Hampton Roads seeking provisions and water, that she captured the privateer *Sans Culotte*, that more British warships are expected from the West Indies, that he encloses the consul's letter and his response, and that instructions would be gladly received. (2) John Hamilton to Newton, 27 Aug. 1793, requesting that the British warship be permitted to obtain water and provisions and be accorded every assistance consistent with the Procla-

mation of Neutrality (printed in CVSP, VI, 500-1, which incorrectly dates the first enclosure; see Wood to Newton, 29 Aug. 1793, in Vi: Executive Letterbook).

17TH. ARTICLE OF THE COMMERCIAL TREATY WITH FRANCE: see note to Document II of a group of documents on the referral of neutrality questions to the Supreme Court, at 18 July 1793. The PECULIAR SITUATION which led to doubts about the applicability of this clause to the *Orion* was the status of its prize, the *Sans Culotte*, as an illegally commissioned privateer officially banished from American ports (TJ to Edmond Charles Genet, 5 June 1793).

To Samuel Biddle

SIR   Philadelphia Aug. 30. 1793.

I duly received your letter of the 1st. inst. I expect to leave this place on the 5th. or 6th. of October and to be on the afternoon of the next day at Mr. Hollingsworth's at Elkton, where I shall be glad to see you. I shall then proceed directly home, and wish you to take measures for meeting me there as quickly after my arrival as possible, because, instead of remaining there as I expected, I find that after about three weeks stay I shall be obliged to come back to Philadelphia, and shall not be fixed at home again[1] till the new year. It will be important for your own settlement, as well as for arranging the crop of the ensuing year, that you should pass as much as possible[2] of the three weeks stay I make at home. I am Sir your obedt. servt   TH: JEFFERSON

PrC (DLC); at foot of text: "Mr. Samuel Biddle." Tr (MHi); 19th-century copy.

[1] Word interlined.
[2] Preceding two words interlined.

To George Buchanan

Aug. 30. 1793.

Th: Jefferson presents his compliments to Dr. Buchanan and returns him many thanks for the pamphlet he has been so kind as to send him, and particularly for the partialities expressed toward himself. He concurs sincerely in the general sentiments of the pamphlet and can say with truth that no man in the United states more ardently wishes to see some plan adopted for relieving us from this moral reproach, and at the same time preventing the physical and political consequences of a mixture. Among the latter will certainly be a second chapter of the history of St. Domingo.

PrC (DLC).

From J. P. P. Derieux

Charlottesville, 30 Aug. 1793. Only great worry at TJ's silence and his own distressful situation can overcome his fear of bothering him again when he may barely have leisure for his own affairs. Since TJ's letter of 10 Mch., he has written on 25 May and 19 July asking what success he could count on from his merchandise and whether TJ could get Vaughan to send the amount from the sales. He begs for a few lines of reassurance, having reached his creditors' limit of indulgence. Colonel Bell told him he received a letter from TJ saying that his merchandise was sold and Vaughan was going to remit the profits at once, but he thinks Bell, not having shown him the letter and now very preoccupied with his own affairs, lost sight of what TJ wrote about him, otherwise TJ would have relayed him this good news. He awaits a response with equal impatience and respect.

RC (MHi); 1 p.; in French; endorsed by TJ as received 9 Sep. 1793 and so recorded in SJL.

To Richard Dobson

Sɪʀ   Philadelphia Aug. 30. 1793

When I last wrote to you I expected that I should have been permanently fixed at home this autumn. I have been obliged however to defer it to the winter. But I shall make a visit there about the middle of October, and therefore will be obliged to you to lodge there for me in the mean time a statement of the paiments made on my bill of exchange and bond, and of the balance due, and I will see that provision be then made for the speedy discharge of it. As there is a weekly post from Richmond to Charlottesville, the conveyance of a letter there will be certain. Only be so good as to note on it 'to await my arrival at Monticello,' lest they should send it on here, while I am on my way there. I am with great regard Sir your most obedt. servt   Tн: JEFFERSON

PrC (DLC); at foot of text: "Mr. Dobson." Tr (ViU: Edgehill-Randolph Papers); 19th-century copy.

From George Hammond

Sɪʀ   Philadelphia 30th August 1793

Several communications having at different times passed between you and myself, both in conversation and in writing, on the subject of the prizes made by the French privateers, fitted out in the ports of the United States; I have thought it expedient, for the sake of perspicuity and of avoiding future misunderstanding, to reduce the result of those communications under one point of view, and to request you, Sir, to have the goodness to inform me, whether my conception of the intentions of this government in this respect be accurate.

I understand—that all captures, made subsequently to the 7th. of June and *antecedently* to the 7th. of August, by any vessel, fitted out, armed and equipped, in the ports of the United States, are either to be restored by the captors, or a compensation for their full value, is to be paid, to their owners, by the government of the United States—and that all prizes, made by vessels of this description *subsequently* to the 7th. of

August, are to be seized and immediately restored by the government of the United States, or, if the restitution cannot be effected, a compensation for their value is to be paid in the same manner as in the former case.

If this statement be correct, I wish, Sir, farther to be acquainted—whether an official communication of any capture, that has been or may hereafter be made under the circumstances abovementioned, will be necessary on my part to substantiate the fact—or whether the circular instructions, which, as I infer from the public prints, have been transmitted to the Collectors of the Customs in the different ports of the United States, will obviate that necessity. [1]

There is another point, connected with the foregoing, upon which also I am extremely solicitous to obtain some early information. Being convinced that the determination of the government upon these subjects has been dictated by a sincere desire to redress, as far as was possible, the injuries that individuals might suffer from acts of rapine and plunder committed by the privateers, which have been fitted out in its ports, in violation of it's authority—I presume that the effects of that desire are not to be limited to the simple restitution of the prizes, but are farther to be extended to the procuring of [2] a reparation for any loss, which the vessels captured or their cargoes [3] may sustain, from detention, waste, or spoliation. Under the influence of this conviction therefore, I shall be infinitely obliged to you, Sir, if you will prescribe the mode, that may appear to the executive government of the United States the most satisfactory, and the best adapted to the ascertainment of the real amount of the damages, which may, in any instance, arise from the causes I have just recited.

I annex to this letter a list of privateers, which, according to the information I have received, have been all fitted out, armed and equipped in ports of the United States; and I have the honor to be, with sentiments of great respect, Sir, your most obedient, humble Servant,

GEO. HAMMOND

RC (DNA: RG 59, NL); at foot of first page: "Mr Jefferson"; with penciled marginal notes by TJ; endorsed by TJ as received 31 Aug. 1793 and so recorded in SJL. FC (Lb in PRO: FO 116/3). Tr (same, 5/1). Tr (Lb in DNA: RG 59, NL).

TJ submitted this letter to the President on 2 Sep. 1793 (Washington, *Journal*, 236).

[1] Opposite this paragraph TJ penciled in the margin: "His notification would be an additional means to us of obtaining knolege of captures and of timely interference. If he is dispensed from notifying altogether, it will leave an opening for claims to be raked up at a future day, which if now brought forward might be repelled."

[2] Next to the preceding three words TJ penciled in the margin: "We will in this govern ourselves by the rule which shall be observed by Gr. Br. If they pay for detention, spoliation &c. we will.

"Or will it be better to do it, as our cases are few, in order to found a claim more strongly against them, in our cases which are many?"

[3] Preceding three words interlined.

List of French Privateers Outfitted and Armed in the United States

List of privateers, fitted out, armed and equipped, in Ports of the United States.

L'Anti-George*	Savannah
Le Citoyen Genet	
Le Sans culotte	Charleston.
Le Vainqueur de la Bastille	
La Caramagnole	River Delawar.
Le petit Democrat	Philadelphia
Le Republicain⊕	Boston.
Le Roland	

* lost
⊕ taken

MS (DNA: RG 59, NL); in Hammond's hand. FC (Lb in PRO: FO 116/3). Tr (same, 5/1). Tr (Lb in DNA: RG 59, NL).

To Montgomery & Henry

GENTLEMEN   Philadelphia Aug. 30. 1793.

I have duly received your favor of Aug. 19. and can with truth assure you that it is the first information I have ever recieved of the existence of such a debt as is therein mentioned. On my annual visits to Monticello, my chief object has been to make an exact statement of every debt great or small due to and from my estate. This I have done chiefly by the information of Colo. Lewis: and thereby made provision for the discharge of them. I have here the statements of the two last years, in neither of which this debt is mentioned. I only repeat to you these circumstances to shew that I was uninformed of it, and that it did not proceed from a want of enquiry. I imagine that Mr. Lewis must have relied on some means of payment which have failed without his knowing it. Be this as it may, the dispositions already made of the monies due to me will oblige me to rely for discharging this on the crop of the present year. I shall be settled at home in the course of the winter, and will take effectual measures for the discharge of it as early as the produce of the year will permit. I am with great regard Gentlemen Your most obedt servt

TH: JEFFERSON

PrC (DLC); at foot of text: "Messrs. Montgomery & Henry." Tr (ViU: Edgehill-Randolph Papers); 19th-century copy.

Alexander Montgomery (b. ca. 1757)

was a merchant in Richmond; his partner has not been identified (Marshall, *Papers*, I, 366n). The firm's FAVOR OF AUG. 19, recorded in SJL as received from Richmond on 26 Aug. 1793, has not been found. TJ's letter to it of 9 May 1794, also recorded in SJL but missing, probably related to the order on James Brown for £83.5.3 with which TJ succeeded in DISCHARGING this debt on 5 June 1794 (MB, 5 June 1794).

From John Nixon

SIR   Philadelphia 30th: August 1793

The merchants of Philadelphia received your communication, as one proof among the many of the attention of Goverment to the Commerce of the United States, which involves in it every other important interest of our Country.

They will avail themselves of the invitation given, to convey all such information as they may obtain respecting the Vexation and Spoil Committed by the Privateers of the Powers at War upon the trading Vessels of America. And they doubt not upon representation being made, those Powers will shew the best disposition to restrain aggressions, which, being exercised against a People, Who, in maintaining a Strict Neutrality, have manifested a friendship for all, and ought to exempt them from such depredations. I am with perfect Esteem, by Order of the Committee, and on behalf of the merchants of the City of Philadelphia, Sir, Your Most Obedt. Servt.   JOHN NIXON

RC (DNA: RG 76, France, Unbound Records); in a clerk's hand, signed by Nixon; at foot of text: "Thomas Jefferson Esquire"; endorsed by TJ as received 31 Aug. 1793 and so recorded in SJL.

A missing letter of 13 Dec. 1793 from Nixon is recorded in SJL as received from Philadelphia a day later.

From Abraham Runnels & Son

SIR   Philadelphia Market Street, No. 222, 30th: August 1793.

When I took the liberty of addressing you on the 5th. Instant, Relative the Captured American Brig, with my Property on board, I could not doubt but that some enquiry would have been made, as to the Propriety of the Capture and the objects either Condemned or Acquitted; it is not necessary to prove that I suffer serious Inconveniencies, and disappointments, by the Detention of my Property (for 'tis too manifest) as a reason of my Application to you; but it is at least necessary that I should be satisfied, as to the Right in those who Detain and possess it, of doing so. The vessel which I allude to, I chartered and Freighted at St. Bartholomew, a swedish Island, where I then Traded and Resided; the Captain of her William Clarke a Citizen of the united States, did let her to me as an American vessel Navigating with a Register from the

State of Pensylvania owned by Jehu Hollingsworth & Co. Merchants and Citizens of this city of Philadelphia; the principal Inducement, to me to Charter a Vessel of that Description in preference to any other, was the Neutrality of the Power, to which she belonged, and the Security she thereby gave to my Person and Property; she was nevertheless Captured by a French Privateer, on the 16th. June, under pretences to which I am even at this moment a Stranger, and brought into this Port on the 23d. of last Month; and hath ever since been in Possession of the Captors.

That she is Truely an American Bottom, is a matter of Publick Notoriety; if she was not Truely So, I have not a doubt but that the Captain, would have been prosecuted, for navigating his vessel under American Colours, and register, if found to have been otherwise obtained, than is prescribed, by the navigation Laws of America.

That the Property on board of her, belongs to Swedish Subjects, is also a Matter of such Publick Fact, as not to be Controverted; yet in despite of these Truths, my Property is withholden, from me, and will no doubt be never restored (if 'tis left to the option, and descretion of the Possessors, to do so), but for the Interposition of Legislative Authority; had I freighted a Vessel belonging to Citizens, and navigating with a register, of any of the Powers at War with France, I could suffer no more manifest Injury, than I do, though I freighted an American Bottom, which at least might and ought to be Exempt from Captures, if any Regard be had to Existing Treaties.

Whether it does, or does not belong to the Executive Department, of your Government, to take Cognizance of, and enquire into this business, I can have no True information of, but from you Sir, as I can have no Communication with that Power but through you, and 'tis therefore necessary to Address you, and to Crave of you decidedly, your Answer, whether or not, the Executive will take Cognizance and Redress the Injured Party.

As a Subject of Sweden, if the Benefits of the Commercial Treaty between her and America, are extended to me, I see no reason to Apprehend, any difficulty with the Executive, (if the Preservation of Treaties belong to that department) to order my Property to be Forthwith restored; and though I may have misapplied the Treaty, and I were a Subject of any of the Powers at war with France, any Property I now have, or in future may have, in an American Bottom, as long as America Continues in Peace, with France, is free and Exempt, from French captures; by the 23d: Article of the Treaty Existing between the two Powers, under these Circumstances then, to whom Sir must I Apply? If 'tis manifest (as it really is) that the vessel now in Question is Truely an American Bottom, owned by American Citizens, the Property Loaded on board of her, is therefore Entitled to the Security given to such Property and Exempted from the Common Fate of War, provided by that Treaty; and who are guarantee's for the Treaty and for the benefits of it, is it, or is it not, the Executive, of the Power in whose Dominions, any part of that Treaty, should happen to be abused or Contravened; I say, does it belong to them to Correct the abuse's. May I be allowed Sir, to Remonstrate to you, that I suffer such Inconveniencies, and disappointments, by my Property being thus unlawfully with-held from me, as nothing scarsely can Atone for; that Property was intended as remittances to Mercantile Houses in Europe, to whom my faith and Credit as a Merchant is Solemnly Pledged and at Stake; the Mortification of the Disappointment, to a Man disposed to do Honor to and Fullfill his engagements is in itself sufficient (tho he should ultimately Suffer no Dimunition of property) to make him Lament the Situation and Languish for redress.

Therefore Sir, if it does belong to the Executive, to take Cognizance of this Case and to redress the Injuries, I suffer, let my situation plead with you, to use some Expedition to bring it before them; beside what I Suffer, in not having the use of my Property, the loss of my time, which now would have been devoted to Salutary objects of business, is another Important Consideration. Whatever Proofs you may need Sir, to Establish the Truth, of the vessel's being an American Bottom, and the Actual Property of American Subjects, I have, and they shall be forth coming and produced, when and wheresoever you require them, as also that the Cargo on board is bona fide, the Property of Subjects of Sweden.

I hope Sir you will Pardon me for the liberty I take in thus Troubling you, and that you will do me the Honor, to Acquaint me with your determination, as Soon as it may be Convenient, with your other weighty Occupations; I have the Honor to be most Respectfully Sir your very Obedient & very Humble Servt.   A RUNNELS & Son

RC (DNA: RG 59, MLR); at foot of first page: "The Honorable Thomas Jefferson Esquire Secretary of State &c. &c. &c."; with marginal notation in an unidentified hand: "Claim of a Swedish subject on the US."; endorsed by TJ as received 31 Aug. 1793 and so recorded in SJL.

For the 23D. ARTICLE of the 1778 commercial TREATY between France and the United States, which Runnels assumed would apply by implication to citizens of neutral third-party nations, see note to Gouverneur Morris to TJ, 20 May 1793.

To George Washington

Aug. 30. 93.

Th: Jefferson has the honor to inclose to the President a letter received from Mr. Maury, Consul at Liverpool, inclosing a copy of the order of the British government for intercepting our commerce in Grain. We shall doubtless receive it authentically and soon from Mr. Pinckney. In the mean time Mr. Maury's information seems sufficient foundation to instruct Mr. Pinckney *provisionally* to make proper representations on the subject, and to return an answer by the meeting of Congress. For this however Th:J. will await the pleasure of the President.

RC (DNA: RG 59, MLR); addressed: "The President of the US."; endorsed by Bartholomew Dandridge, Jr. PrC (DLC). Tr (Lb in DNA: RG 59, SDC). Recorded in SJPL. Enclosure: James Maury to TJ, 4 July 1793, and enclosure.

From George Washington

Augt. 30th. 1793

The President returns to the Secretary of State the letter from Mr. Murry with its enclosure—and observes, that if the Secretary is clear in the propriety of proceeding on the subject in the manner stated in the Secretary's note, he wishes the Secretary to do so; but in case he is not, the President thinks it would be best to have a consultation upon it.

RC (DLC); in Tobias Lear's hand; endorsed by TJ as a letter from Washington received 30 Aug. 1793. Recorded in SJPL.

Cabinet Opinions on the *Roland* and Relations with Great Britain, France, and the Creeks

At a meeting of the Heads of departments and Attorney General at the President's on the 31st. day of Aug. 1793.

A letter from Mr. Gore to Mr. Lear dated Boston Aug. 24. was read, stating that the Roland,[1] a privateer fitted out at Boston and furnished with a commission under the government of France, had sent a prize into that port, which being arrested by the Marshal of the district by process from a court of justice, was rescued from his possession by M. du Plaine Consul of France with an armed force from one of the ships of his nation. It is the opinion that the Attorney of the district be instructed

[795]

to institute such prosecution as the laws will authorize against the said du Plaine; and to furnish to the government of the US. authentic evidence of the facts beforementioned, whereon if it shall appear that the rescue was made by the said Duplaine, or his order, it is the opinion that his Exequatur should be revoked.—Also that the Attorney of the district be desired to furnish copies of his applications or other correspondence with the Governor of Massachusets relative to the several privateers and prizes which have been the subjects of his letters to Mr. Lear.

A letter from Mr. Maury Consul of the US. at Liverpool dated July 4. 1793. was read, covering an inauthenticated copy of certain Additional instructions from the court of St. James's to the Commanders of their ships of war dated June 8. 1793. permitting them to stop the vessels of neutral nations laden with corn, flour or meal and bound to any port of France, and to send them into British ports, from whence they are not to be permitted to proceed to the port of any country not in Amity with Gr. Britain. Whereupon it is the opinion that Mr. Pinckney be provisionally instructed to make representations to the British ministry on the said instruction as contrary to the rights of neutral nations, and to urge[2] a revocation of the same, and[3] full indemnification to any individuals, citizens of these states, who may in the mean time suffer loss in consequence of the said instruction. Also that explanations be desired by Mr. Pinckney of the reasons of the distinction made in the 2d. article of the said instructions between the vessels of Denmark and Sweden and those of the US. attempting to enter blockaded ports.

Information having been also received thro' the public papers of a decree passed the National assembly of France revoking the principle of free ships making free goods and enemy ships enemy goods, and making it lawful to seize neutral vessels bound with provisions to any other country and to carry them into the ports of France, there to be landed and paid for, and also of another decree excepting the vessels of the US. from the operation of the preceding decrees, it is the opinion that Mr. Morris be provisionally instructed, in case the first mentioned decrees have passed and not the exceptions, to make representations thereon to the French government as contrary to the treaty existing between the two countries and the decree relative to provisions contrary also to the law of nations[4] and to require a revocation thereof and full indemnification to any citizens of these states who may in the mean time have suffered loss therefrom, and also in case the said decrees and the exceptions were both passed that then a like indemnification be made for losses intervening between the dates of the said decrees and exceptions.

A Letter from the Governor of Georgia of the 13 instant covering the proceedings of a Council of War relatively to an expedition against certain towns of the Creek Nation was communicated for consideration.

It is the opinion that the Governor of Georgia be informed that the President disapproves the measure as unauthorised by law as contrary to the present state of affairs and to the instructions heretofore given and expects that it will not be proceeded in . . that requiring the previous consideration of Congress it will be submitted to them at their ensuing session, if circumstances shall not then render it unnecessary or improper:[5] that the Governor of South Carolina be also informed that the cooperation desired of him by the Governor of Georgia is not to be afforded; and that the Agent for procuring supplies of provisions for the service of the United States in Georgia be instructed that no provisions are to be furnished on their account for the purpose of the said expedition.

TH: JEFFERSON
ALEXANDER HAMILTON
H KNOX
EDM: RANDOLPH

MS (DLC: Washington Papers); with first four paragraphs in TJ's hand and last two paragraphs in Hamilton's hand, signed by TJ, Hamilton, Knox, and Randolph; ellipsis in original; endorsed by Washington.

The letter of AUG. 24. from Christopher Gore, the United States District Attorney in Massachusetts, to Tobias Lear, which Lear had submitted to the President the previous day, is in DNA: RG 59, MLR. See also Washington, *Journal*, 235. According to this account and other evidence Gore subsequently submitted to TJ, on 20 and 21 Aug. two prizes arrived in Boston that had been captured by the *Roland*, a French privateer recently fitted out there: the *Greyhound*, a schooner owned by the Nova Scotian merchants Alexander Brymer and Andrew Belcher; and the *Flora*, another Nova Scotian schooner. Soon after Deputy Marshal Samuel Bradford took possession of the *Greyhound* on the 21st in the course of serving a writ of replevin obtained by local friends and relatives of its owners, Vice-Consul Antoine Charbonnet Duplaine seized the schooner with an armed force from the *Concorde*, a French warship from Boston harbor, and had it brought under the protection of the frigate's guns. By the time Gore wrote to Lear, Bradford had managed to regain possession of the *Greyhound* because of the *Concorde*'s departure, but in the meantime an armed force from the *Roland* had prevented the service of a writ of replevin on the *Flora* and Duplaine was claim-

ing exclusive admiralty jurisdiction over it (Gore to Lear, 24 Aug. 1793; TJ to Duplaine, 3 Oct. 1793, and enclosures; Boston *Independent Chronicle: and the Universal Advertiser*, 26 Aug. 1793; Helen R. Pinkney, *Christopher Gore: Federalist of Massachusetts, 1758-1827* [Waltham, Mass., 1969], 53-4). See also TJ to Gore, 2 Sep. 1793.

The provisional instructions to Thomas PINCKNEY in accordance with the Cabinet's directions are in TJ's letter to him of 7 Sep. 1793. For the 9 and 23 May 1793 decrees of the NATIONAL ASSEMBLY OF FRANCE, see note to Gouverneur Morris to TJ, 20 May 1793. No provisional instructions were written to Morris on this subject, no doubt because of the receipt on 5 Sep. 1793 of his letter to TJ of 1 June 1793 and its enclosures.

Governor Edward Telfair's 13 Aug. 1793 letter to Secretary of War Knox and the enclosed proceedings of the council of war five days earlier with various state militia officers, which recommended an expedition against five hostile Creek towns by "At least two thousand horse, and three thousand foot," to be supplemented if necessary by Federal troops in Georgia and militia units from South Carolina, are in ASP, *Indian Affairs*, I, 370-1. Knox set forth the President's objections to the proposed expedition in a letter to Telfair of 5 Sep. 1793 (same, 365; see also Notes on Cabinet Meetings, 4 Sep. 1793). For the INSTRUCTIONS HERETOFORE GIVEN, see note to Cabinet Opinion on the Creek Indians and Georgia, 29 May 1793.

¹ TJ here canceled "a ⟨pr⟩ French."
² Word interlined in place of "insist on."

³ TJ here canceled "satis."
⁴ Preceding thirteen words interlined.
⁵ Preceding two words interlined by Hamilton.

From Dennis Griffith

Sir   Elk Ridge Landing 31st. Augt. 1793

I have been engaged for almost two years past in measuring all the principal Waters and Public Roads in the State of Maryland and am laying down a Map thereof: upon measuring the Sea coast very carefully from the line which divides Delaware and Maryland, (the Latitude of which has been, I believe, very accurately ascertained by Messrs. Mason and Dixon) to the place where we were shewn as the dividing line between Virginia and Maryland, and calculating from the above mentioned Gentlemens measurement of a degree of Latitude which is 68.896 miles to a degree; I make the latitude of this last line 38 miles and some few seconds. I observe in your notes on Virginia that you place this line in the Latitude of about 37d.57′ and being diffident of my abilities, have taken the liberty to address you and to request the favor of you to inform me whether I ought in the work I am engaged in, to abide by my own Latitude, or yours; all my enquiries have hitherto furnished me with no satisfactory information. The Public Offices in Maryland contain none. I am ignorant of the manner that I ought to have pursued, perhaps in this application, but from your Character and writings I have taken up an opinion that nothing more was necessary than to state the want of information, to you, in order to obtain it. I am with the highest respect Yr. most Obedient Servant   D Griffith

RC (DLC); endorsed by TJ as received 4 Sep. 1793 and so recorded in SJL.

Dennis Griffith (1759-1805) was a surveyor who served as an ensign in the Continental Army and as a vestryman and justice of the peace in Anne Arundel County, Maryland (Charles F. Stein, Jr., *Origin and History of Howard County Maryland* [Baltimore, 1972], 99, 216). He completed his MAP in 1794 and it was published a year later (Griffith, *Map of the State of Maryland Laid down from an actual Survey . . . and of the Federal Territory; as also a Sketch of the State of Delaware* . . . [Philadelphia, 1795]). TJ had used a LATITUDE OF ABOUT 37D.57′ for part of Virginia's border with Maryland in *Notes*, ed. Peden, 3.

From Thomas Mann Randolph, Jr.

DEAR SIR   Monticello Aug: 31. 1793.

Mr. Randolph arrived yesterday with the packet for Mr. Madison which I delivered immediately to a trusty messenger, charging him to put it into no hands, but those of Mr. Madison himself. The messenger was directed to go first to Colo. Monroes and afterwards to Wilson Nicolases, as I knew Mr. Madison was in the county but knew not which of these places he was at. My Brother, who came yesterday evening to visit us with his wife and Mrs. Beverley Randolph, informed me that he had travelled some time in company with them on his return from Mr. Nicolases to Colo. Monroes which satisfies me that the packet has reached its destination in safety before this, alltho' the servant has not returned. Mr. D. M. Randolph has been at Presquisle since his return from Philada. He says that there is a letter and a box, containing probably the model of the threshing-machine, for you, at Bermuda-hundred, in the custom-house. It will be necessary, he tells me, for the box to be opened that its contents may be valued to ascertain the duty, if there is no note of the price in the letter. It will give him pleasure to execute any orders you may give concerning it. If you wish it brought to Monticello, I can take any extraordinary precautions you think adviseable for its safe-carriage.

This letter is borne by the person who carries your horse to Georgetown. Having reason to think upon farther trial that he will not suit you, there being little prospect of his recovering his health perfectly, I must beg that you will use him as your own untill your return to Virginia, when I shall have a better one ready to exchange for him. If I could have procured a good substitute this should not have been sent, but the time since I was fully convinced of his unfitness would not admitt of it in the present scarcity.

M. De Rieux desires me to ask if you have received a letter from him, written late in the last month. Your most sincere & affectionate friend & hble Servt.   TH: M RANDOLPH

N.B. Mr. Madison and Colo. Monroe have just called on us. The packet was delivered last night as I expected.

RC (MHi); endorsed by TJ as received 8 Sep. 1793 and so recorded in SJL.

The PACKET was TJ's second letter of 11 Aug. 1793 to James Madison. The package

AT BERMUDA-HUNDRED actually contained an orrery (James B. M. Adair to TJ, [ca. 28 Aug. 1793]; TJ to Patrick Hart, 14 Nov. 1793; Hart to TJ, 1 Dec. 1793).

To John Suter

SIR Philadelphia Aug. 31. 1793

Having occasion to send a horse from this place to my own house in Virginia, and to receive another from thence, I have directed a servant to come from thence and be at your house on Wednesday the 4th. of Sep. where another will meet him from this place, to exchange horses, and each return. Both will be furnished with money for their expences: however as accidents may detain one or both on the road, and it is necessary that he who arrives first should wait for the other, which would cause them an expence at your house more than they are provided for, be so good as to debit me with it, and I shall discharge it as I pass on to Virginia, which will be within a few weeks. I am Sir Your obedt servt

TH: JEFFERSON

PrC (DLC); at foot of text: "Mr. Shuter. George town." Tr (ViU: Edgehill-Randolph Papers); 19th-century copy.

John Suter (d. 1794) had operated a farm near Rockville, Maryland, in April 1770, but from 1783 until his death he was the proprietor of Suter's Tavern in Georgetown (MB, 18 July 1792, and note; Oliver W. Holmes, "The Colonial Taverns of Georgetown," *Records of the Columbia Historical Society*, LI-LII [1951-52], 15, 17-18).

INDEX

bald eagle: and maces for Va. General Assembly, 236

Ball, Joseph: and circular letter to merchants, 768n

Ballard, Robert: death, 733-4

Baltic sea: freight charges for, 8; and U.S. trade, 77

Baltimore: customs collector (*see* Williams, Otho H.); French vice-consul at (*see* Moissonnier, F.); passports for U.S. ships at, 57; and French privateering, 68n, 152, 285, 296, 432, 461, 497, 601n, 728; allied ships armed at, 359-60; trade with Jamaica, 379n; trade with France, 388n, 433, 564n; Edward Thornton appointed British vice-consul at, 398; and use of U.S. ports by armed allied ships, 418n; trade with St. Barthélemy, 432; trade with Saint-Domingue, 459n; trade with Barbados, 461; and alleged French refugee plots against Saint-Domingue, 612n; George Buchanan seeks appointment as port inspector of, 733-4; and relief of Saint-Domingue refugees, 740; and circular letter to merchants, 768n

Banfill, Samuel: appointed consular agent by Elias Vanderhorst, 251

Banister, John Farley: death of, 250

Bank of North America: and TJ's salary, 569

Bank of the United States: TJ's draft on, 171n; loan to U.S., 280; U.S. debt to, 304; payment to James Blake, 483n; act for, 523; and TJ's salary, 569; TJ's proposed congressional declaration on, 651; John Taylor of Caroline's pamphlet on, 654-5

Banning, Jeremiah: and case of *Eunice*, 67; described, 68n

Barbados, W.I.: U.S. trade with, 461

Barbary States: maritime insurance against, 94; relations with U.S., 94, 112

Barbeyrac, Johannes: cited by E. Randolph, 33, 35n

Barcelona, Spain: Spanish fleet at, 94; demand for flour and wheat at, 647

Barclay, John: and Barclay's mission to Morocco, 58; mentioned, 124n, 379n

Barclay, Mary (Mrs. Thomas Barclay): letter to, 58-9

Barclay, Thomas: mission to Morocco, 58; mission to Algiers, 751; mentioned, 433n, 662

Barden, Richard: and case of *Jane* schooner, 726-7

Barham Downs (Robert Bage), 779

Baring, John & Francis, & Co.: and bills of exchange for Department of State, 332, 430, 679

bark: importation by Great Britain, 683; Sinclair's views on, 683

barley: experiment of T. M. Randolph, Jr., with, 87; and TJ's crop-rotation plan, 402, 422, 423; and crop-rotation plan of T. M. Randolph, Jr., 471, 593

Barnard, Timothy: and Spanish relations with Southern Indians, 412n

Barnes, Joseph: letters from, 715, 716; and steamboat, 108

Barnes, Timothy: relations with Creeks, 16n

Barnwell, John: and fugitive slaves, 12n

Barret, John: debt to TJ, 189-90, 381, 551; and circular letter to merchants, 768n, 769n

Barriere, Pierre: and cases of *Active* and *William*, 282n

Barry, John: impressed by British, 753n

Barry, William: letter from, 418-20; plans to settle in U.S., 418-20

Barton, Benjamin Smith: letters to, 744, 763; invited to visit TJ, 744, 763; TJ asks for books from, 744

Barton, William: and Currie v. Griffin, 187

Bartram, William: garden of, 122; Kentucky coffee tree seeds for, 168, 274

basins: TJ's sent to Monticello, 19

Basseterre, St. Christopher: and British privateering, 459n

Bassett, Capt. (master of *Active*): ship captured by *Citoyen Genet*, 218

Bastard, M.: and case of *Fury*, 576n

Batton, John: and case of *Peggy*, 712n

Bauló, Juan: and fugitive slaves, 12n

Bautier (Beustier), G.: and case of *Regulator*, 459n, 557

Bavay, France: and War of First Coalition, 69

Baxter, Capt. (commander of *Sudden Death*): and case of *Prosperity*, 389n

Bayley, Mr.: plans to practice law in Va., 105

Bayonne, France: expected Spanish siege of, 223; and French privateering, 388

Beach, Mr. See Bache (Beach), Benjamin Franklin

beans: Petit's recipe for preserving, 618

beans, horse: threshing of, 249

Bear Creek, 118

Beaumarchais, Pierre Augustin Caron de: claim on U.S., 243-7, 277

Beaver (ship): and southern whale fishery, 23n
Beckley, John: and Sir John Temple's consular commission, 27; *Examination of the Late Proceedings in Congress*, 62, 553; relations with Monroe, 137; intelligence about Federalists, 219; and Hamilton's alleged plan for monarchical government, 220-1; TJ's view of, 220; supports William Lambert for House of Representatives clerkship, 234; and case of Andrew G. Fraunces, 267; and "Veritas" essays, 522
beds: TJ's sent to Monticello, 19, 20
Bee, The: sent to TJ, 551
beef: price, 9; captured by British, 337, 436n, 646; captured by Algerines, 421
beeswax: captured by French, 726-7
Belarosi: and Moroccan civil war, 163
Belcher, Andrew: and case of *Greyhound*, 797n
Bell, Thomas: letter to, 386; letter from, 258-9; recommended by TJ, 61; J. G. Jefferson declines to deal with, 214, 258-9, 386; TJ's account with, 259; and wine for TJ, 746; and Derieux's business affairs, 788-9
Bellanger, Mme. *See* Plumard de Bellanger, Mme
Bellegarde, France: Spanish siege of, 223
Bellona (ship): and impressment, 753n
bells: TJ's sent to Monticello, 19
Belvedere (ship): and impressment, 753n
Benasser. *See* Abderhaman Benasser
Bentalou, Paul: letter to, 357; and issuance by foreign officials of passports for U.S. ships, 357; letter from cited, 357n
Bentinck, William: and impressment, 753n
Bergere (dog): offspring, 53
Berniaud, M.: plundered by British, 761n
Bernoulli, Daniel: and steamboat, 108
Berry & Rogers: and inkstand for TJ, 599
Bertrand de Molleville, Antoine François, Marquis de: and U.S. aid to Saint-Domingue, 348, 352n
Berwick (H.M.S.): damaged by storm, 645
Betsey (ship): captured by *Citoyen Genet*, 432, 453-4, 792-4
Betsy (brig): wreck of, 78
Betsy (brigantine): captured by *Sans Culottes*, 624-5
Beustier, G. *See* Bautier (Beustier), G.
Biddle, Charles: and case of *Little Sarah*, 449n; mentioned, 679

Biddle, Clement: letters to, 386, 642; letter from, 630-1; and case of *Suckey*, 376n, 386; letters from cited, 376n, 386n; and case of brigantine *Betsy*, 625n; and British captures of U.S. prizes, 630-1; and restoration of British prizes, 642; mentioned, 633n
Biddle, James: letter from, 147; and case of *Amiable*, 147; identified, 147n
Biddle, Samuel: letter to, 788; letter from, 596; agreement with, 308; overseer for Monticello, 308, 318, 355-6, 397, 401, 422, 428, 445, 596, 657, 788
bills of exchange: and Genet's mission to U.S., 83n; for Department of State, 94-5, 332-3, 354, 430-1, 516, 546, 551, 563, 589-90, 679, 742
Billy. *See* Gardner, William (Billy)
Bingham, William: sale of lands of, 162n; dines with TJ, 241; mentioned, 743
Birch, Joseph: and bills of exchange for Department of State, 431, 679
Birch, Richard: and case of *Catharine* of Jamaica, 666-7n
Birmingham, England: copper coinage in, 779; and counterfeiting of U.S. currency, 780
Biron, Armand Louis de Gontaut, Duc de: defeat of, 69
Biscay: Spanish army in, 223
biscuits: captured by British, 337
blacks: unrest in Martinique, 595; impressed by British, 753n
Blackwood, John: and stolen slaves, 14n
Bladensburg, Md.: Thomas Digges's farm at, 779
Blair, Capt. (master of *Active*): ship captured by *Thought*, 646; mentioned, 147
Blair, James, 575
Blair, John: letters to, 488, 520; and referral of neutrality questions to Supreme Court, 488, 520, 526, 550; letter from Washington, 550
Blake, James: letter to, 483; U.S. courier to Madrid, 474, 476, 483-4, 485, 488-9, 505, 506, 510; identified, 483n; letter to submitted to Washington, 483n; passport for, 484; passport for submitted to Washington, 484n
Blanchard, Jean Pierre: aeronautical experiments, 105n
blockades: British policy toward, 377n
Blodget, Samuel, Jr.: and Thornton's Capitol plan, 425-6
Bloody Fellow (Cherokee chief): Caron-

329; possible U.S. attack on, 375n; U.S. invasion of in Revolutionary War, 375n; French plan to liberate, 438-9; mentioned, 755n

canals: for Monticello, 65, 317, 667; for Federal District, 426n

Canard, Juan: relations with Creeks, 17n

Canary Islands: U.S. trade with, 614

candelabra: TJ's sent to Monticello, 20

candleholders: TJ's sent to Monticello, 19

candles: TJ's sent to Monticello, 19; for TJ, 189, 247

cannon: for Mud Island, 508-9

Cano, Vincente: and case of *Maria*, 455n

Cape Henlopen, 31, 34

Cape Henry, 378, 381

Cape May, 31, 34

Cape May County, N.J., 34

Cape of Good Hope, 388

Cap-Français, Saint-Domingue: destruction of, 456n, 710, 761n

Capitol, U.S.: Thornton's plan for, 425-6, 455, 462, 489-95, 500, 517-19; marble for, 490; Hallet's plan for, 519n; drawings of, 671-2; masonry, 671-2

Capricieuse (French frigate): captures *Juno*, 664n

Caramagnole (French privateer): and French right to fit out privateers in U.S., 708, 791

Carbonnel, Joseph Hilary: oath of allegiance to Pa., 308n

Carew, Mr. *See* Carey (Carew), John

Carey, James: and Spanish relations with Southern Indians, 414n

Carey (Carew), John: *Official Letters to the Honorable American Congress*, 288; described, 289n

caricatures: for Anne Cary Randolph, 617

Caritat, Louis Alexis Hocquet de: and case of *Republican*, 282n

Carmichael, William: letters to, 148-9, 405-12, 485-6, 510; letters from, 206-12, 668-70; account with Willink, Van Staphorst & Hubbard, 73; and case of Joseph Ravara, 104; letter from submitted to Washington, 141n; letter to submitted to Washington, 150n; letter to cited, 163n; and Spanish relations with Southern Indians, 168, 205, 211-12, 328, 405-16, 668-71; and navigation of Mississippi, 206, 210, 485-6; and U.S. boundary with Spain, 206, 210; and Spanish relations with Great Britain, 207-10; and Spanish finances, 224; alleged jealousy of Short, 384-5; and

Spanish seizure of French property on U.S. ships, 430; dispatches for, 483, 484, 573-4; and case of *Dover Cutter*, 510; correspondence with TJ, 510; and case of *Bacchus*, 758; mentioned, 140, 222, 226, 420-1, 428

Carnes, Burrill: absence from France, 743

Carnot, Citizen: and case of *Fame*, 266n

Carolina Packet (ship): fired on by British privateer, 753

Caroline County, Va.: address on neutrality, 766

Carondelet, Francisco Luis Hector, Baron de: and Spanish relations with Southern Indians, 118-20, 148, 263-6, 314, 316-17, 407, 408-9, 414n, 415n, 670-1n; and Spanish relations with Western Indians, 120; fortifies Ecores à Margot, 416n

Carott, M. *See* Caro y Suedra (Carott), Pedro

Caro y Suedra (Carott), Pedro: and Spanish war with France, 223

carpenters: for Monticello, 64, 171; for Mint, 185

carriages: cost of, 29

Carroll, Daniel: letter to, 671-2; letter from, 357; and map of Federal District, 357. *See also* Federal District Commissioners

Carrollsburg, Md.: and Federal District, 425

Carstairs, Thomas: letter to, 500; and Thornton's Capitol plan, 500, 517-19; identified, 500n; estimate of masonry cost for Capitol, 671-2

Cartagena, Spain, 89, 163

Carthage, 736n

Cary, Archibald: and Wayles estate debt, 544

Cary, Wilson Miles: and proposed purchase of lumber for France, 107

Case-Navira, Martinique: and slave rebellion, 164

Cashen, James: store reportedly attacked by Creeks, 15n; mentioned, 16n

Castelfranco, Prince of: and Spanish war with France, 223

Castels, Peter: oath of allegiance to Pa., 308n

Catalonia, 223

Cathalan, Stephen, Jr.: letters from, 93-4, 112; security for, 63n; and case of *Aurora*, 93; letter from submitted to Washington, 94n; and olive culture in S.C., 112

cloth: for slaves, 113; market for in Richmond, 538

clothing: for TJ's slaves, 18, 380, 540, 576, 721; TJ's sent to Monticello, 20

clover: as food for livestock, 356; and TJ's crop-rotation plan, 397, 402, 422, 423; and crop-rotation plan of T. M. Randolph, Jr., 471; hay produced from, 681

clover, buffalo: in Ky., 680, 681; Sinclair's views on, 681

clover, red: and TJ's crop-rotation plan, 397, 422, 470, 576, 577, 578, 657; and crop-rotation plan of T. M. Randolph, Jr., 471, 592

clover, white: at Monticello, 87-8; and TJ's crop-rotation plan, 397; and crop-rotation plan of T. M. Randolph, Jr., 470

clover seed: British taxes on, 682; in Scotland, 682; Sinclair's views on, 682

Cobourg, Prince of. *See* Saxe-Coburg, Friedrich Josias, Prince of

Cockcroft, James: memorial from, 369-74; and case of *York*, 369-74

coffee: price, 94; captured by British, 459n, 564n, 565n, 626, 646; captured by French, 625n; exportation from France forbidden, 744

Coffyn, Francis: and case of *Little Cherub*, 364, 662

Cogdell, John, & Co.: and case of *Commerce*, 251

coinage. *See* copper coinage; Mint, U.S.

Coke, Mr., 779

Colchester, Va., 504

collectors of customs, U.S.: and enforcement of neutrality, 790

Collin, Nicholas: letter to, 631; as patent arbitrator, 631; identified, 631n

Columbia (brigantine): captured by *Fanny*, 459n

Columbia (ship): captured by British privateer, 564n

Commerçant (ship): detained at Madeira, 556

Commerce, Report on: preparation of, 442-3, 546-7

Commerce (schooner): detained at New Providence, 567n

Commerce (ship): captured by *Tyger*, 251; recaptured by British, 251

Commissioner of Loans, Va. *See* Hopkins, John

Commissioner of Revenue, U.S. *See* Coxe, Tench

Commissioners of Accounts: and final settlement of state accounts, 343, 403, 585, 666; letter from Washington, 343; letter from cited, 343n

Commissioners of the Federal District. *See* Federal District Commissioners

Commissioners of the Sinking Fund, U.S.: meetings, 661. *See also* sinking fund

Commissioners of the Treasury, French: and U.S. debt to France, 351

Commissioners to Spain. *See* Carmichael, William; Short, William

Committee of Public Safety. *See* France: Committee of Public Safety

common law: and case of Gideon Henfield, 145-6; and enlistment of U.S. citizens in French service, 383

Communications from the Secretary of the Treasury, to the House of Representatives: and new foreign loan, 304, 307n

compasses: TJ's sent to Monticello, 19

Comptroller of the Treasury, U.S. *See* Wolcott, Oliver, Jr.

Concorde (French frigate): captures *Jupiter*, 746; captures prizes, 746; and case of *Greyhound*, 797n

Condé, France: allied siege of, 68, 69, 164, 166-7, 427, 539, 542, 545; captured by allies, 614

Condorcet, Marie Jean Antoine Nicolas de Caritat, Marquis de: and steamboat, 108; *Plan de constitution présenté à la convention nationale*, 400; flees from Jacobins, 723

Congress, Continental: and Beaumarchais's claim on U.S., 243-6; French attitude toward, 478-9n

Congress, U.S. *See* United States: Congress

Connecticut: and printing of laws, 5; and circular letter to merchants, 767-8; counterfeiting of currency of, 780

Connell, Capt. (master of *Hannah*): ship detained at New Providence, 567n

Connoley, Capt.: privateering activities, 25n

consoles: TJ's sent to Monticello, 19

Constable, James: and circular letter to merchants, 768n; letter from quoted, 769n

Constable, William: business trip to Europe, 769n

Constitutional Interests of Ireland: requested by T. M. Randolph, Jr., 88

Constitution of the United States: and Proclamation of Neutrality, 273, 324; Genet's misunderstanding of, 465, 513,

Courtenay, George William Augustus: battle with *Embuscade*, 582, 608; and case of *Catharine* of Jamaica, 667n

court of admiralty, U.S. *See* district courts, U.S.

Coutinho, Diogo Pereira Forjaz: and case of *Commerçant*, 556, 557

cows: in Va., 29

Cox, Albion: appointed assayer of Mint, 4, 37-8, 191, 676; payment for, 676, 734-5, 737

Coxe, Daniel W.: described, 765n; possible recipient of report on W. Fla., 765n

Coxe, Tench: letters from, 4, 37-8, 45, 56, 57, 94-5, 354, 516, 551, 563, 589-90, 590, 763; and Mint, 4, 37-8; and status of U.S. debtors on French prizes, 45; and eligibility of U.S. citizens to act as French prize agents, 56; and passports for U.S. ships, 57; and bills of exchange for Department of State, 94-5, 354, 516, 551, 563, 589-90; and opposition to excise in Ky., 507; sends report on W. Fla. to TJ, 763-5

Craig, John, 420n

Crammond, Mr.: and case of Joseph Ravara, 118n

Crawford, James: and circular letter to merchants, 768n

cream: used to produce butter in England, 681

Creek Indians: relations with Spain, 9-10, 78-9, 118, 148, 211, 408, 412n, 413n, 476n, 670-1n; hostilities with Ky., 15n; relations with Shawnees, 15n, 16n; alliance with Shawnees, 16n; conflict with Chickasaws, 16n; conflict with Choctaws, 16n; hostilities with Ga., 78-9, 138-40, 148, 151, 156-7, 168, 188, 275, 287, 293, 393, 409, 412n, 615, 671n, 796-7; war with Chickasaws, 156-7, 313-14, 315n, 409, 411; relations with U.S., 313-14; corn for, 315n, 408; relations with Cherokees, 316; relations with W. A. Bowles, 407, 414n; and Treaty of New York, 407; hostilities with U.S., 408, 413-15n, 476n, 670-1n; U.S. aid to, 409; boundary with Ga., 414n

Crèvecoeur, Michel Guillaume St. John de: loses consular office, 157

Critta (Kritty) (TJ's slave), 65

crosses: TJ's sent to Monticello, 19

crotalus horridus. *See* rattlesnake

Crousillat, Lewis: petition and memorial from, 631-2; and case of *Flora*, 630-1, 632, 639-40, 642-3; and case of *Sophia*, 630-1, 640, 642-3; oath of allegiance to Pa., 632, 633n; oath of allegiance to U.S., 632, 633n; identified, 633n

Cruger, Henry: and case of *York*, 142-3, 185, 191, 248, 256

Cruger, Nicholas: memorial from, 369-74; and case of *York*, 142, 369-74, 486-7; letter from cited, 142n; identified, 374n

Cruzat, Francisco: Spanish commandant at St. Louis, 413n

Culloden (H.M.S.): stops *Peggy*, 712n

Culpeper Court House, Va., 622

cultures: TJ's sent to Monticello, 19

Culver (Curvan), William: carries dispatches to G. Morris, 759

Cumberland: settlement at, 316; and Creek hostilities with U.S., 413n; French interest in, 522; hostility to Spain, 522; mentioned, 118

Cumberland river: and Cherokee boundary with U.S., 414n

Cunard, Juan: relations with Creeks, 16n

Cunningham, John: and circular letter to merchants, 768n

cupboards: TJ's sent to Monticello, 20

Curaçao, W.I.: B. H. Phillips not recognized as U.S. consul at, 221-2; U.S. trade with, 370; reinforcements for, 575

Currie, James: letter to, 187-8; letters from, 21, 173, 242; financial affairs, 21, 187-8, 242, 292n; letter from cited, 243n; mentioned, 64

Curvan, Capt. *See* Culver (Curvan), William

Cushing, William: letters to, 488, 520; and referral of neutrality questions to Supreme Court, 488, 520, 526, 550; letter from Washington, 550

cushions: TJ's sent to Monticello, 19

Cusseta king. *See* Fat King of Cussitah (Cusseta king) (Creek chief)

Custine, Adam Philippe, Comte de: reported military actions, 122, 124, 132; arrest of, 723

customs collectors, U.S.: and enforcement of neutrality, 26, 582-3, 610n, 649n, 721n; and passports for U.S. ships, 57, 355

Cutting, Mr., 463

Cutting, Nathaniel: letter from, 229-30; and Humphreys's mission to Algiers, 60, 140, 238, 331, 332, 427, 440, 542, 614, 673, 755; arrives in England,

229; payment to, 286; appointed consul at Le Havre, 743, 783

cutting presses: TJ's sent to Monticello, 19

dairies: Sinclair's views on, 681

Dalbarade, Jean: and case of *Little Cherub*, 663-4n; and case of *Lawrence*, 664n

Dale, Robert: memorial from, 369-74; and case of *York*, 369-74

Dallas, Alexander J.: letter from, 467; and address to Genet, 61; and case of Joseph Ravara, 103; and case of *Little Sarah*, 448n, 464; and Genet's threat to appeal from Washington to American people, 448n, 466, 678n, 694; and case of George Allison, 467; identified, 467-8n

Dandridge, Bartholomew, Jr.: letters from, 319-20, 578; and pardons, 319-20; identified, 320n

Dannery, Thomas: appointed French consul at Boston, 80; exequatur for, 80n

Dauphin (ship): captured by Algerines, 116n

Davidson, Capt. (master of *Eliza*): ship detained at New Providence, 567n

Davis, Augustine: described, 137n; and postal service in Va., 137, 380

Davis, James, Jr.: and circular letter to merchants, 768n

Davis, Richard H.: appointed consular agent by Elias Vanderhorst, 251

Davis, William James: plunders *Rainbow*, 666-7, 758, 761

Davy (TJ's slave): and remodeling of Monticello, 326

Deane, Silas: as English pensioner, 219; and contract with farmers-general, 243; arrival in France, 246n

Dearment, James: relations with Creeks, 16n

Deas, William A.: and bills of exchange for Department of State, 332

Deblois, Lewis: and case of Gideon Henfield, 41

debtors: status of U.S. on French prizes, 45

debt payment act: and new foreign loan, 201, 294, 307n

debt redemption act: and new foreign loan, 201, 294, 307n

debts to British creditors: and Ware v. Hylton, 109-10, 166, 302, 327; obstacles to payment of, 330

Decatur, Stephen: ship captured by *Union*, 433

Declaration of Independence, 682

De Dominio Maris Dissertatio (Cornelius van Bynkershoek): cited by E. Randolph, 33, 35n

deerskins: captured by French, 251

Defiance (ship): captured by British privateer, 626

Deforgues, François Louis Michel Chemin: and U.S. aid to Saint-Domingue, 662, 663n; and case of *Little Cherub*, 663-4n; and case of *Juno*, 664n; and case of *Lawrence*, 664n; and case of *Patty*, 664n; and case of Thomas Toby, 664n; and Genet's recall, 692

De Jure Belli ac Pacis (Hugo Grotius): cited by E. Randolph, 32-3, 34, 35n

Delamotte, F. C. A.: letters to, 574, 737-8, 759; letters from, 166-7, 783; letters from cited, 167n, 783n; and case of *Jay*, 436n; and books for TJ, 737; security for, 783

Delany, Sharp: and enlistment of U.S. citizens in French service, 41; and payment of duties on prize goods in U.S., 620, 621n

Delaware: and printing of laws, 5; and French privateering, 708; and addresses in support of Proclamation of Neutrality, 717n; and circular letter to merchants, 767-8; boundary with Md., 798; mentioned, 31, 32

Delaware Bay: U.S. jurisdiction over, 31-5, 39; mentioned, 532

Delaware river: and French privateering, 791

Delozier, Charles: and case of *Maxwell*, 728

Delozier, Daniel: and case of *Trusty*, 418n

Democratic Society of Pennsylvania: and Hamilton's proposed appeal to American people, 601-2, 652; foundation of, 603n; relations with Genet, 652, 688

Demourier. *See* Dumouriez (Demourier), Charles François du Périer

Denmark: mercantile failures in, 77; and British privateering, 78; and French privateering, 78; neutrality, 78, 214, 460; abolishes certain trade duties, 214-15; U.S. trade with, 276, 442-3, 546-7; and free ships and free goods, 332, 673-4; trade duties in, 442-3, 547n; trade with Great Britain, 442; trade with Netherlands, 442; ambassador to Great Britain, 547n, 673-4

INDEX

organization of British consular service, 220n; and restoration of French prizes, 287; and infractions of peace treaty, 329; and case of *Suckey*, 377n; supports W. A. Bowles, 415n; approves TJ's response to Hammond, 440; and British trade restrictions, 440-2, 673-4, 776-7; and Proclamation of Neutrality, 441n; and case of Philip Wilson, 770-1

Grey, Sir Charles: and British West Indian expedition, 777

Greyhound (ship): escapes capture by French privateer, 36n; seized by Duplaine, 795-6, 797n; captured by *Roland*, 797n

Griffin, Cyrus, 292

Griffin, John Tayloe: letter to, 312-13; letter from, 292; financial affairs, 21, 188, 242, 292n; requests loan from TJ, 292, 312-13; identified, 292n

Griffin, Samuel: and U.S. guarantee of French possessions in America, 121

Griffith, Dennis: letter from, 798; *Map of the State of Maryland*, 798; identified, 798n

Gros-Morne, Martinique: and slave rebellion, 164

Grotius, Hugo: *De Jure Belli ac Pacis*, 32-3, 34, 35n; mentioned, 512

Grouvelle, Philippe Antoine: and Genet's letter of credence, 48-9

grubs: damage crops, 278

Guadeloupe, W.I.: murders in, 122

Guel le Sieur, M.: and case of *Ranger*, 564n

Guernsey, Channel Island: and British privateering, 331, 564n

Guilford Court House, N.C.: battle of, 219-20

Guion, Isaac: and circular letter to merchants, 768n

gunpowder: captured by French, 370, 371

Gurney, Francis: and circular letter to merchants, 768n

Gustavus III, King of Sweden, 733

gypsum: Sinclair's views on, 680, 681

Habersham, John: and Creek hostilities with Ga., 139n

Hale, Capt. *See* Hall (Hale), John

half disme: coinage of, 676

Hall (Hale), John: and case of *Trusty*, 417-18; mentioned, 360

Hall, Parry: letter from, 566; proposed

edition of *Notes on the State of Virginia*, 566

Hallet, Stephen: memorandum from, 468-9; and Thornton's Capitol plan, 425-7, 455, 489-95, 517-19; and plaster of paris, 468-9; dismissal of, 519n; plan for Capitol, 519

ham: captured by British, 337

Hamburg: trade with Le Havre, 368n; U.S. consul at, 539; embargoes grain exports to France, 540; requests departure of French minister, 540; ships captured by French, 540; U.S. trade with, 540; trade with St. Barthélemy, 625n

Hamilton, Alexander: letters to, 161, 321, 361; letters from, 22-3, 99, 173, 243-4, 355, 437, 460, 571, 661, 759; memorandum from, 24; and Genet's recall, xxxix-xli, 448n, 499, 503, 554-5, 598, 652, 688-91, 693-4, 713-14n, 720, 730-1, 745, 752, 759; portrait of, xl, 340 (illus.); and southern whale fishery, 22-3; and TJ's letter to Ternant, 24, 44n, 55; and enforcement of neutrality, 26, 582-3, 610n, 649n, 721n; and restoration of French prizes, 51-2n, 72, 186, 260, 603-4, 607-8, 620, 621, 627; and passports for U.S. ships, 57, 355; and excise act, 62; and withdrawal from U.S. ports of French privateers commissioned by Genet in U.S., 72, 161, 196n, 199n, 296, 321, 327, 498, 620; and exchange rate with France, 84n; and U.S. debt to France, 84n, 179-80, 204, 283-4, 320n, 321, 347-52, 553-4; and duties on wine, 99, 105; letter to cited, 99n; and accounts of Grand & Cie. with U.S., 114, 116, 354; and case of Gideon Henfield, 131n, 160n, 161, 173; and new commercial treaty with France, 132, 748n, 749-50; and proposed purchase of provisions in U.S. for France, 132, 146, 174-84, 252, 283-4; and Creek hostilities with Ga., 138-40, 796-7; offered French citizenship, 142n; and Spanish relations with Southern Indians, 150n, 161, 206n, 328; and sale of French prizes in U.S., 152n, 155-6n, 161, 498, 528, 529; and Chickasaw-Creek war, 156-7, 173; health, 157n, 161n; and enlistment of U.S. citizens in French service, 160n, 161, 173, 498-9, 693; letters from Washington, 176-7, 582-3, 611, 752; and Mint, 186n; conflict with TJ, 193-4, 201-5, 206, 219, 241, 267, 293-5, 303-7, 545, 601-2,

INDEX

Hamilton, Alexander (*cont.*)
606, 652, 689-90; and foreign loans,
193-4, 201-5, 206, 241, 293-5, 303-7,
352n, 545, 606; John Beckley's intelligence about, 219; status in eyes of Pitt
ministry, 219; alleged plan for monarchical government, 220-1; and Beaumarchais's claim on U.S., 243-7, 277;
and case of *Catharine* from Halifax,
258, 260; and French right to commission privateers in U.S., 259-60, 296,
327, 446-52; and French captures of
British prizes, 260; and French captures of prizes in U.S. territorial
waters, 260, 358, 620; alleged favoritism to Baron de Glaubeck, 267-8; dispute with Andrew G. Fraunces, 267;
alleged favoritism to Mrs. Greene,
268n; and John Cleves Symmes's application for land patent, 269; and loan
from Bank of United States, 280; and
case of *Citoyen Genet*, 296, 569; and
case of *Republican*, 296, 620; and case
of *Sans Culotte*, 296, 569; and U.S. aid
to Saint-Domingue, 310n, 352n;
Jacques Odier recommended to, 319;
and infractions of peace treaty, 328,
333; attitude toward Genet, 342n, 602;
and final settlement of state accounts,
343, 666n; and case of *William*, 358,
361; and detention of French prizes in
U.S. ports, 358, 484; and case of
Suckey, 361; and British relations with
Western Indians, 362n; relations with
Nicholas Cruger, 374n; and British neutrality policy, 377n; resides outside
Philadelphia, 401; seeks house in Philadelphia, 401; "Pacificus" essays, 403,
404n, 444, 521, 549, 553, 585-6, 606,
623, 624n, 650, 654-5, 741; and Proclamation of Neutrality, 403, 650; and
U.S. guarantee of French possessions in
America, 403; and suspension of payment on bills drawn to supply Saint-
Domingue, 437-8; and case of *Little
Sarah*, 438, 446-52, 460, 463-4, 467,
482; and case of *Swallow*, 438, 620;
and arming of French privateers in
U.S., 446-52, 528; and Short's business affairs, 460, 571; letter from cited,
473-4n; and referral of neutrality questions to Supreme Court, 484-5, 524,
525, 527-9, 537; and arming of allied
ships in U.S. ports, 485, 498, 528,
579; and case of *Jane*, 485; and arming
of French ships in U.S., 498, 527; and
enlistment in belligerent service of belligerent citizens in U.S., 499, 529,
579, 609; and French use of French
arms in U.S., 499; and sale of U.S.
ships built for war, 499; proposed appeal to American people, 503, 554-5,
598, 601-2, 606, 652, 689-90, 720;
and opposition to excise in Ky., 507n;
and cannon for Mud Island, 508-9; and
purchase of saltpeter, 508-9; Federalist
attitudes toward, 523, 552; and French
right to fit out privateers in U.S., 527,
528, 620, 693; questions for Supreme
Court, 527-9, 537; and use of U.S.
ports by armed allied ships, 527-8,
620; and allied right to fit out privateers in U.S., 528; and French consular
admiralty jurisdiction in U.S., 528,
529, 554, 693, 795-6; and belligerent
captures of prizes in U.S. territorial
waters, 529; and enlistment of U.S. citizens in belligerent service, 529; and
maritime jurisdiction of U.S., 529;
method of addressing Genet, 545; unpopularity in Va., 545; and British seizure of French property on U.S. ships,
554; and relief of Saint-Domingue
refugees, 554, 555n; and early meeting
of Congress, 555, 608, 615n, 650;
and Pascal's contribution to *General
Advertiser*, 555, 694; and arming of belligerent ships in U.S., 579, 608; and
neutrality rules, 579-80, 608-9; proposed neutrality rules, 579; and repair
of belligerent ships in U.S., 579; and
U.S. treaty obligations and neutrality,
580-1, 588, 609; and compensation for
French prizes, 603-4, 607-8, 627; and
use of U.S. ports by French privateers
commissioned in U.S., 604; and War of
First Coalition, 606-7; and use of U.S.
ports by French privateers fitted out in
U.S., 607-8; and battle between *Boston*
and *Embuscade*, 608; and equipment of
belligerent ships in U.S., 608; and
equipment of merchant ships in U.S.,
608-9; and equipment of allied privateers in U.S., 609; and equipment of
allied ships in U.S., 609; and equipment of French ships in U.S., 609; and
alleged French refugee plots against
Saint-Domingue, 620; and case of
Roland, 620, 795-6; and payment of
duties on prize goods in U.S., 620,
621n; plans to retire, 627, 629; "No
Jacobin" essays, 650, 651n; relations
with E. Randolph, 652-3; and sinking
fund, 661; and Genet's threat to appeal

U.S., 682; Sinclair's views on, 682-3; importation by Great Britain, 683

Henfield, Gideon: prosecuted for enlisting in French service, 41n, 81n, 130-1, 145-6, 154, 159-61, 173, 198, 382, 499, 502, 689, 702, 714n; acquitted by jury, 611, 653-4, 702, 713n

Hénin, Etiennette Guignot de Monconseil, Princesse d': letter from Lafayette, 723-4

Herring, Mr., 504

Hervey, John Augustus, Lord: opposes Tuscan neutrality, 674, 675n

Hervieux, François Henri: and detention of *Vainqueur de la Bastille*, 452-3

Hesse-Cassel: hires soldiers to Great Britain, 440

Hesse-Cassel, George William, Prince of: treaty with George III, 440

Hessian fly: damages crops, 276, 288

Hickling, Thomas: and case of *Maria*, 455n; acting consul at St. Michael, 613, 614; visited by Moors, 613; mentioned, 543n

hides: captured by British, 436n; importation by Great Britain, 683

Higginson, Stephen: and circular letter to merchants, 768n

High Court of Admiralty, British: and British trade restrictions, 6, 441n, 776-7; and impressment, 6n; and case of *Jay*, 436n; and British captures of U.S. prizes, 753; and case of Philip Wilson, 771n

Hill, Ebenezer: and circular letter to merchants, 768n

Hirland, Mr.: and case of *Trusty*, 360

Hoban, James: memorandum from, 462; and Thornton's Capitol plan, 425-7, 462, 495, 506, 507n, 517-19; identified, 462-3n; observations submitted to Washington, 463n

Hoffman, Zachariah: agent for Richard Harison, 330

hogs: TJ's views on, 356

hog's lard: captured by British, 337

Holebroke (ship), 88

Holland, Benjamin: letter to, 132; memorial from, 106; and case of Joseph Ravara, 105n; and case of *Little Sarah*, 106, 121, 132, 558; identified, 107n

Hollingsworth, Jacob, 788

Hollingsworth, Jehu, & Co.: and case of *Betsy* brigantine, 793

Hollingsworth, John, & Co.: and case of *Betsy* brigantine, 625n

Hollingsworth, Zebulon: letter to, 363;

letter from, 728; and enlistment of U.S. citizens in belligerent service, 117; and case of John Hooper, 363; identified, 363n; and case of *Maxwell*, 728, 740

Hollins, John: and case of *Betsey*, 432n, 454

Holloway, Thomas: and Mint, 191, 192-3

Holmes, John M.: relations with Creeks, 15n

Holy Roman Emperor. *See* Francis II, Holy Roman Emperor

Homassel, Charles: and Derieux's business affairs, 719

honey: importation by Great Britain, 683; Sinclair's views on, 683

Hood, Samuel, Viscount: naval operations in Mediterranean, 89, 421, 427, 435, 496, 542, 587-8, 751; and recaptured Spanish register ship, 230; fleet damaged by storm, 645

Hoop, Mr., 124n

Hooper, Mr.: owner of *Eagle*, 36n; prize master of *Eunice*, 36n; prosecution of, 76

Hooper, John: and enlistment of U.S. citizens in French service, 363

Hooper, Stephen: dispute with Thomas Pagan, 724-6

Hope (ship): detained by Dutch trade embargo, 91, 143-4, 146-7

Hope (sloop): captured by French privateer, 722n

Hopewell (British privateer): and case of *Prosperity*, 389n

Hopewell, Treaty of: and Indian land cessions, 316

Hopkins, John: and Short's business affairs, 460, 571n

Horse-Hoeing Husbandry (Jethro Tull): recommended by TJ, 241, 303

horses: cost of, 29; for TJ, 66, 325, 424, 504, 657, 721, 757, 799, 800; food for, 356, 578; and TJ's crop-rotation plan, 423, 577, 658

Hortalez, Roderigue, & Cie., 246n

hospital, marine: and relief of Saint-Domingue refugees in Va., 456

Hotham, William: naval operations in Mediterranean, 496

Hough, George: letter from, 539; copyright for, 539; *The Female Guide*, 539; identified, 539n

House, Mrs. Mary: death, 168; mentioned, 133

house joiners: for Monticello, 18, 26-7, 65, 92

INDEX

Jefferson, Peter (TJ's father): death, 235; mentioned, 109

JEFFERSON, THOMAS

Agriculture

and Arthur Young's queries on, 28-31, 353, 396-7; and threshing machine, 62, 66, 141, 169, 241, 249, 356, 658, 742; plans for tenant farmers, 318, 355-6, 386, 596, 657; crop-rotation plan, 396-7, 401-3, 422-4, 428, 470, 576-8, 591-3, 657-8; views on in Va., 622-3

Architecture

house plan for William Madison, 61, 62n, 324, 403; and Thornton's Capitol plan, 425-6, 455, 462, 489-95, 500, 517-19

Business and Financial Affairs

account with J. W. Eppes, 7-8; account with Fenwick, Mason & Co., 46; unable to lend money to J. G. Jefferson, 60-1; sale of tobacco, 93, 171, 239, 738-9; account with Grand & Cie., 115, 116; endorses E. Randolph's note, 146; John Barret's debt to, 189-90, 381, 551; account with Thomas Bell, 259; declines loan to John Tayloe Griffin, 312-13; and Short's finances, 472, 571; Wayles estate debt, 544; sells slaves, 551; salary as Secretary of State, 569-70; declines to endorse note for E. Randolph, 624; account with Donald & Burton, 737-8; account with Adam Lindsay, 765-6; account with Richard Dobson, 789; debt to Montgomery & Henry, 791

Economic Theories

on trade with Great Britain, 275

Governor of Virginia

seeks copies of records as, 153

Personal Affairs

and case of Richard Randolph, 53-4; and J. G. Jefferson's education, 60-1, 213-14, 258-9, 386; plans to visit Monticello, 756, 757, 788, 789

Political Theories

on allied coalition, 26; on French Revolution, 26; on neutrality, 26; on Great Britain, 77; on monarchism in U.S., 100, 101-2, 169, 628, 731; on republicanism, 101-2; on freedom of press, 102, 505; on parties in U.S.,

190; on public service, 239-40; on natural law and peace, 300; on corruption, 306; on diplomatic immunity, 363; on slavery, 503, 504, 788; on expatriation, 701-2

Portraits

by William Joseph Williams, 20

Residences

house on Schuylkill, 247, 445-6, 638, 744

Scientific Interests

telescope, 92, 170-1; steamboat, 108; linguistics, 237, 256; asphyxia, 256; weather, 279, 326; cotton gin, 334; propulsion machine, 353-4; mold-board plow, 586; waterwheel, 631; orrery, 799n

Secretary of State

and Genet's recall, xxxix-xli, xlii-xliii, 448n, 499, 503, 554-5, 561-2, 569, 594, 598, 606, 611, 616, 652, 685-715, 720, 722, 730-2, 745, 747, 752, 759, 760, 762; and new commercial treaty with France, xli, 61, 72, 96-9, 132, 134, 168, 602, 691, 743, 747-50, 751, 754; and Ternant's recall, xli-xlii, 57, 90, 92, 101, 110-11, 274; and French plan to liberate Louisiana, xlii, 393-5, 438-9, 771-4, 785-6; and Mint, 4, 37-8, 185-6, 191, 192-3, 269, 676, 734-5, 737; and printing of laws, 4-5; and impressment, 6n, 191-2; and relations with Southern Indians, 9-10, 78-9, 100; and Spanish relations with Southern Indians, 9-10, 78-9, 118-20, 148-50, 154, 161, 168, 205, 263-6, 313-15, 328, 346, 405-16, 473, 474-6, 497-8, 505; and fugitive slaves from E. Fla., 10-12, 78-9, 89; and slaves stolen from E. Fla., 13-14, 78-9, 89; and Creek hostilities with Ga., 15-17, 78-9, 138-40, 148, 151, 168, 188, 275, 287, 393, 409, 796-7; and foreign loans, 17, 193-4, 201-5, 206, 241, 293-5, 303-7, 401, 545, 606; and public securities, 17; plans to retire, 18, 27, 66, 133, 215, 235, 239-40, 472-3, 584, 593-4, 606-7, 624, 627-30, 659-60, 738, 742, 752, 756, 757, 788, 789; and southern whale fishery, 22-3; and case of *Eunice*, 25, 36, 67, 77, 117; and French privateers commissioned by Genet in U.S., 25, 36, 40, 43, 67, 71-3, 75,

[832]

Juno (ship): captured by *Capricieuse*, 664n; compensated for damages sustained through French detention, 664n

Jupiter (French warship): and Saint-Domingue refugees, 456n

Jupiter (ship): captured by *Concorde*, 746

Jupiter (TJ's slave): and horse for TJ, 504, 657, 721; and canal for Monticello, 667

Justice, John: and case of *Citoyen Genet*, 728n

Justice, Richard (Cherokee chief): relations with Spain, 317

Kean, John: and final settlement of state accounts, 343; letter from Washington, 343; letter from cited, 343n; letter to cited, 570n

Kentucky: and printing of laws, 5; Creek hostilities with, 15n; and possibility of U.S. war with Spain, 375n; and French plan to liberate Louisiana, 393-5, 438-9, 774, 785-6; opposition to excise in, 507

Kentucky coffee trees: seeds for William Bartram, 168, 274; in Va., 274

Kerrener, Peter W.: and case of *Fury*, 576n

Kilty, John: and alleged French refugee plots against Saint-Domingue, 612n

King, Miles: and proposed purchase of lumber for France, 107

King, Nicholas, 354n

King, Rufus: John Beckley's intelligence about, 219; and criticism of Washington, 555; considered as Secretary of State, 629; and Genet's threat to appeal from Washington to American people, 678n, 766

Kingfisher (Indian), 413n

Kingston (ship), 271

Kingston, Jamaica: trade with Philadelphia, 106; and British privateering, 375-7, 632, 640

Kingston, Stephen: and status of U.S. debtors on French prizes, 45; and bills of exchange for Department of State, 563

Kinsley, Apollos: applies for patent, 631n

Kitty. *See* Church, Catherine (Kitty)

Klingham, Mr. *See* Clingman (Klingham), George

Knox, Henry: letters to, 75, 321, 342-3, 361, 648-9, 739-40, 740; and Genet's recall, xl, 448n, 499, 554-5, 598, 652, 688-91, 714n, 730, 745, 752; portrait

of, xl, 340 (illus.); and TJ's letter to Ternant, 24; and restoration of French prizes, 51-2n, 72, 186, 260, 603-4, 607-8, 620, 621, 627, 739-40; and withdrawal from U.S. ports of French privateers commissioned by Genet in U.S., 72, 161, 196n, 296, 321, 327, 498, 620; and enforcement of neutrality, 76, 257n, 437n, 582-3, 610n, 621n; and privateers commissioned by belligerents in U.S., 117; and new commercial treaty with France, 132, 748n, 749-50; and purchase of provisions in U.S. for France, 132; and Creek hostilities with Ga., 138-40, 796-7; and sale of French prizes in U.S., 155n, 498; and Chickasaw-Creek war, 156-7, 315n; and case of Gideon Henfield, 161; and Spanish relations with Southern Indians, 161, 206n, 328; and infractions of peace treaty, 166n, 328, 333; and case of *Catharine* from Halifax, 258, 260; and French right to commission privateers in U.S., 259-60, 296, 327, 446-52, 532; and French captures of British prizes, 260; and French captures of prizes in U.S. territorial waters, 260, 358, 620; and John Cleves Symmes's application for land patent, 269; and case of *Republican*, 270, 296, 620; and case of *Citoyen Genet*, 296, 727-8; and case of *Sans Culotte*, 296; and U.S. debt to France, 320n, 321; and case of *William*, 342-3, 358, 361; and U.S. jurisdiction over belligerent prize cases, 342-3; criticism of Genet, 342n; and detention of French prizes in U.S. ports, 358, 484; and case of John Hooper, 363; and military appointments, 385; and relations with Spain, 408, 413n; and proposed attack on New Orleans by U.S. citizens, 412-13n; and Spanish fortification of Walnut Hills, 412n; and case of James O'Fallon, 413n; and Treaty of New York, 414n; and U.S. aid to Chickasaws, 415n; and case of *Trusty*, 418n; and suspension of payment on bills drawn to supply Saint-Domingue, 437-8; and case of *Little Sarah*, 438, 444-5, 446-52, 463-4, 467, 482; and case of *Swallow*, 438, 620; and arming of French privateers in U.S., 446-52; letter from cited, 473-4n; and referral of neutrality questions to Supreme Court, 484-5, 525, 532-3, 537; and arming of allied ships in U.S. ports, 485, 498,

Mediterranean sea: Roman jurisdiction over, 35; and demand for corn, 77; U.S. trade in, 93
Medoc wine: for TJ, 718
Mentor (ship): destroyed by *Centurion* and *Vulture*, 771n
Mentz. *See* Mainz (Mentz)
Mequinez, Morocco: and Moroccan civil war, 88, 405, 613
merchants, British: influence in U.S., 52n; opposition to French Revolution, 54
merchants, Irish: and neutrality, 26
merchants, U.S.: letter to (circular), 767-8; and British trade restrictions, 5-6; and neutrality, 26, 61, 62n, 382; and restoration of French prizes, 52n; criticism of, 102n; TJ's views on, 190; notified by Hammond of British neutrality policy, 377n; letter to submitted to Washington, 762
Mercié, Jean: and case of *Columbia*, 459n
Meredith, Samuel: and Mint, 185, 676; mentioned, 295
Merlino, Jean Marie François: conversation with G. Morris, 364; mentioned, 369n
Merrideth, James: and patent for John Clarke, 515
Mexico: coinage in, 224-5; and U.S. right to navigate Mississippi, 477
Meyercourt, Mme: murder of, 122
Michaud, Mr. *See* Michaux (Michaud), André
Michaux (Michaud), André: and French plan to liberate Louisiana, xlii, 393-5, 438-9; proposed western expedition, xlii, 393-5; consular commission requested for, 438-9
Mifflin, Thomas: letter from, 444-5; and case of *Amiable*, 158; and case of *William*, 342-3; and case of *Little Sarah*, 438, 444-5, 446, 447n, 448n, 464, 467, 476, 506; and case of *Jane*, 457-8, 480, 481n, 485; absence of, 467; and cannon for Mud Island, 508-9; and case of *Citoyen Genet*, 727-8
militia, French: spirit of, 69
militia, U.S.: and enforcement of neutrality, 75, 270-1, 437n, 508; and Creek hostilities with Ga., 139; Washington's views on, 219-20
milk: and TJ's crop-rotation plan, 577; used to produce butter in Ireland, 681
Miller, George: and French consular admiralty jurisdiction in U.S., 38-9
Miller, John: and detention of *Hope*, 91

Miller, Magnes: and circular letter to merchants, 768n
Miller, Phineas: letter from, 134; partnership with Eli Whitney, 134, 334n
Miller & Whitney: and cotton gin, 334n
Millet, Thomas: observations on Saint-Domingue, 754-5n, 763; described, 755n
mills: in Va., 59; for Monticello, 190, 386; absence in Albemarle County, 259; rental of TJ's, 289, 317
millwrights: for Mint, 185
Milrae, Thomas: ship captured by *Sans Culotte*, 740
Milton, Va.: trade, 259
Minbielle, Capt. (commander of *Medie*): captures *Maria*, 455n, 542
Minerva (ship): sale of, 78
Minister of Finance, French. *See* Clavière, Etienne
Minister of Foreign Affairs, French. *See* Deforgues, François Louis Michel Chemin; Lebrun-Tondu, Pierre Henri Hélène Marie
Minister of Interior, French. *See* Roland de la Platière, Jean Marie
Minister of Justice, French. *See* Gohier, Louis Jérôme
Minister of Marine, French. *See* Bertrand de Molleville, Antoine François, Marquis de; Dalbarade, Jean; Lacoste, Jean de
Minister of Public Contributions, French. *See* Clavière, Etienne
Minister of War, French. *See* Pache, Jean Nicolas
Ministry of Foreign Affairs, French: and U.S. debt to France, 83n
Ministry of Interior, French: and U.S. debt to France, 83n
Ministry of Marine, French: and U.S. debt to France, 83n
Ministry of War, French: and U.S. debt to France, 83n
Mint, U.S.: assayer for, 4, 37-8, 676, 734-5; copper for, 185-6, 288, 598, 674, 753, 777; money for, 185-6; salaries for, 185-6; workmen for, 185-6; engraver for, 191, 192-3, 367; chief coiner and engraver for, 734; and coinage, 734, 737
Mint, U.S., director of. *See* Rittenhouse, David
Minturn, William: memorial from, 369-74; and case of *York*, 369-74
Minturn & Champlin: memorial from, 369-74; and case of *York*, 369-74

Miranda, Francisco de: and French plan to liberate South America, 394n

mirrors: TJ's sent to Monticello, 20. *See also* looking glasses

Mississippi river: Spanish fortification of, 168; U.S. right to navigate, 206, 210, 375n, 412n, 477-9, 485-6, 509, 551; reported British agreement with Spain on, 551; mentioned, 764

Mitchell, James: and case of *Prince William Henry*, 461-2n

Mobile: captured by Spanish, 764

Mobile river, 764

mockingbirds: at Monticello, 88; TJ's views on, 250

Mogador, Morocco: U.S. trade with, 614

Mohairs, W.I., 370

Moissonnier, F.: and case of *Embuscade*, 172; and arming of allied ships in U.S. ports, 359-60; and case of *Betsey*, 432n, 454n; and alleged French refugee plots against Saint-Domingue, 612n

Mollinery, Capt. *See* Mulrinez (Mollinery), Capt. (commander of *Sans Culottes*)

Molloy, Patrick: impressed by British, 753n

Molly (ship): captured by British privateer, 566-7, 568, 574; and restoration of British prizes, 640

monarchy: prospects for in U.S., 100, 101-2, 109-10, 169, 220-1, 628, 731; and parties in U.S., 190; and Proclamation of Neutrality, 273

money, paper: in France, 389, 635-8; in Great Britain, 389, 401; counterfeiting of state in England, 779-82

Monge, Gaspard: and Genet's letter of credence, 48-9; and U.S. debt to France, 82, 86

Monroe, Eliza: narrowly avoids riding accident, 784

Monroe, Elizabeth Kortright (Mrs. James Monroe): health, 137; M. J. Randolph visits, 326; narrowly avoids riding accident, 784; mentioned, 190, 393, 503

Monroe, James: letters to, 189-90, 392-3, 501-3; letters from, 101, 135-7, 381-5, 551-3, 735-6; and proposed purchase of flour for France, 101; and relations with France, 135-6, 551-2; and relations with Great Britain, 135-6, 382-3, 385, 551-2; views on French Revolution, 135; views on neutrality, 135-6; contribution to *National Gazette*, 137; and John Barret's debt to TJ, 189-90;

and British retention of western posts, 382; and enlistment of U.S. citizens in French service, 382-4; and Proclamation of Neutrality, 382-3, 551; and U.S. guarantee of French possessions in America, 382-3; and expatriation, 384; and privateering, 384; and relations with Spain, 384-5, 551-2; and public debt, 385, 551-2; and relations with Western Indians, 385; house for in Philadelphia, 393, 503; purchases slaves from TJ, 551; views on Federalists, 551-2; and "Pacificus" essays, 553; relations with Madison, 651, 654-5, 720, 766; Madison visits, 729, 735, 741; and TJ's criticism of Genet, 735; health, 784; visits Monticello, 799; mentioned, 25, 133, 799

Montesquieu, Charles Louis de Secondat, Baron de: and "Helvidius" essays, 655

Montgomery, Alexander: described, 791n

Montgomery, Robert, 427

Montgomery & Henry: letter to, 791; TJ's debt to, 791; letter from cited, 791n; letter to cited, 791n

Monticello: TJ's furniture shipped to, 8, 18-20, 171, 239, 250, 380, 540-1, 576, 757; house joiner for, 18, 26-7, 65, 92; mason for, 18, 26-7, 65, 92; TJ's housewares sent to, 19-20; trees, 53, 65, 380; garden, 54, 380; remodeling of, 64-6, 325-6; canal, 65, 317, 667; porticoes, 65; potash at, 65; tenant farmers for, 65, 190, 355-6; window frames for, 65, 326; carpenter for, 171; stonemason for, 171; mill, 190, 289, 317, 386; overseer for, 308, 318, 355-6, 397, 401, 422, 428, 445, 657, 788; joists for, 326; timber for, 326; triangular sleepers for, 326; wheels for, 326; Scottish workmen for, 667; stables, 667

Montmorin de Saint-Hérem, Armand Marc, Comte de: and U.S. right to navigate Mississippi, 477, 485, 509, 551

Moore, J., 88n

Moore, James: relations with T. M. Randolph, Jr., 88n

Moore, Sir John, 88n

Moore, William: and case of *Catharine* of Jamaica, 667n; appointed British vice-consul in Rhode Island, 752; exequatur for, 752

Moors: expulsion from Portugal, 613; visit Lisbon, 613, 673

Morgan, William: and case of *Jane*, 469-70

Polverel, Etienne: conflict with Galbaud, 555n; grants freedom to certain Saint-Domingue slaves, 555n; alleged British influence on, 755n

Pope, Nathaniel: as attorney for TJ, 101, 190, 381, 551

Pope, William, 214

poplar trees: at Monticello, 65

pork: price, 9; captured by British, 337, 436n, 646

Port-au-Prince, Saint-Domingue: U.S. ships seized at, 142-3, 185, 229-30, 369-74, 486-7; trade with Philadelphia, 337; council, 371; court of admiralty, 371; destruction of, 504

porter, 213

Porter, Mr., 504

Porter, Andrew: letter from, 641; servant enlists in French service, 641; identified, 641n

porticoes: at Monticello, 65; proper proportions of, 403

Portland (ship): captured by *Thought*, 646

Portsmouth, N.H.: and circular letter to merchants, 768n

Portugal: French ambassador to (*see* Arbot, M. d'); demand for corn in, 77; fleet movements, 140, 427; army, 331; relations with France, 331, 541, 556; and naval protection against Algiers, 421, 614; dispute between minister of marine and naval commanders, 427; sends troops to Spain, 541, 673, 755; and free ships and free goods, 558; expels Moors, 613; treaty with Morocco, 613; Dutch minister to, 614; reportedly enters war against France, 741. *See also* Humphreys, David

postal service: in Va., 325, 380, 784

potash: at Monticello, 65

potatoes: for livestock, 356; and TJ's crop-rotation plan, 397, 402, 422, 423, 577, 658; and crop-rotation plan of T. M. Randolph, Jr., 471, 592; for oxen, 578; and Washington's crop-rotation plan, 658

Potter, Capt. (master of *Union*): detained by *Sans Culotte*, 25n

Powel, Elizabeth Willing (Mrs. Samuel Powel), 522

Powhatan (ship), 21-2

Pragers & Co.: and bills of exchange for Department of State, 94, 354, 516, 546

Prance, Capt. (master of *Joseph*): ship captured by *Sans Culotte*, 218

Prato, Giovannini da: claim on Mazzei,

188; seeks to be tenant farmer at Edgehill, 668

Preble, Capt. (master of *Commerce*): ship captured by *Tyger*, 251

Preble, Edward: quarrel with crew, 587

President, U.S. *See* United States: President

press, freedom of: TJ's views on, 102, 505

Price, David: partner of Robert Leslie, 463

Price, George: ship captured by British privateer, 632, 640

Price, Moses: almost killed by Creeks, 413n

Priestley, Henry: plans to settle in U.S., 679-80

Priestley, Joseph: plans to settle in U.S., 679-80, 716; relations with Thomas Cooper, 715

Priestley, Joseph, Jr.: plans to settle in U.S., 679-80, 716; introduced to TJ, 716

Prince Edward County, Va.: corn crop, 746

Prince William Henry (ship): captured by *Citoyen Genet*, 461-2; and detention of French prizes in U.S. ports, 484, 487; and restoration of French prizes, 620, 621, 634-5

privateering: Monroe's views on, 384

privateers, allied: forbidden to fit out in U.S., 50, 71, 581, 609; forbidden to be commissioned in U.S., 75-6n; forbidden to arm in U.S., 76; forbidden to bring prizes into U.S. ports, 231-2

privateers, British: molest Danish ships, 78; capture U.S. prizes, 165, 336-9, 375-7, 379-80, 387, 433, 435-6, 454-5, 459n, 566-7, 574, 595, 626, 632, 639-40, 646, 753; fitted out in U.S., 165, 344, 359; seize French property, 280; and letters of marque, 387; damage U.S. ships, 388-9n; and British trade restrictions, 440-2; forbidden to fit out in U.S., 700

privateers, Dutch: capture U.S. prize, 221; forbidden to fit out in U.S., 700

privateers, French: capture British prizes, 7-8, 25, 36n, 50-2, 67, 72n, 77, 117, 199-200, 218, 230, 260, 270-1, 335n, 378-9, 398-9, 461-2, 584-5, 600-1, 703, 728, 744-5, 797n; commissioned by Genet in U.S., 25, 36, 40, 43, 51-2n, 67, 71-3, 75, 77, 125-6, 137-8, 167, 195-6, 216-17, 336n, 501, 572,

ment of merchant ships in U.S., 579, 608-9; and neutrality rules, 579-80, 608-9; proposed neutrality rules, 579; and U.S. treaty obligations and neutrality, 580-1, 588, 609; letters from Washington, 582-3, 611, 752; and Hamilton's proposed appeal to American people, 598, 652, 689-90; and compensation for French prizes, 603-4, 607-8; and use of U.S. ports by French privateers commissioned in U.S., 604; and use of U.S. ports by French privateers fitted out in U.S., 607-8; and arming of belligerent ships in U.S., 608; and early meeting of Congress, 608, 615n, 650; and equipment of belligerent ships in U.S., 608; and enlistment in belligerent service of belligerent citizens in U.S., 609; and equipment of allied privateers in U.S., 609; and equipment of allied ships in U.S., 609; and equipment of French ships in U.S., 609; and French right to commission privateers in U.S., 616; and alleged French refugee plots against Saint-Domingue, 620; and case of *Republican*, 620; and case of *Roland*, 620, 795-6; and case of *Swallow*, 620; and French captures of prizes in U.S. territorial waters, 620; and French right to fit out privateers in U.S., 620; and payment of duties on prize goods in U.S., 620; and use of U.S. ports by armed allied ships, 620; TJ declines to endorse note for, 624; considered as Secretary of State, 629; and judicial tenure in Northwest Territory, 643, 644n; relations with Hamilton, 652-3; relations with Washington, 652-3; alleged newspaper essay on case of Gideon Henfield, 653; and sinking fund, 661; and interest payments on debt, 665; allows Genet to remain in U.S., 692; letter from G. Wythe, 717; and Richmond address in support of Proclamation of Neutrality, 717-18; and Pagan v. Hooper, 724-6; and circular letter to merchants, 762; and case of *Jesse*, 782; and case of Duplaine, 795-6; and British trade restrictions, 796; and French trade restrictions, 796; mentioned, 133n

Randolph, James: distributes medals to Indians, 263

Randolph, Martha Cocke (Mrs. Beverley Randolph), 617, 658, 721, 799

Randolph, Martha Jefferson (Patsy, Mrs.

Thomas Mann Randolph, Jr., TJ's daughter): letters to, 18, 122, 250, 445-6, 546, 617, 721; letters from, 53-4, 380-1; and father-in-law's health, 21; and case of Richard Randolph, 53-4; health, 55, 88, 101, 153, 278, 471, 541; TJ's affection for, 66, 169, 424, 504, 546, 578, 617, 658, 757; education in Paris, 122; riding habits, 325; visits Mrs. Monroe, 326; recipes for, 617-18; watch for, 617, 658; affection for sister, 785; entertains guests, 785

Randolph, Richard: alleged incest and infanticide, 53-4

Randolph, Thomas Jefferson (TJ's grandson): health, 53, 55, 88, 153, 278, 380, 471, 541; TJ's affection for, 66, 122, 169, 424, 446, 546

Randolph, Thomas Mann, Jr. (TJ's son-in-law): letters to, 64-6, 169, 307, 355-6, 422-4, 503-4, 576-8, 657-8, 659, 757; letters from, 54-5, 87-8, 153, 278-9, 325-6, 470-1, 540-1, 591-3, 667-8, 784-5, 799; correspondence with Mary Jefferson, 18; and TJ's packages, 18; and father's health, 21; and case of Richard Randolph, 53-4; reconciliation with David Randolph, 53; and French Revolution, 54; and War of First Coalition, 54; manages TJ's affairs, 64-6, 325-6; purchases horse for TJ, 66, 325, 504; experiment with barley, 87; medical education, 88n; health, 101, 110, 137, 541, 578; and TJ's reported resignation from office, 153; and TJ's furniture, 171; TJ's affection for, 250, 546, 578, 617; agricultural observations, 278; entomological interests, 278; weather diary, 279, 326; letters misplaced, 380; and TJ's crop-rotation plan, 403, 422-4, 445, 470, 576-8, 657-8; letter from cited, 504n; crop-rotation plan, 591-3, 657-8; and remodeling of Monticello, 667; and horse for TJ, 721, 757, 799; dines with Monroe, 736; visited by Madison, 784, 799; affection for Mary Jefferson, 785; visited by brother, 799; visited by Monroe, 799; mentioned, 122, 137n, 655

Randolph, Thomas Mann, Sr.: health, 21, 64, 242, 278; and family quarrel, 53

Randolph, Va.: suitability for sheep, 30

Ranger (pilot boat): and *Greyhound*, 36n

Ranger (ship): captured by British privateer, 564n

matic appointment, 517; letter from cited, 517n

Schneider, Mr. *See* Shnydore (Schneider), Ignatius

Schuyler, Robert, 354n

Schweitzer, Jeanneret & Cie.: and U.S. debt to France, 179-80

Scot, James: letter from, 418-20; plans to settle in U.S., 418-20

Scotland: impressment in, 6; watering of meadows in, 681; clover seed in, 682

Scott, James, & Co.: memorial from, 369-74; and case of *York*, 369-74

Scott, William: and case of *Sally*, 388n

Scott, Sir William: and case of Philip Wilson, 770-1

Seagrove, James: and fugitive slaves, 10-12; and Creek hostilities with Ga., 15-17; relations with Creeks, 78-9, 140n; and relations with Spain, 408, 413n; and Spanish relations with Southern Indians, 412n, 414n, 415n; and Treaty of New York, 414n; Spanish complaints about, 671n; letter from submitted to Washington, 737; letters from cited, 737n; and slaves stolen from E. Fla., 737n; mentioned, 416n

Seagrove, John: misidentified by TJ, 737n

Seagrove, Robert: store attacked by Creeks, 15n

sea letters. *See* passports (sea letters)

seals: TJ's sent to Monticello, 19

seamen: changes of allegiance by, 587, 662-3; and French fleet at N.Y., 619; U.S. aid for, 635, 770

seamen, impressment of: in Leith, 6; T. Pinckney's negotiations with Grenville on, 6, 191-2; and case of *Jay*, 436n; in Falmouth, 646; P. Bond's expected information on, 674; in London, 753; in Plymouth, 753n

seed: cost of, 29

Ségur, Louis Philippe, Comte de, 46-7n

Selden, John: *Mare Clausum*, 33, 34, 35n

Senate, U.S. *See* United States: Senate

Sergeant, Jonathan Dickinson: and address to Genet, 61; and case of Gideon Henfield, 131n, 653-4; and Currie v. Griffin, 187

servants: cost of, 29; enlistment of U.S. in French service, 641

Service, Capt. (master of *Camilla*), 92

Seton, William: and Mint, 4

Seven Mile Beach, N.J., 261n

Sevier, John: and Spanish relations with Southern Indians, 414n

Seymour, Richard: detained in Ga., 736-7

Shackerly, John H.: ship captured by *Young Mary*, 55, 74

Shackleford, Tom (TJ's slave): and horse for TJ, 504, 657, 721

Shadwell (Jefferson estate): proposed overseer for, 657

Sharpe, William: and U.S. trade with Canary Islands, 614; and U.S. trade with Morocco, 614; appointed U.S. consul in Morocco by Moroccan emperor, 614n

Shauia, Morocco: and Moroccan civil war, 163, 405, 751

Shaw, Leonard D.: and Creek hostilities with U.S., 413n

Shawnee Indians: relations with Creeks, 15n, 16n; hostilities with U.S., 407-8

Sheddin, Patrick & Co.: memorial from, 369-74; and case of *York*, 369-74

sheep: in Va., 29, 30, 397; and TJ's crop-rotation plan, 428, 578; flax seeds for, 682; rape seeds for, 682; and tallow production, 683

Shelby, Isaac: letters to, 393-4, 785; and French plan to liberate Louisiana, xlii, 393-5, 439, 785-6; draft letter to, xlii, 340 (illus.); and Michaux's proposed western expedition, xlii, 393-5; letter to submitted to Washington, 786n

Shelton, Mr.: J. G. Jefferson's account with, 60-1, 213-14, 258-9

Sheppard, Mr.: and circular letter to merchants, 768n

Sherman, Roger: death, 575

Shewrey, Guillermo (Cherokee chief): relations with Spain, 317

Shippen, Elizabeth Carter Farley Banister (Mrs. Thomas Lee Shippen): son's death, 250

Shippen, William, 256n

ships, Danish: and British trade restrictions, 441n, 674, 796

ships, Swedish: and British trade restrictions, 441n, 674, 796

ships, U.S.: sale of those built for war, 26, 499; passports for, 57, 187, 239, 247, 275-6, 286, 355, 392-3, 434, 542, 645; arming of in France, 96n; sale of in France, 96n; scarcity of, 136; seized at Port-au-Prince, 142-3, 185, 369-74, 486-7; captured by Algerines, 163, 421, 427, 757; captured by British privateers, 165, 336-9, 375-7, 379-80, 387, 433, 435-6, 454-5, 459n, 564-5n, 566-7, 574, 595, 632, 639-40, 646,

INDEX

A comprehensive index of Volumes 1-20 of the First Series has been issued as Volume 21. Each subsequent volume has its own index, as does each volume or set of volumes in the Second Series.